Genealogical and Personal History

OF THE

Allegheny Valley

PENNSYLVANIA

UNDER THE EDITORIAL SUPERVISION OF

JOHN W. JORDAN, LL.D.

Librarian of the Historical Society of Pennsylvania, Philadelphia

LLUSTRATED

NEW YORK
LEWIS HISTORICAL PUBLISHING COMPANY
1913

FOREWORD

412216

THE present work, "Genealogical and Personal History of the Allegheny Valley, Pennsylvania," presents in the aggregate an amount and variety of genealogical and personal information and portraiture unequalled by any kindred publication. No similar work concerning Allegheny Valley Families has ever before been presented, and it contains a vast amount of ancestral history never before printed. The object, clearly defined and well digested, is threefold:

First. To present in concise form the history of Allegheny Valley Families of the Colonial Days.

Second. To preserve a record of its prominent present-day people.

Third. To present through personal sketches the relation of its prominent families of all times to the growth, singular prosperity and wide-spread influence of the Allegheny Valley, Pennsylvania, and its tributary region.

There are numerous voluminous histories of the State, making it unnecessary in this work to even outline its annals. What has been published, however, relates principally to civic life. The amplification necessary to complete the picture, old and nowaday, is what is supplied by these Genealogical and Personal Memoirs. In other words, while others have

COURTHOUSE, FRANKLIN

SOLDIERS' MONUMENT, FRANKLIN.

FOREWORD.

written of "the times," the province of this work is to be a chronicle of the people who have made this magnificent region what it is.

Unique in conception and treatment, this work constitutes one of the most original and permanently valuable contributions ever made to the social history of an American community. In it are arrayed in a lucid and dignified manner all the important facts regarding the ancestry, personal careers and matrimonial alliances of those who, in each succeeding generation, have been accorded leading positions in social, professional and business life. It is not based upon, neither does it minister to, aristocratic prejudices and assumptions. On the contrary, its fundamental ideas are thoroughly American and democratic. The work everywhere conveys the lesson that distinction has been gained only by honorable public service, or by usefulness in private station, and that the development and prosperity of the region of which it treats have been dependent upon the character of its citizens, and in the stimulus which they have given to commerce, to industry, to the arts and sciences, to education and religion—to all that is comprised in the highest civilization of the present day—through a continual progressive development.

The inspiration underlying the present work is a fervent appreciation of the truth so well expressed by Sir Walter Scott, that "there is no heroic poem in the world but is at the bottom the life of a man." And with this goes a kindred truth, that to know a man, and rightly measure his character, and weigh his achievements, we must know whence he came, from what forbears he sprang. Truly as heroic poems have been written in human lives in the paths of peace as in the scarred roads of war. Such examples, in whatever line of endeavor, are of much worth as an incentive to those who come afterward, and as such were never so needful to be written of as in the present day, when pessimism, forgetful of the splendid lessons of the past, withholds its effort in the present, and views the future only with alarm.

Every community with such ample history, should see that it be worthily supplemented

COURTHOUSE AND JAIL, WARREN COUNTY.

FOREWORD.

GEN. EDWARD BRADDOCK.

by Genealogical and Personal Memoirs of its leading families and prominent citizens. Such a work is that which is here presented. And it should be admitted, the undertaking possesses value of the highest importance—in its historic utility as a memorial of the development and progress of the community from its very founding, and in the personal interest which attaches to the record made by the individual. On both these accounts it will prove a highly useful contribution to literature, and a valuable legacy to future generations. Out of these considerations the authors and publishers have received the encouragement and approval of authorities of the highest standing as genealogists, historians and litterateurs. In the production of this work, no pains have been spared to ensure absolute truth—that quality upon which its value in every feature depends. The material comprising the genealogical and personal records of the active living, as well as of the honored dead, has been gathered by men and women experienced in such work and acquainted with local history and ancestral families. These have appealed to the custodians of family records concerning the useful men of preceding generations, and of their descendants who have lived useful and honorable lives. Such custodians, who have availed themselves of this opportunity of having this knowledge placed in preservable form, have performed a public service in rendering

CHAPEL AND SCIENCE HALL, CLARION STATE NORMAL SCHOOL.

FOREWORD.

honor to whom honor is due, and in inculcating the most valuable and enduring lessons of patriotism and good citizenship.

No other region in the United States presents a field of more peculiar interest for such research. Its history reaches back to the beginning days of the Nation. It is exceedingly rich in Indian antiquities, and here the aborigines have left many of their most indelible marks. It was the scene of historic events during the French occupation, and here the Great Washington, as a young man, came to take part in scenes which led to the French expulsion. The immigrant settlers in this region were of the best blood and sinew. They fought valiantly and endured the most dreadful privations in the early days, and later they were a part of the very backbone of the Patriot Army in the Revolution. Later yet, the sons of these worthy sires bore their full share in the maintenance of the Union, shedding their blood upon many a glorious field, including that of Gettysburg, in their own State, destined to form a brilliant page in the history of the Nation to the end of time. The restoration of peace after the close of the Civil War witnessed a remarkable development, and has made this region one of the most wonderfully valuable in the whole land, its natural resources and the products of its labor entering into every phase of commercial and industrial life.

These records are presented in a series of independent genealogical and personal sketches

STATUE OF GEN. JOSEPH WARREN.
Inscribed to the Memory of Soldiers of the Revolution buried in Warren County. Erected at Warren by the Tidioute Chapter of the D. A. R.

SOLDIERS' AND SAILORS' MONUMENT, WARREN.

FOREWORD.

relating to lineal family heads, and the most conspicuous representatives in the present generation. There is an entire avoidance of the stereotyped and unattractive manner in which such data is usually presented. The past is linked to the present in such style as to form a symmetrical narrative exhibiting the lines of descent, and the history of distinguished members in each generation, thus giving to it a distinct personal interest. That these ends have been conscientiously and faithfully conserved is assured by the cordial personal interest and recognized capability of the supervising editor, and his associates, all of whom have long pursued historical and genealogical investigations with intelligence and enthusiasm.

In this connection the publishers express their obligations to Dr. John W. Jordan, LL. D., Librarian of the Historical Society of Pennsylvania, supervising editor; also to Mr. William Temple Bell, of Venango county; Mr. Rufus Barrett Stone, of Warren county; the Rev. Andrew A. Lambing, LL.D., of Allegheny county; and the Rev. Benjamin F. Delo, of Clarion county.

A special feature has been made of the illustrations—portraits, etc. In these respects much of the adornment of the pages of the proposed work is entirely original with this publication.

This work comprises a carefully prepared genealogical history of several hundred representative families of the region treated. The editors and publishers desire to state that they have adopted a different method for collecting and compiling data than has heretofore been pursued in this country. Time and expense have not been spared in making the publication a valuable work for reference. The value of family history and genealogy depends upon accuracy, and the thoroughness of research in public and private records; also, upon the use of old and unpublished manuscripts, supplemented by a careful gleaning and compiling of information to be found in the various printed works in public and private libraries. It has been the aim of editors and publishers to utilize all such material, connecting the same with the American progenitor, where possible, and present in a narrative form the family line down to and including the present generation, weaving in the military and civic services of the subject treated.

In order to ensure greatest possible accuracy, all matter for this work, after careful preparation, has been submitted in typewritten manuscript to persons most interested, for revision and correction.

If, in any case, a narrative is incomplete or faulty, the shortcoming is usually ascribable to the paucity of data obtainable, many families being without exact records in their family line; while, in some cases, representatives of a given family are at disagreement as to the names of some of their forbears, important dates, etc.

COURTHOUSE AND SOLDIERS' MONUMENT, CLARION.

FOREWORD.

It is believed that the present work, in spite of the occasional fault which attaches to such undertakings, will prove a real addition to the mass of annals concerning the historic families of the Allegheny Valley, and that, without it, much valuable information would be inaccessible to the general reader, or irretrievably lost, owing to the passing away of custodians of family records, and the consequent disappearance of material in their possession.

THE PUBLISHERS.

ALLEGHENY VALLEY

MELVIN This name occurs in early Massachusetts records as Melvin, Melvil and sometimes as Melville. There is a record of John Melvin, a tailor of Charlestown, Massachusetts, in 1684, when he was then twenty-eight years of age. He moved to Concord, married (first) Hannah Lewis, (second) Margaret Shannesburg. It is no doubt from this ancestor that Patrick Melvin sprang, but no connection can be shown from existing records. John seems a persistent name in the family, which fact proves nothing except to show a desire to perpetuate a name honored in the family. John seems to be with but little doubt the grandfather of Patrick, probably the son of a second John Melvin, born August 29, 1679.

(I) Patrick Melvin's name first appears on the records of Chester, New Hampshire, as a signer of the Presbyterian protest of June 10, 1735, though probably he was in that town earlier. His will was proved April 28, 1759. He devised to his wife Mary and children Benjamin, Abraham, Elizabeth, Mary, John and Jane. Mary, his wife, died October 1, 1795.

(II) Benjamin, son of Patrick Melvin, was born December 9, 1733, died December 29, 1802. He married, July 13, 1762, Mehitabel, born December 27, 1745, daughter of Samuel Bradley, who was killed by the Indians at Concord, August 11, 1746. She survived her husband and married (second) Deacon John S. Dearborn. She died February 14, 1825. Children: 1. Anna, born March 27, 1763; married Lieutenant Joseph Underhill. 2. Samuel, born 1765; settled in Maine. 3. Sarah, married James Orr. 4. Polly, born 1770, died 1824. 5. Benjamin, married Elizabeth Sargent and settled in Maine. 6. John, of whom further. 7. Josiah, married Sally Blanchard. 8. Mehitable, born April 14, 1781; married John Folsom. 9. William, born 1783; went south. 10. Richard, born February 14, 1786; married (first) Ann Patten, (second) Jane D. Carr.

(III) John, son of Benjamin Melvin, was born January 8, 1776, in Chester, New Hampshire, died there June 11, 1814. He lived on the old homestead and served in the war of 1812. He married, November 13, 1800, Susannah, daughter of Abraham Sargent, who survived him and married (second) Richard Dearborn. Children of John Melvin: Luther, born 1801; John F., of whom further; Lydia R., married David Currier; Thomas J., born April 11, 1808, married Harriet Tenney.

(IV) John F., son of John Melvin, was born in Chester, New Hampshire, December 2, 1802, died in McKean county, Pennsylvania. He was educated in the country schools, settled in New York state, and in 1826 came to McKean county, Pennsylvania. He was a prominent man in the early days of the county; a pioneer merchant and an extensive dealer in lumber. He owned large tracts of land and also engaged in agriculture. Few men did more for the early development of McKean county than Mr. Melvin. Although he had no known oil property, after his death his land was part of the extensive Bradford oil field. He married, July 12, 1828, Lucretia Farr, born at Bellows Falls, Vermont, October 11, 1810, daughter of Isaac and Pantha (Clark) Farr, both of Scotch-Irish descent. Six children reached maturity, four dying in childhood. The former are: Charles C.; Adaline E., married Judge Loyal Ward; Evaline A., married Hon. C. H. Foster; Thomas Jefferson, of whom further; John S., who was killed in the civil war; Mary L., married L. A. Smith, and died in Dunkirk, New York.

(V) Thomas Jefferson, son of John F. Melvin, was born in Bradford township, McKean county, Pennsylvania, August 18, 1847, died February 29, 1904. He acquired a good education in the country schools, finishing with a course at Bryant and Stratton's Business College at Buffalo, New York. He began business life as a clerk, continuing until 1869, when he established a mercantile business in his own name, which he successfully operated until 1876, when he became an oil operator and producer. He was one of the founders of the Alunninia Shale Brick Company and engaged in many of Bradford's earlier enterprises, including the organization of the First National Bank of Bradford. He was a Mason, an Elk and a member of the Edgewood and Country Clubs.

He married, September 28, 1869, Marian Belle, born at Russellburg, near Warren, Pennsylvania, 1850, daughter of Horatio Nelson Parker, a merchant and large lumberman of New York and Pennsylvania. She was educated at Irvine Mills, New York, and Warren, Pennsylvania, finishing at boarding school in Clinton, Oneida county, New York, in 1867. She survives her husband, a resident of East Bradford, Pennsylvania, a member of the Universalist church, the Woman's Literary Club and the Country Club, all of Bradford. Children of Thomas Jefferson Melvin: 1. John Parker, of whom further. 2. Charles C., born in Limestone, New York, June 10, 1872, now (1912) treasurer of McKean county, Pennsylvania; he resides in Bradford with his parents, unmarried. 3. Milton F., born in Bradford, May 10, 1876; founder of a sanatorium for tuberculosis patients at Bradford; married, February 13, 1898, Mabel L. White, and has a son, Milton F., born April 9, 1908. 4. Thomas Jefferson, born in Bradford, July 29, 1878; he prepared for the profession of the law, but is now superintendent of Melvin & Peterson's brick works at Bradford. Two other children died in infancy.

(VI) John Parker, son of Thomas Jefferson Melvin, was born July 17, 1870, at Limestone, Cattaraugus county, New York, the home of his grandparents. The home of his own parents at that time being Bradford, Pennsylvania, where he attended the public school. He entered Phillips Exeter Academy (New Hampshire) whence he was graduated, class of 1888. After a year spent at Harvard University he began the study of law, under George A. Berry, of Bradford, Pennsylvania. He passed the necessary examination and in 1893 was admitted to the bar. He at once began the practice of his profession in Bradford, where he is firmly established as a brilliant and reliable attorney and counsellor. He is interested in business outside his profession, being a director of the Alunninia Shale Brick Company, and a partner of Melvin & Peterson, brick manufacturers. In politics he is a Republican; was chairman of the McKean county Republican committee in 1898; in 1899 was elected district attorney; re-elected in 1902, serving most efficiently for six years. He is prominent in the Masonic order; is past master of Bradford Lodge, No. 334, Free and Accepted Masons, and now district deputy grand master of the twenty-second district of Pennsylvania. In Capitullar Masonry he is past high priest of Bradford Chapter, No. 260; in Cryptic Masonry he is past thrice illustrious Master of Bradford Council, No. 43, and deputy grand master of Council District, No. 3. He is also a devotee of Templar Masonry, and is an officer of Bradford Commandery. He also belongs to the Independent Order of Odd Fellows, Heptasophs and the Royal Arcanum. His club is the Bradford Country; his church: Universalist.

He married, at Bradford, Pennsylvania, July 5, 1892, Adda Laney, born at Spartansburg, Pennsylvania, April 19, 1871, was graduated from the Bradford high school, later entering Lake Erie Seminary at Painesville, Ohio, continuing until 1890. Mr. and Mrs. Melvin have a son, Parker L., born May 27, 1895, now a student in Bradford high school.

Adda (Laney) Melvin is a daughter of William K. Laney, born in Germany in October, 1844. When he was a mere infant his father died, and when but six months old his mother came to the United States, settled in Venango county, Pennsylvania. He remained with her until his fourteenth year, then left home and began working in the oil fields during the summer, obtaining his education during the winter months in the public schools. He was careful of his earnings which he invested in oil wells, and was also engaged in contracting for drilling of wells, having fulfilled large contracts in different states. In 1862 he enlisted in Company I, One Hundred and Forty-second Regiment, Pennsylvania Volunteer Infantry, serving until the close of the war. He participated in many of the famous battles fought by the Army of the Potomac, including Antietam, Chancellorsville and Gettysburg. He was captured on the first day of the Gettysburg fight, but shortly afterward released. He rejoined his company and was present at the surrender of General Lee. After the war he returned to Bradford, where he died in February, 1892. He was an active member of the United Veteran Legion, which he served as lieutenant-colonel of Bradford Post. He was a member of the Masonic Order, belonging to

Lodge, Chapter, Council and Commandery. He married, in Meadville, Pennsylvania, in July, 1870, Flora, daughter of Charles Huntley, who survives him, a member of the Presbyterian church of Bradford, her home. Children: 1. Adda, of previous mention. 2. Grace E., born at Parkers Landing, Armstrong county, Pennsylvania, now resides at Palo Alto, unmarried. 3. Charles W., born November 11, 1878, married Effie Smith, resides at Independence, Kansas, and has Elizabeth, born June, 1907. Grandfather Laney lived and died in Bremen, Germany, where his children were born. Charles Huntley was of Welsh descent. He married ———— Catlin; he died in Pittsburgh, Pennsylvania, leaving two children: Flora, married William K. Laney, and Elsie.

The emigrant ancestor of the POTTER Potters of Bradford, Pennsylvania, was John Potter, born in England in 1607, died in Fairfield, 1643. He came to America in 1632. He was granted a tract of land in Fairfield, Fairfield county, Connecticut, provided he would build a mill and grind mace. His widow Elizabeth married (second), in 1646, Edward Parker.

(II) John (2), son of John (1) Potter, the emigrant, was baptized at New Haven, Connecticut, October 17, 1641, died December 24, 1706. He married, 1661, Hannah Cooper. Children, all born at East Haven: Hannah, born 1661, died young; John, born June 13, 1663, died August 10, 1664; Hannah, born June 26, 1665; John, of whom further; Samuel, born July 23, 1669, died November 16, 1669; Samuel, born December 25, 1670, died January 1, 1671; Samuel, born February 1, 1672, died same month; Mary, born March 6, 1673, died in childhood; Samuel, born January 2, 1675, died November 26, 1707, married Abigail Hill.

(III) John (3), son of John (2) Potter, was born at East Haven, Connecticut, August 14, 1667, died March 12, 1712. He married, February 23, 1691-92, Elizabeth, daughter of John and Elizabeth (Thomas) Holt. Children: 1. Joseph, of further mention. 2. John, born June 14, 1695; married Abigail ————. 3. Elizabeth, born September 12, 1697, married John, son of William and Mary Luddington. 4. Gideon, born June 3, 1700, died December 30, 1756; married Mary, daughter of Nathan and Mary Moulthrop. 5. Daniel, born June 15, 1701-02, died January 20, 1747; married, September 12, 1728, Hannah Holbrook, who died 1742. 6. Enos, born December 12, 1706, married (first) Hannah Robinson, (second) Sarah Hemingway. 7. Samuel, born 1708, married, 1738, Dorothy, born 1712, daughter of Nathan and Mary Moulthrop.

(IV) Joseph, son of John (3) Potter, was born at East Haven, Connecticut, October 6, 1691. He married, March 11, 1729, Thankful Bradley. Children, born at East Haven: 1. Joseph, born August 9, 1730, died April 10, 1800; married Jemima Smith, who died 1801, aged sixty-six years. 2. Timothy, born February 17, 1732, died aged sixty years; married, August 2, 1795, Susanna Penderson. 3. Titus, born April 1, 1734. 4. James, of whom further. 5. Philemon, born March 31, 1738. 6. Thankful, born August 6, 1739. 7. Sybil, born September 1, 1741. 8. Jesse, born May 21, 1743. 9. Elizabeth, born August 1, 1745.

(V) Dr. James Potter, son of Joseph Potter, was born at East Haven, Connecticut, September 26, 1736, died February 10, 1804. He was a practicing physician of Fairfield county and prominent in the public life of his town. He married Abigail ————, born 1744, died 1817. Children: 1. Meranda, born November 2, 1760, died December 21, 1782. 2. Milton, born March 6, 1763, died July 2, 1840. 3. Armido, born June 4, 1765, died August 7, 1798. 4. Abigail, born July 27, 1767. 5. Libertus, born August, 1769, died December 8, 1769. 6. James Addison (Honorable), born January 23, 1771, died January 11, 1809. 7. William Cicero, of whom further. 8. Philomela, born January 28, 1776, died August 17, 1836. 9. Joel Baldwin, born October 20, 1778, died October 7, 1806. 10. Jared C., born June 18, 1781, died 1857. 11. John Lock, born December 27, 1783, died July 28, 1784. 12. Herman B., born October 23, 1785, died January 30, 1804.

(VI) William Cicero, son of Dr. James Potter, was born in Fairfield county, Connecticut, August 22, 1773, died August 21, 1826. He married, July 20, 1793, Nancy Anna Hubbell, born 1776, died 1854, daughter of Eleazer and Anna (Noble) Hubbell. Children, all born in Sherman, Connecticut: 1. Charles F., born March 8, 1795, died February 3, 1881; married (first), March 20, 1816, Hettie, born 1793, died 1843, daughter of David and Jerusha (Bull) Noble; married (second), April 17, 1844, Caroline Noble, born 1803, died 1864; married (third), August 27, 1864, Amelia Stewart. 2. Lucretia Emma, born February

27, 1797, died November 14, 1857; married, January 8, 1818, Simon, son of John Lyman. 3. James Addison, born July 10, 1798, died November 25, 1878; married (first), December 11, 1821, Phoebe Gelton, born 1803, died 1841, daughter of Rev. Maltby Gelton; married (second), August, 1841, Mrs. Mary (Denio) Atkin, daughter of John A. and Harriet (Stiles) Denio. 4. Laura Ann, born November 18, 1800, died February 12, 1837. 5. Mary Abby, born September 27, 1802, died March 13, 1868; married, April 20, 1828, Matthew Gregory. 6. Herman B., born June 9, 1804, died March 19, 1880; married Mary La Homidee. 7. Eleazer, of whom further. 8. William Burr, born May 11, 1808, died February 17, 1877; married, February 17, 1836, Marcia, born 1808, died 1879, daughter of Amos and Mary Gregory. 9. Joel Baldwin, born July 25, 1810, died November 30, 1880; married, July 13, 1836, Adeline, born 1813, daughter of Adgate and Martha (Moss) Lathrop. 10. Henry N., born October 28, 1812, died November 3, 1814. 11. Jane Eliza, born October 27, 1814; married, June 14, 1855, Henry, born 1804, son of Adgate and Martha (Moss) Lathrop. 12. Henry Noble, born April 16, 1817, died September 3, 1862; married, June 12, 1854, ———— Fontaine. 13. Mark Milton, born May 2, 1819, died October 5, 1863; married Helen S., daughter of Judge John F. Errett.

(VII) Eleazer, son of William Cicero Potter, was born in Sherman, Connecticut, April 23, 1806, died in Rockford, Illinois, September 1, 1861. He was educated at Medina, New York, moving from there to Rockford, where he engaged in mercantile business until his death. He was a Republican and a Congregationalist. He married (first) Adeline, born 1806, died 1839, daughter of Edward and ———— (Williston) Eells. He married (second) Mary Morrell, born in New York City, died at Oak Park, 1899. She was educated in New York City and moved to Rockford, Illinois, in 1840. Children by first wife: 1. Edward Eells, born in Medina, New York, May 9, 1833. He entered the navy as a midshipman, February 5, 1850, served on the "Decatur" of the home squadron and on the "Constitution" and "Marion" on the African Station, promoted past midshipman, June, 1856; master, 1858, and lieutenant, June, 1858. He served on the coast of Brazil on the brig "Perry" in the Paraguay expedition, and came home in the "Atlantic." 1859, ordered to the steamer "Fulton," which was wrecked in September, 1859, on the Santa Rosa Island; ordered to the "Pensacola," which went out of commission in 1860; ordered to the "Rhode Island," Admiral Palmer's flagship. When the "Rhode Island" went out of commission he was detached and ordered to the "Franklin," Admiral Farragut's flagship, and promoted commander; ordered to the "Shawmut," which went to the West Indies; detached and on leave and various shore duties until ordered to the "Constellation" to take supplies to famine-stricken Ireland; promoted captain and ordered to the New York navy yard; detached and ordered to the European squadron. After sixteen months' service the "Lancaster" was ordered to the South Atlantic Station; ordered home and on continuous duty until his retirement, May 9, 1895, after forty-five years' service. He married (first), 1861, Harriet L. (Raymond) Blackmer, born 1833, died 1873, daughter of Lyman Blackmer; married (second), March 18, 1875, Harriet L., born 1849, daughter of William C. Grant. 2. Sarah Adeline, born March 19, 1836, at Medina, New York; married, June, 1857, Hon. William Lathrop, born 1825, son of John and Martha Lathrop. Children by second wife: 3. Andrew Morrell, born in Rockford, Illinois, March 8, 1843, died March 30, 1900; veteran of the Seventy-fourth Regiment Illinois Volunteer Infantry; enlisted September, 1862; severely wounded at the battle of Mission Ridge; promoted to the adjutancy of his regiment with rank of first lieutenant; after the war he came to the oil region and died in Bradford, Pennsylvania. He married, October 21, 1869, Clementine S. Perkins, born 1850, died 1888, daughter of Henry Perkins. 4. George Hubbell, of whom further. 5. Mary Elizabeth, born Rockford, Illinois, November 27, 1849; married, October 29, 1875, Cedric G. Marsh.

(VIII) George Hubbell, son of Eleazer and Mary (Morrell) Potter, was born at Rockford, Illinois, July 12, 1847. He was educated in the public school at Rockford, and in 1864 enlisted in the United States navy, serving about one year on the "Winnebago," of Admiral Farragut's fleet, and fought with him at Mobile Bay, August 5, 1864. After the war he came to the oil region of Pennsylvania, and in 1867 settled at Petroleum Centre, where he remained five years, going from there to Butler county, and in 1877 settling in Bradford, his present home. He has been very successful as an oil producer and ranks as one of Bradford's most respected and substantial citizens. He is a director of the Bradford National Bank, president of the Bradford Electric Light and Power Company, and president of the Bradford Garage Company. In politics Mr. Potter is a Democrat, and has given much of his time and ability to the service of his city. He has served on the poor board, the board of health and from 1902 to 1905 was mayor of the city. He is a member of the Benevolent and Protective Order of Elks and of the Merchants' Club. He married Elizabeth Mickels, born 1859, daughter of William M. and Louisa R. Mickels. William M. was a farmer of Lawrence county and a veteran of the civil war, serving three years. He died 1907. Only child of George Hubbell and Elizabeth Potter, Louisa, born in Lawrence county, Pennsylvania, April 5, 1880, resides with her parents in Bradford.

FISHER The Fishers of Bradford, Pennsylvania, descend from Joseph and Catharine (Minegar) Fisher, natives of Germany, he born April, 1734, she August, 1746. They were married June 5, 1764. They came to America and settled near the site of Catawissa, in what is now Columbia county, Pennsylvania, but prior to that they evidently lived in Bradford county, Pennsylvania, as their son Henry was born there July 25, 1767. Their other children were born in Columbia county. Children: Catharine, married Nicholas Shipman; Henry, built a grist mill and tavern in Columbia, which he operated for many years, died 1825; Mary, married Samuel Mutchlu; Hannah, married Caleb Farlee; Elizabeth, John, Moses, David, Jacob, Joseph, of whom further.

(II) Joseph (2), son of Joseph (1) Fisher, was born in Columbia county, Pennsylvania, near Catawissa, about 1780. He located in Northumberland county, near Milton, Pennsylvania, where he died. He was a farmer and a man of some means and influence. He married Sarah Heatherton, and among his children was a son Tunis, of whom further.

(III) Tunis, son of Joseph (2) Fisher, was born near Milton, Pennsylvania, 1801, died at Lewisburg, Pennsylvania, 1877. He was educated in the district school, and worked at farming several years. He left home and eventually became the owner of and ran a line of boats on the Pennsylvania canal. He was a Lutheran and a Democrat. He married Elizabeth, born at Reading, Pennsylvania, died 1899, daughter of Daniel Strohecker, of German descent, who was a farmer and owned a tract of land, part of which is now opposite Lewisburg. He married Leah Garrer. Children of Tunis Fisher. 1. Jasper S., of whom further. 2. Frank, born at Lewisburg, Pennsylvania, died in childhood. 3. Louisa, married ——— Maynard, at Rome, Bradford county, Pennsylvania, and now resides at Haddon Heights, New Jersey; has one son, William, also a resident of Haddon Heights. 4. Sarah J., born at Lewisburg; married H. F. Mann, resides at Sunbury, Northumberland county, Pennsylvania; children: Jesse M., of Williamsport, and Grace M., of Sunbury. 5. Clara, born in Lewisburg; married Wilbert Wendell, of Montgomery. 6. Mary, died young. 7. Joseph G., born at Lewisburg, died at Fort Wayne, Indiana, 1899. 8. Charles S., born at Lewisburg, died at New Orleans, 1901. 9. Tunis, born at Lewisburg, died at Brooklyn, New York, 1908.

(IV) Jasper Strohecker, son of Tunis Fisher, was born at the homestead on the banks of the Susquehanna at Lewisburg, Union county, Pennsylvania, September 3, 1836. He was educated in the public school at Lewisburg and attended a private academy one term. At twelve years of age he was driving a team on the Pennsylvania canal, and later spent a year in Georgia, located at Atlanta, clerk in a boot and shoe store. At the outbreak of the civil war he came north and secured a position with the Pennsylvania railroad, first as clerk, later as station agent. He was located at Titusville, Pennsylvania, with the Pennsylvania railroad until the New York Central secured control of that branch in 1865. He then went to Pitthole, Venango county, Pennsylvania, then to Petroleum Centre in the employ of the Ocean Oil Company, remaining until 1866. He then purchased an interest in the firm of Fisher, Norris & Company, manufacturers of tools used in the production of oil, continuing until 1870. He then spent a year in Butler county; then located in Bradford and took a position with Howe & Cook. He remained with them three years, then established a hardware store with T. M. Griffith as partner. He was so engaged until 1878 when the firm dissolved. He then spent a year in New Jersey, returning to Venango county, Pennsylvania, and entered the employ of his old partner, T.

M. Griffith, continuing until his election to the office of city treasurer in 1907. He is a Democrat in politics and has served as burgess, city assessor from 1904 to 1907, city treasurer from 1907 to 1911, and in November of the latter year was elected to fill another term of four years in the same office. He holds the high regard of his townsmen and has earned their esteem by a rigid adherence to honorable conduct and strict attention to duties of his office. He is a member of the Knights of the Maccabees, and with his family attends the Methodist Episcopal church.

He married, September 5, 1859, Mary Elizabeth Van Ormer, born in Thomsontown, Juniata county, Pennsylvania, in 1839, daughter of James Van Ormer, who died in Juniata county, near Lewistown, which is but a few miles across the line in Mifflin county. He married Elizabeth Graham, who died in the same locality. Their children: 1. Sarah, who survives her husband; resides at Milton, Pennsylvania. 2. Lucy, married J. Levi Bosslee, a marketman of Camden, New Jersey. 3. Caroline, deceased. 4. Mary Elizabeth, married Joseph S. Fisher as stated. Children of Mr. and Mrs. Fisher: 1. Alma L., born 1862, at Lewisburg, now living in Bradford with her parents. 2. Grace Evangeline, born in Petroleum Centre, 1873, died in infancy. 3. Charles V., born 1874, at Petroleum Centre, Pennsylvania; he is an engineer on the Buffalo, Rochester & Pittsburgh railroad and resides in Bradford; married and has a son Henry, born 1905.

LEASURE The Leasures of Bradford, Pennsylvania, are descended from the ancient French family of Le Sueur, who were of royal origin, and have frequently appeared in later French history. Eustache Le Sueur was, in 1617-55, one of the founders of the French Academy of Painting, and was the son of Catherine Le Sueur, a turner and sculptor in wood. He became one of the famous painters of France, and left numerous paintings and drawings that are highly valued and carefully preserved. A latter day artist of the family, Eugene, and a relative of the branch that came to America, amassed a large fortune through his art. A brother of Eustache was Francois Le Sueur, a French Huguenot, who came to this country, and in 1659 was living in Kingston, New York. He married Willdebrand Patterson, of Amsterdam, Holland, and is the American ancestor of the Lasher family of New York. The name in early colonial records is spelled in every conceivable way, and from Le Sueur has come both the Lasher, Loescher, Le Chaire, Lashier and Leasure families in the United States.

This branch of the family were Huguenots and held prominent positions. They were Masters of Horse and held their positions until the persecutions became so fierce that they were obliged to flee. They came to Pennsylvania with the DuPont family, of Philadelphia and Delaware. The name became quickly anglicized, but just when the present form Leasure became generally used does not appear. The emigrants settled on the shores of the Susquehanna, where they farmed, and made salt, furnishing the colonial forts and posts with that article, and sending their product as far west as Fort DuQuesne. The great-grandfather of James W. Leasure of Bradford received his grant of land at Blue Ridge directly from the government, and the patent bore the name of George Washington.

The farm at Blue Ridge, Pennsylvania, was the family homestead for many years, and there John Thorley Leasure lived to the great age of one hundred and four years. He lived in perilous times and reared a large family amid frontier dangers. One of his daughters was slain and scalped by Indians, and danger lurked in every quarter. But in time peace came and the old Blue Ridge farm became a scene of peace, prosperity and happiness. John Thorley Leasure reared a family of thirteen children. One of his sons, Colonel Daniel Leasure, was a brave and daring officer of the civil war. The family were members of the Dutch Reformed church, of which the father was a deacon for many years.

(III) George, seventh son of John Thorley Leasure, was born at Hansted Farm, in Westmoreland county, Pennsylvania, in 1824, died at Bradford, Pennsylvania, July 2, 1880. He was educated in the schools of Pleasant Unity, and on arriving at manhood went to Ohio, where he owned and operated a grist mill for several years at West Salem. Later he moved to Burning Springs, West Virginia, and later became one of the pioneer oil producers of Calhoun county. He was a Republican in politics, and a deacon of the Presbyterian church for many years. He married Priscilla Fry, born in Pleasant Unity, the oldest of three daughters. She died at Sistersville, West Virginia, in 1907, aged eighty years. Children: Frances Marian, William Jefferson, Margaret, John Thorley, deceased; Eugene, deceased; Charles G., Hiram T., Allen Bales, James W., of whom further; Etta Kate, Jacob Fry, deceased.

(IV) James W., seventh son of a seventh son, George Leasure, was born in Salem, Ohio, February 18, 1864. He was a babe when the family moved to West Virginia, and four years old when he was sent to Greensburg, Pennsylvania, where he was educated in the public schools, and lived until he was thirteen years of age. He then entered the employ of the Standard Oil Company at Bradford, remaining nineteen years, in the meantime learning the printer's trade and also bookbinding. In 1896 he bought the job printing and bookbinding department of the Era Publishing Company, that had been owned by the Standard Oil Company, and operated the plant successfully until 1903. The three following years until 1906 he was engaged in the general insurance business at Bradford, Pennsylvania, also operating in Ohio oil and gas properties. He is interested in many business enterprises both at home and abroad. He has forty-three inventions to his credit, among which may be mentioned a vacuum cleaner, an automobile non-skid tire, a sanitary wind shield and an exceedingly durable railroad tie, which is conceded to be one of great importance and which is fast coming into general use. In politics he is a Republican. He is prominent in the social and beneficial orders of his city and a past officer of the Independent Order of Odd Fellows, Heptasophs, Junior Order of American Mechanics, Benevolent and Protective Order of Elks and the Typographical Union. His club is the Merchants'.

He married, June 26, 1896, Anna, daughter of Franklin A. Moore, a farmer and oil producer of Bradford, Pennsylvania, and a granddaughter of Amos and Cynthia (Gardner) Moore, natives of Massachusetts, who moved to McKean county, Pennsylvania, in 1839, settling on a farm of two hundred and thirty-six acres, where Amos Moore died in 1845, and his wife Cynthia in 1839. Franklin A. Moore was born in Erie county, New York, August 8, 1822, came to Pennsylvania with his parents in 1839, and worked on the farm until the death of his father in 1845, when he succeeded to its ownership. Several oil wells have been drilled on the farm which have produced a large quantity of oil, and are still a source of considerable revenue. In 1888 Mr. Moore built his present residence in Bradford, where he was extensively engaged for many years in coal, lumbering and oil operations. He married Edith, daughter of Abraham and Dorothy (Vanderhoff) Vandine, of New York and New Jersey. Children: 1. Amos T., a merchant of Bradford; married Amanda Potter, of Friendship, New York; children: Charles and Lillian Maude. 2. Anna, married James W. Leasure. They have no children.

HABGOOD This family long seated in England was founded in the United States by William Henry Habgood, father of Robert Patton Habgood, of Bradford, Pennsylvania, of the first generation born in the United States.

(I) Robert Habgood was a carpenter and builder of Gloucestershire, England, died in Cheltenham, England. By wife Mary he had children: William Henry, of whom further; Mary, deceased. His wife survived him and came to the United States, where she died and is buried at Bellefonte, Pennsylvania. Mr. Habgood and his wife were members of the established Church of England (Episcopal).

(II) William Henry, only son of Robert and Mary Habgood, was born in Gloucestershire, England, August 16, 1847. He was educated in a private school at Cheltenham, and learned the watchmaker's trade. He was engaged in Cheltenham as watchmaker and jeweler until coming to the United States in 1870. He was a watchmaker and jeweler in Renovo, Pennsylvania, and subsequently employed by the railroad in machinery department. He is now living in Bradford, Pennsylvania. In England he was conservative in politics and in Pennsylvania has always acted with the Republican party. Both he and his wife are members of the Presbyterian church of Du Bois. He married, in England, Sarah Sircombe, born in Bristol, England. Of her brothers and sisters Thomas is a merchant of Detroit, Michigan, while William, Elizabeth and Mary are deceased. Children: 1. Robert Patton, of whom further. 2. Charles William, born 1873, died in infancy. 3. Marian, born August 19, 1875; married C. E. Cosolowsky and resides at Crafton Station, near

Pittsburgh, Pennsylvania; children: Carl, born 1900, and Marion, died at age of two years. 4. William, born 1877, died in infancy. 5. Minnie, born 1880, died in infancy.

(III) Robert Patton, only living son and eldest child of William Henry and Sarah (Sircombe) Habgood, was born at Bellefonte, Centre county, Pennsylvania, May 21, 1871. His early years were spent in Renovo, Clinton county, Pennsylvania, where he was graduated from the high school, class of 1887. In 1888 he came to Bradford, where he was employed in railroad work in various capacities until appointed general timekeeper in 1891, and continued in railroad positions until 1898. He was for one year engaged with a New York tea and coffee house as salesman, and in 1899 became associated with the *Bradford Evening Star* as advertising solicitor. In 1900 he became editor and business manager, and in 1903 secured a controlling interest, becoming president of the company, editor and publisher. In 1909 he merged the *Star* with the *Bradford Record*, and continued the publications as the *Star-Record*. He has made this paper a power in the county and a welcome visitor to the homes of a large list of subscribers. Since 1905 he has been secretary and treasurer of the Pennsylvania State Editorial Association, and holds a prominent position among his editorial brethren. He is also a director of the International Advertising Association, National counsellor of the American Institute of Civics, and has been secretary and manager of the Bradford Board of Trade. Since becoming a voter Mr. Habgood has been active in the Republican party and is a leader in his county. In 1906 he was elected a member of the house of assembly, serving during the session of 1907 as chairman of the committee on printing, and as a member of compare bills, judiciary general, labor and industry, military, public health and sanitation committees. In 1908 he was a delegate-at-large in the National Republican Convention that nominated President Taft. In 1908 and 1909 President of the Pennsylvania Republican State League, and April 1, 1911, was appointed postmaster of Bradford. He is also prominent in fraternal life, being a member of Blue Lodge, Chapter and Commandery of the Masonic Order, the Independent Order of Odd Fellows, the Benevolent and Protective Order of Elks, Improved Order of Red Men and Knights of Pythias. He has held official positions in all these bodies and is the present exalted ruler of the Elks. In religious faith he is a Presbyterian.

He married (first), November 3, 1897, Daisy M. Heffner, born at Parkers Landing, Pennsylvania, 1873, daughter of Samuel Dean Heffner, superintendent of Bradford water department, and Mary I. (Peightal) Heffner. They also have a son, Henry Clay Heffner. He married (second), June 6, 1911, Mary Ann Sheaffer, born in Bloomfield, Perry county, Pennsylvania, June 6, 1882, daughter of Singleton and Margaret (Fisher) Sheaffer, whose children are: James, Harry, deceased; William, Mary A., Lila, Emily. Children by first marriage: Stuart, born 1900; William, born 1902, died in infancy; Samuel, 1904, died in infancy; Dorothy, 1906. Child by second marriage: one son, Robert Jr., born May 25, 1912.

HARRIS The Harris family, originally of Massachusetts and Connecticut, send out many branches to other states. The family of Asa (3) Harris largely settled in New York state in Niagara, Chautauqua and Cattaraugus counties. Descendants of these found their way to Pennsylvania, settling in Fayette, McKean and other counties.

The name Harris is of Welsh origin and means "The son of Harry." The name is found in "A list of sixty of the most common surnames in England and Wales in 1838", and is now found in every county in England. The name is very common in the United States and cannot be traced to a common ancestor, as many distinct emigrations of persons bearing the name appear at a very early period in New England.

(I) The family herein recorded spring from James Harris, whose nativity, parentage and date of coming to America is unknown. He was born about 1640. He married, in 1666, Sarah Denison, of Boston. He moved to New London, Connecticut, about 1690, and died there in 1715. His will, dated June 14, 1714, probated September 13, 1715, bequeathed to his widow Sarah his entire estate during her lifetime. Children: Sarah, born March 2, 1668; Deborah, July, 1670; James, April 4, 1673, married (first) Sarah Rogers, (second) Sarah (Harris) Jackson; Margaret, January 16, 1675, died in infancy; Mary, February 3, 1677, died aged six years; Elizabeth, June, 1678, married William Rogers; Asa, of whom further; Hannah, April 22, 1682; Ephraim, died in infancy; Mary (2), June, 1686; Ephraim (2), July 11, 1688, died 1710, unmarried.

(II) Asa, son of James Harris, was born in Boston, Massachusetts, November 10, 1680, died in Preston, Connecticut, August 20, 1715. He married, March 17, 1709, Elizabeth, daughter of Samuel Rogers and sister of Sarah, second wife of his brother James. Children: Asa, of whom further; Amah, born March 27, 1711, married Samuel Beebee; Ephraim, December 28, 1712; Mercy, November 14, 1714, married John Waterhouse.

(III) Asa (2), son of Asa (1) Harris, was born in Preston, Connecticut, November 27, 1709. He moved to Saybrook, Connecticut, where he was living as late as 1767, and probably died. He married (first) ———, who bore him a son Asa, of whom further. Married (second) Mary ———, by whom he had three children: May, Ely, Alpheus.

(IV) Asa (3), son of Asa (2) Harris, was born in Saybrook, Connecticut, May 21, 1737. He settled in Lebanon, Connecticut, later in Massachusetts at or near Pittsfield. He married, July 22, 1761, Faith McCall, born February 12, 1737. Children: Asa, of whom further; Hannah, born September 16, 1763; Eli, settled in Niagara county, New York, later in Terre Haute, Indiana; Ann Mercy, born March 19, 1769; James, married Polly Roach; Daniel, married Amanda Miller; John C., born December 16, 1774; Nathaniel, March 4, 1778; Levi, August 19, 1779; Polly, February 9, 1782; Rachel, December 7, 1784.

(V) Asa (4), son of Asa (3) Harris, was born in Lebanon, Connecticut, April 18, 1762, and baptized the same day. It is not sure, but the presumption is that he joined other members of the family of his father who settled in New York state. He married Elizabeth Wright and left issue.

(VI) William Asa, son of Asa (4) Harris, was born in Connecticut, about 1783. He settled in New York state and in 1823 his name appears on a list of settlers in Farmersville, Cattaraugus county, New York. He was a farmer. He was a member of the Presbyterian church as was his wife, Marjorie Harris, who was also his cousin. Children: William, died in Wisconsin; Alva, died in Wisconsin; Delpha, of whom further; Golpha, died in Wisconsin; Ira, died in Illinois; Parley, died in McKean county, Pennsylvania; Rebecca and other daughters died in Wisconsin.

(VII) Delpha, son of William Asa Harris, was born in Connecticut, 1808, died in Bradford, Pennsylvania, December 19, 1884. He learned the trade of shoemaker. In 1884 he settled in Bradford, where he continued in business until his retirement from active life. He was a member of the Methodist Episcopal church, a Republican in politics, and a man of sterling character. He married Anna Moore, born May 25, 1811, died in Bradford, April 4, 1902, youngest daughter of Asa Moore (see Moore V). She was a woman of lovable disposition, very charitable and a devoted Methodist. Children: 1. Marshall Delos, of whom further. 2. Louisa Elvira, born in Chautauqua county, New York, 1835, died December 13, 1909; she married Oscar Howe, of Cattaraugus county, killed in the civil war, a descendant of General Howe of the revolution; children: i. William, deceased. ii. Pherson, resides in Bradford, Pennsylvania. iii. Frank, resides in Marietta, Ohio. iv. Llewellyn, resides in Bradford, Pennsylvania. v. Luella, resides in Freedom, Pennsylvania. 3. Victoria Leona, born in Chautauqua county, New York, 1837; married Rev. Almond Horton, a minister of the Methodist Episcopal church, now living retired at Wellsville, Ohio; children: i. Abby, resides in Ulysses, Pennsylvania. ii. Clement, deceased. iii. Mary, deceased. iv. Arthur, resides in Wellsville. 4. Sarah, born 1839, died 1845. 5. Frederick James, born in Bradford township, McKean county, Pennsylvania, 1841; now a farmer and oil producer of Great Valley, New York; married Emily Howe; children: i. Allen, resides in Great Valley. ii. Mary, resides in Kennedy, New York. iii. Orphia, resides in Watts Valley, New York. iv. Milton, a Baptist minister at Shingle House, Pennsylvania. 6. Nancy Belma, born 1843; married James Malona, born in New York state, now engaged in the oil business at Kennedy, New York; children: i. Wilma, residing in Moosejaw, Canada. ii. Lulu, resides in Kennedy, New York. iii. Paul, resides in Youngstown, Ohio. 7. Fernando Cortez, born 1845; resides in Independence, Kansas, engaged in the oil business; married Clara Inglesby; children: i. John, resides in Independence. ii. Delpha, deceased. iii. Ruth, resides in Tacoma, Washington. iv. Alice, resides in Cœur d'Alene, Idaho. v. Leslie, resides in Pittsburgh, Pennsylvania. vi. Fernando, deceased. 8. Mary Rebecca, born June 7, 1848; married Emory Slocum, of Sagaerstown, New York, now deceased; she is now living in Buffalo, New York, but has a residence in Bradford, Pennsylvania; children: i. Carrie, deceased. ii. Harry, resides in Copan, Oklahoma.

(VIII) Marshall Delos, eldest child of Delpha Harris, was born in Frewsburg, Chautauqua county, New York, June 7, 1833. He was ten years of age when his parents moved to Bradford township, McKean county, Pennsylvania, where his education was completed in the public schools. He early became engaged in lumbering, the splendid forests of McKean county affording ample scope for his energy. He owned timber lands, which he cleared, converting the logs into lumber in his own sawmill. In 1854 he began speculating in real estate, buying and selling improved farms and timber lands. He was also for nine years employed by the Erie Railroad Company. In 1874 he engaged in the drug business in Bradford and continued successfully in that line of activity until his retirement from business in 1909. He has spent an active, useful life, and now, respected and honored, resides in his comfortable home, No. 87 High street, Bradford. He has always voted the Republican ticket, and has been a pillar of strength to his party. He has held the offices of justice of the peace, school director for many years, constable, and is now poor master. In religious belief he is a Methodist, his wife also belonging to that denomination. He is a member of Bradford Lodge, No. 334, Free and Accepted Masons.

He married, January 23, 1861, Abby Edson, born in Bridgewater, Massachusetts, May 14, 1837, daughter of Nathaniel Edson (see Edson). Children: 1. Luella Alzina, born in Limestone, New York, October 26, 1862; now a teacher in the schools of Kane, Pennsylvania. 2. Anna Dorothy, born at Bradford, Pennsylvania, January 12, 1867; married Samuel F. Neill, a draughtsman; now resides in Denver, Colorado; children: i. Dorothy, born July 21, 1897. ii. Loraine, born 1900, died in infancy. iii. Cecil Luella, born January 28, 1906. 3. Inez Abby, born in Bradford, June 10, 1873; married George F. Robinson, now in the insurance business at Wilkes-Barre, Pennsylvania. 4. Mary Elizabeth, born in Bradford, May 30, 1875; married Louis Langworthy, born January 1, 1877, in Hornellsville, New York, now an electrician of Bradford; children: i. Lawrence, born September 13, 1900, died December 12, 1906. ii. Kenneth Louis, born August 14, 1903. iii. Martha Deloris, born February 1, 1909.

(The Moore Line).

(I) Deacon John Moore, the first of the line here under consideration, landed in Massachusetts and crossed to the Connecticut river with the early settlers of Windsor, Connecticut. He married and had a son, Joseph, of whom further.

(II) Joseph, son of Deacon John Moore, married and had a son, Joseph, of whom further.

(III) Joseph (2), son of Joseph (1) Moore, was born in 1716, died May 3, 1790. He married Elizabeth Allen, born 1716, died May 10, 1790. Twelve children, among whom was Joseph, of whom further.

(IV) Joseph (3), son of Joseph (2) Moore, married (first) Margaret Kellogg, (second) Hannah Phillips. Children of first wife: Margaret, Asa, of whom further; Joseph. Children of second wife: Orpheus, Seth, Ebenezer, Abigail, Hannah, Mary, Anna.

(V) Asa, son of Joseph (3) Moore, was born June 20, 1762, died in the town of Carroll, Chautauqua county, New York. He served in the revolutionary war from July 1, 1780, to December 16, 1780, as a private in Captain Prior's company, Fifth Regiment Connecticut Line. He married, November 1, 1790, Huldah King, born 1767, died 1840. Children: Joseph K., Amanda, Asa, Roderick, Jesse, Huldah, James, David, Nancy, Frederick, Anna, married Delpha Harris (see Harris VII).

(The Edson Line).

(I) Deacon Samuel Edson, the emigrant ancestor, traced his ancestry in England to Thomas Edson, born 1480, twelve years before the discovery of America. Deacon Samuel Edson arrived at Salem, Massachusetts, in July, 1639. He was then twenty-five years of age, and was accompanied by his bride, Susanna (Orcutt) Edson, aged twenty-one years. He resided in Salem until 1651, when he moved to Bridgewater, Massachusetts. He was one of the fifty-six original proprietors of that town, and one of the earliest if not the first settlers. Besides his own original share in the town, he purchased other land and became a very large landowner and prosperous farmer. He owned two sawmills and built the first corn-mill there. The site of his mills has been continuously occupied by a mill ever since. He was most active in town affairs;

was selectman nine years; was representative to the general court and filled other important offices. He was one of the first deacons of the Bridgewater church, elected in 1664, and so continued until his death. Although not liberally educated, he was of keen intelligence, enterprising, and essentially a man of affairs. He died July 19, 1692. His wife, Susanna, had a happy disposition, modest deportment, dignified presence and graceful manners. Her education and natural abilities were said to be fully equal to his own. She died February 20, 1699. In the old burying-ground at Bridgewater the oldest monument of the kind is that standing over their graves. They had three sons and five daughters. Susanna, their oldest daughter, married Rev. James Keith, the first minister in Bridgewater.

(II) Joseph, son of Deacon Samuel Edson, married Experience Field, and among their children was Samuel, of whom further.

(III) Samuel, son of Joseph Edson, married Mehitable Brett, and among their children was Nathaniel, of whom further.

(IV) Deacon Nathaniel Edson, son of Samuel Edson, married Joanna Snow, and among their children was Nathaniel, of whom further.

(V) Nathaniel (2), son of Deacon Nathaniel (1) Edson, married Betsey Howard, and among their children was Nathaniel, of whom further.

(VI) Nathaniel (3), son of Nathaniel (2) Edson, born April 6, 1803, died June 6, 1881. He married, May 9, 1827, Dorothy Ingalls, born October 29, 1802, died April 3, 1868. Children, all born in Bridgewater, Massachusetts: 1. Dolly Ophelia, born August 29, 1828, died September 9, 1851. 2. Elizabeth, born September 27, 1829, died February 23, 1892; married Royal Baron, a farmer, and died in Erie county, New York; no children. 3. Samuel, born October 30, 1832, died the following day. 4. Adelia, born February 15, 1835; married Rev. Reuben Du Bois, of Friendship, New York, a Methodist minister; no children. 5. Abby, married Marshall Delos Harris (see Harris VIII). 6. Huldah, born October 26, 1841, died in Eldred, Pennsylvania; married Truman Bennett; children: Walter, Evie, resides in Eldred, Pennsylvania; Wellman, deceased; Dolly, deceased; Lowell, resides in the west.

Dorothy (Dolly) (Ingalls) Edson was a descendant of Henry Ingalls, "one of the twelve men who came from Lynn to Andover and bought that town for five pounds sterling and a few articles of clothing." Henry was a son of Edward and Ann Ingalls, who came from Lincolnshire, England, and settled at Lynn in 1629. The line of descent from Edward and Ann Ingalls to Dorothy is as follows: Henry (1), Henry (2), Francis, Elijah, Ezra, born April 12, 1773, died March 6, 1828, married Dolly Wilson, of Andover, born April 29, 1777. Children: 1. Dorothy (Dolly), born October 29, 1802, died April 3, 1868; married Nathaniel (3) Edson. 2. Ezra Jr., born January 7, 1804, died March 6, 1828. 3. Lucy Foster, born September 18, 1807, died August 10, 1839; married, November 28, 1826, Adoniram Whiting. 4. Wilson, born March 25, 1809. 5. Harriet, born March 12, 1814, died June 7, 1839; married, May 26, 1836, John Burrell. 6. Maria Caroline, born April 3, 1817; married, November 15, 1839, Thomas Cunningham. 7. Mary, born September 9, 1819; married April 9, 1836, Ezra Abbott.

SCHERMERHORN This family was established in the Mohawk Valley of New York state by Jacob Janse Schermerhorn, born 1622 in Waterland, Holland. Although in 1654 his father was a resident of Amsterdam, Holland, Jacob Janse died in Schenectady, New York, 1689. At an early day he settled at Beverwyck (Albany), where he became prosperous as an Indian trader and brewer. He made his will, May 20, 1688, and in it devised property worth 56,822 guilders (about $23,000). His estate was considered very large at that time and was exceeded by few except the patroons and men of high official rank. He married Jannetje Legers, daughter of Cornelius Legers Van Voorhoudt. He mentions in his will, May 20, 1688, children: Ryer, of whom further; Symon; Helena, married Myndert Hasmense Van Der Bogart; Jacob; Machledt, married Johannes Beekman; Cornelius; Jannetje, married Caspar Springstein; Neeltje, married Barent Ten Eyck; Lucas.

(II) Ryer, eldest son of Jacob Janse Schermerhorn, settled in Schenectady, New York. He was one of the five patentees named in the patent granted in 1684, and in 1700 was the sole survivor of the original owners of the township. There were about eighty thousand acres of land in the Schenectady patent, all of which, after the death of the other four patentees, came under his charge and management as trustee, except a few farms that had been granted before. This one man power became distasteful to the people, who petitioned for a new charter which should give them the power of choosing five trustees to hold office three years. The new charter was granted, but Schermerhorn paid no attention to it, nor to his newly appointed trustee. He still continued to act as sole trustee for the town in receiving rents and profits thereof and in prosecuting suits-at-law in his own name only, with out giving any account thereof; this too in spite of his suspension from office by the governor. The secret of his stubborn persistence in the duties of the trusteeship was the fact that the first patent of 1684 was still binding and he as the sole survivor of the trustees was vested with all the power and authority originally granted to the five trustees named in the first patent. The fee of the land was in him, his heirs, assigns and successors, and could only be alienated by death, or release in due form. The secured charter was amended and on May 25, 1714, he appeared before the governor and council and after a full hearing for all matters against him was suspended from "acting further as trustee of the said towne", but he continued obstinate and disregarded the demand of the new trustees for an accounting to them of his official acts. They then commenced suit against him in the court of chancery, he and his friends in turn instituting counter suits in the same court. These several suits and others continued down to the death of the second Ryer Schermerhorn in 1795, a period of nearly one hundred years, and were only settled by the New York legislature passing an act, March 26, 1797, which took all powers and duties in relation to the common lands, conferring them upon the mayor, aldermen and commonalty of Schenectady. A commission was appointed under the act which finally settled all claims and closed their accounts, August 10, 1798. In 1690 he was a member of the provincial assembly from Albany county and justice of the peace. In 1700 he was appointed assistant to the judge of the court of common pleas. He was a man of unusual ability, firm will, undaunted courage, great strength and powers of endurance. His mills on the Schuylenburg Kill, together with Farm No. 4 of Van Cuyler's "Bouwerie" was held in the family two hundred years. He made his will, April 3, 1717, and died February 19, 1719, leaving two daughters and three sons, all of whom had families.

He married, July, 1676, Ariantje Bralt, widow of Ulmer Otten, who had left a daughter Tryntije (Catherine), and also property in Holland and America. This caused special contracts and agreements at the time of her second marriage safeguarding her interests and those of her child. Children mentioned in will: Jan (John, Johannes), inherited the homestead; Catalina, married Johannes Wemp; Jannetje, married Volkert Simonse Veeder; Jacob, of whom further; Arent.

(III) Jacob, son of Ryer Schermerhorn, died July 4, 1753. He inherited "8 Morgens (16 acres) of the Hindmost Bouwery, 215½ morgens of woodland" and a lot of land in the village of Schenectady. He married, October 20, 1712, Margarita ———, died May 22, 1741, daughter of Johanna Teller, and granddaughter of William Teller, the first settler of the name in New Amsterdam, and a trader in Albany for fifty years, removing thence to New York. In 1692 he was one of the associate trustees with Ryer Schermerhorn under the famous first patent of Schenectady and the last but him to survive. Children: Ryer, Johanne, Jacobus, of whom further; William, Arent, Andries, Simon, Susanna, married John Visger.

(IV) Jacobus, son of Jacob Schermerhorn, was born January 3, 1720, died July 28, 1782. He was a farmer and owned land in different parts of the town. He married, September 4, 1762, Annatje, died September 7, 1770, daughter of Peter Vrooman. Children: Jacob, born July 21, 1763, died April 26, 1787; John (Johannes), of whom further.

(V) John (Johannes), son of Jacobus Schermerhorn, was born January 29, 1765, died January 7, 1814. He married Catharine Bratt (Bradt), born June 29, 1764, died September 13, 1817, daughter of Jacobus and Elizabeth Bratt, a descendant of Arent Andries Bratt, an early settler of Schenectady. Children: Jacob, of whom further; Elizabeth, died in childhood; Annatje, died in infancy; Eva, died in infancy; Jacobus Bratt; Annatje, married Anthony Van Slyck; Elizabeth, died in infancy; Simon, born April 23, 1802; Arent Bratt, May 4, 1804; Peter Vrooman, May 11, 1806, died May 26, 1853, married Catharine Clute.

(VI) Jacob (2), son of John (Johannes)

Schermerhorn, was born in Rotterdam, Schenectady county, New York, March 26, 1789, died there April 20, 1849. He inherited part of the old Schermerhorn estate and added to it by purchase. He was a farmer, a strong Democrat and a member of the Reformed Dutch church, as had been his ancestors. He married Maria Vedder, who died August 19, 1832, aged forty-five years. Children: John, of whom further; Simon, Catherine, Anna, Sarah, Alida.

(VII) John (2), son of Jacob (2) Schermerhorn, was born in Rotterdam, New York, 1815. He settled in Herkimer county, New York, where he spent his life engaged in farming, dying at an advanced age. He and his wife were Methodists. He married Sybill Brown, born in Herkimer county, New York, where she died. Children: George, Jacob, Lansing, John, Orville, of whom further; James. All born and spent their lives in Herkimer county.

(VIII) Orville, son of John (2) Schermerhorn, was born in Herkimer county, New York, died there in October, 1869. He was educated in the public schools, and was a farmer all his life. He was a Republican in politics, and a member of the Baptist church. He married Mary Elizabeth Harder, born at Rossie, St. Lawrence county, New York, April 24, 1842, who survives her husband, a resident of East Bradford, Pennsylvania. She is a daughter of Jacob Harder, born in St. Lawrence county, New York, 1807, died 1891. He was a stone-cutter and passed his entire life in his native county. He married Jane Ann Collins, born in Amsterdam, New York, died in St. Lawrence county. She had brothers and sisters: James Collins, deceased; William Collins, now living in Tonawanda, New York; Morgan Collins, of Dunkirk, New York; Elizabeth Collins, deceased; George Collins, died in Jersey City, New Jersey, 1910. Child of Orville Schermerhorn, Edward Edgar, of whom further.

(IX) Edward Edgar, only child of Orville and Mary Elizabeth (Harder) Schermerhorn, was born at Sprague's Corners, St. Lawrence county, New York, December 15, 1867. He was educated in the public schools of St. Lawrence, finishing at Lawrenceville Academy, of which he is a graduate. He supplemented his academic study with a course at the New York State Normal School at Potsdam, whence he was graduated, class of 1889. This qualifying him to teach in the New York public schools, he passed two or three years engaged in that profession before his graduation. After leaving normal he secured a position in a graded school in McKean county, Pennsylvania, teaching there from 1889 until 1891. In the latter year he was appointed principal of the borough school of Kendall, which borough is now included in the city of Bradford, Pennsylvania. He continued in that position until 1899, when he was appointed principal of the third ward school of Bradford, remaining there until 1908. In that year he was elected superintendent of schools for the city, a position he now fills (1912). The school system of Bradford—already an excellent one—has been placed upon a still higher plane of efficiency by Superintendent Schermerhorn, who is not only a most efficient teacher but an official of unusual executive ability. He is well known in educational circles and stands among the leaders in his profession. He is a constant student, and since graduation has systematically followed courses of study and reading, thus making his mind a storehouse of knowledge and keeping pace with modern thought, invention and discovery. He is a Republican in politics, and an attendant of the Methodist Episcopal church. He has been financier of the local lodge of the Ancient Order of United Workmen for the past ten years; is a member of Union Lodge, No. 334, Free and Accepted Masons, and of the Knights of Maccabees.

He married, July 24, 1887, Minnie Adelle Gillespie, born at Pike farm, Venango county, Pennsylvania, April 15, 1868, daughter of Robert B. Gillespie, now a resident of Sistersville, West Virginia, engaged in the production of oil. Children: 1. Vivian, born at Red Rock, Pennsylvania, May 20, 1891; married, July 1911, Owen A. Fleckenger, a teacher of manuel training in the schools of Bradford. 2. Victor E., born at Bradford, November 18, 1894, now a student in high school. 3. Dorothy B., born at Bradford, December 5, 1906.

Robert B. Gillespie first came to Pithole, Venango county, at the time of the excitement caused by the discovery of oil, and has since been engaged in oil production in various fields as discovered. He was born in New Athens, Clarion county, Ohio, November 2, 1835, married Julia Lucetta House, born in Macomb, St. Lawrence county, New York, March 21, 1840, died October 22, 1909. Their children: 1. Minnie Adelle, of previous mention. 2. Norman L., born 1870, died in 1872. 3. Frank J., born June 2, 1872, at Millerstown, Perry county, Pennsylvania; married Delpha Mason, at Hebron, West Virginia; children: Naomi, born December 5, 1903; Fred, September 23, 1905; Esther, September 30, 1906; Frank J. Gillespie is an oil well contractor in West Virginia. 4. Blanche, born in Millerstown, Pennsylvania, February 26, 1877; married Rev. Gregory Blakeley, a minister of the Methodist church, now stationed at Parsons, West Virginia; child, Gregory Jr., born September 24, 1901. John J., father of Robert B. Gillespie, was a native of Bellair, Ohio, where he died at the age of seventy-two years. He had four children, two of whom are living—John, at Woodsfield, Ohio, and Robert B., as stated. Julia Lucetta House is a daughter of Isaac House, who married Mary Tamar and died at Pope's Mills, St. Lawrence county, New York.

The name of Holbrook is HOLBROOK ancient and distinguished, and is frequently met with in England and the United States. As early as the reign of Richard II, of England one of that name was admitted to the order of Knighthood and "A chevron between three mallets" assigned as his coat-of-arms. Many Holbrooks were early in New England. The name first appears at Weymouth, Massachusetts, 1640, when Thomas Holbrook settled in that part of Weymouth called "Old Spain." His will, dated December 31, 1668, mentions wife Jane and children: Thomas, John, William, Ann, Elizabeth, Jane.

(II) Thomas (2), son of Thomas (1) Holbrook, died 1697. He resided in Scituate, Weymouth and Braintree, and was a man of wealth and influence. His wife, Joana, survived him. Children: Thomas, Mary, John, Peter.

(III) Deacon Peter Holbrook, son of Thomas (2) Holbrook, was born 1655, died May 3, 1711. He was an important man for his day. He owned lands and lived near Mendon, Massachusetts. He married (first) Alice ———, who died April 29, 1705; (second) Elizabeth Pool. Children: John, Peter, Joseph, Silvanus, Joanah, Richard, Eliphalet, William, Samuel, Mary.

(IV) Peter (2), son of Deacon Peter (1) Holbrook, was born in Mendon, Massachusetts, October 16, 1681, died at Bellingham, Massachusetts, December 24, 1728. He was a weaver by trade. He married, March 23, 1713, Hannah Pool, who survived him. Children: Peter, Isaac, Daniel, Elizabeth, Abigail, Elizabeth, Oliver, Abigail.

(V) Peter (3), son of Peter (2) Holbrook, was born at Mendon, November 26, 1713. He married Sarah ———, and lived in Bellingham, Massachusetts. Children: Stephen, Sarah, died young; Sarah, Peter, Simeon, Elizabeth, Jemina, Timothy.

(VI) Stephen, eldest son of Peter (3) Holbrook, was born April 30, 1737. He married Rachel, daughter of Walter Cook, of Mendon. Children: Sarah, Stephen, Amasa, Simeon, Peter.

(VII) Stephen (2), son of Stephen Holbrook, was born September 29, 1767. He settled in Tolland county, Connecticut. He married ——— Griggs, and had six children, including a son Stephen G.

(VIII) Dr. Stephen Griggs Holbrock, son of Stephen (2) Holbrook, was born in Tolland county, Connecticut, May 1, 1798. His parents moved to Ohio in 1800, where he was educated and prepared for the profession of medicine. He located at Kelloggsville, Ohio, where he was in the active, successful practice of his profession until death there, September 22, 1875. He was a supporter of Horace Greeley when a candidate for president on the Democratic ticket, but always was a Republican. He married (first) Charlotte Kellogg, (second) September 12, 1842, Caroline Kneeland, born at Franklin, New York, January 3, 1815, died July 13, 1875, daughter of Daniel Kneeland (see Kneeland IX). Children of first wife: 1. Celestine, now living at Ashtabula, Ohio. 2. Laura E., a resident of Cleveland, Ohio. 3. Martin, died in Boulder Colorado. Children of second wife: 4. Flora, born August 18, 1846; married, June 30, 1867, Sanford L. Fobus, deceased; she resides with her brother, Stephen A. 5. Stephen Abernathy, of whom further.

(IX) Stephen Abernathy, only son of Dr. Stephen Griggs Holbrook and his second wife, Caroline (Kneeland) Holbrook, was born at Kelloggsville, Ohio, September 7, 1851. He was educated in the public schools at Kelloggsville, finishing his studies at the State Normal School at Geneva, Ohio. He began business life as a clerk in a boot and shoe store at Painesville, Ohio, later, with his brother-in-law, engaged in the drug business in Geneva, Ohio, remaining there until 1881. During the following year he resided in Bradford, Pennsylvania, going from there to Belmont, New York, where he engaged in the manufacture of tooth picks until 1886. From that date until 1905 he was engaged in the same business in Bradford, Pennsylvania. Since the latter year he has been engaged principally in the real estate business, being trustee in several land companies in Buffalo, New York, and in two that operate in British Columbia. He is also associated with F. W. Davis (formerly president of the First National Bank of Bradford) and F. P. Shoemaker (city attorney), in the management of a tract of one hundred thousand acres of timber land in British Columbia. He is a Republican in politics, and is a member of the Methodist Episcopal church. He belongs to the Benevolent and Protective Order of Elks and the Merchants' Club of Bradford.

He married, November 15, 1876, Phœbe Ellen Chapman, born at Conneaut, Ohio, daughter of William B. Chapman, born at Cleveland, Ohio, October 8, 1826, died at Bradford, Pennsylvania, October 27, 1895. He was an attorney-at-law, and a veteran of the civil war, in which he was captain of the Twenty-ninth Regiment, Ohio Volunteer Infantry, organized at Ashtabula. He married Cynthia Olds, born July 30, 1829, who yet survives him. Children of Stephen A. Holbrook: 1. Laura Ellen, born August 13, 1879; married, June 21, 1905, William Angus Donald and resides at Olean, New York; child, Betsy, born May 15, 1907. 2. Sarah Chapman, born July 7, 1881; married, November 10, 1909, Dr. Granville Hunt Walker, of Bellevue, Pennsylvania. 3. Elizabeth Flora, born March 2, 1885; married, October 30, 1907, Homer Samuel McKay; children: Martin Holbrook, born July, 1908; Stephen, March 16, 1910. 4. Helen Cynthia, born August 9, 1886, died January 19, 1900. 5. Ruth Caroline, born August 26, 1893. 6. Dorothy Louise, born January 12, 1897. 7. Marian, born August 18, 1898.

(The Kneeland Line).

Tradition says the Kneelands were among the ancient Vikings that overran northern Europe prior to the tenth century and finally settled in Scotland. Burke in his "Landed Gentry" says: "The family of Cleland (formerly spelled Kneeland) is of great antiquity in Scotland." Anderson in his "Scottish Nation" says: "Kneeland the first of his family on record—Alexander Kneeland living in the time of Alexander III. of Scotland, married Margaret Wallace, daughter of Adam and sister of Sir Malcolm, father of Sir William Wallace." Burke says further: "William Cleland, the tenth of that ilk, eminent for his loyalty to Queen Mary, etc." Both he and his son, Captain John, were eminent in their devotion to this luckless queen. The Kneelands of America use the coat-of-arms granted Major William by Queen Mary: "A lion rampant holding a cross. Crest: A demi lion rampant holding a cross." The Clelands use the original coat-of-arms, which has probably been in the family since the days of Bruce.

The American ancestor of Caroline (Kneeland) Holbrook was a son of Captain John Kneeland, the second son of Major William Kneeland, born at Kneeland Manor, in Lanarkshire, Scotland, about 1550. He was a brave soldier and sailor and commanded several vessels, surviving shipwreck and battle to die peaceably in his own cabin and finding a sailor's grave in the sea. He was a loyal follower of Queen Mary, and inherited from his father the possessions and coat-of-arms bestowed on him by "Her most gracious Catholic Majesty" for gallant services. He married Mary Dunbar, of Dunbar Castle, a descendant of the then extinct peerage of that name, and had several children, all of whom came to America.

(III) Edward, second son of Captain John Kneeland, came to Ipswich, Massachusetts, about 1630, with his brother John. Edward Kneeland had sons: Edward and Benjamin.

(IV) Edward (2), son of Edward (1) Kneeland, was born in Ipswich, Massachusetts, 1640, died 1711. His will dated January 5, 1711, was probated in Salem, Massachusetts. He was a soldier in King Philip's war and is of frequent mention in the early records of Essex and Salem. He married Martha Fowler. Children: John, Martha, Edward, Benjamin, Lydia, Philip.

(V) Benjamin, fourth child of Edward (2) Kneeland, was born in Ipswich, Massachusetts, July 7, 1699. He removed in 1725 to Framingham, Massachusetts, later to Hebron, Connecticut, where he died February 18, 1743. He lived in other places, however, viz.: Oxford, Massachusetts, and Glastonbury, Connecticut. In 1736 he joined with his sons, Benjamin, John, Joseph and Isaac, in a petition for a new town to be made up of parts of Glastonbury, Hebron and Colchester. He married Abigail, whose surname does not appear in the records. Children: Benjamin, Abigail, Elizabeth, John,

Joseph, Ebenezer, Isaac, Deborah, Hezekiah, Edward. In his will he desired his children to live in unity and be content with their father's will, an injunction tradition says was faithfully observed.

(VI) Isaac, son of Benjamin Kneeland, was born at Hebron, Connecticut, May 15, 1716. He was a farmer of Hebron, and was one of the petitioners for the setting off of the new town of Marlboro. He married (first) November 8, 1738, Sarah Beach. She died March 7, 1741. Married (second) November 12, 1742, Content Rowley, a sister of Sarah Rowley, and a "Mayflower" descendant. Three of the sons of Isaac Kneeland, Benjamin, Isaac and Jesse, served in the revolutionary war. Content, second child of John and Deborah (Fuller) Rowley, was born at East Haddam, March 26, 1719. She was a daughter of John Fuller, born about 1655, son of Samuel and Jane (Lathrop) Fuller. Samuel Fuller came over in the "Mayflower" with his father, Edward Fuller, and uncle, Dr. Samuel Fuller. He was married April 8, 1635, by Captain Miles Standish, to Jane, daughter of Rev. John Lathrop, the famous minister of London, England, and of New England. Child of Isaac Kneeland by first wife: Isaac. By second wife: Content, Sarah, Benjamin, Joseph, David, Mindwell, Jesse, Ellis.

(VII) Joseph, fifth child of Isaac Kneeland, was born at Hebron, Connecticut, August 13, 1749, died September 7, 1799. He was a wealthy farmer, and gave his children a liberal education for that day. He married, November 5, 1772, Ruth Pratt, born in Colchester, Connecticut, March 25, 1754. Children: 1. Ruth, married her cousin, James Loveland, and resided in Franklin, Pennsylvania. 2. Molly, married and moved to Ohio. 3. Joseph, a successful farmer of Marlboro, Connecticut; married (first) Elizabeth Eels, (second) Dolly Crocker. 4. Benjamin, born at Hebron, died at Franklin, New York. 5. Daniel, of whom further. 6. Sophia, born at Hebron, December 15, 1782. 7. Eunice, married Jedediah Elderkin and settled in western New York. 8. Denice. 9. Sally, married Nelson Elderkin and lived in Franklin, New York. 10. Denice (2), married Elizah Crocker, of LeRoy, New York. 11. Moses, married Mary Alden and settled in the State of Mississippi, where he died.

(VIII) Daniel, son of Joseph Kneeland, was born in Hebron, Connecticut, March 2, 1781, died at Franklin, New York, May 28, 1842. In the spring of 1802 he settled at Franklin, Delaware county, New York, with his brother Benjamin; took up two hundred acres of land, part of which they cleared and erected thereon a log cabin. After this much had been accomplished, Benjamin sent Daniel back to Marlboro to bring back Benjamin's promised bride, while he remained behind to prepare the cabin for her coming. Late in the autumn, after a tedious journey, much of the way marked only by blazed trees, they arrived at the forest home, but no welcome awaited them, as Benjamin was dead. Grace Williams, the bride-elect, seems to have found equal favor in Daniel's eyes for they were at once married, October 23, 1803, and lived out their joint lives on the forest homestead, which Daniel cleared and made one of the best farms in the country. He died May 28, 1842, Grace, his wife, October 24, 1845. Children: 1. Sophia, born September 29, 1804; married Arastarkus Mann, of Owego, New York. 2. Dr. Daniel, born December 22, 1805; graduate of Cleveland (Ohio) Medical College; practiced at Penn Line, Crawford county, Pennsylvania, until 1855, when he settled at Conneaut, Ohio, where he had a large practice until his death; married (first) Susan Vaughn, (second) Olive A. Brown. 3. Benjamin, born November 13, 1807; married Minerva N. Hine and lived on the old Franklin homestead farm. 4. Williams, born April 29, 1809; married Phœbe Kellogg. 5. Anna H., born February 5, 1811; married a Mr. Armstrong and moved to Canada. 6. Caroline, of whom further. 7. Dr. Isaac, born August 26, 1821; graduate of medicine, practiced at Berea, Ohio, until 1857, when he moved to Charlton, Iowa, where he was in good practice for twenty years; he was a great student and reader, being it is said the best informed botanist in western Iowa; later he moved to Burr Oak, Kansas, where he died in March, 1886; he married (first) Eliza S. Proctor, a descendant of John Alden and Miles Standish, (second) her sister, Susannah Church Proctor. 8. Grace Melissa, born December 7, 1826, died unmarried.

(IX) Caroline, sixth child of Daniel and Grace (Williams) Kneeland, was born in Franklin, Delaware county, New York, January 3, 1815, died at Kelloggsville, Ohio, July 13, 1875. She married Dr. Stephen G. Holbrook (see Holbrook VIII).

DURFEY The Durfey family herein recorded spring from the Rhode Island family of Durfee. The first of record was Thomas, born 1643, died 1712. He was of Portsmouth, Rhode Island, 1664, constable, 1687-88, licensed to run the ferry between Rhode Island and Bristol. August 2, 1698. In his will proved July 14, 1712, he devised lands, money and a negro slave named Jack. He married (first) —— ——, (second) Deliverance, widow of Abiel Tripp. His children: Robert, married Mary Sanford; Richard, married Ann Almy; Thomas, married Ann Freeborn; William, married (first) Ann ——, (second) Mary ——; Ann, married William Potter; Benjamin, of whom further; Patience, married, September 23, 1708. Benjamin Tallman; Deliverance.

(II) Benjamin, son of Thomas and Deliverance Durfee, was born 1680, died January 6, 1754. He married Prudence Earl, born in Portsmouth, Rhode Island, 1681, died in Westport, Massachusetts, March 12, 1733, daughter of William Earl and granddaughter of Ralph Earl, the emigrant ancestor of the Earles of Groton, Connecticut. They lived in Tiverton and Newport, Rhode Island. Children: James, born August 28, 1701; Ann, January 11, 1703; Pope, January 7, 1705; William, December 5, 1707; Benjamin, January 5, 1709; Mary, January 30, 1711; Susanna, January 28, 1713; Martha, July 15, 1710; Thomas, of whom further.

(III) Thomas (2) Durfey, youngest son of Benjamin Durfee, was born in Rhode Island, November 5, 1721. He married Abigail ——. Among his children was a son Joseph, of whom further. With this generation the family appears in Connecticut, and the name seems to be written both Durfee and Durfey.

(IV) Joseph, son of Thomas (2) Durfey, was born in Connecticut. He married Lucy Barnes, of Preston, later of Griswold, Connecticut. He is buried with wife and mother in the cemetery two miles from Jewett City, Connecticut. Children: Alice, married Joseph Latham; Joseph, married (first) —— ——, (second) Lucy Burnham, children: John B.; Charles H.; Benjamin, of whom further; four daughters.

(V) Benjamin (2), son of Joseph Durfey, was born in Connecticut, 1804, died May, 1876, at Greenville, New London county, Connecticut, now a part of the city of Norwich. He spent most of his life in New London county, which he represented in the state legislature. He was a close, personal friend of Governor Buckingham, of Connecticut, and was influential in public affairs. He was a manufacturer and in charge of a plant in New London county, operated by water power. After the formation of the Republican party he was affiliated with that organization, having previously been a Whig. He married (first) Ardelia Avery, (second) Harmony Kingsley, born in Brooklyn, Connecticut, January 14, 1817, died in Norwich, Connecticut, March 28, 1892, daughter of Jabez and Dolly (Averill) Kingsley (see Kingsley). Children of first marriage: 1. Joseph Prentice, died in Brooklyn, New York; married Lucretia Thorp; their only child, William, now engaged in the jewelry business in Brooklyn, New York. 2. Henry M., deceased; was a veteran of the civil war; he married Lucy A. Grey and had Harry, born 1868, and Lucy, 1872, both now residing in Norwich, Connecticut. Children of second marriage: 3. Charles Averill, of whom further. 4. Susan Kingsley, born 1839, became the second wife of Edward Luce and resides at Niantic, Connecticut. 5. Edward, married Louise ——, and resides in Brooklyn, New York. 6. Frank B., married Margaret Foster and both died in Norwich. 7. James Walter, born 1852, died in Palestine, Texas, where he was manager of the International Hotel. These children were all born in Norwich and are all deceased except Edward, of Brooklyn, and Susan K. Luce, of Niantic, Connecticut.

(VI) Charles Averill, son of Benjamin (2) Durfey, was born in Norwich, Connecticut, April 19, 1836, died May, 1896. He was educated in the Norwich schools, and later learned the trade of blacksmith. During the civil war he was employed in the manufacture of firearms by the government in the armory at Springfield, Massachusetts. In 1865 he came to western Pennsylvania as superintendent of the Prescott and Seymour Oil Companies, making his headquarters in Venango county for twelve years. He then changed his field of operations to McKean county, settling in Bradford, where he resided until his death. He acquired personal oil and real estate interests that are now owned and under the management of his son, Frank E. Durfey. In 1877 Mr. Durfey was appointed state oil inspector, a position he held until his death. He built the Durfey block in Bradford, and otherwise aided in the upbuilding of that city. He was a Democrat and served in the Bradford city council and on the school board. He was a deacon of the Congregational church, of which his wife was also a member. He married, in 1864, Elizabeth V. Bowles, who died in 1872, aged twenty-three years. She was a daughter of William and Elizabeth (Moore) Bowles, and granddaughter of Thomas and Elizabeth Bowles, of Worcester, Massachusetts. Children: 1. Frank Edward, of whom further. 2. Gertrude S., born August 20, 1872, at Titusville, Pennsylvania; married (first) in 1893, Charles Rudd; no issue; married (second) in 1901, John G. Hart, of New York City; no issue; she died May 19, 1905.

(VII) Frank Edward, only son of Charles Averill Durfey, was born at Miller farm between Oil City and Titusville, Venango county, Pennsylvania, March 20, 1869. He lost his mother when he was but three years of age, and was reared under the kindly care of his paternal grandparents. He was educated at Norwich, Connecticut, and is a graduate of the high school of that city, class of 1886, later for one year attending Norwich Free Academy. He began business life with the Standard Oil Company at Lima, Ohio. From there he went to Cygnet, Ohio, and Whiting, Indiana, engaged in the construction of oil tanks for the company. He left Whiting in 1892 and came to Bradford, entering the employ of the Erie Railroad Company as fireman, continuing until the death of his father in 1896. Since then he has been in charge of the extensive oil and real estate interests which he inherited. He is a Democrat and for four years was a member of Bradford select council and now is a member of the board of water commissioners. He is past master of the local lodge, Brotherhood of Locomotive Firemen, having previously filled every subordinate office. His clubs are the Bradford, Edgewood and Gun, all of Bradford. In religious faith he is a Congregationalist.

(The Kingsley Line).

Harmony (Kingsley) Durfey was a descendant of John Kingsley, born in Hampshire, England, who descended from Randulphus de Kyngesleigh, of Chester, England, 1120. Arms: "Vert a cross engrailed ermine." Crest; "In a ducal coronet gules a goat's head argent." John Kingsley, (also Kyngesley and Kinsley) according to Savage, was of "Dorchester, Massachusetts, 1635, came probably with some friends of Mather, and was here before him. At any rate was one of the seven pillars on formation of the new church for him, August 23, 1636, and was the last survivor. He removed to Rehoboth after 1648, when he was in office and in 1658, there lived and suffered the Indian hostilities, in which in a letter of supplication for relief under date of May 5, 1676, a most sad picture is given (see Trumbull Colonial Records, vol. ii, p. 445). His will of November 2, 1677, mentions only three children: Edward, Enos and Freedom." A John Kingsley (supposedly the same John) died in Rehoboth, January 6, 1678, and Mary his wife on the 14th of the same month, 1673. They had besides the children mentioned in the will; Eldad, born 1638; Renewal, born March 19, 1644. Another daughter married John French, of Northampton, and perhaps another married Timothy Jones, from Massachusetts. A branch of the family settled in Connecticut, where Jabez, of the fifth generation, served in the war of the revolution. He resided in Canterbury, Connecticut. In 1832 his name is borne on the revolutionary pension rolls as residing in Windham county, Connecticut. He married Dolly Averill, of Griswold, Connecticut. After their marriage they resided in Brooklyn, Connecticut, where Harmony Kingsley, their daughter, was born January 14, 1817, died March 28, 1892. Harmony Kingsley became the second wife of Benjamin Durfey (see Durfey V).

EBY-CALDWELL The Eby family trace descent to Theodore Eby, who emigrated from the "Pflaz," in Germany, in the year 1717, settling in Lancaster county, Pennsylvania.

(II) Christian, son of Theodore Eby, married Elizabeth Meyer, and died September 15, 1756. His wife died December 12, 1787. Children of Christian and Elizabeth Eby: Christian, born February 22, 1734, died September 14, 1807; John, September 28, 1737; Barbara, December 14, 1740, married Jacob Hershey; Peter, November 11, 1742; Anna, January 4, 1745, married Christian Stauffer; Andrew, January 11, 1747; George, December 11, 1748; Elizabeth, August 12, 1751; Samuel, of whom further; Michael, December 29, 1755.

(III) Samuel, son of Christian and Elizabeth (Meyer) Eby, was born in Lancaster county, Pennsylvania, December 20, 1752. He grew to manhood in his native county, then migrated to the then far west, becoming a pioneer settler of Stark county, Ohio, where his after life was spent engaged in farming and in ministerial work. He was a duly licensed preacher of the German Baptist church, and like the preachers of that denomination received no salary but preached for the love of souls and a sense of duty. He cultivated his own acres and prospered in all his doings. He was twice married, having eighteen children, nine by first wife, namely: 1. Samuel, of whom further. 2. Daniel, a farmer, died in Bristol, Elkhart county, Indiana; married Esther Shellenbarger, of St. Joseph county, Michigan; children: Adeline, resides in Rochester, Indiana; Elias, deceased; Octavia, deceased; Owen; Olivia; James, resides in California. 3. Michael, a farmer of Wabash county, Indiana, until his death; married Susan ——, 4. Mary, died at Elkhart, Indiana; married Peter Frank, a farmer of Elkhart until death; children: Joseph, deceased; David, now living in Grand Rapids, Michigan, married and has a son Frank, also a daughter. 5. Peter, died in Cass county, Michigan, where he was engaged in farming; he left a wife Margaret, also children: Peter and Cassius, both living in Cass county. 6. Gabriel, died in Cass county, Michigan, where he was engaged in distilling; he married, in Ohio, Caroline Wagner; children: David, Daniel, Samuel, Christian, Catherine, William and several others. 7. David, died in Bristol, Indiana, where he followed his trade of carpenter; he married Catherine Shellenbarger; children: Rachel, Elias, James and Amanda. 8. Joseph, died in Ohio, a farmer; his wife Margaret survived him as did children: Sarah, Mary, Sidney and another. 9. John, died in Ohio at age of nineteen years, having been an invalid all his life.

(IV) Samuel (2), eldest son and child of Samuel (1) Eby, was born at Canton, Stark county, Ohio, March 30, 1807, died in Elkhart county, Indiana, April 15, 1880. He grew to manhood amid the surroundings of Ohio pioneer days and received a limited education in the public subscription schools. He remained with his father caring for the home farm until his majority, then after his marriage and birth of one child, moved to Elkhart county, Indiana, where he purchased land and was a prosperous farmer until his death. He was a Whig in politics until the birth of the Republican party, which he ever afterward supported by vote and influence. He served as school director, assessor and in other township offices. In religious faith he was a Presbyterian, his wife also being of that faith. He married Elizabeth Kirstetter, born in Northumberland county, Pennsylvania, October 20, 1810, died in Elkhart county, Indiana, December 27, 1881. Children of Samuel and Elizabeth Eby: 1. Caroline, born in Stark county, Ohio, August 4, 1836; married Jesse Meyers, born in Pennsylvania, died in Waverly, Iowa, in 1903, a farmer; children: i. Ann Elizabeth, born 1859, died young; ii. Delilah Catherine, born 1861, died 1901, married William Hursh, in Waverly, Iowa, where he now resides, a farmer; iii. Samuel, born 1863, resides in Colorado, unmarried; iv. Benjamin, born 1865, resides in Waverly; v. Rhoda, born 1867, married William Waterman, a farmer of Waverly; vi. Margaret, born 1869, died 1889, unmarried; vii. Jesse, born 1871, now a farmer of Waverly; viii. Edmund, born 1873, married and a farmer of Waverly. 2. William, born in Elkhart county, Indiana (the birthplace of all his younger brothers and sisters), November 16, 1838, died 1880, a farmer; he married Mary Holmes, born in Pennsylvania; children: Samuel, born 1862; William, 1864; Charlotte, 1865; Benjamin, 1867; George, 1869. 3. Delilah, of whom further. 4. Elizabeth, born January 20, 1842; married James Hass (or Hess), born in Pennsylvania, now a farmer and proprietor of a summer boarding resort at Waloon, on Lake Michigan; child, Alfred, born 1872, unmarried. 6. Samuel, born March 3, 1846, died in his native county in 1877, a farmer; he married Sarah Boyd, born in Pennsylvania; child, Lewis, born 1872. 7. Edmund, born November 24, 1848; married Rhoda Mitchell; child, Frederick, born 1876. 8. Harrison, born January 27, 1850, died in his native county in 1881, a farmer; he married Elizabeth Carrick, born in Michigan, who survives him, residing in Illinois; children: Ada, deceased, and Carson, living in Colorado. 9. Mary Ellen, born March 3, 1852; married Daniel Franks, a teamster, born in Indiana, died in California; children: i. Grace, married —— ——, has two children and lives in Goshen, Indiana; ii. Jessie, married Clark Rice and lives in Elkhart, Indiana; iii. Robert, lives in Goshen, Indiana; iv. Catherine, married James Matthews; v. Ralph, living in Ligonier, Indiana.

The father of Elizabeth (Kirstetter) Eby

died in Stark county, Ohio; her mother, Elizabeth, born 1792, died 1847, in Elkhart county, Indiana. Their children were: 1. Elizabeth, of previous mention, wife of Samuel Eby. 2. Peter, born 1812, died in Goshen, Indiana; a traveling commercial salesman; married Mary Rogers; children: James, deceased; Edmund, living in Elkhart, Indiana; Chauncey, deceased. 3. Jacob, born 1814, died in Kansas City, Missouri, leaving wife and family. 4. George, born 1816, died in Kansas, where he was a farmer for many years; he married Jemima Thompson; children: Joseph, Daniel W., Elizabeth, Lewis, Lydia, George R., Franklin P., Delilah J. and Ellen. 5. Benjamin, born 1818, was killed in a steamboat explosion on the Mississippi river during the civil war; he enlisted from Indiana. 6. Lydia, born 1820, died in Stark county, Ohio, leaving husband and family. 7. Eliza, born 1822, died in Ohio, married and had issue.

(V) Delilah, third child and second daughter of Samuel (2) and Elizabeth (Kirstetter) Eby, was born in Elkhart county, Indiana, at the village of Vistula, February 29, 1840. She was educated in the public school and until her marriage resided at home. Since becoming a widow she has continued her residence at Bradford, Pennsylvania. She is a member of the Presbyterian church and a lady of womanly grace and gentle, kindly manner. She is highly regarded and with her daughter and son is happily passing her declining years. She married, March 14, 1861, Robert R. Caldwell, born in St. Joseph county, Michigan, November 29, 1837, died in Bradford, Pennsylvania, February 16, 1908, son of William Caldwell, born in Pennsylvania, settled in Elkhart county, Indiana, died in Bristol, Indiana, November 22, 1877, a farmer. He married Sarah Wilson, born in Pennsylvania, died in Elkhart county in 1847. Children of William Caldwell: 1. Robert R., of whom further. 2. David, born 1839, enlisted in the Eleventh Regiment Indiana Volunteers, and died while in the army during the civil war. 3. Ann Elizabeth, born 1841, married, December 29, 1863, Lewis Emery, born at Cherry Creek, Chautauqua county, New York, August 10, 1839, now living in Bradford, having large oil interests; children: Delevan, born September 26, 1867; Grace Elizabeth, January 27, 1874; Earle Caldwell, December 12, 1875; Lewis (2), August 27, 1878. 4. Sarah G., born September, 1842; married Lewis E. Hampsher, born December 31, 1843, a prominent oil producer, now deceased.

Robert R. Caldwell was educated in the public school of Elkhart county, Indiana, became a farmer, continuing in that county until 1881. He then moved to Bradford, Pennsylvania, where he became a successful oil producer. He was a Republican in politics, an attendant of the Presbyterian church, and a man highly regarded by all. Children of Robert R. and Delilah (Eby) Caldwell, all born in Elkhart county, Indiana: 1. Sarah Elizabeth, born February 4, 1862, died November 22, 1866. 2. Margaret, born June 3, 1865, now with her mother in Bradford, a loving, cherished companion; she is a member of the Presbyterian church and interested in many good works. 3. Edmund Robert, born November 22, 1868, now proprietor of a machine shop and foundry in Bradford; he is unmarried and resides at home.

AUERHAIM This is an old German family name and has a somewhat peculiar origin. It was first spelled Auerhann, named from a bird which inhabits the Black Forest of Germany, called the "Capercaillie" or "Auerhann." The family might have taken its name from an ancestor being an unusually successful hunter of this winged denizen of the forest or it might have become entangled in the family traditions in some other way.

(I) The family home for the last three generations has been in Province of Posen, Prussia, Germany, where Grandfather Auerhaim conducted a grain business and also a hotel. He was a staid, sober-minded gentleman, living a simple, pious life, and, with his wife, belonged to the Synagogue, which received his sincere and hearty support. His racial characteristics of industry and thrift have descended to his posterity and this accounts in great measure for their successful business careers. He married and had issue: 1. Moses M., of whom further. 2. Lena, married ———— Goldstecker, a storekeeper of Posen, Prussia. 3. Teressa, married and had two children: Celia and Dora, both of whom died in California.

(II) Moses Mordecai, son of Grandfather Auerhaim, was born in Kozmin, Province of Posen, Prussia, in 1811, and died there April 12, 1856. He obtained his education in the public schools of his native village and later in life followed the business of merchant, having a large and lucrative trade. With his wife he was a member of the Orthodox Synagogue. He was twice married, his first wife Sarah, born 1814, died in Prussia, December 25, 1850, daughter of Jacob Aerlich, a hotel proprietor of Kozmin, where he died. Children of first marriage, all born in Kozmin, R. B. Posen, Prussia, Germany: 1. Solomon, of whom further. 2. Lena, born May 6, 1840, married Louis Moses, a cigar manufacturer of her native village, who died in Cincinnati, Ohio; she is living in Buffalo; children: Marcus, Selma, Isadore, Augusta, living in Buffalo; Clara, married Albert Strauss and lives in Erie, Pennsylvania; Bertha, Frances, Samuel, Mamie and Teressa, also living in Buffalo. 3. Amelia, born 1842, married Morris Herron, of Poland, who died in Bradford, Pennsylvania; she now lives at Poughkeepsie, New York; children, all living at Poughkeepsie, New York: Bertha, Mollie, married George Cohen, in the motion photography business, has a child, Harold; Frances. 4. Yeta, born 1844, married ———— Michaelski, of Poland, now a retired business man of Buffalo; children: Sarah, married a produce dealer and lives in Buffalo; Marcus, married and is in the shoe business in Buffalo; Joseph, manager of the Regal shoe stores in New York City, married and has one child; Samuel, proprietor of a shoe store in Buffalo: Frances, married ———— ————, a bookkeeper, and lives in Buffalo; Clara, a bookkeeper in Buffalo. 5. Bernard, born 1846, married Celia Basch; he emigrated to America, but returned to his native country and now lives in the Hartz Mountains, where he is a merchant. Children of Moses M. Auerhaim by second marriage: 6. Louise, lives in Hamburg, Germany. 7. Leopold, lives in Posen, Prussia, Germany.

(III) Solomon, son of Moses Mordecai and Sarah (Aerlich) Auerhaim, was born in Kozmin, R. B. Posen, Prussia, Germany, November 27, 1838, died in Bradford, Pennsylvania, December 27, 1911. His boyhood days were spent and his education received in his native village. Leaving school he entered the dry goods business, beginning at the very bottom and laying deep, sure and strong the foundation on which he was to erect his future business career. In 1855 he came to the United States, settling in New York City, and engaged in cigar manufacturing until 1864, when he moved to Petroleum Center, establishing there in the dry goods business. He conducted this same line of business in Oil City and Erie, Pennsylvania, coming to Bradford in 1881 and opening a store on Main street. The business of which he was the founder has grown until it now occupies four floors of the New Auerhaim building, which he erected. This building is a fine fireproof structure with modern equipment, including one of Bradford's few elevators. It is a splendid monument to the memory of a sincerely mourned citizen, who through his perseverance, industry and untiring zeal, built up a large and substantial business at a time when the oil craze was the principal business interest of the section. He was a devoted member of the Reformed Synagogue, Temple Beth Zion, and his fraternal order was the Independent Order of Odd Fellows.

He married, in Brooklyn, New York, March 23, 1862, Fannie Kuntz, born in Dobrzyca, R. B. Posen, Prussia, Germany, July 4, 1843, daughter of Joseph Kuntz, a baker, born in Rushkoff, Prussia, died in Dobrzyca, January 15, 1877, and Leah (Simon) Kuntz, born in 1804, in Dobrzyca, where she died July 19, 1887. Simon Simon, the father of Leah Simon, lived to attain the wonderfully great age of one hundred and sixteen years, and received recognition from the Royal Court of Prussia in the shape of a congratulatory medal from the king. Children of Joseph and Leah (Simon) Kuntz, all born in Dobrzyca: 1. Esther, born 1824, died in New York City; married Abraham Galla, deceased, a rabbi of the Orthodox Synagogue; children: Isadore, a musician of New York City; Jacob, a clothier in New York City; one child, deceased. 2. Samuel, born 1826, an orchestra leader, died in Chicago, Illinois, November 17, 1889; he changed his name to Frankenstein, married and had issue: Isadore, a merchant tailor of Chicago, Illinois; Esther, lives in Reading, Pennsylvania; Samuel, lives in San Francisco, California. 3. Celia, born 1834, died in New York City, January 6, 1903; married Samuel Lobel, a retired merchant from Kozmin, R. B. Posen, Prussia, Germany; children: Eli, deceased; Isadore, Abraham, Lazarus, Ida, Henry, Joseph, Jacob, Teressa, deceased; all lived in New York City. 4. Fannie, of previous mention. 5. Simon, a merchant tailor, born October, 1844, died in Chicago, Illinois, January 10, 1905; he also changed his name to Frankenstein, married Rachel Phillips, living in San Francisco, California; children: Victor, a physician of Chicago; Rudolph, a lawyer of Chicago; Samuel, a salesman; Harry, a salesman; Ida, lives in San Francisco. 6. Hannah, born 1847, married Samuel Michael, retired and lives at McKeesport, Pennsylvania; children, all living in McKeesport: Joseph, Samuel, Rufus, Ida and Esther. 7. Adelaide, born 1849, lives in New York City. 8. Bertha, born 1853, died in Chicago, Illinois, 1910; married Jacob Bosky, engaged in the cloth dyeing business at Chicago, Illinois, and had five children. Children of Solomon and Fannie (Kuntz) Auerhaim: 1. Selma, born in New York City, September, 1863, married, March 11, 1890, Aaron Goodman, who died at Niagara Falls, New York, June, 1911; he was a merchant tailor at Niagara, where his widow now lives; child, Leona, born March 23, 1894. 2. Ida, born in New York City, September 3, 1865, married, February 27, 1884, in Bradford, Pennsylvania, Lewis Goldstein, a shoe merchant of Buffalo, where he died May 7, 1899; children: Stella E., born in Bradford, Pennsylvania, November 30, 1884, married, April 4, 1909, Irwin Cohen, a surgical chiropodist; Harry, born in Bradford, Pennsylvania, March 30, 1886, died 1887; Joseph H., born in Buffalo, New York, August 6, 1888, graduate of Bradford high school and Dickenson Law School, resides in Buffalo, New York, a lawyer; Harold C., born in Buffalo, New York, January 5, 1892; he is a graduate of Bradford high school. 3. Bertha, born in Petroleum Center, Pennsylvania, November 1, 1866, married, February 4, 1890, Abraham Cohen, a merchant of Kane, Pennsylvania; children: Leona, born November 10, 1891; Florence, born February, 1901; Hyman Joseph, born February 18, 1907. 4. Emma, born in Petroleum Center, Pennsylvania, August 25, 1867, married, at Bradford, Pennsylvania, March 17, 1891, Isadore Sobel, postmaster at Erie, Pennsylvania; children: Jeffrey, born January 22, 1893; Norman, born February 15, 1899; Sidney, born November 27, 1902; Samuel, died in infancy. 5. Clara, born Petroleum Center, Pennsylvania, August 8, 1872, married, at Bradford, Pennsylvania, November 6, 1894, Lewis Leopold, a clothier at Lock Haven, Pennsylvania; child, Raymond, deceased. 6. Martin Moses, born in Erie, Pennsylvania, August 11, 1874, died September 27, 1878. 7. Joseph, born in Oil City, Pennsylvania, September 18, 1876, died in Bradford,

October 10, 1881. 8. Samuel, born in Oil City, Pennsylvania, November 23, 1878, obtained his education in the public schools and is a graduate of Bradford high school and Bryant & Stratton College; he now conducts the business inherited from his father; he has attained high honors as a Mason, holding the thirty-second degree, and has been past high priest of Bradford Chapter, No. 260, and past illustrious grand master of Bradford Council, No. 43; his other fraternal order is the Benevolent and Protective Order of Elks, Bradford Lodge, No. 234, and he also belongs to Zem Zem Shrine, Erie, Pennsylvania, Consistory of Coudersport, Pennsylvania, and the Bradford Club. 9. Moses M., born May 6, 1881, graduate of Bradford high school and Penn State College; he is conducting in partnership with his brother, the business of his father; his club is the Merchants' Club of Bradford, and he is a member of the Masonic order, in which he holds the thirty-second degree, and the Benevolent and Protective Order of Elks, Bradford Lodge, No. 234.

FREDERICK The Fredericks of Bradford, Pennsylvania, descend from an ancient family of Germany, who may be traced to a remote period. The progenitor of the branch herein traced was Leonard Frederick, born in Germany in 1810, died at Millerstown, Pennsylvania, 1891. He came to the United States, settled at Millerstown on a farm and spent the remainder of his life there; he married, in Germany, Elizabeth ———, born 1814, died 1889, at Millerstown. They were both German Lutherans and thrifty industrious people. Children: 1. John, of whom further. 2. George, born in Germany, now a farmer of Butler county, Pennsylvania; he married Lavinia Shackley, died 1907. 3. Catherine, married Henry Swaitz, whom she survives, a resident of Olean, New York, with her children. 4. Mary, married George Arnold, also deceased. 5. Elizabeth, married Charles Diver, deceased; she is living at Chicora, Pennsylvania. 6. Adam, died at Harmony, Butler county, where he followed his trade of shoemaker; he married Hannah Aldinger, who survives him, a resident of Chicora. 7. Philip, died at Harmony, Pennsylvania, a shoemaker; he married Roxanna Hemphill, now living in Chicora. 8. Christina, died in Millerstown; she married Charles Oesterling, now a farmer of Chicora. 9. Henry; a farmer; his widow is yet living in Butler county.

(II) John, son of Leonard Frederick, was born in Germany in 1833, died in July, 1902. He was educated in his native land and served five years in the German army. He came to the United States in 1854 and settled at Millerstown, Butler county, Pennsylvania, where he followed his trade of shoemaker. He enlisted in 1861 in Company I, Seventy-fourth Regiment Pennsylvania Volunteer Infantry, serving three years and six months; he was engaged with his regiment in the first battle of Bull Run, Antietam, the Wilderness, Chancellorsville, Gettysburg (where he lost a thumb), the battles of the Shenandoah campaign and many others. After the war he returned to Millerstown, where he died; he was a good soldier and an honorable citizen; he was a Republican, and a member of the German Lutheran church. He married Elizabeth Hemphill, born April 8, 1836, died December 23, 1911, daughter of Samuel Hemphill, born in Scotland, came to the United States, settled at Millerstown, Butler county, where he engaged in farming and died. He married Susanna Stewart, born in Scotland, died in Millerstown. Children of John Frederick, all born in Millerstown: 1. John H., of whom further. 2. Adam, born 1863, now a resident of Pleasantville, Venango county, Pennsylvania; married and has four children. 3. Charles C., born 1868, now an oil-well worker living at Oil City, Pennsylvania; married and has two children. 4. Susan, now residing at Normansville, Clarion county, Pennsylvania, unmarried.

(III) John H., son of John Frederick, was born in Millerstown, now Chicora, Butler county, Pennsylvania, March 23, 1858. He was educated in the public school, and after finishing his years of study began following the oil fields of Butler and McKean counties. He finally in 1881 made permanent settlement in Bradford, where he now holds the important position of superintendent of the South Penn Oil Company; he is an Independent in politics, and a member of the German Lutheran church. He is a member of Bradford Lodge, No. 334, Free and Accepted Masons; Chapter No. 260, Royal Arch Masons; Council No. 43, Royal and Select Masters; Commandery No 58, Knights Templar; Zem Zem Shrine (Erie); Nobles of the Mystic Shrine; Tent No. 4,

Knights of the Macabees, and Lodge No. 411, Independent Order of Odd Fellows.

He married, February 20, 1878, Sarah A. Carnahan, born on the home farm near Old Stone House, Butler county, Pennsylvania, November 28, 1860, but spent her early years and attended school in Kittanning, Armstrong county, daughter of Thomas Carnahan, and granddaughter of Alexander Carnahan, whose father came from Ireland. Children of John H. and Sarah A. (Carnahan) Frederick: 1. Mary Magdalene, born June 15, 1879, died September 6, 1879. 2. Elizabeth Ann, twin of Mary M., died September 8, 1879. 3. Charles Thomas, born in Millerstown, Pennsylvania, August 14, 1880, now a foreman in the employ of the South Penn Oil Company and resides in Ormsby, McKean county; he married, March 2, 1902, Violet Gee; children: Helen Sadie, born in Degolia, Pennsylvania, June 27, 1903; Clifford Hey, born in Ormsby, November 29, 1906; John Leonard, born in Ormsby, September 22, 1909. 4. Ethel, born at Millerstown, August 16, 1881; married Thomas Frederick Duck, born in Southern Pennsylvania, April 14, 1875, now a foreman for the South Penn Oil Company, residing at Degolia; child, Anna Elizabeth May, born in Bradford, March 20, 1907.

(The Carnahan Line).

(I) Alexander Carnahan was born 1806, died near Muddy Creek, Pennsylvania, November, 1858. He was a stone mason and followed that trade all his active years. He married Elizabeth Anderson, born near Muddy Creek in 1811, died 1857. Ten children: 1. Washington, died in Butler, Pennsylvania, and followed the trade of his father, stone mason; he married Melissa Davis, who died in Kittanning; children: Josephine, Elizabeth, Prush, Margaret, Abigail, Samuel and Thomas. 2. Thomas, of whom further. 3. Mary, deceased; married John Moore, of Tatentum, Pennsylvania. 4. Samuel, deceased; was a stone mason and resided in Butler county, Pennsylvania; he married Margaret Mangel, born in France; children: Mary, Joseph, Catherine, Adalaide, Arthur and Claude. 5. Phoebe, deceased; married Joseph Tait, at one time a wholesale liquor dealer of Bradford, now deceased, no issue. 6. Nancy, died in Colorado; married (first) George Hagen, (second) Joseph Sanderville from Mexico;

children: David, by first husband and Julia by second husband, now living in California. 7. Betty, born in Millerstown, Pennsylvania; married Prush Double, a farmer; children: Zephenia, Mary, Sarah, James, Thomas, Ella, Arthur and Anna. 8. Catherine, now residing at Millerstown, Pennsylvania, unmarried. 9. Sarah, married and lives on a farm near Petersburg; has children. 10. James, a stone mason, now living at Parker's Landing, Pennsylvania; married Julia Naukler; children: Rose, Ella and Frederick.

(II) Thomas, second son of Alexander Carnahan, was born in Westmoreland county, Pennsylvania, March 4, 1833, died in Seattle, Washington, December 25, 1905. After his marriage he settled on a farm in Armstrong county, late in life moving to Seattle. He married Mary Ann Double, of German ancestry, born near Muddy Creek, Pennsylvania, August 1, 1837, who survives him, a resident of Seattle. Twelve children: 1. James W., born at Conneautville, Pennsylvania, 1856, died 1858. 2. Jane, born in Butler county, January, 1858; married Michael Gamble and resides in Tarentum; children: Samuel, William, Arthur, Laura, Sarah, Mary, Edith, Joseph, Charles, Ernest, Clarence. 3. Sarah A., of previous mention, married John H. Frederick. 4. Joseph, born at Old Stone House, Butler county, October, 1862; he married (first) Ruth Shreves, of Kansas, (second) Bertha Hill; children of first wife: Ellsworth, Frederick, Ralph; by second wife: Cronjie and Ruby; Joseph is a bricklayer, residing in Sarver. 5. Mary Prusha, born near Kittanning, Pennsylvania, November 4, 1865; married (first) Hilt Miller, (second) John Williamnee; children of first husband: Ida May, Iva Jane, Charles Thomas and Ethel Matilda; children of second husband: Gertrude, deceased, and Willa. 6. William, born near Kittanning, February, 1867, now an oil well worker living in Bridgeport, Illinois; he married Mardie Boher, of Millerstown, four children. 7. John, born near Kittanning, April, 1869, now a farmer of Bolton, California; has family. 8. Zephenia, born August 10, 1871, now a fruit grower near Seattle, Washington; he married (first) Mary ———, of Kansas; (second) Clara ———; children by first marriage: Earl, born 1897, and Erma, born 1899. 9. Samantha, born April 22, 1874, now a fruit grower of Seattle; he married Melten Case, of Kansas, six children. 10. Matilda, born June 28, 1877; married Charles Case, of Kansas, now engaged in fruit growing at Seattle, no issue. 11. Charles Thomas, born February 7, 1880, died 1881. 12. Michael, born August 6, 1882, now a hardware merchant of Cotton, California; he married Lizzie ———, and has four children.

DOWREY-FITZGERALD The first ancestor of this branch of the Dowrey family of whom we have any record is William Dowrey, a master mechanic of Scotland, who emigrated to the United States, settling in Mason City, West Columbia county, Ohio, where he died in 1854. His political preference was strongly Democratic, and in religious faith he was a Presbyterian. He was a member of the Masonic order, having attained the Knight Templar degree. He married Agnes ———, born in Scotland, died 1892, at the very remarkable age of one hundred and three years, four months and fourteen days. She was graduated from the medical college in Dundee, Scotland, with the degree of M. D., and for thirty-three years subsequent to her husband's death she practiced medicine in the city of Cincinnati, Ohio. Children: 1. James, of whom further. 2. John, born and died in Scotland; he was a traveling salesman; married and had a family. 3. Daniel, a traveling salesman, born and died in Scotland. 4. Ellen, born in Scotland, died in Cincinnati; married William Howard, a clerk in a mercantile house; children: Mary, born in Cincinnati, where she lives; Edward, born in Cincinnati, where he lives. 5. Jane, born in Scotland; deceased; married William Sloan, a mechanic of Scotland; son Thomas, lives in Cincinnati.

(II) James, son of William and Agnes Dowrey, was born in Scotland, 1818, died in Plummerville, Pennsylvania, October 22, 1864. He attended the public schools of his native country and was graduated from an advanced school in the city of Dundee, Scotland. In this city he also served his apprenticeship at the trade which he later followed, becoming an expert machinist and master mechanic. In 1837 he emigrated to the United States and pursuing his trade made the first set of drilling tools that were manufactured in Franklin, Pennsylvania. During the civil war he was drafted, but was granted exemption because of his age. He married, at Harrisville, Pennsylvania, Martha McCoy, born in Harrisville in 1818, died in Coyleville, Butler county, Penn-

sylvania, April 6, 1890, daughter of Thomas McCoy, died in 1874. He settled on three hundred and sixty acres of land in Harrisville, on which he built a sawmill and a gristmill, to which the inhabitants of all the country around brought their timber to be made into workable lumber and their grain to be made into edible meal and flour. He fought in the second war with England in 1812 and all throughout the war was stationed at Fort Erie, Pennsylvania. He and his wife were Presbyterians, but at the age of seventy-two she became a follower of Catholicism. He married Jane Parks, born in Ireland, died in Harrisville, Pennsylvania, in 1868. Children: 1. Eleanor, born at Harrisville, deceased, married George Reed, deceased, who was a farmer; they had several children. 2. Mary, born and died at Harrisville, Pennsylvania; married ——— Dunlap, native of the same town; they had two sons, Samuel and ———. 3. Parks, a farmer, born and died in Harrisville, Pennsylvania; married Sarah Taylor and had several children. 4. Sarah, born and died at Grove City, Mercer county, Pennsylvania, married a farmer and had children. 5. Julia, born and died at Grove City, Pennsylvania; married John Dougherty, a farmer, and had a large family. 6. Hugh, born and died at Grove City, Pennsylvania; married ———
———, deceased, and had two children. 7. Jane, born and died in Grove City, unmarried. 8. Martha, of previous mention. Children of James and Martha (McCoy) Dowrey: 1. Agnes J., of whom further. 2. William Taylor, born in Gallipolis, Ohio, in 1847, died April 6, 1908; a merchant; he married Elizabeth Scott, of Fort Scott, Pennsylvania, who lives at Grand Junction with her three children: Martha, Richard and Scott. 3. Thomas, born January 5, 1850, died in Hamilton, Ohio, November 17, 1908; he followed the oil business, was a traveling salesman and belonged to the Masonic order, holding the degree of Knight Templar; married Agnes Hewlings; children: Maud, a resident of Philadelphia, Pennsylvania; Mary, a resident of Joplin, Missouri; Margaret; Alice, lives with her mother in Ohio; Robert, lives with his mother in Ohio. 4. Anna, born in Indianapolis, 1852; married Patrick H. McBride, a contractor of Coyleville, Pennsylvania; children: Harry and Edith, both living in Butler, Pennsylvania. 5. Emma, born in Pomeroy, Ohio, 1854; married Ogg Johnson, a farmer and collector of taxes in Chandlers Valley, Pennsylvania, where they now live; child, Margie, married ——— Miller, a mechanic of Corry, Pennsylvania. 6. Elizabeth, born in Mason City, West Columbia county, Pennsylvania, 1855; married Joseph Redd, an oil pumper of Butler county, Pennsylvania, now living in Pittsburgh; they have five children. 7. George, born 1856, died 1872.

(III) Agnes J., daughter of James and Martha (McCoy) Dowrey, was born in Harrisville, Butler county, Pennsylvania, March 19, 1845, where she was educated in the public schools. She is a member of the Bradford Mutual Benefit Association and a Roman Catholic in religion. She married, October 22, 1864, in Ellicottville, New York, Robert Fitzgerald, born in Rochester, New York, August 27, 1842, died November 4, 1909. When he was but sixteen years of age he was employed in a freight house at Toledo, Ohio, and for two years held a position with the steamship company owning the boats plying between Buffalo and Duluth. When the oil discoveries were making Pennsylvania the cynosure of the financial world, he caught the fever and prospected in Plumer, Pit Hole, Rouseville, Petrolia and other localities in the region in which the strikes were being made, but with only moderate success. In 1881 he moved to Four Mile, New York, where he remained until 1891, while there forming the Howe Oil Company, which from the date of its corporation has proved a remarkable financial success. On May 6, 1900, Mr. Fitzgerald moved to Bradford, Pennsylvania, where his death occurred. Children of Robert and Agnes J. (Dowrey) Fitzgerald: 1. Martha Agnes, born in Plumer, Venango county, Pennsylvania, July 30, 1865; married Henry Johnson, of Youngsville, Warren county, Pennsylvania, a farmer; children: Edna, born 1891; Herbert, born 1895; Agatha, born 1901. 2. Robert, born April 15, 1869, at Plumer, Pennsylvania; an oil operator of Tulsa, Oklahoma; married Margaret Currens, of Montreal, Canada; children: Robert, born 1900; Margaret, born August 3, 1904. 3. William J., born at Petroleum Center, Venango county, Pennsylvania, August 25, 1873; married Catherine Franks, of State Line, Franklin county, Pennsylvania, and lives at Knapp Creek, Pennsylvania, where he follows the business of oil operator; children: John, born 1900; Leo, born 1902; Robert, born 1906; Agnes, 1908; James, 1911. 4.

Nellie M., born May 10, 1876, at the town formerly called Millerstown, Pennsylvania; married John W. Johnson. 5. Margaret, born at Four Mile, Cattaraugus county, New York, August 18, 1883; she married Arthur Ash, a native Canadian, who was graduated from Queens Medical College, Kingston, Canada, with the degree of M. D.; he then specialized in diseases of the eye, ear, nose and throat at the Manhattan Institute of New York City, and is now a recognized authority on this subject; he lives at Weehawken, New Jersey; children: Frances Agnes, born 1905; William, born 1907; Gordon, born 1910.

Robert Fitzgerald, father of Robert Fitzgerald, was born in Ireland in 1810, died in Ellicottville, New York, in 1878. He emigrated to the United States and made his home in Rochester, New York, where he carried on a large and profitable contracting business. He married Ellen Coughlan, born in Ireland, died in Ellicottville, 1893. Children: 1. Robert, of previous mention. 2. John, born in Rochester, New York, 1844, died in Ellicottville, about 1900, unmarried; was a merchant. 3. Michael, born in Ellicottville; never married. 4. Mary, married Albert Monroe, of Massachusetts, a retired oil operator of Ohio; children: Ellen, born in Petrolia, lives in Ohio; George, born in Petrolia, lives with parents. 5. Ellen, born in Ellicottville, 1850; married Cornelius Moynahan, died in 1910; he was a stone mason by trade and served through the civil war attaining the rank of captain; children: John R., lives in Philadelphia; Cornelius, lives in Buffalo; James, lives in Buffalo; Henry, lives in Buffalo; Daniel, lives in Jamestown, New York. 6. Margaret, born in Ellicottville, 1852; married Thomas Kelly, of Bradford, Pennsylvania, a contractor and operator of Findlay, Ohio; children: Thomas, Ethel and Margaret.

SUTTON-PROSSER The Sutton family are of English lineage and are found seated in that country through many centuries. The first of this branch of the family to settle in the United States was Elihu Sutton, born in England, settled on a farm at Sparta, New York, with his wife Eliza. They lived and died there; she in 1843, aged seventy-five years. He was a member of the Methodist Episcopal church and a Whig in politics. Their children, all born in Sparta, New York: 1. John, of whom further. 2. David, married Polly Dieter, both deceased; their children: William, Wilson, David, died young; David (2), George and May; all deceased except David (2), who resides in Scottsburg, New York, and Mary, who lives in Livingston county, New York. 3. Abigail, died in Sparta; married David Kuhn; their children: Mary, of Sparta; John, of Potter county, Pennsylvania; Simon, deceased; Eliza, of Sparta; Margaret, of Sparta; Lucinda, deceased; Elizabeth, deceased; Jonathan and William, both living in Sparta.

(II) John, eldest child of Elihu Sutton, was born in Sparta, New York, in 1803, died there March 22, 1877. He received a public school education, learned the blacksmith's trade and carried on that business in connection with farming all his life. He was a Republican and a member of the Methodist Episcopal church. He married, in 1836, Sarah Hoffman, born in Milton, Northumberland county, Pennsylvania, February 25, 1816, died at Sparta, April, 1881. She was a Methodist. Her father, John Hoffman, was born near Bremen, Germany, died in Sparta. He emigrated to the United States and settled in Sparta, New York, where he prospered, owning two good farms. He married Mary Kline, whose brother David was a school teacher in Milton, Pennsylvania. Her sister Elizabeth married Adam Smith, of Milton, and died in Sparta; another sister, Susan, married Henry Shaffer, also from Milton. Children of John Sutton, all born in Sparta, New York: 1. Mary Cordelia, of further mention. 2. Lucy Ann, born 1840, died 1855. 3. George, born 1842, died 1844. 4. Lamira, born 1843, married Joseph Steffey, of Dansville, New York, and resides on the old Sparta homestead; their children: Sarah, born February 14, 1871, died in Groveland, New York, in 1911; John, resides in Sparta, unmarried; Josephine, married a Mr. Jackson. 5. Frances Elizabeth, born February 11, 1849; married (first) Wilbur N. Corwin, deceased, leaving Grace J., born in Bradford, Pennsylvania, August 24, 1884, married Vernon Drake and has Wilbur A., born December 16, 1902; married (second) Robert George. 6. John, born 1851, died 1867, of diphtheria, which dread disease carried off four of the family in the same year. 7. William, born 1854, died 1867. 8. Caroline, born 1858, died 1867. 9. Jesse, born 1861, died 1867.

(III) Mary Cordelia, eldest child of John

Sutton, was born in Sparta, New York, December 25, 1838. She was educated in the public schools and at Mount Pleasant Academy. After completing her studies she returned home, remaining until her marriage. She is an attendant of the Methodist Episcopal church of Bradford, and a member of the Ladies' Auxiliary of the Union Veteran Legion. She married Lorenzo Barton Prosser, born in Clarksville, New York, March 3, 1835, died February 27, 1909, aged seventy-three years, eleven months, twenty-four days.

Mr. Prosser received his education in the public schools of Clarksville. He decided upon the profession of law, but after a course of reading and study of Blackstone he settled down to a life devoted to agriculture. He moved to Bradford when still a young man, and during his long life there held many town offices. He was assessor, collector of taxes, constable and held other offices of lesser importance. He made a fine record during the civil war. He was mustered into the service of the United States at Harrisburg, Pennsylvania, May 30, 1861, as a sergeant in Company I, First Regiment of Rifles Pennsylvania Reserve Volunteers (the famous "Bucktail" Regiment, so called from each soldier wearing in his hat the tail of a deer) for a term of three years, and was discharged June 11, 1864, at Harrisburg, on expiration of term of service, having served "honestly and faithfully" as his discharge testified. He saw hard service, this regiment being one of the hard-fought regiments of the Army of the Potomac. He participated in various important battles, among them Drainesville, Harrisonburg, Antietam, Fredericksburg, Slaughter Mountain, Gettysburg, Mine Run, Catlett Station, Bristol Station, and all the engagements in the Wilderness campaign. At Fredericksburg, Virginia, he was taken prisoner, and was taken to Libby Prison, Richmond, Virginia, where he was held for three months before exchange. During his long service Sergeant Prosser never received or asked for a furlough, his service being continuous.

After the war Mr. Prosser purchased a farm at Mineral Run, Pennsylvania, on which he lived for about one year. At the beginning of the oil strikes he returned to Bradford, where he purchased another farm, and also engaged in the production of oil. This Bradford farm was his home during the remainder of his life with the exception of three years spent in Nebraska, where he took up a quarter section under the homestead laws, which he sold later and returned to Bradford. He was a member of the Masonic order and past master of Bradford Lodge, No. 334. Children of Lorenzo Barton and Mary Cordelia (Sutton) Prosser: 1. Myrtie Marion, born in Bradford, August 9, 1865, died August 12, 1870. 2. John Eldridge, born in Bradford, November 27, 1868; now an oil producer; resides with his mother in care of the Prosser estate; he is unmarried. 3. Grace May, born in New Lexington, Nebraska, May 20, 1876; married Wesley Allen, a native of Tennessee, and now resides at Alma, New York, twelve miles south of Buffalo; no issue.

Lorenzo Barton Prosser was the son of the Rev. Holden Prosser, who was born in Connecticut, going from there to Clarksville, New York, and thence coming to Bradford, Pennsylvania, where he died in March, 1879. He was an ordained minister of the Baptist church and a tireless worker in his Master's cause. He married Penelope Satterlee, born in Munda, New York, died in 1879, aged sixty years. Their children were: 1. Fannie, born in Clarksville, New York, died in Savona, New York; married Cornelius Storms, deceased, of Bradford. 2. Lorenzo, now a resident of Savona. 3. Mary, deceased. 4. Millard, resides in Nebraska. 5. Charles, resides in Savona. 6. Minnie, resides in Savona. 7. Holden Levi, born December 5, 1832, in Locke, Cayuga county, New York; he was a carriage maker by occupation; he enlisted in the service of the United States, July 15, 1862, in Company H, Nineteenth Iowa Volunteers, and died August 4, 1864, in the hospital at Vicksburg, Mississippi, aged thirty-two years; he married, July 6, 1858, at Farmington, Lee county, Iowa, Mary Elizabeth Eager, born April 9, 1837, in the town of Kirtland, Ohio, daughter of Lewis and Mary Eager, the ceremony was performed by the Rev. Goldwin, of Farmington; children: i. Mary Adella, born June 14, 1859, in Keosauqua, Van Buren county, Iowa, married, April 9, 1886, Louis Satterlee, and has children: Levi H. and Clara L. Satterlee; ii. Clara Elizabeth, born June 23, 1861, in Keosauqua, Iowa, married, April 16, 1896, William Gilbert, and their children are Mary E. and Marjorie E. Gilbert. 8. Lorenzo Barton, of previous mention. 9. Lafayette, born in Bradford, in 1844, died 1889; married Myra Seward, of Bradford, deceased. 10. Emily, deceased. 11. Lucina, died young.

MURPHY This ancient family which from its original home in the Green Isle has sent many of its members to render valuable assistance in the development of our industries, is represented in Custer City, Pennsylvania, by Timothy B. Murphy, one of the most progressive and prosperous business men of that community. The history of Mr. Murphy's family is traced through the following generations:

(I) Timothy Murphy, born in county Cork, Ireland, where he passed his entire life as a farmer. He married ———— Callahan, a native of Fernoy, county Cork, and two children were born to them: Patrick, of whom further; Margaret, born in 1829, married Patrick Golden, like herself a native of county Cork, and emigrated to the United States, where her husband found employment at railroad work. Two of their six children ———— Daniel and Ellen ————, are now living in St. Paul, Minnesota. Mr. and Mrs. Golden, both of whom are deceased, were members of the Roman Catholic church. Timothy Murphy and his wife were of the same communion, and died at Fernoy, county Cork, Ireland.

(II) Patrick, son of Timothy and ———— (Callahan) Murphy, was born in 1827, in Ireland. He lived for a time in Wales, and in 1861 emigrated to the United States, settling in Wilcox, Elk county, Pennsylvania, where he was employed by different railroads, helping to build the Erie branch from Carlton to Mount Alton. In 1867 he recrossed the ocean his wife having died the year before in Ireland) and returned with his two sons. He afterward went to Minnesota, still working as a railroad employe, and subsequently removed to Custer City, where he lived for twenty years. He was a Democrat, and a member of the Roman Catholic church. He married, in Ireland, Margaret Barry, born in 1828, in county Cork, where both her parents were born and died. Mr. and Mrs. Murphy were the parents of two sons: Timothy B., of whom further; James, born in 1864, in Wales, died on Ward's Island, New York, having contracted a fever on shipboard while his father was bringing him to this country. The mother of these two sons died in 1866 in Ireland. Like her husband she was a member of the Roman Catholic church. Mr. Murphy married (second) Mrs. Mary Wall, by whom he had no children. He died May 16, 1897, at Big Shanty, Pennsylvania, where he had at one time lived.

(III) Timothy B., son of Patrick and Margaret (Barry) Murphy, was born April 8, 1862, in Wales, where his parents lived for several years, his father being employed as a coke manufacturer of Wilcox, Pennsylvania. Timothy B. Murphy obtained his education in the public schools, the father and son lived in various places until the former married a second time. Timothy B. Murphy was then thrown on his own resources and accordingly found employment at the oil business to which, with commendable pluck and perseverance, he steadily adhered, gaining as the years went by not pecuniary profit alone, but much valuable experience, and building up a reputation for ability and integrity which laid the foundation of his success. He came to Custer City when that place was in its infancy and was called Shep's Crossing, and as the result of a long period of wisely directed enterprise is now, as an oil producer, at the head of a large and lucrative business. In addition to this he has interests of considerable magnitude in the Pennsylvania Mutual and the Metropolitan Insurance companies. In politics Mr. Murphy is an Independent, holding himself aloof from partisanship, but giving his vote and influence to the man whom he deems best fitted for the office. Like his ancestors he is a member of the Roman Catholic church.

Mr. Murphy married, January 19, 1898, Ellen C. Sullivan (see Sullivan III), and they are the parents of two children: Frederic, born October 15, 1901; Helen, born August 7, 1902. Both were born in Bradford and attended school in Custer City.

(The Sullivan Line).

(I) James Sullivan, grandfather of Mrs. Ellen C. (Sullivan) Murphy was born in 1800 in county Kerry, Ireland, died in 1870 in Genesee, New York. He married Margaret Lake, born in 1791 in Ireland, and died in 1881 in Wellsville, New York. Their children were: 1. James, deceased; was a farmer; married Bridget Cavanagh, from Coudersport, Pennsylvania, and their children, the eldest now of Olean, New York, and the others of Roulette, Pennsylvania, were: Mary, James, Timothy, Ellen, Margaret, Michael. 2. Michael, of whom further. 3. Ellen, married Morris Conover, a grocer of Wellsville, New York, and died there, leaving Thomas, Patrick and Nellie, all of that place, and another daughter, Mary, of Bradford, Pennsylvania. 4. Ann, married Patrick Shannon, a farmer of Roulette, Pennsylvania, where they both died, leaving a son, John, of East Hebron, Potter county, Pennsylvania, and a daughter, Ellen, of Roulette. 5. Thomas, deceased, was a railroad employe of Wellsville, New York; married Kate Furlong from Coudersport, Pennsylvania, and left John, Thomas and Mary, of that place, a daughter, Margaret, of Buffalo, New York, and a son, Michael, of Hornellsville, New York. 6. John, a farmer of Genesee, New York; married Mary Durkin, a native of Ireland, and their children are: Annie and Nellie, of Buffalo, New York; Mary, of Texas, and James and Michael, of Genesee.

(II) Michael, son of James and Margaret (Lake) Sullivan, was born May 13, 1827, in county Kerry, Ireland. In 1851 he emigrated to the United States and is now a farmer of Roulette, Pennsylvania. He married Ellen Callahan, born December 25, 1832, in county Kerry, died April 29, 1911. Mr. and Mrs. Sullivan were the parents of the following children: 1. Margaret, born January 15, 1853, in Coudersport, near Roulette; married Henry Bannister, from Wellsville, New York, now a contractor and oil producer of Washington, Pennsylvania, and has two children: Irene, born October 18, 1887, and Helen, born July 28, 1889. 2. John, born April 7, 1854, in Coudersport, now a stone mason of Roulette; married Kate Young, from North Hortons, Pennsylvania, and has four children: Robert, William, Thomas and Mabel, all living in Costello, Potter county, Pennsylvania. 3. Joanna, born May 28, 1856, in Coudersport; married the late Benjamin Ongerham, an oil gauger from Lima, Ohio, and has had two children: Florence, deceased, and Benjamin, born February 22, 1895, now living with his mother in Roulette. 4. Mary, born November 16, 1858, in Roulette; married Frank Frantz from Bradford, Pennsylvania, now a contractor of Roulette, and their children are: Lee, Florence, Edith, Raymond, Eleanor. 5. James, born October 11, 1859, in Roulette, now a stone mason of that place; married Bessie Mahon, from Costello, Pennsylvania and their children are: Mary, wife of P. Myers, of Roulette; Elizabeth, wife of Edward Cock, of Kansas; Grace, wife of Thomas Cullen, of Roulette; and Florence and Maude, of the same place. 6. Michael, born September 26, 1860, in Roulette, now a stone mason of Olean, New York, unmarried. 7. Thomas, born October 26, 1861, in Roulette, a stone mason of Bogalusa, Louisiana, unmarried. 8. Ellen C., of whom further. 9. Catherine, born August 30, 1864, in Roulette; married Michael Fitzsimmons from Sartwell, McKean county, Pennsylvania, now a contractor and lumberman of Roulette, and their children are: Harold, Howard, Homer, Albert, Marie, John, Edna, Roderick. 10. Edith, born July 12, 1865, at Roulette; married Elmer White, a civil engineer of that place, who died at Newport News, leaving the following children, who live with their mother in Roulette: Louise, born October 27, 1892; Marjorie, September 19, 1893; Ronald, September 18, 1895; Ruth, June 12, 1897; Elmer, born May 6, 1898. 11. Florence, born November 26, 1867; married William Williams from Franklinville, Huntingdon county, Pennsylvania, now a real estate agent of Buffalo, New York. 12. Edward, born August 3, 1869, in Roulette, where he is now a stone mason; married Katie Eymer, of that place, and they have one child, Raymond.

(III) Ellen C., eighth child of Michael and Ellen (Callahan) Sullivan, was born November 20, 1862, in Roulette, Potter county, Pennsylvania. She received her education in the public schools of Port Allegany, McKean county, of the same state, and became the wife of Timothy B. Murphy (see Murphy III).

MORRIS This family name is well known and highly honored in both England and America. In this country Robert (2) Morris, "the financier of the revolution," son of Robert (1) Morris, was born in London, 1734, died in America in 1806. He was brought by his father to America in 1734, and settled first in Maryland, later in Philadelphia. He is not connected with the Anthony Morris family of Philadelphia, nor with the Massachusetts family of Lieutenant Edward Morris. Robert Morris was a member of the continental congress, signer of the Declaration of Independence in 1776, and during the revolution gave the government the full benefit of his credit; he was also a member of the first constitutional convention and the first United States senate.

(I) Lieutenant Edward Morris, son of Thomas and Grissie (Hewsome) Morris, was born in Nazing, Essex county, England. August, 103—, died September 14, 1689. His grave, the oldest one in Windham county, Connecticut, is marked by a stone inscribed: "Here lies buried the body of Lieutenant Edward Morris, deceased September 14, 1689." He came to the American colonies settling at Roxbury, Massachusetts, where he was constable, selectman 1674 to 1687, and representative 1677 to 1687. He later was one of the early settlers of Woodstock, Connecticut, where he was the first military officer, a selectman and a leader among the early settlers. He married Grace Belt, September 20, 1655. Children, all born in Roxbury, Massachusetts: Isaac, Edward (2), Grace, Ebenezer, Elizabeth, Margaret, Samuel, of whom further; Martha.

(II) Samuel, son of Lieutenant Edward Morris, was born in Roxbury, Massachusetts, April 19, 1671, died at "Myanexit Farm," in Thompson, Connecticut, January 9, 1745. He bought from Governor Dudley a large tract of land in Connecticut, lying along the Myanexit or Quinebaug river, on which he settled. He became of great prominence in that section and was greatly respected and obeyed by the Indians. He married (first) Mehitable Mayo, died in Roxbury, February 8, 1703, aged thirty-three years, daughter of John and Hannah (Graves) Mayo; (second) Dorothy ———, died July 28, 1742. Children by first wife, all born in Roxbury, Massachusetts; Samuel (2), of whom further; Benjamin, born October 18, 1696; Mehitable, June 25, 1698; Rebecca, September 15, 1699; Hannah, November 9, 1700; Dorothy, February 7, 1702; Prudence, January 31, 1703. Child of second wife: Abigail, born February 1704 or 1705.

(III) Samuel (2), son of Samuel (1) Morris, was born in Roxbury, Massachusetts, August 13, 1695. He succeeded his father at "Myanexit Farm," and established business as a trader, buying up produce and exchanging it in Boston. He married Abigail Bragg, their intentions being published September 7, 1728. Children: Mehitable, died young; Samuel, born March 18, 1731, a revolutionary soldier, married Hannah Child; Mehitable, died aged nineteen years; Henry born April 18, 1734, a revolutionary soldier, married Hannah Frizzell, had sons, Samuel, born 1774, and Simeon; John, born September 5, 1735, married Rebecca Gore; Lemuel, of whom further; Anne, born March 11, 1739, married James Bugber; William, born November 28, 1740, a revolutionary soldier, married Sarah Bowman; Abigail, born April 29, 1742, married Ebenezer Lillie; Susanna, born September 1, 1743; Lieutenant Edward, born August 19, 1745, married Dorcas Corbin; Elizabeth, born May 16, 1747; Hannah, twin of Elizabeth, married Daniel Marcy; Lucretia, baptized June 4, 1749.

(IV) Lemuel, son of Samuel (2) Morris, was born July 29, 1737. He married Lydia Wilkinson and had a son Samuel (3).

(V) Samuel (3), probably son of Lemuel Morris, was born about 1767, died 1858. When only a boy he served in the revolutionary war. It is not possible to state which of the sons of Samuel (2) Morris was his father, but the strongest belief is that he was a son of Lemuel and that his birth date was 1767. His revolutionary service must have been very slight and only such as a boy of twelve or fifteen years could perform. He settled in Ontario county, New York. He married, and among his children was a son Simeon Mills, of whom further.

(VI) Simeon Mills, son of Samuel Morris, was born in ———, Massachusetts, 1787, died in 1865. He was a farmer and after reaching manhood settled at Springwater, Ontario county, New York, and later at Mill Grove in the same county. He moved afterward to Pennsylvania, purchasing a farm at Toad Hollow, now South Bradford, which he cultivated until his death. He married Louise McCrea, born in New England in 1797, died at Toad Hollow, now South Bradford, Pennsylvania, 1872, a relative of the unfortunate Jane McCrea who was murdered by the Indians during the revolution. They were both members of the Methodist Episcopal church, Simeon M. Morris being an exhorter. Children: 1. William Schuyler, of whom further. 2. Emmeline, born at Mill Grove, New York, October, 1817, died at Toad Hollow, November, 1879, married Lyman Innus, of New England; had children: i. Amanda Lyman, born 1838, died 1873, unmarried. ii. Mary Melissa, born 1840, died 1873, married David Brown, who survives her, a resident of Clare county, New York; child: Eveline, born April, 1860, married a Mr. Keck, deceased. iii. James, born September 13, 1842, now living in Warren, Pennsylvania, married Lily ———. iv. Francis Abner, born September 1847, now residing at Jamestown, New York, married and has children: Adeline, Clarence and Francis Abner (2). v. Charlotte Louise, born February 10, 1857. 3.

Durcy, born in Mill Grove, New York, March 19, 1819, died May 1882, married in 1842 David Degolia, born ——, died January 12, 1895, had children: i. Sylvester, born August, 1843, married Julia Storms, has children: a. Elva, born July 13, 1872. b. Earl, August 27, 1875, married Flora Long; child: Margaret, born May 2, 1906. c. Caroline, born 1877, died 1882. d. Ruth, October, 1883, married L. Bassage. ii. Samuel Morris, born July, 1845, died September 30, 1911, in Wisconsin, was twice married and had a son Charles. iii. Wilber Fisk, born December, 1847, died 1893, in Florida; married Lucy Jacobs; son Miles, born 1871, died 1905. 4. Sally, born 1821, died April 13, 1839.

(VII) William Schuyler, son of Simeon Mills Morris, was born near Mill Grove, Ontario county, New York, October 15, 1815, died February 26, 1859. He was educated in the public schools. He was nineteen years of age when the family settled at Toad Hollow, now South Bradford, where he engaged all his life in lumbering and farming. He was a Republican, and in 1846 collector of taxes for Bradford township. In religious faith he was a Methodist, as was his wife. He married Eliza Pauline Seamans, born in Westfield, Tioga county, Pennsylvania, February 24, 1822, died in Degolia, June 12, 1895, daughter of Jonathan Seamans, born 1795, died in Westfield, August, 1867, a farmer, who married Rebecca Tuttle, born May 16, 1803, in Westfield, died there September, 1873. Children of William Schuyler Morris, all born in South Bradford, except the last, who was born in Degolia, Pennsylvania: 1. Emma, born in South Bradford, Pennsylvania, September 16, 1844, resides in Bradford. She married John Bell, born in Scotland, 1835, died March 22, 1902, a molder by trade. He joined the Twenty-first Regiment New York Volunteer Infantry, in the first company leaving Buffalo, his place of enlistment, and served two years; then transferred to the Second Regiment New York Artillery. He was wounded at a fight near Richmond, Virginia, again at the battle of the Weldon railroad, and a third time at Hatch's Run; was honorably discharged October 21, 1865, and was in receipt of a government pension until his death. Children: An infant, died unnamed; Marian, born June 6, 1874, died aged three months. 2. Jasper Levi, of whom further. 3. Alice, born February 26, 1850, died March 4, 1850. 4. Robert O., born March 9, 1851, died September 13, 1907, a rauchman at Roscoe, Montana, married Nancy Brown, of Missouri, no issue. 5. Julia, born June 2, 1853, married William Hellenbrook, born in Buffalo, New York, May 4, 1844, died February 27, 1905, whom she survives, a resident of Degolia, Pennsylvania; children, all but first two born in Degolia: i. Ella, born April 24, 1874, in Olean, New York, married James B. Brown, children: George Dewey, born June 23, 1899; Doris Lucille, February 7, 1900; Adis Edgar, December 9, 1901, died April 27, 1903; Frederick William, October 22, 1903; Marjorie Buene, September 18, 1905; Vera Rometta, September 24, 1907; Edna Ruth, August 20, 1910. ii. Roy W., born in Olean, New York, June 2, 1877, married Florence Palmeter, born also in Olean; child: Laura, born February 10, 1907. iii. Ray, born November 24, 1879, unmarried. iv. Iva, born February 5, 1882, married Roy Thompson, of Big Shanty, Pennsylvania; son, Frederick, born May 19, 1906. v. Ralph J., born August 26, 1883, married Bessie Jones. vi. Eliza Pauline, born August 19, 1885. vii. Leona Ruth, born August 15, 1887. viii. Robert, July 23, 1891. ix. Lajune, June 2, 1894. x. Walter Valentine, October 10, 1899. 6. Charles William, born October 9, 1855, now a farmer of Minard Run, Pennsylvania, married Elizabeth Young, born September 17, 1864; children: i. Harry, born January, 1884. ii. Carl, June, 1885. iii. Hugh, 1887; married Ethel Fonda; children: Dorthey and Robert. iv. Neoma, born September 13, 1893. 7. Adaline, born March 16, 1859, married Ira H. Burton, of Maine; children: Gertrude and Theodore.

(VIII) Jasper Levi, son of William Schuyler Morris, was born in South Bradford, Pennsylvania, January 1, 1846. He was educated in the public schools of Degolia, where his early years were spent, and of South Bradford and Minard Run. He has followed farming and lumbering all his life, and is now located on a large farm that he owns at Degolia. He is one of the pioneer farmers of that section and rated as a successful business man. He is a Republican, has always taken an active part in local affairs, and was elected supervisor, serving thirteen consecutive years. In 1885 he was elected collector of taxes and served twenty-one consecutive years. In 1893 he was elected assessor, a position he still holds (1912).

He was also elected school director in 1885, serving two years. In religious faith he is a Methodist.

He married, July 9, 1876, Alice B., born in Hinsdale, New York, April 15, 1858, daughter of John Hellenbrook, born in New York state January 1, 1839, died in Olean, New York, June 26, 1895. He was a molder, but later purchased a farm near Olean. He married Harriet Witter, born in New York state July 18, 1843, died April, 1903, daughter of Pardon Witter, died at Olean aged about eighty-five years, and Laura (Bradley) Witter, died 1885. Their second daughter, Jane, married William Taylor, and lives in the west. Children of John and Harriet (Witter) Hellenbrook, all born at Olean, New York: 1. Alice B., of previous mention. 2. William, born April 27, 1860, died August 29, 1896; married Rose Robbins; children: Leo, Carrie, Edna, Mable, Hazel and Arthur, all living near Westfield, Pennsylvania. 3. John, died in infancy. 4. Nellie, born January 8, 1864, married Arthur Wallace, an engineer on the Delaware & Hudson railroad, now living in Binghamton, New York; children: Percy, Eva, Donald and Mildred. 5. Caroline (or Carrie), born March 8, 1866, married Albert Shankel, a farmer of Kansas; children: Floyd, living in California; Daisy, in Colorado; Dale, in Rew City, Pennsylvania. 6. Harriet, born February 14, 1869, married Thomas Bailey, born in Marion, Virginia, January 16, 1862; children: i. Ethel, born October 13, 1880, married Adolphus Bryant, born February 14, 1888. ii. Bessie, born October 20, 1892, married Norman Wilcott, of Duke Center, Pennsylvania. iii. Frances, May 5, 1894. iv. Fae, February 14, 1903. v. William T., July 13, 1908. 7. Frances, born October, 1873, married Louis Billings, of Canada, now a farmer at Olean; children: Frank, born July, 1895; Florence May, 1907 8. Frederick, born April, 1878, a stone mason, married ———— Witter, of Rochester, New York; child: Cecelia. Children of Jasper Levi and Alice B. Morris, all born at Degolia, Pennsylvania: 1. William John, born June 29, 1877, now a farmer and oil producer of Degolia; married Lucy Nippert, of Songberg, Pennsylvania; children: Helen, born August 28, 1902; Ruth, December 28, 1907. 2. Minnie M., born March 8, 1879; married Robert Howard; children: Wilma, born November, 1897; Wayne, June 29, 1899; Clifford, 1902; Alice, October, 1904. 3. May, born May 16, 1882, died June 2, 1882. 4. George, born July 10, 1883, now of Rochester, New York, unmarried. 5. Earl, born January 14, 1886, now in the oil well business at Bradford; married April 12, 1911, Gladys Thomas. 6. Claude, born August 2, 1887, married, August 24, 1912, Elizabeth Scidmore, of Custer City, now living in Franklinville, Pennsylvania. 7. Frank, born October 7, 1892, now living in Bradford. 8. Fleury, October 27, 1896. 9. Carrie, August 29, 1899. 10. Clayton, March 12, 1903.

FISHER-LAIN The name of Fisher being that of one of the employments of men is found in all nations. This family descends from Anthony Fisher who lived in the latter part of Queen Elizabeth's reign, in the parish of Syleham, county of Suffolk, England. He had four sons and two daughters. His will was admitted to probate in England in December, 1641.

(II) Anthony (2), son of Anthony (1) Fisher, of Syleham, Suffolk, England was baptized there April 2, 1591. He came to New England with his first wife Mary, and children, in 1637, settling in Dedham, Massachusetts, where he had land allotted to him. His wife Mary joined the Dedham church in 1642, but he was not "Comfortably received into ye Church," "On account of his proud and haughty spirit," until March 14, 1645. He was made freeman in May, 1645; selectman, 1646-1647; county commissioner, September 3, 1660, and deputy to the general court, May 2, 1649. He owned a good deal of property, nearly all of which he gave to his sons, they binding themselves to support their mother if she were left dependent. After the death of his first wife Mary, he married, November 11, 1663, Isabella, widow of Edward Breck, of Dorchester, Anthony being then seventy-two years of age. He died April 18, 1671. Children by first wife, all born in England: Anthony (3), of whom further; Cornelius; Nathaniel; Daniel; Lydia; John.

(III) Anthony (3), son of Anthony (2) Fisher, was born in England and came with his parents to New England. He was a member of the Ancient and Honorable Artillery, 1644; freeman, 1646; joined the Dedham church, July 20, 1645; surveyor, 1652-1654; removed to Dorchester, where he died, February 13, 1670. He married, in Dedham, September 7, 1647, Joanna, only daughter of

Thomas and Joanna Faxon. She died October 16, 1694. Children: Mehitable, died young; Experience, died young; Josiah, twice married; ———, married Benjamin Coburn; Sarah, married John Guild; Deborah, married James Fales; Judith; John Bullen; Eleazer, of whom further.

(IV) Eleazer, youngest son of Anthony (3) Fisher, was born in Dedham, Massachusetts, September 18, 1669, died there February 6, 1722. He married, October 13, 1698, Mary Avery, born August 21, 1674, died March 25, 1749, a daughter of William Avery. Children: Eleazer (2), married Mary Penniman; William, married Elizabeth Daniels; Jeminia, married Ezekial Gay; David, of whom further; Ezra, married Mary Fenton; Nathaniel, died unmarried; Mary, married William Alexander; Ezekial, married (first) Susan Wadsworth, (second) Experience Blackman; Timothy, married Thankful Daniels; Stephen, died young; Benjamin, married Sarah Everett.

(V) David, third son of Eleazer Fisher, was born in Dedham, Massachusetts, June 21, 1705, died July 30, 1779. He married (first) at Walpole, February 16, 1732, Deborah Boyden, (second) November 7, 1770, Elizabeth Talbot. His descendants, many of them, settled in New Hampshire. Children: David (2), of whom further; Thomas, married Mary Pettee; Jacob, married (first) Elizabeth Holmes, (second) Sarah Hodges, (third) Elizabeth Brooks; Deborah, married John Lewis; Hannah, married Nathaniel Kingsbury; Nathan, married Esther French; Oliver, married Sarah Morse; Abigail, married William Starrett; Mary, died aged sixteen years; Abner, married Sophia Hibbard.

(VI) David (2), eldest son of David (1) Fisher, was born in Dedham, January 22, 1733. His will was probated September 1, 1812. He was a lieutenant in Captain Savil's company, Colonel Lemuel Robinson's regiment, that marched from Stoughton on the Lexington alarm, April 19, 1875, and also saw other service. He married, September 21, 1758, Abigail, daughter of Isaac and Mary Lewis. Children: David, married Mehitable Hewins; Moses, unmarried; Aaron, of whom further; Ebenezer, married Nancy Morse; Catherine, married (first) Elihu Onion, (second) John Smith; Rebecca, married Nathaniel Morse; Mary, died in infancy; Mary, married Oliver Gay.

(VII) Aaron, son of David (2) Fisher, was born at Sharon, December 16, 1762. His will was probated June 6, 1809. He married Elizabeth Estey. Children: Aaron; William, of whom further; Daniel; Betsey; Abigail.

(VIII) William, son of Aaron Fisher, was born in 1782, in New Hampshire, where he grew to manhood and learned the cooper's trade. He came to western Pennsylvania, being the third white settler to locate in McKean county, where he died in 1860. He was a Whig in politics, and both he and his wife were members of the Presbyterian church. He married ———, born 1785, died in Bradford in 1860. Children: William Rowell, of whom further; Zera, married a Miss Beardsley; Horace; Sallie, settled in Nebraska, where she was three times driven from her home by the Indians, narrowly escaping capture and death; Betsey; Cynthia, married a Mr. Beardsley; Bolina, married Seth Scott, and died in Wisconsin in 1911, the last survivor of the family.

(IX) William Rowell, son of William Fisher, was born in Connecticut, February 13, 1810, died in May, 1889. When he was nine years of age his parents moved to State Line, Franklin county, Pennsylvania, where the lad was educated in the public schools. He became interested in lumbering and always was engaged in some form of that business. After his removal to Bradford he built and operated a grist mill, which is now owned by C. L. Douglass. He was a Republican and served for many years as justice of the peace. In religious faith he was a Methodist. He married, at Tuna, Pennsylvania, Briceus Pantha Farr, born in New Hampshire, January 8, 1818, died in April, 1885, daughter of Isaac Farr, born in 1781, a farmer of New Hampshire, came to Bradford and took up land, which he cultivated until his death in 1852; married Pantha Clark, who possessed considerable medical skill and practiced locally. Their children were: Assal, died at East Bradford; George, died at East Bradford; Lydia, married John Hutchinson, both deceased; Lucretia, born October 11, 1810, married John F. Melvin (see Melvin); Olive Livonia, married Sidney Wheaton; Briceus Pantha, of previous mention; Daphana Dorleski, married Joseph Steven Seaward (see Seaward). (For extended notice of these children see sketch of Herbert E. Allen in this work).

Children of William Rowell and Briceus

Pantha (Farr) Fisher, all born in Bradford, five dying in infancy: 1. Orpha, born October 10, 1838, died February, 1896; married James R. Dart, of Lansing, now of Mason, Michigan; children: Nellie, died young; Gertrude, born January 24, 1866, married Doctor Campbell; Roland, married and has Clizbee, Doctor, William Fisher; Orpha Dorothy; James; Alfred, born May, 1879, married Harriet Lee. 2. Mary C., born March 17, 1840, died September 18, 1901; married Moses P. Woolley, who survives her living near Buffalo, New York. 3. Olive M., of whom further. 4. Ida, died December 3, 1874, unmarried. 5. Alice, born October 7, 1852; married Charles L. Ackley and resides in Grand Rapids, Michigan; children: Clara, born 1875, deceased; Maud, born 1877, married Emil E. Ganser. 6. Nellie, born 1857, died unmarried in June, 1873.

(X) Olive M., daughter of William Rowell Fisher, was born at Bradford, McKean county, Pennsylvania, October 20, 1843. She was educated in Bradford, where she was married and yet resides. She is vice-president of the Ladies Auxiliary of the Union Veteran Legion, also served two terms as president; director of the Benevolent Committee of the Woman's Literary Club; member of the Country Club, and attends the Universalist church. She married, January 26, 1865, Robert Thompson Lain, born in Mount Hope, Orange county, New York, November 3, 1837, died in Bradford, December 13, 1909 (see Lain).

(XI) William Fisher, only child of Robert Thompson and Olive M. (Fisher) Lain, was born in Bradford, Pennsylvania, September 28, 1866. He was educated in the public schools, and graduated from Nazareth Hall Military School in 1882. He is now foreman of the Emory Alkali Acid Company. He is a member of the Universalist church and a Republican in politics. He married, November 12, 1902, Myrtle Stevenson, born at Mill Hall, Clinton county, Pennsylvania, January 31, 1880. Children: Clara, born March 17, 1904; Olive, April 4, 1905; Roberta, July 10, 1906.

(The Lain Line).

Doctor Joseph Lain was a practicing physician at Mount Hope, Orange county, New York, where he died about the year 1840 comparatively a young man. He married and was the father of five children, three sons and two daughters, all deceased.

(II) Robert Thompson, son of Doctor Joseph Lain, was born at Mount Hope, Orange county, New York, November 3, 1837, died in Bradford, Pennsylvania, December 13, 1909. He was educated in the public schools of Otisville, Orange county, New York, and fitted himself for the profession of civil engineer; later he came to western Pennsylvania and was one of the engineers employed in the construction of the branch of the Erie railroad, between Bradford and Alton. He enlisted, August 13, 1861, in the Pennsylvania Bucktail Regiment, and went to the front in the civil war; was wounded in his first battle and after partially recovering was assigned to duty in the office of the hospital steward. His duties consisted in accompanying the surgeons with the ambulance, medicines, etc., to the battlefields and administering to the wounded. After receiving an honorable discharge from the army when the war closed, he came to Bradford in 1865. He next removed to Alton, Pennsylvania, where he was postmaster and engaged in mercantile business in partnership with Charles Melvin, continuing until their store was burned in 1867. He then removed to Wilcox, Pennsylvania, where he was manager of a general store until 1869. In that year he went to Dunkirk, New York, returning to Bradford in 1873 and engaging in the production of oil and the real estate business, continuing until his death. He was a member of the Grand Army of the Republic; the Union Veteran Legion; the Heptasophs; the Country Club, and was the second oldest member of Bradford Lodge, No. 334, Free and Accepted Masons, at the time of his death. He married, June 26, 1865, Olive M. Fisher, who survives him with one son, William Fisher Lain (see Fisher X).

McCREA The emigrant ancestor of this family, William McCrea, descended from a line of honored forbears long seated in county Donegal, Ireland.

(I) William McCrea was born in that county, married, and with his wife emigrated to the United States, secured employment on the canal being constructed in Westmoreland county, Pennsylvania, and died there soon after, in 1826. Both he and his wife were members of the Roman Catholic church. He married Mary Harkins, born in county Donegal, Ireland, died in Donegal township, Butler county, Pennsylvania, 1866, at the remarkable age of one hundred and one years. Children: 1. Eunice, born in county Donegal, Ireland, died in Sugarcreek township, Armstrong county, Pennsylvania; married James Lacey, a school teacher; children: Patrick, resides in Brady's Bend, Pennsylvania; James, lives in New Castle, Pennsylvania; Katherine, and others. 2. William, born in Westmoreland county, Pennsylvania, died in Sugarcreek township; a farmer; married and had a large family; among his children was a son John, who served in the civil war. 3. Hugh, born in Westmoreland county, died in Butler, Pennsylvania, 1898; married Mary Sheridan, from Clearfield township, Pennsylvania, died in Butler, 1911; children: John S., deceased; William S., lives in St. Petersburg, Florida; Catherine, also lives in St. Petersburg; Bernard, Hugh, Daniel, Frank, Mary Ellen, James, and George McClellan, all living in Butler; Hiram, living in St. Petersburg, Florida. 4. Daniel, of whom further. 5. John, born in Westmoreland county, Pennsylvania, died in Canton, Ohio; a cabinet-maker; married and had issue: William and Jane, living in Canton, Ohio; and Hugh D., deceased. 6. Belle, born in Westmoreland county, Pennsylvania, died in Butler, Pennsylvania; married John O'Neil, a farmer, who also died in Butler; children: William; Mary, lives in Butler. 7. Mary, born in Westmoreland county, Pennsylvania, died in Butler, Pennsylvania. 8. Michael, born in Westmoreland county, Pennsylvania, died in California; married Jane Hazlett; he was a carpenter, and went to California in the gold rush of 1849.

(II) Daniel, son of William and Mary (Harkins) McCrea, was born in Westmoreland county, Pennsylvania, March, 1815, died in Donegal township, Butler county, in 1888. He obtained his education in the public schools of his native township, and later became a furnace boss at the Buffalo Furnaces, Armstrong county, Pennsylvania. Abandoning this occupation he engaged in farming in Donegal township, Butler county, where the remainder of his life was spent. He was one of the old type of Jeffersonian Democrats, and for three years was school director of Donegal township. He was a member of the Roman Catholic church, as was his wife. He married Sarah Coyle, born in Pittsburgh, Pennsylvania, April 20, 1822, died in Donegal township, Pennsylvania, 1890, a school teacher of Clearfield, Pennsylvania, daughter of John Coyle, born in Coyleville, Pennsylvania, 1781, died in Donegal township, 1865, a blacksmith and farmer. He married Margaret Dougherty, born in Westmoreland county, Pennsylvania, 1800, died in Donegal township, Pennsylvania, surviving her husband but a short time. Children of John and Margaret (Dougherty) Coyle, all born in Coyleville: 1. Thomas, died on the old farm in Donegal township, 1878; an oil operator in Venango county, from 1860 to 1878. 2. Sarah, mentioned above. 3. Elizabeth, died in Butler, Pennsylvania; married James Tracy, of that town, where he also died, a carpenter; children: Mary, lives in Youngstown, Ohio, and another daughter. 4. Patrick, an oil well worker and coal miner, died in Butler, Pennsylvania. 5. Hannah, died in Clearfield township; married Dennis McBride, a farmer and oil producer of Butler, and had several children. 5. Henry, superintendent of a rolling mill in Philadelphia, Pennsylvania, where he died; married (first) a Miss Downey, of Johnstown, Pennsylvania, now deceased, (second) —— ——, who lives in Philadelphia. 7. John, a rolling mill worker, died near Pittsburgh, served in a Pennsylvania regiment during the civil war; married and had children. 8. William, died on the old homestead in Donegal township; married Sarah Nolan, from Donegal township; children: Maud, and one other daughter. 9. Mary, died in Butler, 1907; married Frank Slator, a retired farmer and school teacher from Donegal township, and now lives in Pittsburgh, Pennsylvania.

Children of Daniel and Sarah (Coyle) McCrea: 1. John Chrysostom, of whom further. 2. Hugh, born in Franklin township, Pennsylvania, November 30, 1845, died in infancy. 3. William H., born in Franklin township, Pennsylvania, May 30, 1847, an oil operator, died near Rangoon, India, 1907; married Margaret Forquer, from Donegal township; she died in Pittsburgh; they had two daughters, both married, and now living in Pittsburgh. 4. Thomas E., born in Franklin township, Pennsylvania, April 2, 1848; he was an oil worker; came to Bradford, Pennsylvania, where he served on the police force for seven years, and was appointed chief of police by Mayor Edward McSweeney; for a time he was a hotel proprietor in Buffalo, New York, and was afterwards deputy sheriff at Erie, Pennsylvania, being killed while taking prisoners from Erie to the penitentiary at Pittsburgh. He married Margaret Duff, from Butler township, died in Erie; children: i. Harry J., an employee of the Buffalo, Rochester & Pittsburgh Railroad Company, lives in Rochester, New York, married; ii. Albinus W., a commercial traveler in the employ of the Watson Paper Company, of Erie, Pennsylvania, married; iii. Rose, married Christopher Shaker, a carpenter, and lives at Edgely, North Dakota. 5. Margaret, born in Franklin township, May 18, 1850, died in Donegal township, 1900; married Jeremiah Johnson, a farmer of Donegal township, and had eight children. 6. Mary Catherine, born in Franklin township, Pennsylvania, March 22, 1852; married Joseph Benson, from Donegal township, and lives near Saint Joseph, Butler county, Pennsylvania; they have four children. 7. Bridget J., born in Donegal township, June 25, 1854; married William Eminger, an oculist of Kittanning, Pennsylvania, and has a large family. 8. Elizabeth, born in Donegal township, August 16, 1856; married Thomas Nolan, a millwright of Donegal township; children: John, Timothy and Bernard, all of whom were employed with their father at Natrona, Pennsylvania, in the mill. 9. Daniel F., born in Donegal township, Pennsylvania, October 10, 1858; an oil operator of Pennsylvania and California, at present proprietor of the Hotel Butler at Butler, Pennsylvania; married Mary (Garble) Stehle, widow. 10. Joseph B., born in Donegal township, June 6, 1861, died in Butler, 1910; an oil-well worker; married Annie Burns, from Donegal township, and had three children. 11. James H., born in Donegal township, July 27, 1863, died 1906; an oil-well worker; married Jennie Logue, from Clearfield, Pennsylvania, where she now lives. 12. Sarah E., born in Donegal township, December 26, 1865; married William J. Keast, of Pittsburgh, an insurance agent.

(III) John Chrysostom, eldest son and child of Daniel and Sarah (Coyle) McCrea, was born in Franklin township, Armstrong county, Pennsylvania, August 31, 1843. When he was nine years of age his parents moved to Donegal township, Butler county, Pennsylvania, where he obtained his education in the public schools. After leaving school his first position was in the employ of his uncle, Thomas Coyle, and John Hohn, in Petroleum Center, Pennsylvania, where he drilled oil wells. Until 1877 he followed the oil fields in Venango, Armstrong and Butler counties, and for one year was chief of police in Millerstown (Chicora), Pennsylvania. In 1879 he came to Bradford, Pennsylvania, and there was chief of police until 1887, in the latter year accepting a position with the Buffalo, Rochester & Pittsburgh railroad, and special agent and claim adjuster. He remained with that company until 1912, and thus his thirty-three years of his service were years of faithfulness, loyalty and fidelity. In all that time he neither had a vacation nor was away from his desk a single day. He capably filled his extremely important position, and was considered one of the company's most valuable men. He has recently opened an investigating and adjusting agency in Bradford, but will accept no cases against the railroad, from whom he receives a liberal pension and free transportation for himself and his wife for life. This is a splendid testimonial of the regard in which he is held by the company. He is also connected as a stockholder with the Kinzua Petroleum Company of Mt. Jewett, and the Kane Petroleum & Gas Company. He is a regular attendant and member of the Roman Catholic church. He belongs to the Benevolent and Protective Order of Elks, No. 234; Catholic Mutual Benefit Association, No. 13; Protected Home Circle, Business Men's Association, and the Bradford Club, all of Bradford, Pennsylvania.

He married (first) at Oil City, Pennsylvania, June 1, 1869, Mary Forquer, died at Millerstown (Chicora), Butler county, Pennsylvania, September, 1878, daughter of William and Rebecca (Marsh) Forquer, both of whom died at Millerstown, (second) in Genesee, Potter county, Pennsylvania, July 24, 1884, Katherine McMurray, born in Scranton, Pennsylvania, September 14, 1863, a daughter of Patrick McMurray. He emigrated to the United States in 1854, and became a miner in Scranton, later purchasing a farm in Genesee, Potter county, and married Sarah Gilmartin, January 28, 1852. Children of Patrick McMurray: 1. Annie, born in Scranton; married ———— Howe, an employee of the traction company in New York City. 2. Michael, born on a farm near Genesee, Pennsylvania, now an employee in the paper mill at Johnsburg, Pennsylvania; married and has several children. 3. Patrick, born near Genesee, Pennsylvania; married, has children, and lives in St. Mary's, Pennsylvania. 4. John, a machinist of Erie, Pennsylvania, married and has children. 5. James, an engineer on the Buffalo, Rochester

& Pittsburgh railroad; married, has a family and lives in East Salamanca, New York. 6. Katherine, mentioned above. 7. Sarah, married John Moran, a switchman on the Buffalo, Rochester & Pittsburgh railroad at East Salamanca, and has two children. 8. Frank, a switchman at East Salamanca, married and has two children. Children of John Chrysostom McCrea, by his first wife: 1. Stephen J., born in Millerstown (Chicora), Pennsylvania, April 10, 1870, now a hotel clerk in Chicago, Illinois. 2. Mark C., born in Fagundus, Pennsylvania, July 5, 1871, a veteran of the Spanish war, now a hotel clerk in Chicago, Illinois. 3. Laura, born in Millerstown (Chicora), Pennsylvania, December 7, 1873; married John Kragel, a carpenter of Chicago, Illinois. Children of John Chrysostom McCrea, by his second wife: 4. George, born in Bradford, Pennsylvania, 1886, died when thirteen months old. 5. Daniel F., born in Bradford, 1887; learned the trade of machinist in East Salamanca and Dubois. He joined a special force of police in Buffalo, and was shot in the temple June 20, 1908, while pursuing some freight-car robbers, and died four days later. 6. Clara, born in Bradford, April 28, 1892; a graduate of St. Bernard's School, class of 1909; married, May 10, 1911, Oscar Johnson, a machinist of Bradford.

DRAKE Members of this family have been prominent at all periods of English history, many having received official recognition from the throne. The earliest record of this branch of the family is of Jacob Drake, who emigrated from England to the American colonies, settling in Morristown, New York. He attained the rank of colonel in the American army during the war of the revolution. He married, and among his children was a son Silas.

(II) Silas, son of Jacob Drake, was born in Roxbury, New York, April 10, 1790, died 1858, at Degolia, Pennsylvania. He was educated for the medical profession, but was disinclined to follow the career prepared for him and became a farmer. In politics he was a Republican, and he and his wife were in belief Universalists. He married, March 13, 1814, Sarah Hamilton, born in Morris, Tioga county, Pennsylvania, April 15, 1788, died in Degolia, 1862. Children: 1. Esther, born March 15, 1815, died in New York state; married ——— Price, deceased; children: i. Charles, died from the effects of disease contracted while in the union service during the civil war; ii. Sarah, deceased, married Dennis Niles, deceased, of Bradford, Pennsylvania; children: Deleven, died in Hornell, New York; Charles, lives in Arcadie, New York. 2. Sarah, born in Roxbury, New York, May 23, 1817; married Christopher Young, deceased, a farmer; children: Christopher, deceased; Adelaide, married David McClure, and lives in Los Angeles, California. 3. Lorenzo Dow, of whom further. 4. Clarissa, born in Roxbury, New York, January 12, 1822, died in Erie, Pennsylvania; married John Rutherford, from near Binghamton, New York, died in Erie, Pennsylvania, a retired farmer. 5. Theodore F., born in Catlin, Tioga county, New York, August 11, 1824, died in Salamanca, New York; a farmer near Great Valley, New York; married Jane ———, died in Salamanca, New York; children: Eva, lives at Perry, New York; Howell, lives near Springville; Hamlin, deceased; Ella, lives at Great Valley, New York; Luella, deceased; Carrie, lives in Nebraska; Gertrude, lives near Great Valley, New York. 6. Joshua, born in Catlin, New York, December 16, 1827; was a soldier during the civil war and died in a camp hospital; married Elizabeth Haiter, deceased; children: Lou; Ellet; Grant, living in Beatrice, Nebraska. 7. Eliza, born in Catlin, New York, March 31, 1830, died in Degolia, Pennsylvania, December 24, 1860; a teacher for several years about Bradford.

(III) Lorenzo Dow, son of Silas and Sarah (Hamilton) Drake, was born September 20, 1819, in Roxbury, New York, died in Degolia, Pennsylvania, October 18, 1900. When he was two years old his parents moved to Degolia, Pennsylvania, where his entire education was received in the public schools. He worked on his father's farm after leaving school, and afterward owned his own land, following the occupation of a farmer all his life. He was a strong Republican in politics, and was elected to the office of school director, which he held for thirty years. He was also elected and appointed to several other town offices, which he filled zealously and efficiently. He was an earnest public-spirited man, giving freely of his time, labor and substance for the advancement of his town. He and his wife were members and regular attendants of the Universalist church. He married, December 5, 1845, Rhoda Bassett Tuttle, born in Westfield, Tioga county,

Pennsylvania, April 16, 1824, died in Degolia, August 19, 1906, daughter of Sheldon Tuttle, a farmer of Westfield, where he died (see Jewett sketch). Children: 1. Silas, born in Westfield, Pennsylvania, November 30, 1846; now living at Kearney, Nebraska, where he has a general store, but he is also a banker and a ranch-owner in Colorado; served two years in the civil war with the Bucktail Regulars; married and has children: Elmer, May and Leroy, all three living near Sumner, Nebraska; Florence; Charles, deceased; Frank; Mabel and Dewey, living with their parents. 2. Ralph, born in Bradford, Pennsylvania, March 13, 1848; is a farmer living in Elm Creek, Nebraska; married Cordelia Wood, of Nebraska; children: i. Nellie, born in Nebraska, June 8, 1880, died July 18, 1908; married, November 20, 1900, Samuel F. Fleming (see Fleming sketch), born in Allegheny county, Pennsylvania, July 21, 1875; children, all born in Degolia; Bernice E., born September 4, 1901; Margaret D., October 12, 1906; Nellie S., July 3, 1908; ii. Charles, deceased; iii. Maud, lives in Sumner, Nebraska; iv. Harry, married; v. Anna, lives with parents. 3. Leroy, born in Bradford, February 25, 1850, a farmer and property owner of Ponca City, Oklahoma; married Jennie Parks, a native of Illinois; children: Guy, an electrical engineer, lives in Wyoming; Mabel, married Raymond West, lives in Wood River, Nebraska; Edith, a nurse; Earl; William; Howard and Irene, living with their parents. 4. Russell, born in Bradford, January 12, 1852, a farmer of Easton, Maryland; married and has children; Neva and Willis, both married and living in Easton, Maryland; Leona, died young; Carl in the United States army; Lee, living with parents. 5. Guy, born in Bradford, February 25, 1854, a farmer and stock raiser of Whitman, Nebraska; married Anna Schoonmaker, of Limestone. 6. Millie C., born in Bradford, March 11, 1856; married Frank D. Smith, of Franklinville, New York, who is engaged in business in Springville, New York, where Mrs. Smith is connected with and a worker in the Universalist church. 7. Ebenezer, born in Bradford, January 30, 1859, died in infancy. 8. Sarah Alice (twin), born in Bradford, January 30, 1859; married Eli Sherman, of New Jersey, an editor of the *Palisades Tribune*, Palisades, California; child: Mildred, born November 28, 1898. 9. Ida Eliza, of whom further. 10. Charles, born in Bradford, April 10, 1865; a civil engineer in the employ of the South Pennsylvania Oil Company at Mannington, West Virginia; married (first) Clara Slingerland, of South Bradford, who died December, 1910, (second) Sarah Jenks, of Mannington, West Virginia, October 11, 1911; children by first wife: Ada, born November, 1892; Hazel, born December, 1893, died August 12, 1908; Harold, born January, 1904, died in infancy; Clara, born December, 1907; Mildred, born April, 1909. The five younger children all attended the Franklinville Academy at the same time for three years. Charles, Sarah and Ida attended the college at Ada, Ohio.

(IV) Ida Eliza, daughter of Lorenzo Dow and Rhoda Bassett (Tuttle) Drake, was born in Degolia, McKean county, Pennsylvania, October 20, 1860. She was educated in the public schools of Degolia and in the academy at Franklinville, New York, later attending the Normal School at Ada, Ohio. After her graduation she taught school for one year at Rutherford Run, Pennsylvania, but with the exception of that year has remained on the old homestead at Degolia. She is a member of the Ladies' Aid Society of the Universalist church of Degolia, and interested in all good works.

HAGGERTY Henry Haggerty, the American progenitor of the family of that name, now living in Bradford, Pennsylvania, and herein recorded, was born in Belfast, Ireland, about the year 1788. He was a well-to-do Irish farmer and cattle dealer, buying and selling cattle and speculating in all forms of standard farm products. In 1835 he came to America, settling in Mountain township, Dundas county, Canada, not far from Matilda, where he purchased land and lived until his death in 1863. He was a Conservative in politics and a man of some prominence. He married, in Ireland, Mary McFadden, who died in Mountain township. He and his wife were members of the Presbyterian church. They were the parents of three sons and three daughters; of these the only survivor is Henry, aged eighty-five years, now living at Irkerman, Canada.

(II) John, son of Henry Haggerty, was born in Belfast, Ireland, in 1812, died at Matilda, Canada, in 1860. He was educated in his native city, and on arriving at a suitable age was apprenticed to a contractor and builder, with whom he served seven years, learning the stonemason's trade and carpentering. In 1830 (five years before his father) he came to Canada, settling at Matilda, Dundas county, where he bought a farm and engaged in buying and selling live stock, the same business which his father conducted in Ireland. He was a Conservative in politics, and a member of the Presbyterian church. He married Nancy Greyband, born in Belfast, Ireland, died on the farm at Matilda, Canada, in 1870, daughter of William Greyband, a cattle dealer of Belfast, where he lived and died. A sister of Nancy, Betsy Greyband, married a Mr. Money, and died in Quebec, Canada. Children: James, born May 5, 1834; Elizabeth, 1836; Hugh, 1838; John, of whom further; Henry, born 1842; Robert, 1844; David, 1846; Alonzo, 1848. All of these are deceased except John.

(III) John (2), third son of John (1) Haggerty, was born at Matilda, Dundas county, Canada, August 8, 1840. He attended the school in Matilda and Branchton, Canada, until he was sixteen years, also helping on the home farm. After his school days were ended he learned the harness maker's trade at Matilda, and later came to the United States, following his trade at Ashtabula, Ohio, and Springfield, Pennsylvania. In 1870 he located at Corry, Pennsylvania, where he remained until the autumn of 1877, when he moved to Bradford, which has ever since been his home. He engaged in the baking business for two years, then became interested in oil production, later became a refiner and is now practically sole owner of the Journal Oil Company, a very successful and well-established refining and manufacturing company of Bradford, Pennsylvania. For a time he also held an interest in the McKean Refining Company. He has always been a supporter of the Republican party; is a member of the Methodist church and of the Masonic order. He has been very successful in business and is one of the highly esteemed, substantial men of Bradford.

He married, January 19, 1862, Margaret Jane Johnson, born near Inkerman, Canada, July 5, 1840, daughter of Simon Johnson, born in Belfast, Ireland, about 1805, died June 16, 1898; married (first) Susan Kitchen, born 1810, in Belfast, died May 12, 1854. Their children: John, James, Simon, William, George, Ellen, Mary Ann, Margaret Jane, Susan, Catharine. He married (second) a Miss Munroe, who died without issue, September 12, 1882.

Children of John (2) and Margaret Jane Haggerty: Emma Alice, Mary Louise, Harvey, John, Arthur Johnson.

Another branch of this family was founded in Clearfield county, Pennsylvania, by William Haggerty, who owned considerable amount of land at Coalport, in that county, and at his death left a large sum of money to the Presbyterian church there, of which they were to have the income so long as they continued the Psalms of David as part of their musical service. Descendants of William are prominent in business and professional life in Clearfield and Clearfield county, Pennsylvania.

ARTLEY This family has been in Pennsylvania since the middle of the eighteenth century, the earliest records obtainable being of Abraham Artley, born in Liberty, Tioga county, Pennsylvania, in 1783, where he died in 1855. He was a farmer all his life and actively interested in politics, being an ardent Democrat. He was a member of the German Lutheran church, his wife belonging to the same denomination. He married Elizabeth Long, who died in Liberty when over seventy years of age. Children: 1. William, a farmer, died in Liberty, Pennsylvania; married Lucretia ———, deceased; children: Frank, Laura and Clara. 2. Jonas, of whom further. 3. Christie Ann, lives at Williamsport, Pennsylvania; married George R. Sheffer, deceased, and had a son Charles, deceased. 4. Cassie, married ——— Weaver, deceased, and lives with her sister in Williamsport, Pennsylvania. 5. Abraham, died in Liberty, Pennsylvania; married Margaret ———, deceased, and had among their children a son William, who lives in Liberty. 6. George, married Margaret ———, and lives on a farm in Liberty. Children: Elizabeth, lives in Elmira, New York; Bertha, lives in Williamsport, Pennsylvania; John, deceased; Charles and Miles, live in Elmira, New York.

(II) Jonas, son of Abraham and Elizabeth (Long) Artley, was born in Liberty, Tioga county, Pennsylvania, June 20, 1830, died at Bradford, Pennsylvania, in March, 1905. He obtained his education in the public schools of his native town and later engaged in the hotel business. In 1860 he moved to Lycoming county, Pennsylvania, and established a hotel at Linden, which he conducted for six years; also establishing one near there, whose existence covered a period of two years. He then moved to Jersey Shore, Pennsylvania, continuing in the same business, coming to Kendall Creek in 1877 and becoming proprietor of the American; in addition, engaging in the oil business. The numerous hotels which he conducted had reputations for uniformly good service and courteous treatment. His political party was the Democratic; his religion, Presbyterian. He was a member of Labelle Valley Lodge, No. 232, Free and Accepted Masons, and the Equitable Aid Union of Kendall Creek.

He married, January 6, 1859, Sarah Elizabeth Sheffer, born in Liberty, Pennsylvania, March 31, 1837, daughter of John Sheffer (2), born in Williamsport, Pennsylvania, December, 1803, died in Liberty, Pennsylvania, December 31, 1876, son of John (1), of English descent, and Susan (Reynolds) Sheffer, of Lancaster, Pennsylvania. John (2) married Sarah Shaffer, born in Whitedeer Valley, Pennsylvania, 1804, died in Liberty, Pennsylvania, in March, 1877. Their children: 1. George, a farmer, born in Liberty, Pennsylvania, in 1828, where he died; children: Clara, lives in Bowling Green; Susan; Cora, lives in Williamsport, Pennsylvania; Nellie, lives in Liberty; Belle, lives in Elmira, New York; Eliza, lives in Williamsport, Pennsylvania; Elizabeth, deceased. 2. Henry, a wagonmaker, born in Liberty, Pennsylvania, in 1830, died in Williamsport, Pennsylvania; married (first) Sarah Levergood, deceased, and had one child, Sarah; married (second) Sheneth Beck, now living in Montoursville, Lycoming county, Pennsylvania; children: Viola, lives in Montoursville; Adele, deceased; Lurella, lives in Virginia. 3. Martin, a farmer, born in Liberty, Pennsylvania, in 1832, where he died; married (first) Henriette Fick, and had one child, Clement, deceased; married (second) Margaret Beck; children: Elmer, lives in Jersey Shore, Pennsylvania; Filmore, deceased; Ida and Frank, living in Liberty, Pennsylvania. 4. Susan, born in Liberty, Pennsylvania, December, 1834; married Charles Hagenbush, deceased, a furniture maker of Allentown, Pennsylvania; children: John, lives in Batavia, New York; Eva, lives in Evanston, Illinois. 5. Sarah Elizabeth, of previous mention. 6. Philip, born in Liberty, Pennsylvania, 1839, died in Nebraska, a wagon maker and farmer; he married Miss Ault, deceased, and had one child, Hattie, living in Pasadena, California. 7. Washington, born in Liberty, Pennsylvania, in 1841, a hotelkeeper in Blossburg, Tioga county, Pennsylvania; married (first) Eliza Kinsman, deceased; children: Annie, lives in Elmira, New York; Charles and Lilly, live in Blossburg; John, lives in the south; he married (second) Margaret Moreland. 8. Alpheus, born in Liberty, Pennsylvania, in 1845, a blacksmith in his native town; married Jennie Kohrback; children: Katherine and Carrie, live in New York City; Harry, lives in Blossburg, Pennsylvania; ———, deceased. 9. Elvina, born in Liberty, Pennsylvania, in 1845, where she still lives. 10. Adeline, born in Liberty, Pennsylvania, 1847; married Jabez Hancher, a farmer, and lives in her native town; children: Gertrude, deceased; Charles, lives in Liberty, Pennsylvania; Nellie, lives in Roaring Branch, Pennsylvania; Harry and William, live in Liberty, Pennsylvania.

Children of Jonas and Sarah Elizabeth (Sheffer) Artley: 1. Philip Sheffer, born in Lock Haven, in 1860, died in Bradford, Pennsylvania, August 10, 1896; married Annie M. Karns; their son, Roy Stephen, born in Bradford, Pennsylvania, August 14, 1887, lives in Wichita Falls, Texas, managing a store for the Atlas Supply Company. 2. Carrie Blanche, born in Lock Haven, Pennsylvania, August 9, 1864; married Joseph Ellsworth, of Holton, Maine, who died in West Virginia, November 15, 1911, was an oil producer; she and her daughter, Pauline, born August 9, 1892, live in Bradford. 3. John Huling, of whom further.

(III) John Huling, son of Jonas and Sarah Elizabeth (Sheffer) Artley, was born in Jersey Shore, Lycoming county, Pennsylvania, July 2, 1872. Here he lived until he was five years of age, moving with his parents to Bradford in 1877, where he attended the public schools, and completed his education at the Bradford Business College. His first position after leaving school was with the Tyler Tube and Pipe Company of Washington, Pennsylvania, with whom he remained five years, returning to Bradford at the end of that time and establishing in the oil producing business. He has ever since continued in that business with great success, owning valuable properties in the oil fields of Pennsylvania and West Virginia. He is a member of the Knights of the Maccabees, Tent No. 5, Bradford, and the Bradford Gun Club. In politics he is a Democrat, in religion a Presbyterian, which church his wife also attends, although she is an Episcopalian. He married, November 24, 1896, Georgia Nina Cowan, born in Farmers Valley, McKean county, Pennsylvania, February 23, 1872, a graduate of Limestone high school, New York, (see Cowan line). Children: 1. Phyllis Huling, born in Babcock, Pennsylvania, July 18, 1902, attends school in Bradford. 2. John Carlton, born in Bradford, Pennsylvania, August 11, 1904.

(The Cowan Line).

(II) William Carl Cowan, son of Isaac Cowan, was born in New York state, 1808, died August, 1871. He was proprietor of the first store in Fullerton (now Limestone), New York, and married Abigail Cramer, born 1818, died in Whitesville, New York, 1900. Children: 1. Fannie, born in Candor (?), New York, 1846, died 1907; married William Matterson, a farmer, deceased; children: George, lives in Lima, Ohio; Nellie, lives in Pasadena, California; Abigail, deceased. 2. Mary, born in Candor (?), New York, 1848; married William Burleu, deceased, a painter of Ithaca, New York; son, Guy. 3. George J., of whom further. 4. Nathan, born in Candor (?), New York, 1852, a shoemaker and farmer of Elkland, New York; married Phœbe Dennis; children: Eva, deceased, and Bertha. 5. Isaac, born in Candor, New York, 1854, a contractor; married Annie ———, and lives in Webb City, Missouri; children: Frank, Jessie, Thaddeus, Thomas, Alice; all live in Webb City except Jessie, who is a resident of Niagara Falls, New York.

(III) George J., son of William Carl and Abigail (Cramer) Cowan, was born in Candor. Tioga county, New York, June 7, 1850, died in Limestone, New York, January 28, 1903. He was a carpenter by trade, a Republican in politics and a survivor of the civil war, having served in Company C, One Hundred and Ninth Regiment New York Infantry Volunteers, enlisting in 1861 and being honorably discharged in 1864. He married Anna Hill, born in Hamburg, New York, March 17, 1850, daughter of Albert Vedder Hill, born in Schenectady, New York, died in Limestone, New York, March 9, 1882, a gunsmith, son of Henry and Ann (Vedder) Hill. He married Catherine Paff, born in Holland, 1822, died in Hamburg, New York, March 2, 1855. Their children: 1. Nicholas, born 1842, in Hamburg, New York, died in infancy. 2. William, born 1846, lives in Olean, New York; married Catherine (Zeliff) Fisk, a widow of Limestone, New York, the second white child born in Cattaraugus county, New York; children: Clara, born July, 1868, married Peter Daly; Henry, born January 18, 1870, lives in Olean, New York; Judson, born September 3, 1872, lives in Bradford, Pennsylvania. 3. Anna, of previous mention. 4. Frederic, born in Hamburg, New York, 1854, died in St. Paul, Minnesota.

Children of George J. and Anna (Hill) Cowan: 1. Frederick, a carpenter, born in Candor, New York, November 6, 1866; married, January 1, 1890, Lina Besson; children, born in Limestone, New York: Arlene, born December 16, 1891; Alan, born February 16, 1904; Georgia, born October 26, 1910. 2. Georgia Nina, of previous mention. 3. Lucy Mary, born in Limestone, New York, March 2, 1875; married, December 12, 1895, George Knight, born December 13, 1873, an oil well driller of Bradford, Pennsylvania. 4. John, born in Limestone, New York, October, 1878, died April, 1879. 5. Lottie Ethel, born in Limestone, New York, April 17, 1880, died March 2, 1882.

ASH

This family traces to Germany where Dunham Ash was born in 1806. He was educated in the excellent German schools, and when a young man emigrated to America, settling in Kingston, Canada, where he died in 1879. He also lived in the United States, having a son born in Erie county, Pennsylvania. Dunham Ash was a veterinary surgeon. He married, in Kingston, Canada, Margaret Breden, born in the North of Ireland in 1807, died in Kingston in 1893, daughter of Thomas Breden, born in Ireland, a cattle dealer and a protestant in religion. He had children: John, William, Robert, Samuel, Margaret and Bessie. Children of Dunham Ash: 1. Thomas, born 1839, in Waterford, Pennsylvania. 2. Catherine, born in Kingston, Canada, 1841, married, in 1870, a Mr. Snyder; child, Bayard. 3. William Breden, born 1843. 4. Margaret, born in Waterford, Pennsylvania, 1845, now residing unmarried in Kingston, Canada. 5. John Breden, born in Waterford, 1849. 6. Dunham E., of whom further. 7. Susan, born in Kingston. 8. Jane, born in Kingston.

(II) Dr. Dunham E. Ash, son of Dunham Ash, was born in Waterford, Erie county, Pennsylvania, April 4, 1852. He was educated in the public schools, later entering the University of Ohio, at Cincinnati, where he obtained his medical education and was graduated with the degree of M. D. He came to the oil country in 1865, and later entered the oil business, which he has engaged in throughout his life in connection with his medical practice. In the year 1887 he began the practice of medicine in Bradford and is now well established as a skillful and thoroughly reliable practitioner. For the convenience of his large clientele Dr. Ash maintains two offices, one on Main street, Bradford, the other in East Bradford. Associated with him is his son, Dr. Garrett G. Ash, an eye, ear, nose and throat specialist. Dr. Ash Sr. is a supporter of the Republican party, and in 1890-91 was burgess of the borough of Kendall, now a part of the city of Bradford. He also served for eight years as a member of the school board of Bradford and since 1899 has been a member of the city council. Prior to coming to the United States Dr. Ash served in the Canadian army, enlisting in the Forty-seventh Battalion Canadian Volunteers. He is a member of the Masonic order, belonging to lodge, chapter and commandery, and is also a member of the Independent Order of Odd Fellows. His clubs are the Country and Edgewood.

He married, March 7, 1878, Mattie Garrett, born in Kingston, Province of Ontario, Canada, July 25, 1858, graduate of the Kingston high school and prior to her marriage a teacher in the public schools of her native province. She is a member of the Methodist Episcopal church, worthy matron of Bradford Lodge, Order of the Eastern Star, and a member of the Country Club. She is the daughter of Jonathan Garrett, born in the North of Ireland, August, 1817, died 1907. He emigrated to America, finally settling in Kingston, Canada, in 1831, continuing there until his death. He married Elizabeth Conner, born in Scotland in 1828, died in Kingston, Canada, in 1886. Children of Mr. and Mrs. Garrett: 1. William, now a resident of North Dakota; married Elizabeth Hunter, deceased; children: Alice, Mary, Alfred and Annette. 2. John, married Jeannette Brevnor and lives on the old homestead farm at Kingston; children: Frederick and Elmer. 3. Mary, born 1847, died 1907; married Thomas Blacklock, deceased, children: Elizabeth and Thomas, both residents of Buffalo, New York; Jonathan Otis, resides in the west; Maud, William and Helen, all residents of Buffalo; Oliver, resides in Clearfield, Pennsylvania. 4. Eliza, born 1850, married a Mr. McClaren and resides in Nelson, British Columbia. 5. Thomas, resides in Toronto, Canada. 6. Mina, born 1854, married a Mr. Woods, a farmer of Ontario, Canada; children: Elmer, deceased; Ethel, and another. 7. Margaret, born 1856, married Joseph Stocks, born in England, died in San Diego. The above children were all born in Menicksville, Canada, those following in Kingston, Canada: 8. Mattie, previously mentioned as the wife of Dr. Dunham E. Ash. 9. Marie, born October, 1861, married William Quincey, born in Canada, whom she survives, a resident of Prescott, Canada; no children. 10. Harriet, born August, 1863, married Sheldon Ward and resides in Delmar, California; children: Margaret and George. 11. Sarah, born October, 1866; married George Conner, of Kingston, and resides with three children at Winnipeg, Canada. 12. Emma, born 1869, died 1891, at Winnipeg, Canada.

Child of Dr. and Mrs. Dunham E. Ash: Garrett Guy, born in Dallas City, McKean county, Pennsylvania, June 23, 1882; he was educated in the public schools of Bradford and is a graduate of the high school; he then entered Washington and Jefferson College, remaining two years; he then matriculated at the University of Pittsburgh (medical department), from whence he was graduated M. D., class of 1907; he immediately associated with his father in the practice of medicine, making a specialty of the diseases of the eye, ear, nose and throat; he is a member of the Masonic order of Bradford, belonging to lodge, chapter and commandery; his clubs are the Country and Bradford.

HAWKINS This family came from Pittsburgh to Bradford, but for two or more generations had been residents in Westmoreland county, Pennsylvania. Originally an agricultural family, the next generation followed the holy calling of the minister, while the present representative has passed a long and useful life in business pursuits. The family records give no trace of the ancestry, nor do Westmoreland county records.

(I) Thomas Hawkins settled at an early day in Westmoreland county, on a farm at Youngstown, where he passed the greater part of his life, died and is buried in the Youngstown cemetery with others of his family. He married, November 29, 1803, Jane Riley, who also died and is buried in Youngstown. They were both members of the Presbyterian church. Children: 1. James, born October 13, 1804; married Jane Boyd. 2. Matthew, born February 17, 1806; married Mary Boyd. 3. Thomas, born October 3, 1807; was an itinerant decorative painter, finally settling in Arkansas. 4. David Riley, of whom further. 5. Ann, born June 27, 1812; married Alex Ross.

(II) David Riley, son of Thomas and Jane (Riley) Hawkins, was born at Youngstown, Westmoreland county, Pennsylvania, February 22, 1810. He learned the tailor's trade, continuing until twenty years of age in his native town. He then began studying for the ministry and was ordained, joining the Pittsburgh conference of the Methodist Episcopal church. He filled many charges most acceptably, his last being Asbury Chapel in Pittsburgh. He died in July, 1850, at the age of forty years. He was an earnest, faithful minister and pastor, greatly beloved by his congregations and useful in his Master's cause. He was a Whig in politics and strongly opposed to human slavery. He married Charlotte Boyd, born in Westmoreland county, Pennsylvania, November 3, 1807, died in Pleasantville, Pennsylvania, 1897, a farmer's daughter, a faithful devoted Christian and a great help to her husband in his pastoral work. She remained his widow twenty-nine years. Children: 1. Adam Clarke, of whom further. 2. Richard Watson, born in Youngstown, Pennsylvania, March 16, 1835, now deceased; he followed in his father's footsteps, studied theology and was a regularly ordained minister of the Methodist Episcopal church; he married, March 19, 1856, in Pittsburgh, Laura H. Smith, who died in Buffalo, New York, in January, 1912, leaving issue. 3. Emma Jane, born in Canton, Ohio, December 19, 1840, died in Greenville, Pennsylvania; married George Kerr Anderson, of Rochester, Pennsylvania, an oil producer and a prominent public man, serving as state senator; children: Lottie, born June 24, 1860; Luella, August 8, 1861, died February 2, 1864; Emma Laura, born May 8, 1863; Olive, July 23, 1864. 4. David Riley, born in Bridgewater, Pennsylvania, November 24, 1842, died in San Francisco, California; he served in the civil war, later becoming an oil operator; he married, in Meadville, Pennsylvania, Harriet Kirly, who died in Philadelphia in 1911; children: Fred W., now living in New Jersey; Bessie, now living in New York City.

(III) Major Adam Clarke Hawkins, eldest son of David Riley and Charlotte (Boyd) Hawkins, was born in Youngstown, Westmoreland county, Pennsylvania, September 23, 1833. He attended the public schools until thirteen years of age, but was a student and reader all through his early manhood and middle life, acquiring in the great school of experience an education that now bespeaks him the cultured, refined gentleman. His first position was as a boy of thirteen in a store at Freeport, Armstrong county, Pennsylvania, where he remained three years. At age of sixteen years he was a salesman for the large iron and machinery house of Scafe & Atkinson in Pittsburgh. He later became bookkeeper for Young, Stevenson & Love, a Pittsburgh firm. He had widely improved his opportunities during these years and built up a good reputation as a trustworthy, capable, young business man. He now graduated from land employment to the river boats, plying the Ohio and Mississippi rivers, between Pittsburgh and New Orleans. He continued as clerk on the "Paul Jones" and other river boats for six years, then located in Rochester, Pennsylvania, again becoming a merchant, going thence to New Brighton, Beaver county, Pennsylvania, in the same business. About 1865 he engaged in mercantile business in Pittsburgh on his own account, continuing successfully until 1879. In the latter year he disposed of his Pittsburgh interests and settled in Bradford and began his long and successful career as an oil producer. He was one of the original stockholders of the Tide Water Pipe Line Company and has been connected with many of the corporate oil enterprises of Bradford as well as conducting large private operations. He has now practically retired from active business, but views with satisfaction a long and well spent life of honorable business activity. His commercial career has only been interrupted by his service during the war between the states with the Ninth Pennsylvania Regiment. He has been an active Republican all his life, and may claim to have been one of the founders of that great party. having cast his first presidential vote for General John C. Fremont. He has served with honor in many political offices and positions of trust, including that of delegate to many state conventions and alternate and regular delegate to national conventions of his party. Major Hawkins has taken an active interest in educational matters and has been a member of the Bradford school board for the past fifteen years and for ten years the president of the board. He is a prominent member of the Masonic order, belonging to lodge, chapter and commandery. He is also a member of the Benevolent and Protective Order of Elks. His clubs are the Merchants and Country of Bradford. In religious faith he is an Episcopalian.

Major Hawkins married (first) January 10, 1855, Elizabeth Stiles, born in Rochester, Pennsylvania, died December, 1893, daughter of John Stiles, of Beaver county, Pennsylvania, and his wife Jane (Pollock) Stiles, a native of Allegheny county, both deceased. He married (second) April 27, 1904, Cora Belle Sweet, born at Alfred Center, New York, daughter of Dr. Nathaniel Sweet, a practicing physician. Children by first marriage: 1. Harry Stiles, born May 14, 1857, now superintendent in charge of his father's business; he married, May 11, 1880, Elizabeth Babbett, born November 11, 1857; two children: Adam Clarke, born February 11, 1882, now engaged in the oil business near Lepulpa, Oklahoma; Howard, born May 10, 1884, died February 11, 1889. 2. Frank Watson, born 1859, now in the employ of the Hope Gas Company of Pittsburgh; his wife died without issue. 3. George Kerr, born in 1860, died in Bradford, 1889, unmarried.

MALLORY

This was an ancient and distinguished family long seated at Studley Royal, in Yorkshire, England. Of this family was Captain Roger Mallory, who founded a line in the Virginia colony about 1660, and some of whose descendants located in Pennsylvania.

(I) Nathaniel Mallory, born at Middletown, Dauphin county, Pennsylvania, was undoubtedly a descendant of Captain Roger Mallory, of Virginia. After growing to manhood he removed to western Pennsylvania. He married and left a son John, of whom further.

(II) John, son of Nathaniel Mallory, was born in western Pennsylvania, in 1794, died at Cambridge Springs, Pennsylvania, in 1880. He was a farmer of Erie county, Pennsylvania. He was a Whig, and later a Republican. He and his wife were members of the Christian church. He married Anna Irish, born near Cambridge Springs, 1794, died there in 1879. Children, all born at Cambridge Springs: 1. Harriet, died at McKean, Erie county, Pennsylvania; married David Greenlee; children: Allen, William, Mary Ellen, Andrew, Hiram, Anna, Jane and Evalina; of these, Andrew lives in Colorado, the last three in Erie, Pennsylvania; the others are deceased. 2. Huldah, died near Cambridge Springs; married Seymour Thorpe, a farmer of that section; children: Anna, deceased; Mary Ellen, living near Cambridge Springs; John, deceased. 3. Truman, of whom further. 4. William, died at the old homestead; married Drucilla Stafford; children: Adelaide, Huldah, Hiram, the latter the only survivor. 5. Hiram, now living at Charlestown, West Virginia; an oil producer; married Lettie Colvin, deceased, of Waterford, Pennsylvania; children: William, living in Charlestown; Mary and Susan, of Edenboro, Pennsylvania. 6. Sarah, died at Waterford, Pennsylvania; married Daniel Rullins, of Union City, Pennsylvania; no issue.

(III) Truman, son of John Mallory, was born in Le Boeuf township, Erie county, Pennsylvania, April 12, 1824. He was well educated in the schools of McClellan Corners, Conneaut Valley, Pennsylvania, and began active life in the lumber business, in which he continued until the oil business attracted him, when he located at Mecca, Ohio. He continued in oil production for many years, and died at Phelps Corners, Pennsylvania, March 17, 1899. He was a Republican in politics, and was actively interested in political affairs, holding many town offices. He was a man of industry and highly respected for his many estimable traits. He married Charlotte Lydia Phelps, born at Phelps Corners, February 15, 1829, died there March 27, 1903, eldest daughter of Theodore Phelps, a wealthy farmer and a noted hunter, who died at Phelps Corners at the age of fifty years; his wife Lydia died there, aged seventy-eight years. Children of Mr. and Mrs. Phelps, all born at Phelps Corners: 1. Charlotte Lydia, of previous mention. 2. Polly, died at Rice Lake, Pennsylvania; married Alonzo Hillyer, a blacksmith of Rice Lake; children: Webb, Julia, James, Lydia, Eliza and Selden. 3. Cenia, died at Phelps Corners; married Hiram Cook, a farmer, later an oil producer of Union City, Pennsylvania, also deceased; children: William, of Los Angeles, California; John, of Corry, Pennsylvania; James, of Los Angeles; Maria, deceased. 4. Lucinda, drowned in French Creek, near

Franklin, in 1850, unmarried. 6. William, died at Phelps Corners, a lumberman, farmer and stock-breeder; married Juliette Fish; children: Frederick, deceased; Emma, living in Waterford, Pennsylvania; Frank, deceased; Lillian, living in Phelps Corners; Ruth, deceased; Willis, living in Phelps Corners. 6. Wesley, killed in the battle of the Wilderness during the civil war, a private of the Eighty-third Regiment Pennsylvania Volunteer Infantry; unmarried. 7. Eliza, living in Edenboro, Pennsylvania; married James McCurry, deceased; son, Vincent, living in Edenboro. Children of Mr. and Mrs. Mallory: 1. Lewis Elmore, of whom further. 2. Frederick Eugene, born at Cambridge Springs, Pennsylvania, February 5, 1851; now living in Los Angeles, California, an oil producer; married Jennie Rittenhouse, of Spartansburg, Pennsylvania; children: George, deceased; Roy, born 1887, operates a poultry farm at Los Angeles, married and had a son Eugene, born 1907. 3. Emma, born near Erie, Pennsylvania, February 15, 1853; married (first) Sidney Chase, an oil producer, deceased; no issue; she married (second) Henry Tracy, a farmer, and resides at Phelps Corners; no issue. 4. John Franklin, born near Erie, 1855; married (first) Susan Shaffer; child, Ernest, born 1880, now a prominent oil producer of Parksburg, West Virginia, married Creta Hutchinson; married (second) Beatrice ——; child, John, born 1908. 5. Sidney Truman, born in Phelps Corners, 1857; now an oil producer of Tulsa, Oklahoma; married Ellen Bushfield, of St. Mary's, West Virginia; child, Ethel, born 1898. 6. Lydia, born in Phelps Corners, February 15, 1859; married James H. Williamson, of Waterford, Pennsylvania; now living at St. Mary's, West Virginia; he is a grocery man and engaged in oil production; children: Mildred, born 1897; Herbert, 1899; Genevieve, 1902; Helen, 1908.

(IV) Lewis Elmore, son of Truman Mallory, was born at Cambridge Springs, Pennsylvania, April 6, 1849. His early education was obtained in the public schools at Phelps Corners, Washington township, but his school attendance ceased when he was fifteen years of age. He then began work in the oil fields, going first to Bull Run in the oil creek district of Venango county. He continued in that field ten years, finishing up his work at wells on the John Steel farm. In 1863-64 he was at Pleasantville in the same county, going thence to Foster, Venango county, where he was a contractor. At the time of the Angel and Prentice developments, he went to Bully Hill and there drilled the first oil well with five and five-eighths casing and drilled to sand without water; this was the first well of its kind below Oil City.

In 1876 he located in Bradford, but has not confined his operations to that city or section. He is known as one of the largest and most successful operators of the oil and gas country, and has been constantly engaged in the development of oil properties, both as an individual operator and in corporate enterprises. He opened up the Watsonville Oil Pool, near Marshburg, in McKean county; the abundant pool in Chipmunk and Second Sands, on Nicholas Run, Cattaraugus county, New York, and the Turkey Mountain Pool, in Tulsa county, Oklahoma. In the Ohio field he operates through the Ohio Fuel Supply Gas Company, of which he is a director; also is a director and member of the executive committee of the Ohio Fuel & Oil Company, a company now actively operating on Blue Creek, Kanawha county, West Virginia. The vastness of his oil interests is best explained by the fact that he owns entirely or partially over a thousand producing wells, many of them in the Bradford fields. His experience covers all branches of oil and gas production, beginning as a boy of fifteen when he took up life's battles. He has been nobly seconded in many of his enterprises by his son, Lewis Elbert. His success has been fairly earned and comes not through fortune's favor, but through energetic, well directed, constant effort and wise management.

He is a Republican in politics, but has never actively entered public life, devoting all his energy to his large business interests. He is a member of the Presbyterian church, the Duquesne Club of Pittsburgh, the Bradford Merchants, Country and Bradford Gun clubs. In the latter he enjoys his favorite recreation, shooting, and with his son has helped make and maintain the high reputation the club has made in marksmanship against picked clubs of the United States and Canada. He is prominent in the Masonic order, belonging to all bodies of the York and Scottish Rites, holding in the latter the thirty-second degree. His memberships are in Bradford Lodge, No. 334, Free and Accepted Masons; Bradford Council, Royal and Select Masters; Bradford Chapter, No. 260, Royal Arch Masons; Trinity Commandery, No. 58, Knights Templar; Syria

Temple, Nobles of the Mystic Shrine, of Pittsburgh, and Pittsburgh Consistory, Ancient Accepted Scottish Rite. He also is a member of the Benevolent and Protective Order of Elks.

Mr. Mallory married, January 1, 1873, Emma Jeannette Crawford, born in Emlenton, Venango county, Pennsylvania, May 23, 1853, where she was educated in Emlenton Seminary. She is a member of the Presbyterian church and Bradford Country Club. She is a daughter of Ebenezer Crawford (see Crawford V). Children of Mr. and Mrs. Mallory: 1. Lewis Elbert, born in Emlenton, Pennsylvania, May 18, 1874; now engaged with his father in oil production in Pennsylvania and New York, maintaining his residence in Bradford; he married Mabel DeHart, born May 17, 1881; children: John Truman, born December 14, 1903, died March 30, 1908; Thomas DeHart, born November 5, 1906; Marjorie Crawford, born May 14, 1910. 2. Nellie Emma, born in Emlenton, Pennsylvania, December 2, 1875; married, March 3, 1903, Frederick G. Crittenden, born May 23, 1867, at Phelps, New York; he is a graduate M. D., but does not practice, being engaged in oil production; child, Janet Mallory Crittenden, born April 5, 1911, at Buffalo, New York. 3. Maude, born August 2, 1881, died October 12, 1881.

(The Crawford Line).

(I) Emma Jeannette (Crawford) Mallory is a descendant of John Crawford, a native of the North of Ireland, of Scotch parentage, who emigrated to America about 1728, settling in Hanover township, Dauphin county, Pennsylvania. With him came several other members of the family, brothers, no doubt; James, who located in Paxtang township; Robert and Hugh, who settled in the same neighborhood. John Crawford married and had at least three sons: James, John and Richard, of whom further.

(II) James, son of John (1) Crawford, the emigrant, was born in Hanover township, Dauphin county, Pennsylvania, in 1730, but in 1770 was a resident of Northumberland county, living along the west branch of the Susquehanna. He was a member of the convention of July, 1776, which framed the first constitution of the state and served in the revolution. He was commissioned major, October 8, 1776, of Colonel William Cook's regiment of the Pennsylvania line; resigned October 12, 1777, and afterwards filled the offices of sheriff, commissioner and justice of the peace. He died about 1812-13 and was buried in the old Pine Creek burying ground, near Jersey Shore. Major Crawford married (first) Rosanna, second daughter of John and Jane Allison, of Lancaster county. Her sister Margaret married Colonel Hugh White, of the revolution. Children: John, served in the revolution, died unmarried; Robert, married Elizabeth Quigley; Thomas, removed to Erie county, Pennsylvania; Ann, married Benjamin Walker. Major Crawford married (second) Agnes, daughter of Captain McDonald, of Cumberland, who survived him. Child, Elizabeth, died in Erie county, Pennsylvania, unmarried.

(II) John (2), son of John (1) Crawford, was born 1736, died April 8, 1789, and is buried in the old Hanover church-yard. He married and left children: William, married Patty Crain; Ann, married Samuel Finney; Violet; Mattie (Martha); John, of whom further.

(II) Richard, the last son of John (1) Crawford of whom there is record, was born 1740, married, 1765, Elizabeth ———, born 1745, died June 12, 1810. After the death of his wife he resided with his daughter Ann, in Anthony township, Columbia, now Montour township, Pennsylvania, where he died about 1813, and is buried at Warrior Run graveyard. Children: Paul; James, married Mary Finney; Ann, married Hugh Wilson; Elizabeth, married Rev. John Moody. Another daughter married a brother of Rev. John Moody.

(III) John (3), son of John (2) and grandson of John (1) Crawford, settled in Greene county, going from thence to Butler county, Pennsylvania, in 1707, thence to Venango county, where he died at Emlenton, February 12, 1812. He married Mary Parker and left issue.

(IV) Ebenezer, son of John (3) and Mary (Parker) Crawford, was born about 1803, died near Emlenton, Pennsylvania, in 1859, on the farm settled by his father. He married Janet Grant from Crofort, Scotland, died in Bruin, Butler county, Pennsylvania. Children (not known to be in order of birth): 1. Ebenezer, of whom further. 2. Alexander, married Margaret Anderson; children: Ebenezer and Anderson. 3. John, married Barbara Hicks; children: Meade, Carlisle, Ida, Mary and Estella. 4. Robert, died unmarried. 5. William, married Jane Herr; children: Zelia, Jessie, Jane and John. 6. Elihu, died unmarried. 7. Harvey, married Martha Ross; children: Lewis, an electrician of Chicago; Lillian, resides in Chicago; Frank, an electrician in the west. 8. Samuel, an oil producer, married Jane Truby, who survives him, a resident of Emlenton; children: Harry, a bank president of Emlenton; Edward and Gertrude. 9. Isabelle, married Harvey Gibson, a miller; children: Sarah, William, Janet, Zera, Ebenezer and Samuel. 10. Matilda, died March 7, 1912, at age of ninety-three years; she married Harvey Crawford, deceased, her cousin from Akron, Ohio; children: David, Janet, James, Lucy and Samuel. 11. Emmeline, now living in Starke, Florida; married George Livingston, deceased; children: Samuel, George and Kate. 12. A daughter, who died at the old homestead.

(V) Ebenezer (2), son of Ebenezer (1) and Janet (Grant) Crawford, was born at the homestead near Emlenton, Pennsylvania, August 26, 1821, died there August 26, 1897. He grew to manhood at the home farm and in 1849 joined the gold-seekers in their rush to California. He prospered and later returned to Emlenton. In his latter years he was engaged in banking. He married Elizabeth Wilson, born in Elizabethtown, Pennsylvania, June 30, 1833, died in Buffalo, New York, June 19, 1906. Children: 1. Clare Minerva, born in Emlenton, January 5, 1851, died at East Brody, Pennsylvania, April 3, 1885; married Milo C. Treat, born April 5, 1842, in Leon Center, New York, who survives her and married (second) Sarah Hicks; child by first wife: Ellis Milo, born November 27, 1872; by second wife: Milo, born 1896. 2. Emma Jeannette, of previous mention, wife of Lewis Elmore Mallory (see Mallory IV). 3. James Burton, born October 5, 1855; now living in Oil City, Pennsylvania, engaged in the oil and gas business as general manager of the National Fuel and Gas Company of New Jersey; married Nellie Comstock; children: Edith, born August 20, 1881; Robert, 1885; Helen, 1887; Ronald, 1890. 4. Lewis, born August, 1857, died 1861. 5. Mary, born 1859, died 1859. 6. George W., born June 4, 1861; now president of the Ohio Fuel Supply Gas Company of Pittsburgh, unmarried. 7. Frederick W., born December 19, 1864; now president of the Ohio Fuel Oil Company, and resides in Columbus, Ohio; married Elizabeth Dreibellis; children: Catherine, born 1896; Jean, 1900. 8. Carroll E., born May 29, 1873; now living in Emlenton, where he is engaged in oil and gas production; married Susan Kribbs, born 1872, died February, 1907; children: Elizabeth, born August, 1897; Gertrude, October, 1901; Richard, August, 1905. These eight children were born in Emlenton, Pennsylvania.

CATLIN-STANTON The surname Catlin is of ancient English origin. In the early records it is spelled Catelin, Cattling, Cattell and Catlin. The name is found frequently in records of county Kent, England, where the family has held property since the Norman Conquest. R. de Catlin was one of the followers of William the Conqueror and is mentioned in the Domesday Book as having two knights fees of land. Sir Catlin was knighted for honorable service at the battle of Agincourt, under Edward, the Black Prince, and the Catlin coat-of-arms was granted him, viz.: "Per chevron or azure three lions passant gnardant in pale, counter charged in chief argent. Crest: A leopard's head couped at the neck argent, ducally collared and lined or reguardant." Motto: *Semper fides*.

(I) Thomas Catlin, emigrant ancestor of the American family, was born in 1600, according to a deposition in court in 1687, giving his age as eighty-seven years. He was in Hartford about 1640 and is mentioned in colonial records in 1644. He was chimney viewer, surveyor of highways, selectman and constable, holding the latter then important office from 1662 to 1674. He married (first) Mary ——, who died before 1675; he married (second) Mary Elmer or Elmore, whose first husband, Edward, was killed by the Indians in King Philip's war. Children: Mary and John.

(II) John, son of Thomas Catlin, was born prior to 1640 in England. He married, July 27, 1665, Mary, daughter of Captain Samuel Marshall, of Windsor, Connecticut. She died in Hartford, October 20, 1716. Children: John, Mary, Samuel, Thomas, Benjamin.

(III) Samuel, son of John Catlin, was born in Hartford, Connecticut, 1672. He married Elizabeth North. Children: John, Thomas, Samuel, Isaac, Abigail, Job, Mary, Adam, Ebenezer.

(IV) Isaac, son of Samuel Catlin, was born in Hartford, Connecticut, November 11, 1712, died May 5, 1803. He married (first) Betsey (Elizabeth) Kilbourn; (second) a widow, Abigail (Ives) Tuttle. Children by first marriage: Isaac, Elisha, Charles, Irene, Polly, Betsey, Ruth, Sarah, Bradley.

(V) Elisha, son of Isaac Catlin, was born in 1745. He married, January 8, 1784. Roxanna Dewey, born January 5, 1763. They lived in Harwinton, Connecticut. Roxanna was a daughter of Eli Dewey, of Westfield, Massachusetts, and Harwinton, Connecticut, where he was a farmer and had a whetstone quarry. He married (first) Abigail Gillett, (second) Mrs. Mary (Dewey) Sloan, widow of John Sloan, and daughter of James Dewey, a kinsman. They had seven children of whom Roxanna was the second. Eli Dewey was the son of David (2), son of David (1), son of Israel, son of Thomas Dewey, emigrant ancestor of the large and influential Dewey family of the United States of whom Admiral George Dewey, the hero of Manila Bay, is a conspicuous member as was Rev. Jedediah Dewey, the "fighting parson," who adjourned a service in his church to go out one Sunday morning to fight the British at Bennington and returned to the house of worship, took up his sermon where he had left off when interrupted and finished it to the end. Thomas Dewey came to Massachusetts in 1633 from Kent, England, married a widow, Frances Clark, and had sons, Israel, Thomas (2), Josiah, Jedediah. Admiral George Dewey descends through Josiah and Roxanna Dewey, through Israel, their third son. Among the children of Elisha and Roxanna (Dewey) Catlin was Dewey, of whom further.

(VI) Dewey, son of Elisha Catlin, was born in Harwinton, Connecticut, died in Buffalo, New York, about 1843. He lived in Connecticut until he was a young man, then went to Buffalo at an early day before railroads crossed the state and the only conveyance was canal boat or team. He was the proprietor of a hotel at Buffalo and a well known citizen. He was an active Democrat and influential in the party. He married Dolly White, who died in Buffalo. They were both members of the Congregational church. Children: Florella; Adaline, married Charles Huntley; Minerva, Samantha, Eli, Oren, of whom further.

(VII) Oren, son of Dewey Catlin, was born at DeRuyter, New York, January 26, 1821, died in Portsmouth, Ohio, March, 1885. He was educated in the public schools of Buffalo, New York, and began business life in that city. He was a traveling salesman for hardware firms of Buffalo, R. L. Howard and George L. Squire, later with D. M. Osborn, of Auburn. He was active in politics, a Democrat, for many years justice of the peace. He married Eliza Ann Tallman, his cousin, born in Buffalo, New York, February 23, 1824, died there February 14, 1872, a member of the Congregational church. She was a daughter of Elijah Tallman, born at Evans, New York, ten miles west of Buffalo, in 1788, died there in 1870, a farmer of Evans throughout the active years of his life. He married Florella Catlin, born in Connecticut, daughter of —— Catlin and sister of Dewey Catlin. Children of Oren and Eliza Ann (Tallman) Catlin: 1. Ellen Virginia, of whom further. 2. Cassius M. Clay, born in Buffalo, September 18, 1849, died October 29, 1908; he was educated in the Buffalo public schools and was a traveling salesman; he married Emma Woodward, of Buffalo; no issue. 3. Mary Minerva, born in Buffalo, July, 1859, died in infancy.

(VIII) Ellen Virginia, daughter of Oren Catlin, was born September 16, 1846, at Buffalo, New York. She was educated in the city schools at Westfield, New York, finishing her studies at Medina Academy at Medina, New York. She later pursued a course of musical study at the Cleveland (Ohio) Conservatory of Music. After completing her studies she taught music until 1872. She married, July 31, 1872, Norman Jacob Stanton, born at Milford, New Jersey, June 17, 1841, died February 19, 1897. He was educated in the different schools, finishing at Syracuse, New York. In 1861, at the age of twenty years, he enlisted in the Fifty-eighth Regiment Pennsylvania Infantry, served his first term, reënlisted and served until the close of the war. His regiment was attached to the Army of the Potomac and participated in many of the hard-fought battles of the civil war. He attained the rank of sergeant under Captain Burnham, witnessed the surrender of General Lee at Appomattox and received an honorable discharge. After the war he lived in Buffalo, New York, going thence to Richmond, Virginia, where he engaged in the lumber business. In 1877 or 1878 he located in Bradford, Pennsylvania, where he held several important city offices. He served as tax collector eight years, was secretary to the board of water commissioners, and for about nine years was chief of police, from 1884 to 1893. He was a capable and trustworthy public official and was held in highest regard. He was a Republican in politics, and a prominent member of the Masonic order, holding the highest degrees of the Scottish Rite. He left no issue. Norman J. was a son of John Stanton, who after enlisting as a soldier in the Mexican war, never returned. He left a widow, Bridget, and children: William, married Salome Bush and now lives on a farm near Smithport, Pennsylvania; Susan, James, Maria and Norman B., all deceased but William. Mrs. Bridget Stanton died in Buffalo, New York, 1844. Mrs. Ellen Virginia (Catlin) Stanton survives her husband and is now (1912) residing in Bradford. She is a member of the Presbyterian church and well known for her benevolences and kindly heart.

IRVINE-ANDREWS The Irvine family herein recorded is of Scotch descent, the great-grandfather of Mary A. (Irvine) Andrews, of Bradford, Pennsylvania, emigrating to this country from Ireland, where the family had settled on leaving Scotland. The family seat was nine miles from Enniskillen, on the banks of Lough Eine, at a little village of thirteen hundred people called Irvinestown, also Loutherstown. Here lived John Irvine, a justice of the peace and deputy lieutenant of the county of Fermanagh. Among the physicians of the village was Gerard Irvine, and among its merchants was William Irvine. This was the family from which sprang the Irvines of Pennsylvania.

(I) Of the brothers that came to America may be named William, Andrew and Matthew. William was born in Enniskillen, Fermanagh county, Ireland, in 1740, and was appointed a surgeon in the British navy. In 1763 he emigrated to America, settling at Carlisle, Pennsylvania, where he practiced his profession with success until 1774, when he was appointed one of the representatives in the provincial convention which met at Philadelphia in that year. In January, 1776, he was appointed colonel of the Sixth Battalion, afterward the Seventh Regiment, Pennsylvania Line. On March 8, 1782, he was ordered to Fort Pitt to protect the frontier, then threatened with British and Indian invasion. He was also employed in settling the boundary dispute between Pennsylvania and Virginia. In 1794 he was appointed with Andrew Ellicott to lay out the towns of Erie, Warren, Waterford and Franklin, in which service they were accompanied by a military escort under Colonel Irvine's command. He was a member of the convention to form a constitution for the state of Pennsylvania, and was commander-in-chief of Pennsylvania troops during the whiskey insurrection, and was appointed by Chief Justice McKean to treat with the insurgents.

General Irvine married Anne, daughter of Robert Callender, of Middlesex, near Carlisle, Pennsylvania, an extensive Indian trader, and who commanded a company of Pennsylvania militia at Braddock's defeat. One of his sons, Callender Irvine, born in Carlisle, 1774, was president of the Hibernia Society of Pennsylvania, and of the State Society of the Cincinnati. Elizabeth Irvine married Dr. Reynolds, a United Irishman of '98, who came to this country and practiced successfully in Philadelphia. In Warren county, Pennsylvania, is the village of Irvine, named in honor of General William Irvine. Andrew, a brother of General Irvine, was also a brave soldier of the revolution, serving as captain. Matthew Irvine, a younger brother of General William and Andrew, came to this country when a boy. He studied medicine at Carlisle and Philadelphia under his brother and the famous Dr. Rush, but imbibing the patriotic ardor of his brothers he left his studies to join the army of Washington. One of these brothers was the father of Andrew, of whom further.

(II) Andrew Irvine was born in Northumberland county, Pennsylvania, on the west bank of the Susquehanna river, in 1787, died in Warren, Pennsylvania, in January, 1851. His parents were obliged to leave Northumberland county on account of the Indians, fleeing to Cumberland county. His father had three wives and twenty-two children, having issue by each wife. A half-brother of Andrew, Welsh Irvine, was a farmer and boat-builder of Bradford county. Another half-brother, George, settled in that county in 1813. Andrew Irvine settled at Towanda, Bradford county, in 1812, where he erected and operated a tannery until 1836, then moved to Warren, Pennsylvania, where he bought property and engaged extensively in farming and lumbering. On the property which he owned and which is now in the possession of his heirs are several productive gas and oil wells. He was a Democrat in politics, and a member of the Presbyterian church, as was his wife. He married Catherine McAffee, born in Bradford county, Pennsylvania, 1791, died in Warren county, Pennsylvania, in May, 1862. Children, all born in Towanda, Pennsylvania: 1. James D., born 1813, died 1884, unmarried. 2. Mary Ann, born 1815, died April, 1876, unmarried. 3. Benjamin F., of whom further. 4. Rosanna, born 1823, died 1826. 5. Infant, died unnamed. 6. Catherine, deceased; married Nelson Parker. 7. Guy C., born 1833, died January, 1903, unmarried; was a wealthy farmer of Warren county, Pennsylvania. 8. Thomas Jefferson, born 1834, married Ursula Brand, born 1837; they now reside in Warren.

(III) Benjamin F., son of Andrew and Catherine (McAffee) Irvine, was born at Towanda, Pennsylvania, August 12, 1820, died at Irvine's Mills, September 10, 1878, leaving a record of a life well spent. He attended the public schools there until his parents moved to Warren, Pennsylvania, where he completed his studies. He worked in his father's tannery and engaged in lumbering on the Alleghenmy river, his father having large lumbering interests. In 1843 he moved to Irvine's Mills, in Cattaraugus county, New York. He there bought five thousand acres of land, much of it heavily timbered, erected saw mills, and caused a village to spring up that was named in his honor. He was a Democrat in politics, and a church member. He married, January 1, 1847, Rebecca Leonard (see Leonard), born in Warren, Pennsylvania, July 12, 1830. She was educated in the public schools of Ellicottville, and Great Valley, New York, finishing at Ellicottville Seminary. She survives her husband, a resident of Bradford, Pennsylvania, with her daughter, Mrs. Mary A. Andrews. Children of Benjamin F. Irvine, all born at Irvine's Mills, New York: 1. Mary A., of whom further. 2. Guy C., born March 21, 1850, died at Bradford, Pennsylvania, January 23, 1912; was a lumberman; married Mildred Beardsley, of Limestone, New York, born November 14, 1850; no issue. 3. Andrew, born May 29, 1854, died November 26, 1855. 4. Leonard Clarence, born March 27, 1856, died at Gardean, McKean county, Pennsylvania, February 4, 1897; an accountant; unmarried. 5. Jerome Nelson, born October 27, 1857, died in infancy. 6. Benjamin Franklin, born September 30, 1859, died August 10, 1910; a tobacco merchant; married Mary Clark, born in Farmer's Valley, Pennsylvania, March 31, 1874, died March, 1905; child: Rebecca Lydia, born in Bradford, Pennsylvania, May 16, 1902. 7. Dewitt Clinton, born February 23, 1866, died in infancy.

(IV) Mary A., eldest child of Benjamin F. and Rebecca (Leonard) Irvine, was born at Irvine's Mills, Cattaraugus county, New York, May 5, 1848. She was educated at the Union School in Tonawanda, New York, and resided at home until her marriage, May 4, 1869, to Harper G. Andrews, and lives at Bradford, Pennsylvania, the family home. She is an attendant of the Universalist church and a member of the Ladies' Auxiliary, No. 4, Union Veteran Legion. Children: Rebecca Irvine, born at Irvine's Mills, New York, January 27, 1870; Robert Irvine, May 10, 1877; Benjamin Franklin Irvine, September 18, 1879; all of whom died in infancy.

Harper G. Andrews was a son of Robert Harper Andrews, born in Plymouth, Connecticut, in 1800, moved to Windsor, New York, and after his marriage was engaged in farming there until his death, September 25, 1872. He married (first) Thiolelia Guernsey, died in Windsor, in 1842; (second) Julia Wilmoth, born in Great Bend, Pennsylvania, 1808, died there, 1878. Children by first wife: 1. Ansel, born 1826, died 1898; married Mary Scott; child, Frank, a farmer of Hollywood, California. 2. Alma, born 1828, died in Windsor, New York; her birthplace, 1896; married David Wilmoth, a farmer, also deceased; children: William, lives in Great Bend, Pennsylvania; Sarah, Kate and Daniel, the last three living in Harpersville, New York. 3. Stella, born 1830, now living in Susquehanna, Pennsylvania; married John Tiffany, a retired engineer; child, Flora, married Nathaniel Decker, and lives in Susquehanna; children: John, Flora and Nathaniel. Children of Harper G. Andrews by second wife: 4. Harper G., of whom further. 5. Robert A., born December, 1847; a real estate agent in Hollywood, California; married Tillie Burt, of Bradford county, Pennsylvania; children: Harper, Howard, Henry, Fred, Grace, Maude, Earl, Mildred. 6. Edna, born 1851; married Bert Bell, of Windsor, New York, now a farmer at Hollywood, California; children: Jesse, a professional educator, New York City; Mina, of Windsor, New York; Lena, of Hollywood, California; Bradley, of Windsor, New York.

Harper G. Andrew, son of Robert Harper Andrews and his second wife, Julia (Wilmoth) Andrews, was born in Windsor, New York,

February 14, 1846, died in Bradford, Pennsylvania, August 30, 1904. He was educated in the public schools of Binghamton, New York, finishing with a course at a commercial college. He began his active career as a farmer near Windsor, continuing until his enlistment, July 25, 1862, in Company B, One Hundred and Thirty-seventh Regiment New York Volunteer Infantry. He enlisted as a drummer, being only sixteen years old, and served until honorably discharged with the rank of first lieutenant, April 14, 1865. He was a brave soldier and saw hard service with the armies of Grant, Rosecrans and Thomas, marched with Sherman "from Atlanta to the Sea," and won his several promotions for bravery on the field of battle. After the war and his marriage in 1869, he settled in Limestone, New York, where he was engaged in a mercantile business. He later engaged in lumbering, and in 1896 moved to Bradford, Pennsylvania, where he continued until his death. He was a member of the Masonic order, affiliated with lodge, chapter, and St. John's Commandery, Knights Templar; and also of Tent No. 4, Knights of the Maccabees, Limestone, New York. He always retained a great affection for his army comrades, and until his death was a member of the Grand Army Post at Bradford, and the Union Veteran Legion. He attended the Universalist church. He was held in high esteem by his business and social acquaintances, and was a true sympathizing friend, and in every walk of life a courteous gentleman.

(The Leonard Line).

(I) Levi Leonard, grandfather of Rebecca (Leonard) Irvine, was born in Montrose, Susquehanna county, Pennsylvania, died in Warren, Pennsylvania, in 1823. He was a lawyer by profession. He married Rebecca Griffith, born in Montrose, died in Warren in 1828. Children of Levi Leonard: 1. Calvin, born 1803; a carpenter; died in Limestone, New York; married Jemima Cogswell; children: i. Samuel, married Valona Fuller, who survives him, living in Limestone; ii. Andrew Jackson, a leather finisher, now residing in Limestone, married Margaret Stevens; iii. Lettie, married and died at Beaver Falls, Pennsylvania; iv. Anna, married and died at Beaver Falls; v. Celinda, married and died at Limestone, New York; vi. Jane, married John Bassett, died at Bolivar, New York; vii. Cynthia, married Squire Chappell Vibbard, both now living in Limestone, New York. 2. Arnold, born 1805, died at Spring Creek, Warren county, Pennsylvania; married Emeline Gillis, who also died there; he was engaged in the lumber business; children: i. Levi, a justice of the peace of Spring Creek; ii. Malvina, married Zal Jobes, a lumberman of Warren county, whom she survives, residing at Spring Creek. 3. Levi, of whom further. 4. Warren, born in Montrose, Pennsylvania, where he died; married Anna Morrison, of Warren; children: i. James, living in Kinzua, Pennsylvania, unmarried; ii. Rose, living in Kinzua, married; iii. Adelaide, living in Kinzua, married. 5. Susan, born 1812, married a Mr. Daly. 6. Robert, born 1814; a farmer; married Mary Oliver, of Jamestown, New York; ten children. 7. Patty, born 1816; married Joseph McMullin, a lumberman; one child. 8. Betsey, born 1818; married Percy Lefevre, a foundryman from Butler county, Pennsylvania; children: Adelaide and Sophia, both living near Pittsburgh.

(II) Levi (2), son of Levi (1) Leonard, was born February 22, 1807. He was a farmer and lumberman near Limestone, New York, where he died September 12, 1879. He married Elizabeth Cargill, born in Maine, December 25, 1805, died in November, 1902. Among their children was Rebecca, of previous mention. Elizabeth Cargill had brothers and sisters, of whom she was the eldest, all born in Maine: 1. John, born 1807; a farmer near Poughkeepsie, New York, where he died; married Nancy Cooper. 2. Albert, born 1809, died in Warren county, Pennsylvania, 1901; married Mary Webb, of Fredonia, New York; followed farming all his life; children: i. William, married, and lives at Corydon, Pennsylvania; ii. Mary, married (first) William Andrus, (second) Mr. Ackly; now living a widow in Jamestown, Pennsylvania. 3. Nancy, born 1811; married James Lowry; both deceased; no living issue. 4. James, born 1814. deceased; a farmer and lumberman of Corydon, Pennsylvania; married Jane Strickler; no living issue. 5. Nathan, born 1817; a farmer of Corydon, where he died unmarried. 6. Sarah, born 1828, died 1910; married Dr. Hollister; no issue.

OLDS-CHAPMAN The earliest record obtainable of the Olds family is of Thomas Olds, of New Hampshire, who spent the greater part of his life and died in Alstead in that state in 1792. He was a farmer and landowner, a Whig in politics and a man of influence. He married Mehitable Pike, who survived him. Children: 1. Ezekiel, of whom further. 2. Ruth, died in Vermont; married a Mr. Pomeroy and left issue. 3. Cynthia, died in Alstead; married a Mr. Jenny and left issue, including a son Chauncey, now deceased. 4. Thomas, a farmer, died in Williams county, Ohio; married Margaret Kennedy; children: Samuel, Mary, Thomas, William, John, Harvey, Justice, Harriet. Harvey is the only one of this family known to be living; he resides in Ohio. 5. Mehitable, died in Conneaut, Ohio; married Thomas McNear; no issue.

(II) Ezekiel, son of Thomas and Mehitable (Pike) Olds, was born in Alstead, New Hampshire, January 27, 1784. He received his education and lived in Alstead until nearly twenty-one years of age. His father died when he was about eight years of age and then he was indentured to an uncle, Benjamin Wood, to serve during his minority. Three months before coming of age, however, he left Alstead and made his way westward to Conneaut, then called Salem. He bought wild land, built a log cabin and cleared a farm on which he lived many years. Later he moved to Como, Illinois, where he died May 5, 1866. He was a Whig in politics, later a Republican, serving as school director and in other town offices. He was a member of the Methodist Episcopal church.

He married (first) Betsey Pitney, born in Crawford county, Pennsylvania, April 29, 1789, died at Conneaut, Ashtabula county, Ohio, January 25, 1832, daughter of Lewis Pitney, a farmer who died in old age in 1848, at Conneaut, outliving by several years his wife Sarah Davis, who also died in Conneaut; their children were: 1. Davis. 2. Elijah. 3. Betsey, first wife of Ezekiel Olds. 4. Ebenezer, a ship carpenter, died in Iowa, married Mary Snow and had Owen, living in Iowa; Marcia, deceased, and Helen, living in the west. 5. Polly, married Charles Beardsley; children: Emily, Charles, Lewis and Laura; parents and all four children are deceased. 6. Lucinda, married William Adams, and had one child, Catherine; all deceased. 7. Melinda, married a Mr. Taylor and had a daughter and son, Lucinda and Pitney; all deceased. 8. Jonathan, deceased, married and left issue.

Ezekiel Olds married (second) Margaret Johnson, who died in Conneaut, in 1852; no issue. Children by his first marriage: 1. Cynthia, born March 12, 1811, died young. 2. Lewis, November 9, 1813, died in Conneaut. 3. Phebe, born February 28, 1815, died in Conneaut, March 10, 1904, married James Press, deceased, a teamster and farmer; children: Mary, John, now living in Gowanda, New York; Ezekiel, James, deceased; Henry, deceased; Jennie, living in Conneaut; Frank, living in Canton, Ohio. 4. Ezekiel, born July 18, 1817, a farmer; married Roxanna Wilcox, both died in Como, Illinois; children: Roxanna, living in Como, Illinois; William C., deceased; was a soldier of the civil war, buried in Marietta, Ohio; Harriet, living in Iowa; Delos, living in Sterling, Illinois; Frank, deceased; Nettie and Charles, also living in Sterling. 5. Sarah Ann, born October 9, 1819, died April 17, 1910, at Hickman's Mills, Missouri; buried in Conneaut; married Isaac Judson, a harness-maker; children: Mary, now living at Hickman's Mills; Frank, Fred, twin of Frank, and Sarah, all deceased. 6. Louisa, born February 10, 1822, died in Kingsville; married Charles Demarandille, a farmer; children: Calvin, lives in Kingsville, Ohio; Betsey, lives at Conneautville, Pennsylvania; Ruth, deceased; Sarah, lives in Ashtabula, Ohio; Charles, deceased; Cynthia, lives in Conneaut; married William Walling, a farmer. 7. John, born June 26, 1824, died in Conneaut, a farmer; married Harriet Laughlin; children: Nettie and Wilson, living in Conneaut; Alfred, living on the old homestead; two others died young. 8. Ruth, born March 16, 1827, now living in Marshalltown, Iowa; married Sylvester Rhoads, deceased, a farmer of Conneaut; children: John, Ezekiel and Charles, all living in Missouri; two daughters, died young. 9. Cynthia, of whom further. 10. Betsey E., born January 6, 1832, died in Geneva, Ohio; married Byron Pettey, a captain on the Great Lakes, who died in Belvidere, Illinois; children: Frank, deceased; Lillian, lives in Belvidere, Illinois; Adelaide and Carrie, live in Elkhart, Indiana; Jennie, deceased; John and Glen, both living in Belvidere.

(III) Cynthia, ninth child of Ezekiel Olds and his first wife, Betsey (Pitney) Olds, was born in Conneaut, Ashtabula county, Ohio, July 30, 1829. She was educated in the public schools of her native town, finishing at Conneaut Academy. She now resides in Bradford, Pennsylvania, a widow, greatly loved and admired by her many friends. She is a member of the Methodist Episcopal church; Ladies' Auxiliary of the Grand Army of the Republic; the Women's Relief Corps; the Ladies' Auxiliary of the Union Veteran Legion, and Willard Union of the Women's Christian Temperance Union, the latter a work in which she has long been interested. She has resided in Bradford since 1877 and after forty-eight years of married life was left a widow in 1895.

She married, October 14, 1847, William Brooke Chapman, born in Cleveland, Ohio, October 8, 1826, died in Bradford, Pennsylvania, October 27, 1895; son of Daniel Chapman, born 1796, a shoemaker, served in the war of 1812, receiving a wound at the battle of Lundy's Lane, died in Bradford, May 22, 1882, a son of a revolutionary sire. Daniel Chapman married Margaret Burt, who died in Conneaut. Children: 1. Uriah, born January 1, 1825, married Rebecca Forsythe; children: Asa, Hannah, B——, William, Catherine, Uriah, Roxy, Daniel, Rebecca, Mary, Isaac and twins Jacob and Olive. 2. William Brooke, see forward. 3. Mary Ann, born October 21, 1828. 4. John Reed, June 14, 1829. 5. Louisa, October 23, 1831. 6. Jane S., October 3, 1833, now living in Conneaut, Ohio, a widow; married James Guthrie. 7. Hannah, born July 5, 1835. 8. Rebecca, October 12, 1841. 9. Thomas Corwin, born November 12, 1844, married and with his wife resides in California. Thomas C. and Jane S. are the only living children of this family. In 1888 eight of them met, the youngest then being fifty-six years old, and had a family picture taken.

William Brooke Chapman was of English and French descent. He grew to manhood and was educated in Ashtabula county, Ohio, graduating from the Conneaut Academy in 1846. He at once began the study of law in the office of General Brewster Randall, at Conneaut; was married in 1847, and in February, 1852, at Columbus, Ohio, was admitted to practice in the Supreme Court of Ohio, having previously been admitted to the Ashtabula county bar. He at once began the practice of his profession, and was becoming well established when the war between the states broke out. He did not hesitate when duty called, and in July, 1861, enlisted in the Second Ohio Light Artillery. He was chosen first lieutenant of his battery and won a promotion to captain. He was wounded at the battle of Pea Ridge, which so incapacitated him for further duty that he resigned his commission, received honorable discharge and returned to Conneaut. He there resumed legal practice, continuing until 1873, when he moved to Erie, Pennsylvania, and in 1877 located in Bradford. Here his talents as an attorney and counsellor brought him quick recognition, and he built up a large, lucrative practice of the best class. He was learned in the law, skillful in its application and thoroughly honorable in all his dealings. He was originally a Whig, but later a Republican and an active worker in the party. He was an ardent advocate of the cause of temperance, but opposed to making it the basis of a third party movement. He belonged to the Masonic order, affiliating with both blue lodge and chapter. Children of Captain William Brooke and Cynthia (Olds) Chapman, all born in Conneaut, Ohio: 1. Sarah Margaret, born June 8, 1849; married in Conneaut, September 28, 1870, Charles Haywood, whom she survives. He was a harness-maker, but during the last twenty years of his life was cashier of a Conneaut bank. Children: 1. Clara, born June 28, 1877; Edna, March 16, 1880. 2. Phoebe Ellen, born August 13, 1851; married November 15, 1876, at Erie, Pennsylvania, Stephen A. Holbrook (see Holbrook). 3. Henry William, born April 6, 1854; married in New York City, December 5, 1889, Louisa Dillon; no issue. They reside in New York City, Mr. Chapman having, for a number of years, traveled for the firm of Mills & Gibbs, corner of Broadway and Grand street, New York City. 4. John Burtt, born June 29, 1856, now a practicing lawyer of Cleveland, Ohio, but resides in Northfield, Ohio; married in Cleveland, Ohio, October 20, 1880, Nellie Stanley, of Ohio; children: Hazel, May and Henry Stanley, a traveling salesman. 5. Will B., born February 8, 1866, now a practicing lawyer with office in Pittsburgh; lives in Crafton, Pennsylvania. He married in Buffalo, New York, November 25, 1896, Margaret Kennedy; children: Margaret, born September 25, 1897; William Kennedy, January 20, 1911.

FREEMAN-EVANS (II) Edmund (2). eldest son of Edmund (1) Freeman (q. v.), the emigrant, was born in England, died March 29, 1673. He resided in Sandwich and for seven years represented that town in the general court. He married (first) Rebecca, daughter of Governor Thomas Prence, by his first wife, Patience Brewster, daughter of Elder William Brewster, of "The Mayflower." Children: Rebecca, Margaret, Edmund, of whom further; Alice, Rachel, Sarah and Deborah.

(III) Edmund (3), son of Edmund (2) Freeman, was born October 5, 1655, died May 18, 1720. He married Sarah ———, mentioned in his will. Children, all born in Sandwich: Edmund, of whom further; Benjamin, Mary, John, Thomas, Joseph, William, Sarah, Isaac.

(IV) Edmund (4), son of Edmund (3) Freeman, was born August 30, 1683, died June 1, 1766. He moved from Sandwich to the state of Connecticut, settling in Mansfield, where he died. He married Kezia Pressbury, who died in Mansfield, April 20, 1764, aged seventy-seven years. Children: Edmund, died young; Lydia, married Benjamin Nye; Edmund, of whom further; Prence, married (first) Ruth Hall, (second) Elizabeth Stetson, (third) Rebecca Johnston; Stephen, married Hannah Jenkins; Silvanus, married Mary Dunham; Nathaniel, married Martha Dunham; Keziah, married (first) ——— Snow, (second) ——— Shaw; Sarah, married Malachi Conant; Deborah, married Zachariah Paddock; Skeefe, married Anna Sargeant; Thomas, died young; Abigail, married William Johnson; Margaret, died young.

(V) Edmund (5), son of Edmund (4) Freeman, was born in Sandwich, Massachusetts, September 30, 1711. He graduated from Harvard College in 1733, taught school, and in 1741 or 1742 moved to Mansfield, Connecticut. He married, August 7, 1736, Martha Otis. Children: Edmund, of whom further; Nathaniel, died young; Nathaniel, twice married; Abigail, married Aaron Harvey; Jonathan, married Sarah Huntington; Otis, married Ruth Ricknell; Russell, married Abia Denkee; Moody, married Kezia Freeman; Frederick, married (first) Abigail Thompson, (second) Abigail Dimmick; Martha, married Roger Harvey.

(VI) Edmund (6), son of Edmund (5) Freeman, was born in 1737 in Dennis, Massachusetts, removed to Mansfield, Connecticut, thence to Hanover, New Hampshire. He was first known as "Captain," then "Colonel" Freeman, and commanded a company in the revolution. He died in Lebanon, New Hampshire, August 6, 1813. He married (first) Sarah Porter, died September 13, 1777, (second) Mrs. Theoda (Porter) Esterbrook, widow of John Esterbrook, of Lebanon. Children, first five by first wife: Sarah, married Daniel Wright; Edmund, of whom further; Otis, married Theoda Capron; Nathaniel, married Martha Hall; John Porter, married (first) Martha Larkins, (second) Rachel R. Nye; Theoda, born April 4, 1779, died unmarried; Joseph, married (first) Nancy Estabrook, (second) Sally Hopkins; Luther, married (first) Roxanna Spence, and a second and third wife.

(VII) Edmund (7), son of Edmund (6) Freeman, was born in Connecticut, August 29, 1764. He moved to New Hampshire and to Hartland, Vermont; was captain in the war of 1812 and major of militia. He married Zilpah Poole. Children: Edmund, of whom further; Zilpah, died August, 1813; Sarah, married Rev. Jacob Scales; John, Elizabeth, married ——— Parmalee; Theoda, Otis, Louisa, Russell.

(VIII) Edmund (8), son of Edmund (7) Freeman, was born in Vermont, January 13, 1793, died in Custer City, Pennsylvania, March 4, 1853. After his marriage he settled in McKean county, Pennsylvania, where he followed agriculture. He married, February 14, 1822, Elizabeth Chadwick, of New Jersey, born April 21, 1799, died July 1, 1882, daughter of Elihu Chadwick, a revolutionary soldier of early New England and English ancestry. Children: 1. Edmund Allen, born March 16, 1823, died unmarried, February 18, 1840, at Custer City. 2. William Chadwick, of whom further. 3. Sabra Calista, born January 15, 1827, died July 5, 1865, unmarried. 4. Dr. Silvanus D., born January 29, 1829, died August 9, 1894; he was a graduate of the medical department of the University of Buffalo, 1856, and began the practice of medicine in Smithport, Pennsylvania, continuing until the civil war, when he went to the front as surgeon of the Pennsylvania "Bucktails," Forty-second Regiment, Colonel Kane; in October, 1862, surgeon to the United States Volunteers, continuing until the war closed; he was brevetted lieutenant-colonel, and resumed practice until the Mexican trouble of 1876, when he was sent to Mexico as correspondent for the committee on foreign relations; on returning he again took up his profession, practicing until his death; he stood high in the profession, was a member of the county, state and national medical societies, prominent in the Grand Army of the Republic, and a thirty-second degree Mason; he married, January 24, 1855, Lucretia A. Reisdorph, now deceased; three children: i. Kate, married Frank Taylor, of Smithport; child: Bessie, married Dr. Hamilton; ii. Ella, married H. C. Wells; iii. Bessie Kane, deceased. 5. Mary Jeffrey, born March 7, 1831, died at Custer City, January, 1840. 6. Melinda Corbit, born March 18, 1833, married, April 30, 1856, Maynard Inglesby, a farmer at Minard Run, Pennsylvania; child, Maynard Jr. 7. Francis Hallock, born December 6, 1836, died June 14, 1908; he was a blacksmith and served throughout the entire civil war in a Pennsylvania regiment, working at his trade; he married, June 14, 1876, Liza Augusta Wood, who survives him, living in Michigan. 8. Mary Elizabeth, born May 13, 1840, deceased; married David Brown, of Custer City, Pennsylvania, a miller, who survives her, and with son Miles, resides in Minard Run.

(IX) William Chadwick, son of Edmund (8) Freeman, was born in Custer City, McKean county, Pennsylvania, August 17, 1824, died on his farm there, June 24, 1855. He was educated in the public school, and on finishing his studies at once began farming, a business he followed without interruption all his active life. He owned a good farm on which his daughter, Effie E., now resides. He was a member and trustee of the United Brethren church, and a Republican. He married, June 24, 1855, Mary Catherine Hammond, born in Herkimer county, New York, June 18, 1829, died in Custer City, December 10, 1811, daughter of Simon Hammond, who came to Custer City when a boy and spent his life on the farm that he inherited from his father, dying at Degolia, 1871. He married Harriet Frazee, who died in Vermillion, South Dakota, in 1886. Their children: 1. Cyrus, died at Bolivia, McKean county, Pennsylvania. 2. Eleasor, died in Ohio. 3. Mary Catherine, of previous mention. 4. Henry, a veteran of the civil war (Pennsylvania Bucktails), now living in Los Angeles, California. 5. Cynthia, residing in Vermillion, South Dakota. 6. Susan, died at Lewis Run, Pennsylvania. 7. Hannah, died young. Children of William Chadwick Freeman: 1. Effie Evangeline, of whom further. 2. William Henry, born in Custer City, October 30, 1858; a merchant of Emporium, Cameron county, Pennsylvania; he married Rose Russell, of Emporium, Pennsylvania; children; Floyd, born in Sherman, New York; Russell, in Emporium.

(X) Effie Evangeline, only daughter of William Chadwick Freeman, was born in Bradford township (now Custer City), August 13, 1856. She received a public school education. She is a member of the United Brethren church of Custer City. She married, September 9, 1880, Thomas Eugene Evans, of Welsh and New England ancestry, born in West Valley, Cattaraugus county, New York, March 8, 1854, son of Benjamin Evans, born in Massachusetts, January 1, 1814, took up a farm in Cattaraugus county at an early date and died there March 19, 1884. He was a Republican and a member of the Methodist Episcopal church. He married, March 4, 1844, Sarah Conrad, born April 1, 1826, near Syracuse, New York, died at Phoenix, New York, June 13, 1885. Their children: 1. Benjamin Franklin, born February 26, 1845, died in Ashford, New York, June 18, 1871, unmarried. 2. Jerome D., born November 21, 1851, married Chloe Proctor, born July 4, 1878, deceased. 3. Thomas Eugene, of further mention. 4. Mary Evangeline, born January 1, 1859, died in the west in 1889; married John Off, born in Germany. 5. Angeline, born January 8, 1862, died January 15, 1874.

Thomas Eugene Evans was educated in the public schools of Ashford, New York, and the United Brethren Seminary at Sugar Grove, Pennsylvania. He studied with a particular view to the ministry and was regularly ordained a minister of the United Brethren church. He was pastor of the church of that denomination at Bradford, Pennsylvania, one year; at Machias, New York, one year; at Port Allegany, McKean county, three years; at Eldred, McKean county, one year; at Sugar Grove, Warren county, three years; at Findlay Lake, New York, one year; at Degolia, Pennsylvania, three years; at Sartwell Creek, McKean county, three years; at Farmers' Valley, McKean county, one year; at Custer City, one year; at Sartwell, New York, one year, and at Diamond, Venango county, three years. At all these charges he served his people acceptably and left behind him a record of faithful and Christian effort. In 1893 he was compelled by circumstances to abandon regular ministerial work to take charge of the old homestead farm of his father-in-law, William Chadwick Freeman, which he has since conducted, and on which the family now resides. Mr. Evans is also engaged in photographic work. Child of Thomas E. and Effie E. (Freeman) Evans, Bessie May, born February 13, 1889, residing with her parents.

CHATLEY   The Chatley family was founded in the United States by Francis Chatley, of Scotch-Irish descent, born in Londonderry, Ireland, in 1764, and died in Beaver county, Pennsylvania, in 1841. He emigrated to America, settling in Beaver county, and becoming a member of the Disciples of Christ. In Ireland he had been a Covenanter, and extremely active in religious circles. He married, in Ireland, Rebecca Spear, who was born in Ireland, and died in Beaver county, Pennsylvania, in 1843, aged seventy-seven years. Children, all born in Beaver county, Pennsylvania: 1. Polly, born in 1799, died in Mercer county; married James Steen, a farmer, who was killed by a bolt of lightning; children: Joseph and Frank, both deceased. 2. Samuel, born in 1801, died in Mercer county, Pennsylvania, a farmer; married Catherine Carr, who died in Mercer county; children: i. John, living in Mercer county; ii. Jane, living in Crawford county, Pennsylvania; iii. Francis, deceased; iv. Griffith, living in Mercer county; v. Catherine. 3. Andrew, born in 1803, and died in Mercer county, Pennsylvania, a farmer; married Ruth Robbins, from Mercer county, where she died. Children: Milton, Irenens, Usiverus, Irene, Clara, Jerome, Lucinda and Mary. 4. Elizabeth, born in 1805, died in the west; married John Campbell, a farmer, from Beaver county; children: Ross, a daughter, Frank, died while in army service; Samuel, deceased; John, deceased; James, living in Arkansas. 5. Jane, born in 1807, died in Mercer county, Pennsylvania; married William Andrews, a native of Ireland, who died in Mercer county, Pennsylvania; children: Mary and Frank, both living in Mercer county, and a daughter. 6. Martha, born in 1809, died in Beaver county, Pennsylvania; married Joseph Clintock, from Beaver county, where he died. 7. John, of whom further. 8. Abijah, born in 1813, died in Beaver county; married and had two children: Milton, a minister in Ravenna, Ohio, and a son. 9. Nancy, born in 1815, died while young, in Beaver county, Pennsylvania.

(II) John, son of Francis and Rebecca (Spear) Chatley, was born in Beaver county, Pennsylvania, October 3, 1811, and died in Mercer county, May, 1887. He obtained his education in the public schools of his native county, also graduating from the academy there. He purchased a farm near Milledgeville, Mercer county, Pennsylvania, which he operated with much success until his death. He and his wife belonged to the Disciples of Christ church. He married Catherine Eleanor Bowman, who was born in Venango county, Pennsylvania, May 10, 1817, and died near Milledgeville, Mercer county, April 24, 1860, daughter of Alexander Bowman, born in Venango county, Pennsylvania, in 1791, died in Illinois in 1885. He married Sarah Crane, who died in Venango county in 1840. Children of Alexander Bowman, all born in Venango county, and went west: 1. Harvey, deceased; a farmer; married and had children. 2. Steven, deceased; a farmer; married and had children. 3. Hiram, deceased. 4. Catherine Eleanor, mentioned above, married John Chatley. 5. Alexander, married and had several children.

Children of John and Catherine Eleanor (Bowman) Chatley, all born near Milledgeville, Mercer county, Pennsylvania: 1. Alexander, born in February, 1842, an oil well worker in Kane, Pennsylvania; married Ella ———, a school teacher in Forest county, Pennsylvania; she was born in Clarion county, Pennsylvania; child: Mary, born in March, 1890. 2. Cyrus, born in February, 1844, a school teacher and farmer; married (first) Rebecca May, deceased, from Crawford county, and had one child, who died young; married (second) Mary Hibbard, from Crawford county, Pennsylvania. 3. Homer, of whom further. 4. Addison, born in March, 1848; married, in 1876, Sarah Burch, from Erie county, Pennsylvania; children: Stella, born in 1877, living in Erie; Bertha, born in 1879, living in California. 5. Adoniram, born in September, 1850, a lumberman; married Eva Seaman, from Mercer county; children: Charles, living in Alabama; and a daughter. 6. Adeline, born in April, 1853; married David Bortz, a farmer of Mercer county; child, Clyde, born in 1884, in Mercer county, where he is a farmer. 7. Caroline, a twin of Adeline; married Walter Davis, from Mercer county, an employe in the steel plant at Ensley, Alabama. 8. Albert, born in October, 1855, a school teacher, died in Sioux City, in 1892. 9. Charles, born in April, 1860, an employe in the Ensley, Alabama, steel plant; married Mary Walker, from Erie county, Pennsylvania; children, both living in Ensley, Alabama; Addison, and another son.

(III) Homer, son of John and Catherine Eleanor (Bowman) Chatley, was born near Milledgeville, Mercer county, Pennsylvania, January 27, 1846. Here he obtained a public school education and later graduated from the Normal School at Edinboro, Pennsylvania, following after his graduation the profession for which that fitted him, teaching. He was a teacher at the following places at different periods from 1866 to 1879: Deer Creek township, Shakleyville, Borough New Lebanon; North East township, Hickory township, French Creek and Belles Camp. After thirteen years as a school teacher he retired from the profession and has since engaged in oil producing in Sawyer City, Pennsylvania, until 1887, and in Bradford, Pennsylvania, from that date up to the present time (1912). He has been successful, both as a teacher and in business, and is an honored, respected member of the community. With his wife he is a member of the Presbyterian church, and is a Republican in politics. Both in Sawyer City and in Bradford he has been a member of the Republican town committee, a position he now holds in the fourth ward, also serving on the election board. He is a member of Bradford Post, No. 141, Grand Army of the Republic, of which he is past junior vice-commander. He married, May 18, 1888, Martha J. Alexander; she was born in Franklin county, Pennsylvania, February 3, 1856, daughter of Watson Stewart Alexander, born in Franklin county, Pennsylvania, July 24, 1824, and died January 1, 1879. He was educated in the public schools; became a carpenter and finisher, later a farmer and was a member of the Democratic party. He was twice drafted for service during the civil war, but exempted each time. He married Elizabeth Brown, born in Franklin county, March 11, 1818, she died there April 9, 1882, daughter of Joseph Brown, born in Germany, 1800, died in Franklin county, 1871. Watson Stewart Alexander was a son of George Alexander, who was born in Franklin county, and died there in 1860; he married Nancy Stewart, of Franklin county, whom he survived. George Alexander was a son of Randall Alexander. Children of George Alexander: 1. Randall, a farmer, died in Burnt Cabins, Fulton county, Pennsylvania; married Martha Kuntzman, from Franklin county, Pennsylvania; she died in Burnt Cabins, Pennsylvania; children: Rachel, Catherine, George, William, Mary, Margaret, Nancy, Martha, Matthew C., John, Rose and Sarah. 2. Martha, died in Dry Run, Pennsylvania; married Samuel Elder, a carpenter and cabinet-maker from Franklin county, Pennsylvania, where he died; children: Nancy, Elizabeth, Ford, Robert. 3. Margaret, died in Franklin county, Pennsylvania. 4. Watson Stewart, mentioned above. 5. Robert, a farmer, died on the homestead in Franklin county; married Mary Taylor, from Doylestown, Pennsylvania, living in Spring Run, Pennsylvania; children: Clara, Emma, Frank and Etta. Children of Joseph Brown, all born in Franklin county, Pennsylvania, probably not in order of birth: 1. Maria, died in Franklin county; married Amos Shear, deceased; a farmer; children: a son, Joseph Brown, died in army service; McGinly, Amanda, Montgomery, Susanna, Lucinda, William West. 2. John, deceased. 3. Joseph, a farmer, died in Ohio; married Martha Shear, deceased; children: Sarah, Jane, Ida, Catherine, Augusta, Elmer and Clara. 4. Elizabeth, mentioned above, married Watson Stewart Alexander. 5. Annie, died in Franklin county, Pennsylvania; married William Ellicott, a storekeeper from Franklin county, where he died; children: Wilson, Joseph, Jennie, Frank and Belle. 6. Amos, a farmer, died in Knox county, Illinois; married Mary Ryan, from Franklin county, and had twelve sons. 7. William, a farmer; married, and died in Illinois; children: Martin, John, Elmer and William. 8. David, a farmer, died in the west; married Margaret Stewart, from Franklin county; all children deceased with the exception of Susanna, who lives in the west. 9. Susanna, died in Juniata county, Pennsylvania, 1903, aged seventy-three years; married John Crouse, from Franklin county, where he died on his farm; children: Mary, William, Emma, Ida, Carrie, Sadie. 10. Rebecca, died in Franklin county; married George Neal, a farmer, from the same county, where he died; children, both farmers of Franklin county: John and William. Children of Watson Stewart and Elizabeth (Brown) Alexander: 1. Joseph Brown, born in Franklin county, December 18, 1848, a merchant and farmer of Dry Run, Pennsylvania; married Paulina Gamble, from Franklin county, Pennsylvania; children: Elizabeth, lives in Dry Run, Pennsylvania; Matthew

Gamble, lives in Willow Hill, Pennsylvania; Jessie, lives in Maryland; Mary and Frances, living in Dry Run, Pennsylvania; Clarence, lives in Willow Hill, Pennsylvania; Watson Irving, Glenn and Lois, live in Dry Run, Pennsylvania; Randall Pomeroy, deceased. 2. Nancy Elizabeth, born in Franklin county, Pennsylvania, July 25, 1851; married Clement McDonald, an oil-well worker in Findlay, Ohio; children: Joseph, born 1874, lives in Rudolph, Ohio; Nora and Nancy, both deceased; Frances Josephine, married ——— McDowell, and lives on a farm in Findlay, Ohio. 3. Mary Susanna, born in Franklin county, Pennsylvania, October 25, 1853; married John Mowers, from Mowersville, Pennsylvania, a coachmaker, and lives at Clear Ridge, Fulton county, Pennsylvania. 4. Martha Jane, mentioned above, married Homer Chatley. 5. John Shear, born in Franklin county, Pennsylvania, October 23, 1858, an oil-well worker in Findlay, Ohio; married Belle Everett, from Franklin county, Pennsylvania; child: Ethel, deceased. 6. James Kirkpatrick, a farmer at Bear Lake, Michigan; married Catherine Brown, from Mount Gilead, Ohio, died in 1910.

Children of Homer and Martha Jane (Alexander) Chatley: 1. John Alexander, born in Sawyer City, Pennsylvania, May 18, 1889, an employe of the Buffalo, Rochester & Pittsburgh railroad in Bradford, Pennsylvania; married, June 21, 1911, Ruth Sliger, born in Paulding, Ohio, December 28, 1892. 2. Albert Homer, born in Sawyer City, Pennsylvania, April 15, 1892, employed by the American Express Company in Bradford, Pennsylvania. 3. Rodney Ellsworth, born in Sawyer City, August 10, 1894, a student in Bradford high school. 4. Otho Brown, born in Sawyer City, Pennsylvania, September 13, 1898, attends school in Bradford.

BACKUS The Backus family is one of the oldest families in this country and in England is traced to Egbert, first King of England, from him to Cedric, first king of the West Saxons, and tradition says that Cedric was a lineal descendant of Woden (or Odin), who was supposed to be a descendant of the eldest son of Noah. There have been many distinguished men in the American family, including Dr. Charles Backus, a president of Yale; Rev. Dr. A. Backus, a president of Hamilton College, New York; Rev. Backus, a noted minister of New England during the revolution; Rev. Simon Backus, who married a sister of the celebrated Jonathan Edwards, and others equally noted. The Smethport family came to Pennsylvania from Berkshire county, Massachusetts, their ancestors going there from Connecticut before the revolution.

(I) William Backus is supposed to have come to this country from Norwich, England, his name appearing as crossing in the "Rainbow" in 1637. The town of Norwich, Connecticut, was so named as a mark of respect and esteem for William Backus, Norwich, England, having been presumably his birthplace. The fine Backus Hospital at Norwich also commemorates the early settler, William Backus. He was at Saybrook, Connecticut, in 1638, and was one of the thirty-five proprietors of Norwich who established the town in 1660. He died prior to May 7, 1664. He married (first) Sarah Chodes, (second) Ann (Stenton) Bingham, and had issue by both.

(II) Lieutenant William (2) Backus, son of William (1) Backus, the emigrant, died in 1721. He ranked high in the public life of Norwich, was lieutenant of the train band and representative many years. He married Elizabeth Pratt and left male issue. Three more generations of the family lived in Norwich, all conspicuous and honored.

(V) One of the fifth generation, Lebbeus Backus, born 1750, moved to Berkshire county, Massachusetts, settled in the town of Lee, married and had issue. He served in the revolutionary war from Pittsfield, attaining the rank of lieutenant.

(VI) Thomas L., son of Lieutenant Lebbeus Backus, was born in Berkshire county, Massachusetts, in 1785. He moved to Lansing, New York, where he became a farmer and landowner. He married Rebecca Couch. Children: Cornelia, Mary, William, of whom further; Seth A.; John Couch, a sketch of whom follows.

(VII) Rev. William Backus, son of Thomas L. and Rebecca (Couch) Backus, was born in Lee, Massachusetts, where he was educated, died in Oklahoma in 1888. He studied for the ministry and became a regularly ordained clergyman of the Presbyterian church. He filled many pastoral charges in the west and gave his entire life to this holy calling. He had four wives. The first, Frances (Ward)

Backus, who died May 14, 1842, six days after the birth of her fourth child, Frank Ward Backus. Children of Rev. William Backus by his first wife: 1. Frederick, born 1838, died in Cleveland, Ohio; was an oil operator, married and left issue. 2. Fanny, born 1840, died in New York City in 1902; married and no issue. 3. William, twin of Fanny, died in Colorado in 1911; was a miner, married and left issue. 4. Frank Ward, of whom further.

(VIII) Frank Ward, son of Rev. William and Frances (Ward) Backus, was born in the state of Connecticut, May 8, 1842. He was early adopted by his uncle, Seth A. Backus, who was childless, and his wife, Matilda (Goodwin) Backus, who brought Frank W. to Smethport when a child of six years. He was educated in the public schools, and has spent his life engaged in farming in the vicinity of Smethport, where he now resides. He is a Republican in politics, a member of the Presbyterian church, his wife of the Episcopal. He married Flora A. Hamlin, born in Smethport, October 22, 1852, now residing in Smethport, daughter of Asa Darwin Hamlin, born February 16, 1820, died in Smethport, February 2, 1880, was a civil engineer, son of Dr. Asa Hamlin, born in Sharon, Connecticut, March 30, 1786, died there December 26, 1802. Children of Frank Ward and Flora A. Backus: 1. Harry Llewellyn, of whom further. 2. Mattie, born in Smethport, July 28, 1874; was educated in Smethport high school and now assistant to her brother in the *Miner* offices.

(IX) Harry Llewellyn, son of Frank Ward and Flora A. (Hamlin) Backus, was born in Smethport, Pennsylvania, September 13, 1872. He was educated in the Smethport public schools, and when fifteen years of age was obliged to leave school and go to work. In June, 1888, he began learning typesetting and printing in the office of the *McKean County Miner*, then under the editorship of Colonel Lucius Rogers, who founded the *Miner* in 1863, but later disposed of it to Bert Olson. Mr. Backus continued with the *Miner* several years, then spent one year on the *McKean County Democrat*, then returning to the *Miner*. He thoroughly mastered the mysteries of the printer's art and continued an employe in various capacities until February 1, 1900, when he purchased the entire *Miner* plant and became sole owner and editor. Under his able management the paper has been not only a financial success, but has taken high position among the papers of Northern Pennsylvania, and is a source of weekly pleasure and profit to its many readers. The politics of the paper reflects the personal views of its owner, and has been a tower of strength to the Republican party of McKean county. Is now Progressive. Mr. Backus is interested in other Smethport enterprises and serves as a director of the Backus Novelty Company. Originally a Democrat, he lost faith in that party during the Cleveland administration and panic of 1892-96 and allied himself with the Republican party, and supported the Republican party up to the time of the Republican national convention in Chicago in June, 1912, could not stand for this convention and joined the Progressives. In 1905 he served as secretary of the judiciary general committee, continuing one term, and is now chief burgess of Smethport. He stands high in the Masonic order, belonging to McKean Lodge, No. 388, Free and Accepted Masons, and holding all degrees of Coudersport Consistory, Ancient Accepted Scottish Rite, including the thirty-second degree. He is also a Noble of the Mystic Shrine, belonging to Zem Zem Temple, Erie, Pennsylvania. He is a member of Bradford Lodge, No. 284, Benevolent and Protective Order of Elks. He is a member of the Smethport fire department and is an exempt in that organization, also a member of the Central Club. He is also a charter member of the beneficial order, Modern Woodmen of America. In religious faith he is an Episcopalian, having been baptized in that faith in early boyhood.

He married, September 11, 1907, Lillian Winifred Shattuck, born in Wellsville, New York, December 22, 1883. She was educated at Cherry Creek, New York, and Oberlin Conservatory of Music, Oberlin, Ohio. She is a member of the Order of Eastern Star and of the Presbyterian church. Children of Harry L. and Lillian W. Backus: 1. Clarissa Grace, born in Smethport, September 26, 1909. 2. Harry Llewellyn, born in Smethport, November 25, 1911. Mrs. Backus is the daughter of Frederick J. Shattuck, born in Oswayo, Potter county, Pennsylvania, September 22, 1862, now a merchant of Linesville, Crawford county, Pennsylvania. He married Clarissa Richmond, born in the town of Independence, New York, November 3, 1863, now living in Linesville. Children of Frederick J. Shattuck: 1. Lillian Winifred, of previous mention. 2. Mabel, born at Cherry Creek, New York, August 25, 1893. 3. Grace M., born at Cherry Creek, January 17, 1897.

Frederick J. Shattuck is the son of John Shattuck, of Potter county, Pennsylvania, a carpenter and a veteran of the civil war, now living in Oswayo, Pennsylvania. He married Clementine Graves, born 1841, died in Wellsville, New York, 1894. Children of John Shattuck: 1. Frederick J., of previous mention. 2. Mabel, born in Oswayo, Pennsylvania, 1868, married William Phillips, of the firm of Shattuck & Phillips, dry goods merchants of Linesville, Pennsylvania; children: Wallace, born 1886; Marguerite, 1887; Glenn, 1891.

Clementine (Graves) Shattuck had three sisters: 1. Ann, born in Wellsville, New York; married (first) Ephraim Powers, (second) George Jones, a farmer, who survives her. 2. Sarah, died in Wellsville in 1908; married R. A. Wells, a clothing merchant, who survives her. 3. Phrone, died in Wellsville; married a Mr. Shattuck, a carpenter, who survives her.

Clarissa (Richmond) Shattuck is a daughter of Henry A. Richmond, born in Allegany county, New York, 1832, now a retired farmer, living in Whitesville, New York. He married Salina Jacobus, born 1841, now living in Whitesville. Children of Henry A. Richmond: 1. William, born 1859, now an optician of Wellsville, New York; married Nettie Baker and has children: Andrew, Sadie, Harry and Gladys. 2. Anson, born 1861, now a merchant of Whitesville, New York; married Oretta Potter and has children: May, married Dr. Probasco; Clara, Henry and Leland. 3. Clarissa, of previous mention. 4. James, born 1865, now a farmer of Genesee, Pennsylvania; married Orpha ———, and has four children. 5. Lena, born 1867, married G. F. Chapman, a merchant of Genesee, Pennsylvania; children: Norman, born 1900; Leona, 1903; Laura, 1906; Lois, 1907. 6. Lloyd, born 1869, now a merchant of Genesee, Pennsylvania; he married Maud ———; no issue.

WINDSOR-BACKUS The grandfather of Mrs. Mary Almira (Windsor) Backus was a farmer of Franklinville, Cattaraugus county, New York, where most of his life was spent. He married and had children: Marvin, Barnet, Ebed and others.

(II) Ebed Windsor was born in Franklinville, New York, where he was educated and grew to manhood. After his marriage and the birth of some of his children he moved to Smethport, Pennsylvania, where he was a farmer until his death in 1845 at the age of forty-three years. He was a member of the Methodist Episcopal church, as was his wife. He married Mary Ann King, who died in Smethport in 1865, aged fifty-five years, daughter of Isaac King, a farmer near Smethport, where he died. He married Phoebe Love. Children of Isaac King: 1. Horace, died in Smethport, a farmer; married Jerusha Rice, who died near Eldred, Pennsylvania; child, George, now living in East Smethport. 2. Joel, died in the west, a farmer; married Eveline Tubbs, deceased; children: Daelli, deceased, and Fred, living in Chicago, Illinois. 3. Olive, died in Chicago, unmarried. 4. Sarah (Sally), died in Smethport; she married Solomon Sartwell; children, all deceased: Chester, George, Roswell, Mary, Samuel. Besides rearing her own family Mrs. Sartwell provided a home for her niece, Mary Almira, of farther mention. 5. Mary Ann, of previous mention, married Ebed Windsor. 6. Huldah, died near Binghamton, New York; married a Mr. Hibbard, a farmer, and left issue. 7. Joshua, died in Smethport, a farmer; he married and had children: Chester, now living in Port Allegany, proprietor of the Sartwell House; Elmira, living in Bradford. Children of Ebed and Mary Ann Windsor. 1. James, born about 1840, was drowned at Smethport; a lumberman; married Mary Ann Gage, of McKean county; two daughters, both deceased. 2. Mary Almira, of whom further. 3. Isaac, born about 1844, died in Smethport; married a Miss Hall, of McKean county; no issue. 4. Phoebe, born 1846, died in Smethport; married Eben Gallup, of Potato Creek, McKean county, Pennsylvania, a farmer; children: Emma M., married Warley J. Gifford, and Carrie. 5. Wesley, born 1848, now living in Boiseville, Wisconsin, a farmer, married and has issue. 6. Sarah, born 1850, now living in Rochester, New York; married Rood Bowers, of near Cuba, New York; child, Verdine, married a Mr. Merriman, deceased. 7. Anthony, born in 1853, now living in Bellefonte, Ohio, formerly a Methodist minister, now a farmer; married ——— ———; children: Frank, Kate and others. 8. Esther, born 1855, died in Iowa, married Cornelius Peet, deceased, an attorney, twice elected to the Iowa legislature;

children: Lyle and a son. 9. Forbutus, died in Port Allegany, Pennsylvania, a wealthy farmer; married Matilda Abbey; no issue.

(III) Mary Almira, daughter of Ebed and Mary Ann (King) Windsor, was born in Franklinville, Pennsylvania, December 27, 1842. She was educated in the public schools of Smethport and the high school at Alfred Center, New York. She married, June 18, 1860, Major John Couch Backus, born at Lee, Massachusetts, March 13, 1817, died at Smethport, October 26, 1888. She survives him, a resident of Smethport. Children, all born in Smethport: 1. Frank, March 11, 1862, resides in Smethport, unmarried. 2. Alice Bell, born October, 1864, died February 5, 1866. 3. John Clayton, born March 14, 1866, now president of the Novelty Works Company of Smethport; married Lucy Blake, of Eldred, Pennsylvania. 4. George Anthony, born June 12, 1868, died unmarried, June 14, 1905; was a merchant. 5. Frederick William, born November 22, 1870, now a lawyer of Smethport; married Carrie Schott, of Olean, New York. 6. Lucy Mygatt, born November 11, 1873; married William Seger, of Emporium, Pennsylvania, now in the music business in New York City; child, Arthur Edward, born January 29, 1907. 7. Nellie Almira, born April 19, 1876; married Dr. Arthur Ward Cutler, a leading physician and surgeon of Oneonta, New York. 8. Ralph Eugene, born March 19, 1880, died November 14, 1880. 9. Merle Edwin, born April 19, 1882, resides at home. 10. Harold Eugene, born October 2, 1886, died June 26, 1910. Both parents being members of the Episcopal church, all the foregoing children were baptized in that faith.

Major Backus was the son of Thomas L. Backus, a farmer and landowner of New York state, who made a wager that he could mow a certain field in a given time, won the wager, but died as a result of the over-exertion necessary to perform the feat, aged about forty years. His wife, Rebecca (Couch) Backus was also born in Massachusetts, died in Smethport, a very old lady. Children of Thomas L. Backus: 1. Cornelia, died in New York state; married a Mr. Davis, a farmer; children, all deceased: Fred, Charles, Louisa, married Samuel Sartwell; Mary, married a Mr. Jennings. 2. Mary, died in Smethport in 1880; married John Melliken; their only living child is W. J. Melliken, an attorney of Bradford, Pennsylvania. 3. Rev. William, a sketch of whom precedes this. 4. Seth A. 5. John Couch, of whom further.

Major John Couch Backus was born in Massachusetts, but in his fourth year his parents moved to Lansing, New York, where his childhood and youth were spent and early education obtained. He was a graduate of Oberlin College (Ohio), and began life fully equipped educationally. After attaining his majority he engaged with his brother, Seth A., in the lumbering business at Wellsville, New York, and in 1845 moved to Tuttle Point, McKean county, Pennsylvania. There they purchased a sawmill and combined their lumbering operations until 1848, when becoming tired of the business and aspiring to a professional career, John C. moved to Smethport and began the study of law with N. W. Goodrich, then a prominent lawyer of the county. In 1851 Mr. Backus was admitted to the McKean county bar and in 1856 to practice in the supreme court. He at once began the practice of his profession in Smethport and for over twenty-five years was engaged in nearly every important case tried in the county. At the time of his death he had been in practice longer than any other lawyer. He also took an active part in politics. He was a life-long Democrat and in 1851 was elected register and recorder of McKean county; was a member of the state legislature in 1875 and 1876, and for ten years was chief burgess of Smethport. He was a veteran of the civil war, enlisting in 1861, and in December of that year was commissioned captain of Company E, Fifty-eighth Regiment Pennsylvania Volunteer Infantry. He fought in all the battles participated in by his regiment until compelled by his failing health to resign. He had risen through successive promotion, and at the time of his resignation was holding the rank of major. In 1877 he formed a law partnership with Sheridan Gorton, of Friendship, New York, which continued until the death of Major Backus. He was a member of the Episcopal church, McKean Lodge, No. 338, Free and Accepted Masons, and of the Grand Army of the Republic.

Major Backus was noted for his generosity, and none ever appealed to him in vain. Positive and energetic by disposition, he pursued with untiring zeal every cause he championed and every work he undertook. He held a high place in the esteem of his townsmen and ever labored for the welfare of Smethport and its inhabitants. He was a prominent member of the Masonic order and was buried by his brethren according to the beautiful Masonic ritual. No more fitting tribute can be paid to his memory than that tendered by one of his brethren of the bar: "In him his country has lost one who proved by his acts that he fully appreciated the duty of a good citizen and a true patriot. In him his wife lost a kind husband, children, an indulgent father, and kin of every degree a generous friend." He always held his army comrades in highest regard and was a charter member of the Smethport Post, Grand Army of the Republic, which post passed fitting resolutions of respect to his memory.

He married (first), in 1857, Mary, died 1860, only daughter of Solomon Sartwell, one of the oldest residents of the county. Children: Frank, died in infancy; Cora, died in 1880. He married (second) Mary A. Windsor, of previous mention.

The earliest records obtainable McVAY of this family are of Patrick McVay, although the family is an old one and has been seated in Ireland for many generations. Patrick McVay was born in Londonderry, Ireland, where his entire life was passed as a farmer. He was a Roman Catholic in religion and a member of the Masonic order. He married and had issue, all born in Londonderry, Ireland: 1. Hugh, born in 1800, died in North Chili, New York, 1880; married Miss Borland, a native of Londonderry, Ireland, died in North Chili, New York. Children: Hugh and Bridget (both deceased). 2. John, of whom further. 3. Patrick (2), a farmer, died in Londonderry, Ireland; married and had issue: i. Sarah, living in Rochester, New York. ii. Jane, lives in Ontario, New York. iii. Hugh, died in 1875. iv. Daniel, lives in Philadelphia, Pennsylvania. 4. Mary, born in 1806, died in Londonderry, Ireland, 1907, having attained the wonderful age of one hundred and one years.

(II) John, second child and son of Patrick McVay, was born in Londonderry, Ireland, June 21, 1802, died in Bradford, Pennsylvania, November, 1900. He obtained his education in his native country and when he was thirty-eight years of age emigrated to the United States, settling in Rochester, New York; later purchasing a farm in Ontario, Wayne county, New York. He and his wife were members of the Roman Catholic church, while in politics he was a faithful adherent to the principles of Democracy. He married Elizabeth McKuhn, born in Londonderry, Ireland, 1814, died in Bradford, Pennsylvania, September 1, 1901, daughter of Patrick McKuhn, a native farmer of Londonderry, where his entire life was spent. Children of Patrick McKuhn: 1. John, born 1806, died in Geneva, New York; married Miss Higgins, from Londonderry, Ireland, she died in Geneva, New York. Children, all living in Geneva, New York: John, Peter, Jane and Sarah. 2. Peter, born 1808, died of yellow fever in New Orleans, Louisiana. 3. James, born 1810, a bricklayer, died in Edinburg, Canada. 4. Susan, born 1812, died in Ontario, Wayne county, New York; married Edward McWilliams, a mason, from Londonderry, Ireland. Children: i. John, has been a member of the Cleveland (Ohio) fire department for many years. ii. James, killed in the service of the United States during the Spanish war. iii. Ellen, lives in Oklahoma. 5. Elizabeth, of previous mention, married John McVay.

Children of John and Elizabeth (McKuhn) McVay: 1. Daniel, born in Geneva, New York, 1838, died in infancy. 2. Hugh, born in Geneva, New York, 1840, died in infancy. 3. Ellen, born in Geneva, New York, April 1, 1842; married James G. O'Dwyer (deceased), a merchant from the south of Ireland. Children: Jennie (deceased), Mary, Ellen, Willis, James, Robert, Margaret and Ruth, all seven living in Jackson, Michigan. 4. William James, of whom further. 5. John, born in North Chili, New York, May 10, 1849, died in Kansas City, August, 1899; married Catherine Hurley, a native of Pennsylvania, died in Bradford, Pennsylvania, 1897. John McVay was an oil producer and ranchman. 6. Sylvester, born in Ontario, Wayne county, New York, 1851, died there in 1863. 7. Charles, born in Ontario, Wayne county, New York, a contractor for artesian and oil wells, and lives in La Junta, Colorado. Children, all living in La Junta, Colorado: Gertrude, Ellen, Sylvester and John. 8. Mary, born in Ontario, Wayne county, New York; married Edward Quigley, from North Chili, New York, a foreman in the employ of the Standard Oil Company in Sistersville, West Virginia. Children: Edward, a bank cashier in Sistersville, West Virginia; William, lives in Sistersville,

West Virginia; Frank, lives in Youngstown, Ohio; Emmet, Elizabeth and Mary, living in Sistersville, West Virginia.

(III) William James, fourth child and third son of John and Elizabeth (McKuhn) McVay, was born in North Chili, Monroe county, New York, January 10, 1844. He obtained his education in the public schools of Ontario, Wayne county, New York, and in 1863 moved to Oil Creek, Crawford county, Pennsylvania, engaging in the oil business as a well-driller; later following the same business in the fields of Venango county for ten years. At the end of that time he was offered a position as foreman of the Indian Rock Oil Company, which was owned by the Webb Shipbuilding Company, a corporation which built many of the Union vessels during the civil war. In 1875 he came to Bradford, Pennsylvania, where he was employed by Whitney & Wheeler as superintendent, meanwhile becoming an oil producer independent of his connection with the firm. He remained with the firm of Whitney & Wheeler for over eighteen years, resigning to accept a position as foreman for Senator Emery, which he held for three years. Since that time he has been an independent oil producer, engaging in contracting in the fields of Ohio and Kentucky. In politics he is an Independent and he was a member of the first common council after the incorporation of Bradford. He is a communicant of the Roman Catholic church and a member of the Catholic Mutual Benefit Association. He was one of the organizers of the H. P. Whitney Volunteer Hose Company, No. 3, and for many years was a member. At his resignation he was presented with a handsome gold watch by his fellow members in recognition of his services both as a fire fighter and as an organizer. He is one of Bradford's most substantial citizens, and is always deeply interested in any plan for its betterment or advancement. He has seen the town develop from a village, with infant or unborn industries, to a city which has large, flourishing mills and factories of considerable importance in the industrial world, and he has taken much honest pride in the transition.

He married, September 21, 1871, Jennie Cummings, born in Burlington, Vermont, in June, 1850, daughter of Patrick Cummings, born in County Wixford, Ireland, died in Painesville, Ohio, and Sarah Cummings, born in County Wixford, Ireland, 1816, died in Bradford, Pennsylvania, 1881. Children of Patrick and Sarah Cummings, all born in Burlington, Vermont: 1. Patrick, enlisted in an Ohio regiment during the civil war, and was among the thousands who lost their lives at the battle of Gettysburg. 2. Mary, married Mr. Fitzgerald. 3. Margaret, died in Painesville, Ohio; married Mr. Manrey, a farmer, and had children. 4. Jennie, of previous mention, married William James McVay.

Children of William James and Jennie (Cummings) McVay: 1. John James, born in Titusville, Crawford county, Pennsylvania, November 24, 1872, an artesian well contractor in La Junta, Colorado. 2. William Legorn, born in Millerstown (Chicora), Pennsylvania, March 4, 1874; an oil producer and contractor of Bradford, Pennsylvania. 3. Charles B., born January 13, 1879, an oil producer and contractor in Bradford, Pennsylvania. 4. Frederick, born December 25, 1882, an oil producer in Bradford, Pennsylvania.

McINTYRE   The branch of the McIntyre family herein recorded is of Scotch descent. The list of their ancestors would contain the names of some of Scotland's most honored and revered citizens, foremost in any line of endeavor in which they were engaged. The emigrant ancestor was Grandfather McIntyre, born, of course, in Scotland, died in Sugargrove, Pennsylvania, 1852. Upon landing in the United States he journeyed by team through the forests to Amboy, New York, from there to Jamestown, New York, finally coming to Sugargrove, Pennsylvania, where he settled on a farm. He was a Whig in politics, and he and his wife were members of the New Light sect in religion, later joining the United Brethren church. He married, and had issue: 1. Nathaniel, of whom further. 2. William, a minister, died in Centreville, Pennsylvania; married Belinda Hill, deceased; children: Jane, Julia, Joan and Alanson. 3. Eleanor, married Calvin Wood, and lived on a farm in Herkimer county, New York; child: John, lives in Herkimer county. 4. Alanson, a minister, died in Sugargrove, New York; married Polly Sullivan, deceased. 5. A daughter, deceased. 6. John, married, had children, and from the latest reports was a cattle dealer in Amboy, New York.

(II) Nathaniel, son and eldest child of Grandfather McIntyre, was born in Utica,

New York, January 4, 1804, died in Bradford, Pennsylvania, May 28, 1892. He obtained his education in the public schools, and later studied for the ministry of the United Brethren church, and had parishes in Warren, Crawford and Erie counties. He was an honorable, upright, God-fearing man, abounding in good works and a veritable angel of mercy to needy ones. His warm heart and generous nature responded quickly to any one in less fortunate circumstances than himself, and his purse always obeyed the impulses of his high strung, emotional nature. He was largely responsible for the building of the United Brethren church at Sugargrove. He married (first) Phœbe Kinney, died in Warren county, Pennsylvania, 1835; (second) Rebecca Harmon, born in Sugargrove, Warren county, Pennsylvania, died in July, 1857, daughter of William Harmon; (third) Elizabeth Sheldon Lytle. Children of William Harmon: 1. William. 2. John, a farmer; married, had children and died in Wisconsin. 3. Hosea, a cattle dealer, lumberman and oil producer; died in Sugargrove, Pennsylvania; married Sally Johnson, deceased, from Sugargrove. Children: Emma and William, both deceased. 4. Sarah, died in North Warren, Pennsylvania; married Amasa Baker, a hotel proprietor from Chautauqua county, New York. 5. Rebecca, mentioned above, married Nathaniel McIntyre. 6. Hulda, died in Sugargrove, Pennsylvania; married Joel Cady, a farmer, from Sugargrove. Children: Hosea, Thomas, William, Laura, Harry, John, Susan.

Children of first marriage of Nathaniel McIntyre: 1. Sally Elizabeth, born in Herkimer county, New York, died in Pittsfield, Warren county, Pennsylvania, 1895; married James McGuire, a lumberman from Warren county, Pennsylvania, died in Pittsfield, same county; one daughter, Jennie, married Charles McKinley, and lives on a farm at Corry, Pennsylvania. 2. Silas, a farmer, born in Herkimer county, New York, died in Pittsfield, Pennsylvania; married Harriet Alger, from Warren county, Pennsylvania; children: Levi, Jerry, Frederick, Phœbe, Charles, Wesley. Children of second marriage of Nathaniel McIntyre: 3. Eleanor, born in Sugargrove, Pennsylvania, July 5, 1842, died in Bradford, Pennsylvania, January 11, 1908; married Andrew D. Hervey, born in Allegany, New York, December 11, 1824, a retired merchant of Bradford. Children: i. Verna, born in Spartansburg, Pennsylvania, December 10, 1868, died August 28, 1900, married William Roden, an oil producer of Titusville, Pennsylvania; children: Jessie, born July 4, 1887, lives in Bradford, Pennsylvania; Eleanor, born in Titusville, May 31, 1892. ii. Maud, born in Spartansburg, Pennsylvania, February 2, 1873; married John L. Mead, born in Pittsfield, Pennsylvania, November 15, 1871, where he is employed by the railroad as ticket agent. iii. Lillian, born in Spartansburg, November 1, 1877, married Herman Girard, born in Elmira, New York, May 24, 1877, a linotype operator in Bradford. 4. Emeline, born in Sugargrove, Pennsylvania, 1845, died in Centerville, Pennsylvania, 1879; married Simon Huckleberry, deceased, a farmer from Crawford county, Pennsylvania. Children: Minnie, Frederick, Archibald and James, live in Crawford county, Pennsylvania. 5. Richard E., of whom further. 6. William, born in Sugargrove, Pennsylvania, November, 1853, a farmer near Warren, Pennsylvania; married Martha Jaquay, deceased, from Sugargrove. 7. Alice, born in Sugargrove; married (first) Zell Weaver, deceased, a minister of the United Brethren church; (second) Frank Allen, a tank builder in Warren, Pennsylvania. Children, all by first marriage: Birdie and Della, both deceased; Elizabeth; Snow, deceased, and Clair. The death of Zell Weaver and three of his children was caused by black diphtheria. 8. Lansing, born in Sugargrove, July, 1856, a minister at Diamond, Pennsylvania; married (first) Myra De Pew; (second) Clementine Wright; son of second marriage: Horace, born February, 1901. Children of third marriage of Nathaniel McIntyre: 9. Eugene, born in Grand Valley, Warren county, Pennsylvania, 1862, died in infancy. 10. Albert, born in Grand Valley, Warren county, Pennsylvania, February 19, 1867, died in Bradford, Pennsylvania, May 17, 1898.

(III) Richard E., son of Nathaniel and Rebecca (Harmon) McIntyre, was born in Sugargrove, Warren county, Pennsylvania, August 16, 1847. He attended the public schools until he was fourteen years of age, when he left to become a teamster in Grand Valley and Titusville. He drew the first load of oil taken from the Maple Shade wells of Oil Creek, and carted the first lumber to Pithole, Pennsylvania, for the oil tanks, the lumber being valued at seventy-five dollars per thousand feet. Until 1881 he engaged in various occupations, cattle driving at Triumph, Pennsylvania; lumbering at Spring Creek, Pennsylvania; teaming in New London, Pennsylvania, and Edenburg, Pennsylvania; farming in Ohio and Crawford county, Pennsylvania, and in that year he began at Mount Alton, Pennsylvania, in the occupation in which he has had the most success, that of butcher. He supplied the meat for the company which erected the Kinzua Bridge, said to be the highest in the world. In 1883 he moved to Lafayette Corners, Pennsylvania, where he conducted a hotel and meat market, leaving that town to go to Bradford, Pennsylvania, establishing what is now one of Bradford's most popular meat markets. He is a member of the United Brethren church, and takes an active interest in all its affairs, having been trustee and treasurer. He belongs to Tent No. 4, Knights of the Maccabees, Bradford; Knights of St. John, and the Independent Order of Odd Fellows, having been a charter member of the Mount Alton Lodge of that order.

He married, September 11, 1871, Lydia Sheldon, born in Pleasantville, Pennsylvania, December 4, 1855, daughter of Allen Sheldon, born in Vermont, a farmer, Republican, and member of the Methodist Episcopal church; married Elizabeth Lytle. Allen Sheldon was a son of Isaac Sheldon, born in Vermont, died in Pleasantville, Pennsylvania. Children of Isaac Sheldon: 1. Allen, mentioned above, married Elizabeth Lytle. 2. Jonathan, died in Warren county, Pennsylvania, 1911, a lumberman and farmer; married Ann Lytle, deceased. 3. Harrison, enlisted in Pennsylvania Bucktail Regiment; was captured and sent to Libby prison, and was lost track of after the war. 4. Mary, married Willard Burton, from Riceville, Pennsylvania, and lives in Titusville, Pennsylvania; Mr. Burton is the owner of a grist-mill. Children of Allen and Elizabeth (Lytle) Sheldon: 1. Frances, born in Pleasantville, Pennsylvania, June 10, 1848, died 1855. 2. John, born in Pleasantville, Pennsylvania, June 24, 1851, a retired oil producer of Bradford; married June 25, 1878, Caroline Hewlings, from Clarion county, Pennsylvania, born May 2, 1859. Children, all born at Edenburg, Pennsylvania: Myrtle, born April 13, 1880; married Ernest Jackson, July 4, 1912; Don, born December 17, 1881, an oil well driller in Bradford, Pennsylvania; Jennie, born June 17, 1884; Jed, born November 12, 1886, a chauffeur, in Bradford, Pennsylvania. 3. Jennie, born in Pleasantville, June 20, 1852, died December 9, 1883; married John King, an oil well driller from Jefferson county, Pennsylvania. Children: Anna, born July 20, 1878; Frank, born April 2, 1880, married, January, 1912, Cary Marshall. 4. Lydia, mentioned above; married Richard E. McIntyre.

Children of Richard E. and Lydia (Sheldon) McIntyre: 1. Lee, born in Centerville, Pennsylvania, April 25, 1875, a minister in Milwaukee, Wisconsin; married Lillian Corry, from Coryville, Pennsylvania. Children: i. Mazie, May 1, 1896. ii. Paul, born April 3, 1901. iii. Lee (2), born October 7, 1910. 2. Snowy, born Edenburg, Pennsylvania, May 9, 1877, died there in May, 1878. 3. Pearl, born in Edenburg, May 29, 1880; married Harry Blanchard, born in Bradford, Pennsylvania, January 20, 1881, son of Charles K. and Laura V. (Slade) Blanchard. He engages in the butcher business with his father-in-law; is a member of the Independent Order of Odd Fellows of Bradford, the United Commercial Travelers, the Western Travelers and the Protected Home Circle. Pearl (McIntyre) Blanchard is a member of the United Brethren church.

BENNINGHOFF The Benninghoffs of Bradford, Pennsylvania, descend through four generations in the United States from an old and honored family of Germany, seated there for centuries. The American ancestor, whose Christian name is unknown, was born in Wittemburg, Germany, died in Clearfield county, Pennsylvania, removing thence from Lehigh county, same state. He married, and among his children were Frederick, of whom further, and George, who, tradition says, went west. There is a family of the name in Tiffin, Ohio, and another in St. Louis, Missouri, who are probably descendants of George Benninghoff.

(II) Frederick Benninghoff was born in Lehigh county, Pennsylvania, in 1760, died in Venango county, Pennsylvania, in August, 1856. Between the years 1810 and 1812 he removed to Union county, Pennsylvania, about 1828 removed to Clearfield county, and between the years 1830 and 1832 removed to Venango county, where he spent the remainder of his days. For several years prior to his death he resided with his son John. He was a member of the Lutheran church, and a man of strict integrity and upright character. He married and among his children was John, see forward.

(III) John, son of Frederick Benninghoff, was born in Lehigh county, Pennsylvania, December 25, 1801, died in Greenville, Mercer county, Pennsylvania, March 20, 1882, and is buried in the family lot in Shenango Valley cemetery. He accompanied his father to Union, Clearfield and Venango counties, Pennsylvania. In the latter-named county he rented a farm known as the Henry farm, a mile or two west of Cherrytree, where he resided for several years, and then purchased what is known as the Benninghoff Oil Farm, which he sold in 1868 and removed to Greenville, where the remainder of his life was spent. He was a man of wealth and became the victim of the "Great Benninghoff Robbery," which is recorded among the great crimes of Pennsylvania. His farm of three hundred acres was located on the famous Oil Creek. An oil well was drilled on his farm which, starting off with three hundred barrels daily, produced great excitement, and he was besieged by operators to whom he leased one and two acre lots, receiving a bonus and one-fourth royalty. He soon became one of the richest men in the oil region, and having no faith in banks in this neighborhood had transferred his funds to New York and Pittsburgh banks; the amount in his private bank was there only waiting such time as it could be transferred to the other banks. He and his son Joseph had each purchased an iron safe in which they placed their money prior to removal to banks. Mr. Benninghoff was warned of the danger of this, but would not pay heed, although he did place a night watchman on the premises with orders to admit no one to the house after dark except members of the family. Notwithstanding this precaution the house was entered on the night of January 16, 1868, the old man bound, the safe broken open and robbed of a large sum, which was carried away in two pillow cases. The amount stolen has been variously stated at from two to five hundred thousand dollars, the former amount being correct. Three of the criminals were found, tried and convicted. Saeger, the chief of the gang, however, never suffered the penalty of his crime. Although badly beaten in his fight with the thieves, Mr. Benninghoff was not seriously injured, and the following year removed to Greenville, as stated.

Mr. Benninghoff married, in Union county, Pennsylvania, in 1823-24, Elizabeth Heise, of Hartleton, Union county, Pennsylvania, daughterter of Martin and Mary (Wagoner) Heise, who were married in 1799, and whose children were: George, born February 12, 1800; Joseph, February 22, 1802; Elizabeth, mentioned above, November 5, 1804; Patience, March 27, 1806; Martin, May 31, 1808; Polly, May 5, 1810, died in infancy; Christina, August 3, 1812; John, June 26, 1815, died in infancy; Catherine, August 10, 1817; Sarah, February 1, 1819; Solomon, July 7, 1821; Mary, April 5, 1823; John, May 4, 1825. Martin Heise, father of these children, was born in Baltimore, Maryland, 1760, died in the fall of 1867, in his one hundred and seventh year; he was a cooper by trade and worked in Philadelphia during the revolutionary war; his first vote was cast for George Washington, and his last for Abraham Lincoln in 1864, and it is said the only time he rode in a buggy was when he went to the polls to vote for Mr. Lincoln when he was one hundred and four years old. He had two brothers, George and Solomon, the former of whom lived in Clearfield county, Pennsylvania, and the latter was a well-to-do farmer in Lancaster county, Pennsylvania. His wife was a native of England. Children of Mr. and Mrs. Benninghoff: 1. George, of whom further. 2. Charles, married Sarah Yates; died March 10, 1890. 3. Martin, married Mary Gehring; died March 3, 1898. 4. Amelia, married Jacob Gehring; died March 28, 1882. 5. Elizabeth, married Sproul Howe, now deceased. 6. John E., mafried Julia Gehring; died March 11, 1888. 7. Catherine, married Horace Duke; died April 9, 1883. 8. Frederick, married Julia Holmes; he died March 15, 1907; his widow survives him, a resident of Greenville, Pennsylvania. 9. Mary Jane, married Eli J. Keep, who resides at Fairview, Pennsylvania; she died January 18, 1898. 10. Jeremy, died April 3, 1903; his widow resides in Leon, Kansas. 11. Joseph, an attorney-at-law, residing in Greenville, Pennsylvania. 12. Milton, died February 11, 1909; his widow resides near Rochester, New York. John Benninghoff and his wife were members of the Lutheran church, and were faithful, consistent Christians. Mrs. Benninghoff died July 26, 1872, buried in the family lot in Shenango Valley cemetery.

(IV) George, son of John Benninghoff, was born in Clearfield county, Pennsylvania, in 1825, and was accidentally killed at Meadville, Pennsylvania, February 5, 1909. He was but a youth when his parents moved to Venango county, where his after life was spent. He engaged in farming after completing his studies in the Venango county schools, and later in the production of oil. He was successful in his business operations, and became one of the substantial men of his township. He was a director of the Benninghoff Oil Company, and interested in other enterprises in the oil country. He was a member of the Presbyterian church and a Republican in politics. He married Julia, born in Cherrytree township, 1830, died February, 1893, daughter of John and —————— (Stevenson) Baney; John Baney was a farmer of Cherrytree township during the greater part of his life, was a member of the Presbyterian church, as was also his wife, and died in 1886, aged ninety-eight years. Children of Mr. and Mrs. Benninghoff, born in Cherrytree township, Venango county, Pennsylvania: 1. Minnie, born November, 1849; married E. L. Affantranger, of Meadville, deceased; children: Nellie, married (first) Joseph Bowes, (second) ——————, 2. Lewis Nelson, born 1850, married Mary McClintock; children: Harry, now in Japan; Homer; Comer, and three others. 3. Livingston, born 1852, deceased; married Emma Cole; children: George, Norman and a daughter. 4. George Edward, of whom further. 5. Julia Minerva, born November, 1863, married Charles E. Morgan, of Meadville; one child.

(V) Dr. George Edward Benninghoff, son of George Benninghoff, was born in Cherrytree township, Venango county, Pennsylvania, February 10, 1854. His early education was obtained in the public schools of the township; at the age of thirteen he went to Meadville and attended the schools of that city for two years, and the following year he was a student at Chamberlain Institute, Randolph, New York. He then entered Oberlin College, (Ohio), remaining one year. Deciding upon the profession of medicine, he entered the Western Reserve Medical College, from which he was graduated with the degree of Doctor of Medicine in 1879. He then located in Bradford, and is now (1912) firmly established in that city in a lucrative practice. He makes a specialty of surgical cases, and is a most skillful and successful practitioner. He is sought for in consultation, having the confidence of his brethren of the profession to a marked degree. He is a member of the state and county medical societies and other professional, social and fraternal organizations. He belongs to Lodge, Chapter, Council, Commandery and Shrine of the Masonic order; the Bradford Club, Merchants' Club, Lafayette Gun and Fishing Club and the Country Club, all of Bradford. He is a Republican in politics, and since 1883 has been president of the United States pension board excepting four years under President Cleveland's second administration.

Dr. Benninghoff married, January 1, 1880, Nancy Jane, born September 1, 1858, in Monterey, Pennsylvania, daughter of James McKee and Priscilla (Sheppard) Hogan, and granddaughter of James and Lydia (McKee) Hogan. James Hogan was born in 1774, died in Clarion county, Pennsylvania, November 7, 1846; his wife was born in 1784, died July 31, 1855. James McKee Hogan was born in West Monterey, Clarion county, Pennsylvania, February 17, 1818, died March 24, 1905; his wife was born in Armstrong county, Pennsylvania. Children of Dr. and Mrs. Benninghoff: 1. Walter Garrett, born September 1, 1887, died March 28, 1903. 2. Julia, born in Bradford, September 3, 1893, now a student of the Colonial School, Washington, D. C.

SLOAN This branch of the Sloan family came to Bradford from Washington county, Pennsylvania, the family having been founded there by James Sloan, born in 1776 in County Tyrone, Ireland, where there were other branches of the Sloan family. The family originally is said to have come from Wales. James Sloan married, in Ireland, Martha Sloan, a distant relative. They were fairly well-to-do, farming good land under a favorable lease. About 1804 they came to the United States, finally settling on a farm in Hopewell township, Washington county, Pennsylvania. He died there in September, 1851; his wife, August 18, 1865, aged eighty-five years. Among their children were the following: 1. John, of whom further. 2. William, died in Allegheny county, Pennsylvania, near Pittsburgh; a blacksmith; married Rebecca ——————. Children: i. George, lives in Uniontown, Pennsylvania. ii. Eli, deceased. iii. Elizabeth, lives in Canonsburg, Pennsylvania. iv. James. 3. Margaret, died unmarried in Allegheny county. 4. Sarah, died in Allegheny county; married George Beyers; no issue. 5. Eliza, died in Allegheny county; married James Wallace, a farmer; one of their children, James (2), now resides in Library, Pennsylvania.

(II) John, eldest son of James Sloan, was born in 1803. He learned the shoemaker's trade, which he followed in earlier life, later becoming a farmer of Washington county, Pennsylvania, where he died in June, 1875. He married Sarah Murphy, born in Washington county, Pennsylvania, in 1813, died in Library, Allegheny county, Pennsylvania, in February, 1899. She was the daughter of James Murphy, born in the North of Ireland, emigrated and settled in Washington county, Pennsylvania, where he became a prosperous farmer; married Mary Goldstone, born in England, died in Butler county, Pennsylvania, about 1862, aged ninety-nine years; both were members of Peters Creek Baptist Church. None of Mary Goldstone's immediate family came to the United States. The children of James and Mary (Goldstone) Murphy were all born in Washington county: 1. John, died in Library, Pennsylvania, aged ninety-one years; was a farmer and merchant; also for many years justice of the peace; married Betsey Long, of Mercer county, Pennsylvania, also deceased. Children: i. Derthula, now living in Library. ii. Robert, deceased. iii. Mary, now living in Library. iv. Josephus, now living in Crawford county, Pennsylvania. v. Nancy, also living in Crawford county. 2. James, died in the west, leaving a family. 3. William, married and left a family. 4. Sarah, mentioned above, married John Sloan. 5. Elizabeth, married James Donnelly, of Pittsburgh, a contractor; had issue. 6. Archibald, lives in Butler county, Pennsylvania, a farmer; married Jane Rysor, and had issue, all now living at Prospect, Butler county, Pennsylvania; Oliver, James, Mary and two other daughters.

Children of John and Sarah (Murphy) Sloan: 1. Mary, born August 14, 1837; married June 12, 1862, William Wagers, a farmer, died at Finleyville, Washington county, Pennsylvania, in 1903; no issue. 2. John, born May 30, 1839, died in Monongahela City, Pennsylvania; a farmer; married Miss Hamilton, of Washington county; also deceased. Children: Emerson; Charles, deceased; Leonard, now living in Philadelphia; a daughter, died young. 3. Elizabeth, born February 27, 1841, died October 13, 1843. 4. Margaret, born December 27, 1842, died in Pittsburgh, 1909; married James Kennedy, of Washington county, a farmer; no issue. 5. William, born March 5, 1845, died in New Kensington, Pennsylvania, 1905; married Mary Grubb, also deceased; had children, Hannah, Elmer, Walter and Sadie. 6. Archibald, born February 21, 1847; now living in Finleyville, Pennsylvania; a farmer and justice of the peace; married Ann Mowrey. Children: Waldo, died August 8, 1912; Maud; Margaret, deceased. 7. Henry, born February 17, 1849, died in New Kensington, 1887; married Elizabeth Fisher, who survives him, living on the home farm at New Kensington. Children: John and Lettie. 8. George, born February 14, 1851, now a rancher at Blythe, California; unmarried. 9. Sarah, born April 16, 1854; married Charles Phelan, a carpenter now residing at Finleyville, Pennsylvania; child, Lillian. 10. James Mitchell, of whom further. 11. Daniel, born March 27, 1858, died in Monongahela City, Pennsylvania, 1904; a farmer; unmarried.

(III) James Mitchell, tenth child of John and Sarah (Murphy) Sloan, was born in Allegheny county, Pennsylvania, near Pittsburgh, February 14, 1855. He attended the public schools, then worked at farming for two years, later moving to Butler, Pennsylvania, where he learned the carpenter's trade. He continued working at his trade until 1878, then became an oil producer in the McKean county district, making his home in Duke Center. He also owned oil rights in the state of Kentucky, and was constantly engaged in the oil business until 1906, when he sold his principal interests. In 1904 he established in Bradford as undertaker and funeral director; in 1910 so greatly had his business increased that he disposed of all his oil properties and interests, giving since then all his attention to his undertaking establishment. He has been a very successful business man and owes his prosperity to his own energy and forcefulness. He is a Republican in politics, but strongly in favor of prohibition, as a party principle, but not as an independent political movement. He was a school director in Duke Center, and in Bradford has served on the common council, also for many years as inspector representing the First Ward in councils. For thirty years he has been an official member of the Methodist Episcopal church, active and helpful in all its work. He is also a member of the Heptasophs. Mr. Sloan is a public-spirited and progressive man, contributing his full share to the upbuilding of his city. He is honored and respected by his townsmen, while in his professional capacity he is most sympathetic, thoughtful and considerate.

He married, February 23, 1888, Ana (or Anna) MacKenzie, born in Brighton, Province of Ontario, Canada, October 20, 1858, daughter of Colin MacKenzie, born in New York state, and when a babe taken to Canada by his parents. Colin MacKenzie was the son of a Scotch emigrant, a scion of the famous Clan MacKenzie, of Scotland. Colin inherited a large farm from his father, and lived to a good old age; he married Amanda Clute, who died in Brighton, Canada, in 1880, a very old lady; their children, all born in Brighton: 1. Wellington, born 1852, no further record. 2. Emma, died at Trenton, Canada, in 1912, unmarried. 3. Wesley, born 1856, now a cigar manufacturer of Montreal, Canada; unmarried. 4. Ana (or Anna), mentioned above, wife of James Mitchell Sloan. She was given a liberal education, and received a teacher's certificate, entitling her to teach in the Canadian schools. She is a member of the Methodist Episcopal church, and with her husband an active worker in its different departments. 5. Donald, born in 1862, no further record. 6. Carlotta, born 1864, now living in Saskatchewan, Canada; unmarried. 7. John, born 1866, now engaged in the insurance business in San Francisco; married Lena Martin, of Belleville, Ontario, Canada; no issue.

Child of James Mitchell and Ana (or Anna) (MacKenzie) Sloan: James MacKenzie, born in Duke Center, Pennsylvania, August 21, 1891; now a student in the forestry department of the University of Toronto.

WAGNER   This name is also found as Waggoner and Wagoner even in the same family. The branch herein recorded descends from the German emigrant, John Wagoner, who first settled in Connecticut, where he married, later going to Central New York, and ending his days in Schenectady. He was a soldier of the war of 1812, serving at the battle of Sackett's Harbor and on the Niagara frontier. He was a farmer and lived on land leased from the Van Rensselaer estate. He was one of their tenants during the anti-rent war in New York state, and was a witness if not a participant in some of the armed conflicts incident to that period. He was an active member of the German Methodist church, and a man of strong character. At one period of his life he lived and farmed in Allegany county, New York. He had four sons and two daughters. The second generation spelled the name Waggoner.

(II) John Henry Waggoner, son of John Wagoner, was born either in Caroline or Dryden, Tompkins county, New York, in 1800, and died in 1857. He followed farming all his active life, which was spent in western New York. When a boy he worked on a Van Rensselaer farm, and witnessed the Case land riot. He was a Whig in politics, and a Methodist class leader. He married (first) Mary Grout; (second) Elizabeth Unsauzant; (third) Eleanor Sears, born on the Genesee river, at Oramel, New York, in 1810, died 1896, daughter of Nehemiah Sears, born in 1755, came with Colonel Gail Brooks Cole to Oramel when a young man, married a widow Hoffman, of Connecticut, and settled on a farm, where he died in 1852. Children of John Henry Waggoner by first wife: Henry and Hannah, both deceased. Children by second wife: John James, Sarah Jane and Martha Elizabeth, all deceased. Children by third wife: Frank, born October 14, 1840, died in Minnesota, January, 1907, married Alice Repenbark; Charles, born March 6, 1842, died 1908, married Lucinda Dake, deceased, leaving children: John Henry, now of Buffalo, New York, and Miles, now of Oramel, New York; Martin Ward, of further mention; Clark W., born September, 1845, died 1853; George E., born September 10, 1846, died August 20, 1909, married Martha Smith, and left children: Lena, now of Wellsville, New York, and Clark, of Chicago, Illinois.

(III) Martin Ward Wagner (as he spelled the name), son of John Henry and Eleanor (Sears) Waggoner, was born in Oramel, Allegany county, New York, November 28, 1843. He attended the public schools, and early in life learned the trade of carriage-maker, which he followed until 1860. He was then seventeen years of age and started out to fight life's battle with little equipment beyond his trade and a sturdy, well-developed body. In 1861 he was at Oil City, Pennsylvania, engaged in oil production. In 1866 he was at Bradford,

Pennsylvania, and for a number of years was engaged in farming at Custer City, McKean county, Pennsylvania. Later he settled in Bradford, Pennsylvania, where in 1876 he built the Wagner Opera House, a house of entertainment that he personally managed until 1903. In 1879 he so enlarged, beautified and improved the opera house that it was considered one of the best houses for dramatic and operatic purposes in the state. During these years he became associated with Moses Reis, forming the partnership of Wagner & Reis. They gradually extended their operations until they had a circuit of playhouses in western and central Pennsylvania and western New York. They were a successful theatrical firm, and continued together until 1903, when Mr. Wagner disposed of the greater part of his interest in the firm, retaining only the theater at Olean, New York, which he still owns. Since 1903 he has been engaged in farming, and a real estate business assisted by his sons Fred and Charles A. In 1882 Mr. Wagner purchased the Moses farm at Limestone, New York, on which in 1875 the first oil well was drilled in the Tuna Valley by William Barnsdall, father of T. N. Barnsdall, of Pittsburgh, and yet known as the "Moses well." During these years Mr. Wagner has had other and varied interests, being a man of great energy, initiative and clear foresight. He is a Republican, and as the candidate of that party has twice been elected to represent his ward in the Bradford city council. He is very prominent in various fraternal circles, a member of Bradford Lodge, No. 334, Free and Accepted Masons; Trinity Commandery, Knights Templar; Ismailia Temple, Buffalo, Nobles of the Mystic Shrine; past exalted ruler of the Benevolent and Protective Order of Elks; past master, charter member and first secretary of Bradford Knights of Pythias; first master of Grange, No. 1182, New York State Patrons of Husbandry, an office he still holds. His clubs are the Merchants' and Country of Bradford, having been a governor and chairman of the house committee of the latter.

Mr. Wagner married, April 28, 1869, Mary Dette Frank, born in Busti, Chautauqua county, New York, January 3, 1850. She is a member of the Universalist church of Bradford, the Woman's Literary Club and the Country Club. Children: 1. Frank Martin, born in Bradford, September 28, 1871, died August 21, 1908; married Lillian Johnson; no children. 2. Maud Eleanor, born in Bradford, October 18, 1874, died 1875. 3. Fred Ward, born in Bradford, December 7, 1876; graduated from Bucknell Academy, 1893, and Bucknell College, 1897; is associated in business with his father; married, November 4, 1910, Effie Eaton, born November 14, 1876; one child: Effie Eaton, born December 7, 1911. 4. Charles Augustus, born in Bradford, January 17, 1880; associated in business with his father; married, April 6, 1902, Gertrude Margaret Lindsay; no children. 5. Mary Isabel, born in Bradford, October 18, 1882, died February 21, 1884. 6. Harry W., born in Bradford, August 29, 1882, died January 25, 1883.

(The Frank Line).

There were two distinct families bearing the name Frank, both coming from Germany and both came to Frankfort, New York, from Pennsylvania, just before the revolution. There is no evidence that they were related prior to intermarriage. Henry Frank and his brother Christopher emigrated from Germany to America before the "Old French War." They landed at Philadelphia and remained in the state of Pennsylvania for a number of years, then settled on the Mohawk river at Frankfort, Herkimer county, New York. Henry Frank's sons, Henry, Laurence and Jacob, were killed in the revolutionary war. His daughters were Eva and Mary, twins, and Margaret. Eva married John Frank, son of Stephen, who was the head of the second Frank family indicated above. During the French war the wife and children of Henry Frank were captured by Indians, taken to near Montreal, but the twin sisters at least were returned, perhaps all.

Second family: Stephen Frank emigrated from Germany to America about 1750. The place of his first settlement is not known, but is believed to have been Pennsylvania. He settled at Frankfort, Herkimer county, New York, before the revolution.

(II) John, son of Stephen Frank, was born in Germany about 1763, and settled with his father at Frankfort, New York, where he died November 5, 1853. He, with Laurence, Eva and Mary Frank, children of Henry Frank, of previous mention, were captured in the "Old French War" by the French and Indians on the Mohawk, and taken prisoners to Canada, where they were kept several years among the Indians before they were ransomed. John Frank was again taken prisoner in the revolutionary war. At Oneida Lake the first night after his capture he escaped and by the aid of friendly Indians among the Oneidas reached in safety his home at German Flats on the Mohawk. In 1817 John Frank with Stephen, his son, and his family and his wife's maiden sister moved down the Ohio river, and stopped at Galliopolis, Ohio, where John (1) Frank died. The others proceeded to Columbus, Indiana, where the maiden aunt died. Stephen Frank with two of his sons went with a flat-bottomed boat loaded with produce to New Orleans, and on his return died on the Mississippi and was buried on the shore. His brother, John (2) Frank, went to Indiana and brought his mother back, who died at his house many years after at an advanced age. Mary Frank, the maiden sister, on her return from captivity among the Indians, had forgotten her mother tongue and was taken from the Indians much against her will. Thus it will be seen the Franks suffered greatly from the Indians during their life on the Mohawk.

John Frank married Eva, twin sister of Mary Frank of previous mention, and with her shared the Indian captivities. They were both daughters of Henry Frank, of previous mention. Three of her brothers were killed in the revolutionary war, and if suffering for one's country be patriotism, then was she the greatest of patriots. She accompanied her husband down the Ohio until death took him, then went with her son Stephen (2) to Indiana, later returning to Herkimer county with her son John (2). Children: 1. Stephen (2), married Margaret, daughter of Laurence (1) Frank; children: Nicholas, Matthew, Polly, Stephen D., Hiram Ava, Solomon, Elizabeth, Jacob and Joseph, twins. 2. Nicholas, of further mention. 3. John (2), married Elizabeth Diefendorf, of German Flats, New York; children: Abraham, John D., died young; Margaret, Harriet, Perry, Christina and Elizabeth. All the children of John (2) were living at Frank's settlement in 1859.

(III) Nicholas, second son of John (1) Frank, was born at Frankfort, Herkimer county, New York, died in the town of Busti, Chautauqua county, New York. Members of the Frank family settled in Busti, John (2) leaving a statement in his own handwriting that he came there February 1, 1812, that his brother Nicholas came in 1816, and that his brother Stephen left Busti in 1807 and died at Fort Pekin, Tennessee, on the Mississippi river, on his return from New Orleans. Nicholas was a farmer of Busti for the remainder of his life. He married Thankful Landon. Children: William, of further mention; Andrew, Stephen, David and Mary.

(IV) William, son of Nicholas Frank, born in Herkimer county, settled in Busti, Chautauqua county, New York, where he died. He was a farmer of Busti, and formed a part of the influential colony of that name. He married (first) Ursula Busbnell; children: Darius, of further mention; Emma Dette, married Sylvester Abbott; Nicholas, died aged seventeen years. He married (second) Christiana Diefendorf; child: John D.

(V) Darius, son of William Frank, was born in the town of Busti, Chautauqua county, New York, June 1, 1824, died in Bradford, Pennsylvania, 1879. He married Arvilla Maria Watkins, born at Locke, Cayuga county, New York, December 14, 1825, died at Bradford, Pennsylvania, April 27, 1899. Children: 1. Derenzel Jefferson, born April 5, 1845, at Busti, New York, died February 18, 1867, married Abbie Hanson and left a daughter Gertrude, born at Bradford, March 11, 1856. 2. Mary Dette, married Martin Ward Wagner (see Wagner III). Arvilla Maria Watkins, wife of Darius Frank was the daughter of Thomas J. Watkins, born at Milton, Cayuga county, New York, May 23, 1801, died May 16, 1847. He married Mary Austin, born at Cambridge, Washington county, New York, April 3, 1801, died 1830. Children: 1. Volney, born at Dryden, Tompkins county, New York, February 17, 1829, died August 6, 1854. 2. Arvilla Maria, married Darius Frank, mentioned above.

JAYNES The Jaynes trace their ancestry to Henry DeJeanne, a graduate of Oxford in 1611, later a lecturer on theology and divinity at the same university.

(II) William, son of Henry DeJeanne, was born in Bristol, England, January 25, 1618. He entered Oxford, but in 1639 was expelled under the decree of uniformity, which required all students of the university to subscribe to all the articles of the Westminster creed. William dissented from several of them and after his expulsion became chaplain in Cromwell's army. After the restoration of Charles II.

William DeJeanne sought safety in flight, changing his name to Jayne and securing passage on a vessel bound for America. He landed at New Haven, Connecticut, remaining there until after his marriage. He then joined a party of ten others, crossed the sound to Long Island, where they purchased from the Nassau Indians the tract of land on which the town of Brookhaven, Suffolk county, now stands. He was one of the original trustees of the village, serving until 1709, when he was succeeded by his eldest son, William (2). He married Anna Briggs, reared a family of six sons and three daughters, and died March 24, 1714.

(III) William (2), son of William (1) Jayne, was born 1678. He was a resident of the town of Brookhaven, Long Island, succeeding his father as trustee in 1709. He married and left issue.

(IV) William (3), son of William (2) Jayne, was born 1712. He resided on Long Island at Brookhaven; married and had sons: Timothy, of whom further; John, Isaac and Ebenezer.

(V) Captain Timothy Jayne, son of William (3) Jayne, was born 1741, died 1799. He held a captain's commission in the continental army, as did his brother Captain John Jayne. Timothy was captain of the famous Jayne company, of which his brother Isaac was lieutenant, and his brother Ebenezer ensign. At the battle of Long Island this company was captured by the British, confined on the prison ship "Jersey," but fifteen of them surviving their incarceration. The parole ticket given to the last survivor was issued to Samuel Jayne, September 1, 1778, and bears the autograph signature of William Tryon, governor. Captain Timothy Jayne married and had sons: David, William, John and Timothy, of whom further. They all settled in Pennsylvania, the first three in what is now Wyoming county.

(VI) Timothy (2), son of Captain Timothy (1) Jayne, was born September 4, 1777, and was thirteen years of age when his father died. After reaching manhood he came to Pennsylvania, settling at Saltsburg, Indiana county. He married Isabelle Trimble, and left issue.

(VII) William (4) Jaynes (as he spelled the name), eldest son of Timothy (2) Jayne, was born December 15, 1803, died at Saltsburg, Pennsylvania, December 11, 1862. He was a man of education and ability, devoting his energy mainly to selling goods and traveling as agent. For many years he was traveling agent for Dr. David Jayne and his then famous remedies. He resided in Saltsburg until his death. He was a Whig in politics and strongly opposed to human slavery. He married, May 1, 1827, Margaret Henderson, who died at Saltsburg, five years after her husband. They were both members of the Baptist church. Children: 1. Lovinia, married Samuel Anderson, deceased, a one-time sheriff of Jefferson county, Pennsylvania; children: Miles, a deputy sheriff of Jefferson county; Annie, Harry and Melissa. 2. Joseph Wallace, of whom further. 3. Caroline, died unmarried. 4. Julia, died in Sistersville, West Virginia; married Abner Cason, a farmer of the old homestead, died 1911; children: Matilda, deceased; Charles O., Frank M. and William. 5. Timothy, a veteran of the civil war, serving from Pennsylvania; now living in Oklahoma.

(VIII) Joseph Wallace, son of William (4) and Margaret (Henderson) Jaynes, was born in Indiana county, Pennsylvania, November 23, 1829, died in Bradford, August 24, 1882. He was educated and grew to manhood in his native county, choosing the trade of blacksmith, serving a regular apprenticeship, and following that trade as a business all his active years in different parts of Pennsylvania. He was a resident of Bradford for many years, and at the time of his death was a member of the poor board. During the civil war he was in the employ of the government as a blacksmith, working at the arsenal in Pittsburgh. He was a Republican in politics and with his wife was a member of the Baptist church. He married, April 28, 1852, in Westmoreland county, Melvina Larimer, born in Pennsylvania, September 28, 1828, died in Pittsburgh, Pennsylvania, December 16, 1908, daughter of James, son of William Larimer. James Larimer was a merchant and justice of the peace for many years, being known far and near as "Squire" Larimer. He died at Grapeville, Westmoreland county, Pennsylvania, in 1854; he married Delitha Bigelow, born in New York state in 1805, died in Derrick City, Pennsylvania, 1888, daughter of Dr. Lebeus Bigelow, a well-known physician of Westmoreland county. Children of James and Delitha Larimer: 1. Melvina, of previous mention. 2. Lizzie, born 1830, died unmarried.

3. Terissa, born 1842, married Thompson England, a farmer; moved to Nebraska, where she now lives near Lincoln, a widow; children: Laura, Samuel, George, Emma and James. 4. Sarah. 5. Milton. 6. Alice. All three latter died in Grapeville in 1854, unmarried. 7. Alvira, born 1846; married George W. Baldwin, a farmer of Washington county, Pennsylvania. Children: i, Jonathan, married Vesta Baue, of Washington county, and now resides at Pleasant Grove, Pennsylvania; children: Oliver, Mary, Gladys, George, Milton and others. ii. Lizzie, unmarried, resides in Washington county, Pennsylvania. Children of Joseph Wallace and Melvina (Larimer) Jaynes: 1. Delitha Alice, born in Westmoreland county, March 19, 1853, died February 2, 1854. 2. James Milton, of whom further. 3. Lizzie Alphina, born March 18, 1858, died at Gilmore, Pennsylvania, February 6, 1904. 4. Willie, died June 18, 1862, four months old.

(IX) James Milton, eldest son and second child of Joseph Wallace Jaynes, was born in Adamsburg, Westmoreland county, Pennsylvania, November 12, 1854. In 1855 his parents moved to Pleasant Grove, Pennsylvania, and in 1866 to Vineland, New Jersey, where he received his public school education, finishing at Beaver Seminary, Beaver, Pennsylvania. After leaving school he entered the oil fields in Butler county, coming to Bradford in 1879, which has since been his home and place of business, excepting three years, 1905 to 1908, spent in Washington, Pennsylvania, and the few years he was engaged in merchandising. He followed the oil strikes in various capacities until 1888, then became a producer, continuing successfully until he had acquired sufficient capital to engage in mercantile business. He had a general store at Summit City, which he sold at a profit, reopening in the same line at Gilmore, Pennsylvania. He continued there until 1904, then sold and the same year established a general insurance business in Bradford. He has also important holdings of oil and bank stock and real estate. He is a Republican in politics, a member of Tuna Lodge, No. 411, Independent Order of Odd Fellows; Fosterbrook Lodge, No. 11, Knights of Pythias, and the National Protective Legion, No. 266, of which he is secretary. Mr. Jaynes is unmarried.

Members of the family of HATFIELD Hatfield were early settlers in Massachusetts and Connecticut. The first record of this branch is of Matthias and Thomas Hatfield, the former a settler at Elizabethtown, New Jersey, the latter at Mamaroneck, New York. They were supposed to be sons of Thomas Hatfield, of Leyden, Holland, a native of Yorkshire, England, and a member of Rev. John Robinson's church at Leyden, Holland. Matthias Hatfield came from New Haven, Connecticut, where he took the oath of fidelity, May 1, 1660, to Elizabethtown, where in the record of surveys, August 29, 1676, his name is spelled Hatfield. He signed his will "Hatfield." He was a weaver and landowner of considerable means. He died in December, 1687, his wife Maria, born in Holland, surviving him with sons Abraham, Isaac and Cornelius. Thomas Hatfield, brother of Matthias, settled in Mamaroneck about the same time the latter settled in Elizabethtown. Descendants of both settled in the Hudson river counties of New York, and from them spring the many families of the name in New York, New Jersey and Pennsylvania. The records fail to show the connection between these early emigrants and Gilbert Hatfield, of White Plains, New York. The family in the early generations were farmers and boatmen and usually men of means and influence.

(I) Gilbert Hatfield was born in White Plains, New York. His occupation was that of farmer, which he followed all his life in the town of his birth. His political party was the Whig. He married Martha Townsend, born at Harts Corners, New York, near the hill which was the scene of General Putnam's famous ride. They were both members of the Methodist Episcopal church. She survived him several years and died at White Plains, New York, over seventy years of age. Children, all born at White Plains: 1. Daniel, of whom further. 2. Rederick, a mechanic, born 1801; married and had two children, both deceased; Mary Eliza and Ann Rederick. 3. Benjamin, born 1811, died 1871, a farmer; married and had children: Edgar and Leonard, deceased; Mary Elizabeth, married John Crafts, a broker and lives in Buffalo. 4. Edward, a farmer, died in Philadelphia, Pennsylvania; married (first) Clarissa ———, and had several children, among them Rederick; married (second) ———, and had one child, Edward, who lives in Philadelphia, Pennsylvania. 3. Ann, died in Peekskill, New York; married Steven Shelley, a farmer, died in Peekskill, New York; children: Teressa, Jane, Ann, Matilda, Maria, Elizabeth, Henry, Ezra, Enos, George, who lives in Port Chester, New York; Isaac, and four others. 6. Jane, died in New York. 7. Margaret, died in White Plains, New York; married Isaac Wooster, died same place; had three daughters. 8. Mary, died in Wellsville, New York; married Joseph Fields, deceased, a farmer of Port Chester. 9. Elizabeth, died in White Plains, New York.

(II) Daniel, son of Gilbert and Martha (Townsend) Hatfield, was born in White Plains, Westchester county, New York, December 7, 1807, died in Bradford, Pennsylvania, June 21, 1885. He obtained his education in the public schools of his home town and when a young man learned the ship carpenter's trade, which he followed all his life. In politics he was a Republican and in religion a Methodist. He married Annie Bailey, born at Mount Pleasant, New York, March 18, 1806, died in Bradford, Pennsylvania, December 18, 1878. She was a member of the Society of Friends and daughter of Elihu Bailey, a farmer of Mount Pleasant, where he died 1847; he married Catherine ———, whose death occurred only a few weeks after his, and had five children. Children of Daniel and Annie (Bailey) Hatfield: 1. Catherine Griffin, born in Mount Pleasant, New York, December 26, 1836; married Dennis Hess, of Herkimer county, New York, a lumber contractor, born in February, 1828, died October 4, 1865. Children: i. Frank, a gas and steamfitter of New York City, born July 24, 1854; married Mary Hanley, born in New York City; children: Annie, Mary, Edward, Florence, Francis. ii. Catherine, born September 7, 1856, died November 14, 1861. iii. Annie, born December 18, 1859, married Henry Belton, deceased, a miner and native of England. iv. Roswell, born November 16, 1863, died in 1864. v. Child, died in infancy. 2. Samuel, an oil-well operator, born in Mount Pleasant, New York, December 16, 1838, died in Derrick City, Pennsylvania, January 5, 1906; married Mary McMurray, a native of Scotland, now living in Derrick City, Pennsylvania. Children: Nellie, lives in Lima, Ohio; Belle, a resident of Titusville, Pennsylvania; Guy, resides in Los Angeles, California; Harry, lives in Lima, Ohio; Roy, a resident of Newark, New Jersey; Murray, lives in California; Ray, lives in Kane, Pennsylvania; Griffin, lives in Olean, New York; Ann, lives in Watkins Glen, New York; Catherine, a resident of Derrick City, Pennsylvania; Daniel, deceased. 3. Griffin, of whom further. 4. Mary Jane, born in New York City, June 23, 1842, died there 1847. 5. Isabelle, born in New York City, March 7, 1848, married Charles Rothwell, deceased, a groceryman.

(III) Griffin, son of Daniel and Annie (Bailey) Hatfield, was born in Mount Pleasant, Westchester county, New York, September 24, 1840. Here he lived until he was five years of age, when his parents moved to New York City. His public education was obtained in New York City, Buffalo and Great Valley, New York, after which he attended Chamberlain Institute at Randolph, remaining there until 1860, and completing his education in a private Friends' school in New York City. He began his business life in the employ of the Bay State Lumber Company in 1862. In 1864, he established in the grocery business at Holyoke, Massachusetts, remaining there until 1867, when he moved to New York City, continuing in the same line. Bradford obtained one of its best citizens and business men when he came there in 1877 and became identified with A. B. Smith & Company, a relation he has continued, both as stockholder and as an official for twenty years. For the past fifteen years he has been engaged in oil producing, remarkable success attending all his operations. In religion he is a member of the Methodist Episcopal church, and in politics a Republican, having held the office of school director for twenty-one years, and was supervisor and auditor for six years. He married in December, 1875, Addie Clark, born in Bradford, Pennsylvania, in August, 1846, daughter of David Clark, a farmer, born in Massachusetts, February 7, 1811, died in Bradford, September 15, 1890; married Mary McKean, born at Black Creek, New York, 1821, died in Bradford, January 15, 1892; their children were: 1. Edwin F., born January 5, 1843, died in Bradford, Pennsylvania, January 11, 1903; married Flora Marsh; children: Russell, born January 2, 1879, married Gene Patterson; Harry, born February 9, 1883. 2. Almira, married George Lawrence, lives in West Virginia; children: Frank and Fred, live in West Virginia. 3. Addie, of previous mention. 4. Marietta, married Washington Cosper, an oil-well operator of Kinzua, Pennsylvania, and lives in West Virginia; they have one son. 5. Mary Elizabeth, married Philip Knight, deceased, and lives in Bradford, Pennsylvania; children: Edwin, Lewis, Harry and Maud. 6. Lucy, married William Pratt, a farmer of Jamestown, where she lives; children, Alice and Grace. 7. Grace, married Judson Cosper, an oil-well operator of Kinzua, Pennsylvania, and lives in Sistersville, West Virginia.

DEMPSEY The American ancestor of the Dempsey family of Bradford, Pennsylvania, herein recorded, was Lawrence Dempsey, born in Ireland, of Scotch ancestors. He first became a resident of Center county, Pennsylvania, soon after the close of the revolution. In 1797 he penetrated the wilds of the Upper Allegheny Valley to the lands open to settlement on the general terms presented by the state. He was the first settler in the region and made his first improvement on the "Cauvel" farm, not far from the old graveyard near Dempseytown, a hamlet named in his honor. Here he planted an orchard, one of the first in the county, and certainly the first in what is now Oakland township. He had two sons, Peter and David. Lawrence Dempsey died in one of the eastern counties of the state, but his wife and one son are buried in the family graveyard at Dempseytown. The name of his wife was Mary Kafman and she was of German origin, coming from the eastern part of the state. They had two sons: Peter, of whom further and David.

(II) Peter, son of Lawrence Dempsey, was born in Center county, Pennsylvania, and came with his father to Venango county, where they settled on the site of the present town. Peter spent his life after 1797 in Venango county, engaged in farming and lumbering. He was a Democrat and a man of strong, upright character. His brother David was also a man of prominence in the county, and served for a time in congress. While Lawrence Dempsey, was the first settler in Dempseytown, Peter Dempsey, his son, laid out the town, employing Samuel Dale who surveyed for him, September 2, 1800, four hundred and one acres of land lying next to the tract owned by his father. On it he built a house, and on the same site later built a hotel that he kept for many years. The old tavern stood until about 1885, when it was destroyed by fire. Peter Dempsey married Susanna, daughter of Thomas Carter, who was the first white child born in Pittsburgh, and who served in the revolutionary war when a young man. He was in the military service at Pittsburgh, also at Fort Franklin, and he settled on Sugar Creek, near Cooperstown. In 1803 he settled at Dempseytown, where he died at an advanced age. Children of Peter Dempsey were: Thomas C., of whom further; Cicero T., born December 18, 1808, married Nancy Kelley; Maria, September 16, 1810, married James Reed; David, October 8, 1813, married Jane Arters; Washington, February 5, 1816, lost on the Ohio river in 1844; Hetty C., April 3, 1818, married Robert Kelley; John C., April 5, 1820, married Jemima Reninger; Sally, April 5, 1820 (twin), married John Kelley; Isabel, February 7, 1823, never married.

(III) Thomas Carter, son of Peter Dempsey, was born at Dempseytown, Venango county, Pennsylvania, October 13, 1806, died in Springboro, Crawford county, January 27, 1884. He received his education in the district school, and learned the carpenter's trade, which he never followed but became a farmer. In 1848 he moved to Kaneville, Venango county, later to Crawford county, where he died. He was a Democrat until the Fremont campaign, when he transferred his allegiance to the Republican party, and ever afterward supported that party. He married Mary Ann, born at Tidioute, Pennsylvania, April 26, 1807, died in 1866, daughter of John Arthurs, then of Tidioute, later of Brookville, Jefferson county, Pennsylvania, where he died. His wife was a Miss Clover. Mary Ann (Arthurs) Dempsey had four brothers: Richard, John, Samuel and James. The children of Thomas Carter and Mary Ann (Arthurs) Dempsey were: 1. Richard Arthurs, of whom further. 2. Carter G., born in Ravenna, Ohio, April 13, 1839, deceased; married Rhoda Clover; four children: i. Carter G., deceased; ii. Harry, now of Erie, Pennsylvania; iii. Benton Thomas, resides in Michigan; iv. Mary, now of Erie, Pennsylvania. 3. Joanna, born in 1845, on the Venango farm; married Harvey Knickerbocker, deceased, who was a merchant and farmer; two children: i. William, a farmer of Glendon, Crawford county, Pennsylvania; ii. Anna, also a resident of Glendon.

(IV) Richard Arthurs, son of Thomas Carter Dempsey, was born in Dempseytown, Venango county, Pennsylvania, April 26, 1837. He was educated in the public schools of Oakland township, Venango county, and of Cornplanter township, Venango county, Pennsylvania. After his school days were over he worked at farming during the summer, and in the winter months in the lumber woods, continuing this until 1862, when he enlisted as a private in Company E, One Hundred and Twenty-first Regiment Pennsylvania Volunteer Infantry. His regiment was attached to the Army of the Potomac, and with it he fought in many of the historic battles of the civil war, under Generals McClellan, Burnside, Hooker, Meade and Grant. He was captured by the enemy near Petersburg, Virginia, October 1, 1864, and for three months and three weeks was held a prisoner at Salisbury, North Carolina, and being detailed to cut wood for the use of the camp he found opportunity to escape January 25, 1865, and after many adventures joined the Union army in Tennessee. His military record is an enviable one. He was advanced successively to the rank of corporal, sergeant, first sergeant and was commissioned first lieutenant of Company E to date from January 1, 1865. With his regiment he fought in Virginia, at Fredericksburg, Spottsylvania Court House, North Anna, Totopotomy, Bethesda, Cold Harbor, around Petersburg, and at Peebles' farm. In 1864 he was under fire every day from May 5, to October 1, the day he was captured. On June 16, 1864, a comrade, William McKenzie, was shot by his side and instantly killed at Petersburg. Sergeant Dempsey with a few men was detached and sent to reconnoitre at North Anna. During the night a staff officer visited them and gave orders for them to remain where they were until further orders which did not arrive until late the next day, the little squad having been without food since noon of the previous day. When he was captured he was stripped of all his belongings, and with ten thousand other Union prisoners endured the intense suffering of a southern prison pen. After making his escape five hundred miles of hostile country lay between him and the Union army. He accomplished this distance in the dead of winter in thirty-six days, finally reaching the Union army in Tennessee. After the war ended he returned to Pennsylvania, where for a time he engaged in mercantile business, and later in the production of oil, and since 1871 has owned and operated an oil refinery. In 1877 he came to Bradford, bringing his family in 1880. In 1882 he became a member of a company in Custer City extensively engaged in the manufacture of high explosives used in the oil field. He retired from that company in 1902. He also owned a large tract of land in Kansas operated as a cattle ranch. At present (1912) he is president of the Pure Carbon Oil Company, president of the Hubbs Oil Company, president of the Dempsey Oil Company, manager of the Lafayette Oil & Gas Company, and of the Holly Oil Company. He is an energetic, capable man of affairs and is held in the highest esteem in business circles. He has given much of his time and ability to the public service, first appearing in public life as the successful candidate for mayor of Bradford. This was in 1886, and his first term covered the years 1887-88; five years later he was again elected mayor, serving in 1893-94-95. He has also filled the elective offices of supervisor of Bradford township, school director, water commissioner, coroner of McKean county, member of the house of assembly (two terms), 1897 to 1900, and served his party as chairman of McKean county Republican committee. Before coming to Bradford he was postmaster at Kane City one term, and Custer City one term. He is past noble grand of Bradford Lodge, Independent Order of Odd Fellows; past master of the Ancient Order of United Workmen; past commander of Bradford Post, No. 141, Grand Army of the Republic, having held that office many times, and belongs to the Union Veteran Legion of Bradford. He is an attendant of the Methodist Episcopal church, and interested in church and charitable work.

He married Martha Emmeline, born in Wallaceville, Venango county, Pennsylvania, June 8, 1843, daughter of Joseph Campbell, of Scotch parentage, born in Mercer county, Pennsylvania, November 4, 1811, a miller and farmer in both Mercer and Venango counties (see Campbell). Martha Emmeline (Campbell) Dempsey is a member of the Bradford Methodist Episcopal Church and of the Ladies Union Veteran Legion. Children of Richard Arthurs Dempsey: 1. Nettie Gertrude, born in Venango county, April 29, 1861, died August 8, 1883; married, January 3, 1883, D. H. McCullough. 2. Mary Ann, born September 6, 1866, in Kane City, Pennsylvania; married, May 10, 1887, at Bradford, Frank Howard, a merchant of Steamburg, New York; deceased; children: i. Charles Dempsey, born April 7, 1888, now a carbon manufacturer at Wellsville, New York; ii. Lois, born June 15, 1891. 3. Carrie J., April 11, 1868, died in Kane City, August 31, 1898. 4. Lissa M., born in Kane City, July 6, 1869, resides with her parents in Bradford. 5. Nora E., born in Kane City, February 2, 1871, married Orville B. Cutting, a contractor, builder and oil producer, now living in Monticello, Kentucky; children: i. Richard H., born July 4, 1901, at Woodsfield, Ohio; ii. Martha, born March 16, 1911, at Monticello. 6. Dick S., born July, 1875, died July 31, 1876. 7. Lulu C., born March 30, 1879, at Kane City, now residing with her parents in Bradford.

(The Campbell Line).

Joseph Campbell married Mary M. Patterson, born in Butler county, Pennsylvania, May 30, 1818, died December, 1909, and their children were: 1. William, born in Mercer county, February 2, 1838, married Louise Smith, who died March 2, 1858. 2. Thomas Patterson, born in Mercer county, October 15, 1839, died April, 1899; he served four years and three months in the civil war and at the time of his death was superintendent of water works at Sistersville, West Virginia; he was a member of the Grand Army of the Republic, belonging to Post No. 68, at Sistersville. 3. Mary E., born in Venango county, July 27, 1841; she married William Wenton, a machinist, now living in Warren county; children: Mina, Adda, Susan, Mary, all living, and Samuel, deceased. 4. Martha Emmeline, married Richard A. Dempsey (see Dempsey IV). 5. Sarah R., born in Venango county, June 5, 1844, married Alfred Flyte, whom she survives, a resident of Rixford, McKean county; children: Pride and Emma. 6. Margaret R., born in Venango county, March 17, 1846, died 1906; she married Nelson Fleeger, of Butler county, who died in 1908; child, Albert, a machinist, living in Indiana. 7. Melissa M., born in Venango county, December 26, 1847, married James P. Boggs, of Butler county, now residing at Evans City, Butler county; children: Mary, Frank, Nettie, Carrie, Zora. 8. William Filmore, born in Venango county, May 25, 1850, died June 11, 1910; he married the widow of Captain Knight; child, Maud, married Edwin L. Bliss, of Lynn, Massachusetts. 9. Bruce M., born in Venango county, May 20, 1852, now a contractor of Morcroft, Wyoming, married Zora Williamson; children: Gertrude and Bertha. 10. Ida Alice, born in Venango county, July 4, 1854, died at Mount Pleasant, Michigan, March, 1883; married Wilson Hunter; child, Grace, now living at Evans City, Pennsylvania. 11. Wallace R., born in Warren county, November 24, 1856, married Ruth Parke, and now resides on their farm at Forestville, New York.

Mary M. (Patterson) Campbell, the mother of these children, was a daughter of Thomas Patterson, born in Ireland in 1759, died 1840. He was the son of William Patterson, who married Sarah Douglass, born in Scotland. Thomas Patterson came to America at an early day and drifted westward joining a company of scouts in 1775, under Daniel Boone at Boonesboro, Kentucky. He served in the revolution under General Greene and was at Valley Forge the dreadful winter of suffering endured by Washington's army. He married (first) Nancy Blakeley, (second) Martha McVannan, in the Ligonier Valley of Pennsylvania, in 1810. The latter was born in 1784, died in 1864. She was in receipt of a revolutionary pension of four dollars monthly on account of the patriotic services of her husband, which was sent to her at Plain Grove, Lawrence county, Pennsylvania, care of Hutchinson Bovard, until her death.

COFFIN The family of Coffin in England was seated at Portledge, in the parish of Alwington, in the northern part of county Devon, and has been in England since the Norman conquest. There are various branches of this family in the county. The Portledge family of Coffin bore these arms: "Vert, five cross-crosslets argent, between four plates". These arms are also used by the American families.

(I) Tristram Coffin, the earliest English progenitor of whom there is authentic record, lived in Brixton, county Devon, England. His will was dated November 16, 1601, and was proved at Tetness in 1602. He left legacies to Joan, Anna and John, children of Nicholas Coffin; to Richard and Joan, children of Lionel Coffin; to Philip Coffin, and his son Tristram; and appointed Nicholas Coffin his executor.

(II) Nicholas, son of Tristram (1) Coffin, lived at Butlers, county Devon. His will was dated September 12, 1613, and proved November 3, 1613. It mentions his wife Joan; sons,

Peter, of whom further, and Tristram, Nicholas and John; daughter, Anna; and Joan, daughter of one of his sons.

(III) Peter, son of Nicholas Coffin, married Joan Thember. He lived at Brixton, and died in 1628. His will was dated December 21, 1627, and proved March 13, 1628. It provides that his wife shall have the estate during her life, and that it then goes to his son Tristram, "who is to be provided for according to his degree and calling." He mentions daughters, Joan, Deborah, Eunice and Mary, as being under twenty years of age. He refers to his tenement called Silfernay, in Butlers, and to his brother Nicholas. In 1649 his widow with her son Tristram and two daughters, went to Salisbury, Massachusetts, and thence to Haverhill and Newbury, Massachusetts. She died in Nantucket or Boston in May, 1661, aged seventy-seven years. She was said to possess remarkable strength of character, and on the occasion of her death Rev. Mr. Wilson preached a funeral sermon. Children: John, born in England, died in Plymouth Fort; Tristram (2), of whom further; Joan, probably died in England; Deborah, probably died in England; Eunice, born in England; Mary, born in England.

(IV) Tristram (2), son of Peter Coffin, was born in England in 1609, died in Nantucket, Massachusetts, October 2, 1681. He married, in England, Dionis, daughter of Robert Stevens, of Brixton, county Devon. He was the immigrant ancestor, and came to Salisbury, Massachusetts, in 1642, with five children. He removed in a short time to Haverhill, and was witness to an Indian deed of that place November 15, 1642. About 1648 he moved to Newbury, Massachusetts, where he kept an ordinary, and thence to Salisbury again in 1654 or 1655 and was commissioner there. In 1659 he was one of the company of Salisbury men who bought land at Nantucket Island, where he removed in 1660 with his wife, mother, and some of his children, and there he died. He was one of the first magistrates of the island and a capable officer. Children: Hon. Peter, born in England, 1631; Tristram (3), of whom further; Elizabeth, born in England; James, born August 12, 1640; John, born in England, died in Haverhill, October 30, 1642; Deborah, born in Haverhill, November 15, 1642, died December 2, 1642; Mary, born in Haverhill, February 20, 1645, mother of the first white child born in Nantucket; John, born in Haverhill, October 30, 1647; Stephen, in Newbury, May 11, 1652.

(V) Tristram (3), son of Tristram (2) Coffin, was born in England, in 1632, died at Newbury, Massachusetts, February 4, 1704. He settled in Newbury and was admitted a freeman April 29, 1668. He is the ancestor of all the Newbury families of the name. His house, which at last accounts was still occupied by his descendants, was built about 1659, and is therefore over two hundred years old. He married, in Newbury, March 2, 1652-53, Judith (Greenleaf) Somerby, born 1625, died at Newbury, December 15, 1705, daughter of Edmund and Sarah Greenleaf, and widow of Henry Somerby. Children, born at Newbury: Judith, born December 4, 1653; Deborah, born November 10, 1656; Mary, November 12, 1657; James, April 22, 1659; John, died September 8, 1700; Lydia, born April 22, 1662; Enoch, January 21, 1663; Stephen, of whom further; Peter, July 27, 1667; Hon. Nathaniel, born March 22, 1669.

(VI) Stephen, son of Tristram (3) Coffin, was born in Newbury, August 18, 1664, died August 31, 1725. He married, October 8, 1685, Sarah Atkinson, born November 27, 1665, daughter of John and Sarah (Mirick) Atkinson. Children, born at Haverhill: Sarah, born May 16, 1686; Tristram, January 14, 1688, died March 9, 1688; Tristram, born March 6, 1689, died at Newbury, January 23, 1718; Lydia, July 21, 1691; Judith, February 23, 1693; John, January 20, 1695. Children, born at Newbury: Abigail, born September 25, 1696; Stephen, 1698; Daniel, September 19, 1700; Abner, April 29, 1702; Mary, September 26, 1704, died January 18, 1717; Joseph, December 26, 1706; Benjamin, of whom further.

(VII) Benjamin, son of Stephen Coffin, was born at Newbury, Massachusetts, June 14, 1710, died April 30, 1784. He married, October 28, 1731, Miriam, daughter of Jonathan Woodman, of Newbury. Children, born at Newbury: Miriam, born August 22, 1732; Abigail, July 29, 1734; Benjamin, September 6, 1735; Moses, January 30, 1737; Sarah, October 12, 1740; Stephen, July 25, 1743; Anna, October 2, 1745; Jonathan, of whom further; Amos, October 5, 1749; Lemuel, November 27, 1751; Mary, March 12, 1754; Jacob, June 11, 1756.

(VIII) Jonathan, son of Benjamin (1) Coffin, was born at Newbury, October 1, 1747.

died at Alton, New Hampshire, in 1813. He married Jane Flanders, who died in 1818. He settled at New Durham Gore, now Alton, New Hampshire, before or during the revolution. In 1782 he was selectman of that town. In 1790 he was living there, according to the first federal census, and had in his family two males over sixteen, four under that age, and five females. Children, born at Newbury and Alton: Benjamin (2), of whom further; Jonathan, Moses, Samuel, Stephen, Sarah, Jane, Miriam and Anna.

(IX) Benjamin (2), son of Jonathan Coffin, was born about 1770, at Newbury, Massachusetts, died at Alton, New Hampshire, in 1858. He came to Alton when a child and was educated there in the public schools. He followed farming for his occupation, and lived at Alton. He and his family were Free Will Baptists in religion. He married ———, died in 1860, and had three sons and three daughters, among them Joseph M., of whom further.

(X) Joseph M., son of Benjamin (2) Coffin, born in 1820, at Alton, New Hampshire, died at Gilmanton in 1887. He was educated in the public schools of his native town. He followed farming most of his life at Alton and Gilmanton, New Hampshire, and was also a dealer in cattle. In politics he was a Republican, and was supervisor for several years. He was prominent in the Free Will Baptist Church and deacon. He married, in 1845, Dorothy S. Gale, who was born at Gilmanton, New Hampshire, and died there in 1867, aged eighty-four years, daughter of Abram S. and Martha (Moulton) Gale. Her father was a blacksmith and dealer in horses at Gilmanton. Joseph M. Coffin had one child, Smith Gale, of whom further.

(XI) Smith Gale, son of Joseph M. Coffin, was born at Gilmanton, New Hampshire, October 17, 1847. He lived in his native town during youth, worked on his father's farm and attended the public schools in Gilmanton and Pittsfield, New Hampshire. After leaving school he was for one year a conductor on a street car in Boston, and afterward was in the employ of C. Morrison until the spring of 1870, dealing in wholesale produce. He removed to Brady's Bend, Armstrong county, Pennsylvania, and had charge for three years of a store owned by the Brady's Bend Iron Company. He resigned to become manager of a feed and grain store in the same town. Thence he moved to Petrolia, Butler county, Pennsylvania, and engaged in business as proprietor of a livery and sale stable. In the fall of 1880 he removed to Bradford, McKean county, Pennsylvania, and started a livery stable, and has continued in this business to the present time. At the present time he owns very spacious and finely equipped stables on Barbour street. He has been prosperous in this business and has also been successful in numerous oil ventures and as an oil producer. In politics he is a Republican, and while living at Petrolia was a member of the city council, but has never sought public office. He is a member of a Lodge of Free Masons; Chapter of the Royal Arch Masons; Council, Royal and Select Masters; Commandery, Knights Templar; and Lodge, Benevolent and Protective Order of Elks; the Merchants' Club, the Edgewood Club, and the Lafayette Gun and Fishing Club. He has been president of the Edgewood Club, and is a director of the Merchants' Club. His wife is a member of the Methodist Episcopal church.

He married, June 24, 1874, Flora M. Fleming, who was born at Fair View, Butler county, Pennsylvania, daughter of William A. Fleming, a native of Butler county. Her father was superintendent of an iron furnace in that county, but afterwards lived at Petrolia, where he held the office of justice of the peace, and where he died in 1906. Her mother, L. J. Graham, was born in Clarion county, Pennsylvania, not far from Foxburgh. Mrs. Flora M. Coffin had two brothers, George and Edward, both now deceased, as her parents had four children, one of whom died in infancy. Children of Smith Gale Coffin: 1. Claudia Dorothy, born June 1, 1876; married (first) V. Oxley, (second) Calvin Watson; child by first marriage, Gale C. Oxley; none by the second; she now resides at Bradford, Pennsylvania. 2. George Ralph, born August 29, 1878; married, October 17, 1911, Grace Renderneck; resides at Bradford. 3. Charles Joseph, born September 4, 1880, an oil producer, living at Robinson, Illinois.

LINDSLEY This family probably came from near London, England. Francis Lindsley is said to have come to the American colonies in 1639, and to have been on the first vessel which anchored in New Haven bay. This is, however, not beyond question. It is certain that he was living at Branford, Connecticut, in

1645, and his brother John signed the oath of fidelity to New Haven in 1641. Francis Lindsley removed to New Jersey in 1667, going from Branford with the Milford, Connecticut, company.

(I) Eleazer Lindsley, the first member of this family about whom we have definite information, was born December 7, 1737, died June 1, 1794. There is divergence about the colony of his birth, whether it was Connecticut or New Jersey; if the latter, he was probably a descendant of Francis Lindsley. Before the revolution he was living in New Jersey, and in that war he was an officer in the regiment called the Jersey Blues. From the church records of Morristown, New Jersey, although his parentage is not disclosed, we learn that he had brothers, Timothy, died June 5, 1787, aged fifty-seven, and Benjamin, born February 22, 1731, died November 8, 1815, married Sarah ———. After the revolution he rode through the Genesee country to find a tract of land. In 1789 he bought at least one-half of township number one, range two, Phelps and Gorham purchase; some hold that he bought the whole township. In the spring of 1790 a party left New Jersey to settle on this new land. The party was of about forty persons, of whom seven were slaves. There were Colonel Lindsley, two sons, Samuel and Eleazer, and several sons-in-law, with other men; nearly all brought their families. The journey was made by wagons and horseback to the Susquehanna river at Wilkes-Barre, thence they went in boats to the purchase, and landed at the Tioga Flats, June 7, 1790. The new town was called Lindsley, but by a mistake the name was changed to Lindley, and this name has been preserved. Here he built the first saw mill; after his death his wife kept the first tavern, and she entertained Colonel Williamson and his company. In 1793 Colonel Lindsley was elected to the legislature. He was a worthy leader of the community, kind and generous, public-spirited, and an earnest Christian. At Morristown he had been a member of the Presbyterian church, as also his wife; in the new settlement, when there were no traveling ministers, he would himself read sermons on the Sundays. He married Mary, born August 23, 1738, died November 20, 1806, daughter of Thomas and Margaret (Wallace) Miller. Children: 1. Samuel, of whom further. 2. Anne, born July 24, 1762, died March 10, 1764. 3. Elizabeth, born July 17, 1764, married John Seely. 4. Mary, born July 17, 1764, died July 29, 1784. 5. Anna, born July 3, 1767, died in January, 1813; married Ezekiel Mulford. 6. Eleazer, born July 4, 1769, died May 11, 1825; married, April 23, 1787, Eunice Halsey. 7. Jemima, born January 28, 1772, died August 16, 1830; married Stephen Hopkins. 8. Micajah, born June 23, 1774, died young. 9. Sarah, born June 8, 1776, died in 1859; married Ebenezer Backus. 10. Phebe, born August 16, 1780, died January 21, 1814; married David Paine.

(II) Samuel, son of Eleazer and Mary (Miller) Lindsley, was born September 6, 1760, died May 1, 1805. He accompanied his father in the migration to Lindley. He married Lois Bradley, who died June 18, 1814.

(III) William, probably son of Samuel and Lois (Bradley) Lindsley, was born in 1786, died at Lindley, in 1840. At that place his life was passed; he was a farmer, and served as a captain in the state militia. He was at least an attendant of the Presbyterian church; his wife is known to have been a devout member. He married Catharine Piquet, born, probably in Virginia, about 1794, died at Lawrenceville, Tioga county, Pennsylvania, about 1878. Children: 1. Abram Bradley, of whom further. 2. Alexander, born in 1814, died during the civil war in Mississippi, opposite Helena, Arkansas; planter; married ——— Brown; no children. 3. Lois, born in 1816, died at Lawrenceville, 1906; married Parday Damon, deceased; he was a lawyer; no children. 4. Catharine, born in 1817, died at Lawrenceville, 1907; married ——— Butts, of Arkansas, deceased; he was a lawyer; children: Katharine, residing in Boston; Lindsley, deceased; Augustus, deceased. 5. Eleazer, born in 1819, deceased; married Delia (Boyer) Harrower, of Lindley; no children. 6. Phineas, born in 1821, died at Lawrenceville, 1890; married Rosetta Wescott, of Caton, New York; children, all residing at Lawrenceville: Mary, Eugene, Frederick. 7. Walter, born in 1823; died in Mississippi, unmarried; was a planter. 8. Margaret, born in 1830, deceased; married J. H. Middlebrook, of Lindley, deceased; he was a merchant; children: William, residing at Manistee, Michigan; May, Blanche; they reside in Boston. 9. Eugene, died at Lawrenceville; he had been a planter in Arkansas; married, had daughter, Lucilla, deceased.

(IV) Abram Bradley, son of William and Catharine (Piquet) Lindsley, was born at

Lindley, March 12, 1812, died at Lawrenceville, June, 1894. Although it is in another state, Lawrenceville is but one and one-half miles from Lindley. His whole life was passed at Lindley. There he attended public school in his boyhood; there he was a farmer, and served as assessor of the town, as supervisor, and in other town offices. He was a Democrat. He attended the Presbyterian church, and his wife was a member thereof. He married Anna Maria, born at Athens, Bradford county, Pennsylvania, January 25, 1815, died in March, 1879, daughter of Michael R. and Emily (Lindsley) Tharp. Her father was born while his parents were on their way to America, in 1775, and lived mainly at Athens and Lindley. He was a surveyor in the northern tier of Pennsylvania counties. He died at Tioga, Pennsylvania, in 1869. His wife was born at Lindley, and died, rather young, at Athens. Children of Michael R. and Emily (Lindsley) Tharp, all born at Athens: 1. Anna Maria, married Abram Bradley Lindsley. 2. Emily, born in 1818, died at Lindley, 1883; married Rev. ——— McCullough, of Tioga county, Pennsylvania, a Presbyterian minister, deceased: children: Henry, residing at Lawrenceville; Samuel, residing in Kansas. 3. Harriet, born in 1826, died in Wilkes-Barre, 1902; married H. M. Fuller, of Wilkes-Barre, a lawyer, deceased; children: Maria, deceased; Emily, Grace, May, Henry, John, deceased. All the living children reside in Wilkes-Barre. Children of Abram Bradley and Anna Maria (Tharp) Lindsley, all born at Lindley: 1. Clarence, born in 1834, died at Emporium, Pennsylvania, 1881; he was a carpenter; married Eliza Clark, of Corning, New York, deceased; children: Harry, born in 1860, resides at Corning; Rue, born in 1879, married Arlie Darling, a physician; they reside at Lawrenceville. 2. Rue, born in 1836, died at Elizabeth, New Jersey, 1879; married Dr. E. B. Miner, of Wilkes-Barre, deceased; no children. 3. George H., born in 1838, resides at Lawrenceville, farmer; married Mary Waldron, of Caton, New York, deceased; several children. 4. William, born in 1840, a carpenter at Corning; married, has children. 5. Joseph, born in 1842, died at Emporium, 1867; was a farmer. 6. Henry, born in 1844, resides at Corning, employed in the glass factory; married Mary Collins, of Erwin, New York; children: Frank E., born in 1872, deceased; Anna, born in 1874, married David Dunkle; they reside at Norwich, Pennsylvania. 7. Halsey, born in 1847, died at Corning, 1906; married Lamira Lane, of Driftwood, Pennsylvania, now residing at Corning; children: John, deceased; Charles, resides at Berea, Kentucky. 8. ——— born in 1850, died at Emporium, 1874; was druggist; unmarried. 9. Sterling Ross, of whom further.

(V) Sterling Ross, son of Abram Bradley and Anna Maria (Tharp) Lindsley, was born at Lindley, Steuben county, New York, June 18, 1853. He attended public school at Lawrenceville. Immediately after leaving school he went to Wilkes-Barre, and began to learn the printer's trade. There he remained three years. In 1872 he went to Lawrenceville, where he worked in a printing office until 1874. Having secured a position with the Mansfield *Advertiser*, he removed to Mansfield, Tioga county, Pennsylvania; two years later he went to Cuba, New York, where he worked for one year on the *Herald*. Two years were then spent at Elmira, New York, with the *Gazette*, and a few months, in 1879, in New York City. In 1882 he took a position on the *Reporter*, of Port Allegany, Pennsylvania. From 1884 to 1889 he was in Smethport, first on the *Democrat*, afterward on the *Miner*. After a year at Bradford, with the Bradford *Star*, he returned to Smethport and for a little more than one year managed the *Democrat*, then becoming editor, manager and part proprietor of this paper. This has been his permanent station, and he is still conducting this paper in a creditable manner. He is a member of Smethport Lodge, No. 389, Independent Order of Odd Fellows, and of the McKean Encampment of the same order. Mr. Lindsley's religion is the Presbyterian, but as Smethport has no Presbyterian congregation he attends different churches and has not connected himself with any one. He married, November 6, 1884, Myra, born at Summerhahoning, Pennsylvania, January 25, 1863, daughter of John and Ann Berfield. Child, Russell Ross, born June 7, 1889; he attended public school at Smethport; having learned the trade of printer, he is now assisting his father with the Smethport *Democrat*.

DEVINE One of Bradford's best known and most highly respected citizens was the late William Francis Devine, for many years the proprietor of a popular and admirably conducted hotel and in his youth a brave soldier in the Union army. Mr. Devine was of Irish ancestry, a stock which has given to the United States many of her best and most useful citizens.

(I) Thomas Devine, father of William Francis Devine, was born in Ireland, emigrated to the United States and became a merchant tailor in Pittsburgh, where he passed the remainder of his life. He married Mary Gilner, who was like himself a native of Ireland, and died in Pittsburgh several years after the decease of her husband in that city. Of the thirteen children born to them the following grew to maturity: 1. Margaret, born in Ireland, married John Feneran, of the same country, now of Baltimore, and had three children: John, deceased; Lauretta, of Philadelphia, and Mayne, of Baltimore. 2. Mary Ann, born in Pittsburgh, died there unmarried. 3. Martha, born in Pittsburgh, is unmarried and lives in Chicago. 4. William Francis, of whom further. 5. Jennie, married Edward Cassidy, a bridge builder of Pittsburgh, and died there as did her husband, leaving two children, Mercedes and Edward, both of Chicago. 6. Ella, now lives in Pittsburgh, widow of Anthony Urban, who was a druggist in Chicago and died there, leaving five children: Ella, Stella, Antoinette, Graham, all of Chicago, and one who died young. 7. Thomas, unmarried, in business in Butler county, Pennsylvania. 8. James, died unmarried in Pittsburgh, in which city all these eight children, with the exception of the eldest, were born.

(II) William Francis, son of Thomas and Mary (Gilner) Devine, was born March 12, 1845, in Pittsburgh, where he received his education in the public schools, afterward finding employment as a puddler in his native city. While still hardly more than a boy the course of his life was changed by the outbreak of the civil war, for he was quick to feel the military ardor which inspired so many youths of that stirring period. In 1861, being then but sixteen years old, he enlisted from Pittsburgh in Colonel Black's regiment and served throughout the entire four years of the war. His regiment did gallant service in the hottest of the fight at Gettysburg and also participated in many other important engagements. After the close of the war Mr. Devine went into the hotel business in Butler county, in what was known as the Bullion District, meeting with an encouraging measure of success. In 1879 he came to Bradford, where he became the proprietor of one of the city's most prominent hotels, the prestige of which he steadily maintained, both by his able and enterprising method of administration and by his personal popularity, continuing in this business until the close of his life. He belonged to Bradford Lodge, Knights of Pythias, and also to the Maccabees, and like his father followed the standard of the Democratic party. He was a member of the Roman Catholic church.

Mr. Devine married, June 12, 1878, Sarah Louise Donahue (see Donahue III), and they became the parents of the following children: 1. Edith, born September 10, 1880, in Butler county, Pennsylvania, married Clifford Bauer, of Bradford, owner of a planing mill in the west. 2. Ella, born December 15, 1882, in Bradford, married Jesse McFarland, foreman of a mill in Oil City, Pennsylvania, and they have four children: Louise, born September 12, 1899; William, born February 22, 1903; James, born November 22, 1906; and John, born 1910. 3. James Marshall, born September 7, 1885, in Bradford, now the proprietor of a hotel in Clarksburg, West Virginia, married Alice Lowe, of Bradford.

The death of Mr. Devine, which occurred March 12, 1898, his fifty-third birthday, was a distinct loss to Bradford, removing as it did one of her most useful and popular citizens, a man of whom it may be truly said that he was loved by his family and friends and sincerely respected by the entire community.

(The Donahue Line).

(I) James Donahue, grandfather of Mrs. Sarah Louise (Donahue) Devine, was born in county Tyrone, Ireland, where he passed his entire life on his farm. His wife was a native of the same county, and one son was born to them, William, of whom further. James Donahue and his wife were members of the Roman Catholic church, and both died on the farm.

(II) William, only child of James Donahue, was born in 1831, in county Tyrone, Ireland, where he received an excellent education. At the age of twenty-one he emigrated to the United States, settling in Butler county, Pennsylvania, where he engaged in the coke and coal business, his superior education enabling him to take charge of the books and at the same time manage the furnaces as overseer. He was a staunch Democrat, and a member of the Roman Catholic church. Mr. Donahue married, in Ireland, Mary Jane, born in 1835, in county Tyrone, daughter of James and —— (Armstrong) McClintic, both natives of that county, where the former was a farmer. Mr. and Mrs. Donahue were the parents of the following children: 1. Sarah Louise, of whom further. 2. Margaret, born in October, 1853, in Butler county, now lives in Cleveland, Ohio, unmarried. 3. Elizabeth, born in 1855, in Butler county, now lives, unmarried, in Buffalo, New York. 4. Cecilia, born in 1857, in Butler county, as were all the younger children, married Patrick B. Hanlon, an oil producer of that county, and died November, 1910, leaving four children: Edith, born 1877, died November, 1910; Harry, born 1879; Frances, born 1881, married George H. Hyde, a millionaire speculator of Ridgeway, Pennsylvania; and Raymond, born 1883. 5. Susanna, born 1859, married William Doughty, of Butler county, now the proprietor of a hotel in Fulton, Ohio, and has one child, Charles. 6. William, born 1861, now in business in Sistersville, West Virginia, married Hattie Patterson, of Clarion county, Pennsylvania, and has one child, Charles, born 1891. 7. Mary, born 1863, died 1864. The mother of these children died in 1865 in Butler county. Like her husband she was a member of the Roman Catholic church.

(III) Sarah Louise, eldest child of William and Mary Jane (McClintic) Donahue, was born March 17, 1852, on the ocean, while her parents were making the voyage to this country. Her education was obtained in the public schools of Butler county, and she became the wife of William Francis Devine (see Devine II). Mrs. Devine is a member of the Roman Catholic church, and belongs to the Ladies' Catholic Benevolent Association of Bradford, having been the first president of this organization.

GALLUP The Gallups of America descend from John Gallup (also Gollop and Gallop), who came to this country from the parish of Nosterne, county Dorset, England, son of John Gallup, whose wife was a daughter of Thomas Crabbe, of Nosterne. He was a grandson of Thomas and Agnes (Watkins) Gallup, of North Bowood and Strode, whose descendants yet own and occupy the Manor of Strode.

(I) The American ancestor, Captain John Gallup, came to America from the parish of Nosterne, county Dorset, England, in the year 1630. He sailed from Plymouth, England, March 20, 1630, in the ship "Mary and John," arriving at Nantasket, now Hull, May 30. His wife Christobel and children came in 1633. He settled first at Dorchester, but was soon afterward a resident of Boston. He was a skillful fearless mariner, and achieved great distinction by piloting safely through a newly found channel the ship "Griffin," having on board Rev. John Cotton, Rev. Thomas Hooker, Rev. Mr. Stone and two hundred others. His most notable adventure was an encounter with a boatload of Indians, whom he destroyed and captured off Block Island, with the aid of his two sons and a hired man. This has been called the first naval battle on the Atlantic coast, and gave Captain Gallup colonial, and later national, reputation. It was one of the first skirmishes of the great Pequot war. He died in Boston, January 11, 1650, his wife, September 27, 1655. Children, all born in England: 1. John (2), of whom further. 2. Joan, married, in 1637, in Boston, Thomas Joy. 3. Samuel, came in 1633, died before 1670; married Mary Phillips, in 1650, at Boston. 4. Nathaniel, came in 1633, died before 1670; married, at Boston, April 11, 1652, Margaret Evetery (?).

(II) Captain John (2), eldest son of Captain John (1) Gallup, was born in England, and came to this country in 1633 with his mother and her other children. He won renown by his bravery against the Indian foes of the colony; had large grants of land, and in 1654 moved with his family to the east side of the Mystic river, now Stonington, Connecticut. He was representative from 1665 to 1667. He was engaged with his company in the Great Swamp Fight, December 19, 1675, and was one of the six captains who fell in that memorable battle, bravely leading their men. He married, in 1643, at Boston, Hannah, daughter of John and Margaret Lake. Margaret (Read) Lake was the daughter of Edmund Read, esquire, of Wickford, Essex county, England, and sister of Elizabeth Read, who married John Winthrop (2), governor of Connecticut. Children of Captain John (2) Gallup: 1. Hannah, born at Boston, September 14, 1644; married Stephen Gifford, of Norwich, Connecticut, June 18, 1672. 2. John (3), of whom further. 3. Esther, born in New London, Connecticut, March 24, 1653; married, December 17, 1674, Henry Hodges, of Taunton, who died September 30, 1717. 4. Benedam, born in Stonington, 1655, died August 2, 1727; married Esther

Prentice, born July 20, 1660, died May 18, 1751. 5. Lieutenant William, born in Stonington, 1658, died there May 15, 1731; married Sarah Cheesebrough, who died September 9, 1729. 6. Samuel. 7. Christobel, married, December 31, 1677, Peter Crary. 8. Elizabeth, married Henry Stevens, of Stonington. 9. Mary, married John Cole, a schoolmaster of Boston. 10. Margaret, married Joseph Culver, of Groton, Connecticut.

(III) John (3), son of Captain John (2) Gallup, was born 1646, died April 14, 1735. He settled in Stonington, and represented that town in the general court in 1685, 1686, 1687 and 1688. He served with his father in King Philip's war and is supposed to have been with him in the "Swamp" fight. He married, in 1675, Elizabeth Harris, born at Ipswich, February 8, 1654. Children: 1. John (4), of whom further. 2. Thomas, baptized April 30, 1682; married Hannah French, January 4, 1721 or 1722, no issue. 3. Martha, baptized April 2, 1683; married John Gifford, of Norwich, Connecticut. 4. Samuel, baptized October 9, 1687; married Mehitable Blount, May 11, 1727. 5. Elizabeth, baptized July 14, 1689. 6. Nathaniel, baptized July 4, 1692, died April 3, 1739; married Margaret Gallup, who died March 2, 1761. 7. William, baptized May 26, 1695, died at Voluntown, Connecticut, August 18, 1735. 8. Benjamin, baptized November 1, 1696; married, May 22, 1735, Theody Parke.

(IV) Captain John (4), son of John (3) Gallup, was born at Stonington, Connecticut, 1676, die.' December 29, 1755. He moved to Voluntown about 1710, being one of the early settlers of that town, taking up a large tract of land, part of which was still in the Gallup family as late as 1891 and perhaps is yet. At the first town meeting held in Voluntown, June 20, 1721, he was chosen one of the selectmen and was ever thereafter active in town and church affairs. He was chosen in 1726 captain of the first military company organized in Voluntown. He married, in 1709, Elizabeth Wheeler, of Stonington, born May 22, 1683, died April 14, 1735, daughter of Isaac and Martha (Park) Wheeler, and granddaughter of Thomas Wheeler, born in England, 1602, came to America 1630. Children of Captain John (4) Gallup: 1. William, born at Voluntown, September 2, 1710, died February 10, 1734. 2. Isaac, born February 24, 1712, died August 3, 1799; married, March 29, 1749, Margaret Gallup, of Stonington, born October 12, 1730, died December 9, 1817. 3. Elizabeth, born April 9, 1714; married Zachary Frink. 4. Martha, born September 3, 1716, died May, 1786; married, January 4, 1737, Thomas Douglass. 5. Hannah, January 29, 1719; married, 1741, Manuel Kinne. 6. Dorothy, born March 22, 1721; married, 1744, John Reed. 7. John (5), of whom further.

(V) John (5), youngest son of Captain John (4) Gallup, was born June 9, 1724, died in Voluntown, April 6, 1801. He married, April 9, 1747, Hannah Frink, and settled in Voluntown, where she died in 1773. Children: 1. Hannah, born February 15, 1748; married John Cogswell, of Griswold, Connecticut. 2. William, born October 8, 1749. 3. John (6), born July 23, 1751, died January 7, 1789; married, October 24, 1773, Lydia Randall. 4. Elizabeth, born June 2, 1753; married William Briggs. 5. Daniel, born March 7, 1755. 6. Wheeler, of whom further. 7. Jabish, born May 12, 1759. 8. Samuel, born April 7, 1761, settled at Voluntown, now Sterling, Connecticut, where he died October 13, 1856; married, December 15, 1785, Lucy Averill, died February 21, 1846, no issue. 9. Nathan, born February 11, 1763, died in Voluntown, June 1, 1829; married, January 19, 1786, Zerwich, died October 31, 1838, daughter of Benjamin and Amy (Kinne) Gallup. 10. Dorothy, born January 11, 1765, died September 20, 1786.

(VI) Wheeler, son of John (5) Gallup, was born January 25, 1757, died December 23, 1796. He married Elizabeth Cogswell, May 2, 1782, Rev. Levi Hart, of Griswold, officiating. She was born October 11, 1754, at Griswold, Connecticut, daughter of Nathaniel Cogswell and his first wife, Huldah Kinney, granddaughter of Edward and Hannah (Brown) Cogswell, great-granddaughter of William (2) and Martha (Emerson) Cogswell, great-great-granddaughter of William (1) and Susanne (Hawks) Cogswell, great-great-great-granddaughter of John Cogswell, the American ancestor, born in England, who married Elizabeth Thompson, September 16, 1615, and came to America, settling at Ipswich, Massachusetts. Children of Wheeler Gallup: 1. Dolly, born in Voluntown, April 1, 1783, married, in 1801, John Cogswell. 2. Elizabeth, born March 6, 1785, married John Colgrove. 3. Nathaniel C., of whom further. 4. Huldah, born March 7, 1789, died May 2, 1872. 5. Sallie, born March 17, 1791; married, November 23, 1813,

PENNSYLVANIA

Gilbert Brown, and settled in Pennsylvania. 6. Wheeler (2), born in Voluntown, September 30, 1793; married (first) Mary Gallup, July 2, 1815; later moved to Pennsylvania, and married (second) Edith Arnold.

(VII) Nathaniel C., son of Wheeler Gallup, was born in Voluntown, Connecticut, March 15, 1787. He moved to McKean county, Pennsylvania, about 1815, and there died, a farmer, founding a numerous family. He married (first) March 3, 1808, Dinah Edmunds, of Griswold, Connecticut, who died April 30, 1826. He married (second) Indiana Arnold. Children of first marriage: 1. Jabez I., born at Voluntown, March 19, 1809, died in McKean county, Pennsylvania, 1891; married Docia Irewer. 2. Andrew, born September 18, 1810; married Harriet Denning. 3. Orin W., born July 17, 1812, died September 7, 1887; married Nancy Corwin. 4. Nathaniel C. (2), born March 14, 1814; married Alsena Derby. 5. Daniel, of whom further. 6. California, born in McKean county. 7. Eben, born in Norwich township, McKean county, March 17, 1821, died in Smethport, August, 1896; married Phœbe King Windsor, born October 26, 1830, died June, 1905. 8. Orlando, born in Norwich, died December 8, 1888; married Floretta Comes. 9. Philetus E., died September 30, 1878; married, December 20, 1844, Laura A. Colgrove. 10. Alfred D., married Ellen Brewer. Child of second marriage: 11. Arnold, married —— Beckwith.

(VIII) Daniel, son of Nathaniel C. Gallup, was born in Norwich, McKean county, Pennsylvania, died there August 8, 1892, a farmer of Norwich township all his life. He married (first) Lucina Dennison, who died January 22, 1848. He married (second) Clara C. Lucore, died 1890. Children: 1. Nathaniel C. (3), of Norwich, McKean county, born January 22, 1844; married, in 1870, Ann Evans; children: Edwin, and Emma. 2. William D., of whom further.

(IX) William D., younger son of Daniel and Lucina (Dennison) Gallup, was born in Norwich, McKean county, September 11, 1846, died in Smethport, September 11, 1900. He was educated in the public schools, and began business life as an employee in the mercantile house of Henry Hamlin, in Smethport, remaining four years. He was then employed in Emporium, Pennsylvania, the succeeding four years; after which he returned to Smethport entering the employ of A. N. Taylor, continuing until the decease of the latter, and then for another year with Frank N. Taylor. In 1877 he purchased the old Sartwell store on Main street, Smethport, continuing there in general merchandising until 1881, when he moved to a new location, where he continued in successful business until his death. He was a Republican in politics and in 1877 was elected treasurer of McKean county. In 1885 was elected county commissioner, filling both these important positions with dignity and honor. He was prominent in the Masonic order, belonging to McKean Lodge, No. 388, Free and Accepted Masons; Bradford Chapter, No. 260, Royal Arch Masons; and Trinity Commandery, No. 58, Knights Templar. In religious faith he was a member of St. Luke's Protestant Episcopal Church, Smethport, Pennsylvania. He was a man of integrity and held in highest esteem by his townsmen.

He married, May 24, 1871, Harriet Elizabeth Sheppard, born in Bradford, Pennsylvania, November 10, 1846, daughter of Darius Sheppard, born in Herkimer county, New York, 1815, died in Smethport, Pennsylvania, December 23, 1879, a wagon-maker. He married Abigail Barrett, born April 21, 1825, who survives him, a resident of Smethport, the loving charge of her daughter, Mrs. Harriet E. Gallup. Children of Darius Sheppard: 1. Harriet Elizabeth, of previous mention, now widow of William D. Gallup, residing in Smethport. 2. George, born in Farmer's Valley, McKean county, January 3, 1855, now a livery man of Port Allegany; married Mina Allen, of Liberty township; children: Lena, residing in Cuba, New York; Nellie, residing in Fredonia, Kansas; Ruth, residing in Port Allegany, Pennsylvania. 3. Dr. Wesley Barrett, born in Smethport, June 10, 1866, now a practicing physician of Peoria, Illinois; married Alice Cook, of Cook, Nebraska; no issue. 4. Frank, died in infancy. 5. Fred, died in infancy. Abigail (Barrett) Sheppard is a daughter of Thornton Barrett, born in New Hampshire, died in Smethport, a farmer. He married (second) Abigail Barrett, also of New Hampshire, dying in Smethport. Children: 1. Henry, died in Farmer's Valley, McKean county, a farmer; married Elizabeth Lasher; children: i. Lelia, resides in Belfast, New York; ii. Nellie, resides in Woodstock, New York; iii. Melvin, resides in Buffalo, New York. 2. George, died in Farmer's Valley, a lumberman; married Palmyra Crandall, who survives him a resident of Farmer's Valley; children: Georgia, deceased, and Ardella. 3. William, now a retired lumberman of Grand Rapids, Michigan; married and has issue. 4. Wesley, died in Seward, Nebraska, a lawyer; married Anna Chase, of Oskosh, Wisconsin; children: Arthur and Grace. 5. Laura, died near Oskosh, Wisconsin; married Jason Blanchard, born in Pennsylvania, a farmer, also deceased; children: Ida, George, Gifford and Charles. 6. Abigail, of previous mention, widow of Darius Sheppard. 7. Adelia, married Ichabod White, of Pennsylvania, deceased, a minister of the Free Methodist church; she survives him a resident of Forestville, New York; children: Frank, Jennie, Mary, Nellie, Laura, Corliss, Gilbert and George. Children of William D. and Harriet Elizabeth Gallup: 1. Fred D., of whom further. 2. Rena Mary, born in Smethport, September 13, 1881; married J. S. Walker, secretary and treasurer of the Smethport Glass Company.

(X) Fred D., only son of William D. and Harriet Elizabeth (Sheppard) Gallup, was born in Smethport, Pennsylvania, June 16, 1872. His early and preparatory education was obtained in the public schools, continuing until 1889 when he was graduated from the high school with the class of that year. He then studied for one year under a private tutor, then entering Trinity College, Hartford, Connecticut. In 1892 he entered Yale as a junior, and was graduated A. B., class of 1894. He then returned to Smethport and began the study of law under the preceptorship of Judge J. W. Bouton, continuing until 1896, when he was admitted to the McKean county bar, later was admitted to practice in all state and federal courts of the district. He formed a law partnership with his old preceptor, Judge Bouton, and as Bouton & Gallup they continued in successful practice until 1900. He practiced alone for six months, then formed a partnership with V. B. Bouton, continuing until 1905. He then practiced alone until 1910, when he became associated with C. W. Shattuck, as partner, under the firm name Gallup & Shattuck, which still continues.

Mr. Gallup is one of the successful lawyers of the McKean county bar, learned in the law and skillful in its application. He has always had a good practice and represents several of the best corporations. He is local solicitor for the Buffalo, Rochester & Pittsburgh Railroad, a position he has held since 1903. About five years ago when McKean county was made a separate legal district (36) by the Pennsylvania railroad he was appointed their solicitor. He is attorney for the Hamlin Bank & Trust Company, Smethport, Pennsylvania, and also a director of that institution since its organization. He is treasurer and director of the Smethport Gas Company, and since 1900 director of the Smethport Water Company, and a director of the Mount Jewett National Bank.

He is an independent, progressive Republican, believing in clean politics, good government and a "square deal" for all. He has served as school director for fifteen years, and president for several years of the McKean County School Directors' Association. He served for six years as a member of the borough council, and in 1908 was chairman of the Republican County Committee. He is a member of Lodge, Chapter and Commandery of the York Rite, and a thirty-second degree Mason of the Ancient Accepted Scottish Rite, Coudersport Consistory. His York Rite bodies are: McKean Lodge, No. 338, Free and Accepted Masons, of which he is past worshipful master; Bradford Chapter, Royal Arch Masons; Bradford Council, Royal and Select Masters; Trinity Commandery, Knights Templar. He is also a noble of Zem Zem Temple, Nobles of the Mystic Shrine, Erie, Pennsylvania; a member of the Benevolent and Protective Order of Elks, Bradford; the Independent Order of Odd Fellows; Smethport Lodge and Encampment, and Phoenix Chapter, Order of the Eastern Star. His club is the Central, and he is a fireman of Smethport Hose Company. In religions faith he is an Episcopalian, belonging to St. Luke's, Smethport.

He married, September 22, 1896, Margaret Mary McKean, born in Kane, Pennsylvania, January 8, 1873, daughter of James A. and Julia (Fox) McKean. Children, both born in Smethport: 1. Marion Gertrude, July 5, 1897. 2. William D. (2), June 7, 1903.

GIFFORD
The family of Gifford is of high antiquity and was seated at Honfleur, Normandy, three centuries before the conquest of England by Duke William, the Conqueror. At the battle of Hastings in 1066 "Sire Rumdolph de Gifforde" was one of the conqueror's standard bearers, and was rewarded by him with estates in Somersetshire and Cheshire, which were

created into a barony from which his descendants had summons to parliament. In the reign of King Henry II., Sir Peter Gifford married Alice, daughter and heiress of Sir Grey de Corpuchim, with whom he had the lordship of Chillington, in Cheshire, which was the seat of the Dukes of Buckingham of this family. Sir Stephen Gifford was one of the barons accompanying Richard Coeur de Lion to the Holy Land, and was killed at the siege of Jerusalem; his son, Sir Stephen, was also wounded there. The family enjoyed great distinction at the English court for several centuries, and at one time five peerages existed in the family name. Baron George Gifford was made Earl of Buckingham by King Henry V., but joining the House of York against that of Lancaster, during the "War of the Roses," and being one of the prime favorites of King Edward V., he was created Duke of Buckingham, and married the Princess Maude Van Plantagenet, cousin of the King. His son, George Gifford, Duke of Buckingham, was one of the favorites of the Duke of Gloucester, afterward King Richard III., and being detected by that tyrant in the act of corresponding with the Earl of Richmond, afterward King Henry VII., he was attainted of high treason and beheaded by Richard's orders. The Duke left several small children, but as they had been deprived of their lands and titles, the king, Henry VII., found it more convenient not to restore them, and Humphrey Stafford, a powerful noble, having married the oldest daughter of Henry, was created by him Duke of Buckingham. The Staffords followed the fate of their maternal ancestor; the grandson of Humphrey was beheaded, and his family deprived of their vast estates. Of the sons of the last George Gifford, Duke of Buckingham, George continued the first line, and continually solicited the crown and parliament for his restoration, but on account of the powerful opposition of his brother-in-law, Stafford, was always defeated. The Giffords in the reign of King Henry VIII., and queens, Mary and Elizabeth, put their claims before the English parliament, never, however, successfully. In the reign of James I., Sir Ambrose Gifford claimed before the house of peers to be the Duke of Buckingham, and in the second year after the reign of Charles I, his claims were disallowed on account of his politics. Walter Gifford, the son of Sir Ambrose, emigrated from England to Massachusetts Bay Colony in 1630, and was the progenitor of the American branch of this ancient family. Noted descendants are: The celebrated critic, Sir John Gifford; and Lord Gifford, master of the rolls, who prosecuted, while attorney-general of England, the wife of George IV., Queen Caroline, upon a charge of high crimes and misdemeanors. Coat-of-arms: Gules, three lions passant, argent; crest, an arm couped above the elbow, vested or charged with two bars wavy, azure, cuffed white, holding in the hand a stag's head, cabossed, gules. Motto: "Nothing without the Divinity."

(II) Walter, son of Sir Ambrose Gifford, emigrated from England to the Massachusetts Bay Colony in 1630, and was the progenitor of the branch of the Gifford family in America herein traced. While there are many who will controvert the statement above, there are many others who accept the fact that Walter Gifford was the son of Sir Ambrose, and the father of William. Walter Gifford married and had a son William, of whom further.

(III) William, son of Walter Gifford, was, according to Huntington's History of Stamford, Connecticut, before the court of that settlement in 1647. The sentence of the court against him was, that he be whipped at the court's discretion and banished. The supposition is that this William Gifford is the same William Gifford we find in Sandwich, Massachusetts, and a member of the grand inquest at Plymouth in 1650. He continued to reside in Sandwich until his death, with the exception of five years, between 1665 and 1670, when he, with George Allen and the sons of Peter Gaunt, all of Sandwich, together with others, were the first proprietors and settlers of Monmouth, New Jersey, having purchased the land from the Indians; and to them the Monmouth patent was granted, April 8, 1665. They were adherents of the Quaker faith, both in Massachusetts and New Jersey. William Gifford owned land in Massachusetts, Rhode Island and Connecticut. His Massachusetts possessions consisted of lands in Sandwich, Falmouth and Dartmouth. The facsimile of the deed exists, of a forty-acre parcel, purchased of a Suckanessett (Falmouth) Indian named, Joh Attukkoo, July 24, 1673. He gave by will to his sons, Jonathan and James, lands in Falmouth, Massachusetts. He also deeded to his sons, Robert and Christopher, lands in Dartmouth, Massachusetts, both of whom erected homesteads upon their estates. Robert continued to live in Dartmouth, while Christopher moved later to Little Compton, Rhode Island. Both have many descendants now living in southern Massachusetts and Rhode Island. William probably deeded his Connecticut lands to his son, John, who gave by will one hundred acres in the colony of Connecticut, to his son, Samuel, and two hundred acres to his grandsons. He died April 9, 1687. Children: John; Hannaniah, living in Monmouth county, New Jersey, in 1700; William, died 1738, married (second) Lydia Hatch, born 2, 1, 1711; Christopher, born 1658, died 11, 22, 1748, married Deborah Perry; Robert, died 1730, married Sarah Wing; Patience, died 1678, married Richard Kirby; Mary; Jonathan, born 5, 4, 1684, married Lydia ———; James, born 3, 10, 1686, married 3, 30, 1710, Deborah Lewis.

(IV) Robert, son of William Gifford, was born in 1660, died in 1730. He lived at Dartmouth, Massachusetts, and married Sarah, daughter of Stephen and Sarah Briggs. Children: Benjamin; Jeremiah; Stephen; Timothy, and Simeon.

(V) Simeon, son of Robert Gifford, married Susannah ———. Children: Job, born May 28, 1725; Sarah, July 1, 1728; Simeon (2), October 29, 1730.

(VI) Job, son of Simeon and Susannah Gifford, was born May 28, 1725. He lived in Salem county, New Jersey, where he married and had issue, including a son, Job (2), with whom the history in McKean county begins.

(VII) Job (2), son of Job (1) Gifford, was born in Salem county, New Jersey, April 20, 1796, died in Keating township, McKean county, Pennsylvania, on his farm, January 11, 1874. He was educated in Salem county, and there conducted farming operations until after his marriage. He resided at Norwich, Pennsylvania, then bought a farm in Keating township, which he cultivated until his retirement from active labor. He was a Democrat in politics, and an active worker, with his wife, in the Baptist church. He married in Salem county, May 5, 1816, Nancy Woodruff, born in Cumberland county, New Jersey, December 21, 1796, died in Keating township, September 9, 1878. Children: 1. Jonathan, born in Salem county, New Jersey, December 21, 1817, died in Emporium, Pennsylvania, a journalist; married Elizabeth Taylor, of New Jersey; children: John T., resides in Lock Haven, Pennsylvania; and Louis, deceased. 2. David, born in Norwich, Pennsylvania, January 17, 1819, died in Corry, Pennsylvania, a farmer; married Sally Curtis, and left issue. 3. William, of whom further. 4. Sarah (Polly), born in Norwich, April 11, 1822, died in Keating township; married Moses Hackett, a farmer, son of Seth Hackett. 5. Job, born in Norwich, March 14, 1824, died in Smethport, a veterinarian and butcher; married Emmeline Cobb, and left issue. 6. Alexander, born in Norwich, July 21, 1825, died in Keating township, a farmer; married Harriet Hackett; children: Duello, lives in Crosby, Pennsylvania; and Ella, in Keating township. 7. Henry, born in Sergeant, Pennsylvania, August 30, 1827, died in Emporium, Pennsylvania, a farmer; married Rachel Morrison; child: Elizabeth. 8. Harriet, born in Sergeant, August 21, 1829, died in Keating township; married James Hackett, a farmer, deceased, and left issue. 9. Rejoice, born in Sergeant, August 6, 1831, died in Emporium, Pennsylvania; married David Morrison, a farmer; no issue. 10. Leander, born in Norwich, Pennsylvania, April 16, 1834, died in Washington, D. C., an employee of the government in the treasury department; married Letina Hyde; child: Cora, living in Washington, unmarried. 11. Alonzo, born in Norwich, October 3, 1838, died unmarried in Keating township. 12. Jane, born in Keating township, April 21, 1840; married John Duntley. Children: i. Jeremiah, of Keating township. ii. Mildred, of Punxsutawney, Pennsylvania. iii. Gertrude, deceased. iv. Emma, married Mr. Hartmeyer, and lives in Buffalo, New York. v. Bessie, married Charles Curtis, and lives in Keating township.

(VIII) William, third son of Job and Mary (Woodruff) Gifford, was born at Bunker Hill, McKean county, Pennsylvania, October 8, 1820, died in Smethport, June 19, 1889. He was educated in the public schools, remained on the home farm until his marriage, then settled on a farm of his own at Gifford Hollow, about two and a half miles from Smethport, where he found a ready market for his farm products. He was a Democrat in politics, and was school director and supervisor of Keating township for many years. He was a consistent Christian and with his wife belonged to the Baptist church. He married at Liberty, McKean county, September 3, 1843, Louisa F. Hackett, born in Chemung county, New York, February 11, 1823, died at Smethport, September 7, 1892, daughter of Seth Hackett, born in Hillsdale, Columbia county, New York, July

4, 1796, died at Gifford Hollow, 1882. His wife, Electa, was born August 12, 1798, at Oxford, Chenango county, New York. Children of Seth Hackett: 1. Moses, born June 10, 1818; married Sarah Gifford, of previous mention. Children: i. Lavinia, deceased. ii. Justina, of Emporium, Pennsylvania. iii. Alice, deceased. iv. Lelia. v. Albert. vi. Nancy, who lives in Potter county. 2. Charles, born July 16, 1820, died May 19, 1848. 3. Louise F., of previous mention. 4. Pamelia, born November 7, 1825; married Samuel Thompson, a farmer; both deceased. 5. Seymour, born March 2, 1828, deceased, a lumberman of Emporium, Pennsylvania. 6. Margaret, born October 6, 1830; married Miles White, a hotel keeper of Coudersport, Pennsylvania; both deceased; children: Milart, Carrie and Michael. 7. Mary, born May 25, 1832, died June 15, 1880; married Isaac Duntley; children: Edgar, deceased; Monte, Cora, Electa and Ross. 8. Sarah Ann, born January 25, 1836; married John Goodwin, a mill worker of Emporium; both deceased; children: Clara, deceased, and Stella, married a Mr. Parks, and lives in Albuquerque, New Mexico. 9. Henry, born September 11, 1838, a merchant of Philadelphia; married and has issue.

Children of William and Louisa F. Gifford, all born near Smethport, Pennsylvania: 1. Zavalia Depew, of whom further. 2. Seth J., born December 27, 1847, now a retired lumber man, living in Carthage, New York; married Nellie Dunbar; child: Myrtle, born 1877, married William A. Ostrander (see Ostrander). 3. Warley, born January 31, 1853, an oil speculator and operator; married Emma D. Gallup; child; Roy, born 1879, now an electrical engineer in Chicago, married Mary Ryan (see Ryan). 4. Leander, born November 6, 1855, a glass worker; married Ellen Bennett, of Smethport; child: Theo, born September 3, 1885, resides in Williamsport, unmarried. 5. Jennie E., born May 28, 1862, died February 3, 1873. 6. William, born April 17, 1865, a mill worker in Randolph county, West Virginia.

(IX) Zavalia Depew, eldest child of William and Louisa F. (Hackett) Gifford, was born in Smethport, Pennsylvania, September 3, 1845. He attended the public schools until he began work as clerk in a hotel, where he remained but a short time. He next became a saw mill worker at Emporium, Pennsylvania, remaining two years, returning to Smethport, and continuing in the same line of work until 1900. Since that date he has been employed by F. D. Gallup, C. D. Comes and Charles McKean on special work, being now (1912) in the employ of the latter. He is a Democrat in politics, and a member of the Ancient Order of United Workmen. He married, December 26, 1868, Emma Bishop, born in Port Allegany, Pennsylvania, October 9, 1849, coming to Smethport with her parents in 1858, and obtaining her education in the public schools of that borough. She is a member of the St. Luke's Episcopal Church. She is the daughter of Amos Bishop, born in 1816, of the New England Bishop family, who died in Smethport, September 22, 1900, a carpenter. He married Adeliza Arnold, born in Otsego county, New York, at Whitestone, in 1818, died in Smethport, January 1, 1891. Children of Amos Bishop: 1. Adelbert, born in Otsego county, New York, July, 1839; married in Smethport, Ellen McCoy, and is now living in Bradford, Pennsylvania, an architect. 2. Ann, born April, 1844, in Otsego county, now living in Smethport, unmarried. 3. Emma, of previous mention, wife of Zavalia D. Gifford. The foregoing are grandchildren of Samuel Bishop, born in New England in 1778, died in Smethport in 1863, a farmer of Cooperstown, New York, where his wife, a Miss Curtis, born in New England, died. Children of Samuel Bishop: 1. William, deceased. 2. Eleazer, a physician for a time in Potter county, Pennsylvania, who moved, and nothing further is known of him. 3. Mary, died in Knoxville, Pennsylvania, in 1859; married Wells Bellows, a physician of Knoxville, deceased; children: Clarence, deceased, and Newton, a farmer of Knoxville. 4. Amos, of previous mention, father of Mrs. Z. D. Gifford.

Adeliza Arnold, the mother of Mrs. Gifford, was the daughter of George Arnold, who lived in Whitestone, New York, and married a Miss Hafford and had issue: 1. Aaron, died in Port Allegany. Pennsylvania, a lumberman and merchant; married Ellen Midberry, of Otsego county, New York; children: Fitz Henry, and Violetta, both deceased. 2. John, died in Illinois, a farmer; married Ruth Brown of Otsego county. Children: i. Frank, a banker of Seattle, Washington. ii. Fitz James, deceased. iii. Angelia, resides in New York City. iv. Augusta, resides in Wyoming. v. George, deceased. 3. Emmeline, died in Port Allegany, Pennsylvania; married Elias Shurtz, a farmer.

Children: i. Orsino. ii. Henry, deceased. iii. Melvina, deceased. iv. John, lives in Williamsport. v. Fitz Allen, resides in Port Allegany. vi. Josephine, resides in Port Allegany. vii. William, resides in Minnesota. viii. Ellen, deceased. ix. Emma, deceased. 4. Edith, died near Smethport; married Wheeler Gallup, deceased, a farmer; children: Elizabeth and Viola, both deceased. 5. Adeliza, mother of Mrs. Gifford.

Children of Zavalia Depew and Emma (Bishop) Gifford: 1. Guy, born in Emporium, Pennsylvania, December 17, 1871, now a car inspector at Olean, New York, unmarried. 2. Gretchen, born in Smethport, April 5, 1876, a graduate of Smethport high school; married Harry Weaver, an engineer, now living in Davis, West Virginia; children: Dorothy, born December 18, 1899; and James, born October 15, 1907. 3. Beatrice, born June 3, 1883, in Smethport, where she now resides, a graduate of high school, unmarried.

(IX) Warley, son of William and Louisa F. (Hackett) Gifford, was born in Keating township, McKean county, Pennsylvania, January 31, 1853. He was educated in the public school, continuing until of sufficient age and attainment to become himself a teacher. He only taught, however, two terms in McKean county, but in 1873 entered the employ of Henry Hamlin in his store. In 1879 he purchased from Mr. Hamlin this Smethport store, in partnership with Mr. Haskell, and continued two years, when he sold his interest and retired from the firm. He then formed a partnership with C. S. King, and until 1884 was engaged with him in mercantile business. In the latter year he became a partner with his brother Seth in the lumber business, continuing successfully until 1906. Since the latter date he has been engaged in the manufacture and sale of window glass. He is a director of the Tuna Glass Company, of Clarksburg, West Virginia, and of the Oswayo Chemical Company, having interests in other enterprises of a minor nature. He is a lifelong Democrat, and has given freely of his time and ability to the public service. He was commissioner of McKean county one year, by appointment of the government to fill a vacancy; chief burgess of Smethport one term, borough councilman two terms, and borough auditor several terms. His fraternal orders are: the Ancient Order of United Workmen, of Smethport; the Benevolent and Protective Order of Elks, of Morgantown, West Virginia; and his clubs: the Central, of Smethport, and the Merchants, of Bradford. In religious faith he is a member of St. Luke's Episcopal Church.

He married, June 6, 1876, Emma A. Gallup, born in Keating township, McKean county, January 24, 1852. She was educated in the public school, finishing in a private school at Cuba, New York. She then taught school for a few years, in the McKean county schools. She is a member of the patriotic order Daughters of the American Revolution; of the Travelers Club, of which she was president for two years; and of St. Luke's Episcopal Church. She is a daughter of Eben Gallup, born in Norwich township, McKean county, March 17, 1821, died in Smethport, August, 1896. He was a farmer of Keating township, a Democrat, and held many offices including county commissioner and school director. He married Phoebe King Windsor, born in Smethport, October 26, 1830, died in June, 1905, daughter of Eben Windsor. Children of Eben Gallup: 1. Emma A., of previous mention. 2. Carrie, born in Keating township March 16, 1857; married (first) Fred Smith, a farmer, killed by his own horses, no issue; married (second) U. D. Fisher, of Mount Vernon, Ohio, a publisher's agent, living in Smethport, no issue. Eben was a son of Nathaniel C. Gallup (see Gallup VII).

Children of Warley and Emma A. (Gallup) Gifford, both born in Smethport: 1. Roy, born September 24, 1878, now an electrical engineer, residing in Illinois; married Mary Ryan, of Kane, Pennsylvania. Children: Edmund Warland, born April 16, 1906; John McDonald, October 24, 1907; William Carleton, 1912. 2. Ethel, born February 22, 1880; married Louis H. Marks, born June 23, 1876, in Jackson, New Jersey, a glasscutter, now living in Smethport. Child: Emma Agnes, born June 16, 1910.

(The Cogswell Line).

(I) John Cogswell, born in England, married, September 16, 1615, Elizabeth Thompson. He emigrated to America, settling in Ipswich, Massachusetts, and is the founder of this branch of the Cogswell family.

(II) William, son of John Cogswell, was born in Melbury, Leigh, England, in 1619, and came to America where he married, in 1649, Susanne Hawks, born in Charlottetown, Massachusetts, in 1633. They resided in Ipswich,

PENNSYLVANIA

Massachusetts, where he died September 15, 1700.

(III) William (2), second son of William (1) Cogswell, was born in Ipswich, Massachusetts, December 4, 1659, died April 14, 1708. He married, October 9, 1685, Martha Emerson, born November 28, 1662, daughter of Rev. John and Ruth (Symonds) Emerson.

(IV) Edward, son of William (2) Cogswell, was born in Gloucester, August 13, 1686, died April 17, 1773. He married, in 1708, Harriet Brown, and lived in Chebacco parish, Ipswich. His wife died in June, 1771.

(V) Nathaniel, son of Edward Cogswell, was born in Ipswich, Massachusetts, February 13, 1714. He married (first) December 8, 1739, Huldah Kinney, or Kinne, born in Preston, Connecticut; (second) 1757, Mrs. Bridget Wedge Cleveland; (third) Mrs. Eunice Williams. Children by first marriage: 1. Eunice, born October 22, 1738. 2. Huldah, May 10, 1740. 3. Nathaniel, May 16, 1742. 4. Louis, April 17, 1744. 5. Judith, January 30, 1746. 6. John, December 28, 1747. 7. Martha, February 9, 1749. 8. Zerviah, July 14, 1752. 9. Nathan, October 11, 1754. 10. Elizabeth, twin of Nathan. By his other marriages he had nine more children. The history of Haverhill, Massachusetts, says eight of his sons served in the revolution.

(VI) Elizabeth, daughter of Nathaniel Cogswell, by his first wife, Huldah Kinney, was born October 11, 1754. She married, at Griswold, Connecticut, Rev. Levi Hart, officiating, May 2, 1782, Wheeler Gallup (see Gallup VI). The following act of the Connecticut assembly, May, 1763, is recorded: "This assembly do establish Mr. Nathan Cogswell to be lieutenant of the second company or train band of the town of Preston." Again, in 1778, as follows: "To be ensign of the 10th company or train band in the 21st regiment in this state." From records of the State of Connecticut, volume 2, page 31.

Children of Wheeler and Elizabeth (Cogswell) Gallup: 1. Dolly, born in Voluntown, Connecticut, April 1, 1783, married in 1801, John Cogswell. 2. Elizabeth, born March 6, 1785, married Jonathan Colegrove. 3. Nathaniel C., born March 15, 1787, married Dinah Edmunds. 4. Huldah, born at Voluntown, March 7, 1789, died at Plainfield, Connecticut, May 2, 1872. 5. Sallie, born in Voluntown, March 17, 1791; married, November 23, 1813, Gilbert Brown, and lived in Pennsylvania. 6. Wheeler (2), born in Voluntown, September 30, 1793; married (first) Mary Gallup, July 2, 1815; later moved to Pennsylvania, and married (second) Edith Arnold.

It is from Nathaniel Cogswell, the revolutionary soldier, through his daughter Elizabeth who married Wheeler Gallup, her great-grandfather, that Mrs. Emma A. (Gallup) Gifford gains one line of revolutionary descent.

KING This family came to McKean county, Pennsylvania, from Rhode Island in 1816. They spring from Clement (2) King, died 1694, who was of Marshfield, Massachusetts, prior to settling in Providence, Rhode Island, where he was made a freeman 1682. His wife, Elizabeth, died November 27, 1708, survived him and married (second) November 12, 1694, Thomas Barnes. Children: 1. John, of whom further. 2. James, died November 19, 1756, married (second) Persis Brooks and had issue. 3. Thomas, died October 10, 1723. 4. Ebenezer, married and had issue. 5. A daughter, married Richard Harris.

(III) John, son of Clement (2) King, died in Providence, Rhode Island, September 18, 1723. He was a landowner and is of record in several transactions. His first wife was Hannah; his second, Elizabeth, died November 27, 1754. Children: Sarah, born April 1, 1703; John, March 13, 1705; Hannah, February 28, 1706; Fearnot, 1708; Abadiah, 1712; Isaac, of whom further; Josiah, 1717; William, 1719; Jemima, 1721; Sarah, 1723.

(IV) Isaac, son of John King, was born in Providence, Rhode Island, in 1715. He was a farmer of Rhode Island, twice married, and had a large family including a son Isaac (2), who was the founder of the family in McKean county, Pennsylvania.

(V) Isaac (2), youngest son of Isaac (1) King and his second wife, was born June 23, 1776, died in Smethport, Pennsylvania, 1845. He grew to manhood in Rhode Island, where he was educated and did farming until his fortieth year. He settled in Pennsylvania on East Potato Creek, McKean county, in 1816, and there spent the remainder of his active life engaged in farming. He and his wife were members of the Methodist Episcopal church. He married Phœbe Love, who died in Smethport about 1859, having lived to be over eighty years of age. She died at the home of Judge

Sartwell. Children: 1. Sally, born October 16, 1802, in Rhode Island, died in Smethport; married Solomon Sartwell, a lumberman, who owned a large store and was judge of the court at Smethport. Children, all deceased: Rosell, Chester, George, Samuel, a daughter who married John Backus. 2. Huldah, born June 26, 1804, died in Chenango county, New York, married and left issue. 3. Harry, died young. 4. Horace Brown, of whom further. 5. Mary Ann, born October 3, 1812, died in Smethport, married a Mr. Windsor and left issue. 6. Joshua, born June 2, 1815, died at Smethport, a wagon-maker, married; children: Chester S.; Mary Ellen, deceased; Almira, who resides in Bradford, Pennsylvania. 7. Chester B., born October 2, 1819, died young. 8. Joel S., born at East Potato Creek, October 2, 1823, died in Wisconsin, a contractor, married a Miss Tubbs; children: Frederick, Luellen.

(VI) Horace Brown, son of Isaac (2) and Phœbe (Love) King, was born in Rhode Island, August 22, 1808, died in Smethport in 1880. He was eight years of age when his parents settled in McKean county, where he resided on the farm at East Potato Creek for over twenty-one years. He became a farmer and a lumberman, being successful as both. Later he was appointed crier of district court at Smethport, a position he held over thirty years. He was a Democrat originally, but voted for Abraham Lincoln and ever afterward acted with the Republican party. He was an active member of the Methodist Episcopal church of Smethport for over a half a century, his father having been a class leader, steward and trustee of the same church for many years. Horace B. King joined the church when very young and all his life bore a full share of church burdens.

He married Jerusha B. Rice, born in Eldred, Pennsylvania, July 4, 1812, died in Smethport, January 27, 1862, a daughter of Justus Rice, a farmer, born about 1780, died about 1860. He married and had children: 1. Almond, deceased, leaving children: Esther, Adalaide, Beverly, Hyde, Hendricks. 2. Richard, a lieutenant in the Pennsylvania Bucktail Regiment, serving three years in the civil war, commissioner of McKean county, and a man of prominence, owning a large farm opposite Eldred; his wife died in 1911; children: A son, Allen, William and Adalaide. 3. Justus, died in Eldred, leaving a large family. 4. Jerusha B., of previous mention, wife of Horace Brown King. 5. Mary, born and died in Eldred, married Rev. Thompson Carpenter, a Methodist preacher and a farmer; children: Florence, Bertha and Lillian. Children of Horace B. King: George W., of whom further, and several others who all died young.

(VII) George W., son of Horace and Jerusha B. (Rice) King, was born in Smethport, August 8, 1844. He was educated in the public schools and immediately after completing his studies became a farmer. In the fall of 1861 he enlisted in Company E, Captain John C. Backus, One Hundred and Fourteenth Regiment Pennsylvania Volunteers. He served four months and was honorably discharged on account of disability caused by severe illness. After recovering his health he resumed farming until 1880, when he removed to Mount Jewett, Pennsylvania, where he engaged as a merchant for two years. He then returned to his farm in Smethport, at Kings Corners, continuing there until 1897. In that year he purchased an established general store business at East Smethport, was appointed postmaster, a position he yet holds. He is a Republican in politics, has served as school director for three years, and was mercantile appraiser of McKean county for one year. He is a member of the church; Smethport Lodge, No. 39, Independent Order of Odd Fellows, and for many years was a member of the Encampment of the same order.

He married, December 19, 1881, Clara Elizabeth Hauer, born in Berks county, Pennsylvania, June 30, 1858, where she was educated in the public schools. She is a member of the Lutheran church, the Protected Home Circle and the Daughters of Rebekah. She is the daughter of John H. (1) Hauer, born in Lebanon county, Pennsylvania, January 28, 1830, died in Schuylkill county, Pennsylvania, January 7, 1898, a miller. He married Lavina Hollenback, born in Berks county, December 11, 1835, died in Schuylkill county, October 8, 1898. Children of John H. Hauer, first six born in Berks, others born in Schuylkill county: 1. John H. (2), born October 18, 1855, now an electrician in Lebanon, Pennsylvania; married Emma Bensing; children: Titus; Ida. married Professor White; Lillian; Harry; Sadie. 2. Clara Elizabeth, of previous mention, wife of George W. King. 3. Wallace C., born June 18, 1861, now a farmer of Lebanon county; married Louise Hummel; children: Vincent, Vertes and Roxana L. 4. Mary Ida, born February 19, 1863; married (first) Uriah Christ, (second) James Stemer, a brick contractor, and lives in Allentown, Pennsylvania; children, all by first marriage and all deceased: Louis, Florence and Augusta. 5. Grant K., born August 25, 1865, died 1872. 6. Irena, born May 2, 1867; married Louis Nye, a mine foreman, and resides in Pine Grove, Pennsylvania; no issue. 7. Kate L., born February 6, 1869; married Walter Hicks, a baker, and lives at Pine Grove; children: Roy, Mary, Pearl, Robert, Clara and Charles. 8. Emma L., born April 28, 1871; married Harrison Zimmerman, a farmer, and resides at North Pine Grove, Pennsylvania; children: James, Lewis, Ruth and Emma. 9. Frank K., born September 1, 1874, died December 21, 1876. 10. James N., born August 18, 1877, now a belt manufacturer of Lebanon, Pennsylvania; twice married, and has sons, Arthur and Walter. John H. (1) Hauer was a son of Henry Hauer, who died in Fredericksburg, Lebanon county, Pennsylvania, in 1864, very old, a cigar-maker. He married Kate Grumbine, who died in 1861, an old lady. In addition to the children of Henry Hauer, mentioned below, five died in infancy: 1. Jacob, died in Lebanon, a wholesale cigar dealer; married a Miss Lonser; children: Jacob, John, William, Harry, Susan, Eliza, and Anna, all living in Lebanon. 2. Samuel, died in Lebanon, a business partner of his brother Jacob, married and left issue. 3. George, a farmer, died in Brownsville, Pennsylvania; had three wives and left issue. 4. Isaac, died in East Hanover, Pennsylvania, a farmer, married and had issue. 5. Peter, now living in Lebanon, Pennsylvania, a lawyer, married and has issue. 6. Elizabeth, died in Lebanon in 1910; married Isaac Wagner, deceased, a cigarmaker; children: Harry, Milton and Belle. 7. Katherine, died in Fredericksburg, Pennsylvania; married a Mr. Klincfelter, a farmer, also deceased, leaving issue. 8. John H. (1), of previous mention. Children of George W. and Clara Elizabeth (Hauer) King, all born at Smethport, Pennsylvania: 1. Horace B., born May 26, 1883; graduate of Smethport high school, 1899; Bucknell University, 1908; Dickinson law school, 1911; was admitted to the bar in Harrisburg, Pennsylvania, July 7, 1911, now a practicing lawyer; he married, August 30, 1911, Rose McKeean, of Carlisle, Pennsylvania. 2. Roxy L., born April 14, 1885; graduate of Smethport high school; a graduate nurse of Allentown hospital, November, 1911; residing with her parents. 3. Lloyd L., born December 28, 1886, died September 20, 1900.

CAMP Nicholas Camp, American ancestor, was born in England, and came to this country in 1638 from Nasing, county Essex. He was at Watertown, Massachusetts, for a time, then at Wethersfield, Connecticut, and in 1639 appears at Guilford, Connecticut. As early as 1646 he had a house and lot of six hundred acres, one right and two parcels at Milford, Connecticut, although his name appears on the list of "free planters" of Milford dated November 20, 1639. In 1686 he was taxed on one hundred and ninety-nine pounds of property at Milford, and died there in 1706. He joined the Milford church, November 2, 1643. His first wife, Sarah (Beard) Camp, died September 6, 1645. He married (second) Mrs. Katherine Thompson, July 14, 1652. Issue by both.

(II) Samuel, son of Nicholas Camp and his second wife, was born in Milford, Connecticut, September 15, 1655, died at Durham, Connecticut. He married (first) November 13, 1672, Hannah Betts, (second) January 6, 1681, Mercy Scoville, and left issue.

(III) John, son of Samuel Camp and his second wife, was born at Milford, Connecticut, March 1, 1700, died at Durham, 1754. His wife was living in 1754. They had issue.

(IV) Israel, son of John Camp, was born in Durham, Connecticut, February 16, 1723, died January 6, 1778. His second wife was Mary (Guernsey) Camp, of Milford, Connecticut. One of the sons of Israel Camp settled in Camden county, New Jersey, and is the progenitor of the Camps of Smethport.

(V) ———, son of Israel Camp, was born in 1750, in Connecticut. He married and left sons: Daniel, of whom further; William, settled in New York City; Ephraim, in Cincinnati, Ohio; John, in New Jersey. These sons all married and left issue.

(VI) Daniel, grandson of Israel Camp, was born in Connecticut, 1778. He moved to New Jersey and settled in Gloucester township, Camden county. He married Ruth Pheffer, who bore him two sons: John, who left no descendants, and Ephraim, of whom further.

(VII) Ephraim, son of Daniel and Ruth (Pheffer) Camp, was born near Winslow, New Jersey, about 1806. He learned the trade of glassblower and spent his active years employed in the glass factories of Winslow. He was a Whig in politics, and a member of the Methodist Episcopal church. He married a widow, Mrs. Rebecca Wescott, whose first husband died shortly after the birth of their only child, David Wescott, who married and left two children: a son Harry, now a glassworker in West Virginia, and a daughter. Children of Ephraim and Rebecca (Wescott) Camp, all born near Winslow, New Jersey: 1. Benjamin Clark, born November 21, 1828, now living in Monongahela City, Pennsylvania, aged eighty-four years; he married Rachel Haines, of Millville, New Jersey, born December 23, 1828, also aged eighty-four years; children: i. Catherine Josephine, married R. E. Byers; ii. Rev. Henry W., deceased, a minister of the Methodist Episcopal church, married Sarah Power, living children; Gail Power Camp, now residing in Monongahela City, Pennsylvania, and Eugene W. Camp, a druggist of McKeesport, Pennsylvania, married and has Walter and Eleanor Camp; iii. Benjamin Edwin, now a druggist at Elizabeth, Pennsylvania, married Emma Wolf, children: Rachel and Josephine. 2. Thomas W., died in Iowa; married and left children: Henry and Frances. 3. John, died in West Virginia in 1910; married Isabella McGrath, who died in 1906; children: William, deceased; Joseph, deceased; Ann; Ida; Sadie. 4. Ephraim, died in Pittsburgh; married and left issue: John, Elizabeth, Rebecca. 5. William Davis, of whom further. 6. Daniel, died in Ottawa, Illinois; married and had two daughters. 7. George, for many years connected with the fire department of Pittsburgh; married and has a son Harry, also connected with that department. 8. A daughter, died in infancy. The seven sons of Ephraim Camp all learned their father's trade of glassworker and followed glassblowing or glass cutting as a business, except George.

(VIII) William Davis Camp, son of Ephraim and Rebecca (Wescott) Camp, was born at Winslow, New Jersey, July 2, 1841. When nine years of age his parents moved to Pittsburgh, Pennsylvania, where he attended the public schools. He early learned the glassblower's trade and in the pursuit of his calling traveled around among the glass manufacturing cities. He worked in Pittsburgh and New Castle, Pennsylvania, and Bellaire, Ohio, for several years, finally locating at Mount Vernon, Ohio, where he is now factory manager of the Camp Glass Company. He is a Republican in politics, and while resident of Bellaire served in the common council of that city. He is a member of the Baptist church which he serves as deacon.

He married Mary Ann Lloyd, born in New Castle-on-Tyne, England, October, 1840, died in Mount Vernon, Ohio, October, 1909, daughter of George Lloyd, born in New Castle-on-Tyne, an iron worker in his native land and in Pittsburgh, Pennsylvania, later a farmer in Lawrence county, Pennsylvania. He died in New Castle, Pennsylvania, 1898. His wife, Rebecca (Fellows) Lloyd, born in England in 1814, died in New Castle, Pennsylvania, 1873. Children of George Lloyd: 1. Edward, died in infancy. 2. Mary Ann, of previous mention, wife of William D. Camp. 3. George, born 1842, now living in Lawrence county, Pennsylvania, an iron worker, now a farmer; married Martha ———, and has issue: George, Rebecca, Mattie, Harry and others. 4. William, born 1844, died in New Castle, Pennsylvania; married Elizabeth Cecely, who survives him; children: Carrie, William, Samuel, George, Grace. 5. Samuel, born 1847, married and resides in the south, a fruit farmer of Louisiana; no living issue. 6. James, born 1854, now a cattle dealer; wife died leaving children: Benjamin and Rebecca. 7. Ellen, born 1856, married Calvin Irwin, a farmer near New Castle; children: Lottie and another. Children of William Davis Camp, first five born in Pittsburgh: 1. George, born January, 1859, died in Bradford, Pennsylvania, 1906; was a partner with his brother, Thomas Wescott Camp, in the glass business; he married in New Castle, Pennsylvania, Emily Barnett; children: i. Harry, born 1883; ii. Pearl, 1890; both living in New Castle. 2. Thomas Wescott, of whom further. 3. Daniel, born April 2, 1863, a glassblower and a stockholder of the Camp Glass Company, Mt. Vernon, Ohio; married Ella Scott, of Terre Haute, Indiana; child, Scott, born 1892. 4. Rebecca, born 1865; died March, 1892; married John Bowden, who died March, 1912; no living issue. 5. Elizabeth, born July, 1867, married (first) William Wilkinson, deceased, a farmer; children: Elsie, married a Mr. Cramer; Carrie, married a Mr. Stanley, both living at Shingle House, Pennsylvania; she married (second) Norman Kiefer, a lumberman, and resides at Smethport, Pennsylvania; no issue. 6. Carrie, born June 16, 1869, married Robert Colderwood, and resides in New Castle, where he is engaged in the tinning business; they have a large family. 7. Ruth, born in Bellaire, Ohio, 1871, married Frank Riggall, of Bolivar, New York, now secretary and bookkeeper with the Camp Glass Company, Mount Vernon, Ohio; children: Howard, born 1901; William, 1903; Archibald, 1905. 8. Nellie, born in Bellaire, Ohio, 1873, married (first) Archibald, Madison, of Bradford, Pennsylvania, a wool worker, now deceased; child, Ruth; she married (second) a Mr. Wescott, of Winslow, New Jersey, a glasscutter, now of Mount Vernon, Ohio. 9. Harry, born in New Castle, Pennsylvania, 1881, now a glasscutter of Mount Vernon, unmarried.

(IX) Thomas Wescott, son of William Davis and Mary Ann (Lloyd) Camp, was born in New Castle, Pennsylvania, June 8, 1861. He attended the public school of Pittsburgh until he was nine years of age, then began working in a bottle making plant, remaining one year. His parents then having moved to Bellaire, the lad followed and until 1881 was employed in a glass manufactory. In the latter year he continued in the same business in New Castle, Pennsylvania, where he remained until 1895, becoming thoroughly familiar with every detail of the glass trade. He spent the years of 1895 to 1898 in Bradford, Pennsylvania, thence going to Du Bois, Pennsylvania, where he engaged in glass manufacturing for himself in a small plant. In 1900 he moved to Smethport where he has engaged extensively in glass manufacture, now being president of the Smethport Glass Company; president of the Camp Glass Company of Mount Vernon, Ohio; president and general manager of the Empire Glass Company of Shingle House, Pennsylvania, also having business interests of lesser importance. He is a thoroughly capable man of affairs, energetic and straightforward in the conduct of his business, serving in the interests of the companies over which he presides with fidelity and zeal. He is a Free Mason of high degree, belonging to McKean Lodge, No. 388, Free and Accepted Masons, and Coudersport Consistory, Ancient Accepted Scottish Rite, in which he has attained the thirty-second degree. He is also an Odd Fellow, belonging to Chenango Lodge and Lawrence Encampment of New Castle, Pennsylvania. In politics he is a Democrat, and in religious belief a Methodist.

He married, November 7, 1882, Sarah Catherine Barber, born in New Castle, Pennsylvania, August 19, 1863. Child, Mabel Claire, born in New Castle, Pennsylvania, February 28, 1884; married, in Smethport, Mark Pomeroy, assistant cashier of the Port Allegany National Bank and resides at Port Allegany, Pennsylvania; child, Catherine, born July 24, 1908.

John Benjamin Barber, father of Mrs. Camp, was born July 6, 1835, at Hammersmith, London, England, died at Smethport, February, 1908. He was a nail manufacturer. He married Mary Ann Scott, born in Staffordshire, England, March 17, 1834, died in Smethport, May 27, 1906. John Benjamin Barber was a son of Charles Walker Barber, born in London, November 18, 1778, died in New Castle, Pennsylvania. He married, August 23, 1834 (being then fifty-six years of age), at St. Martin's Church, London, Sarah Catherine Cole, born June 30, 1818, died in New Castle. They emigrated in 1836, settling near Pittsburgh, Pennsylvania. Children of Charles Walker Barber: 1. John Benjamin, of previous mention. 2. George Stafford, born November 12, 1836, died in Monongahela, Pennsylvania, September 17, 1841. 3. Christopher William, born August 23, 1838, died in New Castle, 1911, a nail worker; married Elizabeth Scott, who survives him, a resident of New Castle; children: Harry, Kate, Mary, Clara, William, Lillian. 4. Catherine B., born December 28, 1840, deceased. 5. Johnson Smith, born January 11, 1844, now a steel worker in New Castle; married and has a family. 6. Ann Louisa, born July 25, 1846, died in New Castle, 1909; married Henry Emery, an iron worker, who survives her with issue. 7. Elizabeth McDonough, born October 10, 1848, married John Shealer, whom she survives, a resident of New Castle, with several children. 8. Charles Walker, born August 12, 1851, died in New Castle, 1894; married and left issue: Earl and Iva. Children of John B. and Mary Ann (Scott) Barber, all born in New Castle, Pennsylvania, except the first: 1. James, born in Niles, Ohio, 1856, now a restaurateur of Cleveland, Ohio; married (first) Grace McCrea, who left children: Nettie and Roy, the latter deceased; by second wife Catherine no issue. 2. Elizabeth, born 1858; married John Walker, now shipping clerk for the Smethport Glass Company; children: Scott, Edward, Gertrude, married Bernard Gurlock. 3. Benjamin, born December, 1860, now a groceryman of New Castle; married Emma Edwards; children: John, born 1878; Carrie, 1883, both living in Cleveland, Ohio. 4. Sarah Catherine, wife of Thomas Wescott Camp; she is a member of the Episcopal church of Smethport, and the Order of the Eastern Star. 5. Harry, born 1874, now a glass worker of Smethport; his wife died shortly after her marriage. 6. George, born 1873, now a baker of New Castle; married Lena Zimmerly; children: Adelaide, born 1899; Sadie, 1901; Melva, 1903, died 1906; daughter, born 1909.

Mary Ann (Scott) Barber, mother of the foregoing six children, was a daughter of Jonathan Scott, born in Staffordshire, England, September 25, 1809, died April, 1892. His wife, Mary (Jones) Scott, born November 8, 1808, in England, died November 4, 1888. Children: Salina; Emma; Mary Ann, of previous mention; James W., born June, 1836, died June, 1889; John Jones, born October 6, 1838; Elizabeth E., March 2, 1841; Henry John, October 16, 1843, died December 14, 1885; Hannah Lloyd, April 22, 1846; Emily Jane, October 14, 1848; Samuel Jones Tyler, June 6, 1850.

WEBSTER This is one of the most distinguished names in the annals of North America, having been especially honored by that famous statesman and patriot, Daniel Webster, Noah Webster, the Lexicographer, and a long list of others noted in all works of life. Daniel Webster was the son of Colonel Ebenezer Webster and half-brother of David Webster, sixth generation of this sketch.

(II) Thomas (2), son of Thomas (1) Webster, American ancestor of this branch of the family, was born in Ormsly, Norfolk county, England, November, 1631, died at Hampton, New Hampshire, January 5, 1715. He came to America in company with his mother Margaret, and her second husband, William Godfrey, settling at Watertown, Massachusetts. He settled in Hampton, New Hampton, with the pioneers of that town, which was thereafter his home. He married, November 2, 1663, Sarah, daughter of Thomas Brewer, of Roxbury, Massachusetts. Children: Mary, Sarah, Hannah, Thomas, Ebenezer, Isaac, John, Joshua, Abigail.

(III) Ebenezer, son of Thomas (2) Webster, of Hampton, was born August 1, 1667. He served in the Indian war and was pilot to Captain Gilman's company which went in pursuit of the Indians. He was one of the proprietors of Kingston, New York, and an early settler there. He married, July 25, 1709, Hannah Judkins, who died February 21, 1756. Children: Rachel, Susannah, Ebenezer, William, John, Hannah, Mary and Joseph, twins.

(IV) Ebenezer (2), son of Ebenezer (1) Webster, was born October 10, 1714. He lived in Kingston, New Hampshire, and was identified with the progress of that town all his life. He married, July 20, 1738, Susan Batchelder, born at Hampton, May 28, 1713, youngest child of Benjamin and Susanna (Page) Batchelder, of Hampton. She was a woman of marked ability and great strength of character, robust in form and black hair, dark complexion and piercing black eyes. Benjamin Batchelder served in many of the campaigns against the Indians, often as a soldier and at other times as a scout and messenger. He was a son of Nathaniel (2), son of Nathaniel (1), son of Rev. Stephen Batchelder, a leading "Nonconformist," born in England, 1561, came to America, 1632, preached in various churches in New England, returned to England about 1654, died there in 1660.

(V) Ebenezer (3), son of Ebenezer (2) Webster, was born in Kingston, April 22, 1739, died April 14, 1816. He grew up without a day's schooling knowing almost nothing of books, but fully equipped physically to fulfill the mission of life on the frontier where strong bodies, sound sense and courage were required to cope with the lurking foes of the forest. He came of age during the great French and Indian war, and about 1760 enlisted in the famous corps known as "Rogers Rangers." In the dangers and successes of desperate fighting the "Rangers" had no equals and in their hard perilous experiences Ebenezer Webster had his full share. He served under General Jeffrey Amherst and returned to his native town with the rank of captain. In 1763 he settled in Salisbury, New Hampshire, there then being no white man's abode between him and Montreal. He spent eleven years there. The revolution broke out and at once enlisted his active support. He raised a company of two hundred men and at their head marched to join the forces at Boston. He served at White Plains, and at Bennington was one of the first to scale the breastwork and came out of the battle with his swarthy skin so blackened with dust and gunpowder that he could scarcely be recognized. He was at West Point at the time of Arnold's treason and when on guard at the general's tent Washington said "Captain Webster I can trust you". He rose to the rank of colonel, and on his return home was elected to every office his neighbors could confer, including representative, state senator, judge of the court of common pleas and presidential elector.

He married (first) January 8, 1761, Mehitable Smith, born at Kingston, died March 28, 1772. Children: Olle, born January 28, 1762, died young; Ebenezer, born July 16, 1764, died young; Susanna, born October 25, 1766, married John Colby; David, of whom further; Joseph, born March 25, 1772, died 1810. He married (second) October 13, 1774, Abigail Eastman, born July 19, 1737, died April 14, 1816. Children: Mehitable, Abigail, Ezekiel, Daniel, "The Statesman" and Sarah.

(VI) David, son of Ebenezer (3) and Mehitable (Smith) Webster, was born May 1, 1769, died 1823. He was a farmer and large land owner at Stamstead, Canada, where he died. He was a merchant in New Hampshire and supplied the American army with provisions, etc., during the war of 1812. He married Rebecca Huntoon, born November 28, 1769. Children: Abigail, born September 5, 1790, married Moses Sargent; Hannah, born December 7, 1792, married Cyrus Bates; Ebenezer, born April 6, 1795, married Betsey Jewett; Philip Huntoon, of whom further; David, born March 25, 1799, married Betsey Blake; Rebecca, born August 15, 1801, married John Perkins; Ezekiel, born July 12, 1803, died July 14 or 18, 1816; Daniel, born September 17, 1805, married Mary Kilborn.

(VII) Philip Huntoon, son of David Webster, was born March 13, 1797, died December 7, 1830. He was a farmer, and a deacon of the Presbyterian church. He married Lucy Jane Dix, born April 8, 1804, died 1858, a sister of Governor and General John A. Dix, of New York state, whose famous utterance: "If any man attempts to tear down the American flag, shoot him on the spot" will long be remembered among the many patriotic expressions of the civil war period (see Dix VI). His wife survived him and married (second) Colonel L. C. Little. Children of Philip H. Webster: Charles Dix, of whom further; Philip Leavitt, of whom further.

(VIII) Charles Dix, eldest son of Philip Huntoon Webster, was born June 18, 1828, died March 3, 1907. He served in the civil war in the Fifty-eighth Regiment Pennsylvania Cavalry, was promoted second lieutenant, July 11, 1862, first lieutenant, 1863, and quartermaster with the rank of captain with headquarters at Fortress Monroe, Virginia. After the war closed he resumed his profession of civil engineer, continuing until 1883, when he located in Florida where after three years as a civil engineer he engaged in the drug business at Tarpon Springs. He continued there successfully until his death in 1907. He married, in 1855, Orpha Jane, daughter of Loren and Mary (Phetterplace) Gleason, who survives him, a resident of Tarpon Springs, Florida. Their only child died in 1871.

(VIII) Philip Leavitt, second son of Philip Huntoon Webster, was born August 6, 1830, in Danbury, New Hampshire. He was taken to Lebanon when two and one-half years old. He was but an infant when his father died and in 1837 his mother married Colonel L. C. Little, agent for the Boston United States Land Company, the owners of one hundred and sixty-five thousand acres of land in Jefferson, Clearfield and McKean counties, considerable of it being in McKean county, Pennsylvania. Soon after his marriage Colonel Little came to Pennsylvania with his wife and two stepsons, settling at Bradford, then called Littleton, making the trip westward through the forest by team. The boys were given the best of treatment by their stepfather, who gave them all the advantages of the early school and an academic course at Springville, Erie county, New York. He died in 1854, his wife in 1858. After the death of his stepfather Philip L. was employed by the Land Company in settling up their business in McKean county. He also worked for a time at the carpenter's trade, and later became an undertaker and for more than a quarter of a century was the leading undertaker and funeral director of Bradford. He withdrew from that business and for more than twenty-five years has been engaged in the real estate business. He was at Fortress Monroe during the war serving as military storekeeper, and after the war was sent to Concord to close up the military post there. He owned orange groves in Florida and for many years passed his winters there. He laid out and placed upon the market Oak Hill cemetery, of which he had charge for many years. Later he formed and incorporated the "Oak Hill Cemetery Association," of which he is president. He is a member of the Independent Order of Odd Fellows and of the Order of Ben Hur. He is a strong Republican. Now eighty years of age Mr. Webster is active, alert and attends daily to his business affairs. He is a man of strong character and highly regarded in his town.

He married, December 17, 1874, Ellen (Johnson) Morrison, born at Fredonia, New York, died April 18, 1898, daughter of Rufus Johnson, a farmer of Forestville, New York, who married Dorcas Keach. Ellen Johnson at the time of her marriage was the widow of Archie Morrison. By her first marriage she was the mother of Frank Morrison, born May 15, 1866; Mr. Webster adopted him legally and changed his name to Webster; he married, 1888, Jennie Nichols and has: Philip Leavitt, born September 25, 1891; Frank Meredith, October 22, 1895; Donald James, May 18, 1900. The home of Mr. Webster is one of the very few structures that were erected in Bradford between 1850 and 1860, at which time the city was but a backwoods town.

(The Dix Line).

Lucy Jane (Dix) Webster was the sister of Governor John Adams Dix, of New York, and aunt of Rev. Morgan Dix. The Dix family came from Holland originally, the name being probably derived from the Dutch word "Dyck" or "Dijck," a bank or dyke. Four branches of the family were founded in America at an early day by Leonard Dix, of Wethersfield, Connecticut, Anthony Dix, of Plymouth, Massachusetts, Edward Dix, of Watertown, Massachusetts, and Ralph Dix, of Ipswich; no relationship is proved but they were undoubtedly from the same English stock. Edward Dix was the ancestor of the present governor of New York, John Alden Dix (1912), while a former governor of the same state, General John Adams Dix, descended from Ralph Dix, of Ipswich, Massachusetts, also the ancestor of Rev. Morgan Dix, rector of Trinity Church, New York City. This branch of the family settled in New Hampshire where they were influential and prominent. Two of this family, Colonel Timothy and John A., are famous in military history, the first in the war of 1812, the latter in both the war of 1812 and the civil. While treasurer of the United States in 1861, he issued the famous order, previously mentioned, "If any man attempts to tear down the American Flag, shoot him on the spot."

(I) Ralph Dix, one of the early settlers of Ipswich, a fisherman, moved to Reading in 1662 and was made a freeman of Malden, 1685, but died at Reading, Massachusetts, in 1686. He married Esther ———. Children: John, of whom further; Samuel, born 1661; Stephen, 1664, died young; Stephen, 1672; Sarah.

(II) John, son of Ralph Dix, was born 1659, died March, 1745. He lived on the old Dix homestead in Reading, Massachusetts. He married (first) Lydia ———, (second) in 1700, Anna, widow of Joseph Fitch. Children of first wife: John and Lydia, twins, born and died 1693; Lydia, born 1695, died 1709; Sarah, 1697; Elizabeth, 1699. Children of second wife: Anna, born 1702; Samuel, 1706; Mary, 1708, Jonathan, of whom further; James, born 1712; Edson, 1714.

(III) Jonathan, son of John Dix by his second wife, was born at Reading, Massachusetts, April 11, 1710. He was a tanner of Littleton, Massachusetts, moved to Boscawen, New Hampshire, where he died at the residence of his son Timothy, December 24, 1804, at the great age of ninety-four years, eight months and thirteen days. He was a member of the church more than seventy-five years. He married (first) June 28, 1739, Sarah, who died at Littleton, Massachusetts, September 30, 1775, in her fifty-sixth year, daughter of Rev. Benjamin Shattuck, of Littleton. He married (second) Miriam Leland, of Hollis, New Hampshire, who died there about 1833 aged nearly ninety years. Among the children by first wife was Timothy, of whom further.

(IV) Timothy, son of Jonathan Dix and his first wife, was born December 7, 1743, died 1824 at Pembroke, New Hampshire. He settled in Boscawen, New Hampshire, where he was postmaster for many years. He later moved to Pembroke where he died. He raised a company of soldiers during the revolution and was familiarly known as Lieutenant Dix. He was noted for integrity, faithfulness, firmness, decision and strong attachment to the cause of his country. He married (first) August 13, 1769, Rachel Burbank, of Bow, New Hampshire, (second) Mrs. ——— Brown, (third) Mrs. Eliza Cunningham, of Pembroke. Children of first wife, Rachel

Burbank; Timothy, of whom further; Josiah Brown, died in childhood.

(V) Colonel Timothy (2) Dix, son of Timothy (1) Dix, died at French Mills, Canada, November 14, 1813. He passed several years in a mercantile house at Amherst, New Hampshire, and with his father and grandfather settled in Boscawen about 1790. He purchased a township in the northern part of the state which bears his name. At the commencement of the war of 1812 he was appointed major of a New Hampshire regiment which was afterwards transferred to the Fourteenth Regiment United States Infantry, a regiment that was recruited under his supervision in Maryland. Early in the spring of 1813 he marched from Baltimore to Sackett's Harbor, but during the summer was prostrated by fever. He accompanied the expedition down the St. Lawrence in the fall against the advice of his physician, but having been promoted lieutenant-colonel and placed in command of the regiment, he would not remain behind. On the 10th of October he was seized with a violent attack of pneumonia and borne from the camp at Chrystters Fields, Canada, by his son, John A. Dix, and two officers of his regiment, placed on his boat and died two days afterward. He was a man of strong character, of fine presence and courteous manner, greatly beloved by all.

He married (first) Abigail Wilkins, of Amherst, March 20, 1791, who died December 3, 1808; married (second) Lucy Hartwell, of Littleton, Massachusetts, July 3, 1809; she died December 30, 1863. Children of first wife: 1. Wilkins, born November 19, 1792, died May 9, 1852; married General Moody A. Pillsbury. 2. Rachel Burbank, born April 18, 1794, died January 15, 1827; married Rev. Daniel Temple and with him sailed as missionaries to Malta, January 2, 1822. 3. Timothy Fuller Shattuck, died young. 4. John Adams, born July 24, 1798, served in the war of 1812 under his father, Colonel Dix; was lieutenant and acting adjutant; studied law and admitted to practice; appointed adjutant-general of New York, 1831; in 1845 elected United States senator from New York; in 1853 assistant treasurer of the United States at New York City, appointed by President Pierce; postmaster of New York City, 1860, appointed by President Buchanan; resigned 1861 to become treasurer of the United States in place of the absconding Treasurer Cobb; it was while in that position that he gave his famous order previously quoted; May 16, 1861, he was appointed major-general of United States Volunteers and after superintending the raising of eleven regiments in New York was assigned to the command of the department embracing the states of Pennsylvania, Maryland and Delaware; he was in command at Baltimore and was instrumental in holding that state in the Union; he served with distinction until the close of the war, then resigned and returned to private life; he was later minister to France and governor of New York; he was a deep scholar and an accomplished linguist, few men being so conversant with the Latin authors in the study of whose works he took the greatest delight; he married, May 29, 1826, Catharine Morgan; children: Morgan, born November 1, 1827, rector of Trinity Episcopal Church, New York, married Emily Woosley Souther; Baldwin, John Wilkins, Elizabeth Morgan, Charles Temple, Catharine Morgan, Anna Morgan. 5. Sophia Wilkins, born May 1, 1800, died January, 1865, at Portland, Maine; married, December 25, 1828, Joshua C. Plummer, of Boscawen, New Hampshire. 6. Marion Means, born April 17, 1802, died July, 1860; married, December 15, 1825, John W. Sullivan. 7. Lucy Jane, of further mention. 8. Frances Louisa, born July 22, 1806; married (first) November 25, 1852, General Moody A. Pillsbury, (second) December 29, 1871, Rev. Buxton. 9. Martha Sherman, died in infancy.

(VI) Lucy Jane, daughter of Colonel Timothy (2) Dix, was born April 8, 1804, died February 9, 1858, in Bradford, Pennsylvania. Married (first) May 31, 1826, Philip H. Webster (see Webster VII); married (second) June 30, 1837, Colonel L. C. Little. Children by second husband: 1. Ellen, born May 4, 1838 (was the first white child born in Bradford, Pennsylvania), died 1911; married Emmett Mix. 2. John Sullivan, born December, 1839. 3. Susan, died aged ten years. 4. Sarah, married Robert Davis, moved to Urbana, Illinois, where she yet resides.

RAYMER Schuylkill county, Pennsylvania, has been the seat of a German population, probably from the early years of the eighteenth century, although the early history of white settlement in this region is obscure. The names

Raymer and Ramer are found in several instances in the Pennsylvania archives, yet it may be doubted whether these references are to members of the present family. The probability favors such a connection, but it is not clear.

(I) Nicholas Raymer, the first member of this family about whom we have definite information, was born, probably on the Mahantongo road, which is in Schuylkill county, Pennsylvania, and the adjacent parts of the state, about 1770, died on the Mahantongo road, about 1854. His life was spent near the place of his birth, and his occupation was farming. He was a Whig. In the work of the Methodist church he took an active interest, and his wife also was a member of that church. The name of his wife is not known; she died on the Mahantongo road, before her husband's death. Children: 1, George, died on Mahantongo road; farmer; married Sarah ———; children: George and others. 2. Joshua, died at Pine Grove, Pennsylvania; wheelwright; married Harriet Sibert, deceased; children: William, deceased; Charles, residing in Virginia; John, deceased. 3. Joseph, lived at McVeytown, Pennsylvania; married, had large family. 4. William, of whom further. 5. Isaac, died at Mifflin, Pennsylvania; farmer; married Mary ———; had a family. 6. Caroline, died on Mahantongo road; married Joseph Wolfgang; he was a farmer; children: Catharine, Mary, Salome, others. 7. Salome, died on Mahantongo road, unmarried. 8. Magdalene, died on Mahantongo road; married George Bensinger, deceased; he was a farmer; children: George, policeman in Buffalo; at least one other. 9. Catharine, died on Mahantongo road; married George Bensinger, deceased; had children.

(II) William, son of Nicholas Raymer, was born in Schuylkill county, Pennsylvania, April 20, 1825, died at Smethport, about 1899. In his native place he received a district school education. He was a wheelwright and wagonmaker at Pine Grove, Schuylkill county, about twenty-two miles from the place of his birth, until 1856, when he removed to Smethport. In 1858 he purchased a farm in Keating township, McKean county, where he carried on farming, raising of stock and dairying. He was a Republican. He was a member of the Methodist church; his wife attended this church also, though she was a Lutheran. He married, at Pine Grove, Matilda, daughter of Jacob and Elizabeth (Ludwig) Fry, who was born in Berks county, Pennsylvania, March 6, 1829, died at Smethport, July 10, 1904. Children of William and Matilda (Fry) Raymer: 1. Lewis, born at Pine Grove, January 4, 1848; he received a public school education at Smethport, then worked on his father's farm at that place until March, 1883; removing to Port Allegany he took a farm on shares for Fitz-Henry Arnold; in 1887 he went into the butcher business, in which he continued for twelve years, but sickness prevented his active work for the next two years; in 1901 he took a position as foreman in the sawmill of S. J. Gifford, at Smethport; after three years he re-entered the butcher business, and he continued until June, 1909, then opened pool and billiard parlors opposite the Smethport postoffice, where he is doing a flourishing business, and has an excellent class of trade; he is a member of the Maccabees, Tent No. 9, Smethport; he is a Republican; for two years he was street commissioner and for two years councilman, and in 1911 was elected again to the latter office for a term of four years from January 1, 1912; he married Florence, born in Norwich township, Pennsylvania, May 31, 1851, daughter of Orrin Wilson and Nancy (Corwin) Gallup; for her ancestry see sketch of Warley Gifford in this work; children: Octavia, born June 4, 1873; Ward W., born April 29, 1883, married Ethel Lund, has two children, Lewis Lund, born October 16, 1907, and Florence, born June 29, 1910. 2. Alice, of whom further. 3. Henry, born at Pine Grove, March 5, 1852, died at the age of eight months. 4. Nathaniel, born at Smethport, September 8, 1858; farmer and general workman, residing at Smethport; married Jane Lambert; child, Elmer, born May 5, 1884, married Sadie Hall. 5. John, twin of Nathaniel, born September 8, 1858, died under one year old. 6. Samuel, born at Smethport, November 14, 1860; farmer and carpenter, residing at Smethport; unmarried.

Jacob Fry was a native of Berks county, born about 1788, was a farmer near Pine Grove and there he died in 1872. His wife was of German extraction, born in 1793, died at Pine Grove in 1865. Children of Jacob and Elizabeth (Ludwig) Fry, all born in Berks county, order uncertain: 1. Samuel, died at Pine Grove; farmer; married Susan Snyder, deceased; children: Malinda, deceased; Maria.

residing at Pine Grove; Rose, residing at Pine Grove. 2. Jacob, died at McVeytown; married Mary Kymes, deceased; children, perhaps not all: Clara, Ella, Charles, Harry. 3. George, died at Pine Grove, unmarried. 4. William, died at Pine Grove; married Rachel Swartz, deceased; he was a paperhanger; children: James, deceased; William, Samuel. 5. John, died at Pine Grove. 6. Isaac, died at South Bend, Indiana; a contractor; married Anna Keefer, who resides at Pine Grove; child, Vitalis, resides at South Bend. 7. Matilda, married William Raymer. 8. Elizabeth, born in 1833, died at Pine Grove, July 7, 1888; married Philip Landenberger, deceased; children: Sarah, born January 20, 1856, deceased, married Frank Vickery; Louis, born May 1, 1858, resides in Reading, married Kate Hane; Catharine, born February 3, 1860, married John Bender; William, born May 12, 1862, resides at Perkasie, married Sarah Sattigan; Anna, born October 31, 1864, married Washington Starks, deceased; George, born August 27, 1866, resides at Fremont, married Emma Kopp; Clara, born June 27, 1868, married Clifford Burlingame; Mary, born July 10, 1871, married C. M. Colegrove.

(III) Alice, daughter of William and Matilda (Fry) Raymer, was born at Pine Grove, May 17, 1850. At an early age she was sent to a select school at Pine Grove; she was only eight when her parents settled at Smethport, and her education was there continued in the public school. At Smethport she has continued to reside to the present. She is a member of the Protected Home Circle, and attends the Methodist Episcopal church. She married (first) November 1, 1867, Robert, born near Smethport, February 26, 1846, died at Kane, Pennsylvania, October 14, 1879, son of Augustus and Minetta (Weber) Walters. His father was an immigrant from Germany, who settled in Philadelphia, but removed to Sergeant township, McKean county; he was a cabinetmaker. She married (second) at Smethport, November 13, 1883, Samuel, born at Franklinville, Pennsylvania, May 3, 1835, died at Smethport, December 31, 1903, son of Joseph and Patty (Long) McClure. He was a carpenter and tool dresser. He was the third of eight children, as follows: Charles, resides at Delevan, New York; Pauline, died in Washington, married Samuel Bly; Samuel, married Alice (Raymer) Walters; William, deceased; Seymour, died in Canada, a machinist; Francinia, died at Sardinia, New York, married Delos Rice, deceased; Edwin, died at Wellsville, New York, unmarried; ———, died in young manhood. Children of Alice (Raymer-Walters) McClure, four by first, three by second husband: 1. Frederick, born at Smethport, June 5, 1868, died at Smethport, August 25, 1879. 2. Leon A., born at Smethport, December 9, 1871; resides in Chicago; married Harriet Canfield, of Manistee, Michigan; children: Elizabeth, born March 6, 1906; Augustine, born December 5, 1907. 3. Addie, born at Smethport, January 9, 1875; married F. E. Baldwin, of Duke Center, Pennsylvania; he was very seriously affected by the Austin flood; at this time (1912) he is state senator, and has been renominated by a handsome majority. 4. Robert Raymer, born at Smethport, September 17, 1879; hardware dealer at Manistee, Michigan; married Margaret Vincent, of Manistee; children: Mary, born January 28, 1910; Alice, born October 23, 1911. 5. Edwin, born at Smethport, July 22, 1884; works on the state highway; unmarried. 6. Frances, born at Smethport, April 25, 1886; married Louis A. Kenyon, from Canastota, New York; he is now a machinist in Buffalo, New York; children: Alice, born March 3, 1907; Louise, born July 9, 1911. 7. Scott A., born at Smethport, March 21, 1890; works on the state highway; unmarried.

GARLICK A Connecticut family of this name was apparently settled at Milford in the early years of the eighteenth century. Yet the family is to the present day small and scattered. Henry Garlick, who came from England was in Milford in 1718, and in New Milford, Connecticut, in March, 1721. He had a large family, including seven sons. In England also the name seems to be rare and to belong especially, if not exclusively, to Lancashire. In the revolution Captain Samuel Garlick, a native of Huntington, Connecticut, was a soldier; he afterward lived at Rose, Wayne county, New York. It remains to say that despite the great similarity of name there is a quite distinct family, Garlock, of Palatine descent, their founder having been one of the leading spirits among those early German immigrants to New York state. Usually variations in surname, of so slight character, indicate nothing else than divergence in spelling; in this case, if the two spellings have been preserved unconfused, there is a wide racial distinction, and it is natural to suppose that any one of the name Garlick is descended from Henry Garlick, of Milford and New Milford.

(I) Truman Garlick, the first member of this family about whom we have definite information, was born in Otsego county, New York, died at Kasson, McKean county, Pennsylvania, in December, 1878. Beside having a farm and residing at Wilcox, Pennsylvania, he was a teamster, going between Smethport and Buffalo and between Smethport and Pittsburgh. He was a Republican. He married Katharine Rifle, born in Tioga county, Pennsylvania, died at Wilcox. Children: 1. Charles, died young, unmarried. 2. Henry, died young, unmarried. 3. George Orson, of whom further. 4. Elizabeth, died at Hazelhurst, Pennsylvania; married Horace Stark, of McKean county, a farmer; children: Dora, deceased; Lucy, resides in Buffalo. 5. Phoebe, died at Stillwater, Minnesota; married Truman McFall, deceased; large family. 6. Lucy, died at Kasson; married Joseph Barnes, of McKean county, deceased; he was a carpenter and a Union veteran, having served throughout the war in the "Bucktail" Regiment; children: Myra, deceased; Katharine, married Thomas Reed, resides in Buffalo; Elizabeth, died young.

(II) George Orson, son of Truman and Katharine (Rifle) Garlick, was born in Hamlin township, McKean county, Pennsylvania, June 8, 1839. His boyhood days were spent on the farm with his father, and his schooling was received in his native township at the public school. After his marriage he went to Minnesota, but he remained there only one year. Although he had never learned the trade of shoemaker, he then went to Wilcox and engaged in that work. This he continued at that place for ten years, when he settled on a farm in Hamlin township, where the greater part of his adult life has been passed. He still resides at Kasson, of which he was postmaster for twenty-six years. He is a Republican. Beside the postmastership he held for six years the office of school director, and for an extended period that of poor master of Elk county. He attends the Methodist church. He married Phoebe, born on Long Island, New York, March 24, 1843, daughter of Bernard and Bridget (Graham) McKean. She is a communicant of the Catholic church. Her father was born in Ireland, 1810, died at Smethport, December 8, 1890. His home was near Smethport, and he was a farmer. His wife was born in the North of Ireland, 1819, died at Smethport, July 13, 1888. Children of Bernard and Bridget (Graham) McKean: 1. Phoebe, married George Orson Garlick. 2. Thomas L., twin of Phoebe, born March 24, 1843; a traveling salesman, residing at Wilcox; married Lena Weidert, of Wilcox; children: Mamie, a nurse in Philadelphia, unmarried; Katharine, residing at Wilcox, unmarried. 3. James A., born August 11, 1845, at Glen Cove, Long Island; farmer and lumberman; he was three years old when his father removed to McKean county; having received only a common school education, he has improved every opportunity to acquire a knowledge of the higher English branches; at the age of eighteen he entered the employment of James E. Butts, at Buttsville, and during the two years spent in his service had charge of the building of the high dam across Three-Mile Run; afterward he worked at the carpenter's trade, and was later employed at Kane in the car shops of the Pennsylvania & Erie Railroad Company; in 1874 he bought the farm adjoining his father's to the southward, and he has since that time been extensively engaged in the lumber and bark business, often in the season employing one hundred men; having built one of the most imposing residences in Smethport, he now lives there; his first presidential vote was cost for Grant in 1868, and he is a staunch Republican; for two terms he has been supervisor of his township, and in 1887 was elected a member of the county board of supervisors; among his business interests are the Hamlin Bank and Trust Company and the Smethport Water and Gas Company; he married, in January, 1869, Julia (Fox) Hubbard; her first husband, Simon Hubbard, died February 2, 1866, at Johnsonburg, and by him she has one son, Simon William, born March 6, 1865, employed by the Smethport Water and Gas Company; he married Nettie Parsons, from LaPere, New York, born there March 26, 1865, died at Smethport, February 17, 1901, and has children, Margaret C., born at Newton, Pennsylvania, January 26, 1896, and James W., born at Smethport, February 23, 1898; Mrs. McKean was born at Windsor, Ontario, in 1837; child of James A. and Julia (Fox-Hubbard) McKean: Margaret Mary, born January 8, 1873, married, September 22, 1896, Frederick

D. Gallup. 4. Mary, born at Smethport, March 28, 1850; married Henry Gallup; they reside at Smethport, and he has a dry goods store; child, William Henry, born at Smethport, April 1, 1880, married Teresa Heinemann, of Colegrove, Pennsylvania; they have a daughter, Julia Belle, born June 3, 1911. 5. William, twin of Mary, born at Smethport, March 28, 1850, died at Smethport, April 16, 1864. 6. Charles, born October 22, 1854; oil producer; lives at Smethport; married Catharine Daly; no children. 7. Edward, born at Smethport, April 20, 1858; married Elizabeth Haffner, of Clermont, Pennsylvania; children: Carlton, born in October, 1889; Charles, born in October, 1890; Helen, born December 25, 1892; Katharine, born July 15, 1894; Lena, born April 1, 1898; Robert, born February 3, 1901. Children of George Orson and Phœbe (McKean) Garlick: 1. Alberta, born at Wilcox, in 1866, unmarried, residing with her parents. 2. Eva, born at Wilcox, in 1868, unmarried, residing with her parents. 3. Bernard Truman, of whom further.

(III) Bernard Truman, son of George Orson and Phœbe (McKean) Garlick, was born at Kasson, Pennsylvania, September 20, 1878. There he was sent to the district school, and he also attended the Smethport high school. In 1900 he took a course at the Westbrook Commercial College, at Olean, New York. He then took a position in the lumber offices of McKean Brothers, at Smethport, in which he remained until 1905. In that year he was appointed to the responsible position of manager of the Smethport Water and Gas Company, which he has acceptably filled from that time. He is also a partner in the hardware firm of Daly & Garlick with an extensive business through this section of the county, and a director of the Taintor Chemical Company at Taintor, Pennsylvania. His political party is the Republican, and his church the Protestant Episcopal, he being a member of St. Luke's, of Smethport. He married, September 25, 1907, Gertrude, born at New Castle, Pennsylvania, January 30, 1883, daughter of John E. and Elizabeth (Barber) Walker. She attended public school at New Castle, and the high school at Smethport. Children of Bernard Truman and Gertrude (Walker) Garlick: 1. Bernard, born at Smethport, December 14, 1908. 2. George Edward, born at Smethport, January 13, 1911. John E. Walker, a nail manufacturer at Smethport, was born at New Castle, March 10, 1853. His wife was born at New Castle, April 18, 1858. Children of John E. and Elizabeth (Barber) Walker: 1. Jonathan Scott, born at New Castle, October 28, 1877; secretary and treasurer of the Smethport Glass Company; married Rena Gallup, of Smethport; no children. 2. Charles Edward, born at New Castle, November 17, 1879; a bottle blower at Smethport; unmarried. 3. Gertrude, married Bernard Truman Garlick.

COLEGROVE The Colegrove family of Pennsylvania descends from the old Welsh family of that name. The emigrant ancestor, Francis Colegrove, was born near Swansea, Wales, and came from London, England, to Warwick, Rhode Island, as early as 1680. The descendants in this country are through his five sons: Eli, Stephen, Francis (2), John and William. It is from the second named son that the family of Smethport has descent.

(II) Stephen, son of Francis Colegrove, was born in 1695 in Foster, Rhode Island, died in 1787. In 1737 he was made "a freeman of the colony" of Providence, Rhode Island, according to the town records. He was chosen town councilman at the first town meeting, which formed the town of Foster in 1781. In 1754 he purchased some land in the town of Scituate where his later years were passed. He married (first) —— Taylor; (second) Phœbe Millard, born 1707, died December 29, 1775. Children of first marriage: 1. Stephen, a farmer of Foster, Rhode Island, born 1722, died 1811; married 1748, Judith Aylesworth. 2. Thomas, of Brattleboro, Vermont, born April 23, 1724; married December 2, 1753, Rachel Aylesworth; he was admitted a freeman of Warwick, Rhode Island, in 1746. 3. William, a farmer of Scituate, Rhode Island, born 1726; married Anna ——. 4. Benjamin, of Windham county, Connecticut, born 1729, died 1820; married October 21, 1759, Sarah, daughter of Eleazer Colegrove. He served in King George's war, and in the Revolution, entering Captain Branch's company of Col. Johnson's regiment of Connecticut militia. He was present at the capture of Louisburg on Cape Breton Island. 5. Mary, born 1731; married (first) in 1750, Samuel Colegrove; (second) in 1773, Richard Nichols. Children of second marriage: 6. Nathan, one of the first settlers of Middletown, Rutland county, Vermont, born 1741; married Miriam Fillmore. 7. John, a farmer of Coventry, Rhode Island, born 1744, died 1817; married (first) Martha ——, who died in 1793; (second) Nancy Corwin, born 1758, and died 1820. 8. Jonathan, of whom further. 9. Isaac, a farmer of Northwest, Connecticut. 10. Phoebe, born 1749, died 1839; married 1779, Phineas Bridgewater, of Bridgewater, New York. 11. Lotta, born in 1751; married —— Shepardson, of Fairfax, Vermont.

(III) Jonathan, third child and son of Stephen and Phoebe (Millard) Colegrove, a farmer of Plainfield, Connecticut, and Norwich, New York, was born in 1745, died in 1812; married Jemima Park, born in 1745, died in 1800. Children: 1. Olive, born May 1, 1774, died 1859; married Edward Corwin. 2. Phoebe, born November 6, 1776; married John Monroe of Norwich, Chenango county, New York. 3. Esther, born January 10, 1778; married Elijah Gibbs of Norwich, Connecticut. 4. Park, a blacksmith, born December 27, 1779, died February 5, 1846; married Margaret M. Lindsey, born November 9, 1790. 5. Jonathan (2), of whom further. 6. Jemima, born December 12, 1783; married Luther Havens. 7. Benjamin, born June 16, 1787, died April 4, 1875, moved to Morenci, Lenawee county, Michigan; married in 1815, Lucy Garlick, who died in 1847. 8. Mary, born May 5, 1790; married (first) Israel Green; (second) Daniel Burbank.

(IV) Jonathan (2), son of Jonathan (1) and Jemima (Park) Colegrove, was born in Norwich, Connecticut, July 25, 1782, died in Pennsylvania April 11, 1872. He was a farmer and surveyor all his life, spending the greater portion of his years in Norwich, Pennsylvania, although for a time he lived in Norwich, New York. Being one of the first settlers of these towns he used his influence in having them named for the town in Connecticut in which he was born. He experienced a short military career during the war of 1812-1814, when he held the rank of lieutenant at Sacketts Harbor a position he was obliged to resign because of ill health. A Whig in politics, he was one of the first county commissioners in McKean county after its organization, and served as treasurer and state representative for one term each. The postoffice and village of Colegrove were named in his honor.

He married in Griswold, Connecticut, Elizabeth Gallup, born in Norwich, Connecticut, March 6, 1785, died in Norwich, Pennsylvania, February 27, 1859. Children, all born in Norwich, Pennsylvania: 1. Eliza Florilla, born June 18, 1809; married Daniel Rifle, a farmer; children: Andrew S.; William Henry Harrison: Samuel and Olive; all are deceased with the exception of William H. Harrison, who lives in Kane, Pennsylvania. 2. William W., born 1810, died 1817. 3. Horace, a farmer in Colegrove, Pennsylvania, born June 30, 1818, died January 16, 1888; married in Norwich, Pennsylvania, Emily Burlingame, died November 14, 1892. Children: i. Jonathan, a merchant of Smethport, Pennsylvania, born November 16, 1843; married Hattie M. Purple, of Troy, Pennsylvania and had two children: Samuel P., and Albert L. ii. Mary E., married Jonathan Greely, of Newerf, McKean county, Pennsylvania, and lives at Colegrove, Pennsylvania. iii. Theron, deceased. iv. Bella D., lives in Smethport, Pennsylvania. 4. William Jonathan, of whom further. 5. Laura Ann, born June 28, 1823, died in Smethport, Pennsylvania, 1896; married Philetus Gallup, a native of Connecticut. Children: Eliza, deceased; J. C., postmaster of Smethport, Pennsylvania; Dorothy, deceased; a daughter, deceased; Albert, deceased; Abraham Lincoln, lives in Los Angeles, California. 6. Laurette, born June 28, 1823, died in Smethport, Pennsylvania, March 23, 1850; married William Burlingame, a lumberman, died in Smethport, Pennsylvania. Children: Amelia, born 1842, lives in Wisconsin; Cornelia, born 1844, deceased; a daughter, died young.

(V) William Jonathan, son of Jorathan (2) and Elizabeth (Gallup) Colegrove, was born in Colegrove, Pennsylvania, March 17, 1821, died in Smethport, Pennsylvania, May 26, 1893. He obtained his education in the public schools of his native town, and became a school teacher, later following the farmer's occupation. In 1852 he succeeded his father in a land business which the latter had built up, and from that time had the exclusive management of the forty thousand acres of land embraced in the Ridgeway estate, being authorized to sell, collect and make titles. He built up and added to the business, and at his death left property amounting to one hundred thousand dollars. One of his outside business interests was as stockholder in the Smethport Water Company. In politics he was a Republican, and he'd numerous offices. He was elected justice of the peace in 1842, was commissioner of McKean county for two years, and a member of the board during the erection of the present court-house which was erected during his term, extending from 1879 to 1881. He was instrumental in obtaining a new postoffice at Colegrove and was postmaster until 1880. He also served part of a term as sheriff of McKean county. He had a wonderful record as a member of the Methodist church which he joined in 1836, holding every possible relation, exclusive of that of minister. For fifty-one years he was steward, for fifty-five years a class leader, for twenty-five years Sunday school superintendent, and was president of the board of trustees for nearly twelve years. His life was exemplary in all respects, and contact with him in all departments of his busy life was free from any ordinary or sordid relation.

He married, January 20, 1841, Eunice Hayford Wright, born in Kanona, Steuben county, New York, November 1, 1821, died in Smethport, Pennsylvania, March 11, 1907, daughter of Erastus Wright, a farmer, born in New York State, January 17, 1787, died in Kanona, New York, January 9, 1858, and Lydia (Wheeler) Wright, born in Steuben county, New York, September 2, 1789, died there in 1860. Children of Erastus and Lydia (Wheeler) Wright, all born in Kanona, New York: 1. Alpha, born April 16, 1813; a Methodist minister, died in Missouri; married Charlotte Holman and had a daughter, Lottie, living in Rochester, New York. 2. Freeman, born August 1, 1815, died young. 3. Hezekiah W., a farmer, born September 21, 1816, died in Missouri; married Miss Holman, sister of Charlotte, who married his brother, Alpha; children: Charles, born 1842, lives in Missouri; Alpha H., born 1844, lives in Dakota; Ettie, born 1846, deceased; George, born 1848. 4. Mary J., born July 31, 1818, died in Steuben county, New York; married Mr. Case, a farmer of Steuben county; children: George, born 1842, deceased; Ellen, born 1844, living in Canister, New York; Lydia S., born 1850, deceased. 5. Eunice Hayford, of previous mention; married William Jonathan Colegrove. 6. George W. E., born October 29, 1824, a medical student in Buffalo, accidently drowned in Buffalo Creek. 7. Lydia J., born August 31, 1828, deceased; married Leroy A. Anderson, from Allegany county, New York, a hardware merchant, oil operator and lumberman. 8. Catherine S., born September 19, 1831, died in Steuben county, New York, a school teacher.

Children of William Jonathan and Eunice Hayford (Wright) Colegrove, all born in Colegrove, Pennsylvania: 1. Harriet Amelia, born February 28, 1842; married Thomas C. Saunders, deceased, a lawyer, from Connecticut; and lives in Boston, Massachusetts; children: Marian, born 1867, married Ralph E. Howard, from Massachusetts, a buyer for a silk and lace firm, and lives in Boston, Massachusetts; William J., born 1876, a real estate agent of Portland, Oregon. 2. Alpha William, of whom further. 3. Lydia Sophia, born January 19, 1849; married (first) John S. Ross, deceased, a real estate merchant, from Coudersport, Pennsylvania; (second) Willis J. Lewis, from Coudersport, Pennsylvania, attorney for the Tide Water Pile Company, and lives in New York City. 4. Clarence Melville, born July 9, 1852, county surveyor; married (first) Lydia S. Case, deceased, from Steuben county, New York; (second) Mary Landenberger, from near Wilkes-Barre, Pennsylvania; children, both of second marriage: William Howard, born November 9, 1893; and Martha Eunice, born August, 1900. 5. Wilmot, born August 14, 1858, died September 28, 1862.

(VI) Alpha William, second child and eldest son of William Jonathan and Eunice Hayford (Wright) Colegrove, was born in Colegrove (formerly Norwich), McKean county, Pennsylvania, June 5, 1844. He attended the public schools of his native town, and although but seventeen years of age at the outbreak of the civil war, enlisted in the Forty-second Regiment, Thirteenth Pennsylvania Reserves, nicknamed the "Bucktail Regiment." On December 17, 1861, he took part in the battle of Gainesville, the first victory gained by the Army of the Potomac. The rigors of strenuous campaigns, however, was too much for his youthful strength, and in December, 1862, he was discharged for physical disability, and for two years was in ill health. He then returned to school, graduating from the Smethport academy, later attending Lima College at Lima, New York. His education was completed by a business course in Eastman's College, Poughkeepsie, New York. During the year, 1866, he worked on his father's farm and the following year was employed as a mercantile clerk in Westfield, Pennsylvania. In 1868 he engaged in the hardware business in Port Allegany, Pennsylvania, and until 1873 was a surveyor on an engineer corps in the West, again establishing in the hardware business in the latter year, this time at Sardinia, Erie county, New York, where he continued until 1880. For the fifteen following years he was employed by the Standard Oil Company, for five years acting as foreman, with headquarters at Colegrove; and in 1895 he opened a drug store in Smethport, selling out two years later. Since then he has been actively interested in politics as a Republican, has been justice of the peace, court crier and road supervisor in Norwich township. He holds the thirty-second degree in the Masonic order, belonging to McKean Lodge, No. 388, Free and Accepted Masons, of Smethport; Arnold Chapter, Royal Arch Masons, and Coudersport Consistory. He is also a member of the Central Club of Smethport.

Mr. Colegrove married (first), December 24, 1868, Ellen L. Burdick, born in Norwich, Pennsylvania, November 19, 1846, died in Port Allegany, Pennsylvania, October 6, 1869; (second) Anna E. Pevey, born in Erie county, New York, died in 1888, daughter of James Pevey, born in Portland, Maine, died in Sardinia, New York, and Laura (Steele) Pevey, born in New York State, now living in Aurora, New York; (third) Hannorah G. Higgins, born May 1, 1871, in Corry, Pennsylvania, daughter of Michael Higgins, born in Ireland, 1844, died in Corry, Pennsylvania, January, 1908, and Bridget (Richards) Higgins, born in County Mayo, Ireland, 1845, died in Corry, Pennsylvania, January, 1908, four days separating her death from that of her husband. Children of Michael and Bridget (Richards) Higgins: 1. Bridget, born in Corry, Pennsylvania, 1867; married James O'Connor, a liveryman of Corry, Pennsylvania, where they reside; children: James, deceased; Edward, lives in Corry, Pennsylvania; and three others. 2. Margaret, born in Corry, Pennsylvania, 1869; married William B. Joiner, a pumper employed by the Standard Oil Company in Chipmunk, Cattaraugus county, New York; children: Melvin, born 1890; Harry, born 1893; Lillian, born 1899; Marguerite, born 1905; all live in Chipmunk, New York, with the exception of Harry, who is a resident of Bakersville, California. 3. Hannorah G., of previous mention; married Alpha William Colegrove. Children of second marriage of Alpha William Colegrove: 1. William Ross, a glass blower, born in Colegrove, Pennsylvania, September 27, 1878; married Lelia Palmeteer, from Potter county, Pennsylvania, and lives in Canandaigua, New York; daughter, Harriet Lydia, born May 9, 1910. 2. Roy Clare, born in Colegrove, Pennsylvania, April 19, 1881, a glass worker in Smethport. Children of third marriage of Alpha William Colgrove: 3. Ellanorah Eunice, born in Colegrove, Pennsylvania, January 20, 1893. 4. Alpha Willis, born in Smethport, Pennsylvania, March 27, 1907.

ADAMS The first record of this branch of the family is of Great-grandfather Adams, who served in the revolutionary war, probably enlisting from New York state. He married and had issue, see below.

(II) Grandfather Adams was a farmer in Ossian, Livingston county, New York, where he spent most of his life and where he died about 1845. He married and had four children: 1. Calvin, a millwright, born 1821, died in Russell, Warren county, Pennsylvania; married Marilda Crocker, of Ossian, died in Russell, Pennsylvania. Children: Lydia, lives near Boston, Massachusetts; Amy, lives in Warren, Pennsylvania; Milo, deceased; Eugene, lives in Russell, Pennsylvania; Roy, lives in Russell, Pennsylvania. 2. Leonard, of whom further. 3. Nelson, died when young at Ossian, Livingston county, New York. 4. James, married and lives in Wisconsin.

(III) Leonard Adams was born near Syracuse, New York, died in Rushford, New York, September 2, 1908. He was educated in the public schools of his native town and when he became of age settled on a farm in Rushford, Allegany county, New York. At the outbreak of the civil war he enlisted in the Fifth Regiment New York Cavalry and served for two years, when because of ill-health he was compelled to retire from the service. In politics he was always a Republican, and with his wife a member of the Methodist Episcopal church. He married Amy Crocker (sister of Marilda Crocker of previous mention), born in Ossian, Livingston county, New York, daughter of Samuel Crocker, a minister of the Methodist faith at Ossian, where he died. Children: 1. James L., of whom further. 2. Edwin L., born in Ossian, Livingston county, New York, in September, 1849, died in New Orleans 1900;

PENNSYLVANIA

served during the civil war in the One Hundred and Fourth Regiment New York Infantry Volunteers. 3. Humphrey, born at New Hudson, Allegany county, New York, in 1851, where he died in 1859. 4. Alice N., born in New Hudson, Allegany county, New York; married —— Bumpus, a rural free delivery postman of Warren, Pennsylvania. Children: Glen, and a daughter. 5. Frank, born in Rushford, New York, in 1871; married and he and family live in the west.

(IV) James L., son of Leonard and Amy (Crocker) Adams, was born at Ossian, Livingston county, New York, October 31, 1847. As a youth he was educated in the public schools at Rushford and completed his education at the academy in the same town. At the outbreak of the civil war he was not old enough to enlist, but waited in feverish impatience for the long years to roll by until he should attain the required age. On September 2, 1864, nearly two months before he was seventeen, he enlisted as a private in Company I, One Hundred and Twentieth New York Infantry Volunteers, serving through the arduous campaign terminating in the battles around Petersburg, and being with General Grant at Lee's final surrender at Appomattox. He received honorable discharge June 21, 1865, and immediately entered Eastman's Business College to prepare himself for the business career in which he has been so justly successful. He was graduated in March, 1866, returning to Rushford where he occupied a position as school teacher for a short time. In 1872 he moved to Bradford where for two years he was manager of a cheese factory, then a bookkeeper, and until 1892 was manager of Swift & Company's beef house. In that year he became a member of the Rock Glycerine Company, dealers in high explosives, who furnished most of the well drillers of that section with the torpedoes used in opening the wells, later entering the firm of the Bradford Torpedo Company. In 1899 he established as an oil producer and has met with unusual, although certainly well deserved, success. He is high in control of several of Bradford's most vigorous and prosperous industries. Although past the prime of life Mr. Adams still retains his personal interest in all his business affairs and each day finds him at his desk. He is one of Bradford's most progressive and esteemed citizens and is always on the alert to take advantage of any plan which will result in the benefit of the town. He is a director and second vice-president of the Keystone United Oil & Gas Company, with offices at Kane, Pennsylvania; vice-president of the Kinzua Petroleum Company, whose offices are at Mount Jewett, Pennsylvania, and president of the Tuna Oil & Gas Company. He holds the office of past commander of Bradford Post No. 141, Department of Pennsylvania, Grand Army of the Republic, and for many years has been a delegate to the department encampments. For the past twelve years he has been a delegate from Pennsylvania to the national encampments. His fraternal order is the Knights of Pythias, and his club the Merchants of Bradford.

He married, July 4, 1871, Emma M. Tyler, born in Farmersville, Cattaraugus county, New York, January 17, 1851, where she was educated. After her marriage she became a member of the following Bradford societies: Women's Relief Corps; Women's Christian Temperance Union; Political Equality Club, and Protected Home Circle. She was also an energetic and devoted member of the Presbyterian church. She died January 23, 1911, at Bradford, Pennsylvania. She was the daughter of Jamin, a farmer of Farmersville, New York, and Melona (Taylor) Tyler, who had the following children: 1. Frank, deceased; married and had a family in Wisconsin. 2. Albert, deceased, was an oil worker at Knapps Creek, New York; married and had one child. 3. Emma M., of previous mention. 4. Truman, deceased, a furniture dealer in Kansas; married. 5. Clayton, deceased, a hotelkeeper of Silver Lake, New York; married but had no children. 6. Verna, died in Buffalo, New York; married David Thomas, an employe of the Pullman Car Company; they had three children. 7. Carrie, died in Sandusky, New York; married Fred. Blackman, of Sandusky.

Children of James L. and Emma M. (Tyler) Adams: 1. Myrtie M., born in Rushford, New York, April 9, 1872; married Clarence B. Van Schoick, a glassblower at Bradford, Pennsylvania. 2. Carrie L., born in Bradford, Pennsylvania, February 7, 1875; married William T. Lane, a jeweler of Bradford, Pennsylvania, born in Friendship, New York, April 7, 1867.

WRIGHT This name, which is probably a name of occupation, is common in various parts of the United States.

(I) Andrew Hamilton Wright, the first member of this family about whom we have definite information, was born in New York state, about 1803, died in Peoria, Illinois, about 1868. As his parents were buried at Groveland, Livingston county, New York, that was probably the place of his birth. He was a farmer at Lima, Livingston county, New York. He married Louisa Ogden, born probably in New York state (the family was a New York state family), in 1809, died at Lima, in 1861. Children, all born near Madison, Madison county, New York: 1. Joseph, died at Lexington, Kentucky; married and had a family. 2. Harriet, died in Illinois; married Jacob Deitz, deceased. 3. Amelia, died at Lima; married, at Madison, William Excell; he was a farmer; only one child reached adult years, Millie, died in the Klondike. 4. Benjamin Franklin, of whom further. 5. Lavinia, died at Smethport; married, in Colorado, —— Schultz, deceased; no children. 6. George, died in Peoria, unmarried. 7. Frederick, enlisted from New York state in the civil war, died in camp near Washington, in 1861. 8. William, resides at Renovo, Pennsylvania; engineer on the Pennsylvania railroad; married Belle Hyde, of Emporium; children: Alice, married —— McCloskey, resides in Pittsburgh; Lina, married John Robbins, resides in Renovo; Louise, married a Mr. Wright, resides in Washington, D. C.; William, an insurance agent in Pittsburgh; Donald, resides at Renovo.

(II) Benjamin Franklin, son of Andrew Hamilton and Louisa (Ogden) Wright, was born at Madison, November 2, 1835, died at Smethport, December 18, 1909. His education was completed in the seminary at Lima. After finishing his schooling, he worked on his father's farm until marriage, and after his marriage he opened a grocery store at Smethport, but he returned to his father's farm before the civil war. In September, 1861, he enlisted in the Forty-Second Pennsylvania Infantry, or First Pennsylvania Reserve Volunteer Corps, the famous "Bucktail" Regiment, and he served in this until the end of the war, thus having part in several important engagements. From private he was promoted to the rank of lieutenant. A wound received at South Mountain incapacitated him for several months. He was also a prisoner, being confined in Libby, afterward in Salisbury, exchanged after about six months' confinement. At Spottsylvania Court House, in 1864, he was wounded a second time. He was mustered out July 3, 1865, and returned to Smethport. Shortly after this he removed to Lafayette, having accepted a position with the Lafayette Coal Company. In the fall of 1866 he was elected sheriff of McKean county, in which office he served one term of three years. In 1875 he built the Wright Hotel at Smethport, and while he conducted it it was the best known hotel at this place, and it enjoys to the present day an excellent reputation. After thirty years he retired from this business. He was a member of McKean Lodge, No. 388, Free and Accepted Masons, Smethport; the commandery at Bradford; and Ismailia Shrine, in Buffalo, New York; also of the Ancient Order of United Workmen, Lodge No. 183, and of the Grand Army of the Republic. He was also a member of the Central Club, Smethport.

He married, in 1859, Catharine L., born at Smethport, March 15, 1838, daughter of Oshea R. and Lucy Green (Warner) Bennett (see Bennett III). Children: 1. Franklin O., born at Smethport, October 20, 1858; a veterinary surgeon, residing at White Plains, Westchester county, New York; married May Parker, of New York City; no children. 2. Allan L., born at Smethport, October 21, 1860, died in Rochester, New York, July 17, 1880. 3. Hamilton, born at Lafayette, September 13, 1866, died at Smethport, February 12, 1867. 4. Ella, born at Smethport, April 28, 1868; married Clinton Foster, of Bradford, Pennsylvania; they reside at Independence, Kansas, where he is a mill worker; no children. 5. Lena H., born at Smethport, November 2, 1870; unmarried; she has a variety store in Erie, Pennsylvania. 6. Lucy B., born at Smethport, September 22, 1877; married F. M. D. Watkins, of Wellsburg, New York; their home is in Binghamton, and he travels for the Shawmut Coal Company; children: Francis, born at St. Mary's, Pennsylvania, March 6, 1906; Hamilton W., born at St. Mary's, August 5, 1908; Catharine, born in Binghamton, March 12, 1911. 7. Elida Taylor, twin of Lucy B., born at Smethport, September 22, 1877; married Samuel Powell, of Bradford; he has a moving picture show in Seattle, Washington; children: John F., born at Smethport, August 20, 1900; Frank Wright, born March 22, 1907, at Ridgeway, Pennsylvania.

(The Bennett Family).

There is a family of this name, long established in Columbia county, New York, which is said to be of Scotch ancestry, but its genealogical history is not clearly known. From this family the present family is probably derived.

(I) Elijah Bennett, the first member of this family about whom we have definite information, was born in March, 1776, died at Smethport, January 2, 1850. The place of his birth is supposed to have been Canaan, Columbia county, New York. His life was passed at Canaan and at Lima, Livingston county, and he was a farmer. He was a Whig. He married Persis ———. Children: William, Phœbe, Electra, Anna, Salva, Oshea R., David R.

(II) Oshea R., son of Elijah Bennett, was born in New York state, probably at Canaan, April 29, 1806, died at Smethport, April 19, 1858. He was educated in the public school at Canaan, but continued his studies by his own efforts after leaving school, and became a well educated man, cultured beyond most of his time and place. He was a lumberman and hotel keeper, and also owned several farms in the vicinity of Smethport, and a sawmill. In politics he was actively interested and was a Republican. He attended the Baptist church, and his wife was a member. He married Lucy Green, born at Lima, July 5, 1808, died at Smethport, daughter of Daniel and Sarah (Green) Warner. Her father was probably a native of Canaan and born about 1783; he died at Lima, about 1858. His wife also died at Lima, about five years later, and her age was then about seventy-five. Children of Daniel and Sarah (Green) Warner, all born at Lima: 1. Edwin, was a farmer, died at Lima; married Helen Dennison; children: Arthur, deceased; a daughter, deceased. 2. Hiram, lived and died in the west, a farmer; married and had a family. 3. Lucy Green, married Oshea R. Bennett. 4. Harriet, died in Wisconsin; married, at Lima, Ezra Richmond; he was a farmer; children: Caroline, deceased; Edwin, deceased; Ezra. 5. Burchard, died in Dakota; farmer; married and had one son. There were perhaps other children of Daniel and Sarah (Green) Warner, beside these five. Children of Oshea R. and Lucy Green (Warner) Bennett, all born at Smethport: 1. Darius, died at Smethport, aged three. 2. Sarah, born October 26, 1834; resides at Smethport; married Judson Eaton, who was born at Springville, Erie county, New York, August 19, 1823, died at Smethport, May 11, 1888; he was a hardware merchant; children: i. Nina L., born November 7, 1857, married Frank Rumsey, deceased; she resides at Smethport. ii. Lucy, married Sheridan Gorton; iii. Guinevere, born January 21, 1869, married Daniel Brasted, a merchant at Smethport. 3. William Henry Harrison, died young. 4. Catharine L., of whom further. 5. Julia, born April 18, 1839; resides at Smethport; married Edwin Richmond, who died at Smethport, in October, 1911; he was a farmer; children: Harry, resides at Colorado Springs, Colorado; Rena, married Charles Balsley, lives in New York City. 6. Edwin, died at Smethport, in infancy. 7. Oshea, died at Smethport, in infancy. 8. Eveline, died at Smethport, in infancy. 9. Charles, died in Dakota, unmarried. 10. Rosina, died in Wisconsin; married Manford Comes, of Smethport; he now resides in Minneapolis, Minnesota; children: Nettie, resides in Minneapolis; Ethel, resides in Minneapolis; Oshea, deceased. Two other children died in infancy, both sons.

(III) Catharine L., daughter of Oshea R. and Lucy Green (Warner) Bennett, was born at Smethport, March 15, 1838. There she attended public school, and this schooling was supplemented at Lima Institute, Lima. For two terms she taught school in McKean county, Pennsylvania. She married, in 1859, Benjamin Franklin Wright (see Wright II). Mrs. Wright now makes her home at Smethport, and is a member of the Travelers' Club.

STEWART-RICHMOND These families are of Scotch and French origin, the Stewarts of this branch coming from Yorkshire, England, the Richmonds also coming from England, but originally from France. The English ancestor, Roaldus Musard De Richmond, coming over with William the Conqueror, is said to have ridden and fought by his side during the battle of Hastings. In England the family early settled in Yorkshire. The Stewarts were also a family renowned in English and Scotch history.

(I) John Stewart, of Yorkshire, was the first to come to America. He settled near St. Thomas, Canada, about 1834, on a farm where his after life was spent, and he died in middle age. He married Ann Moss, born in England 1780, one of the heirs to a large eslate that was settled in the English court of chancery; she died in St. Thomas in 1866. Both were members of the Church of England. She was an only daughter, but had a brother who remained in England. Children of John and Ann Stewart, all born in Yorkshire, England: 1. John, died in Ontario, Canada, a farmer; his wife Mary also died there. Children: Alexander and James, living in Canada. 2. Ann, married James Bell, a farmer, both died in Ontario. Children: John, deceased; James, residing in Finegal, province of Ontario, Canada; Sarah; Jane; Betsey; William, deceased; Joseph; Maria, deceased; Eliza; Frederick, now living in Golden, British Columbia. The other children live in Seattle, Washington. 3. George, came to the United States; no further record. 4. Elizabeth, died near London, Canada; married John Cavanagh. Children: Maria and Esther. 5. William, of whom further. 6. Mary, died in Ontario, unmarried. 7. A daughter, who did not emigrate.

(II) William, youngest son of John and Ann (Moss) Stewart, was born in Yorkshire, England, September 6, 1820, died at Frome, near St. Thomas, Canada, June 15, 1897. He was fourteen years of age when brought by his parents to Canada. He attended the public schools in England, and finished his education in Quebec, Canada. He became a farmer, owning his own farm near St. Thomas. He was a Conservative in politics, and a member of the Episcopal church. His wife was a Presbyterian, later a member of the Methodist Episcopal church. He married, December 14, 1850, Rebecca Jaggers, born at Port Stanley, Canada, March 1, 1833, died on the farm at Frome, May 22, 1895. She was the daughter of Daniel Jaggers, born in Philadelphia, Pennsylvania, a cooper of Port Stanley. He married Mary Fisher, born in Edinburg, Scotland, in 1798, died in Port Stanley, Ontario, Canada, 1882. He had a brother, John Jaggers, who also died in Port Stanley, unmarried. Children of Daniel Jaggers: 1. Rebecca, of previous mention. 2. John, died in London, Canada, a farmer and owner of considerable property in British Columbia. His wife died in 1865 leaving issue: Lola, deceased; Munson, deceased; Margaret, living in London; William, deceased. 3. Mary, married Frederic Bartlett, a carpenter; both died in Port Stanley, leaving a son Charles, now deceased, and a daughter. 4. Eliza, died in Port Stanley;

married John McIntyre, a sailor, born in Scotland, now living in Port Stanley. Children: Mary Jane, Charles, Emma and several others. Children of William and Rebecca Stewart, all born near St. Thomas, Ontario, Canada: 1. Mary Jane, born July 3, 1851, died March 11, 1854. 2. John William, born January 16, 1853; married Lucy Tully, of Kansas City, Missouri, whom he survives, a rancher of New Mexico. Children: Maud, living in El Paso, Texas; Walter and Charles, both living with their father. 3. Martha Ann, born August 9, 1854; married William Moore, a farmer, and resides on their farm in Ontario, Canada. Children: Edgar Charles and Frederick William. 4. Rebecca Jane, born November 3, 1855; married Henry Down, and lives in London, Canada. Children: Ida May, Susanna, Edith and Herbert. 5, David Edwin, born November 1, 1857, died at place of birth May 31, 1879, unmarried. 6, Mary Sarah, of whom further. 7. Frederick Charles, born June 24, 1861, now a brass finisher; married (first) Nellie Silcox, child: Mortimer; (second) Martha Scott; child: Charles Edward, born 1910. 8. Louisa Maria, born May 25, 1863, died June 13, 1893; married Oscar Glendenning, an architect, and settled in Winnipeg, Canada, where she died, without issue. 9. Lydia Emmeline, born August 18, 1865; married (first) Charles Horton, no issue; (second) John Welch, a bookkeeper of Denver, Colorado, their home, no issue.

(III) Mary Sarah, sixth child of William and Rebecca (Jaggers) Stewart, was born at the home farm near St. Thomas, province of Ontario, Canada, July 21, 1859. She was educated in the public schools of Paynes Mills and Frome, Canada. She then lived for four years at Las Cruces, New Mexico, and three years at El Paso, Texas, going thence to San Francisco, California where she was married. She is a member of St. Luke's Episcopal Church and the Order of the Eastern Star.

She married, November 14, 1889, Thomas Franklin Richmond, born in Smethport, Pennsylvania, May 17, 1860, died there January 14, 1908, only child of William Richard Richmond, born in McKean county, Pennsylvania, died in Minneapolis, Minnesota, November, 1894. He served four years in the civil war, enlisting in a Pennsylvania regiment. He married Helen Rebecca Milliken, born July 8, 1834, died September 19, 1864, daughter of John Milliken, born June 19, 1807, died November

4, 1849, and his wife, Mary Elizabeth Backus. William Richard was the son of Nelson Richmond, who died at the age of thirty-two years. He was judge of the court at Smethport, and married Melvina Chapin. Children, all born in McKean county, Pennsylvania: 1. William Richard, of previous mention. 2. Edwin, died September, 1911, a farmer and landowner; married Julia Bennett. Children: Harrie, of Colorado Springs, Colorado; Rena, of Brooklyn, New York. 3. Franklin, died August 31, 1907, a railroad conductor; married Mary Emorette Curtis, of New York, no issue. 4. Emma Jeannette, married Myron Sprague, whom she survives, a resident of Buffalo, New York; he was a dentist, later a hardware merchant. Children: Carlton, of Galveston, Texas; Rose Amanda, of Collingswood, Ohio.

Judge Nelson Richmond was the son of Thomas Richmond, who died in Fredonia, New York, a descendant of the early Richmond family of New England.

Thomas Franklin Richmond spent his boyhood days and obtained his public school education in Smethport, Pennsylvania. When seventeen years of age he entered the college at Lawrence, Kansas, whence he was graduated in 1884. He studied law both before and after his college course, was admitted to the McKean county bar, and began the practice of law in Smethport. About 1886 he went West, located in Lincoln, but unfortunate investments caused him to seek another location. He traveled over a large portion of the western states and territories, stopping in many places and locating for short periods in El Paso, Texas; Tacoma, Washington; Billings, Montana, and San Francisco, California. From the latter city he returned to Smethport and resumed the practice of law. He rose to prominence in his profession and in public life, continuing most successful until his death. His practice was large and was conducted in partnership with Sheridan Gorton (see Gorton sketch). In November, 1898, Mr. Richmond was elected to the Pennsylvania house of assembly, and the same month his partnership with Mr. Gorton began. This was a most effective combination and, as a law firm, compared favorably in ability and success with any legal firm at the McKean county bar. Mr. Richmond served very efficiently in the legislature, and later he received the endorsement of McKean county for state senator, but a candidate was chosen by the convention from another county in the senatorial district. For twelve years prior to his death he was attorney for the McKean county board of commissioners. He was an enthusiastic volunteer fireman, a member for several years of Smethport hose company and president of that organization. When the Northwestern Pennsylvania Volunteer Fireman's Association was formed he was one of the hardest workers for its success, serving as secretary and later as president. He was prominent in the Masonic order, holding the thirty-second degree in the Scottish Rite, and was a noble of Zem Zem Temple, of Erie, Pennsylvania, Nobles of the Mystic Shrine. He also belonged to McKean Lodge, No. 388, Free and Accepted Masons; Bradford Lodge, Benevolent and Protective Order of Elks; the Protected Home Circle, and the Order of the Eastern Star. He was also a member of the Central Club, a Republican in politics, and a communicant of St. Luke's Episcopal Church. He was held in high esteem and in every walk of life was always the true friend, good citizen and christian gentleman. Adopted child of Thomas F. and M. Sarah (Stewart) Richmond: William, born December 10, 1895. Mrs. M. Sarah (Stewart) Richmond continues her residence in Smethport, where she is highly esteemed by a wide circle of friends.

WAITE Waite is an English name, found in Boston before 1640, and from New England it has spread to other parts of the United States. It has been made illustrious by a chief justice of the supreme court of the United States. The name was found in Pennsylvania by 1734.

(I) Franklin Waite, the first member of this family about whom we have definite information, was born in Huntingdon county, Pennsylvania, died at Salona, Clinton county, Pennsylvania. Most of his life was passed at Lamar, Clinton county, and he was a teamster for iron furnaces. In the affairs of the Evangelical church, of which his wife also was a member, he took an active interest, and he held at one time or another most of the church offices. The name of his wife is not known; she died at Milesburg, Pennsylvania, in 1875, at the age of about eighty. Children, probably all born in Huntingdon county: 1. Bartlett, died at Danville, Pennsylvania; contractor; married and had children. 2. Alexander, died in Danville; served throughout the civil war;

was a recruiting officer; married and had children. 3. William, died at Beech Creek, Pennsylvania, dealer in produce; veteran of the civil war; married and had children. 4. John Franklin, of whom further. 5. Sarah, resides at Salona; married Jacob Miller, of Salona; he is a carpenter; children: Mary, Alfred, deceased; William, two others.

(II) John Franklin, son of Franklin Waite, was born in Huntingdon county, Pennsylvania, January 18, 1825, died at Rebersburg, Center county, Pennsylvania, in October, 1904. He received a common school education in Huntingdon county, and became a carpet weaver at Rebersburg. He was a Democrat. For many years he served as school director, and he was constable for about ten years. In the Evangelical church he was for many years a deacon, and his wife was a member. He married Mary Magdalena, born at Rebersburg, August 6, 1825, died at Rebersburg, in August, 1902, daughter of Jacob Gramley. Children: 1. Sarah Elizabeth, born at Salona, December 16, 1846, died at Rebersburg, in 1865; unmarried. 2. Elmedia Frances, born at Rebersburg, June 15, 1849, died young. 3. Samuel Washington, born at Rebersburg, July 4, 1851; resides at Pleasant Gap, Pennsylvania; retired farmer; married Alice Loneburger, of Center Hall, Pennsylvania, deceased; children: Amy, deceased; Pearl, Paul. 4. Harvey Elray, born at Rebersburg, December 30, 1853, died at Rebersburg, in 1874. 5. Mary Catharine, born at Rebersburg, September 24, 1856; married C. L. Beck, of Rebersburg; he is a carpenter, and they reside at Smullton, Pennsylvania; children: Maud, Carrie, John. 6. Franklin Hilbish, born at Rebersburg, January 4, 1858; carpenter, residing at Rebersburg; married Clara Sholl, of Rebersburg; children: Mamie and Charles. 7. Emma Theresa, born at Rebersburg, August 1, 1861; married William Breon, of Mill Hall, deceased; he was an ax-grinder; she resides at Mill Hall; children: John, deceased; Roy, Hayes, Carl, Lois. 8. Lester Ann, born at Rebersburg, November 24, 1863, died in infancy. 9. George Benjamin McClellan, born at Rebersburg, December 17, 1866; farmer, resides at Rebersburg; married Adda Neese, of Rebersburg; child, Jessie. 10. John Wesley, of whom further.

Jacob Gramley was a native of Center county, born January 1, 1786, died at Rebersburg, January 12, 1871; he was a manufacturer of cloth. His wife was also a native of Center county, born in 1787, died December 6, 1861. Children of Jacob Gramley: 1. George, died at Lewisburg, Union county, Pennsylvania; unmarried. 2. Sarah, died at McElhattan, Pennsylvania; married ——— Snyder, of McElhattan; he was a farmer; had children. 3. Levi, died at Lewisburg; hotel keeper; twice married, had children. 4. Kate, died at Rebersburg; married John Hafer, deceased; he was a dentist; children: John and Wesley. 5. Philip, died at Rebersburg; married Kate Fullmer, deceased; children: Isaac, Clare, Daniel, John, Elmira, Anna, Tillie, married ——— Ziegler; Matilda. 6. Mary Magdalena, married John Franklin Waite. 7. Harriet, resides at Woodward, Pennsylvania; married George Vonada, deceased; he was a farmer; children: Emanuel, Rebecca, Emma, deceased; Frank, deceased; Fietta. 8. Rebecca, died at Rebersburg; unmarried.

(III) John Wesley, son of John Franklin and Mary Magdalena (Gramley) Waite, was born at Rebersburg, May 9, 1869. There he attended public school. In 1896 he graduated from the State College, dairying department. Having had two years' experience before entering the college in creameries at Loganton and Coburn, Pennsylvania, he was well qualified on his graduation both theoretically and practically to take the management of the Nunundah Creamery Company's creamery at Smethport, and he has filled this position successfully from that time. He is also a stockholder in this company. Further, he is a stockholder in the Grange National Bank, Smethport. For four years he was chief of the fire department at Smethport, and he is still a member. He is a member of the Smethport Lodge, Modern Woodmen of America. He is a Republican, and has been a councilman at Smethport or nearly four years. He married, March 21, 1895, Gertrude, born at Woodward, Pennsylvania, January 7, 1873, daughter of Thomas William and Rachel (Vonada) Hosterman (see Hosterman III). Children: Lowell, born at Coburn, September 8, 1895; Leroy Arlington, born at Smethport, September 10, 1901.

(The Hosterman Line).

(II) Thomas Hosterman, of German extraction, son of Jacob Hosterman, was born at Woodward, about 1819, died at Woodward, about 1881. He was a farmer. He married Hannah Yearick, born at Woodward, died at

Woodward, about 1874. She was of German descent. Children: 1. Thomas William, of whom further. 2. Pauline, died at Millheim, Pennsylvania; married Thomas Moyer, deceased; he was a miller; children, both deceased: Thomas, Ammon. 3. Amelia, died at Woodward; married Jeremiah Vonada, of Woodward, deceased; he was a farmer; child, Hannah, deceased. 4. Charles, hotel keeper at Woodward; married Salida Reish, of Union county; children: Willard, Thomas, Wesley, Ada, Charles, Verna, Oliver, Herbert, Alida. 5. Elizabeth, died at Woodward; married William Wolf, of Woodward, deceased; he was a farmer; children: Robert, deceased; Thomas, Charles, Sumner, Anna. 6. Clara. 7. Diana, died at Woodward; unmarried. 8. Emanuel, died young. 9. Anna, married Howard Musser, of Aaronsburg; he is a carpenter, and they reside at Woodward; children: Charles, Roy.

(III) Thomas William, son of Thomas and Hannah (Yearick) Hosterman, was born at Woodward, January 15, 1845. Having been a farmer he is now retired, and is postmaster at Coburn. He is a Republican. He married Rachel, born at Woodward, March 15, 1844, daughter of Philip and Mary (Harbach) Vonada. Children: 1. Phoebe Armada, born March 25, 1864, died at Coburn, May 2, 1897; unmarried. 2. Ida Zipporah, born July 19, 1865; married Thomas H. Motz, of Woodward; they reside at Woodward, on a farm; children: Nora, Lodie. 3. Warren Ellsworth, born February 7, 1867; resides at Woodward, on a farm; married Susan Orndorff, of Woodward; children: Maud, John, Blaine, Sarah, Moran, Ellsworth, Earl, Velona, Morris. 4. Anna Manora, born July 6, 1868, died at Fiedler, November 9, 1900; married Clayton Bower; he resides at Aaronsburg, a retired farmer; no children. 5. Edith Mayme, born February 18, 1870; married Bigler Shaffer, of Zion, Pennsylvania; they reside at Center Hall, Pennsylvania, on a farm; children: Roy, Paul, Clara, Thomas, Mary, Nevin. 6. Luther Curtis, born June 27, 1871, died at Rebersburg, May 15, 1898; he was a farmer; married Cora Hazel, of Madisonburg, Pennsylvania; children: Lulu, Estella; his widow married ——— Smith, has no children by him, resides at Center Hill. 7. Gertrude, married John Wesley Waite (see Waite III). 8. William Grant, born May 6, 1874; farmer, residing at Fiedler; married Elsie Krape, of Fiedler; children: Ward, Orvis. 9. Tome Alberta, born April 15, 1876; married John Krumrine, of Millheim; they reside at Weikert, Pennsylvania, on a farm; no children. 10. Thomas Ammon, born August 12, 1877; school teacher; resides at Coburn; married Ella Corman, of Coburn; children: Rachel, Tona, Lodie, Thomas. 11. Nathan Dubbs, born November 28, 1878, died at Coburn, April 29, 1902; he was a postoffice clerk; married Maggie Leitzell, of Millheim; children: Randall, Stewart; she married (second) ——— Boob, has no children by him, resides at Millheim. 12. Hannah May, born March 18, 1881, died September 14, 1881. 13. Elizabeth Amelia Pauline, born November 19, 1882, died at Coburn, March 13, 1902. 14. Mabel Clara, born September 6, 1884; married Harry Snyder, of Spring Mills; they reside at Mifflinburg, Pennsylvania, and he is a telegraph operator; children: Dean, Pauline, Grace. 15. Bertha Caroline, born February 8, 1886, died at Coburn, February 3, 1904. 16. ——— (son), born August 6, 1887, died August 6, 1887.

Philip Vonada was born at Woodward, and died there about 1878; he was a farmer. His wife Mary (Harbach) Vonada, came from Clinton county; she died at Woodward, 1900, aged eighty-seven. Children: 1. Rachel, married Thomas William Hosterman. 2. George, a farmer, resides at Madisonburg, Pennsylvania; married Matilda Musser. 3. Anna, resides at Union City, Pennsylvania; married ——— Boob; he is a farmer. 4. Catharine, resides at Woodward; unmarried. 5. Lydia, resides at Woodward; married (first) Israel Vonada, (second) David Mingle; children, all except the last-named by first husband: Kate, Ida, Cleveland, Miranda, Ammon. 6. Sadie, married Harvey Wise, of Woodward; he is a farmer, and they reside at Woodward; children: Tammie, Mabel. 7. William, a farmer, resides at Coburn; married Aria Jamison, of Spring Mills, Pennsylvania. 8. Almeda, married Thomas Vonada, of Woodward; he is a farmer, and they reside at Woodward; children: Mabel and another daughter.

SPECHT The Spechts of Smethport are of pure German lineage, descending from a long line of ancestors native to that land.

(I) Eingenhaus Specht was born in Germany, 1758, died there, 1831. He was a cabinetmaker and spent his entire life in the town of Deuderstadt. He married, when he was sixty years of age, Hannah Louisa Halmir, who died aged fifty-eight years. Both were members of the Roman Catholic church. Children: 1. William, of whom further. 2. Theresa, born 1827, died in Germany. Hannah Louisa Specht married (second) Jacob Sasse and had a son Carl.

(II) William, only son of Eingenhaus and Hannah Louisa (Halmir) Specht, was born in Deuderstadt, Kingdom of Hanover, Prussia, Germany, September 12, 1825. He received a good education in the public school, and in 1851 came to the United States settling in Smethport, Pennsylvania, where he worked at cabinetmaking, then established and still conducts a large, successful furniture and undertaking business, under the firm name of Specht & Sasse, his partner being his half-brother, Carl Sasse. He is a Republican in politics and for two terms served as borough councilman. He married, December 3, 1854, Elizabeth Heinemann, born in Deuderstadt, 1827, died in Smethport, aged fifty-four years. She was a member of the Protestant Episcopal church. She was the daughter of John Heinemann, born and died in Deuderstadt and at one time held the position of overseer of the jail. His wife was a Miss Autler, born in Deuderstadt, came to the United States in 1851, died in Smethport, Pennsylvania. Their children, all born in Deuderstadt: 1. John, a machinist, died in Germany, unmarried. 2. Catherine, died in Smethport, unmarried. 3. Louisa, died on the farm at Potato Creek, McKean county; married Robert Marsh, born in England, a farmer of McKean county; children: Stephen and William, both farmers of McKean county, also daughters. 4. Elizabeth, of previous mention, wife of William Specht. Children of William and Elizabeth Specht: 1. Carrie, born in Smethport, April 9, 1856, died there December 23, 1886; she married Franklin Corwin. 2. William Frederick, of whom further.

(III) William Frederick, only son of William and Elizabeth (Heinemann) Specht, was born in Smethport, October 15, 1857. He was educated in the public schools, continuing school attendance until he was sixteen years of age. He then secured a position in the drug store of Armstrong, Rogers & Company, also learning telegraphy under the instruction of M. L. Armstrong. In 1875 he entered the employ of Western New York and Pennsylvania railroad, a branch of the Pennsylvania railroad system, as exchange man, filling temporarily vacant positions along the line. In 1876 he entered the employ of Hamlin & Townsend at Clermont, Pennsylvania. In 1877 he was located in Bradford as assistant in a flour, feed and coal business. There he was stricken with typhoid, and as a result was compelled to remain idle until January 1, 1878. He then entered the grocery and drug store of Hamlin & Sartwell at Eldred, Pennsylvania, remaining until their store was destroyed by fire in October, 1878. In 1879 he returned to Smethport and entered the employ of Haskell & Gifford, general merchants. When Mr. Gifford sold out his interest and retired from the firm, Mr. Specht became manager of the store, continuing until 1881, when it was also destroyed by fire. In 1892, after becoming familiar with the insurance business with Haskell & Burdick, Mr. Specht having secured agencies from several companies, opened an office for the transaction of general insurance business. He has been very successful and has one of the largest underwriting agencies in the borough. For twenty years he was deputy prothonotary of McKean county, serving as such under four prothonotaries, regardless of politics, only resigning the position on account of the pressing demands of his growing insurance business.

He is a Republican in politics, served four years as councilman, one year as chief burgess, and school director many years. He is prominent in the Masonic order: is past master of McKean Lodge, No. 388, Free and Accepted Masons, and the present secretary; member of Bradford Chapter, No. 260, Royal Arch Masons; Bradford Council, Royal and Select Masters; Trinity Commandery, No. 58, Knights Templar; Zem Zem Temple, Nobles of the Mystic Shrine, and a thirty-second degree Mason of Coudersport Consistory, Ancient Accepted Scottish Rite. He is also past master of Select Knights, Ancient Order of United Workmen, Smethport Lodge, No. 182. In religious faith he is an Episcopalian, member of St. Luke's Parish of Smethport.

He married, May 15, 1889, Adelaide Octavia Brownell, born in Smethport, October 10, 1864, daughter of William Shaw Brownell (see Brownell VI). Children: 1. Frederick, born in Smethport, July 15, 1890, now a senior at State College, Pennsylvania. 2. Edna, born in Smethport, May 21, 1893, now a student at Rochester Mechanic Institute.

(The Brownell Line).

(I) The emigrant ancestor of all of the name Brownell in the United States, claiming New England ancestry, was Thomas Brownell, of Derbyshire, England, born about 1619, died 1665. He was living at Aquilneck, Rhode Island, now Portsmouth, in 1647, where he had a farm and lived until his death. He was made freeman in 1655, was deputy to the general assembly, 1655-61-62-63. He married, about 1638, Ann ———. Children: Mary, born 1639, married Robert Hazard. 2. Sarah, died September 6, 1676, married Gideon Freeborn. 3. Martha, born May, 1643, married (first) Jeremiah Wait, (second) Charles Dyer, son of Mary Dyer, the Quakeress who was hanged on Boston Common, June 1, 1660. 4. George, born 1646, married Susanna Pearce. 5. William, born 1648, married Sarah Smiton. 6. Thomas, of whom further. 7. Robert, born 1652, married Mary ———. 8. Ann, born 1654, married Joseph Wilbur.

(II) Thomas (2), son of Thomas (1) Brownell, was born 1650, died May 18, 1732. He married, 1678. Mary, born May 6, 1654, died May 4, 1736, daughter of Richard and Susanna (Wright) Pearce. Children: 1. Thomas, born February 16, 1679, married Mary Crandall. 2. John, born February 21, 1682, married Mary Case. 3. George, born January 19, 1685, married Mary Thurston. 4. Jeremiah, born October 10, 1689, married Deborah Burgess. 5. Mary, born March 22, 1692, married E. Carr. 6. Charles, of whom further.

(III) Charles, son of Thomas (2) Brownell, was born December 23, 1694, died February, 1774. He married (first) July 6, 1717, Mary, born January 4, 1696, daughter of Joseph and Ann (Brownell) Wilbur. Children: 1. Samuel, born October 12, 1719, died 1780. 2. James, born May 30, 1722, died December 29, 1736. 3. Mary, born November, 1724. 4. Ruth, born December 29, 1727. 5. Phoebe, born September 22, 1730. He married (second) Mary Wood. Child, Charles, of whom further.

(IV) Charles (2), only son of Charles (1) and his second wife, Mary (Wood) Brownell, was born April 13, 1745. He married, February 22, 1770, Content Shaw, and moved from Rhode Island to Trenton, Oneida county, New York, where he died. She was a daughter of Israel and Sarah (Wilbur) Shaw. Children: 1. Thomas, born January 2, 1771, married Milly Grey. 2. Phoebe, born December 13, 1772, married Peter Garrett. 3. Jedediah, of whom further. 4. Elizabeth, born March 8, 1776. 5. Aaron, January 27, 1778. 6. Ephraim, March 27, 1779. 7. Priscilla, June 4, 1783. 8. Borden, December 18, 1787. 9. Charles, November 18, 1789. 10. Isabel, either she or her sister Priscilla married John Hicks.

(V) Jedediah, son of Charles (2) Brownell, was born in Little Compton, Rhode Island, October 11, 1774, died in Trenton, New York, February 20, 1847. He married, August 5, 1803, Emma Williams, born February 6, 1782, died September 6, 1872. Children: 1. Jedediah, born August 25, 1811, died November 9, 1834. Eunice, born October 19, 1813, died October, 1815. 3. Mary Porter, born September 23, 1815, married Rasselas Brown. 4. William Shaw, of whom further.

(VI) William Shaw, youngest son of Jedediah Brownell, was born in Trenton, Oneida county, New York, October 27, 1818, died in Smethport, Pennsylvania, July 21, 1900. In 1838 he moved to Elk county, Pennsylvania, and began clearing a farm in Jones township, later moving to Sergeant township, McKean county, where he taught school for some time at Bunker Hill. Shortly after his marriage in 1852 he moved to Alden, Henry county, Illinois, where he bought a farm and remained four years. He then returned to Elk county, locating at Ridgway. In 1857 he moved to Smethport, where he bought out a mercantile business and established a store in the old Brownell homestead on State street. Later he moved to a store on Main street. He was twice elected associate judge of McKean county, serving ten years. He was a member of the Masonic order, and at the time of his death was one of the oldest Free Masons in the county.

He married, in Clermont, McKean county, Pennsylvania, August 22, 1852, Octavia C. Howard, born in Adams, Jefferson county, New York, October 13, 1822, died in Smethport, November 21, 1882, daughter of Eliphalet Morgan and Patty (Hinds) Howard. Children: 1. Fitz William, born in Alden, Henry county, Illinois, May 1, 1853, died in Smethport, January 7, 1863. 2. Mary Albina, born in Alden, November 13, 1854, died in Chemung, Illinois, September 25, 1856. 3. George Raleigh, born in Smethport, October 8, 1857, died there December 16, 1904. 4. Fred William, born in Smethport, November 20, 1859, now cashier in the Grange National Bank of Smethport; married Hester Adelaide Foote. 5. Adelaide Octavia, of previous mention, wife of William Frederick Specht.

LILLIBRIDGE The present family was in Rhode Island, prior to its establishment in Pennsylvania. The name was very common in Richmond, Washington county, Rhode Island, in the eighteenth century, yet was apparently not found in the county until about 1725.

(I) Lodowick Lillibridge, the first member of this family about whom we have definite information, was among the first settlers in Port Allegany, McKean county, Pennsylvania, to which he came with the Stantons. From this it is supposable that he had formerly lived at Mount Pleasant, Wayne county, and some slight corroboration of this may be found in the early history of that place, though the family seems to have been there but a short time. He married, April 28, 1814, Anna Carpenter, daughter of Samuel and Martha Carpenter (Morse) Stanton, who was born February 9, 1795 (see Gleason). Children: Elias, of whom further; Samuel, married Louise Wilkin; Alva N., born August 19, 1823, married, June 24, 1847, Leona S. Viner; Phebe A., married Van Rensselaer Vanderhule; Hannah, married Terrence Green; Amy, married Hiram Baker; Lucy, married George M. Hull; Lowell L., married (first) Jennie E. Steele, (second) Sue E. Wilkin.

(II) Elias, son of Lodowick and Anna Carpenter (Stanton) Lillibridge, was born at Port Allegany, about 1817 (one of the first white male children born in the county), and died at Port Allegany in 1887. At this place his life was spent. He was a farmer and lumberman. In politics he was a Whig. There was but one church at Port Allegany, a Union church; this he attended, and he was active in its work. He married Jane Grimes, who was born at Port Allegany, about 1819, and died at Port Allegany in 1899. Children: 1. Annette, born in 1849; married Irvin Stone; children: Ernest; Edwin; Mildred. 2. Wilbur Stanton, of whom further. 3. Ada, born in 1853; married George Baxter, from London, England, deceased; children: Christopher, Frederick, Mary. 4. John, born in 1855, died in March, 1909; married Elma Stone; children: Nora; Clara; Clyde; Zora; Georgia; Frank.

(III) Wilbur Stanton, son of Elias and Jane (Grimes) Lillibridge, was born at Port Allegany, September 17, 1851, and died at Port Allegany, February 9, 1909. There he attended public school. He was a farmer and lumberman, afterward a mail carrier. In political life he was a Republican; for three terms he was school director, and he was road supervisor for one term in Liberty township. His church was the Methodist Episcopal, but his wife was a member of the United Brethren. He married Eva, daughter of Philander and Jeanette (Fay) Webster, who was born at Hinsdale, New York, July 10, 1853, and died at Port Allegany, January 5, 1912. Her father was a native of New York state, where the family have lived for several generations; her mother was the daughter of a Revolutionary soldier, who is buried at Hinsdale. Children: 1. Charles Wesley, of whom further. 2. Rafa, born at Port Allegany, October 16, 1879; married William Martin, of Armuchee, Georgia; there they reside, and he is a planter, and storekeeper and justice of the peace; child: Lucille, born at Armuchee, in 1910.

(IV) Charles Wesley, son of Wilbur Stanton and Eva (Webster) Lillibridge, was born at Port Allegany, February 17, 1878. He attended the graded school and high school, graduating from the latter in the class of 1895. Thereafter he studied at the normal school at Clarion, graduating in the class of 1899; and he had a brief course at Grove City College, Grove City, Pennsylvania. Teaching was to be his permanent profession, not a means to something else, but his personal choice for life work. The first year he taught in Liberty township, McKean county, commencing in the fall of 1899. For a year he taught in Clara township, Potter county. The next fall he assumed charge of the school at Coal Glen, Jefferson county. After one year he was, in 1902, appointed principal of the school at Custer City, McKean county, and there he remained for two years. In 1904 he went to Eldred where he taught for seven years. In the spring of 1911 he was elected county superintendent of schools for McKean county, for a term of three years, commencing with the first of June in that year. He is a member of Eldred lodge, No. 164, Independent Order of Odd Fellows, and is past grand, having occupied all the chairs. In politics he is independent. He is a member of the Methodist Episcopal church at Smethport, and is a trustee thereof.

Mr. Lillibridge married, August 14, 1907, Lucy, daughter of William and Mary (Smith) Knowlton, who was born at Dayton, New York, July 14, 1882. Her father is the son of Lyman and Lucy (Daly) Knowlton, and was born at Dayton, New York, June 22, 1859; he is now an oil producer at Warren, Pennsylvania. Her mother was born at East Concord, New York, October 26, 1859. Children of William and Mary (Smith) Knowlton: 1. Clyde, born at Dayton, June 17, 1881; married Louise Butler, of Bradford, Pennsylvania; is an oil producer at Warren: children: Russell, born December 6, 1905; Lois, born January 29, 1908; Clifford, born March 12, 1911. 2. Lucy, married Charles Wesley Lillibridge. 3. Iva, born at Dayton, January 22, 1885, died at Custer City, October 25, 1907. 4. Lloyd, born at Custer City, August 28, 1892; a grocery clerk at Warren. 5. Gladys, born at Custer City, May 6, 1896; residing with her parents.

Children of Charles Wesley and Lucy (Knowlton) Lillibridge: Mary, born at Eldred, December 29, 1908; Stanton, born at Eldred, February 1, 1911.

SHERMAN The Shermans are of German origin. In the fatherland the name Sherman, Schuman, Schearmaur, or Scherman often occurs, and was no doubt transferred by Anglo-Saxon emigration many centuries ago to the vicinity of London, England, where it still remains numerous. From this stock a scion was transplanted to Dedham, Essex, England. The name is derived from the original occupation of the family, who were cloth dressers, or shearers of the cloth. The family at Dedham retained the family occupation and also the coat-of-arms worn by those of the family residing in and about London. Arms: Or, a lion rampant sable between three oak leaves vert: on the shoulder an amulet for difference. Crest: A sea lion sejant per pale or and argent guttee de poix finned of the first: on the shoulder a crescent for difference. Motto: Conquer death by virtue. In New England are found two distinct families bearing the name Sherman. One of them descends from William Sherman, who came to Plymouth with the Pilgrims about 1630, and settled at Marshfield, Massachusetts. The other is the Dedham stock, a branch of which immigrated to New England, and settled in the vicinity of Boston. The first of the name of that line of whom we have knowledge was Henry Sherman, but few dates are given, and the early records of the family are scanty. In the United States Sherman is an honored name. General William Tecumseh Sherman and his brother John, one the greatest soldier of his age and the other a great statesman, have made the name illustrious. Roger Sherman was a devoted patriot and one of the most prominent signers of the Declaration of Independence. These men were all descendants of Henry of Dedham.

(I) Henry Sherman, of Dedham county, Essex, probably removed hither from the county of Suffolk, as he bore the Suffolk Sherman coat-of-arms. The christian name of his wife was Agnes, who died 1580. Henry died 1589. Children: Henry, of whom further; Edmond; Judith; John; and Doctor Robert, baptized February 6, 1560.

(II) Henry (2), son of Henry (1) Sherman, was a clothier in Dedham, England, died 1610. He married Susan Hills. Children: Henry, born 1571, died 1645; Samuel, born 1573, died 1615; Susan, born 1575; Edmond, 1611, married Judith Angier; Nathaniel, died 1580; Nathaniel, born 1582, died 1615; John, of whom further; Elizabeth; Ezekiel, born July 25, 1589; Mary, July 27, 1592; Daniel, died 1634.

(III) John, son of Henry (2) Sherman, was born in Dedham, England, August 17, 1585. He came to America in 1634, and settled in Watertown, Massachusetts, but returned to England later. He married and had a son, Captain John.

(IV) Captain John (2), son of John (1) Sherman, was born in England in 1604. He came to America with his father in 1634, and settled at Watertown, Massachusetts, where he died January 25, 1691. He was a well educated man and held a high position. He was made a freeman May 17, 1637; town clerk in 1648, and often afterward held the same office; surveyor and selectman many terms; representative four years; ensign in 1654; steward of Harvard College in 1662; and captain of militia. He married Martha, daughter of William and Grace Palmer. Children: 1. John (3), born October 1, 1638, served in King Philip's war, and was killed in the Great Swamp Fight at South Kingston, December 19, 1675. 2. Martha, born February 21, 1641, married Francis Bowman. 3. Mary, born March 26, 164—, married Timothy Hawkins.

4. Sarah, born January 17, 1648, died 1667. 5. Elizabeth, born March 15, 1649, married Samuel Gaskell. 6. Joseph, of whom further. 7. Grace, born December 20, 1653, unmarried.

(V) Joseph, son of Captain John (2) Sherman, was born in Watertown, Massachusetts, May 14, 1650, died there June 30, 1731. He was a blacksmith by trade. He was often chosen selectman and assessor; was representative to the general court 1702-1705 inclusive, and influential in the town. He married Elizabeth, daughter of William Winship, of Cambridge. Children: 1. John, born January 11, 1675, was one of the first settlers of Marlboro. 2. Edward, born September 2, 1677, died 1728, in Wayland. 3. Joseph, born February 8, 1680, a surveyor of Watertown. 4. Samuel, born November 28, 1681. 5. Jonathan, February 24, 1682. 6. Ephraim, March 16, 1685, died young. 7. Elizabeth, born July 15, 1687, married ———, of Stephens township. 8. Martha, born September 1, 1689, married Rev. Benjamin Shattuck. 9. William, of whom further. 10. Sarah, born June 2, 1694. 11. Nathaniel, born September 19, 1696.

(VI) William, son of Joseph Sherman, was born in Watertown, Massachusetts, June 28, 1692. He married (first) Rebecca Cutter, of Charlestown, Massachusetts; (second) September 13, 1715, Mehitable, daughter of Benjamin Wellington. Child by first wife: 1. William, died at the age of sixteen months. Children of second wife: 2. William (2), born March 30, 1716 or 1717, died April 20, 1796; moved to New Milford, Connecticut, in 1740, and engaged as a merchant and farmer; he married Ruth Terrill April 18, 1743; without issue. 3. Mary, married John Brattle, of Dedham, Massachusetts. 4. Roger, born April 19, 1721, at Newton, Massachusetts; settled in New Milford, Connecticut, in 1743. He was a man of education, and took a leading part in the events preceding the revolution; was a member of the continental congress, signer of the Declaration of Independence, and later United States senator and one of the famous men of his day. He married (first) Elizabeth, daughter of Deacon Joseph Hartwell, of Stoughton, Massachusetts, November 17, 1749. She died October 19, 1760, aged thirty-four years. He married (second) in New Haven May 12, 1763, Rebecca, daughter of Benjamin Prescott. Of his thirteen children: Elizabeth married Samuel Baldwin, afterwards a member of congress and mayor of New Haven; Mehitable, married Jeremiah Evarts, and was the mother of William M. Evarts, a lawyer and statesman of international fame; Martha, married Jeremiah Day, president of Yale College from 1817 to 1846; and Sarah, married Samuel Hoar, of Concord, Massachusetts, and was the mother of Senator George Hoar whose long term in the United States senate was of inestimable value to this state and country. 5. Elizabeth, born July 17, 1723, married James Buck, of New Milford, Connecticut. 6. Rev. Nathaniel, of whom further. 7. Rev. Josiah, born March 5, 1726, died at Woodbridge, November 24, 1797; graduate of Nassau Hall in 1754, received the honorary degree of Master of Arts at Harvard 1758, and at Yale 1765. He was settled as pastor over the church of Woburn, Massachusetts, for fifteen years; then at Milford, Connecticut, and Goshen, where he remained until 1788. He married Martha, daughter of James Minot, a graduate of Harvard and a very distinguished man. Children of Rev. Josiah Sherman: Roger Minot, Doctor of Laws, one of the most brilliant and successful lawyers of the Connecticut Bar; Martha, married Rev. Justus Mitchell; Elizabeth, born February 3, 1763, married John Mitchell; Susanna, born April 7, 1765; Josiah, of Albany, New York. 8. Rebecca, married Joseph Hartwell, of New Milford.

(VII) Rev. Nathaniel, son of William Sherman, was born in 1725. He prepared for the ministry and preached in Massachusetts and Connecticut. He married and had children: Edmond James, of whom further; and eight daughters.

(VIII) Sergeant Edmond James Sherman, son of Rev. Nathaniel Sherman, was born at New Haven, Connecticut, in 1755, died at Hadley, New York, in 1839, aged eighty-four years. He was a Democrat in politics and spent nearly his entire life in Connecticut. Edmond J. Sherman served in the revolution as private in the Fifth Company, First Regiment, Connecticut troops, May 18 to December 20, 1775, and as a private in Colonel Lamb's regiment of artillery, enlisting at New Haven April 4, 1777. He was promoted sergeant, served all through the war, and witnessed the surrender of Cornwallis at Yorktown. He married Hannah Wise, of New Haven, who died at an advanced age at Corinth, Saratoga county, New York. They were both members of the Presbyterian church. Their only son was Edmond Jay.

(IX) Edmond Jay, son of Sergeant Edmond Sherman, was born in New Haven, Connecticut, March 10, 1795, died at Hadley, Saratoga county, New York, April 2, 1864. He was educated in the New Haven schools, and was possessed of more than the usual amount of learning for that day. He settled in Saratoga county, New York, where both before and after marriage he taught school and also carried on farming operations. In politics he was an Abolitionist, and was the candidate of his party for member of the house of assembly, but abolition was not popular in that day and he was defeated. He was a member, like his wife, of the Wesleyan Methodist Church. He married, November 11, 1818, at Hadley, New York, Susan Wilcox, born in Lucerne, Warren county, New York, June 17, 1800, died January 6, 1858, at Hadley, daughter of Tyle Wilcox, a farmer of Lucerne, who married a Miss Baker. Children of Edmond Jay Sherman: 1. Eliza, born December 13, 1819, died June 8, 1850; married Nelson Le Baron; children: Harriet, a resident of New York City; George; Fanny; Jane, resides in Hoboken, New Jersey; Delia, resides in Beachburg, Canada; Eliza, resides in Hoboken; and Wilson. 2. Harry, born February 22, 1821, died August 21, 1898; married Lucretia Gilbert; had several children, among them a son William H. 3. Myra Ann, born April 2, 1822, died September 21, 1879; married Nathaniel Chamberlain. 4. Jane, born November 8, 1823, died April 20, 1855; married James Orr; children: Minnie, and William. 5. George, born March 15, 1825, died March 10, 1839. 6. Lydia F., born June 4, 1826; married William H. Kilby, who served for fifteen years in the legislatures of Maine and Massachusetts; survives her husband with two sons, Henry and John Quincy; resides in Roxbury, Massachusetts. 7. Hannah, born August 11, 1827, died August 9, 1828. 8. Myron J., born January 13, 1829, died January 1, 1866; married, in Virginia, Lucy Jones; children: i. Charles Orr, born April 5, 1863, married Bessie Moot; children: Martha E., born June 20, 1897; Myron G., April 3, 1906. ii. Susan, born March 1, 1865, married Gus Forbush; children: Lloyd, Lucy, Charles, William, Gus, Alice, and Susie. 9. Joel Wood, born June 29, 1830, died May 30, 1894; married Louisa Akin; children: Elwy, Hattie and Hawley 10.

Lloyd W., born April 25, 1832, died November 16, 1860. 11. Charles P., born December 25, 1833, died June 11, 1859. 12. Sarah C., born December 5, 1836, died April 6, 1902; married George H. Davis. 13. Edward C. Delevan, born May 23, 1838, died April 14, 1840. 14. Edward Roger, of whom further.

(X) Edward Roger, fourteenth and youngest child of Edmond Jay Sherman, was born at Hadley, Saratoga county, New York, March 28, 1840. He was educated in the public schools, and lived in Hadley until April 13, 1861, when he enlisted in Company F, Twenty-second Regiment New York Volunteer Infantry, winning a promotion to sergeant. He was wounded at the second battle of Bull Run August 30, 1862, and was honorably discharged for disability April 26, 1863. After his return home he took a course of study at Eastman's Business College, Poughkeepsie, New York, being graduated September 18, 1863. He taught school the following winter, and in the spring of 1864 having partially recovered from his wounds returned to Washington, where he received an appointment as first lieutenant of the One Hundred and Sixteenth Regiment United States Infantry (colored), then stationed at Lexington, Kentucky; but his wounds had left him in such physical condition that he could not satisfactorily meet the requirements, and he was obliged to give up all hopes of active service in the field. He was appointed clerk in the office of the provost marshal at Washington, which position he held until Christmas, 1865, when he resigned. He located in Bradford, Pennsylvania, where he engaged successfully in the oil business. He is a Republican in politics; has served several years as coroner, and in 1911 was again elected for a term of four years. He is a member of the board of directors and is treasurer of the Pennsylvania Memorial Home, at Brookville, Clearfield county, and is now serving his third year in the latter office. He is now also president of the poor and charity department and overseer of the First Ward, Bradford. He is past commander of the Knights of the Maccabees; past commander of John S. Melvin Post, No. 141, Grand Army of the Republic, and is now quartermaster; past president of the Protected Home Circle; and an attendant of the Methodist Episcopal church. He is a man of high character and much esteemed in his city.

He married, October 1, 1868, Martha Norton, born in Panama, Chautauqua county, New York, April 13, 1852, died April 3, 1902, daughter of David Norton, of Panama. He was a millwright, died 1909, and married Susan White, born in Toronto, Canada, 1830, died in Boone, Iowa, 1880. Children of David Norton: 1. Jane, born in Toronto, Canada; carried (first) Alonzo Murphy, (second) William Bozarth; resides in Garden City, Kansas. 2. Martha, mentioned above. 3. Susan, born in Toronto, 1854; married Joseph Standeven, deceased; she resides in Omaha, Nebraska; children: Walter, of Hobart, Oklahoma; Bert, of Omaha, Nebraska; Josephine, of Hobart, Oklahoma; Frank, Simpson and Edith, the latter three of Omaha, Nebraska. 4. Isaac Eli, born in Toronto, 1856, died about 1896; married Mary Caskey, of Philadelphia; children: David Joseph and Benjamin Roy, both living in Philadelphia, Pennsylvania. 5. Edith, born in Toronto, 1860; married (first) A. H. Wilson, (second) W. W. Lewis, and resides in Titusville, Pennsylvania; no issue. Children of Edward Roger and Martha (Norton) Sherman: 1. Winifred Laura, born at Pit Hole, Pennsylvania, July 18, 1869; married Simeon Lambright, M. D., of Dennison, Ohio. Children: John Sherman, born August 4, 1904; Edwin, born August 9, 1905. 2. Charles Norton, born August 28, 1870, in Pleasantville, McKean county, Pennsylvania; married Martha Dunkle, of the state of Michigan. Child: Edward Roger, born September, 1897. 3. Susan Louise, born in Titusville, Pennsylvania, June 13, 1877; graduate of Bradford high school and Pittsburgh Kindergarten Training College. For four years she held a position in the Homestead, Pennsylvania, public library; since July, 1905, has been librarian of the Carnegie Public Library of Bradford.

GLEASON

While this name is not common, it is the name of one of the earliest immigrants to America. Thomas Gleason was probably in Massachusetts by 1653; he lived in several of its settlements. From him perhaps all the early Gleasons were descended. The present family, according to tradition, was formerly settled in Vermont; and it is a very probable conjecture that its descent is from this Massachusetts pioneer.

(I) Amos Gleason, the first member of this family, about whom we have definite information, removed from Livingston county, New York, to Warsaw, Wyoming county, New York, about 1835; but, after the death of his wife, he returned to Livingston county, and there lived for the rest of his life, making his home with his daughter. He married Polly Sias, who died at Warsaw, in 1843. He had at least two children: the daughter with whom he lived in Livingston county; and Ira Sylvenus, of whom further.

(II) Ira Sylvenus, son of Amos and Polly (Sias) Gleason, was born in Livingston county, New York, August 5, 1828, and died at Smethport, McKean county, Pennsylvania, December 30, 1896. He had but a limited education. In 1844 he became an apprentice in a harness shop at Warsaw where he remained until January, 1851. On the eleventh of that month he removed to Smethport, and entered the employment of Steele and Johnson, with whom he remained for three years. Then he went into the harness business for himself. He was also a stockholder in the Smethport Water Company. He was a Republican, and held the office of school director and other town offices. In the Methodist Episcopal church, both he and his wife were members, and he was constantly in some important position, holding at one time or another, nearly all; he was steward, class leader, treasurer, and superintendent of the Sunday school. He married, at Smethport, May 31, 1854, Emily Arminia, daughter of Samuel and Weltha (Copeland) Stanton, who was born in McKean county, January 13, 1833, and died at Smethport, November 8, 1898. In her infancy she was adopted by Ghordis and Armenia (Sartwell) Corwin (see Stanton). Children: Dora, born at Smethport, August 2, 1857, died July 26, 1877; Ralph Corwin, of whom further.

(III) Ralph Corwin, son of Ira Sylvenus and Emily (Stanton) Gleason, was born at Smethport, July 2, 1874. There he received his education, attending the common school and the high school. In order to perfect himself in the art of photography, he took a technical course at the Oberlin Retouching School. Immediately after finishing this course, he opened a photographic studio at Smethport where he has been, and is at the present time, a successful photographer. While this is his principal, it is not his sole business interest, for he has interests outside of Smethport; he is a stockholder in the Smethport Water Company, in the Hamlin Bank and Trust Company and in the First National Bank at Eldred. He is a member of the Smethport Central Club. He is past grand of Smethport Lodge, No. 389, Independent Order of Odd Fellows, and is now its recording secretary. Since 1902 he has been a justice of the peace, and since 1903 tax collector for the borough. His party is the Republican.

Mr. Gleason married, June 28, 1905, Harriet Marsh, daughter of Thomas Henry and Harriet (Marsh) Ryan, who was born at Kane, Pennsylvania, October 7, 1881. She is a communicant of St. Luke's Episcopal church. Mrs. Gleason has a very interesting ancestry, and, on her mother's side, is descended from prominent New England families. Her father was the son of John Ryan; both were born in County Limerick, Ireland, and both came to North America. Her grandfather died at Guelph, Ontario, Canada; he was a grain and fur dealer; and he married Mary Maguinn, of County Clare, Ireland, who also died at Guelph. Thomas Henry Ryan was born August 26, 1841, and now resides at Kane; he is an oil producer. At the age of seventeen he left home in Canada, and, coming to the United States, he enlisted in the "Bucktail" regiment, officially the Forty-Second Pennsylvania Reserves, and served in the Civil war for three years. At the battle of Antietam, he was severely wounded in the shoulder. Harriet (Marsh) Ryan was born at Rockingham, Vermont, May 14, 1842, and died at Kane, Pennsylvania, June 7, 1904. Her first American Marsh ancestor was Lieutenant Alexander Marsh, of Braintree, Massachusetts, who died March 7, 1698. He married, October 19, 1655, Mary Belcher, also of Braintree. Their son John, born February 17, 1678, and died in 1747, was prominent in town affairs; he married, August 28, 1701, Sarah Wilson, of New Haven. Their son Moses, living at Braintree, was born in 1714, and died at Greenbush, New York, in the provincial army; he married, September 5, 1739, Sarah Crosby. They had a son, also named Moses, born at Braintree, February 5, 1744, died at Rockingham, Vermont, in 1828; his name is given in the New Hampshire Revolutionary rolls, as a private in Colonel Samuel Ashley's company, at Chesterfield. He married Jerusha Owen, who was born at Braintree, June 16, 1747, and died at Rockingham, in 1828. Among their children was Joseph, born at Braintree, August 3, 1760, died at Rockingham, March 14, 1846. Joseph married, at Rockingham, May 10, 1793, Joanna Pierce, born April 10, 1776, died at Marshall, New York, April 4, 1873. She was descended from John Pierce, freeman of Watertown, Massachusetts, 1638, the line being: John; Anthony; Joseph; Joseph; John; Anthony; Ebenezer (fought at the battle of Bennington, in the Revolution, and was killed there ten days later, while engaged in a scouting expedition); Joanna. Charles Pierce Marsh was son of Joseph and Joanna (Pierce) Marsh, born July 20, 1820; married at Keene, New Hampshire, Celina Thayer Locke. Among their children was Harriet (Marsh) Ryan. Children of Thomas Henry and Harriet (Marsh) Ryan: 1. Kate, born April 21, 1867, a trained nurse at Kane, and graduate of Bellevue Hospital, New York. 2. Benton Charles, born August 17, 1868; married (first) Agnes Marr; (second) Margaret McCarty. 3. Josephine, born May 16, 1871; married Ralph P. Verdon. 4. Myra, born March 23, 1873; married John K. Morrison. 5. Edmund Locke, born February 18, 1875; married (first) Della Hicks; (second) Lillian May Patterson; he is a lawyer, at Buffalo, New York. 6. Ruth, born in 1877, died in 1880. 7. Mary Louise, born January 17, 1879; married Roy Carleton Gifford. 8. Harriet Marsh; married Ralph Corwin Gleason. 9. Florence, born November 20, 1883, died in 1900. 10. Jane (Jennie), born August 15, 1887, unmarried.

Ralph Corwin and Harriet Marsh (Ryan) Gleason have no children.

(The Stanton Line).

This name is said to be derived from two Anglo-Saxon words meaning Stone-town. It is often spelled Staunton, and in the present family some of the descendants spell it the one way, some the other.

(I) Thomas Staunton, the founder of this family, was born about 1614, and died December 2, 1676. January 2, 1635, he took passage for Virginia in the merchantman "Bonaventura." If he ever went to Virginia, in the modern sense of the term, his stay was very short; yet there is some slight indication of such a residence. In 1636 he was a magistrate in Boston. In the Pequot war, he acted as interpreter and was a brave soldier, and after this war, he returned to Boston, but settled soon in Hartford, Connecticut. He acted as interpreter in the treaty of purchase of New

Haven from the Indians. At Hartford, he was an official of the court. He was appointed in 1650 to assist, presumably as interpreter, in preaching among the Indians. In 1650 he also established a trading house at Stonington, Connecticut. It was probably in 1651 that he removed with his family to Pequot (New London), Connecticut, and in 1658 that he finally settled at Stonington, or rather, two and a half miles east of the village; this settlement was then in the jurisdiction of Massachusetts, but was given to Connecticut in 1662. He was the first white inhabitant on the Pawcatuck river. At Stonington, especially, he was much employed about Indian affairs, his knowledge of their tongue making him a valuable citizen. Whenever a court, conference, or treaty was to be held, his services were indispensable, and he was connected with almost every Indian transaction on record. Uncas visited him in 1670 with a train of warriors and captains, to get him to write his will. He was also prominent in other public affairs, and received large grants of land; in October, 1667, the general court granted him, for his services, two hundred and fifty acres in what became the town of Preston, New London county. He took an active part in King Philip's war; served as commissioner of Indian affairs; in 1665 was made a commissioner of Stonington, with authority to hold a semi-annual court at New London, to which office he was annually re-elected until his death, twelve years later. In 1666 he was elected a member of the general court of Connecticut, and he was repeatedly re-elected until 1675. He held other offices beside these. In the organizing of the First Congregational church at Stonington, he was a leader, and his name was the first on its roll. He married Ann, daughter of Thomas and Dorothy Lord, who was born about 1621, and died in 1688. Her father received, in Connecticut, the first license to practice medicine which was granted in New England. Children: Thomas, born in 1638, died April 11, 1718, married Sarah Denison; John (1), of whom further; Mary, born in 1643, married, November 17, 1662, Samuel Rogers; Hannah, born in 1644, married, November 20, 1662, Nehemiah Palmer; Joseph, died in 1714, married (first), June 19, 1673, Hannah Mead, (second), August 23, 1677, Hannah Lord, had two other marriages; Daniel, born in 1648; Dorothy, born in 1651, died January 19, 1742, married, September 11, 1674, Rev. James Noyes; Robert, born in 1653, died October 25, 1724, married, November 12, 1677, Joanna Gardiner; Sarah, born in 1655, died in 1713, married (first) Thomas Prentice, (second) William Denison; Samuel, born in 1657, married June 10, 1680, Borodell Denison.

(II) John (1), son of Thomas and Ann (Lord) Stanton, was born at Hartford, in 1641, and died at Stonington, October 31, 1713. In 1654 he was sent by the court of commissioners to be educated for a teacher of the Gospel to the Indians, but he did not finish his studies. In 1664 he was the first recorder of Southertown (Stonington). He was captain of one of the Connecticut regiments in King Philip's war, and was in command when Canonchet was captured. He married, in 1664, Hannah Thompson. Children: John (2), of whom further; Joseph, born January 22, 1668, married, July 18, 1696, Margaret Cheseboro; Thomas, born in April, 1670, married, in 1692, Anna Stanton; Ann, born October 1, 1673, died March 23, 1680; Theophilus, born June 16, 1676, married, June 5, 1698, Elizabeth Rogers; Dorothy, born in 1680, died April 28, 1699.

(III) John (2), son of John (1) and Hannah (Thompson) Stanton, was born May 22, 1665, his will was dated February 13, 1747, probated July 8, 1755. He lived on lands given him by his father at Preston. He married Mary ——. Children: John, born November 13, 1706, married, in 1735, Desire Denison; Daniel, born June 8, 1708, married, in 1737, Dinah Starke; Joseph, born February 11, 1710, married, in 1737, Abigail Freeman; Lydia, born July 15, 1712, married, August 9, 1734, Daniel Leonard; Robert, born February 20, 1714, married, in 1741, Mary Lester; Hulda, born June 3, 1716; Jabez, born December 10, 1718, married, in 1745, Sarah Morse; David, born October 22, 1720, married, in 1755, Sarah Kimball; Mary, born September 11, 1722, Sarah, born January 20, 1724; Samuel (1), of whom further.

(IV) Samuel (1), son of John (2) and Mary Stanton, was born at Preston, June 26, 1726, and died at Preston, in March, 1803. His home was at Preston. He married, at Voluntown, Connecticut, November 1, 1754, Mary Palmer, who was born about 1737, and died January 20, 1815. Children: Mary, born March 15, 1756, died in 1763; Samuel (2), of whom further; Lydia, born February 24, 1761; Daniel, born October 14, 1762, died in 1769;

Rebecca, born April 7, 1765; Mary, born March 22, 1767; Freelove, born January 19, 1770, died in 1775; Daniel, born in January, 1776, married Catharine F. Roth.

(V) Samuel (2), son of Samuel (1) and Mary (Palmer) Stanton, was born at Preston, April 17, 1759, and died at Bellefonte, Center county, Pennsylvania, April 15, 1816. In June, 1789, he bought a tract of three hundred and twenty-two acres in Wayne county, Pennsylvania, and became the first actual settler in Mount Pleasant township; he had previously done some surveying in that section. The day following his purchase he bought nearly three thousand acres more. About a year later he began to work this land, and he brought his family here in April, 1791. During the following winter he and his family nearly died of starvation. When they were almost beyond hope, a passing hunter killed a deer near their cabin; then discovering their plight, he generously and effectually relieved them. In 1796 Mr. Stanton was appointed justice of the peace in Northampton county. When Wayne county was organized, two years later, he was a commissioner to build the court house, and he was engaged in many enterprises in Wayne county. In October, 1814, he was appointed associate judge of that county. Near the close of his life, however, he removed westward, and purchased seventeen hundred acres of land on Marvin creek, in what is now Hamlin township, McKean county, and three or four hundred acres in Liberty township. In the latter township he erected a store and log house; he also planned for many buildings. His project was, to bring two hundred families to what is now Port Allegany. In this new home he was commissioner of a state road; business growing out of this position called him to Harrisburg. Taking his family, he went as far as the west branch of the Susquehanna; and it was while stopping at Bellefonte to visit a friend, as he was making his journey to Harrisburg, that he died. When he had started with his family, they had just had a visitation of typhoid in which seven of his children had been sick. Mrs. Stanton, after his death, continued the journey to Port Allegany. The main body of the intended colonists settled in Ashtabula county, Ohio. Judge Stanton was a pious Christian man, a member of the Free Communion Baptists, and was the author of about fifty hymns. He was a man of lively imagination, well developed intellect and unusual power of concentration. It is said that he read over two thousand books, and could discourse intelligently about their contents. In disposition he was cheerful, entertaining, yet not jovial, and with a thirst for information which made him alert. He married, at Preston, December 3, 1786, Martha Carpenter, daughter of Daniel and Anna (Carpenter) Morse, who was born at Preston, October 15, 1764, and died at Port Allegany, May 8, 1830. Children: Martha, born November 18, 1787, married, May 12, 1806, William Green; Samuel (3), of whom further; Polly, born August 26, 1791, married, March 31, 1808, Thomas Lillibridge; Rebecca, born June 1, 1793, married, December 10, 1809, William Haines; Anna Carpenter, born February 9, 1795, married, April 28, 1814, Lodowick Lillibridge (see Lillibridge); Lucy, born January 5, 1797, married, February 11, 1819, Elias Morse; Daniel, born June 18, 1799, married, January 29, 1824, Lydia Chadwick; Thomas, born November 15, 1801; Lydia, born June 16, 1803, married, February 11, 1819, Horace Morse; Abel, born June 30, 1805, married, in 1837, Sarah Scott; Hannah, born July 18, 1807, married, September 12, 1824, James Steele.

(VI) Samuel (3), son of Samuel (2) and Martha Carpenter (Morse) Stanton, was born at Preston, February 26, 1789, and died in Minnesota. He married (first), in 1826, Weltha Copeland, (second), in 1851, Polly Rolland. Children, all except the last-named by first wife: Marietta, born April 26, 1829, married, March 10, 1847, Thomas Horton; Mary Ann, married ——— Green; Pauline, married Luther Lucas; Emily (the second name, Arminia, we suppose to have been later conferred by her adopted parents, Ghordis and Armenia Corwin), married Ira Sylvenus Gleason (see Gleason); Betsey Ann.

CORWIN Matthias Corwin was born in England between the years 1590 and 1600, died September, 1658. He came to New England and in 1634 received a second grant of land at Ipswich, Massachusetts. He joined a company under Rev. John Young and settled in Southold, Long Island, in October, 1640. There he lived for eighteen years, until his death. He owned considerable land and held town offices. His wife was named Margaret ———. Children: John, Martha and Theophilus.

(II) Theophilus, son of Matthias Corwin,

was born in 1634, died before 1692. In 1655 he had lands at Southold, Long Island. He married Mary ———. Children: Daniel, Theophilus, David, Mary, Mehitable, Bertha, Phebe.

(III) Daniel, son of Theophilus Corwin, was born between 1660-70, died before 1719. He married Mary, daughter of Simon and Mary Ramsay. Children: Daniel, Henry and Simeon.

(IV) Daniel (2), son of Daniel (1) Corwin, was born about 1690, died September 7, 1747. He was a freeholder of Southold, Long Island, in 1737. He married January, 1722-23, Elizabeth Cleaves. Children: Nathan Peletieh, Mary, Michal (feminine), Lucas, Jedediah, Silas, John Daniel, Edward.

(V) Edward, son of Daniel (2) Corwin, was born 1710, died March 16, 1732. He married and had sons Edward and Separate, who are mentioned in the will of their grandfather, Daniel Corwin, as his grandchildren.

(VI) Edward (2), son of Edward (1) Corwin, was born about 1731. About 1760 he was taken from his family in the night by a press gang, put on a ship where he died four or five years after, without ever getting back to his family. He married, in Mattituck, Long Island, Hannah Horton. On July 29, 1764, Widow Hannah Corwin had three children baptized: Hannah, Edward and Sarah. Previous to February 22, 1756, Phineas and Elizabeth were baptized. Phineas and his brother Edward were in mercantile business in New York City for a time under the name Currin, but soon altered the spelling to Corwin, the proper name.

(VII) Edward (3), son of Edward (2) Corwin, was born on Long Island, New York, February 13, 1759, died at the farm of his son on Potato Creek, McKean county, Pennsylvania, September 15, 1849. He moved to Connecticut about 1775, and after the revolutionary war was a merchant in New York City, then moved to Cazenovia, Madison county, New York, thence about 1822 to Norwich township, McKean county, Pennsylvania. He enlisted in the continental army at the age of seventeen years and served six years. He received a pension for his revolutionary service until his death in 1849. During the revolution he was taken prisoner by the Indians, who delivered him to the British, they holding him twenty-two months. He also received five hundred acres of bounty land, which, however, he was cheated out of by agents and a lawyer. He had many thrilling experiences during his military career; was in the battle of Monmouth, at the surrender of Burgoyne, saw Major Andre hanged and was with General Sullivan in his expedition up the Susquehanna after the Wyoming massacre. He lived to the great age of ninety years. He was a farmer, and he and his wife were for over forty years members of the Baptist church. He married (first) November 4, 1784, Yet-once Barstow, of Franklin, Connecticut, born May 9, 1766, died August 20, 1797. He married (second) March 4, 1798, Olive Colegrove, born in Rhode Island, May, 1775, died December 31, 1859. Children of Edward (2) Corwin: 1. Harry, died in infancy. 2. Ghordis, died in Smethport, a saw and grist mill owner; married Armenia Sartwell. 3. Benjamin, of whom further. 4. Philetus, died in Corwin Center, a farmer; married California Gallup. 5. John, died in Friendship, New York, a carpenter, farmer and oil producer; married Julia Robbins. 6. Edward, died in Norwich township, McKean county, unmarried. 7. Esther, died in Ohio; married Jonathan Southwick, a farmer. 8. Eliza, died in the west; married Andrew Still. 9. Nancy, died in Smethport; married Orrin Gallup, a farmer. 10. Diana, died in the west; married Warren Edson, a shoemaker. 11. Olive, died in Norwich township; married Loren Wilcott.

(VIII) Benjamin, son of Edward (3) Corwin, was born in McKean county, Pennsylvania, April 27, 1807, died in Smethport, December 9, 1881. He was a carpenter by trade, also a farmer, owning a good farm about one mile from Smethport. In later life he sold his farm and moved to Smethport. He married Betsey Chapin, born in Connecticut, July 4, 1812, died in Smethport, November 18, 1886, daughter of Phineas Chapin, who died in New York state, and his wife ——— (Hazleton) Chapin. Children of Phineas Chapin: 1. Sarah ("Sally") married George Allen. 2. Sophronia, married Levi Coates. 3. Lucena, married Elbert Freeman. 4. Lorenzo, died aged twenty-one. 5. Electa, married Joseph White. 6. Betsey, of previous mention. Children of Benjamin and Betsey Corwin: 1. Theodore, born February 22, 1833, died in infancy. 2. Violette, born July 21, 1836, died in infancy. 3. Helen Electa, born in Smethport, Pennsylvania, August 28, 1838; married Arnold Nelson McFall. 4. Ghordis, born May

31, 1842, died in infancy. 5. Estella, born June 6, 1844, died at Marvin's Creek, June 30, 1865. 6. Althea, born May 1, 1847, died in infancy. 7. Alice, born April 15, 1849, died November 21, 1883, at Smethport, unmarried. 8. George, born March 19, 1852, died August 15, 1887, at Smethport; a carpenter; married Adelaide Oakes, of Silver Creek, New York, who survives him, a resident of Erie, Pennsylvania. 9. Franklin, of whom further.

(IX) Franklin, youngest child of Benjamin and Betsey (Chapin) Corwin, was born at Marvin's Creek, McKean county, Pennsylvania, May 26, 1854, died at Smethport. May 21, 1899, by drowning. He was educated in the public schools, and learned the carpenter's trade. His home was in McKean county, but he was largely engaged in the erection of chemical works and tanneries (which he made his specialty) and was obliged to be out of the county a great deal. He was a Republican in politics. He married Carrie, daughter of William Specht. She was born in Smethport, April 9, 1856, died there December 23, 1886. Children: 1. Ghordis Burdette, of whom further. 2. Harry, born in Smethport, December 13, 1887; a graduate of The Case School of Applied Science; is a chemist in the employ of the Erie railroad; married Nina Hosmer, of Cleveland, Ohio, and resides in Youngstown, Ohio.

(X) Ghordis Burdette (called Corte B.), eldest son of Franklin and Carrie (Specht) Corwin, was born in Smethport, Pennsylvania, April 24, 1880. He was educated in the public school, finishing at Smethport high school. He enlisted, April 27, 1898, in Bradford in Company C, Pennsylvania National Guard, later being assigned to Company I of Warren for service in the Spanish-American war. He was discharged in the same year without seeing actual service. He entered the employ of the Camp Window Glass Company, of Smethport, continuing nine years, having the contract for packing the glass made by the company when he left them. In 1907 he engaged with Holmes & Gilfillan, remaining eighteen months, then located in Mount Jewett with the Consolidated Window Glass Company, continuing until December 19, 1904. He then returned to the employ of Holmes & Gilfillan in Smethport, where he is now engaged. He is a Republican in politics and was elected borough auditor, 1908-11. He is a volunteer fireman, belonging to both the Smethport and Bradford departments. He attends St. Luke's Episcopal Church.

He married, September 8, 1903, at Smethport, Edna Lorena Hafner, born in Kasson, McKean county, Pennsylvania, May 20, 1881, educated in the public school there and in Smethport high school, a member of the Baptist church. She is the daughter of William Hafner, of Clermont, Pennsylvania, a farmer, later a merchant of Smethport, now and for the past four years an employe of the McKean County Home for the Poor. He married Melissa Jane Potter, born at Larry's Creek, near Jersey Shore, Pennsylvania. Children, all born in Kasson, Pennsylvania: 1. Margaret Idella, married Frank M. Spanogle, a telegraph operator, and resides in North Girard, Pennsylvania; children: Holmes Hafner, Charlotte Lorena, Margaret, William. 2. Edith Alverna, married Herman Frederick Grabe, an undertaker, and resides at State College, Pennsylvania. 3. Edna Lorena, of previous mention, wife of Corte B. Corwin. 4. Earl Potter, now an attendant in the Insane Asylum at Willard, New York.

VAN DYKE That the present name is Dutch is sufficiently evident on first aspect, and also well known to all, for the name has won distinction in Europe, in the person of the great artist. In America the most eminent of the name is Rev. Dr. VanDyke, preacher, poet, writer and professor. According to its tradition the ancestor of the present family came to America with Stuyvesant, but afterward lived in New Jersey. His name was Nicholas.

(I) Augustus VanDyke, the first member of this family about whom we have definite information, was born in Pennsylvania, about 1824, died at Irvington, Warren county, Pennsylvania, 1874. A large part of his life was passed at Irvington; he was a bridge carpenter. Both he and his wife were Lutherans. He married Mary Sterner, who was probably born at Lancaster, about 1815, died at Irvington, about 1891. Children: 1. Hannah, resides at Petrolia, Pennsylvania; married Frederick Hinman, deceased; he was a manufacturer of nitro-glycerine; children, all living at Petrolia: Fanchon, Roy, Christine. 2. Abram, of whom further. 3. John, died in Peoria, Illinois; brakeman; married ——; children: Elizabeth, residing at Oil City, Pennsylvania; James, residing at Oil City. 4. Mary, died in Kansas; married (first) James Beaumont, of Paterson, New Jersey; married (second) ———; one daughter by first marriage, Lillian, residing at Irvington. 5. Amanda, died young. 6. Sarah, died young. 7. William, died at Irvington, 1909; a car inspector; married Ida ———, deceased; two children, both residing in Washington; Maud, Mary.

(II) Abram, son (Sterner) VanDyke, was born in Montoursville, Pennsylvania, May, 1846, died at Bradford, Pennsylvania, January 17, 1908. He attended public school in his native county. By trade he was a machinist. At a later time he worked for the Standard Oil Company at Bradford for a period of thirty years. He was a Democrat. He married Marinda Jane, born near Smethport, September 17, 1847, daughter of Lyman and Mary (Aldrich) Stark. Her home is now at Bradford. Her father, who died at Tuna Creek, Pennsylvania, 1901, was born near Smethport; he is thought to have been descended from Philander Stark, a near relative of General John Stark, the victor at Bennington. Children of Abram and Marinda Jane (Stark) VanDyke: 1. Augustus, born at Kane, Pennsylvania, August, 1868, died at Smethport, 1870. 2. William Elmer, of whom further. 3. Irma Esther, born at Kane, October 25, 1872; married (first) Leonard Flagg, from Tuneassa, New York; he was a farmer; she married (second) Harry Campbell, of Tuneassa; there they live, he being a farmer; children, two by first, three by second, husband: Mortimer, born in November, 1896; Leonarda, born in September, 1898; Josephine, born July 25, 1905; Richard, born April 10, 1907; Winifred, born December 5, 1910. 4. Frederick, born at Oil City, October 30, 1874; foreman, at Olean, New York, for the Standard Oil Company; married Ethel Fee, of Bradford; child, Fannie. 5. Mortimer, born at Oil City, November 2, 1876; foreman at Olean for the Standard Oil Company; married Minnie Shaffer, of Olean; children: Irma Marinda, Lawrence Donald, Wava Audrey, Bessie Elaine, Jessie Eileen (the last two twins, born April 21, 1905). 6. Winfield Abram, born at Tuna Creek, October 3, 1883; resides with his mother at Bradford, unmarried.

(III) Rev. William Elmer VanDyke, son of Abram and Marinda Jane (Stark) Van-Dyke, was born at Kane, December 25, 1870. He received a public school education in McKean county, and attended Limestone Academy, Limestone, New York. When he was eighteen years of age he took a position as clerk in the general store at Mount Alton, Pennsylvania, and there he remained until he was twenty-one. From 1892 to 1896 he was manager of the Helvetia Supply Company, at Helvetia, Pennsylvania, and assistant postmaster of Helvetia. Having, however, become a member of the Protestant Episcopal church, and desiring to live a life of Christian devotion, he spent three years with the Order of the Holy Cross, while the Fathers were still at Westminster, Maryland. After this he studied privately for orders, and on April 23, 1903, he was ordained deacon by Bishop Whitehead at Ridgway, Pennsylvania. For two years he was in charge at Osceola Mills. Then he came to Smethport and was assistant for two years. During this period, September 16, 1906, he was ordained priest at Smethport by the same bishop. For a year and a half he had charge of the Episcopal church at Kane. For a year, thereafter, he was vicar of St. Mary's Memorial Church, in Pittsburgh. In 1909 he was made rector of St. Luke's, Smethport. He is a member of the Central Club at Smethport. He is a Republican.

He married (first) June 3, 1899, Blanche (Packer) Donnelly, born at Beech Creek, Pennsylvania, November 16, 1866, died at DuBois, Pennsylvania, October 2, 1901; married (second) June 25, 1907, Helen Eliza, daughter of Frederick Arthur and Leone (Huenerfeld) McCoy, who was born at Ellicottville, New York, April 1, 1878. She is a member of the Daughters of the American Revolution and a communicant of St. Luke's Episcopal Church. Her father was the son of Stephen and Eliza (Vinton) McCoy, and her mother was daughter of Peter Joseph Huenerfeld, a native of Germany. Children of Frederick Arthur and Leone (Huenerfeld) McCoy: Eugene, died young; Guy, married Edna Dunbar; Grace, married H. H. Redfield; Helen Eliza, of previous mention; Mary, deceased; Robert, deceased; Allen, deceased. Children of Rev. William Elmer VanDyke, one by first, two by second, wife: Howard Sutton, born September 20, 1901, died at DuBois, September 25, 1901; Jane, born at Bradford, July 25, 1908; Andrew McCoy, born at Smethport, November 30, 1910.

GREEN The Greens of this record descend from an ancient English family, and only claim residence in the United States since 1872, when William A. (2), father of Samuel Green, of Smethport, came to this country.

(II) William A. (2), son of William A. (1) Green, was born in Birmingham, England, February 28, 1841, died in Smethport, September 1, 1902. He was the only child of his parents, who were both members of the Established Church of England. He was educated in the English schools and became a butcher by trade. After the birth of seven of his twelve children he came, in 1872, to the United States. He settled first in Wellsboro, Tioga county, Pennsylvania, where he was joined by his wife and family in February, 1873. In 1878 he came to Smethport. He was a Republican in politics and a member of the Episcopal church.

He married Sarah Field, born in Birmingham, England, December 23, 1840, who survives him, now a resident of Seattle, Washington. Children, first seven born in Birmingham: 1. William, died young. 2. Ebenezer, now a poultry farmer at South Park, Washington; married and has children: Lawrence, deceased; Robert; Lucy; Eben Jr., born at Seattle, Washington. 3. Henry, now a poultry farmer at South Park, Washington; married Nellie Smith of Tylersburg, Pennsylvania. Children: Iva; Ruba, died in infancy; Edith, died young; Ruby. 4. John A., now a poultry and garden farmer of South Park, Washington; married Minnie Smith of Tylersburg, Pennsylvania. Children: Arthur, born 1894; Forest, 1896. 5. Joseph, died in infancy. 6. Moses, died in infancy. 7. Samuel, of whom further. 8. Mary, born September 9, 1874, in Wellsboro, Pennsylvania; married George H. Denning, born in Eldred, Pennsylvania, March 31, 1872, now proprietor of a meat market in Smethport. Children: Rita, Gerald. 9. Lucretia, born in Wellsboro in 1876, died in England 1870, while there with her mother visiting. 10. Phoebe, born in England, 1878; married (first) Leon Grigsby; (second) in Seattle, Emmett Miller, and now resides in Peoria, Illinois; child: Harriet Elsie, born July 31, 1912, in Peoria. 11. Gertrude, born in Smethport, 1880; married Orson Kimball, and resides in Seattle, Washington, no living children. 12. Mountford J., born in Smethport 1883, now a groceryman in Seattle, Washington, unmarried.

(II) Samuel, son of William A. (2) and Sarah (Field) Green, was born in Birmingham, England, November 2, 1872. He was three months old when brought to the United States by his mother, and from that age has resided in McKean county with the exception of one year. He was educated in the public schools and the State Normal School at Edinboro, leaving school in 1901. He spent the next year in Seattle, Washington, working at carpentering. In 1902 he returned to Smethport and finished learning his trade, at which he has since been employed as journeyman and contractor. He also has a general teaming business. One of the public buildings that he helped to erect was the Bradford Theatre. He is a Republican in politics, serving on election boards and in other minor offices. He is a member and trustee of the Baptist church, and belongs to the Smethport Volunteer Fire Department and to the Protected Home Circle. His wife attends the Baptist church, and also belongs to the Protected Home Circle.

He married, April 20, 1893, Mittie Elizabeth, born in Smethport, January 16, 1876, daughter of William Robert Taylor, born in Smethport, 1843, died there October 29, 1882, son of John B. Taylor, son of Deacon James Taylor, son of Robert Taylor, the immigrant. William Robert Taylor married Caroline Provin, born March 4, 1853, died in Smethport January 22, 1891. Children: 1. Harriet Estella, born October 29, 1874; married Charles G. Mesler, and resides in Williamsport, Pennsylvania. Children: i. Paul, born November 27, 1894, resides in Fremont, Ohio. ii. Emmett, born March 27, 1896, now attending the Industrial School at Williamsport. 2. Mittie Elizabeth, of previous mention. Caroline (Provin) Taylor survived her husband and married (second) in 1886, James Moses, a farmer of Allegany county, New York, who died in 1890; no issue. Caroline was a daughter of Samuel Provin, born in Westfield, Massachusetts, 1825, died in Farmer's Valley, Pennsylvania, November 18, 1892. He was a soldier of the civil war, serving in the Pennsylvania Bucktail Regiment. He married Harriet Coon, of Steuben county, New York, born September 22, 1829, now residing in Olean, New York. Children of Samuel Provin: 1. Sanford, born February, 1848, in Addison,

New York, now a farmer of Farmer's Valley, Pennsylvania, owning a large farm. He married (first) Ellen Hamlin, who died in Ridgway, Pennsylvania, in 1873, leaving a daughter: Mary. He married (second) Catherine Coates; children: Jennie, Charles, Sanford (2), William, Rhoda, Alice, Leona, Donald. 2. Alfred L., born in Westfield, Tioga county, Pennsylvania, August 30, 1849, now a farmer and lumberman of East Smethport. He married (first) Nellie Taylor, born 1864, in Coryville, Pennsylvania, died 1887, no issue; married (second) Desire Betts, born in Riceville, Pennsylvania, December 1842, died January 1908; married (third) Ella J. Churchley, born in London, England, November 13, 1868, no issue. 3. Alonzo, born 1850, died 1861. 4. Lucy, born 1851, died 1852. 5. Caroline, of previous mention. 6. Duella D., born 1855; married (first) Alty Sloan. Children: Nina and Harry. He married (second) Annie ———, and resides in Jamestown, New York. 7. Willis V., resides in Olean, New York, a baker; married Sarah McCarthy. Children: Bessie, William, Roxanna. 8. Charles, died aged sixteen years.

John B. Taylor, grandfather of Mrs. Mittie E. (Taylor) Green, died in Smethport about 1879. He was a blacksmith. He married Elizabeth Holcomb, born in Connecticut, died in Smethport, September 23, 1901, aged about seventy-eight years. Both were members of the Baptist church. Children of John B. Taylor, all born in Smethport, where four died young: 1. Victor, now a farmer of Danville, Illinois, married and has a large family. 2. Leroy, a farmer of Iowa, married and has issue. 3. Mary, died in Kilbourne City, Wisconsin; married a Mr. Pike, also deceased, leaving issue. 4. Matilda, married Nathaniel Cummings, whom she survives, a resident of Bloomington, Illinois. Children: Carrie; Lulu, deceased. 5. Maria, died in a hospital in Buffalo in 1892; married a Mr. Harm and resides in Bradford, Pennsylvania. Children: Lewis and Frederick, both living in Pittsburgh. 6. William Robert, of previous mention. 7. Edward, died in Johnsonburg, Pennsylvania, married Lottie Reynolds, also deceased. Children: John H., Robert E., Frederick E., Laura Reynolds, Edna Matilda. 8. Ezra, joined the gold hunters in the Klondike and has never since been heard from. Elizabeth Holcomb, mother of the foregoing children, was a cousin of John Howard Payne, the composer of "Home, Sweet Home."

Children of Samuel and Mittie Elizabeth (Taylor) Green, all born in Smethport: 1. Hazel Estella, born April 10, 1894, married W. P. Mitchell, born in Raleigh, North Carolina, a printer, and lives in Olean, New York. Child: Norma Kathleen, born June 12, 1912. 2. Noal Everett, born September 12, 1896. 3. Milton Taylor, October 1, 1899. 4. Homer Samuel, February 19, 1908.

HOLMES-CARTER The surname Holmes is of ancient English origin and most of the American families of the name are descended from three brothers, emigrants, who came to New England before 1650.

(I) Francis Holmes, immigrant ancestor of the line following, was an inhabitant of Stamford, Connecticut, as early as 1648. His will dated September 6, 1671, is recorded in Fairfield, Connecticut. In it he mentions wife Ann and four children.

(II) John, second child of Francis Holmes, was born in England. He married, 1659, Rachel Waterbury, of Stamford; ten children.

(III) Stephen, son of John Holmes, was born January 14, 1665, died in Greenwich, 1710. He married, November 18, 1688, at Stamford, Mary Hobby; nine children.

(IV) Benjamin, son of Stephen Holmes, was living in Greenwich, May 18, 1721. He served in Captain Clark's company, Eleventh Regiment Connecticut Militia, and died soon after his second marriage. The name of his first wife is unknown; his second was Susanna Reynolds. By first wife he had sons: Israel and Reuben.

(V) Reuben, son of Benjamin Holmes and his first wife, was born in Greenwich, Connecticut, about 1732. He chose as his guardian, February 4, 1746, Nathaniel Mead, and in the proceedings at that time was called fourteen years of age and the minor son of Benjamin Holmes, of Greenwich, deceased. He married (second) (first wife unknown) in 1762, Ruth, daughter of John Wood, of Long Island; eight children.

(VI) Abel, son of Reuben Holmes, was born in Greenwich, Connecticut, 1760, died in Unadilla Center, Otsego county, New York, a farmer. He married (first) Esther ———, (second) Mary Canfield. All were members of the Universalist church. There were eight children by first wife, names not given, and ten by second wife, six of whom are given. Children: 1. John, of whom further. 2. Seeley, died in the west; married and left children: Joseph and Betsey. 3. Rizpah. 4. Amos, died in Unadilla, New York, a farmer; married and had issue: Esther, deceased; Fanny, married William Ballister (second wife); Mary, married William Ballister (first wife); John. 5. Charlotte, married Abel Palmer; both died in Unadilla; children: Esther, Mary, Abel, all deceased. 6. Ira, married twice, one of his wives being Phebe Richmond; he had three children by first wife and two by second, namely, Phebe and Kneeland.

(VII) John (2), son of Abel Holmes, was born in Welling, Tolland county, Connecticut, October 12, 1790, died August 2, 1865, at Smethport, which had been his residence since 1832. When nine years of age he was taken to Chenango county, New York, by his father, and there owing to the death of his mother was adopted by General Robert Morris, of Gilbertsville. When he took the lad General Morris promised him a public school education and that when he became of age would present him with a yoke of two year old oxen. These promises were faithfully kept. Shortly after becoming of legal age the second war with England broke out and the young man was drafted for military service. He was at Sackett's Harbor, and when the British and Indians burned Buffalo was stationed at Port Erie. After the war he became a tanner and currier, owning a tannery at Marvin's Creek. He was also a boot and shoe manufacturer. He prospered in business and became a man of prominence. He had as partner his brother Ira, and they erected a tannery at Latham's Corners in 1827. In 1846 he was appointed judge in McKean county to fill the place of Judge Nelson Richmond. He was a Democrat in politics, and a member of the Universalist church.

He married Nancy Richmond, born in Chenango county, New York, at Guilford Center, September 27, 1802, died in Coryville, October 14, 1887, cousin of the wife of Ira Holmes. She was a Methodist in early life, later an Episcopalian. Her father, Thomas Richmond, was born in Rhode Island, March 12, 1778, died in Smethport, July 2, 1864, a carpenter and farmer. He married Lucy Durand, born in Rhode Island, 1778, died at Latham's Bridge, May 12, 1854. Children of Thomas Richmond: 1. Nancy, of previous mention, wife of John Holmes. 2. Seth D., born at Latham's Bridge on the Unadilla road, died at Latham's Corners; married Maria Cornwell; children: Catherine, married Nelson Green; Orson; Henry, married Sarah Coon and had: Marion, Leroy, Minnie, Olin and another daughter. 3. Nelson, born at Latham's Bridge; married Melvina Chapin; was a business partner of John Holmes and died in Smethport; children: i. William Henry, married Nellie Milliken, of Smethport, child, Thomas; ii. Edwin, married Julia Bennett; children: Harry and Rena; iii. Frank, married Emerett Curtis; iv. George, died young; v. Mary, died young; vi. Emma, married Dr. Myron A. Sprague, deceased; children: Carlton and Rose. Children of John and Nancy Holmes: 1. Lucy, born at Latham's Corners, New York, 1822, died at Coryville, Pennsylvania, 1880; married Captain A. C. Cory, an officer of Company I, Fifty-eighth Regiment of Pennsylvania; he was a printer and published the first newspaper printed in Smethport; later a farmer; died in Corryville, 1892; children: i. Orson, born June 13, 1840, married Lucina Tuttle, child, John, born January, 1862; ii. Nancy, died in infancy; iii. Ella, born April 1, 1858, married Frank Holmes, a farmer of near Rochester, New York, children: John, Orra, Lucy, Leonard, Homer, deceased at age of twelve years. 2. Harriet, born January 7, 1825, at Latham's Corners; married Byron D. Hamlin, a prominent citizen of Smethport. 3. Ormond A., born July, 1827, at Latham's Corners, a merchant; married Mary A. Scull, both deceased; no issue. 4. Thomas, born 1828, died 1851, unmarried. 5. Maria, of whom further.

(VIII) Maria, youngest daughter of John (2) and Nancy (Richmond) Holmes, was born at Smethport, Pennsylvania, December 27, 1842. She was educated in the public schools, finishing at Smethport Academy, under Professor Forest A. Allen. She married (first) January 26, 1859, A. J. Nourse. Children: 1. Fred H., born in Smethport, February 5, 1861, now a farmer and contractor of East Smethport; married Cora, daughter of James H. Stull; children: Forest, Lavida and Louis. 2. Ormond Grant, born in Smethport, April 15, 1865, a saw mill builder now residing in Tomola, Mississippi; married (first) Mattie Simmons, of Smethport; child, Alcene born February 6, 1892; married (second) Hannah Conrad, of Grompion Hills, Clearfield county, Pennsylvania, child, Orrene, 1903. 3. Orson Delano, born in Smethport, November 15, 1871, a farmer near Smethport; married Phoebe Hyde; children: Gladys Marie, born May 30, 1901, and Paul, September 9, 1910. Maria Holmes married (second) Egbert P. Carter, born in Victor, Ontario county, New York, April 21, 1826, died in Smethport, April 18, 1904. He was the leading jeweler of Arcade, New York, for thirty-five years, moved to Smethport, October 16, 1882, continuing there in the same business until his death. He was a Democrat in politics and while living in Arcade was prominent in civic affairs. He married (first) Eliza Ann Brooks, who bore him Albert H., deceased, leaving a son Roy, now serving in the United States navy.

Mrs. Maria (Holmes) Carter is very prominent in fraternal circles. She is past worthy matron of Phoenix Chapter, No. 15, Order of the Eastern Star; past noble grand of Ideal Lodge, Daughters of Rebekah; lecturer in the Patrons of Husbandry, belonging to the McKean county, Pennsylvania, State and National Grange of that order, and is an honorary member of the Protected Home Circle. She is a writer and speaker of pleasing attainment and a local historian of note. Her history of "Early Days in McKean County," published in the *Bradford Independent* in 1911, was valuable historically and most entertaining. She was baptized in the Episcopal church.

JOHNSON Captain Edward Johnson was born in Canterbury, county Kent, England, son of William (1) Johnson. He came first to Charlestown, Massachusetts, with the first emigrants, returned to England and came again in 1636 or 1637 with wife and seven children. He was an influential man, active in the first church, and captain of the first military company at Woburn. He married Susan ———, and left issue.

(III) William (2), son of Captain Edward Johnson, was baptized at Canterbury, Kent, England, March 22, 1628, or 1629, and came with his parents to New England. He was a military officer of every rank from ensign to major, and prominent in public affairs. He married Esther Wiswall, and had issue.

(IV) William (3), son of William (2) Johnson, was born February 26, 1656. He married and left issue.

(V) Thomas, son of William (3) Johnson, was born about 1680. He married and had issue including a son, John.

(VI) John, son of Thomas Johnson, born about 1705, married and left issue including a son, Haynes.

(VII) Haynes, son of John Johnson, born about 1743, died in Concord, New Hampshire, September 2, 1775. He was one of the original grantees of the town of Newbury, Vermont. He married Elizabeth Elliot. Children: Jonathan, married Hannah Sawyer; Jesse, married Elizabeth Sawyer; Haynes (2), of whom further. Mrs. Elizabeth (Elliot) Johnson survived her husband, and married (second) Colonel Remembrance Chamberlain, born December 19, 1747, who served in several of the campaigns of the revolution and was colonel of militia. They were the parents of several sons and daughters.

(VIII) Captain Haynes (2) Johnson, son of Haynes (1) Johnson, was born in Newbury, Vermont, August 13, 1775. He moved to Bradford, 1798, where he followed agriculture until his death November 1, 1863. He was a Whig politically, and connected with the Bradford Congregational Church, as was his wife. He married, April 8, 1802, Jane Sawyer, died May 21, 1869, daughter of Captain Ezekiel Sawyer, born in Rowley, Massachusetts, May 9, 1743, died January 13, 1817. He settled in Bradford, Vermont, 1795, and married Mary Payson, who died July 6, 1819. They had three sons and seven daughters, and of the latter: Hannah married Jonathan, Elizabeth married Jesse, and Jane married Haynes (2) Johnson, the three brothers mentioned above. Children of Captain Haynes (2) Johnson: 1. Ezekiel, of whom further. 2. Mary, born September 26, 1803, twin of Ezekiel, died in Charlestown, Massachusetts, February 7, 1844; married, September 2, 1830, William Peters, born December 14, 1803, who married (second) her sister Hannah. Children: i. William Francis, born 1836, died 1908, a veteran of the civil war, serving four years in a Vermont regiment; married Mary Burt, who survives him residing in Denver, Colorado. ii. Charles Edward, born 1837, died 1902; married Lucinda E. Ho'gdon, of Piedmont, New Hampshire, and had: a. Charles Henry, a real estate agent of Denver, Colorado; b. Lily May, a widow since 1905, now residing in Burlington, Vermont. iii. Mary Jane, widow of Thomas H. Moore, also resides in Denver. 3. Eliza, born February 18, 1808; married, April 26, 1835, Earl Paine, of Washington, Vermont. Children: i. Haynes J., now a farmer of Vermont. ii. Helen E., died in Washington, Vermont, 1886; married, June 6, 1868, Daniel Grant, died 1874; children: a. Anna Evadne, now of Buffalo, New York; b. Aliza Emma, deceased. 4. Haynes C., born April 4, 1811, died 1882; married, February 9, 1843, Harriet, born December 26, 1816, daughter of Captain Israel Willard, of Bradford, Vermont. Children: i. Walter Haynes, born July 15, 1847; married (first) Lizzie Whitcomb, child: a. Mabel Lizzie, born September 7, 1872; married (second) ——— Norton, child: b. Walter. ii. Arthur Franklin, born December 16, 1849; married ——— Carlton; children: Haynes, a daughter, Carlton and Thomas. 5. Hannah, born October 10, 1813; married William Peters, whose first wife was her sister Mary. Children: i. Henry, now of Boston, Massachusetts. ii. Nellie, deceased at the age of eighteen years. 6. Thomas, born December 13, 1816; married Harriet Avery, both now deceased. Children: i. Frank, now a lawyer of New York City. ii. Charles, now a furniture dealer in New York. iii. Herbert T., now a railway mail clerk of Bradford, Vermont. 7. Jane Ann, born February 22, 1819; married Dan W. Shaw, born March 12, 1816, a manufacturer of furniture of North Cambridge, Massachusetts. Children: i. Ella J., born July 19, 1846, died 1902. ii. Emma L., born November 29, 1848, died January 22, 1854. iii. Susie E., born November 30, 1854, died 1905; married, June 4, 1874, George A. Keeler, a hotel proprietor of Boston. iv. Adna B., born December 8, 1858, now a prominent business man of Cambridge, Massachusetts. v. Edward L., born January 24, 1860, in business with his brother Adna. 8. Clarissa P., born July 18, 1825; married, November 10, 1858, John Richardson, of Orford, New Hampshire. Children: i. Clara Alice, died 1897, married ——— Batchelder. ii. John Fred, deceased. iii. Arthur Johnson. iv. William Martin. v. Emma Louise, married Mr. Batchelder, whose first wife was her deceased sister Clara Alice. 9. Edmund Elliot, born November 27, 1827; married (first) Mary Smith, child: i. Elizabeth, now living in Penn Yan, New York. He married (second) Elmira ———, child: ii. Louise, married Charles Brook, advertising agent for the Southern Railroad, now living in Washington, D. C. 10. A daughter, died in childhood.

(IX) Ezekiel, son of Captain Haynes (2) Johnson, was born September 26, 1803, died in Bradford, October 9, 1880. He was reared and educated in Bradford, Vermont, and was a farmer all his days, a Republican and an official member of the Methodist Episcopal church. He married, February 27, 1827, Nancy Corliss Rogers, born in Newbury, Vermont, December 12, 1807, died September 11, 1850 (see Rogers). Children: 1. Mary Elizabeth, born January 19, 1828, at Bath, New Hampshire; married, at St. Albans, Vermont, December 25, 1849, Hon. Roswell Farnham, born in Boston, Massachusetts, July 28, 1827, an attorney from Bradford, Vermont. He served in the civil war in the First and Twelfth Vermont Regiments, being lieutenant colonel of the latter. In 1868 and 1869 he was state senator, and in 1880 was elected governor of the state of Vermont for two years. Children: i. Charles Cyrus, born May 9, 1864. ii. Florence Mary, October 30, 1866. iii. William Mills, July 5, 1869. 2. Ruth Ann, born January 26, 1830, died December 15, 1897; married, April 11, 1850, Benjamin B. Chadwick, a lumberman of Bradford, who died 1903, no issue. 3. Jane, born January 14, 1832, died February 19, 1834. 4. Nancy Jennie, born April 19, 1835; married, March 27, 1856, John H. Ruckel, of Buffalo, New York, their present home. Children: i. Mary E., born 1859, died January, 1870. ii. Herbert, born 1863, died 1870. iii. Adelaine M., born 1867, died 1907. iv. John B., born in Buffalo, 1868, where he is in business as coppersmith and steam fitter, married, but has no children. v. Louise Johnson, born 1872. vi. Ella Shaw, born October 31, 1875. vii. Ruth, born 1877; the three last now reside in Buffalo. 5. Harriet, born December 19, 1836, died July 7, 1891; married, June 6, 1867, Mortimer Bradley, who died in 1882. Children: i. Jennie Louisa, born June 12, 1868, resides in Kane, Pennsylvania, married ——— De Golia; son: Albert Johnson De Golia. ii. Henry Hobart, born April 17, 1870, now a physician on board the English steamer "Verdi" plying between New York and South America; married Nina Tracy, of Buffalo, New York. 6. Ezekiel Thomas, of whom further. 7. William Henry, born at Bradford, Vermont, March 7, 1843; married (first) Virginia, daughter of Dr. W. H. Hartley, of New York City, child: i. Ann Evadne, born in 1867, married Benjamin L. Love, of Buffalo. He married (second) Mary Adelia Lord, who died at Buffalo, July 27, 1874, leaving an infant son: ii. Harrison Foster. He married (third) Mary Hill, of Buffalo, New York; children: iii. Roswell Hill, born 1877. iv. Grace Louise, born 1887. v. Paul Rogers, born 1890.

(X) Lieut. Ezekiel Thomas Johnson, son of Ezekiel Johnson, was born in Orange county, Vermont, May 19, 1839. He was educated in the public schools of Bradford, Vermont, and while still a minor entered the offices of the *Windsor* (Vermont) *Journal*, where he thoroughly mastered the printer's art as then practiced. He continued working there at the printer's trade until the outbreak of the civil war, except a year and a half spent in Boston. He enlisted as a private August 6, 1862, in Company H, Tenth Regiment Vermont Volunteer Infantry, soon afterward being promoted to be corporal. On December 28, 1862, he was promoted to be sergeant; March 4, 1864, to be first sergeant; and December 19, 1864, commissioned second lieutenant of Company E, but for some reason was not mustered. On March 22, 1865, he was commissioned first lieutenant, Company G, and transferred to Company E, Tenth Vermont. He was a good soldier and saw hard service, the Tenth bearing the brunt of battle in several hard fought battles, and he was highly rated for bravery and efficiency. Out of one hundred and one men who enlisted with Lieutenant Johnson, but thirty-five returned to their homes. The Tenth Vermont, with the Fourteenth New Jersey, the One Hundred and Sixth and One Hundred and Fifty-first New York, and the Eighty-seventh Pennsylvania, formed the First Brigade of the Third Division, Sixth Army Corps of the Army of the Potomac. Lieutenant Johnson was engaged with his regiment in the following engagements with the enemy: Kelley's Ford, November 7; Orange Grove, November 27; Mine Run, November 30, the Wilderness, May 5 to 8; Spottsylvania, May 10 to 17; North Anna River, May 23 to 26; Hanover Court House, May 30; Totopatomy Creek, May 31; Cold Harbor, June 1; Cold Harbor, June 3, and 6 to 12; Bermuda Hundred, June 17; Weldon Railroad, June 22 and 23; Monocacy, July 9, 1864; Petersburg, March 25; Petersburg, April 2; Deatonsville Road, April 6; Sailors Creek, April 6; Appomattox Court House, April 9, 1865. At the battle of Monocacy Junction, Maryland, July 9, 1864, he was in charge of the skirmish line on the north bank of the river, under command of Captain George E. Davis, and performing the duties of second lieutenant, a rank for which he had already been named. Here he was severely wounded by a minie ball, which struck the top of his head, cutting through the scalp and scraping the bone, inflicting an ugly wound. He was in the hospital several months, but finally was so far recovered as to rejoin his regiment, yet in the Shenandoah Valley, Virginia, in December, 1864. He did a soldier's duty and was spared to see the final surrender at Appomattox and to march in the grand parade of the victorious army down Pennsylvania avenue in the city of Washington. He was mustered out June 22, 1865, and settled in Buffalo, New York. Later he came to Bradford, Pennsylvania, where he is heavily and successfully engaged in the oil business, as president of the Test Oil Company, and in other companies. He is a Republican in politics, and a member of the Methodist Episcopal church, of which he has been treasurer for many years. He is a member of the Union Veteran Legion and maintains a lively interest in all that concerns his old army comrades.

He married, January 31, 1867, Sophia Louisa, daughter of Colonel Jeffrey Amherst Bayley (see Bayley VII). Two children, died in infancy.

(The Rogers Line).

Nancy Corliss (Rogers) Johnson, mother of Lieutenant Ezekiel Thomas Johnson, claimed descent from Rev. Thomas Rogers, "the martyr," some of whose children settled in Wales, where a century later Stephen Rogers was born. He came to America, settled in Newburyport, Massachusetts, and later in Hampton, New Hampshire. A descendant of his, bearing the same name, married Mary Nichols, from England, whose forbear was high sheriff of Massachusetts colony. This Stephen Rogers died when a young man, leaving a son and daughter, the latter marrying a Morrill.

(I) Lieutenant Josiah Rogers, born about 1747, a descendant of Stephen, was one of the pioneers of the town of Newbury, Vermont. He married Hannah Woodman, of Hampton, whose sister married Deacon William Carter. They were descendants of Hilton Woodman, who came to America in 1635. Josiah Rogers came to Newbury, Vermont, probably about 1784, but the first recorded mention of him is in 1785. He settled on what was later known as "Rogers' Hill," where with the aid of his sons he cleared and cultivated a fine farm. His mother came to Newbury with him, and despite her dread of the wild surroundings lived to the unusual age of ninety-nine years and eight months, dying in 1816, having survived her husband, who died young, eighty years. Josiah Rogers died in 1816, aged eighty-one years. On his tombstone in the old burial ground on Rogers' Hill he is styled "Lieutenant Josiah Rogers." Children of Lieutenant Josiah Rogers: 1. Stephen, born February 5, 1771, lived in Topsham, died in Newbury, Vermont, October 7, 1857; married a Miss Carter. 2. Moses, a tanner and currier, moved to Kingston, Ontario, Canada, where he married a daughter of Colonel O'Neil, of the British army; both died young. 3. Samuel, of whom further. 4. Levi, born October 12, 1776, died September 22, 1839. 5. Lydia, married John True, a plowmaker, and died at North Haverhill, New Hampshire. 6. Hannah, married Oliver Barrett (2), and died at Zanesville, Ohio, in 1858. 7. Mary, married James Smith. 8. Ruth, died at the great age of ninety-eight years; married (first) Mr. Ferrin, a school master; (second) Peter Powers. 9. Josiah (2). 10. Nancy, married (first) Bliss Corliss, of Corinth; (second) Mr. Eastman. 11. Robert, married, March 19, 1812, Mary, daughter of John Johnson, and settled in the south.

(II) Samuel, son of Lieutenant Josiah and Hannah (Woodman) Rogers, was born in Hampton, New Hampshire, February 5, 1773, died in Newbury, Vermont, September 8, 1857. He inherited a part at least of the old homestead on Rogers' Hill, where for a time he kept a tavern and was active in town affairs, being a strong Whig. He married, in 1799, Ruth Stevens, died January 10, 1864, daughter of Daniel Stevens, of Haverhill, New Hampshire. Children: 1. Josiah W., died February 17, 1846. 2. George, died in Boston, Massachusetts, married Eliza Blake. 3. Harriet, married John Bayley, and died in Buffalo, New York, in 1901, aged ninety-eight years. 4. Samuel Frank, lived at West Topsham, married Augusta Sawyer. 5. Nancy Corliss, married Ezekiel Johnson (see Johnson IX). 6. Oliver B., married Polly Ann Carleton. 7. Horace G., married Lucy Clapp, and lived in Milton, Massachusetts. 8. Lucia, died 1843, married Michael Carleton, of Haverhill. 9. Azro B., born March 28, 1823.

(The Bayley Line (also Bailey)).

Sophia Louisa (Bayley) Johnson descends from John Bayley, a weaver of Chippenham, England, and his wife Eleanor Wright. The two Johns, father and son, sailed for America in the ship "Angel Gabriel," from Bristol, England, June 4, 1635, leaving the wife and mother in England, where she died, never venturing across the seas to join her husband. He never dared again to trust himself to the fury of the Atlantic, the "Angel Gabriel" having been wrecked on Pemaquid Island in the great storm of August 14 to 18, 1635. John Bayley (1), after spending two years in Newbury, Massachusetts, moved to what is now Salisbury, where he is said to have been the first settler. He died there November, 1651. He left issue: John (2), of whom further; Joanna, married William Huntington; Robert, remained in England with his mother and one or more sisters.

(II) John (2), son of John (1) Bayley, and fellow emigrant to America in 1635, was born in Chippenham, England, 1613, died in Newbury, Massachusetts, 1691. He settled at Newbury, 1650. He married Eleanor Emery. Children: Rebecca, married Isaac Brown; John (3), died aged twenty years; Sarah, married Daniel Cheney; Joshua, died young; Joseph, married Prescilla Putnam; Rev. James, graduate of Harvard, minister and physician; Joshua, died aged eleven years; Isaac, of whom further; Joshua, married Elizabeth Putnam; Rachel, married Samuel Poor (2); Judith, died young.

(III) Isaac, son of John (2) Bayley, was born in Newbury, Massachusetts, July 22, 1654, died April 26, 1740. He married (first) January 13, 1683, Sarah, died April 1, 1694, daughter of John Emory. He married (second) September 5, 1700, Rebecca Bartlett. Children, all by first wife: Isaac, married Sara Tilcomb, who survived him and married (second) Richard Bartlett; Joshua, of whom further; David, married Experience Putnam; Judith, married James Ordway; Sarah, married (first) Benjamin Chase, (second) Richard Carr, as his second wife.

(IV) Joshua, son of Isaac Bayley, was born October 30, 1685, died October 6, 1760, a farmer of Newbury, Massachusetts. He married Sarah, died November 27, 1768, daughter of Stephen and Sarah (Atkinson) Coffin. Children: 1. Stephen, born March 1, 1708, died July 2, 1707, married Hannah Kelley. 2. Joshua, born 1712, died September 29, 1786, married Elizabeth Morse. 3. Abner, born January 15, 1715, died March 10, 1708, married Mary Baldwin. 4. Enoch, born September 10, 1719, died 1757. 5. Sarah, born February 15, 1721, married Edward Taplam. 6. Judith, born February 13, 1724, married Stephen Little. 7. Abigail, twin of Judith, died February 6, 1815, married Colonel Moses Tuttle. 8. Jacob, of whom further. 9. John, born May 4, 1729, died July 13, 1819.

(V) General Jacob Bayley, son of Joshua Bayley, was born in Newbury, Massachusetts, July 1, 1726, died at Newbury, Vermont, March 1, 1816. He settled in Hampstead, New Hampshire, where he raised a company, of which he was captain at the commencement of the French and Indian war in 1756. He was at the capture of Fort William Henry, but escaped massacre and safely reached Fort Edward. He was made colonel by General Amherst, and accompanied him at the taking of Crown Point and Ticonderoga in 1759. In 1763 he obtained a charter for a township of land in Vermont, where he moved 1764. He was there appointed brigadier general by the state of New York; and by General Washington commissary general of the northern department, a position involving great responsibilities and subjecting him to great danger. A reward of five hundred guineas was offered for him dead or alive by the British, and it required constant vigilance to escape the scouts and enemies sent against him. He made a treaty with the St. Francis tribe of Indians, and was held in great respect by them and by the other friendly Indians. By means of these friends and spies he acquired important intelligence concerning the movements of the British, and rendered great service to his country with purse, pen and sword. He was a factor in the movements that finally penned in Burgoyne, and compelled him to battle at Saratoga and finally to surrender to the victorious Americans. Several of his sons also served with him against the English. He held important public offices, besides military. He was delegate to the continental congress of 1777, member of the constitutional convention that drafted a constitution for Vermont in 1777, member of the first council in 1778, member of constitutional convention 1793, judge of probate for Newbury district 1778, and judge of Orange county, Vermont, from 1781 to 1791, excepting the years 1783 and 1784. He has been most justly called the "Father of Newbury," as he was not only an original grantee but a prime factor in its development. He married, October 16, 1745, Prudence, born April 10, 1725, daughter of Ephraim and Prudence (Stickney) Noyes. Children: 1. Ephraim, born October 5, 1746, died July 7, 1825, a revolutionary soldier. 2. Abigail, born January 16, 1749, died young. 3. Noyes, February 16, 1751, died young. 4. Joshua, June 11, 1753, died July 3, 1841, a revolutionary officer. 5. Captain Jacob, October 2, 1755, died June 28, 1837, a revolutionary officer. 6. James, October 1, 1757, died April 19, 1784, a revolutionary soldier, taken prisoner by a party sent to capture his father, carried to Canada and kept until the close of the war. 7. Amherst, January 16, 1760, died January 6, 1783. 8. Abner, December 10, 1763, died 1783. 9. John, of whom further. 10. Isaac, June 28, 1767, died August 30, 1850.

(VI) Colonel John Bayley, son of General Jacob Bayley, was born at Newbury, Vermont, May 20, 1765, died July 26, 1839. He married Betsey Bailey, died 1788. Child: 1. Prudence, born April 28, 1786. He married (second) November 19, 1789, Hannah, born at Haverhill, May 13, 1772, daughter of Ezekiel and Ruth (Hutchins) Ladd. Children: 2. Betsey, born October 30, 1790; married Dr. Samuel Putnam. 3. George, born June 15, 1792. 4. Jeffrey Amherst, of whom further. 5. Hannah, born June 10, 1796; married Dr. John Stevens. 6. Lucia, born June 8, 1798, died August 28, 1864; married Tappan Stevens. 7. Adaline, born April 25, 1800, died April 20, 1803. 8. John H., born February 25, 1802; married February 27, 1823, Harriet, daughter of Samuel Rogers. 9. Adaline (2), born July 10, 1804; married December 11, 1828, Moses Rogers. 10. Jane, born October 15, 1806; married Arnold Johnson. 11. Mary, born December 24, 1808.

(VII) Col. Jeffrey Amherst Bayley, son of Colonel John Bayley, was born in Newbury, Vermont, February 21, 1794, died October 12, 1858. He was first a wheelwright. He served in the war of 1812, and was colonel of militia. He married December 2, 1819, Melissa, born

October, 1798, died at Evanston, Illinois, September 9, 1885, and is buried in Newbury. She was the daughter of Colonel Simon Stevens. Children: 1. Hannah Stevens, September 6, 1820; married, October 26, 1842, John Alonzo, born September 8, 1818, son of John and Hannah (Putnam) Pearson. Children: i. Henry Alonzo, born August 14, 1843, enlisted in the Eighth Illinois Cavalry, served 1861 to 1865, attaining the rank of lieutenant; married, January 3, 1867, Catherine J. West; child: Henry Putnam, born January 15, 1873. ii. Lucy Isabella, born March 9, 1848; married Rev. Arthur F. Tappan; children: Alice and Lillian. iii. Charles Edward, born May 6, 1862, died October 15, 1862. iv. Helen M., born December 4, 1865, died March 27, 1893; married, July 8, 1860. Rev. Harry P. Calkins. 2. Betsey, December 2, 1822, died December 11, 1822. 3. Marian Wallace, born October 12, 1824; married, January 2, 1843, Rev. Zadoc Seymour Haynes, born May 15, 1816, a minister of the Methodist Episcopal church until death. Children: i. Emory J., born February 6, 1846; married (first) May 6, 1869, Jennie Crowell, died April 26, 1873; married (second) Grace Farley. ii. Carlos J., born June, 1849. iii. Albert, March 9, 1855. iv. Harriet, April, 1857. 4. Sarah, born March 25, 1826; married, December 13, 1848, Daniel Wooster Stevens. 5. Melissa, born April 4, 1828, died October 16, 1887; married, July 22, 1850, Rev. Joseph Elijah King. 6. William Little Stevens, born March 5, 1830; married (first) August 15, 1854, Maria Louisa, daughter of David Goodall; married (second) Ellen Hewes. 7. Harriet Amelia, born July 3, 1833, died October 14, 1898; married, November, 1868, George Shuttleworth. 8. Ellen Augusta, born August 22, 1836; married, October 15, 1857, George Batchelder. 9. Charles Francis, born September 12, 1839, a veteran of the civil war, died unmarried September 19, 1874. 10. Sophia Louisa, born in Newbury, Vermont, October 14, 1843, died May 17, 1870; married Lieutenant Ezekiel Thomas Johnson (see Johnson X).

GILLETT Gillett is the surname from Guillot, the French diminutive for William. It is found spelled Gillett, Gillette, Gillott and Goelet. The ancestors of the branch herein recorded descend from French-ancestors, the first of whom we have record being Montague Gillett, who came to the United States from France, settling in New England.

(II) Jonathan, son of Montague Gillett, settled in Vermont, married and had issue, including a son Martin Luther, of whom further.

(III) Martin Luther, son of Jonathan Gillett, born in Vermont about 1819, died in Bath, New York, January 27, 1896. He was a farmer by occupation in Vermont and Steuben county, New York, where he settled when a young man. He was a Republican, and a member of the Baptist church which he served as deacon many years. He married Catherine Elizabeth Thompson, born in Rensselaer county, New York, died in Bath, November 12, 1910, a Methodist and an active church worker. Children, all born in Steuben county, New York: 1. James Selah, of whom further. 2. Frances E., died in Bath; married Norman H. Daniels, now a merchant of Bath; children: Lewis M., deceased, and Katherine, married John Wellington, a publisher, and lives in Rochester, New York. 3. Mellville H., a merchant of Bath; married Frances Daniels; child, Elizabeth, married Adrian Thurston, also of Bath.

(IV) Dr. James Selah Gillett, eldest son of Martin Luther Gillett, was born in Bath, New York, April 30, 1843. He received his early and preparatory education in the public schools, later entering Cornell University. Deciding upon the profession of medicine he entered Albany Medical College, Albany, New York, whence he was graduated M. D. He practiced for a time in Olean, New York, then moved west, practicing in the states of Iowa, California and Missouri. At the time of his death he was living at Rich Hill, Missouri, assistant surgeon for the Missouri-Pacific and of the Kansas City, Fort Scott & Memphis railroads. He enlisted as sergeant of Company F, One Hundred and Sixty-first Regiment New York Volunteers, but was detailed as assistant surgeon and so served during three years of the civil war. He was a member of the Masonic order, belonging to Lodge, Chapter and Commandery. In religious faith both he and his wife were members of the Episcopal church. He was a skillful physician and surgeon and a man of high mental attainment.

He married Frances Katherine Ayres, born in Henrico county, Virginia, October 24, 1844, died in Newark, Ohio, November 11, 1907, daughter of William Francis Ayres, son of

Francis Henry Ayres, of Virginia. William Francis Ayres was born in Henrico county, Virginia, about 1800, died in Des Moines, Iowa, 1870. He was a surveyor, a landowner and delighted in raising fine horses. He was at one time sheriff of the county in Virginia in which the city of Richmond is located. He married Katherine Delilah Kirkbride, born in Pennsylvania, 1814, died in Rich Hill, Missouri, 1901. He was an Episcopalian in religious faith, she a Carmelite. Children of William Francis Ayres: 1. Giovanni B., an engineer, now residing in Des Moines, Iowa; married Elizabeth Hatter, born in Ohio; children: Lillian, Jessica and another daughter, all living in Des Moines. 2. David K., a ranchman at Mountain View, Santa Clara county, California; has wife Rosa and children: Rosa and Chadbourne. 3. Eleanor, died in Girard, Kansas; married Edwin Howard Brown, of Bangor, Maine, a wealthy coal operator and railroad official, also deceased; children: Frank, Edwin, Frederick H., Lulu, Grace. 4. Henry, a civil engineer of Nevada, Iowa; married and had children; Gertrude and Harley. 5. Frances Katherine, of previous mention, wife of Dr. James Selah Gillett.

(V) Mellville, only child of Dr. James Selah and Frances Katherine (Ayres) Gillett, was born in Iowa Center, Iowa, June 30, 1872. When he was two years of age his parents moved to Oakland, California, and later to Carthage, Missouri, where he attended school. In 1880 the family moved to Rich Hill, Missouri, and while living there he entered the University of the South at Sewanee, Tennessee. He later took a course at Westbrook Academy at Olean, New York, there finishing his education. During these years he had gained considerable experience in civil engineering, but deciding upon a legal career he entered Georgetown University, Washington, D. C., remaining for one year. On leaving the University he entered the service of the government with the geological survey, resigning in 1898 for service in the Spanish-American war by telegraph from his station in the field. He enlisted in Company I, Third Regiment New York Volunteers, as sergeant at Olean, New York, but on July 6, 1898, was detailed for topographic duty on the staff of the Chief Engineer of the Second Army Corps, serving until September, 1898, when he was honorably discharged.

In November, 1898, he located his home and business in Newark, Ohio, and became prominently identified with the natural gas and electrical development of that city as well as prominent in public affairs. In 1909 he selected Smethport as his permanent residence, but retains interests in Newark, Ohio, retaining official connection in but two of the many companies in which he is interested, being president of the Goften Manufacturing Company and vice-president of Burke-Golf Shaft Company, both Newark companies. He was secretary, treasurer and general manager of the Newark Natural Gas and Fuel Company, president of the Newark Gas Light and Coke Company, president for six years of the Licking Light and Power Company, and for three years vice-president of the Augusta (Georgia) Gas Light Company. He was also a prominent figure in Ohio state politics. From 1900 to 1904 he served upon the staff of Governor George K. Nash, as aide-de-camp with the rank of colonel, and in 1900 was the Republican candidate for congress from the Newark district. In 1903 he was candidate before the Republican State convention for the nomination of state auditor and in 1908 for state treasurer. Among five candidates for the latter office he received the second highest number of votes in the convention. He was one of the influential leaders of his party and rendered efficient service during his entire residence in Ohio.

He is a member of the Masonic order, belonging to Lodge, Chapter and Commandery at Olean, New York; Council of Royal and Select Masters at Newark, Ohio, and Nobles of the Mystic Shrine at Columbus, Ohio. He also is a thirty-second degree Mason of the Ancient Accepted Scottish Rite, belonging to Scioto Consistory, of Columbus, also to the Fraternal Order of Eagles, of Newark, and Benevolent and Protective Order of Elks. His clubs are the Central of Smethport; Columbus of Columbus, Ohio; Union League of Chicago, Illinois; Ohio of Columbus; Metropolitan and Chevy Chase of Washington, D. C. In religious faith Mr. Gillett is an Episcopalian, belonging to St. Luke's Church of Smethport.

He married, October 24, 1898, at Smethport, Harriet Forbes Redfield, born in Smethport, August 4, 1874. Children, all born in Smethport: Bernice, February 12, 1901, died February 5, 1903; Redfield Byron, born May 1, 1904; Phylis Katharine, April 13, 1911.

SANBORN-KREINER All the Sanborns in America are descended from two of the three brothers who came to New England in 1632 with their grandfather, Rev. Stephen Bachiler, and were sons of John Sanborne, who about 1609 married Anne Bachiler. For the first hundred years in America the name was written "Samborne" or "Sanborn." How or where the present spelling "Sanborn" was introduced, is not known. Of the three Sanborne brothers, John (2), William and Stephen, the first two only left male issue. The Sanborns of this record descend from John (2) Sanborne, son of John (1) and Anne Bachiler. For convenience the name will be written Sanborn.

(I) John (1) Sanborn was born about 1600, married Anne Bachiler, and lived and died in Derbyshire, England. There is doubt as to whether his widow ever came to America. Sons: John (2), of whom further; William, and Stephen.

(II) John (2), son of John (1) Sanborn, was born about 1620. With his brothers and grandfather Bachiler (who later returned to England, where he died aged one hundred years) he came to New England in 1632, landing at Boston, later living in Lynn, Newbury, and in 1638 at Hampton, New Hampshire. John (2) was a lieutenant, and many years a selectman and representative to the general court from Hampton, ensign in King Philip's war and otherwise prominent. He married (first) Mary, daughter of Robert Tuck, of Hampton, (second) August 2, 1671, Margaret (Page) Moulton, a widow, daughter of Robert Page. Children by first wife: 1. John, born 1649, died 1723; married Judith Coffin. 2. Mary, born 1651, died 1654. 3. Abigail, born February 23, 1653, died 1743; married Ephraim Marston. 4. Richard, of whom further. 5. Mary, born 1657, died 1660. 6. Joseph, born March 13, 1659; married Mary Grove. 7. Stephen, born 1661, died 1662. 8. Ann, born 1662, died 1745; married ———. 9. Dinah (no record). 10. Nathaniel, born January 27, 1666, died 1723; married (first) Rebecca Prescott, (second) Sarah Nason. 11. Benjamin, born December 20, 1668; married (first) Sarah ———, (second) Meribah Tilton, (third) Abigail Dalton. Child by second wife: 12. Jonathan, born May 25, 1672, died 1741; married Elizabeth Sherburne.

(III) Richard, second son of Lieutenant John (2) Sanborn, was born in Hampton, New Hampshire, 1655. He married (first), December 5, 1678, Ruth Moulton, (second), 1693, Mrs. Mary (Drake) Boulter, a widow. Children: Mary, born September 30, 1679; John, of whom further; Shuabel, died May 3, 1759, married Mary Drake.

(IV) Ensign John (3), son of Richard Sanborn, was born November 6, 1681, died September 3, 1727. He lived in North Hampton, New Hampshire, and perhaps in Exeter. He married Sarah, daughter of James Philbreck. Children: 1. Daniel, of whom further. 2. Benjamin, born November 8, 1703; married Elizabeth Gilman. 3. Phebe, born February 6, 1706; married Nathaniel Pease. 4. Richard, born May 27, 1708; married Elizabeth Batchelder. 5. Nathan, twin of Richard; married Elizabeth Pearson. 6. Elisha, born April 1, 1710; married Lydia ———. 7. Ebenezer, born March 4, 1712; married Ruth Sanborn; he died April 9, 1794. 8. Abigail, October 24, 1717. 9. Sarah, born March 18, 1719. 10. Ruth, born March 18, 1719. 11. John, born May 5, 1721. 12. Hannah, born February 3, 1723; married Stephen Dudley. 13. James, born April 5, 1724. 14. Mary, born March 1, 1726.

It is said all of these children married and brought up families; that at the time of their mother's death in 1761, the whole number of descendants was two hundred and thirty-nine, of whom one hundred and eighty-two were then living.

(V) Deacon Daniel, eldest son of Ensign John (3) Sanborn, was born in North Hampton, New Hampshire, February 17, 1702, died in Sanbornton, New Hampshire, February, 1798. He was fifth on the list of petitioners for the establishment of the town of Sanbornton in 1748. There were twelve Sanborns who signed this petition, the town being named in their honor. Daniel was a leading man of the new town, held public office and was a deacon of the church. He married, January 14, 1725, Catherine Rollins. Children: 1. Phebe, born December 13, 1725, died 1707; married Reuben Gove. 2. Anne, born February 21, 1727; married a Mr. Thomas. 3. Catherine, born June 1, 1728; married a Mr. Foss. 4. Daniel, born May 17, 1731, was one of the grantees of Sanbornton. 5. Sarah, born November 2, 1733, died in childhood. 6. Rachel, born April 25, 1736; married Gideon Piper. 7. Thomas, born May 17, 1738; married Anna Marston. 8.

Moses, born June 8, 1740. 9. Sarah (2), born February 24, 1745; married a Mr. Jewell. 10. Captain Aaron, born February 8, 1746; married (first) Molly Barter, (second) Susanna Gale. He served in the revolution. 11. Abijah, of whom further.

(VI) Abijah, youngest son of Deacon Daniel Sanborn, was born, March 4, 1748, died in Sanbornton, New Hampshire, March, 1790. He was an early member of the Congregational church, joining by letter, January 2, 1772, and with his two brothers being among the original members a few weeks previously. He was a farmer all his life. He married, August 17, 1768, a relative, Mary Sanborn, who was a woman of great bravery, known locally as the "heroine of the bears." Children: 1. Sarah, born October 9, 1769; married Josiah Critchett and moved to Ohio. 2. Enoch, born February 24, 1773; married Miss Boyington and moved to Vermont. 3. Thomas, of whom further. 4. Molly (Mary), born February 23, 1780; married a Mr. Ellsworth.

(VII) Thomas, second son of Abijah Sanborn, was born in Sanbornton, New Hampshire, August 2, 1777. He married Mehitable Gilman, and after a residence in Vermont located in New York state, where he died at Allen, Allegany county, in 1853. Children: 1. Bijer (or Abijah), of whom further. 2. Edward, died in the west, a farmer; married Betsey Ingham; children: Lawrence, Celeste and Bijer, all living in Michigan. 3. Gilman, died in Illinois, a farmer; married and had issue. 4. Justice, died in Michigan, a farmer; married Temperance Ingham; no issue. 5. Enoch, died in Michigan, a farmer; married Fanny Ingham; children: Mehitable and another daughter, all living in Michigan. 6. Lodema, died in Warsaw, New York; married Orrin Marchant, a farmer; no issue. 7. Mary, died in Granger, New York; married Ruel Comstock and had issue.

(VIII) Bijer (Abijah), son of Thomas Sanborn, was born in Vermont, 1800, died in Allegany county, New York, in 1882. He settled in New York state when a young man, and spent the greater part of his life engaged in farming in Cayuga and Allegany counties. He was a Democrat in politics, always interested in public affairs, but not an office seeker. He married Hannah Parsel, born in Cayuga county, New York, in 1800, of German parentage, died in Allegany county, 1845. Both were members of the Baptist church. Children, first four born in Cayuga county: 1. Thomas, born 1818, died 1888, a farmer; he married Hannah Oakes, of Allen, New York; child: Llewellyn, now living in Belmont, New York. 2. Delilah, born 1820, died in Allen, New York; married Joseph Wilson, a farmer, deceased; no issue. 3. Rosanna, born 1822, died in Cuba, New York; married Amassa Wilson, a merchant, deceased; children: Darrow, living in Buffalo, New York; Florence, living in California; Mina and William, living in Cuba, New York. 4. Polly, born 1824, died in Venango county, Pennsylvania; married James Hooker, a farmer, deceased; children: Julia, living in Buffalo, New York; and Deborah, deceased. 5. Elias, born in Allegany county, New York, 1826, died in Binghamton, New York, in 1907, a farmer; married Ellen Chase, deceased; children: Coello, living in Binghamton; Frank, living in Buffalo; Vienna, living in Angelica, New York; Emma, deceased; Florence, living in Binghamton. 6. Squire S. A., born in Cayuga county, September 15, 1828, now residing in Bradford, Pennsylvania. He married Jane Wood, born in Batavia, New York, June 13, 1827, died in Bradford, September 13, 1907. Children: i. Nettie, born in Erie county, New York; died aged twenty-two months. ii. Frank, born in Wyoming county, New York, in 1853, died in 1855. iii. William, born March 10, 1855, died in North East, Pennsylvania, September, 1908, a journalist; married Mary E. Kingsley, of Venango county, Pennsylvania; children: Perry Alvord, born in 1876, and George, born in 1878. iv. Fred, born in Angelica, New York, May 10, 1863, now living in Bradford, a painter and decorator; married Florence Little; children: Alfred W., born April 28, 1887, and Lee Squire, born December 6, 1890. 7. Wallace, born in Allen, Allegany county, New York, 1830, now living retired on his farm at Howell, New York; married a Miss Kelly; no issue. 8. Washington, twin of Wallace, died in infancy. 9. Marks B., of whom further.

(IX) Marks B., youngest son and child of Bijer and Hannah (Parsel) Sanborn, was born in Allegany county, New York, near Belvidere, May 14, 1833. He was educated in the public schools and spent his early life in his native town. He learned the blacksmith's trade at which he worked all his active years, both in New York, Michigan and Pennsylvania. He now resides at East Bradford, Pennsylvania. He is a Republican in politics, and an attendant of the Methodist Episcopal church, of which his wife is a member. He married (first) Jennie Pettis, born in 1840, died in Sweden, April 2, 1874. He married (second) in Hudson, Maria Van Epps, born in Hudson in 1847, died in East Bradford, March, 1896, daughter of Peter Van Epps, who lived and died in Hudson. Children of Marks B. Sanborn and his first wife: 1. Alfred, died in infancy. 2. Minnie, of whom further. 3. William, born in Hudson, Michigan, March 26, 1869, now superintendent of the Tide Water Pipe Company at Bradford; married in Mount Jewett, Pennsylvania, Lina Campbell, born in Canada; child: Shirley, born in Mount Jewett, March 23, 1893. Children of Marks B. Sanborn and his second wife: 4. Grace, born in Hudson, Michigan, November 26, 1877; married Harold Slocum, an oil driller of Oklahoma; child: Romayne, born December 12, 1911. 5. Romayne, born in East Bradford, Pennsylvania, February 9, 1885, now a stenographer in the employ of the Tide Water Pipe Company at Bradford, unmarried. 6. Darwin, died aged six months.

(X) Minnie, eldest daughter and second child of Marks B. Sanborn and his first wife Jennie Pettis, was born in Pioneer near Titusville, Pennsylvania, April 6, 1866. She was two years of age when her parents moved to Hudson, Michigan, where she received her early education. In 1879 the family located in East Bradford, Pennsylvania, where she finished her public school studies, later taking a course at the Normal college at Ada, Ohio. After leaving Normal she taught for eight years; five at Kendall Creek (now East Bradford), and three in Custer City. She is a member of the Presbyterian church and interested in church and society work. She married, January 2, 1892, Ferdinand Kreiner, born in Cattaraugus county, New York, February 28, 1857, died in Bradford, June 12, 1896, son of Adam and Otille (Wenzel) Kreiner, of German parentage (see Kreiner family in this work). Ferdinand Kreiner was well educated in the public schools, working on the farm in summers and attending school during the winter months. In 1877 he came to Bradford, securing a position as clerk in the dry goods house of Katz and Simons. In 1879 he entered the employ of the National Transit Company, a branch of the Standard Oil Company. His services were so well appreciated that he was soon made superintendent of a division. He held this position until receiving an offer of the managership of the Connemaugh Gas Company of Pittsburgh, which he accepted and held until his death. He was an active member and worker in the Methodist Episcopal church, being superintendent of the Sunday school and teacher of a class of young men, a form of Christian work in which he took a deep interest. He was an active worker in the labor party, was chairman of the state executive committee, and the candidate of his party for the state assembly from McKean county, failing of election by only a few votes. He was a man held in high esteem by his business associates, and respected by all. Children of Ferdinand and Minnie (Sanborn) Kreiner: 1. Irene, born at Saltsburg, October 30, 1892, educated in the public schools, a graduate of Bradford high school and now a student at Pratt's Institute, Brooklyn, New York. 2. Marian, born at Saltsburg, October 24, 1893, a graduate of Bradford high school, class of 1911. 3. Joseph, born in Saltsburg, December 28, 1894, now a student at Bradford high school.

GORTON The Gortons of Smethport descend from Samuel (1) Gorton, a clothier of London, England, born in Gorton, now incorporated in the city of Manchester, Lancaster county, England, 1592, "where the fathers of his body had lived for many generations, not unknown to the Heraldry of England." The heraldic seal of the early Gortons was: Gules, ten billets of the chief of the second; crest: a goat's head erased ducally gorged. In a semicircle over the design, Gorton. *Vitam impendere vero;* under the design, Gorton. Samuel Gorton was trained in the doctrine of the Established Church and his reason for leaving his native land, as told by himself, was "to enjoy liberty of conscience in respect to faith toward God, and for no other end." He landed at Boston in March, 1636, with his wife Mary, daughter of John Maplet, "gent," and Mary Maplet, of St. Martins le Grand, London, and several of his children. Owing to the religious persecution in Boston, he took up his residence in Plymouth, a more liberal colony, where he joined one of the military companies which was being formed in response to the call of the state for aid to repel the charge of the Pequot Indians. In 1638 he led the opposition to the illiberal changes, delegate representation, etc., thrust into the government by Prence, the new governor of Plymouth, and was unwittingly led into Prence's court and banished from the colony for expressing his contempt of it. In 1639, at Pocasset, Aquidneck Island, he was a freeman and a member of the second or civil compact of government, although in 1640, with many other members of that organization, he was driven from the island by the former deposed ruler, Judge Goddington, who had violently reassumed the reins of government. In the latter part of that year he settled on land purchased from Robert Cole at Bapaquinapang near Massapand Pond, adjoining Providence. Owing to the search for a place where he could find freedom of thought he was compelled to change his residence several times. He grew in importance and held many positions of honor. He was assistant to Governor Roger Williams; elected to the assembly in 1649, and in 1651 was chosen president of the colony, serving as governor in the absence of Governor Williams. From 1664 to 1667 he was chosen deputy and again in 1670, but declined to serve on account of his age. He died in December, 1677 (probably December 10). He was buried in the Gorton burial ground at Warwick, where it is supposed his wife Mary also found her last resting place. The date of her death is unknown.

Samuel Gorton was one of the most prominent men in the early colonial history of New England. A lover of religious liberty he was always foremost in defending the people of the Providence and Rhode Island plantations from the drastic effects of the religious intolerance and grasping tyranny of the Puritans of the Massachusetts and Plymouth colonies. His banishment from the Plymouth Colony was under the following circumstances: A widow, Ellen Aldridge, a woman of good repute, who had lately come over, was employed by his wife as a domestic. It was alleged of her, that "she smiled in church." For this offense Governor Prence commanded, after punishment as the bench see fit, her departure, and also anyone who brought her to the place from whence she came. They proposed to deport her as a vagabond. Gorton appeared at court December 4, 1638, in her defense and undertook to show that the offense was not recognized in the English law, to the protection of which he appealed; that she was no vagabond; was a woman of good report, and by diligent labor earning her bread. He was charged with deluding the court of her and was bound to answer for this contempt at the next sessions. He appeared at the next sessions, and in his defense, seems to have still further antagonized the court. "All his defense and attempted defense" was pronounced to be "turbulent and seditious;" and so on the 4th day of December, 1638, he was sentenced "to depart from Plymouth, his home, his hired house, his wife and children, and to be beyond the utmost bounds of it within fourteen days." His departure from Plymouth was in the extremity of New England winter, and happened in the midst of the greatest tempest of wind and snow recorded of the times. After great exposure and suffering he with his family arrived on December 18, at the nearest settlement on an island in Narragansett Bay. Here he soon came to the front in the struggle by the people against the policy of the judges and elders, who had established a government and court, which was of fidelity, not known to the civil laws, but to the laws of Moses. Gorton was a student of law. His library which he brought from England contained the standard authorities, and he understood his own and the people's rights better than did these judges and elders. Massachusetts claiming a prior charter to the Narragansett territory, Gorton was chosen by the assembly of the Providence plantations as their commissioner to England, and departed on his mission in August, 1645. His work with and before the parliament commissioners in England was continuous and severe, and it was over two years before he succeeded in his efforts for his people. He did not reach home till May, 1648. He was a writer of ability, leaving many valuable state papers and several published works. That he must have been possessed of great and shining virtues is sufficiently evident from the fidelity with which his early adherents followed through life his changing fortunes, and by their never failing confidence in his worthiness to fill public office of the highest trust and of the greatest importance to the general weal. He was their chosen representative to the assembly in the years 1649-51-52-55-56-57-58-59-60-62-63-64-65-66; served a number of years in the upper house, corresponding to the present senate; was associate judge of their highest court, and was their president or governor for the term beginning in 1651 and ending in 1652. He was a multitude of times selected to audit the accounts of the colony, and more than any other man in the colony was called upon to draw up important state papers, and in his old age was continually honored by the gift of the most important civil offices. Sidney S. Rider, whose knowledge of these early men, obtained from a lifelong study of their works, is not exceeded by any one living says that Gorton was "one of the most learned men then living in New England." In the languages, in the law, and in letters, he was exceedingly proficient. His early associations were good; his wife was as tenderly reared as any lady in the colony; his family educated and refined; her brother a college professor, and an excellent Latin poet. He was possessed of more literary education than any of the founders save Williams. In law and politics he understood his rights better than did the elders and magistrates of Massachusetts, and he at all times showed the courage of his convictions and he appeared to have asserted no propositions which he could not legally maintain. Samuel G. Arnold regarded him as one of the most remarkable men who ever lived. John M. Mackey says of him: "His astuteness of mind and Biblical learning made him a formidable opponent of the Puritan hiearchy. By his bold example, by his written and spoken word he did much that should make his name ever freshly remembered by the friends of religious liberty throughout the wide world." Rhode Island may well be proud of his record and of his distinguished services.

His children were: 1. ———. 2. Samuel (2), of whom further. 3. Mary, married (first) Peter Greene, (second) John Sanford. 4. Maher, married Daniel Cole. 5. John, married Margaret Weeden. 6. Benjamin, married Sarah Garder. 7. Sarah, married William Mace. 8. Ann, married John Weaver. 9. Elizabeth, married John Crandall. 10. Susanna, married Benjamin Barton.

(II) Samuel (2), son of Samuel (1) Gorton, was born at Gorton, Lancaster county, England, 1630. He came with his father to New England in 1636, lived with him at Warwick and received from him a deed for his interest in the property. He, like his father, gained the friendship and goodwill of the Indian tribes around them. He was captain of the military company of the town and in 1678 was a member of the court at Newport to try cases against the Indians for depredations committed during King Philip's war. During the years 1676 to 1683 he was a member of the upper house of assembly. He also filled the office of assistant judge two terms; was elected for a third term but declined to serve. He married, December 11, 1684, Susannah Burton, born 1665, daughter of William and Hannah (Wickes) Burton. Samuel (2) Gorton, died September 6, 1724, and his widow married (second) Richard Harris. She died June 25, 1737. Children of Samuel (2) Gorton: 1. Samuel (3), of whom further. 2. Hezekiah, born January 11, 1692, married Freelove Neason. 3. Susannah, born June 4, 1694, married Joseph Stafford.

(III) Samuel (3), son of Samuel (2) Gorton, was born in Warwick, Rhode Island, January 9, 1690. He moved from Warwick to Swansey, Massachusetts, where his last five children were born. He married, June 1, 1715, Freelove, daughter of Elder Joseph and Lydia (Bowen) Mason. Children: 1. Samuel (4), born in March, 1717; married (first) Ruth Slade; (second) Frances (Rice) Graves. 2. Freelove, born August 27, 1718. 3. Ann, September 7, 1721. 4. Lydia, February 1, 1723. 5. Benjamin, July 2, 1725, married Avis Hulett. 6. William. 7. Joseph, of whom further. 8. Susanna, born June 6, 1734. 9. Hezekiah, July 9, 1736. He died in January, 1784, and was buried from the home of his son, Deacon Benjamin Gorton, January 23; funeral sermon by Elder John Gorton.

(IV) Joseph, son of Samuel (3) Gorton, was born probably in Swansey, although his birth is not recorded there. He served in the revolution in Esquire Millard's company, Colonel Waterman's regiment, Rhode Island militia, November 21, 1776; December 4, 1776, and January 9, 1777, length of service not stated. He married, January 1, 1762, Mary Barton, born November 20, 1740, daughter of Benjamin and Mary (Harte) Barton, a sister of General William Barton, who captured the British General Prescott at Newport. Children: 1. Hezekiah, born November 21, 1763, married the widow of Asa Potter. 2. David, of whom further. 3. Mary, born March 4, 1770, married Levi or Sevin Kinnecot.

(V) David, son of Joseph Gorton, was born at Warwick, Rhode Island, November 24, 1768, died at Mansfield, New York. He was married by Elder John Gorton, March 19, 1789, to Alice Whitford, born July 16, 1770, daughter of George and Hannah (Wickes) Whitford, of Warwick. Her name is written alternately, Alice and Elsie. They settled in

Mansfield, New York, but after being left a widow she lived with her daughter Rachel in Bloomfield, Connecticut, where she died in July, 1855. Children: 1. Mary, born 1790, married Philip White. 2. Joseph, of whom further. 3. Hannah, born July 7, 1795, married William Haswell. 4. Susan, born May 12, 1799; married (first) Henry Baxter, (second) Ransom J. Greene. 5. John, born April 19, 1801, married Johanne Sheldon. 6. Silas C., born 1803, married (first) Diadama Meade; married (second) Lucy Steel. 7. Rachel, born December 14, 1805, married William Gillette. 8. Phebe S., born July 1, 1811, married John Robinson. 9. Hezekiah, born 1814, married Sallie A. Edmonds. 10. Alpha, died in infancy. 11. Betsey E., born January 21, 1818; married (first) James Brown, (second) William Henry.

(VI) Joseph (2), son of David Gorton, was born at Warwick, Rhode Island, November 7, 1792, died in December, 1872, at Friendship, New York. He was a cooper by trade. He was named after his grandfather, Joseph Gorton, who gave him a tract of one hundred acres of land at or near where the city of Bennington, Vermont, now stands. This he sold for a few hundred dollars and settled in Friendship, Allegany county, New York, where he married, lived and died. He served in the war of 1812, under Colonel Brockway. He married, January 5, 1814, Phebe Baxter, born October 5, 1795, at North Salem, Westchester county, New York, daughter of John (2) and Dorcas (Whitlock) Baxter. Captain John (1) Baxter came to America in 1664 with the Irish Volunteers, as captain. He received for his services the island of Throggs Neck. He had eight children, among whom was Petit Baxter. Petit Baxter, born December 16, 1732, died February 5, 1809, married Sarah Brush, born November 9, 1738, died February 5, 1823. They had twelve children, the eldest being John Baxter. John (2) Baxter, born September 24, 1760, died November 28, 1841, was a soldier of the revolution. He married Dorcas Whitlock, born June 4, 1776, died April 25, 1839. They had nine children, one of whom was Phebe Baxter Gorton, of previous mention.

Children of Joseph (2) Gorton: 1. Alpha Ann, born November 16, 1814, died August 8, 1815. 2. Sarah H., born March 16, 1816, died April 4, 1816. 3. Harriet Ann, born September 17, 1817, married Levi Horner. 4. Sheridan, of whom further. 5. Joseph, born October 12, 1821, died February 16, 1822. 6. Fanny, born January 12, 1824, married Abel T. Reynolds. 7. Orpha E., born April 25, 1826, married Samuel E. Latta. 8. Phebe F., born May 30, 1828, married John C. Colwell. 9. Susan M., born July 9, 1830, married Robert E. Middaugh. 10. Henry Baxter, born December 27, 1832, married Flora Horner. 11. Josephus, born February 21, 1835, married Ellen M. Church. 12. Erastus, born February 4, 1837, died March 3, 1837. 13. Thaddeus Hezekiah, born March 5, 1839, died January, 1848.

(VII) Sheridan, son of Joseph (2) Gorton, was born in New York state (probably in Friendship), December 21, 1819, died in Friendship, May 23, 1848. He was a musician and during the summer months traveled in that capacity with Van Amberg's circus. He also learned and worked at harnessmaking. He died at the early age of twenty-nine years. He married, August 12, 1847, Abigail Norton, born in Washington county, New York, in May, 1829, died in Friendship, December 22, 1910. They had one child, Sheridan (2), born October 1, 1848. Mrs. Gorton married (second) Walter D. Renwick, a teacher and farmer, who died in Friendship in 1908. She was a Congregationalist, later a Methodist. She was the daughter of Joseph B. Norton, born in Washington county, New York, in 1800, a farmer, also a lumberman, and one of the first settlers of what was then Phillipsville, Allegany county, New York, settling there with wife and one child Abigail. He died in Friendship. By a first marriage there was no issue; he married (second) Prudence Hall, born in Walpole, New Hampshire, in 1806, died in Friendship, in 1900; she was of a prominent family, her grandfather Hall was an officer of the revolution. Children of Joseph B. Norton and his second wife Prudence Hall: 1. Abigail, of previous mention, wife of Sheridan (1) and mother of Sheridan (2) Gorton. 2 David, born 1831, died at Friendship, a harnessmaker and farmer; married (first) a Miss Harrison, who left a son Harry, born 1856; married (second) Libby Bradley, also of Friendship; children: Carrie; Frederick; a daughter; Mary, and Martin. 3. Miriam, born in 1833, in Phillipsville, New York; married William McCracken, of Farmington, Oakland county, Michigan, where they reside on their farm. Children: i. Harry, a farmer and an ex-member of the Michigan legislature. ii. Mary, married William Hewitt, a lawyer of Detroit. iii. Stella, resides in Oakland county, Michigan. iv. Arthur, a lawyer in Indiana. 4. Rhoda, born 1835, married James Hyde, a clerk; they reside in Belmont, New York: no living children. 5. Sheridan McArthur, born 1848, thirteen years after his sister Rhoda; died in Friendship, in 1896; he married Mary Robinson, who survives him; one child: George, an electrical engineer. 6. Clara, born in 1850, at Phillipsville, Allegany county, New York, died in East Lexington, Massachusetts, about 1890; married Edward Spalding, a prominent farmer and citizen of East Lexington.

Children of Abigail (Norton) Gorton by her second husband Walter D. Renwick: 1. Ellena, born in Cuba, New York, 1854; married F. L. Dayton, deceased, a real estate and insurance agent of Friendship, whom she survives; one child: Lolo. 2. Elizabeth, born in Belmont, New York, 1861, married William H. Flint, a mechanic, residing in Friendship; children: i. Jessie, married Roy Glover. ii. Carl, an engraver of Buffalo, New York. iii. Mary, a teacher in Bradford (Pennsylvania) high school. iv. Howard, a student at Michigan University. 3. Walter N., born in Belmont, 1865, now a lawyer of Cuba, New York; married and has: Walter, born 1903; Robert, 1909. 4. Edward M. (Ned), born in Belmont, 1870, a traveling salesman; married Ruth Newton and resides in Cuba, New York; has one daughter Irene.

(VIII) Sheridan (2), only child of Sheridan (1) and Abigail (Norton) Gorton, was born in Belmont (then called Phillipsville), Allegany county, New York, October 1, 1848. He there received a public school education, and became a teacher, following that profession in Allegany county and in Oakland county, Michigan, until 1872. He was then advance agent for a theatrical company four years until 1876. In the latter year he began the study of law, under the direction of S. McArthur Norton, of Friendship, New York. He had previously read and studied law under the direction of Hon. Wilkes Angel and George S. Jones, at Belmont, New York, and now continued under Mr. Norton's preceptorship until June 15, 1877, when he was admitted at Buffalo, New York, as a member of the bar of the state of New York. He located in Smethport, Pennsylvania, July 3, 1877; was admitted to the McKean county bar, September 24, following, formed a partnership with John C. Backus (see Backus), and together they practiced very successfully until the death of Mr. Backus. In November, 1898, he entered into a law partnership with Thomas R. Richmond (see Richmond), then a member of the Pennsylvania legislature. This was a very effective combination and they transacted an enormous business until the death of Mr. Richmond in 1908. Since that time Mr. Gorton has practiced alone, retaining and satisfactorily serving the former firm clients. He is an able lawyer, thoroughly informed in the law and skillful in legal procedure. He is a Republican in politics and has held many town and county offices, including the board of council, school director, district attorney for McKean county (1894-1897), and numerous conventions which he has attended as delegate. He is president of the Smethport Water Company and has large business interests outside his profession. He has given a great deal of attention to fraternal societies and has attained prominence in all. He is past master of Smethport Lodge, No. 182, Ancient Order of United Workmen, and past grand master of the Pennsylvania State organization (1892 and 1893), the Pennsylvania jurisdiction including West Virginia; past noble grand of Smethport Lodge, No. 389, Independent Order of Odd Fellows; past worshipful master of McKean Lodge, No. 388, Free and Accepted Masons; is a companion of Bradford Chapter, Royal Arch Masons; a sir knight of Trinity Commandery (Bradford), Knights Templar; a noble of Zem Zem Temple (Erie), Nobles of the Mystic Shrine, and a thirty-second degree Mason of Coudersport Consistory, Ancient Accepted Scottish Rite. His club is the Central of Smethport. During his long professional and public career, Mr. Gorton has fairly won the confidence and esteem of his townsmen and brethren of the bar, and as a man, a citizen and a lawyer bears a character beyond reproach.

He married, June 29, 1878, Lucy C. Eaton, born in Smethport, April 1, 1859. She was educated in the public schools and has been a lifetime resident of Smethport. She is a daughter of Judson Galusha Eaton, a descendant of John Eaton, the emigrant, of Watertown and Dedham, Massachusetts (see Eaton). Mrs. Gorton is a member of the Travelers' Club and of St. Luke's Episcopal Church. Children of Sheridan and Lucy C. (Eaton) Gorton, all born in Smethport: 1. Sheridan

(3), born September 22, 1879, now a publisher of New York City; married a widow, Mrs. Edith (Case) Montgomery; no issue. By her first husband she had a daughter Marjorie, living in Massachusetts. 2. E. Rex, born June 14, 1881; now in charge of a large garage in Patterson, California; married March 19, 1911, Matilda Nieman, of Cincinnati, Ohio. 3. MacArthur, born February 4, 1889; graduate of Bucknell University, class of 1910, now a civil engineer in São Paulo, Brazil, South America; unmarried. 4. Elva Rita, born May 8, 1893, graduate of Smethport high school and resides with her parents.

(The Eaton Line).

John Eaton, the emigrant, was an early settler of Watertown, Massachusetts, where he was admitted a freeman May 25, 1636; lived there another year and shared in several land distributions. He joined the Dedham church in 1641 and took active part in the public affairs of Dedham, serving on committee to lay out lands; as surveyor of highways, and as wood reeve several years. He died October 9, 1658. His wife Abigail survived him. Children: 1. Mary, baptized at Dover, Kent county, England, March 20, 1631. 2. John, died young. 3. Thomas, born 1633, died 1659. 4. John (2), of whom further. 5. Abigail, born January 6, 1640, died February 13, 1711. 6. Jacob, born June 8, 1642, in Dedham, died young.

(II) John (2), son of John (1) Eaton, born 1636, died April 23, 1684. His wife Alice, died March 8, 1694. Children: 1. John, died young. 2. John, married Ann Whitney. 3. Thomas, married Lydia Gay. 4. William, married Mary Starr. 5. Judith, died young. 6. David, died young. 7. Ebenezer, died young. 8. Judith, born May 17, 1680. 9. Jonathan, of whom further.

(III) Jonathan, son of John (2) Eaton, was born at Dedham, Massachusetts, September 3, 1681, died in Killingly, Connecticut, June 25, 1748. He moved to Connecticut in 1701 and was the first permanent settler at Putnam village, where he built a mill. He attended church in Killingly in 1730, and was chosen deacon. He married Lydia Starr, in 1706, second daughter of Comfort and Mary Starr. She died in March, 1751. Children: 1. Lydia, born November 5, 1707, twice married. 2. Keziah, May 24, 1710, married Deliverance Cleveland. 3. Alice, November 28, 1712, married Joseph Lawrence (2). 4. Susanna, in April, 1715; married Thomas Grove. 5. Jerusha, April 16, 1717; married John Bucklin. 6. Hannah, August 17, 1719; married Seth Johnson. 7. Jonathan (2), November 10, 1721, married Sarah Johnson. 8. John (2), of whom further. 9. Penelope, born March 21, 1729. 10. Comfort, September 25, 1730, married Mehitable Whitmore. 11. Marston, October 21, 1731, married Elizabeth Lyon.

(IV) John (3), son of Jonathan Eaton, was born May 13, 1724, died while on a visit to his son in Eatonville, New York. He lived in North Adams, Massachusetts, and married Hannah Johnson. Children: 1. John (4), married Mehitable Richardson. 2. Elisha, married Sally Case. 3. Wyman, married Mary Knight. 4. Rufus, of whom further. 5. Comfort, married Polly Griffith. 6. Rhoda, married Jeremiah Bucklin. 7. Esther, married Jonathan Richardson. 8. Lydia, married Abijah Richmond. 9. Keziah, married a Mr. Knapp. 10. Mehitable, married Donald Bensley. 11. Hannah, married Chad Brown.

(V) Rufus, son of John (3) Eaton, was born June 16, 1770, died in Springville, Erie county, New York, February 7, 1845. He was but a lad of sixteen years, when with four brothers he emigrated to the site of Eatonville, Herkimer county, New York, and helped to found the town that bears the family name. At the age of forty years he moved with his wife and eight children to the vicinity of Buffalo, New York, but finding it unhealthy, again moved, settling at Springville, Erie county, near the southern boundary of the county. He located there in 1810, obtained a great deal of good land, on which Springville was later largely built, he being one of the first settlers there. He built the first saw mill in the town, was the first justice of the peace, and with his brother Elisha built, in 1824, the old Springville Hotel. He donated land for the village park; the cemetery; the academy; the First Presbyterian Church, and for other charitable and religious purposes. He may be called the father of the town, so intimately is his name associated with its early history. He married, in 1791, Sally Potter, who died November 15, 1843, aged seventy-six years. Children: 1. Sylvester, of whom further. 2. Waitee, married Frederick Richmond. 3. Sally, twice married. 4. Rufus C., born 1796, married Elizabeth Butterworth. 5. Mahala, married Otis Butterworth. 6. Elisha, born 1800, married Betsey Chapee. 7. Harriet, married Dr. Carl Emmons. 8. William, died young.

(VI) Sylvester, eldest son of Rufus Eaton, was born in Little Falls, New York, June 17, 1792. He married (first) Lydia Gardner, (second) Nancy Wilkes. Children by first wife: 1. Peregrine, married (first) Alice Tailor, (second) Phebe Starkweather. 2. Judson Galusha, of whom further. 3. Mary L. Children by second wife: Waitee, Lucinda, and Rosalie, who married a Mr. Rice, of Osago, Iowa.

(VII) Judson Galusha, son of Sylvester Eaton, was born in Springville, New York, August 19, 1823, died May 7, 1888, a tinsmith. He married, September 4, 1856, Sarah Electa Bennett, who survives him a resident of Smethport, where they settled after marriage. She is a daughter of Oshea Rich Bennett, born near Albany, New York, April 20, 1806, died in Smethport June, 1858, a merchant; married Lucy Green Warner, born July 5, 1807, at Lima, New York, died in Smethport, May 11, 1887; they were the parents of twelve children, of which Sarah Electa was the second.

(VIII) Lucy C., daughter of Judson Galusha and Sarah Electa (Bennett) Eaton, married Sheridan Gorton (see Gorton VIII).

STULL This name, originally Stoll, was borne by John Stoll, a Hollander and a resident of the township of Frankford, Sussex county, New Jersey. Many Dutch and German families settled at an early day in Sussex, coming from the eastern part of New Jersey, the lower counties of New York state, Long Island, and in some cases from New England.

(I) John Stoll is the first of whom record is found in Sussex county, where he married and had male issue. He was the father of Captain Jacob Stoll or Stull, of whom further.

(II) Captain Jacob Stoll or Stull, son of John Stoll, was born in Sussex county, New Jersey, 1741, died at Elmira, New York, November 14, 1809. He served in the revolutionary war, first as assistant of the Second Regiment, Sussex county, New Jersey, troops; later was promoted captain. He was engaged at the battles of Quinton's Bridge, Three Rivers, Hancock's Bridge, Connecticut Farms, Van Nest's Mill, Long Island, Trenton (Assanipink), Princeton, Germantown, Springfield and Monmouth, serving with distinction. He was accompanied to the war by his son John, a lad of twelve, who served in the wagon trains as packhorse boy. Captain Jacob Stull was at this time a resident of New Jersey, but after the war moved to New York state settling at Elmira, where he owned a good farm of over two hundred acres. Descendants of Captain Stull are yet found in that locality. He is buried by the side of his wife in the family plot on the old farm. He married Sarah Pipenger, born 1743, died in Elmira, New York, November 2, 1830. She was of English descent, and until her death drew a pension from the government on account of her husband's patriotic service in the revolution.

(III) Joseph, son of Captain Jacob and Sarah (Pipenger) Stull, was born in Sussex county, New Jersey, January 18, 1777; died on his farm in Eldred township, McKean county, Pennsylvania, December 2, 1866. He was a farmer of Chenango and Steuben counties, New York, until 1808, when he came to Pennsylvania, settling in what is now Eldred township, McKean county. He was accompanied by his brother John and they at once began a clearing. Each had a ten-acre lot well cleared, when they discovered they were on another man's property. Joseph moved to what is now Stulltown, McKean county, where he cleared a farm and lived until his death. He married, January 18, 1802, Delinda Brewer, born in Dutchess county, New York, April 17, 1782, died in Eldred township, June 6, 1862, daughter of Abraham and Eunice (Griswold) Brewer, a union with two of the old colonial families. Children of Abraham Brewer: 1. Delinda, of previous mention. 2. Abraham, died in Chenango county, New York, a farmer, married and left issue. 3. Abigail, married John Stull, brother of Joseph, a farmer. She died on the homestead at Elmira, New York.

Children of Joseph and Delinda (Brewer) Stull, first four born in the town of Starka, Chenango county, New York: 1. Alma, born August 15, 1804, died in Scioto county, Ohio; married Lynds Dodge, died in Eldred township, McKean county, Pennsylvania, a farmer and a lumberman; children, all deceased: Eulalia, Mary, Eliza, Matilda, Luman, Joseph and Henry. 2. Abraham, born August 21, 1806, died in Eldred township, McKean county, a farmer; married Philena Green, who died in Eldred township; children, all deceased: Handford, George, Philista and Alice. 3. John, of whom further. 4. Abigail, born August 23, 1811, died at Port Allegany, Pennsylvania; married (first) David Groman, (second) Joseph Long, a farmer and a soldier in the war of 1812; children of second marriage: George, deceased; Joseph, now living at Port Allegany. 5. Camilla, born in Eldred township, McKean county, Pennsylvania, October 12, 1813, died in Harrisonville, Scioto county, Ohio; married John L. Daniels, of Marietta, Ohio, a school teacher, died in Harrisonville. Children: i. James, died in the Union army during the civil war. ii. Artemesia, died in 1912. iii. Mary, now living in San Bernardino, California. iv. Camilla, living in Ohio. v. Alma, living in East Liverpool, Ohio. vi. Lee Quincy, deceased, a veteran of the civil war. 6. Caleb Baker, born in Eldred township, March 16, 1816, died there a farmer; married Caroline Boorhees (?), of Farmer's Valley, Pennsylvania. Children: i. Ridgway, deceased. ii. Orsarilla, living in Olean, New York. iii. Cynthia, deceased. iv. Arthur, living in Eldred, Pennsylvania. v. Ann, deceased. vi. John, living in Coveyville, Pennsylvania. vii. Daniel, living in the state of Washington. viii. Grant, deceased. ix. George, deceased. 7. Laurinda H., married Arthur Young (see Young). 8. Mary Delinda, born in Eldred township, March 10, 1820, died there after two marriages; married (first) Rev. Charles Coe, a Methodist minister; child, Cyrenus, a captain in the civil war, deceased; married (second) John Nolan, a farmer of Emporium, Pennsylvania; children: John, living in Cameron county, Pennsylvania, and Merrick, deceased. 9. Jerome K., born in Farmer's Valley, Pennsylvania, April 21, 1822, died there a farmer, married Ann Maria Kent. Children: i. Dulcina, deceased. ii. Joseph C., now living in Portville, Pennsylvania. iii. Baker J., deceased. iv. Flora, living at Turtle Point, Pennsylvania. v. Sylvester, deceased. 10. George R., born in Farmer's Valley, March 3, 1824, died there a merchant; married Catherine Lewis, of New York City; children: George and Joseph, both deceased. 11. Joseph, born in Farmer's Valley, April 21, 1826, died in Eldred township, a farmer; married Lucinda Myers; children: Favoretta, living in Wayland, New York; Cameron, living in Eldred township.

(IV) John (2), second son of Joseph and Delinda (Brewer) Stull, was born in Brading, Steuben county, New York, December 31, 1808. When an infant he was brought to McKean county, Pennsylvania, by his parents who settled at Stulltown on a farm. He was educated in the public school and became a carpenter, working in New York and Pennsylvania, later a farmer. In 1883 he moved to Smethport, where he died. He and his wife were members of the Baptist church. He married Phœbe Wright, widow of Samuel E. Windsor, who died in Franklinville, New York, by whom she was the mother of Orlando, deceased; William E., died in 1911, in Larrabee, Pennsylvania, and Lewis, deceased. Phœbe Wright was born in Ceres, Pennsylvania, March 1, 1814, died in Eldred township, McKean county, September 17, 1883, daughter of Rensselaer Wright, born about 1791, a farmer and hotel keeper of Eldred, where he died about 1871; he married and reared a family of ten. Children of Rensselaer Wright, not known to be in exact order of birth: 1. Phœbe, of previous mention. 2. James, died in Honeoye, Potter county, Pennsylvania, a lumberman; married Mary Estey, of Ceres; two children. 3. Phelps, died in Michigan, a lumberman; married a Miss Brown; two children. 4. John, died in Eldred, Pennsylvania, a lumberman and farmer; married Editha Moses, of Cuba, New York; children: William, of Olean, New York; Edick, lives at Eldred, on the old homestead; John, of Olean. 5. Carl, now living at Coles Creek, Pennsylvania, a lumberman, farmer and oil producer; married (first) Jerusha Dennis, deceased, who was the mother of his children: Burt, and others; no issue by second marriage. 6. George, died in Eldred township in 1867, a lumberman; married a Miss Paine, who survives him with issue, a resident of Eldred. She married (second) Williard Cummings, also deceased. 7. Junius, died in Eldred, a farmer; married Elizabeth Moddy, of Coveyville, Pennsylvania, who survives him residing in Eldred. 8. Sarah (Sally), died in Smethport, Pennsylvania; married Nathan Palmer, of Ceres, a hotel keeper of Port Allegany, Pennsylvania; children: Adelbert, and three others. 9. Martha, died in Smethport; married a cousin, —— Wright, a journalist; no issue. 10. Maria, died in Michigan; married Russell Miller, a farmer; left issue.

Children of John and Phœbe (Wright-Windsor) Stull, all born in Eldred township, McKean county: 1. James H., of whom further. 2. Maria, born April 10, 1841, died in Duke Center, Pennsylvania, April 10, 1891; married

Randall Middaugh, of Portville, New York, also deceased; children: Nettie, now living in Ohio, married; Lily, died aged twenty months. 3. Almeda, born November 15, 1843; married Dana Nichols, of Eldred township, where they reside on their farm; child: Mellie, born 1870. 4. John E., born November 8, 1845, now a retired farmer of East Smethport; married Adelaide Higgin, of Warsaw, New York; child: Clyde, born August 5, 1881, freight agent at Smethport Depot, unmarried. 5. Leroy, born February 28, 1854, now a farmer near Cuba, New York.

(V) James H., eldest son of John (2) and Phoebe (Wright-Windsor) Stull, was born in Eldred township, McKean county, Pennsylvania, November 14, 1839. He was three years of age when his parents moved to Portville, New York, where he was educated in the public school, finishing in the high school. His first work was on a farm, later under his father's instruction he learned the carpenter's trade. After he returned to Pennsylvania, he taught one term in the Stulltown public school. After his military service he returned to Pennsylvania, and followed his trade in Eldred township, McKean county, where he later purchased a farm. He continued carpentering and farming until October 1, 1883, when he moved to Smethport, where he still resides.

He enlisted in 1861 in Company H, One Hundred and Tenth Regiment, Pennsylvania Volunteer Infantry, which was shortly afterwards consolidated with the Fifty-eighth Regiment. On November 7, 1862, he was transferred to Company D, Fourth Regiment, United States Light Artillery, in which he served until his term of enlistment expired. He reënlisted February 1, 1864, in the same battery, continuing in the service until the close of the war, receiving honorable discharge, February 1, 1867, serving two years after the war in Texas. He took part in nineteen battles, among which were: Black Water Run, ten miles from Suffolk, Virginia, fought between the forces commanded by General Corcoran and General Smith during the siege of Suffolk. In that engagement his battery was hard pressed and lost many men. He was with Grant in front of Petersburg, where his battery was engaged, May 9, 1864, and again on May 13, 1864, they were sharply engaged eight miles from Richmond, suffering severe loss. They crossed the Appomattox, June 14, 1864, took the heights of Petersburg and placed forty-eight pieces of artillery in position on the crest of the hill. His services continued through the battles before Richmond until the final surrender of General Lee, April 3, 1865. He is a member of Knights of the Maccabees, the Grand Army of the Republic, the Methodist Episcopal church, and in politics is a Republican.

He married, March 8, 1870, Ann Eliza (Terry) Keyes, born in the village of Greene, New York, February 4, 1841. At nine years of age her father gave her to her uncle Salmon Montague Rose, with whom she lived five years in Smethport, Pennsylvania, where she was educated in the public schools. She is a member of the Maccabees and of the Methodist Episcopal church. Her father Thomas Terry was born in Connecticut, about 1806, died at Afton, in Chenango, county, New York, July 1, 1851, a cloth manufacturer; he married Mary Rose, born in Binghamton, New York, 1808, died in Afton, August 10, 1849. Mary Rose was the daughter of Salmon Montague Rose, a root and herb doctor, who died in Smethport, Pennsylvania, 1847. He married and had issue: 1. Hinsdale, a farmer died in New York; married Sophronia Barrett; children: Henry, Marian, Lucy, William, Emory and Amelia. 2. John, died in Canastota, New York, an official of the Erie railroad; married and had a family. 3. A son. 4. Salmon Montague, a lumberman, died in Auburn, New York; married Eliza Burdick, from Potato Creek, Pennsylvania; no issue. 5. Mary, of previous mention, married Thomas Terry. 6. Lucy, died in the west; married Asa Sartwell, a lumberman of McKean county and left issue. 7. Sherland, died in the west, a merchant. Children of Thomas Terry, all born in New York state: 1. Violetta, born 1832; married Ferris Loop, of Windsor; died in Savannah, Illinois, a school teacher and bookkeeper; children: Edwin, deceased; Mary, living in Iowa; Alice, living in Savannah; Flavia, living in Savannah, and Kate. 2. John, born 1834, died in Warren, Pennsylvania, in 1897; a veteran of the civil war serving from New York; married a widow, Mrs. ——— (Freeman) Middaugh; no issue. 3. Annetta, born 1836, died in Iowa, in 1902; married (first) a Van Valkenburg; children: Mabel; Anna, and five others; married (second) a Lewis; no issue. 4. Silas, born in July, 1838, now a retired merchant of Harmony, Clay county, Indiana; married Acena Smith, a native of Indiana; no issue. 5. Ann Eliza, of previous mention, wife of James H. Stull. 6. Mary, born in January, 1847, died in January, 1852. Ann Eliza Terry was a widow at the time of her marriage to James H. Stull. She married (first) September 10, 1859, Melvin Keyes, born December 15, 1838, in Portage, New York, died September 14, 1869, in Pike, Wyoming county, New York, a farmer of Eldred township; children: 1. Mary, born in Eldred, February 7, 1861; married Nathan Miller, of Centerville, New York, where they reside on their farm. Children: i. Elma, married Carl Whitney, a farmer of Centerville. ii. Bertha, married Howard Hamer, a farmer of Centerville. iii. Ernest, a farmer of Centerville, married Ethel Hamer. iv. Earl, a farmer of Centerville; married ———. v. Myrtle, married a farmer of Centerville. vi. Clarence, unmarried. 2. Annette, born in Eldred, April 1, 1863, died in February, 1873. 3. Franklin Augustus, born in Eldred, October 21, 1864, died February, 1873.

Children of James H. and Ann Eliza (Terry-Keyes) Stull, all born in Eldred, Pennsylvania: 1. Myrtle Rose, born August 10, 1874; married George Howard, of Arcade, New York, now an oil well driller and foreman for the Crosby Chemical Company, of the gas wells, and is also a contractor; living at Smethport, Pennsylvania. Children: i. Nettie Elizabeth, born August 20, 1896. ii. Harold, January, 1898. iii. Ernst, December 25, 1901. iv. Ralph, January, 1904. 2. Cora Mundane, born October 31, 1876; married Fred Nourse and resides on their farm near Smethport; children; Forrest, born March 3, 1896; Loida M., October, 1898; Lois, December 17, 1906. 3. Grace Belle, born July 11, 1878; married Alfred Hoskins, a farmer, now living near Centerville, New York; children: Raymond, born December, 1897; Sylvia, September, 1899; Robert, 1900. 4. Hattie May, born March 7, 1882; married Clayton Wales, of Friendship, New York, now living in Bolivar, New York, a teamster, following the oil fields.

HOUGHTON The family of Houghton is of very ancient origin in England, and the name, which was originally De Hocton, is supposed to be derived from the Anglo-Saxon word, Hocton or Hoctune, signifying "Hightown," or "High place," and was taken from one of the manors of the family in Lancashire, England, which was remarkable for its lofty situation. The first to assume the name of this manor was Willus De Hocton, or as sometimes written, Willus Dominus De Hocton. This was in the year 1140, very shortly after surnames were first introduced. A son or grandson changed the spelling to De Hoghton and about the middle of the seventeenth century we find the "u" introduced.

Among the Norman barons who came over to England with William the Conqueror was one named Herverus, and after the battle of Hastings, lands were apportioned him in Norfolk, Suffolk and Lancashire. In the time of Hamo, the grandson of this Herverus, the Manor of Hocton came into the possession of the family, and it was Hamo's son, Willus or William, who first assumed the name of De Hocton. The family continued to be a distinguished one, taking an active part in many stirring historical episodes and holding offices and titles of conspicuous distinction. In the eighteenth generation from Herverus, the Norman progenitor, Thomas Hoghton built during the reign of Queen Elizabeth Hoghton Tower from the stone of a quarry in the hill on which the tower stands. This is one of the most splendid specimens of the Tudor architecture that is extant, and it was here that James I. was entertained by Sir Richard Houghton in 1517 with a lavishness that impoverished the house for many years. Sir Richard had, upon the institution of the order six years earlier, been made a baronet, ranking second in sequence of creation. A long list of Houghtons after his time sat in parliament for county Lancaster.

(1) Ralph Houghton, the American progenitor of the family, was born in Lancaster, England, in 1623, died in Milton, Massachusetts, April 15, 1705. He was a man of much larger property than was common among the colonists of the time, and the tradition is that he was the younger son of Sir Richard Houghton, who in the parliamentary wars was a zealous adherent of the King. According to the story, Ralph became a Puritan and took a prominent part in Cromwell's forces, actually leading on one occasion the assault of the Roundheads upon his ancestral home. For this treason his name was dropped from the rolls of the family. He, thereupon, came to this country, probably about the year 1647, and with several others bought of the Indians a tract of land and organized the town of Lan-

caster. This place was repeatedly the scene of savage Indian attacks until the death of King Philip. Ralph Houghton took a leading part in all the activities of the newly organized town, and was a man of unusual ability and force. He married Jane Stowe, born in England, in 1626, died in Milton, January 10, 1700. The children of Ralph and Jane (Stowe) Houghton were: 1. Ralph, born probably in 1648. 2. James, of whom further. 3. Mary, born April 11, 1653, died in Charlestown, October 8, 1679; married, January 20, 1675, William Bently, of Harvard, Massachusetts; children: triplets, William, Henry, and Hannah. 4. John, born February 28, 1655, died October 1, 1679, at Charlestown, Massachusetts. 5. Joseph, born May 1, 1657, died March 22, 1737; married (first) 1693, Jane Vose, (second) Margaret Redding. 6. Experience, born August 1, 1659, in Lancaster; married, as second wife, May 12, 1684, Ezra Clapp, of Dorchester, Massachusetts. 7. Sarah, born December 17, 1661; married, December 28, 1687, Caleb Sawyer; child, Beulah, born in 1699. 8. Abigail, born May 15, 1664; married, May 14, 1688, John Hudson; child, John, born in 1690. 9. Hannah, born October 16, 1667, died October 8, 1679.

(II) James, son of Ralph and Jane (Stowe) Houghton, was born in 1651, probably in Charlestown, or Woburn, Massachusetts, died in 1711. In 1697 he moved to that part of Lancaster now called Harvard, and with his brother-in-law, Caleb Sawyer, built a homestead or garrison house on the land given him by his father near Still River, which house is still in the possession of his descendants. This is for many reasons one of the most interesting historical houses in that part of the state. He married Mary, born in Lancaster, February 14, 1653, presumably the daughter of Thomas and Mary (Prescott) Sawyer. Their children were: 1. James, born in 1690; married Sarah Sawyer. 2. Ralph, date of birth not known. 3. John, born in 1697-98; married, November 18, 1718, Mehitabel Wilson. 4. Ephraim, of whom further. 5. Edward, born in 1705, died March 17, 1777; married, November 16, 1727, Abigail Coye. 6. Hannah, married T. Sabin. 7. Experience, married William Houghton.

(III) Ephraim, son of James and Mary (Sawyer) Houghton, married, December 10, 1725, Hannah Sawyer. Their children were: 1. Ephraim, born December 1, 1727. 2. Joseph, born October 12, 1731. 3. Elisha, of whom further.

(IV) Elisha, son of Ephraim and Hannah (Sawyer) Houghton, was born July 20, 1746. He resided at Fitchburg, Massachusetts. Children: 1. Maria, born 1777. 2. Moses, of whom further. 3. Aaron, twin of Moses, born March 22, 1781, died November 24, 1842; married, September 13, 1804, Martha Eaton.

(V) Moses, son of Elisha Houghton, was born in Fitchburg, Massachusetts, March 22, 1781, died at Lock's Mills, in the town of Greenwood, Maine, sometimes called Woodstock, October 31, 1847. He married, in 1802, Martha Haskell or Gaskell, born February 15, 1780, died April 14, 1823. Children. 1. Richard, born in Acton, Massachusetts, June 9, 1804; married Lucinda Barrows, of Hebron, Maine; occupation, cooper and gunsmith; died at Mechanic's Falls, Maine. 2. Martha, born September 4, 1805; married Nathaniel Knight, of Paris, Maine. 3. Samuel, born September 5, 1837, died April 9, 1809. 4. Samuel H., born July 20, 1809; married Betsey Tuell. 5. Elijah, born May 15, 1811, died July 30, 1830. 6. Maria, born in Norway, Maine, April 6, 1813; married Gillman Tuell, of South Paris, Maine. 7. Sally, born in Norway, Maine, March 1, 1815; married James Dunham. 8. Ruth, born February 22, 1817; married Horatio Russ. 9. Susan, born February 22, 1819; married (first) Henry Russ, (second) a Mr. Tuell. 10. Moses, of whom further. 11. Aaron, born March 25, 1823; married Martha Farris, of Paris, Maine; died in Augusta, Maine.

(VI) Moses (2), son of Moses (1) and Martha (Haskell or Gaskell) Houghton, was born in Waterford, Maine, October 21, 1820. He lived for many years in Greenwood, Maine. He moved from there to West Paris, Maine, and then to Norway, where he died in 1877. He married, in 1840, Lucy Ann Smith. Children: 1. Charles Remington, born October 17, 1841, died November 7, 1907; married (first) March 15, 1868, Mary H. Bolster, died November 27, 1881, (second) Sylvia Fogg, of Hartford, Maine. Children of first wife: i. Jennie Mary, born November 11, 1869, married Harry Cole; ii. Bessie Anna, born November 14, 1874, died April 21, 1883; iii. Charles Frederick, born 1878, died November 25, 1881. Child of second wife: Alice Bessie, born February 2, 1886. 2. Mary Ellen, born January 23, 1844; married, in 1866, George W.

Bryant. 3. Rev. Moses Henry, of whom further. 4. Hannibal Hamlin, born February 16, 1848; married Laura A. Willis; children: i. Winifred Laura, born January 11, 1881, died in December, 1888; ii. Izah Lucinda, born April 29, 1872; iii. Nellie Agnes, born September 14, 1874; iv. Frederick Mason, died 1896; v. Nina Hortense. 5. Etta J., born January 17, 1854; married George A. Brooks, died in Norway, Maine. 6. Rev. Frederick Mason, born October 20, 1855, at Bethel, Maine, died at Deering, Maine, December 30, 1898; he graduated at Tufts College and Divinity School; he married Alice Josephine Buckman, born February 9, 1855; they had two children; Louise Etta, born May 6, 1888, and Charles Frederick. 7. Lucy Emma, born May 28, 1858, in Bethel, Maine; married, June 20, 1889, J. Clinton Harris, born March 25, 1862; children: i. Ersel Dawn, born December 19, 1890, graduate of Brookline high school, June 1916; ii. Carmen, born August 16, 1895, and now (1912) a senior in the Brookline high school. 8. Nina Hortense, born September 14, 1861, at Lock's Mills, Maine, died November 12, 1904; married, May 12, 1904, Hudson Knight.

(VII) Rev. Moses Henry Houghton, son of Moses (2) and Lucy Ann (Smith) Houghton, was born at Locks Mills, Oxford county, Maine, March 17, 1846, died in May, 1910. His early education was acquired at the Academy at Norway, Maine, going from there to the Harvard Divinity School, from which he was graduated in 1873. He entered the ministry at Bath, Maine, taking the pastorate of the First Universalist Church. His charge, which lasted for three years, marked a period of great prosperity for the church, a handsome parsonage being erected during the time at a cost of $3,000. He then organized the Universalist church of Grand Haven, Michigan, and was its pastor two years. He was also pastor of the Universalist church of Hyannis, Massachusetts, for three years, and of that of New Haven, Connecticut, for six years. His health becoming impaired he went west and served as pastor at Storm Lake, Iowa, for three years, and at Dubuque, Iowa, for two years. He was pastor of the church at Titusville, Pennsylvania, for two years. For eight years he was pastor of the Universalist church in Bradford, Pennsylvania, and during this time a beautiful church was erected and equipped with a pipe organ at a cost of $25,000. Owing to failing health he retired from the ministry, and was for eight years collector in the United States internal revenue department. He then returned to the ministry and was pastor of the Springville, New York, congregation, his last ministerial work. He was an eloquent pulpit orator, and a man whose blameless life attracted many to the cause he championed. "Possessing a sunny disposition, a sympathetic heart and a strong intellect, he made a marked impression wherever he labored, and was one of the most popular pulpit orators of the day".

He married (first) January 1, 1865, Agnes Abbott, and they had one child, Clifton Elwell, born October 12, 1868, now living in Erie, Pennsylvania. He married (second) Ida, daughter of Woodbury Langdon and Julia (Estes) Martin (see Martin IX), now a resident of Bradford, Pennsylvania. She is a member of the church whose service claimed the best years of her husband's life, also belonging to the Ladies' Literary Club, of Bradford, of which she was president, and for five years was one of the vice-presidents of the State Federation of Women's Clubs.

(The Martin Line).

The name Martin is not only of frequent occurrence in the old world, but became common in America from an early period, being found in the early lists of settlers in Massachusetts, Connecticut, New Hampshire, Virginia and other colonies. The name is variously spelled even in the records of the same family as: Martin, Marten, Marttin, Marteen, Martain, Martine and Martyn. As it is common to all countries there is nothing in the name to determine the nationality of the family bearing it. It is found in England as early as the Conquest and was the surname of the Lords of Cemmes for seven generations. In America the name is a respected one and has been borne by men and women who have been good and useful members of society, acting well their part in the sphere in which they were placed.

(I) Richard Martin, the progenitor of the family in this country, married (first) February 1, 1654, Sarah Tuttle (see Tuttle), born 1633, died 1666. Their children were: 1. Mary, born June 7, 1655. 2. Sarah, born July 2, 1657, married John Cutt. 3. Richard, of whom further. 4. Elizabeth, born 1662. 5. Hannah, born 1664, married Richard Jose, a sheriff, and they had six children. 6. Michael, born in 1666. Richard Martin married (second) Martha, widow of John Dunnison; (third) Elizabeth, daughter of Henry Sherbourne; and (fourth) Mary Denning, widow of Samuel Wentworth.

(II) Richard (2), son of Richard (1) Martin, was born in 1659, and graduated from Harvard College in 1680. He was a school teacher and preacher, but was never ordained. He preached at Wells, Maine.

The records of the three succeeding generations (III), (IV), and (V) are lost so that the names cannot be given. The dates are 1684, 1709, 1734.

(VI) Richard (3), the great-great-grandson of Richard (2) Martin, was born in Portsmouth, New Hampshire, in 1756, died at Guilford, New Hampshire, October 17, 1824. During his early years he had some opportunities for obtaining an academic education, serving later an apprenticeship to the ropemaking trade. When he arrived at the age of twenty-one the revolutionary war was in progress and Burgoyne had landed in the north, and, relying on the skill and valor of his well-trained troops, had boasted that they would sweep through the whole land, vanquishing everything that opposed. Young Martin, with others in Portsmouth and the vicinity, enlisted in the service of his country. He was at Saratoga on that day, October 17, 1777, when the haughty British general, Burgoyne, surrendered his whole army of 5,752 men as prisoners of war to the American commander, General Gates. Richard Martin after serving his term of enlistment returned to Portsmouth. November 29, 1778, he married Hannah Faxon. He died at the age of sixty-eight years, his widow living until November 11, 1834. He was buried in Guilford and the following is the inscription on the marble at the head of his grave:

> Eld. Richard Martin
> died Oct. 17, 1824.
> aged 68.
> That death might be easy and quick
> In life was my fervent request;
> I died, and without being sick
> Escaped to and welcomed this rest.

The children of Richard and Hannah (Faxon) Martin were: 1. Hannah, married a Mr. Langley. 2. Christopher. 3. Betsy, married a Mr. Blaisdell. 4. Thankful, married a Mr. Jackson. 5. Richard Jr., died May 15, 1860. 6. John Langdon, of whom further.

(VII) John Langdon, son of Richard (3) Martin, was born in New Hampshire, 1782, died September 16, 1856. He was well educated, read medicine and became a well-known and popular practicing physician of Jefferson, New Hampshire. He died in Holyoke, Massachusetts, and is buried in Guilford, New Hampshire. He married (first) Sarah Marston, born in 1790, died in 1866, in Jefferson, New Hampshire. Their children were: 1. Serena, born January 17, 1812, married, in 1831, Aaron Potter, a farmer of Jefferson, and they had nine children: Elizabeth, Mary, George, John Henry, Serena (2), Annette, John Langdon, and two that died in infancy. 2. Sylvester, born in Jefferson, New Hampshire, August 20, 1817, married, January 9, 1842, Euphemia Stillings; their only son, Albert, succeeded his father as a farmer of Jefferson. 3. Woodbury Langdon, of whom further. 4. Willis B., born June 3, 1828, in Hartford, Massachusetts, married Ledora Smith, and both are buried in the same cemetery in East Hampton, Massachusetts; they had six children: i. Adella, born 1853, died 1854; ii. Fred Pierce, born in 1855, living in Holyoke, Massachusetts; iii. Lizzie Jane, born in 1857, deceased; iv. Mary Ella, born in 1863, living in Hartford, Connecticut, unmarried; v. Franz Irvine, born 1867, living in Northampton, Massachusetts, married Jessie Rush and had three children: Glen, deceased; Prudence and Priscilla; vi. Alice Belle, born 1871, married Edward Putnam, a manufacturer, residing in Hartford, Connecticut, with children: Dorothy and Elizabeth.

(VIII) Woodbury Langdon, son of John Langdon and Sarah (Marston) Martin, was born in Guilford, New Hampshire, February 4, 1822. He was educated in the public schools of Jefferson, New Hampshire, and in early life was a farmer. He followed several occupations in early life, finally settling in Holyoke, Massachusetts, where he established a retail coal and wood yard. He was very successful in business, continuing there until 1860, when he retired with a competence. He was a Republican in politics, and a Universalist in religious faith. He was a capable and energetic man of business and a citizen of high standing. He married (first) Julia, daughter of Timothy Estes (see Estes II). She was born in Jefferson, New Hampshire, August 22, 1824, died at New Haven, Connecticut, September 4, 1875. Children: 1. Elnora, born in South Hadley Falls, Massachusetts, December 18, 1846, died March 12, 1851, in Chicopee, Massachusetts. 2. Isadore, born July 12, 1852, died in Chicopee, August 17, 1852. 3. Clarence, born in Holyoke, Massachusetts, June 8, 1855, died there August 28, 1855. 4. Ida, of whom further. 5. Irvin, born in Holyoke, December 7, 1862, died there December 8, 1864. 6. Mabel, born in Springfield, Massachusetts, May 8, 1867, died May 18, 1867. Woodbury Langdon Martin married (second) Mrs. Mary (Fuller) Latham, who survives him, now residing in Bristol, Connecticut, without issue.

(IX) Ida, only child of Woodbury Langdon and Julia (Estes) Martin to survive infancy, was born in Holyoke, Massachusetts, February 1, 1861. When she was four years old her parents moved to Springfield, Massachusetts, and in 1870 moved to New Haven, Connecticut, where she attended private and boarding schools until she was fourteen years of age. She then entered Dean Academy, at Franklin, Massachusetts, continuing until her graduation in 1879. She married, June 19, 1883, Rev. Moses Henry Houghton (see Houghton VII).

(The Tuttle Line).

John Tuttle came from Wiltshire, England, and joined the settlement at Ipswich, Massachusetts, 1635, the same year that he arrived in the ship "Planter" as appears by the town record. His wife was Joanna, who before her marriage John Tuttle was a Widow Lawrence. John Tuttle was made a freeman, March 13, 1639, and a representative in 1644. In 1651 he was called "Mr." He went to Ireland about the time the disheartened colonists at New Haven were negotiating for the purchase of the city of Galloway in Ireland for a future home. He established himself advantageously there and never returned. He died at Carrickfergus, December 30, 1656. His wife Joanna followed him to Ireland in 1654. Their children were: 1. Abigail, born 1629. 2. Simon, born 1631. 3. Sarah, born 1633, married Richard Martin (see Martin I). 4. John, born 1634, married Mary ―――― and had one child, Mary, born April 23, 1663. 5. Simon, born 1637, married (first) in 1659, Joan Burnham; (second) in 1663, Sarah Cogswell.

(The Estes Line).

(I) Benjamin Estes married Sarah Littlefield, of a family distinguished in Maine from revolutionary days down to the present. Their children were: Tabitha, Sarah, Annie, Mary, Katurah, Lydia, Benjamin, Timothy, of whom further; Davis.

(II) Timothy, son of Benjamin and Sarah (Littlefield) Estes, was born in Jefferson, New Hampshire, 1797, died at South Hadley Falls, Massachusetts, 1870. He was a well known contractor and builder. Among his operations was the erection of the hotel on the summit of Mount Washington. He married (first) Mary Low, born in 1806, died in 1858, and is buried in the cemetery at South Hadley Falls. Their children were: 1. Julia, married (first) Charles Latham and they had one daughter, Lucy Ann, who died in 1876, married George W. D. Upton, who survives her and resides at Springfield. Julia (Estes) Latham married (second) Woodbury Langdon Martin (see Martin VIII). 2. Lydia Jane, died in Bradford, Pennsylvania, January 5, 1899; married Noah D. Folsom, a lock and gunsmith, who died in Bradford, January 30, 1900; child, Estes A., deceased. Timothy Estes married (second) Ruby Reynolds and their only daughter Mary, deceased, married Clifford Tily, a furniture dealer, now living in Holyoke, Massachusetts.

Mary (Low) Estes, the first wife of Timothy Estes, was a daughter of Levi and Mary (Soper) Low, of Westerville, Maine, and a granddaughter of Salter Soper. Levi and Mary (Soper) Low had seven children: 1. Levi, a sea captain, died at sea, married and left two children: Eugene and Florence, now living in Maine. 2. Justis, married Lois Watkins, both deceased; their children were: Levi, Pearl, Amos, John, and Mary, all died at Randolph, New York; Anna, the only survivor, married Dwight Phelps, of West Winsted, Connecticut. 3. Clovis, married Apple Green, both deceased; their children were: Electra, Perceval, Oscar, Thaddens, who constructed the railroad up Mount Low in California; Pembroke. 4. Amos, deceased, married and left a son Eugene. 5. Almond, married Olive Starboard; their children were: Charles, George Timothy, Nathaniel, Sylvania, Elvira, Emmeline. 6. Mary Low, married Timothy Estes, of previous mention. 7. Diana, married Anson Stillings and left children: Lyman, Paris, Caroline, Alden.

CLARK It is a confirmed tradition that this family came from Devon, England, from near Plymouth. Burke says: "The Clarks of Buckland were from the north, I believe from Elgin. They settled down in Devon some time in 1500, are worthy upright people". From another source: "The Clarks have never been an uppish pretentious people; most of them farmers; plain, simple honest people, always well enough off in a worldly sense to show them able to take care of themselves without following mean occupations and poor enough to show they are not grabbers of everything in sight".

(I) Samuel Clark was born in 1619 in Devonshire, England, came to Wethersfield, Connecticut, in 1636, and was one of twenty men who settled at Ripponwams, now Stamford, Connecticut, May 16, 1640, having become dissatisfied with the Wethersfield Colony. They purchased lands of the Indian chiefs, Ponus and Tognamske, for thirty pounds in July, 1640. He appears in the list of pioneers to the end of 1642. He is believed to have lived in Milford, Connecticut, in 1669, then moved to Hempstead, Long Island, and to have lived in New Haven, Connecticut, in 1685, died 1699. He married Hannah, daughter of Rev. Robert Fordham.

(II) William, son of Samuel Clark, was born in 1645 in Stamford, Connecticut, died in Bedford, New York, 1712. He removed to Bedford, Westchester county, New York, where he was one of the sixteen men who on December 23, 1680, purchased from the Indians the present township of Bedford, then called the hop lands. A part of this purchase is yet held and resided upon by a descendant, John Green Clark. They organized a Congregational church in 1680. On April 8, 1704, Queen Anne confirmed the town of Bedford twenty-three thousand acres to its twenty-nine land holders, three of whom were two Williams and Nathan Clark. He married and had sons: 1. William, married Hannah ———— and had John, William, Ebenezer, David and Joseph. 2. Nathan, of whom further. 3. Joseph, born about 1680; his name is found on several conveyances including a deal to twelve acres of upland, November 26, 1703, "upon ye Ridge called Clark's Ridge, part of ye land laid out to ye said Clark's honoured father William Clark, senior".

(III) Nathan, son of William Clark, was born at Stamford, Connecticut, 1676. His will is dated April 29, 1726. He came to Bedford with his parents when he was five years of age. He is said to have lived several years after making his will in 1726 and during his last illness made a new will which was worthless, he being too feeble to affix his signature. He was one of the twenty-nine land holders of Bedford to whom Queen Anne confirmed twenty-three thousand acres of land, April 8, 1704. He held several town offices and was a large land owner. His first wife Clemence died about 1709. He married a second wife whom he probably survived as she is not mentioned in his will. Children named in will are Stephen, born 1701; Nathan; Sylvanus, died a young man; Jehiel, born 1711; Joseph, of whom further; Nathaniel, 1714; Elizabeth; Deborah, 1718; Abigail; Esther; Comfort, 1722.

(IV) Joseph, son of Nathan Clark, was born in Bedford, Westchester county, New York, in 1713, died there April 18, 1791. He and his wife were brought up near neighbors in Bedford, and after their marriage settled on the farm at Copps Bottom about one mile west of the village where they spent the remainder of their lives. He married Sarah, daughter of Jacob Smith. She died of palsey, April, 1796. Children: 1. Ezra, died a young man. 2. James, a land surveyor, married Betsey Boulton and had twelve children; he settled in Western New York. 3. Abigail, married John Mills and had ten children; one child settled in Sullivan county, New York. 4. Anna, born July 1, 1742, died August 26, 1802; married Moses St. John, an elder of the Presbyterian church; eleven children. 5. Joseph, of whom further. 6. Nathan, born December 19, 1754, was a revolutionary pensioner; married Lydia, daughter of Joseph and Deborah (Clark) Holmes.

(V) Joseph (2), son of Joseph (1) Clark, was born in Bedford, Westchester county, New York, 1753, died 1821. He lived on the Clark homestead all his life. He married Hannah Clock, of Connecticut, born 1760, died 1825. Children: 1. Ezra, of whom further. 2. Lewis, married Catherine Whitney. 3. Bertha, married Jebiel Canfield. 4. Clara, married Caleb K. Hobbs. 5. Phoebe, married John Bussing. 6. Hannah, married Abial Raymond. 7. John, married Lucy Mead, his son, John Green Clark, now lives on the old homestead farm at Bedford which has been in the family over two hundred years; the home in which he lives is over one hundred years old and there have been eight generations of Clarks baptized in the Presbyterian church at Bedford. 8. Anna, married James Horne. 9. Joseph, had three wives. 10. Ira, married Eliza Backby.

(VI) Ezra, son of Joseph (2) Clark, was born in Bedford, Westchester county, New York, September 11, 1779, died 1858 in Sydney, New York, or Pennsylvania. He was a farmer and a lumberman. After leaving Bedford he settled in Bainbridge, New York, afterward moving to Sidney where he spent the greater part of his life. He married (first) ——— Banks; married (second) April 26, 1807, Mary Foote, born September 24, 1776, died May 8, 1858, in Bainbridge, New York, a member of the Presbyterian church. She was a daughter of a West Point officer serving on the staff of General Washington. Children by first wife: 1. Mary, married Roland Brown. 2. Sallie, married a Mr. Northup. 3. Samuel. 4. Edward, twin of Samuel. Children by second wife: 5. Eliza, married (first) Samuel Porter, no issue; married (second) Dr. William Purington and had a daughter Georgianna. 6. Joseph Foote, of whom further. 7. Susan, married William Wier, of Elmira, New York, and had a daughter Kate Ellen. 8. Henry, who died in 1907, aged over ninety; married Ellen Curtis, of Bainbridge, New York, who still survives him; children: George, Charles, Josephine. 9. Catherine, married William Wier; children: Alice, William, Fred. These children of second wife were all born either in Bainbridge or Sidney, New York.

(VII) Joseph Foote, son of Ezra Clark, was born in Bainbridge, Chenango county, New York, July 1, 1810. He was educated in the public schools finishing with a course at Sidney Academy. He early entered mercantile life, and at the time of his marriage owned and was conducting a dry goods store at Sidney, Delaware county, New York, about 1831 or 1832. He was also proprietor of a store at Smethport, Pennsylvania. At the time of the oil discoveries in Pennsylvania he owned land at Bradford which became oil property. He was very successful and continued his operations in oil until his death. He owned at one time over eght hundred acres of land in Bradford and vicinity, and at his death this was amicably divided among his heirs. The old homestead in Bedford is now occupied by his daughter, Mary Elizabeth Clark. In his final sickness he returned to Binghamton, New York, where he died June 25, 1877. He was a Democrat in politics and for many years a justice of the peace.

He married Laura Louisa Phelps, born in Hebron, Tolland county, Connecticut, August 29, 1809, died 1883, daughter of Roger Phelps, son of a revolutionary soldier, born October 7, 1762, on a farm at Hebron, Connecticut, which is now and has been for seven generations owned in the Phelps family. He died September, 1846. Roger Phelps married Anna Jones, born March 20, 1765, died February 2, 1821. Their children, all born in Hebron, Connecticut: 1. Anna, born November 29, 1787, died September 9, 1850; married Andrew Mann. 2. Betsey, born September 25, 1790, married Allan Knapp, of Colchester, Delaware county, New York. 3. Maria, born March 8, 1793, died April 25, 1848; married Reuben Mann, of Hebron. 4. Henry, born December 1, 1795, died April 6, 1852; married (first) ——— Way; married (second) Ellen Hodges. 5. Rachel, born January 16, 1799, died unmarried, 1868. 6. Clarisa, born October 31, 1801, died June 29, 1861; married Edward Way. 7. Roger L., born April 12, 1805, died March 2, 1863; married Elizabeth Strong. 8. Laura L., born August 29, 1809, a member of the Episcopal church, died at Binghamton; married Joseph Foote Clark. Children of Mr. and Mrs. Clark: 1. Theodore Mortier, born at Smethport, Pennsylvania, October 10, 1834, died at Kendall Creek, now a part of Bradford, Pennsylvania, June 9, 1882; he was a lumberman and a school teacher; served three years during the civil war in Company E, Fifty-eighth Regiment Pennsylvania Volunteer Infantry. 2. Junius Randolph, born at Smethport, July 24, 1836, died February 12, 1912; he was a lawyer; married (first) Ann Eliza Viely, of Jordan, New York; (second) Mary Morse, of Elmira, New York; children by first wife: Frederick, died young; Mortimer, married Claude Dorn and had Lawrence, deceased; Sarah, born 1900; Fred, 1902; Junius, 1907; child by second wife: Paul, born 1877. 3. Charles Randolph, born in Smethport, August 1, 1838, died at Jefferson City, Missouri, May, 1904; he was a speculator and jobber; during the civil war he served in the Pennsylvania "Bucktail" Regiment. 4. Edward Kissam, born at Smethport, January 1, 1841, died at Binghamton, New York, May 30, 1912; married Martha Jane Seymour, of Binghamton, New York; children: i. Roger Phelps, resides in Binghamton, unmarried; an attorney; was assistant counsel to Governor Hughes until the latter was appointed to the supreme court; ii. Laura Louise, married Franklin Morgan and resides in New London, Connecticut; iii. Charles Seymour, deceased; iv. Anna Whitman, a teacher at Lakewood, New Jersey; v. Joseph Foote, superintendent for Pruitt Brothers, leather jobbers of Binghamton, New York, married Grace Van Wormer; vi. Edward Kissam, auditor of a street railway company at Worcester, Massachusetts, married Carrie Emerson; vii. Vernon Seymour, an attorney of New York City, married Laura Mahan; viii. Florence, deceased; ix. Mary Elizabeth, now taking a library course in Brooklyn, New York; x. Louis, now a student at Albany Law School. 5. Ellen Clarissa, born in Bradford, Pennsylvania, July 31, 1843, died April 4, 1912; married William M. Hanna; children: i. Genevieve, born December 9, 1881; ii. Junius Robert, born November, 1883; at the time of the great earthquake in San Francisco he was a student at Stanford and the only person from that institution who lost his life in that disaster. 6. Mary Elizabeth, of whom further.

(VIII) Mary Elizabeth, daughter of Joseph Foote Clark, was born in Cameron county, Pennsylvania, then McKean county, September 11, 1845. She was educated in the public schools at Smethport, Pennsylvania, Bradford Academy and Elmira Female College (New York). After completing her studies she resided with her brother until 1878, then until 1880 sojourning with her mother, an invalid, at Saratoga Springs, New York. Miss Clark has traveled extensively, both at home and abroad, spending the year 1883 in Germany, and since making a more extended tour of Europe. Her American travel included a trip to California and other points of interest in the far west. She resides in Bradford at the old homestead surrounded by her share of the paternal acres.

BOARDMAN

The family of Boardman had its origin in England from William, surnamed "Le Bois de Main," or "of the wooden hand," a Norman and a follower of William the Conqueror. This William had a grant from his monarch, of two knight's fees of land in the county of Suffolk, as is mentioned in "Domesday Book." From him descended Sir Andrew Boardman, the favorite of King Henry VIII., who gave him in marriage the hand of his ward, Lady Katherine Howard, daughter of the Earl of Berkshire, and ultimately sole heiress of her father. During the reign of Queen Elizabeth, two of the sons of Sir Andrew Boardman held command under the Earl of Leicester in the expedition to Ireland, against "the Desmond," one of them having a grant of forfeited land, settled there, and was the progenitor of the Irish line of Boardmans. The English branch of the family is settled in Suffolk. Arms: Argent a chevron vert bordered, gules, ducally gorged and chained or. The chevron shows that he to whom the arms were granted had been present at the siege of a city, the lion in the crest shows that he commanded, and that the enemy retreated leaving him master of the field, and the ducal coronet shows that the enemy was one of the sovereign Dukes of France, and that he or one of his family had been taken prisoner is shown by the chain. The arms of Boardman were all quartered with those of Howard in right of the wife of Sir Andrew. By this marriage they are descended from Edward the Confessor, Hugh Capet, King of France, and Rudolph, the first Emperor of Germany.

The American history of the family begins in 1635. The name in early colonial records is spelled Boreman, Borman, Bordman, Bourman and Boardman. Two of the English emigrants, Thomas and Samuel, were of Ipswich, Massachusetts, 1635. They are not known to have been related.

(I) Samuel Boreman, the progenitor of the line herein recorded, moved to Wethersfield, Connecticut, where he was a man of importance, eighteen times elected deputy to the general court and held many other offices. He died aged fifty-eight years, in April, 1673. His widow, Mary (Betts) Boreman, survived him eleven years and died in August, 1684; ten children.

(II) Nathaniel Boreman, son of Samuel Boreman, was born in Wethersfield, Connecticut, April 12, 1663. He married, late in life, April 30, 1707, Elizabeth Strong, born February 20, 1670, daughter of Lieutenant Return Strong; one child.

(III) Sergeant Nathaniel (2) Bordman (as he spelled the name), only child of Nathaniel (1) Boreman, was born February 19, 1711-12. His father died when he was nine months old, in 1712, making provision in a hastily drawn will of three days before that his wife should bring up his son "to good learning". The widowed mother married, two or three years later, Captain William Warner, and is found again a widow in 1726. Sergeant Bordman's home was the farm, one and one-half miles west of Rock Hill, Connecticut. He died of pleurisy, May 12, 1776. His widow, Ruth (Parker) Bordman, died May 17, 1799, aged eighty-four years; five children.

(IV) Nathaniel (3) Bordman, son of Sergeant Nathaniel (2) Bordman, was born at Rocky Hill, Connecticut, January 25, 1734, died May 4, 1776, of pleurisy, eight days prior to the death of his father of the same disease. He married Mabel Holmes, born September 16, 1736, died November 14, 1777, leaving eight children, the youngest an infant.

(V) Levi Boardman (as he spelled the name), son of Nathaniel (3) Bordman, was born at Rocky Hill, Connecticut, September 21, 1759, died January 16, 1818. He married, January 4, 1789, Rachel, daughter of David and Rachel (Curtis) Riley, who died in 1847, at the home of her son Eleazer in New York state; four children. In this generation the spelling became Boardman in this branch.

(VI) Eleazer, son of Levi Boardman, was born March 24, 1794. He settled in New York state, where he married and reared a family, his wife being a woman of Scotch descent. Children: 1. John. 2. Polly, died in Freehold, Pennsylvania; married Amos Carpenter, a farmer; children: Lucy, deceased; a son, deceased; Adelbert, living in the west; Velorous, deceased. 3. Levi, died in Freehold, a farmer; married and left a family. 4. Sarah (Sally), died in Lottsville, Warren county, Pennsylvania; married Jared Lathrop, a farmer; no issue. 5. Lovena, married a Mr. Sweetland and left three sons: William, now living at Bear Lake, Pennsylvania; Josiah, died in Wrightsville, Pennsylvania, where his widow and children reside, and Jeremiah. 6. Samuel, killed in battle during the civil war; he served in a Pennsylvania regiment with his two sons and brother Jared, the latter being the only one who returned from the cruel struggle between the North and South. 7. Jared, of whom further.

(VII) Jared, son of Eleazer Boardman, was born in Cherry Valley, New York, September 8, 1817, died in Wrightsville, Pennsylvania, June 5, 1882. He grew up on the home farm, and on arriving at man's estate came to Pennsylvania, settling in Wrightsville, Freehold township, Warren county. He was a farmer all his life and a man of considerable importance. He enlisted and served three years in the civil war in a Pennsylvania regiment, receiving honorable discharge in 1864. He received injuries that incapacitated him for field service, but was assigned to lighter duty at Fortress Monroe during the remainder of his term of enlistment. At the time of Lincoln's assassination he was in Pittsfield, Pennsylvania, and walked six miles to Wrightsville, carrying the sad intelligence to that village, there being then no telegraph communication. After the war was over he returned to the farm at Wrightsville, continuing its cultivation until his death. He was a Republican in politics and for many years served as school director. In religious faith he was a Methodist as was his wife.

He married Viletta Wyman, born in New York state, April 11, 1819, died October 21, 1832, at Derrick City, Pennsylvania, daughter of Eli Wyman, born 1796, died in Wrightsville, Freehold township, Warren county, Pennsylvania, September, 1872. He was a farmer, and during all his later years an elder of the Presbyterian church. He married Polly Heather, born in Vermont, 1797, died in Wrightsville, 1884. Children of Mr. and Mrs. Wyman: 1. Alzina, born 1816, died 1903; married Samuel Boardman, a farmer, who died in the Union army during the civil war; children: Andrew, now living at Columbus, Warren county, Pennsylvania; Polly, now living at Sugar Grove, Pennsylvania; Charles, died in the army; Eli, died in the army; George, now living in Corry, Pennsylvania; Minerva, now living in the west; Byron, now living in Wrightsville, Pennsylvania; Bruce, now living in Columbus, Pennsylvania. 2. Viletta, of previous mention, married Jared Boardman. 3. Horace, born 1821, died in Greeley, Colorado, in 1909; he was engaged in mercantile business; married Fidelia Mead, of Youngsville, Pennsylvania; son, Frank, now a jeweler of Warren, Pennsylvania. 4. George, born 1823, died in Greeley, Colorado, where he was engaged in merchandising; he married Algiva Hubbard, of Ohio; children:

Fred, Iva and a son, all living in Greeley. Children of Jared and Viletta Boardman, all born in Warren county, Pennsylvania: 1. Betsey, born August, 1845, died in Wrightsville in 1884; married Philander Wright, now a retired merchant of Seattle, Washington; children, all born in Wrightsville: i. Clara, born July, 1866, married William Wilcox, a merchant of Corry, Pennsylvania, children: Mary, born October, 1886, in Wrightsville, and Donald, 1891, in Corry; ii. Mary, born March, 1875, died January, 1882; iii. Charles, born April 24, 1878, now a watchmaker and jeweler of Seattle, married and had a son Lester. 2. Alphonso Marcellus, of whom further. 3. Horace Edgar, born August 20, 1850, now proprietor of a bakery in Bolivar, New York; he married Mary Price; children: i. Belle, born February 2, 1876, married Elmer Krugh, of Sistersville, West Virginia, a merchant, child, Alice, born January, 1907; ii. Fon W., born June 3, 1884, married Lena Steinberger and is a baker in Bolivar, child, Fon, born June 28, 1911. 4. Artemesia, died in infancy. 5. Arthur W., born August 3, 1860, now manager of the Gas Company at Sheffield, Pennsylvania; married Mattie Blood; children: Fred, born September 12, 1884; Ora, June, 1887; Lottie, all living in Sheffield. 6. Mary, died in infancy.

(VIII) Alphonso Marcellus, eldest son and second child of Jared and Viletta (Wyman) Boardman, was born in Wrightsville, Freehold township, Warren county, Pennsylvania, April 30, 1848. There his early years were spent and his education secured in the public schools. After completing his years of study, he engaged in farming. In 1871 he secured a lease on the Beatty farm at Fagundus, Warren county, and there for seven years was engaged in oil production. He then for two years was engaged in the grocery business at Fagundus, then for five years, beginning in 1880, he conducted a grocery store in Allegheny county, near the McKean county line at a place called State Line. In 1885 he sold his store and purchased land, oil and gas leases at Four Mile, New York, remaining in business there two years. His daughter having arrived at an age that her education became an important consideration he purchased a home at Sugar Grove, Pennsylvania, and made it his residence while she attended the excellent seminary located there. In the autumn of 1890 he moved to Derrick City, Pennsylvania, and spent the ensuing nine years in the management of his oil properties. In addition to his private oil interests he formed the mercantile firm of Boardman & Johnson and conducted a profitable general merchandising business. In 1899 he was elected commissioner of McKean county and during his three years in that office resided in Smethport, the county seat. In July, 1902, he located his residence in Bradford where he established and has ever since conducted a most profitable insurance business.

He is a Republican in politics, and besides his three years as county commissioner served as supervisor for five years and school director four years, being secretary of the board for three of these years. He was made a Mason in Olean Lodge, Free and Accepted Masons, in 1884, demitting in 1899 to Bradford Lodge, No. 334. He is also a member of Coudersport Lodge of Perfection, and Consistory, Ancient Accepted Scottish Rite, holding the thirty-second degree. He is also a noble of Ismailia Temple, Ancient Arabic Order Nobles of the Mystic Shrine, located at Buffalo, New York. His other fraternal orders are: Tent, No. 1101, Independent Order of Odd Fellows, of Derrick City; Fosterbrook Lodge, No. 11, Knights of Pythias, at Gilmore, Pennsylvania, and the Protected Home Circle, No. 68. His religious faith is Presbyterian, as is his wife, who belongs to the Eastern Star.

He married, August 5, 1869, Alice Kay, born in Sugar Grove township, Warren county, Pennsylvania, February 26, 1849, and there educated in the public schools, daughter of William and a granddaughter of John Kay.

Children of Alphonso M. and Alice (Kay) Boardman: 1. Lida Pearl, born at Stetson Hill, Pennsylvania, October 23, 1872; married George Washington Jude, born at Findlay Lake, New York, February 22, 1866, now a lawyer of Jamestown, New York; child, Robert Boardman, born in Bradford, November 8, 1906. 2. Dora, born in Fagundus, Pennsylvania, September 22, 1876, died at State Line, New York, November 17, 1881. 3. Earl W., born in Fagundus, Pennsylvania, March 15, 1878, died December 11, 1881. 4. Rhea Kay, born at State Line, New York, February 12, 1885, now a teacher in Jamestown, New York.

(The Kay Line).

(I) John Kay, born near Manchester, England, died at Sugar Grove, Pennsylvania. He married ———— ————. Children: William, of whom further; Robert, born 1812, died in Manchester; James, born in Manchester, 1815, died in Ashville, New York, being then a retired farmer, married without issue.

(II) William, son of John Kay, was born at Oldham, near Manchester, England, July 17, 1809. He came to the United States in 1846, settling in Pennsylvania in Sugar Grove township, Warren county. He there built a saw mill, superintending its operation until his death, April 2, 1895. He married Mary Hilton, born March 27, 1815, in Oldham, England, came to the United States with her husband, died in Sugar Grove, January 5, 1892. Children: 1. Thomas, born in England, May 8, 1835, now a retired miller of Youngsville, Pennsylvania; married Lizzie Gray, born in England, deceased; children: Charles, born September 27, 1860, lives in Youngsville; Frank, May 16, 1862, deceased; Christy, November, 1863, deceased; Fred, June 17, 1865, lives in Youngsville; Edward, December 31, 1868, deceased. 2. Ann, born March 14, 1837, now living in Jamestown, New York; married Jeremiah Nuttle, of English birth, a farmer of Sugar Grove; children: Ina, born June 5, 1865, married Levant Ricker and lives in Jamestown, New York; William L., born February 2, 1860, lives at Findlay Lake, New York, married (first) Grace Duryea, (second) Ruth Campbell. Grace, born June 7, 1878, married Elmer Wilson and has two children: Gladys and Helen. 3. Mary, born February 16, 1839, lives at Ripley, New York; married her cousin, James Kay, deceased, and settled in Chautauqua county, New York; children: Nellie, born November, 1861; William, May 8, 1865, deceased, and Sophrona, born March, 1876. 4. Elizabeth, born May 1, 1845, died April, 1909, in New York City; married David N. Stilson, of Warren county, Pennsylvania, a merchant of Sugar Grove, Pennsylvania; child, William Earl, born Stetson Hill, Warren county, Pennsylvania, May 15, 1870, married Amy Short, daughter of a prominent banker of Sugar Grove; children; Alden, born January 15, 1901; Earl, born May 1, 1907. 5. Alice, of previous mention, wife of Alphonso M. Boardman. 6. Eliza, born January 20, 1851; married G. Wallace Shutt, of Warren, Pennsylvania, a farmer; children: Mary, born September 30, 1875, married William Bovee, an oil contractor of Grand Valley, Pennsylvania; Broe, born August 30, 1880, now a store manager, married Bess Daley and lives in Sugar Grove. 7. Melvina, born October 5, 1854, died March, 1855. 8. Armina, born May 18, 1856; married George Murray, born 1850 in Glasgow, Scotland, now a retired merchant in Bradford; children: Maud, born May 25, 1879, married Frank Demmick; Stuart, born February 1, 1884, married Jennie Thompson; Stanley, born March 4, 1887, now a chemist of Utica, New York. The last four of these children were born at Stetson Hill, Warren county, Pennsylvania.

HOGARTH The Hogarths of Smethport are of pure Scotch blood, the father and many preceding grandfathers of Leon Keating Hogarth having been born in Scotland.

(I) William Hogarth was an engineer in the English army in India, and met his death in the great Sepoy rebellion. He married and left issue: 1. Cordelia, lived in London, England. 2. Harriet, married Rev. Mr. Hewitt, a Presbyterian minister and emigrated to Canada; one of their children, Harriet, married W. E. Jordan, and is living at No. 623 Cherry street, Erie, Pennsylvania. 3. Mary, married Mr. Pierce, and lived at 4 Waterloo Place, Pall Mall, London, England. 4. Emma, no further record. 5. Thomas, no further record. 6. Frederick William, of whom further. Parents and children were all members of the Church of England.

(II) Dr. Frederick William Hogarth, son of William Hogarth, was born in Glasgow, Scotland, February 14, 1840, died in Port Allegany, Pennsylvania, December 13, 1887. His parents lived in London at the time his father enlisted and was sent to India, and the lad was educated in the old Blue Coat School, founded in 1545 by Henry VIII of England. This is a famous school supported by the British government, the distinctive uniform for the boys being a blue coat. Later he entered a university in Dublin, Ireland, whence he was graduated in pharmacy in 1858. He then came to the United States, settling in Rochester, New York, where he secured employment as draughtsman with the company then building the first railroad between Rochester and Buffalo. In 1861 he enlisted in a New York regiment, serving three months as hospital steward. He then enlisted with the famous Pennsylvania Bucktails, serving in the same capacity until April 12, 1864, when he was transferred to the northwestern territory as assistant surgeon. He saw active service there against the Indians, accompanying his regiment on their expedition into the Black Hills of Wyoming, and on other hazardous marches. After the war he continued medical study, and was graduated Medical Doctor from the University of Buffalo. In 1866 he established in Smethport the first drugstore in McKean county; later moved to Port Allegany, establishing a drugstore there and practicing his profession until his death. He was a successful pharmacist and skillful physician, lovingly remembered by the early settlers as their rock of refuge in times of illness and trouble. He was a member of the Episcopal church and a man of unblemished character.

He married, in Smethport, November 15, 1868, Florence Marian Bennett, born there April 22, 1847, who survives him, a resident of Smethport, a lady of refined and Christian character, educated in the seminary of Lima, New York, and a member of St. Luke's Episcopal Church. She is a daughter of David R. Bennett, born in New York state, January 28, 1810, died at Port Allegany, Pennsylvania, March 23, 1876, at one time sheriff of McKean county. He married, August 14, 1835, Corinna Nana Chapin, born in Chenango county, New York, August 10, 1817, died February 14, 1893, daughter of Henry Chapin and his first wife Johanna Kimball. Children of Dr. Frederick W. Hogarth: 1. Leon Keating, of whom further. 2. Ruth, born at Port Allegany, Pennsylvania, September 23, 1871, died there August 26, 1890.

(III) Leon Keating, only son of Dr. Frederick William and Florence M. (Bennett) Hogarth, was born in Port Allegany, Pennsylvania, September 9, 1869. He was educated in the public schools of Port Allegany and Smethport. After leaving school he entered the drugstore of Alvin B. Armstrong, who had married Caroline E. Bennett, sister of Mrs. Hogarth, and who succeeded Seems & Hogarth in the business established by Dr. Frederick W. Hogarth in 1866, the oldest drug business in McKean county. Mr. Hogarth has since remained in Smethport, prosperous and rated among the town's best citizens. He is a member of the Smethport Tribe, Improved Order of Redmen. He is special deputy game warden of the state of Pennsylvania; secretary and treasurer of the Olds Rod and Gun Club; and a member of St. Luke's Episcopal Church. In politics a Republican, holding for one term the office of chief burgess.

He married, May 16, 1892, Etta Powell, born May 21, 1871, in Foxburg, Venango county, Pennsylvania. She grew to womanhood in Oil City, where her parents moved when she was an infant. She was educated in the public schools, finishing at Bradford high school, and taught in the public schools of McKean county until her marriage in 1892. She is a member of St. Luke's Episcopal Church and of the Travelers' Club, both of Smethport. Children of Leon Keating and Etta (Powell) Hogarth: 1. John Donald, born in Coudersport, Pennsylvania, September 8, 1893, now a junior at Pennsylvania State College, preparing for a career in law. 2. Leona Florence, born in Smethport November 8, 1895, a student at Smethport high school in her senior year, and organist of St. Luke's Episcopal Church. 3. Dorothy Lavinia, born in Smethport, December 26, 1900.

The Powell Line.

The first of this line was Benjamin Powell, of Welsh descent, born May 28, 1764, at Concord, New Hampshire, died August 15, 1852. He married Betsy Bradley, born in Concord, New Hampshire, April 19, 1765, died May 1, 1812. Betsy or Elizabeth Bradley was a sister of Captain Sam Bradley, killed in the massacre of all his company by Indians at Concord, behind a rock which is now a monument with the names engraved thereon of all who fell that day. Benjamin Powell served as a drummer boy in the revolution, though he must have been very young. Among his children was a son, Peter, of whom further.

(II) Dr. Peter Powell, son of Benjamin Powell, was born in Concord, New Hampshire, July 19, 1803, died in Edenburg, Pennsylvania, June 24, 1878, aged seventy-five years. He was a practicing physician. By his first marriage Dr. Powell had a daughter, Amanda, married Mr. Beck, and lives in Ten Mile Bottom, Venango county, Pennsylvania. She has six living children, forty-nine grandchildren, and fifty-one great-grandchildren. He married (second) March 22, 1840, Louisa Blakeslee, born in Crawford county, Pennsylvania, September 14, 1820, died at Dayton, Iowa county, Iowa, November 30, 1863, daughter of John and Nancy (Ward) Blakeslee. John Blakeslee was born in Granville county, Pennsylvania, 1793, died April 8, 1867, at Ridgefield, Illinois, and was the son of Captain ——— Blakeslee, who served in the revolutionary war. Children by second wife: 1. Leona, living in Chicago, widow of Captain Wilson, an officer of the civil war, interested financially in the Chicago stockyards. Children: Harry, Hazel, Edith and Mazie. 2. Alice, died in Minneapolis, Minnesota, married in Edenburg, Pennsylvania, Mr. Galbraith, an oil well worker. Children: William, James, Jennie, and Sylvia, all deceased; Harry, living in Los Angeles, California; Charles O., living in Knox, Pennsylvania. 3. John Henry, of whom further. 4. Delia, died in Chicago; married Mr. Atkinson, an oil well driller, also deceased. Children: Alice, Laura, David, and James. 5. Minnie, died in Duke Center, Pennsylvania; married Mr. Snedecker, an oil derrick builder, also deceased, leaving two sons.

(III) John Henry, son of Dr. Peter Powell, was born March 7, 1846, died in Bradford, Pennsylvania, July 8, 1883. When but fifteen years of age he enlisted in the Twenty-eighth Regiment Iowa Volunteers, and served three years of the civil war as orderly for Captain Wilson. After the war he came to McKean county, following the oil fields until his death. He married, March 3, 1869, Lavinia Weaver, born in Nickleville, Venango county, Pennsylvania, March 3, 1849, who survives him, a resident of Seattle, Washington. Children: 1. Archibald, born in Foxburg, Pennsylvania, March, 1870, died in Oil City, 1875. 2. Etta, married Leon Keating Hogarth (see Hogarth III). 3. Vinnie, born in Oil City December 1, 1872; married Charles F. Schwab, born in Wilkes-Barre, now living in Bradford, Pennsylvania, an oil producer. Children: Frederick, born September, 1902; Richard, November, 1903; Louise, October, 1906. 4. Samuel, born in Oil City August 12, 1874; married Elida Wright, daughter of F. B. Wright, colonel of the famous Bucktail Regiment that won renown in the civil war, and founder and former proprietor of the Wright House, Smethport. This family now resides in Seattle, Washington. Children: John Franklin, born August, 1900; Frank Wright, February, 1908. 5. Katherine, born in Oil City, June 17, 1877; married R. A. Stewart, of Bradford, a telegraph operator, now living in Seattle, Washington, no issue.

Mrs. Lavinia (Weaver) Powell is of German descent, and her father, speaking German as his usual speech, was probably the emigrant. Mr. Weaver was a minister of the Evangelical Lutheran church, and left good estate at Nickleville, Pennsylvania. He married a Miss Gilbert, of French extraction. His family consisted of twelve children: 1. Joshua, a farmer, died at East Sandy, Venango county, leaving a large family. 2. "Cooney," yet living in Venango county, an oil producer, wife deceased, leaving issue. 3. Elizabeth, died in Franklin, Pennsylvania, twice married. Children: Elmer, Charles, and James McKee, all living in Franklin. 4. Margaret, married William Todd, and resides on the old Weaver homestead. Children: Laura, William, and Andrew. 5. Jane, died at Nickleville; married Solomon Myers, a farmer and miller, who survives her with issue. 6. Lavinia, of previous mention, wife of John Henry Powell. 7. Samuel, now a fruit farmer, of Los Angeles, California; married Ella Hall, and has issue. 8. John Oliver, went west and was last heard from in the Black Hills, Wyoming. 9. George, a physician of Nickleville, married and has a family. 10. William, now living in Oil City, a contractor; married Molly ———. Children: Forest, and Winifred. 11. Katherine, died in Oil City; married Dr. Dunlap, no issue. 12. No record.

There are many branches of the BARR Barr family in Pennsylvania, not all springing from the same source. The branch herein recorded cannot be definitely placed, but it is supposed they are of German descent. They were in Lancaster county prior to 1790 and lived near Quarryville where stands the famous "Ark" built in that year by Martin Barr, a wealthy distiller, as a residence. This house, at the time it was built, was not only the largest in that locality, but it was one of the finest and best. The main house was sixty-five by fifty-five feet and thirty feet high from the foundation wall to the eaves. The walls were two feet thick, built of stone. Not a nail was used in its inside finish, wooden pegs and pins being used instead. The hall, twelve feet wide, runs through the centre and the stairway is winding, continuing to the garret. This stairway is a mechanical marvel and has not been improved on by modern stair builders.

The Barrs were good farmers and the land always improved under their farming methods. They fed a large number of cattle and had large flocks of sheep. Martin Barr, builder of the "Ark," had four sons: Abraham, Christian, Martin, Jacob, and two daughters, one, Christina, married John Mowrer; she was the first child born in the "Ark" and lived to be one of the oldest residents in her community. Martin Barr, the father, lived to be a very old man, dying early in the nineteenth century. He was buried in the Barr graveyard, one of the oldest burying grounds in the country. He and wife Elizabeth were Mennonites.

(II) Martin (2), youngest son of Martin (1) Barr, was born in 1773, died in 1826. His father built him a substantial house and barn in 1792. These were of stone, well finished, and are yet in use. He married and had issue, but after the death of their parents the children left Lancaster county and settled in Western Pennsylvania and Ohio.

(III) Jacob, son of Martin Barr, was born in Quarryville, Lancaster county, Pennsylvania, where he resided until well along in life. He spent the last years of his life as a collier in Bruin, Butler county, Pennsylvania, where he died. He was a communicant of the Methodist Episcopal church. He married and had issue: 1. Jacob, died in Bruin, Butler county, Pennsylvania; he was a collier; he married and had a family. 2. Samuel, a lumberman, died in Clarion county, Pennsylvania, leaving issue. 3. John, a collier, died in Oil City, Pennsylvania; married —— ——, deceased, and had children. 4. Katherine, deceased, married —— ——, deceased, and had issue. 5. Christian, of whom further.

(IV) Christian, son of Jacob Barr, was born in Bradford county, Pennsylvania "East of the Mountains," April 6, 1806, died in Bruin, Butler county, Pennsylvania, August 23, 1862. He followed the business of a collier all his life. He settled in Bruin, Pennsylvania. He was a Republican in politics. He married (first) Christiana Stull; (second) in 1830, Sarah Bossard, born in Woodcock township, Crawford county, Pennsylvania, February 28, 1808, died in Meadville, Pennsylvania, in August, 1876. One child by first wife. Children by second wife, born in Woodcock township, Crawford county, Pennsylvania, six miles north of Meadville: 1. Anna Catherine, born June 22, 1831, died in Union City, Pennsylvania, January 6, 1893; married (first) Garrett Davison, deceased, and (second) —— Morton, deceased; children, all by first marriage: John, deceased; Addie, married Albert Wales, and lives in Corry, Pennsylvania; Charles, lives in Union City, Pennsylvania; Laura, deceased. 2. John Henry, born in Crawford county, Pennsylvania, June 20, 1833, died September 10, 1905, at Union City; was a cooper; married Jane Floyd, of Blooming Valley, Pennsylvania; children: Christian, Minnie and Ellen, all deceased; and Catherine, married Max Cottrel, an employee in a chair factory at Union City. 3. Thomas Jefferson, born October 6, 1834, died in Meadville, Pennsylvania, June 2, 1886; was a cabinetmaker; married Margaret Briggs, living in the west; they had a large family. 4. Rosanna, born June 13, 1836; lives in Hayfield township, Crawford county, Pennsylvania; married Harrison Deross, of Crawford county, Pennsylvania, a farmer. 5. Mary Anjeline, born May 2, 1838. 6. Samuel, born June 8, 1839. 7. Jacob, born December 13, 1840, unmarried, died in 1862 at Bakersburg, Maryland, from effects of a fever incurred shortly after enlistment in the army during the civil war. 8. William G., born September 7, 1842; a cooper of Blooming Valley, Pennsylvania; he fought through the civil war in Company C, One Hundred and Fiftieth Regiment Pennsylvania Infantry Volunteers; he was taken prisoner and kept in the Confederate prison pen at Andersonville for seven months and seven days; he married Matilda Brown, of Blooming Valley. 9. Sarah Elmina, born July 12, 1844; lived at Blooming Valley; married Samuel P. Gilmore, a farmer of Blooming Valley, where he died in 1908; children: Lynn, of Crawford county, Pennsylvania; Lyle, deceased; Hugh; Grove and Harry, living in Mason City, Iowa. 10. Jonathan David, born September 15, 1846; a merchant living in Blooming Valley, Pennsylvania; married (first) Anna Thompson, deceased, (second) Stella Hayse, (third) Hester Dewey, of Blooming Valley; child of first wife: Lulu, married Oscar Rondebush, sheriff of Crawford county; child by second wife: Hayse, of Blooming Valley; children by third wife: Dewey, Elizabeth and Douglas, all living with their parents. 11. Charles C., born January 29, 1851; a farmer of Erie, Pennsylvania; married Florence McKelvy, of Bruin, Pennsylvania, and has two children: Harry E., a consulting engineer in Erie, Pennsylvania; Brendis, lives with parents. 12. Christian S., of whom further.

(V) Christian S., son of Christian and

Sarah (Bossard) Barr, was born in Woodcock township, Crawford county, Pennsylvania, September 8, 1853. When he was very young his parents moved to Bruin, Butler county, Pennsylvania, and when he was but nine years of age his father died and he then made his residence with his oldest brother, John, in Blooming Valley, Crawford county, Pennsylvania, where he was educated in the public schools. In 1877 he began working on an oil lease in Butler county, Pennsylvania, where he remained until January 1, 1881, when he moved to Derrick City, McKean county, Pennsylvania, taking a position with the Tide Water Pipe Company, with which company he is still employed. His career with them has been a series of promotions, each one coming from merit recognized. He began with the company on construction work, at which he remained for fifteen months, was promoted to guager, a position he held until 1902, when he was advanced to the office of district foreman, and on July 1, 1908, he received his final promotion, becoming superintendent of the local lines of the company with his office at No. 14 South avenue, Bradford.

Mr. Barr is one of the leading and most enterprising and energetic citizens of Bradford, held in high regard throughout the community. His political sympathies are with the Republican party, although he has never held any office. He is a regular attendant of the Methodist Episcopal church. His club is the Merchants of Bradford, and he is a member of the Bradford Lodge, No. 334, Free and Accepted Masons; Chapter, No. 260, Royal Arch Masons, at Bradford; Commandery, No. 58, Knights Templar, and Zem Zem Temple, Nobles of the Mystic Shrine.

He married, July 24, 1880, Elizabeth Ellen Marshall, born near Wilmington, Lawrence county, Pennsylvania, January 11, 1858. She was educated in the public schools of Venango county, Pennsylvania. She is a member of the Methodist Episcopal church of Bradford, and belongs to the McKean County Historical Society.

Child of Christian S. and Elizabeth Ellen (Marshall) Barr: Gretchen Freda, born in Derrick City, Pennsylvania, May 9, 1891; she was graduated from Bradford high school, class of 1907, of which she was valedictorian, and later attended Mount Holyoke College, from which she was graduated, class of 1911, holding the office of treasurer.

(The Marshall Line).

(I) Samuel Marshall was a farmer of Beaver, Pennsylvania, and died at the age of eighty years. He married Elizabeth Swager, a native of Pennsylvania. Children: 1. Catherine, died in Bradford, Pennsylvania; married ——— Johnson, of New Castle, Pennsylvania, and had one son, Marshall, deceased. 2. Belle, died in New Castle, Pennsylvania; married Samuel Duncan, a merchant tailor of New Castle, where he died. 3. Hugh, of whom further. 4. John, a merchant, died in Oil City, Pennsylvania; married Mary Zuver.

(II) Hugh, son of Samuel and Elizabeth (Swager) Marshall, was born in Beaver, Pennsylvania, January 28, 1826, died in Pleasantville, Pennsylvania, December 8, 1898. He married Susanna Zuver, born June 9, 1831, in Mercer county, Pennsylvania, died in Pleasantville, December 25, 1904. She was a granddaughter of George Zuver, who fought during the revolutionary war, and a daughter of William Zuver, born in Mercer county, Pennsylvania, in 1790, died in Pleasantville, Pennsylvania, 1869. He married Mary Sampson, born in Lawrence county, Pennsylvania, 1800, died in Pleasantville, 1879. Children of Mr. and Mrs. Zuver: 1. George Emery, an oil producer, died in Pleasantville; married Susan Turner, deceased; children: George Quincy, lives in Tionesta, Pennsylvania; Mary, lives in Butler, Pennsylvania; Lewis, lives in Butler, Pennsylvania; Jennie, lives in Martinsburg, Pennsylvania; Thomas, deceased; Leander, lives in Tionesta, Pennsylvania. 2. Sampson, a lawyer, died at Sandy Lake, Pennsylvania; married Nancy Musser, deceased; children: Nancy, lives in Franklin, Pennsylvania; Joseph, deceased; Amanda Alice, lives in Jamestown, New York; Mary, deceased; Florence, lives in Sharon, Pennsylvania; Sampson, lives in Sharon, Pennsylvania; William, deceased; Emma, lives in Franklin, New York. 3. Elizabeth, died in Sandy Lake, Pennsylvania; married Lewis Patterson, deceased, a farmer; children: William, deceased; Lewis, lives at Sandy Lake. 4. Mary, died in Oil City, Pennsylvania; married John Marshall, deceased, a merchant; he was a brother of Hugh Marshall, of previous mention. 5. William, an officer of the Eighty-third Regiment Pennsylvania Infantry Volunteers, was killed in the battle of Gettysburg; married Sarah Culbertson. 6. Susanna, of previous mention. 7. Andrew, died in Conneautville, Pennsylvania, where he was sheriff and justice of the peace; he married Nancy Mars. 8. Brownlee, died in Franklin, Pennsylvania; married Martha Hammel, living in Pleasantville; children: Audley, lives in Pittsburgh, Pennsylvania; Berdina, lives near Pittsburgh, Pennsylvania; Clyde, lives in California; Harry, lives in Pleasantville; a son, who lives in Pleasantville. Children of Hugh and Susanna (Zuver) Marshall: 1. John, born in Mercer county, Pennsylvania, July 17, 1849, died in Pleasantville, October, 1881; married Elizabeth McGinley, of Pleasantville, who has remarried; children: Mirl, married and living in Pleasantville; Minnie, lives in Pleasantville, married James Rumbaugh, a contractor of Pleasantville, Pennsylvania; they have two children, both living at home: Roland and Lloyd; Hugh, unmarried, lives at Pleasantville. 2. Curtis Sanford, born in Mercer county, Pennsylvania, February 26, 1851, and is engaged in the oil business in California; he married Cecelia Stevens, of Oil City; children: Claud, born 1880, engaged in the oil business; Catherine, born 1882, married Lester Buck, a merchant from Sistersville, West Virginia, and they have one child: Talmadge, born 1889, lives in Sistersville. 3. Isabelle, born in Mercer county, Pennsylvania, June 19, 1853, died in October, 1882; married Ralph Pyle, of Forest county, Pennsylvania; children: Charles, Lois, Edith, Roy. 4. Mary, born in Mercer county, Pennsylvania, February 26, 1856, died August, 1883; married Daniel Brown, of Connecticut, who is engaged in the oil business; child, William A., born in 1873, lives in Virginia. 5. Elizabeth Ellen, born January 11, 1858; married Christian S. Barr (see Barr V).

MORRISON Hugh Morrison, the first of the line here under consideration of whom we have definite information, emigrated from the North of Ireland to this country, died in Pleasantville, Pennsylvania. He married Isabella ——— and left issue: Hugh, Thomas, Joseph, William, James, John, all of whom married and left issue.

(II) William, son of Hugh and Isabella Morrison, was born in Center county, Pennsylvania, died in Derrick City, Pennsylvania, in 1885, aged over seventy years. He became a prominent farmer of Pleasantville. He married Elizabeth McMaster, born 1815, in Pennsylvania, died in Forestville, New York, 1869. Children, all born in Pleasantville: 1. Mary, born 1838, died in Titusville, Pennsylvania, 1911; married James Farrell, who died in 1907, a retired oil producer; children: Bertha, Harry, deceased; Sarah, deceased; George, of State Line, New York. 2. Thomas Anderson, of whom further. 3. Isabella, born 1841, died in Forestville, New York, 1892; married Milton Hyde, who survives her, a farmer, with issue. 4. William C., born 1843, now living in Illinois, an oil well worker; twice married and has a son William, an express agent in Chicago. 5. Fidelia, born 1846; married Albert McQuiston, whom she survives, a resident of Rexford, Pennsylvania; children: Ira, of Erie Pennsylvania; Blanche, married George Zilafro; Jennie. 6. Adelaide, born 1848, died at Friendship, New York.

(III) Judge Thomas Anderson Morrison, son of William and Elizabeth (McMaster) Morrison, was born in Pleasantville, Venango county, Pennsylvania, May 4, 1840. He was educated in the public school, Pleasantville Academy and the Pennsylvania State Normal College. He became a very learned man, his lifetime being devoted to study, and to this habit more than any institution of learning his later successful career may be ascribed. At eighteen years of age he began teaching school during the winter months, working during the summer months on the home farm. In July 1862, he enlisted as a private in Company A, One Hundred and Twenty-first Regiment Pennsylvania Volunteers. He went to the front with his regiment and at "bloody" Fredericksburg, December 13, 1862, was borne from the field of battle with one arm shot off and a bullet in his left knee. He was supposedly fatally wounded, but youth and a strong constitution triumphed and after a long term in Washington Hospital he was honorably discharged and mustered out in April 1863. He returned to Pleasantville minus an arm but plus an experience that was perhaps worth the loss as he never faltered in any crisis of his after life, but with the same dauntless courage that carried him up the bullet swept slopes of St. Mary's Hill, the Confederate breastworks, he meets every emergency and presses ever onward. He held the office of justice of the peace in 1864-65. In 1867 was elected treasurer of Venango county holding that office two years. In 1871 was appointed United States deputy collector of Internal revenue and moved to Oil City, Pennsylvania, where he was married, later returning to Pleasantville. He now decided to study law, although at an age where many lawyers have their reputations established. He began to study under Hon. M. C. Beebe and in 1875 was admitted to the Venango county bar and began practice. In 1879 he moved to Smethport, where he established a successful law practice and gained so favorable a reputation that in 1887 he was appointed judge of the fourth judicial district of Pennsylvania, composed of the counties of McKean and Potter, and at the following election held November 13, 1887, he was elected to the same high office for a term of ten years. His judicial record was so flawless that at the expiration of his term he was re-elected for a second term of ten years, which began January 1, 1898. Before the completion of his second term he was appointed by Governor William H. Stone in 1903 (to fill a vacancy) judge of the superior court of Pennsylvania. At the ensuing election he was elected to the same office, his term beginning in 1904 and expiring in 1914. The record Judge Morrison has made as a jurist has won him the high regard of the members of the Pennsylvania bar, and especially those of McKean and Potter counties, with which he was so long associated. He is a member of many legal and other societies, prominent in Grand Army circles, and a lifelong Republican.

He married, March 31, 1870, Helen S. Gardner (see Gardner IV) and maintains his permanent residence in Smethport. Children: 1. Mary Elizabeth, born in Pleasantville, Pennsylvania, October 8, 1874; educated in the high school of Smethport; married, April 18, 1894, Samuel E. Bell, an oil producer; children: Morrison Donovan, born April 3, 1896; Mortimer Elliott, born July 27, 1903. 2. Thomas H., born in Pleasantville, March 11, 1877, graduate of Williams College, Massachusetts, now a practicing attorney of Smethport; he married, June 18, 1904, Maud Davis, of Bradford; child: Thomas F., born September 3, 1905.

(The Gardner Line).

(I) This branch of the Gardner family in the United States descends from Nelson Gardner, born in the North of Ireland, came to the United States, settling in Rhode Island, where his active years were mainly spent. Later in life he joined his son in North Wethersfield, New York, where he died July 30, 183—, aged about seventy-six years. He was a member of the Protestant church, and a Democrat in politics. He married a Miss Larkins, who died in New England. Children, all born in Rhode Island: 1. Edwin, died in Warsaw, New York, a well-to-do farmer. 2. Easton, of whom further. 3. Nathaniel, died in North Wethersfield. 4. Mary, married Dr. John Tibbitts.

(II) Easton, son of Nelson Gardner, was born in Rhode Island, 1801, died in Orion, Michigan, March, 1872. He grew to manhood in Rhode Island and there gained a manufacturing experience and became a master mechanic. He later located at North Wethersfield, New York, where he established woolen mills, being the pioneer woolen manufacturer of that section, there being then no other mills of that nature in New York outside of Buffalo. He spent the greater part of his life in North Wethersfield, but later in life went to Michigan, where he died. He was a Democrat, and a member of the Methodist Episcopal church, as was his wife.

He married Hannah Tift, born 1801, in New England, died in Orion, Michigan, 1870. Children: 1. James, born in Rhode Island in 1824, died in Jackson, Michigan, 1906; a weaver in the woolen mills; had wife Martha and daughter Alice, born December 1, 1849, now living in Jackson, Michigan. 2. John, of whom further. 3. Abby, born 1828 in North Wethersfield, married a Mr. Bradshaw, whom she survives, residing in Detroit, Michigan; no living issue. 4. Albert, born 1830, ran away from home when sixteen years of age and was never heard from. 5. Charles, born 1832, in North Wethersfield, died in Pasadena, California, 1910; he married Della Tibbitts, deceased; child, George, deceased, married Sarah Webster, who survives him, a resident of Pasadena. 6. Richard, born 1835, died in Chicago; was a photographer; he had wife Pruella; children: Richard and Frank. 7. Mary, born 1837, died in Kalamazoo, Michigan; married Rosewell Warren, a farmer, also deceased, leaving issue. 8. Clark, born 1839, died in Los Angeles, California, January, 1890, unmarried; he was ticket agent in Chicago for the Baltimore & Ohio railroad a great many years and at the time of his death was the oldest employee of the road.

(III) John, son of Easton Gardner, was born in North Wethersfield, New York, December 5, 1826, now (1912) under treatment in the hospital at Wellsville, New York. He is well educated, and learned the cabinetmaker's trade. He also for many years was interested in the operation of the Gardner Woolen Mills in North Wethersfield, owned by his father, the only woolen mills in New York outside of Buffalo at that time. He held the office of postmaster at North Wethersfield many years, was school director and filled many other town offices, being always an active leader in party and civic affairs. He enlisted during the civil war but was rejected by the examining surgeons; later he again tried to enter the army but was again rejected by the examiners for physical reasons, he not being either robust or in good health. He is a Republican in politics, and a member of the Congregational church of Warsaw, as was his wife. In 1863 he located in Warsaw, New York, which town was the family home for several years. He married, September 25, 1849, Hannah Elizabeth Stevens, born in Mayfield, New York, March 30, 1828, died in Warsaw, November 19, 1889, daughter of Ira H. Stevens, born in Chester, Massachusetts, October 10, 1790, died in Mayfield, October 5, 1831, a carpenter; he married, October, 1818, Sarah Matthews Rust, born August 16, 1793, died September 10, 1831, a descendant of Henry Rust, the emigrant (see Rust VII). Ira H. Stevens was a son of John and Ruth (Moore) Stevens, all coming from the North of Ireland. Children of John Gardner: 1. Helen Sophia, of whom further. 2. Eva Stevens, born February 5, 1853, died October 4, 1854.

(IV) Helen Sophia, daughter of John Gardner, was born in North Wethersfield, New York, July 7, 1850. She was thirteen years old when her parents moved to Warsaw, New York, where her education was continued in the public school and finished at Warsaw Academy. Through her revolutionary and colonial ancestry she has been admitted a member of the Colonial Dames of America and of the Patriotic Order Daughters of the American Revolution. She is also a member of the Woman's Relief Corps, Grand Army of the Republic; Travelers' Club and St. Peters' Episcopal Church. She married Judge Thomas Anderson Morrison (see Morrison III.)

(The Rust Line).

(I) The American ancestor of the branch herein recorded was Henry Rust, who came from Hingham, Norfolk county, England, between the years 1633 and 1635, settling at Hingham, Massachusetts, being the first of the name to settle in America. In 1661 he was of Boston where he purchased the property later known as the "Seven Star Inn." In 1677 he is mentioned in Boston records as "deponent." He died in 1684 or 1685. His only daughter was named Hannah and from this it is inferred that Hannah was the given name of his wife. Children: 1. Samuel, baptized in Hingham, Massachusetts, August 5, 1638; married Elizabeth Rogers. 2. Nathaniel, baptized February 2, 1639; married Mary Wardell. 3. Hannah, baptized November 7, 1641; married Robert Earle. 4. Israel, of whom further. 5. Benjamin, baptized April 5, 1646.

(II) Israel, son of Henry Rust, was baptized in Hingham, Massachusetts, November 12, 1643, died in Northampton, Massachusetts, November 11, 1712. He moved to Northampton when a young man, took the oath of allegiance, December 8, 1678, and the freeman's oath, March 30, 1690. He married, December 9, 1669, in Northampton, Rebecca, sixth child of Lieutenant William Clark, born in England, 1609, came to America, 1633, settling in Massachusetts. She died February 8, 1733. Children: 1. Son, born and died September, 1670. 2. Nathaniel, of whom further. 3. Samuel, born August 6, 1673, died January 1, 1701; unmarried. 4. Sarah, born May 29, 1675; married, February 20, 1699, Samuel (2) Allen, deacon in the church of which Rev. Jonathan Edwards was pastor. 5. Experience, born July 30, 1677, died young. 6. Israel, born July 15, 1679; married Sarah North, April 3, 1704. 7. Jonathan, born June 11, 1681; married (first) Elizabeth Allen, (second) Anna Lyman. 8. Rebecca, born 1683; married, December 31, 1702, Robert (2), son of Robert (1) and Elizabeth Danks. 9. John, born 1685.

(III) Nathaniel, son of Israel Rust, was born in Northampton, Massachusetts, November 11, 1671. In 1700 he built the first house in what is now South Coventry, Connecticut, on the west side of a beautiful little lake. He did not remove his family there until 1709. Not only was he the first actual settler in Coventry, but as long as he lived was prominent in town affairs. He was chosen selectman, December 5, 1715; chosen to keep the town "Inn," December 3, 1716, and again, December 10, 1717; chosen "Moderator" at a "Legall town meeting," January 5, 1732; again December 11, 1732 and December 10, 1733;

selectman, December 6, 1736; moderator again, January 24, 1737. He married (first) May 17, 1692, Mary or Mercy Atchinson, "from Hatfield," born 1673, died January 21, 1754. He married (second) "Widow" Mary Rose, September 9, 1754. Children, some born in Northampton, some in Coventry: 1. Experience, born November, 1693, died July 10, 1768; married Samuel Gurley. 2. Nathaniel, married Hannah Hatch. 3. Margaret, born May 11, 1698, died 1712. 4. Lydia, died young. 5. Samuel, born May 10, 1703; married Sarah Hawkins. 6. Mary, born July 7, 1705, died 1706. 7. Noah, married Keziah Strong. 8. Daniel, of whom further. 9. Elizabeth, born June 11, 1713; married, 1731, Daniel Herrick. 10. Lydia, born May 9, 1716; married Joseph Herrick.

(IV) Daniel, son of Nathaniel Rust, was born in Coventry, Connecticut, February 18, 1711. He was elected to several town offices in Coventry, including constable, collector, highway surveyor, 1744, and in 1745 was chosen by the town to "keep up the stock of ammunition." He married (first) April 26, 1732, Anna White, died July 23, 1747. He married (second) October 27, 1748, "Widow" Mary (Wilson) Mead, who died in Coventry, September 23, 1775, aged sixty-two. Anna White was the daughter of John White, third of the children of Captain Nathaniel White, son of Elder John White, who was born in England in 1600, arrived in Boston, 1632, located in Hartford, 1639, in Hadley, 1659, returning to Hartford, Connecticut, 1670; married Mary Levit in England, six children. Captain Nathaniel White, eldest son of Elder John White, was born 1624, married Elizabeth ———, and in 1650 moved to Middletown, Connecticut; eight children. John, son of Captain Nathaniel White, was born at Middletown, Connecticut (Upper House), April 9, 1657, died July, 1748. His wife was Mary ———. Children of Daniel Rust, all born of his first wife, Anna White, except the last: 1. Nancy, born June 11, 1733, died 1739. 2. Daniel, born April 16, 1734; married Mary Parker. 3. Anna, born September 26, 1736, died 1739. 4. Gershom, of whom further. 5. Nancy, born August 15, 1739; married, November 23, 1763, Abner Clapp. 6. Lemuel, born February 11, 1741; married Azabah Kingsley. 7. Zebulon, born in Coventry, January 5, 1742; enlisted as a private, January 1, 1777, and served on the brigantine, "Independence," Captain Simeon Samson, until July, 1777, served on same ship from November 7, 1777, one month and twenty-four days; he enlisted again in Springfield, Massachusetts, May 28, 1781, as a private, discharged August 28, 1781. 8. Mary, born December 27, 1744. 9. Anna, born March 14, 1747; married, 1768, John (2) Strong. 10. Nathaniel Wilson, born April 25, 1751; married Rachel Babcock.

(V) Sergeant Gershom Rust, son of Daniel Rust, was born in Coventry, Connecticut, or Southampton, Massachusetts, about March, 1738. After his marriage he moved to Chester where he died October 8, 1823. He was a carpenter and farmer. He served in the revolutionary war with the rank of sergeant, marching from home, October 21, 1776, in Captain Shepard's company, Colonel John Moseley's regiment, under command on the march to Mount Independence of Lieutenant-Colonel Timothy Robertson. He again marched in the same company on the "Bennington Alarm." He married, in Springfield, October 28, 1761, Mary Cooley, who died about 1829, in Mayfield, New York. Children: 1. Anna, born November 1, 1762, died in Norwich township, June 6, 1808; married, in Chester, Elisha, son of Daniel and Dinah (Stark) Stanton, born in Preston, Connecticut, 1754, died in Norwich township, February 13, 1813; a farmer. 2. Justin, born April 23, 1764; married Margaret Clark. 3. Quartus, born January 30, 1766; married (first) Lois Terre, (second) Anna Rust. 4. Gershom, of whom further. 5. Joseph Ashley, born April 27, 1778; married Louise Bonner.

(VI) Gershom (2), son of Sergeant Gershom (1) Rust, was born in Chester, ———, March, 1770, died in Shelby, New York, August 27, 1851. He was a carpenter. He married Sarah Matthews, born in Cheshire, Connecticut. Children: 1. Sarah Matthews, of whom further. 2. Polly Cooley, died in Shelby, New York, February 21, 1872. 3. Lucy Curtis, born February 22, 1798, died May 12, 1849; married, July 10, 1828, Robert Martin Smith, born July 17, 1802, died October 13, 1865; children: i. Lucy Ann, born June 10, 1830, died October 1, 1886; married, June 25, 1850, John G. Mitchell, a surgeon in the civil war, detailed for duty at the hospital in St. Louis where he contracted dysentery and died without seeing actual service. ii. Gershom Stephen, born April 3, 1833, died June 29, 1856. iii. Frances Lodema, born September 3, 1836;

married, November 25, 1856, Andrew Jackson Culver, born August 4, 1829, died at his home in Pontiac, Michigan, August 12, 1889, having served the nine years preceding his death as supervisor of the fourth ward of Pontiac. iv. Octavia Minerva, born November 26, 1838, in Macomb, New York; married, August 19, 1856, Hial Mitchell (brother of John G., previously mentioned), born in Macomb, July 13, 1833. 4. Elisha Converse, born June 21, 1801; married Minerva Baker. 5. Lodema Delight, born February 4, 1804; married, July 20, 1824, Joseph, son of Moses and Mehitable (Walton) Warner, of Suffield, Connecticut. 6. Octavia Hall, born July 5, 1807, died October 30, 1832. 7. Ann Maria, born July 21, 1809; married, in Mayfield, New York, March 9, 1837, Amos Potter, a farmer of Mayfield, born June 3, 1809; she died at Theresa, New York, March 12, 1882. 8. Gershom Cooley, born about 1810; married Hannah Dye.

(VII) Sarah Matthews, eldest daughter of Gershom (2) Rust, was born August 15, 1793, died September 10, 1831. She married Ira H. Stevens. Children: 1. Sarah Matthews, born September 4, 1819, died in Northampton, November 28, 1883; she married, at Chester, August 18, 1842, Hopkins Clapp, born November 12, 1810; children: i. Adelaide L., born in Williamsburg, September 13, 1843, married, June 30, 1864, Lucius Steele, no issue. ii. Mary M., born in Northampton, March 14, 1846, died at Hadley, November 30, 1867. iii. Hopkins, born January 18, 1848, married, August 26, 1874, Jennie A. Beardsley, of Cheshire, Connecticut; children: Mary S., born in Wallingford, Connecticut, June 26, 1875; Bertha L., born in Cheshire, November 17, 1879; Edwin L., born in Northampton, October 12, 1880; Luriah, born in Northampton, November 22, 1888, died in Goshen, October 2, 1891. 2. Lucy Maria, born June, 1821, died November 24, 1831. 3. Hannah Elizabeth, of whom further. 4. Ira Henry, born in Mayfield, New York, May 31, 1830; married, September 11, 1855, Melvina Cornelia Bulkeley, born August 20, 1829, died February 8, 1858, daughter of Roger Griswold and Sally (Taylor) Bulkeley, of Vermont.

(VIII) Hannah Elizabeth, daughter of Ira H. and Sarah M. (Rust) Stevens, was born March 30, 1828, died in Warsaw, New York, November 19, 1889. She married, September 25, 1849, John Gardner (see Gardner III).

(IX) Helen Sophia, daughter of John and Hannah Elizabeth (Stevens) Gardner (see Gardner IV), married Judge Thomas Anderson Morrison and resides in Smethport, Pennsylvania.

BOUTON It is claimed that the Bouton-Boughton race has a traditional record or history dating back to the fifth century, when ancient history tells that clans or tribes of Gauls inhabited the country bordering on the river Rhone and extending from Lake Geneva to the Mediterranean sea, but that they were more particularly identified with the Visigoth clan, the head of the Salian tribe under King Hilderi, A. D. 481, who at his death left his son Clovis king of the tribe.

The "Dictionnaire des Generoux Francais" says: "From A. D. 1350, the military and court records abound with the Bouton name for two centuries. Nicholas Bouton, who bore the title of Count Chantilly; Baron Montagne de Naton, born it is supposed about 1580, was the father of Harard and John (twins) and Noel Bouton, who were Huguenots and refugees during the violent persecutions of the Protestants by the Roman Catholics during the predominance of the Guises in France. At length the intolerance of the Roman Catholic bigots was overcome and the refugees many, returned—among them the aforesaid Boutons. Noel Bouton distinguished himself and was Marquis de Chantilly and was subsequently made Marshal of all France. A life size portrait of him was placed in the gallery of French nobles at Versailles, France, where it is still to be seen. The French historians, speaking of the Boutons says, that it is accorded to a noble ancestry that a proclivity for patriotism, education and religion is seen in the race all down the ages."

(I) The founder in America, John Bouton, son as is supposed of the Count Nicholas Bouton, was a Huguenot, and during the great persecution fled to England, where the government was offering to send emigrants to America on condition they would swear allegiance to the crown of England. John Bouton embarked from Gravesend, England, in the bark "Assurance," July, 1635, and landed at Boston, Massachusetts, in December, following, aged twenty years. As he is the only Bouton that is registered as sailing for America from England, between the years 1600 and 1700, it is believed he was the ancestor of all the Boutons or Boughtons in this country prior to the year 1700. He had three wives and eleven children including six sons. The line herein recorded springs from John Bouton, the emigrant, through his son John (2), a child of his second wife, Abigail Marvin.

(II) John (2), son of John (1) Bouton, was born in Norwalk, Connecticut, September 30, 1659. He inherited land from his father, and settled at Norwalk, Connecticut, later at Danbury, and is of record as one of the settlers of New Canaan, Connecticut. He married, at Norwalk, about 1685, Sarah, born 1667, daughter of John Gregory, of Norwalk. Children: Abigail; Mary; Nathaniel, born 1691; Joseph, 1693; Eleazer, of whom further; John (3), born about 1701; Daniel, 1705.

(III) Eleazer, son of John (2) Bouton, was born in Norwalk, Connecticut, 1696. He married Elizabeth Seymour and lived in Norwalk and Stamford, Connecticut. Children: Ezra, of whom further; Hezekiah, born November 2, 1725; Eleazer, January 22, 1728; Elizabeth, February 8, 1730; Sarah, December 19, 1733; Matthew, March 10, 1735; Ruth, July 16, 1737; Hannah, October 2, 1739; Seymour, June 28, 1742; Nathan, March 4, 1745; Simon, April 11, 1748; Levi, October 15, 1750; all born at Norwalk.

(IV) Ezra, eldest son of Eleazer and Elizabeth (Seymour) Bouton, was born at Norwalk, Connecticut, November 18, 1723. He married, June 28, 1749, Mary, daughter of Jachin Bouton, a descendant of John Bouton, the emigrant, through his third wife, Mary Stevenson. They settled in North Canaan, Connecticut. Children: Seth, born 1750; Enoch, of whom further; Ezra; Elizabeth; Jachin, born 1767.

(V) Enoch, son of Ezra and Mary (Bouton) Bouton, was born in Norwalk, 1752. He married (first) Deborah Smith, (second) Patience Newman. He had issue including a son Ezra, of whom further.

(VI) Ezra (2), son of Enoch Bonton, settled in western New York, where he died in 1820. He was a member of the Methodist Episcopal church. He married and left issue: William, a lawyer, died in Brooklyn; Seymour, died in Allegany county, New York, a lumberman and farmer, married Catherine ——, also deceased; Enoch Edwin, of whom further; and others.

(VII) Enoch Edwin, son of Ezra (2) Bouton, was born in western New York, in 1816. He probably lost his parents very young, as at age of four years he was being cared for in the family of a Mr. Sill, of Franklinville, Cattaraugus county. He was educated in the public schools at Franklinville, and became a farmer and lumberman of Cattaraugus county. He was a Democrat and held prominent position in civic affairs, filling many public offices in Portville, Cattaraugus county, where he died March 15, 1888. He was a member of the Methodist Episcopal church, as was his wife. He married Mary Lucinda Crandall, born in Dorietta, New York, in 1822, died in Olean, New York, March, 1909, daughter of Joseph Crandall, born in Rhode Island, in 1796, a descendant of Rev. John Crandall, of Providence, Newport and Westerly, Rhode Island, the first elder of the Baptist church at Westerly, died 1678. Joseph Crandall died at Portville, New York, aged seventy-five years, a farmer. His wife, Susan (Main) Crandall, was born in Rhode Island, in 1797, died in Portville, in 1878. Susan Main had two brothers, Milton and Sheffield, both died in Portville; also sisters. Children of Joseph Crandall: 1. Russell A., died at Portville, New York, 1908; was a farmer; married and left issue: Henry, H. A., Adella and Minnie, all living in Cattaraugus county, New York. 2. Mary Lucinda, of previous mention; married Enoch Edwin Bonton. 3. Rosetta, died in Portville, unmarried. 4. Palmyra, now living at Farmers Valley; she married (first) a Mr. Barrett, (second) George Rice, a farmer of Farmers Valley, Keating township, McKean county. 5. Sarah, died in Brockton, New York; married Galen B. Everts, deceased, a railroad conductor; children: Edward E. and William. 6. Ira B., died in Portville; a farmer; he married Rebecca Babbitt, deceased; children: Elmer, Alfred N., Susan, Carl, a physician. 7. Jonas, died in Bolivar, New York; a farmer; married (first) a Miss Andrews, (second) a widow, Mrs. Buckley. 8. Hiram, died at Portville; a farmer; married Maria Main, deceased. 9. Sardinia, now living in Fredonia, New York; married Isaac Bennehoff, a clergyman; no issue. 10. Maria, died in Olean, New York; married Charles Cotton, of Olean, a mechanic. 11. Julia, died in Portville, March 30, 1912; married Rev. P. W. Crane, deceased; child, Emma. 12. Rosina, died at Olean, New York; married John Adams, deceased, a blacksmith; children: Frank, George, Henry, Elizabeth, Hiram. Children of Enoch Edwin Bouton, all born in Portville, Cattaraugus county, New York: 1.

Charles, born December, 1852, died in Portville, in 1877; was a school teacher; unmarried. 2. Carrie, born 1854; married C. W. Webb, of Rochester, New York, a purchasing agent for the Pennsylvania railroad, residing in Olean, New York; no issue. 3. Joseph William, of whom further.

(VIII) Judge Joseph William Bouton, youngest son of Enoch Edwin and Mary Lucinda (Crandall) Bouton, was born in Portville, Cattaraugus county, New York, November 20, 1856. His preparatory education was obtained in the public schools of Portville, New York, and Ceres, Pennsylvania, and when a young man he began his legal education under the direction of Judge Thomas A. Morrison, an eminent lawyer, now one of the judges of the superior court of Pennsylvania. Mr. Bouton was admitted to the bar and at once began the practice of his profession at Smethport, McKean county, Pennsylvania, where he has attained high position at the bar and on the bench. In 1903 he was elected president judge of the court of common pleas of McKean county for a term of ten years, expiring 1914. Previous to his elevation to the bench Judge Bouton served a term as district attorney of McKean county, proving a fearless but honorable prosecutor. As a judge he has won the respect and loyal support of his brethren of the profession by his fairness and the justice of his decisions. He is a member of county and state bar associations, is a Republican in politics and a member of the Episcopal church. His fraternal orders are: McKean Lodge, No. 338, Free and Accepted Masons, and Smethport Chapter, Order of the Eastern Star.

He married, February 3, 1878, Julia A. Eastman, born in Ceres, New York, August 21, 1860, daughter of Luther Eastman. She was educated in the public schools, is a member of the Order of the Eastern Star, the Travelers Club and of the Episcopal church. Children of Judge Joseph William Bouton: 1. Victor Burdette, of whom further. 2. Edwin E., born in Smethport, Pennsylvania, August 10, 1895; now a student in Smethport high school. 3. Helen A., born August 21, 1902.

(IX) Victor Burdette, eldest son of Judge Joseph William and Julia A. (Eastman) Bouton, was born in Port Allegany, Pennsylvania, December 14, 1879. He was educated in the public schools of Smethport and was graduated from the high school, class of 1899. He chose the profession of law, and after a year's study under the direction of his father entered Dickinson Law School, at Carlisle, Pennsylvania, whence he was graduated LL. B., class of 1903. He at once began the practice of law in Smethport and for three years practiced with Fred D. Gallup as partner. He is now located in the Grange Bank building, alone and well established in public favor. For the past seven years he has been attorney for the borough of Smethport and for the county of McKean for three years. He is a Republican in politics, and a member of St. Luke's Episcopal Church. His club is the Central of Smethport.

He married, April 20, 1902, Genevieve Gertrude Hussey, born April 6, 1880, in Keating township, McKean county, Pennsylvania. She was educated in the public schools of Glen Hazel, Pennsylvania, was graduated from Bradford Business College in 1907, and is now deputy recorder of McKean county with office at the court house in Smethport.

(The Hussey Line).

(I) James Hussey, grandfather of Mrs. V. B. Bouton, was born in county Kerry, Ireland, died on his farm near Smethport, in 1890, an Irish patriot whose family was closely associated with Daniel O'Connell in the cause of Irish freedom. James Hussey married Bridget Green, born in county Donegal, Ireland, after both had emigrated to this country. They were married at Great Bend, Susquehanna county, Pennsylvania, settled in Keating township, McKean county, where he died in 1861, aged seventy-one years. Both were Roman Catholics. Children of James Hussey, all born in Keating township: 1. Thomas, born January 15, 1848; now engaged in the meat business at Du Bois, Pennsylvania; married Mary Mahoney, of Mount Alton, Pennsylvania; children: Kathryn and Myrel. 2. William John, of whom further. 3. Francis Eugene, died unmarried, aged twenty-one years. 4. Kathryn, born November 10, 1860; married John German, of near Allegany, New York, now residing on the old Hussey homestead on Marvin creek; child: Alice, born January 5, 1890; married John Cunningham, of Rixford, Pennsylvania, an oil driller and contractor; child, Kathryn Margaret, born October 8, 1910.

(II) William John, second son of James Hussey, was born in Keating township, McKean county, Pennsylvania, November 17, 1850, died in Bradford, Pennsylvania, November 23, 1897. He was a lumberman. He married, February 17, 1876, at Newell Creek, Pennsylvania, Mary Hungerford, born in Keating township, August 14, 1855, who survives him, a resident of Smethport. Both were members of the Roman Catholic church. Children of William John and Mary (Hungerford) Hussey: 1. Bessie, born in Keating township, January 13, 1877; married John Joseph Miller, of New York City, now a lumber inspector, resides in Buffalo, New York; child, Elizabeth Catherine, born June 12, 1911. 2. Genevieve Gertrude, of previous mention; wife of Victor Burdette Bouton. 3. Francis William, born July 14, 1882, in Keating township; now a glass blower and painter, residing in West Virginia; he married Maud, daughter of Thomas Ray, a veteran of the civil war, serving from Pennsylvania; children: Francis Gerlad, born November 28, 1902; John Ray, December 11, 1904.

Mary Hungerford is the daughter of Thomas Hungerford, born in 1820, in county Kerry, Ireland, by the lakes of Killarney, died in Smethport, Pennsylvania, September, 1893, a farmer. He married Hannah Shea, born in Tralee, county Kerry, Ireland, in 1829, died at the Keating township farm, in 1891. Thomas was a son of Michael Hungerford, a business man who spent his life in Ireland. He married Hannah Fitzgerald, of Scotch-Irish descent, who lived and died in Ireland. Children of Michael Hungerford (not in order of birth): 1. Maurice, died in Ottumwa, Iowa, having moved west after a residence in Keating township, Pennsylvania, settling at the latter point immediately after his emigration; he married Mary Cavanaugh, born in Ireland, died in Ottumwa; children: Thomas, Mary, Kate, Bridget, Maurice, John, Edgar, Julia. 2. Mary, came to the United States; married (first) a Mr. Horn; child, Maurice; she married (second) a Mr. Sullivan, also deceased; she died in Detroit, Michigan, very wealthy. 3. Bessie, died in Smethport, Pennsylvania, in 1895; married (first) Thomas Stark; children: Kate and Thomas; married (second) a Mr. Marks, who died without issue. 4. Catherine, deceased. 5. Bridget, died in Smethport, Pennsylvania; married (first) a Mr, McCarthy; children: Julia, Callahan, Jerry, Timothy, Margaret; married (second) a Mr. Murphy, who died in Ireland. 6. Thomas, grandfather of Mrs. Bouton.

Children of Thomas Hungerford: 1. Mary, mother of Mrs. Bouton, wife of William John Hussey. 2. Maurice, born August 28, 1857; now an oil producer, living at Rixford, Pennsylvania; he married Mary McNally; children: Fred, Bernard, Hazel, Bessie, Robert, Maurice, Emma, Margaret. 3. John, born February 26, 1860; now a carpenter, living in Rochester, New York; married and has a child, Donald Joseph Vincent, born March 16, 1894. 4. Michael, born July 14, 1862; now engaged in the bottling business in Smethport, Pennsylvania; he married (first) Teresa Klyseth, of Rasselas, Pennsylvania; children: John, died young; Thomas, born December 20, 1901; Clara, January 8, 1903; Helen, April 6, 1905; William, March 26, 1909; he married (second) Catherina Gallagher, of Rixford; child, Edmond Maurice, born June 11, 1911. 5. Thomas, born January 11, 1864; now a traveling bridge contractor, residing in Smethport; he married Carrie Hoffman, of Belmont, New York; children: Edna, born May 16, 1890, married John Saulpaugh, a machinist; Floyd, April 9, 1893, died March 5, 1896; Margaret, September 16, 1866, a student at Smethport high school. 6. William, born April 29, 1866; married Catherine Russell, of Newell's Creek, Pennsylvania, and resides in Smethport, an oil producer; children: Ruth, born April 16, 1893; Russell William, June 9, 1896; Catherine, March 3, 1904; John Joseph, September 18, 1909. 7. Edmund, born June 18, 1868; now engaged in the bottling business in Bolivar, New York, and is also an oil producer; he married Mary Cantwell, of Newell's Creek; children: Francis Gerald, born February 21, 1895; Edmund, February 21, 1866; Thomas, March 17, 1897. 8. Clara, born December 7, 1872, died October 10, 1908, in New York City; she married William H. Miller, of New York City, a hardwood inspector; children: William Hungerford, born February 20, 1901; Lucille, November 1, 1904.

EASTMAN
The first Eastman in New England, Roger Eastman, was born in Wales, England, 1611, died in Salisbury, Massachusetts, December 16, 1694. He came from Langford, Wiltshire, England, sailing from Southampton, in April, 1638, in the ship "Confidence." He received lands in the first division in Salisbury, 1640-1643. The name of his wife is not known, but tradition says it was Smith. Children: John, born January 9, 1640; Nathaniel, March 18, 1643; Philip, October 20, 1644; Thomas, September 11, 1646; Timothy, September 29,

1648; Joseph, born November 8, 1650; Benjamin, December 12, 1652; Sarah, July 25, 1655; Samuel, of whom further; Ruth, January 21, 1661.

(II) Samuel, son of Roger Eastman, was born in Salisbury, Massachusetts, September 20, 1657, died February 27, 1725. He took the oath of allegiance in Salisbury, in 1677, and was admitted a freeman in 1690. He moved from Salisbury to Kingston, New Hampshire, about 1720, being a grantee of the latter place. He was dismissed by the church at Salisbury, September 26, 1725, to join the church at Kingston. He married (first) November 4, 1685, Elizabeth Scriven, baptized and admitted to the Salisbury church, October 8, 1699; he married (second) September 17, 1719, Sarah Fifield, who died in Kingston, New Hampshire, August 3, 1726. Children, all by first wife: Ruth, born January 5, 1687; Elizabeth, December 1, 1689; Mary, January 4, 1691; Sarah, April 3, 1694; Samuel, January 5, 1695-1696; Joseph, January 6, 1697; Ann, May 22, 1700; Ebenezer, January 11, 1701; Thomas, January 21, 1703; Timothy, March 29, 1706; Edward, March 30, 1708; Benjamin, July 13, 1710.

(III) Joseph, son of Samuel Eastman, was born in Salisbury, Massachusetts, January 6, 1697. He settled at Kingston, New Hampshire, on Green Brook; later at Concord, in the same state. It is supposed that later he moved to Hopkinton, as the deaths of his wives are recorded there. He married (first) February 9, 1729, Patience Smith, (second) Tamison Woodwell, who died May 26, 1750, (third) Hannah ———, who died August 24, 1756. Children: Joseph, born 1730; Hannah; John, of whom further; Ann, February 6, 1742; David, May 4, 1746, died young; Benjamin, August 26, 1747; David, August 17, 1749.

(IV) John, son of Joseph Eastman, was born in Kingston, New Hampshire, May 11, 1739. He married Judith ——— and settled in Hopkinton, New Hampshire, where the births of the children are all recorded: Joseph, born September 22, 1763; Henry, April 12, 1765; Abel, of whom further; Judith, March 27, 1770; John, March 27, 1772; Anna, January 1, 1773; Abigail, April 4, 1775.

(V) Abel, son of John Eastman, was born in Hopkinton, New Hampshire, October 11, 1766. He moved to the state of Vermont, where others of the family had settled near Bristol. He was a farmer, married and left issue including a son Abel (2).

(VI) Abel (2), son of Abel (1) Eastman, was born in Vermont, 1806, died in Marietta, Ohio, 1848. He was a lumberman by occupation and with his wife was a member of the Methodist Episcopal church. In politics he adhered to the old Whig party. He married, at Springwater, New York, in 1826, Elizabeth (Betsy) Shattuck, born in Geneva, New York, August 11, 1811, died in Wellsville, New York, January 14, 1895. Children: 1. Paschal, a lumberman and farmer, born in Oswayo, Pennsylvania, 1828, died at Cambridge Springs, Pennsylvania, 1910; served in the Union army during the civil war; married and had issue: George, lives in Cambridge Springs, Pennsylvania; Ira, deceased; Frederick, lives in Cambridge Springs, Pennsylvania; William, a resident of Chautauqua county, New York; and another son. 2. Luther, of whom further. 3. Leander, born in Oswayo, Pennsylvania, in 1833; a farmer and civil war veteran; resident of Bells Run; he has married twice. 4. Thomas, born in Kings Run, Pennsylvania, 1835; a veteran of the civil war; married Judith E. Hill, deceased; children: Mary (Holly), deceased, and Dorr W.; lives in Shinglehouse, Pennsylvania. 5. Bertha, born in Kings Run, Pennsylvania, 1837, died in Wellsville, New York, in March, 1808; married O. H. Perry, deceased, from Wellsville, New York, a grocer; no children. 6. John Q. A., a farmer, born in Kings Run, Pennsylvania, November 21, 1844, died in Myrtle, Pennsylvania, December 16, 1901; enlisted in the Union army from Pennsylvania and served throughout the war, receiving severe wounds in the battle of Gettysburg; he married Martha A. Maxson; children: i. Nelson F., born August 8, 1869; married Lydia Burdick, March 25, 1895; one child, Clifford. ii. Laura B., born August 11, 1872; married Lister Terett, July 3, 1890; died August 11, 1899; one child, Down, deceased. iii. Frank L., born April 27, 1879; married Tessie Carpenter, May 21, 1898; they have three children.

(VII) Luther, son of Abel (2) and Elizabeth (Shattuck) Eastman, was born in Oswayo, Pennsylvania, February 3, 1831, died in Ceres township, McKean county, Pennsylvania, December 13, 1905. He obtained his education in Mrs. Chevalier's select school, at Kings Run, Pennsylvania, and in later life followed the farmer's occupation. In politics he was a Republican and held the offices of judge of election and school director in Ceres township for many years. He was a regular attendant and member of the Methodist Episcopal church, in which his wife was especially active. He married, at Ceres, New York, September 29, 1850, Sophia Ann Maxson, born in Portville, New York, July 16, 1835, died in Ceres township, McKean county, Pennsylvania, July 1, 1892, daughter of Varnum Maxson, a farmer, born in Delhi, Delaware county, New York, died in Portville, New York, December 29, 1883, and Lura Ann (Maxson) Maxson, born in Rockville, New York, October 24, 1816, died in Portville, New York, January 28, 1902. Varnum Maxson, was a son of Phineas V., born June 9, 1776, died October 6, 1833, and Sophia Maxson, born October 1, 1785. Children of Phineas V. and Sophia Maxson: 1. Ira, born October 19, 1805. 2. Varnum, of previous mention. 3. Elizabeth (Betsey), born February 23, 1810. 4. Benjamin, born May 1, 1812, died July 27, 1830. 5. Reynolds, born April 23, 1815. 6. Phoebe, born March 18, 1816. 7. Nelson, born February 3, 1818. 8. Alton S., born April 11, 1820. 9. William C., born June 1, 1822, died November 28, 1826. 10. Demoris, born June 6, 1824. 11. William, born November 3, 1827, deceased. Children of Varnum and Lura Ann (Maxson) Maxson: 1. Sophia Ann, of previous mention. 2. Phoebe E., born March 12, 1837; married Thomas A. Pratt, a farmer, deceased, from Steuben county, New York; children: Emerson A., Martin E., Clara A., all living in Olean, New York, and another daughter living in Kane, Pennsylvania. 3. Phineas V., born February 18, 1839, in Portville, New York; married and lives in Myrtle, Pennsylvania. 4. Benjamin F., born in Portville, New York, September 9, 1842; a farmer. 5. William N., born in Portville, New York, May 5, 1844; was killed in battle, September 14, 1862. 6. Orson F., born in Portville, New York, May 3, 1847; a farmer of Portville, New York; married Rhoda Wilber, and among their children are Brayton and Grace, living in Portville, New York. 7. Martha A., born in Portville, New York, July 4, 1849; married John Q. A. Eastman, of previous mention. 8. Alton W., born in Portville, New York, May 13, 1851; a farmer of Bell's Run, Pennsylvania; married Jennie Grow, deceased, from that place, and has several children. 9. Reynolds M., born in Portville, New York, March 15, 1853; married and has one son, Barton, with whom he lives in Angelica, New York. 10. Horace G., born in Portville, New York, July 17, 1855; a farmer; married and residing near Milton, Wisconsin. 11. Hartley H., born in Portville, New York, July 14, 1858; a hardware dealer in Rochester, New York; married and has one daughter.

Children of Luther and Sophia Ann (Maxson) Eastman: 1. Alvira L., born in Portville, New York, October 30, 1851; married D. L. Wilson, a retired contractor, and lives in Olean, New York; children: i. Volney J., born 1872; married Alice De Groff, have one son, Roy, and live in Olean, New York; ii. Frank L., born 1874; married, has three children, and lives in Olean, New York; iii. Lucy, born 1880, died 1902. 2. Almira D., born in Portville, New York, July 1, 1854; married F. E. Tull, from Ceres, Pennsylvania, tipstaff of the court at Smethport, Pennsylvania; children: Herman E., born December 16, 1873, lives in Smethport, Pennsylvania; Ethel A., born October 24, 1885, lives in Buffalo, New York. 3. Julia Almina, born August 21, 1860; married Judge Joseph W. Bouton (see Bouton). 4. Emma M., born in Ceres township, McKean county, Pennsylvania, July 29, 1863, died at Ceres, Pennsylvania, June 9, 1890; married H. N. Holmes, a farmer of Ceres, Pennsylvania; children: Jennie, born December 10, 1882, lives in Shinglehouse, Pennsylvania; Minnie, born February 8, 1884, married Claude Mulkins, of Shinglehouse, Pennsylvania, and with their children, Claude and Anna, they reside there; Mattie, born May 28, 1888, died May 6, 1909. 5. Henry A., a physician in Jamestown, New York, born in Ceres township, McKean county, Pennsylvania; married Lilla K. Field, from Jamestown, New York, born 1876, died March 16, 1908; their only child, Phillip, died in infancy. 6. John Boothe, of whom further.

(VIII) John Boothe, son of Luther and Sophia Ann (Maxson) Eastman, was born in Ceres township, McKean county, Pennsylvania, September 26, 1870. He obtained his education in the public schools of Smethport and attended the high schools in Eldred and Shinglehouse, Pennsylvania, finishing his education by taking a course in Bryant & Stratton's Business College, in Buffalo, New York, from which he was graduated in 1890. For seven years he was employed as bookkeeper by

E. C. Wolcott & Company, of Eldred, Pennsylvania. In 1896 he was appointed deputy in the office of the register of wills in Smethport, a position he ably filled until 1903, when, in recognition of his efficient and faithful service, he was elected register of wills and clerk of the orphans' court of McKean county. Since then he has been thrice reelected to these offices, which he fills in such a capable manner as to gain the approbation and esteem of all his associates. As a Republican he has held the office of auditor for two terms, tax collector for one term and member of the board of education for one term. He owns the farm of his birthplace and takes great interest in agricultural work. He is a member of McKean Lodge, No. 388, Free and Accepted Masons, of Smethport; Knights of Pythias, No. 278, of Eldred; the Knights of the Maccabees, Tent No. 10, of Smethport; McKean County Grange and the Smethport Hose Company.

He married, October 5, 1893, at Eldred, Pennsylvania, Evalyn Squires (see Squires), daughter of Alson N. and Frances M. Squires, born in Pompey, New York, May 13, 1870. She obtained her education in the public schools, graduating from the Eldred high school in the class of 1888, and was a successful teacher in the public schools from that time until her marriage. Children of John Boothe and Evalyn (Squires) Eastman: 1. Dorothy, born in Smethport, January 9, 1899. 2. John Francis, born in Smethport, July 4, 1910.

(The Squires Line).

The earliest record of the Squires family, whose name was formerly spelled without the final "s," is of David Squire, born December 24, 1743, died February 18, 1821; married, November 24, 1765, Mary Bunker, born May 18, 1747, died September 26, 1812. Children: 1. Elizabeth, born July 24, 1766, died October 3, 1812. 2. Love, born August 13, 1768, died November 26, 1768. 3. A son, born June 25, 1770, died on day of birth. 4. Reuben, of whom further. 5. Love (2), born May 23, 1775, died May 6, 1797. 6. David Bunker, born July 7, 1777, died October 7, 1778. 7. Mary, born January 23, 1780, died October 29, 1794. 8. Nancy, born July 8, 1783, died July 24, 1783.

(II) Reuben, son of David and Mary (Bunker) Squire, was born November 9, 1771, died June 1, 1841; married Anna Tousley, born April 23, 1782. Children: 1. David Reuben Bunker Squire, born April 1, 1803, died July 4, 1804. 2. Alexander Hamilton, of whom further. 3. Alva Bosworth, born March 6, 1805, died March 20, 1880. 4. Mary Ann, born April 16, 1806, died May 11, 1810. 5. Mary Ann (2), born May 13, 1810, died February 13, 1825. 6. Elizabeth Eliza, born April 2, 1812, died May 31, 1878; married Rev. Paul Cossett. 7. Clarissa Tousley, born April 16, 1815, died March 22, 1816. 8. Henry Tousley, born November 8, 1817, died February 3, 1818. 9. Sylvanus Philip, born December 3, 1818, died March 3, 1819. 10. Harriet Maria, born February 8, 1820, died December 8, 1881; married, at Manlius, New York, August 30, 1848, Cyrus O. Phillips; one child, Charles R. Phillips, living at Youngstown, Ohio. 11. Sarah Lowe, born November 18, 1822, died November 25, 1874; married Dr. A. D. Merritt, of Woodstock, Illinois, and had two children: Charles and Frederick. 12. Mary Bunker, born May 26, 1825, died 1870; married Dr. Pettingill, and had one son, Arthur, died in California.

(III) Alexander Hamilton Squires, son of Reuben and Anna (Tousley) Squire, was born August 29, 1804, died in Pompey, New York, February 20, 1870. He married, at Pompey, New York, April 30, 1834, Sarah Nearing, born May 18, 1817, died November 20, 1890. Children, all born in Syracuse, Onondaga county, New York: 1. Ann Elizabeth, born August 23, 1836, died October 21, 1839. 2. Lucian B., born June 13, 1839, died from burns received in an explosion at Triumph Hill, Pennsylvania, March 23, 1871; married Marian Jaquins, deceased. 3. Alson, born August 8, 1840, died May 10, 1841. 4. Alson N., of whom further. 5. Hamilton, born October 8, 1843, died December 4, 1861, at Upton Hill, while in the Union service. 6. Meredith B., born May 28, 1845; an oil producer of Casey, Illinois; married, in Pompey, New York, Lucia A. Robinson, born January 13, 1850; a son, William Hamilton, born at Triumph, Pennsylvania, August 23, 1877. 7. George H., born October 20, 1850; married, at Babylon, Pennsylvania, November 25, 1875, Ella Hyatt, born March 25, 1858; lives at St. Marys, Pennsylvania, a retired liveryman; children: Irvin H., born December 6, 1878; Lucian B., born July 3, 1881; Laverne W., born January 6, 1884; Edith, born September 18, 1887, died Septemher 14, 1888; Lottie A., born April 18, 1889; Frederick M., born August 8, 1892. 8. Charlotte E., born July 24, 1858; married (first) Robert Franklin Sullivan, born August 21, 1861, died October 29, 1899, a member of the Unadilla Academy (New York) faculty; married (second) January 3, 1901, George Frederick Dunbar, born September 6, 1865, a musician.

(IV) Alson Nearing, son of Alexander Hamilton and Sarah (Nearing) Squires, was born in Onondaga county, New York, June 6, 1842, died in Port Allegany, Pennsylvania, December 18, 1906. He was a mechanic, merchant and lumberman. He enlisted, December 1, 1861, as a musician in the Twelfth New York Infantry Volunteer band and received an honorable discharge in August, 1864. He married, at Conneautville, Pennsylvania, January 20, 1867, Frances Maria Brown, born in Sardinia, New York, June 12, 1842, daughter of George Witheral and Amanda Wilkes (Francisco) Brown. George Witheral was the son of Josiah (2) and Millicent (Wright) Brown. Josiah (2) was the son of Josiah (1) and Sarah Brown. Josiah (1) was the son of John and Elizabeth (Patten) Brown. The emigrant ancestor of the Brown family was Josiah (1), who served as lieutenant in Captain Marston's Vermont militia and in Captain John Powell's company, Fletcher's regiment, Vermont militia, during the revolutionary war. The records of the war department giving the rolls of the companies show that he saw much active service.

Children of Alson Nearing and Frances Maria (Brown) Squires: 1. Vinnie, born July 29, 1868; married, January 8, 1894, at Westfield, New York, James B. Doolittle, from North Java, New York, born April 18, 1869; Mr. Doolittle engages in the insurance business; children: Arthur Squires, born in Gowanda, New York, October 15, 1896; Vinnie Evalyn, born in Eldred, Pennsylvania, June 2, 1901. 2. Evalyn, of previous mention; married John Boothe Eastman. 3. Clarence Elmer, born in Tidioute, Pennsylvania, October 3, 1874; married Emma Ward and lives on a farm in Calhoun, Georgia; one son, Alson, born 1900. 4. Eugene Bennett, born in Tidioute, Pennsylvania, April 19, 1878; married, September 20, 1911, Nina Jennie Reisinger, born in Meadville, Pennsylvania; he is engaged in the insurance business and resides at Port Allegany, Pennsylvania.

This family springs from French
DANA ancestors long seated in Alsace, that much disputed province which France and Germany have owned alternately, but which is now a part of the German Empire.

(I) Anthony Dana was born of French parents in Alsace, in 1793. He came to the United States and settled in East Eden, Erie county, New York, where he died in 1865. He was a glazier by trade, but later bought a farm in East Eden. He was a Democrat, but lived a quiet life devoid of participation in public affairs, and was a member of the Roman Catholic church, as was his wife. He married Annie ———, born in Alsace, in 1794, died in East Eden, in 1859. They had ten children: 1. Anthony, left home when a boy and all trace of him has been lost. 2. John, born 1819, died in Fond du Lac, Wisconsin, in January, 1911; married Louisa ———, and had issue, including: Rose, now living in Duluth, Minnesota; Frank, deceased; Mary, now living in New York City. 3. Lawrence, drowned in 1848, while engaged in steamboating on the Great Lakes; married Mactolana Phol, born in Alsace, also deceased; children: Kate, now of Newark, New Jersey; Elizabeth, died 1910; George, now of Findlay, Ohio; Lawrence, now of Kane, Pennsylvania; Emelia, now of Newark, New Jersey. 4. Kate, died in East Eden, New York, 1897; married Nicholas Bettinger, born in Alsace, now deceased, a farmer of East Eden; child, Mary, now lives in East Eden. 5. Elizabeth, died in 1904; married Phitail Cetroick, born in Alsace, now living in Buffalo, New York; seven children: i. Lawrence Lewis, born in Buffalo, August 10, 1845; married, August 9, 1868, Cloe A. Wilcox, born August 30, 1850, at Angola, New York, and has three children: a. Pearl, born in Angola, December 23, 1871; married Manfred Albert, born in Alabama, and has Robert, born March 9, 1893; b. Louis, born in Bradford, Pennsylvania, February 23, 1877; married Grace Park, and has: Ruth, born May 8, 1906; Dorothy, February 5, 1908; and Matilda, February 16, 1911; c. Frank Eugene, born April 28, 1886; now living with his parents; ii. Frank, living in Rochester, New York; iii. Emil, deceased; iv. William, deceased; v. Charles, deceased; vi. John, lives in Cattaraugus county, New York; vii. George, living in Hamburg, New York. 6. George, of whom further. 7. William, born

1829, died in Oil City, Pennsylvania, 1871; was a hotel proprietor; married Caroline Roth, deceased, without issue. 8. Peter, born 1835, died January, 1911; was a farmer of East Eden, New York; married Abbie Gasper, deceased; children: Charles, now of Derrick City, Pennsylvania; Mary, living in Cattaraugus county, New York; John, deceased; Delia, now living in Elmira, New York; Henry, now living in Minnesota; George, residing in the west; Lucy, now of Elmira, New York; Elizabeth, now living in East Eden; Peter, now living in East Eden. 9. Blass, born 1837, died 1872; was a merchant of East Eden; married Eliza Nolan, deceased; children: Elizabeth, William, Albert, Belle, Clara, all living in Hamburg, New York, except Albert, who is deceased. 10. Nicholas, died in 1900, at Jamestown, New York; was a pensioned veteran of the civil war from New York state.

(II) George, son of Anthony Dana, was born in Alsace, now in Germany, December 27, 1824, died in Bradford, Pennsylvania, February 10, 1910. He was four years of age when his parents came to the United States, settling in East Eden, New York, where he was educated and grew to manhood. He secured a position as steward on a lake steamer, sailing out of Buffalo, a position he held several years; afterwards, until 1877, he was engaged in farming. In the latter year he located in Bradford, where he kept a hotel and was interested in the production of oil. He was a member of the Roman Catholic church, as was his wife.

He married Elizabeth Fisher, born February 14, 1826, in one of the Rhine provinces, Germany, died March 13, 1893; she was brought to the United States when young by her father, who settled in Buffalo, where he died in 1840. Children: 1. George Henry, of whom further. 2. Frank William, born December 5, 1846, died October 9, 1890, at Knapp's Creek, New York; was a hotel proprietor; married Kate Warner, born in Canada; children: i. Minnie, born March 17, 1873, in St. Petersburg, Pennsylvania; married a Mr. Megill, of Bradford, now an architect of Newark, New Jersey, and has Isabella, born October, 1893; ii. Susan, born in April, 1874, died in Bradford, in October, 1891; iii. Frank, born April 4, 1880, at Rixford, Pennsylvania; now in the oil business in California; unmarried; iv. Ivy M., born in Rixford, 1884; married John Bushard, of Erie, Pennsylvania, a draughtsman; children: Margaret, born in April, 1903; Frances, July, 1907; John, October, 1911; v. Warner John, born in Gilmore, Pennsylvania; now engaged in the oil business in Illinois; married Ruth Schreiber, of Derrick City, and has: Catherine Mary, born February 28, 1911. 3. Nicholas, born in Buffalo, New York, 1850, died in East Eden, 1862. 4. Lawrence John, born in Buffalo, April 12, 1852; an oil producer at Derrick City, Pennsylvania; belongs to the Roman Catholic church, and Derrick City Lodge, No. 1101, Independent Order of Odd Fellows, and Fosterbrook Lodge, No. 11, Knights of Pythias; married (first) April 6, 1875, Louisa Nabor, born in 1854, died November 7, 1886, (second) Margaret Frank, born January 6, 1869, in St. Petersburg, Clarion county, Pennsylvania, daughter of Martin Frank, who served in civil war, was burned to death in March, 1872; married Rachel Perry, born in Mahoning, Pennsylvania, in 1849, died in Derrick City, March 11, 1899; children, all by first wife: i. Lawrence George, born in East Eden, New York, March 17, 1876; now an oil producer of Derrick City; married Mary Canfield, of Allegany, New York; children: Milton Lawrence, born in Goodell, McKean county, Pennsylvania, August 18, 1901; Helen, born in Derrick City, September 1, 1904; Richard, born in Derrick City, December 30, 1907; Margaret, born in Derrick City, August 12, 1910; ii. Ida Carrie, born at Eden Center, New York, October 6, 1877; married Louis Mack, an oil producer of Bradford; iii. Milton, born in Derrick City, December, 1878, died November, 1880. 5. Elizabeth M., born in East Eden, New York, December 20, 1861; now residing unmarried in Bradford. 6. Anne, born in East Eden, New York, March 20, 1864, died June 3, 1905; married Norman Stewart, who survives her, a resident of Robinson, Illinois; children: Dana, born January 19, 1889, at Duke Center; Ray, February 14, 1891, at Gilmore, Pennsylvania. 7. Emma, twin of Anne, married Elmer Howe, of Elmira, New York, now an oil producer at Red Rock, Pennsylvania, where the family resides; children: Emma, born March 13, 1887; Elmer, November 18, 1890; Elizabeth, January 1, 1894; and George, April 9, 1900.

(III) George Henry, eldest son of George and Elizabeth (Fisher) Dana, was born in Buffalo, New York, January 1, 1844, died in

Los Angeles, California, February 5, 1905. He obtained his education in the public schools of his native county, and later learned the tinner's trade at which he worked until 1897, when he moved to Bradford, Pennsylvania, becoming an oil producer and glycerine manufacturer. In the latter business he was very successful and became a director and manager of the High Explosive Company. He was a highly respected, popular member of the community, kind, considerate and generous in all his actions. He married Louise Bergein, born in Boston, Erie county, New York, July 30, 1848, living in Bradford, Pennsylvania, daughter of George "Buergin" (the German form of spelling), born May 6, 1809, in Baden, Germany, emigrated to the United States in 1846, settling on a farm in Hamburg, New York, died in Duke Center, Pennsylvania, May, 1892. He married Mary Wurslin, born in Baden, Germany, 1821, died in Hamburg, New York, July, 1884. Children of George and Mary (Wurslin) "Buergin:" 1. Mary, born in Baden, Germany, 1844, died in Canada; married William Young, deceased, a tanner from Baden, Germany; daughter, Henrietta, lives in Hamburg, New York. 2. Frederick, born in Baden, Germany, 1846; came to the United States with his parents. 3. George, born in Hamburg, New York, died there in 1856. 4. Louise, of previous mention; married George Henry Dana. 5. Amelia, born in Hamburg, New York, 1849, died there 1850. 6. Charles, born in Hamburg, New York, 1851, died there the same year. 7. Julia, born in Hamburg, New York, 1852; lives in Lewis Run; she married (first) George Platt, deceased, an oil well shooter from Oil City, Pennsylvania, (second) William C. Decker, an oil well pumper from Elmira, New York. Children of George Henry and Louise Dana: 1. Louisa Henrietta, born in North Collins, New York, March 28, 1870; married Joseph Dean, a shoe dealer in Bradford, Pennsylvania ; child, Shirley Bernice, born in Batavia, New York, August 23, 1895. 2. Arthur George, born in North Collins, New York, January 7, 1872; an oil well producer; married Edith Murray and lives in Sedan, Kansas; daughter, Dorothy Murray, born in Butler, Pennsylvania, May 10, 1894. 3. Frederick Wurslin, of whom further. 4. Earl Newton, born in Duke Center, Pennsylvania, April 11, 1881; an oil producer of Bradford; married, in Bradford, Pennsylvania, Lillian Crooker; children: Helen Aline, born April 18, 1910; Marian Louise, September 18, 1911. Mrs. Louise Dana survives her husband, a resident of Bradford, and a member of the Presbyterian church.

(IV) Frederick Wurslin, son of George Henry and Louise (Bergein) Dana, was born in Titusville, Pennsylvania, August 10, 1873. When he was six years of age his parents moved to Duke Center, where he was educated in the public schools. After completing his studies he began working in the oil field as a pumper, continuing until he was twenty-four years of age, residing at Duke Center. In 1897 he located in Bradford and engaged in oil production, a business he has successfully followed until the present date (1912) in the Bradford field. He is a member of Bradford Tent, No. 104, Knights of the Maccabees, and in political action is thoroughly independent. He married, March 24, 1898, Anna X. Caswell, born in New Castle, Pennsylvanic, June 1, 1874; educated in the public schools of Duke Center and in the New Castle high school. Children: Reva May, born in Sawyer City, October 13, 1900; George William, born in Bradford, July 13, 1905.

William Homer Caswell, father of Mrs. Dana, was born in Richmond, Virginia, January 6, 1848, now a retired oil producer living in Bradford. He married Melissa Loraine Clark, born in Leesburg, Pennsylvania, December 29, 1851, died in Bradford, July 30, 1906. Children: 1. Anna M., of previous mention; wife of Frederick W. Dana. 2. Charles Homer, born in Millerstown, Pennsylvania, February 23, 1878; now a contractor in the Oklahoma oil field, married Leonora Dele, of Duke Center, and resides at Bartlesville, Oklahoma. 3. An infant, died unnamed. William Homer Caswell is a son of George Caswell, born in Wareham, Massachusetts, died in Richmond, Virginia, in 1854. He married Anna Morse, born in England, died in Sharon, Pennsylvania, August 30, 1908, aged eighty years. Children: 1. George, born 1846, in Richmond, Virginia; now living in Ellsworth, Kansas, retired; married Lavinia White, of New Castle, Pennsylvania; children: Alma, George, Charles, May, Margaret, Annie and William, the latter five now living in Ellsworth. 2. William Homer, of previous mention. 3. Elisha, born 1850, in Richmond, Virginia; married Emma Fisher, deceased; children: Guy, now living in Sharon; Bertha, now living in New Castle, Pennsylvania; Belle, now living in Youngstown, Ohio; Annie, now living in New Castle. 4. Charles, born 1852, died in infancy.

The progenitor of the Seaward family of Bradford, Pennsylvania, was Amos Seaward, a farmer at Almond, Allegany county, New York, where he died about 1848, aged seventy-five years. He married Sarah Stevens, born 1777, died 1852, near Corning, New York. They were both members of the Presbyterian church. Children, all born near Corning: 1. Oren, married Jane Pond; children: Carrie; Alvira, married Hiram Jewett; Almira, twin of Alvira; Eli. 2. Enos, went west where he married. 3. Amos, died at Alfred, New York. 4. Joseph Stevens, of whom further. 5. Nioma, died in the west. 6. Sarah, married Clement Curtis, both died in Almond, New York, leaving a daughter Emma, now residing in Almond.

(II) Joseph Stevens, son of Amos Seaward, was born in Corning, Steuben county, New York, August 7, 1818, died at Tarport, Pennsylvania, August 6, 1906. He was educated in the public schools of Almond, New York, where he grew to manhood. After completing his studies he taught school in Tuna Valley, Pennsylvania, and in February, 1843, settled on a farm at Tarport, McKean county, Pennsylvania. He was a Whig in politics, later a Republican, and served many years as assessor at Tarport, and for several terms as tax collector. He married Daphana Dorleski Farr, born March 24, 1822, died in Bradford, February 13, 1878, daughter of Isaac and Pantha (Clark) Farr. Isaac Farr, born in 1781, was a farmer of New Hampshire, but came to Pennsylvania and took up land near Bradford, on which he lived until his death in 1852. He married Pantha Clark, who was well versed in medicine and practiced locally. Children of Joseph Stevens Seaward: 1. Levi, of whom further. 2. Adaline Amelia, born in Bradford, Pennsylvania, August 5, 1844; married Absalom Boyd, born June 20, 1846; the family live in Bradford; Mr. Boyd enlisted in Company I, One Hundred and Second New York Infantry Volunteers during the civil war; he is now engaged in oil operations in Missouri; children: i. Steven, born October 6, 1867, died September 13, 1868; ii. Clinton, born July 20, 1869; married Blanche Payne; iii. Ann, born March 17, 1871; married John Machale; iv. Leward, born December 22, 1872; v. Frank, born March 28, 1874; vi. John, born September 20, 1876; vii. Clement, born January 1, 1878. 3. William H., born in Bradford, September 1, 1846; married Anna Martin, a native of Sweden; children: i. Leonard lives in Kingsburg, Fresno county, California; ii. Sophia, lives in Los Angeles, California; married Joseph Roens; no children; iii. Gail; iv. Lizzie; both living in Kingsburg, California. 4. Melvin, born in Bradford, December 25, 1848, now deceased; married Philena Whittaker, of Limestone, New York; children: Olive, Myrtle, Clementine and Edna. 5. Clementina, born in Bradford township, Pennsylvania, January 26, 1850; married, July 15, 1885, Herbert Eugene Allen, born in Napoli, Cattarangus county, New York, December 4, 1856; he is engaged in the real estate business in Bradford, Pennsylvania. 6. Martha Jane, born in Bradford, September, 1852, died 1865. 7. Alice Eveline, born in Bradford, April 19, 1854, died January 16, 1905; married (first) Nelson H. Hastings, of Necoda, Wisconsin; child, Guy, born 1880, died March 23, 1909; she married (second) Jerome Hodges, of McKean county, Pennsylvania; now resides in Bradford; no children. 8. Sydney W., born August 20, 1856, in Bradford; now an oil operator there; married Augusta Conklin, born October 28, 1854, of Damascus, Wayne county, Pennsylvania; children: Clarence Wheaton, born October 7, 1885; Boyd Absalom, April 18, 1888; Daphana, February 2, 1890; Ethel, March 1, 1895. 9. Albert Jerome, born in Bradford, June 1, 1860, died February 15, 1909; he was engaged in mercantile life, and a member of the Asbury Methodist Church, at Bradford. 10. Freemont, born in Bradford, November 12, 1862, died February 14, 1895; married, at Bradford, Susan Bigler, who now resides in Clarksburg, West Virginia; children: Evaline Amelia, born August 25, 1890; Albert Jerome, September 26, 1891; Madaline, December 9, 1892; Pearl R., September 29, 1894, died April 13, 1896. 11. Lincoln, died in infancy. 12. Mildred, died in infancy.

(III) Levi, son of Joseph Stevens Seaward, was born in Almond, Allegany county, New York, December 16, 1842. When he was but a few weeks old his parents moved to Tarport, McKean county, Pennsylvania, now a part of the city of Bradford. He was educated in the public schools, and when but nineteen years of age enlisted as a private in Company B, under Captain Leghorn Wooster, Thirteenth Regiment Pennsylvania Reserves. He saw hard service with the continuously fighting Army of the Potomac, and participated in many of the historic battles of the civil war. He was engaged in the seven days' fight before Richmond, under General McClellan, and in the battles of the Wilderness, Chancellorsville, around Pittsburgh and at Weldon railroad. Upon the expiration of the first term of his enlistment he reenlisted February 1, 1864, and was honorably discharged December 30, 1864. After returning from the war he cultivated his farm, and for a time was employed by the Erie Railroad Company in clearing its right of way through McKean county. He is a Republican, and served as tax collector one term, was a member of the election board for two years, and of the common council of the borough of Kendall. His farm at Tarport is that purchased by his father on coming to Pennsylvania, in 1843. He recently sold about one hundred acres of the old homestead farm reserving the mineral and oil rights. He now resides in the old home with about five acres of land, living practically a retired life.

Levi Seaward married, December 12, 1867, Mary Jane Cole, born in Damascus, Wayne county, Pennsylvania, December 24, 1842, daughter of Moses Cole (see Cole III). Children, all born in Tarport, Pennsylvania: 1. Martha Zeruba, born September 20, 1869, died April 12, 1874. 2. George Algernon, born March 15, 1871; now a resident of Bradford, engaged in the oil business; married Jane Rider, of North Baltimore, Ohio; children: Alton Leroy, born September 1, 1892; Nina Vera, May 2, 1894; Earl Forrest, July 31, 1896; Leland Kenneth, July 25, 1898; Garrett Donald, May 30, 1902; Mildred Freda, November 14, 1904; Chester Devon, May 25, 1906; Wayne, November 15, 1911. 3. Levina Amelia, born August 8, 1872, died November 22, 1876. 4. Fred Terry, born March 2, 1874; now an employee of the Erie Railroad Company, and resides in Buffalo, New York; married Emma B. Grant, of Tarport, born October 8, 1873; child, Gladys, born January 19, 1904. 5. Joseph Redman, born November 15, 1875, died February 22, 1877. 6. Alma Jeannette, born September 3, 1877; married Arthur P. Blair, of Kendall, now a telegraph operator of Bradford, Pennsylvania; child, Robert Arthur, died May 31, 1908. 7. Beulah Elmira, born April 12, 1879; married Morris A. Caverly, of Grand Rapids, Michigan, now a pressman at Bradford; child, Dorothy Ruth, born November 1, 1910. 8. Paul Levan, born December 1, 1884; now a bookkeeper in Bradford; unmarried.

(The Cole Line).

Moses Cole, father of Mrs. Mary Jane (Cole) Seaward, was the son of John Cole, who died near Philadelphia, as did his wife Sally Ball. Through this marriage the Coles became heirs to the famous Ball property, on which a part of the city of Philadelphia now stands. Children, all deceased: 1. Phoebe, married John Francisco, of Beaver Kill, Sullivan county, New York, where both died; children: John and Lorenzo, both deceased. 2. Paulina, married Daniel Cook; children: John Chester, Delinda and Hannah, all deceased, and Prudence, who lives in Sullivan county, New York. 3. Barbara, married Moses Hendricks, and left a son, Moses (2). 4. Delinda, who married a Mr. Davis. 5. Sarah, married Henry Gardiner. 6. Moses, of whom further. 7. William, who died lacking only four months of reaching the age of a century; married Sarah Grippen; children: John, Alonzo, Theron, Roswell, Miranda, Levanda, Polly, George, James and William.

(II) Moses Cole, born at Bristol, Pennsylvania, 1793, died in Tarport, January 25, 1873, was a lumberman and farmer. He married Susanna Evaline Price, born in eastern Pennsylvania, in 1802, died at Tarport, March 5, 1876, whose family came from England. Children, born in Damascus, Pennsylvania: 1. John Ball, died at Whitney's Point, New York; married Mary French, of Owego, New York; children: Leslie, of Whitney's Point; Charles, of Shenango Forks, New York; Willis, deceased. 2. William, a lumberman; resides at Farmers Valley, Pennsylvania; married Susan Andrews, of Owego, New York; children: Charles, living in Michigan; Daniel; Elizabeth; Susan, deceased; Mary, deceased. 3. Lavinia, died at Owego, New York; married William Lawrence, and left a son, Lester, who resides at Forestville, New York. 4. Hiram, died September 25, 1857, at Tarport; a lumberman and a veteran of the civil war, serving in Company B, One Hundred and Ninth Regiment New York Volunteer Infantry; his widow survives him at Turtle River, Minnesota, with a daughter Susan. 5. Moses, born 1835; now a carpenter and builder at Deposit, New York; married Mary Busby, deceased; children: Minnie, Clinton, George, Emma and Harry. 6. Mary Jane, of whom further. 7. George Washington, born 1844; enlisted in Company K, Fifth Regiment New York Cavalry; died September 24, 1864, of fever while serving in the army during the civil war; unmarried. 8. Albert P., born 1845, died in Tarport, April, 1902; married Phoebe Briggs, also deceased, without issue. 9. Sally, who died aged eight years.

(III) Mary Jane, daughter of Moses Cole, born December 24, 1842, in Damascus, Wayne county, Pennsylvania; married Levi Seaward (see Seaward III).

JAMES Francis James with wife and two servants, Thomas Sucklin and Richard Baxter, came from Hingham, England, in 1638, and settled in Hingham, Massachusetts, of which he became a proprietor and he was admitted a freeman, May 10, 1643. His house was burned in May, 1647, and he died December 27 of the same year; his widow, Elizabeth, was appointed administratrix and July 12, 1688, she administered on the estate of her son Philip. Francis James owned land at Conihasset.

Philip James, brother of Francis James, was born in England and came thither with wife and four children and two servants, William Pitts and Edward Mitchell, from Hingham, England, to Hingham, Massachusetts, in 1638. He died soon afterward. His widow, Jane, married (second) February, 1640, George Russell.

Francis, son of Philip James, named for his uncle, according to the weight of evidence, was probably born in England. He died in Hingham, Massachusetts, November 29, 1684, intestate. His widow Elizabeth was administratrix of his estate. He was a farmer at Hingham Center. Children, born at Hingham: Elizabeth, died April 11, 1660; Sarah, born February 27, 1661-62; Jane, November 6, 1664; Francis, January 25, 1666-67; Thomas, December 7, 1669; Philip, died February 15, 1687-88; Samuel, born April 6, 1676.

Francis James, a descendant several generations later of Francis James (II), was born about 1760. The vital records of the town of Sherburn, now Nantucket, Island of Nantucket, show that he married, February 3, 1783, Elizabeth Milton. She died about 1850, aged ninety-one years. In 1790, according to the first federal census, he had two sons and a daughter under sixteen years. The census shows but two other families on Nantucket in 1790, Abigail, whose family consisted of three females, and Hart whose family consisted of four females. Abigail was the widow of Robert Alsop James, whom she married at Sherburn, Nantucket, May 15, 1777. All three families were probably closely related.

Edwin James, son or grandson of Francis James, was born on the Island of Nantucket, April 10, 1808, and there spent his life. He attended the public schools and learned the trade of ropemaker, following it with industry and skill. In early life he was a Whig, later a Republican. He died at Nantucket, August 14, 1868. He and his family were Methodists. He married (first) August 30, 1826, Sarah G. Cash, born December 27, 1807, died December 27, 1833. He married (second) at Nantucket, Sarah G. Sandbury, born at Nantucket, September 13, 1815, died March 21, 1902. Children by first wife: 1. Edwin, born at Nantucket, August 30, 1827, died in infancy. 2. Edwin C., born at Nantucket, March 10, 1829, died in 1871; was a whaler and cooper by trade; married Charlotte R. James, a consin, who died in Nantucket; children: Nellie, lives at Nantucket, unmarried, and Eveline, married John Smith, foreman of a lumber company at Nantucket. 3. Roland B., born July 17, 1830, died in infancy. 4. Phoebe Ann, born May 5, 1832, died in infancy. 5. Sarah G., born December 11, 1833, died in 1834. Children by second wife: 6. Walter Bunker, born September 2, 1836, died at Nantucket, in 1905. 7. Alexander, August 5, 1838, died April 6, 1912; was a cooper in Fair Haven, Massachusetts; married Nellie Haskill, of New Bedford, who died in 1900. 8. Lydia C., born June 22, 1840; married Benjamin B. Long, of Nantucket, a painter by trade, who died in 1904, at Nantucket, where his widow lives with two children: Carrie J., born 1866, unmarried, and Anna T., born 1869, unmarried. 9. Henry F., born December 5, 1841, died November 7, 1911; married Susan Hunter, of Nantucket; he was a whaler and afterward an oil producer at Franklin, Venango county, Pennsylvania, where he died; his widow lives at Franklin, Pennsylvania; their children: Bertha, born 1866, married Charles Hollister, of Franklin, Pennsylvania, an oil worker and storekeeper, and has a child. Henry James, born June 1, 1901; Frank, born 1871, an oil producer, married Louise Holman, of Franklin. 10. Obed Sandsbury, of whom further. 11. Isabelle L., born May 23, 1845, died in 1908; married William

180 ALLEGHENY VALLEY

H. Gibbs, of Nantucket, a seaman and merchant, who died in 1904; two children died young, and Alice, born 1862, married Charles Marks, of Vineyard Haven, Massachusetts, now a farmer on Nantucket, children: Mary, born 1888; Harold, 1893; Horace, 1896. 12. Sarah E., born April 11, 1847, died in 1892; married George Andrews, of Nantucket, a painter, now living at Chelsea, Massachusetts, and had two children: Charles Andrews, born 1874, married and has children, lives in Boston, engaged in the automobile business, and Dwight Andrews, born 1876, a resident of Boston. 13. Andrew C., born November 1, 1849, died December 6, 1852. 14. Ferdinand, born October 12, 1851, died December 19, 1852. 15. Clarence A., born November 28, 1853, died June 17, 1865. 16. Horace A., born February 6, 1856; unmarried; lives at Plainville, Connecticut, where he is in the dry goods business. 17. Carrie H., born May 28, 1857, died February 26, 1865.

Sarah G. Sandbury's father was James Sandbury, who was born July 2, 1782, in Sweden, whence he came to Nantucket and settled, following the occupation of whaler and mariner. He began in early youth to follow the sea as cabin boy for Captain West. He died at Nantucket, in 1860. He married, October 18, 1808, Anne Cleveland, born February 7, 1789, at Nantucket, died there about 1850.

Obed Sandbury James, son of Edwin James, was born in Nantucket, Massachusetts, September 18, 1843. He attended the public schools of his native place, and at the age of fourteen began to follow the sea in a whaling vessel, the "Mohawk," on which he remained for two and a half years. On account of the brutality of the mate, he ran away from the ship while it was in an Australian port and traveled several hundred miles on foot through wild and unfrequented portions of the country to reach Melbourne where he believed he would be able to get an opportunity to return home. After a month of hardship and suffering he joined the crew of the ship "Almira," at Melbourne, and made his way back to Nantucket. Mr. James' experiences at sea and particularly in Australia left a deep impression upon his mind and character. He has always been mindful of others and sought the good rather than the evil in their acts, his experiences teaching him that the good predominates in human nature and that the worth of a man is not to be measured by his misfortunes. He enlisted, August 10, 1861, in the United States naval service and was mustered out, three years later, August 15, 1864, having taken part in many engagements during the civil war. He was at the capture of New Orleans by Admiral Farragut on the ship "Adolph Hugle," which was under heavy fire. He was for eleven days in the siege in front of Vicksburg. Mr. James was promoted to the rank of sailmaker's mate. He was afterward at Pensacola Bay and at Alexandria on guard duty until he was discharged.

After the war Mr. James became an oil producer, following the development of different fields. In 1889 he located in Bradford, Pennsylvania, where he has since made his home, residing at 238 South avenue. In business he has been fortunate and successful. In the course of business he has had to travel much, making four trips to South America, where he spent nine years altogether, later making a trip to Italy in the interest of his company. He drilled the first oil well ever drilled in South America, in 1865, in northern Peru. Mr. James was a member of Franklin Lodge, No. 3, United Workmen, and was at one time a member of Chrozen Lodge, No. 505, Independent Order of Odd Fellows, at Titusville. He is also a member of Bradford Post of the Grand Army of the Republic. He attends the United Brethren church. In politics he is an uncompromising, stalwart Republican, but has never held any public office although taking a keen interest in all public affairs, never failing to vote either at a primary or regular election unless prevented by some unavoidable circumstance.

Mr. James married, November 10, 1868, Elizabeth C. Russell, born at Titusville, Pennsylvania, February 24, 1850, daughter of John Russell. Children of Mr. and Mrs. Obed Sandbury James: 1. Horace Greeley, born December 31, 1869, in Titusville, Pennsylvania; married Ruth Valjean Murray, a native of Pennsylvania, daughter of Alfred Murray, oil operator; they live at Independence, Kansas, where Mr. James publishes and edits the *Independence Daily Reporter*. 2. Wayland Victor, born near Titusville, November 30, 1871; he is a lawyer at Springfield, Massachusetts; married Ida E. Flower, of Springfield, Massachusetts; have one child, Elizabeth, born January 26, 1901. 3. Ida M., born at Petrolia, Pennsylvania, June 25, 1873, died at Pleasantville, Pennsylvania, November 26, 1878. 4. Gertrude M., born at Petrolia, December 24, 1874; married Charles Eugene Putnam, born February 15, 1873, in Bradford, Pennsylvania; superintendent of an electrical car heating factory in Detroit, Michigan; their children, born at Bradford: Pearl Gertrude, June 24, 1896; Margaret Delphine, February 15, 1898; Wayland Arthur, May 3, 1900; Horace James, August 20, 1904. 5. Edra Mabel, born at Franklin, Pennsylvania, May 20, 1882; unmarried; is assistant superintendent of the Bradford Hospital. Mrs. James is a member of the Protected Home Circle of Bradford and of the Women's Christian Temperance Union in which she has been superintendent of scientific temperance instruction. She attends the United Brethren church.

(The Russell Line).

According to tradition the Russell family is descended from Sir John Russell, of England.

(I) John Russell, the first of the line of whom we have information, was a native of New York state, from whence he removed to one of the western states. He married and had thirteen children, among whom were John, Benjamin and George.

(II) John (2), son of John (1) Russell, was born near Elmira, New York, April 13, 1817, died May 6, 1896, at Sistersville, West Virginia, from injuries received by being struck by a railroad train. He was a farmer, and in politics a Republican. He married (first) February 4, 1840, Content Woodward, who was born September 29, 1817, near Elmira, New York, and died March 8, 1842. He married (second) May 31, 1848, Harriet Matilda Corbin, who was born October 14, 1830, and died April 17, 1902, and was a native of New York state, and a descendant of an old New England family. Child of John Russell by his first wife: 1. Sarah, born 1841, died in Elmira. Children by second wife: 2. Elizabeth C., of whom further. 3. Francis Lafayette, born December 9, 1851, died August 8, 1889; married Hannah Widell, of Buffalo, New York, where she now lives; he was an engineer; their children: Charles, died in infancy; Hattie, lives in Buffalo; Alma, lives in New York City; Myrtie, deceased; William, lives in Buffalo. 4. Marshall Fidelion, born February 28, 1854, near Titusville; married Martha Blystone, of Kittaning, Pennsylvania; he is in the oil business and lives at Sandusky, Ohio; their children: Judson, born 1875; Willis, 1877; Bertha, 1882; Arthur, 1886; Hubert, 1890; Lloyd, 1894. 5. Wallis B., born February 24, 1856, died July 8, 1856. 6. Eber E., born April 1, 1858; married Lizzie Oakes, of Lima, Ohio, and lives at Ada, Ohio, where he is in the confectionery business. 7. Clarence, born June 10, 1860, died in 1898; he was a rigger by trade; married (first) December 12, 1883, Kate M. Higgins, and had two children who died in infancy; married (second) Maude ———, a native of Indiana, where she now resides, and had two children: a son, born in 1900; Gladys, born 1902. 8. Leister Gordon, born March 16, 1862; married, September 16, 1885, Mary E. Courtney, of Pittsburgh; he is a confectioner at Norwalk, Ohio; their children: Merl, born 1888; Myrtle, 1890; Twila, 1894; Dorothy, 1902; Hazel. 9. Fanny Rosella, born September 4, 1864; married, September 14, 1881, Tobias F. Miller, of Pleasantville, Pennsylvania, a painter, living at Franklin, Pennsylvania; their children: Fred, born 1884; Gilbert, 1886; Edna, 1890; Francis, 1897. 10. Myrtle Edith, born January 24, 1867, died unmarried in 1889, at Bolivar, New York. 11. Charles M., born December 25, 1872; a rigger by trade; married and has a family.

ALLEN There were forty different Allens who emigrated at an early day to various parts of this country and founded separate lines, spelling the name variously Allen, Allyn, Allin, Allan, etc. They were found in every colony and usually were men of prominence, as were their descendants. The branch headed by William Allen settled at Portsmouth, Rhode Island. He died in 1685, leaving wife Elizabeth, who died later in the same year, and four sons: William, John, Thomas and Matthew. Another branch, headed by John Allen, who died in October, 1708, settled at Newport, Rhode Island. He married, October 14, 1650, Elizabeth Bacon, and left sons, John and Samuel. There is no authority for determining which of these ancestors rightfully belongs to the Allens of Bradford, Pennsylvania. Definite record can only begin with Paul and Polly (Case) Allen, married in Providence, Rhode Island, May 22, 1774.

(II) Henry, son of Paul and Polly (Case) Allen, was born in Providence, Rhode Island, January 4, 1784. He was a farmer, and served as a private in the second war with Great Britain, in 1812 and 1814. At the age of sixty years he settled in the town of Napoli, Cattaraugus county, New York, remaining there until his death in 1874, aged ninety years. He is buried in the cemetery at Napoli, where his wife Nancy is also buried. Children: 1. James, born near Providence, Rhode Island; married and had children: i. Byron; ii. Anna, married Milo Hall, lives in Randolph, New York, and has a son, Court; iii. Lydia, married ——— Bidwell. 2. Henry, died in Rhode Island. 3. Samuel, born 1810, died about 1890; was a sea captain commanding a vessel trading out of Providence; married (first) ———, (second) Minnie Cooney, of Randolph, New York; child by first wife: Samuel C., married Ida Champlin, and resides in Napoli, New York, children: Norman, Henry and Beulah; children by second wife: Freeman and Amy. 4. Thomas Whitman, of whom further. 5. Louisa, died in Napoli, New York; married Palmer P. Barber, also deceased; children: i. Samuel A., now living in Findlay, Ohio; ii. Susan A. Fuller, deceased, 1900; iii. Dr. Daniel P., died in Salamanca, New York, 1900, without issue; iv. Abbie, deceased; married ——— Matson, who survives her, a resident of Providence, Rhode Island; has a daughter, Mrs. Clara Boardman, of East Greenwich, Rhode Island. 6. Amy, married Freeman Baker, and has children. 7. Daniel, deceased.

(III) Thomas Whitman, son of Henry and Nancy Allen, was born in Providence, Rhode Island, August 23, 1820, died August 6, 1887, at Salamanca, New York. He was educated in the public schools of Providence, where his home was until reaching manhood's estate. In 1852 he went to New York state, settling in the town of Napoli, Cattaraugus county, where he followed the trade of carpenter until his enlistment in Company C, New York Regiment of Heavy Artillery. He served during the last eleven months of the war, stationed at Norfolk, Virginia. After the war he returned to Napoli, where he lived until 1882, moving in that year to the village of Salamanca, New York, where he died five years later. He was a Republican, and a member of the Methodist Episcopal church. He married (first) Lola C. Morse, born in Maine, 1830, died January, 1867, in Napoli. She had three brothers: Seth Morse, living in Maine; George Morse, died in California, 1876, unmarried, and Albert Morse, deceased. Thomas W. Allen married (second) Clara Morey. Children by first wife: 1. Ella Madora, born October 8, 1852, died August 21, 1876; married Levi W. Ziegler; now living in Salamanca, New York; children: i. Lola, died 1907; ii. Jennie, married ——— Gusse, resides in Schenectady, New York, and has children: Beatrice and Allen. 2. James Irwin, born 1854, died 1855. 3. Herbert Eugene, of whom further. 4. Frank W., born October 4, 1866; legally adopted by Rev. E. A. Wheat, is known as Frank W. Wheat; married ——— Hill, and is now proprietor of a shoe store in Alliance, Ohio.

(IV) Herbert Eugene, son of Thomas Whitman Allen, was born in Napoli, Cattaragus county, New York, December 4, 1856. He spent his earlier years in Napoli, attending the public school in winter, and working during the summer months at farming and in the cheese factory of Eben Sibley. Later he purchased this factory and operated it until 1882, when he moved to Bradford, Pennsylvania, selling his factory in 1883 to its original owner, Mr. Sibley. In Bradford he engaged in the grocery business for several years, also in oil operations. He sold his grocery business and became senior partner of Allen & Hodges, establishing marble and granite works. In 1902 he sold his interest and has since been actively engaged in the real estate business in Bradford. He is a Republican, and for ten years served as county assessor and for two terms as councilman of Bradford. He belongs to Bradford Lodge, No. 334, Free and Accepted Masons; Order of the Eastern Star and the Independent Order of Old Fellows.

He married, July 15, 1885, Clementina Seaward, born in Bradford township, McKean county, January 26, 1850, daughter of Joseph Stevens Seaward and Daphana Doreski (Farr) Seaward, daughter of Isaac and Pantha (Clark) Farr. Children of Mr. and Mrs. Farr: 1. Assal, died in East Bradford, Pennsylvania. 2. George, died in East Bradford. 3. Lydia, deceased; married John Hutchinson; had a daughter, Olive, who married ——— Collins. 4. Lucretia, born at Bellows Falls, Vermont, October 11, 1810, died in East Bradford; married, July 12, 1828, John F. Melvin; no children. 5. Olive Livonia, died in California; married ——— Wheaton, deceased, son of Horace Wheaton, also deceased. 6. Brizeus Pantha, born in New Hampshire, January 8, 1818; married, at Tuna, Pennsylvania, William Rowell Fisher, born in Connecticut, February 13, 1810, died May 1, 1889; children, all born in Bradford: i. Orpha, born October 10, 1838, died February, 1896; married James R. Dart, of Lansing, Michigan, now of Mason, same state; ii. Mary C., born March 17, 1840, died September 18, 1901; married Moses P. Woolley, now of Buffalo, New York; iii. Olive, born October 20, 1843; married, January 26, 1865, Robert Thompson Lain; iv. Ida, died December 3, 1874, unmarried; v. Alice, born October 7, 1852, now deceased; married Charles L. Ackley, and resides in Grand Rapids, Michigan; vi. Nellie, born April, 1857, died June, 1873, unmarried; the remaining five children died in infancy. 7. Daphana Dorleski, married Joseph Stevens Seaward, mentioned above, and had a daughter, Clementina, who married Herbert Eugene Allen.

HAMLIN The name of Hamblen is supposed to be of German origin, perhaps derived from the town of Hamlin, in Lower Saxony, at the junction of the river Hamel with the Weiser. The name of Hemelin is still common in France, whence some have come to this country and to Quebec, where they have become numerous. In England the name was spelled Hamelyn, Hamlin, Hamelin, Hamlyn, etc., and in America also spelled Hamlin. As the name is found in the Roll of Battle Abbey it was probably brought to England by a follower of William the Conqueror. Many Hamblen families bore arms. Representatives of the distinguished American family of this name participated in the war of the revolution and subsequent wars. It has produced a goodly number of able men, including clergymen, lawyers, physicians, statesmen and men of affairs. The most distinguished representative in official life of modern times was Hon. Hannibal Hamlin, vice-president of the United States during Lincoln's administration, for a number of years member of the United States senate from Maine, and afterward United States minister to Spain.

(I) John Hamelyn, of Cornwall, was living in 1750. He married Amor, daughter of Robert Knowle, of Sarum.

(II) Giles Hamelin resided in Devonshire and married the daughter of Robert Ashay. He had two sons: Thomas and James.

(III) James Hamlin, or Hamblen, was living in London, in 1623. He came to New England and settled in Barnstable, Massachusetts, where he was a proprietor. He was admitted a freeman, March 1, 1641-42, and was on the list of those able to bear arms in 1643. He was a town officer. He married Ann ———. His will dated January 23, 1683, proved October 22, 1690, bequeathed to wife Anne and children: Bartholomew, Hannah, John, Sarah, Eleazer and Israel. The parish records of St. Lawrence, Reading, Berkshire, England, contain what are the baptisms of his children born in England, as follows: James, October 31, 1630, buried October 24, 1633; Sarah, September 6, 1632, died young; Mary, born July 27, 1634; James, of whom further. Children, born in Barnstable: Bartholomew, baptized April 24, 1642; John, baptized June 30, 1644; an infant, buried December 2, 1646; Sarah, baptized November 7, 1647; Eleazer, baptized March 17, 1649; Israel, baptized June 25, 1652, died young; Israel, baptized June 25, 1655.

(IV) James (2) Hamlin, son of James (1) Hamlin, or Hamblen, was born in England and baptized April 10, 1636, at St. Lawrence, Reading, Berkshire. He came to New England with his mother and sisters prior to 1642. He was a farmer at Barnstable, and resided at first on his father's farm, later removing to West Barnstable. He was a proprietor of Falmouth, but did not live there any length of time. His name appears on a list of freemen, May 29, 1670, and he was appointed as "inspector of ordinarys" for the town of Barnstable. He and his wife were members of the church in 1683. He was deputy to the general court in 1705. Late in life he removed to Tisbury where his will was dated September 13, 1717, and where he died May 3, 1718. He married, in Barnstable, November 20, 1662, Mary Dunham, born 1642, died April 19, 1715, daughter of John and Abigail Dunham. Children, born in Barnstable: Mary, July 24, 1664; Elizabeth, February 14, 1665, or 1666; Eleazer, April 12, 1668; Experience, twin with Eleazer; James, August 26, 1669; Jonathan, March 6, 1670, or 1671; a son, March 28, died April 7, 1672; Ebenezer, of whom further; Elisha, born March 5, 1676, or 1677, died December 20, 1677; Hope, March 13, 1679, or 1680; Job, January 15, 1681; John, January 12, 1683; Benjamin, baptized March 16, 1684, or 1685; Elkanah, baptized March 16, 1685.

(V) Deacon Ebenezer Hamlin, son of James (2) and Mary (Dunham) Hamlin, was born in Barnstable, Massachusetts, July 29, 1674, died in 1755. He was an active man in community affairs, and occupied the old farm with his father at Coggin Pond. He removed to

Rochester, Massachusetts (now Wareham), was one of the original members of the church there, and was appointed deacon in 1705. In 1742 he became one of the early settlers of Sharon, Connecticut. By his will he left £24, old tenor bills, for the support of the gospel in the Congregational society at Hitchcocks Corner. He married (first) Sarah Lewis, of Barnstable, April 4, 1698. He married (second) Elizabeth, widow of Samuel Arnold, of Rochester, Massachusetts. Children of first wife: Ebenezer, born March 18, 1699; Mercy, September 10, 1700, married Experience Johnson; Hopestill, born July 23, 1702, married (first) Jonathan Hunter, (second) John Pardee; Cornelius, born June 13, 1705, married Mary Mudge; Thomas, of whom further; Isaac, born January 1, 1714, died 1805, married Mary Gibbs; Lewis, born January 31, 1718, married Experience Jenkins.

(VI) Thomas, son of Deacon Ebenezer and Sarah (Lewis) Hamlin, was born in Barnstable, May 6, 1710. The date of his removal from Barnstable is not known. He made several removals. The date of his death is uncertain. He married (first) December 10, 1734, at Agawam, Ruth Gibbs, (second) at Albany, New York, Mary Crowell. Children: Jabez, born June 21, 1736, died February 15, 1841; Nathaniel, of whom further; Zilpah, July 22, 1741, died in childhood; Marcia, July 17, 1743; Ruth, July 3, 1745; Thomas, July 24, 1747; John, June 25, 1749, died young; Zilpah, born March 10, 1751; Asa, January 14, 1754, at Oblong, New York. Children by second wife: Jonah, born October 12, 1757, called James in one record; Lewis, July 31, 1759; Polly.

(VII) Captain Nathaniel Hamlin, son of Thomas Hamlin, was born in Agawam, Massachusetts, June 7, 1738, died near Sharon Village, Connecticut. He owned a large farm at Sharon Mountain, where he kept a store and inn for the entertainment of travelers. He was appointed ensign of Third Company in Sharon, October, 1771; lieutenant in May, 1772, and first lieutenant, June, 1776. Asa, Cornelius and Thomas Hamlin were privates in the same company, which was commanded by Captain Edward Rogers and attached to Colonel Fisher Gays' Second Battalion in General James Wadsworth's Connecticut brigade of six battalions. This brigade was raised in 1776 to reinforce General Washington in New Jersey, and fought at the battle of Long Island and was at White Plains in active service until December 25, 1776, when their time expired.

He married (first) at Sharon, Connecticut, Lucy Foster, born 1740, died January 5, 1785. He married (second) 1786, Deborah, born May 15, 1763, daughter of Timothy and Deborah (Ryse) St. John. Children of first wife, born in Sharon: 1. Mason, died in infancy. 2. Sylphia, born 1765; married, in Armenia, New York, January 14, 1788, John Hanchett, of New Haven, Connecticut. 3. Cynthia, born 1768, died August 26, 1859; married John Palmer, of Ashford. 4. Mason, died young. 5. Lucy, born April, 1771, died January 30, 1859; married, in Sharon, November 28, 1792, Elihu Coleman, born in Hebron, Connecticut, May 23, 1762, died July 27, 1825, a farmer, Democrat and Methodist; both died in Northampton; children: Seymour, born December 23, 1794; Asenath, March 3, 1797; Henry Robert, October 9, 1800; Hiram Hamlin, twin of Henry Robert. 6. Nathaniel, born 1773; a tanner and lawyer; twice married; no issue. 7. William, born 1775, died October 22, 1778. 8. Manson F., born 1778, died October, 1830; married (first) April 6, 1808, Mary Warner, (second) Amanda Lyman, of Sharon, born March 2, 1798; he was a graduate of Yale, 1799, and a prominent lawyer of Bridgeport, Connecticut. 9. Dr. Asa L., of whom further. 10. Arallus, born 1782, died at Newton, Connecticut, January 14, 1826; a teacher and cabinetmaker; married (second) February 13, 1816, Jerusha Botsford, born October 25, 1799, died January 16, 1867; children of second wife: May, born November 11, 1817; Julia Ann, April 9, 1820; Carolina, April 7, 1823; Frances, November 8, 1824. 11. Loren, born 1784, died November 15, 1848; a farmer of Rupert, Vermont, where he died; married Lydia Baker, died September 3, 1851, aged sixty-three years; children, all born in Rupert: Jeannette, February 15, 1804; Deborah; Fayette B., 1812. Children of Captain Nathaniel Hamlin by his second wife: 12. Julia, born 1787, died 1818. 13. Erastus, born March 23, 1789. 14. Betsey, born 1791, died May 9, 1800. 15. Richard, born June 1, 1794. 16. Philo, born 1796.

(VIII) Dr. Asa L. Hamlin, son of Captain Nathaniel Hamlin, was born in Sharon, Connecticut, March 30, 1780, died at Smethport, Pennsylvania, September 8, 1835. He was reared on the farm, attended the local schools, securing a good education, and later became a regular practicing physician. He moved to

Fairfield, New York, about 1814, to Salem, Pennsylvania, in 1816, and to Smethport, Pennsylvania, 1833. He was a Federalist in politics and "reared under the puritanical regime of the Connecticut Presbyterians."

Dr. Hamlin married, in Sharon, December 26, 1802, Asenath Delano, born in Sharon, April 6, 1780, daughter of Stephen and Huldah (Doty) Delano. Children: 1. Orlo James, of whom further. 2. Eliza Maria, born October 31, 1806, in Sharon; married, in Salem, Pennsylvania, December 16, 1827, James Madison Noble, born in Norwalk, Connecticut, September 24, 1802, a merchant, lumberman, farmer and Methodist of Sterling, Pennsylvania, where both died; he May 12, 1880, she March 14, 1895; children, all born in Sterling: Orra Miranda, born September 24, 1828; Eliza Maria, April 23, 1831; Thomas Mortimer, July 6, 1832; Marian Asenath, September 18, 1835; Harriet Minetta, May 23, 1836, died February 12, 1838; Harriet Minetta, born November 24, 1838, died February 18, 1839; Adelaide Minerva, born September 6, 1840; Emmeline Marilla, July 15, 1843. 3. Edward W., born January 11, 1809, at Fairfield, New York, died young. 4. William Edward, born June 7, 1811, in Fairfield, New York, died at Sterling, Pennsylvania, January 7, 1888; a merchant and lumberman; postmaster at Sterling from 1849 until his death; an Abolitionist, Republican and Methodist; married, in Sterling, October 18, 1840, Deborah Ann Noble, born in Sterling, May 19, 1817, died there March 24, 1885, daughter of David and Sarah Noble; children, all born in Sterling: Harriet, born November 19, 1842; Ona Jeannette, April 12, 1840; Byron Eugene, October 9, 1852. 5. Asenath Jeannette, born in Salem, Pennsylvania, August 27, 1817, died at Geneva, New York, October 20, 1843; married, in Smethport, Pennsylvania, September 10, 1840, Rev. Moses Crow, a graduate of Allegheny College, Pennsylvania, class of 1840, professor in the same college, 1841-42, when he resigned to enter the ministry; he joined the Genesee conference of the Methodist Episcopal church in 1843, was appointed presiding elder in 1855, and later was principal of the Genesee Wesleyan Seminary, at Lima, New York, died at Geneva, in 1862; no issue. 6. Asa Darwin, born in Salem, Pennsylvania, February 16, 1820, died at Smethport, February 2, 1880; a surveyor and civil engineer; he married, September 3, 1846, Viola Chapin, born in Chenango county, New York, March 13, 1825, died at Smethport, February 22, 1891; children, all born at Smethport: Henry Horton, born December 19, 1847; Ellen Marian, born February 25, 1849; Linda J., March 7, 1850; Flora Asenath, October 22, 1852; Eliza Maria, born February 23, 1857; Nellie O., January 13, 1860; Caroline E., February 3, 1862. 7. Byron Delano, born in Sheshequin, Pennsylvania, May 7, 1824; moved with his parents to Smethport, in 1833; elected treasurer of McKean county, in 1850; state senator, 1852; presiding officer of the same in 1854; a Democrat; married, November 17, 1846, Harriet Holmes, born in Chenango county, New York, January 1, 1826, daughter of John and Nancy (Richmond) Holmes; children, all born in Smethport: Delano Richmond, born August 10, 1847; Jeannette, September 18, 1852; May Holmes, born September 29, 1856.

(IX) Orlo James, son of Dr. Asa L. Hamlin, was born in Sharon, Connecticut, December 2, 1803, died at Smethport, Pennsylvania, February 13, 1889. He was educated in such schools as that early day provided in Wayne and Bradford counties, Pennsylvania, and seems to have so well improved his opportunities that in 1824 he was appointed teacher of the pioneer school at Towanda, Bradford county. While holding that position he read law in the office of Simon Kinney, and two years later was admitted to the bar. In 1826 he was admitted with John W. Howe, *ex gratia* member of the McKean county bar. He at once began practice, locating in Smethport, and rose to the highest distinction in his profession and in public esteem. He began his political life in 1828, when he took a leading part in the campaign. He was elected to the state legislature and made his first great speech in support of a state road through McKean county. In July, 1836, he was admitted to practice in the supreme court of the state, and in 1837 practiced before the United States district court at Williamsport, Pennsylvania.

He was active in public and professional life and writing in 1852 says he has filled the offices of "township collector, deputy postmaster, deputy prothonotary, recorder and register, treasurer of the township road funds for two years, postmaster three years, deputy United States marshal to take the census of 1830, deputy attorney-general for McKean and Potter counties and in 1832 member of the legislature." He makes the further statement:

"Complaint has never reached my ear of mismanagement in any of the offices and I could have held them much longer had I chosen to do so. I have learned to consider office rather as a matter of accident and peculiar fortune than the result of talent and management and I have observed that those who seem most desirous of office are least fortunate in obtaining it—consistency in politics should never be lost sight of." After resigning his seat in the constitutional convention in 1837 (which framed the constitution of the state of Pennsylvania) he partially recovered his health, sadly broken by his labors in the convention. He practiced with great success up to 1851, but for over twenty years prior to his death never appeared in court, his last public case being in 1849, when he aided the district attorney in the prosecution of Uzza Robbins on trial for murder, of which he was convicted. Though physically weak he was possessed of rare mental power; an analyst by nature, he was logical in all things and each proposition submitted for his opinion was subjected to this process of logical dissection, so when the conclusion was reached it was an eminently just and proper one.

During the last twenty years of his life, while barred from professional labor, he took up the study of French, German, astronomy, geology and zoölogy, using in his studies the physical assistance of members of his family. In his early life Mr. Hamlin was skeptical in regard to the immortality of his soul, but in 1845 he became a member of the Presbyterian church of Smethport and was baptized. His faith grew stronger as the years ripened and he died in full confidence of a blessed immortality. He was deeply mourned, his death calling forth most fitting eulogy from his brethren of the profession, the press and private friends. He was a resident of McKean county over half a century, and as pioneer lawyer, public official or friend always measured up to the full stature of manhood.

He married, in Norwich township, McKean county, Pennsylvania, January 13, 1828, Orra Lucinda Cogswell, born in Griswold, Connecticut, September 10, 1804, died in Smethport, April 17, 1880, daughter of John and Dolly Cogswell, of Griswold, Connecticut. Children of Orlo James Hamlin, all born in Smethport: 1. Harriet, born January 3, 1829. 2. Henry, of whom further. 3. John Cogswell, born March 4, 1836, died October 25, 1912; was a merchant; married, October 15, 1857, Charlotte M., daughter of Dr. William Y. and Charlotte A. (Darling) McCoy; children, born in Smethport: William Orlo, born March 2, 1859; Charlotte Aline, December 1, 1860; Mary Eugenia, October 10, 1863. 4. Pauline E., born September 13, 1838; married, January 20, 1858, Robert King, born in Guilford, England, September 30, 1830, educated in Birmingham, England, came to the United States in 1850, a surveyor and draughtsman, Democrat and a member of the Episcopal church, although his parents in England were members of the Society of Friends; children born in Smethport: Mary Luella, a music teacher; Rowena Jeannette, born January 8, 1862, died in Rochester, New York; Eulalia Maria, born November 28, 1864; Orlo William, born April 3, 1868, died September, 1869; Orra Hamlin, October 3, 1875.

(X) Henry, son of Orlo James Hamlin, was born in Smethport, Pennsylvania, April 9, 1830. He inherited his father's love for books and research, and after his preparatory education was obtained began the study of law. Finding his health demanded a less sedentary occupation he engaged as clerk in the mercantile establishment of O. J. and B. D. Hamlin. At the age of nineteen years he was admitted a partner, continuing most successfully until 1878, when he sold out his interest in the business to Mr. Hoskell. His later business life has been spent in oil, timber and banking ventures and have brought him large returns. His holding of timber lands in Pennsylvania and other states was very large, while his oil, banking and commercial ventures have been managed with a wisdom most wonderful. His faculty for acquiring a complete knowledge of the most intricate detail of every enterprise submitted to him has been the great secret of his success, rarely making a mistake or suffering a loss in his investments. He established in 1863 the banking house of Henry Hamlin, in Smethport, which became one of the solid financial institutions of western Pennsylvania. He was one of the original organizers of the Smethport Water Works Company, and has been concerned in the founding of every public enterprise of merit in his borough. He is an ex-president of the First National Bank of Port Allegany, Pennsylvania, and senior member of the banking house of Henry Hamlin & Sons, established 1863, now the Hamlin Bank and Trust Company, of which he is president.

Mr. Hamlin is also director of the Coudersport and Port Allegany Railroad Company; trustee of the Fidelity Trust & Guaranty Company of Buffalo, New York; president of the Buckeye Gas Company of Cincinnati, Ohio; director in the Logan, Newark and other gas companies of Ohio; director of the Fulton & Phoenix Gas Companies in New York state; director of the Conklin Wagon Company of Olean, New York; trustee of the Minona Mining Company of Colorado; president of the Smethport Water Company and director in the Great Southern Lumber Company of Bogolusa, Louisiana. Besides the erection of a handsome bank building and a fine residence, Mr. Hamlin has further beautified Smethport by the erection and endowment of St. Luke's Episcopal Church, of which he and his family are communicants and he senior warden. This is but one of his many benevolences to religious and charitable societies and well illustrates his generous Christian character. He was a Democrat originally, but dissented with his party on the question of human slavery and supported the candidacy of Abraham Lincoln. In 1881 he was elected associate judge of McKean county, holding that office until the abolishment of same by McKean county becoming a separate judicial district.

He married, in Smethport, August 14, 1854, Hannah L., born February 18, 1834, daughter of Dr. William Y. and Charlotte A. (Darling) McCoy. Children, all born in Smethport: 1. Laena Darling, born June 7, 1856; married, September 5, 1877, Robert Hutchinson Rose, born in Montrose, Pennsylvania, in 1848, son of Edward Wallace and Marian (Simpson) Rose; he is a lawyer of Smethport, state senator, a thirty-second degree Mason, a Republican and a member of the Episcopal church; Mrs. Rose is a member of St. Luke's Episcopal Church, the Monday Afternoon Club, the Civic Club, King's Daughters, and deeply interested in church and charitable work; children; Robert Craig, born August 10, 1880; Marion, born June 6, 1885, died August 17, 1897. 2. Emma Marion, born December 26, 1857; married, October 26, 1885, Rev. John Heber McCandless. 3. Eugenia May, born December 2, 1865; married, January 21, 1891, Howard E. Merrell, born in Geneva, New York, June 14, 1862, son of Dr. Andrew and Anna (Cannon) Merrell; he is a graduate of Hobart College, A. B., class of 1883, and member of Magna Ium Sande and Phi Beta Kappa societies; he is a leading nurseryman of Geneva; no issue. 4. Orlo J., of whom further.

(XI) Orlo J., only son of Henry Hamlin, was born in Smethport, Pennsylvania, June 23, 1873. He obtained his early education in the public schools, prepared for college at St. Paul's Academy, Concord, New Hampshire, entered Hobart College, whence he was graduated, class of 1894. He then took a course in business college and at once began an active business life. He was junior member of the banking house of Henry Hamlin & Son, now the Hamlin Bank & Trust Company, of which he has been vice-president since the consolidation with other institutions. He is president of the Buhl Oil and Gas Company, with offices in Bradford, Pennsylvania; president of the United States Electric Company of New York City; vice-president of the Haines Flint Bottle Company, Smethport; director of the Allegany Window Glass Company of Port Allegany; director of the Empire Window Glass Company of Shinglehouse, Pennsylvania; ex-president of the Clarence Stone & Lime Company of Clarence, New York, and ex-director of the Smethport Glass Company. He is an energetic man of business and fully lives up to the high standard set by his forbears in the generations since the Hamlins came to Smethport. His college fraternity is Kappa Alpha, Hobart; his clubs, the Country and Bradford of Bradford, Central of Smethport, Kanadasaga of Geneva, New York, and the Republican of New York City. He is a member of the Masonic order, belonging to McKean Lodge, No. 388, Free and Accepted Masons; Bradford Chapter, No. 260, Royal Arch Masons; Trinity Commandery, No. 58, Knights Templar; Coudersport Consistory, thirty-second degree, Ancient Accepted Scottish Rite, and Zem Zem Temple, Nobles of the Mystic Shrine, of Erie, Pennsylvania. He is also a member of Bradford Lodge, Benevolent and Protective Order of Elks. In politics he is a Republican, and is a member of St. Luke's Episcopal Church, being vestryman of same.

He married, January 4, 1899, Mirabel Depew Folger, born in Geneva, New York, September 23, 1877, daughter of Charles Worth Folger, born in Geneva, 1848, died there January 11, 1886, a retired nurseryman. Mr. Folger married Vashti Susie Depew, born in Peekskill, New York, November 9, 1852, died in Geneva, January 23, 1911, a distant relative of Senator Chauncey M. Depew. Charles

Worth Folger was the son of Charles James Folger, secretary of the treasury under President Garfield, and a judge of the New York supreme court and candidate for governor of New York state. He married Susan Rebecca Worth, who died in Geneva. Children of Judge Folger: 1. Jane Gaitskill, died at Saranac Lake, New York; unmarried. 2. Charles Worth, of previous mention. 3. Susan Worth, married ———— Ouden, an electrician, now residing in Schenectady, New York; children: Charles Folger, Constance and Jane, all living at home. Vashti Susie Depew, wife of Charles Worth Folger, was the daughter of George Washington Depew, who died in Peekskill, and Vashti (Cole) Depew, died 1854. Children of George Washington Depew: 1. George, died in Peekskill, where his widow Julia now resides; no issue. 2. Anne, died in Paterson, New Jersey; married Henry Wooster, who survives her; children: Eugene; Susie, married J. Conklin; all residing in Paterson. 3. Vashti Susie, of previous mention, wife of Charles Worth Folger. Children of Orlo Jay and Mirabel Depew (Folger) Hamlin, all born in Smethport: Mirabel McCoy, September 6, 1901; Hannah McCoy, January 10, 1905; Susan Depew, January 29, 1911.

The Fullers of Bradford descend from the early Massachusetts family through the New York branch.

(I) Chase Fuller was born 1796, died at Limestone, New York, 1870. He came to Limestone in early life, later moved to Humphrey, New York, thence to Virginia, later returning to Limestone. He was always a farmer; supervisor at Humphrey for a number of years and justice of the peace. He married Nancy Kenyon, born in Vermont, January 12, 1801, died at Limestone, December 25, 1887. Both were members of the Methodist Episcopal church. Children: 1. Philetas, born in Erie county, New York, deceased; he was an oil producer in business, and in public life county commissioner and associate judge, also a veteran of the civil war, serving in a Pennsylvania regiment; he married (first) a widow, Cornelia Farrer, (second) Elizabeth Drake, (third) Anna Morris, who survives him without issue at Smethport, McKean county, Pennsylvania; children of first wife: Ophelia, Emily, Truman, deceased; children of second wife: Roy D., Bernice, deceased, and Myrtle, deceased. 2. Lafayette, born in Erie county, New York, March, 1825, died December 7, 1911; he was a farmer at Minard Run, where he died; he married Olivia Kellogg, who survives him; children: George, Arvilla, Lavella, Irene, Jennie, deceased; William, deceased; Lenora, and Rupert. 3. Manly, born in Erie county, New York, died at Rochester, Minnesota, 1876; was a farmer and a member of the Minnesota legislature; married Jane Bisby, of Ellicottville, New York, died 1908; children: Milton, Wellington and Mary. 4. Dolly A., born in Erie county, New York, May, 1830, died June, 1906; married Marcus McMilan, deceased, a carpenter and builder of Olean, New York, where he died; children: Adelbert, Mabel, Lelia and Arthur. 5. Romanzo, born in Erie county, New York, May, 1835, died May, 1904; was a carpenter; married Harriet Leonard, of Limestone, New York; children: Herbert, Angelia, Jerome and Samuel. 6. Elizabeth, born November 3, 1837; married Samuel Huntington, whom she survives, a resident of Custer City, Pennsylvania; he enlisted in a New York regiment, was captured and confined in the Andersonville prison pen; although he survived the horrors of that infamous place, his health was so broken that he died soon after being liberated; children: Adelle, born at Gilmore, Pennsylvania, December, 1854, married Martin McKay; Milford, born 1856, now living near Sawyer City, Pennsylvania, married Martha Etheridge; Ruby, born 1858, died February, 1903, married George Woodward, a bridge builder, who survives her. 7. Velonia, born March, 1839; married Samuel Leonard, of Limestone, New York, a carpenter and builder, who died May, 1907; she survives, a resident of Limestone; children: Grace, Ralph, Roy, Maud, Gertrude, deceased; Belle, and Jennie. 8. Zoroaster Chase, of whom further. 9. Olivia, born in Erie county, New York, May 6, 1844; married Almanzo Jones, of Allegany county, New York, a railroad man, died in Minnesota, whom she survives; children: Millard, Lois, Arthur, deceased; Frank; this family resides in Oklahoma. 10. Millard, born February, 1850, died 1864.

(II) Zoroaster Chase, son of Chase Fuller, was born in Freedom, New York, September 21, 1842. When he was but a child his parents moved to Limestone, New York, where he was educated in the public schools. When he was sixteen years of age he began working in the lumber woods and farming at Humphrey, New

York, where he remained until 1869. He then went to Virginia settling on a farm at Caroline, near Richmond, continuing until 1873. He returned north and in December, 1878, located at Degolia, McKean county, Pennsylvania, where he followed agriculture the remainder of his life. He died at Custer City (near Degolia), April 14, 1910. He was a Democrat until his later years, when he became a Republican. He held the office of constable in Humphrey and was assessor of Bradford township. He enlisted in the Sixty-fifth Regiment New York Volunteers in the spring of 1865, serving until the close of the war. He married, October 8, 1867, Sila G. Wickes, born in Franklinville, New York, January 27, 1850, who survives him, a resident of Custer City, a member of the Methodist Episcopal church. She is a daughter of Charles D. Wickes, born in Delaware county, New York, July 15, 1817, died in Ellwood, Illinois, November, 1896, a farmer, and in later years proprietor of a meat market. He married Emeline, daughter of ——— and Betsey (Daniels) Gleason, who had six other children: Nelson; Lavina, married Ariel Howard; William, married Caroline Blanchard; Franklin, married Celina ———; Eliza, married John Simonson; Sarah, married ——— Alleson; all are deceased. Children of Zoroaster Chase Fuller: 1. Millard C., born at Humphrey, New York. October 20, 1868; now in the oil business at Jamestown, Pennsylvania; he married Lottie Pratt, born 1858, died July 8, 1911; no issue. 2. Allie Lorena, born at Bowling Green, Caroline county, Virginia, May 29, 1870; married Carlton W. Cloud, born January 18, 1872, now a merchant of Custer City, Pennsylvania; child, Frederick Ellsworth, born January 31, 1898. 3. Hattie Emeline, of whom further. 4. Mary E., born in Elwood, Mill county, Illinois, May 23, 1875; married Mertin F. Howard, born January 29, 1873, in Erie county, Pennsylvania, engaged in the oil business at Custer City; child, Maxine F., born July 6, 1899.

(III) Hattie Emeline, daughter of Zoroaster Chase Fuller, was born in Allegany, Cattaraugus county, New York, September 21, 1872. She was a child of two years when her parents moved to Elwood, Illinois, and of six years when they returned to the vicinity of Bradford, at what was then Degolia, now Custer City. There she was educated in the public schools, finishing her studies in 1889. She then qualified as an instructor and taught in the schools of Allen and Hazelton, Pennsylvania, until a short time previous to her marriage. She married, June 15, 1892, Hance Cooper Chesney, son of John Chesney, born in Ireland, 1813, came to the United States in 1822, lived at New Castle, Pennsylvania, where he followed his trade of blacksmith, later purchasing a farm on which he resided until his death in 1903. He married Catherine Stoner, born in Vermont, 1812, died 1901; eight children: 1. James, born in New Castle, Pennsylvania; now an oil producer. 2. Jane, married Alexander Pattison, and resides at Slippery Rock, Pennsylvania; children: William, Kittie, Elizabeth, John and David. 3. William, an oil producer of Butler county, Pennsylvania; married Eunice Elizabeth, daughter of Michael and May Grimm, of Columbiana county, Ohio; children: Margaret, Kittie, May, David and William. 4. Robert, an oil producer of Allegheny county, Pennsylvania; married Belle Patterson, deceased; children: Harry, Frank and Mabel. 5. Jemima, married James Kildoo, deceased; children: Elizabeth, Isabella and Robert; James Kildoo was of Scotch descent, owned a large farm at Portersville, Butler county, Pennsylvania, on which his widow now resides. 6. Hance Cooper, of whom further. 7. Belle, married Smith Patterson, a prosperous farmer of Grove City, Mercer county, Pennsylvania; children: Ethel DeWitt and Emerson. 8. Martha, died aged eighteen years.

Hance Cooper, sixth child and fourth son of John Chesney, was born in Philadelphia, Pennsylvania, November 24, 1862. He was educated in the public schools of Lawrence county, and at Rose Point Academy in the same county. He then began the study of medicine under Dr. J. M. Ralph, of Rose Point, later entered Columbus (Ohio) Medical College, whence he was graduated M. D., class of 1883. He began practice at North Liberty, Mercer county, then for one year (1885) was located at Irvingtbn, Warren county, making permanent location at Custer City, Pennsylvania, in 1886. He was an exceedingly skillful and popular physician, his services being so constantly in demand that he broke down under the crushing weight of his practice and died March 2, 1907. At the time of his death he was an active member in the McKean County Medical Society, and was also justice of the peace for Bradford township, McKean county, Pennsylvania, which office he held for a number of years. He was a Republican. He was a member of the Masonic order, belonging to lodge, chapter, commandery of Knights Templar and Ismailia Shrine of Buffalo. He also held membership in the Knights of the Maccabees and the Methodist Episcopal church. Mrs. H. C. Chesney, who survives her husband and resides in Custer City, is a member of the Order of the Eastern Star and of the Methodist Episcopal church. She has no children, but has an adopted daughter, Nellie Arvilla Chesney.

This name is derived from the ABBOTT Hebrew ab, "father," through the Syriac. It had its origin in the monasteries of Syria, whence it spread through the east and soon became accepted generally in all languages as the designation of the head of a monastery. At first it was used as a respectful title for any monk, but was soon restricted to the superior. The name is spelled in a multitude of ways, but this branch uses the two "t's" as did their American ancestor. The most distinguished member of the English family was George Abbot, born 1562, died 1633, archbishop of Canterbury, a strong manly character who wielded a powerful influence over the English king, James.

(I) Captain Thomas Abbott was born in England about 1632, died in Andover, May 15, 1695. In 1642 he was an inmate of the family of George Abbott, of Rowley, Massachusetts, supposed to have been a near relative. He lived in Rowley until 1659, then went to Concord for a time, settling in Andover, Massachusetts, where he was married. He was a farmer in Andover, where with others he owned a mill privilege. He took the oath of allegiance to the king February 11, 1678, and was styled captain, probably a militia title. He married, December 16, 1664, Sarah Stewart, who died in February, 1715, aged sixty-nine years. Children: Joseph, born 1666, died young; Thomas, 1668; Sarah, 1671; Joseph (2), 1674; Dorothy, died young; Nathaniel, 1678; John, of whom further; Dorothy (2); Mary, 1686; Ebenezer, 1689.

(II) John, son of Captain Thomas Abbott, was born in Andover, Massachusetts, September 23, 1681. He was a weaver and farmer. He married, April 11, 1710, Hannah Chibb, who died May 23, 1733. He married (second) October 29, 1734, Hepzibah Frye. Both he and his second wife were living in Andover, in 1763. Children: Hannah, born about 1711; Sarah, died young; Mary, died young; John (2), of whom further; Sarah, born August 5, 1722, married Timothy Noyes; Mary, born November 12, 1727, married Samuel Griffin.

(III) John (2), son of John (1) Abbott, was born in Andover, Massachusetts, February, 1718, died in Andover, Maine, in 1803. He was a farmer of Andover nearly all his life. He married, in Massachusetts, June 17, 1746, Hannah Farnum. Children: Jonathan, born April 12, 1747; Philip, of whom further; Hannah, married John Johnson; Susannah, married Daniel Stevens; Betsey, married Peter Carlton; John, born January 24, 1769, married Ruth Lovejoy.

(IV) Philip, son of John (2) Abbott, was born in Andover, Massachusetts, October 4, 1749, died May 4, 1840, aged ninety years, in East Andover, Maine. He was a cooper and farmer, and moved to East Andover, Maine, about 1800, where he dealt quite extensively in land. He married, November 20, 1771, Elizabeth Frye, who died September 11, 1834, aged eighty-four years. Children: Olive, born June 1, 1772, died 1809; Holton, born June 20, 1774; Isaac, born 1776; Philip (2), of whom further; Timothy, born February, 1781, married Susan Pillsbury; Nathaniel F., born 1783; Samuel, born 1785; Betsey, 1787; Lydia, 1789.

(V) Philip (2), son of Philip (1) Abbott, was born in Andover, Massachusetts, in 1778. He settled in Yates county, New York, where his children were born. He married ———— Harris. Among his children was a son, Philip Harris, of whom further.

(VI) Philip Harris, son of Philip (2) Abbott, was born in Yates county, New York, in 1816. He moved to Steuben county, New York, where he followed lumbering; later was in McKean county, Pennsylvania, settling in Bradford, in 1848. He was associated there with the Bennett Lumber Company, and later with Daniel Kingsbury, a large landowner and promoter of early Bradford enterprises. He married, in Yates county, New York, in 1836, Eliza, daughter of Abraham Covert. Children who grew to maturity: 1. Philip, died unmarried. 2. Alzina, married Charles Fish. 3. James Polk, of whom further. 4. George, married Silence Cramner. 5. Calvin V., born in Steuben county, July 9, 1850, died October 23, 1912; came to McKean county, in 1857, with his parents; owned a farm on Bennett brook road, Bradford; supplied building stone to contractors; married Lizzie Mulligan; children: Charles W., of Watkins, New York;

Abraham, Thomas, Calvin (2), Harry, Fred, Mrs. A. A. Tibbitts, Mrs. J. V. Wilcox, Mrs. Henry Colley, Grace, Kittie and Estella, all of Bradford. 6. Jane, now living at No. 24 Bennett brook road, Bradford; married William Wilson, deceased. The others are all deceased.

(VII) James Polk, son of Philip Harris Abbott, was born at Ithaca, New York, August 25, 1844, died in Bradford, Pennsylvania, July 11, 1891. He was four years of age when his parents moved to Bradford, where he was educated in the public schools. He learned the shoemaker's trade, which he followed until 1874, and then became proprietor of the St. Nicholas Hotel, one of the best hotels in the city. This was built on the site of the present public square. In 1876 he opened the Bennett Brook Hotel and successfully managed it until his death. He was also interested in real estate and oil production. He was a Republican in politics, and a member of the United Brethren church.

He married, in 1872, Sarah Jane Wagoner, born in Albion, New York, April 3, 1856, daughter of William Henry and Harriet Newell (Piett) Wagoner. Sarah Jane (Wagoner) Abbott survives her husband, and married (second) Byron M. Smith, born in Wayne county, New York. Children of James Polk Abbott: 1. Loyal, died in infancy. 2. James Emoroy, of whom further. 3. William Edward, born in Bradford, August 25, 1876; married, September 18, 1906, Cecil Victoria Landrigan, whose father was a soldier of the civil war in Colonel Kane's Bucktail Regiment. Mr. Landrigan was responsible for the regiment's bearing that singular title. While passing a market he cut the tail from a deer hanging there and stuck it in his cap. Colonel Kane at once noticed the circumstances, and then and there named them the Bucktail Regiment. 4. Albert Polk, born in Bradford, February 3, 1878, died there July 25, 1902. 5. Viola Pearl, born in Bradford, August 20, 1879; married (first) Thomas Powell, at the time of his death first assistant engineer of the Bradford fire department; married (second) Melvin L. Daugherty; child by first husband: James Powell, now a resident of Bradford.

John Henry Wagoner, grandfather of Sarah Jane (Wagoner) Abbott, was born in Germany, emigrated to the United States, and settled in Dansville, Steuben county, New York, and died in 1864, at the age of seventy-seven years. He married Sarah Van Alstyne, born in Germany, died in Dansville, in 1864, four months after her husband. Their children were: Lambert John; William Henry, of whom further; Abigail; Catharine; Jane; George; Carl; and twins, who died in infancy.

William Henry Wagoner was born at Wheeler, Steuben county, New York, 1828, died 1891. He was a carpenter and mason. He married Harriet Newell Piett, and had children: Amanda, married Charles Burton, both now deceased; Mary, married a Mr. Williams, and lives in Bakersfield, California; Sarah Jane, of previous mention; a child, died in infancy; Harriet, now deceased; William; Venus, married Thomas Crosterline, both now deceased; Alida, married Andrew Swanson, and resides in Carnegie, Pennsylvania; William and Josephine, now deceased.

(VIII) James Emoroy, son of James Polk Abbott, was born in Bradford, Pennsylvania, January 12, 1875. He was educated in the public schools of that city, which has always been his home. He began business life as a newsboy, and is directly responsible for the organization of the first newsboys' union in the United States. Although it had but a brief existence of two years an offshoot, the Buffalo Newsboys' Union, has been successful from its inception. Mr. Abbott next ran a small newspaper for a short time. He became correspondent and sales agent for several of the large eastern papers from 1896 to 1903. He then began the business of sign painting, an art in which he is naturally skillful. He is a Republican in politics, and has served on the election board; was a member of the first personal registration board of McKean county; was elected jury commissioner in 1909; and in 1911 was chosen county auditor for a term of four years. He is a member of the Keystone Guards and of the Order of Moose. He is unmarried.

SMILEY This family is of Scotch origin. The first of the name are said to have arrived in New England about the same time and settled in Haverhill, Massachusetts. One of them at least, John Smiley, remained there and was the progenitor of the Smileys of that city. Francis Smiley, emigrant ancestor of the Maine family, was born in the north of Ireland, in 1680, and came to America with others of his family about 1727. He did not settle in Maine, but in 1743 is first found in Windham, New Hampshire, where he lived until his death, March 16, 1763. He married Agnes Wilson and had three sons, William, David and Hugh, who settled in Maine.

(I) Thomas Smiley, direct progenitor of the Smileys of Bradford, Pennsylvania, is supposed to have been a brother of Francis. His ancestors emigrated from Scotland to the north of Ireland, where Thomas was born, near Londonderry, about the time of the close of that famous siege. He came to America, in 1747, and settled in northern New England, supposedly Maine or New Hampshire. He married, and among his children were three sons: Thomas (2), founder of the Venango county family; Charles, founder of the Perry county, Pennsylvania, family; and James, of whom further.

(II) James, son of Thomas Smiley, died at Union City, Erie county, Pennsylvania. He was a farmer of the state of Maine, where he married. He was a soldier of the revolution, and also served in the war of 1812. After the war he came to Pennsylvania, settling at Union City, Erie county, where he built and operated the first mill in the town. He also owned and cultivated a farm. In 1833 he was elected justice of the peace. He was a Democrat and a man of influence. He married and had children: 1. William, died in Union City, Pennsylvania; married ———— Chichester. 2. Moses, of whom further. 3. John, born August 13, 1814, died January 22, 1894; married Rachel Wilson, born May 31, 1814, died December 30, 1906; children: i. Alfred, lives in Foxburg, Clarion county, Pennsylvania; ii. Jefferson, deceased; iii. Matilda, born May 28, 1839, now deceased; married John Needham, March 7, 1805, and has: John (2), and a daughter, who married Thomas E. Cooper; iv. Hannah, lives in Pittsburgh; v. Mina, lives in Union City. 4. A son, died in early youth. 5. George, a farmer near Union City, died unmarried. 6. Robert, died June 27, 1907; a noted hotel proprietor in Union City for many years. 7. Ann, lived with her unmarried brother George in Union City; died unmarried.

(III) Moses, son of James Smiley, was born in Maine, October 5, 1809, died at Union City, Pennsylvania, March 4, 1884. He was educated and grew to manhood in the state of Maine, later settling in Erie county, Pennsylvania, where he purchased and cultivated a farm near Union City. He was an old school Democrat and served his town in many local offices, including that of justice of the peace, an office he held for many years. By a first wife Moses Smiley had two children: John, deceased, and Jane, deceased. He married (second) Margaret Marshall, born in Ireland, October 14, 1820, came to the United States when a child with her parents, died at Union City, April 9, 1898. She had a brother, James Marshall, who died in California, and a sister, Mary Jane, who married John Thompson, at one time associated in the leather business with General U. S. Grant, at Dubuque, Iowa. Children of Moses Smiley, all born near Union City: 1. James Van Buren, born January 20, 1841; a merchant of Union City; married Adaline Perry, deceased, of Union City; children: Eugene, William, Cora. 2. Perry, of whom further. 3. Dallas, born April 19, 1846; now a banker and merchant of Union City, and for the past twenty years a justice of the peace; married Ella Zinn, of Union City; children: Frank, Clyde, Ward, Robert. 4. Addison, born March 24, 1851; now a resident of Bradford, Pennsylvania, engaged in oil production; married, September 10, 1874, Carlettia Lacina Henton, born in Erie county, August 29, 1858; children: i. Nellie M., born March 26, 1876; married L. A. Nash, of Bradford, Pennsylvania; children: Edwin A., born September 29, 1898; Leona, August 16, 1905; ii. Pearl Lillian, born September 16, 1891; iii. Addison H., July 18, 1902. 5. Lilly, born December 27, 1858; married John Wescott, a successful lumberman, of Union City. 6. Emma, born January 27, 1853, died 1858. 7. Ida, born December 17, 1854, died 1857.

(IV) Perry, son of Moses Smiley, was born at Union Mills, now Union City, Erie county, Pennsylvania, May 1, 1843. He attended the public schools and worked on the farm until January, 1862, when he enlisted as a private in Company L, Twelfth Regiment Pennsylvania Cavalry. He saw hard service with the Army of the Potomac, participating in the battles of Second Bull Run, Winchester, Antietam, Harper's Ferry, and was with Sheridan throughout his entire famous campaign in the Shenandoah Valley. At the battle of Winchester his horse was killed under him, and at the battle of Charleston, Virginia, he had the same experience. He had three horses killed during the war. He was promoted sergeant in 1864, and that same year was detached as a scout, under Captain McAllister. He was honorably discharged and mustered out July 20, 1865. After the war he returned to Erie county, and for a few years was variously employed, then came to McKean county and the oil regions. In 1877 he was appointed superintendent of the National Transit Company, a position he still most capably fills. He is a Republican, and served as councilman of the borough of Kendall Creek, now part of the city of Bradford. He is a member of Bradford Post, No. 141, Grand Army of the Republic; Bradford Lodge, Free and Accepted Masons; Trinity Commandery, No. 58, and Chapter No. 260, Royal Arch Masons.

He married, July 6, 1869, Melissa Electa Bacon, born in Bloomfield, Crawford county, Pennsylvania, August 13, 1848. She was educated in the public schools of Union City. She was the first worthy matron of Bradford Chapter, No. 61, Order of the Eastern Star. She is also a member of the Woman's Relief Corps and the Daughters of Rebekah. Her father was Daniel Scott Bacon, born in Phelps, Chenango county, New York, June 25, 1821, died April 27, 1890, a cattle dealer of Waterford, Pennsylvania; later of Union City, where he died. He was a Republican and a Methodist. He married Louisa Drake, born October 12, 1825, in Smyrna, New York, died October 30, 1893, in Union City, Pennsylvania, daughter of Hiram Drake, who was born December 4, 1796, died August 27, 1870, and married Electa Pease, born November 5, 1796, died November 29, 1853. Children of Daniel S. Bacon: 1. Henry L., born in Wayne, Pennsylvania, June 13, 1845; a veteran of the civil war, having served in Company C, Sixteenth Regiment Pennsylvania Cavalry; married a Miss Wade, of Union City. 2. Melissa Electa, of previous mention. 3. Ellen Louisa, born at Rockdale, Pennsylvania, June 22, 1853; married Paul Perkins, of Union City, an engineer; children: Charles, born May 15, 1873; William, lives in Chicago; Lines, deceased; Roy, of Union City; Mina, of Cambridge Springs, Pennsylvania. 4. Estella J., born May 31, 1855; now a resident of Jamestown, New York; unmarried. Daniel Scott Bacon was a son of Henry Bacon, born about 1788, died in Union City, Pennsylvania, 1860, a farmer, and the son of a revolutionary soldier. He married and had children: 1. Daniel Scott, of previous mention. 2. Louisa, married Daniel Phelps, and moved to Kansas; child, Devault, now resides in New York City. 3. Chester, married Roxanna Slocum; children: Charles, of Meadville, Pennsylvania; Jennie, of Union City. 4. Horace, served in a Pennsylvania regiment of infantry during the civil war, married Amelia Fox, who survives him, a resident of Hatch Hollow, Erie county, Pennsylvania; children: Ida and Flora. 5. Wells, married Julia Chafey, who survives him, a resident of Hatch Hollow, Erie county; children: George and Gertrude.

Children of Perry and Melissa E. (Bacon) Smiley, all born at Union City, Pennsylvania: 1. Ida Louisa, born April 24, 1870, died October 18, 1879. 2. Ella Josephine, born August 24, 1871; married, July 30, 1895, William W. Lourey, a railroad employee in Boston, Massachusetts; child, Guy Perry, born November 23, 1899, died April, 1900. 3. Bert Moses, born July 15, 1873; now captain of Hose Company, No. 3, at Bradford; married, May 23, 1909, Nora Elizabeth Murphy, born in Cork, Ireland, January 25, 1886; child, Perry Edward, born August 6, 1910, deceased.

FLEMING The Flemings were a noble family of Scotland high in favor with Robert Bruce whom they assisted in gaining his throne. Sir Thomas Fleming, of ancient descent, emigrated to Virginia, in 1616, and was followed by others of his family. The family took prominent part in early Virginia times and during the revolution many served in the Continental army. From Virginia they spread to Kentucky, North Carolina, Ohio and Pennsylvania. One branch settled in Indiana county, Pennsylvania, and from them sprang the Flemings of Degolia. The earliest record we have is of Thomas Martin Fleming, who spent a great portion of his entire life in Blairsville, Indiana county, Pennsylvania, where he died about the year 1871. He married Sarah Calwell, a native of Plum Creek, Pennsylvania.

(II) William Martin, son of Thomas Martin and Sarah (Calwell) Fleming, was born in Indiana county, August, 1804, died at Natrona, Allegheny county, Pennsylvania, August, 1883. He followed the shoemaker's trade for the greater part of his life in Allegheny county. In politics he was a staunch supporter of the Democratic party, and with his wife a member of the German Lutheran church. He married Mary Calwell, born at Plum Creek, Pennsylvania, September, 1807, where she died March, 1876. Children: 1. Mary Catherine, born in Indiana township, 1840; married David Freshwater, of Armstrong county, Pennsylvania; he is a farmer near Natrona, Pennsylvania; they have a large family. 2. Nancy, born 1842, died in Allegheny, Pennsylvania, 1875; married Samuel Shannon, of Pittsburgh, who died in Allegheny county; children: Mary, lives at Pittsburgh; Sally. 3. Penelope, born 1844, died at Napoli, Pennsylvania; married William Shannon, deceased, a carpenter of Pittsburgh, Pennsylvania. 4. Sarah Jane, born in Indiana township, Pennsylvania, August 19, 1846; married David Fleming, born in Indiana township, Pennsylvania, August 26, 1859, died June 2, 1896, at Degolia, Pennsylvania, where his widow still resides. 5. William Luther, a carpenter of Little Washington, Pennsylvania, was born in Armstrong county, Pennsylvania, October, 1849, died in Little Washington, June, 1908; married Nancy Mitchell, of Natrona; children: Andy, Charles, Mary, Naomie, Warren, Frederick. 6. Martha, born in Armstrong county, Pennsylvania, March, 1851; married David Washbaugh, a farmer who died in Mount Pleasant, Westmoreland county, Pennsylvania, 1907; children: Willard, Wade, Vernon, Beatrice, Mildred. 7. Samuel Martin, of whom further. 8. John M. R., born in Armstrong county, Pennsylvania, 1855, died 1857.

(III) Samuel Martin, son of William Martin and Mary (Calwell) Fleming, was born in Armstrong county, Pennsylvania, March, 1853. He was educated in the public schools of the county and afterward learned the machinist's trade, an occupation he now follows in Wellsville, Ohio. He is a Republican in politics, although the only office he has ever occupied is that of school director, which he has held for several years. He and his wife were members of the Methodist Episcopal church. He married Mary, born 1846, daughter of Jacob Kuhn, of Armstrong county, Pennsylvania, who died April, 1876, in Armstrong county; he was a cooper by trade, and married Mary Kuhn, born in Armstrong county, Pennsylvania, died at Freeport, Pennsylvania. Mary (Kuhn) Fleming had one sister Agnes, who died at Freeport, unmarried; and one brother Harry, who lives at Freeport with his family. Children of Samuel Martin and Mary (Kuhn) Fleming: 1. Charles, born 1873; an employee of the Traction Company of Findlay, Ohio; married Marguerite Clark, of Findlay, Ohio. 2. Samuel M., of whom further.

(IV) Samuel M. (2), son of Samuel M. (1) and Mary (Kuhn) Fleming, was born in Allegheny county, 1875. He received his education in the public schools and afterward graduated from the business college at Bradford. He followed the oil business for several years in Bradford oil fields, Pennsylvania, and then in Nebraska, trying to establish for private family use a crude oil burner. On November 18, 1911, he purchased a grocery store at Custer City, Pennsylvania, where he has milling facilities for grinding and mixing feed. In politics his vote has always been cast for the individual, never for the party. He is a member of Tent No. 4, Knights of the Maccabees, at Bradford. He and his wife attend the Methodist Episcopal church. He married, November 20, 1900, Nellie S. Drake, born in Custer county, Nebraska, June 8, 1880, died at Bradford Hospital, July 18, 1908, daughter of Ralph Drake, a ranch owner of Elm Creek, Nebraska, born March 13, 1848, son of Lorenzo Dow Drake. Ralph Drake married Cordelia Wood, a native of Nebraska. Children of Samuel M. (2) and Nellie S. (Drake) Fleming: Bernice E., born in Degolia, September 4, 1901; Margaret D., in Degolia, October 12, 1906; Nellie S., at Bradford Hospital, July 3, 1908.

KIMMEL-COYNE The Kimmel family, whose members were famous in the history of Germany, was founded in the United States by Tobias Musser Kimmel, born in Germany, in 1805, died in Struthers, Ohio, in 1875. He emigrated to the United States and settled in Coitsville, Ohio, where he followed farming. His tilling of the soil was abundantly rewarded and he became a man of considerable substance. He and his wife were members of the Methodist Episcopal church. He married Lydia Smith, born in Mercer county, Pennsylvania, died in Coitsville, Ohio, in 1864. Children: 1. Joseph, passed his life on the home farm, where he died. 2. Abraham, of whom further. 3. Smith, a farmer, died in Youngstown, Ohio; married Julia Strouble; children: Martin, lives in Poland, Ohio; David, lives in North Jackson, Ohio; and several others. 4. William, a blacksmith, died in Hubbard, Ohio; married Jane Kirk, deceased; children: William (2),

Maud, Calvin, Kirk. 5. John, died on the homestead in Coitsville, Ohio; married Maria White, deceased; children: Luella, Amy. 6. Dwight, a farmer, died in Illinois; married and had one child. 7. Musser, died on the home farm in Coitsville, where his wife, Maud (Gisie) Kimmel, still lives; children: Harry, Wilbur, deceased; Julia; both the living children reside on the home farm. 8. Mary, married D. Stevens, a retired farmer, and lives in Hubbard, Ohio; children: John, Alberton, Maud; the first two live in Hubbard, Ohio. 9. Sarah, died in Youngstown, Ohio; married William Armstrong, deceased, a farmer; children: Inez, lives in Youngstown, Ohio; Mott, lives on a farm near Niles, Ohio. 10. Ruth, died in Youngstown, Ohio; married Luther Stevens, deceased, a carpenter; two children.

(II) Abraham, son of Tobias Musser and Lydia (Smith) Kimmel, was born in Youngstown, Ohio, March 6, 1825, died in Ohio, in 1906. He obtained his education in the public schools and in his late years followed the blacksmith's trade. At the outbreak of the civil war he enlisted from his home state and was engaged in much active service, until captured and confined in the Confederate prison at Andersonville. He was at one time an ardent Republican, but later changed his affiliation and became a Democrat. He once held the office of justice of the peace. In religion he was a firm supporter of the belief of his fathers and belonged to the Methodist Episcopal church, as did his wife.

He married, in Pymatuning, Mercer county, Pennsylvania, December 28, 1844, Elizabeth McCord, born in Greenville, Pennsylvania, June 26, 1848, died in Struthers, Ohio, April 10, 1875. Her father, Robert McCord, a surgeon in the war of 1812, was born in Westmoreland county, Pennsylvania, 1791, died in Brookfield, Ohio, May 1, 1872; her mother, Elizabeth (Snyder) McCord, was born in Westmoreland county, died near Greenville, Mercer county, Pennsylvania. Their children were: William, married Elizabeth Carmichael, and is a farmer in Iowa; Robert, died young; Thomas, died young; Joseph, married and lives on a farm in Iowa; Elizabeth, of previous mention.

Children of Abraham and Elizabeth (McCord) Kimmel: 1. Viola A., of whom further. 2. Albert, born November 16, 1848, died September 20, 1849. 3. Alfred, twin of Albert, died 1849. 4. Adelaide, born in Coitsville, Ohio, July 21, 1850; married, August 17, 1869, Isaac Williams, a farmer, born in Coitsville, Ohio, in 1846, now deceased; children: Nellie, born in Hubbard, Ohio, June 23, 1872, died June 25, 1872; Nettie, twin of Nellie, died June 25, 1872; Chrisse, born October 2, 1874, died same day; Etta; Elsie Dale; Howard, and Harrie. 5. Margaret, born in Coitsville, Ohio, June 25, 1853; married William Carpenter, born in Youngstown, Ohio, where they live; they had one daughter, died when six years of age. 6. Mary, born in Coitsville, Ohio, October 25, 1855; married William Sharp, born near Edenburg, Ohio, lives in Poland, Ohio; children: Elsie, born in Poland, October 22, 1874; Edward, a carpenter, lives in Youngstown, Ohio; Emil, lives in Youngstown, Ohio; Kimmel, lives at home; Dorothy, lives at home. 7. Albin, born in Coitsville, Ohio, March 21, 1860, died in Struthers, Ohio, February 3, 1893, an employee in a sheet mill; married Mary Ditmore, born near Lowellville, Ohio; children: Albin (2) and Ralph, living in Lowellville, Ohio, with their mother.

(III) Viola A., daughter of Abraham and Elizabeth (McCord) Kimmel, was born in Youngstown, Ohio, November 7, 1846. She obtained her education in the public schools of Coitsville, Ohio. After her marriage she moved to Bradford, Pennsylvania, where she is an earnest and devoted member of the Hill Memorial United Brethren Church.

She married, in Sharon, Mercer county, Pennsylvania, October 1, 1868, John Coyne, born in Montreal, Canada, March 23, 1847, died in Bradford, December 1, 1910. John Coyne was a contractor, doing a large business in Ohio and Pennsylvania. In 1870 he settled in Bradford, where he was living at the time of his death. He was the son of Thomas Coyne, born 1816, died near Grove, New York, April 20, 1898, who emigrated from France to Montreal, Canada. Thomas Coyne married Isabel Ferguson, born in 1820, died in Grove, August 22, 1883. Children of Thomas and Isabel (Ferguson) Coyne: 1. Jeannette, born 1845; married Steven Nicholson, deceased, a railroad employee, and lives in Chicago, Illinois; children: John; Patrick, deceased; Joseph; Mary; the three living children are in Chicago, Illinois. 2. John, before named. 3. Duncan, a farmer, born in Canada, 1849, died November 11, 1900; married Bridget Crowe, of Fayetteville, Steuben county, New York, who lives in Grove, New York. 4. William, a teamster, born in Canada, May, 1854, died in Bradford, Pennsylvania, July 8, 1893; married, in Ridgway, Pennsylvania, Ellen Sullivan, born in Ireland, March 10, 1863; children: Mary, born October 8, 1883; Margaret, August 19, 1886; John, September 3, 1890, died December 30, 1891; Helen, born January 9, 1892. 5. George, born in Canada, November 14, 1856; a railroad employee in Bradford, Pennsylvania; married Ellen Luby, of Ridgway, Pennsylvania, born August 22, 1863; children: Margaret, born in Bradford, Pennsylvania, May 24, 1884; Thomas, born in Ridgway, Pennsylvania, April 22, 1886; Michael, Ridgway, May 9, 1888; Florence, Ridgway, April 2, 1890; Francis, twin of Florence; Helena, born in Ridgway, April 26, 1892; Mary, born in Bradford, April 18, 1897. 6. Mary, born in Canada, 1857, where she died.

Children of John and Viola A. (Kimmel) Coyne: 1. Elver, born in Warsaw, Pennsylvania, October 24, 1869, died in Fayetteville, New York, October 24, 1870. 2. Dolly, born in Warsaw, Pennsylvania, March 9, 1873; married, August 21, 1894, Frank Cathan, an upholsterer, of Bradford, and lives in Ballston Spa, Saratoga county, New York; child, Ethel, born July 4, 1898. 3. May, born near Andover, New York, January 27, 1875; married Ford O. Williams, a carpenter, of Youngstown, Ohio; children: Cyril, born July 4, 1902; Ralph, born 1904; Edna, born 1911. 4. Anna, born near Andover, New York, July 20, 1876; married Joseph Madigan, of Bradford, and lives in West Chicago, Illinois, where he is a hammersmith; child, Jack, born 1909. 5. Edna, born in Bradford, Pennsylvania, August 25, 1878; married Clifford Stevens, a grocery clerk, of Bradford; child, Josephine, born July 31, 1901. 6. Thomas, born in Bradford, January 13, 1880, died April 1, 1880. 7. Lillian, born in Bradford, April 5, 1883; married Christopher Burke, of Bradford, an express agent at Beaver Falls, Pennsylvania. 8. Viola, born in Bradford, September 14, 1888; lives with her mother.

REDFIELD This family is supposed to be of English origin. It is hardly possible to doubt this; yet the name is very rare in England, almost nonexistent. In 1860 it was stated that no Redfield appeared in the directories of London, Liverpool, Manchester, Birmingham, Edinburgh nor Glasgow. Similar names are found, though rarely, in old English records, and arms have been granted to a few persons with possibly related names. In America, also, there is an obscurity about the name in the early days, where it seems to have been changed in the second generation from Redfin, almost as uncommon in England as Redfield, to Redfield, the evidence being conjectural, but strong, from the early records. The following account cannot be in all points guaranteed with the same confidence as is possible in some families, but is probably correct, and accords with the records so far as they carry the matter.

(I) William Redfin, the founder of this family, died about May, 1662. He was probably one of the early immigrants from England to Massachusetts. By 1639 he occupied a house and four acres of land on the south side of the Charles river, about six miles from Boston. He sold this place in September, 1646, and from that time his name disappears from the Massachusetts records. With some of his neighbors he probably joined the stream of migration to Pequot, now New London, Connecticut. The first certain evidence of his presence there is on May 20, 1654, at which time he had already built a house. The change of name to Redfield seems to have begun at New London, about the time of his death. He married Rebecca ———, who survived him. Children: 1. Lydia, married (first) January 19, 1655-56, Thomas Bayley, (second) in 1676, William Thorne. 2. Rebecca, died August 16, 1670; married, December 12, 1661, Thomas Roach. 3. James, of whom further. 4. Judith, died April 30, 1678; married, June 17, 1667, Alexander Pygan.

(II) James Redfield, son of William and Rebecca Redfin, was born, it is supposed, about 1646, and was living in 1719. In 1662 he bound himself for five years to learn the trade of tanning. About a year before the expiration of his time his master removed and he became free. For a short time he lived at New London. In 1671 he was an inhabitant of Martha's Vineyard, and five years later was living at Saybrook, where he remained at least ten years. By 1693 he removed to Fairfield, Connecticut. He married (first) at New Haven, in May, 1669, Elizabeth, daughter of Jeremy How, who was born in 1645, (second) at Fairfield, Deborah, daughter of John Sturgis. The order of his children is not quite certain, nor is it in every case certain by which wife. Children: Elizabeth, born May 31, 1670; Sarah, married Daniel Frost; Theophilus, of whom further; Margaret, baptized October 7, 1694; James, baptized October 25, 1696, died in 1743, probably thrice married.

(III) Sergeant Theophilus Redfield, son of James Redfield, was born about 1682, died February 14, 1759. He was a joiner. He probably settled, soon after coming of age, at Killingworth, Connecticut, in the part now called Clinton. About 1718 he moved to North Killingworth, now Killingworth. He is called Sergeant Redfield. He married, December 24, 1706, Priscilla, daughter of Daniel and Lydia Greenel, who was born about 1689, died January 12, 1770. Every one of his children had a family. Children: 1. Daniel, born September 22, 1707, died January 11, 1758; married Elizabeth ———. 2. Elizabeth, born May 8, 1709, died in 1742; married, February 3, 1731-32, Josiah Hull. 3. Richard, of whom further. 4. Ebenezer, born December 3, 1713, died January 4, 1766; married, November 30, 1741, Hannah Colton. 5. Lydia, born February 9, 1715-16, died December 16, 1784; married (first) February 21, 1737, Joseph Hodgkin, (second) November 15, 1753, Levi Leete. 6. Theophilus, born September 6, 1718, died January 30, 17—; married (first) September 4, 1740, Mary Buell, (second) in December, 1749, Martha Gray. 7. Priscilla, born July 20, 1720, died January 12, 1770; married, October 15, 1740, Joseph Bradley. 8. Peleg, born April 2, 1723, died December 5, 1760; married, April 25, 1744, Sarah Dudley. 9. George, born November 7, 1725, died May 30, 1812; married (first) in 1750, Trial Ward, (second) January 8, 1767, Abigail Stone. 10. William, born December 5, 1727, died in July, 1813; married, January 8, 1755, Elizabeth Starr. 11. Josiah, born September 6, 1730, died August 6, 1802; married, December 8, 1757, Sarah Parmelee. 12. Jane, born June 24, 1733, died May 24, 1762; married, January, 1753, Samuel Crane. 13. James, born March 29, 1735, died April 3, 1788; married Sarah Grinnell.

(IV) Richard, son of Sergeant Theophilus and Priscilla (Greenel) Redfield, was born June 18, 1711, died February 2, 1771. His home was at Killingworth, and he was a sea captain. He recognized the church covenant in 1725. He married (first) June 23, 1735, Mary, daughter of George and Esther Chatfield, (second) ——— Wilcox. Children by first wife: 1. Eliphalet, born July 24, 1736; married, June 15, 1767, Anna Stannard. 2. Priscilla, born March 12, 1739; married, October 10, 1759, Rufus Hardy. 3. Reuben, born June 21, 1742, died young. 4. Abigail, born September 21, 1743, died December 25, 1779; married William Pendleton. Children by second wife: 5. Reuben, of whom further. 6. Richard, born April 6, 1768, died March 26, 1851; married (first) Phebe Loper, (second) Lucy Brown.

(V) Reuben, son of Richard Redfield, was born at Killingworth, January 8, 1766, died at Eden, Erie county, New York, January 8, 1835. He lived at Highgate, Vermont, on the international boundary, and in several other places in that vicinity, and removed to Eden about 1832. He married, at Castleton, Vermont, about 1788, Elizabeth Jocelyn, who died February 4, 1829. Children: 1. Hervey, died young. 2. Harriet, died in March, 1854; married William Reynolds. 3. Almeria, married Elias Isham. 4. Alzira, born in 1708, died August 3, 1851; married, in 1821, John Jannays. 5. William Villeroy, married, March 22, 1821, Delana Barr. 6. Elizabeth Jocelyn, born November 21, 1802, died July 25, 1840; married, April 1, 1823, John Proper. 7. Lucy, died young. 8. Horner Johnson, married, September 17, 1844, Ruth Merrill. 9. Horace Linzy, of whom further.

(VI) Horace Linzy, son of Reuben and Elizabeth (Jocelyn) Redfield, was born at Highgate, Vermont, December 23, 1800, died at Eden, December 23, 1849. Eden was his home and he was a physician there. He married, April 28, 1838, Clarissa Jane, daughter of Edwin and Mary W. Forbes, born at Erie, Pennsylvania, June 16, 1816, died in Washington, D. C. For a time after her husband's death she lived at Jasper, Marion county, Tennessee. Children: 1. Edwin Forbes Linzy, born April 22, 1842, died in Texas; lived south; served in the Confederate army; married and had children: Henry L. and Maud, both residing in Dallas, Texas. 2. Horace Victor Eugene, of whom further. 3. Caroline Clarissa, born December 15, 1849, died January 11, 1850.

(VII) Horace Victor Eugene, son of Horace Linzy and Clarissa Jane (Forbes) Redfield, was born at Eden, December 23, 1845, died in Washington, D. C., November 17, 1881. He was a newspaper correspondent; at one time being the Washington correspondent for the Cincinnati *Commercial*. For a time he lived at Chattanooga, Tennessee, and there was an alderman. He was a Republican. Both he and his wife were communicants of the Episcopal church. He married Jeanette, daughter of Byron D. and Harriet (Holmes) Hamlin, who was born at Smethport, McKean county, Pennsylvania. Children: 1. Harriet Forbes, born at Smethport, August 4, 1874; married Mellville Gillett (see Gillett V). 2. Horace Hamlin, of whom further. 3. Scott Forrest, born in Washington, October 5, 1879; married Caroline Larned, of Syracuse, New York; he is a publisher, and their residence is at Smethport; children: Scott Forrest, born May 31, 1908; Janet, born August 29, 1910.

(VIII) Horace Hamlin, son of Horace Victor Eugene and Jeanette (Hamlin) Redfield, was born in Chattanooga, Tennessee, January 10, 1878. His schooling was begun at Smethport and afterwards continued at Augusta, Georgia. From the public school he was sent to St. John's Military School, Manlius, New York, and thence to Hobart College, which he left, however, in 1898. From 1900 to 1907 he was in the hardware business at Smethport. Having sold this business to Daly & Garlick he went into banking at Eldred, Pennsylvania, and elsewhere. But he has retained his residence at Smethport to the present day. He is president of the First National Bank at Eldred; director in the Hamlin Bank & Trust Company, Smethport, and the First National Bank at Bradford, Pennsylvania; a member of the advisory board of the First Mortgage, Guarantee & Trust Company, Philadelphia; and formerly was a director of the Grange National Bank, Smethport. He is a thirty-second degree Mason, belonging to Coudersport Consistory; Zem Zem Temple, Nobles of the Mystic Shrine, Erie, Pennsylvania; McKean Lodge, No. 388, Free and Accepted Masons; Phoenix Chapter, No. 15, Eastern Star. His clubs are the Central, Smethport; the Bradford and the Country Club, Bradford. Mr. Redfield is a Republican. For five years he has been school director of the borough of Smethport, and has served one term as councilman in that borough. At this time he is a candidate for the Pennsylvania assembly. He is a communicant of St. Luke's Episcopal Church, Smethport.

He married, October 10, 1900, Grace Emily, daughter of Frederick A. and Emily Leona (Huenerfeld) McCoy, who was born at Ellicottville, New York, April 1, 1878. She is a graduate of the Smethport high school, in the class of 1895. She is a member of Smethport Chapter, No. 15, Eastern Star. In connection with St. Luke's Church, of which she is a communicant, she is a member of St. Christopher's Guild. Her father is a druggist at Smethport, son of Stephen and Eliza McCoy. Emily Leona, born at Ellicottville, February 3, 1855, was the daughter of Peter Joseph and Emily (Riggs) Huenerfeld. Peter J. Huenerfeld was born at Cochem, Prussia, September 18, 1818, son of Paul and Mary (Gillis) Huenerfeld. Emily Riggs, daughter of John and Melenza (Litchfield) Riggs, was born at North Adams, Massachusetts, March 26, 1827. Children of Peter Joseph and Emily (Riggs) Huenerfeld, all born at Ellicottville: 1. Louise, born April 21, 1849; married H. B. Drown. 2. Jeanette, born October 12, 1852; married C. B. Greene. 3. Emily Leona, mentioned above. 4. Mary, born October 21, 1858; married R. V. Hixson. Children of Horace Hamlin and Grace Emily (McCoy) Redfield: 1. Hamlin Delano, born at Smethport, January 17, 1902. 2. Robert Horace, born at Smethport, March 12, 1905. 3. Louise, born at Smethport, March 16, 1909.

ARMSTRONG The clan Armstrong was famed in Scotland for courage and patriotism. Scott, in the "Lay of the Last Minstrel," makes the chief say, when about to assemble the clans for some daring enterprise:

Ye need not go to Liddisdale,
For when they see the blazing bale
Eliots and Armstrongs never fail.

The family tradition is that the name was originally bestowed upon a Highland chief for his great courage and physical powers. Another and better authenticated tradition is that the name Armstrong is derived from the following circumstances: "An ancient king of Scotland, having his horse killed under him in battle, was immediately remounted by Fairbaim, his armor bearer, who took the king by the thigh and placed him in the saddle, although heavily weighted by armor. For this timely assistance and feat of strength, the king amply rewarded him with lands on the border; gave him the name of Armstrong, and assigned him for crest an armed hand and arm; in the left hand a leg and foot in armor couped at the thigh all proper."

The Armstrongs were early settlers in Connecticut and New Hampshire, in the latter state settling in Londonderry, and coming from Londonderry, Ireland. Stephen Armstrong settled in Windham, Connecticut, in 1710, while an earlier settler was Gregory Armstrong, of Plymouth, Massachusetts, who died in 1650.

(I) The line of descent of the Armstrongs of Smethport, Pennsylvania, is from Benjamin Armstrong, of Norwich, Connecticut, who died January 10, 1710. He married Rachel ———, and had sons: Benjamin, John, Joseph, Stephen.

(II) John, son of Benjamin and Rachel Armstrong, was born December 5, 1678, at Norwich, Connecticut, died March 21, 1749. He married, January 18, 1710, Anne Worth. He had seven sons: John, Preserved, Hopestill, James, Thomas, Jeremiah, Ezra, and six daughters.

(III) Hopestill, son of John and Anne (Worth) Armstrong, was born in Norwich, Connecticut, October 15, 1713. He married, December 22, 1737, Rebecca Durkee, and had six sons: Tibbeus, Solomon, Hopestill, Peletiah, James, Zephaniah, and two daughters. It is from one of these six sons that the Smethport family descend. The name of their grandfather not having been preserved, the connection cannot be definitely shown. The sons of Hopestill Armstrong scattered, some settling in Vermont, thence coming to New York state.

(IV) ——— Armstrong, grandfather of Alvin Backus Armstrong, although very young, served in the war of the revolution, as did two of his brothers. After the Wyoming massacre he was sent north with a reconnoitering party, and was so pleased with the country around Seneca Lake, New York, that after peace was restored he made permanent settlement there. He was a farmer, married and both he and wife lived to advanced ages, members of the Presbyterian church. Children: 1. Martin, died in New York City, a merchant, suffering the loss of his store in the great fire of 1837; married and left issue. 2. George, died in Seneca county. 3. John, died young and unmarried, a victim of the cholera. 4. Caroline, died in Waterloo, New York; married a Mr. Moore and left issue. 5. Alexander McLane, of whom further.

(V) Alexander McLane Armstrong was born in Seneca county, New York, in 1809, died in Kansas, at the home of his daughter, in 1893. He was educated in the public school and resided in Seneca county until 1834, when he moved to Cuba, Allegany county, New York. He was a cabinetmaker and followed his trade in Cuba until 1849, and in Rushford and Houghton, New York, and in 1861 went to Mount Pleasant, Iowa. He was a most excellent mechanic and one whose services were always in demand. He was a Republican, and a member of the Presbyterian church. He married Julia Ann Backus, born in 1813, died in Mount Pleasant, Iowa, 1863, only child of Joseph Backus, born in Massachusetts, 1788, a shoemaker and old time music teacher. He died in East Rushford, New York, in 1853. He married Elizabeth Reynolds, born in Massachusetts, died in Nunda, Livingston county, New York. Her brother, Philetus Reynolds, died in Cuba, New York, where he held a position on the Genesee Valley canal. Both Alexander Armstrong and his wife were of deeply religious temperament, taking an active part in church work, both being devout Presbyterians, he leader of the choir. Children, nine in number, six dying in infancy and childhood, three here of mention: 1. Alvin B., of whom further. 2. Martin Luther, whose sketch follows. 3. Ally, born in Rushford, New York, 1856; married James L. Anderson, a farmer of Beloit, Kansas, whom she survives, a resident of Denver, Colorado; children: Ruby, resides with her mother in Denver; Marian, resides in Seattle, Washington; Ethel, resides in Oregon, an I three others, names unknown.

(VI) Alvin Backus, son of Alexander McLane and Julia Ann (Backus) Armstrong, was born in Cuba, New York, July 26, 1838. He was educated in the "little red schoolhouse" and Rushford Academy, and when fourteen years of age began working on a farm. In 1853 he moved to Ridgway, Pennsylvania, where he was employed in the store owned by Joseph S. Hyde. In 1854 he came to Smethport, where his first position was a booking agent for the Stage Company operating a line between Smethport and Olean, New York. He continued with the Stage Company three years, then for the succeeding three years was a clerk in the mercantile house of Ford & Smith, which later he purchased, and operated with a partner as Irons & Armstrong for two years. He then sold his interest and began the study of law under the preceptorship of John C. Backus. He was admitted to the McKean county bar in 1861, but was not at all in sympathy with his profession, soon returning to mercantile life as senior of A. B. Armstrong & Company. In 1866 he bought out the drug store of Seems & Hogarth, located on Main street, Smethport, which he operated for several years with H. L. McCoy, and still controls, the oldest drug store in McKean county. He has been a very successful business man and has large holdings in the principal enterprises of Smethport. He coöperated with DeWitt C. Young in organizing the Grange National Bank in 1907, and is vice-president of that very successful financial institution. He organized the Smethport Water Company and for many years was its treasurer and managing director. He was prominently connected with the organization of the Smethport Gas Company and was treasurer and manager for several years, also treasurer of Rose Hill Cemetery Association. He owns a fine dairy farm of over two hundred acres located five miles from Smethport, where he gratifies his love for the soil and for fine bred stock. He there maintains a herd of the best Guernsey cows and a dairy perfectly equipped with every sanitary device and modern dairying machines. He also prides himself upon his finely bred Berkshire hogs and his Plymouth Rock poultry.

Notwithstanding his many business engagements and unending demand upon his time, Mr. Armstrong has not neglected his duty as a good citizen. He takes an active interest in civic affairs and the upbuilding of his borough. He has served a great many terms as councilman, and in 1869 represented Clinton, Cameron and McKean counties in the Pennsylvania house of representatives, and for twenty years served as justice of the peace. He is a member of the Presbyterian church; is past master of Smethport Lodge, Free and Accepted Masons, and a Royal Arch Mason of Olean, New York. His club is the Central of Smethport. In politics he is a Democrat.

He married, March, 1860, in Smethport, Caroline E. Bennett, born in Smethport, October 4, 1840, educated in the public schools and Lima (New York) Academy. Child of Alvin Backus and Caroline E. (Bennett) Armstrong: Ethel, born in Smethport, March, 1862, died March, 1894; married William P. Walsh, managing director of the Smethport Water Company; child, Ethlyn, born March, 1894, died August, 1894.

David R. Bennett, father of Mrs. Armstrong, was born in New York state, January 28, 1810, died at Port Allegany, Pennsylvania, March 23, 1876, a hotelkeeper at Smethport, also deputy sheriff, later sheriff, of McKean county. He married, August 14, 1835, Corinna Nana Chapin, born in Chenango county, New York, August 10, 1817, died there February 14, 1893, daughter of Henry Chapin, born in New York state, April 5, 1787, died in Smethport, April 23, 1858, a farmer. He married (first) February 24, 1811, Johannah Kemball, born in New York, November 18, 1792. Children of Henry Chapin, all deceased: 1. Amanda Melvina, born September 1, 1812; married Judge Richmond, of Chenango county, New York, judge of the court at Smethport, Pennsylvania, a man of marked ability and prominence. 2. Arminta, born September, 1814; married a Mr. Boardman. 3. Corinna Nana, of previous mention; wife of David R. Bennett. 4. Oscar, born February 21, 1819, died June 1, 1819. 5. Henry, born October 13, 1820, died June 1, 1827. 6. Thaddeus Lindorf, born April 20, 1823, a farmer; married Betsey Corwin; children: Cynthia and Bertha. 7. Viola Ophelia, born March 13, 1825; married Darwin Hamlin, of Smethport, a civil engineer. 8. Ann Elizabeth, born October 7, 1826; married C. K. Sartwell, of Smethport, a merchant, and one time prothonotary, register and recorder of McKean county; children: Ella, married a Mr. Quackenbush; Henry, married a Miss Coleman; Mary, now matron of an insane asylum at Anna, Illinois. 10. Fitz Henry, born June 17, 1831, died in childhood. Henry Chapin, father of the foregoing ten children, married (second) February 4, 1833, Indiana Hive Arnold, born in Chenango county, New York, September 17, 1799, died in Smethport. Children: 11. Catherine Indiana, born in Smethport, August 27, 1834; married Calvin C. Hooker, a farmer, who died in South Dakota. 12. Joanna Fidelia, born in Smethport, September 19, 1836, died there May 28, 1902; married Samuel C. Hyde, deceased, a lawyer.

Children of David R. Bennett, all born in Smethport, Pennsylvania, but the first: 1. Abrosia (or Ambrosia), born in Port Allegany, Pennsylvania, December 15, 1858, died in Smethport, September 15, 1904; she married (first) Edgar Mason, a hardware merchant of Smethport, (second) a Mr. Crandall, deceased, a merchant in Nebraska; children of first marriage: Elva, born March 21, 1858, died January 8, 1885, and Clayton, born 1863, deceased; child by second marriage: Benjamin. 2. Caroline E., of previous mention; wife of Alvin Backus Armstrong. 3. Frances, born October 3, 1842; married Lynn W. Mason, deceased, a hardware merchant, whom she survives, living in Buffalo, New York; children: Mary Mae, born April 14, 1867; Cora, May 11, 1872. 4. Mary Ellen, born February 2, 1845; married Dudley Gifford, of Smethport, now an employee of the Smethport Glass Works; child, Theo, born September 3, 1884; now a bookkeeper in Williamsport, Pennsylvania; unmarried. 5. Flora, born April 22, 1847; married Dr. F. W. Hogarth, who died in Port Allegany, a practicing physician, whom she survives, a resident of Smethport; child, Leon R., born September 9, 1869, now a druggist of Smethport. 6. Ida, born January 15, 1854; married Anson Burdick, now a plumber of Smethport; no issue.

The foregoing children of David R. Bennett are grandchildren of Elijah Bennett, born March, 1776, died January 2, 1850. His wife Persis was born December 27, 1773, died July 11, 1839, leaving seven children, as follows: 1. Dr. William, born February 28, 1795, died in Angelica, New York, October 11, 1875; was a physician and one of the first settlers of Bradford, Pennsylvania. 2. Phoebe, born July 8, 1796, died August 6, 1840; married a Mr. Wheeler. 3. Electra, born December 17, 1797, died February 12, 1880; married a Mr. Warner. 4. Anna, born October 3, 1800; married a Mr. Moser. 5. Salva, born November 17, 1804, died October 27, 1848; married a Mr. Horton. 6. Oshea R., born April 28, 1806, died April 19, 1858; married Lucy Green Warner. 7. David R., of previous mention; father of Mrs. Alvin Backus Armstrong.

(VI) Martin Luther Armstrong, son of Alexander McLane (q. v.) and Julia Ann (Backus) Armstrong, was born in Cuba, Allegany county, New York, October 6, 1848. When he was seven years of age his parents moved to Houghton, New York, where he attended school until he was thirteen years of age. In 1861 the family moved to Iowa, locating at Mount Pleasant, where he finished his education in the Mount Pleasant schools and the academy at Denmark. After leaving school he secured employment on a cattle ranch, and for three years led the life of a cowboy. In 1865 he came to Smethport where he first secured employment as a clerk. He then began working at the jeweler's trade and in 1868 purchased the jewelry business of F. Seems. He has been continuously in business in Smethport from that date until the present, a period now nearing the half century mark. His store is located on the main street in the heart of the business district and is patronized most liberally by satisfied customers, this being the leading jewelry store of the borough and unsurpassed in equipment and quality of goods by any in the county. Mr. Armstrong is a Republican in politics and has served as councilman and chief burgess. He was baptized in the Presbyterian church and has always maintained a connection with that denomination. His fraternal order is the Ancient Order of United Workmen.

ARMSTRONG

Mr. Armstrong married (first) in June, 1876, Alice Chadwick, born in Smethport, in 1856, was educated in the public schools, finishing at high school, died at the place of her birth in November, 1898. She was the daughter of John R. Chadwick, an early settler at Smethport, born 1815, a farmer and one time clerk of McKean county. He died in Smethport in 1902. He married Jeannette Wright, born in 1817, died in 1882. Children of John R. Chadwick (a partial list only): 1. Alice, of previous mention; wife of Martin Luther Armstrong. 2. Freeman, now a farmer living near Smethport; married Martha Cobb; no issue. 3. John E., now living at Smethport; married; no issue. Children of Martin Luther Armstrong, born in Smethport: 1. Charles Lloyd, now an employee of the American Express Company, located at Buffalo, New York; he married Louisa Tamlin, of Buffalo; child, Louisa, born September 2, 1911. 2. Aletha, married John R. Kelly, of Elmira, New York, now a restaurant proprietor at Shinglehouse, Potter county, Pennsylvania; children: Martin, born in Smethport, 1904; Ellen, born in Elmira, New York, June 24, 1909. Mr. Armstrong married (second) Jannett Ripley. He married (third) June 17, 1911, Sarah, daughter of Joseph B. Oviatt, of Smethport, Pennsylvania.

SHARP

In a record of the Scotch-Irish Presbyterian families who were the first settlers at the "Forks of Delaware," now Northampton county, Pennsylvania, is found the name of Robert Sharp, from Cumberland county, who was a son of Thomas and Margaret (Elder) Sharp. "Covenanters," who because of their religious faith were driven from Scotland to the province of Ulster in the north of Ireland, residing in Belfast, county of Antrim, until 1747, when they came to America, the family consisting of Thomas Sharp, his wife, five sons and four daughters; they settled in the township of Newton, Cumberland county, Pennsylvania.

(II) Robert, son of Thomas Sharp, after coming to this country, later returned and came again bringing the remainder of the family. He located at the "Forks of the Delaware," where he married. This was before the revolution in which he and his brother Alexander served as wagoners. He married Margaret Boyd, a descendant of John Boyd, born in Scotland. Children: James, John, David, Thomas, Margaret.

(III) One of the sons of Robert and Margaret (Boyd) Sharp.

(IV) Robert (2), grandson of Robert (1) and Margaret (Boyd) Sharp, was born about 1820. He was an early settler and a farmer of Lawrence county. He was a prosperous farmer. He was an influential Whig. He served in the Pennsylvania house of assembly and held county office. He died in Lawrence county, aged seventy years. He married Ann Christie, born in Allegheny, died in Lawrence county, long before her husband. Children, all born in Lawrence county: 1. William, born 1837; a farmer and miller; has a grist mill in Lawrence county. 2. Rev. Joseph, born 1839; a minister of the Presbyterian church at New Castle, Pennsylvania. 3. Hess, born 1842; resides in New Wilmington; a farmer. 4. Thomas, born 1843; a carpenter, living in Minneapolis, Minnesota. 5. James, born 1845; a prominent manufacturer of Morehead, Clay county, Minnesota; has served twenty-four years on the school board of Morehead and is now probate judge of Clay county. 6. Martin Luther, born 1847. 7. John, born 1850; when last heard from was prospecting in the Black Hills, Wyoming. 8. Robert C., of whom further.

(V) Robert C., youngest child of Robert (2) and Ann (Christie) Sharp, was born in Lawrence county, Pennsylvania, April 6, 1852, died in Kane, December 9, 1905. His mother died when he was young and he was reared by his brother William. He was educated in the public school and began business life as a tool dresser in the Venango county oil fields. He followed this vocation for several years in the oil fields of Pennsylvania and New York state, coming to Kane in 1885. He became interested in several Kane industries, operated in oil and gas, organized the Valley Gas Company, and was engaged actively in business until his death. He was a Republican in politics, and was reared in the Presbyterian church, but three months prior to his death joined the Roman Catholic church, the faith of his wife.

He married, in Warren, Pennsylvania, Ellen Ramsey, born November 8, 1862, daughter of Owen Ramsey, born in county Cavan, Ireland, in 1832, an Orangeman. He settled in Edinburgh, Scotland, where he married, and prior to 1854 came to the United States and lived in various parts of Pennsylvania, accumulating considerable property. He died in 1907, in Warren, Pennsylvania. He married Rose Glenn, born in Ireland, in 1833. She followed her husband to the United States, in 1854, and died in Warren, in 1908. Rose Glenn, while living in Edinburgh, was the proprietor of a large inn. Living children of Owen and Rose Ramsey: 1. Mary, born in Edinburgh, Scotland; now living in Warren, Pennsylvania; married Patrick Murphy; children: Rose, Cecelia, Anna and others. 2. John, born in Edinburgh. 3. Ellen, of previous mention; married Robert C. Sharp. 4. Owen, born in Warren, Pennsylvania; now living in Youngstown, Ohio. Children of Robert C. and Ellen Sharp: 1. Reuben Johnson, of whom further. 2. Robert Crawford, born in Warren, May 12, 1881; now living in Youngstown, Ohio, an office employee of Republic Iron and Steel Corporation. 3. Mary, born in Warren, May 8, 1883; married Oscar Ford, a merchant, now living in Shinglehouse, Pennsylvania. 4. Josephine, born in Allentown, Pennsylvania, June 22, 1885; married Hugh McAndrew, of Bernhard Bay, New York, now engaged in business with his brother-in-law, Oscar Ford, at Shinglehouse. 5. James Harvey, born in Kane, July 27, 1887; now a shoe salesman of Youngstown, Ohio; unmarried. 6. Rose, born in Kane, January 27, 1891; resides in Youngstown. 7. Edward, born in Kane, January 28, 1893; now residing in Youngstown; a salesman. 8. George Evan, born in Kane, May 14, 1898; resides in Youngstown. 9. Maude, born November 15, 1900, in Kane.

Mrs. Ellen (Ramsey) Sharp, mother of the above children, survives her husband and resides in Youngstown, her unmarried children making their home with her. She married (second) M. O'Byrne, of East Emporium, but separated from him because of friction over her children, Mr. O'Byrne not wishing to have them reside with him.

(VI) Reuben Johnson, son of Robert C. and Ellen (Ramsey) Sharp, was born in Warren, Pennsylvania, June 21, 1879. He was educated in the public schools and was graduated at Kane high school, class of 1896. In September of that year he became clerk in the Kane postoffice, continuing until 1899 when he was appointed assistant postmaster. He was acting postmaster from May 18, 1909, until August 1, 1909, then again assistant until June 22, 1912, and since that time again acting postmaster, October 1, 1912. He is a capable official and a journalist of recognized ability, having for the past two years been one of the editorial writers of the *Kane Daily Republican*. He is president of the Kane fire department, member of the board of directors of the Kane Republican Publishing Company, state consul for Pennsylvania Modern Woodmen of America, venerable consul of Kane Camp, No. 5728, of that order, serving his third consecutive term; grand knight of Kane Council, No. 715, Knights of Columbus, for three terms; delegate to the state convention three years and in 1908 national delegate to the Supreme Council that met in St. Louis, and in May, 1912, was a delegate to the state convention at Harrisburg, serving on the committee on resolutions. He organized Kane Assembly, Knights of Columbus, in 1909, was the first chairman and now is serving as "Active Faithful Admiral." He is one of the energetic, capable young business men of Kane and stands high in his community. In 1912 he was one of the active workers that organized the Kane Board of Trade. He was elected a director of the board, and he was then elected secretary of the board. He is a member of the Roman Catholic church, and politically a Republican, and during the campaign of 1908 and 1910 was one of the regular staff of speakers on McKean county platforms. In June, 1910, he was a delegate to the state convention held in Harrisburg and at that convention was elected president of the Republican organization of the twenty-third senatorial district.

He married, April 3, 1901, Laura Eliza Yount, born in Richardsville, Jefferson county, Pennsylvania, June 12, 1876; educated in the public school, entered the first class for nurses ever formed at Kane Summit Hospital, and was a member of the first class graduated, following her profession one year, until her marriage. She is the daughter of Jacob Yount, born in Clarion county, Pennsylvania. He was a lumberman on the Clarion river in the early days, but during the last fourteen years of his life lived with his son Samuel in Brockport, Pennsylvania, being an invalid nearly that entire period. He died there in 1904. He married Eliza Wilson, born in county Donegal, Ireland, 1830, died in Brockport, December 8, 1905. Their children: 1. Samuel, a merchant and farmer of Brockport; twice married and has a son Raymond. 2. Martha, married Thomas Chamberlain, a farmer, and resides in Pueblo, Pennsylvania. 3. James, a farmer of Richardsville, Pennsylvania. 4. John, in charge of the State Coal and Iron Police at Ambridge, Pennsylvania. 5. Silas, postmaster, merchant and farmer at Pueblo, Pennsylvania. 6. George, a laborer, living in Elk county. 7. Laura Eliza, of previous mention. 8. Melvin, now steward of the Fraternal Order of Eagles Club at Ambridge, Pennsylvania; married a Miss Wildew, adopted daughter of his brother Samuel. Children of Reuben J. and Laura Eliza Sharp, all born in Kane: Virginia, August 25, 1902; Paul Yount, August 13, 1903; Catherine, January 17, 1905; Samuel, October 12, 1906; Mary Martha, August 25, 1912.

WRIGHT The simplest and most natural explanation of this surname is that which makes it a name of occupation, nearly agreeing in meaning with the name Smith. It is said that smith was the general term for a worker in metals, whereas a wright was one who worked in wood and other materials. As is usually the case with surnames, the "authorities" give widely differing explanations, and anyone not satisfied with one interpretation has only to consult another dictionary. Both the simplicity of explanation and the frequent occurrence of the name give strong probability to the explanation here favored.

Characteristics of the family are truth and honor. The word of a Wright would sooner be accepted than to believe most men on their oath. Rare executive ability, strong sense of justice, firmness combined with courtesy and affability, are other traits to which may be added patriotism, military ardor and a self-sacrificing spirit. Length of years have been rewards for upright living, and the Wrights have numbered many centenaries in their ranks. It is recorded of one that when an old man—in the neighborhood of ninety—he went out one day to mow with the young men, but sat down to weep when he found that he could not keep up with the others. The Wrights from the oldest to the youngest are noted for their honesty and uprightness in all their dealings.

(I) Rensselaer Wright, the first member of this family about whom we have definite information, was born in Delaware county, New York, died in 1884. Removing from New York state, he settled at Eldred, McKean county, Pennsylvania, where he was engaged in farming. He was also proprietor of a hotel, and largely interested in lumbering. Emphatically a self-made man, he nevertheless deserved and held a high place among the representative men of his place and time. He was one of the first commissioners of McKean county, and in 1829 was elected sheriff of the county. In the course of his official career he went on horseback to Philadelphia, and brought back with him necessary funds for the erection of the first court house of the county. He and his wife were active members of the Methodist Episcopal church. He married Sarah Moore, who died in 1881. Children: 1. James, deceased. 2. John, deceased; married Editha ———. 3. George, deceased. 4. Phelps, died in the west; he was a farmer and local preacher. 5. Nelson, died young; his death being due to drowning. 6. Junius, deceased; married Elizabeth Moody. 7. Sally, deceased; married Nathan Palmer. 8. Martha, deceased; married Edick Wright. 9. Maria, deceased; married Waterbury Miller. 10. Charles C., of whom further. 11. ———.

(II) Charles C., son of Rensselaer and Sarah (Moore) Wright, was born at Smethport, McKean county, Pennsylvania, in June, 1820, died at Coleville, McKean county, Pennsylvania, September 20, 1909. He was brought up and educated at Eldred. When he started in life for himself he settled at Cole Creek, Keating township, McKean county. Here he erected a steam saw mill, and was one of the leading lumbermen of McKean county. In politics and the questions of the day he was actively interested, and he upheld the principles of the Republican party. Both he and his wife were members of the Methodist Episcopal church and active in its work. He married (first) Jerusha, daughter of Nathan and Tirzah (Knapp) Dennis, born in 1831, died at Moundsville, West Virginia, in 1877, (second) in 1879, ———, daughter of ——— Madison. James Dennis, father of Nathan Dennis, was a soldier in the revolution. He was captured by the Indians; in three months' time he effected his escape, but he died soon after reaching home, in consequence of the hardships which he had endured. Nathan Dennis was a soldier in the war of 1812. In 1822 he settled in Ceres (now Eldred) township, McKean county, Pennsylvania, where he cleared and improved two farms. He was also engaged in mercantile and hotel business, and was for thirty years postmaster at Allegany Bridge (now Eldred). He married Tirzah Knapp. Children of Nathan and Tirzah (Knapp) Dennis: 1. George T., born at Masonville, Delaware county, New York, September 22, 1819; farmer, school teacher, veteran of the civil war; since 1874 he has been engaged in the manufacture of botanical remedies at Eldred; he has been since 1886 a licensed local preacher; a Republican and a Methodist; he married (first) March 13, 1844, Mary Ann Crandall, (second) H. Eliza Barrett; children, all by first wife: Mason G., Matthew N., Clark W., William B., Joseph B., Rosa P., married H. J. Doolittle; Matie, married William Boone. 2. Lucinda, married M. G. Knapp. 3. Susan, married Daniel Crandall. 4. James N. 5. Reuben, born at Eldred, August 27, 1826; farmer, lumberman, hotelkeeper at Eldred, where in 1879 he erected the Central Hotel; once commissioner of McKean county; he was a Democrat until 1856, then a Republican, but from 1884 a Prohibitionist; he married (first) Ruth Barden, (second) Helen Beardsley, (third) Emma J. Belknap; four children by first wife, two by second, two by third. 6. Lewis L. 7. Jerusha, married Charles C. Wright. 8. Jane, married Daniel Blanchard. 9. Washington. 10. Martha, married Thaddeus Royce. 11. Virtue, died at the age of six. Children of Charles C. and Jerusha (Dennis) Wright: 1. Victor C., born in 1854, died at Sawyer City, Pennsylvania, in 1881; oil producer; married Estella Crandall; she now resides at Olean, New York; no children. 2. James Burdette, of whom further. 3. William A., born in 1858, died at Olean, in 1893; a setter in saw mills; married Celia Parrish, deceased; one son, died at two years old. 4. Delano W., born in 1862; resides at Rew City, McKean county, Pennsylvania; oil producer; married Ida Weiner;

child, Maude, born in 1884, married William Ward, they also reside at Rew City, where Mr. Ward is an oil well worker. 5. Lillian J., born in 1868; married Lewis Maynard; they reside at Sumner, Illinois, and he is an oil well worker; children: Lewis, Clyde, Carl, Mary. 6. Milton W., born in 1874; resides at Coleville, Pennsylvania; oil producer; married Anna Wright (not related); children: Carl, Leslie.

(III) James Burdette, son of Charles C. and Jerusha (Dennis) Wright, was born at Coleville, September 4, 1856. There he received a public school education. As soon as he was of sufficient age, he began working for his father in the lumber business, and he worked with him until he was twenty-one. In 1877 he bought sixty acres of timber land at Coleville; from this he cut the timber, had the logs sawed at his father's mill, and sold the lumber in the oil country. Two years later he bought from Henry Hamlin another piece of timber at McCord Hollow, and again he sold his manufactured products in the oil region. After this he bought a much larger tract at Farmer's Valley and another, later, at Rexford. He manufactured the lumber until 1898, when he formed a partnership with D. H. Miller, under the firm name of Wright & Miller. They went to Nansen, Elk county, Pennsylvania, which was named by Mr. Wright in honor of the intrepid Arctic explorer, and here they conducted their business until 1910. The business having greatly increased, they built the Elk and Highland railroad. A large mill which they built was destroyed by fire, but they rebuilt. They cleared several thousand acres of timber, manufactured the lumber, and in two years shipped over twenty-five million feet of hemlock. Meanwhile, they had erected another mill at Springer, McKean county, which manufactured fifty thousand feet of hemlock per day. There they built about three miles of standard gauge railroad. Their next purchase was of nine thousand five hundred acres of timber in Cattaraugus county, New York, and there they built about seven miles of standard guage railroad. This road was incorporated under the name of the Tunasassa and Bradford Railroad Company; Mr. Wright is a stockholder and vice-president, and he holds the same office, with that of treasurer, in the Elk and Highland Railroad Company. Since 1896 he has had his home at Kane, McKean county, and in the present year (1912) he has begun a wholesale lumber business at this place. For thirty-three years consecutively he has now been engaged in the manufacture of lumber. He is a stockholder and president of the Nansen Supply Company, stockholder and director in the Quaker Supply Company and in the Wright and Miller Company. He is a member of the Ancient Order of United Workmen, at Bradford, and of the Independent Order of Puritans, in Pittsburgh. He is a Republican and a member of the Methodist Episcopal church.

He married, January 9, 1877, Kate Helen, daughter of Alfred and Sythere (Snyder) Matteson, who was born at Bradford, Pennsylvania, July 17, 1857. There she attended public school, and graduated in 1874 from the high school. Her father was a native of Pennsylvania, a farmer at Bradford. In 1861 he enlisted in the Union army, and he was drowned in the James river in 1864. His widow was born at Sardinia, New York, May 27, 1829, and now resides at Coleville. Mrs. Wright is their only child. She is a member of the Lady Maccabees, at Kane. Her church is the Methodist Episcopal. Child of James Burdette and Kate Helen (Matteson) Wright: Isabelle, born at Coleville, October 18, 1879; married Henry Curtis; they reside in Pittsburgh, and he is superintendent of a telephone company; they have one son, Lester, born at Kane, June 4, 1900.

HURLEY-BARRY The earliest records obtainable of the Hurley family in Ireland are found in county Cork, where Grandfather Hurley in 1785 was thrown from a horse and instantly killed. He married Johanna Brickley, born in county Cork, Ireland, who soon after her husband's death came to the United States and died in Boston, Massachusetts, three months after landing. They were born Roman Catholics, which is still the family faith. They had two children, one of whom was Jerry of whom further.

(II) Jerry, son of Grandfather and Johanna (Brickley) Hurley, was born in Skebreen, Ireland, died there in 1876. He was educated in the public schools and always followed the occupation of a farmer. He married Ellen Sullivan, born in county Cork, February, 1817, died there in 1882, daughter of Daniel Sullivan, a farmer and commission merchant of Cork, born in 1775, died in 1867. Children of

Daniel Sullivan; 1. Mary, lives in London, England. 2. Katherine. 3. Dennis, served in the English army, died in county Cork, Ireland; he married and had a son Dennis, who died when ten years of age, and a daughter now living in London, England. 4. Daniel, a coachman for the wealthy Townsend family; married Johanna ———, and lives in county Cork, Ireland. 5. Townsend. 6. Ellen, of previous mention. Children of Jerry and Ellen (Sullivan) Hurley, all born in county Cork, Ireland; 1. Mary, deceased; married Thomas Rose, a native of England, holding a government position; they had thirteen sons and one daughter. 2. Jeremiah, married and has children; he is living in England. 3. Dennis, accidentally killed when only twelve years of age. 4. Ellen, died young, as did her younger sister. 5. Katherine. 6. John. 7. Ellen, of whom further. 8. Margaret, born in county Cork, Ireland, 1859; married David Barry, a native of Ireland, who became an oil producer of Pennsylvania; she lives in Buffalo, New York; children: Mary, Margaret and Frances, all living at home.

(III) Ellen, seventh child of Jerry and Ellen (Sullivan) Hurley, was born in Skebreen, county Cork, Ireland, October 1, 1856. She was educated in the public schools of her native country, and in 1872 came to America. She married, December 18, 1873, at Allegheny, Pennsylvania, John Barry, born in county Cork, Ireland, May 12, 1846, died in Bradford, Pennsylvania, February 14, 1904, son of Thomas Barry, born in county Cork, Ireland, 1817, died there May, 1894. Thomas Barry's father was originally a native of England and an officer in the English army. Thomas Barry married Johanna Darley, born in county Cork, 1818, died there April, 1905, and had issue: 1. John, of whom further. 2. Richard, born in county Cork, Ireland, 1848; emigrated to the United States, in 1860, and became an oil producer; he married Ellen Walsh, in Smethport, Pennsylvania, and now lives in Coleville, McKean county, Pennsylvania; children: i. William, a physician of Philadelphia; ii. Agnes, married Leo Herzog, a miller of Smethport, Pennsylvania, and has one child, Virginia, born in 1910; iii. Anna, a school teacher of Pittsburgh, Pennsylvania; iv. Edward; v. Alice; vi. Frank: the last three live on farms in Coleville, Pennsylvania. 3. Katherine, born in county Cork, Ireland, 1851, died there in 1898; she married ——— Connors, a farmer; children: John, lives in New York City; Charles; Anne; Mary; Katherine. 4. Ellen, twin of Katherine, died in county Cork. 5. David, born in county Cork, Ireland, 1854, died in Buffalo, New York, June 5, 1910; an oil well worker; married Margaret Hurley, of previous mention. 6. Thomas, born in county Cork, Ireland, 1856; is pensioned by the government, having been sergeant of police for many years; he married and has: Nora; Thomas; Edward; James; Richard; Patrick; and a boy; all living in Cork, Ireland. 7. Mary, born in county Cork, Ireland, 1858; married ——— Mahoney and lives on a farm; they have six children. 8. Edward, born in county Cork, Ireland, 1861, where he died, 1907; a farmer.

John Barry obtained his education in the public schools, and when he was eighteen years of age immigrated to the United States and was employed on a farm in Rome, New York, for two years, later coming to Erie, Pennsylvania, and obtaining a position in the freight department of the Lake Shore railroad. All his savings were invested in the oil fields, so he soon gave up his situation at Erie, going to Westmoreland county, where he was driller and part owner of the first oil well opened in the county. Later he drilled one of the first wells of the "Gas City," a venture which proved to be such a great success that he formed the firm of Barry & Shirk to further develop the resources of that region. His operations were uniformly successful, and he prospered to such an extent that at his death the value of his estate was estimated at a million dollars. This was indeed a marvelous achievement for a penniless immigrant and farm hand. The secret, however, of his great success lay not in any lucky turn of the wheel of fortune, but in his frugality and saving habits in early years, his pluck and strength of character, his determination to succeed, characteristics, which if rightly and honestly directed, cannot fail to batter down all obstacles, and enable the possessor to reach those heights which only the most deserving can attain. He was an excellent conversationalist, possessed of a keen wit and ready tongue. His power in dealing with and handling men was due largely to his ability to determine their moods, and his tact in dealing with them. He belonged to the United Workmen of America, and other societies. Children of John and Ellen (Hurley) Barry: 1. Thomas, born in Millerstown (now Chicora), Butler county, Pennsylvania, October 23, 1874;

a lumberman; married Laura McMann, from Bradford, and lives in Illinois; children: i. Verna, born August 9, 1898; ii. Helen, born November, 1900; iii. Thomas, born July, 1902; iv. Margaret, born February, 1905, died young; v. Margaret, born May 5, 1906, died November, 1911. 2. Edward David, born in Millerstown (Chicora), Pennsylvania, May 10, 1876; an oil producer in Bradford, Pennsylvania; married, October 18, 1905, Emma Allen, born in Derrick City, Pennsylvania, February 23, 1882; children: i. Mary Josephine, born in Bradford, Pennsylvania, May 30, 1907; ii. Helen Gertrude, born in Bradford, Pennsylvania, August 24, 1909; iii. Frances Elizabeth, born July 2, 1912. 3. Nora Ellen, born in Millerstown (Chicora), Pennsylvania, March 11, 1878; married Peter A. Nash, born in Crawford county, Pennsylvania, now engineer in a horseshoe factory in Erie, Pennsylvania; children: i. John Barry, born in Bradford, Pennsylvania, November 18, 1907; ii. Mary Catherine, born in Bradford, Pennsylvania, September 16, 1909. 4. Mary Margaret, born in Coleville, Pennsylvania, October 7, 1882; married James Donavan and lives at Duquesne, Pennsylvania. 5. James Richard, born in Coleville, Pennsylvania, October 22, 1884; an electrical contractor; married Margaret Warren from Winona, Michigan; son, James Warren, born September 11, 1909. 6. Alexander, born in Coleville, Pennsylvania, March 15, 1886, died August 25, 1888. 7. Francis Joseph, born in Bradford, Pennsylvania, January 24, 1891; attends college in Allegany, New York. 8. John Clarence, born in Bradford, Pennsylvania, April 3, 1893; an oil producer in Bradford. 9. George Albert, born in Bradford, February 12, 1895, where he attends school. 10. Leo Alphonso, born in Bradford, Pennsylvania, December 9, 1897.

WILLIAMS
The name of Williams is very ancient and probably extends throughout the civilized world. Most of the original members of the family were doubtless of Welsh extraction. They form a large part of the principality of Wales in England, somewhat like the O's in Ireland and the Mac's in Scotland. "Burke's Peerage" says of Sir Robert Williams, the ninth baronet of the house of Williams of Penryhn, that "His family is lineally descended from Marchudel of Cynn, Lord of Abergelen in Denbighshire, of one of the fifteen tribes of North Wales, who lived in the time of Roderic Mawr (Roderic the Great) King of the Britons, about the year 849. From him was descended the royal house of Tudor. The lineage of Marchudel is traced from Brutus the first King of the Britons."

The family is one of the most notable in New England, where over forty families of the name settled before 1700. The branch herein recorded springs from the Connecticut family located at Lebanon, who descend from Rev. Solomon Williams, D. D., of Lebanon, who was a half-brother of Elisha Williams, of Wethersfield, born in Hatfield, August 24, 1694, son of William Williams. The founder of the family in Pennsylvania is Shuabel Williams, who is the grandfather of George D. Williams, of Bradford, Pennsylvania.

(I) Shuabel Williams was born in Lebanon, Connecticut, died in Ararat, Susquehanna county, Pennsylvania, May 14, 1867, after a residence in the latter town of fifty-five years. He was an old man at the time of his death, had been a pillar of the Methodist Episcopal church for over a half a century; cast his first presidential vote for Thomas Jefferson, and his last for Abraham Lincoln. He was a farmer by occupation, both in Connecticut and in Pennsylvania. He moved to Ararat, Susquehanna county, Pennsylvania, where he was engaged in farming until his death. He settled in Ararat, in September, 1812, going there from Lebanon, Connecticut, with his wife and one child. He and his wife were of the number who first united to sustain the gospel there, and for over fifty years nearly every Sunday he could be found in his seat at church. He married ———, who died in Ararat, October 10, 1871. Children: 1. Samuel, died in Binghamton, New York; married and had a family; his son, Wellington W., was station master in Susquehanna county, Pennsylvania, for twenty years, then was transferred to Binghamton. 2. Oliver, died in the west; married. 3. Ralph, of whom further. 4. Sherman, died in Ararat, Pennsylvania; a farmer; married Miss West, of Susquehanna county; children: Emeret, deceased; Dwight, deceased; Judson, lives in Scranton, Pennsylvania. 5. Jane, died in Ararat; married Jones West, deceased, a farmer; children: Melissa; Abbie, resides on the old homestead; Emerson, lives in Scranton. 6. A daughter, died in Ararat; married David Avery, of Susquehanna county, a farmer; children: Eli, died in Ararat; Albert, living in the west; Olive, married Peter Dunn, and lives in Ararat; Susan, married Clarence Mumford, and lives in Starrucca, Pennsylvania; Ada, deceased; a daughter.

(II) Ralph, son of Shuabel Williams, was born in Ararat, Pennsylvania, September 8, 1822, died in the hospital at Suffolk, Virginia, February 1, 1863. He was educated in the public school and became a farmer of the town of Thompson, Susquehanna county, Pennsylvania. He was a Republican in politics, serving as constable and tax collector of the township. He was a soldier of the civil war, serving in Company E, One Hundred and Seventy-seventh Regiment Pennsylvania Infantry, and was confined in the hospital at Suffolk, Virginia, where he died of typhoid fever. He was an active official member of the Methodist Episcopal church, his wife also being a member. He married (first) in Lebanon, Connecticut, September 3, 1848, Abbie E. Davis, born there March 12, 1831, died in Thompson, Pennsylvania, April 12, 1860. She was the daughter of Daniel Davis, a farmer of Connecticut and New York. He died in the town of Napoli, Chautauqua county, New York, about 1865, aged sixty-nine years. His wife, Hannah Holland, born in Rhode Island, died in Napoli, in 1873, aged seventy-five years. Hannah Holland had three brothers: 1. Nicholas, a farmer, died in Napoli; married Lydia Pierce and left a daughter. 2. Weager, died in Rhode Island; a farmer; married a Miss Gardner; children: John, living in Wakefield, Rhode Island; Lillian, living in Randolph, New York; Abbie, living in Wakefield. No record of the third brother.

Ralph Williams married (second) September, 1860, Lydia E. Wright; no issue. Children of Ralph Williams and his first wife: 1. Chauncey, born in Lebanon, Connecticut, December 29, 1849, died in Brooklyn, New York, March 9, 1907; a carpenter; married Mary Ann Gardner, born in Rhode Island; children: i. Fannie A., born October, 1876; a teacher in the Pennsylvania State Normal School at Clarion; unmarried. ii. Rodney Ralph, born 1881; a practicing physician of Binghamton, New York; unmarried. 2. George Davis, of whom further. 3. Mary E., born in Lebanon, Connecticut, October 3, 1854, died in Napoli, New York, August 3, 1860.

(III) George Davis, son of Ralph Williams and his first wife, Abbie E. Davis, was born in Lebanon, Connecticut, November 3, 1851. His parents moved to Susquehanna county, Pennsylvania, in 1856, settling in Thompson township, where he attended the public school. After the death of his mother in 1860 he went to relatives in Napoli, New York, where he completed his education in Chamberlain Institute. After leaving the institute he began work on a farm in Conewango, Cattaraugus county, continuing one year, and working the following two years in the creameries and cheese factories of Conewango. In 1874 he began working in the cheese factory at Elm Creek, Cattaraugus county, and in 1875 in association with his brother Chauncey, he purchased the plant. They continued together in successful business for two years, then George D. purchased Chauncey's interest and alone conducted the cheese-making business until 1888. In the spring of that year he was sent to Kansas as superintendent of a creamery and cheese factory there. Six months later he sold his Elm Creek factory, and in the spring of 1890 returned to Cattaraugus county, working as clerk in the store of F. W. Adams, at East Randolph. In the autumn of 1890 he moved to Bradford, forming a partnership with Eugene J. Boyle, and until 1900 conducted a successful grocery business under the firm name of Boyle & Williams. Since 1900 the firm has been manufacturing table syrups and confectionery, and has won an assured position in the market. Mr. Williams is also vice-president and treasurer of the Eagle Oil Company. He is a Republican in politics, and while in New York was tax collector for the town of Conewango, and for two terms was assessor. In religious faith he is a Presbyterian. He is a member of the Heptasophs and Independent Order of Odd Fellows of Bradford, and the United Commercial Travelers' Association of America. His club is the Merchants.

He married, February 19, 1876, Emir Belle Helmes, born in East Randolph, Cattaraugus county, New York, March 21, 1853. She was educated in the public schools, finishing with a course at Chamberlain Institute. She is a member of the Presbyterian church. Her father, Chauncey C. Helmes, was born near Rochester, New York, and was one of the pioneer merchants and farmers of his section of Monroe county. He died in East Randolph, January, 1859. He married (first) Sabina Jeffords, born near Rochester, New York, July 31, 1803, died in Randolph, January 4, 1848. Children of Chauncey C. Helmes, all born in

East Randolph: 1. Saphrona, born February 16, 1825, died in Ohio; married Samuel Eggleston, in Randolph, New York, also deceased, a blacksmith; children, all living in Ohio: Mary, Sharp, Clyde and Legrand. 2. Cornelia, born February 10, 1827, died March 8, 1843, in Randolph; unmarried. 3. Mary, born February 3, 1830, died in Randolph, May 22, 1848; married Charles Hubbard, a blacksmith; no issue. 4. George W., born January 29, 1832; enlisted in the One Hundred and Fifty-fourth Regiment New York Infantry, and was one of the many "missing" when the roll was called after the battle of Chancellorsville; unmarried. 5. Delilah, born May 6, 1838; lives in East Randolph; unmarried. 6. Charles H., born September 2, 1840; enlisted in Ninth Regiment New York Cavalry, serving three years; now living in East Randolph; a painter; child: Walter, born September 19, 1842. 7. Eliza, born September 19, 1842; married her cousin, Adelbert Helmes, deceased, a decorator, whom she survives, a resident of East Randolph; child, Claire, also living there. 8. James, born January 12, 1846; a veteran of the civil war, serving in the One Hundred and Fifty-fourth Regiment New York Volunteer Infantry; now living in East Randolph; he married (first) Susan Curtis, (second) the widow of Byron Helmes; no issue; children of first marriage: Nellie, living in Tionesta, Pennsylvania; Chauncey and Lee. 9. John C., born January 4, 1848; married Luella Sloan, of Salamanca, New York, and resides in East Randolph, a blacksmith; children: Floyd, deceased, and George, living at Frecks Mills, New York. Helmes married (second) January, 1849, in East Randolph, Laura A. Hovey, born October 21, 1821, in Warsaw, New York, died in Bradford, December 17, 1905; two children. 10. Mary, born July 20, 1850; educated at Chamberlain Institute, Randolph; now residing in Bradford; a member of the Presbyterian church; unmarried. 11. Emir Belle, of previous mention; wife of George Davis Williams. Chauncey C. was a son of Robert Helmes, who died July 22, 1844, in East Randolph, a farmer. His wife Betsey died January 29, 1853, at a good old age.

Children of Robert Helmes, all born in East Randolph, New York: 1. Albert, died in East Randolph; a farmer and general merchant; married (first) a Miss Jeffords, (second) a Miss Harding, (third) a Miss Longstreet; children of first wife: Mortimer, Emily and Rumina; children of second wife: Eunice, Acena and Mary Ann; children of third wife: Adelbert, Gaylord and Cordelia. 2. Robert, died in Madison, Wisconsin; a farmer; married Jane Benson; children: Robert, Lyman, Abraham and others. 3. Homer, died in Madison, Wisconsin; a farmer; married Melinda Hovey; children: Frank, Virgil, Laura, Mary, Helen and Robert. 4. Chauncey C., of previous mention; father of Mrs. George Davis Williams. 5. Millie, died at East Randolph; married John Benson, a farmer; children: Marcus, Van, Matilda, Sophrona and Maria. 6. Sarah, died in East Randolph; married Daniel Dixon; children: Charles, Daniel, Henry, Homer, Eliza and Andrew. 7. Aurelia, died in East Randolph; married William Foy; no issue. 8. Henry, died in Wisconsin; a farmer; married Caroline Kingsley, and left issue. 9. Salina, died in East Randolph; married William Calhoun, a railroad employee; children: Agnes, Marian, John, Thaddeus, William, Eliza and others.

Laura A. Hovey (second wife of Chauncey C., and mother of Mrs. George Davis Williams) was a daughter of Ziba Hovey, whose father was born in Mansfield, Connecticut, in 1747. He moved to Warsaw, New York, in 1804, died April 24, 1820, leaving issue: Orra, Simeon, Gordon, John, Luel, Theodora, Ziba (see forward), Eliphalet, Alvin, Lura and Tina.

Ziba Hovey was born in Connecticut, lived in Warsaw, New York, and spent his latter years in East Randolph on his farm, where he died a very old man. He married Sophia Metcalf, born in New Hampshire, died in Randolph, very old. Children, all born in Warsaw, New York: 1. Jackson, died in Iowa; a farmer; married and left issue. 2. Ziba (2), died in East Randolph; a carpenter; married Charlotte North, of Cattaraugus county; children: Horace, Laura and Richard. 3. Franklin, died in East Randolph; a lumberman; married Harriet Hall; children: Della, Nelly and Kitty. 4. Lafayette, now living at Cold Spring, New York; a carpenter and farmer; married Lovisa Case, deceased; children: Carrie, Ferdinand and Nettie. 5. Emily, now living near East Randolph; married Daniel Spalding, a farmer, deceased; children: Betsey, Sarah, Emma, Keziah and Sophia. 6. Melinda, died in Madison, Wisconsin; married Homer Helmes;

no issue. 7. Laura A., of previous mention. 8. Clarissa, died at Cold Spring, New York; married (first) John Helmes; child, Orphelia; married (second) a Mr. Town; child, Diette. 9. Amelia, died in Nashua, Iowa; married Erastus Rathbone, born in Canada, a cooper; children: Frank, Belle, Grace, Charles and Dolly.

Children of George Davis Williams: 1. Marguerite Louise, born in East Randolph, New York, November 18, 1890, died in Bradford, Pennsylvania, January 18, 1893. 2. Lawrence George, born in Bradford, October 31, 1895; now a student in high school.

CAMPBELL A family of this name in Scotland can be traced to the beginning of the fifth century, and the name has become one of prominence, especially in military affairs. At Balhaldie, Scotland, there is an old church, whose churchyard can never be sold and in which no one not a Campbell can ever be buried.

(I) Prince Campbell, the first member of this family about whom we have definite information, was a Scottish Jacobite, and was therefore exiled with his wife to France. He married Lady Elizabeth Stewart. Children: 1. Patrick, commissary for the British army; bought cattle all over the world to supply the army; stock farmer at Perth, Scotland; removed to Australia; he died, leaving a fortune of half a million pounds in the Bank of England, besides real estate; although this should belong to the Campbell family, it cannot be claimed, as the letters of proof have been destroyed by fire. 2. Dougall, of whom further.

(II) Dougall, son of Prince and Lady Elizabeth (Stewart) Campbell, was private secretary to the Duke of Richmond. He became captain of the old Forty-second Highlanders, known as the "Black Watch." This company was disbanded after the Ashburton treaty, and officers and men received grants of land in New Brunswick, Canada; Captain Dougall Campbell received one thousand acres. He married ———— Drummond. Children: Alexander, of whom further; Patrick, married Ann Ross Monroe; Ludlow, married Sarah ————; Jacobina, engaged to Sir Colin Campbell; Ann.

(III) Alexander, son of Captain Dougall and ———— (Drummond) Campbell, married Carolina Frederica Hoffman. Children: Thomas Dougall, married Margaret McCloud; Alexander Neil, of whom further; Patrick Wirtle; Carolina Frederica, married George Armstrong; Mary, married W. J. Shaw; Ludlow; Richard, married Susan Morley; Jacobina, married James Moore; Edwin Jacob, married Eliza Shaw; Frederick, died young.

(IV) Alexander Neil, son of Alexander and Carolina Frederica Hoffman, was born at Taymouth, New Brunswick, November 29, 1820, died at Bradford, Ontario, January 22, 1877. He was a lumberman in Canada and Maine. He was a member of the Church of England. He married (first) Mary Ann Casey; she also was a member of the Church of England, (second) Mary Jane Arnold. Children, all by first marriage: 1. Collin Drummond, born at Taymouth, May 8, 1844, died at Mount Jewett, Pennsylvania, in 1894; hotelkeeper; married Francis Nogar; she now resides at Mount Jewett, and keeps the Hotel Campbell; children: Linna; Frederica; Alexander, deceased; John; William; Frances, deceased; Huston. 2. Randolph McGibbon, of whom further. 3. Allen Douglas, born at Taymouth, January 21, 1848, died at Elmira, New York; machinist; married Elsie J. Ames; she resides in Elmira; children: Daisy, Elsie, Anna, Arthur. 4. Frederick Alexander, born at Stanley, New Brunswick, June 8, 1850; grocer; lives at Winnipeg, Manitoba; married Janet MacDonald; children: Mary P., MacDonald, Lillias, Duncan, Randolph, Kathleen, Kenneth. 5. Arthur Edwin, born in Aroostook county, Maine, February 1, 1853, died in Chicago; band saw filer; unmarried.

(V) Randolph McGibbon, son of Alexander Neil and Mary Ann (Casey) Campbell, was born at Taymouth, February 11, 1846, died at Kane, McKean county, Pennsylvania, November 22, 1892. At that place he had at the time of his death been assistant railroad yardmaster for twenty-three years. In the civil war he enlisted in Company A, One Hundred and Sixty-ninth New York Volunteer Infantry; for about one and one-half years he was in the Army of the Potomac, about Richmond, but he was stationed at Raleigh, North Carolina, at the time of Lee's surrender. In political and civic affairs he was prominent; he was a Republican, and held the offices of school director and tax collector. He married Laura Clementia, born at Springfield, Bradford county, Pennsylvania, October 30, 1845, now resides at Kane, daughter of John D. and Emily (Stacey) Leonard. Springfield, Bradford county, Pennsylvania, was named after Springfield, Massachusetts, because a majority of its inhabitants came from that city. In June, 1803, Austin and Ezekiel Leonard came from West Springfield, Massachusetts, under the auspices of the Susquehanna Company, to make a home in Northern Pennsylvania. John D. Leonard was born at Springfield, Pennsylvania, February 3, 1816, and was one of the first settlers of Kane. At the time of his death, July 14, 1888, he was with one exception the oldest citizen of the borough. Here he was a merchant, although he had retired from business life before his death, and for twenty-one years he was postmaster, holding this position until February 22, 1886. He married (first) Emily Stacey, who died January 3, 1856, (second) Betsey E. Fuller, born at Springfield, November 3, 1837, died November 2, 1859, (third) Susan M., daughter of Nicholas B. Smith, who was born at Alba, Bradford county, Pennsylvania; she now lives in California. Children of John D. Leonard, three by first, one by second wife: 1. Evaline, born at Springfield, February 4, 1839; resides at Kane; married, at Springfield, March 10, 1859, Philip F. Whiting; he was killed in the civil war; no children living. 2. Maria, born at Springfield, October 26, 1842; married, at Erie, Pennsylvania, July 12, 1869, J. C. Malone; he is a retired jeweler; child, Maud. 3. Laura Clementia, aforementioned, married Randolph McGibbon Campbell. 4. Edith May, born at Springfield, September 28, 1859, deceased. Children of Randolph McGibbon and Laura Clementia (Leonard) Campbell, all born at Kane: 1. Claude, born December 16, 1868, died at Kane, April 19, 1883. 2. Norma, born April 5, 1874; married, at Chautauqua, New York, July 2, 1896, Willard P. Merrell; he is a jeweler at Kane; child, Willard Randolph. 3. Frederick Randolph, of whom further. 4. Eva, born April 7, 1880; resides with her mother at Kane; graduate of Kane high school, in the class of 1898.

(VI) Frederick Randolph, son of Randolph McGibbon and Laura Clementia (Leonard) Campbell, was born at Kane, June 4, 1877. After graduating from the Kane high school, in the class of 1896, he took a year's work at Bucknell University. In 1897 he accepted a position with the National Food Company at Niagara Falls, New York, but he returned the next year to Kane. Here he worked until 1905 in a jewelry store. Then he started out for himself with a news store, books, and phonographs. He has practically a monopoly of the newspaper business at Kane, and is also manager of the jewelry store. In college he became a member of the Sigma Alpha Epsilon fraternity. He is a member of Kane Lodge, No. 566, Free and Accepted Masons; Kane Chapter, No. 279, Royal Arch Masons, of which he is past high priest; and the Benevolent and Protective Order of Elks, at Kane. Formerly he was a member of the Independent Order of Odd Fellows, at Kane. He is a Republican, and attends the Methodist Episcopal church. He married, December 5, 1901, Jessie Clarina, born at Bradford, Pennsylvania, June 17, 1880, daughter of John C. and Rosetta (Mapes) Breneman. Her father was born near York, Pennsylvania, in 1850; he now keeps the county home at Smethport, which office he has held for many years. His wife was born in 1852. Children of John C. and Rosetta (Mapes) Breneman: Jessie Clarina, married Frederick Randolph Campbell; Walter Asper, born at Bradford, April 10, 1889.

ECKELS This family is of north of Ireland stock, and its first American home was at Baltimore, Maryland. Like many other families found in the north of Ireland, Scotland was the country of its origin, and the family had gone to Ireland at the time of the political and religious troubles.

(I) James Eckels, the first member of this family about whom we have definite information, was born probably in the Cumberland Valley, died at Clarksville, Greene county, Pennsylvania, about 1858, having attained an advanced age. A large part of his life was passed at Sawmill Run, Pennsylvania, near Pittsburgh. He was a farmer. He married ———, who died at Clarksville. Both were members of the Presbyterian church. Children: 1. James, died at Clarksburg; cabinet maker; married ———; children: Edwin, Fannie, John, Frank, Mabel. 2. John, of whom further. 3. Robert, died at New Wilmington, Pennsylvania; a farmer; married ——— and had children. 4. Esther, deceased. 5. Ann, died near Conneautville, Pennsylvania; married Donaldson, deceased; he was a farmer.

(II) John, son of James Eckels, was born at Sawmill Run, in 1821, died at Reno, Pennsylvania, September, 1888, being killed by the cars. In early boyhood he attended the district school near the place of his birth, but he was still young when he went to Greenville, Mercer county, Pennsylvania, and there learned the blacksmith's trade, at which he worked until 1866. He then became a Methodist minister; he preached in Venango, Mercer, Crawford, Erie and Lawrence counties. In politics he was a Republican, and he served as a burgess at Greenville. Mr. Eckels married (first) Martha Walker, (second) Caroline, born in New York state, in 1835, died at Cambridge Springs, Pennsylvania, in 1907, daughter of Samuel and Jane (Alexander) Leech. She also was a member of the Methodist Episcopal church and prominent in Women's Christian Temperance Union work. Her father was a preacher in New York state; he settled on a farm at Leech's Corners, near Greenville, where he died about 1869. Children of Samuel and Jane (Alexander) Leech: 1. Alexander, died at Greenville; stonemason and quarryman; married Phoebe Freeman, deceased; children: Addie, married Henry Homer, children: Ralph, Harriet, Nelson; Harry; Frederick; Jennie. 2. Caroline, married John Eckels. 3. Mary, died near Bethel Church, Mercer county, Pennsylvania; married David Baxter, from Fairview, Pennsylvania, deceased; had children. 4. Plimpton, died at Greenville; stonemason; married Charlotte Bond, of Greenville, deceased; children: May, married Charles Granel; Jessie; one son. By his first marriage John Eckels had no child that lived. Children of John and Caroline (Leech) Eckels, all born at Greenville: 1. Ellen, died young. 2-3. Daughters, died in infancy. 4. Emma Jane, died at Greenville, young. 5. William Plimpton, of whom further. 6. Sadie, born in 1857; married A. R. Bullock; they live at Cambridge Springs, and he is a retired meat merchant; children: Ruth, married Victor R. Shanberger; Arza; Esther; Hazel; Perry. 7. Clark, born in 1859; resides at Cambridge Springs, where he is postmaster; by trade he is a printer; married Mary Perry, of Warren, Pennsylvania; child, Perry. 8. Charles, born in 1861; resides at Erie, Pennsylvania; formerly a printer, now promoter of a land company in Texas; married Eva Morris; children: Mildred and Morris. 9. Arthur, born in 1863; resides at Wellsville, Ohio; road foreman of engineers on the Fort Wayne & Chicago railroad; married Ella Kincaid, from New Castle, Pennsylvania; child, Bessie.

(III) William Plimpton, son of John and Caroline (Leech) Eckels, was born at Greenville, May 22, 1853. There he began his public school education, but this was completed in Venango and Crawford counties. In 1876 he graduated from Allegheny College, Meadville, Pennsylvania, with the degrees of Bachelor of Arts and Master of Arts. For the next two years he taught at North East, Pennsylvania, and for two years after this at Spartansburg, Crawford county, Pennsylvania. In the winter of 1881 he taught at Guy's Mills, also in Crawford county. Then he came to Kane, and for six years was principal of the graded school, which he brought up to the rank of a high school. In 1887 he was elected county superintendent of schools, and he held this office for nine years, but in 1896 he returned to teaching, and for four years was principal of the school at Smethport, McKean county, Pennsylvania. From 1900 to 1909 he was treasurer of the Kane Window Glass Company. He then entered mercantile business as a member of the firm of Leonardson Company, of which he is now secretary and treasurer. He is a stockholder in the Kane Bank and Trust Company, the Kane Window Glass Company, the Kane Supply Company, and the A. W. Leonardson Company, of Clearfield, Pennsylvania. He is a member of Kane Lodge, No. 566, Free and Accepted Masons; Kane Chapter, No. 279, Royal Arch Masons; Bradford Council, Royal and Select Masters; Trinity Commandery, No. 58, Knights Templar, at Bradford. In these lodges he has been through all the chairs, and he is a member of Williamsport Consistory, Thirty-second Degree Masons. He is a member of the Royal Arcanum also, at Warren. While he is a Republican, he is independent in political action. In the Congregational church at Kane, of which his wife also is a member, he has for some time been trustee, and for the past three years one of the deacons.

Mr. Eckels married, at Kane, December 30, 1885, Mary, born at Ebensburg, Cambria county, Pennsylvania, December 8, 1859, daughter of Thomas M. and Ann (Williams) Jones. She received a public school education at Ebensburg. Children: 1. Martha, born at Kane, May 19, 1887; graduate of Kane high school; for two years she studied music at the conservatory, Oberlin, Ohio, and then went to the Warren Conservatory of Music, from which she graduated; she is now teacher of vocal music at Broaddus Institute, Philippi, Barbour county, West Virginia; unmarried. 2. Claude Alan, born at Smethport, Pennsylvania, September 10, 1891; member of the class of 1913 at Allegheny College, Meadville, Pennsylvania.

NELSON This is a name of distinction both as an English and as a Scandinavian name. The most noted person who has borne this name was an English sailor, Admiral Lord Nelson, but in our country the best known Nelson is probably the honored senator from Minnesota, Knut Nelson, a Scandinavian. The present family is supposed to have been settled in Varmland, Sweden, for generations.

(I) Nels Nelson, the first member of this family about whom we have definite information, was born in Varmland, Sweden, and died in Varmland. He was a farmer, and a member of the Lutheran church of Sweden. Whom he married is not known. Child, Nels, of whom further.

(II) Nels (2), son of Nels (1) Nelson, was born in Varmland, in 1835, died at Mount Jewett, McKean county, Pennsylvania, February, 1909. In Sweden he received a common school education. Coming to America he settled in 1879 at Mount Jewett, where he purchased a farm. His sons helped in the management of the farm, while their father followed his trade, that of carpenter and builder. He was a Republican. In the work of his church, the Swedish Lutheran, he was very active; for many years he was a deacon, and he used to teach in Sunday school. Also, though not an ordained minister, he used to preach in the church at Kanesholm, Wetmore township, McKean county, Pennsylvania. He helped to build the Swedish church at Mount Jewett, and contributed liberally toward its cost and maintenance. He married (first) in Sweden, ———, (second) in Sweden, Betty ———, born in Varmland, in 1834, died at Mount Jewett, in 1904. Children, three by first, four by second wife, all born in Varmland, but all coming to America: 1. Anna, born in 1852; married Nels Hanson; they reside on a farm near Mount Jewett; children: Henry, John, Hulda, Esther, Mildred, Selma, Olga. 2. Mary, born in 1855, died at Mount Jewett, McKean county, Pennsylvania, in 1889; unmarried. 3. Olaf, born in 1859; a farmer near Mount Jewett; unmarried. 4. Kate, born in 1863; married Andrew Anderson, from Smoland, Sweden; he is a carpenter, and they reside at Mount Jewett; children: Carl, Gertrude. 5. John, born in 1866; he has bought a farm near Erie, Pennsylvania, and contemplates removing with his family to that place; married Hannah Lantz, from Lafayette Corners, McKean county, Pennsylvania. 6. Nels August, of whom further. 7. Ellen, born in 1873; married Magnus Sylvander, born in Varmland; he is a railroad clerk, and resides at McKeesport, Allegheny county, Pennsylvania.

(III) Nels August, son of Nels (2) and Betty Nelson, was born in Varmland, October 1, 1869. He came over with his mother in 1880, his father having come in the preceding year, and they settled at Mount Jewett; there he received a public school education. He helped his father on the farm, and from the time when he was twelve years old until he was fourteen worked in a basket factory. After this he worked at different occupations, mainly carpentering and working on a farm at Mount Jewett until 1889. At Bradford, Pennsylvania, he learned photography, which he followed with success, first at Mount Jewett for four years, then at Kersey, Elk county, Pennsylvania, until 1907. At Kersey, in 1900, he entered into the hotel business without, however, giving up his photographic studio. At this he has been very successful and in it he has prospered. Since 1907 he has been landlord of the Lamont Hotel, one of the leading houses at Kane. He is a member of Olympia Lodge, No. 667, Independent Order of Odd Fellows, at Kersey, of which he is past grand; of Kane Lodge, Scandinavian Brotherhood of America, of which he is past president; of Lodge No. 130, Loyal Order of Moose, at Kane, of which he has held the treasurership since the lodge was established in 1909; the Fraternal Order of Eagles, at Kane; and the Benevolent and Protective Order of Elks, at Kane. In politics he is independent. While living at Kersey he was for ten years auditor of Fox township, and for one term he was township treasurer. Although he left for Kane before his term in this office had expired, his constituents insisted on his finishing his term, being thoroughly satisfied with his conduct of the office. He is a member of the Swedish Lutheran church.

Mr. Nelson married, December 23, 1893, Hulda, born in Smoland, Sweden, February 22, 1875, daughter of Sven August and Christine Swanson. She is also a Lutheran. Children: 1. Clyde, born at Mount Jewett, February 22, 1896; a sophomore in the Kane high school. 2. Mildred, born at Kersey, July 8, 1901. 3. Gwendolyn, born at Kane, August 15, 1909.

MALTBY This is an old English family early transplanted to America. William Maltby, Esq., the emigrant ancestor, was born in England, 1645. He came to America with his elder brother John from Yorkshire, England, both with the rank of "gentlemen." They settled in New Haven colony about 1670. They are the founders of the various Maltby families of the United States, found as Maltby, Maultbey, Maltbie, etc. William Maltby was deputy to the general court at Hartford several sessions, and died at Branford, Connecticut, September 1, 1710, aged sixty-five years. His first wife Hannah joined the church with him at Branford, 1688. His second wife was Abigail Bishop. Children: John; William (2), born January 9, 1673; Elizabeth, married Abraham Hoadley; Daniel, of whom further; Captain Samuel, one of the two graduates of Yale College, 1712; Jonathan, born July 26, 1698; a daughter, married Daniel Parker.

(II) Daniel, fourth child of William and Abigail (Bishop) Maltby, was born May 19, 1679, died December 26, 1731; married, October 27, 1702, Esther Moss, who survived him and married (second) June 20, 1739, Samuel Todd; children: May, born 1703; William, February 17, 1705; Daniel (2), June 16, 1708; Joseph, May 11, 1712, a sea captain; Abigail, March 16, 1713; Daniel, October 29, 1715; Benjamin, of whom further; Martha, September 10, 1720; John, April 25, 1722.

(III) Deacon Benjamin Maltby, seventh child of Daniel and Esther (Moss) Maltby, was born June 20, 1717, died July 9, 1796. He married (first) Sarah, daughter of Deacon Samuel Harrington, (second) 1753, Elizabeth, born October, 1728, died December 31, 1820, daughter of Josiah and Hannah (Baldwin) Fowler, of Durham, and sister of Captain Josiah and Jonathan Fowler, of White Hollow. Children of second wife: Elihu, died in infancy; Benjamin (2), born January 10, 1755; Corporal Thaddeus, December, 1757, revolutionary soldier; Rev. Jonathan, May 2, 1759, graduate of Yale; Elizabeth, April, 1761; Sarah, May, 1763; General Isaac Maltby, of whom further; Colonel Stephen Maltby, born July, 1769, an eminent teacher, died January 22, 1812.

(IV) General Isaac Maltby, fourth son of Deacon Benjamin Maltby, was born November, 1767, died September 9, 1819. He was an officer of the war of 1812-14. In the summer of 1814 many portions of the militia of Massachusetts were called into actual service for the defence of the seaboard, especially in and near Boston. Another brigade of the volunteer militia was organized and placed under the command of Brigadier-General Isaac Maltby, of Hatfield. The regiment went into camp at Cambridgeport for a few days, but was soon removed to Commercial Point, Dorchester, where there were better accommodations. General Maltby was a representative to the legislature prior to his removal to Waterloo, New York, where he died in 1819. He published "Elements of War" (1812), and "A Treatise on Courts Martial and Military Law" (1813). He was a graduate of Yale College, 1786, and an eminent teacher and scholar. He married Lucinda, only child of Brigadier-General Seth Murray, of the revolution, and his wife, Elizabeth White. Sons: Zaccheus, Jonathan and Samuel.

(V) Zaccheus, son of General Isaac Maltby, was born in Connecticut, about 1801. Early in life he removed to Evans, Erie county, New York, following his trade of shoemaker at Evans and Eden until his death in 1871. He was a Whig and later a Republican, and both he and his wife were members of the Congregational church which he served for several years as deacon. He married Elizabeth Gifford, born about 1804, died 1864, at Evans, where both are buried. She was a native of Lee, Massachusetts, where her family had lived for several generations. She had a brother Lewis who came to Erie county, a farmer, and is buried at Eden, New York. Zaccheus Maltby had two brothers, Jonathan and Samuel, the latter settling at Evans, New York, where he and several of his children are buried. Children of Zaccheus and Elizabeth Maltby, all born in Evans, New York: 1, Frederick Lewis, of whom further. 2, Johanna, 1823, died in Angola, New York, 1883; married Nelson Wood, deceased; their only child, Nelson Bradley Wood, resides in Buffalo, New York. 3, Nathaniel Bradley, born about 1834, died 1899. He was a deputy sheriff of Erie county, serving under Sheriff

Grover Cleveland. He married Frances Slater, who survives him, resides in Buffalo with her only daughter, Johanna, born 1855; a son William, born 1869, also resides in Buffalo.

(VI) Frederick Lewis, son of Zacchens Maltby, was born in Evans, Erie county, New York, March 31, 1822. He was reared on the farm and educated in the public schools. He was a farmer all his life, and a salesman of agricultural implements. He was a Republican, and a member of the Congregational church. He died at Eden, New York, September 6, 1898. He married Harriet Lathrop, born in Canandaigua, New York, March 9, 1823. When seven years of age her parents, Rufus and Betsey (Lovejoy) Lathrop, removed to Eden, New York, where Rufus died at the age of sixty years, and is buried in the cemetery there. Betsey Lovejoy was born in New Hampshire, a descendant of the ancient Lovejoy family of Massachusetts, whose heirs claim ownership of the land in Cambridge upon which the buildings of Harvard University are standing. Children of Frederick Lewis Maltby: 1. Frederick Rufus, born in Evans, Erie county, New York, March 29, 1849; now a resident of Buffalo in the employment of the Lake Shore railroad. He married (first) Mary Fairbanks, of Evans, who died without issue about 1900; he married (second) a widow, Grace (Wilson) Morton, of Niagara county, New York. 2. Sarah Elizabeth, born in Evans, 1852; married Thomas Piper, born in England, died in Buffalo, 1906; children; Jennings, died at age four; Harriet, proprietor of a millinery store in Buffalo, New York, married Charles Kruger; Adalaide, a graduate of Syracuse University, afterward taught school, now a partner with her sister Emma in the millinery business in Buffalo; William S., graduate of Harvard College, now a civil engineer in Pittsburgh, Pennsylvania, married a Miss Vandewater and has William T.; Arthur L., a practicing physician of New York City; Archie, with his brother, William S., in Pittsburgh. 3. Harriet Sophia, born 1856; married Frank M. Phelps, a farmer, who died in 1909; she survives him, a resident of Eden, New York. 4. Lewis Lathrop, of whom further. 5. Mary, died 1902; married Willis G. Clark, who survives her, a resident of Springville, New York; their children: Fred, resides in Buffalo, New York; Beulah, manages a millinery store in Cattaraugus, New York; Walter, a student of Syracuse, New York; Erma, resides in Buffalo; Norma, twin of Erma, resides in Buffalo; Wilma and Willis.

(VII) Lewis Lathrop, son of Frederick Lewis Maltby, was born in Evans, Erie county, New York, November 9, 1859. He was educated in the public schools, finishing his studies in the academy at Angola, New York. He resided in Evans until his eighteenth year, when he came to the Bradford oil field, where he was employed until 1881. In the latter year he purchased a stock of merchandise and opened a general store at Wyandale, New York, where he continued in successful business until 1889. In 1890 he came to Bradford and opened a grocery store; since then he spent five years as traveling salesman for William Elwood & Company, of Buffalo, New York, wholesalers of men's furnishing goods. Then for about eight years he was with Brewster, Gordon & Company, wholesale grocers, of Rochester, New York. He then returned to the grocery business in Bradford, and is now so engaged with William H. Freemeyer as partner, located at 1-3 Summer street. He is an Independent in politics, dividing his allegiance between the Republican and Prohibition parties. In 1910 he was the nominee of the Prohibitionists for councilman from the fourth ward of Bradford. He was beaten by the Republican candidate by only ten and by the Democratic candidate by only eight votes. In 1911 he was the Prohibition candidate for city treasurer. He is the member of the First Methodist Episcopal Church of Bradford; Tent No. 4, Knights of the Maccabees; and Tuna Lodge, No. 411, Independent Order of Odd Fellows.

He married, June 9, 1881, Nora Alice Martin, born at North Bay, Oneida county, New York, February 28, 1860. She was educated in the public schools and resided with her parents until her marriage. She was a daughter of John Caleb Martin, and a granddaughter of Thomas Martin, who was born September 5, 1780, and died January 22, 1865. He was born in England, where he lived and married his first two wives. In 1829 he emigrated to the United States, settling at McConnellsville, New York. He married (first) Mary West, June 28, 1804, born February 6, 1778, died January 8, 1827; children: Mary, born August 3, 1805, died in Philadelphia; Thomas, born December 29, 1807, died in England; Jabez, born July 8, 18—, died in England; Ann, born March 15, 1811, died in Philadelphia;

Joseph, born October 10, 1812, died February 19, 1813; William, born August 4, 1816, died in Sherburne, New York; John Caleb, of whom further. Thomas Martin married (second) February 7, 1828, Frances West, born August 17, 1789, died March 5, 1847; children: Fannie A., born December 12, 1828, died in Wisconsin; Frances A., born April 7, 1832, died May 10, 1832; Stephen, born September 6, 1834, now living in Oneida, New York, married Etta Yeager, deceased, and has three living children: Chester, Orissa and Adelbert. Thomas Martin married (third) April 9, 1842, Sarah Crippen, born March 13, 1788.

John Caleb, seventh child of Thomas Martin, was born in the town of Stoke Brewing, Northamphshire, England, September 30, 1822. He was brought by his parents to the United States in 1829, the family settling at McConnellsville, New York. Later he moved to North Bay, New York, where he was engaged in the milling business until his death, December 31, 1891. He married, September 25, 1842, Margaret Bristol, born in McConnellsville, September 20, 1823, died May 16, 1875. Children: 1. Laforest J., born April 13, 1844, died December 13, 1862; he enlisted in the Sixteenth Regiment New York Volunteers, and was killed at the battle of Fredericksburg. 2. Cordelia M., born December 21, 1846; married J. D. Bodine, now a retired employee of the Tide Water Oil Company; children: Laforest John, lives in Illinois; Lewis, deceased; Harry M., enlisted in Sixteenth Pennsylvania Regiment, served in the Spanish-American war, died while in the army at Ponce, Porto Rico; Angie Beatrice, resides with her parents in Simpson, McKean county, Pennsylvania. 3. David Thomas, born October 11, 1849; married Cora Brainerd, of Fredonia, New York; both living; children: Odella, lives in Fredonia; Laforest, lives in Seattle. 4. Mary Emily, born February 19, 1852; married (first) William Godfrey, who died at North Bay, New York, leaving a son John, who resides at Rew, McKean county, Pennsylvania; she married (second) John Walters, retired, living at Rew; no issue. 5. Olive Huldah, born May 3, 1854, died December 2, 1889; married Andrew Kittell; their only child, Zela, is deceased. 6. Henry B., born January 8, 1857, died November, 1909; married Flora Kittell; children: Dora, of Buffalo, New York; Flora, of Tonawanda, New York; Olive, of Tonawanda; Herbert, of Duke Center, Pennsylvania; Henry, resides in Buffalo; Joseph, also resides with his mother. 7. Nora Alice, born February 28, 1860; married Lewis L. Maltby, of previous mention. 8. Harriet Ann, born March 18, 1862, died 1883; married M. L. Acox, a hotelkeeper of Pittsfield, Pennsylvania; children: James, lives in Ohio; Clarence, deceased. 9. Angie J., born November 22, 1864, died October, 1906; married (first) Alfred Roberts, (second) James Griffin; children: Thomas, Charles and Harry, all residents of North Bay. 10. John William, born November 11, 1866, died September 17, 1867. Children of Lewis Lathrop Maltby: 1. Olive Harriet, born at Eden Centre, New York, September, 1882; married, March 5, 1902, Wesley J. Benjamin, of Bradford, born February 20, 1879; children: Myron L., born February 14, 1903; Aletha, September 26, 1906. 2. Frederick Valors, born at Wyandale, New York, March 22, 1884; married, June 9, 1909, Nelle Brown. 3. Bessie Lathrop, born in Wyandale, New York, April 22, 1887; married Norman Rathfon, born November 19, 1884; children: Griffith Lewis, born February 12, 1906; Ruth Louise, September 21, 1907; Norman L., September 12, 1909; Donald Lathrop, December 8, 1910. 4. Clara Belle, born in Wyandale, New York, December 25, 1889, died January, 1890. 5. Sarah Alice, born in Bradford, Pennsylvania, December 28, 1892, died September 25, 1893. 6. Louise Irene, born November 9, 1894, in Bradford; a student in Bradford high school. 7. Margaret Beatrice, born November 28, 1897, in Bradford; a student in the high school, passing her entrance examinations with the highest general average ever given a student in similar examinations.

BEATTY
The Beattys came to the north of Ireland from Scotland, and after several generations there a descendant, William Beatty, born 1783, came to the United States. He was a good blacksmith, but seems to have been an equally good teamster and driver. He spent most of his life in this country in Armstrong county, Pennsylvania, and was one of the old stage coach drivers running from Philadelphia to Pittsburgh. He was a strong Democrat, and a Presbyterian. He died in Armstrong county, in 1867. He married Isabella Colwell, born in Ireland, in 1789, died in Armstrong county, 1873. Children, all born in Armstrong county: 1. James, deceased, a cabinetmaker and mer-

chant; married Catherine Richards; children: William, Mary, Michael, Miles, John, Samuel, Daniel, Ruth and Catherine. 2. William, died in Manorville, Pennsylvania, a blacksmith; married Jane Patterson; children: Hamilton, Hannah, John K., deceased; Isabella, Mary, William. 3. Absalom, of whom further. 4. Isabella, married Jacob Brewer, a farmer, both deceased; children: Matilda, William, Samuel and Daniel. 5. Robert, died in Manorville, a blacksmith; married a Miss Grim, also deceased; children: Mary, Jane, James, Milton and Robert. 6. Margaret, died in Pittsburgh; married Samuel Patterson; children: Miller, James, Mary, Anna, Mary Ellen, James and Henry. 7. Jane, died in Pittsburgh; married William Bollman; children: James, Agnes, Robert, Emma, Mattie and Samuel. 8. Samuel, died in Tarentum, Pennsylvania; a farmer; married Mary Mott; children: David, Noah, Mary, Sarah, William (twin of Sarah), Absalom, Samuel, Howard, Martha, Nancy and Margaret.

(II) Absalom, son of William and Isabella (Colwell) Beatty, was born in Armstrong county, Pennsylvania, in 1819. He attended the public school for a few years, but at an early age left school to become a bread winner. He learned the shoemaker's trade, which he followed several years, but later became a farmer of Manor township, continuing until his death, October 2, 1882. He was a man of influence in the Democratic party, and held several township offices. He was a lifelong member of the Presbyterian church, and from 1854 until his death in 1882 held the high office of elder. His wife was also a faithful active member. He married Sarah Patterson, born in Wilmington, Delaware, in 1812, died in Leeper, Clarion county, Pennsylvania, October, 1895, daughter of William Patterson, born in Derry, Ireland, where he followed the trade of weaver until shortly after his marriage, when he came with his bride to the United States, settling in Wilmington. In 1813 he moved to Manor township, Armstrong county, Pennsylvania, bought a farm and there ended his days. He married Sarah Henry, born in Derry, Ireland, died in Manor township. Children: 1. Sarah, of previous mention; married Absalom Beatty. 2. William, born 1814, in Wilmington, Delaware, died in Indiana county, Pennsylvania; a carpenter; twice married; a son William now lives in Indiana county. 3. Samuel, born 1816, in Nobleston, Allegheny county, died in Pittsburgh; a wagonmaker; married Margaret Beatty, a sister of Absalom. 4. Jane, born 1818, died at Manorville, Pennsylvania; married William Beatty, brother of Absalom. 5. Robert, born 1820, died in Allegheny, Pennsylvania; blacksmith; married Martha Mahaffey; children: James, Lewis, Margaret, Anna, Catherine and Emma. 6. Mary, born 1822, died in Kittanning, Pennsylvania; married Noah Wolf, a farmer; children: Sarah Jane, married William Huston; Finley, an attorney of Kittanning; Perry, deceased; Wesley, a physician of Allegheny, Pennsylvania; Dorcas, unmarried, resides with her brother Dr. Wesley Wolf.

Children of Absalom and Sarah Beatty, all born in Manor township, Armstrong county: 1. William James, born 1838, died young. 2. Mary, born 1840; resides in Dayton, Pennsylvania; unmarried. 3. Isabella, died young. 4. Robert E., born 1844, died in Dayton, Pennsylvania, 1910; a veteran of the civil war; married Anna Stewart, who survives him, residing on the farm at Dayton; children: Perry, Ella, Minnie, Percy, McCurdy, Maude, George, Thomas, Ellis, Marlin, and Sarah, died young. 5. Joseph, died young. 6. James, died young. 7-8. Died at birth. 9. Lizzie, born February 14, 1848; married Squire Calvin Wilson, and resides at Callensburg, Clarion county; "Squire" Wilson has been justice of the peace for forty years; is postmaster, and a veteran of the civil war; no issue. 10. Smith Graves, of whom further.

(III) Dr. Smith Graves Beatty, youngest child of Absalom and Sarah (Patterson) Beatty, was born in Manor township, Armstrong county, Pennsylvania, December 23, 1854. He obtained his education in the public schools, finishing at Freeport Preparatory School. In 1870 he taught the public school at Pine Creek Furnace, and in 1871 became a clerk in a Manorville store. He also clerked in Youngstown, Ohio, and Parker's Landing, Pennsylvania, continuing in that line of work until 1877. He then sold pianos on the road for Washburn & Shaffer for a short time, then in 1878 became clerk in a drug store at Millville, now Hawthorne, Pennsylvania, continuing until 1880. During the years spent in the drug business he had been reading and studying medical works, and in 1880 entered the College of Physicians and Surgeons at Baltimore, Maryland, whence he was graduated M. D., class of 1882. He at once began practice in

Clarion county, Pennsylvania, continuing until December 1, 1907, very successfully. He then located in Kane, Pennsylvania, where he is now well established in practice, and prosperous. He was physician to the board of health of Clarion county several years, is now medical examiner for several old-line insurance companies, and is regarded as a particularly skillful, honorable physician and surgeon. He is a member of the State Medical Society and of the County Medical Society of Clarion and McKean counties. He is a member of Kane Lodge, No. 329, Benevolent and Protective Order of Elks, and a member of the Presbyterian church, which he has served as trustee.

He married, December 20, 1882, at Scotch Hill, Clarion county, Sarah Thompson, born there September, 1857, obtaining her education in the public school. She is a daughter of William Thompson, born near Clarion, Pennsylvania, in May, 1816. He resided at Thompson's Eddy, on the river, in Clarion county, until 1865, then moved to Scotch Hill, where he died February 8, 1895, a lumberman and farmer. He married Levina Confer, born near Fryburg, Clarion county, February 22, 1826, died in Kane, August 23, 1908. Children, all born at Scotch Hill: 1. Clarence, 1849, died young. 2. Mary, born March 22, 1850; married Manus Henry, whom she survives, residing at her farm near Scotch Hill; children: Ella, Ethel and Edna. 3. Milton, born 1851, died young. 4. Perry, born March, 1853; a farmer; married Mabel Reynolds, who survives him, residing in Corsica; children: Blanche, Walter and Charles. 5. Theophilus, born February, 1855; married Flora Carley, and resides on his farm at Scotch Hill; children: John, William, Alberta, Joseph, Olive, and an infant. 6. Sarah, of previous mention; wife of Dr. Smith Graves Beatty. 7. Benton, born 1859, died near Scotch Hill, 1874. 8. Anna, born 1862; married Martin Spence, a carpenter, and resides at Brownsville, Fayette county, Pennsylvania; children: Reynolds, Lee, Alice, Manda, deceased; Sarah, deceased; Samuel Harold, and Rose, deceased. 9. Rosa Belle, born June, 1864; married George W. Kerr Jr., and resides in Forest county, Pennsylvania; children: Sadie, Willa, Theodore, Flora, Ella, Elder, Grace and William. 10. Melissa, born 1866, died young. 11. Samuel, born July, 1872; married Letitia Carl, and lives on his farm at Scotch Hill; children: Claire, Geraldine, Clifford, Frank and an infant.

William Thompson, father of Mrs. Dr. Beatty, was the son of Samuel Thompson, born near Harrisburg, Pennsylvania, a lumberman, who spent his adult life near Scotch Hill, Clarion county. He was born 1790, died 1870. His wife, a Miss Cathers, was born in Reynoldsville, Pennsylvania, 1790, died in Fisher, Pennsylvania, 1867. Their children, all born near Scotch Hill: 1. Rosanna, born 1810, died 1907; married Thomas Dougherty, born in Ireland; children: Samuel; Josephine, married G. W. Fuller; Dallas; James; Jennie, married a Reynolds, of Reynoldsville. 2. Joseph, born 1812, died in Condor, Iowa, 1900; a farmer; married Nancy Fulton; children: Sarah, Edith, Charles and others. 3. Alexander, died young. 4. William, of previous mention. 5. Cyrus, born 1825, died at Scotch Hill, 1912; married Mary Harvey. 6. Jane, born 1827, died at Fisher, Pennsylvania, 1910; married Adam Potter, a farmer now living at Fisher, aged ninety-one years; no children. 7. Nancy, born 1829, died at Shippensville, Pennsylvania; married William Lawhead, a farmer; children: Nancy, Edith and others. 8. Catherine, born 1830; married Robert Hindman, a farmer, whom she survives, residing in Brookville, Pennsylvania; children: Clara, Thompson and Blanche, all deceased. 9. Clara, died unmarried.

Children of Dr. Smith G. and Sarah (Thompson) Beatty: 1. De La Rue, born at Scotch Hill, October 18, 1883; mechanic; married Olive Rogers, of Tionesta, and resides in Kane; children: Angela, Sarah, Charles, Lee, Rogers and Lloyd. 2. Orah T., born at Scotch Hill, July 16, 1885; a telegrapher; married Mildred Millet, and resides at Lamont, Pennsylvania; children: Donald, born 1905; Dwight, 1908. 3. Charles McIntosh, born in Clarion, Pennsylvania, April 24, 1888; graduate of Dechman Preparatory School, Baltimore; now a student at College of Physicians and Surgeons, Baltimore. 4. Smith Graves (2), born in Leeper, Pennsylvania, August 9, 1895; student in Kane high school. 5. Pearl Kathleen, born in Leeper, October 14, 1897.

RYAN The Ryans herein recorded descend from Irish forbears of county Limerick, Ireland, where the family lived for many generations. The grandparents lived and died in Ireland, devoted members of the Roman Catholic church. Their children: 1. John, of whom further. 2. Michael, died in Canada; was a farmer, living near Dunville; married Margaret Hayes, from near Niagara Falls, also deceased; children: Thomas and James, the former living in Buffalo, a grocer, the latter living in Canada. 3. ———, married a Mr. Reagan. 4. James, died in Buffalo, New York; married and had issue: John and James, living in Buffalo; Margaret, married Albert Hett, of Buffalo; Mary, living in Cleveland, Ohio; Nellie, living in Buffalo, unmarried; Annie, deceased.

(II) John Ryan was born in the parish of Caharass, county Limerick, Ireland, in 1807. He was well educated in the schools of Ireland. He married, and in 1837 emigrated to Canada, settling first at Lundy's Lane, later at Robinson's Road, where he and his two brothers bought a large tract of land. He, however, only remained there two years, then moved to Arthur, and later to Guelph, Canada, where he purchased a smaller farm, which he cultivated until his death, about 1875. Both he and his wife were members of the Roman Catholic church. He married Mary McGuaine, born in county Clare, Ireland, in 1813, died in Guelph, Canada, 1889. Brothers and sisters of Mary McGuaine: 1. John, was a soldier in the British army before coming to Canada, and at the time of his death was proprietor of the Prince Albert Hotel, Niagara Falls, Canada. 2. Owen, sailed for Trinidad, South America, and all trace lost. 3. Frank, died in Toronto, Canada; married and had issue: Kate, married Thomas Nolan, a grocer, living in Toronto; Frank; James; Lucy; Dora, and probably others. Children of John and Mary Ryan, all born in Ireland: 1. Thomas Henry, of whom further. 2. Michael, born 1843, died July 3, 1863, in Baltimore, Maryland. 3. James, born 1847, died in Guelph, Ontario, Canada, July, 1910; a commission merchant; married Margaret Waldman, of Guelph; child, James H., born 1891, a market gardener, resides in Guelph with his mother.

(III) Thomas Henry, eldest son of John and Mary (McGuaine) Ryan, was born on the Browning estate nine miles from the city of Limerick, Ireland, August 26, 1841. He was six years old when his parents emigrated to Canada, settling at Lundy's Lane, thence at Robinson's Road, two and a half miles from Dunville. Here he attended the public school. His father then moved around, living in different places, finally settling at Guelph in the province of Ontario in 1858. Thomas H. received little more schooling, but early became a worker on his father's farm. Later he went to St. Mary's, Canada, and began driving a team for a contractor, who was constructing a section of the Grand Trunk railroad. He remained with him until 1859, when he came to the United States, settling at Brandy Camp, Elk county, Pennsylvania, where he drove a team until April 19, 1861, when he enlisted in Company G of the Pennsylvania "Bucktail" Regiment, serving three years. He saw hard service, was wounded at Antietam, September 16, 1862, and again at Gettysburg, July 3, 1863. He was honorably discharged and mustered out July 11, 1864.

After his war experience he returned to Brandy Camp, where until the autumn of 1864 he was in charge of the farm of Mrs. B. P. Little. He then during the winter of 1864-65 was employed skidding logs for Chauncey Brockway. In the spring of 1865 he was rafting on the river and worked in the saw mills until August of that year. He then entered the oil fields, working in Titusville and through the Venango field, finally in September, 1865, settling in Kane, which has ever since been his home. For a time he was in the employ of General Kane, and in 1868 entered the service of the Pennsylvania railroad, continuing with them eighteen and a half years. From 1893 until 1903 he was superintendent in charge of the McKean county poor farm, a period of about nine years that he was away from Kane. In the meantime he had secured oil leases and after leaving the superintendency devoted himself to oil production, in which he was very successful. He is an independent Republican; was township treasurer for several years and for two years councilman of Kane. He is an attendant of the Episcopal church. He is an ex-member of the Union League Club of Philadelphia, and a member of the Grand Army of the Republic. He stands high in the Masonic order; is past worshipful master of Kane Lodge, No. 566, Free and Accepted Masons, having been made a Mason at Smethport in McKean Lodge, No. 388, in 1868, forty-four years ago. He is a companion of Kane Chapter, No. 279, Royal Arch Masons; a knight of Trinity Commandery, No. 58, of Bradford, Knights Templar, and in the Scottish Rite he longs to Presque Isle Lodge of Perfection at

Erie, Pennsylvania, and to Coudersport Consistory, holding the thirty-second degree. He is highly regarded among his brethren and held in the greatest esteem by his business associates and social acquaintances.

He married, June 3, 1866, Harriet Marsh, born in Rockingham, Vermont, May 14, 1843, died in Kane, June 7, 1904 (for Marsh family see Davis sketch in this work). Children, all born in Kane: 1. Catherine Marsh, born April 21, 1867; graduated from Lock Haven Normal School, 1887, and from Bellevue Training School for Nurses, 1898; resides in Kane with her father; member of the Episcopal church. 2. Benton Charles, born August 17, 1868; now a conductor on the P. S. & N. railroad; married (first) June 14, 1893, Agnes Marr, born in Tamaqua, died in Renova, Pennsylvania, April 24, 1894; child, Agnes, born April 1, 1894; married (second) October 11, 1899, Margaret McCarthy, of Smethport, and resides at St. Mary's, Pennsylvania; children: Robert, born in Kane, September 14, 1900; Marian, born in Kane, January 6, 1902; Alice, born in Smethport, June 5, 1904; Timothy, born May 31, 1906. 3. Josephine, born May 16, 1871; married, August 21, 1895, Ralph P. Yerdon, traveling salesman for the Cary Safe Company of Buffalo, New York, and resides in Kane. 4. Myra, born March 23, 1873; married John K. Morrison, a farmer of Emporium, Pennsylvania; children, all born at Emporium: Kendall, April 9, 1896; Thomas Cyril, November 29, 1897; Clyde, January 28, 1900; Maxwell, August 26, 1902. 5. Edmund Locke, born February 18, 1875; an attorney at law, practicing in Buffalo; married (first) Della Hicks, of Des Moines, Iowa; child, Thomas Henry, born in Kane, February 11, 1900; married (second) Lillian May Patterson, of Connaught, Ohio; children: Dorothy, born in Kane, July 13, 1903; Catherine Marsh, born in Olean, New York, December 28, 1908. 6. Ruth, born March, 1877, died 1880. 7. Mary Louise, born January 17, 1879; married Roy Carleton Gifford, son of Warley Gifford, a sketch of whom appears elsewhere in this work. 8. Harriet, married R. C. Gleason, a sketch of whom appears elsewhere in this work. 9. Florence, born November 29, 1883, died March 31, 1901. 10. Jennie, born August 15, 1887; graduate from Kane high school, class of 1906, now living with her father at the family home in Kane. The mother of these children was a devoted Christian woman, a member of the Episcopal church.

GILLIS The ancestors of the present family were members of the Gillis clan, who moved from Scotland to the north of Ireland at the time of the persecutions.

(I) Robert Gillis, the first member of this family about whom we have definite information, was born in Boston, Massachusetts, in 1740, three days after the landing of his parents, and died at Hebron, Washington county, New York, in 1836. His young manhood was spent as a sailor on coasting vessels running between Boston and New Orleans and other American ports. He married (first) Jerusha Clark, of New Hampshire, (second) Sarah Stewart. Of the five children by the first wife all lived to at least eighty years of age, and one, John, died at the age of ninety-three. Children of second wife: 1. Enos, died at Ridgway, Elk county, Pennsylvania, aged sixty-seven; a tanner. 2. Samuel, died at Wasseon, Ohio, aged eighty-four; a tanner. 3. James Lyle, of whom further. 4. Thomas, born June 10, 1794, died at Warren, Warren county, Pennsylvania; a tailor; married, had at least one child. 5. Elizabeth, died at the age of fifty-five; married Elisha Ingersoll. 6. Hugh, deceased.

(II) James Lyle, son of Robert and Sarah (Stewart) Gillis, was born at Hebron, October 2, 1792, died at Mount Pleasant, Iowa, July 8, 1881. He received a good education, attending the common school three months in the year. Although his educational opportunities were meager compared to those offered in our time, he made the most of them. In 1808 his parents went to Argyle, New York, and here he served an apprenticeship of three years at the tanner's trade. In 1812, immediately after the declaration of war between Great Britain and the United States of America, he enlisted in the mounted dragoons, commanded by Captain C. V. Boughton. This was an independent company, and served as the escort of General Hull. When the regiment went into winter quarters, James Lyle Gillis enlisted again, this time under the command of Colonel Stone. During the year he was at Fort George with General McClure; after the abandonment of this fort he was sick and was sent to Batavia, New York. In the meanwhile Buffalo, Lewiston, Youngstown, Black Rock, and Manchester were captured and burned, and in the winter of 1813-14 Captain Boughton's company was discharged. In the following spring Mr. Gillis again enlisted for one year, and he was in the battles of Chippewa and Lundy's Lane. He was wounded at Lundy's Lane and his horse was shot from under him. On the seventh of August he was in charge of sixteen men sent on a foraging expedition; they were surprised and four were killed; nine, including Mr. Gillis, were captured, and they were confined at Toronto, Kingston, Prescott and Montreal. Mr. Gillis with twenty-five others was put on board the transport "Stately," November 14, 1814, which was about to sail for England, but he and five others escaped in a boat and landed near Quebec. After wandering in the woods three days they met a Frenchman, who agreed to conduct them to a place of safety, but they were again taken by the British and kept at Halifax until peace was made in the spring of 1815. For some time after the war Mr. Gillis lived at Victor, New York, and worked with his brothers, Enos and Samuel, at tanning. In 1822 he came to Jefferson, now in Elk county, Pennsylvania, and settled in the wilderness, seventy miles from the nearest postoffice, and with no neighbor nearer than sixteen miles. Here he cleared what is now the Montmorenci farm, and built a saw mill and grist mill three miles west of Montmorenci. He was the first to manufacture lumber on a large scale in this district. In the new community he became a leader. Being appointed associate judge of Jefferson and Franklin counties, he held this office for two terms. In 1840 he was first elected to the state legislature, in which he served three terms in the house and three terms in the senate. Then in 1856 he was elected to membership in the United States house of representatives. In the same year he was a delegate to the convention which nominated James Buchanan for president of the United States; President Buchanan and James Lyle Gillis were intimate friends. The last office which he held was that of agent for the Pawnee Indians, to which he was appointed in 1859. Three years later he went to Iowa and there lived with his son, Charles B. Gillis, until the latter's death. James Lyle Gillis was thus a leading figure in the affairs of his time and in the pioneer activities of Elk county. He was a Democrat. He attended the Methodist Episcopal church, of which his second wife was a member.

He married (first) in 1816, Mary Ridgway, of Philadelphia, who died in 1826, (second) Cecilia Ann, born in Walton, Cattaraugus county, New York, 1806, died at Ridgway, Elk county, Pennsylvania, April 25, 1855, daughter of Henry Berray, who was a farmer in Cattaraugus county, New York, died there when over eighty years old. Children of first wife: 1. Ridgway B., born at Victor, New York, February 15, 1818, died at Mount Pleasant, Iowa; he was with his father in the lumbering business; moved to Mount Pleasant in 1848; the next year he went to California as a prospector; returned to Mount Pleasant and lived on his farm; he was accidentally shot; married Margaret Bain, from Elk county, deceased; children: James R., Mary, Hudson B., Wade, Andrew Jackson, Charles. 2. Jeannette Caroline, born at Victor, May 2, 1820, died at Ridgway, February 22, 1892; married Jacob V. Houk, from Beaver county, Pennsylvania, deceased; he was a lumberman and merchant; child, Son, died young. 3. Charles B., born at Victor, April 1, 1823, died at Mount Pleasant, Iowa, February 23, 1881; he was a farmer at Mount Pleasant, and was murdered by a tramp, as he was standing in his own doorway; the murderer confessed in 1911, explaining that he mistook Mr. Gillis for the marshal; he married Emma J. Howard, from McKean county, Pennsylvania; child, Emma, died young. Children of second wife: 4. Mary B., born at Montmorenci, Pennsylvania, August 23, 1829, died at Brockton, New York, February 8, 1895; married Samuel Porter, from Chautauqua county, New York, deceased; he was a carpenter; children: Anna, James, Augustus, Claude, another daughter. 5. James H., born at Montmorenci, May 14, 1831, died at Melbourne Beach, Florida; a commodore of the United States navy; married (first) Lydia Alexander, (second) Ursula Z. Canfield; she is living, and resides in Syracuse, New York, in the summer and at Melbourne Beach in the winter; children, all by first wife: Harry A., graduate of Annapolis; Lyle; Irwin, a commander in the navy; Carrie. 6. Bosanquet W., born at Ridgway, August 8, 1835; resides in Brooklyn, New York, and is a proof reader for the *New York Times*; married Martha Radcliffe, deceased; children: Frank, Martha, Cecilia, Roberta, Arnold. 7. Emma Augusta, born at Ridgway, March 7, 1837; resides at Portland, New York; married James Noxon, from Chautauqua county, New

York, deceased; he was a farmer; children: Mary, Seaborn, Sophia, Cecilia. 8. Robert S., born at Ridgway, May 1, 1840, died at Mount Pleasant, Iowa; president of a bank and had a large farm; married Sophia Whiting, from Mount Pleasant, and now living there; children: James, Sarah, Henry, Hugh, Ansel. 9. Claudius Victor Boughton Goodrich, of whom further. 10. Cecilia A., born at Ridgway, April 3, 1844; married Henry Whiting; he is a retired mechanical engineer; a few years ago he became blind; they spend the winters in Florida; no children.

(III) Claudius Victor Boughton Goodrich, son of James Lyle and Cecilia Ann (Betray) Gillis, was born at Ridgway, September 14, 1841. Having attended public school at Ridgway, he was afterward graduated from White Hall Academy, in Cumberland county, Pennsylvania, with the class of 1859. Immediately after leaving school in that year, he took charge of building the Pittsburgh & Erie railroad, from Sunbury to Erie. He then went out among the Pawnee Indians, one hundred and twenty miles west of Omaha, on the Loup fork of the river Platte; here he spent the summer of 1861 with his father, who was then Indian agent at this place. On June 21, 1861, he witnessed a victory in battle of the Pawnees over the Sioux; about two thousand were engaged. In the fall of 1861 he was clerk in a store in Omaha, and he remained until the following year, when he went to Mount Pleasant, Iowa, and in the autumn of 1862 he returned to Ridgway. Then he became captain's clerk on the United States gunboat, "Commodore Morris," and was at Norfolk, Virginia, until May 3, 1864, or cruising on the James river. Then he went to Alexandria, Virginia, as clerk for Joe Styles, a government scout. Sickness necessitated his return to his home in Elk county, Pennsylvania, and he entered mercantile business. He served one term as county treasurer in Elk county, and one term as deputy county treasurer. January 18, 1876, he came to Kane, McKean county, Pennsylvania, and here he has lived from that time, being for many years engaged in the drug business. He has acquired extensive interests in oil leases; was a stockholder in and director of the Temple Theater Company until July 16, 1912, when he sold this interest. He is still a stockholder and director in the Kane Bank and Trust Company, and was stockholder and director in the White Rock Land Company.

In Masonry he has reached the thirty-second degree, being a member of Caldwell Consistory, Bloomsburg, Pennsylvania. His other Masonic bodies are: Kane Lodge, No. 566, Free and Accepted Masons, of which he is past master by service; Elk Lodge, No. 379, of which he was secretary and past master by service; Kane Chapter, Royal Arch Masons; also Elk Chapter, of which he is past high priest; Bradford Council; Orient Council, No. 40, he having one term been illustrious grand master; Knapp Commandery, No. 40, Knights Templar, at Ridgway, of which he is past eminent commander; Trinity Commandery, No. 58, at Bradford; Syria Temple, Nobles of the Mystic Shrine, Pittsburgh; and he has been district deputy high priest. He is a member of the Benevolent and Protective Order of Elks, at Kane; the Grand Army of the Republic, Charles J. Biddle Post, No. 226, at Kane, and the Kane Country Club. He is a Democrat. Beside the political offices already mentioned, which he held in Elk county, he has for three years been school director in Wetmore township, McKean county, and he has now for twenty-five years, been a justice of the peace of the borough of Kane, having been elected to this office the first Monday in May, 1887.

Mr. Gillis married, December 30, 1864, Anna D., daughter of Abram and Lucy A. H. Overholtzer; she was born in Lancaster county, Pennsylvania, July 2, 1838, died at Kane, July 24, 1897. She was a college graduate, and for a number of years before her marriage she taught school in Cumberland county, Pennsylvania. She was a member of the Eastern Star. Her church was the Baptist. Abram Overholtzer was born in Chester county, Pennsylvania, September 9, 1812, died at Whitehall, Cumberland county, Pennsylvania, March 7, 1883. His wife, a native of Lancaster county, died at Kane, aged eighty-three. Children of Abram and Lucy A. H. Overholtzer, all born in Lancaster county, Pennsylvania: 1. Henry F., born August 17, 1836; tailor; resides at Seguin, Texas; married Eunice Benson, from Elk county, Pennsylvania; children: Dora, Daisy. 2. Anna D., married Claudius V. B. G. Gillis. 3. Louisa E., born August 12, 1841; married Isaac Wolf, from Cumberland county; they reside in that county on a farm; no children. 4. Regina D., born February 9, 1844; resides in Philadelphia; married Ezra P. Dickenson, deceased; he was a contractor; child, Blanche I. 5. Clementine, born August

18, 1847, died December 24, 1849. 6. George W., born August 24, 1850, died at Kane, December 27, 1885; unmarried. Children of Mr. and Mrs. Gillis: 1. James H., born at Ridgway, March 11, 1866; druggist; resides at Kane; married Jennie O'Day, from Kane; children, all born at Kane: Marian, born June 27, 1890; Lucille, born in October, 1891, deceased; Leonora, born August 17, 1894; Marguerite, born August 17, 1894; Francis, born June 4, 1896. 2. Claudius B., born at Ridgway, December 30, 1868; graduate of Lock Haven Normal School, class of 1889; a general insurance agent at Kane; married Lillian E. Warner; no children. 3. Anna C., born at Kane, October 20, 1877; graduate of Kane high school, class of 1896; resides with her father; unmarried.

SHRIEVER That women have a legitimate place in the business world has been so often proven by their success in many fields that there should be none to controvert the statement. The business career of Miss Marie Shriever is another perfect illustration of feminine capacity, as she has risen solely by her own ability and intelligence.

She is the daughter of Jacobus Shriever, born July, 1813, in Aachen (the German name for Aix La Chapelle), a frontier city of Rhenish Prussia, a capital of Aix La Chapelle province. He was a University graduate and a man of a high order of intelligence. In 1835 he came to the United States, settling in Jefferson county, Pennsylvania, at Brookville, where he died in May, 1876. He was a manufacturer of woolens and a merchant of Brookville; was ill for several years prior to his death. He was a Democrat in politics, and became prominent in civic affairs. He was a Catholic in religious faith and one of the pioneers in the county, the first Catholic service in the county being held at his house.

He married (first) in Alsace, Loraine, his wife coming to Brookville with him, and there died without issue. He married (second) Veronica Sehmandt, of St. Mary's, Pennsylvania, born February 2, 18—, died in Kane, June 23, 1911. She was the daughter of Boniface Schmandt, a merchant of Hessen Cassell, Germany, came to the United States, settled at St. Mary's, Pennsylvania, where he lived, retired later, moved to Emporium, Pennsylvania, where he died aged eighty-seven years. His wife, Frances (Koenig) Schmandt, born in Germany, died in St. Mary's. Children of Boniface Schmandt: 1. Catherine, born in Germany, died in Erie, Pennsylvania; married John Singer, a marble cutter; children: Frank and John, deceased. 2. Veronica, of previous mention. 3. Louisa, born in Hessen Cassell, Germany, came with her parents to America when four years old; married Edmund Huff, a carpenter and lumberman, who died in Emporium, Pennsylvania, 1911; she still surviving; children: Augustus, a conductor on the Pennsylvania railroad; Mary, now Sister Christopher of St. Joseph's Convent, Buffalo; Bertha, deceased; Kate, deceased; Elizabeth, deceased; Dora, resides in Coudersport; Edward, deceased; William, deceased; Charles, a railroad employee; Edward, a hotel proprietor; Carrie, assistant postmaster at Emporium. 4. Mary, born at St. Mary's; married Joshua Bair, a contractor, and resides in Emporium; children; Edward, deceased; Albert, resides at Jersey Shore; Matie, married B. Egan, a furniture dealer and undertaker of Emporium; Kate, married P. Burke, of Emporium; Minnie, deceased; Rose, married a Mr. Green, superintendent of the Iron Works, at Emporium; William, a photographer of Emporium, married Harriet Auchue; Bertha, of Emporium; Leo, deceased; Frank, deceased. 5. Matilda, died young. Children of Jacobus and Veronica Shriever: 1. Marie, of whom further. 2. Elizabeth, born in Greenville, Pennsylvania, March 8, 1863; she was educated at the Brookville parochial school and St. Elizabeth's School, Allegany, New York; she is partner with her sister in the firm of M. Shriever & Company, merchants, and of the firm of M. and E. Shriever, real estate; she is a lady of great force of character and business ability, very fond of travel, spending her hours "off duty" in European and American journeyings; she visited California and Yellowstone in 1901 and toured Europe in 1905. 3. Gertrude, born in Greenville, February 8, 1864; married, October 13, 1888, Joseph Kavanagh, employed in the traffic department of the Erie Railroad Company. 4. Dorothy, born 1866, died the same year and is buried in Brookville. 5. James Boniface, born in Brookville, April 30, 1868; he was educated in the parochial school, taking the commercial course, and at fifteen years of age was graduated with highest honors. He then came to Kane where he was a bookkeeper for the Pennsylvania railroad two years; at age of eighteen years he opened a photographic studio at Emporium, became quite noted for the quality of his work, then was in the same business in Elmira, New York, a few years, then located in Scranton, Pennsylvania; he there organized and financed the American School of Photography, and was its president for many years; he is acknowledged an artist of the very highest class, his studio in Scranton being one of the finest equipped in the United States and the quality of his work of the very highest artistic merit; his photograph of the Madonna has received favorable comment from the artists of the United States and from the famous Berlin (Germany) photographers; he married Katie Zarps, of Emporium, Pennsylvania; child, Irene Marie, born June 21, 1895. 6. Julia F., born in Brookville, June 19, 1871; educated in the parochial school and Clarion State Normal; she is now manager of the millinery department of M. Shriever & Company and like her sisters possesses rare business ability; she accompanied her sister Elizabeth in her European trip in 1905 and has toured California, Florida, Cuba and the West Indies, being in Kingston, Jamaica, shortly after the earthquake.

The father of Jacobus Shriever never came to the United States, but died in Aix La Chapelle, Germany, when comparatively a young man. His widow came with her son Jacobus, dying in Brookville. They were both members of the Roman Catholic church. Their children, all born in Alsace, Loraine: Gertrude, Elizabeth, Agnes, Jacobus and others.

(II) Marie, eldest daughter of Jacobus and Veronica (Schmandt) Shriever, was born in Frenchville, Clearfield county, Pennsylvania, August 3, 1861. She was educated in the public schools at Brookville and the parochial school of the Church of the Immaculate Conception. She absorbed all learning so quickly that at thirteen years of age she was granted a teacher's certificate, with the proviso that she should not use it until she was sixteen. Being barred by her youth from teaching, she worked for a time in a store at Du Bois, Pennsylvania. Her health becoming impaired, she took an outside position, continuing for eighteen months, traveling as saleswoman for a book publishing house. She was a successful agent and during the eighteen months saved from her earnings a sufficient sum to enable her to start a small store in Kane. She began business in March, 1876, in a small room twelve by twenty-eight feet, stocked with ladies goods. Her little venture was a successful one and at the expiration of two years her business warranted her removal to a larger store. The death of her father in 1876 left her the head of the family and with her business success she was able to continue the education of the younger children and to provide positions for her sisters on their leaving school. After twelve years successful business in millinery and ladies wear at Kane, she extended her field of operation and opened a similar store at Union City, Pennsylvania. Having proved her own powers and established a reputation as a capable, successful business woman, she still further enlarged, opening a store in Emporium and later another in Cambridge Springs, Pennsylvania. These four stores were successfully operated until 1894, when she sold the outlying stores, retaining only the parent store at Kane. She admitted her sister Elizabeth to a partnership and another sister Gertrude as a department manager. After centering all her energy in the Kane business, she enlarged and strengthened her lines until now hers is the leading and largest millinery and ladies furnishing store in the city.

Her acute business instincts quickly saw the opportunity for a real estate firm to profitably operate, and with her sister Elizabeth she formed the firm of M. and E. Shriever and since has added to her mercantile line a very successful real estate business. Like all children of foreign born parents, she had a great desire to visit the land from which her parents came and of which she had heard so much. In 1900 her opportunity came; she joined a Christian Endeavor party going to Oberammergau to witness the Passion Play there performed by the villagers every ten years. After witnessing their wonderful portrayal of the life of Christ, she toured the continent of Europe, visiting Italy, Belgium, Germany, Switzerland, Bavaria, Holland and France, also the British Isles. She has also spent her vacation periods in American travel visiting the Pacific States and British Columbia. She was in Seattle during the chase of Tracy, the outlaw, and saw something of the intense excitement caused by the plucky but unsuccessful fight for liberty of that desperado.

While thoroughly capable and entirely devoted to her business enterprises, Miss Shriever is not a mere dollar coining machine. She enjoys the fruits of success in many ways and is highly regarded in her community. She is devoted to the church of her fathers and takes active part in parish work. She was a member of the Ladies' Catholic Benevolent Association of Union City, being the first unmarried member of that branch. No. 1, now transferred to No. 13 of Kane, Pennsylvania. She is a member of Court No. 2, Daughters of Isabella, organized in Meadville, the first established in Pennsylvania. In 1907 she organized a court of the same order in Kane. Perhaps when the school board refused the girl of thirteen authority to teach, they rendered her a greater service than they knew, as it drove her into the world of business, where she is a shining example of feminine business ability, while as a teacher the confinement in a school room would assuredly have resulted in a broken constitution, although she would no doubt have won fame as an instructor. She has nobly won fame, fought the battle of life and fairly won success from all adverse circumstances.

MARSH-LONG[*] The first ancestor of Abbie Louise Marsh-Long to arrive in America, Boston, Massachusetts, was William Locke, an orphan, six years of age.

From the "Gentlemen's Magazine," vol. 62, part 2, page 789, A. D. 1792, we find that tradition considers the name of Locke of Scotch extraction, but if so it must have been in very early times, for when Alfred divided this kingdom into parishes the dwelling of a great man by the name of Locke was called after him Lockstown, where the family at one time became numerous. The Locke family consider themselves descended from a very ancient house, arguing that they gave the name to the parishes where they lived before the conquest, and do not derive their names with a De from the parishes, as is commonly the case.

In 1460 we find John Locke sheriff of London. Thomas, his son, was a merchant in London, who died *anno* 1507, and by Joan, his wife, left three sons, John, William and Michael. John died without issue, and was buried in Mercers chapel in 1519, with his arms in the window, a proof that the family bore arms before those granted by Queen Mary, 1555.

William, the second son (Henry VIII.), undertook to go over to Dunkirk and pull down the "pope's bull," which had been there posted up by way of a curse to the king and kingdom. For this exploit the king granted him a freehold of a hundred pounds per annum, dubbed him knight, and made him one of the gentlemen of his privy chamber. "He had alsoe the speciall favor of the kinge to come to him when he would; the kinge dined at his house, he being the kinge's mercer."

Sir William lived to be an alderman of London, and was sheriff of the city. He received his arms (Per fesse oz, and or, in chief three falcons volant of the second; Crest—A hand p. p. r. holding up a cushion or) in the reign of Henry VIII., having reference to his exploit of going to Dunkirk, in France, and tearing down the Excommunication against the king, a deed which at the present time would not be of much moment, but in the age when the pope claimed such great powers, and was dreaded and feared by the people, it might require as much moral courage as to storm a castle.

Sir William was employed by Henry VIII., having charge of his commercial affairs both at home and abroad. In the Cottonian Library, London, there are several manuscript letters from him to the king and to Secretary Cromwell, dated at Antwerp 1533 to 1538. He was, says Collins, particularly employed by Queen Ann Bullen (Boleyn) privately to gather the Epistles, Gospels and Psalms from beyond sea, in which he ran great hazard, some having been secretly made away with for attempting the same thing. He died in 1550, and by his four wives left issue of twenty or more children, and from his sons are descended the Lockes of Stepney Parish, London. John Locke, commonly called "The Great Philosopher," was of the same family as Sir William.

Stepney Parish, anciently written Stebunheath, is one of the largest subdivisions of London. In the records of the parish we find the following baptism, 1628: William, son of William Locke, mariner, and Elizabeth, his wife, 20 December, 1628, seven days old—subsequently—Buried, Elizabeth, wife of William Locke, Mariner, 27 June, 1631. The father was lost at sea.

[*] The Ancestry and Descendants of Abbie Louise Marsh-Long—I consider it a duty of honor and of love to help in the preservation of the virtues and victories of the "Silent Majority;" they have given their lives that we might live. Let us treasure their memories, and record their history upon the tablets of enduring gratitude and fame. The accompanying genealogy is a condensed copy of certified family records in her possession.

The record relating to William Locke, Jr., is as follows: "22 March, 1634, theis underwritten names are to be embarqued in the Planter, Nic Trarice, Master, bound for New England per certificate from Stepney Parish and attestacon from Tho. Jay and Mr. Simon Muskett, two Justices of the Peace: the men have taken the oath of supremacy and allegiance.

Nicholas Davies 40 yeres			Robert Steven
Sarah Davies 38 "		Servants	John Moore
Joseph Davies 13 "			James Haiward
William Locke 6 "			Judith Phippen"

In the will of Nicholas Davies, probated March 12, 1669, he makes a bequest to his "cossen" (nephew), William Locke, Woburn. Where or with whom William Locke resided during his minority is not known. On the 25th of December, 1655, he was married to Mary, daughter of William and Margary Clark, of Woburn.

Concerning William, Senior, he was for many years a distinguished citizen, and deacon of the church of Woburn. From the town records it appears that he had a share in managing town affairs. He was frequently on important committees, Selectman for several terms, grand juror to the supreme court. He was possessed of great wealth his real estate transactions alone cover many pages of court records. To three of his sons he gave homesteads in Lexington, and four others were provided with homes near the Lexington line.

From Bodges "History of King Philip's Indian War," 1676, pages 66 and 91, we learn that William Locke was chirurgeon of the Massachusetts forces at Mount Hope, June, 1676. In vol. 69, page 10, is a letter dated Hadley, May 3, or 30, 1676, from William Locke to Secretary Rowson, requesting the government to forward him with the greatest speed a supply of medicine and other things for the "poor wounded." Attached to it is a long memorandum of the medicines wanted. It is evident he was a man of education.

The following is a partial list of his descendants to the year 1850, who took part in the military duties of their country, and those who followed a professional career.

Soldiers—90, of whom 12 took part in the Lexington fight and 2 at Concord, 6 at Bunker Hill, one of whom, Captain James Bancroft, commanded a company (he was many years in the wars and was one of the original members of "Society of Cincinnati"); 10 were lieutenants, 16 captains, 3 majors, 1 adjutant, 7 colonels, 2 generals. (His female descendants by marriage brought into the family 59 soldiers and 49 officers—1 ensign, 6 lieutenants, 19 captains, 5 majors, 1 adjutant, 12 colonels, 2 generals, 1 commodore and 3 governors). Officers of town and county—50, selectmen 18, deacons of the early church 9, clergymen 20, two of whom were D. Ds., and Rev. Samuel Locke, S. T. D., president of Harvard College. Graduates from College—63. Senators and representatives—26, physicians 29, lawyers 14, judges 3. (Female descendants married 34 clergymen, 15 physicians and 13 lawyers).

Lieutenant Joshua Locke was an ensign in the army under General Winslow at Nova Scotia, May, 1755, and was the Lieutenant Locke who was in the army with General Braddock, and was wounded at the time of "Braddock's Defeat." He was also with Colonel Rogers, the famous Ranger, in New York and Canada. And he was distinguished as the only one by the name of Locke who was a Loyalist, or more generally known by the term, "Tory", and when the British evacuated Boston he left with the army, was in the battle of Staten Island, where he met and recognized his sons, Frederick and Henry, in the American army. He eventually went to England and never returned.

Three of the descendants made unusual marriages. John Fessenden married Abigail Child, of Warren, Rhode Island, the daughter of Colonel Sylvester Child, who married Priscilla Bradford, a lineal descendant of Governor Bradford of Plymouth. Lemuel Pierce married Eliza Mildeberger, whose mother was Mary Magdeline Colon, a descendant of Christopher Columbus. Joseph Lorenzo Locke married Laura J. Bulluck (January 4, 1843), who was born in Savannah, Georgia. Her paternal grandfather was the first colonial governor of Georgia, and her mother was descended from Sir John Allston, of South Carolina.

The Bible which belonged to William Locke is in black letter, and was undoubtedly printed before 1600. His death occurred at Woburn, Massachusetts, June 16, 1720. His wife died in 1716. The "Old Locke Place" is the property of a descendant. A "wing" of the original house is owned by the Historical Society of Woburn. The children were: 1.

William, born 1659; married (first) Sarah Whittmore, 1683, (second) Abigail Haywood. 2. John, born 1661; married Elizabeth Plympton. 3. Joseph, born 1664; married (first) Mary ———, died 1707; married (second) Margaret Mead; married (third) Hannah Pierce, 1743. 4. Mary, born 1666; married Samuel Kendall. 5. Samuel, born 1669; married (first) Ruth ———; married (second) Mary Day. 6. Ebenezer, of whom further. 7. James, born 1677; married Sarah Cutter. 8. Elizabeth, born 1681; married James Markam. All the above marriages were of Pilgrim or Puritan English. The children of William Locke Sr., were intelligent and educated people of their time. Many of their descendants had greater advantages and evidently embraced them.

Lieutenant Ebenezer (2) Locke, son of William (1) Locke, was born in 1674. He was a prominent man in Woburn. A large estate with the homestead included was given him by his father. He was frequently elected to town offices, and was lieutenant of the Train Band. He married (first) Susannah Walker, 1697, daughter of Israel Walker, of Woburn, who died in 1699. One son by this marriage, Ebenezer, born 1699, married Mary Meriam, and is said to have fired the first shot at the battle of Lexington, where he resided. He married (second) Hannah (3) Meads, 1701, born in 1676, whose father, Daniel (2) Meads, was a soldier in King Philip's Indian war. Vide "Hodges History." Children of Lieutenant Ebenezer Locke by second wife: 1. Samuel, born in 1702; married Rebeckah Richardson in 1730. 2. Josiah, born 1705, died 1727; unmarried, a young man of education with a taste for poetry. 3. Joshua (3), of whom further. 4. Nathan, born 1713, died 1723. 5. Hannah, born 1716; married, in 1739, Asa Richardson. Gabriel (1) Meads, Puritan, came over in 1630 with Sir Richard Saltonstall. Resided at Dorchester and Watertown—Freeman 1638. The mother of Hannah (3) Meads Locke was Hannah (3) Warren, daughter of Daniel (2), born in England in 1628, in 1650 married Mary (2) (daughter of Ellis (1) Barron), Watertown—Freeman 1640. Selectman 1680 to 1692. Was in Pequot War and fight at Sudbury.

John (1) Warren, Watertown, married Margaret. Came over in 1630 with Sir Richard Saltonstall. Selectman of Watertown 1636 to 1640. Puritan.

Ellis (1) Barron—Freeman. Watertown, 1640. Selectman, 1668. Wife, Grace, thought to be mother of all his children.

Joshua (3), son of Lieutenant Ebenezer Locke, was born August 21, 1709, at Woburn, Massachusetts. He married (first) Hannah (5) Reade, in March, 1732, daughter of Lieutenant Thomas (4) and Sarah (4) (Sawyer) Reade, of Woburn, born 1687, and sister of James Reade who was a military officer of eminence in French and revolutionary war. In May, 1775, he was colonel of the second New Hampshire Regiment and held the rail-fence with John Stark at Bunker Hill. He was, on the recommendation of Washington, the first brigadier-general appointed by the provincial congress. He married (second) Tabitha Bellows, Boston, April, 1744, daughter of Dr. Isaac Bellows, of Southboro. Resided at Woburn, Westboro, Boston and Southboro. He sold land in Southboro in 1753, was on the alarm list in that town in 1757, and died there in 1767. No children by second wife. His children by Hannah Reade were: 1. Joshua, born 1733; married Abigail Maynard. 2. Josiah, born 1735; married Persis Mathews. 3. Ebenezer, of whom further.

Ebenezer (4), son of Joshua Locke, was born in 1737 at Woburn. He was three years in the French war, and with General Winslow at Nova Scotia in 1755. Resided at Oxford. Rev. Army Records, Washington, D. C., certify: Ebenezer Locke Sr., served in Captain John Wood's company, Colonel Baldwin's regiment. Invalid pensions in state of New Hampshire show Ebenezer Locke in Fifteenth Massachusetts Regiment, and wounded in right thigh, and as fit for duty, vol. III., p. 345. He died September 24, 1812. He married, in 1759, Phoebe Mores. Their children were: 1. Mary, born 1761; married Thomas Laws. 2. Ebenezer, of whom further. 3. Allis, born 1769; married Nathaniel Ford. 4. Collins, born 1771; married Elizabeth Burroughs. 5. Rufus, born 1779; married Lydia Stebbins. 6. Nathan, married Hannah Goodnow. 7. Edward Jewett, born 1778; married Rhoda Laws.

Ebenezer (5), son of Ebenezer Locke, was born 1763, in Ervingshire. After the revolutionary war he purchased land in Rockingham, Vermont, where he lived until his death in 1833. Naturally possessed of a good mind, much practical good sense and good habits, he reared a large family respectably, and accumulated a handsome property, and secured the respect and esteem of all who knew him. His revolutionary service reads: Ebenezer Locke Jr., served in Captain John Wood's company, Colonel Baldwin's regiment, 1775-1779, when he re-enlisted for three years—thirty months as private, three months as corporal. He began his soldier life at the age of twelve years. On February 6, 1783, he married (first) Hannah Gustin (Augustine) of Rockingham, Vermont, born in 1764, died in 1833. Children born at Rockingham, Vermont: 1. John, born 1784; physician; married Hannah Gordon Clark, 1810. 2. Phoebe, married —— Fay. 3. Cyrus, of whom further. 4. Asa, born 1792; married Fanny Prentiss, 1815. 5. Albert, born 1795; married Phoebe Chafin, 1823. 6. Randilla, married Nathaniel Walker, 1813. 7. Oren, born 1798; married (first) Catherine Tyler, 1823, married (second) Nancy Williams, 1841. 8. Lewis, born 1802; married Laura Darby, 1828. 9. Henry, born 1804; married Eliza Prentiss, 1827. He married (second) 1835, Mrs. Susan Campbell. No children.

Cyrus (6), son of Ebenezer Locke, was born April 14, 1789, at Rockingham, Vermont. He was a man of good principles and assured position; of influence in town and county, selectman and magistrate, president of orphans court eighteen years. Bountifully he was blessed in "basket and store" and being of a genial and hospitable disposition his home in "Old Town" was always filled to overflowing with the ever welcome guests. He married, January 14, 1812, Randilla (7), daughter of Captain William (6) Thayer, whose line was: Lieutenant William (5), William (4), William (3), Shadrack (2), Thomas (1), and wife, Susannah (7) Lincoln, whose line was: Elkanah (6), Elkanah (5), Jonathan (4), Thomas (3), Thomas (2), Thomas (1). Their children were: 1. Lucius Elliot, born November 30, 1812; married Louisa Blake. 2. Cyrus Henry, born 1814; married, 1841, Amelia Bailey. 3. Randilla, born 1816; married, 1836, George Marsh. 4. James Leonard, born 1819; married, 1842, Lavinia Russell. 5. Celina Thayer, born 1822; married, 1842, Charles Pierce Marsh. 6, Eliza Maria, born 1824; married, 1845, Isaac Glynn. 7. Martha Jane, born 1826; married, 1847, Thomas C. Wells. 8. Henry Thayer, born 1829; married, 1863, Jane Peterson. 9. Rollin Mallory, born 1832; married, 1858, Marcia Stone. 10. Albert Emerson, born 1834; married, 1860, Emma Sackett. 11. Abbie Louise, born 1837; married, 1859, Charles Pollard. 12. Rush Sylvester, born 1839; married, 1861, Ellen Davis.

(The Reade Line).

Lieutenant Thomas (4) Reade was a prominent man. He was representative to the general court, and for many years connected with the Train Band of Woburn. Vide "Cutter's History of Woburn."

George (3) Reade, born in England in 1629, settled in Dorchester. Married, in 1652, Elizabeth, daughter of Robert Jamison. See "History of Dorchester."

William (2) Reade, son of Thomas (1) Reade, of Brocket Hall, Northumberland, England, and wife, Mary, came to New England in the "Defence," 1635, aged forty-eight years, with wife, Mabel Kendall, aged thirty years. The history of the Reade family has considerable account of him as identified with early history of Dorchester.

The Reades were among the reigning princes of Northumberland, Kent, Wessex and Mercia, and all seem to have been of the same blood and allied politically. Withred was king of Kent in the seventh century. Their seat was at Rede in the hundred of Merdinnie, now Marden. Here many of the kinsfolk by name of Reade resided. Sir Walter Scott in "Rokeby" alludes to a slab in Elsden Church which describes the family as having been seated in Redesdale nine hundred years. The Redes of the Cragg of Redesdale descended from the elder branch of Redes of Troughend Redesdale, and until recent years held lands granted by the crown prior to the conquest.

The original coat-of-arms of the Reades, described in heraldic terms, is "Azure; a griffin sergeant, or rampant, or clowed geles;" this emblem was of great antiquity and was borne by Cerdicus (Cedric), the Saxon, when he landed in Britain. The crest was an eagle sable, with wings extended, beak and claws gold—the heraldic motto, "Avi Numerantur Avorum." (Translated: "They exhibit a long line of ancestors.") Two Saxon ealdormen, Cedric and son Cynric, founded in 495 a settlement on the coast of what is now Hampshire. That settlement grew into the kingdom of England. Twenty-four years after their first landing the two Saxon ealdormen deemed their position strong enough and their conquests wide enough for them to assume the kingly title. Thus began the royal line of the West-Saxons, which became the royal line of England.

Joshua (3) Sawyer, born 1655, married, 1678, Sarah Potter. He was a soldier in King Philip's Indian war. Vide "Bodges History."

Thomas (2) Sawyer, England, was at Lancaster in 1644; was one of the first six settlers. He had before resided at Rowley. He married Mary, daughter of John Prescott. His first son, Thomas, was a captive among the Indians several years, and his second son, Ephraim, was killed by them in 1676.

John (1) Sawyer, born in England in the sixteenth century. He did not come to America.

(The Prescott Line).

The name of Prescott is of very ancient origin, and is composed of two Saxon words "Priest" and "Cottage." The ancestry has been traced back in the English records to Alfred the Great, and the earliest of the Saxon kings. It is certain that they belonged to the nobility of England. There is preserved by the descendants in this country (America) a family coat-of-arms, which was conferred upon one of the remote ancestors for his bravery, courage and successful enterprise as a man and military officer. This coat-of-arms must have been very old, as it was used by the Prescotts of Theobald Park, Hertfordshire, Barts, and by those of the ancient families of that name in Lancashire and Yorkshire. Among the most marked traits of this race, which have remained the same in each succeeding generation for centuries, are independence and great force of character, executive ability, integrity, tenacity of purpose, and quickness to think and act in emergency.

John Prescott, who sold his lands in Shevington, Lancashire, and wife, Mary Platt, who died in 1683, sailed for the Barbadoes, where he landed in 1638, and became an owner of lands there. In 1640 he came to Boston. He then settled in Watertown, where he had large grants of land allotted him. Like most of the early settlers in New England he left his home to escape the relentless religious persecutions in his native land. How much his coming meant to what was then a wilderness!

John Prescott was a pioneer of Lancaster, one of the most interesting and prominent of the early settlers of New England. (See History of Lancaster for above named). His record as a sturdy pioneer is of greater value than any royal descent. Although the leading citizen of Lancaster he was for a quarter of a century without a vote or any voice in the government, not eligible even to serve on a jury. His brave stand for liberty, against the Puritan despotism should offset any Royal descent. (Boston Transcript).

From him have come ministers, scholars, statesmen, soldiers, and brave men and good women filling honorable places in their respective communities—such men as "Prescott, the Historian" and "Prescott of Bunker Hill" are prominent figures in the line of his descendants.

When the "Prescott Memorial" was ready for press, it was withheld until the soldiers were "mustered out" at the close of the "Civil War." Three hundred and sixty of the names responded—also many of the Prescott ancestry.

The first American ancestor of the Prescotts was of fine physique, forceful character, and brilliant mind; he was a remarkable personage, and at once became an influential man in his adopted country.

(The Thayer Line).

"Tayer"; Thayer: The origin of the name is, as of all surnames, signified by the occupation followed by the persons, or signified by the locality or some personal peculiarity.

Judge Horace Metcalf, who has examined the English law on the subject of the "Tayer" name spelled in the different ways in those reports (Thayer, Thear, Theyer, etc.) is of German origin, and in that language signifies an ox or a cow, or dealer in such. Consequently it seems probable that our ancestors took their surname from the continent, and it is synonymous with a bullock in the English language. We do also know that England was over run by the Danes and Saxons one thousand years ago, more or less, and the counties of Kent and Essex on the east coast of England passed into the possession of those marauders composed of intruders from the opposite coast. We next find a coat-of-arms conferred on Augustine Thayor, of Thaydore, a small village in the county of Essex, eighteen miles from London.

The Thayers when coming to this country chose their residence in Braintree, Massachusetts. It has been a great pleasure to many of their descendants to trace back their progeniture in an uninterrupted series, to those who first landed on the unhospitable shores of New England, and it is not improbable that the arrival of the Puritan Fathers of New England will form a more memorable epoch in history than the Conquest of England does in that country, (and that posterity, a few centuries hence, will experience as much pleasure in tracing back its ancestry to the New England colonist as some of the English feel who are able to deduce their descent from the Norman).

Thomas (1) Tayer-Thayer was a shoemaker. He was a progenitor of a numerous offspring, by some said to be a distinct race from Richard, but it is not positively known as to the facts. Both families settled in the same town (Braintree; Mass.) about the same time; and as intermarriage took place, it would make them relatives. He brought with him from England his wife, Margery Wheeler, and three sons: Thomas, Ferdinando, Shadrack, of whom further. Will recorded, 13th of September, 1665. Good Puritan.

Shadrack (2), son of Thomas Thayer, died in 1678. He married (first) Mary Barrett, 1654, and settled in Braintree, Massachusetts. She died in 1658. Child, Rachel, born 1655. Married (second) Deliverance (2), daughter of James (1) and Elizabeth Priest, of Boston and Weymouth. Died 1723, aged seventy-nine. Children: Freelove, born 1662, died 1662; Mary, born 1663; Timothy, born 1666; Samuel, born 1667; Ephraim; Hannah, born 1672; William, of whom further.

William (3), son of Shadrack Thayer, born in 1675. He married, in 1692, Hannah (3) (Hosmer) Heywood, a widow, daughter of James (2) Hosmer and wife Alice, and settled in Braintree, Massachusetts. Children: Bethiah, born 1700; Jonathan, born 1703; William, of whom further; Martha, born 1709. Thomas (1) Hosmer, father of James Hosmer, came from Hawkhurst, county Kent, England, in 1632, to Cambridge, Hartford, Connectient, 1636. Representative. Died 1687, aged eighty-three. Wife Frances died 1675, age seventy-three.

William (4), son of William Thayer, was born 1705, died 1769. He married Abigail, daughter of John (3) Burt, of Buckley, Massachusetts, 1729, died 1790, aged eighty-two. Resided in Old Taunton, Massachusetts. Children: Jacob, born 1730; William, 1732; John, 1734; Abigail, 1737; Elijah, 1740; Sally, 1743.

John (3) Burt, 1671-1767, married Abigail, born 1673, daughter of William (1) Paull and wife Mary (3) Richmond; John (2), John (1), England. "Emery's History" of Taunton, p. 401, says: "The Press Masters returned under their hands, that they impressed for his Majesties service, July 25, 1697, just as the afternoon meeting was done. (When the King of England and the king of France got mad and wouldn't play, then they went to war; and the English provences were brought into the struggle, hence John (3) Burt, paid his fealty to his King.")

Richard (2) Burt, England, 1620-1685: One of the purchasers of the "North Purchase" of Taunton, 1668, and of the "South Purchase", 1672. In King Philip's war, 1675. Married Charity, daughter of George Hall, who died 1711. Surveyor. Took oath of fidelity, 1657. Constable, 1667. Freeman, 1670.

Richard (1) Burt: One of the forty-six "First purchasers" of (Cohannet) Taunton of Massasoit, 1639. Advanced in years; name not in first military company 1643. Died previous to 1647. Date of marriage and name of wife not given. Puritan English.

Lieutenant William (5) Thayer, William (4), William (3), Shadrack (2), Thomas (1), 1732-1779. A gentleman of landed estate, Taunton, Massachusetts. Ensign Fourth Taunton Company: Captain James (3) Leonard, Bristol county regiment: Colonel Samuel White, Mass. archives 99: 47, State House, Boston. Appointed lieutenant Fourth Taunton Company: Captain James Leonard, Third Regiment Bristol county, 1771. Mass. archives 99:47. "Also assisted in establishing American Independence, while acting in capacity of lieutenant in New York, December, 1776, and at different times until he contracted small-pox and died." Emery's "History of Taunton," p. 452. He married, in 1763, a widow, Mary (5) Leonard (Tisdale) 1729-1814, daughter of Captain James (4) Leonard, of Taunton. Children: William, born 1764; Wealthy, 1766; Polly; Lydia.

(The Lenerd, Leonard Line).

James (2), James (3), James (4), Mary (5).

Thomas (1) Leonard, Monmouth, England, was the English ancestor who never came to America, but who is enumerated in the Leonard Genealogy. James (2) Leonard, and brother Henry, were the first representatives of the family in this country, coming from Pontypool, Monmouthshire, England.

They were skilled "Iron Masters" and were interested in the first "Bloomerie" erected in New England, situated at Saugus. In 1651-52 they superintended the erection of the first foundry at Braintree, and in the same year they removed to Taunton and erected their own "bloomerie," which remained in operation in the hands of Leonards and descendants until it was demolished in 1876. James Leonard, Sr., was one of the "Associates" of the North Purchase in 1668 of Philip. The price paid for this tract of land was "the full sum of one hundred pounds."

In 1695 two hundred acres of land were given the Leonards for another forge on the "Stony Brook" in the "North Division," and also the liberty to take their next division of one share in the North-Purchase lands "in the best iron-oare that they can find." They were also allowed the privilege of digging ore in any other man's land, for the use and benefit of said works, by "paying the owner of such land one shilling a tun for every tun of iron-oare they shall dig." At one colonial period they coined money for the realm; certain pieces are on exhibition at the present time in Historical Hall, Taunton, Massachusetts.

By his wife, Margaret Martin, he had a large family of children: Thomas (3), James (3); Abigail (3), who married John Kingsley, of Milton; Rebecca (3), married Isaac Chapman, of Barnstable; Joseph (3); Benjamin (3); Hannah (3), married Isaac Dean; Uriah (3). The two most distinguished were Thomas (3) and James (3).

Captain James (3) Leonard, 1643-1726, was like his father, a "Bloomer." He was selectman (one of the principal offices) of Taunton for many years; representative to the general court of Massachusetts; first lieutenant in the first Military Company of Taunton, 1705; captain in 1713. Vide Emery's "History of Taunton." By his three wives he had thirteen children.

He married (second) in 1675, Lydia, 1658-1705, daughter of Anthony (1) Gulliver, born 1619 in England, died in Milton, 1706, and wife, Eleanor (2), daughter of Stephen (1) Kingsley, England and Dorchester, Massachusetts, representative 1650 to general court; removed to Braintree; ordained "Ruling Elder" of the church, 1639; Representative 1666.

Names of children: Eunice (4), married Richard Burt; Prudence (4), married Samuel Lewis, of Barnstable; Hannah (4), married John Crane; James (4), married Lydia, daughter of Jonathan Gulliver; Lydia (4), married William Britton; Stephen (4); Abigail (4), married Ezra Dean; Seth (4); Sarah (4), married Henry Hodges; Elizabeth (4), married Captain Joseph Hall.

To show the manly and friendly side of James (2) and James (3) Leonard, I will quote from "Abbott's History:" "It is said that Philip had given orders that the town of Taunton should be spared until all the other towns in the Colony were destroyed."

"A family by the name of Leonard resided in Taunton, where they had erected the first forge which was established in the English colonies. Philip, though his usual residence was at Mount Hope, had a favorite summer resort at a place called 'Fowling Pond,' then within the limits of Taunton. In these excursions he had become acquainted with the Leonards. They had treated him and his followers with uniform kindness, repairing their guns, and supplying them with such tools as the Indians highly prized. Philip had become exceedingly attached to this family, and in gratitude, at the commencement of the war, had given the strictest orders that the Indians should never injure a Leonard. Apprehending that in a general assault upon the town his friends, the Leonards, might be exposed to danger, he spread the shield of his generous protection over the whole place." . . . .
"His extraordinary kindness to the Leonards, inducing him to avert calamities from a whole settlement, lest they, by some accident, might be injured develops magnanimity which is seldom paralleled." Francis Baylies "History of Taunton."

Captain James (4) Leonard, 1677-1764, was also a manufacturer of iron; selectman of the town for many years; representative to general court, 1708-1721, 1726-1733, 1735-1739, 1740. Plymouth and Massachusetts Colonial Records. Ensign, lieutenant, captain of Militia Company, 1736. He married (first) 1699, Hannah (Walley) Stone, of Bristol, by whom he had Lieutenant James (5), born 1699, captain and muster-master for Taunton in revolutionary war, died in 1793; Eliphalet, 1702-1786, of Easton; Lydia, married Captain Thomas Cobb and were the parents of David Cobb, lieutenant-governor of Massachusetts, general and aide to Washington in the revolutionary war, judge and member of congress, 1793-95; Sally, married Robert Treat Paine, "Signer of Declaration of Independence." The Daughters of the American Revolution Chapter of Taunton is named for "Lydia Cobb." He married (second) Lydia, widow of John Gulliver, of Milton, and daughter of Jonathan (2) Gulliver and wife, Mary Robinson, by whom he had Jonathan; Mary (5), widow of Loved Tisdale, who married (second) Lieutenant William (5) Thayer; Elizabeth, married Joseph Harvey; Jerusha, married Abijah Hodges. Wife died previous to 1759. He married (third) Mercy ———. "History of Norton," p. 85.

The Leonards claim descent from Leonard Lord Dacre, one of the most distinguished families in the United Kingdom, descended in two lines from Edward III., through two of his sons, John of Gaunt, Duke of Lancaster, and Thomas Plantaganet, Duke of Gloucester. There appears to be ground for this claim from the fact that the arms of Lennerd and Lenord families are the same: Or, on a fesse gules (red) three fleur-de-lis of the first or field. Crest: Out of a ducal Coronet or, a Tiger's head argent. Motto: Pour-Bien-Desirer. To wish well.

Near the close of the last century the last Lord Dacre bearing the name of Lennard died, and it is supposed that the late Judge George Lenerd could have claimed the title, but the judge said "He preferred to be lord of acres in America rather than Lord Dacre in England."

All the foregoing is recorded and part of the History of "Old Taunton."

The third and fourth editions, "Americans of Royal Descent" have "Leonard" pedigree. Leonard belongs to the class of names that originated from the Christian name. The signification is Lion-hearted, from Leo, or Leon and ard. It seems strange that those who attained the honors of knighthood did not adopt a Lion's head for their crest instead of a tiger's! "New England Historical and Genealogical Register," 1848, vol. II, p. 162.

Captain William (6) Thayer, Lieutenant William (5), William (4), William (3), Shadrack (2), Thomas (1), 1764-1830. After the revolutionary war he purchased a thousand-acre estate in Springfield, Vermont, which remained in the family until 1908. "In the spring of 1788 he with his wife removed to their new home; he driving a pair of oxen hitched to a two-wheeled cart, which held their household goods, the wife riding a small horse and carrying their valuables. For seven years they lived in a log house, while the new one was building, which was a fine large mansion, and which is standing today, perfect in every respect. The nails were handmade; the trees were felled, the timbers and material for the entire structure prepared by men employed for the purpose, in the same primitive manner — the shingles were made from the hearts of old pine trees, and lasted for seventy years. He hired the best masons and carpenters at fifty cents per day (or less), and in summer they worked eighteen hours out of the twenty-four. (The night before they left the old house one log rolled out and one rolled in). He was for many years justice of the peace, selectman, captain of militia company, surveyor, and surveyed most of the land in the state of Vermont. The needle of his compass, that is over one hundred and fifty years old, still points to the North pole. His revolutionary war service began in Taunton at the age of sixteen years in Captain Jacobs Hoskins' company, Colonel Isaac Dean's regiment.

He married, January 1, 1789, Susannah (7), 1769-1833, daughter of Elkanah (6) Lincoln, and wife Susannah (4) Torrey, of Norton, Massachusetts. Their children were: Hon. William, born 1790, married (first) Eunice Field, Surry, New Hampshire, (second) Sarah Joslin, Surry, New Hampshire; Susannah, 1792, married David Brown; Randilla (7), 1796, married Cyrus (6) Locke, Rockingham, Vermont; James Leonard, 1799, married Sarah Clapham, Madrid, New York; Selina, 1806, married George Putnam, Rockingham, Vermont; Eliza Maria, 1808, married Ichabod Gibson Adams, Springfield, Vermont.

(The Lincoln Line).

Elkanah (6) Lincoln, 1747-1816, was a man of affairs, and a large land-owner. After the death of his father he was styled "Gentleman." He served in the revolutionary war, first as private, second as corporal, third as sergeant in the Continental Line of Massachusetts. Married, in 1768, at Taunton, Susannah, 1749-1833, daughter of Deacon Samuel (3) Torrey. Children: Susannah, 1769; Micah, 1771; Constant, 1773, married ——— Kendall; Elkanah, 1775; Zebina, 1777; Tisdale, 1780; Catey,

1784, married Abel Gleason; William, 1787. In 1782 he removed to Westmoreland, New Hampshire, where he and his wife died.

Deacon Samuel (3) Torrey, Micah (2), William (1), 1688-1782, Weymouth, Massachusetts, occupation, cooper. Will made 1782; large estate divided among children. Married, 1732, at Taunton, Constant Linkton (Lincoln), daughter of Nathaniel and Alice (3) (Andrews), John (2), John (1) Andrews, Boston, 1656, from Wales, Puritan. Children: Order of birth unknown: Order taken from old deed. Sarah, married, 1754, Joseph Andrews; Daniel, married, 1761, Keziah Stockbridge; Constant, married, 1761, Abiel Eddy; Levi, married, 1778, Elizabeth Arnold; Lois, married ———— Fisher; Rachel, married, 1764, Nathan Franklin; Susannah, married, 1768, Elkanah Lincoln Jr.

Deacon Micajah (2), 1643-1710, Weymouth, married Susannah ————. Children: Micajah, 1673-1722, married Sarah Batt, of "Mayflower" ancestry; Margaret, 1675-1752, married James Humphreys; Mary, 1681-1716; Silence, died 1724, married Samuel French; Joshua, 1686-1752; Susannah, died 1687; Susannah, 1687-1752; Samuel, 1688-1782, married, 1732, Constant Linkton.

England—

(1) Gen'n, d. 1556, William Torrey
(2)   "   " 1604, Philip   "
(3)   "   " 1639, William "
(4)   "   " 1621, Philip   "   m. Alice Richards.

Immigration, 1640.

William (1) Torrey, son of Philip and Alice Torrey. From Combe St. Nicholas, England, and Weymouth, Massachusetts.

Baptized, December 21, 1608, Combe St. Nicholas, died June 10, 1690, Weymouth, Massachusetts; Freeman, 1642; representative, 1642, and often afterward, having special qualifications for that office. He was lieutenant and captain, clerk of the house of representatives and magistrate. (Savage "Geneal. Dic. Papers Pioneers of Mass." Hobart's "History of Obington, Massachusetts"). He married (first) in 1629, at Combe St. Nicholas, Agnes Combe, daughter of Joseph and Winifred (Rossiter) Combe, who died in 1629. He married (second) in 1630, Jane Haviland, daughter of Robert and Elizabeth (Gyse) Haviland, from Hawksbury, Barnes, England, who died in 1639. Children by second wife, Rev. Samuel, childless; Captain William, 1638-1718, married Deborah Green, the lineal ancestor of Louisa Mariah (Torrey) Taft, the mother of William H. Taft, president of the United States. Married (third) Elizabeth, daughter of Edward Frye and wife (name not recorded). Children: Samuel, 1632-1707, married (first) 1657, Mary P. Rawson, married (second) 1694, Mary Symmes, widow; William, 1638-1718, married Deborah Green; Naomi, born 1641, married ————Hayward; Mary, born 1642, married William Downs; Micajah, 1643-1710, married Susannah ————; Josiah, 1650-1732, married Sarah Wilson (Batt), widow; Judith, 1655-1693, married Thomas Hunt; Angel, 1657-1725, married Hannah ————.

Elkanah (5) Lincoln, 1718-1783, married, at Norton, 1744, Lydia Pratt, of Norton. Almost nothing is known of him, except what is revealed by the records of his real estate transactions. There are indications that he received a better education than his father. In early life called yeoman, after 1777 he was styled "Gentleman." He was the first in his ancestral line to take that title, and it indicates quite an advance in public and social life. Their children were: Lydia, born 1745; Elkanah, born 1747, married Susannah Torrey; Enos, born 1749; Samuel, born 1751; Prudence, born 1754; Hannah, born 1757; Amasa, born 1762; Luther, born 1766.

Jonathan (4) Lincoln, 1687-1773, Taunton. He was more successful than his predecessors, and brought together a large estate, and was the first in his family line who could write his name and spell it correctly. He was generous toward his children. Married, 1712, Hannah, born 1690, daughter of Captain John and Alice (3) (Shaw) Andrews. John (2), Abraham (1) Shaw, in Boston, 1639, Good Puritans. Children: Jonathan, born 1713; James, born 1715; Elkanah, born 1718, married Lydia Pratt; Abiel, born 1720; Hannah, born 1723; George, born 1727; Job, born 1730.

"Captain John Andrews was from Wales. Immigration 1663."

Thomas (3) Lincoln, born 1656, Taunton. He accumulated considerable property of his own. In one respect he made a distinct advance over his ancestors, for while he signed his name by a rude S, yet his children received an education. He made no will, instead conveyed his property to his children before his death. Married Mary Stacey, of Taunton, daughter of Richard and Abigail Stacey. Their children were: Thomas, born 1680; Benjamin, born 1681; Nathaniel, born 1684; Jonathan, born 1687, married Hannah Andrews; William, born 1689; Lydia; Hannah, born 1692; Constant, born 1696.

Thomas (2) Lincoln, born in England, 1628. Came to Hingham, Massachusetts, with his father in 1636. He settled in Taunton in 1649, died there in 1695, and was granted a home lot. In 1675, at the breaking out of King Philip's war, he was one of ninety heads of families. In 1687-88, being then senior, he gave five acres of land toward Taunton's first minister, Samuel Danforth. In 1689 when money was raised for the expedition under Colonel Benjamin Church he contributed ten shillings, and during King William's war when money was raised for the expedition to Canada in 1690, he gave two pounds. In 1695 when the Chartley Iron Works were organized and one hundred acres of land was given to it from the North Purchase he was one of those who signed the deed. Member of the Military Company of Taunton in 1682. A large land owner, for in addition to his own rights under the original purchases he also inherited from his father considerable land. In 1658 declared a freeman; in 1677 elected surveyor to set off the common lands. In 1669, 1672, 1677, he with others purchased from King Philip all the land included in the ancient town of Taunton, from which several towns were later carved (except a purchase called the Titicut Purchase). He married, in 1651, Mary Austin, daughter of Jonah (1) Austin Sr. In 1694, instead of making a will he divided his property among his children, only reserving the right to sell a portion for his support. Names of children: Mary, born 1652; Sarah, born 1654; Thomas, born 1656, married Mary Austin; Samuel, born 1658; Sarah, born 1660; Hannah, born 1663; Mercy, born 1665; Jonah; Experience, born 1693.

"Jonah (1) Austin was one of the purchasers of the 'Taunton North Purchase' of King Philip in 1668."

Between the years 1635 and 1640 eight men by the name of Lincoln came to Hingham, Massachusetts, from or near Hingham, England. Four of these were named Thomas, designated by their occupation as the weaver, the husbandman, the cooper and the miller. Three of the eight men were brothers, Samuel, Daniel and Thomas. Immigration 1635.

Thomas (1) Lincoln, born 1603, came to Hingham, Massachusetts, from Hingham, Norfolk county, England; on the 3d of July, 1636, was granted house lots of five acres of land. He was called "Thomas the Miller" to distinguish him from three others by the same name. In 1649 he removed to Taunton; "the town voted him accommodations." He became a large landholder, and died in 1684. The inventory of his estate was two hundred and five pounds and eight shillings. A member of the first train band in 1649.

Iron had been discovered on "Two-Mile River," and other locations in Taunton, and the enterprising Pilgrim settlers considered the field open for the establishment of a "bloomerie." A company was organized in 1653-54, and the name of Thomas Linkon Sr., is among the subscribers. (From "History of Taunton, Mass.," by Samuel Emery Hopkins, D. D.). He was one of "ye associates" of the "South Purchase," a tract four miles square, for which King Philip was paid two hundred and seventy-three pounds. At the time of King Philip's war in 1675 he was reckoned the richest of ninety-six heads of families. A man of no education, could not write his own name, and signed all instruments by mark. Married (first) 1627, in England, name of wife unknown. His first three children were born in England, the others in Hingham. Names of children: Thomas, born 1628, married Mary Austin; John; Samuel, born 1636; Mary, born 1642; Sarah, born 1645. He married (second) in 1665, Elizabeth Street, of Taunton, by whom he had no children.

When he first came to Hingham he was called Junior, his father's name must have been Thomas, and he the eldest son.

The name of Lincoln appears frequently on the records of the sixteenth century in and about Hingham, in the county of Norfolk, and there are many records of baptisms in St. Andrews Church in Hingham with Christian names similar to the names of the Lincolns in this country.

"Fairbain in his 'Crestes of the Families of Great Britain and Ireland,' vol. II, plate 67, No. 5," gives the Crest of "Lincolne" as a Loan Rampant, standing on a wreath facing the left.

Between the years 1635 and 1640 the eight first men in the colony by the name of Lincoln came to Hingham, Massachusetts, from or near Hingham, England. Three of the eight were brothers, and the other five closely related. From Samuel, the weaver, is descended Abraham Lincoln, the president (Lincoln Family Association).

Origin of the Name.

The "Lincolns" have the satisfaction of having a name descended from very ancient times in Britain. When the Romans conquered North Britain about the year A. D. 86 they founded at what is now the city of Lincoln, not a castra or camp, but a colony, naming it Lindum Colonia. The location was a very ancient one, there having been a settlement of the old Britains at this place long before the coming of the Romans. From the abbreviation of the two words—Lindum and Colonia, or Lin-coln—we derive our name of "Lincoln."

The name "Lincoln" is a hybrid of Celtic and Latin. It appears in some very old records as Lindum Colonia and Lindocolina. The "Lindum" is purely Saxon, and exactly describes the early British settlement as "the hill part of the pool."

The name Nicol, Nicole is Norman-French for Lincoln. "In modern history times the earliest record of the Lincolns show them to have been people of wealth and station; the name of Wigod de Lincoln appears as a witness to the charter of Edward the Confessor, in 1060. Alured de Lincoln, who came over with William the Conquerer, held a great barony in Lincoln and Bedford in 1086." "The Doomsday Book," 1086, mentions several men of the same name, more especially Alfred de Lincoln, who, being a Saxon by birth, could not hold lands until after his marriage with a Norman lady.

The Lincoln Impe.

In Lincoln Cathedral, in what is known as the Angel Choir, so called from the numerous figures of angels among the carving, there are at the spandrils of the arches to the windows in the clear story, numerous carvings, among them his grotesque figure.

Memorial to the President.

In the year 1909, the centennial of the birth of President Abraham Lincoln, it was proposed to place in old St. Andrews, Hingham, a memorial to him and his ancestors, for it was in this church that Samuel Lincoln was baptized August 23, 1622, the son of Edward Lincoln, who did not come to this country. "The Lincoln Family Association" responded most generously.

(The Marsh Line).

Charles (6) Pierce Marsh, Joseph (5), Moses (4), Moses (3), John (2), Alexander (1) Marsh, born 1820, Rockingham, Vermont, married, July 5, 1842, at Keene, New Hampshire, Celina (7) Thayer, daughter of Cyrus (6) Locke, Ebenezer (5), Ebenezer (4), Joshua (3), Ebenezer (2), William (1) Locke, and wife, Randilla (7) Thayer, Captain William (6), Lieutenant William (5), William (4), William (3), Shadrack (2), Thomas (1) Thayer.

By this marriage were joined two distinct "Historical" families, originally of Old England, Colonially of New England, and, like Browning's "Happy Warrior," marching breast forward to join in the formation of the thirteen original states, and the birth of our American Republic.

After disposing of the "Marsh Homestead" in 1850 he with his mother, wife and two children removed to Allegany county, New York, and purchased a home in Marshall, where three older brothers (Joseph (6), Orlin (6), Otis (6)) and one sister, (Pamelia, who married Benjamin Whipple) had previously located, having purchased their land from the "Holland Land Company" at a period when the Indians were quiet. (Soon after warfare broke out, and for two years they lived in constant fear of their lives; when a treaty was made to the effect that by paying thirty silver dollars to a certain chief—who desired a necklace—future annoyances would cease. After receiving the silver the Indians left that part of the country and never returned).

Of a versatile disposition he interested himself in different lines of business, agriculture, lumbering, surveying and prospecting for coal, principally in McKean county, Pennsylvania. In 1857-58 he took his family with him and located at Howard Hill, now Mt. Jewett, remaining for a few months, when he returned with his family to Allegany county; the "call of the wild" leading him back each winter to join congenial companions in camping and hunting the wild game, which at that time was abundant; a noted "shot," he rarely failed in a "good bag;" at one time bringing down two deer with one shot. In May, 1864, he removed with his family to Lamont (Kane), Pennsylvania, where, the following September he opened its first hotel, which was the nucleus of the "Old Thomson House."

Charitable, as well as public-spirited, many

of the early settlers of the place remember him with thankful hearts. The township being without school funds, he, with William Carlyle (resident Engineer P. R. R.), organized a select school, engaging Catherine Marsh, of Marshall, New York, as teacher, they paying the greater part of her salary. The school was well attended, as all the little foreign waifs were made welcome.

His wife dying in August, 1864, he sold his hotel interests to a man by the name of Charles Jones, and again returned to Allegany county, where the following year he was one of a company formed to mine for silver and drill for oil in Marshall. The venture was not a financial success.

He married (second) in 1866, Olive, 1840-1910, daughter of Caryl Holden and wife, Randilla Damon, of Marshall, and sister of Judge Lawson C. Holden, of Saginaw and the "Soo," Michigan, also a cousin of Judge Crittenden Marsh, of Warren county. A few years later he removed to Belfast, same county, where he lived a quiet uneventful life, dying in 1892, loved by his family and kin and respected by his townspeople. By his two wives he had eight daughters: Abbie Louise (7), mentioned below; Harriet (7), born Rockingham, Vermont, married Thomas Henry Ryan, born Limerick, Ireland, residence, Kane, Pennsylvania; Mary (7), born Rockingham, Vermont, died Marshall, New York; Mary Jane (7), born Marshall, married William Griffith, born Ebensburg, residence Kane; Flora (7), born Marshall, deceased; Myra Alda (7), born Marshall, married L. Hawes Long, born Huntingdon, Pennsylvania, residence Chicago and Belfast, New York. Children by second wife: Lucy Holden (7), born Marshall; Edna Damon (7), born Marshall.

Abbie Louise (7), daughter by first wife, compiler of the Family History, married William Calvin Long, born Huntingdon, Pennsylvania, journalist, of Chicago, Illinois. Two children survived by this marriage. Suffering from pulmonary trouble, in 1888, she with her daughters took up their residence in Kane, where she remained until 1899, when she accepted the situation as "Instructor of Art" at the State Hospital, Warren, a position she still retains, 1912. Confirmed in 1876 by the Rt. Rev. McLarren S. T. D., Episcopal bishop of Illinois; member of the Cathedral of S. S. Peter and Paul, Chicago; one of the "Founders" of St. Johns Church, 1889, Kane; member of "Old Colony" and other Colonial Societies; member of the "Lincoln" and "Reade" Family Associations, and a "Daughter of the American Revolution;" Charter member of the General Joseph Warren Chapter, Warren, Pennsylvania.

Her education along scholastic and art lines was principally by private instruction; and, as much of the formative period of her life was spent in literary and art circles in Chicago, the advantages derived from such congenial associations were far greater than is received by the average art student. She was also able to gratify her love for travel, which made a desirable prelude to her present "Home Missionary" work among the women of an unfortunate mental condition.

Her elder daughter, Maude, born Chicago, Illinois, married William Herman Davis, Kane, son of Joshua and wife, Hannah (Howells) Davis, of Ebensburg and Kane. Their children: Dorothea (9), Joshua (9).

Her second daughter, Mabell Washington (8), born Chicago, Illinois, married (St. Johns, Kane) Benjamin Howard Patterson, M. D., son of John and Priscilla (Focer) Patterson, of Pittsburgh, Pennsylvania. Their children: John (9), Louisa (9), Thomas (9).

One tradition in the family is that Francisco de Marisco, who went over with the Conqueror, was the founder. When anglicized the name became Marsh. Marais, the French word for Marsh, is now a common name in France. The supposition is that the family are of French origin, and came from low marshy lands. In ancient Latin deeds the name appears as De Marisco. The mecieval form is Ate-Mershi. If the name started as Saxon, March means a boundary, as the marches of Wales, or a landmark. Other forms are Marche and Marisq, and the most familiar derivations are Marshall and Marshman. One branch of the family claim royal blood through descent from Alfred the Great.

The Marshes have helped to make history, and the name is honored for its men of character and renown, its heroes and its pioneers. There was the martyr, George Marsh, burned at the stake during Mary's reign. The list of members of the family who have been archbishops, bishops and priests is an imposing one. One of the foremost men of letters of his day was Herbert Marsh, bishop of Peterborough. Francis Marsh was archbishop of

PENNSYLVANIA

Dublin in the reign of William III., and Narcissus Marsh was archbishop of Armagh.

The Marsh arms: Gules, a horse's head coupled between three crosses bottoine, fitchee argent. Crest: Out of a mural crown gules, a horse's head argent, ducally gorged or.

In the New World the Marshes were men of affairs. John Marshe was one of the first settlers. Jonathan Marsh, another Pilgrim father, lived in Hartford, of which he was one of the founders. The family was represented in the colonial wars, and those of 1770 and 1812. Nathaniel Marsh had charge of the company which escorted Burgoyne to Cambridge after the surrender at Saratoga.

Sylvester Marsh, called "Crazy Marsh," was not so crazy after all. It was he who built the railroad up Mt. Washington. When the legislature granted him a charter willingness was also expressed to give him a charter to the moon if he wished, so impossible a feat was the building of a "Jacob's Ladder" considered.

Joseph Owen (5) Marsh, Moses (4), Moses (3), John (2), Alexander (1), born 1769, Braintree, Massachusetts, died 1846, Rockingham, Vermont, was a "gentleman" of landed estate; educated and provided for his large family as the times permitted. He married, May, 1793, at Rockingham, Vermont, Joanna (8) Pierce, born 1776, at Putney, Vermont, daughter of Ebenezer (7) and wife, Elizabeth (4) Gilson. She had many of the old fashioned graces that stamped the gentlewoman of her time; intelligent and active to the last, and greatly beloved by her descendants, who mourned her passing away in 1872, aged ninety-six years. Their children: Royal, born 1793, unmarried, service in Mexican war, settled in Louisiana, sugar and rice plantations, large slaveholder, Union man in 1863, slaves freed by the North and property confiscated by the South; he died a poor man before the close of the civil war; Joseph, born 1795, married Polly Bailey; Anna, born 1797; Orlin, born 1799, married Fanny Stoddard; Otis, born 1801, married Rossella Holden; Charles, born 1803; George, born 1805, married Randilla Locke; Horace, born 1807; Betsey, born 1809, married Rossiter Crittenden; Sally, born 1811, married (first) Thomas Stoddard, who died, married (second) —— Wilson; Pamelia, born 1813, married Benjamin Whipple; Horace, born 1815, married Julia Ann Studley; John, born 1817, married Lucy Studley; Polly,

born 1819, married Elijah Pratt; Charles, born 1820, married Celina (7) Locke.

The English name of "Peirce" is derived from the word "Peter." When we consider how important has been the position claimed for him we can readily understand the influence that the ecclesiastics of the early days must have had in making it popular.

The Pierce coat-of-arms: Three ravens rising sable; Fesse—hummette. Motto: Dixit et Fecit. (He said and he did). Crest: Dove with olive branch in beak.

Ebenezer (7) Pierce, Anthony (6), John (5), Joseph (4), Joseph (3), Anthony (2), son of John (1). Resided in Westmoreland, New Hampshire, and Putney, Vermont. The history of the Pierce Family says: Ebenezer Pierce was shot by British soldiers just before the battle of Bennington; while another account says he was killed by Tories at Bennington. He was one of the Vermont "Minute-Men" and was shot while carrying dispatches. He married, 1793, Elizabeth (4), daughter of Michael (3) Gilson, born 1741, at Groton, Massachusetts. Their children were: Roswell, born 1764, married Elizabeth Morton; Reuben, born 1766, married his cousin, Arvilla Gilson; Royal, married Azubula Davenport; Elizabeth, married Samuel Chadwick; Millicent, married (first) —— Bunday, (second) —— Crosby; Joanna, 1776, married Joseph (5) Marsh, Rockingham, Vermont.

Michael (3) Gilson, John (2), Joseph (1), 1702-1760. Resided at Groton, Massachusetts. In 1750 he resided above Northfield, Massachusetts, in New Hampshire. He was a soldier in French and Indian war, and was wounded, June 24, 1746. Proprietor in 1752. He married, in Westmoreland, in 1720, Susannah, born 1709, daughter of Zachariah Sawtell and wife Mercy, Groton, Massachusetts. Names of children: Zachariah, 1727-1735; Rachel, 1728; Michel, 1730, married Sarah Sessions, a prominent man in Putney, Vermont, captain in revolutionary war; Jacob, 1732-1735; Benjamin, 1735; Zachariah, 1736; Susannah, 1739; Elizabeth, 1741, married, November 24, 1763, Ebenezer Pierce.

Zachariah Sawtell. His will probated November 29, 1737. In it he mentioned wife Mercy, son Zachariah, and daughters Mary Blanchard, Susannah Gilson, Sarah, Anna and Elizabeth.

John (2) Gilson, died 1707, slain by Indians. He married, at Groton, in 1697, Sarah

———. Children: John, 1698; Sarah, 1700; Michael, 1702, married Susannah Sawtell; Susannah, 1704; Ebenezer, 1707, posthumous.

Joseph (1) Gilson immigrated from North of Ireland previous to 1660. Resided in Chelmsford, Massachusetts, and Groton. Good Puritan. Married (second) November 18, 1660, Mary Caper. Children: Joseph, born in Groton, married, 1667, Hepsibah; Sarah, 1669; John, married, in 1697, Sarah ———.

No data concerning Anthony (6) Peirce, and John (5), of Watertown.

Joseph (4) Peirce, born 1669, Watertown.

Joseph (3) Peirce, Watertown, son of Anthony (2), had wife, Martha, married (second) in 1698, Elizabeth (Kendall) Winship. Freeman in 1690. Joseph (3) Peirce, Watertown, by petition with Daniel Warren, evidences that he was at Sudbury, April 21, 1676, at the fight with the Indians in which Captain Samuel Wadsworth and Broshlesant were slain, together with fifty others. The petition recites their part in the engagement and concerning the burial of the dead. The petition, original, is in Massachusetts Archives, Boston State House, vol. 68, folio 224.

Joseph (3) Peirce, Watertown, appears in company of Watertown men, August 24, 1676, and as receiving for his services. "Bodges History," p. 376.

Anthony (2) Peirce, Watertown; eldest son of John of Watertown, born in England, freeman, 1634. He had two wives, Sarah and Ann, the first died in 1633, and the second 1682. He died 1678. Children: John, "eldest son," born England; Mary, 1636, married Ralph Reed, of Woburn; Jacob, 1637; Daniel, 1639; Martha, 1641; Joseph; Benjamin, 1649; Judith, 1650, married John Swain, 1667.

Many intermarriages took place in early days between the Peirces and Lockes, and the "Locke Book," 1850, claims it is from Anthony Peirce that President Franklin Pierce is descended.

John (1) Peirce, of Watertown, came from England. Freeman in 1638. A man of good estate. Projected settlement at Sudbury and Lancaster. Died May 9, 1661. Will probated the October following. In it he provides for wife, Elizabeth, "Eldest Son" Anthony, and other children, whom he does not name; but his widow, in her will names children: Anthony; John; Robert; Ester Morse, wife of Joseph; Mary Coldham; Judith, who married Francis Wyman; Elizabeth, who married John Ball, Jr.

Moses (4) Marsh, Moses (3), John (2), Alexander (1), born 1774, at Braintree, Massachusetts. Removed to Chesterfield, New Hampshire, where he served in revolutionary war, as private in Colonel Samuel Ashley's company, Chesterfield, New Hampshire. In 1779 he purchased in the town of Rockingham, Vermont, "three ninety acre Lotts, being Lotts Number Eleven, Twelve and Thirteen, in the Fourth Range of Ninety Acre Lotts in said Rockingham, said Land being forfeited to this State by James Rogers, by his Treasonable Conduct—in consideration of six hundred pounds Lawful Money."

He married, in 1764, Jerusha (4), daughter of Joseph Owen, in Braintree, Massachusetts. He was a large landowner, and man of affairs in town, holding different offices. They had numerous offspring. His wife died, and he married (second) Ester Day, of Rockingham. No children. Children by first wife: Joseph (5), born 1769, Braintree, married Joanna Pierce; Thomas; Mariah; Jerusha, married, 1788, Phineas White; Sally; Moses, married, 1799, Betsey Campbell; Betsey, baptized 1779, married ——— Boyington; Daniel, baptized 1779, married Martha Bailey; Polly, baptized 1785, married ——— Burt; Samuel, baptized 1785; Phebe, baptized 1787, married, 1802, Christopher Lovell; John.

Joseph (3) Owen, born 1720, Braintree, Massachusetts. Estate probated 1760, died in Provincial service in Boston. He married, in 1742, Elizabeth (5), daughter of John (4) Newcomb and wife, Mary. Their children: Anne Owen, born 1742-43; Betty, born 1744; Jerusha, born 1747, married, 1764, Moses Marsh; Sarah, 174—, married, 1768, Silas Hollis; Elizabeth, born 1750; John, born 1753.

(The Newcomb Line).

John (3) and wife, Elizabeth; John (2), Francis (1), came in the "Planter" to Boston at the age of thirty years, with his wife, Rachel, who was twenty years old in 1635; settled first in Boston, then in Braintree. He died at the age of one hundred years. See "Savage's Genealogy of Newcomb Family."

Joseph (2) Owen, born 1695, Braintree, married, 1718, Elizabeth, born 1694, daughter of John and Humellis Williams, of Boston.

Their children: Joseph, born 1720, married Elizabeth Newcomb; Elizabeth, born 1722; John, born 1726.

Nathaniel (1) Owen, died 1733, Braintree, Massachusetts. Married Mary ———. Large estate; gave thirty pounds to Harvard College, after providing for his family and giving them a liberal education. Their children: Nathaniel, born 1683 or 1684, married, 1714, Deborah Parmenter; Benjamin, born 1691; Joseph, born 1695, married, in 1718, Elizabeth Williams; William, born 1697, died 1702; John, born 1699; Mary, born 1702, married, 1723, Thomas French; Sarah, born 1708, died young.

The Owen family was of rugged and sturdy Puritan stock.

Moses (3) Marsh, John (2), Lieutenant Alexander (1), born 1713, at Braintree, Massachusetts. He was a man of wealth and prominence; was drafted into "His Majesty's Service," and regardless of influence was obliged to serve, and died from exposure at Greenbush, New York. He married, in 1739, Sarah (4), daughter of Simon (3) Crosby and Rachel, his wife. She married (second) in 1761, William Hayden, of Boston. Their children: Mary, born 1740, died young; Sarah, born 1741, married Samuel Peck; Moses, born 1743-44, married Jerusha Owen; Rachel, born 1746, married Joseph Brackett; Anna, baptized 1749, married ——— Thomas; Phebe, baptized 1753, died 1839, unmarried; Mary, born 1750, married, 1777, Jonathan Damon, of Dedham.

(The Crosby Line—Puritan Strain).

Simon (3) Crosby, Joseph (2), Simon (1), 1688-1755, Braintree. Married Rachel ———. He held property in partnership with his brethren, Joseph, Thomas and Ebenezer. Will proved June 27, 1755. Children: Samuel; Joseph; Simon; Timothy; Richard; Elizabeth; Sarah, married Moses Marsh; Matthew (?) (Martha); Mary; Anna.

Joseph (2) Crosby, 1639-1695, Braintree. He was representative to great and general court in 1689; soldier in King Philip's Indian war, 1675-1676. Vide Bodges History. He went against "Mount Hope," also to defence of Marlborough. He married (first) in 1675, Sarah, daughter of Richard Brackett and wife, Alice. Married (second) Elin ———. Children: Sarah, born 1677; Thomas, born 1688 or 1689, married ———; Simon, married Rachel ———; Joseph, married, 1726, Abigail Adams; Ebenezer, born 1694 (by wife Elin), married Bathsheba Beale.

Richard (1) Brackett, born 1611, in England, was in Boston in 1632; freeman in 1636; member of Artillery Company in 1639. Dismissed, with wife Alice, from Boston church to Braintree, December 5, 1641; ordained deacon in 1642; town clerk for many years; was the third captain of train band of Braintree; he was a magistrate and served the town as deputy to general court. Married Alice ———. Died in 1691. Children: Hannah, baptized 1635, married Samuel Kingsley; Peter, baptized 1637, married Elizabeth Bosworth; John, married Hannah French; Rachel, born 1638, married, July 15, 1659, Simon Crosby; Mary, born 1642 married, 1662, Joseph Thompson; James, married Sarah ———; Josiah, born 1652, settled in Billerica; Sarah, married, in 1675, Joseph Crosby.

Simon (1) Crosby, born 1609, in England, died in 1639, at Cambridge, Massachusetts. Came to the "Susan and Ellen," 1635, freeman in 1636, selectman in 1636, 1637 and 1638. His estate finally passed into the possession of the Brattle family. Brattle House is on a portion of it. He married Anna ———. Children: Thomas, "aged six weeks," born England, or "seaborn," Harvard College, 1653; clergyman; settled in Eastham, Massachusetts; died in Boston, 1702; had several children; Simon, born 1637, married Rachel Brockett, daughter of Richard Brockett (1); Joseph, born 1639, married Sarah Brockett, daughter of Richard Brockett (1). The widow of the emigrant married (second) an early minister in Braintree, which evidences that she was a woman of fine quality. The Bracketts were people of means in Boston and Braintree.

John (2) Marsh, son of Lieutenant Alexander Marsh, 1678-1747, resided at Braintree, "Gentleman" of landed estate, and large business interests bequeathed by his father. His estate was divided among his heirs, June 24, 1747. He married, 1701, Sarah, born at New Haven, 1684, daughter of Dr. John (6) Wilson, and wife, Sarah (2) Newton. Their children: John, born 1702, married Submit Woodward, settled in East Haddon, Connecticut; Sarah, born 1704, married, 1748, John Hall, of Hingham; Alexander, born 1705, died 1706; Alexander, baptized 1707, married Hannah Parmenter, settled in Holliston, Massachusetts; Ambrose, baptized 1709; Wilson, born 1711, married a widow, Abigail Allen, daughter of

Rev. Experience Mayhew, of Martha's Vineyard; Moses, born 1713, married Jemima Spear, settled in 1760 in Nova Scotia; Edmund, born in 1720, died 1728; Mary, born 1722, died 1722; Ezekiel, born 1724, died in infancy.

(The Wilson Family of Boston and England).

Dr. John (6) Wilson, Rev. John (5), Rev. John (4), Rev. William, D. D. (3), William (2), gent., William (1)—born in Midfield in 1666. Educated at Harvard College. In 1692 removed to Braintree, settling on land willed to him by his father. Here he resided, cultivated the farm, practicing medicine and performing legal services until his death in 1728. By reason of his education, large estate, and distinguished ministerial family connections, he occupied a leading social position, and was popular and prominent in town affairs from 1695 to 1710, often serving on committees and as moderator at town meetings, and was representative to the general court in 1698. In 1696 he received a commission as captain of one of the local military companies, and on June 7, 1700, was appointed justice of the peace, offices of distinction at that time. He married, in 1683, his cousin Sarah, born 1662, daughter of Rev. Roger (1) and Mary (Hooker) Newton. Mr. Newton came to New England when a youth, and was educated for the ministry by Rev. Thomas Hooker, whose daughter he later married; was minister at Farmington, Connecticut, 1652-1657; went back to England, but returned in 1660, and was settled over the church at Milford, Connecticut, where he died in 1683. His wife died in 1676.

Rev. John (5) Wilson, born in England in 1621; was brought to New England by his father on the latter's second voyage, 1632. He was graduated in the first class at Harvard College, in 1642, was admitted to his father's church in Boston in 1644, and was freeman in 1647. After preaching several years he became assistant to Rev. Richard Mather, at Dorchester in 1649, and after two years' service here removed to Midfield, soon after the settlement of that place, and in December, 1651, he was installed as the first minister of the town, where he was ordained pastor, October 12, 1652, in which service he continued for forty years, until his death, besides performing the duties of physician and schoolmaster. By a contemporary he is referred to as "gracious and godly, a faithful and useful man, well esteemed." He died in 1691. He married, about 1648, Sarah (2), daughter of Rev. Thomas (1) and Susannah Hooker, of Hartford, Connecticut.

Mr. Hooker, a powerful and distinguished Puritan preacher, was born at Marfield, county Leicester, England, in 1586; educated at Emmanuel College, Cambridge, B. A., 1608, M. A., 1611, fellow of the University, 1612-1620, rector of Esher, county Surrey, 1620-1625; preached at Chelmsford, 1625-1629, where he was silenced for non-conformity; being persecuted he went to Holland, where he preached two years at Delfthaven, and a few months at Rotterdam, as assistant to Rev. Dr. Ames; came to New England in 1633, and located first at Cambridge, whence in June, 1636, he removed to Hartford, Connecticut, where he served as minister until his death in 1647.

Rev. John (4) Wilson—Rev. William (3), D. D., William (2), gent., William (1)—born at Windsor, England, in 1588. After four years' preparation at Eton School, he was admitted to King's College, Cambridge, in 1602. While at the University he became deeply interested in the theological discussion of the day, and under the influence of Rev. Richard Rogers, of Wethersfield, and of the celebrated Rev. William Ames, D. D., he soon became converted to the principles of the Puritans. His non-conformity resulted in his being obliged to leave the University for a time, and he entered one of the Inns of Court to study for the legal profession, but, his disposition for the ministry continuing, by the father's influence, he was returned to the University, where, at Christ College, he obtained the degree of B. A. in 1606 and M. A. in 1609. After preaching in several places and being persecuted and frequently suspended for his nonconformity, he encouraged and supported the colonization of the Massachusetts Bay, and joined the first emigration, coming to New England in the spring of 1630, in the "Arbella," with Governor Winthrop, leaving his wife and children in England. Soon after the arrival of the company the First Church of Boston was organized, on July 30, 1630, John Wilson being installed as teacher. After laboring for nearly a year, and filling an important part in establishing the colony on a permanently prosperous basis, he went back to England, in 1631, returning to Boston in May, 1632, with his wife, son John and daughter Elizabeth. A few months after his return he was installed as pastor of the church, November 23, 1632, being succeeded as teacher by the celebrated Rev. John Cotton. He continued as pastor until his death in 1652.

Many contemporary writers and records bear witness to the high esteem and veneration in which Rev. John Wilson was held. While not endowed with as brilliant talents as the Rev. John Cotton, he was, nevertheless, a devout, learned, zealous and able man, and his sympathetic nature, kindness of heart and generosity to the needy, greatly endeared him to his parishioners. Of his character Cotton Mather says: "If the picture of this good, and therein great, man were to be exactly given, great zeal with great love would be the two principal strokes, that joined with orthodoxy should make up his portraiture." The Rev. John (4) Wilson went as chaplain in the expedition against the Pequot Indians. During his ministry he frequently made visits to the Indian settlements with Rev. John Eliot, the "Apostle" and labored as a missionary to the savages.

Hooker and Wilson created much history. They are "Founders" of Commonwealths. Connecticut and Massachusetts are what these men and their associates proposed and carried out.

Thomas Hooker was author of the first written constitution forming a government, which is the government of the United States. The Rev. Samuel Stone was selected as an "assistant unto Mr. Hooker, with something of a disciple also."

Rev. William (3) Wilson, born 1542, graduated from Merton College, Oxford, B. A., 1564, M. A., 1570, B. D., 1576, D. D., 1607; prebendary of St. Paul's, London, 1595, 1615, and of Rochester Cathedral, 1591-1614; and about 1580 he became chaplain to Edmund Grindall, archbishop of Canterbury, and in 1583 he became canon of Windsor, holding this position for thirty-two years, until his death, in 1615. He was buried in the chapel of St. George, Windsor Castle, where a monumental brass to his memory states that he was "beloved of all in his life, and much lamented in his death." He married (first) 1575, Isabel, daughter of John Woodhall, Esq., of Walden, county Essex, by Elizabeth, his wife, sister of Edmund Grindall, the celebrated Puritan archbishop of Canterbury, described by Lord Bacon as "the gravest and greatest prelate of the land." He married (second) Anne, sister of Rev. Erasmus Webb, canon of Windsor, who died in 1612, without issue.

William (2) Wilson, gent., born 1515, removed from Penrith and settled at Welbourn, county Lincoln. He acquired considerable estate, and on March 24, 1586, had confirmation of the following coat-of-arms, and grant of a crest: Arms, per pale argent and azure three lion's gambs erased fessways in pale counterchanged; crest, a lion's head argent guttee de sang. He died at Windsor Castle (where his son William was prebendary) 1587, and was buried in the chapel of St. George, where a monument was erected to his memory. The name of his wife has not been learned.

William (1) Wilson, of Penrith, county Cumberland, born probably within a decade of 1490, is the earliest ancestor yet known to whom an unbroken line can be traced in the family herein treated.

The last male descendant in America, bearing the family name of Rev. John (4) Wilson, the first minister of Boston, is one, Edward Smith Wilson, a musician living in New York City, married Jennie Stone, and has had no children.

The name Wilson being of patronymic origin, it is evident that numerous distinct family lines bearing the name were founded in England at various times, and places by individuals in no degree related; and as hereditary family names did not come in vogue until about the reign of Edward I. (except among the nobility and landed families) it is not likely that any Wilson family was permanently established bearing the name continuously, until toward the close of the reign of the above sovereign (circa A. D., 1300). "New England Historic Genealogical Society," 1907.

Lieutenant Alexander (1) Marsh, of Braintree, county of Suffolk, within his Maj:s. Province of Massachusetts Bay, in New England, yeoman. Left an estate at his death, 1698, valued at £1290,18.04. His parentage has not been found. He was lieutenant of the Braintree train band, and evidently was a man of affairs and good position, as he married (first) in 1655, Mary, daughter of Gregory (1) Belcher, and wife, Catherine, a leading business man, and in company with him ran a "furnace" in Braintree. From his will we gather that he had other financial interests besides that of smelting iron ore. He married (second) Bathsheba, daughter of Rev. John Letterup, of Barnstable.

Gregory (1) Belcher, born 1605; came into New England before 1637; was a freeman in 1640; was one of the founders of the church in Braintree.

DELO
Among those who peopled North America there are none whose history is fraught with more interest and is more difficult to trace in its genealogy than that of the French Huguenots. For three centuries they were the flower and wealth of the French Empire—the artisans, mechanics and manufacturers, and among the most intelligent citizenship. Yet they were the most persecuted people of almost all history, because of their religion—the purest system of faith and practice, for the time, in all Europe. Contending for religious liberty, they gave their lives and blood on the altar of freedom that they might worship God according to the dictates of conscience, with an open Bible before them. At last, when greatly decreased in numbers, they expatriated themselves, taking refuge in the English Isles, Holland, Switzerland and Germany. Many of them came to the American colonies—to New England, Maryland, Vermont, Virginia and the Carolinas. To trace many of these families is impossible. Names were changed, suffixes dropped, and translations made into other languages. Their descendants are among the best citizens, and have given eminent men to positions of trust and responsibility in church and state.

Before the revolutionary war, three brothers—Michael, Joseph and Charles Delo, Huguenots—came to Westmoreland, Virginia, which then embraced the southwestern part of Pennsylvania. Governor Dunmore held court at Pittsburgh, then Fort Duquesne, in 1774. He changed the name to Fort Dunmore. Joseph Delo went down the Ohio, and Charles went east, possibly into Maryland; Michael Delo located in the vicinity of Greensburg. He was a soldier and was killed in an ambuscade by the Indians, leaving a son, George; his wife was Mary Kiefer. It was about 1773 when Mr. Delo was killed. The widow later married Jacob Smith; they raised a large family of sons and daughters, many of whose descendants are in Clarion county, connected with the Brenemans, McLains, McNaughtons and other families.

George Delo, son of Michael and Mary (Kiefer) Delo, was born in Westmoreland, in 1773, about the time his father was killed. When he came to manhood he married Eve Catherine Kuhns. The Kuhns family is quite numerous in Westmoreland and Clarion counties. In 1807 he moved to a place about four miles southwest of the present location of Clarion. Three years later he sold his land to his half-brother, Henry Smith, and moved to the mouth of Piney, on the Clarion river. Delo's Eddy, on the Clarion, took its name from him. Not long after he moved to a bluff on the Clarion between the mouths of Canoe and Beaver creeks, where he had secured a large tract of land. His wife's brother, John Kuhns, joined lands with him; another, Christian Kuhns, moved in 1813 to a farm joining the present Reedsburg. Mr. Delo erected a sawmill at the mouth of Canoe creek, and about a half mile below a boat scaffold on the river bank, in 1815, and engaged in lumbering and boat-building, at the same time clearing a large and beautiful farm, with large and substantial frame buildings. In 1840 he sold his sawmill to Maxon O'Dell. In 1818 the wife of Henry Smith was killed by a cow. Some time after he visited Mr. Delo, who inquired after his circumstances. He replied that it was hard to get along without a mother in so large a family. Mr. Delo said: "You should get you a wife." He replied: "I have no time to hunt one." Mr. Delo told him he had a neighbor, a widow with a number of children, and "when you come again I will take you up and introduce you." Several years passed. In February, 1820, Mrs. Delo died, and when Mr. Smith came again Mr. Delo had married the widow. She was Eve, oldest daughter of Christopher Hummel, one of the founders of Hummelstown, in Dauphin county, who had been a teamster in Washington's army. They were of German stock. She had married Daniel Loughner, a son of Rudolph Loughner, of Westmoreland. He died at the mouth of the Tiscaminitas in 1812. The widow at once moved to Beaver township, where her brothers, Samuel and Henry, and other members of the family, lived. A sister, Susan Hummel, married William Mays, three of whose sons are living in Clarion county—Samuel H., a veteran of the civil war; David, and John. When Mr. Delo married the widow he had nine children and she had six. Of the Loughner children, Barnet, Michael, Samuel and Daniel, were tradesmen, and all violinists;

their descendants are numerous. Christianna married Daniel Delo, and Susan married Reuben Fowles, a native of Juniata county; two of their sons were veterans of the civil war— A. R., and William. About 1842, Mr. Delo bought three hundred acres of land at Walnut Bend, on the east side of the Allegheny river, in Venango county, including the islands. Here he laid out a town and named it Georgetown. It became considerable of a place during the oil excitement in the sixties. In 1865 land there sold for $1,000 an acre. Indians were often guests of Mr. Delo, but they had no fixed location in the county. The territory seems to have been reserved for hunting grounds. There were many evidences of their camps in earlier times. There was an Indian by the name of Jack Snow, who had been in the habit of coming up the Clarion and camping on its banks for some years to hunt and fish. The last time he came was in the fall of 1809. With his party of hunters and squaws they set their camp at the mouth of Deer creek. After a short time Snow got into a quarrel with some white men who had gone to his camp; after they had left, one threatened to shoot Snow the first opportunity offered. Mr. Delo went over the river and advised Snow to leave, telling him that his life had been threatened. Snow at once left. The camp fixtures, meat, traps, etc., were packed into their canoes, and hunters and squaws, with their boats, went down the river, never again to return and camp along the stream. They, however, for years traveled through the country, it was thought to visit lead deposits. Several of them came at one time and lodged with Mr. Delo one night. In the morning before breakfast they went out into the woods and soon returned with a quantity of lead ore. Mr. Delo was somewhat of a hunter before he left Westmoreland county. From the vicinity of Greensburg, he with two others followed the track of a large panther; on the evening of the second day, at Freeport, they lost the trail. His companions, discouraged, returned home, but Mr. Delo after some effort found the track on the third day. He followed this on a chestnut ridge; after a time he came on his own tracks. The hunter had become the hunted. They soon looked into each other's eyes, and a practiced hand and keen sight laid out the panther. An old physician, Dr. Meeker, said the skin measured eleven feet from point of nose to tip of tail, that it was stuffed and sent to Philadelphia. Possibly true. At the mouth of Canoe creek, Mr. Delo saw a panther on a rock on the opposite side of the river watching for a fish breakfast. He shot her and got twenty dollars for the scalps of the mother and two cubs. Once he shot a bear and gave the skin to a neighbor, who said: "Sure, Mr. Delo, ven you was so gute as to gif me de skin, mebby you gif me de hear too." The skin was of no value, but the meat was a necessity. Deer and bear were to be had at almost any time; fish also, filled the streams, great shoals of them, were in the Clarion river, pike, salmon and bass, with suckers and smaller fry. The creeks were full of speckled mountain trout.

Mr. Delo served two campaigns in Captain Neely's company from Venango county, at Erie, in the war of 1812. He and his family were Lutherans in religious belief. He died March 11, 1848, when he had living nine sons and three daughters. One daughter, Polly Keiser, wife of George Keiser, had died in 1845. The oldest son was Daniel, of whom below.

Joseph, son of George and Eve Catherine (Kuhns) Delo, was born in Hempfield township, Westmoreland county, in 1801. When he came to manhood he married Susan Best, of Beaver township, Clarion county, where he purchased a farm. They had four sons and four daughters when his wife died. He then married Rebecca Wiles, who blest him with three daughters and three sons. Among them were the following: 1. Joseph, married a Miss Ashbaugh. 2. George Adam, was twice married, and lives in Centerville, McKean county. 3. Daniel, married a Miss Lamb, of Clarion township; he died in 1910; they have two daughters living in Warren, Pennsylvania. 4. David, living in Enterprise, Warren county; married, and has a daughter living, a teacher. 5. Mary, married John Black, of Licking township. 6. Susan, married George Baker; she is deceased. 7. Elizabeth, married John Shively; she died without issue. Of the second wife's children: Simeon served in the civil war, married Miss Stover, and have a family; William, lives in Pittsburgh, married a Miss Canan, of Millcreek township; Amos, a local preacher in the Methodist Episcopal church, deceased, married a Miss Barnet.

Jacob Delo, son of George and Eve Catherine (Kuhns) Delo, married a Miss Silvis; they moved to McKeesport in 1840, where he was mine boss for some time; an injury made him a cripple for life; he had a son killed in the civil war, and another son was also in the civil war; a grandson, David Delo, lives in Carnegie, Pennsylvania, and has two sons—John and Albert. George P., son of George and Eve Catherine (Kuhns) Delo, married Betsy Best; they had four sons and a number of daughters; one son, Rev. I. J., is a Lutheran minister. John, son of George and Eve Catherine (Kuhns) Delo, died without issue. David, son of George and Eve Catherine (Kuhns) Delo, married a Miss Logan of Kittanning, Armstrong county; in 1840 he moved to Wheeling, West Virginia; he was a coach maker; during the civil war he was in service, and was superintendent of artillery wagon shops in Chattanooga, Tennessee; his son Watson lost a leg in the civil war; was a printer and was employed in the government printing department; deceased, leaving a widow, four daughters and a son, who reside in Washington, D. C. Another son of David, Rev. Frank Delo, is a Lutheran minister in the west. David Delo died at the age of eighty-five years. Anna, daughter of George and Eve Catherine (Kuhns) Delo, married Daniel Winger, of Beaver township; they had a family of five children when she died. Of the sons, John J. was a minister of the Methodist Episcopal church. He built the first Methodist church building in Kansas City, was a missionary in Arizona and New Mexico. After twenty years of earnest work on the frontier his eyesight failed. He died at Los Angeles, California. Simon, a veteran of the civil war, died in Michigan in 1910; Reuben, another veteran son, lives in Beaver township; Susan McDowell, a daughter, aged eighty-five years, lives in Beaver township; Katharine Murphy, died in Illinois. Esther Fry, another daughter of George and Eve Catherine (Kuhns) Delo, died in Missouri aged ninety-five years and five months, at the home of her son, Isaac Fry. Eve, daughter of George and Eve (Hummel) Delo, married Slocum Kerr, a physician; they went to Cincinnati in 1840; a second husband was Jacob Reiche, who lived near Chicago, where she died. Henry J., son of George and Eve (Hummel) Delo, married Hannah Barr, of Beaver township; for a time they lived at Walnut Bend, and then moved to Elkhart, Indiana, on a farm, where he died; his descendants live in that vicinity. Louis, son of George and Eve (Hummel) Delo, married Caroline Lobaugh, of Licking township. They are both deceased; they have a number of children living: Reuben F. and two brothers live in the Bradford oil field. Rev. Reuben F. Delo, son of George and Eve (Hummel) Delo, a Lutheran minister, was educated in the common schools and Wittenberg College, at Springfield, Ohio; his pastorates were at Elkhart, Indiana, and Three Rivers, Michigan; he died in Colorado; he was chaplain of an Ohio regiment of volunteers during the civil war. All the sons of George Delo were active in church work and liberal in support thereof. Three of them taught in the public schools of the county.

Daniel Delo, first born son of George and Eve Catherine (Kuhns) Delo, was born December 9, 1779, in Hempfield township, Westmoreland county. He was seven years old when he came with his parents to Clarion county, then Armstrong county. A year later he had three months in school, all he ever had. Some time later he went with his father on a flatboat to Pittsburgh, where he purchased a Testament, which became his daily companion and study. When resting his horses in the plow he would sit on the plow beam or under a tree and read until his mind became filled with the wonderful story of the Christ and His tragic death. In his old age he related to his son Benjamin this experience: While resting his horses he sat under a tree reading and in meditation. Suddenly there appeared before him the Christ with the print of the nails in His hands and the thrust of the spear in His side, with a halo of light enswathing His person. He saw the risen Christ as Thomas had seen Him. He had never seen any pictures at any time and there were none about the house. In explanation he remarked that becoming so familiar with the facts impressed upon his mind a mental image was formed and thrust out before his eyes. At the age of fourteen he had his right shoulder dislocated; all efforts failed to adjust it, notwithstanding six months spent under the treatment of Dr. Merchant, of Greensburg. During this period he made his home with his uncle, David Keifer. Not being able to do manual labor, he procured books and gave himself to study. In the evenings a pine torch afforded him light. At the age of eighteen he taught his first school, on Cherry Run, in Clarion county, on the Louis Wilson farm. He subsequently taught at Leatherwood, Churchville, and at Alts, in Beaver township, where for some time he had a select school to which students came from other neighborhoods, boarding in the vicinity. Among those was John Over, who came especially to study German. Mr. Over died in Clarion at the age of ninety-four years, in 1900. He was the father of Judge Over, of the orphans' court of Allegheny county. Mr. Delo served as constable for several years. In 1823 he married his stepsister, Christiana Loughner. They had thirteen children: two died in infancy, one at ten years. In 1828 Mr. Delo was appointed justice of the peace by Governor Shulze, for the townships of Richland, Rockland, Elk, Paint and Beaver, in Venango county. The territory extended on the west side of the river, from the mouth of the Clarion to Horse Creek on the Allegheny, taking in all of what is now Clarion county, west of the Clarion, and part of what is now Venango. He labored especially for the adoption of the common school law. He served one term as auditor of Venango county. After serving fourteen years in the office of justice, he was elected sheriff of Clarion county and served a term, and was deputy for the two succeeding terms. In 1844 he was a campaign speaker for the Democratic party, and was especially sought after for his capabilities as a German orator. He was appointed colonel on Governor Shunk's staff. He had then been captain of a militia company for fifteen years. He was one of the owners and builders of Eagle Furnace on his land, where he had a sawmill, having formerly been engaged in boatbuilding and lumbering. In 1847 he sold his interest in Eagle Furnace and bought the Great Western Hotel in Clarion, which he conducted for three years, when he sold out. In 1853 he was appointed weighmaster on the Pennsylvania canal at Hollidaysburg, and also served three years as cargo inspector; then was for a short time weighmaster for the P. R. R. at Johnstown. Returning to Clarion, he taught school one winter, and in 1860 was elected prothonotary of the county and served one term. In the beginning of the civil war he drilled the first volunteers enlisted in Clarion, and went over the county speaking at mass meetings for enlistments. He subsequently served a term as justice and was for a number of years president of the school board and tax collector. Soon after their marriage Mr. and Mrs. Delo united with the German Reformed church; he was treasurer of the classis of that church in Clarion county. At Hollidaysburg they united with the Lutheran church, and on their return to Clarion became members of the Presbyterian church, of which he was a ruling elder for twenty years. He never departed from one great interest—the education of the people and their religious culture in the Sunday school. He was spiritually minded, and his home was ever open to all ministers of the gospel. Mrs. Delo was an ideal mother and housekeeper, and was of wonderfully well balanced mind, an assistant to her husband in counsel, and of loving and tender heart. Mr. Delo died October 19, 1877, aged seventy-eight years, and his wife went to her reward only six weeks later, aged seventy years. They were buried in Clarion cemetery. Few people were so universally esteemed. All classes gave them honor and their memory abides as ointment poured forth.

Dr. George Washington Delo, son of Daniel and Christiana (Loughner) Delo, was born March 14, 1824, in Beaver township, Clarion county. He was educated in the common schools, and added thereto by close application thereafter. He married Sophia Wheaton, daughter of Charles Wheaton; she was a native of New Jersey, and came to Pennsylvania when she was four years old. They were highly esteemed in the communities where they lived. They had an old-fashioned family of thirteen children; three died in infancy, the living ones are: C. A., a coachmaker in Frisco shops, Springfield, Missouri, is married and has a family of four children. William R., married Sadie Adams, of Rockland, Venango county; he operated in the Bradford (Pennsylvania) oilfield, and state of Indiana, where he died in 1910; his widow lives in Franklin, Pennsylvania, and a daughter, Lenore Coswell, lives in Bartleville, Oklahoma. John A. is a brickmason, in Springfield, Missouri, and has a family. Mary E., widow of Benjamin La Belle, lives in Springfield, Missouri. Wesley B. is a brickmason, and lives in Springfield, Missouri. Maria, wife of George Atterbury, resides on a farm near Springfield, Missouri. George F. is a railroad man of Kansas City. Joshua H. is a carmaker in the Frisco shops, Springfield. Hannah J. is the wife of L. B. Cooper, and lives on the farm with her father, the mother having died a few years ago, aged eighty-two years. George W. Delo, the father, was a carpenter in his early manhood, later he studied medicine. He had taught school for several winters. For some years he lived in the oilfield of Oil Creek, Pennsylvania; then in Clarion county. In 1857 he moved to Elkhart, Indiana, thence to northern Alabama, where he practiced medicine in connection with agricultural pursuits. The Kuklux sent him several death notices. He finally sold out his plantation at a sacrifice and moved to a farm joining the city line of Springfield, Missouri, where he has prospered, and in his eighty-ninth year is a well preserved man, physically and mentally, and has a competence for his old age. He and his wife held membership in the Lutheran and Methodist Episcopal churches in their changes of residence. He is a Prohibitionist.

Rev. John A. Delo, second child and son of Daniel and Christiana (Loughner) Delo, was born April 15, 1826. He had a common school education, and for a time was a clerk at Eagle Furnace. He had united with the Methodist Episcopal church when sixteen years of age, but transferred his membership to the Evangelical Lutheran. Feeling called to the ministry, he studied for a time with his pastor, Rev. Witt, in Shippensville, and finished his course in Wittenberg College, at Springfield, Ohio. During his first pastorate at Marionville, Pennsylvania, he married Amelia Buffon, in 1855. He after had pastorates at North Washington, Butler county, and Apollo, Armstrong county. From Apollo he went into the army as chaplain of the Eleventh Regiment Pennsylvania Reserve Volunteers. He went with his regiment through the Wilderness campaign, to the James river, where they were discharged. He had contracted a chronic disease, and the same fall, November 1, 1864, he died at North Washington, Butler county, Pennsylvania, where he is interred. He was a man of deep piety and much more than ordinary pulpit ability. The veterans of his regiment have spoken of him as an ideal chaplain in camp and in hospital, ever on the lookout for their physical and spiritual good. He and his wife were the parents of one daughter, Alice, and two sons, Alonzo and Howe. Alonzo was an artist in Pittsburgh, died leaving two children; the mother also died, and the children are in the care of Alice Delo, who is unmarried. Rev. Howe Delo, the other son of John A. Delo, was a Lutheran minister at Beaver Falls, Pennsylvania; he had consumption, went to Texas for relief but died there in Austin.

Abigail, daughter of Daniel and Christiana (Loughner) Delo, married Abraham K. Page, of Juniata county, Pennsylvania. She was born in Beaver township, June, 1828, and died in 1907, aged seventy-nine years. Mr. Page was long engaged in the furniture and undertaking business in Clarion. Their children are: 1. William E., married Louisa Brinkley, of Clarion, and has two sons married: William E. and Charles; all are painters and decorators. 2. Benjamin F., married Carrie Fleming, and is the successor of his father in the furniture and undertaking business in Clarion. Their children are: Ora, wife of John W. Cyphert, locomotive engineer of Union City, Pennsylvania; Mary B. Hood, of Seattle, Washington; Ruby, married Charles Wensel, cigar manufacturer of Clarion, they have two children: B. F. Jr., and Paul A. The Flemings are a large connection in Clarion county and are sturdy Scotch stock. B. F. Page also had three other children who are deceased. 3. James, married Erdine Reyner, of Knox, Pennsylvania; they have a son Wayne and a daughter. Mr. Page was engaged in the grocery trade, is now deceased, and his widow carries on the business successfully. 4. George B. is a painter and decorator in Clarion. He married Nora Neely; their children are: Abraham K., Abigail Delo, George Neely, and Harold Earl. 5. Mary, married N. B. Rowley, of Chester, West Virginia. They have two daughters: Abigail, a student in college, and Mary, at home. Mr. Rowley is a general traveling agent. 6. Christiana, married M. L. Longnaker; they have one daughter. Mr. Longnaker is a bookkeeper for the Westinghouse Electric Company, East Pittsburgh. They reside in Wilkinsburg, Pennsylvania.

Mrs. A. K. Page was a Presbyterian, also her son William and Mrs. Longnaker; B. F. and family and the Rowleys are Baptists. George B. and family are Presbyterians, and Mrs. James Page is a Lutheran.

Jeremiah, son of Daniel and Christiana (Loughner) Delo, was born in Beaver township, July 3, 1830. His education was in the common schools of Clarion. In 1850 he united with the Methodist Episcopal church. He then organized the first church choir of Clarion; then went to Meadville, was a carpenter and contractor, choir leader in the First Methodist Episcopal Church, and married Melvina

Lane, whose parents, Mr. and Mrs. Ross Lane, came from Chautauqua county, New York. Their four children are living: Eva Bell, Harriet O., and Charles, in Altoona, Pennsylvania, and William, married, superintendent of pattern department, shops of P. R. R. at Bellevue, Allegheny county, Pennsylvania. In 1858 Jeremiah Delo moved to Altoona, Pennsylvania, and for a short time was carpenter for the P. R. R., when he was appointed weighmaster. When first appointed he had three hours' work in the day and his assistant three at night. After serving forty-one years he was retired on age limit, when superintendent of weighing, with seventeen assistants who were constantly employed. Such was the increase of tonnage in his time of service. His wife died in 1870. In 1872 he married Charlotta Wandel, of Salem, Clarion county, daughter of William Wandel. At once, on moving to Altoona, he took charge of the choir of the First Methodist Episcopal Church. When the Eighth Avenue Methodist Episcopal Church was organized he filled the same position there. He was chairman of the building committee, constructing two successive church buildings for this organization, and on the committee that built the present beautiful and costly edifice. He was a most exemplary Christian, and had the confidence of all who knew him. During his retirement he enjoyed a most happy life for several years, when his health failed and he gradually came peacefully to the translation to the better life.

Herman Levi, son of Daniel and Christiana (Loughner) Delo, was born in Beaver township, Clarion county, Pennsylvania, June 4, 1836. He was educated in the common schools and academy of Clarion. He married Sarah Eliza, daughter of Samuel and Charlotte (Brotherline) Longanecker, of Hollidaysburg, Pennsylvania. He was in the employ of the P. R. R. for fifty-two years and three months, dating from April 1, 1854, to July, 1906, when he was retired by age limit, and was at that time assistant chief motive power clerk of all the P. R. R. lines east of Pittsburgh and Erie. He and his family are members of the Lutheran church. For many years he was the organist of the First Lutheran Church of Altoona, and he is a prominent member of the F. and A. M., and past commander of Mountain Commandery. Herman L. Delo's children are: Herman E., O. Frank, George H., Howard, Sarah Matilda. Herman E.'s children are: Harry C., has a son Joseph C.; Edward F., has children Dorothea L., Harold E. and Lucial B.; Walter H. and Elma R. O. Frank's children are: Rebekah Elizabeth and Sarah Martha. O. Frank Delo is chief clerk of the middle lines of the P. R. R. George H. is chief clerk of Juniata locomotive works of the P. R. R. Co., where they build their locomotives. Howard is electrician of the eastern grand division and branches between Altoona and Philadelphia. Herman E. is chief inspector of the Altoona & Logan Valley Street railway from Hollidaysburg through Altoona to Tyrone.

Samuel Porter, son of Daniel and Christiana (Loughner) Delo, was born May 1, 1839, in Beaver township, Clarion county. He was married twice, and has a son William by his first wife, who lives in North Baltimore; he is a locomotive engineer on the B. & O. R. R. A son by his second wife lives in Los Angeles, California, with his mother. Samuel P. Delo was a violinist and an expert on nearly all musical instruments. He had a common school education, and became a locomotive engineer on the P. R. R. between Pittsburgh and Fort Wayne. In an accident his arm was broken; after recovery he enlisted in Pittsburgh in the first call for volunteers in the civil war. After serving his term he re-enlisted and became a recruiting sergeant, when he was appointed chief clerk in the provost marshal's office in Meadville, where he remained up to the close of the war. He then traveled for a number of years as a canvasser. Last he was employed as timekeeper for the Southern Pacific R. R. at Birmingham, Alabama, where he died in 1893.

Joshua Hunter, son of Daniel and Christiana (Loughner) Delo, was born October 15, 1841. He was educated in the common schools and academy of Clarion. He married Susan Richards, daughter of Abraham Richards, of Clarion. He clerked for his father in the prothonotary's office until 1862, when he enlisted under Captain B. J. Reid, in Company F, of the Sixty-third Regiment Pennsylvania Volunteers, Colonel Hays commanding. In the beginning of the battle of Fair Oaks or Seven Pines he was killed while as first sergeant, he was forming the company for action; he was buried on the battle field. Following is the last letter he wrote to his wife, also extracts from various sources giving testimony as to the esteem and love in which he was held by friends and associates:

12 Miles from Richmond, Henrico Co., Va., May 28th, 1862.

Dear Wife:—When I last wrote, we had just returned from a picket, having been relieved by the 87th Regiment New York Volunteers. They in turn were relieved by the 57th Regt. Penna. Volunteers on yesterday morning. By custom they should have been relieved by the 105th Regt. Penna. Volunteers, but were not, for what reason I cannot tell. Nothing worthy of note or interest has occurred since being on picket. I am in the enjoyment of excellent health today, and have been for sometime past for which I am thankful to my Heavenly Father.

An order was issued on day before yesterday that all knapsacks and contents were to be sent to the rear, keeping nothing but our woolen blankets, and shelter tents. We are to be encumbered as little as possible in view, I suppose, of approaching conflict. I kept my Bible and likenesses of both mother and yourself, all of which I shall carry with me. We had a delightful shower of rain this afternoon which has effectually cooled the scorching rays of Old Sol.

Evening.—The sun is about setting, the beautiful rays flashing in the heavens, and painting the clouds with a beauty and richness the art of which a painter might court to possess. John is very sick, and has been for several days, hardly being able to walk. He will have to go to the hospital. I hope that his sickness will not be of a very serious character. The health of the company generally is good, that also of the regiment. I do not know when we will leave our present camp. I hope and trust that this war will speedily come to a close, as I am tired of it, yet my love for my fallen and bleeding country is such, that unless I have to be discharged on account of sickness or disability, or death should take me, I will remain and share all its privations, hardships and toils, and while I am fighting for my country, may I also fight the battle of the Cross.

May 29th, 1862, 6½ a. m.—I am in the enjoyment of very good health, as also that of the company. I had a very delightful conversation with Rev. Dr. Marks on last night. He says he will give me a certificate of membership, and a letter to Rev. Montgomery, today. I want to send it as soon as possible, for if there was any danger of Mr. Montgomery leaving this world, I want him to know it before he leaves, as his prayers and supplications are at last answered. I am very sorry to hear that the usually very quiet place of Clarion was so excited that a riot almost occurred. I hope that that riot will be last that Clarion shall ever behold. As it is time for company drill I must close, and I want my letter mailed in time. My love to father, mother and the boys, also to Pages. My most sincere love to you and the children, kiss them for me. I remain as ever your loving and affectionate husband,

JOSHUA H. DELO.

Battle Field of Fair Oaks, Va., June 4th, 1862.

My Dear Friend:—My heart almost fails me when I take my pen to speak of what you already know—the early but glorious death of your son, Sergeant Joshua H. Delo, who fell fighting bravely for the flag of his country on the bloody battle field of Saturday last. It is natural that you should grieve—as well as all who were connected with him by family or social ties. In that grief I sympathize with you deeply. But let it be a source of just pride to you that he has acquitted himself well and fell honorably in the very front of the battle. * * * At dusk we were obliged to fall back, our ammunition being exhausted, and there being evident danger of being surrounded and cut off by the superior numbers of the enemy. We got all our wounded that we could find with us, but could not bring off the dead. The next day, Sunday, the rebels returned to the attack, but when they approached our lines Hooker's division on the left and Sedgwick's and Richardson's on the right, who arrived late in the afternoon of Saturday, met and repulsed them at every point. Our division being in the hottest of the fight on Saturday and having lost severely and rendered great service in checking and driving back the enemy when in full pursuit of Casey's flying columns, was held in reserve in the battle of Sunday. We were kept under arms all day, and no man could leave his post. On this account and because the battle field of Saturday was still disputed ground throughout Sunday, it was impossible for any of us to go where Joshua lay, but on Monday morning there was no longer any obstacles, and I sent out a detail to bury the dead and search for three of my company who were missing. * * * They could not find the body of your son. They found some fresh graves near where he had been carried to, and after considerable search in the vicinity they concluded he must have been buried by some of the other search parties then in the field. We were on the point of giving it up about dusk, when Sergeant Kuhns making another circuit through the bushes found your son. * * * His features were natural and calm. He looked as one that slept a peaceful sleep. We buried him where we found him, under a small oak tree, and marked his name on the tree and on a headboard placed at the grave. I cut a lock of his hair which I enclosed the other day in a letter which I wrote to Mrs. Reid; I suppose you have received it before this. We turned from his grave with sad hearts. We all loved him. The whole company mourns his loss. He had won, too, the respect and esteem of the regimental officers, with whom his duties as orderly brought him into frequent contact. It will be gratifying to you to learn that during the last two months Joshua became more and more impressed with religious feelings. I could notice an increasing seriousness of manner, but there are others who knew his mind more intimately on this subject than I did, and who assure me that he took a deep interest in religion. Present my sincerest condolence to his bereaved widow, to his mother, and all your family.

Very truly your friend,
B. J. REID, CAPT.
Co. F, 63d Reg. P. V.

The following is from the obituary published in the Clarion *Democrat*, 1862:

In the battle of Fair Oaks, now historic, many brave men have fallen, fighting manfully the great battle of the constitution and the government, many hearthstones have been made desolate, and many hearts sad, but over no community did the spirit of mourning brood more heavily than that from which went forth the subject of this notice, when on the still Sabbath morning of the 8th inst. the news spread from house to house that he had fallen, nobly battling for the right in the front ranks of our noble army, while cheering them on to deeds of noble daring. Not twenty-one years of age, he thus fell, leaving the bright example of glorious action and a noble death, falling as brave men love to fall, if fall they must, in the din of battle, with their faces to the foe. In this example, although dead, he yet lives. He leaves behind a sorrowing companion and two orphan children, parents, relatives and friends to mourn his early death; yet for them are the consolations of the word of eternal life, and they mourn not as those without hope—they have the comforting assurance from the letters of his brave and excellent captain, himself and others, that the deceased died a faithful soldier of the Cross, as well as a true soldier of the republic, and for those thus dying, death has no sting, the grave no victory. Let his mourning widow remember Him who saith, "I will be the widow's portion and the orphan's stay;" his parents and relations, that the "Lord gave and the Lord taketh away," and let all say, "It is the Lord, he doeth all things well."   G. W. L.

He had a son Joshua Stanley Delo, who resides in Chicago, Illinois, and Mary Hunter Delo, a graduate of Carrier Seminary and Edinboro Normal School. She is a professional teacher and has taught many terms successfully.

Daniel Alvin, son of Daniel and Christiana (Loughner) Delo, was born in Clarion borough, June 28, 1846. He was educated in Clarion common schools and academy. He served three months in Captain B. B. Dunkle's company at the time of Morgan's raid in Ohio, during the civil war. He also clerked in the provost marshal's office at Meadville to the close of the war. He died in 1865 in Meadville.

Thomas B., son of Daniel and Christiana (Loughner) Delo, was born in Clarion, September 17, 1848. He was educated in the common schools, academy, and Carrier Seminary of Clarion. He taught a term of school in Leatherwood; clerked for some time in Thomas Moffit's store, then for Nathan Myers in Clarion, and then worked in the Clarion *Democrat* office at printing. He went to Altoona, Pennsylvania, in September, 1869, as clerk for the P. R. R. Company. He was married in 1871 to Theodocia E. Moore, daughter of Johnston and Maria Moore, of Altoona, Pennsylvania. By this union there were two children: Ray B. Delo, now assistant cashier of the Second National Bank of Elmira, New York, who married Lily Mason, daughter of W. C. Mason; they have one child, Eleanor Louisa. Dr. J. Moore Delo, of Philadelphia, Pennsylvania; married a daughter of Mr. Hadfield, of Philadelphia, no children. After the decease of the mother of these children, Thomas B. Delo married Clara Adell Van Gorder, daughter of Jacob and Amanda M. Van Gorder, of Elmira, New York, and granddaughter of Colonel E. C. Frost, of Schuyler county, New York. There were no children by this union. Thomas B. Delo moved from Altoona, Pennsylvania, to Elmira, New York, as clerk for the Northern Central Railroad, and has continued in the employ of that company. He is a Presbyterian, and has been choir leader in Altoona and Elmira.

Rev. Benjamin F. Delo, son of Daniel and Christiana (Loughner) Delo was born in Beaver township, Clarion (then Venango) county, April 16, 1832. He was only five years old when he went to his first school; his first teacher was Miss Polly Morgan, who married Rev. George F. Reeser, a Methodist Episcopal minister of the Erie Conference. His other teachers were: Rev. Daniel Kuhns; Peter B. Simpson, who died in Helen township, aged ninety-three years; Daniel B. Hays, an attorney, died in Mercer, Pennsylvania; a Mr. Winal, whose father was a minister of Westmoreland county; Mrs. Gardner, a summer school, and Abraham Alabaugh. On April 1, 1844, the family moved to Clarion. he then went to a summer school kept by Rev. George F. Ehrenfelt. In August, 1844, his father apprenticed him to Reid & Alexander, of the Clarion *Democrat*, to learn the art of printing. A year later Alexander purchased Reid's interest and later sold a half interest to George B. Weaver. The office force consisted at different times of John C. Reid, journeyman, James F. Weaver, later editor in Center county, and colonel in the civil war, and J. P. George, later editor and publisher of the Brookville *Jeffersonian*, who were apprentices. At the end of three years in the office he was a journeyman for a few months; he then attended school for the winter, after which he was journeyman on the Clarion *Banner*, A. J. Gibson, proprietor. In February, 1849, he united with the Methodist Episcopal church in Clarion, and for a short time canvassed as a book agent. The first part of 1850 was spent in study with his brother, John A., at Shippensville. The summer was spent in the Clarion

Banner office. In 1851 he clerked for M. S. Adams at Martinsburg (now Bruin), Butler county, Pennsylvania. The winter following he taught school at Attleberger's schoolhouse, in Beaver township, Clarion county; in March, 1852, he received license as an exhorter in the Methodist Episcopal church. The early part of the summer was spent in charge of the store at Martha Furnace, in preparation for closing up the works. In the fall of 1852, after clerking for Richard Richardson in Shippensville for a time, he went to Meadville, and worked as journeyman for J. C. Hays on the Crawford *Journal*, until the spring of 1853, when he entered as a student in Allegheny College. In the vacation of 1855, July 3d, he was licensed a local preacher of the Methodist Episcopal church, on the Shippensville circuit. In the middle of the fall term at college, he was called as second preacher on Pleasantville circuit. In the fall of 1856 he did some speech making for the Republican party, and entered into the lumbering business. On the 1st of January, 1857, Mr. Delo married Phebe Ann, daughter of Daniel Jr. and Phebe Ann (King) Fleming, of West Hickory, Pennsylvania. Daniel Fleming Sr. came from Allegheny county, son of ——— Fleming, whose wife was a Reed. Daniel Fleming Sr. married Nancy Hardy, of Venango county. She had a brother, ——— Hardy, who kept a hotel on the Franklin and Pittsburgh turnpike. The Kings were from Tioga county, New York (Bainbridge). Of the Flemings it is said their progenitors were from the north of Scotland. In August, 1857, Mr. Delo returned to Meadville and worked as a journeyman for Mitchell & Sears on the *Spirit of the Age*. From January 1, 1858, to August, 1859, he was foreman on the Crawford *Democrat*, ——— Wilson was editor and proprietor. He returned then to lumbering on West Hickory. In August, 1859, Colonel Drake struck petroleum oil, two miles below Titusville, on Watson Flat. The influx of population required an additional preacher in the Methodist Episcopal church of Titusville, in the beginning of 1860, and Mr. Delo filled the place. From July, 1860, to July 1862, he was a missionary on Oil Creek, in the oilfields. He did the first Methodist preaching at Rouseville and Plummer. In 1862, in August, he was appointed on Pleasant Valley circuit. In 1863 he was received as a member of the Erie conference of the Methodist Episcopal church, Bishop Simpson presiding, was ordained a deacon, and appointed to Kinzua, where he preached for three years. His pastorates thereafter were Frewsburg, New York; Cochranton, Youngville, Wheatland, Brookville, Greece City, Petersburg; presiding elder of Brookville and Clarion districts in Pennsylvania. Returning to pastorates he served Callensburg, Knox, agent for Carrier Seminary, and pastor at Clarion. During this last pastorate he led the congregation to build a beautiful church building of native stone at a cost of $35,000, at present valued at $60,000. He continued for several years in itinerant preaching, but on account of his wife's illness he could not move. After having served in the conference for thirty-three years he retired. During his retirement he was three times connected with the Clarion *Republican*. The last time in 1901 when he was editor and publisher. Since then he has had no employment and is now in his eighty-first year. He was the father of only three children: 1. Daniel F., who was educated in the common schools, Carrier Seminary and Allegheny College. After studying law he died at the age of twenty-four years. He was born in Meadville, November 22, 1857; married Mary Frances, daughter of Henry Lewis, of Edinboro, Erie county, Pennsylvania. They had one daughter, Flora Winifred, born in Callensburg, see below. 2. William Chester, was born in West Hickory, Venango county, Pennsylvania, November 26, 1859. He was educated in the common schools and Carrier Seminary; was assistant agent at Clarion, of the B. & O. R. R. and agent at West Clarion. He is unmarried. 3. Mary Ella, was born at Kinzua, Pennsylvania, November 16, 1865, and died at Wheatland, Pennsylvania, aged six years, four months, eleven days.

Flora Winifred, daughter of Daniel F. and Mary Frances (Lewis) Delo, was born at Callensburg, Pennsylvania. She was educated in the common and high schools of Clarion, Clarion Normal and Beaver College, and was always at the head of her classes. She taught two years in the model school of Clarion Normal, at Carnegie, Verona high school, and is at present teaching in the high school at Coraopolis, Pennsylvania.

Rev. B. F. Delo is a Mason, being a member of Clarion Lodge, No. 277, F. and A. M., and the Grand Lodge of Pennsylvania; Eden Chapter, No. 259, Royal Arch Masons, of

Clarion, and at present chaplain of the Grand Chapter of Pennsylvania; also a member of Franklin Commandery, No. 44, Knights Templar of Pennsylvania. His wife is living and is in her seventy-seventh year.

(Ancestry of Flora Winifred Delo).

Flora Winifred Delo was a daughter of Daniel F. and Mary Frances (Lewis) Delo; granddaughter of Benjamin F. and Phebe Ann (Fleming) Delo, and Henry and Frances Ellen (Frye) Lewis; great-granddaughter of Daniel and Christiana (Loughner) Delo, Jesse and Sarah (Campbell) Lewis, Isaac and Mary (Petra) Frye, Daniel and Phebe Ann (King) Fleming; George and Eve Catharine (Kuhns) Delo, Daniel and Nancy (Hardy) Fleming, Lot and Jemima (Garwood) Lewis, John and Lucy Frye, David and Mary Petra, John and Mary (Loughery) Campbell; great-great-granddaughter of Michael and Mary (Kiefer) Delo, ——— and ——— (Reed) Fleming, James and Jane (Winters) Campbell, Mediah and ——— (Titus) Garwood, James and Mary Loughery, ——— and Lydia (Squire) Lewis; great-great-great-granddaughter of William and Ann (Boone) Winters, ——— and Anna (Ball) Campbell; great-great-great-great-granddaughter of Squire and Sarah (Morgan) Boone; great-great-great-great-granddaughter of George Boone and Mary Boone.

William Winters' family was in some respects remarkable; there were nineteen children by two wives. His first wife, Ann Boone, was a sister of Colonel Daniel Boone, of Kentucky fame. Their oldest daughter, Hannah, married Abraham Lincoln, the grandfather of President Lincoln, she was the mother of eleven children. The second wife was Eleanor Campbell, she had eight children. One of these, a daughter Mary, married Charles Huston, who was for a number of years a judge of the supreme court of Pennsylvania; another daughter, Ellen, married Thomas Burnside, a member of congress, judge of court of common pleas, and finally justice of the supreme court; Sarah, married Benjamin Harris; Elizabeth, married Thomas Alexander, a carpenter and builder, who erected one of the first dwellings in Williamsport, Pennsylvania; Lucy, died in 1875, married William W. Potter, a prominent politician, he died while a member of congress in 1898.

OSBORNE There were several unmistakable grants of the family of Osborne in New Haven, Connecticut, among the early settlers. Richard Osborne came from England to Hingham, Massachusetts, and thence to New Haven; served in the Pequot war; was a tanner by trade; afterward lived at Fairfield, Connecticut, and Newtown, Long Island. John Osborne, another early settler of New Haven, removed to Fairfield with his father Richard; married Sarah Bennett and had children: Samuel, John, David, Joseph and Elizabeth. Children of Richard Osborne: John, Elizabeth, Priscilla and Daniel.

(I) Thomas Osborne, the pioneer ancestor of this family, from Mardstone, England, was a brother of Richard Osborne, and was also at New Haven among the early settlers. In 1650 he removed to East Hampton, Long Island. He was a land owner in East Hampton and in 1687 conveyed all his remaining lands to his son Benjamin, returned to his old home at New Haven, and died there. Jeremiah Osborne, perhaps a brother of Richard, settled in New Haven; was a tanner, like Richard; served as deputy to the general court, 1672-74; married Mary ——— and had children: Rebecca, Increase, Benjamin, Jeremiah, Mary, Elizabeth, Jeremiah, Joanna, Thomas and Elizabeth. The names of the children of Richard, Jeremiah and Thomas indicate that they were brothers. Thomas was also a turner. Children: Benjamin, Thomas, mentioned below; John and Jeremiah.

(II) Thomas (2), son of Thomas (1) Osborne, was born in England in 1622, came to this country with the family and removed from New Haven, Connecticut, to East Hampton, Long Island, in New York, with his father. He died at East Hampton in 1712, aged ninety years. Among his children was Daniel, mentioned below.

(III) Daniel, son of Thomas (2) Osborne, was born in 1666 at East Hampton, Long Island, died there January 6, 1713. His branch of the family located in the lower part of Main street, East Hampton, and from that fact came to be known in later years as the "Down Street Osbornes." The old homestead of Daniel Osborne was owned in recent years by David E. Osborne. Daniel Osborne married Elizabeth Hedges, daughter or granddaughter of William Hedges, the immigrant ancestor of the Hedges family of New York. Children, born at East Hampton: Daniel, mentioned below; Thomas, Abigail, Rebecca, Mary.

(IV) Daniel (2), son of Daniel (1) Osborne, was born about 1690 at East Hampton, Long Island, died there May 18, 1757. He married, June 10, 1713, Elizabeth Austin. Children: Elizabeth, Daniel, Rebecca, Jonathan, Hannah, David, mentioned below.

(V) David, son of Daniel (2) Osborne, was born May 11, 1720, at East Hampton, Long Island, died December 4, 1792. He married Mary Huntting. They had five children. Their sons were Daniel, and David, mentioned below.

(VI) David (2), son of David (1) Osborne, was born in East Hampton, Long Island, August 22, 1761, died at Kingsbury, Washington county, New York, February 16, 1813. He married, November 20, 1788, at Amenia, Dutchess county, New York, Lucretia Harris, born in Cornwall, Litchfield county, Connecticut, July 30, 1768, died in Kingsbury, January 30, 1813. Children: Cornelia, born October 2, 1789, died December 23, 1821; Maria, April 5, 1791, died same day; John Huntting, November, 1792, died August 13, 1794; Sophronia Lucretia, April 5, 1795, died August 3, 1830; Platt Smith, mentioned below; Harriet Munro, April 13, 1800, died June 5, 1829; Harris Burnett, January 12, 1803, died in 1889; Morris Dickson, December 29, 1805, died July 26, 1808; Cynthia Ann, October 29, 1807, died February 4, 1864.

(VII) Platt Smith, son of David (2) Osborne, was born March 26, 1798, died at Sherman, New York, April 20, 1887. He married Mary A., daughter of Nehemiah and Anna Platt. Children, born at Ripley, New York: Sophia Lucretia, born June 14, 1829, married Dr. Graves; David Cuvier, mentioned below; Platt Smith Jr., April 27, 1834; Harriet, January 20, 1836, married Samuel P. McCalmont (see McCalmont V); Cynthia Ann, April 3, 1838, married Dr. Samuel McNair; Isadore, December 12, 1839; Harris Burnett, August 11, 1841; Samuel Whitehall, February 10, 1843; Mary Ann, July 15, 1845, married Stephen Benedict.

(VIII) Rev. David Cuvier Osborne, son of Platt Smith and Mary A. (Platt) Osborne, was born at Ripley, Chautauqua county, New York, August 3, 1830, died at Kalamazoo, Michigan, October 26, 1912. His father, a tanner by trade, was one of the pioneers of New York state, having taken up his farm from the government in 1820. Their home was the simple, God-fearing home of industrial people of that day. David C. gave early evidence of an active mind and had made such good use of the school privileges in the public school and at the Westfield Academy that, at the age of sixteen, he taught the village school at Sherman, where the family was living at that time. The Osborne family were naturally musicians, and David C. was specially endowed with musical gifts. He spent two years in New York City studying music under the best instructors of that time, and later taught music, both vocal and instrumental. He spent two and one-half years in the study of law in the office of Hon. Abner Lewis in Panama, New York. On New Year's Eve, 1850, while attending evangelistic services he became a Christian and soon thereafter united with the Methodist Episcopal church. His persuasive speech, even at that time, led many of his friends to say that the Gospel ministry would be his life's work. In 1853 he was admitted, not to the bar to practice law, but to the Erie conference to preach the Gospel. Thus began the active ministry of one of the foremost Methodist pastors of the Middle West. He was noted for his work among the young people, it being one of his principles that they should share largely in his responsibility of the church's activity. He kept the spirit of eternal youth in his soul and never grew old. He was noted for the attention he gave to church music. He organized and drilled church choirs and installed pipe organs in many of the churches which he served. He perhaps was still more widely known for the church building enterprises which he conducted. In this connection mention should be made of the First Church, Akron, Ohio, which was the original "Akron Plan" church. This plan was the result of long hours of thought on the part of Dr. Osborne, the pastor, of Louis Miller, the superintendent of the Sunday school, and financier of the enterprise, and of Jacob Snyder, the architect. The pastor's study was the place where most frequently this trio met to compare their ideas. The Akron Plan was one of the fruits of an earnest soul who wanted to see the best sort of a building constructed for Sunday school and church social activities. Dr. Osborne served as pastor of the Methodist church at Randolph, 1853;

Wattsburg, 1854; Dunkirk, 1855-56; Warren, 1857; Franklin, 1858-59; New Castle, 1860-61; Erie, First Church, 1862-64; Akron, 1865-67; Cleveland, Erie Street, 1868-70; Titusville, 1871-72; Cleveland district, as superintendent, 1873-76; Steubenville Kramer Church, 1877-78; Massillon, 1879-80; Canton, First Church, 1881-83; Youngstown, First Church, 1884-86; Painesville, 1887-89; Conneaut, 1890-92; Barnesville district as superintendent, 1893-98; Niles, 1899-1900; Madison, 1901; superannuated, 1902, moved to Kalamazoo, Michigan. While living there he supplied the pulpit at Comstock, Michigan, in 1904-07. Dr. Osborne was one of those with whom Dr. John H. Vincent took counsel in the founding of the Chautauqua movement; and he took an active part in the planning and conducting of the Chautauqua Assemblies. While on the Barnesville district, 1893-98, he was superintendent of instruction in Epworth Park Assembly of Bethesda, Ohio, and those who appeared on the program of that assembly in those years were guests in his cottage. With all his genius in the conduct of large church enterprises he was intensely evangelistic, and very many prominent and useful laymen were converted under his ministry, among them William A. McKinley, who afterward became president of the United States.

He was married to Arvilla Maria Hill, eldest daughter of the Rev. Bryan S. and Mary E. (Sanborn) Hill, October 23, 1856. Children: Bryan Hill, mentioned below; David Winthrop, born at New Castle, Pennsylvania, March 16, 1861; Cyrus Clarke, born at Akron, Ohio, October 19, 1865; Mary, born at Cleveland, Ohio, September 21, 1869; Donald Platt, born at Steubenville, Ohio, October 28, 1878.

Arvilla Maria (Hill) Osborne, wife of Rev. David Cuvier Osborne, was born December 29, 1837. She was a daughter of Rev. Bryan S. and Mary E. Sanborn Hill. The children of Rev. Bryan S. and Mary E. (Sanborn) Hill are as follows: 1. Arvilla Maria, mentioned above. 2. Robert Allen, born March 23, 1839, died April 29, 1858. 3. Mary E., born October 3, 1840, died April 23, 1859. 4. Adeline, born August 20, 1842; married, November 17, 1864, George M. Permer. 5. Julia, born December 20, 1844; married, October 26, 1865, Daniel B. Foote. 6. Emily, born January 17, 1847; married, September 3, 1870, Dr. S. F. Chapin. 7. Stella, born June 8, 1849. 8. Eva Marila, born February 12, 1852; married, June 28, 1881, John C. Compton. 9. Moses Simpson, born February 18, 1854, died October 1, 1857. 10. John Sanborn, born July 26, 1856, died July 16, 1886; married, November 9, 1881, Minnie H. Fritts. 11. Johanna Stewart, born July 26, 1856, died April 28, 1899; married (first) June 28, 1882, Joseph R. Allen, (second) January, 1892, George Sammons.

(IX) Bryan Hill, son of Rev. David Cuvier Osborne, was born at Franklin, Pennsylvania, August 10, 1858. He attended the public school of his native town and the high school at Cleveland, Ohio, where he fitted for college. He entered Ohio Wesleyan University, class of 1880, but did not graduate. He began to study his profession in the law office of McCalmont & Osborne at Franklin, and in 1881 was admitted to the bar. He immediately entered upon the practice of law and has continued to the present time with office at Franklin. In his profession he has attained high distinction. He has also been honored with various offices of trust in the city. For several terms he was a member of the city council, and in 1896 he was mayor of the city. In 1903, 1905 and 1906 he represented his district in the state legislature. In politics he is a Republican. He is also a trustee of the State Hospital for the Insane at Warren, Pennsylvania; president of the board of trustees of the Franklin Hospital; director of the First National Bank of Franklin and of the Union Heat and Light Company, S. T. Karns Sons Company; secretary and director of the West End Water Company, and other companies. In religion he is an Episcopalian and for some years has been vestryman of St. John's Protestant Episcopal Church of Franklin. He is financially interested in various other enterprises in this vicinity and has lent his aid in co-operation in many projects appealing to the men of public spirit in this city.

He married, December 11, 1889, Stella M., daughter of Forster W. and Laura M. (Wilson) Mitchell (see Mitchell III). They have one child, Geraldine, born at Franklin, Pennsylvania.

(The Mitchell Line).

(I) Rev. David Mitchell was a native of the north of Ireland, of old Scotch stock. He settled in Center county, Pennsylvania, and for many years was a preacher in the Methodist Episcopal denomination in that state. He had sons: Thomas, mentioned below, and James.

(II) Thomas, son of Rev. David Mitchell, was born near Bellefonte, Center county, Pennsylvania, about 1800, died in 1870, in Ashtabula, Ohio, whither he had removed. By trade he was a blacksmith. In April, 1836, he settled on a farm in Alleghany township near Pleasantville, Venango county, Pennsylvania, and in addition to the management of his farm he conducted a general store. He married (first) Eliza Lamb, who died in 1851. He married (second) Jane Weir. Children: David H., of Titusville; John L., born April 10, 1826, married, February 21, 1867, Hattie R. Raymond; Forster W., mentioned below; Sarah Jane, married Judge James L. Connely, of Philadelphia, Pennsylvania; Martha, married L. T. Lamberton, of Franklin, Pennsylvania; Melvina; Minerva E., married Alexander W. Brown, of Pleasantville; William; Charles R.; Mary J.

(III) Forster W., son of Thomas Mitchell, was born near Millhall, Center county, Pennsylvania, May 7, 1828. He came with his parents to Venango county when a boy of eight years and was raised on his father's farm at Pleasantville. Forster W. passed his youth and early manhood on the farm, at the same time familiarizing himself with lumbering and mercantile methods. The strenuous school of his earlier life developed the self command, perseverance and courage that were inherent in his disposition, and to these qualities he unfailingly united throughout life the traits that dominated his strong and high character—candor, fidelity to trust and duty— those old fashioned virtues for which, as time goes on, the world is likely to have as much need as ever. In March, 1865, Mr. Mitchell removed to Franklin, which was thenceforth the family home.

Mr. Mitchell was engaged in lumbering and merchandising at Enterprise, Pennsylvania, in 1859, when Colonel Drake struck his well, and was one of the earliest to view the fifteen barrel wonder. Without any delay he secured a lease on a portion of the Buchannan farm on the bank of Oil Creek, and began drilling by the primitive and laborious spring pole method, a well said to be the third to be completed after the Drake venture. It was a success and started at seventy-five barrels per day and flowed for more than six months. From the time of that initial venture until the recent past Mr. Mitchell was an extensive and successful operator for oil. He purchased and developed the Shaw farm near Rouseville; was interested in the Bullion field when in company with John H. Lee and Hon. W. R. Crawford he owned the "Big Injun," a well that made the high record for the district, flowing over 3,000 barrels, June 18, 1877. Mr. Mitchell was also profitably interested in the Bradford oil field in company with Captain J. T. Jones, of Buffalo, New York, and the late George H. Van Vleck, of Toledo, Ohio.

At all times Mr. Mitchell took every means and occasion to conserve or advance the interests of those engaged in the various activities of the oil industry. Being gifted with the initiative faculty, the discernment of what to do and how to do it, he was able to render practical and effective services in times of stress and danger. In the period of haphazard methods and wild fluctuations he was a pillar of strength. He took an active part in all public movements of the producers. In the days of the oil exchange was a heavy operator in the market. The advance in the price of crude oil from 60 cents to $1.27, in 1880, was known as "Mitchell's boom."

While managing his extensive oil interests, Mr. Mitchell at the same time carried on a banking business, in which he was long and successfully engaged. In 1870 he opened a bank at Rouseville with F. H. Steel, row of Toledo, Ohio. In 1873 the business was removed to Oil City, where for over twenty years the firm of F. W. Mitchell & Company was prominent in finance, the company being composed of F. W. Mitchell, F. H. Steel and George V. Forman, the latter giving place in 1882 to W. H. Wise, of Oil City. The banking business was discontinued in 1894 and he retired from active labor. In 1875 he was appointed by Governor Hartranft one of the Centennial Commission of Pennsylvania, and served as treasurer of the board during the historic event of the Exposition.

From the time he took up his residence in Franklin, forty-seven years ago, Mr. Mitchell has devoted largely of his means and energies to the material progress of Franklin and vicinity, and was recognized as one of the leaders of public spirit in this part of the state. Among his benefactions to this community were the lots on which the City Building and the Opera House are erected.

May 17, 1850, Mr. Mitchell was married to Laura M. Wilson, daughter of Alonzo and Lucy (Rowe) Wilson (see Wilson VI), and took up his residence in the village of Enterprise, Warren county, Pennsylvania. She died in 1907. Three children were born to them: Herbert W., who died in his youth; Lottie M., of Paris, France, who married Dilworth Richardson, of Cincinnati, Ohio, deceased; Stella M., wife of Bryan H. Osborne, of Franklin (see Osborne IX).

In his home Mr. Mitchell was a charming host, given to genuine hospitality, always with "holiday in his eye," his conversation at times spiced with anecdotal wit and humor. He was fond of diversions. As late as the 7th of May, 1912, when his daughter, Mrs. Osborne, entertained some of his intimate old friends at a dinner in honor of his eighty-fourth birthday, he closed the festivities by engaging them in the customary bout at whist or euchre.

A striking characteristic of Mr. Mitchell was his faculty of friendship, which he possessed in rare degree. He was happy in his friends, and his loyalty to them, whatever their position or circumstances, was steadfast and lasting. In his choice of them he exercised his keen and correct understanding of men, arising from his ability to look through material possessions, through differences of taste and station, and see the genuine man that abides within. Those friends must with pleasure recall him in the latter years of his long and busy life, the cordial, courteous, alert veteran, of handsome presence, who radiated health and good will and lent a charm to old age.

While retentive of the old time associations and memories, he did not live in the past, but kept in close touch with the present, moving along with the modern march, alive to the pressing questions of the day, interested in men, matters and events. Carrying these habits and qualities into a dignified and serene old age, he was spared the gloom that so often couples long life with decay and settles over it the sense of being helpless and alone. His later years, it is true, were not without sorrows and disappointments, but he resolutely met them with drafts upon his fund of "cheerful yesterdays and confident tomorrows."

The death of Forster W. Mitchell, for nearly half a century a prominent and honored citizen of Franklin, occurred December 15, 1912, at his apartments in the Exchange Hotel. The event followed an invalidism of about four years, during which his fine constitution gradually yielded to ailments of a rheumatic nature. He was clear in mind and serene in spirit to the end.

It is more than a mere formality of phrase to say that in the passing of Mr. Mitchell from life our city suffers a loss that is felt and acknowledged; for a prosperous man, who obtains his wealth honestly and uses it rightly, is a blessing to the community. Such a man was the one whose departure is now mourned.

The remains of Mr. Mitchell will repose with those of his wife in the family mausoleum in the Franklin Cemetery. But a more desirable monument to his memory already stands erected in the honor and respect of the many who knew him well, and the love of the few who knew him best.

(The Wilson Line).

No less than twelve pioneers of the Wilson family came to Massachusetts before 1650 and their descendants have been very numerous. Nathaniel Wilson came early to Roxbury and was a planter in that town and at Brookline. In 1647 he gave a power of attorney to John Wilson, of Halifax, Yorkshire, England, clothworker, to collect a legacy left him by Nathaniel Holgate, of Halifax, deceased. He sold his house in Roxbury, February 16, 1652. He married, April 2, 1645, Hannah, daughter of Griffin Crafts. Children: Hannah, baptized May 2, 1647; Nathaniel, baptized April 30 or May 2, 1653; Joseph and Benjamin, baptized January 31 or February 12, 1655; Isaac, born August 24, 1658; Mary, born May 2, 1661, recorded in Boston; Abigail, baptized April 10, 1664; Samuel, June 10, 1666.

(I) John Wilson, a relative of Nathaniel Wilson, and perhaps the John mentioned in the power of attorney, presumably a brother, settled after 1650 in Woburn, Massachusetts. The names Nathaniel, Benjamin, Hannah, are common to the descendants of both to an unusual extent. Children: John; Dorcas; Francis, born in England, married, March 6, 1683, Ruth Duntlen at Woburn, and she died at Rehoboth in 1700, he died August, 1724, at Rehoboth. Born at Woburn: Samuel, December 29, 1658; Abigail, August 8, 1666; Elizabeth, August 6, 1668; Benjamin, mentioned below; Hannah, May 31, 1672; John, January 3, 1674; Hannah, December 28, 1675; Hannah, March 11, 1677; Susanna, March 11, 1679.

(II) Benjamin, son of John Wilson, was born at Woburn, Massachusetts, October 15,

1670. With others of the family he removed to Rehoboth, Massachusetts. He married Elizabeth ———. Children, born at Rehoboth: Benjamin, mentioned below; Jonathan, December 8, 1698; Rebecca, January 20, 1701; Hannah, October 7, 1702; Francis, September 7, 1704; Elizabeth, July 8, 1706; Samuel, January 5, 1707-08; Ruth, April 7, 1710; Bethia, December 4, 1711; Abigail, August 30, 1713; Mary, October 17, 1714.

(III) Benjamin (2), son of Benjamin (1) Wilson, also lived at Rehoboth, Massachusetts. Elizabeth, wife of Benjamin Jr. died July 10, 1731. He married at Rehoboth, December 15, 1730, Elizabeth Sprague. He must have had a first and third wife also named Elizabeth, unless there were two of the same name at the same time in Rehoboth. But after 1730 there is no positive indication of more than one Benjamin (1730-46), except that the record of birth of Nathaniel states that his father Benjamin was of England. That may mean that the father was then absent in England. The children credited to Benjamin and Elizabeth at Rehoboth are: Sarah, born February 23, 1729-30; John; Nathaniel, mentioned below; Lucas, August 10, 1735; Ammi, April 26, 1737; Benjamin, April 11, 1739; Jonathan, April 7, 1741; Ezekiel, May 11, 1744; Chloe, June 23, 1746.

(IV) Nathaniel, son of Benjamin (2) and Elizabeth Wilson, was born at Rehoboth, Massachusetts, June 10, 1733. The history of West Stockbridge says he was a native of England, but the records of Rehoboth, given above, seem to prove that he was born in Rehoboth, lived in Canada and in Richmond near the Stockbridge line. He served in the French and Indian war in Canada, at which time his life is romantically said to have been saved by a spider's web. "Pursued by Indians he took refuge in a hollow log which being observed the following morning by his pursuers with a spider's web across the end, was supposed to be vacant, they remarking 'no white man there, cause spider's web'" and he was unmolested. He married twice and had twenty-one children. He married, at Rehoboth, June 10, 1756, Jemima Turner (married by Elder Richard Rounds). Children, recorded at Rehoboth: Huldah, born June 30, 1757; Sarah, October 17, 1759; Philanda, June 30, 1761; Shubael, April 8, 1763; Nathaniel, June 24, 1773. Rufus, the youngest, came at the age of six to Stockbridge and succeeded to the farm lately owned by John G. Wilson. The history of Stockbridge says that about the close of the revolution Elisha, Peter, Mary, Phebe and Mehitable Wilson with their mother went with others to the Chenango Purchase, New York. Rufus Wilson built a saw mill and grist mill about the close of the revolution on the site occupied later by a mill built by John G. Wilson at West Stockbridge. In 1790 there were living at Stockbridge, according to the first federal census, Elnathan at West Stockbridge, Mary at Stockbridge, and Farron, mentioned below. None of the family was at Springfield, Massachusetts.

(V) Farron, son of Nathaniel Wilson, was born before 1770, probably at Rehoboth. An effort has been made to find the family name from which Farron was taken. In 1790 Farron Wilson was living at Stockbridge, and had in his family his wife and one son under sixteen. He had daughter Laura, who married Umstead Allen, and they resided in Springfield, Massachusetts; two sons, Uriah and William, the latter a Presbyterian minister, and Elizabeth, who married a Mr. Tremaine, and they also resided in Springfield.

(VI) Alonzo, son of Farron Wilson, was born as early as 1800, died about 1850. He removed from Springfield, Massachusetts, about 1834, to Silvercreek, New York, and afterward to the town of Enterprise, Warren county, Pennsylvania. He married Lucy Rowe. Children: Laura M., married, May 17, 1850, Forster W. Mitchell (see Mitchell III); Delia, married David H. Mitchell and had children; Alonzo, died in infancy; Claude, Frank, Frederick, Jessie, Antoinette, Oscar.

McCALMONT There is a tradition in the McCalmont family that before their Scottish ancestors of whom we have knowledge, their forbears were Irish, descended from Fiack, son of Niall, who was the 126th monarch of Ireland, and that from Fiack they come through nineteen generations to Calma (in Irish, "brave"), from whom came the ancestors of the Scottish clan of MacCalma, or McCalmont. Of the descendants of Fiack, one line comprises the McGeoghagans, lords of Maycassel and Terlulagh, in county Westmeath, Ireland. Of the same stock are the Higgins family, of counties Westmeath and Galway. From Main, son of Niall, of the

Nine Hostages, and brother of Fiack, came Loftus of Meath and Fox, lords of Tiffin. Thus the McCalmonts seem to be descended from kings and princes of Ireland. The family arms in Scotland are: A lion rampant between three dexter hands couped at the wrist gules. Crest: A grey hound standart azure. Motto: *Semper patriae servire presto*. At Dumfries, Scotland, the family name is preserved on a pane of glass in the home of James McCalmont, upon which in July, 1793, Robert Burns inscribed the following verse:

Blest be McCalmont to his latest day;
No envious clouds o'ercast his evening ray;
No wrinkle furrowed by the hand of care,
Nor ever sorrow add one silver hair,
O, may no son the father's honor stain,
Nor ever daughter give the mother pain.

(I) Thomas McCalmont, a Covenanter minister who was persecuted for his faith in the reign of Charles II., made his escape by crossing in a fishing boat to Ireland, where he settled at Cairn Castle, county Antrim. His children were: 1. Thomas, of whom further. 2. James, born 1707, married Hannah Blair. 3. John, born May 1, 1709; emigrated to Pennsylvania, and settled on the Susquehanna; married a Latimer, of county Tyrone, Ireland; died 1779. 4. Robert, of whose descendants there is no trace. 5. Hugh.

(II) Thomas (2), son of Thomas (1) McCalmont, was a resident of county Armagh, Ireland, for a short time previous to 1766. He subsequently joined his brother John in America, and was drowned in crossing a river near Philadelphia, on his way to meet his son Robert, who had come in his ship to conduct him back to Ireland. He married Susan Wallace.

(III) John, son of Thomas (2) and Susan (Wallace) McCalmont, was born in Ireland, in county Armagh, near the town of the same name, January 1, 1750 (old style), and came to America when sixteen years old. He was apprenticed to a clockmaker, and, not liking his master or the trade, entered into an agreement with the captain of the ship "Rose" to serve three years for his passage to this country, with the privilege of selecting the person with whom he should live, and have his indenture cancelled on payment of a certain sum of money. He remained near Philadelphia until 1773, when he married Elizabeth, born 1750, daughter of Henry and Jane (Stroud) Conard (or Kunders), and great-granddaughter of Theresa and Ellen (Streipers) Conard (or Kunders). Thomas Kunders and the eminent Pastorius were the first in America to protest against human slavery.

John McCalmont was out with the militia in the revolution one tour of service under General Lacey, in Captain Alexander Brown's company, and wintered with Washington at Valley Forge. In 1783 he moved to Nittany Valley, having previously for a few years lived in Kishacoquillas Valley, at Greenwood, now Mifflin county, near Lewistown. In Nittany Valley he purchased a tract of land near where Jacksonville is located, his home being a few rods from Lick Run meeting house. He remained there until 1805, when he removed to Venango county and located in Sugar Creek township, about four miles north of Franklin. Children of John and Elizabeth (Conard) McCalmont: 1. Thomas, born October 14, 1774; came to Venango county in 1802. 2. Henry, born March 15, 1776; came to Venango county in 1819. 3. John, born January 15, 1779; drowned when about eighteen months old. 4. James, born May 17, 1781; served in war of 1812, wounded in battle of Bridgewater, and died from wounds about three weeks later. 5. Robert, born August 26, 1783; came to Venango county in 1802. 6. Alexander, of whom further. 7. John, of whom further. 8. Elizabeth, born February 3, 1791; married William Shaw. 9. Sarah, born November 3, 1792; married George Crain. 10. Jane, born October 8, 1794; married James Ricketts. 11. Joseph, born November 23, 1798.

John McCalmont died August 3, 1832, at the home of his son Henry, in Cornplanter township, Venango county, and was buried in the churchyard there. His wife died August 12, 1829, and was buried in the old graveyard at Franklin.

The following are extracts from the notebook of Alexander McCalmont, son of John and Elizabeth McCalmont:

I was born at a place called Greenwood, in Cishacoquillas Valley, October 23, 1785. (Note that date of his birth given in list of John McCalmont's children, is October 13, a discrepancy of ten days; the first date is copied from the family Bible). When about two years old my father moved to Nittany Valley and settled on a place at the head of a spring called Lick Run. The tract of land on which we lived and improved until the spring of 1803, adjoining the tract on which my uncle Thomas settled, and on which Jacksonville is. My father's tract which he purchased was east of the one on which the village of Jacksonville is, and was bounded on the east by a tract owned by Captain Thomas Wilson, on which he was settled before the revolution.

My brothers Thomas, Henry, John, James and Robert were all born in Cishacoquillas Valley. John was drowned when about eighteen months old. My next brother, John, born in August, 1788, was named the same. I recollect the day of his birth, and also recollect seeing the raising of the house in which he was born, and the small shanty without any floor or loft, in which we lived before the house in which he was born was built. It was of hewed logs. Joseph McKibben was one of the corner men and raised the northwest corner. It is strange that he is the only one assisting that I can recollect. I had come near the corner of the house on which he was, and he throwed chips at me and told me to go away. This I never forgot, and his image at the time, and that of the building on the corner of which he was, are still as fresh in my mind as the occurrences of yesterday.

The first school I went to was taught by William Wilson. The schoolhouse was between Thomas Wilson's and William Wilson's. The land on which it stood was afterwards owned by Samuel Beck. This was in 1792. The only persons living in Nittany Valley between where Bellefonte now is and Fishing Creek Narrows, in my earliest recollection, were as follows: William Lamb lived on Spring Creek (now Bellefonte); a German family by the name of Elson lived three miles further down the valley; Thomas Wilson next east of us; Thomas McCalmont around the point or little hill south of us; William Wilson lived down the valley on the next place east of Thomas Wilson's; William Swaney next below; Joseph McKibben next; William Davis lived down near Fishing Creek Gap. There was no mill in Nittany Valley. Robert McClelland built the first mill in the narrows at Lick Run. I remember when he came to my father's. The second time he brought hands with him—Joseph Lucas and Baptist Lucas. They lodged at my father's and sawed the stuff for the mill with a whip-saw. Philip Houses was the millwright whom Joseph McClelland settled on a tract next to my uncle Thomas, up the valley. A number of settlers came in soon after, and a road was opened for wagons down along the sunnier north side of the valley. At the time my father came to Nittany I think there were no improvements on the Nittany below Harbison's Gap. John Harbison lived there at the time my father settled.

In 1794 a school house was erected on my uncle Thomas' land, twenty or thirty perches southwest of my father's. William McGarvey was the first teacher, and taught in it two years. I attended his school most part of the time, and sometimes in winter went barefoot through the snow. McClelland's mill had been burned, and when rebuilding, I recollect Mr. Petit was the master millwright. William Tipton and David Tipton were working at the mill and attended the school in the winter. Thomas Wilson, John Shoup and other young men went from William Wilson's to the school past my father's, and frequently carried me on their shoulders to school. About that time there were frequent meetings to make arrangements for building a meeting house and forming a congregation. The only sermon I had ever heard up till 1794 was preached by Rev. Mr. Grier, in Mr. Wilson's barn. His text was,

"Come unto Me, all ye that labor and are heavy laden" (Matt. xi, 28, 29, 30). I think it was in 1795 or 1796 that arrangements were made to build a meeting house. It was built by Bennet Lucas and his boys, of hewed logs. Pine trees were very plenty at that time, and were not as valuable as at present. The meeting house was covered with lap-shingles. I recollect I carried shingles to the top of the house for amusement. The first year there was nothing done to it but to cover it. It progressed very slowly. The next summer a door and floor were in it. The first sermon I recollect was preached by a Mr. Johnston, a son-in-law of Judge Brown's. It is possible that others were preached there before. Henry R. Wilson took charge of the congregation and continued until I left in the spring of 1803.

(IV) Judge Alexander McCalmont, son of John (I) and Elizabeth (Conard) McCalmont, was born in Mifflin county, Pennsylvania, October 23, 1785. He went with his parents when they removed to Venango county, and there passed the remainder of his life. Having for those times acquired a good practical education, he became a teacher. He later embarked in mercantile pursuits, and subsequently was engaged in the iron business. He was a Democrat, and at one time took active part in local politics. He was sheriff in 1811, commissioner in 1814, and prothonotary in 1818. He also served as deputy surveyor. He became a member of the Methodist Episcopal church in 1820. Having taken up the study of law, he was admitted to practice about 1820, met with considerable professional success, and acquired a reputation as an able attorney. He was appointed president judge of the Eighteenth judicial district in 1839, and served with distinction for ten years. He died August 10, 1857. Judge McCalmont married (first) Margaret, daughter of John Broadfoot, of Franklin, Pennsylvania. She died in 1817 without issue. In 1818 he married (second) Elizabeth Connely, born in Bellefonte, in 1801, but became a resident of Franklin in 1806, with her father, who removed there. Children: 1. William. 2. John Swazey, born April 28, 1822, died 1906; married Elizabeth Stehley. 3. Alfred B., of whom further. 4. Elizabeth, married General Edward Clinton Wilson.

(V) General Alfred B. McCalmont, youngest son of Judge Alexander and Elizabeth (Connely) McCalmont, was born in Venango county, Pennsylvania, April 28, 1825, and died May 7, 1874. He received his education in the local schools, Allegheny College and Dickinson College, and was graduated from the last named institution in 1844, at the age of twenty years. He studied law in his father's office, and was admitted to the Venango county bar May 25, 1847. He afterward removed to Pittsburgh and entered upon the practice of his profession, and his ability soon won for him a satisfactory share of the legal business there. In 1853 he was associated with T. J. Keenan in the newspaper business. In 1855 he was appointed prothonotary of the supreme court of the district of western Pennsylvania, an office always filled by a lawyer. This position he resigned in May, 1858, to accept an appointment as chief clerk to Hon. Jeremiah S. Black, then attorney general of the United States, in the cabinet of President Buchanan, with functions since exercised by the deputy attorney-general. He held that responsible position until the end of that administration, and then returned to Franklin and resumed his law practice, in partnership with James K. Kerr. An ardent patriot, in 1862 he espoused the Union cause and recruited a company of volunteers for the 142d Regiment Pennsylvania Volunteers, which was attached to the Army of the Potomac. He early displayed genuine soldierly qualities, and by successive promotions rose from the rank of captain to lieutenant-colonel in his regiment, and later was commissioned colonel of the 208th Pennsylvania Regiment. He served throughout the war and made a most brilliant record. He commanded a brigade in the assault upon Petersburg, and in recognition of his gallantry in that and other engagements he received from President Lincoln the brevet rank of brigadier-general. At the close of the war he returned to Franklin and resumed professional work, continuing actively employed until his death. He was one of the ablest members of the Venango county bar, winning for himself, by his brilliant oratory and forensic ability, a reputation which, after all these years, is still green in the memory of all who knew him. Judge Heydrick said of him, in an article on the Venango bar, in the "Proceedings of the Celebration of the First Centennial of the Organization of the County of Venango," (and the tribute is as just to him in his professional as in his military career): "General McCalmont was impulsive, and, under a great impetus, just the man to win promotion for a successful assault upon fortifications. Given the opportunity and supposed incentive, he would have led another six hundred at another Balaklava, but might not have been willing to lead a retreat."

General Alfred B. McCalmont married, April 25, 1853, Sarah F., daughter of Evan Reece Evans, of Pittsburgh, Pennsylvania. Children: 1. Lydia Collins, born February 12, 1854; married Thomas McGeough. 2. Sarah Lowry, born June 7, 1856; married W. A. Lewison; children: Sarah McC., and Almina Parker, who married George Hayes, of Boston. 3. Robert, of whom further.

(VI) Robert, only son of General Alfred B. and Sarah F. (Evans) McCalmont, was born in Washington, D. C., while his father was residing there and officially employed, September 18, 1859. He was educated in the Franklin schools and Princeton University, graduating from the latter institution in 1878 at the age of nineteen years, as civil engineer. After finishing his university course he read law in the office of Dodd & Lee, in Franklin, and was admitted to the Venango county bar in 1881, and from that time has practiced law in that city with conspicuous success. In politics he is affiliated with the Democratic party. He is a communicant and vestryman of the Protestant Episcopal church, and is a member of the Masonic order. He married Jessie B. Crawford, daughter of William R. and Jane (Kerr) Crawford.

(IV) John McCalmont, son of John and Elizabeth (Conard) McCalmont, was born in Center county, Pennsylvania, September 9, 1788, and died August 27, 1877. He was one of the early pioneers of Venango county, whither he removed with his parents in 1803, the family locating in the forest of Sugar Creek township. After coming to this region he remained with his parents for a time, assisting in clearing and tilling the homestead farm. He obtained a good education for that early day, and taught in one of the pioneer schools. On attaining his majority he removed to Franklin and engaged in the milling business, and later in the manufacture of iron. He always took an active interest in public affairs, and was county commissioner in 1814 and treasurer of Venango county from 1816 to 1818. He married (first) Maria ———, who died in 1814, without issue. He married (second) January 18, 1818, Mary H., daughter of Samuel Plumer; she died September 3, 1842. Her father settled in Jackson township, Venango county, in 1800. He was a son of Nathaniel Plumer, who purchased four hundred acres of land embracing part of the site of Mount Washington, one of the present wards of Pittsburgh, on the south side of the Monongahela, and settled thereon in 1789, and grandson of Jonathan Plumer, a commissary in Braddock's expedition, and quartermaster of Forbes' army, a native of Newbury, Massachusetts, and descendant of Francis Plumer, one of the founders of that town in 1635. Children of John and Mary H. (Plumer) McCalmont: Patty, married Rev. A. G. Miller; John, Samuel, Margaret; and Samuel Plumer, of whom further.

(V) Samuel Plumer McCalmont, son of John and Mary (Plumer) McCalmont, was born in Sugar Creek township, Venango county, Pennsylvania, September 21, 1823. His boyhood was passed on the farm, assisting his father in the laborious occupation of pioneer farming. After attending the neighborhood school, he took a brief term of study at Allegheny College. He then entered the office of his uncle, Judge Alexander McCalmont, as a law student, and was admitted to the bar of Venango county November 25, 1847, and at once entered upon the active practice of his profession, which he successfully followed without intermission until the infirmities of age compelled his retirement, only excepting a period of three years spent in the California mining region, and a brief term in public service. He was an industrious, vigilant and aggressive lawyer, and one of the best known members of the Venango bar. Politically he was originally a Democrat. He was, however, bitterly opposed to human slavery, was one of the most aggressive pioneer anti-slavery advocates, and devoted much time and liberally of his means to the cause. Even now there are not a few who have distinct recollection of his bold and uncompromising advocacy of abolition. With the opening up of the free soil issue as opposed to slavery extension, in 1856 he became one of the organizing members of the Republican party, to which he ever afterward steadily adhered until 1874, when he aided in organizing the Prohibition party, being for forty years an unswerving enemy of the liquor traffic. In 1855 he was elected to the legislature, and he was twice re-elected. He married, in April, 1859, Harriet, daughter of Platt Smith Osborne, died December 25, 1912 (see Osborne VII). Children: Mary Plumer; Samuel Plumer Jr.; John Osborne; Harriette Osborne; James Donald, born February 10, 1870; Constance Plumer, July 6, 1874; David Burnett, of whom further.

(VI) David Burnett, son of Samuel Plumer and Harriet (Osborne) McCalmont, was born in Franklin, Pennsylvania, December 1, 1876. He was reared in that town, and received his preliminary education in its public school, passing through the high school, afterward entering the Sheffield Scientific School of Yale University, from which he was graduated with the class of 1897. He then studied law under the office preceptorship of Bryan Osborne, and was admitted to the bar of Venango county August 26, 1900, and at once entered upon practice, in which he has been successfully engaged to the present time. For ten years, from 1898 to 1908, he served in the Pennsylvania National Guard, attaining the rank of lieutenant. He is a Prohibitionist in politics, and in 1905 was elected to the state chairmanship of that party, occupying that position until 1909, when he resigned to take charge of the *Venango Herald*, the only Prohibition daily newspaper in the United States. He has been the candidate of his party for local offices on various occasions, and in 1903 was nominated for district attorney, being defeated by only 308 votes, and receiving 3,394 votes.

Mr. McCalmont married, September 26, 1900, Edna Swallow, born December 31, 1878, daughter of Burling E. and Lydia (Schuyler-Jack) Swallow, and a descendant of the famous Schuyler family of revolutionary fame. Children: Virginia Lucretia, born September 10, 1905; Samuel Plumer (2nd), November 11, 1906; David Burnett Jr., August 9, 1909.

BLEAKLEY This family is of excellent Scotch-Irish ancestry, as is attested by the record borne by the immigrant ancestor of the American branch, John Bleakley, of whom further.

(I) John Bleakley, son of James Bleakley, was born in the town of Merley, county Tyrone, Ireland, October 20, 1788. With his wife (name unknown), he came to the United States in June, 1819, bringing an excellent introductory letter from his pastor, Presbyterian, and the following demit from his Masonic Lodge, No. 911, Jurisdictions of Ireland:

To all to whom it May Concern: We the Master Wardens and Secretary of Lodge No. 911, held in the town of Merley, and county Tyrone, and on the Registry of Ireland, do hereby certify that the bearer, Mr. John Bleakley, a regular registered Master Mason in said lodge, and during his stay with us behaved himself as an honest brother. Given under our hands and seal of our lodge in our lodge room, dated this 12th of June, 1819, and of Masonry 5819.

The above is signed by Mathew Hunter, master, James Bleakley, senior warden, James Dogherty, junior warden, John Hanna, secretary. John Bleakley first settled in Berks county, Pennsylvania, and in 1833 removed to Venango county, where he located permanently, and died September 11, 1869. His wife died soon after their arrival in this country, leaving one son, James, of whom further.

(II) James (2), son of John Bleakley, was born near Unionville, Berks county, Pennsylvania, September 13, 1820, died October 3, 1883. At an early age he was apprenticed to the printing business, and after completing a three year term of service he went to Butler, Pennsylvania, where he worked three years. In spite of a rather limited education, by hard work and application he was able to acquire considerable knowledge, as is shown by his next venture, which was in the newspaper publishing field. In 1842 he returned to Franklin, and in company with John Shugert, established the *Democratic Arch*, continuing its publication about two years and a half. The files of this paper from July, 1842, to October, 1843, still in possession of the Bleakley family, are the earliest continuous files extant of any newspaper in Venango county. In the spring of 1844 he engaged in business as a merchant, and through thrift and close application to work was soon able to accumulate a little money, which he invested in real estate in Franklin and throughout the country. In 1849 he erected the building occupied for many years by the International Bank. He continued in the mercantile business for about twenty years. In 1851 and for several years thereafter he was associated with A. P. Whitaker in the publication of the *Venango Spectator*. He was elected county treasurer in 1851, and held that office two years. In 1864 he assisted in organizing the First National Bank of Franklin, occupying the position of cashier until 1867. In 1868 he opened the International Bank, for many years one of the best known financial institutions of the country, and was its president until his death. In addition to his financial interests he was also connected with many other enterprises, among them being a tannery, foundry, oil refinery, and tinning establishment, and in real estate and other transactions. From the year 1859 until his death he was engaged in various branches of the oil business. He was one of the purchasers of the Galloway tract and outlot No. 8, famous for their production of Franklin lubrication oil. The block built by him on Liberty street, Franklin, is one of the most substantial in the city. In politics he was a Democrat until Buchanan's election in 1856, but from that date affiliated with the Republican party. He was burgess of Franklin several terms, and served in the council of both borough and city.

He married Elizabeth, born May, 1822, daughter of Jacob Dubbs, who came from Harrisburg, Pennsylvania, his native place, and was a pioneer merchant in Franklin. Children: 1. Elizabeth, born January 16, 1845; married T. W. Bridgham. 2. Clara, born April 6, 1847; married Alexander McDowell. 3. William, of whom further. 4. Effie, born November 26, 1851; married Dr. E. W. Moore. 5. Orrin Dubbs, of whom elsewhere. 6. Harry, born January 8, 1859. 7. Edmund, born October 30, 1860; married Bertha Legnard.

(III) William James, son of James (2) and Elizabeth (Dubbs) Bleakley, was born in Franklin, July 6, 1849, died September 27, 1908. He was educated in the local public schools, followed by terms in the Waterford Academy and Oberlin (Ohio) College. At an early age he entered upon a business career that was destined to be constant. He was teller in the First National Bank. In 1868, when James Bleakley, his father, established the International Bank, he became his assistant and in 1872 became cashier; in 1883, on the death of his father he became president of the International Bank, and under his management the International Bank continued its career of substantial prosperity. He remained in that position until 1902 when the bank became the Franklin Trust Company, when he retired in order to give his time to other matters of importance, particularly to the extensive and varied interests of the Bleakley estate of which he was the chief executor. At the same time, while managing his personal business, he entered largely upon public enterprises. He was president of the Venango Water Company several years, an organizer and president of the Franklin Electric Company, and helped to organize the Franklin

Steel Casting Company, of which he was treasurer. He was identified with the Marvin Manufacturing Company in its infancy and brought this company from practically nothing to one of the largest manufacturing corporations in the city today. For a number of years and to his death he was a trustee of the State Institution at Polk, and his counsel was highly valued by the board and others connected with the institution. As a business man he was a prodigious worker, yet doing things without noise or ostentation. His impulse toward the practical benefit of others was evinced in his management of the Bleakley estate. He began on a large scale the scheme of building homes for people of limited means, to be acquired on easy payments, and many homes on Bleakley Hill and Oak Hill attest the beneficence of the system.

Added to the multifarious and exacting demands of private business Mr. Bleakley was much in request in public affairs. Politically a Republican, he served twelve terms in the city council and was elected mayor in 1887 and 1888 and 1891. During his administration he succeeded in reducing the debt of the city and establishing a sinking fund for the extinguishment of the bonded indebtedness. In 1908 he was elected a member of the school board, and at the time of his death he was serving his third term as president. In him the public schools and pupils had an active friend. He felt the necessity of lifting the mind out of the levels of mere trade and traffic, and while overweighed with other unavoidable business cares, he still found time to aid most effectively in every detail pertaining to his office as school director. He was largely instrumental in the erection of the present magnificent high school building, in which he had to contend with some opposition, but, as in the case of many other of his enterprises, the results vindicated his judgment. He was one of the best known men in the Pennsylvania oil region, and as a financier had few equals. He measured up to the full stature of a true and good man, and in his doings, large and small, public or private, he exemplified the old fashioned, rock-ribbed virtues of honesty, square dealing and brotherly kindness. He was faithful to every trust, competent and reliable in every duty that devolved upon him. Although his time was fully taken up with business, personal and official, he devoted his considerable attention to his domestic enjoyment. His strong personality, clear mind and fair methods commanded the respect of the many with whom he came in contact, and secured their confidence and friendship. But, successful as he was in his relations with the outside world, he was at his best in his own home. He loved it, and spent with his family all the time he could spare from the unceasing demands of business. In that well ordered home, the haunt of comfort and hospitality, he found the rest, refuge and content that his nature craved. He was a cordial host, the center of cheer among his guests and family. He was an adherent of the First Presbyterian Church, and a member of its board of trustees, always giving the benefit of his counsel and generous support to the building of its temporal interests.

The following resolutions on the death of Mr. Bleakley were adopted by the Franklin School Board:

To the President of the Board of Directors, Franklin School District:

Pursuant to the resolution passed at the special meeting of the School Board held September 28th, your committee has the honor to present the following in memory of our late President, William J. Bleakley:

After a continuous service of more than twelve years as a member of the Board of School Directors, and while serving his twelfth year as its President, William J. Bleakley died September 27, 1908. It is fitting that his long and faithful service deserve recognition by the formal action of the Board. We therefore offer this tribute to his memory, and direct that it be placed upon the record of the Board:

Chosen by his fellow citizens for so many years to fill the office of School Director, though his personal interests seemed to demand his attention, he gave freely of his time, talents and energy to the duties of his office, thus exhibiting in an unusual degree that rare quality of good citizenship which subordinates the demands of private business to the public good.

In all his official acts he ever kept in view the best interests of the schools, fearlessly and conscientiously advocating whatever measures would tend to their improvement, being actuated by a supreme desire to aid in the advancement of the cause of general education in our city.

It is therefore obvious to all who have been more or less intimately associated with him in his work that the Franklin School District in his death loses a staunch supporter in all that could contribute to its advancement in educational matters and that his associates greatly feel the loss that has come to them through his sudden and unexpected death.

(Signed)
F. L. BENSINGER,
NATHAN EVANS,
M. F. ELLIOTT.

William J. Bleakley married, May 17, 1876, Mary S., daughter of John and Mary Anna (May) Lamb (see Lamb). Children: 1. Anna Mary, born February 4, 1877; married February 4, 1903, George B. Woodbrun; one daughter, Margaret, born August 8, 1906. 2. Orrin Louis, born February 10, 1879; married, June 29, 1904, Florence Dickey Campbell; children: Elizabeth Jane, born April 15, 1905, Florence Evelyn, October 2, 1906. 3. Frederick James, born October 23, 1880; married, October 2, 1907, Ethel Niedlander; one son, Frederick J. Jr., born December 25, 1909. 4. Margaret May, born December 16, 1882; married, November 4, 1908, Louis E. Habegger; children: William J. Bleakley, born September 27, 1909; Margaret Louise, born August 7, 1910. 5. Evelyn Elizabeth, born November 26, 1884; married, February 4, 1909, Victor W. Stewart. 6. William Jay, born December 31, 1888. 7. Donald Sherburne, born June 9, 1894. 8. Kenneth Huntington, born December 2, 1896.

(The Lamb Line).

John Lamb Jr., son of John and Nancy (Sparks) Lamb, was born near Bellefonte, Center county, Pennsylvania, June 13, 1806, died November 18, 1863. At an early age he was apprenticed to the tanner's trade. In 1829 he came to Allegheny township, Venango county, and purchased a small piece of land in the woods, on which he built a log cabin, started a tannery, and began clearing up a farm. The farm grew to be one of the largest and finest in Venango county, and the little home a popular and well known wayside inn in the old stage and coach days, and the tannery expanded into an extensive mercantile and lumber business. Through his efforts a postoffice was obtained for the neighborhood, which bore his name and was kept at his house. On the discovery of oil he engaged in the production and refining of that commodity in a limited way, as the oil business was only in its infancy at the time of his death. He was active in politics, and was a Democrat until Lincoln's nomination for president, when he became a Republican.

He married (first) April 23, 1833, Mary Bailey, daughter of Captain William Smith, of Waterford, Pennsylvania; she died November 1849. He married (second) February 1, 1853, Mary Anna, daughter of Rev. Hezekiah and Margaret (White) May; she died November 17, 1877. Children by first wife: William Smith, born September 17, 1834; Alfred, December 28, 1835; David, September, 1840; Nancy Elizabeth, September 28, 1842; Sarah King, October 2, 1844; Henry Rowan, April 14, 1849. By second wife: Mary Smith, April 18, 1854, married William J. Bleakley (see Bleakley III).

Rev. Hezekiah May was born at Haddam, Connecticut, December 25, 1773, died July 4, 1843. He was a graduate of Yale College, and was distinguished for his learning, piety and abilities, and was a licensed preacher of the Gospel upward of forty years. He was extensively acquainted in the states of Connecticut, Massachusetts, Maine, New York, Pennsylvania, in all of which he labored in the Gospel ministry. He was a noted minister in the early days of the Congregational, and later, Presbyterian church. He came to Venango county under the patronage of the New England Society for the Propagation of the Gospel in this country. He secured a tract of one thousand acres of land at Old Town, three miles above Tionesta, Pennsylvania. He was in Franklin in the earliest days of that town, but afterward removed to Tionesta, where with the help of his sons he cleared a large tract of land at Old Town, and erected a large saw mill at the place. Old Town was the remains of an ancient Indian village when he located there. It was called Sa-qua-lin-get, translated, "the place of council." It was purchased by Mr. May from John Ranger, a revolutionary soldier.

PATTERSON This family is of Scotch origin, and the branch here considered has been seated in Pennsylvania for several generations.

(I) Robert Patterson, a native of Scotland, married Mary Ball. They were the parents of three children: Abraham, who married a Miss Gourley, emigrated to the United States and located in or near Bellefontaine, Lyon county, Ohio; David, of whom further, and a daughter who married Thomas Hays, and remained in Scotland.

(II) David, second child of Robert and Mary (Ball) Patterson, was born in Scotland. He was a weaver by trade, and went to Ireland', and made his home in the parish of Kalinsha, county Down. Before he removed there he married, about 1800, Mary, daughter of William and Elizabeth Leslie; children: Robert, born May 31, 1803; William, of whom further; Isaac, Abraham, Jane and David.

(III) William, second child of David and Mary (Leslie) Patterson, was probably born near Belfast, Ireland, about 1804 or 1805, as near as can be ascertained. He married Isabel, daughter of Joshua and Mary (Montgomery) Coleman. In 1822 a passage to the United States was bought for the entire family, but before their arrangements for the voyage had been completed all excepting the father (David Patterson) were taken ill with typhoid fever. To the parents this affliction brought the conviction that their leaving their home was contrary to the wish of Providence, and they abandoned their purpose. However, William and his elder brother Robert were not to be dissuaded, and they proposed that if the father would provide for their passage they would go, and if they were pleased with the new country would send for the remainder of the family. William Patterson settled in Mercer county, Pennsylvania, and became a successful farmer and merchant. He was a Presbyterian of the genuine Scottish type, and was zealous in promoting the advancement of the church at his new home. He assisted in building the first church of his denomination in Mercer county, and contributed liberally to its support throughout his life. In 1873 he removed to Allegheny City, where he died in 1889. To him and his wife were born eleven children.

(IV) Isaac Newton, son of William and Isabel (Coleman) Patterson, was born in Mercer county, Pennsylvania, December 12, 1833. He received his education in the public schools of his native county, and at an academy in Butler county. He began his business career as a clerk in his father's store, where his ability and energy soon placed him at the head of the business, which he continued to carry on for twenty years. He was also engaged in other business enterprises on his own account, and at the beginning of the oil excitement went into partnership with his brother in the production of oil, this partnership continuing for twelve years. In 1872 Mr. Patterson removed to Venango county, and located at Franklin. He became one of the leading oil producers of the county. He was president of the Franklin Savings Bank for a number of years. This bank eventually failed, but not until long after Mr. Patterson had sold out his stock and resigned from the presidency. He has always been a public-spirited man, and interested in all matters affecting the general welfare of the county. In politics he is a Republican, in early life having been an active worker for the party in local issues. He married, July 2, 1873, Ella Donzella, daughter of Hiram Thomas Frame (see Frame III). Children: Helen, married Dr. T. A. Irwin, of Franklin; Edith Melissa, married Dr. Carl D. Foster, of Johnstown, and they have one child, Carl D. Jr., and reside in Denver, Colorado; Charles Leedon.

(The Frame Line).

(I) Thomas Frame, born in Dublin, Ireland, married Lady Mary McNoll, also of Dublin. They emigrated to this country, locating first at Philadelphia and later at Chester, Pennsylvania. Children: James, of whom further; John; Allie, married a Mr. Hoover; Abner; Margaret

(II) James, son of Thomas and Lady Mary (McNoll) Frame, was born in Chester, Chester (now Delaware) county, Pennsylvania, January 24, 1791. He served in the war of 1812, was with Perry in the famous battle of Lake Erie, and served on the brig "Niagara" and the schooner "Porcupine." He was one of the command detailed to shoot Bird for deserting his sweetheart. Bird, who was an intimate friend of his, was buried on the shore of Lake Erie. Frame returned to the spot many years later and finding the waves of the lake had encroached on the grave, he exhumed the body and removed it either to Erie or Northeast, where it was reburied. James Frame settled in Crawford county, Pennsylvania, where he purchased land and became an influential farmer. He was an ardent disciple of John Wesley, and one of the most active workers of the Methodist church in Jamestown, Pennsylvania, where he died about 1868. He married, February 28, 1816, Elizabeth Van Sickle, born December 28, 1793, daughter of Richard and Nancy (Caswell) Van Sickle. Richard Van Sickle was born in Maryland, and Nancy Caswell in Virginia. The Van Sickle family is of Holland origin, and its members who came to this country in the seventeenth century are widely dispersed throughout New York and other states. Various branches of the family use the form Sickles or Syckles, and it has been impossible to trace the present line.

(III) Hiram Thomas, son of James and

Elizabeth (Van Sickle) Franc, was born about 1824, died in Westboro, Kentucky, in March, 1864. He was engaged for many years in the manufacture of wagons and the smithing business. At the time of the gold fever in 1849 he amassed considerable wealth in building wagons for and fitting out those bound for the gold fields in California. He himself made several voyages around the Horn to California, where he had mining interests. Later he moved to New Orleans, and at the outbreak of the civil war, his sympathies being entirely with the North, he was obliged, owing to threats against his life, to leave that city with his family and seek refuge further north. He located in Westboro, Kentucky, where he died before the end of the war. He was a Master Mason, member of Volcano Lodge of Sacramento, and of the Grand Lodge of California, joining the latter December 11, 1856. He married and had children: Edith, married Dr. Newman and had one daughter, Donna Bunnell, wife of H. C. Drake, of Plainfield, New Jersey; Ella Donzella, married, July 2, 1873, Isaac Newton Patterson (see Patterson IV).

McCLUNE ——— McClune, a native of Indiana county, Pennsylvania, and a scion of fine old Scotch-Irish ancestry, was engaged in farming operations in Indiana county during his entire active career. He married ———, and had a son, Reed, of whom further.

(II) Reed, son of ——— McClune, was born in Indiana county, Pennsylvania, in the year 1813. He passed his boyhood and youth on his father's farm in Indiana county, and later learned the trade of millwright. When a young man he came to Clarion county and settled in the vicinity of Sligo, working for the Craigs and making his home with that family for a time. He was engaged in the work of millwright until a very old age. After his marriage he established the family home at the mouth of Piney creek and there resided until the outbreak of the civil war, when he moved to the Corbett farm in Piney township, near Madison Furnace. Subsequently he purchased a farm near Reidsburg and still later bought the McCalmont farm on Piney creek, on which estate he died about 1900. He farmed and worked at his trade of millwright and also was a draughtsman, putting up many barns and repairing blast furnaces. In politics he was a Republican, but never aspired to public office. Mr. McClune married Phoebe, daughter of Edward and Sarah Corbett, who were connected with the early Corbetts of Clarion. There were ten children in the Corbett family, as follows: James, was a cabinet-maker in Clarion county during his active life; John, was a farmer in the vicinity of Asheville, Ohio; Gerardus, was a farmer near Columbus, Ohio; Miles, was a frontiersman and miner in Nevada, where he died; Allen Wilson, killed in the battle of Fredericksburg in the civil war; Phoebe, aforementioned, married Mr. McClune; Sarah Ann, became the wife of Jacob King, and died in Reynoldsville; Phinetta, widow of Robert Mills and lives at Madison Furnace; Susan, married Lindsay Wray and died in Chicago; Wynkoop, was a roamer and died somewhere in the west. Mr. and Mrs. McClune had twelve children: 1. Sarah Ann, died young. 2. John Q., died young. 3. Mary, also died young. 4. James, a farmer and lumberman in Limestone township, Clarion county, Pennsylvania. 5. Charles Reed, mentioned below. 6. Manela, wife of J. O. Delp; they live in Kane, Pennsylvania. 7. Morrison, a machinist and millwright; resides at Galeton, Potter county, Pennsylvania. 8. Craig, a carpenter, now living in Clarion. 9. Phoebe, widow of James Smathers; lives in Monroe township, Clarion county, Pennsylvania. 10. Alla, widow of James Ogden; lives near Pittsburgh, Pennsylvania. 11. Miles, a sawyer and farmer near Clarion. 12. Rosa, died young. Mr. and Mrs. Reed McClune were devout members of the Baptist church in their religious faith.

(III) Charles Reed, son of Reed and Phoebe (Corbett) McClune, was born in Clarion county, Pennsylvania, April 3, 1844. He was educated in the old "8 square" school-house in Piney township. On August 1, 1862, he enlisted in Company E, Tenth Pennsylvania Reserves. Later he was transferred to the One Hundred and Ninety-first Regiment, Company I, and he served in the war until June 1, 1865, when he received his honorable discharge. He participated in the conflicts at South Mountain, Antietam, Fredericksburg, Appomattox Court House, Gettysburg, Petersburg, Welden Railroad, Hatchers Run and the Wilderness campaign. He was wounded by a bursting shell at Fredericksburg and sent to the hospital at Washington, D. C., where he remained for six weeks. He was never captured. After the close of the war he returned to Clarion county and for one year worked at boatbuilding on the Clarion river. In 1867 he went to the oil fields at Pleasantville and from there to Foster Island. In 1871 he came back to Clarion county and from that year until 1905 was engaged in the lumbering business. He operated in the forests of Clarion county, built boats, and with his partner employed an average of twenty men all the year round. In 1904 Mr. McClune removed to Callensburg and here purchased some fine residence property. He has lived retired since 1905, but still retains a moneyed interest in the lumber business with which he was identified for so many years. He is a stockholder in the Citizens Trust Company at Clarion and has some oil interests in this section of the state. In politics he accords an unswerving allegiance to the Republican party, in the local councils of which he is an active factor. He has served on the Callensburg school board for the past five years, and has also been a member of the city council. He and his wife are members of the Reformed church, to whose good works they are most liberal contributors.

Mr. McClune married, July 30, 1871, Levina E. Reese, born in Clarion county, Pennsylvania, November 6, 1844, daughter of Thomas and Mary (Barrett) Reese. The paternal grandfather of Mrs. McClune was Andrew Reese, who was born in Baltimore, Maryland, where he was married and whence he came to Clarion county, Pennsylvania, engaging in agricultural pursuits. The maternal grandparents of Mrs. McClune were old residents of Farmington township, where the Grandfather Barrett was a farmer. Thomas Reese was a Democrat in politics, and he and his wife were members of the German Reformed church. He met death by drowning in the Clarion river, and his widow, who never remarried, died about 1885. There were ten children in the Reese family, namely: John, Susan, Amanda, Mary, Andrew, Levina E. (Mrs. McClune), Sophia, wife of Aaron Hartman, resides in Clarion township; Sarah, married Alexander Over, lives in Licking township; Elizabeth, twin of Sarah, wife of William Clark, of Nebraska; Thomas Jefferson, married Clara Weeter, lives in Ohio. Mr. and Mrs. McClune have two children: 1. Sarah Elizabeth, born June 12, 1873; wife of Elmer Hale, of Licking township; they have three children: Walter, Reed and Herbert. 2. Blanche Irene, born December 22, 1875; wife of Merl Wensel, a railroad conductor; they live in East Brady, Clarion county, Pennsylvania, and have three children: Herbert, DeVere and Elizabeth.

CRISWELL

The early records indicate that this name was spelled variously, as Creswell, Cresswell and Crisswell. The family is of Scotch-Irish derivation.

(I) Elisha Criswell, the first member of this family of whom we have definite information, was born about 1770, died in Kishacoquillas valley, Mifflin county, Pennsylvania, about 1820. He settled with two of his brothers, Benjamin and Elijah, in the Kishacoquillas valley, where he acquired land, which he cleared and tilled. He married Elsie Chesney, born about 1769, died in 1856. Among his children was Robert Chesney, of whom further.

(II) Robert Chesney, son of Elisha and Elsie (Chesney) Criswell, was born in the Kishacoquillas valley, Mifflin county, Pennsylvania, May 6, 1813, died in Richland township, Venango county, Pennsylvania, in March, 1897. He was a substantial farmer and prominent in his neighborhood. He owned land in Richland township, and after first clearing and improving one farm there, he removed to and settled on a larger one where he remained until his death. He married (first) Mary Say, and (second) Hannah, daughter of William Nickle, of the north of Ireland. Children, two by first marriage: 1. Elsie, married Henry Neeley; children: William, David, Harvey, James and Dora. 2. David. 3. William, born in 1845, living in Kansas; married Maria Sheffer; children: George, Lloyd, Walter and Lulu. 4. Nancy, born in 1847, died in 1863. 5. Montgomery, born September 20, 1848; married, September 28, 1874, Ellen Weaver; children: Pearl E., deceased; Blanch P., married Charles F. Beals; Royal G. 6. George Stuart, of whom further. 7. Silas, born February 6, 1852; married, March 30, 1876, Lucinda Reath; children: A child, died in infancy; Myrtle, Fleming, Nellie, Mary and Elizabeth. 8. Mary Elizabeth, born in 1854; married J. J. Weaver; children: Maud, Herbert, William, Wallace, Mabel, Mollie, Blanche, Reuben, a daughter died in infancy, and Mary.

(III) George Stuart, son of Robert Chesney and Hannah (Nickle) Criswell, was born in Richland township, Venango county, Pennsylvania, April 7, 1850. He was reared on the old homestead in Richland township, and was educated in the public schools and in the Emlenton Academy, teaching school for five winter terms. In 1873 he began reading law, and in 1874 entered the office of H. A. Miller, Esq., of Franklin, and was admitted to the bar of Venango county in 1875. From the time of his elevation to the bench he was actively engaged in the practice of law, being associated a portion of the time with the Hon. J. W. Lee, later of Pittsburgh, now deceased, and F. W. Hastings, Esq., of Bradford, Pennsylvania. He is a Presbyterian in religion.

Politically he has always been affiliated with the Republican party. On March 4, 1872, he was appointed deputy prothonotary and held that position for over two years. He represented Venango county two terms in the legislature of Pennsylvania, and during the last term was chairman of the general judiciary committee of the house. Upon the resignation of the Hon. Charles E. Taylor, he was appointed by Governor Hastings, as president judge of Venango county, and took the oath of office on March 7, 1895. He afterward received without opposition the nomination of the Republican party for the judgeship and was elected by a large majority for the full term of ten years. In about 1905 he was re-elected for another term of ten years, beginning the first Monday of January, 1906, upon which he entered and which he is now serving. Since his elevation to the bench he has proven himself to be an ideal judge, and is frequently called to other counties to preside at the trial of important cases. He is by temperament and traits of mind and character as well as by training eminently well fitted for the judiciary. Never a partisan, never rash in deciding a question before a full hearing, he presides at trials with dignity and treats all parties with the greatest courtesy and strictest impartiality and brings to the decision of legal questions a mind naturally clear, calm and judicial, and by training easily able to grasp the controlling question of the case. His decisions are never warped by personal feelings or prejudices and he has also a great capacity for care and painstaking work. As a result his decisions are rarely appealed, and nearly always sustained. Judge Criswell has been a member of the city council and school board of Franklin, and at present is member of the water commission of Franklin, and board of trustees of the State Institution for Feeble Minded, at Polk, Pennsylvania.

He married, November 26, 1879, Flora, daughter of Joseph Harrison and Eliza Margaret (Davis) Smith. Children: 1. Chesney Harrison, born March 25, 1884; graduate of Washington and Jefferson College, and Massachusetts School of Technology; chemical engineer at Greely, Colorado. 2. Elisha Wayne, born November 5, 1885; graduate of Washington and Jefferson College, read law, and was admitted to the Pennsylvania bar in January, 1911. 3. George Stuart (2), born February 6, 1888; graduate of Alleghany College; now teaching in the Franklin high school. 4. Richard Lee, born July 17, 1889, died in January, 1890. 5. Clarence Crawford, born November 21, 1891; a student.

NICHOLS Through marriage this family is connected with the Farwell, Mason and Riddell lines, all three of which are mentioned in this narrative. Nothing is known concerning the immigrant ancestor of this family, and the first representative of the name of whom we have record is John Nichols, of Farmersville, New York. He married Ann Seely. Children: George, Maria, William Wallace, of whom further; Caroline, Benjamin, served in the civil war; Ormes, killed in the civil war; John, served in the civil war.

(II) William Wallace, son of John and Ann (Seely) Nichols, was born in Farmersville, New York, October 27, 1830. He was reared and educated in the place of his birth, whence he removed to Salamanca, New York, where he died July 4, 1895. He was for many years in the employ of the Atlantic & Great Western Railroad Company, which was finally merged with the Erie road. He married, in August, 1857, Mary Victoria, daughter of Lucius and Lucy (Farwell) Durkee (see Farwell X). Lucius Durkee was born in Brandon, Vermont, February 14, 1804, and married Lucy Farwell, February 18, 1830. He was a son of Robert Durkee, born in Brandon, Vermont, in 1780, and married Delight Polly. William Wallace and Mary Victoria (Durkee) Nichols had one son, Hosea Monroe, of whom further.

(III) Hosea Monroe, son of William Wallace and Mary Victoria (Durkee) Nichols, was born in Farmersville, New York, November 26, 1859. He was educated in the public schools and Randolph Academy. On the completion of his education he entered the employ of the Standard Oil Company and worked up to the position of assistant cashier of the Bradford office of that company. In 1885 he went south to Meridian, Mississippi, where he was for four years teller in the National Bank. In 1890 he came to Oil City and again entered the employ of the Standard Oil Company. In 1902 he organized the Citizens' Banking Company on the South Side, Oil City, and was elected its first president, which office he now holds. He is also connected with various other enterprises in this city. He is a member of the Venango and Rockmere clubs, and in his religious faith he is a devout Methodist.

He married, March 31, 1878, Zaidee Lenore Mason, daughter of Augustus C. and Charlotte (Riddell) Mason, born August 12, 1860, died January 4, 1913 (see Mason VII). Children: 1. Lotta May, born January 25, 1879, died March 26, 1881. 2. Ethel Maud, born April 19, 1880, died January 6, 1881. 3. Roy McKay, born March 24, 1881; married, July 24, 1905, Margaret Ellen Touhey; children: Margaret Lenore, born July 13, 1906, died May 29, 1909; Richard McKay, born April 10, 1909; David Monroe, born January 11, 1910.

(The Farwell Line).

The ancestry of this old family is traced for four generations in England prior to the immigration to America of Henry Farwell, in 1631.

(I) Simon Farwell was born and reared in Yorkshire, England, whence he removed, with his wife Dorothy to Bishop Hill, near Taunton, England, in 1500. He had a son George, of whom further.

(II) George, son of Simon and Dorothy Farwell, was born in England. He married a girl whose Christian name was Phillippi and they had a son George, of whom further.

(III) George (2), son of George (1) and Phillippi Farwell, was born in England. He and his wife Mary had a son John, of whom further.

(IV) John, son of George (2) and Mary Farwell, was born in England. He married Dorothy ———, and had a son, Henry, of whom further.

(V) Henry, son of John and Dorothy Farwell, was born in England, in 1596. After his marriage he came to the United States, settling at Concord, Massachusetts, in 1631. In 1630, at Bishop Hill, England, he married Olive ———. He died August 1, 1670; his wife Olive died March 1, 1691. Their children: John, born December 2, 1639; Mary, December 26, 1640; Joseph, of whom further; Olive; Elizabeth.

(VI) Joseph, son of Henry and Olive Farwell, was born at Concord, Massachusetts, where he died December 31, 1722. He served in the French and Indian war and was called Ensign Joseph. August 25, 1702, he conveyed one-third of his property to his son Henry and then removed with his father to Dunstable, Massachusetts. He married, December 25, 1666, at Woburn, Massachusetts, Hannah Larned, born August 24, 1649, died December 31, 1685. Children: Hannah, born January 20, 1668, at Concord, Massachusetts; Joseph, of whom further; Elizabeth, June 9, 1672; Henry, December 18, 1674; Isaac; Sarah, September 2, 1683; John, June 15, 1686; William, January 21, 1688; Oliver, April 25, 1692.

(VII) Joseph (2), son of Joseph (1) and Hannah (Larned) Farwell, married, January 23, 1695, Hannah Colburn. Children: Joseph, born August 5, 1696; Thomas, October 11, 1698; Hannah, May 6, 1701; Elizabeth, December 31, 1703; Edward, of whom further; Mary, February 5, 1709; John, June 23, 1711; Samuel, November 14, 1714; David, May 21, 1717.

(VIII) Edward, son of Joseph (2) and Hannah (Colburn) Farwell was born June 12, 1706. He married Hanna ———. Children: Edward, born November 23, 1731; Submit, December 19, 1733; Hannah, October 3, 1736; David; Abel, of whom further.

(IX) Abel, son of Edward and Hanna Farwell, was a soldier in the war of the revolution, as a private in Captain Thomas Warren's company, Colonel Brooks' regulars, returned October 31, 1776. He settled at Mt. Holly, Vermont, and was one of the pioneers of Rutland county. He married Hannah ———. Children: Lemuel, born January 4, 1771; Solomon, February 29, 1772, died in infancy; Abel, twin of Solomon, died in infancy; Solomon, March 23, 1773; Leonard, April 16, 1776; Russell, of whom further; Hannah, May 17, 1781; Betsey, July 17, 1783; James, December 14, 1784; Lucy, July 1, 1788, died in 1886.

(X) Russell, son of Abel and Hannah Farwell, was born July 4, 1778. He married

———— and became father of Lucy Farwell, who married Lucius Durkee, and they were the parents of Mary Victoria, married William W. Nichols (see Nichols II).

(The Mason Line).

(I) Sampson Mason was the immigrant ancestor of this family in America. The first mention we have of him is in 1649, when Edward Bullock, of Dorchester, in the colony of Massachusetts Bay, New England, being about to depart for England and mindful of the many perils of the voyage, made his will July 25 of that year. In this will his name appears thus: "To Sampson Mason for wife's shoes." The foregoing is the earliest known record to prove the presence of Sampson Mason in New England. Of his early history nothing more is known than is contained in the following extract from the "History of the Baptists in America," compiled by the Rev. Isaac Backus. "Sampson Mason was a soldier in Cromwell's army and he came to America upon the turn of times in England and settled in Rehoboth, Massachusetts."

On the ninth day of March, 1650-51, Sampson Mason, designated shoemaker, purchased from William Betts his house and home lot in Dorchester, the lot containing six acres. The date of purchase of this house probably indicates very nearly the time of his marriage to Mary Butterworth. In February, 1655-56, he sold to Jacob Hewins his house and home lot and some other land. The exact date of his removal to Rehoboth is unknown but the records of the town have the following entry: "1657, December 9, it was voted that Sampson Mason should have free liberty to sojourn with us and buy houses, lands and meadows, if he see cause for his settlement, provided he lives peaceably and quietly."

From the records it is evident that Sampson Mason had acquired considerable property when he removed to Rehoboth and then entered extensively into land speculations. He appears as the holder of one share of the seventy-nine and one-half shares in the Rehoboth North Purchase, which afterward became the town of Attleborough, and also one of the proprietors or share holders of the town of Swansea, in which his descendants for many generations were prominent. He was one of the original proprietors of Swansea and a subscriber to the agreement which took effect when the town was incorporated by the court at Plymouth in an order as follows: "March 5, 1668. The township of Wannamoisett and the parts adjacent are established as Swansey."

It is probable that Sampson Mason became a member of the First Church about this time and the family tradition that he was converted to the Baptist faith by Elder John Myles, the first Baptist minister and founder of Swansea, may rest upon a substantial foundation although the tendency of his religious leaning was manifest prior to this time. During his residence in Dorchester he evidently had some connection with the orthodox church, possibly through his wife, and had not then arrived at the conclusion that infant baptism was wrong, for his son Noah was baptized in 1652 without protest or any evidence of disapproval on his part; but in 1660, when his son John was brought to baptism in the First Church of Dorchester by John Gurnell, he expressed his disapproval while giving his consent.

Though in 1672 Sampson Mason was allotted twelve acres of land in Swansea and erected a house upon this plot, there is no evidence that he removed to Swansea and his burial is recorded in Rehoboth, September 15, 1696. His personal estate was large for his time. During King Philip's war, which broke out shortly before his death, his widow contributed thirteen pounds, five shillings and ten pence, the ninth largest in the list of contributions from Rehoboth.

About 1650 he married Mary Butterworth, who was probably a daughter of John Butterworth, of Weymouth, Massachusetts. She died August 29, 1714. Children: 1. Noah, born between October 26, 1651, and February 8, 1652, died March 2, 1699; married (first) Martha ————, who died February 6, 1675; married (second) December 6, 1677. Sarah Fitch. 2. Sampson, born probably in 1653; married, July 14, 1705, Abigail Ferris. 3. John, born between March 18 and May 12, 1655, died March 18, 1682; married, October 15, 1679, Content Wales. 4. Samuel, born February 12, 1656, died January 25, 1743; married (first) March 2, 1682, Elizabeth Miller, who died March 3, 1718; married (second) November 4, 1718, Mrs. Lydia Tillinghast. 5. Sarah, born February 15, 1657. 6. Mary, born February 7, 1659, died November 15, 1727; married, January 7, 1684, Ephraim Wheaton. 7. Joseph, born March 6, 1662, died May 19, 1748; married (first) March

12, 1683, Anne Daggett; married (second) September 4, 1686, Lydia Bowen. 8. Bethiah, born October 15, 1665, died before 1712; married, May 23, 1688, John Wood. 9. Isaac, of whom further. 10. Pelatiah, born April 1, 1669, died March 29, 1763; married, May 22, 1694, Hepsibeth Brooks; is said to have had three other wives. 11. Benjamin, born October 20, 1670, died in August, 1740; married Ruth Rounds. 12. Thankful, born October 27, 1672; married, June 17, 1689, Thomas Bowen.

(II) Isaac, son of Sampson and Mary (Butterworth) Mason, was born in Rehoboth, Massachusetts, July 15, 1667, died January 25, 1741. He was a shoemaker by trade, and lived in Rehoboth for some years after his marriage. About 1706 he removed to Swansea, where he probably erected the house, still standing, which by tradition was his home. He was chosen deacon of the Second Church of Swansea soon after its organization, in 1693, and continued in that office until his death. His wife Hannah was living when he made his will in 1741, but the date of her death is unknown. He married Hannah ———. Children: 1. Hannah, born January 9, 1694, died February 26, 1697. 2. Mary, born January 26, 1695, died March 4, 1697. 3. Isaac, born December 26, 1698, died in 1732; married, January 29, 1723, Mary Fiske. 4. Sampson, born February 24, 1700, died probably in 1731; married, September 26, 1723, Experience Lewis. 5. Hezekiah, born June 6, 1704, died April 4, 1738; married, July 23, 1730, Rebecca Martin. 6. Nathan, of whom further. 7. Oliver, born August 20, 1706, died December 11, 1787; married, December 19, 1728, Martha Cole. 8. Hannah, born March, 1710; married, December 27, 1727, Samuel Lewis. 9. Benjamin, born April 10, 1711. 10. Mary, born May 21, 1713; married, December 18, 1737, Nathan Bowen.

(III) Nathan, son of Isaac and Hannah Mason, was born in Rehoboth, May 10, 1705, died May, 1758. He was a blacksmith, and lived in Swansea during the greater part of his life. He married, August 26, 1731, Lillis Hale, daughter of John and Hannah (Tillinghast) Hale, born in Swansea, October 2, 1714. After his death, Mr. Mason's widow married, January 30, 1763, Mial Pierce. Children: 1. Sampson, born September 27, 1732, died September 29, 1811; married, August 5, 1751, Hannah Haile. 2. Barnard, born March 13, 1735, died December 6, 1804; married, July 22, 1756, Abiah Eastbrook. 3. Jesse, of whom further. 4. Lillis, born May 8, 1739; married, March 16, 1764, Isaac Fish Jr. 5. Nathan, born February 21, 1741; married (first) March 7, 1765, Mehitable Carpenter; (second) Mrs. Rhode Mason, widow of James Mason and daughter of Nathan Wood. 6. Freelove, born April 25, 1743, died February 23, 1814; married, March 23, 1763, Aaron Wood. 7. Innocent, born August 20, 1745, died in 1778; married, December 2, 1767, Benjamin Kingsley. 8. Mary, born June 30, 1748, died December 17, 1834; married, October 8, 1769, Joseph Cornell. 9. Aaron, born June 29, 1749; served in militia during the revolution. 10. Rosanna, born about 1750, died March 10, 1795; married, July 14, 1776, Joseph Baker. 11. Sibbel, married Levi Wood. 12. Levi, born October 15, 1752, died August 20, 1834; married Amy Tilson. 13. Pardon, born August 14, 1758, died May 18, 1845; married (first) April 24, 1785, Anna Hale; married (second) September 24, 1837, Mrs. Elizabeth Potter, daughter of John Stafford.

(IV) Jesse, son of Nathan and Lillis (Hale) Mason, was born in Swansea, Massachusetts, March 21, 1737, died October 17, 1823. He was a carpenter by trade. About 1770 he removed to Lanesborough, Berkshire, Massachusetts. He served in the revolutionary war as a private in Captain Daniel Brown's company. The company was called into service, August 14, 1777, on an alarm from Lanesborough, Massachusetts, and fought at the battle of Bennington. He served a second time in Captain Daniel Brown's company, Colonel Benjamin Simon's regiment, in October, 1780. The company rendered service at Berkshire, Massachusetts.

He married, March 22, 1758, Lois Mason, daughter of Pelatiah and Hannah (Hale) Mason, born in Swansea, February 23, 1739. He is said to have married (second) in 1813, Mrs. Pratt. Children: 1. Esther, born October 17, 1759; married Simeon Martin. 2. David, of whom further. 3. Nathan, born August 8, 1762, died in Malone, New York; married, January 1, 1784, Mercy Wood. 4. Elizabeth, born October 1, 1763. 5. Lydia, born July 4, 1765, died September 17, 1812; married, December, 1782, Reuben Baker. 6. Zephaniah, born August 29, 1766; married, November 12, 1786, Desire Cole. 7. Daniel, born March 26, 1769, died in 1838; married, November 14, 1788, (possibly) Polly Whitman. 8. Prudence, born July 26, 1770; married, December 22, 1787, Kingsley Martin. 9. Reuben. 10. Lorana, married, August 1, 1789, Stephen Potter. 11. Jesse, born July 24, 1778, died about 1854; married, May 25, 1800, Hannah Brown. 12. Lois, married Stephen Greenman.

(V) David, son of Jesse and Lois (Mason) Mason, was born in Swansea, Massachusetts, April 3, 1761, died March 16, 1817. The family settled in New Ashford, Massachusetts. He married, November 19, 1780, Mehitable Pratt, born September 11, 1762, died in March, 1852. Children: 1. Linda, born August 28, 1781; married, January, 1799, Eliphalet Dean. 2. Benjamin Pratt, mentioned below. 3. Lewis, born May 3, 1785, died September 17, 1786. 4. Jesse, born April 25, 1786. 5. Arvilla, born September 4, 1789; married William Beach. 6. Mehitable, born August 23, 1791; married, March 21, 1811, Dudley Skinner. 7. Achsah G., born March 24, 1793; married, October 31, 1816, Elisha Davenport. 8. Polly, born March 25, 1795; married, December 20, 1815, Julius Hutchinson. 9. Jerusha H., born April 17, 1797; married, May 5, 1816, Samuel Springer. 10. Lewis T., born August 14, 1799, died unmarried. 11. John Luther, born January 9, 1801. 12. Electa Beach, born October 30, 1804; married Asa Skinner. 13. Henry Turner, born July 20, 1807, died September 20, 1873, unmarried.

(VI) Benjamin Pratt, son of David and Mehitable (Pratt) Mason, was born April 23, 1783, died in 1867. He married, in 1805, Rhoda Brown, born in 1785, died December 24, 1846. Among their children was Augustus C., of whom further.

(VII) Augustus C., son of Benjamin Pratt and Rhoda (Brown) Mason, was born in September, 1817, died May 26, 1895. He lived for a number of years in Buffalo, New York, and then removed to Salamanca, New York, where he was engaged in the real estate business. He married, January 1, 1837, Charlotte Riddell, born January 20, 1820, died in February, 1895 (see Riddell III). Children: 1. Albert Woodford, born in November, 1844; married Desdemonia Smith; children: Albertina, married George Eastman; May, married Frank Gardner. 2. Olive Jane, born October, 1847; married Timothy Babbitt; children: Timothy and Jennie M. 3. Perry Foster, born July, 1850; married (first) Evelyn Wilcox, by whom he had one son, Wayne; married (second) Lucy Chamberlain. 4. James Augustus, born May, 1853; married Catherine Wright; children: Verne, Guy, Emma and Ada. 5. Charlotte Idelle, born November 12, 1855; married Charles M. Wenrick; children: Raymond M., Charles M., Albert, Earl, Olive E. and Charlotte M. 6. Zaidee Lenore, born August 12, 1860, died January 4, 1913, married Hosea Monroe Nichols (see Nichols III).

(The Riddell Line).

(I) Thomas Ridel (or Riddell) was born in county Tyrone, Ireland, in 1739. He was brought to this country when a child and grew up in New England. He was a farmer. It is said that he served in the war of the revolution. He married Rebecca Moulton, of Monson, Massachusetts. Children: 1. John, born 1761; married Olive Blodget. 2. Joseph, of whom further. 3. Elijah, born January 27, 1772; married Clarissa Fuller. 4. Mary. 5. Susan, born between 1772 and 1773; married John Squires. 6. Sally, born February 16, 1774. 7. Sally, born February 16, 1778; married Levi Patterson. 8. Thomas, born September 7, 1781; married Minerva Merrick.

(II) Joseph Riddle (or Riddell), son of Thomas and Rebecca (Moulton) Ridel or Riddell, was born in Monson, Massachusetts in 1763. He resided in Monson until 1808, when he emigrated to the "Holland Purchase" in the state of New York, where he settled as a farmer and resided during the remainder of his lifetime. In the summer of 1775 he enlisted under Captain Isaac Cotton, in Colonel David Brewster's regiment. In 1776 he enlisted under Captain Joseph Munger, in the regiment of Colonel Robert I. Woodbridge, "Massachusetts Line." July 1, 1777, he entered the service for three years under Captain Caleb Keen, and Colonel William Shepherd, of the Fourth Massachusetts Regiment, General Glover's brigade, as drum-major; and in July, 1780, was discharged by Captain Simon Larned, who was in command of the regiment at "Robertson Farms," near West Point. He was in a short tour in the militia and at the surrender of Burgoyne, but was not in the decisive battle preceding that event, in consequence of guarding the road to Albany. He was in the battle of Monmouth, New Jersey, June 28, 1778, and with General Sullivan, in Rhode Island, in August, 1778. He married Mary or Polly ———. Children: 1. Rebecca, born March 10, 1782; married Thomas Broadway. 2. Polly, born August 1, 1784; married

Daniel Moulton. 3. Lina, born June 1, 1786; married Maturin Allard. 4. Charlotte, born June 8, 1788; married James McKain. 5. Orrin, born May 18, 1790; married Bertha Chaffe. 6. Freeborn Moulton, of whom further.

(III) Freeborn Moulton Riddell, son of Joseph and Mary Riddle or Riddell, was born in Monson, Massachusetts, September 18, 1793, died March 12, 1877. He was a farmer by occupation. He married (first) Abigail Chaffe, of Alexander, New York. She died March 15, 1829. He married (second) Sarah Smith, of Batavia, Genesee county, New York. He married (third) Jemima Baston. Child by first marriage: Charlotte Riddell, born January 20, 1820, died in February, 1895; she married, January 1, 1837, Augustus C. Mason (see Mason VII).

The Hull family are recorded
HULL. in the "Heralds Distinction" of Devonshire, England, but the original name, De la Hulle, in Shropshire, in the reign of Edward II., indicates they went from the continent to England. Shortly after the Pilgrims landed at Plymouth, five brothers came to Massachusetts from England: John, George, Richard, Joseph and Robert. The family in England bore arms: "A chevron ermine, between the lions or talbots, heads erased."

(I) Rev. Joseph Hull was born in England, 1595, and matriculated at St. Mary's Hall, Oxford, May 12, 1612, and became a B. A., November 14, 1614, being then nineteen years of age. He was instituted rector of Northleigh in 1621, resigned in 1632 and in 1635 with a second wife Agnes, seven children and three servants, and a company of people he had collected, sailed for America. He settled at Weymouth, Massachusetts, but a year later went to Hingham. He was afterwards minister at the Isle of Shoals, York, Oyster River, and again at the Isle of Shoals, where he died November 19, 1675, and is buried at York, Massachusetts.

(II) Captain Tristam Hull, son of Rev. Joseph Hull, was born in 1624, died in 1666. He was a seafaring man and became a sea captain. He was a selectman of Bristol and served on numerous committees. He owned two ships and lands constituting a comfortable fortune for that day. He married Blanche ———.

(III) John, son of Captain Tristam Hull, was a resident of Canonicut, Massachusetts. He held many positions of trust and was representative in 1757. He married a Miss Cary.

(IV) Oliver, son of John Hull, settled in New York City with his wife, Penelope (Pfones) Hull, a few years before the revolution. Though members of the Society of Friends they took an active but quiet part, and aided the efforts of the Quakers to mitigate the sufferings of the American prisoners during the time the British held possession of New York.

(V) John (2), son of Oliver Hull, was born in Canonicut, Massachusetts, August 11, 1762. He came to New York with his father, where in 1781 he married (first) Mary Avery, who died in 1802, in Dutchess county, New York, where they moved in 1800. He married (second) November 23, 1803, Amy Cornell.

(VI) John (3), son of John (2) Hull, was born about 1800, died in Warren, Pennsylvania, August, 1873. He was born in Dutchess county, New York, and lived in New Jersey, where his marriage occurred. He came to Warren, Pennsylvania, during the decade 1840-50, where he engaged in general merchandising. Later he became proprietor of the old Warren House, built in 1819. In 1848 he began the erection of the Carver House, which he opened for the entertainment of guests in 1849. This has always been the leading hotel of Warren. Mr. Hull was its proprietor from 1849 until January 1, 1857, when he leased it, but again resumed its management in 1859, continuing until 1864. The following year his son, Milton W., became its proprietor, continuing until 1867, when it passed out of the controls of the Hulls. Mr. Hull was one of the leading men in the development of Warren, and was influential in public affairs. In 1853 he was elected borough councilman (his son Milton W. being elected chief burgess the same year) and was reëlected 1854-55-56-57-58-62-63-65-66-67-68-69-70-71-72-73, dying in the office in August of that year. He was an able, honorable gentleman and held in the highest regard. He was a member of the Masonic order, holding a high position, and an Odd Fellow of prominence. He married Nancy Gibbs. Children: Cindrella, married Charles Holman; Theodore, married Jemima McGowan; Matilda, married Julius Hall; Milton W., of whom further; Morris, died young while attending school at West Point; Cynthia, married McKinney Mead; Annie E., married Edward E. Mooar.

(VII) Milton W., son of John (3) Hull, was born in New Jersey, died in Franklin, Pennsylvania, and is buried in Warren. He came to Warren, Pennsylvania, with his father and was his assistant in business and his contemporary in public affairs, both working in harmony for the public good. He became proprietor of the Carver House in Warren, June 1, 1805, in association with J. B. Hall, continuing until April, 1867. He then engaged in the oil business and became one of the successful producers of his section. In 1853 he was elected chief burgess of Warren, and in 1856 was elected councilman, reëlected 1857-64-65; with the exception of the year 1864 his father was also a member of council. He was one of the early volunteer firemen of Warren, being a charter member of Vulcan Fire Company, No. 1, organized in 1853. He married Rebecca Jones Conarros. Children: Cora Evelyn, of whom further; Nettie M., married Silas Morton Ross, children: Cora E. and Mildred E.; John H., married Isabel Young.

(VIII) Cora Evelyn, daughter of Milton W. and Rebecca Jones (Conarros) Hull, was born in Warren, Pennsylvania. She married, June 12, 1879, Samuel Young Ramage, son of Benjamin and Almira (Seavey) Ramage, and resides in Oil City, Pennsylvania. Children: Florence E., married Henry Logan Golson; Samuel Young, married Elizabeth D. Saxon, children: Samuel S. and Ruth E.; Ruth E., died young; Louise, died young; Alfred Hull, now (1912) a student at Amherst College; Isabel; Benjamin.

LAY   The earliest record of a Lay in Pennsylvania is of the eccentric Benjamin Lay, of Abington. He was born in Colchester, England, and for a time followed the sea. In 1710 he was in Barbadoes, where he witnessed much of the suffering caused by slavery. He was engaged there as a merchant, but soon left in disgust, coming to Pennsylvania and settling at Abington, ten miles from Philadelphia. He was a member of the Society of Friends, and it is said that at one time he was known to every man and woman in Philadelphia, and to nearly every child. He had two hobbies, hatred of slavery and of animal food. Many interesting stories are related of him, and it would seem that he was a thorn in the side of his Quaker brethren, who kept slaves. He is said to have been but four feet in height, and an ancient print of him shows a full beard. He wrote a book against negro slavery that was printed by Dr. Franklin in 1737. He died in February, 1759, aged eighty-two years, at the residence of Joshua Morris, and is buried in the Friends' burial ground at Abington. There is no mention of his having a family, nor do the records of the Abington monthly meeting bear the name of any other Lay. The census of the United States, taken in 1790, does not disclose the name of any Lay living in Pennsylvania at that date. Histories of York give no one of the name in York township or borough in 1783. Hence the conclusion is irresistible that John Lay, the progenitor of the Lays of Oil City, was a descendant of the Lays of Connecticut, and came to York, Pennsylvania, after the census of 1790 was taken. John was a persistent name in the Connecticut family, and in the absence of any contrary evidence, John of York may safely be considered a descendant of John (1) Lay, of Lyme, Connecticut, who first appeared in (then) Saybrook, later Lyme, in 1648. He had two sons, both named John, one by a first and one by a second marriage. This has led to much conjecture and no little confusion. There were many Johns in each generation, usually bearing a distinctive title, as: "senior," "junior," "second," "third," etc. There are two branches of the family recognized as having separated from each other in the second American generation. The Lays of New York descend from Robert Lay, of Westbrook, Connecticut, a descendant of one of these two sons of John (1) Lay, named John.

(I) The first connected definite record of the progenitors of Charles H. Lay, of Oil City, is of John Lay, who was born on the hillside of the west side of Codorus, and buried in York, Pennsylvania. He was a coppersmith, engaged also in the kindred business of tinsmithing. He married (first) ———. Children: Charles, of whom further; George; Josiah, and Margaret. He married (second) a widow, Mrs. Ruby, of German parentage.

(II) Charles, son of John Lay, was born in York, Pennsylvania, October 3, 1798, died in California. He continued his residence in York until the year 1822, then moved to Erie, Pennsylvania, where he worked at his trades of coppersmith and tinsmith, which he had learned with his father. In addition to this business he also conducted a general store. In 1832 he contracted and built a one mile section of the French Creek canal and moved his residence to Franklin, Pennsylvania. When his contract was completed he again moved, settling in Pittsburgh, where he was engaged in building engines to be used on the inclines by which canal boats were taken over the Allegheny mountains on the old Pennsylvania canal. Afterward he ran the engine at Incline No. 5 for a year, then moved to Columbia, Pennsylvania. When the railroad was built from Baltimore to York, Pennsylvania, he ran the first engine that passed over it. Later he moved with his family to York, Pennsylvania. In 1849 he joined a party of gold-seekers and went to California, where all trace of him was lost. He left Sacramento with considerable gold on his person, and it is supposed he was attacked by robbers and murdered.

He married, February 18, 1824, Ann Catherine Bartols, born in Baltimore, Maryland, February 6, 1799, of German parentage, died in Columbia, Pennsylvania, August 4, 1842. Her twin sister Margaret was the mother of John Randall, of Memphis, Tennessee. Children: 1. Charles Henry, of whom further. 2. William Lambert, born February 18, 1827, died in Oil City, Pennsylvania, December 10, 1896; he married Harriet Lentz. 3. John Columbus, born September 10, 1829; married Mrs. Eliza Jane Erwin, born in 1837, at Scotch Hill, Clarion county, Pennsylvania. 4. Newton, born January 4, 1832, died at Balize, Honduras, August 24, 1858. 5. Oliver, born February 27, 1835, died at Oil City, Pennsylvania, March 10, 1873. 6. Mary Ann, born March 22, 1838; married, February 12, 1863, Andrew Bunker; children: Fannie and Mary.

(III) Charles Henry, son of Charles and Ann Catherine (Bartols) Lay, was born in Erie, Pennsylvania, March 18, 1825, died in Oil City, Pennsylvania. He became a manufacturer of printing inks in Philadelphia, with his brother, William L. Lay, and John R. Campbell. Later he moved to Oil City, where he became engaged in the lumber business. He was a man of wealth and influence; a member of the Episcopal church and a Republican in politics. He married, December 23, 1852, Isabel Rogers Campbell, born February 14, 1830, died November 7, 1908, daughter of Alexander and Abby T. (Russell) Campbell (see Tillinghast VII). Children: 1. Charles Hamilton, of whom further. 2. Russell Campbell, born in Philadelphia, Pennsylvania, November 11, 1855, died in Karns county, Texas, March 27, 1863. 3. William Dennett, born July 31, 1858, in Philadelphia, died there June 15, 1859. 4. William Russell, born in Karns county, Texas, March 18, 1863; married, July 12, 1886, Tirza Leona Hill, born September 3, 1864, in Oil City, Pennsylvania; children: Margaret Isabel, born May 14, 1887; Frances Trask, November 8, 1889; Joseph Hill, March 12, 1896; Lawrence Campbell, March 23, 1904. 5. Alexander, born in Oil City, Pennsylvania, November 19, 1866, died there June 2, 1867.

(IV) Charles Hamilton, son of Charles Henry and Isabel Rogers (Campbell) Lay, was born in Philadelphia, Pennsylvania March 14, 1854. He is a resident of Oil City. Prior to the dissolution of the Standard Oil Company he was treasurer of seven subsidiary companies, and at present is treasurer of the National Transit Company. He married, June 6, 1877, in Oil City, Pennsylvania, Alice Gertrude Colling, born in Medford, Minnesota, October 13, 1858, daughter of W. H. Colling. Child, Russell Colling, born January 3, 1879; married Rebecca White, born November 22, 1880; children: Isabel Priestley, born September 29, 1906; Eleanor Mable, February 9, 1909.

(The Tillinghast Line).

(I) Isabel Rogers (Campbell) Lay, wife of Charles Henry Lay, was a direct descendant of Elder Pardon (3) Tillinghast, a soldier under Cromwell, who was born at Seven Cliffs, near Beachy Head, England, in 1622, son of Pardon (2) and Elizabeth Tichbourne Tillinghast. He came to Connecticut in 1646, thence to Providence, Rhode Island, where he was a proprietor in 1665, having been a resident of Newport in 1663. In 1681, and for many years, he was minister and elder of the First Baptist Church of Providence. In 1711 he gave to the church a deed of the meeting house and lot. He was a cooper and engaged in commerce and storekeeping, owning a storehouse and wharf. He was a deputy to the general court, 1672-80-90-94-96-97. He was overseer of the poor in 1687 and for seventeen years member of the town council, his service being almost continuous. Morgan Edwards asserts that he was remarkable for his plainness and piety. In deeding his property to the church he stated the consideration as "The Christian love good will and affection, which I bear to the Church of Christ in Providence which I am in fellowship with and have the care of, as being Elder of the said Church." His will was proved February 17, 1718. He was buried in his own lot at the south end of the town of Providence.

He married (first) —— Butterworth; children: 1. Sarah, died young. 2. John, a deputy in 1690. 3. Mary, married Benjamin Carpenter. He married (second) April 16, 1664, Lydia, died 1718, daughter of Philip and Lydia (Masters) Taber. Children: 4. Lydia, married John Audley. 5. Pardon, of whom further. 6. Philip, a merchant, in 1690 a soldier in the expedition against Canada, justice of the peace, for twelve years deputy and at the same time member of the town council; his estate inventoried five thousand pounds, a very large fortune for his day; married Martha Thomas, who bore him fifteen children. 7. Benjamin, also a merchant; married Sarah Rhodes and left an estate almost as large as his brother Philip. 8. Abigail, married Nicholas Sheldon. 9. Joseph, a merchant; married (first) Freelove Stafford, (second) Mary Hendon. 10. Mercy, married Nicholas Power. 11. Hannah, married John Hale. 12. Elizabeth, married Philip Taber.

(II) Pardon (4), son of Elder Pardon (3) and Lydia (Taber) Tillinghast, was born in Providence, Rhode Island, February 16, 1668, died in East Greenwich, Rhode Island, 1743. He was a deputy in 1702-04-06-08-14-19-20-22-25. From 1705 to 1710 he was justice of the peace. He left an estate of three thousand pounds; to the Baptist church he left twenty-five pounds "Towards defraying the necessary charge in spreading the Gospel." He married (first) Mary Keech. Children: Mary Philip, John, Joseph and Mercy. He married (second) March 25, 1699, Sarah Ayers. Child, Pardon, of whom further.

(III) Pardon (5), son of Pardon (4) and Sarah (Ayers) Tillinghast, was born at East Greenwich, Rhode Island. He married Avis, daughter of Benjamin and Avis Norton. Children: Pardon, of whom further; William, married Sarah Holmes; Martha, married Benjamin Slucum; Avis, married James Carpenter.

(IV) Pardon (6), son of Pardon (5) and Avis (Norton) Tillinghast, married Abigail, daughter of John and Isabel Rogers. Children: Mary, married John B. Mumford; Abby, married Rev. Caleb Greene, a minister of the Baptist church; Martha, of whom further; Pardon, married Elizabeth ——; William, married Elizabeth Champlin; John, married Mary Ann Sanford.

(V) Martha, daughter of Pardon (6) and Abigail (Rogers) Tillinghast, married Charles Russell, of New Bedford, Massachusetts Children: Mary, died July 26, 1862, married Dr. Peter Van O'Linda; Martha, died November 15, 1845, married James Allen; John Somer; Abby, of whom further.

(VI) Abby, daughter of Charles and Martha (Tillinghast) Russell, was born May 5, 1799, died December 29, 1833. She married Alexander Campbell. Child, Isabel Rogers.

(VII) Isabel Rogers, daughter of Alexander and Abby (Russell) Campbell, married Charles Henry Lay (see Lay III).

CYPHERT The immigrant ancestor of the present family is said to have come from Holland, which points to a Dutch or German origin of this family. The name is a very uncommon one. Yet there is a similar German name. Among English surnames we find the following, apparently all rare, which may well be equivalent one to another and each to the present name: Cypher, Sypher and Syfert. On the whole, a German origin seems to us the most probable for the present family.

(I) Philip Cyphert, the founder of this family, was born in Holland, and died in Berks county, Pennsylvania. In that county he had settled after his coming into the colonies. It is not known whom he married, but he is known to have had ten children, and among these was Anthony, of whom further.

(II) Anthony, son of Philip Cyphert, was born in Berks county, Pennsylvania, in 1789, died in Limestone township, Clarion county, Pennsylvania, in 1873. Here he had settled in 1825, and he had a farm of four hundred acres. He married, in Westmoreland county, Pennsylvania, Mary, born in Westmoreland county, Pennsylvania, in 1788, died in 1882, daughter of Jacob Ringle. Her father had come from England to Philadelphia, and he spent his last days in Berks county. Children: James, deceased; John, deceased; Solomon, deceased; Thomas B., of whom further; William, deceased; David K.; Caroline, married Louis Barr, lives at Brookville, Pennsylvania; Nancy, deceased, married Joseph Reinsel, also deceased, and they lived in Clarion county.

(III) Thomas B., son of Anthony and Mary (Ringle) Cyphert, was born in Westmoreland county, Pennsylvania, February 13, 1829, died in March, 1909. He was a farmer. While he supported the Democratic party, he never sought office. He and his wife were members of the Methodist Protestant church. He married Jane, born in Clarion county, Pennsylvania, March 15, 1830, died in 1907, daughter of Robert and Jane (English) Allison (see Allison IV). Children: Son, died in infancy; Jane, deceased; David Harvey; Wilmer Reid, of whom further; Boyd Allison; Hugh Burton; Mary May, married Warren F. Snyder, lives in Limestone, Clarion county, Pennsylvania.

(IV) Wilmer Reid, son of Thomas B. and Jane (Allison) Cyphert, was born in Limestone township, Clarion county, Pennsylvania, July 18, 1864. He was brought up on a farm. Beside receiving a common school education, he studied at Corsica Academy, at a business college at Titusville, and at the Clarion State Normal School. For thirteen terms he taught school, and for six years he was clerk in a store in Limestone township. On January 1, 1909, he was appointed commission clerk of Clarion county, and he was reappointed January 1, 1912, to hold office for a term of four years. For nine years he was school director in Limestone township. He is a member of the Free and Accepted Masons and of the Order of United American Mechanics, both of the senior and of the junior order. Mr. Cyphert is a Democrat. He is a member of the Methodist Protestant church.

(The Allison Line).

(I) Robert Allison, the first of the line here under consideration, came from Ireland to Bedford county, Pennsylvania. The family were from Scotland, but Robert emigrated from Ireland in 1750. He met his wife, Beckie Beard, on board ship coming over and they were married in 1752. They later removed to Indiana county, Pennsylvania. They had among other children, Fate, of whom further.

(II) Fate, son of Robert and Beckie (Beard) Allison, was born in Indiana county, Pennsylvania, and settled in what is now Clarion county in 1800. He was one of the pioneers to venture into this region and did much to build up and have it made a county. He married Polly Henry. Children: Beckie; Sallie; Robert, of whom further; Henry; John; Jane; Nancy; Thomas; Mary; Fate.

(III) Robert (2), son of Fate and Polly (Henry) Allison, was born in Indiana county, Pennsylvania. He removed in 1800 to what is now Clarion county with his father. He married, in 1820, Jane English. Children: Mary; Beckie; David; Elizabeth; Robert; Jane, of whom further; Fate; Sarah; Harvey; Thomas.

(IV) Jane, daughter of Robert (2) and Jane (English) Allison, was born in Clarion county, Pennsylvania, March 15, 1830, died in 1907. She married Thomas B. Cyphert (see Cyphert III).

FURMAN Many at least of the Foremans, Formans and Furmans in this country are descended from Robert Forman, who was one of the original patentees of Flushing, Long Island, in 1645. He had gone to England from Holland, where he was a member of the congregation at Vlissingen (Flushing), and thence he came to New York; he died in 1671. From him are probably descended the Furmans of Mercer county, New Jersey. At some time before the middle of the eighteenth century, Richard Furman came from Long Island to Lawrenceville, Mercer county, New Jersey, and he died in 1752. Jonathan has been quite a common name among the New Jersey Furmans. In Cooley's "Early Settlers of Trenton and Ewing," there is an account of the Furman family there, and there are two Jonathans named, whose descendants are not traced, and either of whom may have lived at the right time; one of these was son of Richard, he of Jonathan, he of the Richard with whom Cooley's account begins, and this Jonathan Furman may well have been the Jonathan Furman, of whom further.

(I) Jonathan Furman, the first member of this family about whom we have certain information, was born in New Jersey, and died in Clarion township, Clarion county, Pennsylvania, in 1862. He was drafted into the war of 1812, and served three months at Marcus Hook, near Philadelphia, Pennsylvania. He settled in Northumberland county, Pennsylvania, but removed to Clarion township in 1825. He married Sarah Howe, born in Philadelphia, died in 1852 or 1853. Children: William, died young; Nathan, of whom further; Hannah, deceased; Elisha, deceased; Samuel, deceased; Jane, deceased; Pamelia, deceased; John, deceased; Sarah, deceased; Ambrose, deceased; Clara, deceased.

(II) Nathan, son of Jonathan and Sarah

(Howe) Furman, was born in Northumberland county, Pennsylvania, in 1805, died July 13, 1888. Having received a common school education in Northumberland county, and having come with his parents to Clarion county, he became a farmer and lumberman. He was an expert at hewing. In his earlier life he was a Whig, afterward a Republican. He was a member of the Baptist church. He married Isabella, born in Mifflin county, Pennsylvania, April 6, 1805, died January 13, 1893, daughter of William and ———— (Walker) Longwell. Both her parents died in Mifflin county, wherein her father was an early settler. Their oldest son, Matthew, came to Clarion county, and died near Concord church, Perry township, lacking less than two months of being one hundred and one years of age. All the children, of whom there were thirteen, lived to advanced ages. Children of Nathan and Isabella (Longwell) Furman: Alonzo Baldwin, of whom further; Clementine, born May 13, 1838, married W. S. Love, of Jefferson county, Pennsylvania, and they have five living children; William Wallace, born August 10, 1841, died February 25, 1865, enlisted, in 1861, in Company H, Eighth Pennsylvania Reserves, and died in the war.

(III) Alonzo Baldwin, son of Nathan and Isabella (Longwell) Furman, was born in Clarion township, Pennsylvania, August 4, 1836. He was brought up on a farm, and educated at Strattanville, and at public school at Clarion, to which place his father had removed in 1847. Since 1859 he has resided at Strattanville, and he is a blacksmith and machinist. Since 1856, when he cast his first presidential vote for John C. Fremont, he has always been a Republican. At Strattanville he has served on the council, and he has been for a number of years a member of the school board. From 1858 he has been a member of the Baptist church at Strattanville, and he helped in getting out the lumber to build the First Baptist Church. He married (first) March 22, 1859, Ann Catherine, born in Clarion county, Pennsylvania, March 22, 1839, died March 15, 1906, daughter of John and Ellenor (Clough) Lowry. Her father had come, with two brothers, William and Hugh, from Union county, Pennsylvania, at an early time, and all died in Clarion county. Mr. Furman married (second) September, 1906, Anna Wonsettler, a widow, born in Fairfield township, Columbiana county, Ohio, March 26, 1856. Children, all by first wife: James Lowry, born January 14, 1860, died April 25, 1868; Samuel Kerney, May 1, 1862; Ellen Isabel, October 11, 1865, died May 25, 1892; Mary Clemtine, March 15, 1867, married David R. Whitehill; John Charles, November 8, 1868; Hiram Carrier, August 8, 1872; Sarah Elizabeth, May 16, 1876, died March 2, 1904; Cassius Emerson, July 30, 1880.

MEALS

Americans are beginning to realize the moral as well as the historical significance of genealogical foundations. A nation which relies upon the record of its homes for its national character, cannot afford to ignore the value of genealogical investigation as one of the truest sources of patriotism. The love of home inspires the love of country. There is a wholesome influence in genealogical research which cannot be over-estimated. Moreover there is a deep human interest to it.

(I) The Meals family of Pennsylvania is of staunch German extraction, the original progenitor of the name in America having been Samuel Meals, who was born in Baden Baden, on the river Rhine in Germany, and who came to this country in the early colonial days. He located first in York, Pennsylvania, and in 1796 settled in Westmoreland county. Still later he removed to Butler county, where he plied his trade as a blacksmith and where he was likewise a prominent Indian trader. He married a Miss Richardt and they became the parents of six children: George; Samuel, died in Butler county, Pennsylvania; William; Margaret, married George Daubenspeck, and resided in Butler county, Pennsylvania; Jacob; Daniel, of whom further.

(II) Daniel, youngest child of Samuel and ———— (Richardt) Meals, was born in eastern Pennsylvania. He accompanied his father to Butler county prior to 1801. He became a successful farmer and at one time owned a well improved estate of one hundred and six acres. He died during the period of the civil war of typhoid fever. In politics he was a Republican, and both he and his wife were devout Lutherans in their religious faith. He married Catherine Studabaker; children: Samuel, of whom further; Mary M., married Michael Turney, of Clarion, both deceased; Margaret, married (first) James Campbell, and (second) Jacob Daubenspike; David, died in the '60s of typhoid fever; Joseph, married

Mary Pettigrew, he froze to death near Hilliards, Butler county, Pennsylvania.

(III) Dr. Samuel (2) Meals, son of Daniel and Catherine (Studabaker) Meals, was born in Butler county, Pennsylvania. As a young man he began to study medicine in the office of Dr. Joseph Eggert, of Butler county, Pennsylvania, and subsequently he attended a course of lectures in the Western Reserve University at Cleveland. He initiated the active practice of his profession in Butler county, Pennsylvania, where he resided until August, 1859, when he removed to Callensburg, where he maintained his home and office until death called him, October 8, 1884. He controlled a large and lucrative patronage in Callensburg and the country normally adjacent thereto, and in connection with the work of his profession was a valued and appreciative member of the Clarion County Medical Society and the Pennsylvania State Medical Society. He wrote a great amount of valuable medical literature, none of which was ever published, but which is a great help to his son in his research work. In his political convictions he was a stalwart Republican, and he and his wife were devout members of the Presbyterian church.

Dr. Samuel Meals married Hannah, daughter of William and Elizabeth Emery, who were natives of Newcastle, Pennsylvania, whence they removed to Butler county about 1832. Mr. Emery was a farmer by occupation. There were six children in the Emery family: 1. Robert, was a valiant soldier in the civil war; he was a carpenter and farmer; died in Fairview, Pennsylvania. 2. Nancy, widow of James Blaine and lives in Newcastle. 3. Sebastian, twin of Nancy, removed to California in the '50s and is thought to be living there still. 4. Mary, widow of John Hartzell; she lives in Sunbury, Pennsylvania. 5. Joseph, a Methodist minister, and although past eighty years of age is still preaching in California. 6. Hannah, became the wife of Dr. Samuel Meals, as already noted. Children of Dr. Samuel and Hannah (Emery) Meals: 1. Dr. Nelson M., of whom further. 2. Margaret, wife of Walker Pollock; they live near Callensburg, Pennsylvania. 3. Catherine, married William Stoner, a blacksmith in Clinton county, Pennsylvania. 4. Clara, married (first) James French, and (second) Albert Jamison, of Canton, Ohio. 5. Emma, wife of W. L. Elliott, of Clarion county, Pennsylvania. 6. Ella, was the wife of Professor W. A. Beer at the time of her demise; he resides in Oregon. 7. Lottie, wife of Joseph Cochran; they maintain their home in Parkersburg, West Virginia. 8. Samuel W., superintendent of the Carnegie Gas Company in Moundsville, West Virginia.

(IV) Dr. Nelson Monroe Meals, son of Dr. Samuel (2) and Hannah (Emery) Meals, was born in Butler county, Pennsylvania, April 6, 1848. In January, 1859, he removed with his parents to Callensburg where he was educated in the common schools, and in Western Reserve University, in the medical department of which he was graduated as a member of the class of 1874 with the degree of Doctor of Medicine. After graduation he returned to his home state and settled in Callensburg, where he has since resided and where he has practiced medicine for more than a third of a century. He was associated with his father in medical work until the latter's death, in 1884, and since that time has carried on an individual practice. He has won recognition as one of the most skilled physicians and surgeons in Clarion county. He is a member of the Red Bank Physicians Protective Association, the Clarion County Medical Society, the Pennsylvania State Medical Society and the American Medical Association. For many years he was a member of the Callensburg board of health, and he has also served as health officer for district No. 363, including Licking and Perry townships and the borough of Callensburg. He has been incumbent of the latter office since 1908. He is medical examiner for Licking township and for Callensburg, has been on the school board for many years, and is secretary of the city council. Fraternally he is affiliated with the Independent Order of Odd Fellows, and religiously he and his family are devout Methodists.

In 1872 Dr. Meals married (first) Jennie R. Graham, a native of Clarion county, Pennsylvania, daughter of James and Elizabeth (Miller) Graham. She died June 12, 1894. In December, 1895, Dr. Meals married (second) Martha J. Dunlap, born in Clarion county, Pennsylvania, daughter of Samuel and Levina (Slaugenhoupt) Dunlap. Children of first marriage: 1. Elizabeth, wife of Nelson Stover, a prominent lumberman and farmer in Licking township. 2. May, died at the age of two years. 3. Kittie, married (first) Jesse F. Lazear, and (second) Chester Allen, 4. Nora M., wife of John Bunting, of Sisterville, West Virginia. 5. Clarissa, died at the age of twelve years. 6. Mary, wife of John Shaw, of Olean,

New York. 7. Samuel, clerks in a store in Callensburg. 8. Nelson M. Jr., a drug clerk in Silver Creek, New York. One child by second marriage, died unnamed. Dr. Meals' office is on Clarion street and the family home is in a beautiful residence just off that thoroughfare.

WHITE The history of the White family has been traced back into England to Robert White, who served as guardian and church warden in South Petherton, Somerset county, England, in 1578. He had a wife, Alice, buried there August 22, 1596, and he was buried September 7, 1600.

(II) Robert (2), son of Robert (1) and Alice White, was a resident of South Petherton, England, in 1598, and in 1601 he was guardian and church warden. He had a wife, Joan, who died in South Petherton, September 13, 1631, and he died there March 8, 1642.

(III) John, son of Robert (2) and Joan White, was baptized in South Petherton, Somerset county, England, March 7, 1601-02, died in 1673. After his marriage, May 28, 1627, to Joan, baptized April 16, 1606, died in Lancaster, Massachusetts, 1654, daughter of Richard and Maudlin (Staple-Cooke) West, of Burton in Drayton, he resided in Drayton parish, Somerset, England. In 1638 he owned a house in South Petherton parish. It is thought he left England in April, 1639, and reached Salem, Massachusetts, in August, where he was granted sixty acres of land. He appears to have made a trip to England in 1648, returning to Massachusetts in 1653. Shortly after his return he went to Lancaster to live, where he had twenty acres of land allotted to him on the "Neck," which was the family homestead for several generations. He was granted other tracts from time to time in Lancaster and died there, his will being proved May 28, 1673.

(IV) Josiah, son of John and Joan (West) White, was baptized in Salem, Massachusetts, June 4, 1643, died November 11, 1714. He lived on the estate of his father at Lancaster, and his residence there was used as a garrison. He was a soldier in King Philip's war under Major Simon Willard, of Middlesex county, Massachusetts, in 1675, also under Captain Poole (see pp. 122, 260, Dodge's "Soldiers of King Philip's War", "New England Historical and Genealogical Register", vol. 41, p. 274). He married Mary, daughter of Thomas and Mary (King) Rice, of Marlboro.

(V) Josiah (2), son of Josiah (1) and Mary (Rice) White, was born September 16, 1682, died May 5, 1772. He resided upon the homestead in Lancaster. He served as tithingman in 1718, moderator six years, treasurer one year, representative in the general court of Massachusetts in 1728-29-30-31-37, when he refused re-election, selectman for five years, being one of the first seven. He was sergeant in command of the garrison in the war with the Indians in 1704 on the west side of Penicook creek (called the Neck), and was deacon of the first church from 1729 to 1772. He married, June 26, 1706, Abigail, daughter of Josiah and Rebeckah (Waters) Whitcomb. Among their children was Josiah, of whom further.

(VI) Josiah (3), son of Josiah (2) and Abigail (Whitcomb) White, was born in Lancaster, January 3, 1714, died September 1, 1806. He resided in the part of Lancaster which was set off as Leominster where he built the first saw mill in the town, and also the "Old Abbey" in 1738. He later resided in Charlestown, New Hampshire, and Rockingham, Vermont. He married, March 14, 1739, Deborah House, who died September 22, 1768. Among their children was Luke, of whom further.

(VII) Luke, son of Josiah (3) and Deborah (House) White, was born in Leominster, Massachusetts, December 8, 1757, died in Richville, New York, March 17, 1837. He served as a private in Captain William Warner's company, Colonel Thomas Marshall's continental regiment, 1777-79; reported on command with state commissary, January, 1779; private in Colonel Marshall's regiment, 1780 (Continental Army Books, vol. 2, part 1, p. 76; vol. 10, part 2, p. 31). He married, November 30, 1782, Eunice White; children: Betsey, Orson, Eunice, Susan, Luke, Horace, David, Roswell, Asenath, Eusebia, John, of whom further. Eunice (White) White was born in Charlemont, March 29, 1766, died in Heath, Massachusetts, January 30, 1824, daughter of David White, baptized August 29, 1742, in Leominster, settled in Charlemont, and was drowned in Deerfield river in 1768. He married, February 14, 1765, Eunice, daughter of Simon and Anna (Fairbanks) Butler, the latter named having been a granddaughter of Jonas Fairbank, an early settler of Lancaster, and the great-granddaughter of John Prescott, the founder of Lancaster, who came to Boston, Massachusetts, in 1640, bringing with him his armor and coat-of-mail, and he was son of Ralfe and Ellen Prescott, Shevington, Parish of Standish, Lancaster, England, who was a descendant of Alfred the Great through William Fitz Gilbert (governor of Lancaster Castle, fifth baron of Kendal) and his wife, Conred, Countess of Warwick, daughter of William de Warrenne and his wife, Elizabeth de Vermandois. David White was a son of Jonathan White, born in Lancaster, October 4, 1708, died December 4, 1788, son of Josiah (2) and Abigail (Whitcomb) White, aforementioned as generation V. Jonathan White was a large landholder, settling in the northern part of the New Grant, now Leominster, where he lived the greater part of his life. He was also an early proprietor of the town of Charlemont and built a house in the south part, which is now Heath. On March 29, 1755, he was commissioned captain in the Worcester Regiment of Colonel Ruggles, which marched for Crown Point. In this campaign he was promoted to the rank of major and then of lieutenant-colonel; as colonel he fought in the battle of Lake George, 1756, and participated in the Lake Champlain campaign, serving creditably until the end of the war. He married, June 22, 1732, Esther, daughter of James and Abigail (Gardner) Wilder.

(VIII) John, son of Luke and Ennice (White) White, was born in Heath, Massachusetts, June 10, 1805, died in Harmony township, New York, May 23, 1853. He was educated at Canton and Potsdam, New York, taking training for the ministry. However, he taught school for some time, became a merchant and manufacturer of veneering, conducted a saw mill, and later, in 1843, purchased a farm in Chautauqua county, New York. He was a member of the Episcopal church, and highly respected in the community. He married, June 7, 1831, Rebekah Barber, born in Charlemont, Massachusetts, January 16, 1807, died at White's Mills, Carter county, Missouri, November 19, 1881 (see Barber VII).

(IX) John Barber, only child of John and Rebekah (Barber) White, was born in Ellery township, Chautauqua county, New York, December 8, 1847. He was educated in the public schools of the township and Jamestown (New York) Academy. From 1866 to 1868 he taught school in the winter and worked on the farm in summer, and then, in partnership with two Jenner brothers, purchased a two hundred acre tract of pine timber, cut the logs, and had them sawed at a neighboring mill. In 1870 Mr. White bought out the Jenner brothers, and associated with R. A. Kinnear, of Youngsville, Pennsylvania, he opened lumber yards in Brady and Petrolia, Pennsylvania, which he disposed of in 1874. He then moved to Tidioute, Pennsylvania, where he purchased the Arcade Mill, and opened a lumber yard in Scrubgrass, Pennsylvania, and at the same time he assisted in founding the *Warren County News*, a weekly paper, in Youngsville, Pennsylvania, which was later moved to Tidioute, when Mr. White became the sole proprietor. In 1878 he returned to Youngsville and purchased a stave, heading and shingle mill. In 1880, in association with E. B. Grandin, Captain H. H. Cumings, the late J. L. Grandin and the late Jahu L. and Livingston L. Hunter, all of Tidioute, Mr. White organized the Missouri Lumber & Mining Company, a pioneer company in the development of the yellow pine lumber industry. Its mills, which were located at Grandin, Missouri, for over twenty years, are now in operation at West Eminence, Missouri. Mr. White has been general manager of this company since the beginning and president for a number of years, holding both positions at the present time. In 1899 he was associated with O. W. Fisher and others in the organization of the Louisiana Long Leaf Lumber Company, with mills at Fisher and Victoria, Louisiana, having been secretary and director of this company since that time. In 1901, he organized the Louisiana Central Lumber Company, with mills at Clarks and Standard, Louisiana, and he is president of this company at the present time. He is also connected with various enterprises in the following capacities: President of the Forest Lumber Company, which owns a line of retail yards; secretary, treasurer and general manager of the Missouri Lumber & Land Exchange Company, with offices in the R. A. Long Building, Kansas City, Missouri; president of Salem, Winona & Southern Railroad Company; president of the Ouachita & Northwestern Railroad Company; president of the Reynolds Land Company; vice-president of the Grandin-Coast Lumber Company, with timber holdings in the state of Washington; vice-president of the Fisher Flouring Mills

Company, with mills at Seattle, Washington, and Belgrade, Montana; vice-president of the Fisher-White-Henry Company, Seattle, Washington. Mr. White also owns a dairy farm on Chautauqua Lake, New York. He was the organizer and first president of the Missouri & Arkansas Lumber Association, the first organization of Yellow Pine lumber dealers, which was later merged into the Southern Lumber Manufacturers' Association, of which Mr. White was twice elected president. He is now a director of the Yellow Pine Manufacturers' Association, and a member of the board of governors of the National Lumber Manufacturers' Association. He was also president of the Bank of Poplar Bluff, Missouri, from 1886 to 1907, and is a director in the New England National Bank, Kansas City, Missouri.

Mr. White served as president of the board of education at Youngsville, Pennsylvania, from 1876 to 1879 and from 1880 to 1883. He was elected to the Pennsylvania legislature in 1878, and was elected by the legislature of 1878 and 1879 one of a committee of seven to prosecute bribery cases. He served as postmaster at Grandin, Missouri, from 1887 to 1892. In November, 1905, he was appointed by President Roosevelt as his personal representative to investigate as to whether the Cass Lake (Minnesota) Indian reservation should be opened up in part for settlement. Mr. White is deeply interested in the cause of conservation, and has written many papers which have been published in pamphlet form. In 1908 he was appointed by President Roosevelt as a member of the National Commission on the Conservation of Natural Resources. He was appointed by Governor Hadley on the Missouri State Forest Commission. He was chairman of the executive committee of the first, second and third National Conservation Congress, and president of the fourth National Congress held at Indianapolis, Indiana, in October, 1912. He is a director of the National Conservation Association, and also of the American Forestry Association. He is a member of the National Association for Preventing the Pollution of Rivers and Waterways, of the Trans-Mississippi Commercial Congress, the National Irrigation Congress, and the Southern Commercial Congress. He is chairman of the Missouri committee of the National Conservation Exposition to be held in Knoxville, Tennessee, in 1913. He is a member of the advisory committee of National Soil Fertility League. In 1912 he was appointed by Governor Hadley, of Missouri, on his personal military staff with the rank of colonel.

Mr. White also holds the following offices: President of the Kansas City Historical Society, elected October 1, 1912; for fifteen years deputy governor-general of the Society of Colonial Wars from Missouri; fourth vice-president from Missouri of the Sons of the Revolution; trustee of Kidder Institute, Kidder, Missouri; trustee of Drury College, Springfield, Missouri. He is a thirty-second degree Mason, being a member of Mt. Moriah Lodge, Jamestown, New York, and Ararat Temple, Kansas City, Missouri. He is a member of the Missouri Historical Society, Virginia Historical Society, New England Historical & Genealogical Society, Worcester Society of Antiquity, "Old Northwest" Genealogical Society, Heath Historical Society (life), National Municipal League, American Academy of Political and Social Science (life), American Political Science Association, Academy of Political Science of New York, American Civic Association, National Civic Federation, National Geographic Society, Holstein-Friesian Association (life), American Society of International Law. He is also a member of the following clubs in Kansas City, Missouri: City Club, Commercial Club, Mid-Day Club, Civil Service League, Knife and Fork Club, Fine Arts Institute. Mr. White is a student of genealogy, having published four volumes of the "Genealogy of the Descendants of John White of Wenham and Lancaster, Massachusetts, 1574-1909"; "A Genealogy of the Descendants of Thomas Gleason of Watertown, Massachusetts"; "A Genealogy of the Descendants of Thomas Barber of Windsor, Connecticut, 1614-1909, and of John Barber of Worcester, Massachusetts, 1714-1909." Mr. White and his family are members of the Congregational church.

Mr. White married (first) July 22, 1874, Arabell Bowen, born in Harmony township, Chautauqua county, New York, February 22, 1848, died at White's Mills, Carter county, Missouri, November 16, 1881, daughter of Daniel Washington and Eliza (Smith) Bowen, who were the parents of two other children, namely: Hattie E. and Elmina. Daniel W. Bowen was a farmer (see Bowen XI). Mr. White married (second) December 6, 1882, Emma Siggins, born in Chariton, Iowa, February 6, 1857, daughter of Benjamin Baird and Elizabeth Erma (Walker) Siggins (see Siggins III). Children of first wife: 1. John Franklin, born in Tidioute, Pennsylvania, November 9, 1875, died in Kansas City, Missouri, June 11, 1900; he graduated from the Kansas City high school in 1894; taught school one year in Box Butte county, Nebraska; attended the University Medical College of Kansas City for two years, graduated from Missouri Medical College at St. Louis in 1898, and studied in Philadelphia also; in the fall of 1898 he became a member of the staff of the hospital department of the Missouri Lumber & Mining Company at Grandin, Missouri; in 1899 he took charge of the hospital department of the Louisiana Long Leaf Lumber Company, Fisher, Louisiana; he was also local surgeon for the Kansas City Southern Railroad Company. 2. Fanny Arabell, born in Youngsville, Pennsylvania, November 19, 1876; she graduated at Oberlin College in 1902; in 1903 she married Alfred Tyler Hemingway, general manager of the Forest Lumber Company, Kansas City, Missouri; children: Franklin White, born in Alliance, Nebraska, March 4, 1904, and Jane, born in Kansas City, Missouri, April 29, 1908. Children of second wife: 3. Emma Ruth, born in Youngsville, Pennsylvania, October 30, 1884; she graduated at Wellesley College in 1907, and was a post-graduate student at the University of Wisconsin at Madison in 1910 and 1911; in 1911 she made an investigation of the conditions of employment of women in industries for the board of public welfare in Kansas City; in 1912 she is pursuing studies in Berlin, Germany. 4. Jay Barber, born October 2, 1886, died August 2, 1887. 5. Raymond Baird, born in Grandin, Missouri, March 18, 1889; graduated from the Kansas City Westport high school in 1909, and entered the University of Wisconsin in the fall of 1909, where he did three years work; is at present taking a course in agriculture at Cornell University, Ithaca, New York.

(The Barber Line).

(I) Thomas Barber, the emigrant, was born probably in the county of Bedfordshire, England, about 1614, died at Windsor, Connecticut, September 11, 1662. He came to Windsor in 1635 with a party fitted out by Sir Richard Saltonstall, under Francis Stiles, a master carpenter of London. He was the first of the Barber name in New England. Windsor records show he was granted a lot there in 1635, where he resided. He was a sergeant in the Pequot war, and took a fort from the Indians which they considered impregnable. In 1641 he was granted about six hundred acres of land in the vicinity. He married Jane or Joan, surname not known. Among their children was Samuel, of whom further.

(II) Samuel, son of Thomas and Jane or Joan Barber, was born in Windsor, Connecticut, October 1, 1648. His will was proved April 4, 1709. He married Ruth Drake. Among their children was Joseph, of whom further.

(III) Joseph, son of Samuel and Ruth (Drake) Barber, was born in Windsor, Connecticut, 1681. He married Mary Loomis. Among their children was Daniel, of whom further.

(IV) Daniel, son of Joseph and Mary (Loomis) Barber, was born April 23, 1719. He settled in Harwinton, Connecticut, about 1746, and moved to Amenia, New York, about 1750. He married, 1741, Naomi Barber. Among their children was Elizabeth, of whom further.

(V) Elizabeth, daughter of Daniel and Naomi (Barber) Barber, was born in 1749, died April 29, 1789. She married, in Harwinton, Connecticut, Rev. Isaiah Butler Jr., who served in the revolution (see "List & Return of Conn. Men", vol. 12, p. 6). Among their children was Rebekah, of whom further.

(VI) Rebekah, daughter of Rev. Isaiah and Elizabeth (Barber) Butler, was born in Greenbush, New York, April 7, 1779, died August 10, 1858. She married, 1802, Moses Barber, born March 14, 1773, lived in Charlemont, Massachusetts, and died in June, 1825. He was a son of John Barber, born March 12, 1742, in Worcester, married Patience Gleason, died in Guilford, Vermont, May 27, 1776. John Barber was a son of John Barber, born about 1714, lived in Worcester, married Lydia Stimpson, and his will was proved January 7, 1777.

(VII) Rebekah, daughter of Moses and Rebekah (Butler) Barber, was born in Charlemont, Massachusetts, January 16, 1807, died at White's Mills, Missouri, November 19, 1881. She married, June 7, 1831, John White (see White VIII).

(The Bowen Line).

(I) Sir James Bowen, of Wales, married

Mary, daughter of John Hale, Esq. He had a son, Mathias, of whom further.

(II) Mathias, son of Sir James Bowen, of Wales, married Mary, daughter of John Phillips, Esq., of Picton Castle. He had a son, James, of whom further.

(III) James (2), son of Mathias Bowen, of Wales, married Eleanor, daughter of John Griffith, Esq., of Richley, son of Sir William Griffith, Penrhyn Knight. He had a son, Richard, of whom further.

(IV) Richard, son of James (2) Bowen, was born in Wales. He came with his wife, Anne, and children to New England, in 1638; lived a short time in Salem and Boston, Massachusetts, but was of Rehoboth, in 1643, where he died; buried February 4, 1675; will probated June 4, 1675. Among their children was Richard, of whom further.

(V) Richard (2), son of Richard (1) Bowen, was born in Wales, buried in Rehoboth, June 4, 1678; settled with his father in Rehoboth, Massachusetts; married, March 4, 1646, Esther Sutton, died November 6, 1688. Among their children was a son John, of whom further.

(VI) John, son of Richard (2) Bowen, was born in Rehoboth, March 15, 167—; married, in Rehoboth, September 12, 1700, Elizabeth Beckett. No record of deaths. Among their children was a son John, of whom further.

(VII) John (2), son of John (1) Bowen, was born in Rehoboth, Massachusetts, December 19, 1709; married (second) by Rev. John Greenwood, August 17, 1749, Hannah Peck, born in Rehoboth, March 10, 1726, died September 21, 1756. Among their children was a son Bezaleel, of whom further.

(VIII) Bezaleel, son of John (2) Bowen, was born in Rehoboth, August 23, 1754. He was a sergeant in the revolution, enlisted in August, discharged in December. He was a school teacher and farmer. Married, about 1776, in Hartford, Connecticut, Mary Bradley. Among their children was a son, Daniel, of whom further.

(IX) Daniel, son of Bezaleel Bowen, was born in Bristol, Connecticut, March 10, 1785, died in Harmony, New York, May, 1863; married, June 14, 1814, Lucretia Cook, born in 1793, daughter of Titus and Silvia (Kimball) Cook. Among their children was a son, Daniel Washington, of whom further.

(X) Daniel Washington, son of Daniel Bowen, was born in Bristol, Connecticut, September 6, 1816, died in Youngsville, Pennsylvania, July 15, 1902; married Eliza Smith, born April 25, 1822, died in Watts Flats, Chautauqua county, New York, September 6, 1898. They had a daughter, Arabell, of whom further.

(XI) Arabell, daughter of Daniel Washington Bowen, became the first wife of John Barber White (see White IX).

Hannah Peck, wife of John Bowen (see Bowen VII) was a daughter of Nicholas Peck, of Rehoboth, Massachusetts, who was a son of Joseph Peck, also of Rehoboth. Joseph Peck was a son of Lieutenant Nicholas Peck, born in England, baptized April 9, 1630, died May 27, 1710; was an ensign in the Massachusetts militia, 1678; member of the council of war, 1678; lieutenant, 1682. Lieutenant Nicholas Peck was a son of Joseph Peck, the emigrant, baptized in Beccles, county Suffolk, England, April 30, 1587, died December 23, 1663, son of Robert Peck, and a descendant in the twenty-first generation from John Peck, of Belton, Yorkshire, England. Joseph Peck, the emigrant, came in the "Diligent," reaching Boston, August 10, 1638, from Ipswich, Suffolk, England. He settled in Hingham; was representative 1639-40-41-42; moved to Rehoboth, Massachusetts, in 1645; settled in the part now known as Seekonk Plain; was a very active and influential citizen.

(The Siggins Line).

(I) William Siggins was of Sligo county, Ireland; he married Mary Taylor, born in Drumcliff parish, Sligo county, Ireland. Among their children was John, of whom further.

(II) John, son of William Siggins, was born in Sligo county, Ireland. He married there Sarah Hood, said to have been a near relative of Admiral Samuel Hood, of the English navy. She was born in Leitrim county, Ireland, in 1750. In 1793 they came to America, settling successively near Philadelphia at Carlisle, Pennsylvania, and finally in Center county, Pennsylvania, where he died in 1801. She died at Youngsville, Pennsylvania, September 30, 1835. Among their children was Alexander, of whom further.

(III) Alexander, son of John Siggins, was born in 1793, on shipboard en route to America. He married, November 7, 1816, in Venango county, Pennsylvania, Margaret Kinnear (see Kinnear IV). He died April 7, 1858 at

Youngsville, Pennsylvania. He and his wife were members of the Methodist church. One of their sons, Benjamin Baird Siggins, married Elizabeth Erma Walker (see Walker VII) and became the father of Emma (Siggins) White (see White IX).

(The Kinnear Line).

(I) William Kinnear and his wife, Jane (Simpson) Kinnear, lived in Connaught parish, Leitrim county, Ireland.

(II) Margaret, daughter of William and Jane (Simpson) Kinnear, was born in Leitrim county, Ireland. She married there Thomas Kinnear (probably a relative). They came to Philadelphia, Pennsylvania, in 1794 or 1795. She died at Franklin, Pennsylvania, in 1821.

(III) Margaret (2), daughter of Thomas and Margaret (1) (Kinnear) Kinnear, married in Pennsylvania, in 1797, Henry Kinnear (probably a relative). Henry Kinnear was a son of Robert and Elizabeth (Barow or Verow) Kinnear. He was born in Ireland, on Easter Sunday, 1764. He was an officer in the English army (Light Horse) for about thirty years and was sent to America to purchase horses for the English army. After attending to this commission and making shipment of the horses to England, he took up his residence in this country. He obtained certificate of naturalization in Center county, Pennsylvania, July 17, 1803. He became a merchant by trade and settled in Venango county about 1814. He was one of the first commissioners in Warren county, becoming justice of the peace in 1816, an office he held during the remainder of his life. He was an ardent supporter of the Methodist church for many years, but on account of some difficulties was expelled from the church at one time. Seven years later he repented the course he had taken, and requested that he be reinstated as a member, and that it be known and remembered that he died within the pale of the church and at peace with God. He died at Youngsville, Pennsylvania, March 6, 1826. Among the children of Henry and Margaret (Kinnear) Kinnear was Margaret, of whom further.

(IV) Margaret (3), daughter of Henry and Margaret (2) (Kinnear) Kinnear, was born December 1, 1801, died April 16, 1877. She married, November 7, 1816, Alexander Siggins (see Siggins III).

(The Walker Line).

(I) John Walker, the first of this family of whom there is definite information, lived and died in Wigton, Scotland. He married Jane McKnight. Among his children was a son John, of whom further.

(II) John (2) Walker, the emigrant, and son of John (1) Walker, was born in Wigton, Scotland. He moved with his family from Scotland to Newry, Ireland, and probably in May, 1726, sailed from Strangford Bay, landing in Maryland, on August 2, of that year. He settled in Chester county, Pennsylvania, where he died in September, 1734. He had contemplated removing to Virginia, as did many of his relatives, and had bought a farm in Rockbridge county a short time before his death. He married, January 7, 1702, Katherine, daughter of John and Isabella (Allein) Rutherford, who lived on the river Tweed in Scotland (see Allein). They afterward removed to county Down, Ireland, where John Rutherford died in the eighty-fourth year of his age.

(III) Alexander, son of John (2) Walker, was born May 19, 1716, died in Rockbridge county, Virginia, in 1784 or 1785. He served in the colonial war, and an account of his service may be found in "Va. Hist. Mag." (vol. 8, No. 3, at pages 278-9). He married Jane Hammer (or Hummer), on January 8, 1747. Among their children was James, of whom further.

(IV) James, son of Alexander Walker, was born June 29, 1751, in Virginia. He moved from Virginia to Kentucky, where he died April 12, 1800. He was one of the Virginia militia who forwarded "Sentiments" to the legislature, in October, 1776 (see "Amer. Archives," 5th series, vol. 2, p. 815). He married, July 8, 1778, Margaret (Peggy) Gray. Among their children was Alexander, of whom further.

(V) Alexander (2), son of James Walker, was born December 15, 1779, and grew up in Woodford county, Kentucky. He settled in Adair county, Kentucky, where he owned a farm of three hundred acres, and raised large crops of tobacco. He married Elizabeth, born April 6, 1788, in Kentucky, daughter of Samuel and Martha (McCorkle) Scott. Samuel Scott was born in North Carolina, in 1762, died December 12, 1820. He served in the revolutionary war, entering the volunteer service as a minute-man. He took part in the battle of King's Mountain, North Carolina, as did his two brothers, William and Thomas (see "Sumner's History of Southwest Virginia," p. 864). He and his wife moved to Kentucky in 1783 in company with Daniel Boone, making a perilous trip and encountering hostile bands of Indians. His father, John Scott, was born in Scotland, went to Ireland and fought in the Irish rebellion, losing an arm in the service. He married a Miss Thornton, evidently a Virginian, after coming to this country. Among the children of Alexander and Elizabeth (Scott) Walker was Samuel Scott, of whom further.

(VI) Samuel Scott, son of Alexander (2) and Elizabeth (Scott) Walker, was born in Adair county, Kentucky, January 30, 1807, died January 22, 1892. When a young man he emigrated to Illinois, pushing on later to Iowa. At Fairfield, Iowa, he served as sheriff four years. He was noted for honesty and integrity in all his dealings, and also for his interest in the civic welfare of the community. In 1840 he was appointed colonel of the state militia by Governor Dodge. He married, January 24, 1832, Sarah Ann Allen, born and raised in Adair county, Kentucky, died in November, 1882, in Cowley county, Kansas, daughter of William and Elizabeth (Tilford) Allen. William Allen was a son of Malcolm Allen, of Botetourt county, Virginia. The Chalkley Records contain an account of his colonial war service.

(VII) Elizabeth Erma, daughter of Samuel Scott and Sarah Ann (Allen) Walker, was born in Adair county, Kentucky, February 20, 1833, died September 29, 1864, at Cobham, near Tidioute, Pennsylvania. She was educated at a young ladies' seminary in Fairfield, Iowa. She married, February 24, 1856, Benjamin Baird Siggins, born July 27, 1827, at Youngsville, Pennsylvania, died June 14, 1903, at the same place, son of Alexander and Margaret (Kinnear) Siggins (see Siggins III). He attended Allegheny College after which he studied law, and practiced for a time in Chariton, Iowa. He then moved with his family to Colorado, making the trip with teams and covered wagons, and narrowly escaping capture by the Indians. In Colorado he engaged in mining. He also was judge of the probate court in Central City, Colorado. In 1864 the family moved to Pennsylvania where the mother, Elizabeth Erma (Walker) Siggins, died shortly after. Mr. Siggins married as his second wife, Druzilla E. Belnap. They resided in Pennsylvania, living for a good many years at Youngsville, where Mrs. Siggins still lives. By his first marriage Mr. Siggins had the following children: Emma, of whom further; Laura, born August 15, 1859, married, September 19, 1883, J. O. Messerly, of Warren, Pennsylvania; Clinton C., born December 31, 1862, married, April 20, 1890, at Hugo, Colorado, Nellie Cunningham, now living at Twin Falls, Idaho. By his second marriage: Albert B., born 1866, died the same year; Lida B., born February 3, 1867, married, in 1886, George H. Hyatt, of Whitehall, New York, died June 29, 1887.

(VIII) Emma, daughter of Benjamin Baird and Elizabeth Erma (Walker) Siggins, was born February 6, 1857, at Charlton, Iowa. She graduated from the Youngsville (Pennsylvania) high school and also from the pioneer class of the Chautauqua Literary and Scientific Circle of 1882. She subsequently taught school for ten years in Warren county, Pennsylvania. She was married, December 6, 1882, at Youngsville, Pennsylvania, to John Barber White (see White IX). Both before and since her marriage Mrs. White has been prominent in social and club life in the various localities in which she has been resident. She has been a member of the Good Templars Lodge of Youngsville, Pennsylvania; the Athenaeum Literary Club of Kansas City, Missouri, and the "History Class of 82" of Kansas City. Mrs. White at present (1913) belongs to the C. L. S. C. Alumnae Association; is a life member of the Kansas City Historical Society; director in the Juvenile Improvement Club, and chairman of their furnishing committee for the new Boys' Hotel, erected in 1911, at Kansas City, Missouri, and also chairman of their Women's Auxiliary; is a member of the advisory board of the Fine Arts Institute of Kansas City. She was one of the organizers of the Kansas City Chapter, Daughters of the American Revolution, and its historian for seven years, and is at present vice-regent of this organization and chairman of their patriotic education committee, which has accomplished the important work of placing framed copies of the Ten Commandments in the hallways of the eighty public school buildings of Kansas City, December, 1912. She belongs to the Westminster Congregational Church of Kansas City, of which she is also a deaconess. Mrs. White is author of the

Walker genealogy, and is at present compiling histories of the Siggins and Kinnear families.

(The Allein Line).

Tobias Allein was born about 1590. He was descended from the Alleins of Suffolk, and lived in Devizes, Wiltshire, England. He was a tradesman who was engaged by the corporation to take toll of everything sold in the public market, Devizes being the great center of the wool traffic. He was a prominent citizen, his name often appearing in the town records. In 1636 he was sponsor for the equipment of a musketeer in the town train bands. Later he lent the borough three hundred pounds in the time of war. He was a "capital Burgess" of the common council, and was also a devout Puritan. He married, October 11, 1617, Elizabeth, daughter of Edward Northie, who was four times mayor of Devizes. Children: 1. Edward Allein, a clergyman, who died in his twenty-seventh year, said to be a "young minister of rare promise." 2. Joseph Allein, born 1633, at Devizes; he entered Oxford at the age of sixteen; was very studious, became in 1853 a tutor in the college of Corpus Christi, where he also acted as chaplain; he was assistant minister at Taunton, Magdalen, Somersetshire, from 1655 to 1662, when he was deprived for non-conformity; he still continued to preach six or seven, and sometimes fourteen or fifteen times a week; in 1663 he was committed to Ivelchester jail, was convicted for his preaching and remained in prison twelve months; he then renewed his labors, but was so broken down by imprisonment that he died in 1668; he was author of "An Alarm to the Unconverted" and numerous books of a like nature; he died in 1668; he married, about 1655, Theodoshia Allein, a distant relative, who was the daughter of Richard Allein, rector of Dichet, Somersetshire, for nearly fifty years; they had a daughter, Isabella Allein, who married John Rutherford, and had a daughter, Katherine, wife of John Walker (see Walker II).

RODGERS The name Rodgers or Rogers, more frequently written without the "d," was borne by many immigrants to the American colonies and has become very common in New England, Pennsylvania, and elsewhere in this country.

(I) Samuel Rodgers, the founder of this family, was born at Milford, county Down, Ireland, June 29, 1762, died in 1842. In 1792 he came to Delaware, in which state he lived for three years. Then he came to Fayette county, Pennsylvania, where he resided four years. Moving into Mercer county, Pennsylvania, he settled on a farm of about one hundred and eighty acres, which is now owned by a great-grandson. He married, in Fayette county, Mary Henry, born in Fayette county, Pennsylvania, in 1780, died in September, 1865. Children: Betsey, Nancy, Sallie, William, Polly, Jane, Peggy, Robert, James Renwick, of whom further. Of these children, eight lived to be over eighty years of age, and Robert died at the age of ninety-six.

(II) James Renwick, son of Samuel and Mary (Henry) Rodgers, was born at Greenville, Mercer county, Pennsylvania, May 17, 1819, died April 17, 1900. He was a farmer, in politics a Republican, and a member of the Reformed Presbyterian church. He married, in 1843, Sarah Jane, born at Glade Mills, Butler county, Pennsylvania, January 6, 1826, died January 31, 1911, daughter of John and Margaret (Wilson) Love. Her father was born in Ireland in 1788, came to Butler county, Pennsylvania, in 1807, died at Rose Point, Pennsylvania, in 1872. Her mother was a native of Lawrence county, and died at Rose Point in 1849. Children of John and Margaret (Wilson) Love: Ezekiel, deceased; Sarah Jane, married James Renwick Rodgers; David, deceased; John, deceased; William, deceased; Charles. Children of James Renwick and Sarah Jane (Love) Rodgers: 1. Daughter, died in infancy. 2. Margaret Mary, born in 1845, died in August, 1878; married Stewart Wright; children: William Ervin, James Stewart, Sarah, Bennett, Samuel. 3. Martha Jane, born 1847, died in September, 1853. 4. Nancy Caroline, born in 1849, died in September, 1853. 5. Elizabeth Emeline, married Abraham Van Horn Fox, and is now (1913) living at Sharon, Mercer county, Pennsylvania; children: Mary Eva, married William Leisinger, and lives in Brooklyn, New York; James Renwick, deceased; Rachel, died unmarried; Sarah Jane Love, married George McWilliams, living at Seattle, Washington; David Clarkson, lives at Sharon, Pennsylvania; Robert George Geddis, resides at Sharon, Pennsylvania; Willa, deceased; Ada. 6. John Love, born in 1856, died in October, 1865. 7. Sarah Ann, born in 1859, died in

September, 1865. 8. Amanda Jane, married Samuel Rutherford Kennedy, and lives at Detroit, Michigan; children: John Love, George Earl, Margaret, Florence, Sarah Bessie, Walter. 9. Jemima Ann, married James Eli Ramsey, and lives at Rose Point, Pennsylvania; children: Nellie Jane, married Robert Curry; Uriah Clifford; Martha, deceased; Mary Emma; Elsie. 10. David Haxton, of whom further.

(III) David Haxton, son of James Renwick and Sarah Jane (Love) Rodgers, was born in Lawrence county, Pennsylvania, December 13, 1865. He was brought up on the farm and attended public school. For about ten years he was a dealer in machinery and implements at Rose Point. Having sold this business he bought a farm at Warren, Trumbull county, Ohio, remaining but one year. Returning to Pennsylvania, he kept a temperance hotel at Bakerstown, Allegheny county, and for about six months was engaged in the real estate business in Pittsburgh. June 1, 1906, he bought a farm of one hundred and ten acres in Clarion township, Clarion county, Pennsylvania, where he now lives. Since December, 1909, he has been associated with the E. A. Strout Farm Agency, and has been very successful. He is a Republican and a Presbyterian. Mr. Rodgers married, August 31, 1886, Mary Josephine, born at Prospect, Butler county, Pennsylvania, December 11, 1868, daughter of Jacob and Sarah (Henry) Millison. Children of David Haxton and Mary Josephine (Millison) Rodgers: Samuel John, born September 11, 1887; Daughter, born October 24, 1888, died in infancy; William Carl, born September 15, 1889; Charles Herbert, born January 4, 1892; James Anderson, born September 24, 1895, died December 10, 1903; Sarah Eva, born February 14, 1897; Jacob Robert, born March 25, 1899; Mary Ethel, born June 3, 1901; David Clarence, born September 15, 1903; Francis Leroy, born September 18, 1906; Ruth May, born December 6, 1911.

Jacob Millison was born in Butler county, Pennsylvania, January 5, 1836. He married, August 22, 1866, Sarah Henry, born at Castle Ray, county Down, Ireland, in 1825. They settled at Prospect, where Mr. Millison died in 1872. Jacob Millison is still living at Newcastle, Lawrence county, Pennsylvania. He was one of five brothers who answered the call and four of whom mustered out at the close of the civil war. They were Jacob, Hiram, John, Aaron and Elias. Hiram was killed at the battle of the Wilderness. Mr. Millison enlisted at Portsmouth, Ohio, August 5, 1861, and joined Company A, Thirty-third Ohio Volunteer Infantry. He was wounded September 19, 1863, and captured the same day and taken to the prison at Atlanta, Georgia, and later to Nashville, Tennessee. He was exchanged at Evansville, and was discharged at Cincinnati, February 24, 1865, when he returned to Prospect, Butler county, later removing to Newcastle, where he still lives (1913). Children of Jacob and Sarah (Henry) Millison: Llewellyn Telfair, died in June, 1899; Mary Josephine, married David Haxton Rodgers; Daniel Francis; Charles Robert.

REED   In various forms, Reed, Read, Reade, Reid, this is an exceedingly common name in America, and widely scattered. Many men of distinction have borne some form of this surname.

(I) John Reed, the founder of this family, was born in Ireland, and died in Highland township, Clarion county, Pennsylvania. In this township he settled on a farm in the early days of this region. He married ———— Doomy, who died in Highland township. Child, William S., of whom further.

(II) William S., son of John and ———— (Doomy) Reed, was born in Clarion county, Pennsylvania, in 1829, died in 1880. He was a farmer. In politics he was a Democrat, in religion a Presbyterian. He married Elizabeth Burlin, born in Clarion county, Pennsylvania, in 1831. Her parents were early settlers in this county. Children: 1. Nancy Jane, deceased. 2. Arminta, married Edward Bower, lives in Warren, Pennsylvania. 3. Rosella, deceased. 4. Caroline, deceased. 5. Lavina, married S. M. Crook, of Clarion, Pennsylvania. 6. John Paul, lives on the home farm. 7. Gertrude, married William Hasselbach, lives at Falls Creek, Pennsylvania. 8. Albert, lives in Montana. 9. Roland Amos, lives in Welston, Ohio. 10. James Emmerson Clyde, of whom further. 11. Elizabeth May, deceased.

(III) James Emmerson Clyde, son of William S. and Elizabeth (Burlin) Reed, was born in Highland township, Clarion county, Pennsylvania, August 15, 1871. He was raised on a farm, and attended the public school in Highland township. At Kellettville, Forest county, Pennsylvania, he was for some years engaged in the hotel business and in the meat business. November 1, 1904, he returned to Clarion county, and bought his present farm in Clarion township, one mile west of Clarion. It consists of seventy-three acres, and on this he has made many improvements, including the building of a silo in the present year (1912). Making a specialty of dairying, Mr. Reed keeps from twenty to thirty cows. He is a Democrat. In Highland township he held the office of township clerk. He married, in 1896, Elizabeth, daughter of Harrison and Katherine Dotterer, who was born in Forest county, Pennsylvania. Her father, who died in 1908, and her mother were early settlers in that county. Children: Alva Gerald, born June 8, 1899; William Amos, December 15, 1902; Sarah Margaret, June 16, 1911.

MILLER Miller is an exceedingly common name in Pennsylvania and other parts of the country, belonging to many different families and to at least two distinct stocks. For while many families of British origin bear this name, there is a probably smaller but not inconsiderable number of families of German descent whose name was formerly Mueller, but has been anglicized into Miller. In Chester county, Pennsylvania, to which the present family is traced, there were, very early in the eighteenth century, three Miller families, perhaps related, all presumably of English or Irish origin.

(I) John Miller, the first member of this family about whom we have definite information, was born in Chester county, Pennsylvania, in 1773, died in Chester county, Pennsylvania, December 13, 1851. He married ———— Wolf, born in 1773, died July 21, 1841. Child, John, of whom further.

(II) John (2), son of John (1) and ———— (Wolf) Miller, was born in Chester county, Pennsylvania, October 25, 1809, died in Lancaster county, Pennsylvania, in 1889. He married Eliza Ann, born March 10, 1810, died April 20, 1864, daughter of John and Catharine (Baer) Myers. Her father was born in 1784, died in Chester county, Pennsylvania, October 14, 1874; her mother was born in 1791, died in Chester county, September 13, 1875. Children of John (2) and Eliza Ann (Myers) Miller: 1. Abner, born in Lancaster county, Pennsylvania; was a prominent physician; was twice sent to Europe by Pennsylvania State Medical Society; married (first) Mary Longnecker, deceased, (second) Sarah Cooper, deceased; he died in Lancaster, Pennsylvania, about 1903, aged sixty-eight years. 2. John, born in Lancaster county, Pennsylvania; resides there at the present time and is a large landowner; married Margaret Worst. 3. Jacob B., of whom further. 4. Jonathan, born in Lancaster county, Pennsylvania, about 1840, died about 1910; he was a farmer, but lived retired at Honeybrook, Chester county, Pennsylvania; married Anna Irving, who survives him, residing at Honeybrook. 5. Mary Frances, born in Lancaster county, Pennsylvania, 1842; married Klingan Buchanon, a farmer, resides near Lancaster, Pennsylvania. 6. Catharine, born in Lancaster county, Pennsylvania, 1844; married Benson Irving; now living retired at Lancaster, Pennsylvania. 7. Anna Eliza, born in Lancaster county, Pennsylvania, about 1847; married George Given; resides in Montgomery county, Pennsylvania. 8. Sarah, born in Lancaster county, Pennsylvania, about 1854; married George Clendening; resides in Camden, New Jersey. 9. Frank, born in Lancaster county, Pennsylvania, about 1856, a farmer, resides near Honeybrook, Pennsylvania; married Ella Overholtzer.

(III) Jacob B., son of John (2) and Eliza Ann (Myers) Miller, was born in Lancaster county, Pennsylvania, April 5, 1838. He was brought up on a farm in Lancaster county, and received a common school education. In 1855 he came to Curllsville, Clarion county, Pennsylvania, and was clerk in a store. Returning to Lancaster county, he there remained for five years, then came to Madison Furnace, Clarion county, and was again a clerk. After this he was engaged in business at Callensburg for eleven years. At Sligo he then entered into a mercantile business with one of his sons, under the firm name of J. B. Miller & Son. Later the firm became J. B. Miller & Sons, and the business is still continued by the J. B. Miller & Sons Company. Near Sligo he owned about one thousand acres of land, and he had a saw mill on the Clarion river, at Beaver. Another tract of land, which he owned in Forest county, Pennsylvania, has been sold by him to Judge Harry Wilson, of Clarion. He owns a flouring mill also, at Sligo, and was owner of a brick-making plant at this place, which he operated for some years, but recently sold. At a later time he was engaged in coal operation. He has now retired from business, but continues to reside at Sligo. He is a Republican, but has never held office. His religion is the Presbyterian.

He married, in 1859, Sarah Catharine, born in Piney township, Clarion county, Pennsylvania, May 1, 1841, daughter of Jacob and Catharine (Fransue) Mast. Both her parents were natives of Northampton county, Pennsylvania, where her father was born December 20, 1798, her mother May 14, 1803. In 1832 they came to Curllsville. Mr. Mast was a farmer, a Democrat, and a member of the German Reformed church. He died December 4, 1877; his wife had died November 24, 1871. Children of Jacob and Catharine (Fransue) Mast: 1. Isaac, married Sarah Reese; he died aged seventy-nine years, she died aged eighty-one years. 2. Lavina, deceased; married Andrew Reese, deceased. 3. Abram, resides in Nebraska, aged eighty-two years; married (first) a Miss McElroy, deceased, (second) Mary McCord. 4. Jacob, died May 10, 1864; he was a Union soldier, and was killed in the battle of the Wilderness. 5. Sarah Catharine, married Jacob B. Miller. Children of Jacob B. and Sarah Catharine (Mast) Miller: 1. William Montgomery, born September 17, 1860; brought up at Callensburg, and attended public school and the Carrier Seminary at Clarion, Clarion county; he is a farmer and a merchant; he is a member of the Free and Accepted Masons; he is a Republican; both he and his wife are Presbyterians; he married, in 1884, Lucy Gales; children: Harry C., born in 1885; Thomas B., born in 1889. 2. Aldus Portley, born in Lancaster county, Pennsylvania, August 28, 1862, died February 9, 1913, interred with Masonic honors at Sligo, Pennsylvania; educated at Callensburg and Sligo; he was a merchant at Sligo; he was a member of the Free and Accepted Masons; he was a Republican; he married, in 1883, Fanny Lyon Gales; children: Anna May and Benjamin Gales. 3. Anna May, born July 3, 1868, died in 1883. 4. John B., of whom further.

(IV) Dr. John B. Miller, son of Jacob B. and Sarah Catharine (Mast) Miller, was born at Callensburg, Pennsylvania, December 19, 1873. He was brought up at Sligo, attended common school and the Clarion State Normal School, also Westminster College, where he graduated in 1896. Five years later he graduated from the Jefferson Medical College, in Philadelphia, receiving the degree of Doctor of Medicine. One year was then spent in the Methodist Hospital, Philadelphia. In the fall of 1902 he engaged in practice at Sligo, where he has remained, and been very successful. He is a member of the County, State and American Medical societies. He is a member of Clarion Lodge, No. 277, Free and Accepted Masons. Dr. Miller is a Republican. His church is the Presbyterian, and his wife also is a member. He married, 1902, May Leone, daughter of William and Mellisa (Morgan) Hutchinson, who was born at Anderson, Fremont county, Iowa. Child, Connell, born July 21, 1907.

RUTHERFORD James Rutherford, the founder of this family, was born in Scotland, about 1811, died February 15, 1864. He came to Pittsburgh, Pennsylvania, but after his marriage settled on a farm in Farmington township, Clarion county, Pennsylvania. In 1858 he removed to Sligo, also in Clarion county, Pennsylvania. By trade he was a stone-cutter. In the last part of his life he was a Republican. His church was the United Presbyterian. He married Elizabeth McDowell, born about 1804, died in 1886. Children: 1. John G., born November 17, 1842; he received a common school education; in 1858 he came to Sligo, and he hauled the first lumber and stone used in building the first house at this place; on August 15, 1862, he enlisted in Company H, One Hundred and Fifty-fifth Pennsylvania Volunteer Infantry, but he was discharged on account of disability in the following March; at the end of the war he served for four months more, having been drafted; he is a Republican, and his religion is the Presbyterian; he married, in 1864, Nancy Jane, born in Piney township, Clarion county, Pennsylvania, died July 4, 1897, daughter of Nelson and Nancy (Crow) Craig; children: i. Effie, married W. P. Moggey; ii. Robert, married Louisa McCall, children, Pauline, Marie, Robert Jr.; iii. Elizabeth, deceased; iv. Scott, married Alice Murry, one child died in infancy; v. Edward, unmarried; vi. John, married Roxy Reese, children, Alpha and Thomas; he is principal of New Bethlehem schools; vii. Annie, died young; viii. Orrin, unmarried, resides in California; ix. Clyde, unmarried, resides in California. 2. Sarah Jane, married John M. Craig, son of Nelson Craig, who died in 1904; she now lives at Reynoldsville, Jefferson county, Pennsylvania; children: Robert L., James O., Arthur, Harry, F. Burton, Edith, Grace, all are living. 3.

Christina, deceased. 4. Thomas, of whom further. 5. Robert, conductor on a Pullman car, running out of Philadelphia.

(II) Thomas, son of James and Elizabeth (McDowell) Rutherford, was born in Clarion county, Pennsylvania, October 15, 1848, died at Sligo, May 16, 1910. He was brought up in Clarion county, and there received his schooling. At the age of eleven he came to Sligo. For eleven years he lived at Bakerstown, Allegheny county, Pennsylvania; for about nine years in West Virginia; and for three years in Minnesota. He was a lumberman and oil producer. He was a Republican, and a member of the United Presbyterian church. He married, March 3, 1882, Sarah Margaret, born at Shippen's Furnace, Clarion county, Pennsylvania, December 17, 1864, now lives at Sligo, daughter of Samuel and Mary (Slater) Sailor. Her father was born east of the mountains, in Pennsylvania, in March, 1840, her mother in Farmington township, Clarion county, in 1843. They now live near Rimersburg, Clarion county, Pennsylvania. Her maternal grandparents were Christian and Elizabeth (Gold) Slater, pioneers of Clarion county; he died at Salem, in this county; she was born in Ireland, died at Emlenton, Venango county, Pennsylvania. Children of Samuel and Mary (Slater) Sailor: 1. Sarah Margaret, married Thomas Rutherford, aforementioned. 2. William Edward, married Sarah Greenwalt; children: James, Ada, Thomas R., Ruth, Rosa, John, Arnold. 3. Matilda, died in infancy. 4. Daniel C., married Christiana Rapp; children: Walter, Charles, Leona, Samuel, May, Viola, Twilla. 5. Charles, died young. 6. Matilda, died in infancy. 7. Adda, died in infancy. 8. Della, died in infancy. 9. Walter, died in infancy. Children of Thomas and Sarah Margaret (Sailor) Rutherford: 1. James Arthur, born December 3, 1884, died February 15, 1898. 2. Floyd, born in Minnesota, February, 1887, died at the age of three weeks.

WHITMER The Whitmer family are of German origin. The name was originally spelled Widmer and the branches of the family remaining in Germany still retain the original spelling. This family for centuries owned and still own and occupy a patrimonial estate in the province of Hohenzollern, near the town of Sulz, on the river Neckar, in Germany. At the close of the eighteenth century the estate was owned by and in possession of John Whitmer, who married (first) Margaret Stull, by whom he had three children: John, Mathias and Mary; and by his second marriage a son, Jacob. When he died the estate descended, under the laws of that country, to the eldest son, John. Mathias, mentioned below, emigrated to America and became naturalized. John died childless and the estate passed into the hands of Jacob.

(II) Mathias, son of John Whitmer, was born in the old home on the river Neckar, in the province of Hohenzollern, April 2, 1798. His boyhood was spent amid the stirring scenes of that time in a country that was continually at war either with or against Napoleon. After attending the schools of his native place he was registered as a student in the University of Heidelberg. At the early age of seventeen he was called upon to serve in the Prussian army under Marshal Blücher and was wounded at the battle of Ligny; two days later he took part in the battle of Waterloo. Later he was a student in the Prussian military school at Koenigsberg. As part of his education he learned the trade of cabinetmaker and millwright. In 1819, on the death of his father, he emigrated to America, settling in Northumberland county, Pennsylvania. Later he removed to Westmoreland county, living there until 1835, afterwards moving to Allegheny county, and settled finally, in 1838, in Farmington township, Clarion county, Pennsylvania, where he engaged in lumbering and farming. In 1832 he married Mary, daughter of George Rosensteele, of Westmoreland county, Pennsylvania. Her ancestors at a very early date had settled in Maryland, and, as the country became settled, they removed to the Cumberland valley, near Gettysburg, finally settling at Johnstown, Pennsylvania. Her father was killed in 1813 at the battle of Queenstown, where Brock's monument now stands on the Niagara river, Canada. Children of Mathias Whitmer: George Jacob, mentioned below; John; William; Lewis; Mary, and Daniel.

(III) George Jacob, son of Mathias and Mary (Rosensteele) Whitmer, was born in Hempfield township, Westmoreland county, Pennsylvania, August 14, 1834, died in Clarion county, March 8, 1900. He received his early education in the public schools. At the outbreak of the civil war, in 1861, he enlisted at Meadville, Pennsylvania, in the Federal army.

He afterward contracted typhoid fever and was unable to pass the physical examination for active service. He later purchased his father's farm as well as his saw mill and lumber business and was actively engaged in these industries for many years. He married, in 1863, Catherine, daughter of Justice and Catherine (Behrens) Lockhart, born February 19, 1840, and still living. Her father settled first at Lawrenceville, now part of Pittsburgh; later he moved to Washington township, Clarion county, Pennsylvania, where he died in 1856. His children were: 1. Martha, married Henry Herr, a banker of Pittsburgh, Pennsylvania. 2. Mary, who married John Geyer, of Pittsburgh, Pennsylvania. 3. Elizabeth, who married (first) James Martin, who was killed in the civil war, (second) John A. Frank, a banker of Atlantic, Iowa. 4. Catherine, mentioned above. 5. Helmuth W., now living in Clarion county. 6. Louisa.

Children of George Jacob and Catherine (Lockhart) Whitmer: George F., mentioned below; Erwin S., married Emma Coleman, now living at Indiana Harbor, Indiana; Laura, married John Seigworth; Sylvester M., general superintendent and manager of the Mosser Tannery and Lumber Company in Richwood, West Virginia.

(IV) George F., son of George Jacob and Catherine (Lockhart) Whitmer, was born in Farmington township, Clarion county, Pennsylvania, August 16, 1866. He received his early education in the public schools of his native county, Carrier Seminary, Edinboro Normal School, and was graduated from the Clarion State Normal School in 1888. He then took up the study of law in the office of Hon. W. A. Hindman and was admitted to the Clarion county bar on August 11, 1890. After his admission to the bar he went to the state of Washington and was admitted to the superior court of that state; returning later to Pennsylvania, he established himself in the active practice of his profession in Clarion, in which he still continues. He has been admitted to practice law in the superior and supreme courts of his state and the United States courts and is admittedly one of the leading lawyers of northwestern Pennsylvania. Besides his law practice he is and has been engaged in the lumber and oil business. He married, June 10, 1891, Emma, daughter of John A. and Nancy (Roll) McFeatters. Children: Helen, born August 21, 1892; Florence, born November 6, 1900; Robert R., born July 30, 1905.

FASENMYER Baltzer Fasenmyer, the emigrant ancestor of the family, was born in Baden, Germany, died May 3, 1868. He was a soldier in his native land, serving under Napoleon; was captured and confined on the Island of Galarera, but escaped and returned to his home. He emigrated to the United States in the year 1828, locating in Washington township, Clarion county, Pennsylvania. He married in his native land and was the father of seven children, the first four born in Baden, Germany, the others in Washington township, Clarion county, Pennsylvania. Children: Felix; Catharine; Agatha; Jasper, of whom further; Magdelena; Jacob; Joseph, born August 19, 1837, married (first) Francesca Speigle, who died in 1863; married (second) Philomena Doty.

(II) Jasper, son of Baltzer Fasenmyer, was born in Baden, Germany, December 31, 1823. He accompanied his parents to this country, growing to maturity in Washington township, Clarion county, Pennsylvania. After his marriage he removed to Knox township, where he became a man of some consequence in the community, passing the greater portion of his life on a farm there. He was a Democrat in politics, and held a number of township offices. He and his wife were members of the Catholic church. He married, in Washington township, Agatha Seigel, born December 28, 1828, whose father, a native of Germany, came to Washington township about the same time that the Fasenmyers came, and there lived and died. Mr. and Mrs. Fasenmyer were the parents of fourteen children, all of whom are now living in Clarion, Crawford and McKean counties, Pennsylvania, and all of whom have been remarkably successful in life, some as farmers and farmers wives, and others interested in gas and oil. In 1912 they enjoyed a reunion at the old homestead in Knox township. Their names are as follows: 1. John, born February 22, 1849; married (first) Mary Snyder, and (second) Rose Bausinger. 2. Caroline, born October 16, 1850; married Nix Schwang. 3. Frank, born August 23, 1852; married (first) Veronica Bausinger, and (second) Mary Fitzgerald. 4. Mary Magdelena, born July 21, 1854; married Henry Hargenrader. 5. Anna, born June 15, 1856; married John Smith, now deceased; he was a soldier in the civil war. 6. Therese, born March 28, 1858, unmarried. 7. Joseph, born September 20, 1859; married Anna Baper. 8. Anthony, born September 25, 1861; married Fannie Spangler. 9. Bernard, born August 10, 1863; married Frances Hargenrader. 10, George B., of whom further. 11, Jacob, born July 26, 1867; married Agnes Bauer. 12. Mary Agnes, born June 8, 1869; married Paul Guth. 13. Elizabeth, born October 12, 1871; married Joseph Bauer. 14. Frances, born June 19, 1874; married Alphonso Bauer.

(III) George B., son of Jasper and Agatha (Seigel) Fasenmyer, was born in Knox township, Clarion county, Pennsylvania, July 17, 1865. He was educated in the common schools of that township. At the age of seventeen years he left his farm home and went to Bradford, McKean county, Pennsylvania, and secured employment as a pumper for J. M. Stevenson and Louis Hampshire. Later on he became manager of their oil and gas lease. During that time he began operating as partner with companies in Crawford and Clarion counties. At the end of ten years he resigned and located at Venus, Clarion county, where he took charge of one of the leases, remaining nine years. He then moved to Leeper, Farmington township, Clarion county, and took charge of another lease. Since then he has had many extensive dealings in oil and gas production, which have been very successful, drilling and operating continuously. He is the owner of real estate in Farmington and Washington townships, having eighteen acres of land in Leeper, whereon he resides in an attractive house, equipped with all necessary comforts. He and his family are members of the Catholic church, and he is a Democrat in politics.

Mr. Fasenmyer married (first) February 20, 1896, Cecelia Leight, who died February 20, 1908. Children: Austin Henry, born May 9, 1901; Amelia Elizabeth, born October 4, 1907. Mr. Fasenmyer married (second) January 30, 1912, Josephine, only child of William and Minnie Beatty, who for the past three years have made their home at Gulfport, Mississippi. Mr. Beatty is a drummer; he was born September 6, 1866, in Jefferson county, Pennsylvania, son of Henry and Josephine Beatty, who lived near Brookville, Jefferson county, Pennsylvania. Minnie Beatty, born in Clarion county, Pennsylvania, February 5, 1869, is the daughter of David and Mary (Markett) Greenawalt, both living at present (1913) in Clarion county, Pennsylvania. Mr. Greenawalt, who is a stonemason by trade, was born in Lancaster county, Pennsylvania.

COLLNER The founder of the Collner family in St. Petersburg, Pennsylvania, was Lewis Collner, born in Germany about 1810, the only one of his family to come to the United States. He died in St. Petersburg in 1893. He was educated in the States school and learned the shoemaker's trade. He was a soldier in the German army and at the age of twenty-two, he so disliked the idea of compulsory service, that by the influence of friends and officials he took passage for the United States. The voyage consumed sixty days from port to port, but ended in safety. He worked at his trade in New York City for a time, then located in Allentown, Pennsylvania. He then came to western Pennsylvania, and became a traveling salesman in the counties of Mercer, Crawford and Venango. He was a careful buyer and shrewd salesman, and his traveling business was made very profitable. He abandoned travel and in 1846 settled in Richland township, Clarion county, within half mile of the present borough of St. Petersburg. Here he opened a small store, and although at that time there were only two houses in the settlement, yet he prospered, and a few years later erected a store building on the tract on which St. Petersburg now stands. There he conducted a general store, and although as the village increased in importance, other merchants coming in, he retained his position of "leading merchant" until his retirement.

In 1871 he practically retired, turning the business over to his son, who continued under the firm name H. Collner & Brothers. He was active in all departments of village life, and business acumen, wide experience and thrifty nature combined to make this old pioneer merchant a leader. His eighty-three years were well spent, successful ones, made so by his industry and perseverance. He was a member of the German Reformed church; his wife was a Lutheran. In politics he was a strong Democrat. This thrifty merchant did not confine himself to the buying and selling of merchandise. He purchased a large farm near St. Petersburg, and when Pennsylvania "struck oil," he sold the oil right for a generous royalty. Timber lands were also a favored investment and he made large purchases in favorable localities. In all his dealings he was upright and honorable, but always secured a profit. He was honored and respected by all and truly mourned when his long, useful life ended.

He married Sarah Fry, born near Alum Rock, Richland township, about 1818, died in St. Petersburg, 1894, daughter of Samuel and Anne (Neely) Fry, of Richland township, their farm including Alum Rock. Samuel Fry was a soldier of the war of 1812, serving in the company raised in Richland township by Captain Henry Neely, his brother-in-law. Captain Neely and his company saw active service in the war and are commemorated in histories of that period. Children of Samuel Fry: 1. Samuel (2), a farmer of Clarion county. 2. Paul, lived and died on the Richland township homestead farm. 3. Fannie, married Henry Weter, a farmer of Salem township, both deceased. 4. Sarah, of previous mention; married Lewis Collner.

Children of Lewis and Sarah Collner: 1. Levi, now a farmer of Richland township, Clarion county; married Sarah Ashbaugh. 2. William F., deceased; was a veteran of the civil war, enlisting at the age of sixteen years, serving until the end; later was sheriff and prothonotary of Clarion county; after retiring from public life he engaged in the insurance business; he married Cecelia Brannon. 3. Samuel, became a successful merchant of Franklin, Pennsylvania, where he died May 12, 1912. 4. Harrison, associated with his brother Lemuel in business at St. Petersburg; he married Elizabeth Caldwell. 5. Joseph, now a retired merchant of Clarion. 6. Lemuel, of whom further. 7. Calvin, died aged twenty-three years.

(II) Lemuel, sixth son of Lewis and Sarah (Fry) Collner, was born in St. Petersburg, Clarion county, Pennsylvania, February 1, 1854. He was educated in the public school and when but a boy began working in his father's store. When the father retired in 1871, and the brothers, Harrison, Samuel and Joseph, succeeded to the business as H. Collner & Brothers, Lemuel continued in their employ. Later he was admitted to the firm, Samuel and Joseph retiring. In 1875 the firm began the erection of a double two-story brick store, which was finished in 1876 and has since been occupied by H. Collner & Brothers, the firm name remaining unchanged, although the present owners and proprietors are Harrison and Lemuel Collner.

The firm has continued, as always, the leading business house of the section and now transacts a very large volume of business. During the "oil boom," when St. Petersburg was the center of a population of ten thousand people, the firm prospered mightily, those being the years of their heaviest business as merchants. Both brothers inherit the admirable traits of the old pioneer merchant, their father, and have lived up to the high standard of honorable dealing, upon which the business was founded. The Collner brothers are both Democrats in politics. Lemuel Collner is unmarried.

CORBETT (III) Samuel T. Corbett, seventh child of William (q. v.) and Sarah (Clover) Corbett, was born in Center county, Pennsylvania, June 15, 1792, died June 15, 1869. When he was nine years of age his parents moved to Clarion county, Pennsylvania, the journey being made by him on a pack-horse. He obtained a practical education in the schools near his home, and upon attaining young manhood erected the first mill in Clarion county, on Brush Run, which was known as Corbett's Mill, and this he conducted until his death. He was the owner of a farm located in the vicinity of his mill, which he cultivated and on which he resided. He was a member of the militia, in which he attained the rank of major, being known always as "Major Corbett," and he was an important personage at the military reviews. He was a member and elder in the Presbyterian church, of which his wife was also a member, and in politics he was a Whig, later a Republican.

He married Ruth Kirkpatrick, born in Westmoreland county, Pennsylvania, 1807. She was of Scotch-Irish descent, her father being a native of Scotland and her mother of Ireland. Both emigrated to this country early in life, married here and settled in Westmoreland county, Pennsylvania, where they spent the remainder of their lives. Mr. and Mrs. Kirkpatrick were the parents of five other children, as follows: William; Alexander; Jane, married Rev. Dickey; ———, married Robert Henry; Nancy, married William Corbett. Children of Mr. and Mrs. Corbett: 1. Dewitt Clinton, deceased. 2. Charles Lee, a farmer in Clarion township; married Nancy Wilson, deceased. 3. Jerod, resides in Clarion; married Margaret Rankin, deceased. 4. Samuel Bruce, a retired merchant, resides at New Bethlehem; married Susan Space. 5. James M., who served as agent for the Pennsylvania railroad from the time the road was built until he retired from active pursuits; resides at New Bethlehem; married Jennie Space. 6. Nelson, a retired merchant, resides at Corsica, Pennsylvania; married Loretta Ray. 7. Albert G., of whom further. 8. Frank S., a farmer, resides in Clarion township; married Anna Orr. 9. William S., formerly a merchant, now engaged in insurance business; resides in New Bethlehem; married Priscilla McClellan. 10. Sarah, married (first) James Kirkpatrick, (second) ——— Kifer; she died December 25, 1909.

(IV) Albert G., seventh child of Samuel T. and Ruth (Kirkpatrick) Corbett, was born in Clarion township, Clarion county, July 17, 1844. He grew up on his father's farm in Clarion township, and his education was obtained in the public schools near his home and a three years' course at the Glade Run Academy. He then became a clerk in a general store at Corsica, Pennsylvania, and in 1877 he removed to Clarion and opened a drug store on Main street, which he has conducted up to the present time (1912), enjoying the distinction of being the only merchant in the city to continue active operations from that year, 1877, to the present. In addition to this he has been interested in oil and gas ventures at various times, and is serving in the capacity of president of the East Gellico Coal Company of Tinsley, Kentucky. He has always taken an active interest in the welfare and development of the community, and is now acting as president of the board of trustees of the Clarion State Normal School at Clarion. He is a member of the Clarion Presbyterian church, as is also his wife, and he has served as trustee for a period of nine years. He is a Republican in politics, but has never sought elective office.

Mr. Corbett married, June 8, 1870, Clara V., born in Highland township, Clarion county, Pennsylvania, January 26, 1850, daughter of Jacob and Nancy (Cochran) Howe, the father, a lumberman and early settler of Clarion county. Children: 1. Stanley, born October 18, 1871, resides in Pittsburgh, employed in the internal revenue department; married Gertrude Grainor; children: Catherine and Stanley Jr. 2. Lucy, born October 19, 1872, resides at home; unmarried. 3. Edgar J., born October 9, 1878, resides in Du Bois, Pennsylvania; manager of the Corbett Specialty Company, a wholesale drug company; married Maud Bausingauer; no issue. 4. Clifford W., born October 22, 1882, resides in Clarion, Pennsylvania; manager of the Wayne Chemical Company; married Reba Kelly; one child, Albert. 5. Ronald G., born November 29, 1890, resides at Punxsutawney, Pennsylvania; owner of the Granny Coon Mineral Springs; unmarried. 6. Fannie, died aged nine months.

MARSHALL The Marshalls of Pollock, Pennsylvania, descend from Robert and Ann (Douglas) Marshall, both of whom lived and died in England, leaving issue.

(II) George, son of Robert and Ann (Douglas) Marshall, was born in Winloyton, county Durham, England, September 1, 1809, died on his farm one mile south of Emlenton, Pennsylvania, June 6, 1883. He was educated in English schools, learned the trade of blacksmith, married, and in 1840 came to the United States, the voyage from Liverpool consuming seven weeks. He first settled in Pittsburgh, remaining two years, working at his trade. He then moved to Brady's Bend, Armstrong county, where he worked in the rolling mills until 1850, when he purchased a farm at Poplar Bottom, on the line separating Butler and Venango counties, his farm house in Butler, his barn in Venango county. He lived in peaceful prosperity the remainder of his life, thirty-three years, dying at age of seventy-four. He was reared in the Church of England, but died in the Methodist faith.

He married, in Winloyton, county Durham, England, August 6, 1837, Isabella Dickson, born in Winloyton, England, November 7, 1813, daughter of Robert Dickson; she died at the home of her daughter, Mary Cubbison, in Scrubgrass township, Venango county, Pennsylvania, July 16, 1903. Children of George and Isabel Marshall: 1. Thomas, born in England, now a resident of the state of Indiana; he inherited a fortune from England and is now living retired. 2. Robert, a carpenter, now residing in Butler county, Pennsylvania. 3. Douglas, a carpenter, now living in Venango county, opposite Emlenton. 4. John, now living in Butler county, an employee of the South Penn Oil Company. 5. Belle, married William McLaughlin and resides in Ohio. 6. Mary, married William Cubbison, a farmer of Venango county, near Emlenton. 7. Elizabeth, married Jack Smith, a farmer of Venango county. 8. George Washington, of whom further.

(III) George Washington, son of George

and Isabella (Dickson) Marshall, was born at Brady's Bend, Armstrong county, Pennsylvania, October 12, 1842, died in Perryville, Clarion county, Pennsylvania, September, 1911. He was seven years of age when his parents moved to the Butler, Venango county, farm, where he grew to manhood and was educated in the public school. He worked on the farm for some time, then became an oil producer, making and losing a fortune during the Elk City excitement. Later he was gauger in the employ of the Standard Oil Company and engaged in oil production on his own account. He followed the oil fields and resided in different places in Clarion county. He was a man of daring enterprise, very energetic and on the whole successful in business. He was a Democrat in politics, and a Lutheran in religion. His wife, in the absence of a Lutheran church nearby, has affiliated with the Methodist Episcopal church. He was a Mason, and was active with the Knights of the Maccabees, and as member of the Allegheny River Boatmen's Association.

He married Rosella Ogden, born in Venango county, Pennsylvania, 1854, who survives him, residing in Perryville, Clarion county. She is the daughter of Joseph and Eliza Ogden, both deceased. Joseph Ogden was born in Venango county, was a farmer of Scrubgrass township, owning the best farm in that section of the county. Both he and his wife were members of the Methodist Episcopal church. Children of Joseph Ogden: 1. John, now a farmer of Clarion county. 2. Rosella, of previous mention. 3. Dessie, married John Hewitt, an oil producer of Clarion county. 4. Clara, married William Cubbis, an oil producer of Butler county.

Children of George W. and Rosella Marshall: 1. George Wesley, of whom further. 2. Lillian, married William I. Goble, of West Virginia; he is general manager and one of the principal stockholders of the Crude Oil and Gas Company of West Virginia. 3. Della, married Charles Glenn and lives at Mentor, Ohio; he is connected with the Mentor Woolen Mills Company of that place. 4. Flora, married William Burt McGinnis, of Polk, Pennsylvania. 5. Josephine. 6. Pauline. 7. Walter D. The last three are living at home.

(IV) George Wesley, eldest child of George Washington and Rosella (Ogden) Marshall, was born at Fullerton, Richland township, Clarion county, Pennsylvania, January 25, 1873. He was educated in the public schools of Elk City, Shippensville and Clarion, finishing his studies at the Clarion State Normal School. After completing his studies he became engineer at a pumping station of the Standard Oil Company in Butler county, continuing three years in that position. He was then appointed gauger for the same company at East Parker, Pennsylvania, a position he has held since 1896. He has held many positions of trust and at this time is trustee of the Pollock Coal and Lime Company, and one of the prosperous men of his section. He is a member of the Masonic order, belonging to Parker City Lodge, No. 521, Free and Accepted Masons; Clarion Chapter, Royal Arch Masons; and Order of the Eastern Star. He is also a member of the Fraternal Order of Eagles. He is a Democrat in politics.

He married, July 30, 1896, Earla Pearl Ray, born at North Washington, Butler county, Pennsylvania, daughter of Perry Franklin Ray, a farmer and stock raiser, making a specialty of Percheron horses; he married (first) Mary Badger, deceased, by whom he had children: Earla Pearl, aforementioned; Cora Eva, married Edward Kuhn, of Hooker, Butler county, Pennsylvania; William Perry, deceased; Charles Roy, lives at Jerome, Idaho; Mary Estella, married Arthur Cumberland and lives at Hooker, Pennsylvania; Lewis Franklin, lives at Sunny Side, Utah. Mr. Ray married (second) Sarah (Sadie) Campbell; children: Merl, Floyd, Harriet, living at home.

Children of George Wesley Marshall: Osseli Frances, born August 29, 1897; Rosella, November 4, 1903; Georgianna, November 6, 1906.

KEEFER The Keefers came to Clarion county at an early day even before its erection as a county. The earliest definite record found of this branch is of Benjamin Keefer, whose history follows.

(I) Benjamin Keefer was born near Edenburg, Clarion county, Pennsylvania (then a part of Venango county), in 1810, died 1881. He became a farmer, owning his own land. He married Margaret Keefer, born near Edenburg in 1815, died in 1881, daughter of Jacob Keefer, born in Eastern Pennsylvania, where he married, came west and was among the early settlers of Venango county. He was of German descent, and both he and his wife members of the Lutheran church. Children of Jacob Keefer: Henry, a farmer of Clarion county; Sarah, married John Highbarger; Kate; Margaret, married Benjamin Keefer; after the death of her husband in 1851, she returned to her parents, remaining until about 1863, when she afterward resided with her children. Children of Benjamin and Margaret Keefer: George, deceased, a veteran of the civil war; Jacob Marion, of whom further; Jesse, deceased, an oil operator, died in California; Paul H., an oil pumper in Clarion county until 1911, when he moved to Whittier, California; Harriet, died young; Mary Delilah, died young; Clara, married Archie Coventry, and resides in Oil City.

(II) Jacob Marion, second son of Benjamin and Margaret (Keefer) Keefer, was born in Venango county, Pennsylvania, February 19, 1844. He was seven years of age when his father died and afterward worked around among the neighboring farmers for his board and clothes. When he was eighteen years of age he enlisted in August, 1862, in Company K, One Hundred and Twenty-first Regiment Pennsylvania Infantry. He was in the hard-fought and sanguinary battles of Fredericksburg and soon afterward was stricken with a serious illness, and on recovery honorably discharged for disability. He remained at home one year, and in 1864 again enlisted, joining Company G, One Hundred and Fifty-fifth Regiment Pennsylvania Volunteer Infantry, fought with the Army of the Potomac during all their battles to Appomattox and marched with that tattered but triumphant army in the Grand Review before President Lincoln, receiving honorable discharge in June, 1865. Returning to Clarion county, Pennsylvania, he began working in the lumber woods as a saw mill hand and was in the lumber business until 1902 in both Clarion and Forest counties. In 1902 he settled in Clarion, Pennsylvania, where he has since lived a retired life. He had been a hard worker from childhood and has richly earned the comfort and ease he now enjoys. He is a Republican in politics, and he and his wife members of the Lutheran church.

He married, November 23, 1882, Nancy Jane Wiant, born in Porter township, Clarion county, Pennsylvania, June 17, 1858, daughter of William and Elizabeth (Howe) Wiant. William Wiant was born in Clarion county, Pennsylvania, February 23, 1832, died November 15, 1906, son of Jacob and Hannah Wiant, of German descent, early settlers of Porter township. William Wiant was a farmer, living on the Howe farm, and served in the civil war, receiving a wound in the shoulder. About 1890 he moved to Clarion where he lived retired until his death. His wife, Elizabeth (Howe) Wiant, was a daughter of Abraham and Barbara (Yearty) Howe, also early settlers of Porter township, Clarion county, Pennsylvania. Children of William Wiant: Margaret, married McCellan Ferringer, and lives at New Mayville, Pennsylvania; Kate, married Paul Keefer and resides in California; Nancy Jane, of previous mention; John, died in infancy; Martha, married John Corman, and lives in Rimersburg, Pennsylvania; Wallace, now living in Clarion county; Clara, twin of Wallace, married William Gold and lives in Butler county; Rebecca, deceased, married Thomas Hall; Ella, married George Adams, both deceased; Fannie, married Hiram Eiserman and resides in Strattonville, Pennsylvania.

Children of Jacob M. and Nancy Jane Keefer: 1. Frank, born March 10, 1879; attended the public schools at Leepers Mills and other public schools in Clarion county, then entered Clarion high school whence he was graduated class of 1896. After leaving school he became a clerk in Martin's feed store in Clarion, remaining four years. He was then clerk for four years in C. E. Capron's general store, later clerk in the Peter's general store, Carrier Brothers' store, then for two and a half years in Brinkley's general store. In January, 1904, he was appointed deputy treasurer of Clarion county, a position he now holds. He is a Democrat in politics, but chooses his candidates for local office for their fitness, unbiased by political preference. He is a member of the Improved Order of Red Men and keeper of records in the local lodge of Maccabees, an office he has held five years. He is also secretary and treasurer of the Carion County Cemetery Association. Both he and his wife are members of the Lutheran church. He married, May 30, 1899, Kate Hiwiller, born in Toby township, Clarion county, Pennsylvania, March 6, 1880, daughter of George and Frances Hiwiller, both deceased, Mrs. Hiwiller dying in 1908, he February 8, 1913. Children of Frank L. Keefer: Bertha, born October 30, 1900; Kenneth, June 6, 1902; Gladys Lucile, died in infancy; Savila Marie, born February 6, 1907. The family home is at 616 Liberty street, Clarion. 2. William

Evans, born April 12, 1884; is now an engineer on the Pennsylvania railroad, and resides in Clarion. He married Cora Dean; children: Dorothy Dean and Charles William. 3. Bessie, born March 27, 1886; married Kent Logue, a blacksmith, and resides in Clarion; children: Grace, Ethel and Everet. 4. Jesse Earl, born September 22, 1892, a glass worker; married Mabel Wensell and resides in Clarion; child, Earl Clifford, born March 10, 1912. 5. Freda, died in infancy. 6. Orvis Craig, born July 17, 1896; lives at home with parents. The family home of Mr. Keefer is on Fifth avenue, just outside of the Clarion borough line.

SHIREY The progenitor of the Shirey family in Clarion county, Pennsylvania, was Samuel Shirey, whose birth occurred in Berks county, this state. He was a pioneer farmer in Clarion county, and was a stalwart Democrat in his political convictions. In religious matters he was a devout member of the Reformed church. He married Miss Johnson, a native of Berks county, and to this union were born ten children. Those to reach maturity were: William; Rude; James; Joseph; Samuel, of whom further; Katie; Angeline; Jewett, and Polly, married ———— Deitman.

(II) Samuel (2), son of Samuel and ———— (Johnson) Shirey, was born in Clarion county, Pennsylvania, January 10, 1838. He grew up on his father's farm and spent most of his lifetime in Clarion county, where he was the owner of a finely improved farm of one hundred and thirty-three acres, on which he was most successfully engaged in diversified agriculture and stock raising.

He married Mary J. Weeter, born May 10, 1838, on a farm in Clarion county. She was twice married, her first husband having been V. R. Polliard, by whom she had the following children: John, died in infancy; West Anna, December, 1860, married S. S. Carson; Elmer Mead, January 22, 1863. After Mr. Polliard's death she married (second) Samuel Shirey, and to this union were born seven children: Sarah, born December 14, 1870; Mary Ellen, July 14, 1872, died September 2, 1879; Levi, August 20, 1874, died October 7, 1874; Charles, of whom further; Harvey W., December 14, 1876, died September 18, 1879; Naoma, May 5, 1879, died September 2, 1879; and Eva, twin to Naoma, died May 17, 1879. Those of the above children who died in 1879 were carried away by an epidemic of diphtheria. Mrs. Shirey was a daughter of John Weeter, a farmer and stock raiser in Toby township, Clarion county. The Weeter homestead is now owned by Charles Shirey. There were three daughters and two sons in the Weeter family. Mr. Shirey was a gallant and faithful soldier in the civil war, during the greater part of that sanguinary conflict. In politics he owned allegiance to the principles and policies for which the Democratic party stands sponsor, and he and his wife were members of the Reformed church, in the different departments of whose work they were zealous factors.

(III) Charles, son of Samuel and Mary J. (Weeter) Shirey, was born in Toby township, Clarion county, Pennsylvania, November 15, 1875. He was educated in the district schools of his native place and remained on the home farm until he had reached his twenty-first year. His first work after leaving home was on a street car line at Braddock, Pennsylvania. Subsequently he became a carpenter and painter and was engaged in the work of these trades for several years. In 1908 he came to his present farm in Toby township, and after running this place for a short period he worked in the lumbering woods for five months. With the exception of that period he has resided continuously on this estate, which was originally the old Weeter homestead. This farm comprises one hundred and thirty-three acres and is in a fine state of cultivation. Mr. Shirey owns considerable coal deposits under his farm and in connection with his agricultural work runs a coal bank. In politics he maintains an independent attitude, preferring to give his support to men and measures meeting with the approval of his judgment, rather than to vote along strictly partisan lines. He is an unusually affable gentleman, and has scores of sincere friends throughout Clarion county.

Mr. Shirey married, June 23, 1906, Neva Catherine, daughter of Robert E. and Mariette (Coleman) Lee, prominent residents of Sligo, Pennsylvania. There were six children in the Lee family: Neva C., of whom above; Vera Blanche; Alford S.; Jennie R., and Paul C. and Robert, twins, the latter of whom is deceased. Mr. and Mrs. Shirey have three children: Estella, born January 26, 1907; Mary West Anna, October 25, 1909; and Charles Mead, April 12, 1912.

YOUNG The Youngs of Foxburg, Pennsylvania, descend from Robert Young, of Strathmore, Franklin county, Pennsylvania, and West Virginia. He was of English descent and of a good family. Many of this name have been ministers of the gospel, and in this branch the Rev. Lloyd Young is shown to have been a loyal faithful member of the sacred profession. In Clarion county a Young has the distinction of having been the first white male child born in the county, one Thomas Young, born 1802.

(I) Robert Young was born in Massachusetts, died in West Virginia. In 1811 he moved to French Creek, Harrison county, Virginia, where he owned a good farm in Upshur county. He was a man of means and education, giving his children unusual advantages for that early day. He married Lydia Gould, of Massachusetts. Children, all deceased: Festus; Sophronia, married a Mr. Phillips; a daughter, married a Mr. Sexton; a daughter, married a Mr. McAboy; Lyman; Loyal, of whom further; and a son died young.

(II) Rev. Loyal Young, son of Robert and Lydia (Gould) Young, was born in Carlemont, Franklin county, Massachusetts, July 1, 1806. When he was five years of age his parents moved to French Creek, Harrison county, Virginia, where he obtained a good education in the public schools. In 1826 he entered Jefferson College, whence he was graduated in 1828. He tutored in a private family one year, then entered Western Theological Seminary at Allegheny City, Pennsylvania, where he pursued study in divinity until June 21, 1832, when he was licensed by the Presbytery of Ohio, as a minister of the Presbyterian church. Soon after taking Holy orders, Rev. Mr. Young was sent to Butler county, Pennsylvania, where he preached his first sermon August 29, 1832. He preached as a candidate the following summer and was ordained and installed as the third pastor of the Butler congregation by the Presbytery of Allegheny, December 4, 1833. For nearly thirty-five years he served well his Master's cause in that congregation. Although no man can estimate the good he accomplished, figures can be given showing results. During his ministry four hundred and fifty persons were brought into the church, eight hundred adults and children were baptized, and over two hundred couples united in marriage. Of the sick and dying visited and cheered, there is no record, nor of funerals attended, but he was always the faithful pastor, and no feature of his work was neglected. He preached his farewell sermon to the Butler congregation May 10, 1868, and the same month took charge of the French Creek and Buckhannon churches in West Virginia. He remained at French Creek eight years, and was then installed as pastor of the First Presbyterian Church of Parkersburg, West Virginia, remaining five years. His next pastorate was the Winfield Point Pleasant and Pleasant Flats churches of West Virginia, where he labored from 1880 until 1885. He then moved to Washington, Pennsylvania, and became supply for a few years. Here his wife died, and a few months afterward, in 1888, he returned to Butler, continuing ministerial work until shortly before his death, October 11, 1890. He was a man of great ability and learning. Washington College in 1858 conferred upon him the degree of Doctor of Divinity; he was twice moderator of the Synod of Pittsburgh, once of the Erie Synod, and represented the Presbytery in the General Assembly several times. His published works are: "Commentary on the Book of Ecclesiastes," "Hidden Treasures," "Communion," "From Dawn to Dark," and but a few weeks before his death he completed a "Commentary on the Book of Proverbs."

To Dr. Young more than to any other man is due the establishment of Witherspoon Institute at Butler. He was the guiding spirit in calling the convention which brought that school into existence, in preparing the charter, in raising money, and in placing the institution on a solid foundation. He was principal of the institution for a long period, and his name is closely interwoven with its early growth and progress. In a sermon delivered July 2, 1876, Rev. C. H. McClellan paid Dr. Young the following tribute: "A man bold in the defence of the truth, vigorous and active in frame, and indefatigable in promoting the interests of Christ's cause, his life and work in Butler will be remembered long after he himself shall have passed from earth." No better testimony to his ability as a preacher and pastor can be found than the well taught and strongly organized church he left in this place; no better proof of the reality of his piety and good works than the readiness with which all classes young and old, rich and poor, Protestant or Catholic, speaks his praise. He was indeed an Israelite in whom there was no guile.

He married, October 25, 1832, Margaret P. (died in Washington, Pennsylvania, December 29, 1887), daughter of Rev. Robert Johnston, first pastor of the Presbyterian church of Scrubgrass, Venango county, who died aged nearly ninety years, in New Castle, Pennsylvania. Children of Rev. Robert Johnston: 1. Judge Samuel, judge in Warren county, Pennsylvania, two terms. 2. Rev. Watson, a minister of the Presbyterian church. 3. Dr. Robert, a physician of Pittsburgh several years ago. 4. James, a lawyer, practicing in Kansas. 5. Margaret, wife of Rev. Loyal Young. 6. Harriet, married a Mr. Ross, a druggist, both deceased.

Children of Rev. Loyal and Margaret (Johnston) Young: 1. Robert Johnston, died in the state of Indiana, a railroad agent, and a veteran of the civil war. 2. Lydia Ellen, died in 1910, unmarried. 3. Rev. Watson Johnston, a minister of the Presbyterian church, now retired, living in Michigan, a veteran of the civil war. 4. Torrence F., of whom further. 5. James Wright, a veteran of the civil war; a gold seeker in Alaska; died in California. 6. Henry Kirk White, died in Kentucky, an oil driller. 7. Samuel Hall, now a missionary in Alaska. 8. Walter Macon Long, now living in California, an oil operator.

(III) Torrence F., son of Rev. Loyal and Margaret (Johnston) Young, was born in Butler, Pennsylvania, April 9, 1840. He was educated in the public school, and in early life was a farmer. He enlisted in Company D, 100th Regiment Pennsylvania Volunteer Infantry ("Old Roundheads"), and served two years, and was with his regiment at the battles of Spottsylvania Court House, North Ann River, Petersburg, Weldon Railroad, Hatcher's Run, Fort Stedman, and the evacuation of Petersburg. He was wounded in the shoulder by a sharpshooter's bullet in front of Petersburg and compelled to remain in the hospital one month. He received honorable discharge at the close of the war and returned to Pennsylvania. He located at Petroleum Center and worked in the oil field for others until 1870, then moved to Richland township, near Richland, Clarion county, secured leases, and began operating for his own account. He has been a successful operator and so continues, being one of the oldest operators in the county. In 1892 he moved to Foxburg, where he erected a residence on the hill, which he now occupies with his family. He is a Republican in politics, and cast his first vote for Abraham Lincoln. He enjoys the friendship of his old army comrades, and is affiliated with them in the Grand Army of the Republic. Both he and his wife are members of the Presbyterian church.

He married, September 12, 1867, Anna Henry, born in Philadelphia (at the time of marriage living in Armstrong county, Pennsylvania), daughter of James and Rachel Henry, born in Maryland, moved to Philadelphia, later to Armstrong county. Anna Henry Young died November 12, 1910, leaving an only child, Maude Mary, born January 28, 1876, married February 26, 1907, Robert Burney, a railroad engineer. They reside with Mr. Young in the Foxburg home. Their only child, William Torrence Burney, was born April 16, 1909.

CUMINGS Captain Henry Harrison Cumings, son of Charles and Emily (Amsden) Cumings, was born in Monmouth, Illinois, December 1, 1840.

He passed his youth in the middle west. He attended the schools of Madison, Ohio, teaching to help himself along, and at Oberlin College, Oberlin, Ohio, where he graduated with degree of A. M. in 1862. On the eve of graduation he enlisted in the Union army, serving until 1865 with the 105th Regiment Ohio Volunteer Infantry; he was recruiting officer for this regiment. On the day of commencement of his class he stood in line of battle near Lexington, Kentucky, but though absent, was graduated with his class, receiving his diploma at his home on his return from war. Three months after enlisting he was detached from his regiment and assigned to duty as first lieutenant of Parson's Battery, which was practically destroyed at the battle of Perrysville; fifty per cent. of the members of the battery on the field were killed and wounded. Lieutenant Cumings was then assigned to duty on the staff of Colonel A. S. Hall, commanding brigade, and later was assigned to duty on the staff of Brigadier General E. H. Hobson. Returning to his regiment March 1, 1863, he participated in every campaign, skirmish and battle in which it was engaged—Louisville, Perrysville, Milton, Hoover's Gap, Tullahoma, Chickamauga, Lookout Mountain, Missionary Ridge, Tunnel Hill, Buzzard's Roost, Resaca, Burnt Hickory, Lost Mountain, Kenesaw Mountain, Peach Tree Creek, near Atlanta; Jonesboro, and also was with Sherman in his

March to the Sea. He was promoted to a captaincy after the battle of Missionary Ridge, and was assigned to Company K, of the 105th Ohio Volunteers. He remained with his command until it was mustered out in Washington, D. C., June 3, 1865. He was breveted major about the time Lincoln was assassinated, but as he had no active service under that title, refused to acknowledge it.

He settled in Tidioute, Pennsylvania, immediately after the close of the civil war, and has remained there until the present time. Prior to the war he taught school. After the war he entered the business of oil production, and had a small refinery in Tidioute, which he disposed of about 1871, remaining in the oil production business. He has served the town in various offices, being burgess during the time of the great smallpox epidemic there in the early 70's. He has been director and president of the school board from 1880 till 1913, and still has the position. He has held many county and state offices, the last being state senator from his district. He served on the committee or board of directors for the Scotland School for Soldiers' Orphans, and on the board for the Soldiers' Home at Erie, Pennsylvania. He has been faithful and conscientious in upholding only what was for the best interests of his townspeople and constituents in every position he has held. Captain Cumings has been prominently identified with the Republican party. He was delegate to the Republican convention held in Chicago in 1888. He was a member of the state senate of Pennsylvania, 1899, to and including 1903, re-elected 1903, to and including 1906. He has been urged since then to permit his name for this office and others, but feels he is entirely out of politics now, and has earned the rest. He was prominent in the organization of the Grand Army of the Republic, has been several times commander, as well as filling other offices of the Col. George A. Cobham Post, G. A. R. He has served on the staff of state officers in the G. A. R., and in the Northwestern Association, Department of Pennsylvania, G. A. R., as commander, and in 1895-1896 was department commander of Pennsylvania, Grand Army of the Republic. He has also been an officer on the staff of the commander-in-chief of the national organization of the Grand Army of the Republic at various times. He is a member of Olivet Commandery, Knights Templar, Erie, Pennsylvania.

He is president of the Tidioute Savings Bank; a director of the Warren Trust Company of Warren, Pennsylvania; president of the Missouri Lumbering and Mining Company, and has large business interests in Grandin, Missouri, and Clarks, Louisiana. He is interested in the oil development in Oklahoma, and in the gas production in Quebec, Canada, besides business interests in many smaller concerns.

Captain Henry H. Cumings is a lineal descendant from many of the Puritan settlers in Massachusetts, through Isaac Cumings, who settled in Ipswich, Massachusetts, in 1627, and his descendants who have intermarried with children and descendants of other early settlers of those days in Massachusetts. His ancestral line through his father—i. e., the Cumings, follows.

(I) Isaac Cumings, born 1601, died 1677; four or more children.

(II) John Cumings, born 1633, died December 1, 1700; married (first) Sarah, daughter of Ensign Thomas and Alice (French) Howlett. In court John Cunings testified to being forty years old in 1673, and in 1679 again testified, giving his age as fifty years, and again in 1696 as being sixty-three years of age; he had eleven children.

(III) John Cumings, born 1657, married, September 13, 1680, Elizabeth, daughter of Samuel and Hannah (Brackett) Kinsley; they had eight children, of whom

(IV) Samuel Cumings, born in Chelmsford, Massachusetts, October 6, 1684, died in Groton, Massachusetts, 1718. He married, in Charlestown, Massachusetts, before Edward Emerson, justice, January 14, 1708, Elizabeth Shed, of Groton, Massachusetts. They had three children. His widow married a second time.

(V) Samuel Cumings, born in Groton, Massachusetts, March 6, 1709, died in Hollis, New Hampshire, January 18, 1772. He married, in Groton, Massachusetts, January 30, 1732, Prudence, daughter of Thomas and Prudence Lawrence, of Groton, Massachusetts, born September 14, 1715, died March 6, 1797; six children. (See pp. 21-27, Groton Hist. Series, Book X, vol. I, S. A. Green; also Cumings Genealogy, A. O. Cummins, p. 44.)

(VI) Benjamin Cumings (Lieutenant), born in Hollis, New Hampshire, November 25, 1757, died March 8, 1804, in Brookline, New Hampshire, where he then lived. His name appears on the muster roll of Captain Reuben Dow's company of minute-men at the Lexington alarm, and Bunker Hill, who marched from Hollis, New Hampshire, April 19th, 1775. He was one of fifty-three men who remained at Cambridge and who volunteered for eight months in a new company under Captain Reuben Dow. This company was mustered into the Massachusetts regiment commanded by Colonel William Prescott. History of Hollis, New Hampshire, page 164, states, "Benjamin Cumings enlisted for one year in either the 6th Company of the First Regiment, or the First Company of the Third Regiment, New Hampshire Continental Line, and served in the battles and operations about New York, and at Princeton and Trenton, New Jersey." The History of Hollis, pp 203-204-205-206; Rolls of the New Hampshire Continental Line, First and Third Regiments —among the names of the Hollis men shows Benjamin Cumings serving in the Lexington campaign, 1775; Cambridge campaign, eight months, 1775; Continental army, one year. Lieutenant Benjamin Cumings married (first) December 7, 1780, Bridget, daughter of William Poole, a revolutionary soldier, and his wife, Hannah (Nichols) Poole. Bridget Poole, born August 5, 1762, died March 3, 1785. William Poole was a private under Captain John Goss in 1776, and participated in the capture of Ticonderoga. He was born in 1726 in Reading, Massachusetts, died in Hollis, New Hampshire, October 27, 1795; married, June 19, 1751, Hannah Nichols. They had fourteen children.

(VII) Benjamin Cumings Jr., born in Hollis, New Hampshire, August 24, 1781, died in Unionville, Ohio, September 11, 1852. He was known as Major Benjamin Cumings, obtaining the title in service in the war of 1812. He married, in Brookline, New Hampshire, March 6, 1805, Lucy Whitaker, born in Mason, New Hampshire, May 22, 1782, daughter of John and Thankful (Pierce) Whitaker, of Brookline, New Hampshire; she died in Madison, Ohio, June 4, 1861; (both buried in Middle Ridge Cemetery, Madison, Ohio). John Whitaker, a revolutionary soldier, born 1743-44, died October 1, 1829, was a member of Walker's company, New Hampshire militia, which company is said to have been raised out of the Fifth Regiment Militia of the state of New Hampshire, by an order from Major General Folsom, December 7, 1776, to reinforce the Continental army at New York until March 1, 1777. (Record from the Pension Office, O. W. & N. Dep't, Washington, D. C., and vol. XIV. Mass., pp. 438-527, Soldiers and Sailors.) Thankful Pierce, born June 5, 1744, died September 6, 1830, wife of John Whitaker, married, December 23, 1760, was a daughter of Stephen Pierce, of Groton, Massachusetts, and his wife, Rachel. Lucy Whitaker, wife of Benjamin Cumings Jr., was born in Mason, New Hampshire, May 22, 1782; died in Madison, Lake county, Ohio, June 4, 1861. They lie beside each other in the cemetery at Middle Ridge, Madison, Ohio.

(VIII) Charles Cumings, born in Brookline, New Hampshire, September 5, 1814, came from Hollis, New Hampshire, with his parents, to Unionville, Lake county, Ohio, in 1825. At the age of nineteen years, when residing in Unionville, Ohio, he was converted, becoming a minister in the Methodist Episcopal church. For several years he was a circuit rider in Illinois, residing with his first wife and two older children in Monmouth, Illinois. Within a year after the death of his wife, Emily Amsden, he left this work through the persuasion of his relatives in Ohio and returned to them, where he later married his second wife, and settled on a farm in North Madison, Lake county, Ohio, becoming a local preacher at that place. About 1870 his eyesight failed so that he gave up preaching, but he was always active in the church work until the day of his death. He died in Madison, Ohio, October 4, 1900. He married first in Unionville, Ohio, March 25, 1838, Emily (VII) Amsden, born in Stowe, Vermont, June 17, 1816, daughter of Abraham Amsden, born in Sharon, Massachusetts, September 17, 1788, and his wife, Mehitable Currier, born 1787, died April 27, 1840, daughter of Peter Currier, of Stowe, Vermont, and in 1790 of Windsor, Vermont. Abraham (VI) Amsden, father of Emily (VII) Amsden, was born in Sharon, Massachusetts, September 17, 1788, died in Ashtabula, Ohio. He was a son of Abraham (V) Amsden, born February 20, 1752, died in Reading, Vermont, married, April 28, 1773, Submit Morse, born in Sudbury, Massachusetts, died in Ashtabula, Ohio.

Said Abraham (V) Amsden, born February 20, 1752, was a son of Abraham (IV) Amsden, born August 29, 1723, and Hannah Whitcomb, married, February 13, 1746. This Abraham (IV) Amsden was a son of Abraham (III) Amsden, born October 15, 1692, died in Marlboro, Massachusetts, March 7, 1763, aged 73 years; married, November 29, 1722, Hannah Newton, born 1698, died October 9, 1793, daughter of John Newton Jr., and wife, Hannah Morse, of Marlboro, Massachusetts. Abraham (III) Amsden, born 1692, was a son of Isaac (II) Amsden Jr., born in Cambridge, Massachusetts, 1655, a soldier in the Indian wars between 1680 and 1683, removed to Marlboro, Massachusetts, where he was known as Captain Amsden. He was a proprietor of the Ockoocangansett purchase in 1684, a town clerk for a few years, and selectman for fourteen years, and a justice of the peace until after 1717. He died in Marlboro, Massachusetts, May 3, 1727. His wife was Jane Rutter (or Butler), of Sudbury, married, at Cambridge, May 17, 1677; she died in Marlboro, Massachusetts, November 22, 1739, upward of 80 years of age; she left a very interesting will. Isaac Amsden Jr. (II) was a son of Isaac Amsden Sr. (I), the first recorded settler of the name in this country, who appears in Cambridge at the time of his marriage in 1654. He was born in England 1616 (?). He followed the trade of a mason in Cambridge, Massachusetts, where he owned twelve acres of land at the time of his death, April 7, 1659. On June 3, 1654, he married Frances Perriman, who was admitted to the Cambridge church in October, 1661. The following November her two children were baptized. She died in June, 1693, aged about 72 years, according to her gravestone, making her birth about 1621, though Paige's History of Cambridge states her birth about 1625.

Emily Amsden, wife of Charles Cumings, died in Monmouth, Illinois, August 14, 1851, leaving two children: (Captain) Henry Harrison Cumings, and Lucy Mehitable Cumings. Charles Cumings married (second) September 2, 1852, Rebecca Agnes Sullivan, daughter of Patten and Mary (Buel) Sullivan, of Geneva, Ohio, born in Killingly, Connecticut. She died in Madison, Ohio, March 29, 1903.

(IX) 1. Henry Harrison Cumings, born in Monmouth, Illinois, December 1, 1840, resides in Tidioute, Pennsylvania, (the subject of this article).

2. Lucy Mehitable Cumings, born in Monmouth, Illinois, July 22, 1844; married, February 15, 1872, James H. Boyce, of Willoughby, Ohio; she died September 4, 1898, while visiting her parents in Madison, Ohio. James H. Boyce died in Willoughby, Ohio, March, 1909. They left one adopted daughter, Maude Boyce, who married Edward Mosher, and resides with their children in Wickliffe, Ohio.

3. Charles Elliott Cumings, born in Madison, Ohio, June 15, 1853; married, May 8, 1879, Sarah E. Burridge, daughter of Captain Eleazer and Margaret Burridge, of Mentor, Ohio. They reside in East Brady, Clarion county, Pennsylvania. They have two daughters—Margaret Rebecca Cumings, who married Charles Wallace, of East Brady, have one daughter, Margaret Wallace; and Charlotte Sarah Cumings, who married, October, 1912, Frank Hilderbrand, of Butler, Pennsylvania.

4. Francis Asbury Cumings, born in Madison, Ohio, June 10, 1855, married (first) October 6, 1880, Mary Rood, of Madison, Ohio; she died in Madison, Ohio, March 6, 1896. He married (second) July 7, 1897, Winnifred E. Rand, daughter of his cousin, Elmer H. Rand (a granddaughter of Lucy (Cumings) and Martin Rand, born in Mason, New Hampshire). His children are: 1. Walter Cumings, born in Criswell, Butler county, Pennsylvania, September 8, 1881, married, and resides in Madison, Ohio. 2. Bessie Agnes Cumings, born in Criswell, Pennsylvania, May 2, 1888, graduated from Wilson College, Chambersburg, Pennsylvania; resides in Madison, Ohio, a librarian in Cleveland, Ohio.

5. Jane Rebecca Cumings, born in Madison, Ohio, February 1, 1857; married, May 8, 1884, Howard A. Atkinson, of Willoughby, Ohio, where they resided until his death, June 12, 1904, after which Mrs. Atkinson removed with her family to Cleveland, Ohio. Children: Arland Cary Atkinson, born in Willoughby, Ohio, February 9, 1885, married, and resides in Cleveland, Ohio; Ralph Howard Atkinson, born in Willoughby, Ohio, December 2, 1886; William Charles Atkinson, born in Willoughby, Ohio, October 8, 1888, died there January 10, 1892; Raymond Cumings Atkinson, born October 30, 1895. The two unmarried sons reside with their mother.

6. Benjamin Potter Cumings, born in Madison, Ohio, June 30, 1860, died there September 22, 1861.

7. Homer Potter Cumings, born in Madison, Ohio, February 19, 1862; graduated at Union College, Schenectady, New York, class 1885. He was retained there as an instructor

in the college. He later engaged in the business of civil engineer in Painesville, Ohio, and became city engineer. He has been very successful. August 13, 1891, he married Jennie Hills, of Willoughby, Ohio. Children: 1. Mildred Josephine Cumings, graduated from school in Painesville, Ohio, in 1910; she was born February 8, 1893. 2. Homer Harold Cumings, born August 13, 1895.

8. Emily Estelle Cumings, born in Madison, Ohio, January 21, 1864; is unmarried; she is a deaconess in the Methodist Episcopal church.

9. Mary Maria Cumings, born in Madison, Ohio, September 8, 1860; graduated from Oberlin College, Oberlin, Ohio, class of 1889. She taught Latin and Greek languages for eleven years in Ottawa, Illinois, when she accepted a similar position in Painesville, Ohio, that she might be nearer her mother during her remaining years. She still retains that position, and resides unmarried in Painesville, Ohio (1913).

10. Nellie Lavinia Cumings, born in Madison, Ohio, March 2, 1869; attended Oberlin Conservatory of Music, Oberlin, Ohio, 1888-89; married, August 15, 1894, Allen N. Benjamin, of Madison, Ohio, where they reside; two children, living in Madison, Ohio: Mary Frances Benjamin, September 8, 1897; Allen N. Benjamin Jr., born August, 1906.

11. Kate Cumings, born in Madison, Ohio, January 18, 1872; educated in the schools in Madison, and Oberlin College and Oberlin Conservatory of Music, Oberlin, Ohio; married, July 25, 1900, Orlando Pershing, of Madison, Ohio, pastor of the Presbyterian church, Pueblo, Colorado, where they reside; one child, Charles Pershing, born in Ada, Ohio, 1909.

12. Edgar Roscoe Cumings, born in Madison, Ohio, February 20, 1874; graduate of Union College, Schenectady, New York, receiving degrees of Bachelor of Arts and Master of Arts. He was an instructor and did post-graduate work at both Cornell College, Ithaca, New York, and Yale College, New Haven, Connecticut. Yale College conferred upon him the degree of Ph.D. He is professor of geology in the Indiana State University, Bloomington, Indiana, where he resides. He married, in Oak Lane, Philadelphia, Pennsylvania, June, 1907, a sister of his nephew's wife, Lois Crowthers, daughter of Henry H. Crowthers, of Philadelphia; two children: Edith Cumings, born November, 1908; Edgar Roscoe Cumings, born 1910.

Charlotte Jane Sink, wife of Captain Henry Harrison Cumings, was born in Rome, Oneida county, New York, April 25, 1846. She is a lineal descendant from the Earl of Stafford, of Warwickshire, England; from John Billings and Sir Thomas Billings, of Rowell and Northampton, England, through eight generations to the emigrant to America, William Billings; from Sir Thomas Bromley, of Staffordshire, England, through his son, Luke Bromley, and his grandson, Luke Bromley, of Stonington, Connecticut. Thomas Stafford, son of the Earl of Stafford, born in Warwickshire, England. Was in Plymouth Colony, 1626, later of Providence and Warwick, Rhode Island; his wife was Elizabeth. Their daughter, Hannah Stafford, who died before 1692, married Luke Bromley Jr., born 1665, died 1697.

Mrs. Cumings is also a lineal descendant of the noted Willis family of Connecticut. Thus: William Bromley (son of Luke Jr. and Hannah Bromley), born 1668, died 1700, married Lydia Billings, daughter of William Billings and wife Mary, of Stonington, Connecticut, baptized 1672. She died 1747. William Billings came from Taunton, England, appearing in Dorchester, Massachusetts, 1658; he died in 1713. Their son, William Bromley, baptized at Preston (now Griswold), Connecticut, October 21, 1694, married Judith ———, and resided in Preston, Connecticut. He died January 7, 1769, and Judith Bromley, his wife, died September 28, 1776. Their daughter, Bathsheba Bromley, born in Preston, Connecticut, February 12, 1733, married William Willis, of New Haven, March 25, 1750. William Willis, born January 9, 1725, died October 9, 1774. Their daughter, Welthy Willis, born September 18, 1772, died in Cleveland, New York, June 23, 1854, married, in Stockbridge, Massachusetts, January, 1799, James Carroll, who was born in the North of Ireland, 1763, emigrated to America, 1786. He died July 16, 1830. He and his wife are buried in the John Davis Cemetery, Cleveland, New York. Their daughter, Camilla Carroll, born December 3, 1798, in Lenox, Massachusetts, died in Rome, New York, December 28, 1877, married, October 19, 1816, Jacob Sink, of Stockbridge, Massachusetts. Their son, Andrew Jackson Sink, born at Fort Schuyler, near Utica, New York, June 14, 1823, died in

Rome, New York, February 15, 1880, married, in Philadelphia, Pennsylvania, March 4, 1840, Sarah Catherine Rue, of Lockport, New York. Their daughter, Charlotte Jane Sink, wife of Captain Henry H. Cumings.

On her mother's side of the family, Mrs. Cumings is a lineal descendant of Richard Higgins, of Plymouth, and one of the first proprietors of Eastham, Massachusetts, and his second wife, Mary Yates. They removed to New Jersey in 1670. Also a lineal descendant of Richard Stout, who married the famous Penelope Van Princess, in 1624, and also of Matthew Rue, of Staten Island, an early settler; and of George Mount, an early settler and prominent man in New Jersey. Her lines trace through as follows:

(I) Richard Higgins married second wife, Mary Yates, in October, 1651; their son,

(II) Jedediah (Jediah) Higgins, of Hunterdon county, New Jersey, married, April, 1715, Mary Newbold, 1684; their son.

(III) Jedediah (Jediah) Higgins Jr., married Hannah Stout; their son,

(IV) Joshua Higgins, born 1732, died 1804, married, 1755, Mary Quick, born 1726, died 1813; their son,

(V) Peter Higgins, married Elizabeth ———; their daughter,

(VI) Charlotte Higgins, married, 1816, Matthew Matthias Rue; their daughter,

(VII) Sarah Catharine Rue, married, 1840, Andrew Jackson Sink.

Richard Stout was a son of John Stout, of Nottinghamshire, England, born there 1584, married, in New York, 1624, Penelope Van Princess, born in Amsterdam, Holland, 1602. Mrs. Cumings' lines:

(I) Richard Stout, born 1584, married, 1624, Penelope Van Princess.

(II) Jonathan Stout, married Ann ———.

(III) Hannah Stout, married Jedediah Higgins; see generation III. in above Higgins line.

Mrs. Cumings' line from Matthew Rue, of Staten Island:

(I) Matthew Rue came to Middlesex county and Hopewell, New Jersey, from Staten Island about 1702. He died in New Jersey, 1722. His son

(II) John Rue, married Peternella Wyckoff, of Staten Island, removed to New Jersey about the time his father came there; their son

(III) Matthew Rue, died November, 1755; married (second) Margaret (Mount), widow of Rev. James Herbert (or Harbour), of Middletown, New Jersey, October 11, 1749. Matthew Rue was scalped by the Indians in November, 1755. (After his death, Margaret, his widow, married a third husband in 1760—the Rev. James Dey, of Monmouth county, New Jersey). Their son

(IV) John Rue, born 1754, married, January 1, 1777, Annie, daughter of Captain and Judge Jonathan Combs, of Cranbury, New Jersey; their son

(V) Matthew Matthias Rue, born in New Jersey, February 24, 1782, died 1828; removed to Lockport, New York. In 1816 he married as his third wife Charlotte Higgins, of New Jersey; their daughter

(VI) Sarah Catharine Rue, married, 1840, Andrew Jackson Sink.

Mrs. Cumings' line from George Mount is:

(I) George Mount, born in Scotland, died 1705, in New Jersey; he was a state deputy in New Jersey in 1698, and of his time a very prominent man in all state affairs and offices, serving in the assembly; married Catharine ———

(II) Matthias Mount, his son, born in New Jersey, died 1695; married Mary ———; their son

(III) Matthias Mount, born about 1692; married ———; his son,

(IV) Matthias Mount, born 1716, died 1791; was an elder in the Presbyterian church; married Anne ———; his daughter

(V) Margaret Mount, married (first) March 24, 1739, Rev. James Herbert (or Harbour); (second) October 11, 1749, Matthew Rue; (third) November 24, 1760, Rev. James Dey.

(VI) John Rue (see above), born 1754, married, January 1, 1777, Anne Combs, born 1751, died 1789, daughter of Captain and Judge Jonathan Combs, of Middlesex county, New Jersey. Captain Jonathan Combs was in commission as captain in the Third Regiment, Middlesex county, New Jersey, militia, during the revolutionary war (see records on file in office of Adjutant General of New Jersey; also, Stryker's "Officers and Men in the Revolutionary War.")

See now generation IV. in the Rue line just preceding this; here the lines come together and follow:

(VII) Matthew Matthias Rue, son of John Rue, born 1782, married his third wife, Charlotte Higgins, in 1816. They resided in Lockport, New York. Matthew M. Rue died there November, 1828, and Charlotte (Higgins) Rue died there April 14, 1827. Their daughter

(VIII) Sarah Catharine Rue, born in Lockport, New York, March 11, 1823, married, March 4, 1840, Andrew Jackson Sink, born at Fort Schuyler, near Utica, New York, June 14, 1823. Mrs. Sink died in Adams, New York, June 3, 1881; buried beside Mr. Sink in the family plot in the cemetery at Rome, New York. Mr. Sink died February 15, 1880. Mr. Sink was engaged in the hotel business, owning hotels in Rome, New York; Chicago, Illinois; Toledo, Ohio; Titusville and Triumph, Pennsylvania; Adams, New York; and other places. He was an attendant of the Protestant Episcopal church of Rome, New York; and a Democrat in politics. Their children:

1. Charles Melvin Sink, born June 14, 1841, died December 24, 1841; born and died in Philadelphia, Pennsylvania.

2. George Henry Sink, born in Rome, New York, November 4, 1842, died there January 21, 1875; married in Rochester, New York, May 30, 1870, Rose Cassidy, born in Rome, New York, November 24, 1851; their children, born in Rome, New York: 1. Harriet Charlotte Sink, born August 9, 1871, died in Chicago, Illinois, March 1, 1897, married, June 6, 1894, Albert Thomas Trott. 2. Sarah Catharine Sink, born October 4, 1872, married (first) William H. Gers, April 26, 1897, divorced November 2, 1901, married (second) Philip J. Gorman, November 24, 1902, divorced December 14, 1912, one son, George Clarke Gorman, born in Chicago, Illinois, January 8, 1904. 3. Georgiana Helen Sink, born January 11, 1875, died March 7, 1904; married (first) Frank Louis Hopkins, February 26, 1894; he died September 8, 1899. She married (second) July 12, 1900, Charles E. Lyon. Two children, residing in Chicago, 5748 West Ontario street: Frank Harold Hopkins, born December 25, 1894, and George Howard Hopkins, born November 26, 1898, both born in Chicago, Illinois.

3. Charlotte Jane Sink, subject of this sketch, was born in Rome, New York, April 25, 1846; married in Brooklyn, New York, April 17, 1867, by the Rev. George T. Thrall, Captain Henry Harrison Cumings, of Tidioute, Warren county, Pennsylvania. They were married at the home of Mrs. Cumings' cousin, Fanny (Higgins), wife of Joseph Judson.

Mrs. Cumings attended the schools of Rome, New York; Chicago, Illinois; and Notre Dame, in South Bend, Indiana. Mrs. Cumings is a member of the Woman's Relief Corps, having held the positions of president of the Col. George A. Cobham Woman's Relief Corps, and other offices; also has held state offices in that organization, as well as having been the president of the State Department of Pennsylvania, Woman's Relief Corps, 1893 and 1894. She has also held the office of national aide of the Woman's Relief Corps, and other similar offices in the national organization of the Woman's Relief Corps. In this work she was a member of the "Andersonville Prison" Board when it was being restored and was given to the government of the United States. She organized the Tidioute Chapter of the Daughters of the American Revolution, and was its regent for eleven years, when she resigned to accept the regency of the Pennsylvania State Society, Daughters of the American Revolution, where she has successfully served two terms, and has received the nomination for a third term. Mrs. Cumings is also a member of the following local clubs in her neighborhood: The Shakespeare Club, the Mendelssohn, and the Eastern Star, in each of which she was a charter member; she is also a member of the Philomel, of Warren, Pennsylvania. Mrs. Cumings and family are members of Christ Protestant Episcopal Church of Tidioute. Their nine children:

1. Harriet Emily Cumings, born January 9, 1868; educated in the Tidioute public schools; the class of 1890, of Oberlin College; and Oberlin Conservatory of Music, Oberlin, Ohio. She married, in Mayville, New York, August 27, 1888, Theodore Horatio Ellis, born in Oberlin, Ohio, February 20, 1867, son of the Rev. Professor John Millot Ellis, born in Nashua, New Hampshire, March 29, 1831, and his wife, Minerva Emeline (Tenney), born in North Amherst, Ohio, September 19, 1837, she a daughter of Luman Tenney, M. D., born in Orwell, Vermont, April 3, 1809, and his wife, Emeline Charity (Harris), born in Becket, Massachusetts, October 9, 1809. They resided for three years in Grandin, Missouri; ten years in Tiona, Pennsylvania; two and a half years in Reading, Pennsylvania; and since 1904 in Baltimore, Maryland. While residing in Tiona, Pennsylvania, and also in Reading, Pennsylvania, Mrs. Ellis kept up her interests in the clubs of

her old home in Tidioute. She assisted her mother in organizing the Tidioute Chapter, daughters of the American Revolution, and was its treasurer in 1902-03; she was a member of the Shakespeare Club and the Twentieth Century Club of Tidioute, Pennsylvania; also of the Woman's Relief Corps, Col. George A. Cobham Corps, being its president in 1893. She filled different offices of that corps while residing in that place; also, Mrs. Ellis held several state offices, being installing and instituting officer, National Woman's Relief Corps, and the first patriotic instructor. It was due to her efforts that the Flag Salute was first introduced into all the schools of the state. Mrs. Ellis wrote a personal letter to every teacher in the state asking them to use the Salute daily in their schoolrooms. The county and state superintendents furnished Mrs. Ellis with a list of names of every teacher, with their addresses. In this organization Mrs. Ellis served as national aide for three years, and in other offices, such as flagbearer and guard at the national conventions at Indianapolis and Pittsburgh. Mrs. Ellis is interested in the Mothers' Club of Baltimore, the Woman's Club of Forest Park in Baltimore, and was the organizer of the Mordecai Gist Chapter, Daughters of the American Revolution, and is a member of Federated Women's Clubs of Maryland. She also takes an active interest in philanthropic and civic work in Baltimore; and last but not least, does a great deal of historical and genealogical research work, endeavoring to have old and ancient manuscript state records printed and bound and placed where the people of the state will be able to consult them and have a better knowledge of their state history.

Mr. Ellis is a large stockholder and manager of the United States Asphalt and Refining Company, in Baltimore, as his main business, but has an interest in several other business enterprises. He is a member of De Molay Commandery, Knights Templar, Reading, Pennsylvania, and Rajah Temple of the Mystic Shrine, of the same place. He is a member of the I. O. O. F., of Clarendon, Pennsylvania, and Modern Woodmen of America. In Baltimore he is a member of the Maryland Society of the Sons of the American Revolution, and of the Crescent Club and Baltimore Yacht Club. Mr. Ellis and family attend the Associate Congregational Church. Their children are:

(a) Bernard Tenney Ellis, born in Tidioute, Pennsylvania, May 29, 1889; graduated with the class of 1908, Baltimore City College, and was in Johns Hopkins University, class of 1912. He is a small stockholder and interested in the U. S. A. R. business with his father. He is a member and chief petty officer of the Maryland Naval Brigade. He is also a member of the Masonic organization; he is unmarried, and resides with his parents.

(b) Charlotte Cumings Ellis, born in Tidioute, Pennsylvania, July 15, 1895; educated in the public schools of Baltimore; graduated in class of 1913, Baltimore Eastern High School, vice-president of her class; member of the Baltimore Art Institute.

(c) Minerva Tenney Ellis, born in Tiona, Pennsylvania, April 6, 1901; two years in public schools of Baltimore, and a member of the Girls' Latin School, in Baltimore; member of the Baltimore Art Institute.

2. Charles Andrew Cumings, born in Tidioute, Pennsylvania, December 12, 1869; early education in the public school of Tidioute, then at Pennsylvania State College. He settled first in Butler, Pennsylvania, on an oil lease, remaining there for several years. While there he became a member of the Pennsylvania National Guard. He enlisted in the Cuban war, and for the war in the Philippines, where he served as first lieutenant for three years. He voluntarily resigned his commission in 1901. Next he became a government guager, with headquarters in Pittsburgh and in Meadville, Pennsylvania, where he continued for several years. After resigning from this work he removed to Syracuse, New York, for several years, and finally settled in Philadelphia, Pennsylvania, where he is in business. He married, in Ridgewood, New Jersey, November 14, 1901, Helen Ada Crowthers, daughter of Henry H. Crowthers, formerly of Ridgewood, but now of Philadelphia, Pennsylvania. They have one daughter, Margaret Shippen Cumings, born April 26, 1908, in Philadelphia, Pennsylvania.

3. Henry Harrison Cumings Jr., born in Tidioute, Pennsylvania, August 24, 1871; attended and graduated from the public schools of Tidioute; attended Oberlin College, Oberlin, Ohio, one year, and then had three years at Allegheny College, Meadville, Pennsylvania. After leaving college he entered business with his brother-in-law, Theodore H. Ellis, refining oil at Tiona, Warren county, Pennsylvania.

They continued this business until the spring of 1901, at which time they sold out and opened an oil business in Reading, Pennsylvania. The following winter Mr. Cumings was called to Rome, New York, to look after family business there, taking charge of the Stanwix Hall, one of the hotels owned by his grandfather, Andrew J. Sink, leaving Mr. Ellis to look after the oil business in Reading. Finding the hotel business congenial, Mr. Cumings has remained in Rome, New York, in this business. In Erie, Pennsylvania, July 15, 1896, Henry Harrison Cumings Jr. married, at the home of her mother, Mrs. Garetta (Hatch) Pierce, Bertha Garetta Pierce. They have two sons: Henry Harrison Cumings (3d), born June 20, 1897; Pierce Amsden Cumings, born March 5, 1900; both born in Tiona, Pennsylvania.

4. Sarah Charlotte Cumings, born in Tidioute, Pennsylvania, April 15, 1875, died there September 10, 1875.

5. Ralph Hunter Cumings, born in East Brady, Pennsylvania, December 11, 1876; educated in the public schools of Tidioute, Pennsylvania; prepared for college in Kiskiminetas Springs School, of Indiana, Pennsylvania, and of the class of 1898 at Yale College, New Haven, Connecticut. Just before graduation he enlisted for the Cuban war, with the Yale Battery. While the company was held in camp he was acting quartermaster. After the close of the Cuban war he was in the hospital in New Haven for several months. When well, he returned home and engaged in business in Marietta, Ohio. A few years later he sold out his business, returning to Tidioute, and went in with the Union Razor Company, and was their secretary. In 1910 he sold out this business, removing to Baltimore, Maryland, where he formed a company and went into the manufacture of roofing. He married, in East Orange, New Jersey, September 5, 1906, at the home of her sister, Mrs. Woolruff, Elizabeth Harriet Benjamin, of New York City. They had one son, born April 27, 1908; he died the same night.

6. Laura Frances Cumings, born in Tidioute, Pennsylvania, August 27, 1879; educated in the public schools of Tidioute, Pennsylvania, graduated class of 1896; entered Lake Erie College, in Painesville, Ohio, for one year. She married, in the Presbyterian church, of Tidioute, Pennsylvania, by the Rev. Dr. Garrett, of Christ Protestant Episcopal Church, June 15, 1904, Arthur Burt White, of Riverside, California, formerly of Boston, Massachusetts. They resided in Riverside, California, then Corona, California, where Mr. White was the city engineer and civil engineer. When his term of office expired Mr. White removed to Los Angeles, California, where he engaged in the civil engineering business for himself. They own several ranches in California, at Lancaster, Ontario and Corona. Their children: Muriel Burr White, born in Riverside, California, April 13, 1905, died there February 28, 1906; Henry Cumings White, born in Corona, California, November 28, 1906; Laurence Adams White, born in Los Angeles, California, December 6, 1909; baby daughter White, born in Los Angeles, California, November 17, 1911, died there November 18, 1911.

7. Baby daughter Cumings, born in Tidioute, Pennsylvania, February 2, 1883, died there February 16, 1883.

8. Benjamin Rue Cumings, born in Tidioute, Pennsylvania, October 4, 1887, died there December 13, 1890.

9. Abigail Lynch Cumings, born in Tidioute, Pennsylvania, November 17, 1893; attended the public schools of Tidioute, also Westlake School for Girls, Los Angeles, California, and later Miss Marshall's School, Oak Lane, Philadelphia, where she graduated with high honors in the class of 1912. Miss Cumings has been endowed with a beautiful voice and is a great addition to the clubs of which she is a member in her home town. She has traveled extensively with her parents, and resides with them, except when studying music and perfecting her voice with the best teachers in Philadelphia.

The fourth child of Andrew J. Sink and wife, Sarah Catharine Rue:

4. Willard Stockton Sink, born in Stanwix, New York, June 2, 1852; married, at Rome, New York, October 17, 1877, Sarah A. (Hook) Strong, widow of Giles Strong, who died June 22, 1875; she was born January 28, 1855, a daughter of John and Rebecca Hook. Their children:

1. Blanche Emily Sink, born in Rome, New York, August 28, 1879, died there July 6, 1891.

2. Charlotte Frances Sink, born in Rome, New York, November 11, 1883; married, in Toronto, Canada, August 13, 1902, Wilford Meeker St. Auburn; their children: a, Wil-

ford Meeker St. Auburn Jr., born in Wellington, Ohio, April 26, 1903; b. Ernestine Meeker St. Auburn, born in Rome, New York, April 29, 1905; c. Marian Meeker St. Auburn, born in Rome, New York, June 25, 1906; d. Raymond Meeker St. Auburn, born in Yorkville, New York, May 2, 1911.

3. Helen La Rue Sink, born in Tidioute, Pennsylvania, July 10, 1885; married, in Oneida, New York, July 10, 1903, Harry B. West; their children, born in Rome, New York: Harold Bela West, born November 28, 1904; Ben Rue West, born March 23, 1906, died there August 4, 1906; Stewart West, born July 2, 1909; Dorothy West, born February 1, 1911; Marjory West, born July 8, 1912.

4. Willard Stockton Sink Jr., born in Rome, New York, May 17, 1890, died there September 24, 1890.

5. Willard Henry Sink, born in Rome, New York, September 26, 1891; married, in Utica, New York, April 11, 1912, Miss Grace E. Snyder.

6. Harold Hook Sink, born in Rome, New York, February 24, 1896.

5. Harriet Camilla Sink, born in Chicago, Illinois, March 15, 1856; married (first) in Rome, New York, November 11, 1875, Theron La Fora Holley, born 1841, died in Rome, New York, February 16, 1899. One daughter, Blanche Emily Holley, born in Rome. New York, September 10, 1876, resides in New York City, with her mother. Mrs. Holley married (second) in New York City, October 24, 1904, Carl William Klapproth, born in Germany. They reside in New York City.

The name Sibley is believed to SIBLEY be composed of the two Anglo-Saxon words sib and lea. The primary signification of sib is peace; a later signification is relationship. The word lea is field, or in a more general sense, land. The name Sibley may, therefore, be translated either as "Peacefield," "Land of Peace" or "Kinsmen's Land."

In the so-called "Rotuli Hundredorum" of the reign of Edward I. (1272-1307), Sibleys are listed as owners of land in the counties of Kent, Oxford and Suffolk. The family is, therefore, an ancient one, as surnames in England did not come into common use before the twelfth century. Enthusiastic and painstaking antiquarians and genealogists have claimed to be able to trace the line back to the time of William the Conqueror. Two coats-of-arms according to heraldic authorities are now, or have been in former times, borne by certain Sibley families in England. These coats are to be found recorded, the one in Sir William Dugdale's "Origines Juridicales," published in 1671, and the other coat in several editions of Burke's "General Armory."

The one figured by Dugdale and dated 1559, belonged to John Sibley, of Gray's Inn, one of the most renowned seats of English legal learning. The coat is thus described: "A shield quarterly; in first and fourth a tiger, gules, viewing himself backward in a mirror, azure; in second and third a chevron, gules, between three cows' heads caboshed, sable." The coat found in Burke's "General Armory" is described as follows: "Per pale, azure and gules, a griffin passant between three crescents, argent." This coat was, during the reign of George I., confirmed to Henry Sibley, Esquire, and to Thomas Sibley, Esquire, high sheriffs of Hertfordshire. It is possible that these arms had been borne by other Sibleys several centuries earlier. A Sibley crest is given in Fairbairn's "Crests of Great Britain and Ireland" as: "Out of a ducal coronet, or, a swan's head between wings, p. p. r."

However strong the probability, there is no documentary evidence yet submitted to the writer of this sketch to prove that any Sibleys of this country are, according to English rules, authorized to use either of these coats. Arms are not granted to families but to particular individuals and to their descendants. The use of armorial bearings by Americans is being discouraged.

Several facts indicate that the New England Sibleys come from St. Albans, or, at least, from the county of Hertford in which St. Albans is situated. Representatives of the Hertfordshire Sibleys have within the past few years aided in making researches tending to strengthen the probability. They have taken pains to set forth from sundry records certain reasons why it is likely that John Sibley, of Salem, Massachusetts, who took the freeman's oath, September 3, 1634, was a descendant of John Sibley, who was mayor of St. Albans in 1557, 1569 and 1578, and who is believed by them to be the John Sibley who was the eminent barrister of Gray's Inn.

"The names with which John Sibley's is associated in the records of Gray's Inn are among the most eminent in English history, being those of Spelman, Sackville, Lovelace, Walsingham, Lord Bacon, Yelverton and others, all fellows of the same renowned hospice." Another sentence from West's "Life of General Henry Hastings Sibley," first governor of Minnesota, may prove of interest in this connection: "That the Sibleys of Hertfordshire were of the same family as the Sibleys of Somerset, Kent, Middlesex, Sussex, Essex, Leicester and Huntingdon is attested by various genealogists." Other counties in England in which Sibleys were, in 1875, owners of land were Lincoln, Warwick and Devon.*

Several of the Sibley surname in England have achieved distinction and there has been a number of alliances with the nobility. Those who desire to pursue these and kindred subjects further may find additional facts in the "Life of General Henry Hastings Sibley" by Nathaniel West, D. D., published in 1889 at St. Paul, Minnesota, and in the "History of the Town of Union, Maine," by John Langdon Sibley, A. M. The latter work was published in Boston in 1851. The author was a member of the Massachusetts Historical Society, was a diligent gleaner of New England records, published several other works, and was for many years prior to his death librarian of Harvard University. A member of the Sibley family in England, who at the present time has an international reputation, is Walter Knowsley Sibley, M. A., M. D., M. R. C. P., M. R. C. S., etc., of Grosvenor Square, London. He is a member of the senate of Cambridge University, physician to the Northwest London Hospital, and holds several other positions of responsibility and honor. He has made many noteworthy scientific investigations and is the author of a considerable number of highly esteemed writings. Brief particulars concerning him are given in the current volume of "Who's Who."

According to Felt's "Annals of Salem," it seems that the first Sibleys in this country came to Salem, Massachusetts, in the fleet of 1629. Their given names were John and Richard and they are supposed to have been brothers.

(I) John Sibley, who took the freeman's oath, September 3, 1634, is sixteenth on the list of members of the First Church of Salem. The Salem Church in those days had two ministers or spiritual leaders. One of them, designated as pastor, was the Rev. Samuel Skelton, M. A., of whom a few particulars will be given later on; the other one, designated as teacher, was, after the death in 1630 of the Rev. Francis Higginson, M. A., the illustrious Roger Williams, subsequently to be the founder of Rhode Island. The members of the Salem Church zealously championed the cause of Williams in his controversy with the government of the colony concerning religious toleration. They continued to support their leader until they were at last forced into silence by threats of political disfranchisement. John Sibley was selectman of Salem in 1636. He owned land at Winter Island Harbor, at Manchester and also near the present village of Danvers. He was selectman of Manchester in 1645 and 1658. Possibly he served the community in other years and in other capacities, but the town records for a considerable portion of his lifetime are, unfortunately, lost. He died in 1661, an extensive landholder. He had nine children, four boys and five girls. His wife Rachel brought the inventory into court and,—"Ye court doe order that ye estate be left in ye widoe's hands to bring up ye children till ye court take further notice." The names of the children were in order of birth: Sarah, Mary, Rachael, John, Hannah, William, Joseph, Samuel and Abigail. The eldest was baptized in Salem Church in 1642, and the youngest in 1659.

(II) Joseph was born in 1655. Though he was a landowner and husbandman, yet he was, like his father, for a part of his life engaged in the fishing trade, which contributed so materially to the welfare and prosperity of the colony. It is recorded in Felt's "Annals of Salem" that on his return from a fishing voyage to Cape Sable, he was impressed on board a British frigate. His wife petitioned the governor and after a time his release was secured. Little is known of him, though it would appear that he was a man of vigor and of social disposition and that he had influential friends. He was of Lynn in 1715, when he bought land in

---

*Since the above was in type, I am in receipt of a copy of a document showing that under date of September 12, 1642, John Sibley, of Salem, for the sum of three score pounds, paid to him and Nicholas Hallet, sold and conveyed certain life leases held by him and Hallet in Bradpole Manor, county Dorset, England. The document sets forth also that John Sibley and W. Sibley were "sonnes of Wm. Sibley," and that the latter had died prior to the granting of these leases in 1617. (See Aspinwall Notarial Records, page 162). A professional genealogist informs me that he has traced the line in England to 1483, and that for the sum of $500 he sells the information to members of the Sibley family under restrictions not to publish it. I have not seen fit to accept his terms.   E. H. SIBLEY.

Sutton, Massachusetts. His brother, Captain John Sibley, was a selectman of Manchester for many years; was a representative to the general court and leading man generally in town affairs. Joseph Sibley married, February 4, 1683, Susanna Follett. She was the daughter of Robert and Persis (Black) Follett.

Joseph Sibley was the common ancestor of many who have been honored for their character, talents and important public services. Only a few of these can here be mentioned, viz: Henry Hastings Sibley, "The Father of Minnesota," carried through, while a member of congress from Wisconsin, the bill creating the territory of Minnesota; was its first governor when it became a state; put down with raw troops the Sioux Rebellion, was brevetted a brigadier-general by President Lincoln. Subsequently he was brevetted a major-general. He was president of the Minnesota State Historical Society; president of the Board of Regents of the University of Minnesota; he commanded the whole military district of Minnesota during the civil war; was commander of the Loyal Legion; was president of the St. Paul Chamber of Commerce; president of the State Normal School Board, and the recipient of many other state and national honors.

Henry Hopkins Sibley, of Louisiana, was brevetted a major for gallantry during the Mexican war. He was a general in the Confederate army; was the inventor of the Sibley tent. After the close of the civil war he was for some years engaged in engineering work for the Khedive of Egypt.

Hiram Sibley learned several trades. He put through the first line of telegraph from the Mississippi river to the Pacific coast. He was the first president of the Western Union Telegraph Company. He owned forty thousand acres of land and had the most widely known seed raising establishment of any man of his day. He conducted successfully many other great business enterprises. He founded the Sibley College of Mechanical Engineering at Cornell University, and made other noteworthy benefactions.

Solomon Sibley was a member of congress and a member of the first territorial legislature of the northwest. He drafted and carried through the latter body the bill incorporating the city of Detroit, one of the streets of which is named in his honor. He was United States commissioner with General Lewis Cass to treat with the Indians for the cession of territory equal in area to more than three states the size of the state of Rhode Island. He was chief justice of Michigan for twelve years.

Dr. John Sibley, a surgeon in the revolutionary war, was for several years a member of the legislature of Louisiana. Under the administration of Jefferson he was, according to the "History of Sutton, Massachusetts," a commissioner to make treaties with Indian tribes in the lands ceded by Spain. Gallatin stated that Dr. Sibley's account of the tribes between the Mississippi and the Red river was the most complete that had been written.

Jonas Sibley was for seventeen years in succession a representative to the general court of Massachusetts; was also a member of the state senate and a representative in congress.

Jonas L. Sibley, his son, was the recipient of several political honors in the state of Massachusetts. He was an eminent lawyer, and it is recorded that he had eighty-one cases at one term of court.

Mark H. Sibley was a judge, state senator, and a member of congress from New York.

Josiah Sibley, of Augusta, Georgia, was one of the pioneer cotton manufacturers of the south; was widely known and esteemed not only for his business ability, but also for his nobility of character and public spirit.

Major George Champlain Sibley, with a band of one hundred Osage warriors explored the Grand Saline and Salt Mountain, and published an account of the expedition. He was a United States commissioner and made many treaties with Indian tribes. He put through a highway from Missouri to New Mexico. In or about 1838 he with others founded a woman's college at St. Charles, Missouri.

Frederick W. Sibley, lieutenant-colonel of the United States army, was twice brevetted for gallantry, and was recommended for a gold medal. He was in 1910 the commandant at the United States Military Academy at West Point.

Rufus A. Sibley, eminent as a breeder of Jersey cattle, is the head of a firm having stores in Rochester, New York, in New York City, in Chemnitz, Germany, and in Paris, France.

Frank J. Sibley, orator, editor and author, now, or recently, a resident of Los Angeles,

California, has been for over thirty years prominent as a leader in temperance and prohibition work throughout the United States.

Hiram Luther Sibley was judge of the circuit court of Ohio; was appointed in 1906 a member of the commission of three to revise and consolidate the laws of the state of Ohio. He has had several other honors. He is the author and editor of legal works.

From 1755 down through the period of the war of the revolution we find of the descendants of Joseph Sibley conspicuous for their military services: Captain John Sibley, Captain James Sibley, Captain William Sibley, Captain Nathaniel Sibley, Captain Jonathan Sibley, Captain Solomon Sibley and Colonel Timothy Sibley. Ten of Joseph Sibley's descendants were among the minute-men at Concord.

The Sibleys of New England, according to West, "are intermarried with the Putnams and Whipples, the Bigelows and Sumners, the Pierponts and Morses, the Lelands and Wheelocks, the Tarrants and Bancrofts, the Dudleys and Spragues, and, later down in the flow of their generations, with the Wellses and Conklings, the Livingstons and Chases and other influential families."

The Sibley family in this country is a comparatively small one. In 1853 a genealogist estimated that the Sibleys of the male sex, of New England origin, from 1629 to that date, did not exceed five hundred. Their activity, usefulness and prominence as leaders in proportion to their numbers have received many favorable comments.

The Sibleys in the central, southern and western states are, in general, descended from Joseph Sibley. There are, however, certain Sibleys in Florida and in Maryland who are not related to the New England family. Joseph Sibley and wife, Susanna Follett, had six sons and one daughter. Their names were Joseph, John, Jonathan, Hannah, Samuel, William and Benjamin. Five of the sons settled in Sutton, Massachusetts.

(III) The youngest, Benjamin, baptized September 19, 1703, married Priscilla Rich, who was born in Wrentham, September 28, 1706. She was the daughter of Samuel and Hannah (Marsh) Rich. He died in Sutton about 1729. After living a short time in Sutton, Benjamin Sibley and family moved to Ashford, Connecticut. He was a farmer; he died at Willington, Connecticut, November 2, 1789, in his eighty-eighth year, according to his tombstone record. The town records for forty years or more, from 1739 are lost, so there is but little known of his activities. A glimpse at one of the customs of the times is afforded by his cattle mark, which is recorded as "a crop of ye right ear and two slits." His brothers, particularly Captain Joseph Sibley, were shown many evidences of esteem by their fellow townsmen of Sutton, Massachusetts. The children of Benjamin and Priscilla (Rich) Sibley were: Priscilla, Benjamin, Ezekiel, Zurviah, Susannah, Hannah, Ezra, Aaron, Moses, Joseph, Samuel and Jonathan.

(IV) Jonathan Sibley, born March 4, 1750, at Willington, Connecticut, died there, July 31, 1826. Jonathan Sibley was a farmer. He was a member and deacon of the Baptist church. He was selectman for nine years or more; moderator of the town meeting for six years; was representative to the legislative assembly six times and received numerous other evidences of the esteem of his fellow townsmen. His brother, Ezra Sibley, was a sergeant in the revolutionary war. Jonathan Sibley married, November 15, 1774, Patty Brooks, daughter of Deacon Abijah and Lucy (Knowlton) Brooks. Patty Brooks was born January 5, 1755, at Ashford, Connecticut. The children of Jonathan and Patty Sibley were: Patty, Susannah, Jonathan, Polly, Nathaniel, Roxanna, Esther, Benjamin, Abijah, Lucy, Joseph, Orrin and Hannah.

(V) Abijah, son of Jonathan and Patty (Brooks) Sibley, was born November 1, 1788, at Willington, Connecticut, died June 3, 1856. He moved to Concord, New York, where he purchased a farm. He was a contracting carpenter, locally famed for his skill and quickness. His integrity, kindness and marked self-control caused him to be highly regarded by all who knew him. He was a soldier in the war of 1812. He had a twin brother, Benjamin, who died in Wisconsin prior to 1860. Two other brothers, Jonathan Sibley Jr. and Nathaniel Sibley, were representatives to the general assembly of Connecticut. Dr. Joseph Sibley, another brother, moved to Michigan, where he embarked in business. On his death he left an estate that was considered large for the times. Abijah Sibley married, January 1, 1816, at Skaneateles, New York, Lucy Marcy, of Willington, Connecticut, daughter of Zebadiah and Phoebe (Pearl) Marcy. Lucy Marcy was born April 21, 1794. She died March 19,

1859. Their seven children, all born at Concord, New York, were: Adaline, Edwin Hamilton, Joseph Crocker, Anson DeWitt, William Augustine, Clark Carlton and Lucien George.

(VI) Dr. Joseph Crocker Sibley, son of Abijah and Lucy (Marcy) Sibley, was born December 19, 1817. His general education was acquired at the common schools and at the Springville Academy. As a young man he taught school for three or more winters. He read medicine with his cousin, Dr. Lyman Crocker. After taking his degree of M. D. at a medical college, he made a specialty of surgery under Dr. Munn, an eminent surgeon of Rochester, New York. Dr. Sibley practiced medicine in Friendship, Bath, Boston, Springville and Colden, all in New York state. He performed with marked success all the finer operations in surgery known to his day, including the removal of cataract and several other operations now rarely attempted except by specialists. He owned a farm near Colden, New York, and raised choice fruit and improved strains of live stock. He was a Whig and a Republican in politics and made many public addresses. He was an active worker in the cause of temperance. He was a member of the Baptist church and was at one time superintendent of the Sunday school.

Dr. Sibley was a man of kindly impulse, of good humor, of impressive appearance and of excellent physique, and was in the active practice of his profession until about one week prior to his death, which was due to pneumonia, and which occurred March 17, 1866, at Colden, New York. Seldom have there been in that section of the country so great evidences of respect shown any individual as marked the funeral services of Dr. Sibley. His brother, Edwin Hamilton Sibley, M. D., was also a man of commanding presence, noble character and signal ability. He represented Medina county, Ohio, in the legislature in 1854 and 1855. Their youngest brother, Lucien George Sibley, was a volunteer in the civil war and was wounded in the battle of Shiloh.

Dr. Joseph C. Sibley married, October 8, 1845, at Wirt, New York, Lucy Elvira, youngest child of Captain Luke and Betsy (Main) Babcock. Her brother, Raymond P. Babcock, was a member of the New York legislature. Lucy Elvira Babcock was born November 7, 1822, at Colerain, Massachusetts. She was educated at the academies at Homer, New York, and Alfred, New York. Several of her ancestors contributed largely to the public welfare of the New England colonies, particularly to the colonies of Connecticut and Rhode Island. Some of these ancestors will be briefly mentioned: John Babcock, Colonel Oliver Babcock, Colonel Joseph Pendleton, Captain James Pendleton, Captain Edmund Goodenow, Captain James Avery and Major Brian Pendleton, were often members of legislative assemblies and rendered effective military service. Captain James Avery commanded the Pequots of the Indian allies in King Philip's war. Major Brian Pendleton was deputy governor of Maine in 1680, and was also active in public affairs in Massachusetts, New Hampshire and Rhode Island. Joseph Clarke spent fifteen years in public life, six of which were as a member of the governor's council of Rhode Island. He was a brother of Dr. John Clarke whose services to Rhode Island were second in importance only to those of Roger Williams. Dr. John Clarke was four years deputy governor and twelve years the agent of the colony at the English court. He secured from King Charles II. the charter of 1663, which remained the fundamental law of the state until 1843. Dr. John Clarke left no descendants. Lucy Elvira (Babcock) Sibley's maternal grandfather was Captain Amos Main, of Stonington, Connecticut, who during the war of the revolution commanded a company of the militia of the Eighth Regiment. His name and services in connection with revolutionary matters are often mentioned in the public records of Stonington.

The four children of Dr. Joseph C. and Lucy Elvira Sibley were: Ann Adelaide, married Charles Miller; Joseph Crocker, Edwin Henry and Mary Eleanora. The last named died in Franklin, Pennsylvania, April 5, 1881, in her seventeenth year, while a pupil in the high school. Over five years after the death of her first husband, Mrs. Sibley was married to Rev. E. F. Crane, M. D., a Baptist minister of Elmira, New York. He raised two companies for the civil war and was commissioned a captain but resigned to become chaplain of the Twenty-third Regiment of New York Volunteers. His death occurred at Franklin, Pennsylvania, February 11, 1896. She died in Franklin from pneumonia, May 5, 1908, in her eighty-sixth year, with her mental faculties still bright and keen. In particular, her memory was as accurate in regard to recent occurrences as it was in the days of her girlhood. This was the more remarkable inasmuch as since the age of eighty-one she had suffered from three paralytic strokes, any one of which was severe enough to have proved fatal to one not possessed of her unusual vitality. Out of an estate of $30,000, she left a bequest of $2,000 for the foreign missions of the Baptist denomination. Fanny Lormore Crane, the only child of Rev. E. F. and Lucy Elvira Crane, was married to Albert F. Logan, of Franklin, Pennsylvania. Her death took place April 22, 1895, in her twenty-second year.

Dr. Sibley was a direct descendant of several who were distinguished for the value of their services to the New England colonies. A few of these will be named: Rev. Samuel Skelton, M. A., was the first pastor of the First Church in Salem, Massachusetts. He was a graduate of the University of Cambridge, England. He was a friend of Governor Endicott, and as a member of his council, was associated with him in authority. Skelton was one of those who officially welcomed Governor Winthrop on the latter's arrival in America. Skelton was described by Edward Johnson of Winthrop's company as "a man of a gracious speech, full of faith, and furnished by the Lord with gifts from above to begin this great work." He died in 1634. Ezekiel Richardson was an early believer in religious toleration. He was one of the leaders among the colonists of Massachusetts, was one of the founders of Woburn and was a member of the general court from Charlestown, Massachusetts, in 1635. Captain Bozoun Allen, "mercer," came from England in 1638 and was prominent in civil and military matters in Sudbury, Hingham and Boston. Lieutenant Edward Morris was a representative to the general court from Roxbury, Massachusetts, in 1678, and for many years thereafter. He was the first military leader of the settlers of Woodstock, Connecticut. Captain John Johnson and his son, Captain Isaac Johnson, were both members of the general court and both members of the famous Artillery Company. Captain John Johnson was surveyor-general of arms and ammunition of the Massachusetts colony in 1630. Captain Isaac Johnson was killed during King Philip's war while leading his troops at the great swamp fight at Narragansett, December 19, 1675. Captain Timothy Pearl, of Willington, Connecticut, Dr. Sibley's maternal great-grandfather, was fifteen times a representative to the legislative assembly. He was a member of the body which approved for Connecticut the Declaration of Independence. He rendered various other services to the cause of the patriots and was accorded by his fellow citizens many evidences of their esteem.

Dr. Sibley's paternal great-grandmother's maiden name was Lucy Knowlton. She was a sister of Colonel Thomas Knowlton who won imperishable fame at the battle of Bunker Hill. He was a friend of Washington, who showed Knowlton several marks of appreciation and respect. Colonel Knowlton was killed in 1776 at the battle of Harlem Heights. His statue has been erected by the state of Connecticut at the capital at Hartford.

(VII) Hon. Joseph Crocker (2) Sibley, son of Dr. Joseph Crocker (1) and Lucy Elvira (Babcock) Sibley, was born in Friendship, Allegany county, New York, February 18, 1850. As a boy he was strong, active and quick, and like all other normal, healthy boys, fond of play. His father believed in training boys to work and to assume responsibilities, and therefore early assigned him numerous tasks suitable to his years and ability. It is noteworthy that in school he learned his lessons with great ease and that when six years old he was as far advanced in his books as the average child of twice his age. His mother, as well as his father, had been a school teacher and often encouraged him to devote himself to his studies. He had a taste for reading and his mother frequently related with pardonable pride that when nine years old he had on his own initiative read through a two-volume history of the life and campaigns of Napoleon Bonaparte. This love for reading has been a marked characteristic of Mr. Sibley throughout his life. He was fortunate in being endowed with a retentive memory for facts, circumstances, ideas and even for exact words. If his memory for faces had been equally strong, he would in after years as a man in public life have been equipped far beyond the measure of many others who have also been notably successful. It was in his boyhood days greatly to his advantage that he lived in small country towns and that he was often brought into contact with nature on his father's farm and on farms belonging to his uncles. When he was nine years old the family removed from Bath, Steuben county, New York, to Boston, Erie county, New York. As was to be expected, the new boy in the village was at first set upon by those of his own size and age, and when he had successfully defended himself from their attempted drubbings he was then compelled to do the best he could for himself in rough-and-tumble struggles with the elder brothers of those whom he had worsted. The final outcome was that it was generally agreed that the newcomer was made of the right kind of material and could safely be admitted to the inner circles of the royal court of Boyville. Dr. Sibley noticed the ability of the boy to make money and encouraged his sense of responsibility and his pride in ownership by giving him one or more farm animals for his own. When the boy was twelve years old he was entrusted by his father with the sale in Buffalo of a drove of cattle from the farm which was located about twenty miles away. The business was attended to in as satisfactory a manner as it could have been done by one of mature years.

The death of Dr. Joseph C. Sibley occurred in 1866, when his son Joseph C. was sixteen. The boy had previously attended district schools, a German school, and the academies at Springville, New York, and Friendship, New York. He nominally continued to be a student at the Friendship Academy for a year or two longer, but during one winter he taught a country school, so that practically his student days were over some time before he was eighteen. The start he had made together with his fondness for books was sufficient to cause him to become in later years a man of extensive learning. Probably not one in a hundred of college graduates ever attains, even many years subsequent to graduation, the knowledge of history, law, diplomacy, sociology, economics and general literature, which Mr. Sibley by judicious use of his leisure time has acquired. In fact, if Mr. Sibley had not been favored through inheritance with strong vitality and if he had not in his earlier years strengthened his nervous system as well as his muscular system by plenty of manual labor and of outdoor sports, such as hunting, fishing, baseball, riding and driving, it is doubtful if he would have had, as he grew older, the courage to undertake or the ability to assimilate the authors that he so continuously and diligently studied. When, on account of limited funds, he finally decided that it was best for him to give up a college course, to which he had looked forward, he had considerable difficulty in deciding what business, trade or profession he should take up. He clerked for a while in a country dry goods store. At one time he thought of becoming a physician, and while a clerk in a drug store began the reading of medicine. So numerous were his talents that it is likely that he could have made a success in any one of half a dozen lines of worthy endeavor. On the death of his father he had chosen his brother-in-law, Charles Miller (in later years major-general of the National Guard of Pennsylvania), as his guardian. From the inception of this guardianship until the present day the business interests of Joseph C. Sibley and Charles Miller have often been closely identified. His first employment in Franklin was as a clerk in the dry goods store of Miller & Coon. This was in 1869.

For two years prior to 1873 Mr. Sibley was agent at Chicago for the Galena Oil Works of Franklin. He lost all his effects and came near losing his life at the time that Chicago was devastated by its great fire. The beginning of Mr. Sibley's noteworthy success in business may be said to date from 1873 when, having returned to Franklin, he began marketing for railway use a signal oil compounded by him which was superior in illuminating power, in safety and in cold test to any that had ever been previously in use. About this time the Signal Oil Works was formed, with Mr. Sibley as president. A few years later he compounded also the first successful valve oil ever produced from petroleum stocks. Both of these oils after a lapse of over thirty-five years are still considered the standard of excellence. When the Galena-Signal Oil Company was formed, about 1902, General Miller was made president and Mr. Sibley chairman of the board of directors.

When he was twenty-nine years old, Mr. Sibley was, after an exciting contest, elected on a progressive platform, mayor of the city of Franklin. Old residents state that he was the first man in the history of the city who had been elected to this office before he had attained the age of thirty.

The noted stock farm enterprise of Miller & Sibley was inaugurated in 1882. By insisting on the importance of constitution and healthfulness in cattle; by calling attention to the best type for milk, cheese and butter; by emphasizing the necessity for proper feed and care; and, especially, by demonstrating in great competitive contests the correctness and practical value of the propositions which he had advocated, Mr. Sibley has rendered inestimable service not only to the dairy and live stock interests of the country, but also to the general public, the consumers of animal products, as well. A few of the remarkable achievements of the stock farm may be briefly summarized. It produced the Jersey cow, Ida Marigold, that won two sweepstakes prizes at the World's Fair in Chicago in 1893. One of these prizes was in the show ring; the other was in practical contests for thirty days for milk, cheese and butter (open to all breeds). The Miller & Sibley herd won a total of two hundred and twenty-four first prizes and sweepstakes at twenty-two state fairs or greater expositions, a record believed to be unequalled by any other herd of Jerseys in the world. Matilda 4th, the first Jersey cow in the history of the breed to give over sixteen thousand pounds of milk in one year, was owned, developed and made her record at this farm. Mr. Sibley bought her at auction before she had had her first calf, but he stated at the time of purchasing her that she had the making of a great cow. Mr. Sibley was a superior judge of form and a student of pedigrees as well. The success of this particular cow was the more gratifying to Mr. Sibley because, according to the Escutcheon Theory then in vogue, she should have proven a small milker and unprofitable as a dairy animal. In fact, Mr. Sibley had been advised by theorists to get rid of her, as they predicted that she would be unworthy a place in the herd. Adelaide of St. Lambert, another of the famous Prospect Hill Jerseys, gave over one ton of milk (2,005¼ lbs.) in thirty-one days. This constituted at the time, June 24, 1898, the world's record for this period for the Jersey breed, and it is still unequalled. The bull Pedro was purchased by Mr. Sibley for $2,500 and sold the following year for $10,000. This bull, a few years after he had been sold by Messrs. Miller & Sibley, won the sweepstakes prize in the show ring at the World's Fair at Chicago. Stoke Pogis 5th and Ida's Rioter of St. L., two other bulls selected by Mr. Sibley, were esteemed as among the most successful sires in the Jersey breed. Each bull lived until his fifteenth year. Stoke Pogis 5th was bought at auction for $130. Subsequently $15,000 was offered and refused for him. In 1903 he had more granddaughters with standard butter records (14 lbs. of butter or more a week) than any other bull that ever lived. Fawn of St. Lambert, La Petite Mere 2d, and Ida of St. Lambert were also the holders at one time of the world's records for the Jersey breed for milk or for butter. The descendants of the Miller & Sibley herd are to be found in the leading herds of Jerseys throughout the world. Fourteen head of Jerseys from their farm were sold to a breeder in Japan.

In the era for high prices for trotting horses, Miller & Sibley owned as many as two hundred and fifty head. St. Bel, purchased by Mr. Sibley for $10,000, could show when not in training a gait of 2:02. Fifty thousand dollars were offered and refused for him. He was regarded by horsemen as the best son of the famous Electioneer. On the very day that St. Bel was to have been shipped from Franklin, Pennsylvania, to Independence, Iowa, to take a low record, he was seized with a spell of indigestion, which resulted in his death the day following. Many of his get were noted race horses. Conductor, another son of Electioneer, was purchased for $7,500. A short time later, after he had won a hard-fought race in Chicago, he was sold for $35,000. It was not uncommon at Prospect Hill Stock Farm to sell young colts and fillies for from $5,000 to $10,000 each.

Mr. Sibley first became a figure of national importance in 1892 when he was nominated for congress in the Twenty-sixth Pennsylvania district, though he was a resident of the Twenty-seventh. At the outset it looked as if the chances were against him, as his Republican opponent had a regular party majority of over five thousand behind him, and had also an extensive acquaintance throughout the two counties of Erie and Crawford, which constituted the district. Moreover, the Republican nominee had wealth, business alliances and church connections which were supposed to render him an unusually strong candidate. Mr. Sibley was supported by the Democrats, the Prohibitionists and members of the People's party, elements which left much to be desired in the matter of organization and in the unity of interests. A more strenuous or amusing campaign would be hard to imagine. Mr. Sibley worked heroically, sometimes delivering as many as six addresses a day, and succeeded in arousing the highest enthusiasm. It was at once recognized that he was a reasoner, a wit, a man of affairs, an orator, and, best of all, a strong, courageous man with a big heart and helpful impulses. The roorbacks started against him were easily refuted, and merely served to win new friends and to make the old ones more zealous in his behalf. The election returns showed that he had not only overcome the big hostile majority with which at the start he had been handicapped, but also that he had piled up for himself the surprising plurality of three thousand, three hundred and eighty-seven over his principal competitor, and a total majority of three thousand, two hundred and five. Four times subsequently Mr. Sibley was elected to congress, twice being from the Twenty-seventh Pennsylvania district and twice from the Twenty-eighth. At the close of his fifth term Mr. Sibley declined a renomination, stating that he desired to retire from public life. However, four years later, in 1910, yielding to the urgent appeals of hundreds of his former constituents of the Twenty-eighth district, he consented to become again a candidate. In March, shortly after the announcement of his candidacy had appeared, Mr. Sibley underwent in a Washington hospital an operation for the removal of cataract. About the same time he had a recurrence in aggravated form of an organic trouble of the heart, from which, without his being aware of the real difficulty, he had been a sufferer for about two years previous. Mr. Sibley's condition became so serious that for weeks doctors and nurses feared that the end might come at any moment. With the exception of two days when he went by train to two or three places in Mercer county, he was practically unable to give any assistance or advice whatever as to the conduct of the campaign. In fact, for a considerable portion of the time he was in absolute ignorance of anything that was being done in his behalf. Nevertheless, at the primaries in June he won the nomination for a sixth term. He was assured by party managers and friends in various parts of the district that his majority at the November election would be the largest he had ever received. However, as the heart disease, instead of improving as he had hoped, became more and more a fixed certainty, he resigned the nomination, feeling that if elected he could not properly attend to the duties that would devolve upon him.

While Mr. Sibley was a member of the house of representatives, few were more active and few had a wider acquaintance or wielded more influence. He was a ready debater, well fortified with facts, and stated them in an interesting and effective way. Many of his efforts were listened to by immense audiences, and he was often the recipient of congratulations from practically all of his colleagues. During his first term he was a member of the committee on appropriations. He was also for several terms on the committee on post offices and post roads. In this capacity he did much to favor rural free delivery, which has proven such a boon to all farmers wherever it has been put in use. He was chairman of the committee on manufactures and a member of the committee on insular affairs. Mr. Sibley believed in looking at all questions from the standpoint of common sense, of patriotism and of humanity, regardless of the dictates of politicians and party managers. Party names with him counted for but little. As a matter of fact, he was classed in congress as a Democrat prior to 1900; after that time, as a Republican. As early as 1895 he boldly declared that the tariff should no longer be regarded as the plaything of political parties, but should be put into the hands of a commission composed of able and patriotic financiers, who should consider it as the greatest practical business problem with which citizens and the government are called upon to deal. Under President Taft a beginning has been made in this direction. Several measures advocated by Mr. Sibley many years ago and which received scant recognition then, are now generally approved and are likely to become soon the law of the land. One of these was that of changing the presidential term from four to six years and making the holder ineligible to re-election. A bill to this effect was introduced by Mr. Sibley in two or three different congresses, but was not pressed because, in the judgment of his colleagues, the time was not then ripe. Mr. Sibley always desired to do justice to the laboring man and to the one whose condition in life is hard. He, therefore, was an early advocate of the cause of bi-metallism. When the world's stock of gold began greatly to increase through the discovery of new fields and the improvement of the processes for extracting the ore, he ceased to be a champion of the free coinage of silver. While hoping for the day to come when nations shall learn the art of war no more, Mr. Sibley was not so childish and impractical as to suppose that the day was already here. He, therefore, regarded it as the plain duty of the representatives of the people to provide a navy adequate in strength to protect our coasts and to insure the continuance of our welfare and our national independence. Nor did he, like too many others, shrink from this country's bearing the burdens and performing the obligations which the war with Spain imposed upon us.

Toward those who had risked their lives in defense of the nation, Mr. Sibley held that the government should maintain a liberal attitude. He was disgusted with parsimonious and red tape methods which so often prevented the payment of pensions to which soldiers were entitled and of claims which were just and should have been accorded recognition. Largely through Mr. Sibley's efforts legislation was enacted which removed technicalities which had too long debarred many a suffering and worthy veteran from receiving from the government what he and all fair-minded men considered right and due.

Mr. Sibley's talents have in many ways been recognized by those who have had an opportunity to know him thoroughly. He was permanent chairman of the Pennsylvania Republican state convention in 1902. In the national house of representatives he was often called upon to preside when the speaker wished to take part in debates or for other causes could not occupy the chair. At the Democratic national convention in 1896 he received votes for president of the United States, and a large number of votes for vice-president. Probably no other man in Northwestern Pennsylvania has so many warm enthusiastic friends and so few personal enemies as has Joseph C. Sibley. This is due to his kindness of heart, to his frankness, to his integrity, to his courage, and to his loyalty to his friends. Mr. Sibley has often in fires, floods and accidents of various kinds risked his own life to save the lives of others. Franklin feels proud to claim him as a citizen. He was the first man to propose a hospital here and the largest individual contributor to the fund necessary for its construction. While he was mayor he set on foot a movement to replace the city bonds which bore seven per cent interest with an issue bearing only five per cent. Though, owing to legal technicalities, the desired result was not accomplished until after his term of office had expired, yet he is entitled to part of the credit for lightening the burdens of city taxation. The Franklin Opera House was built by a company of which Mr. Sibley was the organizer and the first president. Mr. Sibley gave to the legal fraternity of the county his extensive law library, which is kept in the Court House where it can be readily consulted. He has been a liberal supporter of the churches, also of the Young Men's Christian Association, and for many years past has maintained at his own expense a club for workingmen, where they can meet under wholesome conditions, read the papers, enjoy a chat with their friends, play harmless games, use the baths, and in short be furnished with comforts which in former times were restricted to the rich, or at least were likely to be found only where there was an opportunity and a temptation to indulge in late hours and to use spirituous liquors. For several years, as a commissioner of the public parks of Franklin, Mr. Sibley did much to improve their appearance. He made the largest contribution to the fund for erecting the Egbert Memorial fountain. The Venango County fairs which used to rival the State fairs in the important and excellence of exhibits owed no little of their success to Mr. Sibley's zealous and untiring efforts. Mr. Sibley was formerly a director of the American Jersey Cattle Club and had much to do with framing and introducing a new scale of points which rightly emphasized the practical utility of the breed rather than its gazelle-like appearance, which had previously received too much attention. For a number of years Mr. Sibley was an efficient member of the Pennsylvania State Dairymen's Association, of which he was president for two or more terms. He was also a member of the State Board of Agriculture. He took the initiative in forming the American Trotting Register Association, and also served the organization in the capacity of a director. He was vice-president of the National Half-Mile Track Association, and for many years a member of the Board of Review of the National Trotting Horse Association. He was one of the directors of the Allegheny River Improvement Association. Within the past two years Mr. Sibley was the recipient of a silver platter, suitably inscribed, from the Lake Champlain Yacht Club, of which he has been the commodore. Mr. and Mrs. Sibley were presented during 1911 with a silver loving cup as a testimonial of respect and esteem from the First Baptist Church of Franklin, of which both he and his wife had been members since early life, and of which Mr. Sibley has for many years been chairman of the board of trustees. Mr. Sibley has been honored by the friendship of many of the leading men of the nation, including not only the members of the house and senate, but also officers of the army and navy, ambassadors, members of the cabinet and justices of the supreme court. He received the degree of LL.D. from two colleges and was offered it by a third.

As human nature is at present constituted, no one so conspicuous as Mr. Sibley has been in the affairs of the nation could hope to escape hostile and bitter criticism. It is safe to assume, however, that one whose record in private life is such as to command the respect of all who know him intimately, will not in dealing with greater matters in a public capacity be actuated by a totally different set of motives or principles. During one of his heated campaigns Mr. Sibley repeatedly stated that if he had ever throughout his lifetime taken from anybody one dollar or any other sum wrongfully, he would cheerfully refund it fourfold. It is almost needless to add that no claimant ever appeared to take advantage of the offer.

Mr. Sibley is a man of the progressive, but not of the fanatical or anarchistic type. He does not harbor feelings of hatred or revenge. He believes in dealing fairly and honorably with individuals, with organizations and with all legitimate business interests. Besides those who would for ordinary political reasons be opposed to him, Mr. Sibley has antagonized two other radically different classes of men. These are on the one hand, those who by nature do not favor change of any kind, and on the other hand those who from whatever cause, selfish or otherwise, seek to forward all sorts of wild, impracticable and unjust schemes which tend ultimately to the overthrow of government and of social order itself. Three suits, each of a political nature, have in the course of his lifetime been brought against Mr. Sibley. They were widely heralded in sensational newspapers. When, however, two of the most important suits were dropped on the petition of those instituting them, perhaps not one in a thousand of those who had read of legal proceedings having been entered ever saw any notice of the final outcome of the cases, or came to realize the fact that the charges were baseless and absurd. The other suit referred to was many years ago called for trial in the courts of Crawford county, but before testimony on behalf of Mr. Sibley was fairly under way, the plaintiff by reason of evidence contained in his own letters, which he had forgotten or had supposed were no longer in existence, asked that the case be dismissed.

Mr. Sibley's life has been a most stirring and eventful one, and a large volume would be required to set forth adequately the part he has played. Enough has been said, however, to show that he merits the love and esteem which he at present enjoys from his fellow-citizens, and that he will long be remembered after all that is mortal of him shall have been put underneath the sod.

Mr. Sibley married, March 17, 1870, Metta E. Babcock, born November 28, 1853, daughter of Simon M. and Celia (Kellogg) Babcock, of Friendship, New York. She died July 26, 1911. She was a generous contributor to the poor and unfortunate. The two children of Joseph C. and Metta E. Sibley are: Josephine, born January 16, 1873, at Friendship, New York, and Celia, born September 19, 1874, at Franklin, Pennsylvania. The elder daughter, Josephine, was married, March 17, 1897, at Franklin, Pennsylvania, to William Emerson Heathcote (see below), of Omaha, Nebraska. At present Mr. and Mrs. Heathcote and family reside at St. Petersburg, Florida, where her father has, also, for several years owned an orange grove and a winter home. Celia married, June 5, 1901, at Franklin, Pennsylvania, William McCalmont Wilson, of Washington, D. C. They are now residents of Franklin, Pennsylvania.

William Emerson Heathcote, son of Mathew and Mercy (Stone) Heathcote, both of English descent, was born at Morrison, Illinois, May 12, 1863. He left school when eighteen years of age and began his business career as an accountant. Four years later he entered the employ of S. P. Morse & Company, wholesale and retail dealers in dry goods in Omaha, Nebraska. After remaining four years with this firm, he went to Evanston, Wyoming, as an employee of A. C. Beckwith & Company. This firm was subsequently taken over by the Union Pacific Coal Company. For this corporation Mr. Heathcote served as superintendent of stores for a period of eight years. Among other duties he had charge of purchasing the supplies for the company's stores in Wyoming, Colorado and Utah. During this time he became financially interested in copper mining and certain other investments which proved profitable. In 1897 he came to Franklin, Pennsylvania, as vice-president of the Signal Oil Company, and remained seven years. In the fall of 1904, for the sake of a milder climate, he moved with his family to St. Petersburg, Florida. In that city he has since then been extensively engaged in citrus growing, in real estate and in banking.

(VII) Edwin Henry Sibley, a younger brother of Hon. Joseph C. Sibley, was born at Bath, Steuben county, New York, February 12, 1857. He was prepared for college in the public schools of Franklin, Pennsylvania, and at MacKoon & Waite's Private School, subsequently known as the Cascadilla School at Ithaca, New York. He spent four years at Cornell University, receiving in 1880 the degree of Bachelor of Arts. In certain subjects he had the honor of leading his classes. At the time of the organization of the Student's Guild he was, on motion of one of the professors, chosen chairman of the joint meeting of faculty and students. On the merit of his production he was selected by the faculty as one of the nine members of his class to have a public exercise on commencement day. By his fellow-students he was elected president of the Cornell University Christian Association, Ivy Orator for class-day and one of the board of editors of the *Cornell Review*, the literary magazine published by the students of the institution. When leaving Cornell he made arrangements to pursue his studies further at Harvard and at the University of Leipzig with a view to fitting himself to become a college professor, but a combination of circumstances led him into business. For an outing he went with a railroad surveying corps into the mountains of southeastern Kentucky. From the position of chainman he rose rapidly in succession to transitman, paymaster, purchasing agent, secretary, treasurer and a director of the company, ultimately holding the last four titles simultaneously. As President Charles Miller and other officials were in the east, it fell to Mr. Sibley's lot to look after many of the important interests of the company in Kentucky such as would naturally be attended to by a general manager. All the duties incident to these positions were satisfactorily performed. On one occasion he received the congratulations of the board of directors for the able and judicious manner in which he had conducted an important affair.

He continued to look after a certain part of the company's business until about 1886, when he entered the employ of the Galena Oil Works and the Signal Oil Works of Franklin as local treasurer. A few years later he was elected treasurer, which position he still holds. He was also for over twenty years manager of Prospect Hill Stock Farm of which Major-General Charles Miller and Hon. Joseph C. Sibley were proprietors.

Mr. Sibley has always taken a lively interest in the educational affairs of Franklin. For some years he did a large part of the work necessary to make a success of the courses delivered here by University Extension lecturers. He was a member of the board of school directors during the time that the new high school building was erected. When the citizens failed at the first election to authorize the necessary bond issue, he took pains to see the leading members in the community to insure their aid when the question should be again submitted. He wrote one signed communication and several editorials in the local paper urging the necessity and importance of the building. At the second election the required authority was granted by a vote of approximately three to one. Mr. Sibley also took the leading part in letting the contract for the building, and in arranging with Mr. Charles E. Lord, the principal of the high school, for new courses of study and for additions to the faculty. In particular, Mr. Sibley introduced the teaching of modern languages. He was president of the Franklin Public Library for twelve years and declined a reëlection. When Mr. Sibley severed his connection with the library, in 1912, the number of books owned was approximately seven thousand, among them many valuable historical, scientific and literary works and works of reference. During Mr. Sibley's presidency the library bought what was known as the Bailey property at the southwest corner of Twelfth and Liberty streets. Of the sum raised for the purchase of this property, about one-fourth was secured, principally in small amounts, by Mr. Sibley's personal efforts, supplementing the work of the soliciting committee. A handsome profit was realized by the sale of the land, and the library then acquired what is commonly known as the Judge McCalmont homestead at the southeast corner of Buffalo and Twelfth streets. The fees for maintaining the library have purposely been put low, and tickets are given to all clergymen and teachers in the public schools. Consultation of reference books is allowed to everyone without charge. A large part of the books which have been purchased out of library funds has been those which Mr. Sibley has selected.

Mr. Sibley completed a post-graduate course in modern history and political science assigned him in 1880 by the faculty of Cornell University. For many years he and his wife were attendants at Chautauqua and enjoyed the privileges for education and culture it affords. They were graduates of the class of 1905, of which Mr. Sibley was elected a trustee. In 1886 he was the nominee of the Prohibition party for the state senate. He made speeches throughout the district, not aiming at election, but receiving the largest vote that at that time had been polled for a Prohibition candidate for the same office. Later he spoke at many places throughout Venango county in favor of the proposed amendment to the constitution prohibiting the manufacture and sale of alcoholic liquors.

For scholarly attainments Mr. Sibley was in 1906 given by Bucknell University the honorary degree of Master of Arts. He received from Alfred University in 1908 the degree of Doctor of Literature. Two others who were recipients of honorary degrees at Alfred University at the same time as Mr. Sibley, were Justice Williams of the supreme court of the State of New York, and Dean Bailey, of the department of agriculture of Cornell University, who was the author and editor of many works and who was subsequently the chairman of the Roosevelt commission on country life. From his private library Mr. Sibley has from time to time given to college libraries and public libraries a total of over two thousand carefully selected volumes. He has been president of the Cornell Association of Railway & Supply Men, which meets annually at Atlantic City, New Jersey. He was for seven years president of the Pennsylvania Jersey Cattle Club, whose annual meetings were held in Pittsburgh. He was one of the incorporators and the first treasurer of the Franklin Hospital. He is the author of sundry reports, papers, communications, addresses, literary essays, humorous articles, aphorisms and inspiration mottoes. Some of his humorous productions have appeared in *Puck* and in the *Buffalo Illustrated Express*.

A paper read before the Pennsylvania State Dairymen's Association on "Some of the Elements of Success in Breeding Dairy Cattle" was printed in the *Jersey Bulletin* of Indianapolis and called forth numerous favorable criticisms from the editor and from correspondents. A wall card entitled "Administration of Life" was commended by Bishop John H. Vincent, chancellor of Chautauqua, and by Hon. Andrew D. White, United States ambassador to Germany and president of the American delegation to the Hague peace conference, and by many other men eminent as educators or as leaders in practical affairs. An address delivered at Atlantic City on "Some of the Prizes of Life" was first printed in the columns of the *Cornell Alumni News* and was subsequently reprinted in England in a journal edited by James Allen, author of "As a Man Thinketh," and of many other works widely read in England and the United States.

He married, December 23, 1884, at Dunkirk, New York, Jessie A. Williams, born April 19, 1863, at New Haven, Ohio, daughter of Richard and Rachel Maria (Thompson) Williams. Her father has been master mechanic on a number of different lines of railway. He was a volunteer in the civil war and served on Admiral Porter's flagship. Mrs. Sibley received a superior education in vocal and instrumental music. The three children of Edwin Henry and Jessie A. Sibley, all born in Franklin, Pennsylvania, are: 1. Edna, born December 23, 1885, was graduated with distinction in Franklin from the high school, and in Philadelphia from the Ogontz School for Young Ladies; married, July 17, 1909, at Franklin, Pennsylvania, to Mr. Joseph Clark Tipton, son of Enoch and Martha J. Tipton. He was born August 11, 1868, on Boone Valley Ranch near Watrous, New Mexico; is a graduate of the University of Missouri in both the classical and legal departments, and won the honor of Phi Beta Kappa. He is the manager for South America of the Galena-Signal Oil Company. He and his wife reside in Buenos Aires, Argentina. Their daughter Martha was born July 10, 1911, in New York City. 2. Joseph Crocker Sibley Jr., born January 27, 1888; attended the graded schools and the high school at Franklin, Pennsylvania, and Betts Academy at Stamford, Connecticut. He was graduated A. B. at Cornell University in 1910. He completed the four years course in three and one-half years, spending the last half of his senior year at

Eastman Business College. At Cornell he received numerous honors from his fellow-students; he was assistant business manager of the *Cornell Alumni News;* literary editor of the *Cornell Widow;* president of the Men's Association of Arts and Sciences, and won election to the honorary senior class society known as Sphinx Head. At the University of Wisconsin where he spent a part of a year, he won second prize for an article contributed to *The Badger,* and was chosen one of the board of editors. At Eastman Business College he completed the course in stenography in the shortest time ever made by any student in that institution. He is in the employ of the Galena-Signal Oil Company. He married, July 17, 1911, at Chicago, Illinois, Mahala Rosecrans Holm, daughter of Nils and Sara (Winterbotham) Holm. She was born at Eau Claire, Wisconsin, April 24, 1889. She was for a time a student at the University of Wisconsin in the class of 1912. Their son, Joseph Crocker Sibley IV, was born April 14, 1912, at the Harrington Maternity Hospital, Buffalo, New York. 3. Jeannette, born March 23, 1889; she passed through the graded schools and entered the high school, but left on account of ill health. She completed the Chautauqua course with the class of 1907. Subsequently she continued her studies at Philadelphia at the Ogontz School for Young Ladies. She was graduated from the latter institution in 1910 in vocal music, being one of the four out of hundreds of pupils to whom the American representative of the Lamperti method had ever awarded the distinction of a diploma.

WITHERUP — Among the early settlers of the "Scrubgrass" region in Venango, was John Witherup, probably the only man of English birth in that section in the early day. On coming to the United States he first settled in Trenton, New Jersey, later was in Philadelphia, thence moving to Pittsburgh. He was one of the early freighters between Pittsburgh and Philadelphia, making many trips over the mountains in the pursuit of his calling. He was also engaged in the lumber business in Pittsburgh, and was the contractor selected to furnish the building material for the first Allegheny county court house. He often related with pride that he hewed the first stick of timber placed in position in that structure. In 1800 he settled at the mouth of Big Scrubgrass creek, in Venango county, on a tract of 440 acres, and there built the first saw and grist mill ever erected in Clinton township. In addition to milling, he engaged in farming and lumbering. He continued contracting operations, and was the contractor for the first Venango court house, also superintending its construction. In 1803 he was elected road commissioner, and in 1805 had the distinction of being elected the first sheriff of Venango county. In 1821-22-24 he served as county auditor, and in 1826 was elected county commissioner, serving until his death. He was also elected justice of the peace, serving for over twenty-five years. His long useful life ended in 1843 at his farm in Clinton township.

He married Mary Brockington, also born in England, died in Venango county. Both were members of the Cumberland Presbyterian church. Children: 1. Abraham, of whom further. 2. David, married Jane Dunlap, and moved to Missouri, where both died; children: Alexander, Mary, David (2), Elizabeth, John and James. 3. William, married Jane Ridgway, and moved to Virginia, where both died, leaving issue. 4. John (2), died unmarried. 5. Alexander, a farmer, died in Scrubgrass township, Venango county, married Sarah Tracy, also deceased. 6. Martha, married Colonel William Shorts, of Sandy Creek township; both deceased; they have a son Abraham still living. 7. Robert, died on the Red River, Texas.

(II) Captain Abraham Witherup, son of John Witherup, the emigrant and pioneer, was born in Philadelphia, January 18, 1787. He was taken with his parents to Venango county in 1800 and shared the pioneer burden of clearing and building a home in the wilderness. After marriage he lived for a time in Rockland township, later returning to the old homestead at the mouth of Big Scrubgrass creek, where he engaged in both farming and lumbering. In 1865, on the discovery of oil, he had his farm prospected and found he was over an extensive pool. He began drilling and had forty wells sunk on the farm, which, with very few exceptions, produced from two to one hundred sixty barrels of oil daily for about eight years. He, of course, reaped a large pecuniary benefit from his lumber and oil operations, and became one of the substantial men of the country, and was one of the most progressive enterprising citizens of his day. He was a lifelong Democrat, and held many public positions, including justice of the peace, an office he filled for twenty years. During the war of 1812 he commanded the Seventh Company, 132nd Regiment Pennsylvania militia, recruited in Venango county. When Erie was threatened, he marched with his company to its defense, but for some reason did not arrive on time, which suggested a hint from some one that cowardice was the cause. Stung to the quick by this suggestion, he went into the fight with such reckless daring that he won the admiration of Commodore Perry, who after the battle sent Captain Witherup an invitation to dine with him. He was very proud of the fact that on election day, 1856, he marched to the polls with his eight sons, and all cast their ballots for the Democratic nominee for the presidency, James Buchanan. He died April 4, 1875, loved, honored and respected. He married Elizabeth Phipps, born November 14, 1800, died November 19, 1880, fourth daughter of John Phipps. Children: 1. Mary Ann, born December 3, 1819, died 1887; married, June 19, 1837, James Haslett. 2. John, born February 18, 1821, died unmarried, March 25, 1888. 3. Robert, born 1822, married Sarah McCool; both deceased. 4. David, born March 31, 1824, died June, 1863; married Catherine Webster, also deceased. 5. Catherine, born December 11, 1825, died 1855; married Nathan M. Wasson, also deceased. 6. Joseph, born July 8, 1827; married, November 13, 1856, Eleanor Brandon; both deceased. 7. Abraham (2), born March 30, 1829; married, November 18, 1852, Sarah Porter, and now resides in Akron, Ohio, retired. 8. Samuel P., born January 29, 1831, died January 6, 1894; married Mary J. Porter, September 18, 1862. 9. William, of whom further. 10. Sarah, born June 30, 1835; married, June 28, 1855, Oliver D. McMillen, whom she survives, a resident of Worthington, Armstrong county, Pennsylvania. 11. James B., born June 8, 1838; married, February 18, 1875, Achsah Coulter, whom he survives, a resident of Clinton township. 12. Martha S., born February 10, 1841; married, June 23, 1864, Elliot Davis, whom she survives. 13. Elizabeth Ann, born July 23, 1843; married Alfred Hardwick, whom she survives, a resident of Evans City, Pennsylvania.

(III) William, ninth child of Captain Abraham and Elizabeth (Phipps) Witherup, was born in Rockland township, Venango county, Pennsylvania, August 24, 1832. He was educated in the public schools and grew to manhood on the homestead farm. He spent his active years engaged in farming and lumbering, although after oil was discovered he drilled in 1888 about one hundred wells on his farm, where over thirty are still producing oil, although in much diminished quantities. He has always supported the principles and nominees of the Democratic party, served as school director, and is a member of the Presbyterian church. He married, November 1863, Martha L., daughter of David and Rebecca (Stalker) Eakin, of Clinton township, and a granddaughter of Thomas and Rachel (Baten) Stalker. David Eakin, a farmer, died in Venango county, aged forty-three years; his wife died in 1868; he was a Democrat. Their children: 1. Rachel, married Snowden Porter, deceased, a resident of Akron, Ohio. 2. Samuel J., deceased; married Julia Ann Atwell, who lived in Kansas. 3. Thomas, died in infancy. 4. Thomas Jefferson, deceased; married Adalaide ———, who now resides in Colorado. 5. Mary Jane, married Murphy Lockard, whom she survives, a resident of Venango county. 6. Martha L. (of previous mentioned), wife of William Witherup. 7. Elizabeth, married John Fabian, both deceased. 8. Sarah, married John Myers, whom she survives, a resident of Crawford county, Pennsylvania. 9. David V., an oil well contractor and driller, now residing in New Castle, Pennsylvania; married Henrietta Cross. Mrs. Rebecca (Stalker) Eakin survived her first husband, and married (second) David Phipps, who was associate judge five years. Their only child married Charles Thero. Mrs. David Phipps died February 17, 1878; both she and her first husband were members of the Cumberland Presbyterian church.

Children of William and Martha (Eakin) Witherup: 1. Forest Foster, born January 2, 1865, died unmarried, December 21, 1897. 2. Imelda, born March 26, 1866, resides at the family home in Kennerdell. 3. D. Thomas, born April 2, 1868, an oil producer, now living in Erie, Pennsylvania; married Laura Cox. 4. Harry King, born December 20, 1869; an artist, residing in Buffalo, New York; married Minnie Heible. 5. Joseph Alvin, born August 7, 1872; married (first) Catherine Ryan, (second) Mary Pitchard; now resides in Oklahoma; child by first wife, Gladys, born 1902. 6. Lewis Hudson, born December 5, 1874, died November 12, 1880. 7. Samuel Bennett, born

December 19, 1876; resides in Venango county, an oil producer; married Katherine Shaffer; children: William, born 1902; Winifred, 1903; Almira, 1905; Katherine, 1907; David, 1910. 8. Jesse Lee, born August 7, 1879; resides in New Middletown, an oil contractor; married Georgia McClellan. 9. William Vick, born April 8, 1882; married Madge Boylan; children: Charles Leroy, born 1910; Martha, 1912. 10. Bessie Phipps, born January 17, 1885, residing at home.

Mrs. Martha (Eakin) Witherup, the mother of the foregoing children, is a member of the Presbyterian church, and although advanced in years is in excellent health and interested in all current happenings.

CROSS About the beginning of the nineteenth century, William Cross, born in England, came to the United States, settling first in Pittsburgh, Pennsylvania; later he moved to Butler county, Pennsylvania. He was a furnace builder and a skillful builder of grist and saw mills. He erected many in the western counties of Pennsylvania, became prosperous, and at one time owned seven mills in active operation. He was also engaged in the grocery business, having his son Robert as partner. He experimented and sunk a great deal of money in an effort to refine oil in the early days, skimming it off the surface of the river and creeks. He lost $13,000 in his experiments, and finally, after having been to the river for a supply of oil, died in his wagon on the way home. He was a Whig in politics, and he and his wife members of the United Presbyterian church. He was a soldier in the American army during the war of 1812, and became an ardent supporter of his adopted country's cause. His wife, Jane Merkley, died in Clintonville, Pennsylvania, aged seventy-five years. Children: Samuel, married Jane McCutcheon; Robert, of whom further; Jane, married Nathan Davis; Matilda, married John Maxwell; W. C., married (first) Isabel Cummings.

(II) Robert, son of William and Jane (Merkley) Cross, was born in Pittsburgh, Pennsylvania, March, 1811, died in Clintonville, Pennsylvania, 1873. He was educated in the public schools of Pittsburgh, which he attended until he was eleven years of age. His parents then moved to Butler county, locating at Centerville. He learned the carpenter's trade and became a contractor and builder, and was also engaged in mercantile business with his father and in his attempts at refining oil. He was postmaster of Clintonville forty years, and in mercantile business there for that length of time. He was roadmaster and supervisor, also for one term associate judge. He was a Democrat in politics, and an elder of the Presbyterian church many years. He married Hannah McKissick, born in Maine, died at Sandy Lake, Pennsylvania, aged seventy-five years, daughter of Aaron McKissick, who in his latter life lived in Franklin, but died in Waterloo, Pennsylvania, a general contractor. His wife, Jane Means, lived to be about eighty years of age. Children of Aaron McKissick: Putman; John; Henry; Hannah (of previous mention), married Robert Cross; Jane, married Henry Near; Mary, married Dr. A. J. McMillen; Sophronia, married Henry Snail; Thomas S.; all deceased. Children of Robert and Hannah Cross: 1. Caroline, died aged thirteen years. 2. Mary Jane, married E. P. Newton, both deceased, leaving a daughter Kate, who married, and lives in New Castle, Pennsylvania. 3. Harriet, married Major R. J. Phipps, and lived in Franklin, Pennsylvania; children: Marshall, married Belle Campbell; and Lizzie, deceased. 4. Lovisa, married Rev. James Foster, who survives her, residing at Clark's Mills. 5. William, married Nancy Phipps, and lived on their farm in Venango county; children (not in order of birth): i. Fred A., an engineer, married Laura Irwin, and lives at Hampton Station, Pennsylvania. ii. Hannah, married John A. Proctor, an oil pumper of Evans City, Pennsylvania. iii. Mary Effie, married James I. Black, an oil driller of Brookville, Pennsylvania. iv. Frank, secretary and treasurer of the Sun Oil Company, married Margaret McKee. v. Raymond, superintendent of Oil City Gas Company, married Belle Eakin. vi. Florella. vii. Harriet, married Edson Bymer, a farmer of Scrubgrass township. viii. Robert, an oil operator of Oklahoma. 6. Oliver Byron, of whom further. 7. Emma, deceased, married C. M. Riddle, a carpenter, now residing in Clintonville. 8. Alice, married (first) Dr. Jackson, (second) Joseph Bowman, an oil well driller of Sandy Lake, Pennsylvania. 9. Etta, married D. V. Eakin, a contractor and oil well driller of Newcastle, Pennsylvania.

(III) Oliver Byron, son of Robert and Hannah (McKissick) Cross, was born in Clintonville, Venango county, Pennsylvania, May 14, 1848. He was educated in the public schools and began business life as clerk in his father's store at Clintonville, and later became a partner, continuing until his father's death in 1873. After that date he became sole proprietor and continued there in successful business for thirty years more. He then retired from mercantile life and has since been engaged in the oil business. He is a Democrat and Prohibitionist in politics, and for two years served as constable. In religious faith he is a Presbyterian. He married, December 8, 1870, Elizabeth Davidson, born in Clinton township, Venango county, Pennsylvania, January 12, 1848, daughter of Patrick Davidson, born in Ireland, came to the United States, became a farmer of Clinton township; he married Miss Patterson, also born in Ireland; children: Martha, died unmarried; Nancy, now living at Grove City, unmarried; William, died unmarried; James, died in infancy; Elizabeth (of previous mention), married Oliver B. Cross; their children: 1. Melville, an oil producer, married Jane Jacobs, and lives in Franklin, Pennsylvania; children: Helen, born 1896; Eugene, 1898; Robert, 1904. 2. Leslie, an oil producer and contractor of Clintonville, married Doskey Pearce (or Pierce). 3. Henry, of Franklin. 4. Albert, a merchant of Middletown, Ohio. 5. Jeannette, died aged sixteen years. 6. Julia, living at home. 7. Elizabeth, living at home. 8. A child died in infancy.

The Hutchinson family HUTCHINSON of Clintonville, Pennsylvania, came there from Butler county, after a previous residence in Westmoreland county, Pennsylvania. The family there springs from Irish ancestors in one branch, while another is of English descent, coming to Westmoreland county from the state of Maine. The conclusion is that Fergus Hutchinson was of the Irish family, and the father of Robert, father of Robert A. Hutchinson, of Clintonville. Fergus Hutchinson was a pioneer settler of Butler county, and in religious faith a Methodist. He married and had issue: Thomas, married Rebecca Keim; Robert, of whom further: White, married Sarah Stroup.

(II) Robert, son of Fergus Hutchinson, was born in Westmoreland county, Pennsylvania, died in Butler county, aged seventy-two years. He was educated in the public schools of Westmoreland county, and moved to Butler county, where he purchased a farm, which he cultivated many years. In his latter years he moved to near Annadale, Ohio, where he died. He was a Democrat in politics, and a member of the Methodist Episcopal church. He was a devoted Christian, a class leader, and one to whom disputes were referred for arbitration. He married Sarah Muller (?), who survived him, aged seventy-one years. Children: 1. Andrew J., married Isabel Van Dyke; both deceased; children: Elizabeth, married James Thompson; Jackson; Minnie; Sarah. 2. Alexander, married Mary Young, who survives him, residing in Butler county; child: James. 3. Margaret, married Josiah Dodd, who survives her, residing in Iowa; children: Clarence, Homer R., Anna and Ditemer. 4. Mary, married G. K. M. Crawford; both deceased; children: Anna, married Jared Marsh; Harriet; William and Robert Bruce. 5. Elizabeth, married William Seaton; both deceased; children: Belle, married a Mr. Sloan; Maude, married James Speer. 6. Ellen, married Abner Seaton, whom she survives, living at New Castle, Pennsylvania; children: Anna, John, and Montgomery. 7. Robert A., of whom further.

(III) Robert A., son of Robert Hutchinson, was born in Butler county, Pennsylvania, February 4, 1843. He was educated in the Butler and Venango county public schools, and began business life in Forest county as a lumberman, continuing five years. He enlisted September 13, 1861, in company L, Fourth Regiment Pennsylvania Volunteer Cavalry, and received an honorable discharge February 4, 1865, fourteen months of his term of service being spent in the prisons at Andersonville and Milan. He saw hard service, and was engaged with his regiment at Gaines' Mill, White Oak Swamp, Malvern Hill, South Mountain, Antietam, Culpeper, Middleburg, Rappahannock Station, and Kelly's Ford, where he was taken prisoner. He passed safely through the perils of battle to face the worst, hunger and disease in the awful pen at Andersonville, but survived even that and returned home at the end of his service. He then located at Oil City, Pennsylvania, where for two years he was engaged in the oil business. He again engaged in the lumber business for four years, then again began operating in oil, and is still so engaged, residing in Clintonville. He is a Republican in politics, has been burgess of Clintonville the past six years and is still in office; was school director four years and justice of the peace three years. He belongs to W. B. Mayo Post No. 220, Grand Army of the Republic.

He married, February 8, 1871, Elizabeth Henderson, born in Venango county, March 12, 1842, daughter of Thomas and Catherine (Brenner) Henderson. Thomas Henderson was a farmer of Venango county, died aged seventy-six years. Children of Thomas Henderson by first wife, Catherine Brenner: 1. John B., married Luella Hovis, both deceased; no issue. 2. Amanda, married William M. Blair, a farmer, deceased, she residing in Venango county; children: Thomas, married June Foster; John, married Mary Hoffman; Leonard (?), married Maud Rice; Clyde, married Melda Hovis; Cora, married Daniel Hoffman; Edith, married Charles Allen. 3. Elizabeth, married Robert A. Hutchinson. Children of Thomas Henderson by his second wife, Catherine Keller: 4. Minnie, married Frank Hovis, an oil producer of Clintonville; children: Esther and Margaret. 5. Sarah, died unmarried, aged twenty-five years. 6. Anna, married Albert White, a farmer of Venango county; children: Alphena and Paul. 7. Boyd. 8. Robert, a farmer and oil producer of Venango county, married Nellie Trumble; children: Marie, Neal and Clarence. 9. Margaret, married Edward Eakin, an oil producer of Grove City, Pennsylvania; children: Sarah, married John Thorn; and Georgie Clifford. 10. Homer, an oil pumper and driller of Venango county; married Ethel Barringer; children: Delilah and Eugene.

Children of Robert A. and Elizabeth (Henderson) Hutchinson: 1. Child, deceased. 2. Luella Ann, residing with her parents. 3. Biddie, died in infancy. 4. Thomas Andrew, died aged seventeen years. 5. Mary Ellen, married George Eakin, an oil producer, residing in Clintonville; children: Robert Jackson, William Wayne and Sarah Elizabeth. 6. William, an oil pumper of Venango county; married Malinda Nutt; children: Lewis, Sarah and Sterling. 7. Lloyd L., residing in Clintonville; married Winifred McLallen; child: Imogene. 8. Ralph, a student.

LAMBING Rev. Andrew A. Lambing, LL.D., Roman Catholic clergyman and author, was born at Manorville, Armstrong county, Pennsylvania, February 1, 1842. He is descended from Christopher Lambing, who emigrated to America from Alsace, in the vicinity of Strasburg, in 1749, and settled in Bucks county, where he died about 1817, at the age of ninety-nine years. Some of his family passed to Adams county, where his son Matthew married and settled in New Oxford, where Michael A. Lambing, the father of the subject of this sketch, was born October 10, 1806. The family came west to Armstrong county in 1823. Here Michael married Anne Shields, December 1, 1837. She was descended from Thomas Shields, who immigrated from county Donegal, Ireland, about 1740, and settled in Amberson's valley, Franklin county; but his grandson William came to Armstrong county in 1798 and made his home near Kittanning, where his daughter Anne was born July 4, 1814. Michael was the father of five sons and four daughters, of whom Andrew Arnold was the third son and child. Both parents were remarkable through life for their tender and consistent piety, and for the care they bestowed on the education and training of their children. Three of their sons fought in the civil war, one of them losing his life and another becoming disabled; two of their sons are priests, and a daughter a Sister of Charity.

Trained in the school of rigid poverty, Andrew began work on a farm before he was eight years old, and a few years later found employment in a fire-brick yard, where he spent nearly six years, with four months' schooling in each winter; and two years in the old refinery, a considerable part of which time he worked from three o'clock in the afternoon to six the next morning being at the same time foreman of the works. During this time he managed to steal a few hours as opportunity permitted to devote to study and useful reading, for reading has been the passion of his life. At the age of twenty-one years he entered St. Michael's Preparatory and Theological Seminary, Pittsburg, where he made his course in the higher studies, frequently rising at three o'clock in the morning to continue his course, and being nearly all that time prefect of the students. He was ordained to the priesthood in the seminary chapel by Bishop Domence, of Pittsburg, August 4, 1869. He was then sent to St. Francis College, Loretto, Pennsylvania, as professor, with the additional obligation of assisting the pastor of the village church on Sundays with the exception of one Sunday in each month, when he ministered to the little congregation of Williamsburg, Blair county, about forty miles distant. On the following January he was appointed pastor of St. Patrick's Church, Cameron Bottom, Indiana county, where he remained till the end of April, when he was named pastor of St. Mary's Church, Kittanning, with its numerous out-missions. While there he built a little church a few miles west of the Allegheny river, for the accommodation of the families residing there, and in the middle of January, 1873, he was sent to Freeport, with the additional charge of the congregation at Natrona, six miles distant, but at the end of six months he was appointed chaplain of St. Paul's Orphan Asylum, Pittsburg, with a view of bettering its financial condition. This, however, was rendered impossible by the financial crisis of the fall of the same year, and he was named pastor of the church of St. Mary of Mercy, at the Point, in the same city, January 7, 1874. Here he placed the schools in charge of the Sisters of Mercy, bought and fitted up a non-Catholic church for the congregation, and placed an altar in it dedicated to "Our Lady of the Assumption at the Beautiful River," as a memorial of the one that stood in the chapel of Fort Duquesne during the French occupation, in the middle of the previous century; and also built a residence. But the encroachment of the railroads began to drive the people out in such numbers that he was transferred to St. James' Church, Winkinsburg, an eastern suburb of the city, October 15, 1885, where he still remains. The congregation was then small, numbering about one hundred and sixty families, with a little frame church, but it soon began to increase rapidly. His first care was to open a school, which he placed in charge of the Sisters of Charity, and in the summer of 1888, he enlarged the church, which, however, was occupied only three months when it was entirely destroyed by fire. Nothing daunted, he immediately undertook the present combination church and school building, which was dedicated just a year after the destruction of the other. So rapid has been the growth of the town and the increase of the congregation that an assistant has been required since the spring of 1897; and although parts of four new congregations have been taken from it, it still numbers nearly six hundred families.

As a writer, Father Lambing is the author of "The Orphan's Friend" (1875), "The Sunday-School Teachers' Manual" (1877), "A History of the Catholic Church in the Dioceses of Pittsburg and Allegheny" (1880), "The Register of Fort Duquesne, translated from the French, with an Introductory Essay and Notes" (1885), "The Sacramentals of the Holy Catholic Church" (1892), "Come, Holy Ghost" (1901), "The Immaculate Conception of the Blessed Virgin Mary" (1904), and "The Fountain of Living Water" (1907). Besides these he has written a considerable number of religious and historical pamphlets, and a considerable part of the large "History of Allegheny County, Pennsylvania," "The Centennial History of Allegheny County" (1888), and "The Standard History of Pittsburg" (1898). He was associate editor of "Pennsylvania, Historical and Biographical," 2 vols. (1904); and wrote the history of the western part of the state for it. And was also one of the assistant editors of "A Century and a Half of Pittsburg and Her People," 4 vols., 1908. In 1884 he started the *Catholic Historical Researches*, a quarterly magazine and the first of its kind devoted to the history of the Catholic church in this country, now continued by Mr. Martin I. J. Griffin, of Philadelphia, as a monthly; and he is a constant contributor to periodicals on religious and historical subjects. The editor of "The Standard History of Pittsburgh" says of him, that "he has done more than any other one man to place in permanent form the valuable and fast-perishing early records." For a number of years he was president of the Historical Society of Western Pennsylvania, and he is one of the trustees of the Carnegie Institute and the Carnegie Technical School of Pittsburg.

As a churchman he was for many years president of the Clerical Relief Association of the diocese of Pittsburg, and was president of the board that prepared the diocesan school exhibit for the Columbia Exposition. For nine years he was fiscal procurator of the diocese of Pittsburg, and has long been the censor of books, and is now president of the diocese school board. Of regular habits and inheriting the health of his fathers, standing six feet tall, with heavy frame, he seemed built for labor and endurance, and he was more than thirty years on the mission before he was off duty for a single day on account of ill health, although he has never taken a vacation. In 1883 the University of Notre Dame, Indiana, conferred on him the degree of Master of Arts, and two years later that of Doctor of Laws.

PENNSYLVANIA

CUNNINGHAM Dr. Paul Eli Cunningham, one of the best known physicians of Clintonville, Pennsylvania, is a descendant of Scotch-Irish ancestors who have for at least a century and a half been numbered among the inhabitants of the Keystone State.

(I) Benjamin Cunningham, great-grandfather of Paul Eli Cunningham, was born March 10, 1770, probably in Lawrence or Beaver county, and was presumably a son or grandson of the immigrant ancestor.

(II) William, son of Benjamin Cunningham, was born May 15, 1805, probably in Lawrence county, where he spent his early life, removing about 1858 to Venango county, where he passed his remaining years. He married (first) November 23, 1826, Margaret White, by whom he became the father of the following children, all of whom are deceased, with the exception of the eldest: Eliza, lives at East Brook, near Newcastle; Sarah, Milo, and James. Mr. Cunningham married (second) Polly Weimer, and the following children were born to them: William, deceased, married Mary Walsmith, who lives in Newcastle and is now the wife of John Ross; Henry L., mentioned below; Margaret, married Frank T. Miller, an oil well driller, of Washington, Pennsylvania. Mrs. Cunningham was killed in a runaway accident, and Mr. Cunningham married a third wife, by whom he had no children. He and his second wife were United Presbyterians. Mr. Cunningham died in 1878.

(III) Henry Lewis, son of William and Polly (Weimer) Cunningham, was born May 12, 1848, in Lawrence county, and was ten years old when the family removed to Clinton township, Venango county. His education was received in the public schools of these two counties, and when about sixteen years old he went to Franklin, Pennsylvania, where he learned the shoemaker's trade, which he followed in that place for about twelve years. He then moved to Clintonville, where he engaged in shoemaking and farming. In politics he was a Republican, and for six years filled the office of assessor. He married Mary Elizabeth Hovis, whose ancestral record is appended to this sketch, and their children were: 1-2. Born respectively in 1880 and 1882, dying unnamed. 3. Frank William, born September 6, 1884; married Stella M. Hoffman; children: Howard L. and Harold F.; died April 28, 1911. 4. Paul Eli, mentioned below. 5. Child, died unnamed in 1889. Mr. Cunningham died in Clintonville, June 27, 1902, and his widow now resides in the same place.

(IV) Dr. Paul Eli Cunningham, son of Henry Lewis and Mary Elizabeth (Hovis) Cunningham, was born May 2, 1886, at Clintonville, Pennsylvania, on a farm two miles north of that place. He first attended the public schools of Clintonville, passing at the end of four years to those of Clinton township, and then entering the high school, which closed after he had spent two years there. In 1903 he entered Oil City Business College, graduating in February, 1904, and for two years thereafter was employed in the oil fields. In 1906, deciding to make the practice of medicine his life-work, he matriculated in the Medical Department of the University of Pittsburgh, graduating June 15, 1910, with the degree of Doctor of Medicine. He immediately returned to his native place and there entered upon the active practice of his profession, in which he has ever since been continuously engaged, acquiring a lucrative connection and building up an enviable reputation. Politically, Dr. Cunningham is a Prohibitionist. He was for four years school director, and is now serving a five years' term as president of the board of health. He affiliates with Emlenton Lodge, No. 562, F. and A. M., and Horton Lodge, No. 470, Knights and Ladies of Honor. He is a member of the Methodist Episcopal church.

(The Hovis Line).

John C. Hovis, grandfather of Mrs. Mary Elizabeth (Hovis) Cunningham, married Elizabeth Walters.

Eli, son of John C. and Elizabeth (Walters) Hovis, was a carpenter and married Barbara Monjar. Their children were: 1. John Franklin, a physician of Saginaw, Michigan, married Fanny Cobbet, and has two children, Lyda and Frederick. 2. Mary Elizabeth, mentioned below. 3. Jackson, of Kenosha, married Mattie Crow, and has three or four children. 4. Lydia, married Joseph Osborn, a farmer of Clintonville, and is now deceased. 5. Richard M., of Clintonville, married Frances van Dyke, and their children are: Eli, married Luvisa Murrin, and has two children; Samuel, of Plairsville, married Silvia Vanderlin, and has one child; Wilda; Ollie, widow of Hiram Hilliard, has four children; Elsie, married Warren Kerr, and has one child; Myrtle. Maggie and William. 6. Mary, died at the age of twelve years. 7. Thomas, clerk, at Vandergriff. 8. Philip, mail-carrier of Clintonville, married Irene Duffy; children: Francis, Cathleen, Richard and Duffy. 9. Florence, married William Crile, a railroad detective of Freeport. 10. Barbara, married John Duffy, a coal driller of Murrinsville. 11. John F., a merchant of Clintonville; married Daisy Davies. 12. Lillian, married Bert McKain, a driller of Clintonville; children: Theril and Vivian. 13. Richard, a merchant of Clintonville. 14. Julia. Eli Hovis, the father of this family, is now living in Newcastle, Pennsylvania, his wife having passed away in 1888.

Mary Elizabeth, daughter of Eli and Barbara (Monjar) Hovis, was born March 4, 1839, in Venango county, and became the wife of Henry Lewis Cunningham, as mentioned above.

GRAHAM William Graham, the first member of this family of whom we have any definite information, was born in Scotland. He emigrated to America and the first known record of him is dated 1794 when he took out a patent for a tract of land on Ten-Mile creek, Washington county, Pennsylvania, but he is known to have settled previous to that time on old Chartiers creek, in Washington county, where he built and operated a grist mill and followed his trade as a miller. A few years later he removed to the mouth of Bear creek in Armstrong county, where he built the first grist mill in that section and finally purchased a farm in Perry township, Clarion county, then a part of Armstrong county, below the mouth of the Clarion river and opposite the present town of Parker. It was later made a stopping place for steamboats on the Allegheny and the property became known as Graham's Landing. He resided here until his death in 1835. His wife's name was Sally Rogers and the children were James, Rebecca, William, referred to below; Mary, Samuel.

(II) William (2), son of William (1) and Sally (Rogers) Graham, was born 1796 in Armstrong county, Pennsylvania. He inherited part of his father's farm in Clarion county and purchased the holdings of the other heirs of the estate and lived in the old homestead the greater part of his life, but moved in his later years to East Brady, where he died in 1872. He was a Presbyterian in religion, and a Democrat in politics. Married (first) Janet Wasson in 1826, who died December 28, 1828, leaving a son, Joseph W. Graham. In 1831 he married (second) Margaret, daughter of John Mechling, a Western Pennsylvania pioneer. They had the following children: George, referred to below; Aaron, married Sidney Gibson, now living at Renfrew, Butler county, Pennsylvania; Sarah, married William Jardine, of East Brady, died in 1876; Amanda, married John P. Forcht, now living in Butler, Pennsylvania.

(III) George, son of William (2) and Margaret (Mechling) Graham, was born June 11, 1832, in Perry township, Clarion county, Pennsylvania, died in East Brady, Pennsylvania, March 6, 1899. He grew up on his father's farm, received a public school education, learned the trade of carpenter, and was a pilot on the Allegheny river. He served in the civil war as a member of Company B, One Hundred and Sixty-ninth Pennsylvania Regiment, and after the close of his term of service returned to Brady's Bend, Pennsylvania, where he re-entered the employ of the Brady's Bend Iron Company as a carpenter; was later made master mechanic and superintendent of construction. On the failure of the Iron Company he engaged in the lumber business at Brady's Bend with Judge A. Cook, of Cooksburg, and in 1874 removed to East Brady, where the lumber and planing mill business was operated on a larger scale and under the firm name of Graham, Forcht & Company, later Graham & Cook, until 1890, when he sold his lumber interests to his son, Newton E. He married Margaret, daughter of Daniel Fritz, born in Berks county, Pennsylvania, died at East Brady in 1902. Her father was of Pennsylvania Dutch parentage. The children of George and Margaret (Fritz) Graham are: John William, married Ella Sedwick; Ella Mary, married John F. Neely, now living at New Castle, Pennsylvania; Newton Ellsworth, referred to below; Ida May, born 1864, died 1880; George, married Mollie Young, now living at Butler, Pennsylvania; Celia, married Joseph A. Neely, died 1910, leaving two children, Marion and Joseph Applegate; Frank Fritz, born 1868, died 1897.

(IV) Newton Ellsworth, son of George and Margaret (Fritz) Graham, was born at St. Petersburg, Clarion county, Pennsylvania, July 2, 1861. He moved at an early age with his parents to Brady's Bend. He received a common school education and entered the employ of his father in the lumber business; in 1885 founded the *East Brady Review*, of which newspaper he was editor and publisher until 1890, when he purchased his father's interest in the lumber firm of Graham & Cook at East Brady; in 1902 he purchased the Cook interests and organized the Graham Lumber Company, which still continues; in 1900 he was one of the principal organizers of the People's National Bank of East Brady, of which he was elected president and has held this office continuously since the organization; is president and principal owner of the East Brady Water Works Company, director in the Central Allegheny Valley Telephone Company and interested in oil, gas and other industries. Always an active Republican, has held a number of borough offices, county chairman, delegate to state conventions and delegate to the Republican National Convention at Chicago in 1904; is a member of the Duquesne Club, Country Club, Athletic Association of Pittsburgh; a Knight Templar and Shriner. He married, in 1886, Lenora, daughter of James Young and Mary (Wallace) Foster, and has one daughter, Maurine.

SMITH This branch of the Smith family came to Clarion from Jefferson county, Pennsylvania, where they were early pioneer settlers. A Mrs. Ann Smith was an early teacher in the public schools. She left Ireland when a girl of ten years, worked in the fields with her husband, yet so educated herself that in her latter years she was able to teach.

James and Andrew Smith, father and son, are mentioned as men whose deep thought gave an intellectual tone to discussions. George Smith is named as a mighty hunter, and the Smiths are noted as aiding in the establishment of schools. Washington township, which seems to have been their most favored location, was settled by Scotch-Irish, mostly from the counties of Antrim and Tyrone, Ireland.

(I) The line of descent is supposed to be from James and Eleanor (Kearney) Smith, who came from county Donegal, Ireland, to Philadelphia, Pennsylvania, in 1822, later settling in Washington township, Jefferson county.

(II) Henry, son of James and Eleanor Smith, was born in Jefferson county, Pennsylvania, and about 1849 settled at West Monterey, Clarion county, where he kept a store, continuing there in business until his death. He married Maria Lazure, who also died at West Monterey. Children: Jacob, of whom further; Margaret, now residing in West Monterey, unmarried; William, a soldier of the civil war, killed at the battle of the Wilderness; Samuel Wallace, a soldier of the civil war, killed at the battle of Hatcher's Run; Harriet, now residing in West Monterey, unmarried; Elizabeth, now residing in West Monterey; Sarah, now residing in Washington, Pennsylvania; John, deceased; George, deceased.

(III) Jacob, son of Henry and Maria (Lazure) Smith, was born in Jefferson county, Pennsylvania, January 28, 1841, died September 2, 1901. He was educated in the public school; he grew to manhood in Jefferson and Armstrong counties. After his marriage he settled at once in West Monterey. He was an old time river pilot and during the months of open navigation piloted the Allegheny river craft, laden with oil, coal and lumber to ports below on the Allegheny and Ohio rivers. He owned a small farm of twenty acres which he also cultivated and there made his permanent home. This tract is now partly the site of the village of West Monterey and still owned by his heirs. He was a member of the Methodist Episcopal church, as was his wife. In politics he was first a Democrat, and later a Republican. His fraternal order was the Senior Order of American Mechanics. He died at his home in West Monterey, September 2, 1901.

He married, March 20, 1862, Esther George, born in Armstrong county, Pennsylvania, May 10, 1842, daughter of John George, born in 1812, married in Westmoreland county, Pennsylvania, and at once moved to Armstrong county, where he followed his trade of stone mason until his retirement to a small farm he owned in Perry township, Armstrong county. He died in 1891. He married Susan, born in Westmoreland county, Pennsylvania, in 1816, died in 1903, daughter of David Davis. Children of Mr. and Mrs. George: Franklin, died in infancy; Elizabeth, married William Dort and lives in Mars, Pennsylvania; Esther; William, served four years in the civil war, now residing in Mars, Pennsylvania; Francis, now living in New Kensington, Pennsylvania, a farmer; Sarah Matilda, died in infancy. Children of Jacob and Esther Smith: Ida Mae, married Louis Grossman and resides in Butler county; William, a contractor and oil well driller of Kittanning, Pennsylvania; Samuel Alvin, of whom further; Ella, died in infancy; Charles, now living in West Monterey; Ella, married Curtis McCullough, a farmer of Butler county; Emma, married Harry McMurtry and resides in California; Maude, married Thomas Reichart and lives in Clarion county; Edward, now living in Monterey; Harry, residing at home; Alta, married Rev. Earl Thompson and resides in Erie county, Pennsylvania.

(IV) Samuel Alvin, son of Jacob and Esther (George) Smith, was born in West Monterey, Clarion county, Pennsylvania, August 4, 1869. He was educated in the public schools, and grew to manhood in association with his father and his work. Later he became an oil well driller and a contractor. His field of operations covers Westmoreland, Armstrong and Jefferson counties in Pennsylvania and in this field he has contracted and put down a great many wells, keeping from thirty to thirty-five men constantly employed. He is also an oil producer, owning, with his business partner, William Smith, several good properties. In politics he is a Republican, but has never been an aspirant for public office. He is a charter member of the Monterey Lodge, Senior Order of American Mechanics, and on November 17, 1912, completed a membership in that order of twenty-five years. Both he and his wife are members of the Methodist Episcopal church.

He married, December 24, 1902, Alberta Shoemaker, born in Armstrong county, Pennsylvania, February 1, 1879, daughter of John Henry and Martha (Lemmon) Shoemaker, who were married at Cochran's Mills and now living on their own fertile farm on Crooked Creek, and granddaughter of Daniel and ——— (Kreiger) Shoemaker, who were the parents of nine children, namely: 1. John Henry, of whom further. 2. Isaiah, married Maria McKee; he is a Baptist minister; resides (1913) in Armstrong county, Pennsylvania. 3. Lebbeus, married ——— Coulter; he is a Baptist clergyman; resides (1913) in Butler county, Pennsylvania. 4. Albert D., deceased; he was a teacher in an Indian mission school in Oklahoma. 5. Eliza, deceased; married Thomas Young, deceased. 6. Sarah, married ——— Heckman, deceased. 7. Margaret, married ——— Schaub, deceased; she resides in Philadelphia, Pennsylvania. 8. Lucinda, married Isaac Shoemaker; he is owner of large brick works at St. Charles, Pennsylvania. 9. Mary, married Charles Webster; resides (1913) in Oklahoma; he is engaged in the oil business. John Henry, son of Daniel Shoemaker, married Martha Lemmon, who descends from revolutionary ancestry, and from a soldier of the war of 1812, while her father, John H. Lemmon, was a soldier of the civil war, serving in the Seventy-sixth Regiment Pennsylvania Volunteer Infantry. Children of John H. Shoemaker: 1. Alberta, aforementioned as wife of Samuel A. Smith. 2. Daniel, married Helen McMillen; child, Mary; he is a farmer. 3. Louis, married Eliza Logan; he is an attorney; resides in Pittsburgh, Pennsylvania. 4. Fred, unmarried; is an attorney; resides in Pittsburgh, Pennsylvania. 5. Grace, unmarried; is a school teacher. Children of Samuel A. and Alberta (Shoemaker) Smith: 1. and 2. Anna May and Esther Grace (twins), born June 18, 1906, Anna May died in infancy. 3. John Jacob, born June 30, 1908. 4. Martha Isabel, born July 6, 1911.

SCHETTLER The Schettler family in Clarion county have now been farmers for three generations in Pennsylvania. The first of the name, Joseph Schettler, owned farm lands in Knox township during the middle of the last century, which he successfully cultivated. He married Elizabeth ——— some time prior to the year 1868, and had a son, William A., of whom further.

(II) William A., son of Joseph and Elizabeth Schettler, was born December 31, 1868, in Knox township, Clarion county, Pennsylvania. His education was received at the parochial schools of Lucinda, Clarion county, which he attended as well as the schools of Knox township, and at the conclusion of his studies assisted his father on the farm. At the age of twenty-four years he became a farmer on his own account, farming his father's farm, and continued there for eight years. He then left Knox township and came to Leeper, in 1900. He entered the hotel business which he pursued in Farmington township for a number of years. In 1908 he returned to the farm in Knox township, where he followed the old calling for a year and eight months, and where his son has succeeded him. Mr. Schettler now owns one hundred and seven acres of farm land and also has six lots of ground and the large hotel known as the Leeper House. He is the proprietor of five gas wells in all, four of them being located on the farm, and the remaining one on the lots which he owns. He has become one of the most important and influential men in this locality, and conducts a very prosperous business in general farming and stock raising. He is a Democrat politically, and has been treasurer of Farmington township for a year.

He married, February 2, 1892, Elizabeth Laner, born in Pennsylvania, January 29, 1872, daughter of George and Lena (Huffmester) Laner, her father having been a farmer of Knox township, and later a stone mason at Kane, McKean county, Pennsylvania; her mother is still living. Children of George and Lena (Huffmester) Laner: Elizabeth, married William A. Schettler; John, married Rose Felterman, resides in Brookville, Pennsylvania; Edward, married Rose Schettler (deceased), and resides in Oil City, Pennsylvania; Mary, married (first) Ira Bauer, and (second) Jack Foley, and resides at Woodlawn, Pennsylvania; Emma, married Walter Monery and resides at Ashtabula; Frances, married Harry Agey, and resides at Woodlawn, Pennsylvania; Margaret, married John Clinger, resides at Kane, Pennsylvania; William, resides at Pittsburgh, Pennsylvania; Frank, deceased, married Frances Luken; Arthur, married Belle ———, resides at Kane, Pennsylvania; Curtis, unmarried; Rosa, married James Stratton, resides at Strattonville, Pennsylvania; Christina, married Henry Carson, resides at Kane, Pennsylvania.

Mr. and Mrs. Schettler are members of the Catholic church at Crown, Clarion county; they have eight children: 1. Amanda Catherine, born in 1892; married John Smerker, a barber of Fryburg. 2. Ralph Alexander, born July 5, 1893; unmarried, and lives on the home farm. 3. Earl Leo, born August 25, 1895; resides at home. 4. Olga Elizabeth, born September 17, 1897; resides at home. 5. Grace Helen, born May 31, 1900. 6. Mildred Frances, born in March, 1904. 7. Ruth Marie, born October 12, 1907. 8. William Edward, born October 3, 1909. The younger children live at home with their parents.

PRENTICE Joseph Prentice was a resident of Brooklyn, New York, who went west at an early day and settled at Port Lawrence, now part of the site of the city of Toledo, Ohio. He died May 6, 1845, aged sixty-four years. He was accompanied on his western journey by his second wife Eleanor.

(II) Frederick, son of Joseph Prentice and his second wife Eleanor, was born at Port Lawrence, Ohio, December 6, 1823, and is said to have been the first white child born there. His birthplace is now part of the city of Toledo. He was prominent in the early history of Lucas county, Ohio (Toledo), later residing in Michigan. He married (first) Anna ——— and had a son Joseph. Married (second) ——— Maddox and had a daughter Mary. Married (third) Mary Park and had sons Frederick Ashley and Charles. Married (fourth) Amanda Stillwell. He now resides in New York City.

(III) Frederick Ashley, son of Frederick and his third wife, Mary (Park) Prentice, was born at Coldwater, Michigan, May 18, 1853, died at Guayandotte, West Virginia, April 1, 1885. He grew to youthful manhood in New York City, finishing his education in universities of Europe; at Geneva, Switzerland, and Freeburg, Saxony, taking at the latter a course in mining. After his return to the United States he went to the state of Colorado, where he acquired large mining interests, which he developed. Later he located in West Virginia, where in association with his father he carried on an extensive lumbering business, manufacturing and marketing the lumber obtained from their own saw mills, working in extensive forests which they had purchased. He continued actively engaged in this business until his death. He married, September 24, 1873, Mary Caroline Ulman, who survived him (see Ulman II). Their only child, Mary Frederica, born at Clifton Springs, New York, married, February 12, 1896, Charles Joseph Sibley Miller, son of General Charles Miller, of Franklin, Pennsylvania.

(The Ulman Line)

(I) Simon Ulman, a lieutenant in the Bavarian army, was born in Wiesbaden, Germany, and in the early twenties of the nineteenth century came to the United States. He located in Philadelphia, Pennsylvania, where he was engaged in mercantile business. Later he continued for a time in the same business in Franklin. He married Sarah, daughter of John Nicholas and Elizabeth (Marshall) Moyer (see Marshall). Children: Hiram; Solomon, of whom further; Sarah; Matilda; Leonore and Louise.

(II) Solomon, son of Simon and Sarah (Moyer) Ulman, was born in Philadelphia, Pennsylvania, September 7, 1824, died in Franklin, Pennsylvania, May, 1882. He received a good education in his native city, and was associated with his father in mercantile life. He accompanied the latter to Franklin, but did not return to Philadelphia. He continued in mercantile life and developed the largest business in Venango county and ranked as the leading merchant of his day in Franklin. He was very open handed and generous in his business relations with his customers, always helping those who were deserving through the days of pinching poverty that so frequently overtook the settler at that early day. He was not only the man of business, but catered as well to his fine intellectual taste, having one of the best and largest libraries in Western Pennsylvania. He married, March 18, 1847, Lydia Louisa Eliza Parks (see Parks VII), born October 28, 1825, died October, 1889. Children: Myron Parks; Fannie Louisa, died in Franklin, December 9, 1885; Mary Caroline, married Frederick Ashley Prentice (see Prentice III); Edgar Stone, died in Baltimore, Maryland, January 21, 1885.

(The Marshall Line).

The Marshall family of Virginia descends from Captain John Marshall, born and reared in Ireland, a captain of cavalry in the English army, who came to Virginia in 1650. There is a great similarity of names between the Virginia and the Pennsylvania family, but the latter came at a much later date. They were of Philadelphia and Lancaster county, Pennsylvania, prior to the revolution. Several of the name were prominent in Western Pennsylvania. Colonel James, who always spelled his name Marshel, was of Cross Creek township, Washington county, Pennsylvania, 1778. He owned a large tract of land, which was surveyed to him in 1785, called "Marshel Hall." In 1781 he was appointed by the supreme executive council lieutenant of Washington county. From 1781 to 1784 he was recorder of deeds and register of wills for the county, and again from 1791 to 1795. From 1784 to 1787 was sheriff of the county. He was a prominent actor in the "whiskey" insurrection of 1794. In 1796 he advertised thirteen hundred acres of patented and improved land for sale, and shortly afterward moved to Brooke county, Virginia. Colonel James Marshel's wife was his cousin, a sister of Robert and Captain John Marshall, who spelled his name Marshall. John Marshel, son of Colonel James Marshel, was elected sheriff of Washington county in 1835; resigned in 1836 to become cashier of the Franklin Bank in Washington county. Colonel James Marshel died in Brooke county, Virginia, 1829. Captain, also Colonel John and Robert Marshall were half-brothers and cousins of Colonel James Marshel, whose wife was their sister. Robert purchased land of Colonel James in Close Creek township, on which he lived until his death at seventy-three years of age.

Captain John Marshall was born in Ireland in 1750, came to Pennsylvania and settled in Hanover township, Lancaster, now Dauphin county, Pennsylvania, in 1770. He served in the revolutionary war, holding the rank of captain of a company in Colonel Samuel Miles' rifle regiment, serving in 1776. He was engaged at the battle of Long Island and received serious injuries. He was later captain of a company of the Second Regiment Pennsylvania Line, Colonel Walter Stewart, and on muster roll bearing date September 8, 1778 (reported as severely wounded at the battle of Brandywine September 11, 1777). He received a pension for his patriotic service and was still living and on the pension rolls in 1835, being then eighty-five years of age. In 1779 he appears in Washington county, coming with his half-brother Robert (previously mentioned). In August, 1781, he was appointed a justice of the peace, and associate judge for Hopewell township; in 1802-05 was a member of the Pennsylvania house of assembly. He was also colonel of Washington county militia. In 1820 he sold the two hundred acre tract that he had purchased of his cousin, Colonel James Marshel, and moved to Crawford county, Ohio. He married Hannah Baldwin and had issue. Their daughter, Elizabeth Marshall, married John Nicholas Moyer; their daughter, Sarah Moyer, married Lieutenant Simon Ulman (see Ulman I); their son, Solomon Ulman, married Lydia Louise Eliza

Parks (see Parks VII); their daughter, Mary Caroline Ulman, married Frederick Ashley Prentice (see Prentice II).

John Nicholas Moyer, born December 26, 1769, was a son of Valentine Moyer, an early settler in Berks county, Pennsylvania, where he died in 1799. He was a well-to-do farmer, served in the revolution and was a member of "Host Church." His wife, Margaret Barbara, survived him being generously provided for in his will made April 30, 1797, but all contingent upon her "remaining my widow." By a first wife he had a son Philip; by a second wife eleven children, of whom John Nicholas was the third. He came into possession of the "homestead" in 1797, owning it until 1828. About 1817 he built a large stone farm house and a large barn on the "plantation." He married Elizabeth, daughter of Captain John and Hannah Baldwin Marshall.

(The Parks Line).

(I) This name is spelled in early record, Park, Parke, Peirk, Parks, Park perhaps being the true spelling, but Parks the more general form. Richard Parks was a proprietor of Cambridge, Massachusetts, 1642, died 1665. He married Sarah, widow of Love Brewster, son of Elder William Brewster, and left issue.

(II) Thomas, son of Richard Parks, was born 1629, died August 11, 1690. He owned a six thousand acre tract and house near Bemis Mills on the Charles river. He married Abagail Dix, of Watertown, Massachusetts.

(III) John, son of Thomas Parks, was born in Newton, from Cambridge, Massachusetts, September 6, 1656, died 1718. He married (second) Elizabeth Miller and left issue.

(IV) John (2), son of John (1) Parks by his second wife, was born in Newton, Massachusetts, December 20, 1696. He married Esther —— and left issue.

(V) John (3), son of John (2) Parks, was born in Newton, Massachusetts, May 1, 1719, died at Shrewsbury, Massachusetts, June 8, 1804. He married, at Waltham, Hannah Hammond, November 28, 1748, and left issue.

(VI) Jonathan, son of John (3) Parks, was born in Newton, Massachusetts, 1753, died in North Brookfield, 1847, aged ninety-four years. He had two or three wives, and lived in Sheffield, Massachusetts.

(VII) Myron, son of Jonathan Parks, was born in Sheffield, Massachusetts, July 8, 1797, died at Pittsburgh, Pennsylvania, February 16, 1863. He came to Western Pennsylvania when a young man, settling at Meadville, Crawford county, where he married, September 12, 1821, Lydia Louisa Davis, born in Martinsburg, Virginia, October 1, 1801, died in Franklin, Pennsylvania, March 26, 1877. Children: Mary Caroline, born September 24, 1823, married David B. Hayes; Lydia Louisa Eliza, married Solomon Ulman (see Ulman II); Frederick Horatio, died in 1850; John Pearsall, died March 22, 1890, married Laura Plumer; Myron, died in infancy; Myron L., deceased; Marion Blanche, married John Ramsey Drum.

McKEE   Joseph McKee was born in Clarion county, Pennsylvania, of Irish ancestors. He was reared and educated in his native place, and after reaching his legal majority turned his attention to farming operations on an extensive estate in Piney township. He was a Democrat in his political convictions, and was a loyal supporter of all matters projected for the good of the general welfare. His wife, whose maiden name was Mary Wilson, was a daughter of Lewis Wilson, who was a soldier in the war of 1812. Mr. and Mrs. McKee both lived to a ripe old age. Children: William; Wilson; John; Eliza, died at the age of forty-four years; James; Robert, mentioned below; Hugh, living on the old homestead farm; Thomas; Mary, wife of John Moggy.

(II) Robert, son of Joseph and Mary (Wilson) McKee, was born in Clarion county, Pennsylvania, July 26, 1832, died October 20, 1896. He was a farmer by occupation and owned two hundred acres of the old homestead in Piney township, one mile east of Sligo. He owned allegiance to the Democratic party in his political faith, and was the popular and efficient incumbent of a number of important township offices during the latter part of his lifetime. He was connected with the United Presbyterian church, of which his wife is still a member. Mr. McKee married, January 5, 1859, Elizabeth A. Elliott, born in Clarion county, Pennsylvania, January 1, 1840. The grandparents of Mrs. McKee were George and Elizabeth (Henry) Elliott, the former of whom was born in Ireland and the latter in Pennsylvania. George Elliott immigrated to America as a young man and located on the Juniata river, later settling on a farm near Callensburg, Clarion county, Pennsylvania.

George and Elizabeth Elliott had nine children: 1. James, deceased; married (first) Mary Harshbach, deceased; (second) Rachel Rankin, deceased. 2. William, deceased; married Elizabeth Hogan, deceased. 3. Thomas, deceased; married Jane Wilson, deceased. 4. Harrison, married Jane Watson. 5. John, mentioned below. 6. Anderson, married (first) Mary McCombs; (second) Mrs. Waddell. 7. Preston, twin of Anderson, married Elizabeth Shoup. 8. Matilda, married a Mr. Elliott. 9. Mary Jane, married a Mr. McComb.

John Elliott, fifth in order of birth of the above children, and father of Mrs. Robert McKee, was born in Clarion county, Pennsylvania, in 1816. He was a farmer by occupation, a Democrat in politics, and a member of the Presbyterian church. He was twice married, his first union having been with Mary Core, daughter of Rev. John Core, who was a drummer boy in the British army in 1776 and who later deserted and came over to the American cause. The first Mrs. Elliott died at the early age of twenty-five years; child, Elizabeth A., aforementioned as wife of Robert McKee. For his second wife Mr. Elliott married Elizabeth Wilson, daughter of Alexander Wilson, who died aged one hundred years. John Elliott died in 1867 and his second wife died in 1898. Children of second marriage: 1. Melissa, married William Francis; children: William, John, Joseph, Jessie, Edith, Jennie and James, twins, and Mildred. 2. Margaret, married William Gardner; children: Benjamin, Frank, Paul, Elizabeth, Charles. 3. John, married (first) —— McLughlin, (second) Mrs. Schwab; children: Carl, Grace, Mildred, Marie and two who are deceased. 4. Ora, died in infancy. 5. Marinda, married James Cole, child, Helen. Mrs. Robert McKee survives her husband and is living with her son Leslie R., in 1912. Children born to Mr. and Mrs. McKee: 1. Anna Mary, born in January, 1860, died as the wife of Marion Winkett, a carpenter. 2. Joseph, died as a small child. 3. Arminda, born December 10, 1863. 4. John, born February 26, 1865. 5. Eva, born October 30, 1867, deceased; was the wife of Ambrose Shamer, a jeweler in Sharpsburg, Pennsylvania; child, Gertrude, married Hicks Clinton. 6. Ora, died in infancy. 7. Blanche, born December 2, 1869; wife of Dr. Love, of Verona. 8. J. Willis, born January 14, 1871; married Verda Sloghenhopt. 9. Robert, born March 13, 1876; married Jennie Henry and they reside on the old homestead. 10. Mellissa married William Baldwin, deceased; she lives at McDonald; child, Leslie. 11. Tellford, died at the age of twenty-four years. 12. Clyde, married Oma Wyman; he is a laborer in Sligo. 13. Frank, engaged in railroad work in Sligo; married Edna Craig. 14. Leslie R., mentioned below.

(III) Leslie R., son of Robert and Elizabeth A. (Elliott) McKee, was born in Piney township, Clarion county, Pennsylvania, July 1, 1884. He was educated in the public schools of Sligo, where he attended high school for two years. Subsequently he was a student in the Normal School at Clarion for one year, at the expiration of which he turned his attention to teaching. He taught school for two years and then went to Lancaster, Pennsylvania, where he learned the jeweler's trade. In 1906 he located in Sligo, where he has since been engaged in the jewelry business. He conducts one of the finest jewelry stores in Clarion county and controls a very large and lucrative patronage. He is deeply interested in all that affects the good of his home community, and his political support is given to the Democratic party. In a social way he is affiliated with the local lodge of the Independent Order of Odd Fellows, and in their religious faith he and his wife are devout members of the Presbyterian church, to whose good works they are most liberal contributors.

Mr. McKee married Anna Graff, born September 27, 1886, daughter of William and Lavina (Rowe) Graff. Mr. and Mrs. McKee have one child, Beulah, whose birth occurred May 22, 1908.

WALTER Michael Walter, the founder of the family in this country, was born in Germany in 1812, died in Tylersburg, Pennsylvania, in 1857. In 1830 he emigrated to America and settled first in Albany, New York, where he remained for two years, and then removed to Baltimore, Maryland, where he remained for a time, going from there to Pittsburgh, Pennsylvania, and in 1836 to Clearfield county and then to Clarion county, Pennsylvania. In 1838 he settled in Knox township, where he remained until 1853 when he removed finally to Tylersburg, where he opened a cabinetmaker's shop and conducted a hotel until his death. He was a Democrat in politics, and a Roman Catholic in religion. He married, in Pittsburgh, Pennsylvania, in 1836, Catherine Yost, born in 1818, died in 1894. Children: Joseph, referred to below; Minnie, now living in Grove City, Pennsylvania, married James Wray; Frank, now living in Mill Creek township, married Sallie Ann Smith; Michael, referred to below; Stephen, deceased; John, now living in Tylersburg; Maggie, deceased; Mary, deceased; Jacob H., referred to below.

(II) Joseph, son of Michael and Catherine (Yost) Walter, was born December 28, 1839, and is now living in Tylersburg, Pennsylvania. He received his early education in the public schools, and then learned the trade of a cabinetmaker and also the trade of a wagonmaker, and in 1861, on the outbreak of the civil war, enlisted in Company F, Sixty-seventh Pennsylvania Volunteer Infantry, and served throughout the war, taking part in all of the battles of the Army of the Potomac. He was captured and confined for five months in Andersonville prison and five days in Libby prison and later exchanged and rejoined his regiment. After the war he was for fourteen years in the Golinza Mills, then removed to Tionesta, Pennsylvania, finally settling in Tylersburg, where he is now living, having retired from active business. He is a Republican in politics. He is a member of John Martin Bowman Post, Grand Army of the Republic. He married, in 1882, Alma Smail, of Clarion county, Pennsylvania. Children: Robert, deceased; Viola, deceased; Anson, Curtis, Dona.

(II) Michael (2), son of Michael (1) and Catherine (Yost) Walter, was born October 15, 1845, and is now living in Tylersburg, Pennsylvania. He received his early education in the public schools, and then went to work in the woods as a lumberman and later became a boat-builder and general carpenter, and finally settled in Tylersburg, where he was in the mercantile business for many years. He is a Progressive in politics. He married, in 1869, Sarah Neely, of Clarion county, Pennsylvania. Children: 1. Ernst, born August 26, 1871; educated in the public schools and at E. B. U. College and at G. W. Michaels College in Delaware, Ohio, and at Zanescan College in Columbus, Ohio, and is now engaged in the produce business. 2. Gertrude, now living in Endeavor, Pennsylvania; married Edward Myers. 3. Harry, now living in Elmira, New York.

(II) Jacob H., son of Michael and Catherine (Yost) Walter, was born in Tylersburg, Pennsylvania, July 11, 1855, and is now living in Leeper, Pennsylvania. He received his early education in the public schools, and at the age of fourteen years engaged in general labor, which he followed until he was twenty-six years of age, when he worked at shoemaking for five years; he then bought a farm, which he cultivated for fourteen years and finally, in 1901, settled in Leeper, where he entered mercantile business in which he still continues. He also owns a farm in Farmington township. He is a Republican in politics, and was for several terms the supervisor of North Farmington township. He married, August 24, 1882, Sallie, born in Tylersburg, Pennsylvania, October 25, 1862, now living in Leeper, daughter of David R. and Rowena (Smith) Mays (see Mays III). Children: 1. Alice, born February 11, 1884; married William Slaughenhaupt; child, Walter, deceased. 2. William, born February 19, 1885; married, June 12, 1906, Della Hulings; children: Geraldine, born February 14, 1907; Milton, October 14, 1908; Charlotte, June 28, 1910; Donald, March 4, 1912. 3. David, born July 30, 1891. 4. Evelyn, born March 24, 1904.

(The Mays Line.)

(I) Thomas Mays, the first member of this family of whom we have any definite information, was born in 1753 in South Carolina, died in Clarion county, Pennsylvania, in 1830. He removed to Georgia, later to eastern Pennsylvania, from there to Westmoreland county, and finally about 1820 settled in Clarion county, where he built the first flouring mills west of the Allegheny mountains. He was a soldier during the revolutionary war. He married, in Charleston, South Carolina, Mary Hamilton, born in 1751, died in Forest county, Pennsylvania, in 1850. Children: John, Thomas Washington, James, William, referred to below.

(II) William, son of Thomas and Mary (Hamilton) Mays, was born in Georgia, in 1793, died in Clarion county, Pennsylvania, in 1870. He removed with his parents to Clarion county where he became a farmer and a boatman on the Allegheny river. He, with his three brothers, served in the army during the war of 1812. He married Elizabeth Hummel, born in Westmoreland county, Pennsylvania, in 1799, died in Clarion county, Pennsylvania, in 1840. Children: 1. Mary, married John Long. 2. Thomas. 3. Samuel H., born in Clarion county, 1823, now living at Verona, near Pittsburgh, Pennsylvania; married, in 1848, Sarah Lowry, born 1826, died 1897; children: Mary Heller, Emma, Florence, Judson S., Alice C., William L., George H., Harry M. 4. James, deceased. 5. David R., referred to below. 6. George, deceased. 7. Elizabeth, married John R. Cribbs. 8. Jane, married Samuel Roseman. 9. John, now living in Clarion county, Pennsylvania.

(III) David R., son of William and Elizabeth (Hummel) Mays, was born in Clarion county, Pennsylvania, September 25, 1827, and is living at Leeper. He received his early education in the public schools, and then became a lumberman on the Clarion river, which occupation he followed for forty years and then retired to a farm in Farmington township. He married (first) in 1848, Mary Carbough, died October, 1856, and married (second) December 15, 1858, Rowena, daughter of Philip and Sallie (Brenneman) Smith, born in Clarion county, Pennsylvania, April 30, 1836, died in 1909. Children by first wife: 1. Hester Ann, deceased; married William Smith, deceased. 2. Emma, married Esquire Cook; resides in Cooksburg, Pennsylvania. 3. Loretta, married James Starr; resides in Elk county, Pennsylvania. Children by second wife: 4. Florence, married Joseph McCartney. 5. Alma Lucretia, married Charles Swatziager, deceased. 6. Sallie, married Jacob H. Walter (see Walter II). 7. Alice, married Daniel Carson, who was killed in a saw mill in 1903. 8. Ida, married William Austin, deceased. 9. Samuel, married Effie Dale; resides in Kane, Pennsylvania; employed on the Baltimore & Ohio railroad. 10. Lowella, married B. A. Shotts; resides near Sharon, Pennsylvania. 11. Herbert M., married Emma Ostemyre; resides at Fort Wayne, Indiana. 12. Gertrude, died in infancy.

JAMIESON The Jamieson family in America is of direct Scotch descent. Though many generations separate the members of the American branch from their kinsmen in Bonny Scotland, they still retain an inherent love for the land of their forefathers, and have also inherited the noted Scotch clannishness.

The first of the family to cross the Atlantic in search of religious and political liberty was John Jamieson, who came over about the year 1724, and located in the colony now known as the state of New York. He appears to have been of a wandering nature as he soon afterward went to the Berkshire Hills, Massachusetts, and later removed to Manhattan Island, New York. He was here joined by his cousin, Ailsie Jamieson, and they were married immediately after her arrival. Several children were born of this union, among them John (2), who, following the trend of the times, and being imbued with the pioneer spirit, which Thomas Jefferson said (many years afterward) would be the making, and cause the extension, of the United States (at that time the American Colonies of the English Crown), went farther westward and located in Wyoming, Luzerne county, Pennsylvania. His name, or that of his son John, appears in the list of soldiers, July 3, 1778, who were led by Colonel Zebulon Butler and Colonel Nathan Denison in their historical battle with the British, the Tories and the Indians. The Jamiesons early acquiring a competence (in each family) were among the few Americans who, after the revolutionary war, visited the "Auld Countree" frequently, thus keeping in touch with their trans-Atlantic relatives.

(I) John Jamieson, one of the above-mentioned, became interested in the mills of Paisley, Scotland, during a visit, there married and settled for the time. He was the father of a large family of children, the majority of whom, from time to time, deserted the ancestral home in Scotland and came to the United States. Among his numerous children was Hugh, of whom further.

(II) Hugh, son of John Jamieson, was born in Scotland, married Jeannette ———, in 1823, emigrated from Paisley, Scotland, in 1824, to Hudson-on-the-Hudson, New York, and removed later to Berkshire Hills. During his residence in Berkshire Hills he had charge of the weaving department of the large cotton factories of that place, introducing the latest and most approved European methods of weaving cotton cloths. In the fall of 1843, following in the footsteps of his progenitors, he removed to Pennsylvania, settling in Sugar Grove, Warren county. Here he entered the employ of D. K. Grandin. Retiring from active business life, his latter years were peacefully spent on a farm in Sugar Grove. He was an ardent Presbyterian, as was his good wife Jeannette, and to the end of their days they were both devoted to the "kirk." He died, after a useful life, well and worthily spent, at the ripe old age of ninety-eight; while his wife passed away at the age of eighty-eight years. Hugh and Jeannette Jamieson were the parents of several children, among whom was Hugh A., of whom further.

(III) Hugh A., son of Hugh Jamieson, was born in Berkshire county, Massachusetts, May 31, 1835. With his parents, sisters and brothers he removed to Sugar Grove, Warren county, Pennsylvania, in 1843. He received a common school education, such as was obtainable at that time, but being ambitious and a close student he fitted himself to teach. He taught three winters, the last in Jamestown, New York. In the spring of 1857 he returned to Sugar Grove. Buying out the business interests of Mark Wilson, he formed a partnership with Isaac N. Tider. His business acumen was so pronounced, coupled with his legal knowledge, that he excited universal favorable comment. He was persuaded to study law. He severed his connection with Mr. Tider in 1859, and entered the law office of Johnson & Brown. He was admitted to the bar in 1861. His former interest in commercial life still clung to him, and while practicing his profession he accumulated a large number of business interests. These becoming so financially important and needing his undivided attention, he gave up his legal practice to engage in strictly commercial enterprises. Years before his death he had accumulated a fortune. He successfully established the largest hardware business in Warren county. He was a director and president of the Citizens' National Bank of Warren county. He was an active worker for the Warren Library Association, contending that the reading of books was absolutely essential for the growth and cultivation of the mind and for enlarging a man's outlook on life. He was a loyal Republican, always voting with his party, and was elected burgess of the town in 1882. His religious affiliations like those of his parents, were with the Presbyterian church. He married (first) Julia Crane. To them were born four sons: Hugh and Frank, dying in infancy; Mark W.; Charles Wetmore, of whom further. His second marriage was to Rhoda Hall, now deceased.

(IV) Charles Wetmore, son of Hugh A. and Julia (Crane) Jamieson, was born in Warren, Pennsylvania, July 9, 1867, died July 6, 1912. He was reared in the west under the judicious direction of his mother, and graduated from the public schools and Grinnell College. He returned to his native city about 1895, where he at once entered into business, connecting himself with the Warren Refining Company, in conjunction with his father, Hugh A. Jamieson. He continued a member of the company until the time of his demise. He also engaged in other business enterprises, notably among which were the Floridin Company, of Warren; the Abbott Motor Company, of Detroit, Michigan; in both of which he was serving as president at the time of his untimely taking off. In 1909 Mr. Jamieson succeeded the late Perry D. Clark as president of the First National Bank, and was acting in that capacity at the time of his death. He was a director of the Corn-Planter Refining Company, and of the Riverside Acid Works. For years he was in the forefront of every progressive movement, church, municipal, state and personal business, and was characterized by his fellow townsmen as one of the leading men of his city and section. He was an active member of Trinity Memorial Episcopal Church, and to it was always generous, loyal and helpful. It was largely through his personal efforts that the Brotherhood of St. Andrews was organized, he serving as president, which has been an invaluable aid to the church. He was a constant attendant at the meetings and its staunch supporter. He was a liberal contributor to the Young Men's Christian Association, and was for years president of the local branch of that institution, and was thrice elected member of the state committee. He later resigned the presidency, but retained his position on the board of directors. He established in Warren a high standard of truth and right living, and wielded a powerful and beneficent influence on those with whom he came in daily contact during his life, and this influence will continue for all time, for such an influence does not die with the man. In his death Warren lost one of its foremost, most appreciated and best known citizens. He was of more than local fame as he was a great captain of industry, one who built well and wisely, not for himself alone, but for those around him and for those who come after him. It can be truthfully said of him that the world is better for his having lived in it.

He married (first) in 1894, in Des Moines, Iowa, Lily L. Yoder, a classmate, who died in 1901. On April 13, 1903, he married (second) Wilhelmina D. Schnur. Mrs. Wilhelmina D.

(Schnur) Jamieson is of colonial and revolutionary stock. Her ancestors fought the battles of the colonists against the Indians, helped to conquer the wilderness, and aligned themselves on the side of the continental army in its struggle for independence from England. She is one of the leading members of the General Joseph Warren Chapter, No. 950, of the Daughters of the American Revolution. Her national membership is No. 84106. She is a prominent member of Trinity Memorial Episcopal Church, where she in a measure tries to sustain the work of her husband.

PORTERFIELD This family is of Scotch origin. The emigrant was born in Edinburgh, Scotland, of Scotch-English parentage, and settled in Lancaster county, Pennsylvania. Three sons, Robert, George and John, grew up in Lancaster county, and later all became farmers of Venango county.

(II) Joseph, fourth son of the Emigrant Porterfield, settled in Westmoreland county, Pennsylvania, later moving to Venango county, where he built the first iron furnace in the Mill Creek district. He also engaged in lumbering and milling, owning a saw mill and grist mill on Mill Creek, Richland township. He married Hannah, daughter of James Hall, of Richland township. Children: John C., of whom further; Cyrus, yet living in Venango county; William H., died in Oil City, Pennsylvania; James, twin of William H.; Priscilla, married Captain Alexander Frazier, whom she survives, now living in Cooperstown, Pennsylvania.

(III) John C., son of Joseph and Hannah (Hall) Porterfield, was born in Venango county, Pennsylvania, September 6, 1828, died in Emlenton, Pennsylvania, April 5, 1894. He spent his youth at the home farm, attended the public schools, and for a short time taught school and worked in the store operated by the proprietors of Shippen Furnace. When nineteen years of age he located in Emlenton, Pennsylvania, where he became clerk in the Morgan dry goods store, then situated near the bridge. In 1849 he became manager of the "Iron Store" established by Brown, Phillios & Company, of the Kittanning Iron Works. He continued in that employ until 1857, when he became the senior member of the general hardware firm of Porterfield, Teitzell & Company, John McCombs being the silent partner. In 1860 the firm became Porterfield & McCombs, so continuing until the death of Mr. McCombs in 1890, Mr. Porterfield continuing the business until his death four years later. Under his management the business had grown and expanded from that of the "Iron Store" to one of great proportions, combining four departments. It was not only the oldest business house in Emlenton, but the largest in that section. The stocks in every department were complete and every customer was dealt with in absolute fairness. This policy has been continued by his successor, Howard Hall Porterfield, who in all things has proved a worthy son of his honored father. John C. Porter was a man of varied activities and a most potent factor in the development of Emlenton and Venango county. He maintained a large, general mercantile establishment at Foxburg, and for twenty-four years was a director and stockholder in the Foxburg Bank. He was treasurer of the Emlenton Bridge Company; director of the Emlenton Gas Light and Fuel Company; interested in the St. Petersburg Bank, and in oil and gas properties elsewhere. Another enterprise with which he was connected and one that gave Emlenton its first great impetus was the building of the Emlenton & Shippensville railroad. The corporation was organized June 17, 1875, Mr. Porterfield being chosen a member of the first board of directors. He was a charter member of Allegheny Valley Lodge, 552, Free and Accepted Masons. In politics he was a Republican, and a most liberal, public-spirited and valuable citizen. From an humble beginning he built for himself a name synonymous with integrity and success, leading where others followed and bequeathing to his posterity not only riches, but an honorable name.

He married, in 1851, Susan, daughter of Henry Allebach and granddaughter of Jacob and Verona Allebach, of Germantown and Venango county, Pennsylvania (see Allebach II), Mrs. Susan Porterfield survives her husband and resides in Pittsburgh, Pennsylvania. Children: 1. Emma, married W. S. Watson and resides in Pittsburgh. 2. Howard Hall, of whom further. 3. Jessie A., married P. O. Heasley, whom she survives, a resident of Pittsburgh. 4. Henry A., now manager of the Dexter Oil Company, of Pittsburgh.

(IV) Howard Hall, son of John C. and Susan (Allebach) Porterfield, was born in

Emlenton, Pennsylvania, January 6, 1856. He received his early education in the public schools, then entered Phillips Academy at Andover, Massachusetts, whence he was graduated in 1873. Choosing a business career he entered his father's employ as manager of the Porterfield general store at Foxburg, holding that position until the death of John C. Porterfield in 1894. He then continued in management for the estate, of which he was executor, of both the Foxburg and Emlenton stores until 1905, when he purchased the interests of the heirs and became sole owner. The Emlenton business was diversified to include four principal departments and became the largest general mercantile establishment in the county as well as the oldest. The business done was not only of a retail character, but a large wholesale trade was carried on extending beyond local limits. Since 1905 Mr. Porterfield has been sole owner of the Foxburg store and has proved his excellent business capacity in its management. He is also vice-president of the Foxburg Bank, of which his father was an organizer, and is also interested in the Pennsylvania Fuel Company and other enterprises of lesser importance. He is a past master of Emlenton Lodge, Free and Accepted Masons; a companion of Venango Chapter, Royal Arch Masons; a Knight of Franklin Commandery, Knights Templar; a thirty-second degree Mason of Pennsylvania Consistory, Ancient Accepted Scottish Rite, and a Noble of Syria Temple, Ancient Arabic Order Nobles of the Mystic Shrine; the two latter bodies located in Pittsburgh. He married, October 26, 1900, Anna L., born in Punxsutawney, Pennsylvania, January 6, 1870, daughter of Rev. David Gatshaw.

(The Allebach Line.)

(I) The founders of this family in the United States were Jacob and Verona Allebach, who came from Germany, settling in Germantown, Pennsylvania. During the revolution they were driven out of Germantown by the British and their home burned. They found refuge and safety in Berks county, Pennsylvania. Jacob and family later settled in Venango county, Pennsylvania, where the parents died.

(II) Henry, son of Jacob and Verona Allebach, was born November 5, 1800, in Montgomery county, Pennsylvania, died in Emlenton, Pennsylvania, September 25, 1888, after an illness of but ten days. His early life was spent in Berks county, Pennsylvania, where he worked in a woolen mill. Later he moved to Reading, where he learned the jeweler's trade and carried on business until 1837, when he moved to Beaver township, Venango county, Pennsylvania, where his parents had preceded him. There he bought a farm on which he resided three years, then sold and moved to Emlenton, Pennsylvania, where he was the first jeweler to locate, having his store on Main street. He continued in business until 1852, when his eyesight failing he turned the business over to his son Levi and for five years engaged in a mercantile business less trying to the eyesight. He then returned to the jewelry business, continuing until his retirement in 1872. At his death he lacked but two years of a half century residence in Emlenton. Both he and his wife were members of the Lutheran church and helped organize the first congregation of that faith in Emlenton. He married, November 30, 1823, in Berks county, Pennsylvania, Sarah, daughter of Christian Shaner; she died in Emlenton, January 3, 1888, aged eighty-six years, eleven months and twenty days. The business founded by Henry Allebach continued by his son Levi, is still continued by his grandson under the firm name of Allebach Brothers. Children of Henry and Sarah Allebach: 1. Maria, deceased; married George Truby. 2. Sarah, married John Sloan. 3. Levi, deceased; he was his father's successor in business. 4. Susan, widow of John C. Porterfield (see Porterfield III). 5. Henry, died young.

CARNAHAN The first authentic information relating to this family dates back to the year 1540, when three Irish tribes or clans by the name of Carnochan, Carnaghan and Carnahan, entered into an agreement to unite for self protection. Previous to this time, tradition says, they subsisted by the right of the strong arm, as was the custom of the day, preying upon the weaker tribes and levying tribute in lands, cattle and servants. Inhabiting the rough and stormy coast of the north part of Ireland, one of their chief means of support was from the wreckage of vessels driven ashore, and they were even accused of luring them ashore by means of false lights. When these three tribes had no mutual enemies to assail they fought each other until their numbers were greatly diminished. When the great religious reformation spread over Ireland, they embraced the Calvinistic faith and doctrines, and in 1540 united under the leadership of one James Alexander Carnahan. That they were strong and firm in their beliefs is evidenced by the fact that they met in numerous pitched battles the soldiers of Mary N Tudor (1553-58). In the latter year they were almost exterminated, their chief slain, and goods and lands confiscated to the crown. Many suffered imprisonment or death. Some escaped and of these there are traces of two branches who took refuge in Scotland; one settled at or near Dumfries, and the other at Aberdeen. The Dumfries branch became weavers by occupation; the Aberdeen branch became hewers of stone, or stone masons, and at one time owned and worked large quarries. That they became people of some importance is known, for one John Andrew Carnahan was a delegate to the convention in France from which resulted the celebrated Edict of Nantes (1585).

But little is known of the family again until 1700, when James Alexander Carnahan was born in Aberdeen, Scotland. He is supposed to be the direct ancestor of the branch of the family hereinafter described. He is reputed to have been a man of powerful build, standing six feet four inches in his bare feet, and weighing about two hundred and fifty pounds, of a dark and swarthy complexion, self-esteemed, and very determined in his religious views. He had fourteen sons and five daughters. Of the sons, James, Hugh and John emigrated to America with their families between 1760 and 1770, and settled in the Cumberland valley at Carlisle, Pennsylvania.

(I) Undoubtedly descended from one of the brothers above named was Adam Carnahan, born at or near Carlisle, Pennsylvania, November 22, 1777, died August 25, 1853. He removed to New Lebanon, Mercer county, where he settled on a five hundred acre tract of land for which he had obtained a patent, a document which is still extant. He served in the war of 1812. He married Ruth McElwayne, born January 25, 1781, died June 23, 1853, two months before the death of her husband. Children: Margaret, born February 6, 1804, married Wilkes Walker; Nancy, January 18, 1806, married John Hanna; Maria, July 5, 1808, married ———— Walker; James Madison, of whom further; Elizabeth, April 16, 1813, married Adam Thompson; Adam Jr., October 12, 1816, married Lizzie Moore; Ruth, December 28, 1818, married William Zahnizer; John, April 15, 1821; William, July 19, 1823.

(II) James Madison, fourth child and eldest son of Adam and Ruth (McElwayne) Carnahan, was born near New Lebanon, Mercer county, Pennsylvania, December 3, 1810, died September 12, 1901. He was reared on the home farm, and received such education as the day provided. As he states in an autobiography, his class books were a speller, the New Testament and an arithmetic, with instruction three months in the year in a little log schoolhouse, whose window lights were of greased paper. When he attained manhood he received from his father a portion of the home farm, unimproved, covered with timber. This tract he improved and turned into fruitful fields. By frequent purchases he added to his farm until it comprised more than two hundred acres. Upon it he built a comfortable home for his family. It was built of bricks made from clay dug on the land, and is still standing. He was a devoutly religious man, and was all his life an active church worker. He was received into the Presbyterian church, November 16, 1841, at Fairfield, Mercer county, and was ordained elder, June 13, 1858. In politics he was first a Democrat, was a Republican during the civil war period, and finally joined the Prohibition party, of which he became a strong advocate, and he testified to his fealty by repeatedly being a candidate for the assembly on the Prohibition ticket, when there was no hope of his success. He married (first) in 1837-38, Mary, daughter of Thompson and Margaret (Lindsay) McElwayne; (second) Mary Wilson; (third) Permelia Coulson. Children by first wife: Buchanan H., of whom further; Lacey, married ———— Sponsler; Mary, married Caleb Bailey, children: Oscar and James. By second wife: Melvina, married Joseph Smith; by third wife: Elmira, married Charles Christie; James, married Kate Bird; John, married Lucy Gilmore; Otis, married Florence Simcox; Cassius S., married Florence Mook.

(III) Buchanan H., eldest child of James Madison and Mary (McElwayne) Carnahan, was born on the homestead farm at New Lebanon, Pennsylvania, May 2, 1839. After receiving a good common school education he went west to Missouri, where for a time he taught school. In 1863 he had removed to Boulder City, Colorado, where he engaged in the transportation business. Shortly after his marriage in 1864 he returned east and lived for a year on the old farm. He then removed to Oil City, where he established himself in the transfer business, and erected the comfortable house in which he has resided for the past forty-seven years. He has served the city of his adoption in various responsible positions, aggregating the long period of twenty-four years, a fact amply testifying to his capability and the esteem in which he is held by his fellow-citizens. He was a member of the city council many years, and also of the water board. In 1908 he was elected mayor, and his administration was characterized by signal ability and integrity. He is a member of the First Presbyterian Church, and in politics is a Republican.

Mr. Carnahan married, October 3, 1863, Melinda, daughter of Maxwell Coulson. Children: 1. Nettie G., born July 8, 1864; married (first) Oliver Shook, (second) Newton Ackley. 2. James M., born July 25, 1866, died January 8, 1910; married (first) Lucy Sloper, (second) Susie Runkle. 3. Howard, born October 3, 1873; married Minnie Paul; children: Marion and Christopher Paul. 4. William, born February 2, 1876; married Cora Bannon.

PARKER The name Parker is derived from the Latin parcarius, and means one who keeps a park. It is thus a name of occupation. It is claimed that Danes, Saxons and Normans have borne this name, which thus would not only not be the exclusive name of one family, but would not even indicate common racial origin. The name is frequently met in English history, and is one of the most common surnames in England at the present; it is also found in Ireland.

There are few surnames in America whose bearers are harder to trace. Only for a few families of the name has the overwhelming task been extensively undertaken. Connecticut had the first Parker family, but there were numerous early New England settlers named Parker; Virginia received a number of Parker immigrants in the sixteenth century; New Jersey and New York have notable Parker families. The immigrant ancestors were numerous and widely scattered; the name is common and widely extended, and relatively speaking this has been true from the beginning of white settlement in America. There are coats-of-arms of Connecticut, Virginia and New Jersey Parkers which, while not identical, are similar, probably pointing to original unity of these families in England.

(I) William Parker, the first member of this family about whom we have definite information, died in 1808. Our first clear knowledge of him finds him in Westmoreland county, Pennsylvania, perhaps in the part which is now Washington county. This region is part of that which was disputed territory between Virginia and Pennsylvania, at the time of its early settlement. It is thought probable, though not certain, that William Parker came from Virginia. It is unfortunate, though not curious, that he is not traced back of his settlement in Westmoreland county; in the case of one so prominent, and of so interesting a history, we crave further information, but our ancestors were little concerned with the keeping of records; they were rather making their own history! With several other families he removed from Westmoreland county and settled on Bear Creek, Armstrong county. When they were opposite the garrison at Pittsburgh, one of the boats upset and several persons were drowned, included in this number being a son of William Parker. His son John was in Armstrong county before him. Soon after his arrival he erected a mill. He married a sister of John Moore, who was president judge of Westmoreland county from 1785 to 1791. His parents were William and Jeannette (Wilson) Moore; his father died, his mother married (second) James Guthrie, and it seems more probable that the wife of William Parker was a daughter of this second marriage. Children: Samuel; John, of whom further; Mary, married Thomas McKee, who was one of the first two associate judges of Venango county.

(II) John, son of William Parker, was born in 1766, died July 17, 1842. As deputy under Judge John Moore he came into western Pennsylvania for the purpose of surveying, about 1786. For his services in the survey he received land in this new country; nearly all the site of Parker City formerly belonged to him. About 1797 he removed to his land, settling at Parker's Landing, Armstrong county, Pennsylvania, his house, however, being in Butler county, in the present town of Parker. He was one of the first associate judges of Butler county and held this office thirty-five years. He was a farmer and stock raiser, and very successful in business; he greatly encouraged and promoted the settlement of the surrounding territory. In 1815 he laid out the village of Lawrenceburg, now part of Parker City. Mr. Parker was a man of prudence and sagacity. He married, December 7, 1797, Jane Woods, who died July 5, 1833. Children: 1. James W., born June 14, 1799, died August 24, 1833; married, April 14, 1829, Margaret Hamilton. 2. John W., of whom further. 3. Juliet, born December 29, 1802, died February 13, 1876; married, April 21, 1822, John Gilchrist. 4. William, born February 24, 1805, died November 13, 1848. 5. Fullerton, born December 15, 1806, died December 26, 1883; married, April 5, 1832, Amelie Harris. 6. Washington, born July 11, 1809, died June 25, 1844; married, October 15, 1833, Susan Clark. 7. George, born September 8, 1812, died December 10, 1887; married, June 20, 1843, Jane Pollock. 8. Thomas McKee, born December 17, 1815, died June 17, 1864; married, December 11, 1849, Margaret Woods. 9. Wilson, born June 3, 1821, died January 17, 1845.

(III) John W., son of John and Jane (Woods) Parker, was born October 20, 1800, died July 24, 1861. He married, January 8, 1822, Margaret, daughter of Moses and Sallie (Russell) Perry. Children: 1. William, born May 16, 1823, died July 4, 1893; married Isabelle Pollock; children: Robert Pollock and others who died young. 2. James, born May 4, 1825, died September 8, 1894; married Emma Leonard; children: John D., Mary Jane, Clara, Samuel, Reuben, Elizabeth, William, Keziah, Phoebe. 3. Sarah, born July 18, 1827, died in October, 1903; married Samuel Craig; children: Elizabeth and Miranda. 4. Elizabeth, born in 1829, died June 11, 1851; married Dr. John T. Beatty; children: William and two others who died young. 5. Margaret, born April 18, 1831, died December 11, 1896; married Dr. Joseph W. Eggert; children: John, George L., Elizabeth, Manda. 6. John, born October 9, 1833, died September 15, 1901; married Martha Jane Fitterer; children: Alonzo S., Margaret Ann, Charles A., Katharine D., John W., Ethel. 7. Susan, born August 29, 1835; married (first) W. D. Biddle, (second) George W. Ball. 8. Phoebe, born July 16, 1835, died in December, 1908; married Jason Berry; children: Isabelle, Richard Jason, Charles Parker. 9. George Washington, of whom further.

(IV) George Washington, son of John W. and Margaret (Perry) Parker, was born February 22, 1841. He attended business college in Pittsburgh. In 1861 he came to Oil City. He enlisted and served three months in the civil war. In 1865 he returned to Oil City and founded, in company with a man named Castle, the firm of Parker, Castle & Company; they were large shippers of oil. The firm was changed at a later date to Parker, Thompson & Company. Mr. Parker remained in this business until 1872, when he entered the employment of the Oil City National Bank. He was first teller, was promoted to cashier, became president, and holds this position at the present day, having thus been connected with this bank, in various capacities, for over forty years. He has been a director for fifteen years. When Oil City was incorporated as a city, he was elected to the first city council, and he served in this office for ten years. For four years, also, he was a member of the select council, and for fifteen years a member of the school board. Mr. Parker married, November 4, 1869, Rebecca McCready, born June 19, 1850, died January 8, 1909. Children: William M., of whom further; Edith, born July 13, 1874; Harold Thompson, born October 23, 1884; he is a graduate of Princeton College, and was admitted to the Venango county bar in 1911.

(V) William M., son of George Washington and Rebecca (McCready) Parker, was born December 19, 1870. He is a graduate of Princeton College in the class of 1891. He studied law with F. W. Hays and John S. Mattox, and at the same time taught mathematics in the high school at Oil City. In 1895 he was admitted to the bar, and in the same year he formed a partnership with J. D. Trax. This is one of the leading law firms of Oil City. Mr. Parker is a Republican. He married, April 21, 1898, Helen Innis. Children: Helen Elizabeth, born July 18, 1899; Marian, March 14, 1901; Warren Innis, September 9, 1902; Rebecca McCready, September 2, 1905; William M., November 14, 1907.

LEWIS   Lewis is one of the oldest names in English history, and one of the most frequent and distinguished in America. The name is said to be the same as the French Louis. Many Huguenots of the name Louis went from France to England at the Revocation of the Edict of Nantes, and changed the form of the name to Lewis. However, the name Lewis was common in England, and even in Virginia, before this time. The name is too old and too frequent to allow the supposition of common origin for all who bear it. Its frequency in Wales, for several centuries before the settlement of the United States, is even comparable to the frequency of the name Smith in America today. How many distinct Lewis families are in America is not known.

(I) Enoch Lewis, the first member of this family about whom we have definite information, was born, probably in Wales, about 1743. His father's name was also probably Enoch. A tradition in the family says that the noted Baptist preacher, Christmas Evans, was brought up in South Wales by Enoch Lewis. He came to America and probably settled in Pennsylvania. One of his sons, it is said, was a vice-president of the Pennsylvania railroad in the early days of that company. Mr. Lewis married (first) ———, (second) ——— Gibson. Among his children were: William, Ruth, Philip, of whom further.

(II) Philip, son of Enoch Lewis, was born in 1777 or 1778, and died near Clarion, Clarion county, Pennsylvania, in 1852. He lived at one time in the Juniata Valley, near Tuscarora, Pennsylvania; from this place he removed to Clarion (then Venango) county, and took up a tract of land near Clarion, on which he settled, about 1815. Clearing the timber, he made of this place a valuable farm and lived thereon the remainder of his life. He married Eleanor Williams, who died in 1862 or 1863. Children: Zachariah, of whom further; Philip, Nathaniel, Enoch, Jared, William, Amy, Margaret, Elizabeth.

(III) Zachariah, son of Philip and Eleanor (Williams) Lewis, was born in the Juniata Valley, Pennsylvania, June 5, 1809, died July 12, 1899. He went to Clarion county with his parents, and owned a farm adjoining his father's homestead, which also came into his possession by inheritance. He also learned the trade of a carpenter. In the Baptist church he was a deacon. He married, March 24, 1836, Lydia (King) Cochran, born May 29, 1808, died October 24, 1871. Children: 1. Francis M., born March 25, 1837; in the civil war he served three years, and was first sergeant in Company E, Thirty-ninth Regiment (Tenth Reserves) Pennsylvania Volunteers; he was made prisoner at the battle of Gaines' Mill, and wounded before Fredericksburg; by occupation he was a photographer; he led the first orchestra that ever played in Oil City, Pennsylvania, and took an active part in the early musical life of that city; he married, October 6, 1871, Nettie E. Blackmer; children: Evelyn Frances, Mabel, Lucy, Leon B., Arthur R., Lydia K., Anna C., Madge H. 2. John A., of whom further. 3. Thomas E. H., a private in Company E, Tenth Reserve. 4. Gilbert L., died young. 5. Jackson K. 6. Ellen S. 7. Amy F.

(IV) John A., son of Zachariah and Lydia (King-Cochran) Lewis, was born in Clarion county, Pennsylvania, November 25, 1838. He was brought up on the home farm, and educated at the local schools. For the greater part of his life he has been a farmer. He has also been an architect, contractor and builder. In April, 1861, he enlisted in Company E, Tenth Reserve Pennsylvania Volunteers, was mustered in July 5, of the same year, and was mustered out at Pittsburgh, June 11, 1864. He participated in the following battles: Drairesville, West Virginia; the Seven Days' fight before Richmond; the second Bull Run; South Mountain; Antietam; Meade's Mardi Gras campaign; Fredericksburg; Gettysburg; Catlett Station; the Wilderness; Bethsaba Church; Cold Harbor. At Spottsylvania Court House, May 8, 1864, he was captured by the Confederates, but at Beaver Dam, May 9, 1864, he was released by the Union forces, which overtook the enemy at that place. From the first to the last of his service, Mr. Lewis took part in all the engagements in which his regiment participated. He was never off duty for any period, never spent a day in the hospital, and was only once, and slightly, wounded. Almost immediately upon being mustered out he came to Oil City, Pennsylvania, and has since that time adhered to the occupation of architect, contractor and builder except for a short time during which he was engaged in the oil business. He served on the city council at Oil City for twelve years, and has been justice of the peace for a number of years. He was one of the organizers and is a member of Grand Army of the Republic Post No. 435, at Oil City. For seven years he was its quartermaster, and in 1887 he was its commander.

He married, at Oil City, in 1868, Bessie Porter, died November 25, 1911. Children: Theron Victor; Rena Agatha, married Edward Eichner, and their children are:

Gretchen, Elizabeth, Helen, Edgar; Ora Cecil, married Harry Stephenson, and their children are: Hugh, Betty, Charlotte, Lester Leroy, married Orpah Nail; Walter Everett; child, died in infancy.

HOWE This is a very common name among those of British descent, and has been graced by men of distinction both in Great Britain and in the United States. The present family is said, however, to be of German origin.

(I) Abraham Howe, the first member of this family about whom we have definite information, may be the Abraham Howe who was a weaver, and owned forty acres of land in Derry township, Cumberland county, Pennsylvania, in 1779; nevertheless, this date seems too early. He married Barbara ———. Child, George, of whom further.

(II) George, son of Abraham and Barbara Howe, was born in Huntingdon county, Pennsylvania, July 11, 1823, died in Farmington township, Clarion county, Pennsylvania. He had come into Clarion county in 1837, and settled near Polk Furnace. From that place he removed, in the next year, settling near the mouth of the Piney river. In the year following that he went to Knight's Mills. Finally, about 1844, he settled on a farm in Farmington township. Here he was an industrious and successful farmer, a quiet, unassuming man, a good neighbor. While he was not active in politics, he was a Republican. In religious affairs he was prominent, and he was an elder in the Presbyterian church. He married Janette, daughter of Peter B. Simpson, who was born in Scotland; she died in 1904. With her father she had come to the United States; he settled in Farmington township, and there died. Fifteen children, including James, of whom further.

(III) James, son of George and Janette (Simpson) Howe, was born at Scotch Hill, Farmington township, Clarion county, Pennsylvania, May 22, 1856. In this township he was brought up and attended school, and he learned the trade of carpenter. He now lives at Grove City, Mercer county, Pennsylvania. While he lived in Farmington township he held the office of school director. He is a Democrat, and a member of the Presbyterian church. He married Jane Rea, who was born in Clarion township, Clarion county, Pennsylvania, August 8, 1856. Children: Margaret; John L.; Orin C.; George Jennings, of whom further; Edwin C.; James R.; Norris W., deceased; Mary W.; Jenetta; Florence; Ruth A.; Martha E. and Bertha, twins, Bertha, deceased.

(IV) George Jennings, son of James and Jane (Rea) Howe, was born in Farmington township, Clarion county, Pennsylvania, September 28, 1883. He was brought up on a farm and attended the public school at Scotch Hill, also for two years Grove City College. For one year he taught school. In 1905 he entered into mercantile business at Watterson, Clarion county, Pennsylvania, and from that time has continued in commercial life. His home and business are now at Showers, Clarion county. He is a Democrat. For seven years he has been postmaster. He married, October 23, 1907, Mary, born in Clarion township, Clarion county, Pennsylvania, October 8, 1877, daughter of Christopher and Elizabeth (Wynkoop) Thompson. Children: Jennings Bird, born August 13, 1908, died August 18, 1908; Ruth Elizabeth, born March 26, 1911; Mary Pauline, born February 5, 1913.

KUHNS Kuhns and Kuhn are names of prominence in Westmoreland county, Pennsylvania. The form Kuhns is varied with Kuntz in the same family. The Westmoreland county Kuhns family is possibly of Dutch but more probably of German extraction.

(I) Christopher Kuhns, the first member of this family about whom we have definite information, was born in Westmoreland county, Pennsylvania, died in Clarion county, Pennsylvania. To this region he had come at a very early stage in its settlement, and settled in Monroe township, on the farm now owned by the widow of John Curtis Kuhns. Whom he married is not known, but he had a son, John, of whom further.

(II) John, son of Christopher Kuhns, was born in Westmoreland county, Pennsylvania, in 1793, died in Monroe township, Clarion county, Pennsylvania, January 20, 1881. He married Margaret Ann Delp, born in Armstrong county, Pennsylvania, in 1800, died January 3, 1894. Child, Joseph, of whom further.

(III) Joseph, son of John and Margaret Ann (Delp) Kuhns, was born in Porter township, Clarion county, Pennsylvania, January 5, 1823, died in Monroe township, Pennsylvania,

February 11, 1895. On the death of his father, he received the homestead farm, where he lived and died. He married Amanda, born in Monroe township, March 14, 1834, now lives on the Kuhns homestead, daughter of Adam and Susanna (Drumheller) Kifer. Her father was born in Westmoreland county, Pennsylvania, in 1784, her mother in Luzerne county, Pennsylvania, in 1804; they were early settlers in Monroe township, Clarion county, Pennsylvania, where her father died November 26, 1856; her mother died March 10, 1874. Children of Mr. and Mrs. Kuhns: 1. John Curtis, of whom further. 2. Edwin Hallock, died February 19, 1893. 3. Clara Mary, married J. W. Gibson; they live at Oil City, Pennsylvania; children: Ethel F. and James Leen. 4. Harry, married Ida Lerch; lives at Sligo, Clarion county, Pennsylvania; children: Alda Madge, Ruth Irene, Ethel Ida.

(IV) John Curtis, son of Joseph and Amanda (Kifer) Kuhns, was born on the homestead farm in Monroe township, Clarion county, Pennsylvania, March 13, 1860, died September 28, 1906. He was brought up on the homestead, and attended public school. The homestead farm of one hundred and eighty acres came to him, and here he carried on general farming. He was a Republican. He and his family were Baptists. He married, in 1884, Sara Candace, born in Monroe township, October 1, 1864, living on the Kuhns homestead farm, daughter of Jeremiah M. and Mary Core (Kaster) Corbett. Her father was the son of Isaiah and Sarah (Fox) Corbett. His father spent most of his life in Clarion county, Pennsylvania, of which his mother was a native; in this county he was born, in Monroe township, in 1835; he received a public school education in Clarion county, and was a farmer and a veterinary surgeon, living in Monroe township; on his farm of sixty-five acres his son, John A. Corbett, now lives; here he died, August 24, 1874; his widow is living in Clarion township; he was a Democrat, and both he and his wife were Lutherans; they married November 5, 1863. Mary Core (Kaster) Corbett was born at Curllsville, Clarion county, Pennsylvania, May 30, 1842, daughter of John A. and Susanna (Lobaugh) Kaster. Her father was a native of Westmoreland county, Pennsylvania, born January 8, 1813, her mother of Monroe township. John A. Kaster had come to Monroe township with his parents, Philip and Susan (Fox) Kaster, who settled and died in this township. Philip Kaster was a miller; John A. Kaster was a farmer, a Democrat, and a Lutheran, but his first wife was a Presbyterian. Children of Philip and Susan (Fox) Kaster: Samuel, Jacob, John A., Catharine, Eliza, Mary, Christina. John A. Kaster married (first) Susanna Lobaugh, (second) Eliza Huey. Children, all except last named four by first wife: James Madison, died in the civil war; Jane Elizabeth; Mary C., married Jeremiah M. Corbett; Simon Harty; Nancy Catharine; Philip P.; Ellen; John, deceased; Hannah Belinda; Emma Agatha; Amos Mateer; Christina; Sarah; Susan; Lydia. Children of Jeremiah M. and Mary Core (Kaster) Corbett: Sara Candace, born October 1, 1864, married John Curtis Kuhns; John A., born March 6, 1867, farmer in Monroe township, married Caroline Swetky, and their children are: Charles, Sarah, Merle; Wade H., born September 21, 1869, lives at Spokane, Washington, married Julia Waters. Children of John Curtis and Sara Candace (Corbett) Kuhns: Mary Alice, born August 3, 1885; Clara, born August 21, 1887, died in infancy; Benjamin H., October 23, 1888; Margaret Amanda, August 15, 1890; Susan, March 9, 1892, died April 22, 1894; James Edward, July 7, 1893; Bessie Isabel, December 6, 1894; James Thomas, February 6, 1896; John Harold, April 24, 1898; William Wade, April 10, 1900; George Corbett, June 24, 1902; Sarah C., January 29, 1904.

BYERS This is a German name, which was found in Pennsylvania as early as 1740. The present family, however, is of later American origin.

(I) Charles Byers, the founder of this family, was born in Germany, died in Paint township, Clarion county, Pennsylvania. Having come to Philadelphia while he was young, he married, and settled in Center county, Pennsylvania, from which he afterward removed to Clarion county. He married Mary Glayhop, born in Germany, died in Paint township, Clarion county, Pennsylvania. She also had come to America in her early life. Children: Bastian; Anthony, of whom further; John, deceased; Margaret, deceased.

(II) Anthony, son of Charles and Mary (Glayhop) Byers, was born in Clarion county,

Pennsylvania, in 1852, died in Paint township, December 31, 1876. His schooling was received in Clarion county. He was a pumper in the oil regions, and farmed on the homestead, where he died. He was a Democrat. Both he and his wife were communicants of the Catholic church. He married Sarah Catharine, born March 28, 1856, daughter of James and Jane (McMaster) Coulter. Both her parents were born in Pennsylvania, and they were early settlers in Clarion county, where both died, her father at New Bethlehem, her mother near Corsica, in Clarion township. Children of James and Jane (McMaster) Coulter: John; Elizabeth, deceased; Sarah Catharine, married Anthony Byers; Ella, deceased; James. Child of Anthony and Sarah Catharine (Coulter) Byers, Charles Henry, of whom further.

(III) Charles Henry, son of Anthony and Sarah Catharine (Coulter) Byers, was born in Clarion, Pennsylvania, January 9, 1873. The place is now the corner of South and Fifth avenues, and was owned by Mr. Slick, but is now the property of Michael Henry. Charles Henry Byers was brought up on a farm, received a common school education and also attended Clarion Academy. At first he was a woodsman and saw mill man. On June 6, 1908, he graduated from the Veterinary Science Association's College, at London, Ontario, Canada, with the degree of Doctor of Veterinary Surgery. On September 1, 1908, he bought a farm in Monroe township, Clarion county, of one hundred and six acres; this he still owns and on it he built in 1909 a good house. Here he lives as a farmer, and he has a good local practice as a veterinary surgeon. He is a Republican, and a member of the Baptist church at Reidsburg, Clarion county. He married, June 15, 1897, Rev. Benjamin F. Delo officiating, Lyda E., born in Paint township, February 27, 1877, daughter of Abraham and Eliza (Wyant) Bish. Her parents were early settlers in this township, and her father died in 1900, her mother in 1899. Children of Charles Henry and Lyda E. (Bish) Byers: Amanda, born August 10, 1898; Grace, September 6, 1900; Kenneth, December 10, 1901; Emerson, September 4, 1903; Villard, October 11, 1904; Harold, February 9, 1906; Twila, October 7, 1907, died September 29, 1908; Evelyn, April 20, 1910; Olive, September 28, 1911.

DIXON In surnames not infrequently a diminutive form is used, and this is a frequent cause of the existence of two really equivalent family names. The present name seems to afford an illustration of this, for it is probably equivalent to Richardson. From the thirteenth century there has existed a Scottish border clan of this name, among whose members it is usually spelled Dickson. The present family is perhaps descended from James Dixon, of Scotch descent, who came from the North of Ireland to America about 1735, and settled in Lancaster county, Pennsylvania (as then existing). He had a son John, who was born in Ireland, about 1724, and died in Pennsylvania, in December, 1780. He again had a son John, who served in the revolution, and was apparently lost to his father's knowledge, as he made him a bequest, "if he ever returns." Yet he would probably have lived too early to be John Dixon, of whom further.

(I) John Dixon, the first member of this family about whom we have definite information, died in Clarion county, Pennsylvania. The farm on which he settled is now owned by his grandson, Harry E. Dixon. He married Eliza Layhlin, who died in Clarion county, Pennsylvania. Child, James A., of whom further.

(II) James A., son of John and Eliza (Layhlin) Dixon, was born on his father's farm, in Piney township, Clarion county, Pennsylvania, February 2, 1839. He is a farmer, and was a carpenter by trade. He is a Democrat. His church is the Lutheran. He married Lavina Jane, born in Piney township, May 20, 1845, died October, 1911, daughter of Michael Over. Children: William, Elinor, Effie, Harry E., Anna, Reynolds, Jane, Sarah, Over, Grover, Pearl, deceased.

(III) Harry E., son of James A. and Lavina Jane (Over) Dixon, was born in Piney township, Clarion county, Pennsylvania. July 7, 1869. He was brought up on the farm, and received a common school education. His farm is of one hundred acres extent. For a time he lived in Porter township, Clarion county, Pennsylvania, but is now living on the ancestral farm. He is a Democrat. At the present time he is township auditor; when he lived in Porter township he held the offices of school director and auditor. He is a member of the Lutheran church. He married, in February, 1892, Sarah, born in Monroe township, Clarion county, Pennsylvania, daughter of Adam and Philistin (Delp) Smith. Her paternal grandfather, John Smith, was one of the pioneers of Clarion county, Pennsylvania. Children: Raymond, born October 31, 1894; Mabel, December 28, 1895; Edwin, October 14, 1906; Iona, October 19, 1908.

BOWERSON

Paul Bowersox was born in Eastern Pennsylvania and in an early day came to Clarion county and settled in Porter township on the estate now owned by John L. Hines, whose wife was Mr. Bowersox's daughter. He was engaged in agricultural pursuits there until death called him, in 1877, aged eighty years. His wife bore him nine children, among whom was John, mentioned below.

(II) John, son of Paul Bowersox, was born in Center county, Pennsylvania, and he was twenty-five years of age when he came with his parents to Clarion county, where he was reared and educated. After reaching his legal majority he turned his attention to farming operations and bought a farm of one hundred and twenty-seven acres in Red Bank township. In politics he supported the principles promulgated by the Democratic party, and while he never aspired to public office of any description he was a loyal and public-spirited citizen and one who was ever on the alert to forward all matters projected for the good of the general welfare. Religiously he was a devout Lutheran. He married Mary Weckerly, born in Center county, Pennsylvania, daughter of John Weckerly, a pioneer settler in Red Bank township, Clarion county, Pennsylvania. Mr. and Mrs. Bowersox became the parents of seven children, among whom was Thomas Paul, mentioned below. John Bowersox's death occurred in 1906, and his wife passed away in 1909.

(III) Thomas Paul, son of John and Mary (Weckerly) Bowersox, was born in Red Bank township, Clarion county, Pennsylvania, December 9, 1857. He was educated in the district schools of his native place, and here has resided during the entire period of his lifetime thus far. He is the owner of a finely improved estate of one hundred acres, eligibly located eight miles distant from New Bethlehem. He has gained great repute as a breeder of Black Percheron and Canadian horses and he likewise breeds Guernsey cattle and Berkshire hogs. He manifests a deep and sincere interest in community affairs, and in politics is a stalwart Democrat. In 1886 Mr. Bowersox married Susan, daughter of Daniel Stahlman, and a native of Clarion county, Pennsylvania. Mr. and Mrs. Bowersox are the parents of six children: 1. Arthur W., associated with his father in the work and management of the home farm. 2. Gertie Belle, wife of George G. Weeter, a farmer in Monroe township, Clarion county, Pennsylvania. 3. Henry C., at home. 4. Blaine McKinley, at home. 5. Margaret R., at home. 6. Walter Ray, at home. Mrs. Bowersox is a devout member of the Methodist Episcopal church and in the faith of that denomination is rearing her children. The Bowersox home is one of great comfort and cheerfulness and it is widely renowned for most generous hospitality.

WALKER

The Walker family in Warren, Pennsylvania, is descended from old England stock, there having been several immigrants of this name coming from Great Britain to the new world during the early colonial period. Their descendants are scattered throughout the New England states and the middle states, and the name has been conspicuous in the history of the country both in colonial and later times. The name of Captain Richard Walker, immigrant ancestor of one of the most prominent branches of the family in America, is found on the records of Lynn, Massachusetts, as early as 1630, when he was ensign of the local military company. There is no doubt that he was of English descent. He was made a freeman in 1634, and his burial at Lynn is recorded in 1687. His descendants are to be found throughout New England, principally in Massachusetts, New Hampshire and Vermont. One of the most noted was the Rev. Timothy Walker, who became the first settled pastor of Pennacook, later known as Rumford, now Concord, New Hampshire. He was graduated from Harvard in 1725, and appointed to the pastorate of Concord some years later. His influence was a powerful one because of his ability and learning and his solicitude for the temporal and spiritual welfare of his flock. His son, Colonel Timothy Walker, was active during the revolutionary war and earned distinction in that struggle. From that time until the present the members of this line have ever been patriotic and eminent citizens.

Another immigrant from Great Britain of this name was Andrew Walker who, with wife and two sons, came from Londonderry, Ireland, in 1714, and settled at Billerica, Massachusetts. He was a descendant of the Rev. George Walker, rector of the parish of Donoughmore, and was one of the leaders of the besieged inhabitants of Londonderry in 1689. A man of great force of character, his descendants have been characterized by the same energy and strength of intellect. Another branch of the family was established in Providence, Rhode Island, in 1700, by Archibald Walker, who came from Scotland. His descendants are also to be found throughout New England, mainly in Rhode Island, New Hampshire and Massachusetts, though some have migrated as far west as California. Others of this name have come to America at various periods, have prospered and multiplied, and filled posts of eminence and responsibility in the history of the country within the last two centuries.

(I) John Walker, the immediate progenitor of the Pennsylvania family, was probably a native of Vermont, removing to Delaware county, New York, where he died at Hambletville, about 1866, being then eighty-one years of age. He located on a farm of eighty acres on Cold Spring creek, about one mile from the Delaware river, and was also engaged in the lumber business. A devout member of the Methodist Episcopal church, he was an ardent worker in its behalf and was especially interested in the work of the Sunday school because of his love for children. He was a man of generous build and of most amiable disposition. In public life he was an old line Whig, and was an able and enthusiastic politician. He married Betsey Styles, of Scotch descent and of an old Massachusetts family, and who died at the age of eighty-six years. Her father was in active service during the revolution. Children: Fayette, died at the age of eighty-one; Aaron Styles (see forward); Eunice, Betsey, Darius, Phoebe, Katherine, Esther, Leonard, a daughter, who died young.

(II) Aaron Styles, son of John and Betsey (Styles) Walker, was born on the old homestead in Delaware county, New York, in 1820. Early in life he was a farmer, but later became a successful stone mason. He became employed by the Erie Railroad Company, doing contract work for them, and about 1853 removed to Jamestown, New York, where he made contracts in his line of business for the construction of the Atlantic & Great Western railroad, which today is one of the main Erie lines. At the end of five years he returned to his old home and engaged in the wood business. At this time all locomotives used wood as fuel, and Mr. Walker furnished a large amount of wood for the Erie railroad, in the doing of which he cleared a large tract of land. In 1867 he came to Sheffield, Warren county, Pennsylvania, worked at his former trade, and built the stone work for the erection of the Horton & Crary tannery. For some time he resided at Stoneham, then removed to Warren, where he resumed his contract work. He took part in the Interstate or anti-rate war, and was a Democrat in politics, although never active in political affairs. He was reared in the Methodist Episcopal church, and died about 1895. Mr. Walker married (first) Elizabeth Hamblet, born in Delaware county, New York, daughter of Daniel and Phoebe (Underwood) Hamblet; she died at the age of thirty-five years, and was buried in Hambletville. Mr. Walker married (second) Betsey Lee, of Chautauqua, New York. Children of first marriage: Orrin Elliott, born 1847, married Loretta Whittaker, and resides in Topeka, Kansas; Stella Ophelia, deceased, married George W. Cogswell; Silas Ellsworth (see forward); Mary Ellen, married (first) Henry Palmer, and has a son, George C., (second) John A. Bell; Edward, a sketch of whom appears in this work. Child of second marriage: Elisha D., who is married and has two children: Wallace and Guy I.

(III) Silas Ellsworth, son of Aaron Styles and Elizabeth (Hamblet) Walker, was born May 11, 1851. Until the age of sixteen years he lived on the home farm, then came to Warren county and learned the trade of a plasterer and stone mason at Stoneham. He was thus engaged until 1876, when the oil excitement arose and he entered into the oil business, in which he was engaged for one and a half years, then, after one year spent in Bradford, he left there and entered into the meat business in association with George W. Cogswell. In 1880 he sold his interest in this enterprise and engaged in a contracting oil business in Clarendon. He was elected constable in the borough of Warren in 1883, and served in

1884-85-86. In the latter year he resigned from office and was appointed deputy revenue collector for Warren, Elk, Cameron and McKean counties, and served under the first administration of Grover Cleveland. He was recommended by Congressman W. L. Scott and was appointed under three different collectors. He served three years and ten months as collector of internal revenue. He again engaged in the oil business, in Cherry Grove, and then returned to the contract plastering business.

Mr. Walker commenced the publication of *The Democrat* in 1893, published it until 1903, then sold it to the Sibley Democrats, and August 13, 1900, commenced the publication of *The Times*, which is today the leading publication of its kind in the entire state, and occupies its own building, a fine brick structure. The paper was started by a stock company with $3,000, but has assumed dimensions of considerable magnitude, both as to value and influence. Mr. Walker has purchased and owns the entire stock of the plant, which is equipped with all modern and up-to-date facilities for the getting out of a daily paper. It is also published weekly. They produce a seven-column paper and use a Goss semi-rotary and linotype machine. It has a circulation of between thirty-five and thirty-six hundred. Mr. Walker built up this paper against strong opposition and deserves much credit for the enterprise and perseverance he has shown in this undertaking. The sheet is newsy and fearless, yet at the same time fair. He is a member of North Star Lodge No. 241, F. and A. M.; Occidental Chapter No. 235, R. A. M.; Warren Commandery No. 63, K. T.; Zem Zem Temple, A. A. O. N. M. S.; and the Benevolent and Protective Order of Elks.

Mr. Walker married, August 29, 1878, Cinderella Jane Dalrymple, born in Conewango township, Warren county, Pennsylvania, April 6, 1853 (see Dalrymple V). She was educated at the public schools and at Chamberlin Institute, Randolph, New York, and after graduation taught for several terms in Warren county. Since her marriage she has become one of the most prominent and influential women in this section of the state. She is active in every movement for the advancement of the interests of the county and the preservation of the old traditions. She is a member of Tidioute Chapter, Daughters of the Revolution, in which body she has served as vice-regent, and was one of the prime movers in the organization of General Joseph Warren Chapter, being a charter member. She was elected regent in this chapter, an office she is still holding. She was also one of the prime movers in the erection of the monument to the memory of the revolutionary soldiers, and to General Joseph Warren, and was chairman of the monument committee, and carried to completion the beautiful memorial. The funds were liberally contributed by the citizens of Tidioute and Warren and the country in general. Mrs. Walker is now taking an active part in raising the necessary amount to erect a fountain and beautify the park on the river front. She is a member of the Presbyterian church and of the Blue Stocking Club. Mr. and Mrs. Walker have children: Richard Orrin, born November 1, 1879, is associated with his father as a member of the editorial staff of *The Times*; Ross Aaron, also a member of the editorial staff of *The Times*, was born July 24, 1882, and married Nellie Walsh; William Allen, born August 29, 1885; Sarah Eleanor, born February 4, 1892, is a member of the Daughters of the Revolution.

(The Dalrymple Line).

This is one of the oldest and most famous of the historic families of Scotland, the name being prominent in the civil and military affairs of the country for many centuries. Among the most noted members of the family in the old country was James Dalrymple, first Viscount Stair, who was an eminent statesman and jurist. He was born in Ayrshire, Scotland, 1619, son of James Dalrymple, of Stair, and became the ancestor of many distinguished men. He was appointed judge of the court of sessions under Cromwell, having previously held the chair of philosophy in the University of Glasgow. He published authoritative works on Scottish law and, being exiled in Holland on account of his refusal to take the test oath in 1681, returned with the Prince of Orange in 1688 and was raised to the peerage as Viscount Stair. His son John became the first Earl of Stair, and was made secretary of state, incurring great odium by his complicity in the massacre of Glencoe, of which he was considered the chief author. His son John was known as the great General Dalrymple. He served as aide-de-camp to the Duke of Marlborough in Flanders, succeeded to his father's title as Earl of Stair, and later became commander-in-chief of the forces of Great Britain. He died without issue in 1747.

John Dalrymple, F. R. S., was a celebrated London surgeon and oculist, an authority in natural history, and died in 1852. Sir John Dalrymple, of Cranston, of an earlier period, was a famous Scottish lawyer and author, who died at the commencement of the last century. Alexander Dalrymple, an eminent Scottish hydrographer, of the same period, served in the East India Company and published charts of the sea. David Dalrymple, a celebrated writer and historian, whose title was Lord Hailes, published, 1779, "The Annals of Scotland," a work which Dr. Johnson highly commended. Members of this family have been eminent in many walks and have left their influence upon every branch of public life in the country which gave them birth.

(I) Andrew Dalrymple, the first of the family to come to America, was born near Drummerchut, Scotland, 1684, emigrated to Ireland, then to America, settling in Worcester county, Massachusetts. Children: John, Andrew, David (see forward), Sarah, Barbara, Polly.

(II) David, son of Andrew Dalrymple, was born at Belfast, Ireland, 1709. He emigrated with his parents to America in 1713, became a farmer in Worcester county, and died in 1807. He married Susannah Ellison, of Scotch descent, and his four eldest sons served in the revolutionary war. Children: William, born in Massachusetts, June 4, 1751; John Shepard, born in Massachusetts, September 15, 1753; Susannah, born September 27, 1754; Andrew, born in Massachusetts, September 10, 1756; Dorothy, born in Pennsylvania, May 25, 1759; David (see forward); Hannah, born January 10, 1764; Mark, born at Silver Creek, New York, December 29, 1769; Hercules, born at Silver Creek, October 3, 1771; Luke, born at Stockton, New York, June 6, 1773.

(III) David (2), son of David (1) and Susannah (Ellison) Dalrymple, was born in Pennsylvania, March 12, 1762. He was a soldier in the revolutionary war. He married Mary Corning; children: Hark, Mark, Luke, John, Barbara, Prudie, Annie. David Dalrymple married (second) Polly Richardson Fairbanks; children: William, Lydia, Ephraim, Corning (see forward).

(IV) Corning, son of David (2) Dalrymple, was born in Vermont. He came to Pennsylvania and settled at Yankeebush, in Warren county, purchasing a tract of land which he cleared and on which he resided until his death at the age of seventy-nine. He was married probably a little after 1820, to Polly Goodenough. Children: Truman, Alvina, Clorinda J., Richard William (see forward), Orrin, Lodema, Lavina, Austin (died young), and Austin.

(V) Richard William, son of Corning and Polly (Goodenough) Dalrymple, was born March 12, 1831, and died in 1876. He was reared on the farm, receiving such education as the schools of the day afforded. When thirty years of age he ventured into the oil business and built the first refinery in the Warren oil fields. Previously he had been engaged in the merchant tailoring business at Pithole, Venango county, which he sold out. After some time devoted to oil refining and boating it down the river, he disposed of his interests and entered upon the tobacco trade, having a store, and commenced speculating in oil. He was a member of the Independent Order of Odd Fellows, and of the Methodist Episcopal church.

He married, June, 1852, Sarah Jane Kitchen, born in Scotland, January 1, 1834, daughter of Alexander and Margaret (McLean) Kitchen, the name being a well known one in Scotland, where Alexander was a distinguished civil engineer and a graduate of the University of Edinburgh. One of his brothers was the Rev. James Kitchen, rector of a parish in London, England, and another is John Kitchen, a skilled iron worker. After the death of her husband, Mrs. Kitchen emigrated to America, bringing with her several of her children, and uniting by letter with the Presbyterian church in this country. Two of her sons became residents of Warren county, and the family is well represented in the present generation by several of the county's most esteemed citizens. Among the children of Mr. and Mrs. Kitchen were: Alexander, Margaret, James, John, Charles, William, Robert, and Sarah Jane, who married Mr. Dalrymple at the age of sixteen years, and died April 28, 1901. Mr. and Mrs. Dalrymple had children: Cinderella Jane, mentioned above (see Walker III); Eurial E., born July 2, 1855; and Burt L., November 30, 1869.

WALKER (III) Edward Walker, son of Aaron Styles (q. v.) and Elizabeth (Hamblet) Walker, was born April 21, 1856, at Jamestown, Chautauqua county, New York. He was an infant eleven months old when his mother died; and three months later he was adopted by his uncle and aunt, Mr. and Mrs. Alfred Greeley Hamblet. Mr. Hamblet and his wife, who was Betsey Mills, were second parents to the child, loving and caring for him as if he were their own offspring, and he grew to maturity under their wise guardianship as if he were indeed their son; they were father and mother to him in almost every sense of the word. In 1880 they came to Warren where they made their home; and where on April 5, 1891, Mr. Hamblet died, having been born November 23, 1809, near Montpelier, Vermont. His wife, whom he married on November 21, 1841, was born August 29, 1817, and died November 11, 1912, at the home of her adopted son in Warren.

Mr. Walker's first home with his adopted parents was at Hambletville, in Delaware county, New York; his primary education was received in the public schools of the village of Tompkins, after which he learned the trade of a shoemaker. He then adopted the vocation of farming, and also became employed in a lumber mill, thus beginning his business career. On April 17, 1874, he married and located on a farm, following agricultural pursuits for the following three years. On May 24, 1877, he came to Warren, Pennsylvania, and engaged in the oil business, being employed for four years in pumping on oil wells. In the year 1881 he became associated with his brother, S. E. Walker, in a patent medicine business, in connection with which they conducted a printing department. In this same printing office one of the daily papers of Warren today was first issued. In October, 1882, the brothers established the *Warren Sunday Mirror*, a four-page paper of four columns each; the venture was successful, and in 1886 the paper became a daily, and continued until April 5, 1895, when it was sold to W. J. McLaren.

In 1895 Mr. Walker began the business of manufacturing ice cream. He rented a room in the Steber block, beginning with the very humble method of a hand freezer, and retailed the product. During the winter season he added oysters to his business, and the place which he conducted came to be known as "an Oyster Bay." This was the beginning of the present excellent I. X. L. restaurant, one of the leading institutions of its kind in Warren today. In the spring following the establishment of this business, Mr. Walker sold out, and opened another establishment at No. 4 Water street, where he devoted his entire energies to the manufacture of ice cream, assisted by his wife and a boy; this continued until January 23, 1904, when his place was destroyed by fire. This did not check his ambition; he re-opened on a much more extensive scale at No. 309-11 Union street, the site of the business which he conducts at the present time. In 1905 this was incorporated under the name of the Walker Ice Cream Company, Ltd., the plant having a capacity of a hundred thousand gallons a year. In 1903 also he established a creamery at Akeley station, which he sold in 1906, and then another at Riverside, town of Kiantone, Chautauqua county, New York, in connection with which he conducted the Walker farm, well stocked with a fine lot of cows. In January, 1911, the Sugargrove Canning Factory and the Sugargrove Creamery and Condensed Milk Plant were also founded.

Mr. Walker has become one of the best and most prominent of the business men of Warren, distinguished for his initiative and excellent judgment in mercantile matters; he is a natural leader, never following in the footsteps of others or confining his dealings to antiquated and worn out methods; and in this way he has met with the success which so strongly characterizes his present undertakings. He has also become one of the most prominent citizens here in social and Masonic affairs, being a very active member of the Benevolent and Protective Order of Elks; he is chairman of the building committee in the erection of the beautiful Elk home now under way and nearing completion at the corner of Fourth and Hickory streets, and is a member of the board of trustees. He is also a member of North Star Lodge, No. 241, Free and Accepted Masons, Warren; of Occidental Chapter, No. 235; of Warren Commandery, No. 63; of Zem Zem Temple, Erie, Pennsylvania; Coudersport Consistory; Knights of Pythias; and of the Knights of the Maccabees. He belongs to the Presbyterian church.

On April 10, 1874, Mr. Walker married Frances Loretta Gray, born December 24, 1854, at Parksville, Sullivan county, New

York, daughter of Garrett and Lucy (Joscelyn) Gray. Her father was born at Parksville, having been a blacksmith at the beginning of his career, and later became a farmer in Delaware county, New York; he was a member of the Presbyterian church. His wife was Lucy Joscelyn, born January 27, 1829, daughter of David and Sylvia (Davis) Joscelyn. The Davises were residents of Beaver Kill, New York, the family having a revolutionary history. David Joscelyn lived and died in the state of Michigan; his children being: Halsey, Samuel, Nelson, Sarah, Lucy, Amanda, Agnes. The children of Mr. and Mrs. Garrett Gray, the parents of Mrs. Edward Walker, were: David H., Sylvia, Frances Loretta, Louisa, James, Augusta, deceased, Ernest, Clara, deceased. Mrs. Walker's grandfather, Dr. William Gray, who was of English descent, lived and died at Parksville. His wife was a native of Dutchess county, who lived to the advanced age of eighty-one, surviving her husband who died at seventy years of age. Among their children were: Benjamin; Daniel, who left home and was heard of no more; William; Isaac; DeWitt; Garrett, father of Mrs. Walker; Sarah; Margaret; Leah; Hannah; and another daughter who grew to womanhood and married.

The children of Mr. and Mrs. Walker are as follows: 1. Porter Romaine, born February 16, 1876; he is now a resident of Cleveland, Ohio, having formerly been a member of the company established by his father; he married (first) October 21, 1894, Gertrude Fay; they had two children, William I. and Elizabeth Gray Walker. He married (second) Virginia Flagherty, by whom he has no children. 2. Burr Raymond, born December 12, 1878; now a member of the Walker Company; he married Elizabeth Jane Cohn and has one child, Edward Cambridge Walker.

JORDAN Frederick Jordan, the first member of this family of whom we have any definite information, was of "Pennsylvania Dutch" origin and was born in Union county, Pennsylvania. In 1827 he removed with his family to Armstrong (now Clarion) county, Pennsylvania, and settled in Perry township, where he took up a farm of one hundred and twenty acres on the Allegheny river which is now called "Bartley farm." He married Polly ———. Children: Israel, referred to below; Barbara, married Samuel Barger, of Perry township; Katherine, married David Young; Mary, married Peter Fair; Sophia, married George McCoy; Manuel; David.

(II) Israel, son of Frederick and Polly Jordan, was born in Union county, Pennsylvania, March 3, 1818, and died October 9, 1912, in Perry township, Clarion county, Pennsylvania. He removed with his parents to Clarion county when nine years of age and grew up on his father's farm. He later purchased a farm of one hundred and forty acres on which he worked for many years, and during the winter seasons followed his trade as a shoemaker. He was a Democrat in politics, and a Lutheran in religion. He married Catherine Jordan, born in Union county, Pennsylvania, January 24, 1824, died in Clarion county, in 1892. Children: Polly, died aged eighteen years, unmarried; F. P., referred to below; twins, died in infancy; Sophia, died aged twenty years, unmarried; Eli, died aged five years; John, died aged three years; a son, died in infancy.

(III) F. P., son of Israel and Catherine (Jordan) Jordan, was born on his father's farm in Perry township, Clarion county, Pennsylvania, August 9, 1842, and is now living there. He received his early education in the public schools of his native county, and later worked as an engineer in the coal mines for several years, and then returned home and took up the management of his father's farm. He operated a saw mill on the place and in the woods of Clarion county for four years, and then devoted himself entirely to farming until he retired from active pursuits. He is a Democrat in politics, and served for two terms as tax collector of Clarion county, and has also served as supervisor. He is a member of the Independent Order of Odd Fellows. He married, January 2, 1872, Sarah Estella, born in Elk county, Pennsylvania, daughter of Samuel Sherwin. Children: 1. Samuel, born June 4, 1880; now a machinist in Blue Goose mines; married Ella Karns; children, Arthur, Francis, Mary Viola, Edna, twins, November 19, 1912. 2. Clyde, referred to below. 3. Calvin Henry, born September 23, 1885; now a miner in Black Fox mines; married Eva Everett; no children. 4. Bertha Viola, born December 6, 1887; married Harry Guiste, of Indiana county, Pennsylvania; children, Carrie and Frank.

(IV) Clyde, son of F. P. and Sarah Estella (Sherwin) Jordan, was born on his father's farm in Perry township, Clarion county, Pennsylvania, July 1, 1882. He received his early education in the public schools, and later worked for several years in the coal mines, and then for four years assisted his father and brother in operating a saw mill in the woods of Clarion county, after which he returned to farming on the old homestead in which he is still engaged. He married, August 17, 1910, Catherine, daughter of Reuben and Jane (Houss) Barger, of Perry township, Armstrong county, Pennsylvania. Child, Lester Harry, born July 30, 1912.

LOCKE It is probable that the Locke family is descended from William H. Locke, one of the first settlers in Lawrence county, and a miller by trade. He is supposed to have been born in Westmoreland county, Pennsylvania, and traced his descent to stanch German stock. He died in Lawrence county, Pennsylvania, at the age of sixty-four years. His son Thomas is mentioned below.

(II) Thomas, son of William H. Locke, was born in Lawrence county, Pennsylvania, and during the major portion of his active career was engaged in farming operations in Plain Grove township, that county, where his death occurred in 1844. He was a Whig in his political convictions, but did not take an active part in public affairs. His wife, whose maiden name was Sarah Fox, was a daughter of Peter Fox, a farmer who lived two miles north of Plain Grove, in Lawrence county. Mrs. Locke died in Leesburg, Pennsylvania, May 6, 1887. There were eight children in the Fox family, as follows: Joseph, married a Miss Warner, and they removed to Iowa, where both died; David, married Rachel Van Horn, both deceased; Michael, deceased; John, married a Miss Brian, both deceased; Catherine, became wife of Elijah Morrison, both deceased; Martha, married William Reicher, both deceased; Hannah, married Robert Blair; and Sarah, married Thomas Locke, as already noted. Mr. and Mrs. Locke became the parents of four children: 1. Mary, became the wife of William McCracken; children: William, married ——— Shaw, and he is a farmer in the vicinity of Leesburg, Pennsylvania; Adam, married ——— Crea, he is deceased; Austin, a farmer near Leesburg; also three daughters. Mr. and Mrs. McCracken are both deceased. 2. John, mentioned below. 3. David, lives near Slippery Rock, Pennsylvania; married Catherine Rodgers; children: William; John, married ——— Crees; Frank, married Hattie Shallowtree; Ray; Ernest; Catherine, married Ed. Crocker; Dora, married Harry Rodgers. 4. William, was a soldier in the civil war, and while in service contracted smallpox from which he died January 1, 1863. As the father of the above children died when the oldest was a child of but seven years of age, the widowed mother returned to the home of her parents with her family, and they were reared in the Fox household.

(III) John, second child of Thomas and Sarah (Fox) Locke, was born in Lawrence county, Pennsylvania, April 5, 1837. He grew up and was educated in Lawrence county, and at the tender age of fourteen years was thrown upon his own resources. He worked about as a farm hand until he had reached his seventeenth year, when he entered upon an apprenticeship to learn the trade of carpenter. He was engaged in the work of his trade until 1864, when he enlisted for service in the Union army as a member of Company E, One Hundredth Pennsylvania Volunteer Infantry. He participated in several important campaigns marking the close of the war, and won great admiration for his bravery and daring. Since the close of his military career he has been engaged in the farming business at Clintonville, Venango county, Pennsylvania.

In 1866, Mr. John Locke married Sarah Elizabeth Rodgers, a native of Lawrence county, Pennsylvania, daughter of Nathaniel Rodgers and Catherine (Boozell) Rodgers. Children: 1. Nathaniel, born February 6, 1867, died June 16, 1890. 2. Thomas L., born June 24, 1868; married Alice Hovis. 3. Harry H., born February 21, 1871. 4. Robert W., born February 6, 1874; married Elda Hovis. 5. Mary C., born June 7, 1876; married Frank Cannon. 6. James R., born February 10, 1885; married Sallie Cumings.

LUCART Helwig Lucart, the first member of this family of whom we have any definite information, was born in Washington township, Clarion county, and is now living in Clarion county, Pennsylvania. His parents emigrated to America and settled in Washington township, where they died. He received his early education in the public schools, and then engaged in farming, in which pursuit he still continues. He is a Democrat in politics, and a Free Methodist in religion. He married Martha E., daughter of William and Barbara Fellers, born in Washington township and died there. Her parents came from Westmoreland county and settled on a farm in Washington township and died there. Children of Helwig and Martha E. (Fellers) Lucart: Lillie, married W. H. Sliker; Barbara, married R. C. Glitzinger; John Webster, of whom further; Belle, married G. W. Frill; W. Elmer; Robert Pierce, resides in Aberdeen, Washington (1913).

(II) John Webster, son of Helwig and Martha E. (Fellers) Lucart, was born on his father's farm in Washington township, Clarion county, Pennsylvania, and is now living in Tylersburg, Pennsylvania. He received his early education in the public schools and then worked as a lumberman in the woods for twelve years, and then became a contractor in the oil and gas fields, in which industry he is still engaged as a producer. He is also interested in lands in Farmington township. He is a Democrat in politics. He married, October 24, 1906, Harriet, daughter of J. G. and Alice (Young) Wagner, of Warren, Pennsylvania. Children: Dorothea Claribel and Elton Wagner.

SMITH This name, as an English name, would be very common, for English names frequently represent occupations, and the occupations of smiths are necessary in any state of society, except, perhaps, the purely agricultural. But to this stream of Smiths of English origin, descendants of so many immigrants not related one to another, have been added others of German and of Dutch origin, with similar names, and the Dutch families, at least, have in some instances anglicized the name. It would probably be hard to find today any extensive section of the United States where Smith is not the most common of all names.

(I) John Smith, the first member of this family about whom we have definite information, was an early settler in Clarion county, Pennsylvania, having come from Maryland. Here he was a farmer. It is not known whom he married. Children, all deceased: Daniel, Jacob, Samuel, Elizabeth, John H., of whom further, Susan.

(II) John H., son of John Smith, was born August 26, 1808, died in 1887. He was owner of land, both in Clarion and in Jefferson counties, Pennsylvania, two hundred acres in all, and farming was his principal occupation. He was a Democrat. Both he and his wife were Lutherans. He married Hannah, born in 1812, died in 1870, daughter of George and ——— (Winner) Bashline. Her parents, both natives of Columbia county, Pennsylvania, settled in Monroe township, Clarion county, in 1824; there they lived on one hundred acres of land. He was a Democrat, and a member of the Lutheran church; she was a member of the German Reformed church. Children of George and ——— (Winner) Bashline: Philip, Samuel, Elias, Abraham, a Methodist Episcopal minister; George, Mary, Catharine, Susan, Lavina, Hannah, married John H. Smith. Children of John H. and Hannah (Bashline) Smith: 1. Isaac, a farmer; married three times. 2. Sarah, married David Kline; he is a farmer in Monroe township. 3. Elizabeth, married Josiah Hartman; they live in Toby township. 4. John Adam, of whom further. 5. Jeremiah, a farmer in Madison township; married Nancy Swan. 6. Jennie, married E. E. Henry; he is a farmer in Porter township. 7. Samuel, a farmer in Piney township; married Margaret Magee. 8. David W., of whom further.

(III) John Adam, son of John H. and Hannah (Bashline) Smith, was born May 11, 1848. His education was mainly received in the common school in Monroe township, but he attended also for about five months the old academy. His early days were spent on a farm, and he has continued to follow this occupation. At one time he was a director of the bank at Sligo, Clarion county, Pennsylvania. He is a Democrat. Both he and his wife are members of the Lutheran church. He married, February 1, 1872, Philista M., born February 25, 1855, daughter of Isaac Smith. She is not related to her husband. Her father was a farmer in Piney township, Clarion county, Pennsylvania. Children: 1. Sarah Jane, born in 1872; married Harry Dixson; he is a farmer in Piney township. 2. Mary Ella, born in 1874; married O. E. Barlett; he is a farmer in Monroe township. 3. Caroline, born in 1876; married John Hartman; he is a mason at Rimersburg. 4. Amos, born in 1878; mail carrier; married Maud Sayers. 5. Bertha, born in October, 1880; lives at home. 6. Stella E., living at home. 7. Adam A. Stella E. and Adam A. are graduates of the Clarion State Normal School, and are teachers.

(III) David W., son of John H. and Hannah (Bashline) Smith, was born in Monroe township, on the farm where his widow now lives, August 15, 1856, died April 11, 1900. He was brought up on the homestead farm, and attended the common school of the neighborhood. His land holding was of one hundred and seventeen acres extent. He was a Democrat, but never sought office. Both he and his wife were members of the Lutheran church, and very active therein. He married, December 24, 1878, Emma, born in Piney township, Clarion county, Pennsylvania, January 23, 1861, daughter of John N. and Susanna (Reese) Whitmore. Her grandfather, Jacob Whitmore, was a native of Germany, and one of the first settlers of Licking township, Clarion county, Pennsylvania, where he died; his wife, Catharine, died in Piney township. John N. Whitmore was born in Licking township, October 2, 1818; his wife was born April 30, 1831. They celebrated their golden wedding anniversary, and both were alive for several years after this. Their children: Alice, Sarah, James, deceased; Emma, Amanda Jane, deceased; Leila, Ida, Andrew, Elkanah, Edward, deceased; Charles, deceased; Arminta. One other (the oldest of all) died in infancy. Children of David W. and Emma (Whitmore) Smith: 1. Lillie Arminta, born February 22, 1880; married Robert Sweitzer; they live at New Bethlehem, Clarion county, Pennsylvania; children: Ralph LeRoy and Russell Eugene. 2. Myrna Susanna, born August 18, 1881. 3. Laura Edith, born January 8, 1884. 4. John Emery Orville, born October 9, 1886. 5. Alzora Gertrude, married Grover Dixon; child, Harold Smith. 6. Homer Audley, born August 1, 1892; married December 31, 1912, Lettie Sherman; they reside on the home farm.

HEETER This name is found in Berks county, Pennsylvania, as early as 1767, for in that year Adam Heeter was named in the proprietary return of Eastern District township. He does not seem to have been a landowner, nor was he among the taxables there in 1759, nor in 1779. Others of this name are found in Oley township in 1780, and in Exeter township in 1785. The Heeters probably belonged to the German immigration, which was so prominent among the formative elements of Pennsylvania, but to a rather late part of it, yet the name does not appear among the foreigners who took the oath of allegiance between 1727 and 1775. Finally, there was proved, in Berks county, March 17, 1806, the will of Adam Heeter; he names his wife, Elizabeth, and children, Benjamin, Adam, Jacob, Mary, Odilla, Magdalena; he disposes of one hundred acres of land in Earl, in that county.

(I) William Heeter is the first member of this family about whom we have definite information. He married ———. Child, George W., of whom further.

(II) George W., son of William Heeter, was born in Licking township, Clarion county, Pennsylvania, April 6, 1845. His education was received in public schools. For many years he has been a lumberman, and has been largely interested in the manufacture of lumber and in boat building on the Clarion river. He also owns several fine farms, about four hund'red and fifty acres in all. Since 1902 he has lived at Clarion, and his home is on Wood street. He is a Democrat. For four years he was county mercantile appraiser, and he has held many town offices. Mr. Heeter is a member of the Presbyterian church. He married Rachel A., born in Licking township, in 1851, daughter of William Bell. Her parents were among the early settlers of Clarion county. Children: Harvey B., Phoebe L., William Melvin, Linda L. All are living.

(III) William Melvin, son of George W. and Rachel A. (Bell) Heeter, was born in Licking township, Clarion county, Pennsylvania, April 9, 1874. He was brought up to the lumber business, on the Clarion river, and attended public school, also Rimersburg Academy. At first he was associated in business with his father, but since 1904 he has been in business by himself. Until 1909 he lived at Callensburg; in that year he came to Sligo and there he built a fine residence. Having sold this in 1912, he built another house, also at Sligo. He is a Democrat. At the present time he is serving a term of six years as school director in the borough of Sligo. He is a Presbyterian. Mr. Heeter married, September 27, 1900, Zoe Bell, born in Licking township, May 6, 1877, daughter of James and Louise (Reese) Over. Children: Evelyn Bell, George James, Carle Melvin.

BANNER Joseph Banner, the founder of this family, was born in Germany, about 1813, died in Paint township, Clarion county, Pennsylvania, in

May, 1864. After his marriage he lived for a time at Pittsburgh, and then at Bradys Bend, Armstrong county, Pennsylvania, finally settling in Paint township, Clarion county, where he lived on a farm and practiced the cultivation of the soil for the remainder of his days. He was a Democrat, and a communicant of the Catholic church. He married, in Pittsburgh, Pennsylvania, Kunegunda Heinlein, born in Germany, died in 1899. Children: Mary, deceased; Joseph; George, of whom further; John, deceased; Anna, deceased.

(II) George, son of Joseph and Kunegunda (Heinlein) Banner, was born at Bradys Bend, Armstrong county, Pennsylvania, August 17, 1849. When he was three years of age he was brought by his parents to Clarion county, and finally to Paint township, where he grew to manhood on the home farm and attended the public school. After arriving at years of maturity he soon became interested in the oil and gas business, in which he was a large operator during the remainder of his life. For about thirty years he lived at Clarion, Clarion county, and was superintendent of the Clarion & Tylersburg Gas Company for about eighteen years of that time. He was also one of the leading figures in the creation of the Home Gas Company, of which he was superintendent for a number of years. He followed the varying fortunes of this line of business into different localities, and one of the most successful of his ventures was the oil strike in the Miola field. He owned and lived in a fine residence at the corner of Fifth avenue and South street. While he never sought political preferment he was an ardent Democrat and took an active interest in matters pertaining to the party. He was a member of the Catholic Mutual Benefit Association, and at his death one of the oldest members of his branch.

Mr. Banner died suddenly February 8, 1913, of heart failure after an illness of several months. The funeral services were held in the Church of the Immaculate Conception of Clarion, of which he was for many years a trustee, and requiem high mass was celebrated by Rev. Father Deckenbrock, who officiated. The obituaries of the papers published in the town in which he had made his home for so many years testified to the regard and esteem in which he was held by all in the community. We quote from the Clarion *Democrat*:

Mr. Banner was one of the best and happiest dis-

positioned men in the community. He was a plain, frank, open-hearted man, affable, agreeable and courteous at all times, and bore the reputation of an honorable and just man in all his dealings with men. His children inherit a rich legacy in the name he left with them.

He married, October 15, 1872, Barbara Rebecca, born in Bavaria, Germany, October 27, 1850, daughter of Matthias and Barbara (Herman) Blissel. Her father and mother were both born in Bavaria, Germany, and came to New York in 1853; from that city they removed to Pittsburgh, whence after a short residence they removed to Freeport, Armstrong county, Pennsylvania. For a while after that they lived at Worthington, in the same county, and they finally settled in Clarion county, where both died in 1904, he in April, she in March. Children of Matthias and Barbara (Herman) Blissel: Julia; Barbara Rebecca, married George Banner; Mary, John, Catharine, Frances, George, Anna, James P. Children of George and Barbara Rebecca (Blissel) Banner: Bertha Loretta; Mary Josephine; Georgia Katherine; Mercedes Rosalie; Edward Henry, of whom further; Thomas Leo, of whom further; Edith Christine; Augustine Raymond, deceased.

(III) Edward Henry, son of George and Barbara Rebecca (Blissel) Banner, was born at Elk City, Clarion county, Pennsylvania, June 27, 1882. He was educated in the Catholic parochial school and took a further course in the Clarion State Normal School, graduating from its business department in 1900. Until 1906 he kept books for the Dietz & Mooney Hardware Company, at Clarion. For the next three years he was with the Pearl Glass Company, at Clarion, as assistant manager and secretary. In April, 1909, he entered into the plumbing business at Clarion, with his brother, Thomas Leo Banner, as his partner, under the name of Banner Brothers. During the same period he has been employed by the Dietz & Mooney Hardware Company as clerk. Banner Brothers own the building known as the Alexander Building, and during the year 1912 remodeled it. Part of the building is used as a newsstand. In political affairs Edward Henry Banner is quite active, and he is an upholder of the principles of the Democratic party. During the presidential campaign of 1912 he was county treasurer of his party. He is a member of the Catholic church.

(III) Thomas Leo, son of George and Barbara Rebecca (Blissel) Banner, was born at Clarion, Pennsylvania, September 13, 1884. His education was begun at the Catholic parochial school and continued at the State Normal School at Clarion. By trade he is a plumber. In April, 1909, he entered into partnership with his brother, Edward Henry Banner, to engage in this business at Clarion. He also is a Democrat. He married, November 29, 1911, Letitia, daughter of Charles and Mary (Staab) Maier, of Clarion. Both he and his wife are communicants of the Roman Catholic church. To them was born on February 3, 1913, a daughter, Beatrice Katherine.

McKINLY This branch of the McKinly family was found in the United States in 1833, settlement being made in the state of Michigan after a residence of a few years in New York City. The family was an important one, closely connected with the financial history of Pontiac, Michigan. While there is no connection traced between the McKinlys of Michigan and President William McKinley, they no doubt trace to common Irish ancestry.

(I) Andrew McKinly, born about the year 1800, spent his early life and married in the North of Ireland. In 1833 he came to the United States, living for a time in New York City, where a son was born in 1837; later he moved to Pontiac, Michigan, where he owned considerable land and became a prosperous farmer. His three sons on growing to manhood founded the banking house of McKinly Brothers, and for several years were a well known influential banking house of Pontiac. Later they transferred their interests to the oil regions of Pennsylvania, locating in Oil City, where they were important factors in the development of that section. In 1872 Andrew McKinly joined his sons in Oil City, where he continued his residence until his death in 1893. He married, in Ireland, Margaret Sproul. Children: 1. Charles, a member of the banking house of McKinly Brothers, of Pontiac, Michigan, and of the McKinly Oil Creek Petroleum Company; married Elizabeth Squires; children: Theodore, Charles, Roland and Minnie McKinly. 2. John G., of whom further. 3. Andrew (2), associated with his brothers in the McKinly banking and oil companies; married Irene Spaker; child: Lucille. 4. Margaret, married William Baines, of Pontiac, Michigan; child: Irene.

(II) John G., second son of Andrew and Margaret (Sproul) McKinly, was born in New York City, August 15, 1837, died in Oil City, Pennsylvania, April 27, 1886. He was educated in the public schools of Pontiac, Michigan, and engaged with his brothers in the banking business of McKinly Brothers until 1861, when attracted by the oil discoveries in Pennsylvania he came to Oil City. Here he engaged extensively in oil production, and with his brothers, Charles and Andrew, formed the McKinly Brothers Oil Company. This company was one of the largest producing companies of that section and owned some of the most productive wells in the Oil Creek field. He was a most capable business man and actively interested in many Oil City activities. He was deeply interested in politics, and a member of the Masonic fraternity, the Odd Fellows, and other well known organizations. He married, April 9, 1868, Carrie, daughter of John and Caroline Moore, and granddaughter of George and Margaret Moore, of London, England. Children: 1. Maud, married E. Z. Duncan. 2. J. A. Livingston, of whom further. 3. George, married Josephine Naggette; children: Edmund and Stanley. 4. Louis, married Flora Justice; child, Justice. 5. Grace. 6. Carroll, married Nellie Miller; child: Grace Eldred. George, Louis and Carroll McKinly were all liberally educated, and are members of the Independent Order of Odd Fellows.

(III) J. A. Livingston, eldest son of John G. and Carrie (Moore) McKinly, was born in Pontiac, Michigan. When young his parents came to Oil City, Pennsylvania, where he has since resided. He was educated in the public schools, later entering Colgate University, where he completed his education. After leaving college he engaged in the oil business and carrying forward the enterprises established by his father. He is a member of the Phi Gamma Delta, Beta Delta Beta and Theta Nu Epsilon fraternities, and of the Independent Order of Odd Fellows.

BLOSS Edmund Bloss, progenitor of the family by this name in America, came to Massachusetts before 1634, and his wife Mary, aged forty, and his son Richard, aged eleven, Bond says, in his "History of Watertown," came to join him in the ship "Francis," from Ipswich, in April of that year. He was admitted freeman at

Watertown, May 22, 1639. His wife died May 29, 1675, and he married (second) September 27, 1675, Ruth, daughter of Hugh Parsons. She died December, 1711, and at a meeting of the selectmen of Watertown, December 21, 1711, it was "ordered four gallons of wine also sugar and spice that Ruth Bloss (who lies dead) may have a decent funeral." It is said that Edmund was born in 1587, and died at a great age, believed to have been April, 1681. He was a grantee of five lots in Watertown. Among their children was Richard (see forward).

(II) Richard, son of Edmund Bloss, was born in England, in 1623, died August 7, 1665. He came to this country with his mother in 1634, and took the oath at Watertown, 1652. He married, February 10, 1658, Micael, daughter of Robert Jennison. His widow married, July 11, 1667, John Warren, and died July 14, 1713. Children: Richard (see forward); Mary, born December 11, 1661; Micael, born April 3, 1664.

(III) Richard (2), son of Richard (1) and Micael (Jennison) Bloss, was born December 7, 1659. He was admitted freeman April 12, 1690, and owned land which is now the old or lower graveyard at Waltham. He removed to Connecticut and was one of the original members of the church of Killingly, being admitted by letter from the church at Watertown, May 21, 1716. He married, September 26, 1688, Ann, daughter of James and Lydia (Wright) Cutler, of Cambridge Farms, now Lexington. Children: Richard, born January 25, 1700-01; James (see forward); Samuel, born February 26, 1704-05; Ann, born August 10, 1707, married, January 9, 1723, Isaac Jewett.

(IV) James, son of Richard (2) and Ann (Cutler) Bloss, was born November 3, 1702, died June 3, 1790. By his will recorded in Chepachet, Rhode Island, probated February 7, 1801, it appears that he was twice married, no mention being made of his first wife's name, and only the christian name of his second wife being given, viz., Sarah. Children by first wife: Abigail, married (first) September 30, 1749, John Younglove, (second) September 13, 1770, Ebenezer Atwood; James (see forward); Anne, married Ephraim Ellingwood, of Woodstock; John, married, March 9, 1758, Hannah Allen, of Pomfret. By second wife: Ebenezer; Job.

(V) James (2), son of James (1) Bloss, died at New Rochelle, New York, 1776. He married, June 8, 1756, Elizabeth, born 1733, died June 26, 1803, daughter of Jonathan and Mary Clough. After her husband's death she married ——— Kilbourne. Children: Elizabeth, born September 24, 1757; Joseph (see forward); Sarah, born 1762, died 1840; James, born March 27, 1764, died March 26, 1812, married, July 27, 1797, Rowena Kellogg; Salome, born 1766; Eliza, born November 30, 1769, married (first) ——— Harrison, (second) William Murphy; Anne, born 1772; died 1802, married Ephraim Hubbard; Jesse, born November 10, 1775, at Hebron, Connecticut.

(VI) Joseph, son of James (2) and Elizabeth (Clough) Bloss, was born September 29, 1759, at Thompson, Connecticut. Joseph and his brother James moved from Thompson, Connecticut, to Berkshire county, Massachusetts, about 1789, and established themselves there as merchants. Joseph afterward, in 1816, moved to Brighton, Monroe county, New York, and he was one of the founders of the Congregational church there, and at which place he died February 15, 1838. In the summer of 1776, while living at Hebron, Tolland county, Connecticut, he was called out to go to the defense of New York City, but his father, who was exempt from military service, arranged to substitute himself with his ox-team to be employed in the transportation of baggage. It was while in this service that his father died at New Rochelle, New York, in the fall of 1776. In November, 1776, Joseph was drafted for three months from Hebron, Connecticut. In 1780 he was a substitute for a Mr. Post. He was present at the execution of Major Andre.

He married, October 4, 1790, at New Canaan, Columbia county, New York, Amy, daughter of Andrew and Amy (Wentworth) Kennedy. Children: 1. Harriet Wentworth, born September 26, 1792, died March 20, 1865; married, July 7, 1836, Amos Graves. 2. William Clough (see forward). 3. Sarah Elizabeth, born December 15, 1797, died January 18, 1845; married, June 16, 1817, Samuel Olmstead Cogswell, and had: Polly Ann, born October 18, 1818, died October 7, 1856; Samuel B., born September 17, 1820, died in United States army, 1863; Henry M., born September 2, 1824, died May 19, 1846; Joseph Hubert, born September 2, 1828, was lieutenant-colonel of 150th New York Volunteer Infantry; Charlotte M., born April 23, 1833. 4. Amy Kennedy, born February 6, 1800, died April 4, 1806; married, April 8, 1823, Isaac Moore, and had; Jacob, born May 5, 1825, died June 6, 1831; Amy, born January 14, 1827; Frances, born October 22, 1828, died April 11, 1845; Isaac, born October 10, 1831; Mary, May 20, 1833; Jacob, December 28, 1835; Caleb, April 1, 1840, who was major of Eighth New York Volunteer Cavalry, and died March, 1869. 5. Joseph Bayard, born January 11, 1802, died March 24, 1883; married, April 2, 1828, Caroline A. Bush, and they had; Caroline Louise, born June 15, 1829; John Brown, December 1, 1830; Theodore Edwin, March 3, 1833; Edwin Charles, October 22, 1834; Harriet B., 1837, died 1839; Caroline Frances, born August, 1839, married W. H. McCourtie. 6. Olive Goodwin, born February 4, 1804, died February 5, 1869. 7. James Orville, born November 14, 1805, died December 4, 1869; married, November 11, 1834, Eliza Ann Lockwood, and they had: Sarah Louise, born August 4, 1835, died November 22, 1853; Henry Lockwood, born November 23, 1836, married Annie Moore; Charlotte Sophie, born September 16, 1838, married, March 25, 1868, Rev. James A. Daly, and had Grace Bloss, Merwin Taylor, Warren Cox; James Orville, born June 19, 1840, died November 23, 1847; Charlotte Finney, born January 9, 1842, died young; John Jay, born October 11, 1843, was quartermaster sergeant in Eighth New York Cavalry, and was killed in the battle of Winchester, Virginia, September 19, 1864; Celestia Angenette, born September 1, 1845, married, February 2, 1875, Louis P. Gage; James Orville, born September 30, 1847; Harriet Eliza, born December 28, 1849. 8. Charlotte Maria, born July 11, 1808, died June 20, 1885; married, February 3, 1836, Ezra Rosebrugh. 9. Theodore Edwin, born January 18, 1811, died February 4, 1811. 10. Celestia Angenette, born March 17, 1812; married, March 12, 1849, Isaac Brewster; she was principal of Clover Street Seminary, Rochester, New York, and a woman of considerable literary ability, having written "Bloss' Ancient History," a valuable textbook, also "Heroines of the Crusades."

(VII) William Clough, son of Joseph and Amy (Kennedy) Bloss, was born January 19, 1795, at West Stockbridge, Massachusetts, died April 18, 1863. He was a man of great strength of character, and for years previous to the civil war was prominent as one of the anti-slavery party, esteeming it no dishonor to be called a "Black Republican." He was also a person of deep religious convictions, and in his later years devoted himself to preaching to the prisoners in the jail at Rochester. For three terms, 1845-46-47, he was a member of the assembly of New York from Monroe county. He married, June 19, 1823, at Brighton, New York, Polly Bangs Blossom. Children: 1. Harriet Wentworth, born June 22, 1824, died October 16, 1825. 2. Elizabeth House, born June 24, 1826, died March 3, 1863; married, October 24, 1850, George C. Buell, and had: Edward Norton, born September 20, 1851, died May 28, 1870; Mary Blossom, born June 9, 1853; Paul Clifford, born September, 1857, died young; George C., born July 3, 1859; Elizabeth B., born February 19, 1863, died October 9, 1864. 3. Caroline Augusta, born September 6, 1828, married September 20, 1849, Charles H. Webb, and had: William Watson, born September 16, 1850; Charles Howard, born July 2, 1854, died October 23, 1859; Florence Elizabeth, born June 3, 1856, died October 15, 1859; Amy Caroline, born April 23, 1858, died October 24, 1859; Caroline Bloss, born February 1, 1872, died September 28, 1875. 4. William Wirt, born March 25, 1831; married, June 2, 1855, Louise Kate Skinner; they had: William Wirt, born October 7, 1856; Harry Hubble, January 10, 1860; Violet, June 11, 1869. 5. Henry Culver (see forward). 6. Joseph Blossom, born November 22, 1839.

(VIII) Henry Culver, son of William and Polly Bangs (Blossom) Bloss, was born at Rochester, New York, July 16, 1833, died in Titusville, February 15, 1893. He studied law and was admitted to the bar of Rochester, but followed it as a profession only a few years. Later he was admitted to the Crawford county bar. In 1865 he moved to Titusville, and in company with his brother, Major W. W. Bloss, founded the *Morning Herald*, the first daily paper in the oil regions. In 1883 he became sole proprietor of the paper, and sought always to maintain a sheet free from all innuendoes and aspersions. He was president of the common council and school board, and was interested in every measure which had at heart the advancement of Titusville. He was a graceful and accomplished writer, few excelling him when he set his well stored mind to the task, in producing an article tersely expressed and full of power. He was fond of art, and had a keen eye for the beautiful whenever he saw it. He was a lover of his country, and found pleasure in describing its future splendid possibilities. He possessed a warm and kindly disposition, and those who knew him best admired him most. He was a member of the Episcopal church, and a firm supporter of the teachings of the Master. He married, October 24, 1867, Sarah A. Mackie, of Wareham, Massachusetts. Children: Joseph Mackie, of whom further; Edward Buell, born October 21, 1870; Elinor Elizabeth, born July 19, 1873, died February 12, 1877; Mary Frances Wentworth, born March 2, 1878.

(IX) Joseph Mackie, son of Henry Cuiver and Sarah A. (Mackie) Bloss, was born at Titusville, September 24, 1868. He was educated in the public schools of Titusville, the high school, and at Cornell University, taking a course of three years and a half in that institution. At the death of his father in 1893 he took charge of the *Herald* as managing editor, and has continued since to conduct this paper. In July, 1903, he was appointed by President Roosevelt postmaster of Titusville, has served two terms in that office, and is now entering upon the third. He is a member of the Titusville Board of Trade, the City Club and the Titusville Country Club. In politics he is a Republican, in religion a member of St. James Episcopal Church, its vestryman and secretary. Mr. Bloss married, April 22, 1898, Lizzie Clark, born February 1, 1869, daughter of Charles O. and Elizabeth (Murdock) Rowe.

GILMORE This branch of the Gilmore family descends from James Gilmore, born in Ireland, who came to the United States about the revolutionary period and settled in Pennsylvania, living in Somerset, finally in Washington county, where he died. He had sons Joseph and John.

(II) Joseph, son of James Gilmore was born about 1775. He was a resident of York county, Pennsylvania, until his removal to Western Pennsylvania, where he settled on a tract of wild land lying on the line dividing Butler from Venango county. He cleared his land, converting the timber into lumber as far as practicable. He married, and had children: William, James, John, of whom further; Thomas, Jane and Maria.

(III) John, third son of Joseph Gilmore, was born October 5, 1804, died February 28, 1844. He became one of the prosperous farmers and business men of Irwin township, Venango county, Pennsylvania. He built the second grist mill in that section, and from the time of his settlement in Irwin township in 1832 until his death, was active in business and public life. He was appointed justice of the peace in 1840 by Governor Porter, and was holding that office at the time of his death. He died at the early age of forty years, but they were active busy years and filled with useful and honorable endeavor. He married Nancy Peters, of Mercer county, Pennsylvania, who died about three months after her husband, May 15, 1844. Children: Angeline, married Daniel Hoffman; Lucy A., married Craft Walters; Esther, married James Kimes; Eusebia, married Walter Hovis; Joseph; Alexander, of whom further; Jefferson, married Nancy Yard; William H., married Martha Walters.

(IV) Alexander, second son of John and Nancy (Peters) Gilmore, was born in Irwin township, Venango county, Pennsylvania, May 21, 1832, died August 17, 1888. He attended the public schools, and was his father's assistant at farm and mill. In 1870 he located near the mill, where his family yet reside, and continued in the milling business there until his tragic death eighteen years later. He was a good citizen and held in the highest esteem by his neighbors and patrons. His whole life was spent in Irwin township, where he ranked as one of the most enterprising men of the township. He was twice elected justice of the peace, and was holding that office at the time of his death. He was also county auditor and held several minor offices in the township. He took especial interest in the public schools and did all in his power to increase their efficiency. He was a Republican in politics, and in religious faith a Presbyterian, as was his wife. He met his death while repairing his mill dam, falling into the stream and drowning before rescue could be made.

He married, January 1, 1851, Nancy L. Shontz, born in Harmony, Butler county, October 9, 1833, and brought to Irwin township by her parents at an early age, and there died June 3, 1908. She was the daughter of Amos Shontz (see Shontz). His first wife was Catherine Latshaw, born in Lancaster county, Pennsylvania, her parents later settling in Harmony. Children of Amos Shontz: 1. Amos, deceased; married Mary Shuler, who survives him, a resident of Franklin, Pennsylvania. 2. Nancy L., of previous mention, wife of Alexander Gilmore. 3. Sarah, married Manson Brown, a farmer of Sandy Creek township, where they now reside. 4. Catherine, married Rev. Daniel Blakely; removed to near Kirksville, Missouri, where both died. 5. Hannah, married John Pryor, a farmer of Rockland township, who survives her. Also the following: Aaron, Sidney, Elizabeth, Christian, Ellen, Mary, Augeline, all of whom died unmarried; and Henry B. (half brother), of Sandy Creek township, Venango county, Pennsylvania.

Children of Alexander and Nancy L. Gilmore: 1. John L., now a miller, living at Barkeyville, Pennsylvania; married Mary Kinder; children: Keturah, deceased, married Charles Struthers, a blacksmith, Grove City, Pennsylvania; Lodema, married E. F. Atwell, a contractor, and resides at Grove City, Pennsylvania. 2. Amos, now a farmer and oil producer of Irwin township; married Ellen Yard; children: Clarence, a carpenter, married Sarah Osborn, and moved to Colorado; Sidney J., now a lumberman of Idaho; Lovella, resides in Franklin, Pennsylvania; Mary, married and removed to Colorado Springs, Colorado; Edward, resides in Irwin township, at home; Benjamin, deceased; Almeda, at home. 3. Elma E., married S. B. Hoffman, a farmer of Clintonville; children: Lilias, married John Phipps, an oil well driller of Clintonville; Sylvia, married Roy Hovis, an oil pumper of Clintonville; Caroline, married Henry Gelbach, a farmer and oil producer of Evans City, Pennsylvania; Catherine; William G.; Kelse M., at home; Burwell; Edith; Alexander C.; all deceased, unmarried. 4. Lysander Boyd, an oil well pumper of Irwin township; married Sarah E. Hovis; children: Zola, Selma, Buena (deceased). 5. Dr. William Grant, of whom further. 6. Catherine L., married Lewis S. Martin, oil producer, residing in Clarendon, Pennsylvania; child, Elma. 7. Meona, married G. B. Berringer, a farmer of Sandy Creek township; children: Beulah, married Harry Rice, a farmer of Franklin, Pennsylvania; Ruth; Georgie, living at home; Fay, unmarried, deceased. 8. Jefferson, died unmarried. 9. Alexander, died unmarried. 10. Elizabeth, married Thomas M. George, a machinist of Franklin; children: Thomas M., an infant daughter. 11. Margaret M., deceased, married B. F. Keefer, a furniture dealer of Emlenton.

(V) Dr. William Grant Gilmore, son of Alexander and Nancy L. (Shontz) Gilmore, was born in Irwin township, Venango county, Pennsylvania, March 8, 1864. He obtained his early and preparatory education in the public schools of the township, attending Grove City College. He then entered the Western University of Pennsylvania (now University of Pittsburgh) whence he was graduated from the medical department M. D., 1894. While attaining his college and university education and preparing for the practice of medicine, he taught seven years in the public schools. After securing his degree Dr. Gilmore located in Wesley, Pennsylvania, for a short time, then moved to Clintonville, where he was in successful practice for about ten years. In 1904 he located in Emlenton, where he is well established in public favor as a skillful physician. He is a member and ex-president of the Venango County Medical Society, member of the State Medical Society, and is held in high esteem among his professional brethren, and has the confidence of the entire community. He is an active Republican, and served as school director and burgess of Clintonville, also burgess of Emlenton. He is a member of Emlenton Lodge No. 644, Independent Order of Odd Fellows; Franklin Lodge No. 110, Benevolent and Protective Order of Elks; Oil City Lodge No. 68, Loyal Order of Moose; Emlenton Lodge No. 111, Knights of the Maccabees; Camp No. 6143, Modern Woodmen of America, at Emlenton; Central Encampment No. 206, I. O. O. F., Foxburg, Pennsylvania. He is physician for the Maccabees and Woodmen, and is an attendant of the Methodist Episcopal church.

He married, September 4, 1894, Sarah E. Beighle, born in Irwin township, August 17, 1871, daughter of Milton Beighle, born in Irwin township, where he died at the age of twenty-six years. He married Josephine Hoffman, born in Irwin township. Children: 1. Sarah E. (of previous mention). 2. Sherman M., an oil producer of Grove City, Pennsylvania; married May Berringer, and has a daughter Twila. Mrs. Josephine (Hoffman) Beighle married (second) E. F. Vogan. Their children: 1. Harvey W., a merchant at Sandy Lake, married Verna Gadsby, and has Roland, Alton and Paul. 2. James Martin, station agent at Raymilton, Pennsylvania; married May Davis, and has a son Edward. 3. Cassius Edward, a telegraph operator at Rock, Pennsylvania; married Myra Weber, and has a son

Charles. 4. David Earle, a physician, practicing in Emlenton, with Dr. Gilmore. 5. Guy S., a student living at Sandy Lake. The mother of the above mentioned children resides at Sandy Lake, Venango county, Pennsylvania, aged sixty-two years. Dr. Gilmore has no children.

(The Shontz Line).

The history of Dr. William G. Gilmore's branch of the Shontz family, as written by Ezra E. Eby, of Berlin, Ontario, Canada, is as follows:

(I) Jacob Shontz, a native of Switzerland, came to Montgomery county, Pennsylvania, in 1710. He had the following children: Esther, Susannah, Isaac, of whom further; Christian.

(II) Isaac, eldest son of Jacob Shontz, was born in 1748, died in 1802. He had the following children: Mary; Abraham, of whom further; Christian, Jacob, Isaac, David, Veronica, Samuel, Joseph.

(III) Abraham, eldest son of Isaac Shontz, was born in 1776, died in 1836. He settled in Harmony, Butler county, Pennsylvania, and had the following children: Moses; Aaron; Catherine; Isaac; Elizabeth; Lena; Amos, of whom further; Mary; David; Ellen; Nancy; Sarah; Livy; Abraham; Joseph.

(IV) Amos, fourth son of Abraham Shontz, was born August 23, 1814. On May 18, 1835, he was married to Catherine Latshaw, of Harmony, Pennsylvania, who died December 17, 1870. September 18, 1872, he married (second) Margaret Jane (Beatty) Swartzlander. He died June 7, 1884, aged seventy years. He had the following children: Nancy L., mother of Dr. William G. Gilmore; Catherine; Aaron; Sidney; Elizabeth; Christian; Sarah; Ellen; Amos; Hannah; Mary; Angeline; Henry B. (half brother), living on old homestead in Sandy Creek township, Venango county, Pennsylvania, where Dr. Gilmore's grandfather died.

DITZ John Ditz, the founder of the family in this country, was born in Germany and died in Clarion county, Pennsylvania, on his farm, which is now a portion of the town of Fryburg. On May 28, 1825, he emigrated from Germany to America and landed at New York City, then traveled overland by way of Harrisburg, Somerset and Greensburg to Clarion county, where he arrived October 4, 1825, and where, in 1826, he purchased one hundred acres of land on which he built a block-house and cleared a farm which he cultivated until his death. He married, in Germany, Magdalene Witzigmann, and among their children was Ferdinand, mentioned below.

(II) Ferdinand, son of John and Magdalene (Witzigmann) Ditz, was born in Reuth, Baden, Germany, February 26, 1810, died on his farm near Fryburg, Pennsylvania, August 28, 1881. He received his early education in Germany and in 1825, when fifteen years of age, emigrated with his parents to America and settled in Clarion county, Pennsylvania. He later purchased a farm of one hundred acres adjoining the land of his father and worked in the furnace of Jacob Black, at Shippensville, until he had paid for the land. He married in 1834, and in 1835 built a house on his farm which is still standing and later, in order to educate his children, he drove eighty miles to St. Mary's and engaged Magdalen Buchheid as a teacher and established a school which was later removed to the basement of the church. In 1849 he built a hotel on the westerly portion of his land which he conducted until it was destroyed by fire May 12, 1879. He married, April 9, 1834, Franceska, born in Germany June 22, 1808, died August 4, 1903, daughter of Jacob Eisenman (see Eisenman). Their marriage was the first solemnized in Fryburg. Children: 1. Mary, born 1836, died at Fryburg, Pennsylvania, aged seventy years; married (first) Killean Aulbach, (second) Joseph Buechner. Children: i. Herman, born June 20, 1857; resides at Fryburg, unmarried. ii. Frank, died about 1898; was educated for a priest, and was a member of the Brotherhood of Xavier, at Baltimore, Maryland. iii. Rosa, born 1860, died young. iv. Lena, born 1862, married a Mr. Mayer. v. Lizzie, born 1864, resides at Fryburg in 1913, unmarried. 2. Walburga, deceased, born about 1838; married George Strubler, deceased. Children: i. Elizabeth, married Nathaniel Malrich; children: Mary, married a Mr. Reedy and resides at Oil City, Pennsylvania; Frank, Stella, Anthony, Anna, Elizabeth, John, deceased. ii. Joseph, died in 1898; married Lizzie Siegel, resides at Oil City; children: Beatrice, Elizabeth, Agnes. iii. John, resides at Pittsburgh; married Laura Lampman; children: Harry and Lawrence. iv. Frances, a sister in St. Benedictine Convent, died there. v. Anna, a sister in St. Benedictine Convent, died there. vi. Alfred, resides at Oil City, unmarried. vii.

PENNSYLVANIA

Frank, unmarried. viii. George, Jr., resides at Oil City; in the hotel business. 3. Caroline, deceased, born about 1840; married Patrick Graham, deceased. Children: i. Joseph, married Josephine Keener. ii. Walter, married Stella Ormiston. iii. Augustin, unmarried. iv. Francis, unmarried. v. Agnes, unmarried. 4. Augustin, mentioned below. 5. Veronica, born 1846; married Joseph Bauer. Children: i. Augustin, married Lottie Weaver, one child. ii. Frank, unmarried. iii. Carrie, unmarried. iv. Bertha, unmarried. v. Ferdinand, unmarried. vi. Edward. vii. Andrew. viii. Anthony. ix. Mary. x. Joseph.

(III) Augustin, son of Ferdinand and Franceska (Eisenman) Ditz, was born in Fryburg, Pennsylvania, January 18, 1844, died there September 27, 1897. He received his early education in the Roman Catholic parochial schools and in private schools of Fryburg, and then entered the hotel business with his father in which he continued until his death. He also owned and cultivated a farm. He married (first) November 21, 1871, Agnes, daughter of John and Mary (Fogelbacher) Seth, born at Lucinda Furnace, Clarion county, died in Fryburg, March 17, 1878. He married (second) May 6, 1884, Mary Magdalene, daughter of Lawrence and Mary Magdalene (Leicht) Songer. Mrs. Ditz's grandfather was born in Germany and emigrated to America, being one of the pioneer settlers of Limestone township, Clarion county, and her father was born in Shannondale and died in Corsica, February 4, 1901. Her mother, Mary Magdalene Leicht, was born in Holshonse, Germany, March 15, 1826, and died March 29, 1902. In 1849 she came to America with her parents, locating at Shannondale, Pennsylvania, where in 1850 she married Lawrence Songer, who was born at Shannondale, August 9, 1825. He remained there until 1856, when he and his family removed to a farm near Corsica, Pennsylvania, and here engaged in the lumber business and farming until his death February 4, 1899. Children of Lawrence and Mary Magdalene (Leicht) Songer: 1. Catherine, born September 24, 1851, died August 2, 1864, of diphtheria. 2. Peter, born October 28, 1853, died August 8, 1864, of diphtheria. 3. Theresa, born February 18, 1855, died July 30, 1864, of diphtheria. 4. Mary Magdalene, born October 15, 1856, became the wife of Augustin Ditz, as noted above. 5. Caroline, born April 10, 1858, died August 7, 1864, of diphtheria. 6. Elizabeth, born April 13, 1860, died August 5, 1888. 7. Edward, born May 6, 1863, died August 11, 1864, of diphtheria. 8. Francis Albert, born March 14, 1865; married Cecelia Aaron and lives on the old homestead. 9. and 10. Twins, Sarah Ann and Veronica, born February 16, 1867; Sarah Ann died February 26, 1897, and Veronica married Harry Aaron, of Kingsville, Pennsylvania, a farmer of that place, and they are now (1913) the parents of seven children. 11. Charles Gabriel, born February 14, 1869; he married Ann Newhouse and has three children. He is engaged in the lumber business at Tionesta, Pennsylvania. 12. Lewis Edward, born March 23, 1871; married Catherine Green and has five children; they live at Marienville, Pennsylvania. 13. John, born March 28, 1873; married (first) Rose O'Neil, by whom he had five children, married (second) Josephine Aaron, by whom he has one child; he is superintendent of the steel mills at South Sharon, Pennsylvania. Children of Augustin Ditz (two by first marriage): 1. Anthony F., born June 1, 1873; resides in Cleveland, Ohio; married Anna Curry; children: Augustin, Alice Margaret, Helen, and a son, name unknown. 2. Mary F., born October 10, 1875; resides in Fryburg; married George Fletcher, engaged in the drug business; children: Antoinette, Mabel, Catharine, Alvis, Marie. 3. George A., mentioned below. 4. Aloysius A., born May 17, 1886. 5. Leo M., born October 5, 1887. 6. Frances E., born December 31, 1888. 7. Michael V., born April 5, 1890. 8. Edward L., born October 14, 1891. 9. Irene V., born January 7, 1894.

(IV) George A., son of Augustin and Mary Magdalene (Songer) Ditz, was born in Fryburg, Pennsylvania, February 12, 1885, and is now (1913) living there. He received his early education in St. Michael's parochial schools and later graduated from Holy Ghost College, now Duquesne University, at Pittsburgh, Pennsylvania, and then returned to Fryburg where he took up the cultivation of the old homestead farm, and the management of a large hotel which was built on the property by his father in 1870, and he still continues in those occupations. He is also interested in lumber and gas businesses, and was one of the organizers of the First National Bank of Fryburg, being now cashier and one of the directors of that institution. He is a Democrat in politics. He is president of the Knights of St. George, and was the first president of the branch of the society at Fryburg. He is a Roman Catholic in religion. Mr. Ditz is unmarried.

(The Eisenman Line).

(I) Jacob Eisenman, the founder of the family in this country, was born in Baden, Germany, died in Clarion county, Pennsylvania. He emigrated to America in 1820, and settled near what is now the town of Fryburg where he bought and cultivated a farm of two hundred and sixty acres, a portion of which he later gave to the Roman Catholic church and on which the first church building of that faith in the section was erected, the congregation worshipping in his house until the building was completed. His wife's name is unknown. Children: Jacob; Lambert, mentioned below; Joseph; Barbara; Franceska, married Ferdinand Ditz, referred to above.

(II) Lambert, son of Jacob Eisenman, was born in Germany, died in Fryburg, Pennsylvania. He emigrated to America with his parents, was brought up on his father's farm and later conducted a hotel in Fryburg for many years. He was a Democrat in politics, and a Roman Catholic in religion. He married Catherine Fasenmyer, born in Germany, died in Fryburg. Children: Edward, referred to below; Helen; James, now living in Pittsburgh; Mary Agatha; Francis; Balser; Luke; Veronica; Mary; Catherine; Lambert.

(III) Edward, son of Lambert and Catherine (Fasenmyer) Eisenman, was born on his father's farm near Fryburg, Pennsylvania, June 30, 1841, and is now (1913) living in Washington township, Clarion county, Pennsylvania. He received his early education in the Roman Catholic parochial schools and later engaged in farming in which occupation he still continues. He has developed several oil and gas wells on his property. He married May 10, 1864, Magdalina, born in Lucinda Furnace, Clarion county, June 22, 1841, died July 9, 1911, daughter of John and Mary (Fogelbacher) Seth. Children: Agnes, born April 3, 1865; Clara, born June 9, 1867; Constance; Albert, born February 3, 1871; Frank, born March 14, 1873; Joseph, born March 21, 1875; Anna Mary, born September 2, 1876; Christiana, born January 13, 1880.

McKINLEY James McKinley moved on a tract of land settled by John Donaldson, who was followed by Judge Robert Mitchell, from whom Mr. McKinley purchased in 1834, in Irwin, now Clinton township, was a farmer after coming to this place, but had previously been a carpenter and cabinet-maker. He was born in 1792 and died in 1872, at the age of eighty years. He lived for a while in Beaver county, then in Ohio, coming to Irwin township in Venango county in 1834. In politics he was first a Whig and afterward a Republican, growing to be a man of considerable prominence, and serving as school director in Irwin and Clinton townships. He belonged to the Associated Presbyterian (afterward the United Presbyterian) church, and was a member of session from 1851 until the time of his death. He married Elizabeth McKelvey, and had the following children, all of whom, as well as himself and wife, are now deceased: 1. Mary, married Thomas Baird; children: James, Cyrus, Jefferson, and Calvin. 2. Martha, married Robert Weakley, who is also deceased; no children. 3. John, married (first) a Miss Orr, (second) Elizabeth Moore; he had children by both marriages. 4. James, married twice, his second wife having been a Miss Reimold; the children by this latter marriage were: Elizabeth, married Frank Wiandt; Philip M. and James C. 5. Marvin, married Mary A. Moore, who survived him and now lives in Clinton township; no children. 6. Nathaniel, twin brother of Marvin, who is mentioned further.

(II) Nathaniel, son of James and Elizabeth (McKelvey) McKinley, was born October 26, 1826, in Beaver county, Pennsylvania, where he passed the first two years of his life. He then lived in Ohio until he was eight years of age, when coming to Venango county he remained for the rest of his life in this place. Here he attended the public schools in his youth, and at the conclusion of his studies became a farmer, which vocation he followed until his death. He was a Republican in politics, but never an office holder; he was a sober and respected citizen, living a useful and upright life. He was noted as never having used tobacco in any form, and died September 12, 1881. He married Catherine Daugherty, born June 1, 1825, in Indiana county, Pennsylvania, daughter of William and Elizabeth (Lewis)

Daugherty, whose children were: Anna, died unmarried at the age of eighty-two; Rachel, also died unmarried; Catherine, became Mrs. McKinley; Mary, died unmarried; William, died unmarried when over seventy-nine years of age; Mrs. Daugherty lived to be eighty-four years old, dying in 1871. Mr. and Mrs. McKinley were both members of the United Presbyterian church, of which Mr. McKinley was a trustee for several years; Mrs. McKinley died December 18, 1912. Children: Samuel, died in infancy; H. John, of further mention.

(III) H. J. McKinley, son of Nathaniel and Catherine (Daugherty) McKinley, was born May 21, 1860, in Clinton township, near Clintonville, Pennsylvania, and here his early life was passed, attending the public schools of the township off and on between the ages of seven and eighteen years. He then entered Clintonville Academy, where he remained five terms; after which he attended Grove City College for one term, and then finished his educational career by a course in civil engineering with the International Correspondence Schools of Scranton, Pennsylvania. During his early career he taught school for a while, and also worked on the farm; he then devoted his attention to surveying, in which profession he has been engaged for the past nineteen years with marked success. He was county surveyor for nine years, and has been township auditor at different times for several years. On May 1, 1910, he was commissioned justice of the peace for a six year term, and is now serving in that capacity; he is a Prohibitionist in his political belief. Mr. McKinley is a member of the Engineering Club of Venango county, and belongs to the United Presbyterian church of Clintonville.

Mr. McKinley is the only living descendant of his family on the maternal side, though his mother's parents had six children in all. On July 10, 1884, he married Miss H. Lissa Schrefler, of Barkeyville, Venango county, Pennsylvania.

DALE The Dales came from England to the American colonies at an early period, settling in New England, Virginia and Pennsylvania. The inference is that the Virginia and Pennsylvania families were related. Bishop Meade in his "Old Churches, Ministers and Families of Virginia," says, "I must not forget to mention among the families of Norfolk county, that of Dale, an ancient and respectable one of this and surrounding counties."

Winfield Dale, a "respectable shipwright" of Portsmouth, Norfolk county, Virginia, was the father of Commodore Richard Dale, born in Norfolk county, November 6, 1756, the famous naval hero who fought as first lieutenant with John Paul Jones and was the first Yankee to leap aboard the "Serapis," where he received the sword of the British Captain Pearson.

(I) The earliest ancestor of the Tionesta family of whom record is found, is Christian Dale, of Northampton and Center counties, Pennsylvania. He is believed to be the first of his branch in this country, and on first coming settled in Northampton, where his children were born. He was one of the first settlers in the Buffalo Valley of Center county, obtaining and clearing a farm near Lewisburg. In 1790 he moved to the end of Nittany Mountain, and in 1796 erected a grist and saw mill. These he willed to his son Felix. The name of his wife is not known. His children were: Henry, of whom further; Philip; Felix; Frederick; Mary, married Nicholas Straw; Eve, married Peter Earhart; Rachel, married Louis Swinehart; and Christian, who moved with his brother Frederick to Ohio. Christian Dale, the father, died in Ferguson (now Harris) township, July, 1805.

(II) Henry, eldest son of Christian Dale, was born in Northampton county, 1758, died in Harris township, Center county, March, 1844. He was a farmer of Center county, and served in the revolution, fighting at Trenton and Princeton. In the year 1800 he built a large stone house on the road between Lamont and Oak Hall. He lived to be eighty-six years of age, and was very well to do. He married and left male issue.

(III) Rev. Joseph Dale, son of Henry Dale, was born in Center county, Pennsylvania, 1786, died 1814. He was reared on the farm, obtained a good education, and became a minister of the Methodist Episcopal church. He was at one time superintendent of an iron foundry and works at Bellefonte, Center county, but died at the early age of twenty-eight years. He married Mary Gates, born 1789, died 1872, daughter of Thomas, son of Henry Gates, of an early Pennsylvania family. After the death of her husband she joined her own family in western Pennsylvania (now Forest county), making the long and perilous journey in wagons with her small children. The family home was for several years in a log cabin, but with the aid of her sons all difficulties were surmounted and she lived to see her two sons and daughter grow to be honored members of their community. For a long time prior to the termination of her years, eighty-three, she was tenderly and lovingly cared for by her children, whom she had always shown the example of a Christian life of self-sacrifice and devotion. Children, all born in Center county: 1. John A., November 14, 1808; educated in the public school of Venango (now Forest) county, and for several winters taught school. He also studied medicine, but was never in regular practice. In 1835 he began merchandising in Tionesta, and in 1847 was elected sheriff of Venango county, and later was appointed prothonotary of the county to fill a vacancy. He was active in the formation of Forest county and the selection of Tionesta as the county seat. In 1867 he was appointed associate judge, and filled many positions of trust in the new county. From 1870 he was connected with the Atlantic & Great Western railroad, and until his death, June 25, 1877. He was an honored member of the Masonic order, and was buried with Masonic ceremonies. He married (first) Jane E. Richardson, of Kittanning, Pennsylvania. He married (second) in 1852, Elizabeth E. Watson, who survived him. She was a sister of Lewis F. Watson, who was United States congressman for several terms. Children, all by first wife: Mary Elizabeth, deceased, married Ephraim Davis; James H., deceased; Ellen, married David Hays, deceased, whom she survives, living in Arkansas; Florence, married L. Ross Freeman, a capitalist of Warren; Gertrude, married W. A. Graves, whom she survives, living in Warren. 2. Susan, married William McClatchey; both deceased; children: John, now living in Crawford county; Eliza, deceased, married Mr. Mitchell; Emma, married Mr. Hull, and lives in Iowa; Samuel, now living in Crawford county; Joseph, lives in Kansas; William, resides in New York City. 3. Joseph Gates, of whom further. 4. A son, who died soon after the removal to Venango county.

(IV) Hon. Joseph Gates Dale, son of Rev. Joseph and Mary (Gates) Dale, was born in Center county, Pennsylvania, near Bellefonte, May 15, 1815, died in 1898. He was but one year of age when his widowed mother made the journey from Center county to the home of her father, Thomas Gates, in Venango (now Forest) county. She remained there a few years, then moved to a small improved tract near the mouth of the creek, now known as the Kiser farm. Here the lad spent his boyhood days, becoming familiar with the hardest work and learning all the secrets of the forest and stream. The country at that time was densely covered with timber; even the site of the present borough of Tionesta was covered with a thick growth of hickory, walnut and butternut timber. There were no roads, and the only method of travel was by canoe in summer and over the frozen river in winter. Those possessing horses could travel on horseback after trails were broken, and in this way the old doctors traveled to minister to their widely scattered patients. Amid the rudest possible surroundings he grew to manhood, absorbing all knowledge that it was possible to obtain from the early schools. At the age of fifteen he began working in the lumber works, logging, and later rafting the logs to market. He continued lumbering eight years, and at the age of twenty-one years was appointed lieutenant of militia by Governor Ritner. Two years later, in 1838, he used the little capital he had accumulated and opened a small general store, continuing in successful operation as a merchant for seven years. He then sold out, investing his capital in the lumber business, a line of activity he continued during the greater part of his long and active business life. He was one of the prominent lumber men of the region, and later, after the discovery of oil, he became a large producer, opening his first well on the Blood farm, on Oil creek. Later he purchased the Ball farm, near Pithole, paying therefor $105,000. In the balmy days of Pithole he was a director of the Pithole Valley Railroad Company, the only railroad that ever entered that bubble city. From 1865 to 1873 he was the principal owner of a savings bank in Tionesta, and was the leading business man of the village. He was largely instrumental, in connection with his brother John A., in securing the removal of the county seat from Marionville to Tionesta, and gave much time to the public service. He was postmaster of Tionesta for several years under President Lincoln, resigning in 1867. Under President Johnson he held the position of internal revenue collector, and for five years was associate judge of Forest county. In his conduct of public business he used the same cautious energy as in his private affairs, and was a model public official. He was originally a Whig in politics, later a Republican, but at one time united with the Greenback party as a protest against some of the wrongs he felt were being inflicted upon the people. For three years he owned and published the *Forest Republican*, for many years the only Republican newspaper published in Forest county. He joined the Independent Order of Odd Fellows in 1853. He was a most capable man of affairs, of clear judgment, quick insight, and always had the courage of his convictions. His ruling trait was kindliness of heart and many were his benefactions.

During the eighty-two years spent in Forest county he saw the great changes that time wrought, and could feel a just pride in the fact that he bore a man's part in the great development, settlement and upbuilding of a prosperous community. In the winter of 1897 he wrote and published in the *l'indicator* a history of Tionesta, from which we learn that "Indians were very numerous here at that time along the creek and river, in the summer time, fishing and killing deer. Game of all kinds was plentiful, especially deer, and wolves could be heard howling every night." These conditions he helped to change, replacing the forest with well cultivated farms and prosperous villages, railroads, churches, schools, banks, and all the comforts of modern life. The many positions of honor and trust he filled were well filled, as on a good public school education he built a world of knowledge gained by a lifetime of study and close observation. His library, comprising hundreds of volumes, was not ornamental, but each volume bore evidence of the devotion of its owner to reading and study. As associate judge he was dignified and just to all. He was held in high esteem by his brethren of the fraternities to which he belonged, and as the last mark of respect they could show, buried him with fraternal ceremonies. He took an active interest in the social life about, and was concerned always in all that tended to the betterment of his town and country. His kindly disposition and open, generous, genial nature endeared him to all, and at his funeral there was a great gathering of all ages and conditions of life. He arranged for his funeral, wishing no display, asked that the fifteenth chapter of First Corinthians be read and prayer offered at the house, and that the Odd Fellows have charge of the ceremonies at the cemetery, which was done. In religious faith he was a Universalist.

Mr. Dale married, December 24, 1840, Nancy Agnes Holeman, born at Holeman's Flats, three miles from Tionesta, on the Allegheny river, September 14, 1822, daughter of Alexander and Clarissa (Sexton) Holeman (see Holeman).

Mrs. Dale survives her husband, and in November (1912) is living at Tionesta, enjoying excellent health, although ninety years of age. On December 24, 1890, Mr. and Mrs. Dale celebrated the fiftieth anniversary of their wedding day, and at their home in Tionesta received the congratulations of a very large number of relations and friends. Not until eight years later was this lifetime association sundered by the death of Mr. Dale. She is a member of the Presbyterian church. Children: 1. Belle M., married Colonel Jacob H. Dewees; children: i. Jacob Dale, born November 5, 1867, married Kate Kingsley, and lives in Salem, Ohio; they have a son, Alexander Harry, born November 5, 1890, married, November 29, 1911, Nina Fairfield, and resides in Cleveland, Ohio; ii. Joseph Dale, born June 2, 1892; iii. Howard K., October 25, 1901. 2. Jennie C., married M. A. Patridge, a merchant, residing in Pittsburgh; children: Charles, deceased; Joseph, living in Pittsburgh; Frederick, living in Pittsburgh; Dale, deceased. 3. John Taylor, born February 25, 1849; educated in the public schools, and has been engaged in banking and lumber business and in the public service of Forest county all his life; he was county commissioner three years, county clerk nine years, deputy prothonotary, and member of Tionesta borough council several years; unmarried. 4. Alexander Holeman, born May 11, 1861; educated in the public schools, and Bucknell College; until 1905 a prominent oil operator and lumberman of Forest, Venango and Warren counties. In 1905 he moved to California, where he is still located in the real estate business at Oakland and San Francisco. He was burgess and councilman of Tionesta several years. He is unmarried.

(The Holeman Line).

Mrs. Nancy Agnes (Holeman) Dale is a descendant of Eli Holeman, who came to what is now Forest county about the year 1800, the first *bona fide* white settler in the county. He settled at what has ever since been known as

Holeman's Flat, on the Allegheny river, in the spring of 1800, and there continued to reside until his death. He was born in Chester county, Pennsylvania, about 1755, and during the revolution served with the Pennsylvania militia at the battles of Brandywine, Germantown, and in other battles of the war for independence. His father was also a soldier of the revolution, both receiving as pay the worthless Continental money of that day. After the war he spent five years in Northumberland, which was then on the frontier, and there he was again forced to fight on many occasions the fierce Indians of that section. His father was taken prisoner by the savages, and on one occasion he had barely time to secrete his family and himself in the dense woods surrounding his cabin, before a whooping murderous band of Indians attacked and robbed it, but mercifully spared its destruction. After the county had become a trifle less dangerous he moved further west to Lycoming, and in 1800 to Holeman's Flats. There he took up land and established a ferry across the Allegheny, which was the only ferry north of Kittanning. After the state road was established from Milesburg to Waterford, Holeman's Ferry became quite an important point, as many of the pioneers of western Pennsylvania crossed at that point. His nearest early neighbors were Moses Hicks, who lived near where David G. Hunter now lives, and Patrick McCrea, who settled at what is now known as Eagle Rock. There were, however, a number of "squatters" within a radius of a few miles. There the old pioneer hero lived and prospered until his death in 1825, founding a family prominent in later day county affairs.

He married Nancy Agnes, daughter of Alexander McGrady. Children of Eli and Nancy A. Holeman: 1. Margaret H., married Samuel Rhodes; children: Samuel, unmarried; Nancy, married John Burns; Charles, unmarried; Margaret, married Mr. Collins. 2. Charles H., name of first wife unknown, who bore him a son Eli, who moved to New York. He married (second) a widow, Mrs. Betsey (Dustin) Reynolds; children: Elizabeth, died young; Catherine, died young; Alexander, married in Vineland, New Jersey, and moved to Kansas. 3. Jane, married Moses Pierson; children: Nancy, married Andrew Fleming; Herman, died young; William, married Charlotte Reynolds, a daughter of Betsey Dustin by her first husband; Eli, married Sarah Barr; Rhoda, married Matthew Elder. 4. Alexander, of whom further.

(II) Alexander, son of Eli and Nancy Agnes (McGrady) Holeman, was born December 17, 1790, died in Tionesta, Pennsylvania, February 26, 1874. He was his father's companion in his pioneering experiences in Venango county, later Forest, and spent his life under similar conditions, farming, lumbering, and operating the ferry. He married, December 27, 1815, Clarissa Sexton, born September 6, 1800, died September 15, 1868. Children: 1. Charles, born September 8, 1817; married (first) Jane Hunter, (second) Nancy Strainer. 2. Roswell, born February 14, 1819, died young. 3. Elizabeth, born April 10, 1820; married W. F. Hunter. 4. Nancy Agnes (of previous mention), widow of Joseph Gates Dale. 5. Ashbel, born October 28, 1824; married Nancy Shelmadine. 6. Jane, born May 1, 1827; married Hugh Morrison. 7. Eli, born July 9, 1830; married (first) Lydia McCalmont, (second) Julia Blisdell. 8. John, born February 6, 1833; married Ellen Barr. 9. Mary, born December 5, 1835; married (first) James Cosgrove, (second) Jacob Maye. 10. Richard, born March 27, 1838; married (first) Mattie Scott, (second) Jennie Skellton.

FRILL. Stephen Frill, the founder of the Frill family in this country, was born January 13, 1781, in Germany and died January 13, 1865, in Washington township, Clarion county, Pennsylvania. He emigrated to America and settled at Lucinda Furnace, in Knox township, Clarion county, where he worked for many years. His wife Magdaline was born April 27, 1792, died April 27, 1870. Among his children was Jonathan, referred to below.

(II) Jonathan, son of Stephen Frill, was born in Germany, and died in Washington township, Clarion county, Pennsylvania. He emigrated to America with his parents when ten years of age, and went to work in the furnaces in Lucinda Furnace, Pennsylvania, and later bought a farm in Washington township, which he cultivated until his death. He was a Republican in politics, and a member of the United Brethren church. He married Eliza, daughter of Elihu and Sarah (Fitzgerald) McMichael, born in Washington township, May 15, 1840. Her grandfather was born in Ireland and emigrated to America and was one of the pioneer settlers of Crawford county, Pennsylvania, and married Mary Crawford. Her father Elihu was born in Crawford county, in 1810, and died in Washington township in 1882. He settled near Lickingville in 1838, and was a local minister of the Methodist Episcopal church, and married Sarah Fitzgerald, born in Mifflin county in 1817, died in 1883. Their children were: Alonzo; Eliza, married Jonathan Frill, referred to above; child, died in infancy; Phoebe, George, Margaret, Harvey, Sarah, Diantha, Benjamin F., Edwin H., Milton, Laura E., Charles W. Children of Jonathan and Eliza (McMichael) Frill: Benjamin F., referred to below; Clara, now living in Kellettville, Pennsylvania, married W. J. Deter; Mary, now dead; Jennie, now living in Washington township, married John Ashbaugh; John G., now living in Silam Springs, Arkansas, married Florence Ashbaugh; George W., now living on the old homestead in Washington township, married Bell Lueart; William Penn, now dead; Emma, married Benjamin Weaver; Richard H., now living in Tylersburg, married Mabel Harmon; Edward Howard, Frederick H., and Charles, all now living in West Virginia.

(III) Benjamin Franklin, son of Jonathan and Eliza (McMichael) Frill, was born in Washington township, Clarion county, Pennsylvania, March 26, 1861, and is now living at Newmansville, Pennsylvania. He received his early education in the public schools, and worked on his father's farm until he was seventeen years of age. He learned the trade of plasterer, and later worked for some time in the woods as a lumberman, and then purchased a farm of one hundred acres in Washington township. He also purchased later a residence and six acres of land at what is known as Frill's Corner, in Washington township, where he established a general store which he still conducts. He is a Republican in politics, and has held several local public offices. He is one of the committeemen of Washington township.

He married, November 14, 1882, Susan, daughter of Martin and Victoria (Oxner) Groner, born in Washington township, May 20, 1863. Children: 1. Clarence E., born October 14, 1885; now living on the old homestead in Washington township; married Carrie Kirkwood, of Tylersburg. 2. Loretta V., born January 13, 1887. 3. Martin Van Buren, born April 26, 1891; married Goldie Mealey, and now living in Youngstown, Ohio. 4. Floyd Albert, born June 2, 1893.

McDOWELL The McDowell family is descended from Milesius, King of Spain, through the line of his son Heremon; the founder of the family was Colla Meann, son of Escha Dubhfein, or Doivien, brother of Fiacha Straivetine, first King of Conneaught, of the race of Heremon, and son of Carbre Liffeachair, King of Ireland, A. D. 264. The ancient name was Doill, which signifies "blind." The possessions of the sept were located in the present county of Donegal, many also of the family having settled in Antrim. The McDowells were among the most notable descendants of the royal branch of the Clan Colla. There were many descendants of the Ulster family among the Irish who in the early part of the last century, about 1710, settled in the Blue Ridge mountains of Virginia, in the territory now embraced in the counties of Patrick and Rockbridge.

A prominent member of the old family in Ireland during the last century was Patrick McDowell, R. A., born in Belfast in 1799. He attained highest eminence as a sculptor, among his most notable works being "Virginius and His Daughter," "Eve," "Psyche," and the group typical of "Europe" in the Albert Memorial, Hyde Park, London. He died in 1870.

(I) William McDowell, the immigrant ancestor of the present American family, was born in Ireland, coming to this country in the early part of the eighteenth century and settling first in Chester county, Pennsylvania. In about 1731 he removed to Lancaster county, a part of which later became Franklin county, where he became the owner of an enormous estate, Parnell, upon which a fort was established. He was king's magistrate for that part of the country before the revolution, being arbiter in all disputes between varying sects and between the colonists and the Indians. After having been King George's confidential man, he became a Whig at the outbreak of the war and was a most ardent patriot. He continued in the capacity of recruiting officer for the colonies, and was a man of great prominence in that part of the country which prior to 1784 was embodied in Cumberland county. It was from this section that many members of the McDowell family and their descendants went forth to serve their country in various ways and helped to make its history. William McDowell had to flee his estate finally on account of Indian troubles, and on February 17, 1782, died in York county, Pennsylvania, near the town of Wrightsville, being buried at Donegal Presbyterian Church in Lancaster county. By his wife Mary he had nine children: John, married Agnes Craig; William, mentioned further; Nathan, married Catherine Maxwell, and died June 2, 1801; James, married Jane Smith; Thomas; Jean, married Archibald Irwin; Margaret, married Robert Newell; Sarah, married William Piper; daughter, married John Reynolds.

(II) William (2), son of William (1) and Mary McDowell, was born in 1720, living and dying at l'arnell, in Franklin county, on the vast estate which had been his father's before him; this was at or near Bridgeport, in Peters township. He was a colonial recruiting officer; was appointed ensign, August 13, 1776, under Captain Whitesides, in Colonel Thomas Porter's battalion; and in 1778 became justice of the peace for Peters township, being a man of great prominence in the county. In 1765, during an uprising of the "Black Boys," who besieged Fort Loudon, he was given by Lieutenant Grant, commandant of the fort, the custody of the arms taken from the country people, and rendered a receipt for five rifles and four smoothbore guns to be held by him until the governor's pleasure in their disposition could be known. At the same time four men executed a bond in £200 Pennsylvania currency to protect him against arrest or action at law. William McDowell died September 17, 1812, and was buried at Waddell's graveyard at Lebinarten, Pennsylvania, near the old estate. By his will dated in 1807 and probated in 1812, he left several large plantations to his sons. He married Mary Maxwell, born 1728, died April 9, 1805. Children: William, born 1749, was captain in revolution, married Elizabeth Van Lear, and died June 19, 1835; John, L.L.D. at Johns Hopkins, born 1751, died December 22, 1820, unmarried; Susan, born 1752, married John Martin, died May 17, 1839; James, died young; Mary, married Mr. Magaw, died May 9, 1799; Nathan, born 1758, married Mary McLanahan, died February 1, 1830; Alexander, born 1760, mentioned further; Andrew, born 1762, married Nancy McPherson, died January 10, 1846; Margaret, born 1765, married Matthew Maris, died February 17, 1853; Nancy, born 1767, died June 6, 1848; Patrick, born 1769, married Elizabeth Davidson, died April 24, 1846; Thomas, born 1772, married Mollie Davidson, died August 4, 1851.

(III) Colonel Alexander McDowell, son of William (2) and Mary (Maxwell) McDowell, was born in Franklin county, Pennsylvania, in the year 1760. He was a soldier in the revolutionary war, being then in his early manhood; and some time after the cessation of hostilities with England became agent for the Holland Land Company, receiving the appointment from them of deputy surveyor in the year 1793. He became the most noted of all the surveyors in northwestern Pennsylvania; and was one of the most distinguished members of a family that has been prominent and numerous in the public and social life of that portion of Pennsylvania embraced by the counties east of the mountains since their early settlement. In 1794, after his appointment by the Holland Land Company, he came out to Venango county, Pennsylvania, in their interests, and became one of the earliest pioneers in this region.

Returning east, he was married in 1795 to Miss Sally Parker, a colonial belle of Philadelphia; and in 1797 he brought his young family out to Venango county, making his permanent home in Franklin, where he became one of the prominent men of the town from the first. In 1796 he received the appointment of justice of the peace from Governor Mifflin, and was an arbiter in all cases of difference between the settlers. He became well acquainted with the celebrated Cornplanter, whose land he surveyed and whose home he assisted in establishing to the lasting gratitude and friendship of the Indian chief; and through his kindly spirit and fair dealings won the esteem and loyalty of all the neighboring tribes. He and his little family were thus enabled to live in peace and security, fearing naught, though the Indians were oftentimes noisy and intoxicated in their encampments across the creek, whooping and yelling sometimes half the night.

At the time that Colonel McDowell established his home in Franklin the town had been laid out about a year, and there were but four or five families in the place. The McDowell family at first resided in a log house, the property of the Holland Land Company, which was located on the bank of the creek near the site of the present Venango mills. It was without windows or doors, as there was no carpenter in the place to construct these, and the openings were hung with blankets. Colonel McDowell erected a more commodious log house for his family on Elk street, below

Eleventh, which was later weatherboarded and eventually became comfortably equipped and furnished, and (after the erection of a stone addition about the year 1803) was considered one of the two finest residences in Franklin. The first wall paper in the town was introduced by the McDowells for their home; the paper came from Philadelphia in sheets, and being thick and strong, lasted until the destruction of the old house in 1874; the design pictured boys and dogs in blue upon a light ground, and was greatly admired by the neighbors.

When the county was organized in 1800, Colonel McDowell was appointed one of the trustees to superintend its affairs, until commissioners were elected in 1805; he was then elected first county treasurer. In 1801 he was appointed first postmaster of Franklin. He had been one of the earliest patrons of Edward Hale at his trading post at Fort Franklin in 1798; and in 1801, as one of the town trustees, signed the lease of a part of the public square to him, "at the rate of one dollar a year until the ground which the said Hale has now in cultivation is wanted for public use."

Colonel McDowell died January 4, 1816, at the age of fifty-six years. According to portraits yet extant, he seems to have been a gentleman of the old school, sedate, dignified, and well accustomed to the amenities of life and social usages. He was a Presbyterian, as his ancestors had been, and as many of his descendants have remained, and when as late as 1801 there had been no preacher in Franklin of any denomination he doubtless was instrumental in securing the services of a clergyman, presumably of his own creed, who arrived in the year named and preached at the homes of the citizens until a suitable structure was erected for church and school.

Mrs. McDowell, who had been Miss Sarah Parker, of Philadelphia, survived her husband nearly half a century, dying at the extreme old age of one hundred and two years. She was born in the Quaker City on September 11, 1763, and was the daughter of Captain Parker, who died in her early childhood. Her mother, who was a Miss Elizabeth Adam, and whose mother in turn was a Miss Sarah Jones, married again after Captain Parker's death, her second husband being Thomas Skelly, a sea captain, who died in 1806. Sarah Parker resided with her stepfather in Philadelphia until the time of her marriage, being a noted belle in those days. She was small, slight and graceful, had great personal beauty, and was witty and charming. She exchanged her earlier life of refinement and ease for the privations attending a pioneer's wife with the cheerfulness and philosophy of her courageous character, and lived to see the poverty and hardship of the first few years give way to the rich development of after days; having been at all times equal to the occasion and a helpful and friendly neighbor in her crude surroundings. She had brought with her into the wilderness where she came as a young wife, a chest full of the finery of her former days, silk and velvet gowns, laces and jewelry, keeping these as relics of her earlier life.

In the pioneer days she was energetic and resourceful to a degree; preserving and managing her little household with frugality, bartering with the Indians for provisions and matching her quick wits against theirs, winning their esteem and loyal friendship and that of her white neighbors as well. In the after days she had many reminiscences to relate of the town and its growth, describing the clearing by moonlight of the bushes and stumps from what is now the park; the purchase of fish from the Indian fishermen, and their rooted distrust of the white woman's honesty until it was well proven; and telling how upon one occasion when a hen had eaten the few cucumber seeds which she had drying on a table for the next season's crop, she cut open with a pair of scissors the craw of the fowl, recovered the seed, sewed up the wound with a needle and thread, which was apparently not heeded, and thus preserved both seed and fowl for her future household supplies.

After the death of her husband in 1816, Mrs. McDowell continued to reside in the old home; and in 1823 and 1824 was recorded as keeping house there with her three sons. In 1826 she donated to St. John's Church a lot valued at seventy-five dollars. Her death occurred September 25 (or 27), 1865, at the home of her son (Thomas S.), where she passed the last few years of her life after leaving the old homestead (that was less than half a square away). Only two of her children survived her and she had lived until she was weary of life, peacefully passing away in the third year after she had attained the century mark. The town had grown strange to her and all of her friends were gone; she was undoubtedly the oldest person who ever lived in Franklin.

Colonel and Mrs. McDowell were the parents of nine children: 1. Elizabeth, born 1796; died December 23, 1809. 2. Susan, born 1798; died August 30, 1806. 3. Margaretta, born in Franklin in 1800; died at Warren, January 28, 1825. In December, 1819, married Archibald Tanner, born in Cromwell, Connecticut, February 3, 1786, died at Warren, Pennsylvania, February 15, 1861. Children: (a) Sarah Parker, born July 3, 1821; died June 3, 1849. (b) Laura Margaretta, born September 9, 1823, at Warren; died September 14, 1909; married, November 20, 1845, Judge Glenni W. Scofield, born March 11, 1817, died August 30, 1891. He was graduated at Hamilton College; read law and in 1842 was admitted to practice in Warren county, Pennsylvania; was a Republican, and served as a member of the Pennsylvania legislature; in 1862 was elected to congress and served twelve years; in 1878 appointed by President Hayes as Register of the Treasury, resigning in 1881 when appointed by President Garfield as Judge of the United States Court of Claims; served ten years in this capacity, and resigned in 1891, one month previous to his death. Children: Ellie G., born October 28, 1850; Archibald Tanner, born July 4, 1854, in Warren, married Kate S. Brecht, of that city, born January 3, 1869, and had children: Eleanor Margaretta, born November 10, 1889, died January 3, 1890, Glenni William, born July 19, 1892, Lawrence Stranahan, born March 11, 1894, Herbert Latham, born June 8, 1901, and Archibald Tanner, born January 28, 1909; Mary Margaretta, born May 2, 1857, died February 17, 1887. 4. Thomas Skelly, the first white male child born in Franklin, April 25, 1803, died there February 7, 1876; married January 30, 1825, Emily Nevins Ayres, born at Brownsville, Pennsylvania, March 9, 1808, died in Franklin, June 27, 1862. Children: (a) Margaretta Rachel, born July 11, 1827, at Franklin; died October 10, 1905, at Brooklyn, New York; married at Franklin, August 1, 1850, Elisha Burritt Gray, born April 20, 1823, in Kenton county, Kentucky, died at Franklin, August 5, 1890. Children: (aa) Emily Jane, born May 18, 1851, married May 2, 1872, at Franklin, to Joseph Allen Fleming. Children: (aaa) Burritt Gray, born February 13, 1873, died August 15, 1873. (bbb) John Gray, born August 23, 1874, married Leonore McCarthy, May 17, 1898. Children: Emily Leonore, born August 13, 1900; Burritt Gray, born July 31, 1903; Margaretta Gray, born November 8, 1905; Frederick McDowell, born March 5, 1911. (ccc) Margaretta Anna Fleming, born May 1, 1879, married Marion Ellsworth Lafferty, May 29, 1902. Children: Margaretta Emily, born February 26, 1903; Marion Ellsworth, born May 5, 1905. (bb) Anna Cynthia, born March 14, 1853, in Trigg county, Kentucky; married in Maysville, Kentucky, June 4, 1875, Captain James Patton Newell, born in Center county, Pennsylvania, October 2, 1840, died at Carthage, Missouri, June 4, 1895. Children: (aaa) Emily Jane, born January 9, 1877, at Joplin, Missouri; married December 24, 1900, at Carthage, Missouri, Harry Wallace Blair, born July 7, 1877, at Maysville, Kentucky. Children: Harriet, born October 8, 1903, at Washington, D. C.; Newell, born April 5, 1907, at Carthage, Missouri. (bbb) James Patton, born August 8, 1878, at Franklin, Pennsylvania; married May 8, 1900, at Carthage, Missouri, Jessie Maud Caffee, born September 12, 1877, at Carthage. Children, all born at Carthage; James Patton, September 18, 1902; David Caffee, January 23, 1904; John Warden, December 11, 1907. (ccc) Anna Gray, born February 8, 1881, at Joplin; deaconess in Episcopal Church. (ddd) Julia Porter, born December 22, 1883, at Carthage; married May 8, 1900, at Carthage, Philip W. Chappell. (eee) Margaret Louise, born October 27, 1885, at Carthage; unmarried. (fff) Ella Rebecca, born June 27, 1887, at Carthage, where married, September 18, 1900, Ralph Putman. (cc) William Galbraith, born August, 1855; died October, 1856. (dd) Margaretta Gray, born May 24, 1858, at Portsmouth, Ohio; married (first) at Franklin, Pennsylvania, June 1, 1880, Henry S. Church, born July 16, 1857, at Brooklyn, New York, died at Cheyenne, Wyoming, March 18, 1885. Married (second) August 6, 1891, at Hartford, Connecticut, Albert J. Rothwell, born at Galena, Illinois, February 18, 1854. Children, by first marriage: (aaa) Katharine Gray, born May 6, 1881, in New York City; married November 8, 1909, Theodore Solomons. Children: Susan Eleanor, born February 15, 1911; David Sexius, born June 22, 1912. (bbb) Henry Seymour, born April 12, 1883, at New Brighton, Staten Island, New York; died, Denver, Colorado, February 23, 1909. (b) Emily Elizabeth, born August 16,

1829; died June 18, 1847. (c) Sarah Parker, born at Franklin, August 13, 1831, died at Robins, Iowa, October 14, 1893; married at Franklin, September 24, 1854, Royal Atwater, born in Vermont, April 30, 1829, died in Iowa July 7, 1885. He enlisted in 1861, serving in the Fourth Pennsylvania Cavalry during the civil war. Children: (aa) Elizabeth, born July, 1854, died 1854. (bb) Daniel W., born November 6, 1856, married (first) October 7, 1878, Lillian Kent, who died December 31, 1888, married (second) February 4, 1890, Abigail F. Burns; he lives at Seminole, Pennsylvania, near New Bethlehem. Child by first marriage: Henry K., born February 20, 1883, lives in Pittsburgh. Children by second marriage: Florence, born November 13, 1891; Ralph, born August 7, 1894. (cc) Ayres B., born May 30, 1858; married Chloe A. Marsh, October 12, 1887. He is a farmer at Robins, Iowa. Children: Olive B., born September 14, 1888; Donald, born June 11, 1890; Josephine F., born April 13, 1893. (dd) Louis C., born March 12, 1860; died June 12, 1862. (ee) Laura M., born January 7, 1863; married M. D. Pember, of Woodburn, Washington, October 1, 1884. (ff) Charles S., born November 15, 1866; unmarried. (gg) Louise C., born August 6, 1868; married, April 1, 1900, George Sines, a farmer of Pomerania, New Jersey. Child: Sarah, born August 21, 1904; died same year. (hh) James R., born September, 1870; married, April 9, 1904, Emily M. Hawks, lives at Wessington, South Dakota. Child: Flossie Ellen, born October 1, 1905. (d) Archibald Tanner, born May 31, 1834, at Franklin; died January 19, 1874, at Warren; married at Jamestown, New York, in August, 1860, Mrs. Frank Homer Tiffany, born at Jamestown, April 1, 1842, dying at Philadelphia, April 1, 1895. Children: (aa) Anna D., born May 27, 1863, at Sinclairville, New York; married at Philadelphia, December 22, 1885, B. G. Anderson. Children: Anna Frances, born October 24, 1886; Rose Delia, December 30, 1887; Bertha Gertrude, April 22, 1890; Ida Barr, April 25, 1892; James Archibald, June 28, 1894; Grant Herchelroth, January 21, 1896; Raymond Gray, October 10, 1897. (bb) Bertha G., born at Franklin, May 4, 1866; married at Philadelphia, March 4, 1884, E. L. Weckerly. Child: Anna Ray, born December 29, 1884. (cc) William T., born June 1, 1868. (e) Amy Elizabeth, born August 8, 1836; died September, 1849. (f) Josephine Cecelia, born at Franklin, June 28, 1839; married there, July 19, 1862, Philander Raymond Gray, son of Alanson Gray and Jane R. Tarvin, born January 14, 1837, in Campbell county, Kentucky. Mr. Gray enlisted in Company A, 121st Pennsylvania Volunteers, under Capt. George E. Ridgeway, going to the front with the army in 1862. After serving as first sergeant of the company he was promoted to second lieutenant for bravery at the battle of Fredericksburg, December 13, 1862, and complimented in a general regimental order for his conduct in that hard fought battle. In October, 1863, he was appointed to first lieutenant; was detailed as acting quartermaster of the 121st Regiment and commissioned in November; in February, 1864, was detailed quartermaster of the brigade, serving as such until the close of the war, when he was honorably discharged. In 1865, a few months after his return from the seat of war, he was elected sheriff of Venango county. During his term the Pithole oil excitement had its rise, lawlessness was frightfully prevalent, and the position of sheriff was really the most arduous in the gift of the people. How faithfully the difficult task was performed was familiar to every resident of Oildom. Mr. Gray was one of the pioneer oil refiners, selling his refinery to accept the superintendency of the Eclipse Lubricating Oil Works, Ltd., and remained with this company until January, 1885, when he removed with his large family to Elizabeth, New Jersey, and became identified with the Tide Water Oil Company of Bayonne, New Jersey. Up to the time of his removal from Franklin he was very prominent in the politics of Northwestern Pennsylvania. Mr. and Mrs. Gray's family is somewhat celebrated for its size, there having been eleven children born to them, all of whom lived to celebrate with their parents their golden wedding on July 19, 1912, at Elizabeth, New Jersey. Children: (aa) Elisha Burritt, born June 25, 1865, in Lewis county, Kentucky; married September 3, 1891, Haidee Reed, born September 21, 1854, in Canada, near Buffalo, daughter of Louis Reed and Emma Maywald, of New Brighton, Staten Island. No children. (bb) Philander Raymond, born December 8, 1866, at Franklin; unmarried. (cc) William Ayres, born May 24, 1868, at Franklin; married at Elizabeth, New Jersey, January 11, 1893, Margaret Byers Morrison, born at Elizabeth, January 13, 1873, daughter of James Morrison and Caroline Thompson Farnham, of that city. Child: William Ayres, born September 17, 1894, at Elizabeth. (dd) Frederick Charles, born February 12, 1870, at Franklin; married in New York City, July 6, 1903, Daisy Claire Wallace Huber, born at Harrisburg, Pennsylvania, January 5, 1877, daughter of Philip Allen Huber and Katherine Elizabeth Grover, of Sunbury, Pennsylvania. No children. (ee) Fanny Josephine, born at Franklin, Pennsylvania, December 17, 1871; unmarried. (ff) Alanson McDowell, born at Franklin, October 24, 1873; married at Elizabeth, New Jersey, June 5, 1907, Caroline Henderson Koues, born in New York City, November 9, 1883, daughter of George Ellsworth Koues and Mary Parmly Toby, of Elizabeth. Children, born at Elizabeth: Alanson McDowell, March 15, 1908; Caroline Koues, August 21, 1909. (gg) John Lathrop, born at Franklin, February 6, 1875, married at Elizabeth, New Jersey, June 3, 1901, Harriet Hamilton Tyng, born May 26, 1879, at South Orange, New Jersey, daughter of Russell Degen Tyng and Harriet Matilda Cornell, of Elizabeth. Children, born at Elizabeth, New Jersey: John Lathrop, March 20, 1905; Harriet Mathilde, October 21, 1906; Cecelia, September 16, 1909; Penelope Royal, November 28, 1912. (hh) Emily Jane, born at Franklin, February 11, 1877; married June 24, 1903, at Elizabeth, Charles Douglas Galloway, born January 15, 1881, at Washington, D. C., son of Lieutenant Charles Douglas Galloway, U. S. N., and Anna Louisa Smith, of Washington. Children: Emily Gray, born July 13, 1905, at Camden, New Jersey, died May 15, 1908; Jane Gray, born May 26, 1909, at Elizabeth. (ii) McDowell, born July 17, 1879, at Franklin; married July 20, 1903, Florence Robbins, born December 6, 1883, at Doylestown, Bucks county, Pennsylvania, daughter of William Henry Robbins and Emma Lotte Yost, of Easton, Pennsylvania. Children: Audrey Meda, born January 12, 1905, at Easton; Evelyn Ayres, born November 26, 1912, at Elizabeth. (jj) Thomas Tarvin, born August 29, 1881, at Franklin; married December 6, 1905, at Philadelphia, Ella Moray Watson, born March 21, 1880, at Washington, D. C., daughter of Major Malbone Francis Watson, U. S. A., and Mary Byvane Codwise, of Dayton, Ohio. Child: Ruth Watson, born September 4, 1906, at Elizabeth. (kk) Josephine McDowell, born October 11, 1883, at Franklin; married in New York City, February 12, 1906, Hamilton Wainwright Weeks, born June 9, 1880, at Elizabeth, son of Edward Francis Weeks and Kate Pond, of Elizabeth. Children, born at Elizabeth: Hamilton Wainwright, March 18, 1908; Philander Raymond Gray, March 21, 1910; William Tubbs, July 18, 1912. (g) Jane Houston, born August 6, 1841, at Franklin; married January 27, 1871, at Franklin, James W. Sparks; died at Bayonne, New Jersey, February 23, 1900. Children: William Wylie, born December 6, 1871; Estelle McDowell, born September 22, 1873, died April 27, 1899; Joseph A., born January 12, 1876; Frank Owens, born June 3, 1878, died April 26, 1881; Thomas Ayres, born September 11, 1881; Margaretta C., born May 28, 1885. (h) Helen Delia, born April 6, 1844; married R. Z. Newton; died July 30, 1879. (i) Fanny Galbraith, born August 26, 1846; died October 10, 1910, in Washington, D. C., where she held an important and trusted position in the Treasury Department for more than forty years. (j) Thomas Skelly, 2nd, born at Franklin, April 6, 1849; he has been chief engineer of Lafayette City Waterworks since 1883. At the age of fourteen years enlisted on June 29, 1863, as private in Captain Charles W. Whistle's Company II, Second Battalion of Pennsylvania Volunteer Infantry, serving six months; was discharged January 21, 1864, at Pittsburg, at expiration of term of service, and is now a member of John A. Logan Post No. 3, G. A. R., at Lafayette, Indiana. He married at Dunkirk, New York, July 19, 1865, Jennie Day, born October 2, 1850. Children: (aa) Mary F., born May 24, 1867; married at Lafayette, April 30, 1894, Charles F. Perrin. Children: Mary L., born June 28, 1895; Genevieve E., September 28, 1899; Paul J., December 22, 1902; John A., July 8, 1504; Charles F., July 15, 1908. (bb) William A., born December 20, 1868. (cc) Jennie E., born March 10, 1870. (dd) Emily E., born September 10, 1871; married at Lafayette, July 16, 1895, George F. Long. Children: Helen M., born December 3, 1897; George, born October 7, 1909. (ee) Sarah J., born April 13, 1874; married at Lafayette, July 27, 1898, James E. Duffy. Children: John E., born June 28, 1899; Raymond M., August 16, 1901; Helen E., October 6, 1903; Ruth J., January 31, 1905. (ff) Fanny E., born December 21, 1877; married at Lafayette, September 12, 1906, James Duffy Jr. (gg) Archibald T., born January 10, 1879; married at Lafayette,

November 24, 1903, Mary Marcus. Children: Archibald, born April 17, 1905; Eugene A., born January 14, 1908. (hh) Frank E., born December 1, 1880; married at Lafayette, October 18, 1904, Helen Marcus. Children: Edward F., born January 9, 1906; Robert M., born October 13, 1907. (ii) Thomas Skelly, 3rd, born January 1, 1883; married at Lafayette, June 5, 1912, Florence Grady. (jj) Joseph A., born September 14, 1884. (kk) Irene H., born June 14, 1886. (ll) Vincent P., born March 20, 1892. 5. Parker, born in 1805; mentioned further. 6. Major Alexander McDowell (2d), son of Colonel Alexander, served as a county auditor in 1832; was appointed by Governor Ritner, of Pennsylvania, in 1836, register, recorder and clerk of the courts of Venango county, and served until 1839, and also held a commission as major of state militia; born November 23, 1807, died at Franklin, December 8, 1875; married November 3, 1842, Anna Moffett, born in Philadelphia, August 20, 1821, died at Franklin, June 29, 1889. Children: (a) William Parker, born August 27, 1843; married Lydia A. Fry. (b) Sarah Parker, born at Franklin, July 6, 1845, died August 12, 1911; married at Franklin, September 29, 1864, George B. Fry, born February 18, 1843. Children: (aa) Marcus A., born June 12, 1869; died March 9, 1894. (bb) Amy L., born at Franklin, February 15, 1872; married at Jamestown, New York, December 14, 1899, Arthur T. Hjorth. Child: Sarah Josephine, born July 6, 1902. (cc) George B., born at Franklin, July 10, 1878; married at Jamestown, New York, October 7, 1903, Bertha Alice Wampler, born January 4, 1878. Children: Edith Geraldine, born June 17, 1906; Robert Alden, born February 26, 1910. (c) Eleanor Moffett, born at Franklin, March 31, 1847; married June 12, 1883, at Franklin, Thomas Matthews; she died May 7, 1910. Child: James, born April 14, 1884. (d) Thomas Moffett, born at Franklin, December 25, 1848; died August 30, 1907; married at Emlenton, Pennsylvania, August 24, 1882, Jennie Jones, born March 28, 1858. Children: (aa) Harry Y., born February 26, 1883. (bb) Alfred B., born January 4, 1885, at Franklin; married November 18, 1908, Cora Osborn. Child: James Paul, born November 2, 1910. (cc) Roscoe Richard, born at Franklin, June 4, 1887; married August 3, 1901, Elizabeth Nottrott. Children: Robert R., born August 31, 1910; Grace E., born April 15, 1912. (dd) Emma E., born June 14, 1890. (ee) Anna M., born June 21, 1892. (e) Eliza, born January 31, 1851; died August 3, 1898. (f) Hattie C. born May 1, 1853; died October 23, 1880. (g) Alexander H., born at Franklin, February 24, 1855; married (first) at Franklin, October 21, 1881, Ada T. Lane, born February 25, 1857, died May 25, 1892. Married (second) at Grove City, Pennsylvania, November 29, 1895, May C. Cunningham, born June 27, 1870. Children by first marriage: Hazel May, born November 23, 1882, married Albro C. Holmes, June 17, 1903; Grace L., born February 21, 1886, married Fred Martin, December 29, 1908, having one child, Marjory Martin, born August 16, 1912. Children by second marriage: Kenneth C., born October 16, 1897; Ralph A., born March 11, 1906; Richard Aigner, born February 4, 1908. (h) Margaret J., born April 24, 1857; died December 3, 1909; married Joseph A. Weikal. (i) Robert R., born at Franklin, February 28, 1858; married at Wooster, Ohio, December 20, 1892, Mamie Faber, born at Wooster, December 17, 1872. Children: Robert F., born September 23, 1893; Ruth B., May 16, 1896; Dudley A., December 9, 1902. (j) Charles T., born at Franklin, March 22, 1861; married at Cranberry, Pennsylvania, March 22, 1883, Anna Miller. Children: Simon W., born January 25, 1884, married, August 14, 1912, Lydia Jane Harland, born December 5, 1889; Mary P., April 3, 1885, married April 4, 1906, Arthur Claton Walter, born February 5, 1877, children: Esther Mary, born August 10, 1907, Guy Lowell, October 8, 1910; Gertrude, June 6, 1888; Wilda S., February 21, 1890; Orrin C., January 11, 1892; Glenni S., April 6, 1894; Wilkin T., January 6, 1900; De Wayne, April, 1903. (k) Glenni S., born at Franklin, March 31, 1864, drowned in Conneaut Lake, August 20, 1902; married at Sunville, Pennsylvania October 20, 1886, Cora C. Richey, who died June 20, 1906. Children: Harold R., born October 10, 1887; Laura S., born April 18. 1889, drowned in Conneaut Lake, August 20, 1902. 7. William, born ———; married Elvira McNutt. 8. Mary, born 1813; died March 16, 1821. 9. Sarah, born ———; married Alexander S. Hays, and died July 3, 1821.

(IV) Parker McDowell, son of Colonel Alexander and Sarah (Parker) McDowell, was born in 1805 at Franklin, Pennsylvania, where he died August 16, 1860. He was a merchant, and engaged in this and the lumbering business at or near Titusville, Pennsylvania, for a number of years, however, always making his home in the old homestead at Franklin. He married, May 15, 1839, at Titusville, Pennsylvania, Lavinia Titus, daughter of Jonathan and Mary Martin Titus, her father having been the founder of Titusville. She was born February 22, 1817, at Titusville, dying May 9, 1893, at Cambridge Springs. Children: 1. Mary E., born May 2, 1840; died August 6, 1911. 2. Sarah Parker, born February 7, 1842; married at Titusville, February 20, 1868, James W. Rowland, born April 16, 1838, near Pulaski, Pennsylvania. Children: (a) Harry Willard, born December 25, 1868; married November 21, 1894, Louise C. Grimm, born January 19, 1872. Child: Darthea Louise, born November 27, 1897. (b) Fred James, born July 7, 1870; died February 1, 1892. 3. Alexander, born March 4, 1845; mentioned further. 4. Jonathan Titus, born September 11, 1846, at Franklin; married at Marietta, Ohio, June 1, 1870, Anna M. Jenvey, born at Winchester, England, August 26, 1849, died at Pittsburgh, Pennsylvania, October 31, 1912. Child: Josephine, born October 10, 1871; married, October 15, 1895, Dory A. Smith, having one child, Harold McDowell Smith, born January 20, 1897. 5. Parker, born November 8, 1848, at Franklin; married at Sharon, Pennsylvania, June 4, 1879, Martha A. McClain, born November 7, 1857. Children: William C., born December 21, 1879, married Laura O'Brien, September 6, 1904; Alexander Walter, born August 7, 1883; Sarah Rowland, born June 5, 1898. 6. Lavinia, born January 8, 1850, at Franklin; married there, September 15, 1875, John Patterson, born March 17, 1840, in Mercer county, Pennsylvania, died at Franklin, June 7, 1894. Child: Orrin James, born January 4, 1878, married December 20, 1905, Helen Marie Brannon, born in 1880, having one child, James Alexander, born December 19, 1906.

(V) Major Alexander (2) McDowell, third son of Parker and Lavinia (Titus) McDowell, was born at Franklin, Pennsylvania, on March 4, 1845, the date of President Polk's inauguration. He received his schooling under William Burgwin, a capable teacher, and at the old academy on Buffalo street; at the same time learning the printer's trade in the small establishment of the *American Citizen*, a weekly newspaper of commendable repute in its day. His father's death in 1860 obliging him to quit school in order to assist in the support of the family, he became a clerk in the general store of the late George W. Brigham, an enterprising merchant of early days. Working at his trade in leisure hours fully occupied his time until August 23, 1862, when he responded to the call of his country and enlisted in Company A, of the One Hundred and Twenty-first Regiment of Pennsylvania Volunteer Infantry. Serving in this regiment as sergeant and severely wounded at the battle of the Wilderness, in December, 1864, he was brevetted major of the Twenty-first United States Veteran Reserve Corps, in acknowledgment of his gallant conduct. He continued thus until the close of the civil war when he was honorably discharged. He wore his well-won military honors modestly, sometimes facetiously declaring, "Me an' Grant put down the Rebellion."

Retiring from the army in 1865, Major McDowell became the partner of Nelson B. Smiley, a talented lawyer and journalist, in publishing the *Venango Citizen*, the Republican organ of the county. Mr. Smiley retired in 1867 to attend to his extensive practice, selling his interest to the Major; who also retired, on January 1, 1869, having decided to engage in other business. He wielded a ready pen, printed a vigorous paper, and would certainly have climbed high had he remained in the profession. With the view of adopting a legal career, he read law for a while; but his change of residence to Mercer county prevented the completion of his studies and his admission to the bar. That he would have excelled in the learned profession, particularly as an effective pleader, all who know the Major's ability and temperament feel assured.

Removing to Sharon, Pennsylvania, in 1870, to manage the James Bleakley banking interests, he acquired control in 1872 and built up a strong financial institution. For thirty-five years he conducted the business under the title of A. McDowell, Banker, and in 1907 reorganized it as The McDowell National Bank, with a capital stock of $150,000, Alexander McDowell, president, and Harry B. McDowell, cashier. The history of the bank during its long career has been marked by steady progress, unvarying courtesy, and rigid fidelity. Today it ranks among the most substantial and popular in Northwestern Pennsylvania.

Shortly after locating in Sharon, Major McDowell was elected school director, filling this responsible position acceptably ever since. At the organization in 1886, in his adopted city, of the Protected Home Circle, a mutual benevolent society, he was elected supreme treasurer, holding the office uninterruptedly to the satisfaction of his associates and the great advantage of the order. Its marvelous growth to a foremost place in fraternal systems is largely owing to his competent oversight and sound judgment. From the beginning he took an active part in advancing the best interests of Sharon and of Mercer county, giving liberally of his means and personal efforts to promote the general welfare. Nor has he forgotten his native heath, where no visitor is more welcome, especially those boyhood friends now facing toward life's sunset, who are always delighted to meet and greet one whose genial presence brings a flood of pleasant memories and hearty cheer.

Politically Major McDowell is and has ever been by training, habit, and experience a stalwart Republican, the kind who puts principle above expediency and despises trimmers and parasites. In 1892 he was elected congressman-at-large, serving his term with characteristic sagacity and zeal. Deprived of the nomination two years before by machine jugglery, public sentiment placed him on the ticket at the next opportunity and sent him to Washington by an overwhelming majority. Elected clerk of the House of Representatives in 1895, he served continuously until the Democrats gained the ascendancy in 1911, a record perhaps unequalled in national annals. Men of all creeds, classes, and parties have esteemed him for his staunch integrity, his invincible good humor, his oratorical power, and his splendid courage. He has a most charming personality, is generous and broad-minded, and has an exhaustless fund of pat stories. These qualities have all combined to make him a drawing card on the rostrum in many campaigns, speaking with telling effect, quoting pertinent passages of scripture, clinching solid arguments with apt illustrations, and rivaling Adam Bede's best and brightest effusions.

Major McDowell is a Presbyterian and a Mason, a member of the G. A. R. Post of Sharon, Pennsylvania, and of the committee appointed by congress to take charge of the arrangements for celebrating the fiftieth anniversary of the battle of Gettysburg, in July, 1913. Although his hair is silvered and he is nearing three score and ten, he stands erect, his eye is keen, his hand clasp has lost none of its warmth, and the brave spirit retains its youthfulness and vim. He enjoys his comfortable fortune, helps the poor and distressed, is the soul of the social sphere, and never happier than by his own hospitable fireside. He devotes some time and thought to a big farm, where he raises fine fruits and bountiful crops. He keeps in touch with current events, is a typical American through and through, at peace with God and with his fellows everywhere.

On September 17, 1867, Major McDowell was married at Franklin, Pennsylvania, to Miss Clara Bleakley, who was born at Franklin on April 6, 1847. She is a daughter of Colonel James and Elizabeth (Dubbs) Bleakley, and has proved a worthy helpmeet to her distinguished husband. Major and Mrs. McDowell have had the following children: 1. James Parker, born February 19, 1869. 2. Lizzie, born November 15, 1872; married September 15, 1895, Edward Buchholz, born September 25, 1870. Children: Edward McDowell, born January 22, 1904, died in infancy; Clara Elizabeth, born July 22, 1905; Mary McDowell, born September 3, 1907; Harriet McDowell, born May 31, 1909; Katherine McDowell, born May 24, 1912. 3. Willis, born February 6, 1875. He is a lieutenant commander in the United States navy, stationed at the New Hampshire Navy Yard at Kittery, Maine. On June 14, 1899, he married Grace A. Delamater, born October 29, 1874, and has one child, Percival Eaton, born April 10, 1900. 4. Mary B., born August 22, 1876. 5. Clara, born January 3, 1880; married August 19, 1909, Glenn Carley, born October 23, 1876, having one child, Clara McDowell, born September 6, 1912. 6. Harry Bleakley, born April 19, 1882; married November 22, 1911, Grace Osborne, born April 6, 1883, and has one child, Mary McDowell, born November 6, 1912.

McKELVEY The McKelveys of Warren, Pennsylvania, are of Scotch-Irish descent. There is a tradition that the grandfather of Alexander H. McKelvey came to the United States, but no record of him is known to exist.

(I) George McKelvey, the first of whom we have record, and the founder of this branch of the McKelveys in the United States, was born in county Antrim, Ireland, September 3, 1803, died in Vandalia, Tulare county, California, December 24, 1878, and is there buried.

He was educated in the "boys school" at Belfast, Ireland, and after finishing his studies learned the weaver's trade. He followed his trade in both Ireland and Scotland until 1832, then came to the United States, locating at Haverstraw, New York. He was employed in the calico print factory there for a short time, then came to Pennsylvania, settling about 1834 in Freehold township, Warren county. He purchased fifty acres from the Holland Land Company, later adding another twenty-five acres. He was a pioneer in the district, his nearest neighbors being a mile distant, both east and west. He built a log cabin and began clearing his farm. He later went to West Greenville, Mercer county, where he worked in the soft coal mines for a time. He then returned to his farm which he cleared and cultivated until 1852, when he succumbed to an attack of "gold fever" and sailed for California via Cape Horn, being one of the first gold-seekers to go from Freehold township. The vessel was five months in reaching San Francisco and unfortunately had touched at Rio Janeiro, Brazil, where yellow fever was epidemic. The disease was contracted by some on board, and Mr. McKelvey was stricken with this usually fatal disease; careful nursing, however, brought him back to health and he was able to prosecute his search for gold most successfully until 1855, when he returned to Warren county. He again resumed farming, but the charm of the California climate, and the lure of gold, was upon him and he could not content himself with the, to him, monotonous life of the farm. In 1865 he bade friends and kinsmen in Warren county a final farewell and again departed for California, taking with him a son, Albert C. He located in Porterville, Tulare county, California, where he was engaged in business, retiring prior to his death in 1878. After settling in Porterville he was joined by his entire family except Alexander H.

He married, in Ireland, Mary Kernochan, born February 11, 1811, died in California, January 19, 1876. Children: 1. John, born in Ireland, August 11, 1831, died February 15, 1896. 2. Isabella, born December 4, 1833, in New York state, died December 21, 1907. 3. Andrew, born July 13, 1835, died December 10, 1839. 4. James, born February 2, 1837, died January 31, 1872; was a farmer; served for three years and eight months during the civil war as a private soldier, enlisting in the Forty-ninth New York Volunteers, Company K, in 1861; he married Helen Margaret Abbott, and their daughter, Dell Alberta, married Clyde C. Cooper. 5. George, born November 9, 1838, died September 20, 1871. 6. Alexander H., of whom further. 7. Mary Jane, born June 4, 1842; married John Tyler and resides in Porterville, California. 8. Christopher William, born April 14, 1844; a veteran of the civil war, served in the navy, also in the One Hundred and Fifty-first Regiment Pennsylvania Infantry. 9. Albert Crawford, born December 12, 1846, died in California, August 20, 1869. 10. Eliza Victoria, born October 12, 1850, died February 13, 1891; married Sweezy Mapes. The family religious affiliation is with the Methodist Episcopal church, and Mr. McKelvey Sr. was first a Whig, later a Republican.

(II) Alexander Hugh, fifth son of George and Mary (Kernochan) McKelvey, was born November 4, 1840. He was educated in the public schools of Warren county, and grew to manhood at the home farm. In the fall of 1861 he enlisted in the Union army, serving in Company K, Forty-ninth Regiment, New York Volunteer Infantry, forming a part of the Sixth Army Corps, Army of the Potomac, and saw hard service with that hard-fought army. He was wounded near Culpeper Court House in September, 1863, and there taken prisoner by Confederate pickets. He was kept in Libby prison for a short time, then exchanged and taken to the Naval Academy Hospital at Annapolis, Maryland, from there transferred to Annapolis Junction Hospital and later to Fort McHenry, Baltimore, finally in September, 1864, was mustered out with an honorable discharge, after three years spent in the service. After returning to Warren county he spent a short time in recuperating, then entered Syracuse Business College, whence he was graduated in 1866. He entered business life as clerk and bookkeeper in a Warren dry goods store, continuing until 1867. He was next employed as bookkeeper in the First National Bank of Warren, remaining until January 14, 1870, when he was placed in charge of the books of Brown, Struthers & Company. This firm with which the young man was destined to have long and important association was founded in 1851 by W. F. Kingsbury as a foundry, later Henry W. Brown was admitted a partner and a frame foundry and machine shop was built on the site of the present works in 1855. This building is remembered as having a steam whistle, the first factory plant in Warren to use a steam whistle to summon the workmen.

In 1860 Mr. Kingsbury retired. John and Thomas, brothers of Henry W. Brown, becoming interested with him and operating as Brown Brothers. In 1868 Thomas Struthers acquired an interest in the firm, which then and until 1871 was known as Brown, Struthers & Company. About 1871 Mr. McKelvey became a stockholder and the business was incorporated as the Brown Struthers Iron Works, Mr. McKelvey being elected secretary and treasurer, continuing until 1875, when the company became the Struthers Iron Works, the owner being Thomas Struthers, James C. Wells and Alexander H. McKelvey. This company had a prosperous career and is still in existence, although none of the old partners are connected with it. Mr. Struthers and Mr. Wells are both deceased, and Mr. McKelvey sold his interest in August, 1895, having served as treasurer of the company twenty-five years.

In 1895, after retiring from the iron works, he became interested in life insurance and was manager for one of the leading companies, his territory being the thirty-seventh judicial district of Pennsylvania. When oil was discovered he became interested and has always been a producer, holding at times very large interests in various fields and is still interested in production in Elk and Forest counties, Pennsylvania, as a partner in the South Penn Oil Company, also has oil interests in Warren county. He retains a lively interest in his old army comrades, and is a member of Lieutenant E. N. Ford Post, Grand Army of the Republic. In politics he is a Republican, but has never consented to hold public office. In religious faith he is a Presbyterian, having been an active member of the First Presbyterian Church of Warren, Pennsylvania, since 1868, ruling elder since 1872, for many years was clerk of the session and treasurer of the sessional funds, has served on the board of trustees, and ever since joining the church has been a teacher in the Sunday school. His life has been one of useful activity and no man stands higher in his community.

He married, in 1871, M. Olive James, born in Maine, died January 4, 1905, daughter of David M. and Sophronia James. She was an untiring worker for church and charity, of great public spirit and always interested in those movements tending toward the public good. She was deeply interested in the cause of public education and in 1894 she led in the movement which resulted in women being selected as members of the board of education. She was president of the Ladies Auxiliary of the Young Men's Christian Association, and nobly assisted in raising a goodly sum with which to furnish the association building. She organized the idea of the women in Warren celebrating the one hundredth anniversary of the birth of the town by publishing a "Woman's Centennial Paper." She carried this plan through most successfully as general manager, the issue being the largest ever published in Warren, five thousand copies of a sixteen-page paper. Financially the result was equally striking. She was an active worker in the Presbyterian church, accomplishing great good in her favorite field of work. Children: 1. Hugh K., born August 27, 1876; married Lena Magee, of Scottsburg, New York, July 21, 1909. 2. Kate Winifred, born September 7, 1881, died July 7, 1884. 3. Junius A., born September 24, 1888; he has been in business in Los Angeles, California, since the fall of 1909.

SCHIMMELFENG   Charles Edward Schimmelfeng was born February 28, 1866, at Honesdale, Wayne county, Pennsylvania, son of Henry and Margaret Eliza Schimmelfeng. His father is now one of the most prominent citizens of Ridgway, Elk county, Pennsylvania, being a well known lumberman of the western portion of the state and operating extensively in Elk, McKean and Center counties.

Charles Edward Schimmelfeng spent his childhood and early youth in Elk county, his education being received in the public schools there, supplemented by a course at the Normal School at Lock Haven, and a business college course at the same place. At the age of twenty years, his education being then completed, he began his career in business life by becoming his father's assistant in the lumber business, having charge of the work in the woods and the oversight of the logs and bark there. He was also engaged about the mills in a different capacity. He continued in association with his father in the lumber business for about six years, and in 1892 came to Warren, where he engaged in producing oil, a business which he followed for about seven years. He has also been much interested in horses since coming to this place and has had extensive dealings in this line. At the present time Mr. Schimmelfeng is engaged in the advertising business and has his sign boards distributed throughout the western portions of Pennsylvania and New York. He is a most popular and progressive citizen, and has before him the promise of a very successful and prosperous career; he is one of the most highly esteemed men of Warren and has a very wide circle of friends and acquaintances by whom he is considered a distinct addition to the social and fraternal life of the place. He is a member of a number of fraternal organizations, belonging to the Knights Templar of Ridgway, and having been made a Mason in Elk Lodge, No. 379, Free and Accepted Masons, at Ridgway.

On March 12, 1908, Mr. Schimmelfeng was married at Jamestown, New York, to Lea Eva Munn, daughter of George B. and Eva Munn, of Warren. Mr. and Mrs. Schimmelfeng have a delightful home at No. 11 Central avenue, Warren, where they take great pleasure in dispensing their hospitality and entertaining their many friends. They have no children.

The Cowan family in America COWAN traces its ancestry to the Colquhouns of Scotland. Three brothers, Ephraim, James and John Cowan, natives of Scotland, came to this country in the early part of the seventeenth century and settled in Massachusetts, John locating at Scituate.

(I) Robert Cowan, a grandson or great-grandson of Ephraim Cowan, removed to what was then known as the Camden Patent, Albany county, New York, some time between 1761 and 1763. He was a soldier of the revolutionary war, serving in Colonel Van Wert's regiment of New York troops, and died some time prior to the year 1790. His wife was Joanna Rogers, said to be a descendant of John Rogers, the English martyr; the marriage occurred before the family settled in New York. They had a son, Ephraim, of whom further.

(II) Ephraim (2), son of Robert and Joanna (Rogers) Cowan, was born in the year 1766, at Cambridge, Albany county, now Washington county, New York. He married Sally Wilson, born October 6, 1771, daughter of George Wilson. Children: Samuel, born 1790; Betsy, 1792, at Cambridge; Robert, of whom further; Joanna, 1796; Sally, 1798; George Wilson, 1802; Ephraim, 1804; James, 1807, at Fort Ann, New York; John, 1816, at Westport, Essex county, New York.

(III) Robert (2), son of Ephraim (2) and Sally (Wilson) Cowan, was born in 1794, in New York state. He and his brother Samuel served in the war of 1812, their mother spinning the yarn and weaving the cloth of which she made their uniforms. In 1819 Robert Cowan was commissioned captain of a company in the One Hundred and Seventieth Regiment of New York militia. About the year 1832 he removed with his family to Carroll, Chautauqua county, New York; he and his wife were members of the First Congregational Church at Jamestown. He married (first) Abigail Sabin, in the year 1818; she was born October 11, 1800, daughter of Timothy and Abigail (Heacock) Sabin, and granddaughter of Lieutenant Zebediah and Anna (Dwight) Sabin, and a descendant of William Sabin, of Rehoboth, Massachusetts. Lieutenant Sabin died in 1776 while serving the expedition against Quebec during the revolutionary war. Abigail Cowan died September 7, 1848. Mr. Cowan married (second) August 27, 1857, Mary Barber. He died August 5, 1873. Children by first wife: Ephraim, of whom further; Sally B., born 1824; Robert E., 1825; Abigail Zevier, 1828, married Sergeant John Thomas; Betsy Ann, 1830, married (first) Ephraim E. Eddy, (second) C. W. Eddy; Samuel A., 1834; John H., 1837; James Otis, 1838.

(IV) Ephraim (3), son of Robert (2) and Abigail (Sabin) Cowan, was born in 1821, at Wales, Erie county, New York. When twenty-one years of age he attended the Fredonia Academy for a term, then entered the Jamestown Academy, where he graduated after four years with the highest honors. He then read law for a year, after which he entered the office of the *Jamestown Journal*. In July, 1848, he came to Warren, Pennsylvania, in company with Mr. Warren Fletcher, and started the publication of the *Mail*, as an organ of the Whig party; in 1849 he bought the office and good will of the business and continued in the ownership of the paper, with his sons, Willis and Dwight, as partners, until his death in 1894. In 1856 Mr. Cowan was delegate to the convention which nominated General Fremont as president, and was subsequently elected county treasurer, an office which he held two years. From 1861 until 1862 he represented Warren and Crawford counties in the assembly at Harrisburg, and from 1862 until 1865 he was clerk in the department of the interior at Washington, D. C., and clerk in the house of representatives. He served several winters as clerk of the Pennsylvania state senate, and in 1874 was appointed deputy collector of internal revenue for Warren, McKean, Elk and Cameron counties, Pennsylvania, serving in this capacity for eleven years. For more than four years he acted in the capacity of private secretary to the public printer, Mr. Palmer, and died in Washington, D. C., January 23, 1894. He was a lifelong member of the First Congregational Church of Jamestown, New York, and one of the founders of the Sabbath school of the First Presbyterian Church of Warren, sustaining it until it became an established branch of the church.

Mr. Cowan married (first) April 18, 1850, Melvina Tamar, daughter of John and Betsy (Gilson) King, pioneer settlers in Warren. She was a granddaughter of Tamar Putnam, whose father, Nathan Putnam, was a field officer in the American revolution, and a great-granddaughter of Lieutenant John King, who served in the revolution. Mrs. Cowan's mother, Betsy (Gilson) King, was the daughter and granddaughter of revolutionary patriots, and a descendant of John Whitney, of Watertown, Massachusetts, whose lineage has been traced through the Lancastrian kings of England to the early French monarchs. The line of Nathan Putnam has also been traced back as far as Pepin of Heristal, in France. Mrs. Melvina T. Cowan died April 22, 1868. Mr. Cowan married (second) October 12, 1870, Julia Frances Camp, of Forestville, New York, who died May 18, 1887; no children. Mr. Cowan had three children by his first wife: Willis, born 1851; Dwight, of whom further; Clara Belle, married, January 30, 1879, George P. Orr, of Warren.

(V) Dwight, son of Ephraim (3) and Melvina T. (King) Cowan, was born September 21, 1853, at Warren, Warren county, Pennsylvania. He was educated in the local public schools, and when a very young man assisted his father in the office of the *Warren Mail*, in which paper he is to-day financially interested. In the year 1879 he became a partner with his father, continuing thus until his father's death in 1894, when he and his brother Willis purchased their sister's interest in the enterprise. Mr. Cowan later purchased his brother's interest, and conducted the paper alone until further changes were made in its management. In the year 1900 he became associated with the Pennsylvania Gas Company of Warren in the capacity of collector and clerk. For the past sixteen years he has been a member of the board of assessors, and is a Republican in his politics. From 1887 until 1898 he was a member of Company I, Sixteenth Regiment, National Guard of Pennsylvania, being corporal of the company for three years. At the outbreak of the Spanish-American war most of the married men dropped out of the company, and Mr. Cowan, with others, joined Company D, Twenty-first Regiment Home Guards. At the close of the war he returned to his old regiment and served out his unexpired term. He belongs to several fraternal organizations, being a member of Ramona Council, Royal Arcanum, and past noble guard of the Independent Order of Odd Fellows of Warren. He is a communicant of the Presbyterian church. Mr. Cowan has passed practically all of his life in Warren, having always been identified with the best interests of the city. He is one of the leading citizens, both socially and in business circles, and is esteemed for his talents and public-spirited attitude.

On October 2, 1878, he was married in Warren to Peoria Anna Thomas, born in Warren, October 30, 1858, daughter of John and Frances Harriet (Payne) Thomas (see Thomas III), and received her education in Warren. She taught school in early life, and is a devout member of the Presbyterian church to many of whose societies she now belongs. She has been superintendent of the primary Sunday school, and president of the Ladies' Aid. She has the unique distinction of having served as one of the directors on the Warren school board, being one of the three women who have been so honored. Mrs. Cowan is eligible to membership in the Daughters of the American Revolution, through both sides of her family, and takes a keen interest in the history and genealogy of her people. Mr. and Mrs. Cowan have the following children: 1. Harriet Luella, born July 13, 1880; married Percy Waters Wilkins, and has two children, Richard Cowan and Stanley Cowan Wilkins. 2. Earl Willis, born March 28, 1884; now in the office of the Hope Natural Gas Company at Pittsburgh, Pennsylvania. 3. Ernestine Cowan, born

March 2, 1889; attended Oberlin College of Kindergarten and is now a teacher in Jamestown public school No. 7.

(The Thomas Line).

(I) John Thomas, the earliest recorded progenitor of this family, was a native of New York state, born August 30, 17—, died August 3, 1808. Married, September 10, 1775, Elizabeth Hoff, born January 17, 1750, died August 29, 1805. Children: Jacob, born March 12, 1777; John, November 30, 1778; Isaac, October 25, 1780; Anna, March 24, 1783; Sally, March 12, 1785; Peggy, April 4, 1787; James, September 3, 1789; William, of whom further; Betsy, February 4, 1800.

(II) William, son of John and Elizabeth (Hoff) Thomas, was born November 18, 1791, died April 28, 1853. He was a millwright by trade, and resided at Jackson Run, Warren county, Pennsylvania. He was a Presbyterian. On May 4, 1823, he married Jane M., daughter of William and Elizabeth Hannah McConnell. Her father was a native of Scotland, married in Dublin, Ireland, and died at Warren, Pennsylvania, March 1, 1858; her mother died February 3, 1850. Children of William and Jane M. Thomas: William J., deceased; John, of whom further; Joseph, deceased; Elizabeth; Elisha; Margaret; Sarah, deceased; Mack, deceased; Mary, deceased; Henry, deceased.

(III) John (2), son of William and Jane M. (McConnell) Thomas, was born September 11, 1825, at Schenectady, New York. He came with his parents and six children to Jackson Run, Warren county, Pennsylvania, when he was eight years old. His first pursuit was lumbering. He served a term as treasurer of Warren county (1868-70) and was for a few years proprietor of the "Tanner House," a popular hotel, from 1865 to 1870. He removed from Warren to Falconer, New York, and then to Jamestown, where he followed farming on a large scale until his advanced age made it necessary to retire. In 1861 he enlisted in the Twelfth Pennsylvania Cavalry and served four years and four months, being first sergeant of Company K. He is a Republican. In 1856 he married (first) Frances Harriet Payne, who died in the year 1864. She was a daughter of Nathaniel and Lucinda (Sill) Payne, her father having been a major in the Twelfth Pennsylvania Cavalry, enlisting in 1861. She had three brothers, Hervey, Walter and Calvin. Children of John and Frances Harriet (Payne) Thomas: 1. Peoria Anna, born October 30, 1858; married Dwight Cowan (see Cowan V). 2. Mary Luella, born 1860, died 1880. 3. Berta L., born April 17, 1862; married James W. Kitchen, of Warren. In 1868 Mr. Thomas married (second) Abigail Zervier Cowan, who was the mother of Robert, who died at the age of sixteen years; and Bessie, who married M. A. Bliss, of Jamestown, New York.

(V) Willis, eldest child of Ephraim (3) (q. v.) and Melvina Tamar (King) Cowan, was born in Warren, Pennsylvania, August 14, 1851. He attended the Warren schools, and afterward took a course in a business college in Buffalo, New York. He was taken into partnership in the *Warren Mail* by his father in 1874. After the death of his father he was editor of the same until he sold his share to his brother in 1905. He has for some time been connected with the *Warren Evening Times*. He was a member of the Niagara Hose Company for several years, a member of Company I, National Guard of Pennsylvania, from 1880 to 1887, and a member of the board of assessors until he changed his residence to another ward in 1912. He and his brother were among the public-spirited citizens, who by paying a certain sum every year for five years gave Warren a free library, and is still a member of the Warren Library Association. He is a straight Republican, a Mason and Knight Templar, and a member of the Royal Arcanum, the Warren County Historical Society, a charter member of the Chamber of Commerce, and was one of the organizers of the Warren County Agricultural Society and secretary of the same for ten years. He has a generous, sympathetic disposition, and has always been actively interested in everything concerning the welfare of Warren. He and his family are members of Trinity Memorial Protestant Episcopal Church.

He married, September 24, 1878, Lucy Marie Davis, of Watkins, New York. Children, all born in Warren, Pennsylvania, and all educated in the schools of Warren, graduating from the high school, which is one of the finest in the United States: 1. Clara Belle, living with her parents. 2. Julia Melvina, married, October 11, 1911, William Allen Stover, of Ashland, Pennsylvania, now living in Duluth, Minnesota. 3. Lucy Marguerite, after graduating in the Normal course of Domestic Science at Drexel Institute, Philadelphia, Pennsylvania, accepted the position of dietist in the Fabiola Hospital, Oakland, California, where she remained until July, 1909, when she was sent to Manila, Philippine Islands, the first scientific dietist sent there by the government; she remained there in the Philippine General Hospital until the summer of 1911, reaching home September 15, 1911; on March 11, 1912, she was united in marriage to Leon H. Abbott, of Warren, Pennsylvania; her health failed as a result of the work in Manila, and she passed away August 29, 1912, aged twenty-six years and eight months; she had a lovable disposition, and was always trying to lift up the depressed and unfortunate; she was a charter member of General Joseph Warren Chapter, Daughters of the American Revolution, of Warren. 4. Anna May, married, November 22, 1911, Willis Ray Eysinger, of Warren, Pennsylvania. 5. Dorothy Davis, living with her parents.

Mrs. Lucy Marie (Davis) Cowan was born in Watkins, New York, the only daughter of Lot Barnum Davis and his second wife, Julia (Hudson) Davis. Lot B. Davis was the eldest son of Greley Davis, born in 1787, in Saratoga, New York, and Lucy (Dow) Davis, daughter of John Dow, first settler in Reading, New York, a member of the New York state assembly from Steuben county for three terms, and judge of the court of common pleas for forty years. He was a son of Benjamin Dow, of Voluntown, Connecticut, who served as sergeant in the revolution, son of Ebenezer Dow, one of the founders of Voluntown, one of the founders of the first Presbyterian church in Connecticut, elder in the same until his death, a justice of the peace under King George II. Ebenezer Dow was the son of Thomas Dow, who was in the Great Swamp fight, December, 1675, and grandson of Henry Dow, of Watertown and Hampton. Greley Davis served in the war of 1812, and his father, Alpheus, and grandfather, John Davis, both served in the revolution. Julia (Hudson) Davis was the daughter of Dr. Lemuel and Mary Treadwell (Woodruff) Hudson. Dr. Hudson served in the war of 1812-14 as surgeon, and afterward he was appointed brigadier-general in the New York state militia; he was the son of Asa Hudson, a revolutionary soldier, and his wife, Mary (Scott) Hudson. Mary T. (Woodruff) Hudson was a daughter of Rev. Hezekiah North Woodruff and his first wife, Mrs. Sarah Bartlett (Alden) Woodruff. This is quite a notable line. Mrs. Woodruff was the daughter of Dr. John Bartlett, and his first wife, Susanna (Southworth) Bartlett. Dr. Bartlett served as surgeon in the Indian war preceding the revolution, and as surgeon-general of the northern division of the revolutionary army. He was a son of Josiah Bartlett, who married Mercy Chandler, a descendant of the Alden family, and who was a son of Ichabod and Elizabeth (Waterman) Bartlett. Ichabod was a son of Benjamin and Sarah (Brewster) Bartlett. Sarah was the daughter of Love and Sarah (Collier) Brewster. Benjamin was a son of Robert Bartlett, who married Mary, daughter of Richard Warren. Dr. John Bartlett married Susanna Southworth, at Duxbury, Massachusetts, 1753. He married (second) Lucretia Stewart or Steward, at Stonington, Connecticut, 1761. Susanna (Southworth) Bartlett was a daughter of Jedediah and Hannah (Scales) Southworth, Jedediah being the son of Thomas Southworth and Sarah, daughter of Jonathan (2) Alden. Thomas was the son of Edward (3) Southworth, who married Mary Pabodie, granddaughter of John Alden. Edward (3) was the son of Constant Southworth, an officer in the Pequot war, and treasurer of Plymouth colony for sixteen years. Constant Southworth married Elizabeth Collier, and was himself the son of Edward (2) Southworth, who married Alice Carpenter. Edward (2) was the son of Thomas and Jane (Wynne) Southworth, and Thomas was the son of Edward (1) and Jane (Lloyd) Southworth. Edward (1) was the son of Christopher (2), son of Sir John Southworth, who married Lady Ellen of Walton. Sir John was the son of Sir Christopher (1) Southworth, whose wife was Lady Isabella de Dutton.

Thus Mrs. Cowan can claim as ancestors, Richard Warren, William Molines, John Alden, Elder William Brewster and son, Love Brewster, of the "Mayflower" voyagers. The Southworth lineage has been traced to Charlemagne the Great, Alfred the Great, William the Conqueror, to the earliest of the French and Saxon kings and allied families. Among her English ancestors Mrs. Cowan numbers six Knights of the Garter, including one of the founders, namely: Sir Thomas de Holland, first Earl of Kent; Sir Thomas de Holland, second Earl of Kent; Sir Richard Fitz-Allan, Earl of Arundel, died in 1375; James d'Audley, fourth Baron Audley, of Heleigh, 1316-87; Ralph de Stafford, first Earl of Stafford, one of the founders, born in 1299, and Sir Robert d'Holland, in Parliament in 1314, died in 1328. Also eight Magna Charta Sureties, namely: Sair de Quincy, first Earl of Winchester, died 1219; John de Lacie, Earl of Lincoln, died 1240; Roger Bigod, created Earl of Norfolk, 1189 A. D., and his son, Sir Ralph Bigod, Knight; Gilbert de Clare, Earl of Gloucester; Richard de Clare, sixth Earl of Clare, fourth Earl of Hertford; Robert de Ros, Lord of Hamlake, died 1227; William d'Albini, died 1236.

Although domestic in her tastes, Mrs. Cowan has always taken an active part in the social and church life of Warren, as a member of several clubs, societies, etc. In 1891 she was appointed a member of the county committee on Woman's Work, an auxiliary of the Board of World's Fair Management. She is a life member of the executive committee of Trinity Guild, a director of the Warren County Historical Society, and charter registrar of the General Joseph Warren Chapter, Daughters of the American Revolution. Her membership papers were endorsed by Miss Eugenia Washington, of Washington, D. C., and accepted October, 1892. In 1904-05 she transferred to the Tidioute Chapter, Daughters of the American Revolution, and served as registrar of that chapter for five years, until the organization of the chapter in her home town, 1911.

GOAL John Goal, the progenitor of the Goal family in Pennsylvania, was a native of Alsace-Lorraine, France, coming to America with his young family in the summer of 1851, and locating first in Lancaster county, Pennsylvania. He was a cabinetmaker, which trade he followed all his life, uniting with it the business of local undertaker. After remaining in Lancaster county a few years, he removed to Clarion county and located on a farm near Fryburg, where he died shortly after and was buried there. This was somewhere about the year 1870. Mr. Goal being then sixty-two years of age. His wife, Barbara (Stroeble) Goal, died about 1882, aged seventy-three; no other member of her family ever came to America. Mr. and Mrs. Goal were the parents of about ten children, eight of whom were as follows: 1. John C., born in 1846; now a prominent resident of North Clarendon, Pennsylvania, and one of the first to engage in the petroleum business there, having operated also in Warren and Venango counties; he is vice-president of the Cornplanter Refinery Company of Warren; married Hannah M., daughter of Albert W. Haight, of Pleasantville, having two sons, one deceased in infancy, and the other, Albert W., in business with his father. 2. William. 3. Caroline. 4. Adolphus D., of whom further. 5. David. 6. Frederick. 7. Mary. 8. Kate. The younger members of the family were born in this country.

(II) Adolphus D., son of John and Barbara (Stroeble) Goal, was born February 14, 1851, in Berlin, Germany. He was but three months old when his parents emigrated to America and settled in Lancaster county, Pennsylvania. Here he passed the years of his early boyhood, and when his parents removed to Clarion county he was sent to the public schools of Fryburg. His education was completed at the high school of Pleasantville, Venango county, after which, at the age of fourteen years, he started out upon his business career, working for a year in an oil refinery. He then went to Tidioute, Warren county, where for a year he pumped wells for his elder brother, John C. Goal, removing afterwards to Pleasantville, where he continued at the same work. In 1869 he acquired an interest in his first well, and locating at Fagundus, Warren county, worked as a driller, employing himself afterward in the same way at St. Petersburg, Clarion county; Bear Creek, Butler county, and Martinsburg, Blair county. At the last named town he became a partner in the firm of Hart, Hecks & Company, and operated with them for a period of three years. He then removed to Petrolia, Butler county, and operated alone for four years. His first large strike was at Edenburg, Clarion county, and after having spent eleven thousand dollars before reaching sand, he refused thirty thousand dollars for the well as soon as the bit struck. After this he became interested in a well that started out with a production of several hundred barrels of oil per day, operating here for three years and a half. He then went to North Clarendon and engaged with his brother, John C., in the refining business, continuing for five years. Removing at the end of this time to Forest county, he operated for another eleven years, and is now engaged in operating in Sugargrove and Brokenstraw townships, about four miles from Youngsville. He has eleven new producing wells, and the outlook is a very promising one, as he understands the oil business probably as well as any one in the field.

Mr. Goal is a very liberal and generous man, being popular and well educated, and an extensive reader. His open-handed generosity is a byword in the community, where he has paid for at least a hundred dry wells beside those from which he has obtained oil, and has spent money as freely and lavishly as he has made it. He is known among his intimate friends as "Doc" Goal, having been ambitious as a young man of adopting the medical profession. To this end he employed much of his time while engaged in pumping wells in the study of medical books which he obtained and read voraciously. He acquired a great deal of medical knowledge in this way, and has put several patent medicines upon the market, being probably more competent to practice medicine than many of the present day practitioners. Mr. Goal occupies a very prominent position in the public affairs of the community, having served for twenty-one years on the board of education, eleven years in Forest county, and ten years in Clarendon borough. He is a member of the Coudersport Consistory, No. 481, Independent Order of Odd Fellows, Sheffield, Pennsylvania, and the Free and Accepted Masons at Tionesta, Pennsylvania.

On April 16, 1874, Mr. Goal was married, at Butler, Butler county, Pennsylvania, to Olivia S. Campbell, born in Butler county, August 20, 1855, is daughter of Joseph F. and Elizabeth (Porter) Campbell. Her father is a veteran of the civil war; resides on a farm at Petrolia, Pennsylvania; he is now eighty-four years of age; he was also at one time in the oil business and served as treasurer of Butler county. His wife, Mrs. Goal's mother, died in April, 1912, at the age of eighty-three. They had seven children: Olivia S. (Mrs. Goal), William L., Ambrose, Lulu J., Robert J., Nora, Vetus, deceased. Mr. and Mrs. Goal became the parents of the following children: Clarence W., Joseph A., Lizzie M., Mary D., Lulu J., deceased; Ella R., Ethel L., Franklin, John L., a daughter, died in infancy.

SIGGINS (IV) George Washington Siggins, son of William (2) (q. v.) and Jane (Hunter) Siggins, was born at West Hickory, Forest county, Pennsylvania, October 7, 1843. He received his education at the local public schools, passing his boyhood days on his father's farm, where he assisted in the general work. He afterwards became a clerk in the store of John Siggins and was eventually a partner in the business. He came to Tidioute, Warren county, in 1884, and bought a farm of fifty-five acres in extent from James Wells, and to this he added twenty acres which he bought from John Breitenstine, making seventy-five acres in all. He conducted this farm from the time of its purchase and the property still remains in the hands of his widow. Mr. Siggins had also in early life acquired a knowledge of the milling business with N. G. Ball and he was thus enabled to assume the management of the flour mills of A. Dunn, in Tidioute, and this was conducted by him until March 18, 1911. He seemed to have been a man of great mechanical ability and could turn his hand to anything in that line, being naturally an excellent carpenter, blacksmith, millwright, and even repairer of his own automobile, which he came to own in later years. He prospered greatly in his business undertakings, and about eighteen years ago purchased his late residence on the south side of the Allegheny river, near the Economite bridge which there crosses it. His standing in the community was very high, and he was one of the leading and most influential citizens of this place. He died at Tidioute, Pennsylvania, May 20, 1911, having passed all of his life in Forest and Warren counties, Pennsylvania. He was a Democrat, and served on the school board and was appointed road commissioner. In his religious convictions he was a member of the Methodist Episcopal church, as is also his wife who survived him.

He married, February 17, 1868, Melissa, born November 21, 1850, on Tionesta creek, Forest county, Pennsylvania, daughter of Abraham and Nancy (Whitton) Bean (see Bean). She was educated at Hickory school, Forest county, and in social and church affairs is one of the leading ladies of this city. Children: 1. Georgiana, born November 18, 1868; married Harry A. Walters, August 8,

1907, and has one son, Joseph Harrison; Mrs. Walters is a member of the Daughters of the American Revolution. 2. Elnora, born April 11, 1879; married William Merkle and had three children, Karl, Edward, Ralph. 3. Isaac, born January 4, 1872; now resides at Perry, New York, unmarried. 4. George, born June 22, 1881; he is a physician at Venus, Clarion county, having graduated at Jefferson Medical College in the year 1905. A sketch of Dr. Siggins appears elsewhere in this work. 5. Daisy, born May 3, 1883; married, October 5, 1911, George Clark Nelson; they have one child, George Siggins Nelson, born September 3, 1912. Mr. Nelson was born at Gowanda, New York, September 13, 1880, and is the son of Olaf and Georgiana Nelson. His youth was passed at Gowanda, where he attained his education in the public schools, and where afterward he became employed in the Cutlery Works, learning the finishing business. He later removed to Fremont, Ohio, and from there to Little Valley, New York, following his trade. He then returned to Gowanda, and in 1903 came to Tidioute, Pennsylvania, where he was made foreman of the finishing department of the Tidioute Cutlery Works. In October, 1912, he became general manager of the plant, which position he now holds. He is a member of Phoenix Lodge, No. 262, Free and Accepted Masons, and belongs also to the Little Valley, New York, Lodge of the Independent Order of Odd Fellows. Mr. Nelson's father, Olaf Nelson, was a native of Sweden, emigrating from that country to America, where he settled at Gowanda, New York. He was a skilled mechanic, having acquired a thorough knowledge of the cutlery business in his native land, and held the position of foreman for many years in the Romerax Works. He was a naturalized citizen of this country, as recorded either in Gowanda or Buffalo, and was a member of the Republican party. His death occurred in 1892, when about thirty-eight years of age, and he is buried with his wife at Gowanda. The maiden name of his wife is not known. She was a native of Denmark, coming to this country alone, but a sister now resides in New York. Mrs. Nelson died in 1889, having had three children: George C., of whom we have spoken; Sophia, born September 9, 1884, married Francis Peterson, a resident of Rochester, New York; Harry, born October 31, 1886, now residing in Canton, Ohio.

(The Bean Line)

The name of this family, descended undoubtedly from the old Scottish clan, Vean, has been variously spelled, Bean, Bain and Bayne; in Gaelic the letters B and V are interchangeable, so that Vean and Bean are the same name differently spelled. The origin of the name is a matter of conjecture; by some it is claimed to be derived from the name of the clan's place of residence, "beann," a mountain. But an opinion which seems to have better authority is that it is a name derived from the fair complexion of the earliest progenitor of the old family, "bean" meaning white or fair. This term is often used by highlanders to indicate a man of fair complexion; as "olive," black or swarthy, is used to designate the opposite. The Clan Vean, or as often styled, MacBean, in Scottish history, was one of the tribes of the Chalti, or Clan Chatlan, which occupied the Lochaber territory some time previous to the year 1300 A. D. Three distinct families of this blood came to America: The Bains settled in Virginia, the Banes in Maine, and the Beans in New Hampshire. In what year or in what ship the immigrant ancestor of the Bean family reached these shores is not known and probably never will be.

This ancestor, John Bean, first appears in American history as the grantee of land by the town of Exeter, New Hampshire, in 1660, other grants having been made to him afterward. Tradition has it that his wife died on the passage over, and that he married again, his second wife having been a fellow passenger on the voyage. The name of the first wife is not known; the name of the second, whom he married prior to the year 1661, was Margaret. She joined Hampton Church in 1671; and "goodwife Bean" was among those who were dismissed from that church in 1698, "in order to their being incorporated unto a church state in Exeter." Margaret Bean was one of those who organized the church in Exeter, September 2, 1698. She was a member in 1705, which was the last mention of her; she died before 1718. John Bean died some time between January 24 and February 8, 1718. He divided his property among his children before his death and left no will. He had eleven children; by the first wife there was one, Mary, and by the second wife, ten, born in Exeter, as follows: John, died young; Henry, Daniel, Samuel, John, Margaret, James, Jeremy, Elizabeth, Catherine. One of the descendants of

John and Margaret Bean settled in New Jersey, being the progenitor of Abraham Bean and founding the family in that state.

Abraham Bean, the father of Mrs. George W. Siggins, was born January 5, 1828, died February 3, 1882, aged fifty-four years. He is buried at East Hickory, Forest county, Pennsylvania. Mr. Bean was a well known and successful lumberman of Forest county, doing business on Tionesta creek from the year 1865 until about 1880, when he moved over near Breakston, where he lumbered until his death. He became one of the most influential citizens in the circle in which he moved, and was a prominent man in connection with the Free Methodist church of which he was a member. In politics he was a Republican, taking a deep interest in the integrity of his party and the principles for which it stood. Some time prior to the year 1848 he was married to Nancy Whitton, a native of New Jersey, where his own family had resided for many years. Mrs. Bean, who became the mother of thirteen children, died in April, 1905. The children of Mr. and Mrs. Bean were as follows: 1. Fayette, married Judson Clark. 2. Melissa, married George W. Siggins (see Siggins IV). 3. Albert, who became a minister of the gospel and resides near Fairbanks, Alaska; he married Flora Patterson. 4. Henrietta, deceased. 5. Ellen, married Matthew McCray. 6. Warren, married Della Keiffer; lives in Washington state. 7. Belle, deceased; married William Hall. 8. Laura, married Simon Metzgar. 9. Lincoln, deceased. 10. Mary, deceased. 11. Ida, deceased. 12. Alice, deceased. 13. Kirk, lives in Delaware, Oklahoma.

STILLMAN The immigrant ancestor of the Stillman family in this state was George Stillman, who came to Massachusetts in the year 1680, from Steeple Aspen, England. After reaching this country he became a Seventh Day Baptist, having been a member of the established church while in England. His descendants have with few exceptions clung to the faith of their fathers.

(II) Edwin Amos Stillman, one of these descendants, was born July 19, 1813, at Middletown, Connecticut, being the son of James and Susan (Trench) Stillman. His father died when the boy was very young, and being the son of a widowed mother he began at an early date to support and educate himself, working on a farm before he was thirteen years of age, and taking a trip as cabin boy to Barbadoes and the West Indies. When thirteen years old he went to Meriden, Connecticut, as an apprentice in the Japanned ware business, remaining there for four years. During this time he joined the Baptist church, and distinguished himself as a religious speaker; he obtained a license to preach and was urged to study regularly for the ministry. He therefore spent a year at the Newton Theological Institute, and being then eighteen years of age decided to take a college course before completing his theological studies. Entering Brown University at Providence, Rhode Island, he remained a year, teaching in a classical school in Providence while pursuing his own studies. During the summer of 1833 following, his attention was attracted to the slavery question by an article which appeared in an English magazine, and he became convinced that it was his duty to preach "the deliverance of the captive and the opening of the prison doors to those who were bound." He began writing articles on the subject of slavery; he made the acquaintance of J. G. Whittier, with whom he became associated as a fellow delegate to the general convention of Abolitionists which met at Philadelphia and formed the "American Anti-Slavery Society." He was at this time a resident of Middletown, where there were but three avowed Abolitionists, and invited speakers from abroad whom he entertained, holding meetings in spite of the violence of the opposing mobs. All of this time he was still pursuing his theological studies, but finally he became discouraged by the indifferent attitude of the church toward the slavery question and abandoned his intention of a ministerial career.

In the year 1835 Mr. Stillman turned his attention to the study of civil engineering, and in the following year secured a position with the New York & Erie railroad. Soon afterward he became surveyor and assistant engineer on the Genesee Valley canal, being assigned charge of ten miles of the work from the tunnel below Portage to Hume, Allegany county, embracing some of the heaviest part of the work. Tunnels were a novelty in the country at that time, and his success in constructing this portion, as compared with similar works in Europe, was widely complimented. He was also instrumental in suppressing fraud and graft during the construction of the tunnel, and established a high reputation for personal integrity. In 1845 he removed to North Bloomfield, where he was engaged in locating a line of railroad from Canandaigua to Niagara Falls, and in 1854 he went to Springwater, where he began a career as lumberman, acquiring timber lands and erecting a lumber mill. He served in the engineering corps during the civil war and was engaged in the construction of Block House in Tennessee. He established a home in Canadice eventually, and lived here until his death, June 14, 1892, at the age of seventy-nine years.

During his residence at Canadice he took an active part in politics, being for many years identified with the Republican party. He was postmaster under President Lincoln, and held the office of justice of the peace, having read law and practiced in justice's corps. He was the Republican candidate for member of the assembly in 1861, but was defeated; he was again candidate on the Greenback ticket for the same office, and for that of state engineer and surveyor. His last political affiliation was with the Prohibition party. He also continued to do some work at surveying while in Canadice, and was employed for several years by the Honeoye Millers' Association in their contest with the Rochester Water Works Company. He was a well-informed and public-spirited man generally, taking an active interest in all educational works and being an authority on many points in civic affairs. The lumber and cooperage business, which he established, was continued by his two sons, John C. and Edwin S. Stillman.

On December 20, 1842, he married Jennie, daughter of Rev. James Cochrane, a Presbyterian minister of Rochester, New York, her mother having been Jane Craig, daughter of an Irish nobleman. Mrs. Stillman was born in the north of Ireland, coming to this country with her parents; she died at the age of seventy-nine years, having survived her husband. Mr. and Mrs. Stillman, who began their married life in Rochester, were the parents of seven children, as follows: 1. Ellicott R., enlisted in the Eighty-fifth New York Volunteer Militia, and was in the seven days' battle in the retreat from Richmond with McClellan's army; he was captured at Florence, North Carolina, and was a prisoner at Andersonville for about six months; he was postmaster of the city of Milwaukee for two terms, appointed by President McKinley; he died in 1912. 2. James Amos, of whom further. 3. Alice B., married Charles N. Legg, of Coldwater, Michigan. 4. Florence, married F. F. Betts, of Wellsboro, Indiana. 5. Jennie, died young. 6. John C., who continued in his father's business. 7. Edwin S., who also continued in his father's business. 8. Mabel C.

(III) James Amos, son of Edwin Amos and Jennie (Cochrane) Stillman, was born December 14, 1845, at Lima, Livingston county, New York. There he spent his early years, being educated in the public schools of the locality. When he was twenty years old he bought his time from his father, paying a hundred and fifty dollars, and removed to North Cohocton, Steuben county, New York, where he engaged as head sawyer in a mill. Having made this beginning in business, he later removed to Michigan, where he engaged in the same capacity in a number of the leading lumber mills of the state, spending some time in Central Lake and at Saginaw. After remaining in Michigan for a considerable time he returned home and farmed for a year. He then went to North Bloomfield, where he purchased a water power mill which he operated for five years; returning to Michigan again after this time he spent two years there, after which he came back to Bloomfield. In October, 1884, he came to Tidioute, Pennsylvania, and purchased the James Mill which he remodeled, establishing a planing mill in connection with it, and operating both for fifteen years. The industry was then destroyed by fire, and Mr. Stillman became foreman in a barrel factory at Milwaukee, Wisconsin, where he remained for a year. At the end of this time he came back east and for nine months was employed by Mr. E. D. Collins. He then returned to Tidioute and rebuilt his mill, but it was again destroyed by fire, in July, 1910. Since this time Mr. Stillman has been engaged in concrete work and the building of sidewalks. He resides on Main street, in the house which he purchased in 1884, and is considered one of the leading citizens. Mr. Stillman is a very ardent and active Socialist, wielding a strong influence in the party of which he was one of the organizers. He inherits the enthusiasm and ability of his father who was the subject of mob violence in Connecticut on account of his views as an Abolitionist. He is a member of the Universalist church, in which he has served as trustee. He is also interested and prominent in Masonic matters, having become a Mason at Honeoye Flats, New York, in the order of the Free and Accepted Masons. He is at present a member of the Tidioute Temple Lodge, No. 412, of this organization, having served as worshipful master in 1910.

Mr. Stillman has been married three times. In the year 1869 he married Maria North, born in 1852, died in 1872, being buried at North Bloomfield. To this union was born one son, Frederick J., in 1872. He grew to manhood and married Kate Whitten, having two children, Mabel and Ray. James A. Stillman married (second) May 15, 1879, Emma Commons, a relative of the poet Longfellow; she was born in 1856, died in 1889, being buried at North Bloomfield. One daughter was born of this marriage, Mollie Louise, July 13, 1881; she married Lyle R. Briggs, and has a daughter, Ethel Louise Briggs. On March 9, 1892, Mr. Stillman married (third) Amelia Catherine Turner, born August 21, 1852, at Tidioute, daughter of George W. and Mary J. (McMillen) Turner, and the younger sister of Christy Ann Turner, a sketch of whom appears elsewhere in this work. She has been a lifelong resident of Tidioute and is a member of the Universalist church in this place. She is also a member of the Daughters of the American Revolution, her national number being 36,488. Mr. and Mrs. Stillman are members of the Economite Chapter, No. 144, Eastern Star. There have been no children by this union.

DOWNING This is a prominent family of Western Pennsylvania, the progenitor, George B. Downing, having been a successful and influential lumberman of the region, engaged also in milling. He was a member of the Methodist Episcopal church, and was one of the leading citizens in this locality. On June 23, 1861, he married Elizabeth Ann Hollock, born September 1, 1841, now deceased, as is also her husband. She was a daughter of Jesse J. and Lovina (Van Buren) Hollock, residents of Garland, Pennsylvania, where her father was a farmer. Mr. Hollock was born June 23, 1810, died September 7, 1879. On July 27, 1830, he married Lovina Van Buren, born March 20, 1815, died February 14, 1880. Their children were: Lucy Jane, born January 13, 1832, at Jamestown, New York; Martin Llewellyn, born July 31, 1835, died July 27, 1839; William Reilley, born July 27, 1837, served in the civil war, now deceased; Wyman Hamilton, born October 8, 1839, died March 13, 1843; Elizabeth Ann, born September 1, 1841, married George B. Downing, now deceased; Almon D., born January 10, 1844, served in civil war, and lives at Garland, Pennsylvania; Washington E., born February 13, 1846, lost his life, August 19, 1864, during the civil war; Jesse Leroy, born March 26, 1851, residing at Erie, Pennsylvania; Alice Lovina, born March 13, 1854, married Thomas Sageon, of Tidioute, Pennsylvania. Mr. and Mrs. Downing were the parents of the following children: Nettie May, born May 14, 1862, died March 13, 1865; Walter Hollock, born August 23, 1864, married (first) Effie Proper, and had two children, Sylvia and Cora, married (second) Cora ———, and had two children, Ruth and George; William Frederick, born September 13, 1867, died July 25, 1868; George Halsey, born July 25, 1869, married (first) Harriet Dunn, married (second) Emma ———, has one child, William Downing; Frank Leroy, of whom further; Minnie Alice, born October 21, 1875, widow of M. Burton Lewis.

(II) Frank Leroy, son of George B. and Elizabeth Ann (Hollock) Downing, was born October 13, 1873, in Clarion county, Pennsylvania. He came to Tidioute with his parents when a boy, and received his education in the public schools. He entered upon his business career early in life, engaging with the Tidioute Chair Company as a marker, remaining here for awhile, after which he went to Warren, Pennsylvania, where he entered the employ of the Gale Manufacturing Company. He was employed in the plant of the latter company for about six months, however, when he left Warren and returned to his former position with the Tidioute Chair Company, the plant having changed hands; a history of this business is given in the sketch of Orry Husted Holdridge, elsewhere in this work. Since his return to Tidioute, Mr. Downing has been a member of the firm now known as the Tidioute Furniture Manufacturing Company, and has continued ever since as a resident of this place. He is one of the most influential business men in Tidioute, and is also prominent in the public life of the town, being a member of the Progressive party, and taking a strong interest in the welfare of the state. He is a member of the Methodist Episcopal church, and belongs also to the Knights of Pythias and the Grand Hose Company. On December 29,

1897, Mr. Downing was married at Jamestown, New York, to Bessie Esther Holdridge, born at Port Leyden, Lewis county, New York, September 4, 1878, daughter of Orry Husted and Harriet Amelia (Kellogg) Holdridge, a sketch of her father appearing elsewhere in this work. Mrs. Downing is a member of the Woman's Christian Temperance Union, of the Mendelssohn Club, and of Tidioute Chapter, No. 522, Daughters of the American Revolution. Mr. and Mrs. Downing have three children: Vera May, born April 24, 1901; Harold Halsey, April 30, 1903; Harriet Elizabeth, May 7, 1909.

PARSHALL The Parshall family, representatives of whom are among the most prominent citizens of this portion of Pennsylvania to-day, is one of the oldest families of the country, their English ancestry reaching back in unbroken line to the time of the Norman Conquest of England. The line of descent in this country has been taken from "The History of the Parshall Family, from the Conquest of England by William of Normandy, A. D. 1066, to the Close of the Nineteenth Century," by James Clark Parshall, Syracuse, New York, 1903.

(I) James Parshall, the immigrant ancestor, was born in England about the middle of the seventeenth century, there being no record extant of the exact date. He died at Southold, Suffolk county, New York, September 15, 1701. The fact that he died about twenty-three years after his marriage indicates that in all probability he did not reach a very advanced age. The first record regarding him in the colonies is a deed under date of December 12, 1679, he having been at that time a resident of the Isle of Wight, or Gardner's Island as it is now called, in the township of Easthampton. In about the year 1678 he was married, probably at Easthampton, to Elizabeth, only daughter of David and Mary (Lerringman) Gardner, of Easthampton. Children: Mary, born about 1679; Israel, of whom further; David, born 1683; Benjamin, probably died in infancy; Margaret, married, in 1710, Caleb Howell.

(II) Israel, son of James and Elizabeth (Gardner) Parshall, was born in 1680, probably on Gardner's Island, died at Aquebogue, Suffolk county, New York, April 18, 1738. He married, December 4, 1702, Joanna Swezey, born about 1678, died February 22, 1724. Children: Joanna, born about 1703; James, died April 9, 1719; Elizabeth, born June 27, 1705; Keziah, died in 1771; Israel, of whom further; Jemima, died November 18, 1753; Experience, married Daniel Reeve, November 11, 1736.

(III) Israel (2), son of Israel (1) and Joanna (Swezey) Parshall, was born probably at Aquebogue, Suffolk county, New York, some time between the years 1708 and 1712. He married, November 16, 1732, Bethia Case. Children: James, of whom further; Phineas; Benjamin, born October 6, 1736; Phineas; Benjamin, born September 12, 1744; Jesse; Delilah, married ——— Terry; Bethia, born March 1, 1749-50; Jemima, married David Wells; Joanna, married Joshua Wells; child, deceased; son, deceased.

(IV) James (2), son of Israel (2) and Bethia (Case) Parshall, was born some time between 1733 and 1735, in Suffolk county, New York. The records regarding him are of the most meagre description; it is certain, however, that he removed from Suffolk county to Orange county, New York, prior to the breaking out of the revolutionary war. His signature appears as a member of the association to support the continental congress at Goshen precinct, Orange county, New York, June 21, 1775. He also appears to have been appointed ensign of the Chester company of the West Orange regiment. He was "one of the scouts who served April 5 to 6, being two days in covering certain Tory prisoners from Warwick Mountain to Kings Town" (Kingston). That he served through the revolution is certain, but as there was another James Parshall, born 1762, who served in the later part of the war, it is not always possible to determine from the official records one from the other. It is believed that he removed after the close of the war to western New York and located at or near Palmyra, Wayne county, but as the other James Parshall, previously referred to, located at the same place, the difficulty of distinguishing them is increased. James Parshall was accompanied on his removal by a sister who had previously married a Mr. Terry, and whose daughter, Deliverance, subsequently became the wife of his brother Israel. We have no record of the marriage of James Parshall, but Samuel Parshall, mentioned below, was a son, as can be better explained in the Parshall genealogy from which this record is taken.

(V) Samuel, son of James (2) Parshall, was born March 20, 1757, on Long Island, New York, died at Ellsworth, Ohio. He appears to have removed with his putative father to Orange county, New York, prior to the breaking out of the revolutionary war, and lived with him in Goshen precinct in 1775, when he was in Captain Phineas Rumsey's company and signed with the Association Congress. He appears also as a private in Captain Marion's Company of Colonel Drake's regiment. He was employed in a powder mill in Maryland during the greater part of the war, as is absolutely certain. In about 1778 he married (first) Sarah ———, who died probably about 1786, after the birth of her second child. The two children were: James, born June 6, 1779; Samuel, of whom further. Samuel Parshall married (second) on Long Island, Rachel Stratton, a native of that place, born March 30, 1765, died about 1848. Children: Sarah, born July 29, 1787; Elizabeth, May 6, 1789; John, June 24, 1791; William, November 15, 1794; Daniel, June 9, 1796; Thomas, July 21, 1798; David, October 17, 1800; Jacob, March 15, 1803; Nancy, May 18, 1806; Moses, January 10, 1810.

(VI) Samuel (2), son of Samuel (1) and Sarah Parshall, was born July 6, 1781, probably on Long Island, died at Tidioute, Pennsylvania, in 1840. He married, at Poland, Ohio, Elizabeth, born at Poland, March 20, 1783, died at Tidioute, March 9, 1866, daughter of Henry Goucher. Children: Henry, born February 1, 1807; John Munnell, of whom further; Rhoda Ann, July 22, 1811; Elizabeth, December 12, 1812; Samuel, November 14, 1814; Nancy, November 13, 1817; George Stranahan, January 14, 1820; Jeanette Stratton, February 22, 1822; James, September 19, 1827.

(VII) John Munnell, son of Samuel (2) and Elizabeth (Goucher) Parshall, was born February 23, 1809, probably in Orange county, New York, died at Troyville, Pennsylvania, November 6, 1889. He married, at Tidioute, about 1829, Alice, born at Tidioute, November 10, 1811, died there in April, 1898, daughter of Samuel and Charity (Gilson) McGuire. Children, all born at Tidioute: Samuel, born in 1830, deceased; Rhoda, April 24, 1832; Matilda, February 15, 1835; Elizabeth, 1836; Lucinda Marion, December 5, 1838; William Henry, October 30, 1840; Hugh McGuire, of whom further; Nancy M., October 21, 1844; John Munnell, November 15, 1846, died in Erie, Pennsylvania, June 4, 1905, on March 21, 1869, he married at Greenville, Pennsylvania, Elizabeth, born May 2, 1846, in Venango county, daughter of Jonathan D. and Jane (Walton) Hogan and they had a son, Frank Carlton, born August 30, 1873, married Estella, daughter of Samuel and Elizabeth Johson.

(VIII) Hugh McGuire, son of John Munnell and Alice (McGuire) Parshall, was born July 23, 1842, at Tidioute, Warren county, Pennsylvania. Here he made his home all his life, spending, however, a portion of his time in Mexico and Central America. He was engaged for some years in mercantile pursuits in Tidioute, but for many years represented Reeves, Parvin & Company, of Philadelphia, beside doing considerable outside business in staple provisions. He was a veteran of the civil war, having enlisted at Riker's Island, New York, August 20, 1861, in Company F, Fifth Regiment Excelsior Brigade New York Volunteer Infantry. He was promoted to the rank of second sergeant during service. He fought at the siege of Yorktown, Williamsburg, in the seven days' fight before Richmond, the second battle of Bull Run, Fredericksburg, Chancellorsville, Gettysburg, Mine Run, Wilderness, Spottsylvania Court House, Front Royal, Cold Harbor, and the siege of Petersburg. In August, 1863, he was detailed from Front Royal, Virginia, to repair to New York City as drill sergeant for colored troops; he remained six months, and also did recruiting service. His term of service expired on August 29, 1864, at which time he was honorably discharged at Petersburg, Virginia. Mr. Parshall was a trustee of the Presbyterian church. He was a member of the Grand Army of the Republic, under the auspices of Colonel Cobham Post, being an active and influential member; he spent the last evening of his life with his comrades and associates here, his death occurring suddenly at his home, February 10, 1904. He was a man of fine and strong character, quiet and self-contained at all times, seeming to have uppermost in his mind the two thoughts of duty to his family whom he loved devotedly, and a desire to benefit humanity at large in a manner as quiet and unostentatious as possible. He was a broad-minded and patriotic citizen, and a true friend.

On April 18, 1866, Mr. Parshall was married, at Erie, Pennsylvania, to Sarah West, a native of Harbor Creek, Pennsylvania, where she was born February 17, 1845. She was a daughter of Spencer and Susanna (Morgan) West (see West III). Mrs. Parshall was educated in the public schools of the locality, finishing with a course at Erie Academy, after which she taught for two terms in the district schools prior to her marriage. For the past thirty years she has been a member of the Presbyterian church of Tidioute, having come to this place about forty years ago. She is one of the most esteemed members of the community here, belonging to the Tidioute Chapter of the Daughters of the American Revolution, No. 57,144. She is also very active in the Women's Christian Temperance Union, exerting an influence that is felt very widely for good. Mr. and Mrs. Parshall were the parents of the following children: 1. Harriet May, born February 13, 1867; she was educated in the schools of Tidioute, finishing at the high school here, and taking a subsequent course at the New England Conservatory of Music at Boston, Massachusetts; she then took up evangelical work at Moody Institute, Chicago, Illinois, and is now traveling with the Dr. Edward Brederwolf Company throughout the western states. 2. Frank M., born July 19, 1868, died in March, 1870. 3. Edward E., born April 16, 1871, died February 10, 1896; he became a dentist, being a graduate of the University of Pennsylvania. 4. Allan W., born December 31, 1876, died February 17, 1877. 5. Hugh Raymond, born April 17, 1878; married (first) Ellen Jane Kreer; (second) Helen Marr. 6. Florence, born September 30, 1881; married, June 27, 1906, several years after the death of her father, to Professor Charles M. Freeman, having three children as follows: Sarah Marie, born August 29, 1907; Maxson and Marjorie, twins, born October 28, 1912. Three of Mr. Parshall's children, as mentioned above, were living at the time of their father's death; as was also his brother, John M. Parshall, of Erie, who was for a number of years his partner in business, and who died June 4, 1905. Mrs. Parshall has taken an active interest in the genealogical history of her own and her husband's family.

(The West Line).

(I) The earliest American progenitor of this family was Ebenezer West, who was a soldier in the revolutionary war; he enlisted from Connecticut, as is shown by the records at Hartford.

(II) Joseph, son of Ebenezer West, died August 21, 1847, at the age of eighty-two years. He married Ruth Munson, and they had the following children: Huldah, born September 24, 1784; Ithamar, September 12, 1786; John, June 1, 1789; Lydia, October 1, 1791; Joseph, September 21, 1794; Calvin, October 29, 1796; Spencer, of whom further; Lyman, August 11, 1803; Charles F., March 30, 1807; Sydney C., May 22, 1811; Samuel F., August 10, 1816.

(III) Spencer, son of Joseph and Ruth (Munson) West, was born May 21, 1799, died July 17, 1885. He was a native of Hartford, Washington county, New York, removing with his parents to Essex county, and then to Chautauqua county, in the same state. He finally settled on a farm at Harbor Creek, Erie county, Pennsylvania, and his last years were spent in Corry, Pennsylvania. He was a Republican, and a member of the Baptist church. He married Susanna Morgan, born December 10, 1806, daughter of Medes and Ann (Hall) Morgan; her father died in December, 1849, and her mother in May, 1861. Children of Medes and Ann (Hall) Morgan: Mahala, born November 20, 1799; Electa, August 20, 1804; Susanna, December 10, 1806, married Spencer West; Ezra, June 18, 1809; Huldah, August 12, 1812; Thomas, January 31, 1815; Delatus, October 4, 1817; Anna, March 25, 1820. Children of Spencer and Susanna (Morgan) West: Philetus C., born August 2, 1828, died in Fredonia, New York, March 12, 1913; Adoniram J., February 3, 1831, died 1877; S. Newell, April 22, 1833, died in 1908, in Traer, Iowa; Huldah M., May 31, 1835; Luke M., September 12, 1837; Harriet N., January 26, 1841; Sarah, February 17, 1845, married Hugh M. Parshall (see Parshall VIII); Markham, September 18, 1849, died October 1, 1862. Mr. West died July 3, 1900.

WESTGATE-KING There is a tradition that the first Westgate in this country came from England with the King's troops; was a sailor-soldier, and when the war or the occasion that called for troops was over decided not to return to England with his comrades. It is further believed that this sailor-soldier was Adam Westgate, the first of the name found in colonial records. He is said to have resided at Salem, Massachusetts, 1647 to 1662, but it is probable that his residence there exceeded the fifteen years intervening between these dates. The Christian name of his wife was Mary; his children: Robert, of whom further; a son, who died unmarried; Thomas, born February 12, 1654; two sons, named Joseph, both died young; two daughters named Mary, both died young; Benjamin, born July 26, 1662, died in infancy.

(II) Robert, son of Adam Westgate, was born in Salem, Massachusetts, July 1, 1647, died December 23, 1717. He settled in Warwick, Rhode Island, where he owned and cultivated a farm until his death. In 1687 he was chosen constable for Newport, and in 1700 he is credited with a contribution of twelve shillings toward the erection of a Quaker meeting house at or near Mashapang. His will dated September 1, 1716, probated January 10, 1718, appointed his wife Sarah executrix. She died September 23, 1723. Children: Catherine, born December 23, 1684, married a Northup; John, born April, 1686, died July 24, 1687; George, born April 24, 1688, married, October 5, 1727, Elizabeth Earle, five children; Silvanus, of whom further; Priscilla, born February 26, 1693; Sarah, January 15, 1695; Rebecca, January 8, 1697, married Benjamin Earle, four children; Robert, September 18, 1698, died 1750, a carpenter, married (first) Patience Carr, born February, 1701, died March 27, 1753, married (second) a widow, Mrs. Mary Hawkins, six children by first wife; John, May 19, 1700; James, September 19, 1703; Mary, September 7, 1706, married John Carrder, five children.

(III) Silvanus, son of Robert Westgate, was born in Warwick, Rhode Island, February 19, 1691, was lost at sea, September 27, 1719. He married, September 13, 1711, Jerusha Davis, born January 17, 1690, who survived him and married (second) July 22, 1726, John Stafford. Children of Silvanus Westgate: Sarah, born January 10, 1713; Robert, March 19, 1716, will proved February 4, 1750, mentioned his wife, mother, sister Sarah Rhodes, brother Silvanus and a half sister Amey Stafford; Silvanus, of whom further.

(IV) Silvanus (2), third and youngest child of Silvanus (1) Westgate, was born in Warwick, Rhode Island, July 16, 1719. He moved to Provincetown, Barnstable county, Massachusetts, whose harbor was made famous by the "Mayflower" on her first arrival. He married and left a family including Silvanus, of whom further.

(V) Sylvanus or Silvanus (3), son of Silvanus (2) Westgate, was born August 26, 1766, in Provincetown, Massachusetts. His life was spent in his native state, where he held the offices of justice of the peace and postmaster. He was a highly respected citizen, just and upright in his dealings with his fellowmen, genial and courteous to all. After an epidemic of typhoid fever, about 1855, which deprived him of a son and daughter, he practically retired from all business. This affliction was followed by another, loss of sight, and the last ten years of his life were spent in total darkness. He married Deborah Hammond, born September 27, 1757. Children: Hannah, born December 28, 1789; Polly, July 17, 1791; Prince, May 9, 1793; Benjamin Boles, of whom further.

(VI) Benjamin Boles, youngest son of Sylvanus or Silvanus (3) Westgate, was born July 10, 1795, died at Riceville, Crawford county, Pennsylvania, and is there buried. He was educated in public schools and spent his early life at Fishkill and Providence, Rhode Island, coming to Pennsylvania in 1839 and locating at Riceville. His early business was the manufacture of bent wood ware, cheese boxes, bowls, etc. After coming to Riceville he established a sash, blind and door factory, marketing his products in Erie, Pennsylvania, transporting them from mill to market by teams. He operated his Riceville factory for twenty-five years and was rated one of the substantial men of the town. He was a Whig in politics, later a Republican, holding the office of postmaster and justice of the peace. He was an attendant of the Congregational church, of which his wife was a member. He married (first) February 18, 1819, Abigail, daughter of Matthew and Abigail St. John. He married (second) at Saratoga, New York, August 10, 1828, a cousin of his first wife, Martha St. John, born May 14, 1796, died March 11, 1865, daughter of Josiah and Sabra (Dunham) St. John. Children of his first marriage: Lorenzo, born December 14, 1819; Reuben B., January 9, 1822; St. John, January 24, 1824; Orson, September 2, 1825. Children of his second marriage: Ann Martha, May 30, 1829, married William L. Robinson, children: Cora May, Edgar C., Herbert W.; Mary Jane, October 24, 1831, died 1855; Harriet, February 13, 1835, died 1905, married

C. N. Smith; Ira, October 31, 1837, died 1856; Caroline M., of whom further.

(VII) Caroline M., youngest child of Benjamin Boles and Martha (St. John) Westgate, was born in Riceville, Pennsylvania, January 14, 1841. She married, October 1, 1861, Francis G. King, born in Panama, Chantauqua county, New York, February 26, 1834, son of Harry King, and one of a family of eight, three of whom were living in 1911, namely: Mrs. Catherine Alden, Mrs. H. F. Shaw, and J. H. King. Francis G. King received his education in the public schools of Jamestown, New York. In the spring of 1862, when the oil excitement in Pennsylvania was at its height, he and his brother, Harry J. King, went to Titusville, where they engaged in the hardware business and enjoyed unbounded success. He remained in Titusville three years, and then disposed of his business and removed to Rochester, New York, where he again became actively engaged in business. After nine years in that city his health began to fail and he was compelled to seek a different climate. He accordingly went to Denver, Colorado, which was then a new city, and growing rapidly. Mr. King engaged in the real estate business, besides being largely interested in milling and mining industries. He identified himself with the growth of the city and won prominence in social, as well as business circles. In March, 1885, he returned to Rochester, New York, where he remained until 1896, when he came to Warren, Pennsylvania, where he resided until his death, which occurred June 1, 1911.

Mr. King was possessed of a strong character and was generally known to men of business affairs as one of the strictest integrity. He commanded the respect of all men. His business career for many years was an active one, and it may be said of him that in his dealings with his fellowmen he was always honorable, and the good influence exerted by him will long be remembered, his death depriving Warren of one of its best citizens. Although Mr. King was not a man who took an active interest in politics his strong personality was generally recognized and his interests were always for the uplift of the people and the betterment of the public institutions. He was a member of the Conewango Club since its organization, and also a member of the Conewango Fishing Club. He was a great traveler, having taken a trip around the world in 1890, and many other trips to foreign lands. Children of Mr. and Mrs. King: 1. Bessie, born in Denver, Colorado, March 11, 1876; married J. P. Rogers, of Warren, Pennsylvania; children: Francis King and Catherine King Rogers. 2. Dwight D., born April 9, 1879; married Mrs. Ann Sill; no children; they reside at Mabelle, Colorado.

The ancestors of this HOLDRIDGE branch of the Holdridge family came to Warren county, Pennsylvania, from the state of New York, but it is not known when the original immigrant came to this country nor where he first located.

(I) Perry Holdridge, the first recorded progenitor, was born about the year 1812, the place of his birth not being known. For many years he resided in Schenectady, New York, removing in early life to Chatham, Columbia county, where he was married. He was by trade a carpenter, making doors, sashes and blinds, and everything in the line of his business. He was also an undertaker and was well versed in cabinetmaking, had a furniture store, made coffins, and manufactured everything in the carpentering line that could be used in building. He was a man of more than ordinary ability, being prosperous in his business and greatly respected in the community in which he lived. He was a Republican, and a member of the Dutch Reformed church, and at his death, at about the age of seventy years, was buried with his wife in the cemetery at Nassau, New York. He was married at Chatham to Betsey Husted, born at Nassau, July 17, 1813, died in 1878, daughter of Nicholas and Mary (Waterbury) Husted, who were married in 1795; he was born February 15, 1772, at Nassau, dying November 5, 1815, and she was born September 28, 1774, dying April 5, 1841. Children of Mr. and Mrs. Husted: Mary, born August 15, 1796; Daniel, June 25, 1798; Nicholas, April 27, 1801; Orry, May 18, 1803; Sacket, February 8, 1805; Clarissa, April 11, 1812; Betsey, July 17, 1813, married Mr. Holdridge. Mr. and Mrs. Holdridge had the following children: 1. Electa, died young. 2. Edgar Perry, served during the civil war, dying in a hospital during his service. 3. Mary E., married General Wallace and resides in Los Angeles, California. 4. Loren, served during the civil war and now lives at Ocean Grove, New Jersey. 5. Orry Husted, of further mention. 6. Emma, married James Henderson and resides in Los Angeles.

(II) Orry Husted Holdridge, son of Perry and Betsey (Husted) Holdridge, was born October 20, 1849, in Chatham, New York. His education was received in the public schools of his locality, and in a select school. At the age of sixteen years he removed to Troy, New York, where he obtained employment as a pressman in the office of the *Daily Times*. Here he remained for two years, when he again removed and settled in Port Leyden, New York, where he subsequently married. He became engaged as a saddler, and eventually embarked in mercantile business for himself in this line, opening a harness store at Port Leyden. Later on he conducted a store at Grey, New York; and subsequently located in Philadelphia, where for three years he was established in this business. In 1890 he disposed of his store in Philadelphia and came to Warren county, Pennsylvania, locating first at Kinzua. Here he was in charge of the finishing department of the plant of Hood, Gale & Company, furniture manufacturers. When the Kinzua plant was destroyed by fire, Mr. Holdridge came with the firm to Warren borough, and here was in charge of the same department as formerly, remaining with the firm until 1898, when he severed his connection with them and came to Tidioute. Here the firm of Simmons, Holdridge & Company was established, of which he was one of the promoters and proprietors, later becoming the president when Mr. Simmons withdrew from the firm and the name was changed to the Tidioute Furniture Company. Mr. Holdridge was also one of the directors and president of the new firm, with which he remained until 1910, when he sold out his interests and devoted himself to his original invention, "the Holdridge Folding Crate." This article he is now arranging to manufacture on a large scale as soon as a company can be incorporated for that purpose. He is also the inventor of the Holdridge Fire Escape.

Having prospered in his business affairs, Mr. Holdridge purchased in 1907 his present beautiful residence on Main street, the Hague homestead, where he and his family are comfortably domiciled. He is one of the most prominent citizens in this place, and is a Republican in politics. It was his desire to serve in the civil war, and at the age of fifteen he left home to enlist, being, however, rejected at Albany, New York, on account of his youth. He holds membership in Port Leyden Lodge, F. and A. M., where he was first made a Mason. On March 21, 1869, Mr. Holdridge was married, at Port Leyden, New York, to Miss Harriet Amelia Kellogg, a native of that town, where she was born on August 20, 1851, daughter of Hial Handy and Mary Silvina Kellogg (see Kellogg). Her education was received in the schools of Port Leyden and at Boonville high school, and she is eminently fitted for the prominent position which she occupies in the community. As a member of the Methodist Episcopal church and the various societies connected with it, she has exercised a great influence for good; and is a most influential member of the Women's Christian Temperance Union, of which body in Tidioute she has been president for the past ten years. She has served one year as county president of the same, and is a very active worker in the cause of temperance. Mr. and Mrs. Holdridge are the parents of the following children: 1. Franklin L. (q. v.). 2. Mary Emma, born May 8, 1875, at Port Leyden; married George W. Denham; no children. 3. Bessie Esther, born September 4, 1878, at Port Leyden; married Frank L. Downing, a sketch of whom appears elsewhere in this work; children: Vera, Herold and Harriet E. Downing. 4. Ruey Kellogg, born January 16, 1885, at Port Leyden; married Gaylord Allen. 5. Edgar Leroy, born October 28, 1890, at Kinzua, Pennsylvania.

(The Kellogg Line).

Every tradition in this family points to a British origin, there being extant a number of legends as to the derivation of the name and the ancient home of the first progenitors. Hon. Day Otis Kellogg, formerly U. S. Consul at Glasgow, Scotland, one of the best known collectors of Kellogg history and traditions, enters an able argument for their Scottish origin, claiming that the family were partisans of James VI. of Scotland, and accompanied him to England when he ascended the English throne as James I. From England the first ancestors of the family in America probably came to this country in the seventeenth century. The same authority for this theory suggests also that the name Kellogg was originally derived from the two Gaelic words "kill," a cemetery, and "loch," a lake; the meaning being, the "family of the lake cemetery."

Nicholas Kellogg, the first of the family whose name is found in the public records of England, was born about 1488, as shown by his deposition in 1548. He married Florence, daughter of William Hall, of Debden, Essex county, England. He was buried May 17, 1558; and his wife, November 8, 1571. As the names of his children are not mentioned in his will, their names are not all known. The manorial court rolls indicate that he had at least two sons, William and Thomas.

Thomas Kellogg, son of Nicholas and Florence (Hall) Kellogg, resided in Debden, inheriting his mother's estate and owning much property. He was at Debden in 1571, as he succeeded his mother in the ownership of what was in the possession of her husband, Nicholas Kellogg. Tradition says that he married, and it is supposed that Philip Kellogg was his son, as no other family of this name was resident at that time in this part of England.

Philip Kellogg, probable son of Thomas Kellogg, was the first of the name in England from whom the Kelloggs of the New World can with any certainty trace their descent. He first appears in Bocking, Essex parish, adjoining Braintree, when his son Thomas was baptized, September 15, 1583. Other records of baptism are those of Robert, 1585, and Martin, November 23, 1593; there is burial record of daughter Annis, in Great Lights, May 25, 1611.

Martin Kellogg, son of Philip Kellogg, was baptized November 23, 1595, and married in St. Michael's, Bishop's Stortford, county Hertford, October 22, 1621, to Prudence Bird; she died before May 20, 1671, as her name does not appear in the will. Martin Kellogg died in Braintree, England, some time between May 20, 1671, when his will was made, and September 20 of the same year, when it was approved. By trade he was a weaver of cloth. Children, mentioned in will: Sarah; Joseph, mentioned further; Daniel; Samuel; Nathaniel; Martin.

(I) Lieutenant Joseph Kellogg, son of Martin and Prudence (Bird) Kellogg, was baptized at Great Lights, England, on April 1, 1626. He was the first member of the family to come to America, though the exact date of his arrival is not known. He was in Farmington, Connecticut, however, as early as 1651, being one of the early settlers there, and selectman. He and his wife joined the church October 9, 1653; the children named in his will were John, Martin, Edward, Joanna, Stephen, Elizabeth, Abigail, Prudence, Ebenezer, Nathaniel and Joseph. These probably survived him. He married (first) probably in England, Joanna ———, who died in Hadley, Massachusetts, September 14, 1666; he married (second) Abigail Terry, born in Windsor, Connecticut, September 21, 1646, daughter of Stephen Terry, who was born at Stockton, Wiltshire, England, on August 25, 1608. Lieutenant Kellogg died some time between June 27, 1707, when his will was dated, and October 31, 1726, when it was approved. Children, by first wife: Elizabeth, born 1651; Joseph, 1653; Nathaniel, 1654; John, mentioned further; Martin, born 1658; Edward, 1660; Samuel, 1662; Joanna, 1664; Sarah, 1666. Children, by second wife: Stephen, born 1668; Nathaniel, 1669; Abigail, 1671; Elizabeth, 1673; Prudence, 1675; Ebenezer, 1677; Jonathan, 1679; Daniel, 1682, died young; Joseph, born 1684; Daniel, 1686, died young; Ephraim, born 1687.

(II) John, son of Joseph and Joanna Kellogg, was born in 1656, and baptized December 29 of the same year, at Farmington, Connecticut. His name appears in a list of those owning large estates in Hadley, Massachusetts, in 1720. He married (first) December 23, 1680, Sarah Moody, born 1660, died 1690. Children: Sarah, born 1682; John, born 1684, died 1691; Joseph, born 1685; Samuel, mentioned further; son, born 1689, died in infancy. John Kellogg married (second) Ruth ———; children: Ruth, born 1693; Joanna, 1694; Esther, 1696; Abigail, 1697; John, 1699.

(III) Samuel, son of John and Sarah (Moody) Kellogg, was born April 1, 1687, at Hadley, died May 27, 1761, and is buried at Westfield, Massachusetts, where his gravestone is still standing. He owned several hundred acres of land, and built a saw mill and a grist mill; also the second meeting house, in 1721. He was known as Captain Samuel Kellogg; married (first) July, 1714, his cousin, Mary Ashley, born March 12, 1694, died April 8, 1728; married (second) June 3, 1728, his cousin, Rachel Ashley, born February 14, 1695. Children, by first wife: Josiah, born 1715; Samuel, 1717; David, 1721; Seth, 1723; twin daughters, 1724, died same day; son, 1725; John, mentioned further. Children by second wife: Justus, born 1729; Mary, 1730; Shem, 1732; Sarah, 1734.

(IV) Captain John (2) Kellogg, son of

Captain Samuel and Mary (Ashley) Kellogg, was born July 5, 1727; he resided in Westfield. In 1764 he built a house which was considered the best in the place, and cut a tomb in the solid rock, over which a church was subsequently erected. He was a soldier in the French and Indian war, enlisting April 6, 1759, and serving under General Amherst until December 3 of the same year. He was also a soldier in the revolution, serving on the Lexington alarm at the defense of the town and harbor of Boston and at the capture of Dorchester Heights. He was captain in Colonel Leonard's regiment "to go to Ticonderoga," in 1777. He married (first) (published September 15, 1750) Anne Terry, born August 17, 1732, died October 5, 1764; married (second) (published September 21, 1766) Anna Lord, born about 1725, died September 2, 1781; married (third) July 7, 1791, widow Jemima Ward. Children by first wife: Ann, born 1751; Lovisa, 1753; Josiah, mentioned further; Bassorah, 1757; Lucy, 1759; Aaron, 1762; daughter, 1764, died same day, and was buried with her mother.

(V) Josiah Kellogg, son of Captain John (2) and Anne (Terry) Kellogg, was born May 31, 1755, died January 30, 1814. He resided in Westfield. Married, May 31, 1780, Lois Day, born in Springfield. Children, born in Westfield: Lucy, 1782; John, 1784, died 1785; John, born 1786; Pamelia, 1788; Silas, mentioned further; Polly, 1792; Henry, 1794; Arminta, 1799; Collins, 1802.

(VI) Silas, son of Josiah and Lois (Day) Kellogg, was born February 10, 1791, in Westfield, Massachusetts. In 1823 he removed to Hopewell, New York, and thence in May, 1825, to Port Leyden, New York, where he died April 9, 1876. He married, October 24, 1816, Julia Loomis, born August 6, 1793, daughter of Jonah Loomis, of Westfield; she died in March, 1878. Children: Silas Franklin, born 1817; Julia Ann, 1819, died 1833; Lucy, 1821, died 1844; Henry, 1823, died 1847; Sophia, 1824, died 1855; Marietta, 1826, died 1845; Enos Emery, born 1828; Hial Handy, mentioned further; Clarissa, 1832; Amanda, 1834, died 1837.

(VII) Hial Handy, son of Silas and Julia (Loomis) Kellogg, was born August 20, 1829, in Lewis county, New York. He was a farmer, owning a farm of one hundred acres at Port Leyden. He became a local preacher in the Methodist Episcopal church and was a great advocate of temperance, being active in the cause of the organization of Good Templars. He was a Republican. On October 17, 1850, he married Mary Silvina, born October 7, 1833, daughter of Solomon and Harriet (Pinney) Tyler. Solomon Tyler was born April 10, 1808, at Port Leyden, and his wife was born March 4, 1811, at Westerlo, New York. Children of Mr. and Mrs. Kellogg, all born at Port Leyden: 1. Harriet Amelia, August 20, 1851; married Orry Husted Holdridge (see Holdridge). 2. Henry Franklinton, born April 13, 1855, died December 21, 1860. 3. Elmer Erwin, born October 31, 1862; married Elizabeth (Libbie) Jordan. 4. Lillian May, born January 26, 1871. 5. Herbert L., residing in Ilion, New York.

(II) Franklin Loren Holdridge, son of Orry Husted HOLDRIDGE Holdridge (q. v.) and Harriet Amelia (Kellogg) Holdridge, and grandson of Perry and Betsey (Husted) Holdridge, was born November 19, 1870, at Port Leyden, Lewis county, New York. He was educated in the public schools of Port Leyden, and passed the first eighteen years of his life in that town. He then came to Warren county, Pennsylvania, and was employed for a year in a furniture factory in Kinzua, and then removed to Utica, New York, where he remained for a short while ultimately returning to Warren county and resuming his employment in the factory, on the veneer department. Later on he was made foreman of this department, having completely mastered the business, and, coming to Tidioute, became associated with the Simmons & Holdridge Company as one of the partners. For thirteen years he was foreman of the glue and veneer department of this company, being in charge of the purchasing for the department and having complete oversight. In February, 1910, Mr. Holdridge sold out his interest in the business, and has given his time subsequently to the promoting of his own invention, the F. L. Holdridge Milk Can Lock. He has inherited to the full his father's mechanical ingenuity and inventive genius, and bids fair to make a great success of his invention.

In October, 1912, Mr. Holdridge received the appointment of demonstrator and inspector from the Division of Zoology of the Pennsylvania State Department of Agriculture. He is a prominent and active member of the Republican party, and greatly interested in the welfare of the community in which he resides and the country at large, having shown his patriotism in the good service which he rendered in the borough council. He is distinguished also in Masonic circles, having been made a Mason in North Star Lodge, No. 241, F. and A. M.; he is now a member of Temple Lodge, No. 412, F. and A. M., of Tidioute, and a member of the Lodge of Perfection, Oil City, Pennsylvania. Mr. Holdridge has also been active in the religious affairs of the community, being a member of the First English Evangelical Lutheran Church of Warren, in which he has served as superintendent and librarian of the Sunday school. On September 30, 1896, he was married to Miss Viola Muckle, a daughter of Henry L. and Savilla (Hoover) Muckle, the family being an old one and of Scotch descent. According to tradition the name was originally "McMuckle," or "Muckleheany."

Henry L. Muckle is a son of Benjamin Muckle and his wife, who are buried at Ephratah, in Lancaster county, Pennsylvania. He is a cigarmaker by trade, and is now living at Mill Creek, in Huntingdon county, having had at one time a factory of his own in Lancaster county, at Bellville, where he resided for some time. He was also a resident of Evansville, Pennsylvania, where he was an engineer, removing to Mill Creek about seventeen years ago and being subsequently employed for a number of years as a night watchman. He was a soldier of the civil war, and is a member of the Methodist Episcopal church. His wife was Miss Savilla Hoover, and they had the following children: Amanda, married William Benner; Ella, married John Leiby; Viola, married Franklin L. Holdridge, as previously mentioned; Laura, married Claude McDonald; Austin C., married May Heading; Adam C., unmarried; Emory, married Verna Hohn; Beulah, married Oscar Spece.

Mr. and Mrs. Franklin L. Holdridge are the parents of two children: Vivian Bonetta, born December 5, 1898, in Warren, Pennsylvania; Frederick Burnham, born June 16, 1900, at Tidioute.

NEYHART Adnah Neyhart, one of the most prominent and successful of the old time oil men of the Allegheny Valley, was a native of New York state, having been born at Lansing, Tompkins county, December 20, 1836. He came to Tidioute, Pennsylvania, in 1865, being then a young man of nearly thirty years of age, and having by unfortunate investments in the oil regions lost heavily. Being possessed of an unusual amount of business sagacity, self-reliance and enterprise, he proceeded at once to build up his fallen fortunes and turn his former defeat into a complete and well sustained financial victory. He associated himself with Joshua Pierce, of Philadelphia, in the oil producing firm of Pierce & Neyhart, which became well known throughout the petroleum world, being pioneers in the business of transporting oil in tank cars. Building a number of large iron tanks in which to store their own production during the low prices of 1866, at which time they owned a number of immense wells, they afterwards gave up operating and confined themselves wholly to the shipping business. Mr. Neyhart remained in the oil regions, while Mr. Pierce attended to the business of the firm in the east. This association lasted until about 1870, when the partnership was dissolved and Mr. Neyhart continued to carry on operations independently. He became one of the largest and most successful oil producers in the country, applying himself to business with unremitting zeal and exercising a wisdom and foresight in his dealings which earned for him a wide-spread reputation throughout these regions. He became closely associated with the three Grandin brothers, whose sister he married, and continued operations with them characterized by an unusual degree of mutual profit and esteem. Their confidence in the moral and business integrity of one another was so complete that little attention was given to recording travel expenses when any member of the partnership was abroad in the interests of the work. The close application which Mr. Neyhart gave to the business, however, gradually undermined his health and compelled him to abandon his personal activities and seek rest and recuperation in a different climate. He removed with his family to California, continuing to direct all important movements by letter and telegram from that place. His enterprising spirit would not allow him to be idle, and he engaged in gold mining, purchased a gold mine, and set up the requisite machinery, meeting with his usual success, when he was stricken down by death. He died at San Diego, California, February 17, 1875, and was buried at Tidioute, under the auspices of the Masonic fraternity, of which he was a worthy member. His religious affiliations were with the Presbyterian church, and his personal character was such as to worthily uphold its teachings and tenets in the community in which the most important part of his life was passed. By his own industrious hands, vigorous intellect, and honest principles, he achieved a worldly success that is meted out to but few men who begin life with no other capital save a strong personal character.

On September 17, 1868, Mr. Neyhart was married, at Tidioute, to Miss Maria Jane Grandin, daughter of Samuel and Sarah Ann (Henry) Grandin, and sister of the three oil merchants with whom Mr. Neyhart was in business association; further information in regard to this family will be found in the sketch of William J. Grandin, elsewhere in this work. Mr. and Mrs. Neyhart were the parents of the following children: 1. Emma G., born June 22, 1871, at Tidioute; married Howard Couse, and resides in Cleveland, Ohio, having one daughter, Margaret, born November 15, 1900. 2. Adnah, born December 31, 1872, at Tidioute; married Grace G. Stephenson, and resides at Framingham, Massachusetts; they have two children: Ruth, born November 7, 1896; and Dorothy, born July 11, 1900.

YOUNIE The first member of this family to come to Warren county, was James Younie, born in Scotland, where he married and in the spring of 1834, came to the United States, settling in Sugargrove township, Pennsylvania. He there purchased one hundred acres, the property now owned by Fremont Ellis, on which part of the village of Sugargrove is built. Later Mr. Younie purchased one hundred acres of the old Robert Falconer estate of William Falconer; the original purchase of this land by Robert Falconer was from the Holland Land Company. Mr. Younie was a member of the Presbyterian church as was his wife. He was a Whig in politics, later a Republican, serving the town as road commissioner. He died in Sugargrove aged sixty-nine years. He married in Scotland, Margaret, daughter of John and Christie Stuart, a relative of Robert Falconer. Children: Christie, born on shipboard, while crossing the Atlantic, married Frank Miller; William Alexander, of whom further; Margaret, born October 13, 1838, died 1908, married Joseph Langdon; James, a cavalryman of the civil war, died in Washington, D. C., 1862; John, born September 23, 1844, now of Sugargrove, engaged in the meat business, married (first) Julia Green, (second) Elva Ricker; Eliza, born June 1, 1846, widow of James C. Hamilton, resides in Sugargrove, and has child, Margaret.

(II) William Alexander, son of James Younie, the emigrant, was born in Sugargrove township, Warren county, September 27, 1836, and attended the public schools of Sugargrove where his boyhood and early life was spent at the home farm. He enlisted in 1864 in Company G, 211th Regiment, Pennsylvania Volunteer Infantry, serving nine months, until the close of the war, receiving honorable discharge at Harrisburg, where his regiment was mustered out. He returned to Sugargrove and resumed farming, continuing until the oil excitement drew him to Pithole, Pennsylvania where for two years he conducted a meat market. He next entered partnership with William Weld, built a saw mill and began lumbering in Warren county. After one year he bought Mr. Weld's interest, continuing the lumber business alone for several years. He then purchased the one hundred acre farm first owned by his father and lived there until the purchase of his present farm, known as the old Robert Gray farm, where he now resides. He is a Democrat in politics and has served as road commissioner and constable. He is a member of the Masonic order.

He married (first) Florence E., daughter of Robert M. and Hannah (Weld) Gray. She was born March 8, 1847, died December 8, 1891. He married (second) Della Page, born 1857, died 1897, daughter of Richard and Mary Adeline (Holmes) Page. Children of first marriage: 1. Nellie, resides with her father. 2. Jessie, married, January 30, 1909, Marion L. Daniels. 3. Florence, married William P. Thorpe, September, 1902, and has children: Bertrice and William. Children of second marriage: 4. William Page, born March 12, 1887, now living at Dewey, Oklahoma, in the oil business; married Mabel Welch, April, 1907; children: Gerald A. and Isabel. 5. Gerald William, born February 27, 1889, now a farmer in Sugargrove and a member of the Independent Order of Odd Fellows; married Matilda Soderholm; child, William.

WHELOK
1285

WHEELOCK The Wheelock family of Warren county, Pennsylvania, are the direct descendants of Ralph Wheelock, a Puritan, who was a descendant of Hugh de Wheelock, in the reign of Henry II. The name appears as early as about 1200, sometimes as de Quelok, de Whelok, Whelok, and laterly Wheelock. The Wheelock family has been prominent for several hundred years. In the early days there was a marriage between the Wheelocks and Leversages, and the two families have been associated with the village of Wheelock, in England, from ancient times. The Wheelock coat-of-arms was adopted in 1285, and is described: Argent chevrons between three Catherine wheels, when the name was Whelok, a cut of which accompanies this sketch.

(I) Ralph Wheelock, above referred to, was born in Shropshire, England, in 1600, in the town of parish of Wheelock. He was educated at Clare Hall, Cambridge University, graduated in 1626, taking his master degree in 1631. He was a relative, perhaps a brother, of Abraham Wheelock, who was the professor of Arabic at Cambridge and later the librarian. He held title to the village of Wheelock, Cheshire county, England. He was ordained in the Church of England, but became a Puritan soon after leaving college and joined the ranks of the non-conformists. He doubtless suffered much in the persecutions of the Puritans. In 1637, accompanied by his wife and daughter Rebecca, he migrated to New England, residing first at Watertown, Massachusetts, and later removing to Dedham, Massachusetts, being one of the proprietors of Dedham in 1638-39. His house lot was the first one granted in the town, at the corner of Main and North streets, and contained twelve acres of land. He served as a selectman, 1651-55, for several years was deputy to general court, taught the first public school there, was appointed by the general court a commissioner to end small causes, the local magistrate, and was appointed to join persons in marriage. He was one of the founders of the church of Dedham, learned, devout, unselfish, and practical. He built a house in Dedham in 1652, on the north side of Main street, and became one of the founders of Medfield, an adjoining town, in 1649, and removed there a few years later, continuing his career of usefulness and prominence. He was one of the signers of the famous Dedham Covenant, July, 1637, his being the tenth name on the list of one hundred. This instrument was the constitution of that body of settlers, first colony laws; known as the Body of Liberties, 1641. He was also on the committee to collect funds for Harvard College. He died in November, 1683. His children were: Rebecca, Gershome, Eleasor, Benjamin (of whom further), Samuel, Record, Experience, Mary, and Peregrine.

(II) Benjamin, born in Dedham in 1639-40, was the first Wheelock born in America, son of Ralph Wheelock, married, and his children were: David (of whom further), Jonathan, Paul, and Silas.

(III) David, son of Benjamin Wheelock, married Lydia White, and reared a family, among whom was Abner, of whom further.

(IV) Abner, son of David Wheelock, was born June 19, 1747, and died May 11, 1831, aged eighty-four years. He was one of the first settlers of Charlton, Massachusetts, and marched on the alarm of April 19, 1775, serving in the revolutionary war. He married Mary Blanchard, born March 30, 1754. His children were: Rachel, Lucy, Daniel, Esther, Calvin, Betsy, and Abner (2), of whom further.

(V) Abner (2), son of Abner (1) Wheelock,

was born in Charlton, Massachusetts, October 9, 1796, died May 22, 1886. He migrated to Genesee county, New York, where he married, and located for a number of years. About 1830 he removed to Erie county, Pennsylvania, and settled on a tract of land three miles north of Corry. He purchased a farm of one hundred acres on Hare Creek, now Wheelock, Wayne township, cleared up the place, and resided there till 1850, when he disposed of the same and removed to Sugargrove township, Warren county, Pennsylvania, where he resided, but spent the last fifteen years of his life with his son Edward R., at the village of Sugargrove. He was a member of the Methodist Episcopal church, and a Republican in politics. He married, in the town of Wales, Genesee county, New York, October 29, 1818, Lydia Tillottson, born January 19, 1801, died 1871. His children were: Charles A. (of whom further); George G., born November 23, 1823, died September 7, 1894; Betsy A., born November 21, 1825, died July 24, 1826; Edwin Ruthven (of whom further); Matthew G., born August 22, 1830, died December 20, 1895.

(VI) Charles A., eldest son of Abner (2) Wheelock, was born August 19, 1822, died at Warren, Warren county, Pennsylvania, December 20, 1892. After completing his studies he gave his attention principally to farming, which line of work he followed throughout the most part of his life. He was a resident of Wayne township, Erie county, Pennsylvania, residing on his farm until 1860, when he removed to Meadville, same state, and for one year engaged in the foundry business. The following year he purchased a farm one mile west of Lottsville, in Freehold township, Warren county, Pennsylvania, where he spent the remainder of his days. He was a Protestant in religion, and a Republican in politics, and served in the capacity of constable and supervisor of the township where he lived. He was a member and past master of Freehold Grange, and at the time of his death was secretary of Lottsville Lodge, I. O. O. F. He married, June 7, 1851, Elizabeth M. King, born May 11, 1828, daughter of Ambrose and Dolly (Steele) King, died June 4, 1878. They had one child, De Forest A., of whom further.

(VII) Major De Forest A. Wheelock, son of Charles A. Wheelock, was born in Wheelock, Erie county, Pennsylvania, July 23, 1855. He gained his preliminary education in the common schools, and this was supplemented by a course at the Teachers' Normal Department of Chamberlain Institute, Randolph, New York, from which he graduated in 1877, and he pursued a commercial course at the same institution, completing it in the unparalleled time of four weeks, also a special course of civil engineering, which profession he has since followed. He has devoted his attention to civil engineering, and has repeatedly been summoned to various parts of his and other states to settle land and other important engineering questions and disputes, and is considered one of the most reliable experts on questions submitted to him. Prior to taking up the active profession of civil engineering he was engaged for several years as a teacher in common, graded and union schools, holding a state teacher's certificate entitling him to teach in any part of the state of Pennsylvania. From 1875 until the present (1913), with the exception of six years, he has been the official surveyor of Warren county, Pennsylvania, and since March, 1895, has been the city engineer of Warren, Pennsylvania. At the present time (1913) he is chief engineer of the Hammond Engineering Company, which manufactures and erects water and sewage purification plants. He was for several years employed by the Pennsylvania State Department of Health as special engineer, to examine, report and recommend regarding matters of water and sewage purification that came before the department. He also acted, and does at present, as special engineer for the Pennsylvania State Railroad Commission. He was appointed by Governor Hastings in 1895 on the commission to determine the advisability of forming a new (Grow) county out of parts of Luzerne and other counties in the anthracite coal region. He was also appointed by the courts in 1886 to relocate the dividing line between Warren and Erie counties, in 1887 between Potter and Cameron, and Warren and Crawford, in 1895 between Center and Huntingdon, in 1909 between Crawford and Mercer, and in 1910 between Crawford and Venango counties.

When the United States declared war against Spain in 1898, Major Wheelock, being loyal and patriotic, and also having had a military experience from December 2, 1882, when he enlisted in Company I of the 16th Regiment of the National Guard of Pennsylvania, and having been promoted to corporal, sergeant, first sergeant, second lieutenant, first lieutenant, and captain, he was one of the first to volunteer his services under the call for volunteers, ranking as captain of Company I, which was mustered into the service of the United States, May 10, 1898, after having been on duty at the call of the state authorities since April 27th. His was the only company from the state that volunteered with full ranks to a man. After camping at Mt. Gretna, Pennsylvania, the company started for Chickamauga Park, Georgia, on May 15th, where he was joined by his son, Carl A., as corporal in his company, and subsequently ordered to Charleston, South Carolina, where they embarked July 22nd on the transport "Mobile," No. 21, and arrived at Ponce, Porto Rico, July 28th. The following night Captain Wheelock was ordered with fifty picked men from the 16th Regiment to El Coto, about seven miles distant, with orders to prevent any of the Spanish forces located there from burning the town, which they had threatened to, or from committing any other hostile demonstration. As Captain Wheelock and his men entered the town the rear guard of the Spanish forces retreated from the town. Captain Wheelock immediately took possession of the barracks just vacated by the enemy and captured several prisoners, as well as a large amount of commissary and quartermaster stores. On July 31st Captain Wheelock, in command of his company, and being reinforced by Company A, of Corry, proceeded under orders to Juana Diaz, took possession of the public buildings, telegraph and telephone offices, and at once hoisted the United States flag over the former. While at Juana Diaz, August 2nd, Captain Wheelock learned that at the seaport town of Port San Isabelle was a large amount of commissary stores ready to be delivered to the Spanish forces at Aibonita, and promptly during the night sent a detachment to take possession of the same. The detachment arrived just as the loaded wagons were starting for the Spanish lines. The detachment took the stores and some prisoners, and returned to Captain Wheelock's camp at Juana Diaz during the night, with stores, among which was a large amount of rice, which the captain at once turned over to the quartermaster of the 16th Regiment for the use of the men, which, as rations at the time were short, was a welcome accession. Guard duty was done there and outpost duty for two days, and a quantity of supplies and number of prisoners taken, among the prisoners being the Spanish war secretary from Port San Isabelle, whose commission and saber the captain has ever since retained. The remainder of the 16th Regiment joined Company I and A, and on August 4th moved to a point halfway between Juana Diaz and Coamo, encamping along the military road. During the night of August 8th the regiment made a flank movement to get to the rear of Coamo, camping in the mountains during the night, and the following morning (August 9th) reached the top of the mountain overlooking Coamo, about sunrise, with the battery of the United States troops opened fire on the block house about two miles outside of the town, when the Spaniards retreated through the town and toward Aibonita, opening fire on the United States troops of the 16th Regiment, who were double-timing down the side of the mountain to intercept them. The battle lasted about an hour, when the Spanish forces surrendered. The principal part of the fighting was done by the First Battalion of the 16th Pennsylvania troops, composed of Companies I, A, H, and C. Captain Wheelock after the battle found that he had three men slightly wounded, but otherwise no casualties. When the Spaniards surrendered, Company I, under Captain Wheelock, entered the town of Coamo, took possession of the Spanish barracks and a large amount of government military stores, among which was taken the Spanish flag that floated over the barracks at the time the battle began, and which has ever since been retained by Captain Wheelock, who prizes it very highly. They then went into camp just east of the town, on that part of the battle field occupied by the Spanish forces during the engagement, remaining there until October 1st, when the regiment under orders started to march to San Juan, a seaport city on the north side of the Island, but after three days' marching were ordered back to Ponce. During this three-day period Captain Wheelock, who had just reported for duty from the hospital, was placed in charge of 136 convalescents whom he furloughed home, and rejoined his regiment in time to go with it back to the United States, leaving Ponce October 11th and arriving at New York on October 17th. He reached Warren with his company October 19, 1898, and was mustered out of United States service December 28, 1898. He continued in the service of the National Guard, being elected major October 14,

1907, and served as such till January, 1909, when after over twenty-six years' service he resigned and went on the retired list on account of long service.

Major Wheelock is a member of North Star Lodge, No. 241, Ancient Free and Accepted Masons; Occidental Chapter, No. 235, Royal Arch Masons; Warren Commandery, No. 63, Knights Templar, of which he is past eminent commander; Pennsylvania Consistory, 32nd degree, Valley of Pittsburgh; Presque Isle Lodge of Perfection, 14th degree, of Erie, Pennsylvania; Warren Lodge of Odd Fellows; due to his efforts, Lottsville Lodge, Independent Order of Odd Fellows, was organized, he being its first noble and past noble grand; Warren Lodge, B. P. O. E., of which he is a past exalted ruler, and past trustee. He is a member of the American Society of Civil Engineers, and the Engineers Society of Pennsylvania.

Major Wheelock married, May 1, 1878, at Columbus, Pennsylvania, Sarah Le Ell Smith, born July 11, 1854, daughter of David O. and Emily A. (Walton) Smith, who were the parents of five other children, as follows: Albert J., Eva A., Winnie, Arta W., and Robert W. David O. Smith was a farmer and justice of the peace. Children of Major Wheelock: Carl Ayres, of whom further; Harry O., born June 5, 1881; Bertha E., born August 22, 1882, married, June 25, 1912, Frank J. Lyons, district attorney of Warren county, Pennsylvania; Winnie C., born February 28, 1884, married, February 16, 1907, Kern W. McCray, superintendent of an oil and gas company in West Virginia.

(VIII) Carl Ayres Wheelock, son of De Forest A. Wheelock, was born at Lottsville, Warren county, Pennsylvania, March 8, 1879. He attended the district school at Lottsville until ten years of age, then became a student in the Warren grade and high school, graduating from the latter in 1898, and during the years 1897-98 also attended a business school. In November, 1898, he entered the employ of the Warren Street Railway Company, remaining until July 31, 1899, when he was employed by the Struthers Wells Company, remaining until March 18, 1901, and from that time to the present (1912) has served in the capacity of accountant at the State Hospital for the Insane at Warren, Pennsylvania. During the Spanish-American war he enlisted his services in defence of his country, June 14, 1898, holding the rank of corporal in Company I, Sixteenth Regiment Pennsylvania Volunteer Infantry. He joined the company in Chickamauga, after completing his high school course, went with his regiment to Charleston, South Carolina, where a week later he took transport for Ponce, Porto Rico; he participated in the skirmish at Coamo, went with his regiment to Cayey when they received orders to return to Ponce and subsequently to the United States, arriving in New York City, October 20, 1898, and received his honorable discharge, December 28, 1898. Mr. Wheelock is an attendant of the Presbyterian church. He is a member of North Star Lodge, No. 241, Free and Accepted Masons, of which he is past master; Occidental Chapter, No. 235, Royal Arch Masons, of which he is past high priest; Warren Commandery, No. 63, Knights Templar, of which he is past commander; Venango Lodge of Perfection, of Oil City; Pennsylvania Consistory, of Pittsburgh; Zem Zem Temple, Ancient Arabic Order Nobles of the Mystic Shrine, of Erie; Conewango Council, No. 115, Royal Arcanum, of North Warren, of which he is past regent and treasurer; Conewango Club, of Warren, and Deerhorn Fishing and Hunting Club, of Warren.

Mr. Wheelock married, December 17, 1902, at North Warren, Pennsylvania, Elizabeth, born October 23, 1872, daughter of Robert and Mary (Jackson) Grier. Children: Bertha Elizabeth, born November 1, 1903; Carl Albert, June 26, 1905.

(VI) Edwin Ruthven, son of Abner (2) Wheelock, was born in the town of Wales, Genesee county, New York, August 24, 1827. When he was three years of age his parents removed to Pennsylvania, settling on a farm three miles north of Corry, Erie county, and there he spent his boyhood days. He was educated in the schools of the neighborhood, and later went to Waterford, Pennsylvania, where he attended the State Academy, having for his classmates many who later became prominent in the history of Waterford and whose descendants now reside in that locality. At the age of sixteen years Mr. Wheelock left the old home and took up his residence in Freehold township, locating at Wrightsville, where he became identified with the lumber industries. He boated on the river, and was successful in his various undertakings. He made his home in Freehold township until about 1871, when he moved to the village of Sugargrove and there erected a store, embarking in the general hardware business and later admitting his sons as partners, conducting for many years a successful and remunerative business. He was one of the influential and active citizens of Sugargrove, his residence on Main street being one of the best and most attractive. He retired from active pursuits in 1904 and then went to Decatur, Illinois, where he resides with a son. Almost every year he pays a visit to Sugargrove, where he is a most welcome guest, not only among his relatives, who are numerous, but in almost every home in the entire community. He was reared in the Methodist Episcopal faith, and is a Republican in politics, active in the affairs of his party, having served as county commissioner two terms, burgess of the borough of Sugargrove one term, and served for many years as councilman and school director.

Mr. Wheelock married, September 20, 1853, Betsey Allen, born in Freehold township, Warren county, Pennsylvania, August 28, 1833, died February 18, 1901, daughter of David and Fannie (Abbott) Allen. Children: Frank De Forest, of whom further; George R., born August 26, 1860, in Freehold township; he was educated in the common schools, spent his early life in Warren county, in 1884 went to South Dakota and farmed two years, returned to Sugargrove, Pennsylvania, and engaged in the hardware business, and subsequently removed to Decatur, Illinois, where he is working at his trade of tinsmith; he married Charlotte, daughter of George and Emiline (Green) Reynolds; one child, Bessie May Reynolds Wheelock, born in 1903.

(VII) Frank DeForest, eldest son of Edwin Ruthven Wheelock, was born at Freehold, Warren county, Pennsylvania, August 12, 1854. He attended the public schools of Freehold and Sugargrove, acquiring a practical education. Upon attaining his majority he engaged in the hardware business at Sugargrove, continuing in the same until 1892, when he went to northern Wisconsin and there served as manager for a lumber company until 1899, when he returned to Sugargrove and again embarked in the hardware business, purchasing his father's store, which he has conducted to the present time (1912), being in receipt of an extensive patronage. He carries a full and complete line of hardware, and in addition deals in wagons and buggies, and ranks among the enterprising and successful merchants of the community. He adheres to the principles of the Republican party and has been the incumbent of several township and borough offices, in which he served creditably and efficiently. He is a member of Stillwater Lodge, No. 547, Free and Accepted Masons, of Sugargrove, in which he served as worshipful master for ten years.

Mr. Wheelock married, at Jamestown, New York, January 6, 1896, Rozella (Blodgett) McDonald, born at Sugargrove, Pennsylvania, July 6, 1857, daughter of Alden Divers and Helen (Brands) Blodgett, and widow of Archibald D. McDonald, by whom she had two children: Anna B., born June 4, 1878, at Sugargrove, married, August 1, 1906, Dr. William Hamilton Shortt, one son, William Hamilton Jr., born May 26, 1907, they reside at Youngsville, Pennsylvania; Alden Blodgett, born January 26, 1880, at Sugargrove, is a specialist on diseases of ear, eye, nose and throat, located at Warren, Pennsylvania. Alden D. Blodgett was a farmer and merchant; he and his wife were the parents of three children, as follows: Jane Celia, Robert Brands, Rozella, aforementioned. Mr. and Mrs. Wheelock have no children.

BEMIS Every probable and improbable way of spelling this name seems to have been employed by the twenty-two families, each having a different orthography, but all perhaps springing from a common ancestor. A few of the most distorted spellings are: Beemish, Bemisht, Beamiss, Beeamis, Beamous and Bemass. There is also Bemis, Bemus, Bemos, Bemas and Benes. The name is perpetuated locally by localities in Massachusetts, New Hampshire and New York, the best known, perhaps, being Bemis Heights, Saratoga county, New York, where the battle of Saratoga was mainly fought and where Burgoyne surrendered, September 19, 1777.

(I) The founder of the branch herein recorded was Joseph Bemis, born in England, 1619. He came to Watertown, Massachusetts, as early as 1640, bringing, it is believed, his wife Sarah with him, or as is possible they were married in Boston, 1641, as the birth of their first child is recorded there. He was elected selectman of Watertown, 1648-72-75. He was a farmer and at times seems to have been also a blacksmith. His will is dated the day of his death, August 7, 1684, and proved October 7, following. His widow Sarah died in 1712. Children: Sarah, born January 15, 1642-43, married John Bigelow; Mary, September 10, 1644, married Samuel Whitney; Joseph and Ephraim, twins, October 28, 1647, were buried November 4, following; Joseph, of whom further; Rebecca, April 17, 1654, married (first) John White, (second) Thomas Harrington.

(II) Joseph (2), son of Joseph (1) Bemis, "the emigrant," born at Watertown, December 12, 1651, died at Westminster, Massachusetts, August 7, 1684. He was a soldier of King Philip's war, his name being spelled on the record Joseph Bemish and service credited under Captain James Oliver, March 24, 1675. His wife Anna also died in Westminster. Children: Joseph; Mary; Philip, died 1782; Thomas, of whom further.

(III) Thomas, youngest child of Joseph (2) and Anna Bemis, died in Westminster, Massachusetts, 1788, having settled there about 1738. Children: Anna, born April 22, 1741, said to have been the first girl baby born in Westminster; Thomas, of whom further.

(IV) Thomas (2), son of Thomas (1) Bemis, was born in Westminster, Massachusetts, where he learned the trade of blacksmith. He married, September 3, 1787, Lucy Green, who died September 13, 1824. Children: Daniel; Pearson, married Betsey Jackson; Polly, married (first) Henry Dunster, (second) William Lewis; Reuben, born 1797, died April, 1811.

(V) Daniel, son of Thomas (2) and Lucy (Green) Bemis, was born in Westminster, Massachusetts, 1788, died at Chesterfield. He married Polly Sawin. They lived at Chesterfield and Croydon, New Hampshire. They had issue including a son, Elias H.

(VI) Elias Harrison, son of Daniel and Polly (Sawin) Bemis, was born in Croydon, New Hampshire, 1818, died in the town of Granville, Washington county, New York. He was well educated, and in early life learned and followed the shoemaker's trade, later coming to Granville, New York, where he bought a farm of one hundred acres. He cultivated this farm until late in life, when he sold it and moved to the village of North Granville, where he lived retired until his death. He was a member of the Baptist church, and a Whig, later a Republican in politics. He was twice married, his first wife, a Miss Chase, being the mother of Horace Allen, of whom further, and Silvia (or Sylvia), who married Captain William Thomas, a deep sea mariner, plying between New York and Liverpool, England, they reside in Granville, New York.

(VII) Horace Allen, only son of Elias Harrison Bemis and his first wife, was born in the town of Granville, Washington county, New York, March 29, 1842, died there December 19, 1903. He was educated in the public schools, and when compelled to leave school and commence work he continued study in night schools. He learned the carpenter's trade and became a well known contractor, although his residence was always at Granville he did a great deal of business in neighboring towns and in Massachusetts. He lost his life by a boiler explosion at the plant of the Matthews State Company at Hatch Hill, where he was doing some carpenter work at the time. It was during the noon hour and Mr. Bemis had gone to the engine room to eat his lunch, the weather being too cold to sit outside. He was an active working member of the Baptist church, and a Republican in politics, holding many township offices in Granville. He married Harriet M. Van Gilder, born at Granville, May 17, 1847, died April 29, 1906, daughter of Daniel Van Gilder. Children: William; Horace Allen; Fred; Cora, died young; Harriet, died in childhood; Charles; Flora E.; Elias Harrison, of whom further; Daniel D.; four others who died young.

(VIII) Elias Harrison (2), son of Horace Allen and Harriet M. (Van Gilder) Bemis, was born in Granville, Washington county, New York, April 4, 1870. He was educated in the public schools and North Granville Seminary, taking a full course at the latter institution and receiving a diploma. He began business life as an employe of the Algonquin State Company, continuing with them seven years in the paint department. He was with the Stucco (or Staco) Paint Company for two years, then with the American Seal Paint Company of Troy, New York, where his health failed and he returned to Granville. He next became traveling salesman for the Atlantic Refining Company of Cleveland, Ohio, continuing until 1906, when he returned to Granville and entered the employ of the Borden Condensed Milk Company. He began at the bottom and worked up through all branches and departments, thus gaining a practical knowledge of all phases of the business. He remained with the Borden's in Granville four years. He was then offered and accepted the position of superintendent with the Walker Ice Cream Company at their condensing plant in Sugargrove, Warren county, Pennsylvania, which position he now holds. He is a Republican in politics. In Granville he was a member of both lodge and encampment of the Independent Order of Odd Fellows, transferring his membership to Sugargrove Lodge. He is also a member of Sugar Lodge, Free and Accepted Masons, a member of Modern Woodmen and the Knights of the Maccabees, of Granville. He married, June 8, 1898, Daisy M. Hutchins, born at Middletown, Vermont, June 9, 1882, daughter of Herbert and Susan Hutchins. Children: Mildred H., born December 3, 1899; Herbert H., March 1, 1901; Milton H., October 30, 1905; Viola S., July 4, 1908; Sylvia D., 1910, died aged eleven months.

RICE The Rice family, in early generations, was prominently identified with the history of the state of Massachusetts, five generations having resided there, in the towns of Marlborough, Sudbury, Petersham and Shrewsbury.

(I) Asa Rice, the first of the line here under consideration of whom we have definite information, was a native of Massachusetts, from whence he removed to Caroline Center, Tompkins county, New York, where he spent the remainder of his days, dying at about the age of eighty years. He followed the occupation of farming, which proved a remunerative source of income. He was a member of the Episcopal church, and highly respected in the community where he resided for so many years. He married Polly Reed, who lived to an advanced age. Children: 1. Augusta, deceased, married Harry Grant. 2. Henry, a resident of Missouri; married and reared a large family. 3. William Bigelow, of whom further. 4. Christopher Columbus Titus, was a resident of Missouri; married and reared a large family. 5. Alvin, died unmarried. 6. James H., died in Chicago, Illinois; married but left no issue. 7. Frank, deceased. 8. George R., deceased, resided in Seneca county, New York. 9. Ann, deceased; married Ismond Knapp.

(II) William Bigelow, second son of Asa and Polly (Reed) Rice, was born August 9, 1818, died December 8, 1902. He spent his early life in Caroline Center, New York, obtaining a practical education in its common schools, and later learned the trade of millwright, which line of work he followed for many years. About the year 1840 he removed to Bradford county, Pennsylvania, where he worked at his trade, and six years later removed to Warren county, Pennsylvania, purchasing a farm consisting of one hundred and twenty-five acres in Freehold township. He was a Republican in politics and was a man of integrity and honor, esteemed by all who knew him. He married Mary Ann, born January, 1829, died in 1869, buried at Wrightsville cemetery, daughter of David and Fanny (Abbott) Allen, who were the parents of six other children, as follows: Jane, Betsy Ann, Martha, Desdemona, Medora and David Othello. David Allen was born in Scotland, from whence he was brought to this country at the age of three years; he was reared and educated here and resided the greater part of his life in Freehold township, Warren county, Pennsylvania, where he was the owner of a one hundred acre farm, which is still in the possession of the family, being owned by Leslie Allen. David Allen was a lumberman and farmer by occupation, a Republican and a member of the Wesleyan church. Children of Mr. and Mrs. Rice: Arthur Eugene, of whom further; William Emerson, of whom further; Mary Alline, born November 4, 1869, married Harry Aner and had children, Marjorie and Katherine. The family resides in Corry, Pennsylvania.

(III) Arthur Eugene, eldest son of William Bigelow and Mary Ann (Allen) Rice, was born at Lottsville, Warren county, Pennsylvania, February 9, 1851. He spent his boyhood on his father's farm, attended the common schools of Freehold township and Sugargrove Union School, and learned the trade of carpenter with his father. He taught school for a period of three years, being thoroughly qualified for that vocation. From 1879 to 1898 he was an oil well worker, at first engaged in rig building and later conducting general lease work, and in the latter named year he returned to the homestead farm in Freehold township, which he cultivated and managed until 1906, when he took up his residence in Sugargrove borough, residing there at the present time (1912). He is now actively interested in oil producing in the Indiana oil fields, from which he derives a lucrative income, and in addition to this is serving in the capacity of assistant postmaster of Sugargrove, having been appointed in 1909, and his tenure of office is noted for efficiency. He held the office of assessor of Sugargrove for three years, and borough councilman four years, having been elected on the Republican ticket. He is a member of the United Brethren in Christ church, in the affairs of which he takes an active part. He was made a Mason in Olean, New York, and is now a member of Stillwater Lodge at Sugargrove, having held the office of senior warden and master in that order; he is a member of the Independent Order of Odd Fellows at Lottsville, having served as secretary, trustee and noble grand, and is also a member of the Benevolent and Protective Order of Elks. Public-spirited to the highest degree, he is ever forward in encouraging enterprises which will in any way advance the interests of his adopted borough.

Mr. Rice married, October 3, 1873, at Sugargrove, Pennsylvania, Emma, born July 28, 1853, in Crawford county, Pennsylvania, daughter of Rev. William and Permelia Ann (Houck) Cadman, who were the parents of seven other children, as follows: William Charles, Mary, Luella, Cora, May, Mattie. Rev. William Cadman was a minister in the United Brethren denomination; he served as a soldier of the United States during the Mexican war.

(III) William Emerson, second son of William Bigelow and Mary Ann (Allen) Rice, was born at Lottsville, Warren county, Pennsylvania, December 19, 1860. After attendance at the common schools of his native town, he supplemented the knowledge thus obtained by a course in Chamberlain Institute, Randolph, New York, and Allegheny College at Meadville, Pennsylvania. The first seven years of his active career were devoted to teaching, in which line of work he achieved success. In 1882, having decided to lead a professional life, he became a student in the office of Wetmore, Noyes & Hinckley, of Warren, Pennsylvania, a leading law firm, under whose guidance and tuition he advanced rapidly. He was admitted to the bar of Warren county, April 16, 1885, and immediately began practice in the borough of Warren, continuing to the present time (1912). In 1888 Mr. Rice formed a partnership with Judge Brown and Hon. C. W. Stone, the firm name being Brown, Stone & Rice, which obtained until 1890, when the partnership was dissolved, and Mr. Rice then became associated with W. D. Hinckley, under the firm name of Hinckley & Rice, which connection remained unbroken for a number of years. Mr. Rice now practices on his own account, receiving a goodly share of the patronage in his judicial district. He was elected judge of Warren county, having been a candidate on the Republican ticket, but resigned to accept the position of corporation attorney for the Elk Tanning Company, in which capacity he is serving at the present time. During his judgeship he discharged the duties of that office with fidelity and impartiality, and year by year he has advanced in public estimation, his advice being eagerly sought and earnestly followed in political affairs as well as in legal matters. To a natural dignity of manner Judge Rice added a geniality that has won him hosts of friends and makes him welcome everywhere.

ABBOTT

The Abbott family, represented in the present generation by the sons of Noah Weld Abbott, all prominent and influential residents of Sugargrove, ranks high among the early settlers of Warren county, Pennsylvania. Members of this family have intermarried with about every family represented in Freehold and Sugargrove townships, and descendants thereof hold family reunions, which are well attended and thoroughly enjoyed.

(I) Nathan Abbott, the ancestor of the family, was born August 29, 1765, died September 3, 1841. He married (first) February 28, 1787, Abigail Baldwin, born August 11, 1763, died April, 1799, without issue. He married (second) July 2, 1799, Anna Gibson, born August 2, 1772, died March, 1846. Their children were: Harry, born May 28, 1800, died December 3, 1879; George, March 11, 1802, died August 25, 1869; Fanny F., October 4, 1803, married David Allen; John G., of whom further; Thomas K., February 22, 1808, died September 31, 1873; William K., December 14, 1809, died September 18, 1867; Franklin S., June 4, 1812; Betsey Ann, January 4, 1815, died September 2, 1827.

(II) John G., son of Nathan and Anna (Gibson) Abbott, was born January 26, 1806, died February 17, 1873. He devoted his attention to farming, in which he was successful, providing a comfortable home for his family. He married, October 20, 1829, Nancy Allen, born May 1, 1806, died October 11, 1886. Children: Albinas C., born July 26, 1830, died March 1, 1898; William, September 28, 1832, died unmarried; Charles, April 18, 1834; James H., December 27, 1835, died October 1, 1836; Robert, September 1, 1837; James A., July 6, 1839; Noah Weld, of whom further; Isabel, May 3, 1844, died March 24, 1897; Loretta, August 23, 1845, died March 6, 1897; Jane, born July 9, 1851.

(III) Noah Weld, son of John G. and Nancy (Allen) Abbott, was born March 17, 1841, died July 29, 1910. In early life he was engaged in agricultural pursuits and in lumbering, owning and operating saw mills, which proved highly remunerative, and he became well known throughout his section of Pennsylvania as a prominent lumberman. In his later years he owned and operated a farm in Sugargrove, where he spent the remainder of his life. He and his family affiliated with the Methodist Episcopal church, in which they took an active and leading part, and he was a Republican in politics. He married, June 4, 1864, Mary M., born July 24, 1845, daughter of Thomas and Ann (Heap) Norris. She is living at the present time (1912). Children: John M., Eugene W., Earl T., Lena C., born April 21, 1874, died June 19, 1875; Christopher M., James Edward, Harry A. and Hila Parish. The sons are all mentioned at length in this and succeeding articles.

(IV) John M., eldest son of Noah Weld and Mary M. (Norris) Abbott, was born March 4, 1865. After completing his studies he directed his attention to lumbering, and is now a member of the lumber firm of Abbott Brothers, also a member of the firm of Abbott Brothers Company, merchants, of Sugargrove. He possesses the attributes of a successful business man, is highly regarded in the community and has a host of friends. He is a member and officer in the Methodist Episcopal church, and a member of the Independent Order of Odd Fellows, in the work of which he takes an active interest. He married, April 13, 1880, Matilda J. Eastman, born November 3, 1865, daughter of Charles and Christine (Burdick) Eastman. Children: Jessie, born November 30, 1889; Ralph, born November 9, 1897. The family resides in Sugargrove, Pennsylvania.

(IV) Eugene W., second son of Noah Weld and Mary M. (Norris) Abbott, was born January 31, 1867. He attended the schools in the vicinity of his home, and throughout his active career has been identified in some way in the lumber business. He is at the head of the Abbott Brothers Lumber Company and the Abbott Brothers Company, the brothers also being interested in farm lands and timber tracts. Eugene W. Abbott is one of the best known men in the county, public-spirited and enterprising, a man of the strictest integrity, whose word is as good as his bond, and a keynote to his success is his executive force and mastery of detail in whatever engages his attention. He is a member of the Methodist Episcopal church, and for many years served as superintendent of the Sunday school connected therewith. He casts his vote for the candidates of the Republican party, and has served with credit and ability in various borough offices. He is a member of the local lodge of the Independent Order of Odd Fellows of Sugargrove, the lodge that has a reputation over many states for its degree work and large membership, the members being all men of the highest type of manhood. Mr. Abbott married (first) June 14, 1893, Addie Cooper, born October 13, 1866, died April 18, 1908, daughter of Nathan Joseph and Mary J. (Woodburn) Cooper. A history of the Cooper family will appear in this work. Mr. Abbott married (second) May 18, 1909, Agnes, born April 14, 1869, daughter of James B. and Eliza (Jagger) Abbott, who is descended from the same ancestry as her husband. Children of first wife: Harland Eugene, born August 29, 1897; Laura Belle, born July 20, 1899, died March 3, 1906.

(IV) Christopher M., fourth son of Noah Weld and Mary M. (Norris) Abbott, was born September 22, 1875. Upon the completion of his studies, he at once entered upon an active career and is now serving in the capacity of manager of the general store of Abbott Brothers Company, a position for which he is thoroughly qualified and which he is filling to the satisfaction of all concerned. He is genial and sociable, and is highly regarded by all with whom he is brought in contact. He is a member of the borough council, the Presbyterian church, and the Independent Order of Odd Fellows, in all of which he takes an active interest. Mr. Abbott married (second) June 7, 1905, Arnetta M., born August 16, 1882, daughter of Frederick M. and Augusta (Thorman) Meyer. One child, Frederick Meyer, born March 31, 1912. Mrs. Abbott is secretary of the Abbott Family Reunion Association.

(IV) James Edward, fifth son of Noah Weld and Mary M. (Norris) Abbott, was born December 15, 1878. He was a student in the public schools of the neighborhood, and his entire attention has been devoted to concrete work, in which he excels. Throughout his life he has been a resident of Sugargrove, and is honored and respected by all with whom he has had business dealings. He holds membership in the Methodist Episcopal church, is an active member of the Independent Order of Odd Fellows, and is a Republican in politics. He married, September 28, 1898, Minnie M., born February 2, 1877, daughter of James and Sarah (Sherrard) Moore. Children: Mabel Arlene, born May 28, 1900; Myrtle Altheda, December 4, 1904; Warren Edward, September 21, 1906; Norman Weld, February 4, 1911. The family resides in Sugargrove.

(IV) Harry A., sixth son of Noah Weld and Mary M. (Norris) Abbott, was born May 5, 1882. After completing his studies, he became a rural free delivery mail carrier, in which capacity he is serving at the present time (1912). He resides on the old homestead in Sugargrove. He affiliates with the Methodist Episcopal church, is active in the affairs of the Independent Order of Odd Fellows, and a Republican in politics. He married, December 19, 1902, Ethel, born September 29, 1883, daughter of Zelamon and Sarah (Sheldon) Ball. Children: Dora Katherine, born August 12, 1903; Dorothy Margaret, May 9, 1907; Geneva June, February 16, 1909.

(IV) Hila Parrish, seventh son of Noah Weld and Mary M. (Norris) Abbott, was born March 22, 1887. He was reared in Sugargrove, educated in its schools, and at the present time (1912) is filling the position of shipping clerk in the George Irish Paper Company, of Jamestown, New York. He married, June 25, 1908, Fannie, daughter of Lester and —— (Curtiss) Hoyt. One child, Hoyt Lester, born March 22, 1911.

ABBOTT (IV) Earl T. Abbott, son of Noah Weld (q. v.) and Mary M. (Norris) Abbott, was born in Sugargrove township, Warren county, Pennsylvania, March 17, 1869. He received his education in the public schools, and as soon as he was old enough he engaged in the lumbering business, working in saw and shingle mills until he was thirty years of age. When he was twenty-one he embarked with his brothers in various mercantile pursuits, working at the same time in the lumber trade and doing an extensive business. Among other things they purchased, the Curtis-Davis feed and saw mills, and on April 3, 1899, they bought the mercantile business of D. M. Stillson. At this time Earl T. Abbott took charge of the store end of their business while his brother looked after the lumber interests. On January 1, 1904, Mr. Abbott sold his interest in the lumber business to his brothers and purchased from them the interests in the Abbott Brothers store. Since that time he has been in business for himself alone. He also owns and operates a large feed mill and does an extensive coal business besides. Mr. Abbott pays a mercantile tax of seventeen thousand dollars. He also owns the stage and dray line running between Sugargrove and Jamestown, New York. He is a member of Colebrook Lodge, No. 1124, Independent Order of Odd Fellows, and has been active in the affairs of that lodge, being a member of the degree team. He and his family attend the Methodist Episcopal church. He is a man of high character and strict integrity and has never taken any intoxicating drink. He married, June 13, 1891, Mina Emma, born at Riceville, Pennsylvania, February 22, 1867, daughter of Abraham and Hannah (Crouch) Horton. Children: Ray Augustus, born July 2, 1894; Mary Alfreda, April 16, 1896; Elsa Verna, May 14, 1901; Donald Earl, October 31, 1904.

Abraham Horton, father of Mrs. Mina Emma (Horton) Abbott, was born May 16, 1825, died May 30, 1897. He married Hannah Crouch, born February 15, 1834, died April 16, 1875, daughter of Stephen Crouch. Children: 1. Derestus Spencer, born October 9, 1857, died May 2, 1893. 2. George Morris, born January 1, 1860, died August 24, 1895. 3. Augustus Henry, born January 4, 1862, died January 26, 1894. 4. Keziah Elizabeth, born June 9, 1864, married Frederick Frank; children: Ellen, born March 4, 1889; Jennie, July 5, 1891; Kenneth, June 24, 1893; Margaret, June 5, 1895; William, March 1, 1898; Allan, September 28, 1903; Hortense, July 12, 1905 (twin); Horton, July 12, 1905 (twin); Marion, May 24, 1907; James, May 13, 1910. 5.

Mina Emma, born February 22, 1867, married Earl T. Abbott, aforementioned. 6, Fannie, born August 8, 1870, died in March, 1871. 7. Sarah Lillian, born February 20, 1874; she was adopted by Mr. Cyrus Dupree and goes by the name of Grace; she married Frank Shannon, and resides in Oil City, Pennsylvania.

Abraham Horton was descended from one of the branches of the Horton family in England that settled in this country. The word Horton in the Anglo-Saxon language means an enclosure or garden of vegetables. It is said to be a compound derived from ort and tun, ort meaning plant, and tun, enclosed. The Hortons of England and their descendants in America have generally been cultivators of the soil. They have been almost universally in the middle class of society and it is not known that any royal blood has ever coursed in their veins. They are and have always been producers rather than consumers, and for industry, integrity and piety they will lose nothing in comparison with the renowned of the earth, either in the new or in the old world.

The family bearing the name that emigrated to this country, of whom we have any authentic record, came over from England during the years from 1633 to 1638. Thomas, Jeremiah and Barnabas were among the early immigrants, and old tradition says they were brothers. Thomas came over in the "Mary and John" in 1633, and settled permanently in Springfield, Massachusetts. Jeremiah also settled in Massachusetts. There was a John Horton in New York in 1645, but no one has been found claiming descent from him. He probably returned to England. It is not known from what place in England either Thomas or Joseph came, nor is there any certain evidence that they were brothers of Barnabas, but the fact of the three of them coming at the same time would favor the tradition that they were brothers. The name in olden time was frequently written Orton, and it is highly probable that the Ortons and Hortons bear what was originally the same name and perhaps also the Nortons. The antiquity of the Horton family is established by the fact that one, Robert de Horton, manumitted a bondsman to his manor of Horton, long before the time of Henry Larey, Earl of Lincoln, who died in 1310. It is also mentioned that the Hortons had a manor house in Great Horton, with a mill and certain demense lands therewith, belonging to a very remote period.

A record of strong characters who WELD reached honorable positions in both the old country and the new distinguishes this family of Weld. Both religious bodies, Protestant and Romanist, received adherents of the name of Weld during the period of the Reformation. Many literary men and divines bore the same patronymic, and others of the family gained positions of honor under the civil government.

(I) The American line here given traces its descent from Edmond Weld, of Sudbury, Sussex, England, and the will containing his children's names is found in Windebanck. Among these children are found: Rev. Thomas Weld, a colleague of the Rev. John Eliot who gave the Bible to the Indians, and was also his collaborator, together with the Rev. Richard Mather, in producing the famous first hymnal of the New World known as the "Bay Psalm Book," his pastorate being the First Church, Roxbury, Massachusetts, where he settled before 1635; Joseph, of whom further.

(II) Captain Joseph Weld, son of Edmond Weld, was born in England, died in Roxbury, Massachusetts. He was captain of the training band, and an original member of the Ancient and Honorable Artillery Company of Boston. He acquired the tract still known as the Weld farm in Roxbury, and gained much wealth as a merchant. His estate at his death was inventoried at £10,000 sterling, and was considered as possibly the largest in the colony. He founded the Roxbury Latin School, so that like his brother he evidently was a man of learning. At the present day Harvard University has named one of its buildings Weld Hall, and an addition to its library is called the Weld Collection. In his will, which has been published in the New England Historical and Genealogical Register, he bequeathed "his best tawny cloke" to his friend, the Rev. John Eliot. He married and left a son, John, of whom further.

(III) John, son of Captain Joseph Weld, was born in England in 1623. He emigrated three years after his father and reached Roxbury in 1638. He married in Massachusetts, and left a son, Joseph, of whom further.

(IV) Captain Joseph (2) Weld, son of John Weld, was born in Roxbury, in 1650. He gained his title of captain in state service in the Indian wars. He married Sarah Faxon, November 27, 1679. Children: Sarah, born October 25, 1685; John, August 19, 1689, died

January 11, 1704; Daniel, of whom further; Edmond, born June, 1700, died July 25, 1710; Ebenezer, born October, 1702.

(V) Lieutenant Daniel Weld, son of Captain Joseph (2) Weld, was born August 4, 1697, at Roxbury. He entered the colonial army of the English king, like his father and great-grandfather, and gave faithful service for many years in protecting the infant colonies against the Indians. He spent his life upon the ancestral farm at Roxbury. His grave was made in part of the old Weld farm, a cemetery now near Bussey Park, Boston. He married, January 22, 1720, Elizabeth Tucker. Children: 1. Daniel Jr., born August, 1721; married Joanna Haven; moved to Charlton, Worcester county. 2. Stephen, born July 7, 1723, died August 16, 1745. 3. Noah, of whom further. 4. Job, born August 4, 1730; married Eunice Thayer; moved to Charlton. 5. Edward, born April 1, 1733, died October 13, ———. 6. David, born August 14, 1734, died January 5, 1821.

(VI) Noah, son of Lieutenant Daniel Weld, was born December 7, 1725, at Roxbury, died August 16, 17—. He moved to Charlton, Worcester county. He married Eleanor ———. Children: 1. Calvin, born August 14, 1751. 2. Isaac, of whom further. 3. Luther, born April 14, 1761; he and his brother Calvin married Rogers sisters, and lived for a time in Guilford, Vermont; and some of Luther's sons lived at Cohocton, New York. 4. Kathrin, married a Mr. Porter, of Franklin county, Massachusetts. 5. Eleanor, married a Mr. Wells, and moved to Tennessee.

(VII) Lieutenant Isaac Weld, son of Noah Weld, was born in 1755, at Charlton, Massachusetts, died April 22, 1808. Although a resident of Guilford, Vermont, at the time of the revolution, he is recorded in "Massachusetts Soldiers and Sailors in the Revolutionary War" as from Guilford and serving as a "private, Capt. Moses Draper's Co. Lieut. Col. Wm. Bond's (late Col. Thomas Gardiner's) 37 Regt., company return, dated Camp Prospect Hill, Dec. 30, 1775." He is again recorded on May 15, as a private on the list of "Thomas Newhall, muster master" and "engaged for the town of Petersham, term 8 months." There is also a certificate dated from Petersham, May 23, 1778, in which he was mustered to serve "8 months to the credit of Petersham." In 1782 he served as second lieutenant in the Third Guilford Regiment of Captain Joseph Elliott, from Vermont county. When the war closed he served in 1783 in the boundary war between Vermont and New York, joining the party that defended New York, who were called "Yorkers." He was fined in Guilford two pounds ten shillings for being second lieutenant of a Yorker regiment in this controversy. These men were dispersed by General Ethan Allen. He seems to have the migratory spirit, for he removed from Guilford to Wardsborough in the same county, then to Verona, New York, and again to Sodus Bay, Wayne county, in the latter state. He married Betsey Farrell, in 1780. Children: 1. Catherine, born March 8, 1782; she is lost track of. 2. Robert Farrell, of whom further. 3. Noah, born November 4, 1787; made a distinguished record as a physician; married, in 1815, Huldah Susannah Hoyt, of Danbury, Connecticut, and had issue; died July, 1851. 4. Anna, born October 29, 1789, died unmarried June 6, 1808. 5. Betsey, born November 24, 1792; married a Mr. Pierce; lived at Wales, New York. 6. Jane, born 1795, died unmarried 1854, at Sugargrove, Pennsylvania. 7. Sally, born January 27, 1799; married Amos Moore; died soon after marriage. 8. Roxanna, or Roccena, born November 22, 1803; married John Baker, January 26, 1826; lived at Rices, New York; died November 1, 1891.

(VIII) Robert Farrell, son of Lieutenant Isaac Weld, was born in 1784, in Windham county, Vermont, died in 1870 at Sugargrove, Pennsylvania. He lived at various times in Sodus Bay, New York, and Sugargrove, Pennsylvania. He belonged to the agricultural profession, and was highly regarded by all neighbors on account of his intellectuality and strictest honesty. He enlisted in the defense of the United States during the war of 1812, and served at Black Rock and Buffalo. He married, February 9, 1817, Clarissa Howe, of Brattleboro, Vermont. Children: 1. Theodore Nelson, born November 23, 1817, died June 2, 1862, at Chandlers Valley, Pennsylvania; married Julia A. Jones, January 14, 1848, and left six children, all born at Sugargrove. 2. Susan Ann, born July 25, 1821, at Bath, New York, died at Youngsville, Pennsylvania, in 1894; married Cyrus F. Arters, April 8, 1857, but had no children. 3. Squire Howe, born November 23, 1823, at Bath, New York, died February 18, 1900; lived in Centerville, Pennsylvania, and served in the Two Hundred and Eleventh Pennsylvania Infantry during the civil war; married (first) June 27, 1853, Martha Goodwin, (second) Susannah Dye, November 26, 1884, and had nine children. 4. Sarah McCay, born July 25, 1826, died August, 1905; married Washington P. Cummings, April 13, 1853, and had three children. 5. Lieutenant William Wallace, of whom further. 6. Caroline Howe, born January 4, 1832, at Busti, New York, died January 14, 1832. 7. Jeanette Langdon, born March 16, 1833, at Busti, New York, died October 5, 1833. 8. Mariette, born October 1, 1835, at Busti, died June 11, 1836. 9. Mary Ann, born October 1, 1835, at Busti, twin of Mariette, died in infancy. 10. Clarissa Emaline, born January 18, 1840, at Sugargrove, Pennsylvania, died September 3, 1883; married Enoch Dupree, September 2, 1868, and is said to have had three daughters.

(IX) Lieutenant William Wallace Weld, son of Robert Farrell Weld, was born February 23, 1829, at Bath, New York, died July 16, 1903, at Sugargrove, Pennsylvania. He lived on the Weld farm at Sugargrove except for the period of two years, from 1859 to 1861, which he spent in California working at the trade of painter, and the period spent by him as a soldier in the army. He enlisted in Company B, Ninth New York Cavalry, at Sugargrove, September 23, 1861, and was mustered in as second lieutenant, October 3, 1861, and as first lieutenant, January 16, 1863. He was discharged for disability, March 18, 1863, but again re-enlisted in 1864, in the Two Hundred and Eleventh Pennsylvania Volunteer Infantry, and was promoted to ordnance sergeant, and served until the close of the war. He was a courageous and progressive man, held in warm estimation by his fellow townsmen, and successful in his ordinary profession of farmer. He married, January 1, 1868, Christine Stewart Falconer, born June 24, 1836, at Elgin, Scotland. Children: 1. Robert James, of whom further. 2. Fred Falconer, born at Sugargrove, September 19, 1871; educated at Pennsylvania State College, and is a civil engineer; resides at Seattle, Washington; married, June 27, 1901, Eliza R. Busick, and has children: Alice Christina, born January 29, 1903; Theodore Busick, born at Detroit, Michigan, June 18, 1905; Robert James, born in Seattle, Washington, August 27, 1909; Edwin Stuart, born in Seattle, March 4, 1911. 3. Guy Theodore, born April 25, 1874, at Sugargrove, died February 27, 1883.

(X) Robert James, son of Lieutenant William Wallace Weld, was born at Maple Shade farm, Sugargrove, Pennsylvania, October 27, 1868. He was educated in the public schools at Sugargrove, followed by a course in the Luce Business College at Sugargrove Seminary, and later completed his studies at the Pennsylvania State College. His business life began with a partnership with his father on the farm. January 1, 1893, he entered the employ of the Pennsylvania State College Experiment Station, as he was familiar with the difficult problems that confront the agriculturist, and remained there until March 1, 1894, when he resigned and returned home. He again returned to the Experiment Station during the winters of 1897 and 1898, and added greatly to his scientific knowledge of soils and farm products, and rendered valuable service to the government, especially in the department where feeding experiments were conducted. His knowledge of these subjects, which were of interest and importance to all the farmers of Warren county, was so great that he was induced to enter upon a course of lectures given at the Pennsylvania Farmers' Institute, in 1900. He also went into various parts of Pennsylvania during the next five years to give practical instruction to farmers generally. In 1911 he began a course of work in the Movable Agricultural School, a new method of meeting the most distant farmer on his own ground and teaching him the best way to utilize his farm and its products. Mr. Weld is still engaged in this profitable line of work, and has won for himself the commendation of every hearer, and the admiration of the whole farming class for his success in practical farming and the application of scientific principles thereto. He helps to foster other business interests of the community, and is a stockholder and director in the Sugargrove Savings Bank. He is a member of Sugargrove Grange since its organization, having been the first one to be initiated, and has held the office of master for three consecutive terms. He is also connected with Cold Brook Lodge, Independent Order of Odd Fellows.

Mr. Weld married, June 5, 1902, Fanny Wright, born July 14, 1863, in Cincinnati, Ohio, daughter of Dr. Edward B. and Eliza Wright, whose other children are: Laura, Alice, Lucy, Annie. Child of Mr. and Mrs. Weld, Robert Arlo, born December 17, 1905.

HAGGERTY The members of the Haggerty family residing in Sugargrove and vicinity, noted for thrift and enterprise, trace their descent to an Irish ancestry who came from their native land, locating first in Canada, from whence they removed to Pennsylvania, where their descendants have resided ever since, honored and respected for their many excellent characteristics.

(I) Daniel Haggerty, grandfather of Donald Hector Haggerty, was a successful farmer, conducting his operations on a farm located in the vicinity of Mercer, Pennsylvania, the probability being that he migrated there from Canada. His brother, George Haggerty, was a resident of Mercer. Daniel Haggerty married —————— ——————, who bore him at least three children: William Morrison, of whom further; Sarah and another.

(II) William Morrison, son of Daniel Haggerty, was born March 17, 1830. He was reared on his father's farm near the village of Mercer, Mercer county, Pennsylvania, and obtained a practical education in the common schools adjacent to his home. In young manhood he removed to Warren county, Pennsylvania, locating at Wrightsville, where he was extensively engaged in the lumber business, sending rafts and lumber down the Allegheny river. At first he was associated in partnership with Robert Allen, and later for a number of years with Edwin R. Wheelock. They built and operated a saw mill at Sugargrove, which proved a most successful enterprise. About the year 1897 he went west, locating in North Dakota, where he purchased about five thousand acres of land which he devoted to the growing of wheat, from which he derived a goodly profit. In 1899 he returned to Sugargrove, Pennsylvania, and purchased a farm consisting of one hundred and twenty-five acres from the Clark heirs, on which he made many improvements and on which he resided for the remainder of his days. He was extensively interested in the oil fields of Pennsylvania, operating in the vicinity of Pleasantville and Tidioute, and he also owned and operated oil producing wells in Canada. He was one of the most extensive stockholders in the Farmers' and Mechanics' Bank, Jamestown, owning one-twelfth of the entire stock. He was a member of the Free and Accepted Masons, at Jamestown, and a Republican in politics.

Mr. Haggerty married (first) Harriet Allen, who bore him one child, Ina, born 1858, married Watson Dalrymple; children: Maud, Christy, William, Ralph. Mr. Haggerty married (second) Christy Ann McLean, born February 15, 1846, died November 14, 1902, interred in the cemetery at Sugargrove. Children: Isabel, born May 20, 1880, and Donald Hector, of whom further. The death of Mr. Haggerty occurred at Tibury, Ontario, Canada, thirty miles east of Detroit, September 22, 1906, from the effects of gas asphyxiation He was interested in some oil property at Tibury and was there overseeing the work; one of his men was cleaning a tank and became overcome with the gas; Mr. Haggerty went to his assistance and met the same fate; both men were found lying on their backs in a few inches of oil in the tank, the first mentioned being dead and Mr. Haggerty only lived a short time.

(III) Donald Hector, only son of William Morrison and Christy Ann (McLean) Haggerty, was born in Sugargrove, Warren county, Pennsylvania, May 24, 1885. He obtained his education in the district schools, the United Brethren Seminary at Sugargrove and Betts Academy, Stamford, Connecticut. For a short period of time after completing his studies he was engaged in the oil section of his native state, but then decided to follow agricultural pursuits. He purchased his father's farm, located near the village of Sugargrove, consisting of one hundred and eighty acres, the original farm of Green Clark, which he has brought to a high state of perfection, being practical and progressive in his methods, and his farm takes high rank in the community. Mr. Haggerty is actively interested in all that concerns the betterment and advancement of Sugargrove, contributes liberally to all worthy objects, and has won and retained a wide circle of friends. He is a stockholder in the Farmers' and Mechanics' Bank of Jamestown. He is a member and trustee in the Sugargrove Presbyterian church, and a member of Stillwater Lodge, No. 547, Free and Accepted Masons.

Mr. Haggerty married, June 15, 1905, Minnie Virginia, born June 10, 1884, daughter of Nelson and Minnie Anderson; Mr. Anderson resides in Sugargrove, but was the American emigrant of this branch of the Anderson family, being a native of Denmark. Mr. and Mrs. Haggerty are the parents of two children: Helen Virginia, born at Sugargrove, March 14, 1906; Christy McLean, born at Sugargrove, January 16, 1910.

REISINGER This name is of strictly German origin. Charles Reisinger was born in Lancaster county, Pennsylvania, December 31, 1798, died at Meadville, Pennsylvania, August 22, 1882. He was the son of Peter and Catharine (Heckert) Reisinger, who were natives of York, Pennsylvania. They were married September 3, 1786. Peter Reisinger was born July 11, 1766, died April 24, 1852. His father, John Peter Reisinger, and paternal grandfather, Hans Nicklaus, came to America together in the ship "Dragon," reaching Philadelphia, September 26, 1749. Hans Nicklaus was a widower, and before 1753 he married Eva, widow of Lorentz Schmahl, of York, Pennsylvania, who was born June 10, 1708, in Essenheim, Hessen, Germany (where his ancestors had lived for many generations), and emigrated to America with his family in 1743; he died in 1749. Her maiden name was Eva Ubert. John Peter Reisinger married her daughter, Eva Schmahl. Catharine Heckert was born May 10, 1762, died at Beaver, Pennsylvania, May 10, 1831. Both her father, John Jacob, and her grandfather, Franz, were born at New Bamberg, Hessen, Germany, the latter in 1703, and the former April 13, 1730. They came to America in the ship "Harle," arriving at Philadelphia, September 1, 1736.

Charles Reisinger married Providence, daughter of Isaiah Roberts, October 7, 1829. She was born at Abingdon, Harford county, Maryland, December 3, 1806, died at Franklin, Pennsylvania, May 10, 1894. Her father was of Welsh and English extraction. Her mother, Elizabeth (Standiford) Roberts, was the daughter of Abraham Standiford, who belonged to one of the early Maryland families, and Susan Chamberlain, whose father and grandfather were residents of Harford county, but were of the Virginia Chamberlains, whose ancestor, Thomas Chamberlaine, emigrated from Gloucestershire, England, about the year 1670, and located in Henrico, Virginia, where he married Mary, daughter of Major General Abraham Wood, of that county. He sold lands in Henrico county in 1686, and in 1695 was a member of the house of burgesses for Charles City county. In the early records of Virginia and also in the ancient English records the name is variously spelled, Chamberlaine, Chamberlayne and Chamberlain. Thomas Chamberlaine, the emigrant, was a great-grandson of Sir Thomas Chamberlaine, of Presbury, Gloucestershire, who was ambassador to Henry the Eighth, Edward the Sixth, and Queen Elizabeth. He died in the latter end of Elizabeth's reign. He married Elizabeth, daughter of Sir John Ludington.

Sir Thomas Chamberlaine, otherwise Tankervile, Knight, was a descendant in the tenth generation from John, Count de Tankervile, of Tankervile castle in Normandy, who came into England with King William the Conqueror, but returned again into Normandy. His son, grandson and great-grandson respectively, were Lord Chamberlain to Henry the First, Stephen and Henry the Second. The grandson, Richard de Tankervile, assumed the name of Chamberlaine, "and gave for arms, one and four gules, an inescutcheon, argent, in an orle of eight mullets, or; two and three gules, a chevron, between three escallops, or, which his descendants bear at this day." This is one of the very earliest historically authenticated instances of the bearing of coat armor in England, as it dates from the year 1174. (See below). William Chamberlain, lord of North Riston, was son of Richard; he had taken prisoner Robert de Bellemont, earl of Millain in Normandy, and earl of Leicester in England, commonly called Blanchmains, who had taken part with young Henry, son of King Henry the Second, against his father; and for this service the king granted him to quarter the arms of the Earl of Leicester with the arms of Tankervile, in the year 1174.

(Wotton, 1741). The generations from John, Count de Tankervile to Thomas Chamberlaine, the emigrant are as follows: John, Count de Tankervile; John de Tankervile; Richard Chamberlaine; William Chamberlaine, Lord of North Riston; Robert Chamberlaine; Sir Richard Chamberlaine; Sir Robert Chamberlaine; Sir John Chamberlaine; Sir Richard Chamberlaine; John Chamberlaine; Thomas Chamberlaine; John Chamberlaine; John Chamberlain; William Chamberlaine; Sir Thomas Chamberlaine; Edmund Chamberlaine; Edmund Chamberlaine; Thomas Chamberlaine, the emigrant.

Authorities—Sir Robert Atkyns, "the ancient and Present State of Gloucestershire," p. 365. Thomas Wotton's "The English Baronetage," ed. 1741, vol. 2, pp. 374-378. "The

Visitation of Oxfordshire in 1566 and 1574," publications of the Harleian Society, vol. 5, pp. 235-237.

(II) Roe,* fourth son and sixth child of Charles and Providence (Roberts) Reisinger, was born October 28, 1842, in Fallstown, Beaver county, Pennsylvania. In 1844 his father purchased a large tract of land on Sandy Creek, Venango county, and removed there with his family. For the next six years he followed the business of farming and lumbering, and part of the time doing work as a blacksmith, which was his trade. As the opportunities for educating a family were limited at that time in Venango county, in 1850 he decided to locate in Meadville for the opportunity it afforded to send his sons to Allegheny College. He resided in Meadville, engaged in blacksmithing, and later in farming until his death, in 1882. His determination to give his children the best obtainable education never relaxed, and his life was devoted to unceasing effort to that end. His oldest son, Napoleon B., graduated in 1855, and the second, James W. H., in 1856. Charles Standiford, the third son, began a college course, but not having a strong desire for a classical education, went into other pursuits. Roe Reisinger, the next in age, inherited the literary taste characteristic of his two oldest brothers, and from childhood had an intense passion for reading. He had no decided talent for mathematics, his abilities and inclination being toward philosophy, history and poetry. His education up to his seventeenth year was obtained in the common schools of Meadville and suburbs, and the Meadville Academy. In 1858 he entered Allegheny College and followed an interrupted course until 1861. Owing to the breaking out of the rebellion he finally left college, and after spending a year in the oil regions he enlisted for the war, at the same time with his brothers, James W. H. and Charles S. His oldest brother, Napoleon B., had previously joined the Seventeenth Indiana Volunteers. He became broken in health from exposure in army life, and was discharged for disability, dying soon afterward. He had begun the practice of law in Evansville, Indiana. James W. H. became captain of Company H, One Hundred and Fiftieth Pennsylvania Volunteers, and later lieutenant-colonel, Twenty-fifth United States Colored Troops. Charles S. fought with his regiment (the One Hundred and Fiftieth Pennsylvania) in all the battles of the campaign from the Wilderness to Cold Harbor, rising to the rank of captain. He was wounded in the battle of Cold Harbor, causing the amputation of his left leg.

Roe Reisinger enlisted August 20, 1862, and was assigned to Company H, One Hundred and Fiftieth Pennsylvania (Bucktail) Volunteers. He served with his regiment until disabled by wounds received at Gettysburg, July 1, 1863. He was a corporal and one of the regimental color-guard up to that time, was afterward promoted to sergeant, to date from that battle; was in hospital from his wounds until October 29, 1864, when he was transferred to Company B, Fourteenth Veteran Reserve Corps, and served until discharged by expiration of enlistment, June 26, 1865. He was commissioned as an officer of the One Hundred and Fourteenth United States Colored Troops, July 26, 1865, and served with that regiment in Texas until April 2, 1867, when he was discharged as a first lieutenant, his regiment being disbanded. The desperate defense which his regiment made in the battle of Gettysburg, at the McPherson stone barn, is recorded in history. Its loss was one-third greater than that at Balaklava. Every field officer fell with severe wounds. The color-bearer was killed and all of the color-guard were killed or wounded. As to Corporal Reisinger's conduct in that battle, the best evidence should be the records of the war department and of congress, and these are full and explicit. In his official report of the engagement, Colonel (later General) Huidekoper, who commanded the regiment, said: "Among the many brave, I would especially commend for coolness and courage, Corporal Roe Reisinger." In a subsequent letter to the secretary of war, General Huidekoper gave the following statement of the facts which caused him to make honorable mention of Corporal Reisinger in his official report:

To explain the part taken by Corporal Reisinger in the contest at the McPherson barn, on the Chambersburg pike, I would say that the Corporal was one of the color-guard. He was wounded early in the afternoon by a minie ball penetrating his right

---

*A namesake of Joshua Monroe, a noted Methodist clergyman of Western Pennsylvania, distinguished as a writer for the Christian Advocate. At school and college the name was written J. Monroe, or simply the initials J. M., and in the army, with a single exception, he was borne on the rolls as J. Monroe Reisinger. From childhood he was always familiarly called Roe, and more than forty years ago he adopted that as his formal name, using it ever since.

foot, causing later the removal of two bones from his foot, with the result of permanent lameness because of that injury.

Notwithstanding this severe wound, which would have entitled Reisinger to go to the hospital at that time for treatment—as he was urged to do by his comrades—he continued to perform his duty as a soldier until wounded three times, when weakness from injuries and from loss of blood compelled his retirement.

Further details of the fight at the stone barn were given in an address delivered by Major Chamberlin at Gettysburg. He said:

The afternoon had worn on to 2.45 o'clock. The enemy drew nearer and nearer, firing rapidly as he came, but was met by a resistance which time and again staggered him, though it could not shake him off. Greatly superior in numbers and relying upon his supports, he kept urging the attack, only to find the defense as stubborn as his own advance.

If for a moment our line swayed backward a few steps under the enemy's heavier musketry, it promptly advanced again at the word of command, forcing the enemy to recoil in turn.

This state of things could not long continue. By sheer weight our thinned ranks were pushed some rods to the rear, but without panic. To encourage his command, Colonel Huidekoper instructed the color bearer Sergeant Peifler, of Company I, a man of large stature and boundless courage, to move forward with the colors. This he did without hesitation, in the face of a galling fire, and the line moved automatically with him.

The enemy's advance was stayed, but his firing continued with telling effect. Then again for some moments the opposing ranks beat backward and forward, yielding ground alternately, but recovering it promptly, apparently resolved to lose the last man in defending or winning the position. A storm of lead constantly sought the flag, and such of the color guard as had hitherto been spared were all either killed or wounded, Corporal Reisinger, of Company H, receiving no less than three balls.

A few years ago the surviving field officers of the regiment called the attention of the war department to Corporal Reisinger's conduct at Gettysburg, and asked that the medal of honor should be awarded to him. The case was referred to the attorney general, who decided that under the general law it could not be given to one not then in the military service. The matter was taken up in congress and a special act was passed by a unanimous vote of both the senate and house of representatives, which became a law on February 7, 1907, awarding to Corporal Reisinger the medal of honor. The following is the text of the act:

Resolved, By the senate and house of representatives of the United States of America in congress assembled, That the secretary of war be, and he is hereby, authorized and directed to award the congressional medal of honor to Roe Reisinger, alias J. Monroe Reisinger, late corporal, Company H, 150 Regiment Pennsylvania Volunteer Infantry, for specially brave and meritorious conduct in the face of the enemy at the battle of Gettysburg July first, eighteen hundred and sixty-three.

This is the only instance where it has ever been awarded by a special act of congress to an individual officer or soldier. On his final muster out, after a service as an officer and soldier of four and a half years, he returned to his home at Meadville, and began the study of law. He was admitted to the bar of Crawford county and of the supreme court of Pennsylvania in 1870, and opened a law office at Meadville. After being fifteen years at the bar he left it, and for some time was in the newspaper business. In 1888 he located in Franklin and since that time he has been connected with a business corporation.

He married (first) June 1, 1871, Mary Augusta, daughter of Dr. H. R. Barnes, of Rock Stream, New York. She died April 23, 1875, leaving one child, a daughter, who survives. In 1882 he married (second) Ellen, daughter of Jacob Lieberman, of Meadville. They have one child, a son. The daughter, Austa, is supervisor of drawing in the Franklin public schools. The son, James W. H., Jr., is a graduate of the United States Military Academy, and is a first lieutenant in the Thirtieth United States Infantry, now stationed at Fort St. Michael, Alaska.

www.ingramcontent.com/pod-product-compliance
Lightning Source LLC
Chambersburg PA
CBHW060103170426
43198CB00010B/758